DISCOVER MCGRAW-HILL NETWORKS™
AN AWARD-WINNING SOCIAL STUDIES PROGRAM DESIGNED TO FULLY SUPPORT YOUR SUCCESS.

» Aligned to the National Council for the Social Studies Standards

» Engages you with interactive resources and compelling stories

» Provides resources and tools for every learning style

» Empowers targeted learning to help you be successful

UNDERSTANDING IS THE FOUNDATION OF ACHIEVEMENT

Clear writing, real-life examples, photos, interactive maps, videos, and more will capture your attention and keep you engaged so that you can succeed.

You will find tools and resources to help you read more effectively.

FOCUS YOUR TIME AND YOUR EFFORT

LEARNSMART®

No two students are alike! We built LearnSmart® so that all students can work through the key material they need to learn at their own pace.

YOUR TIME MATTERS

LearnSmart® with SmartBook™ adapts to you as you work, guiding you through your reading so you can make every minute count.

DISCOVER A PERSONALIZED READING EXPERIENCE

Every student experiences LearnSmart® differently. The interactive challenge format highlights content and helps you identify content you know and don't know.

RETAIN MORE INFORMATION

LearnSmart® detects content you are most likely to forget and will highlight what you need to review.

networks

BE THE STUDENT YOU WANT TO BE

STUDENTS WHO UNDERSTAND THE WORLD WILL BE THE ADULTS WHO CAN CHANGE IT.

DISCOVER IT ALL ONLINE!

1. Go to connected.mcgraw-hill.com

2. Enter your username and password from your teacher.

3. Click on your book.

4. Select your chapter and lesson, or explore the Resource Library.

GO ONLINE AND START EXPLORING!

MHEDUCATION.COM/PREK-12

DISCOVERING OUR PAST

A HISTORY OF THE
WORLD

networks™

There's More Online!

Jackson J. Spielvogel, Ph.D.

Mc
Graw
Hill
Education

DISCOVER MCGRAW-HILL NETWORKS™, AN AWARD-WINNING SOCIAL STUDIES PROGRAM DESIGNED TO FULLY SUPPORT YOUR SUCCESS. Networks™.

- Aligned to the National Council for the Social Studies Standards

- Engages you with interactive resources and compelling stories

- Provides resources and tools for every learning style

- Empowers targeted learning to help you be successful

UNDERSTANDING IS THE FOUNDATION OF ACHIEVEMENT

Clear writing, real-life examples, photos, interactive maps, videos, and more will capture your attention and keep you engaged so that you can succeed. You will find tools and resources to help you read more effectively.

Cover credits: (bkgd)Richard Nowitz/Photodisc/Getty Images; (clockwise from top)Library of Congress Prints and Photographs Division [LC-DIG-ppmsca-00957]; (2)Frans Lemmens/Fuse/Getty Images; (3)Hans Wolf/Getty Images

mheducation.com/prek-12

Copyright © 2018 McGraw-Hill Education

Send all inquiries to:
McGraw-Hill Education
8787 Orion Place
Columbus, OH 43240

ISBN: 978-0-07-668388-8
MHID: 0-07-668388-5

Printed in the United States of America.

4 5 6 7 8 9 QVS 22 21 20 19 18

Jackson J. Spielvogel is Associate Professor of History Emeritus at The Pennsylvania State University. He received his Ph.D. from The Ohio State University, where he specialized in Reformation history under Harold J. Grimm. His work has been supported by fellowships from the Fulbright Foundation and the Foundation for Reformation Research. At Penn State, Spielvogel helped inaugurate the Western civilization courses, as well as a popular course on Nazi Germany. His book, *Hitler and Nazi Germany*, was published in 1987 (seventh edition, 2014). He is also the author of *Western Civilization*, published in 1991 (ninth edition, 2015). Spielvogel is the coauthor (with William Duiker) of *World History*, first published in 1998 (eighth edition, 2016). Spielvogel has won five major university-wide teaching awards. In 1988–1989, he held the Penn State Teaching Fellowship, the university's most prestigious teaching award. He won the Dean Arthur Ray Warnock Award for Outstanding Faculty Member in 1996 and the Schreyer Honors College Excellence in Teaching Award in 2000.

Contributing Authors

Jay McTighe has published articles in a number of leading educational journals and has coauthored 10 books, including the best-selling *Understanding by Design* series with Grant Wiggins. McTighe also has an extensive background in professional development and is a featured speaker at national, state, and district conferences and workshops. He received his undergraduate degree from the College of William and Mary, earned a master's degree from the University of Maryland, and completed post-graduate studies at the Johns Hopkins University.

Dinah Zike, M.Ed., is an award-winning author, educator, and inventor recognized for designing three-dimensional, hands-on manipulatives and graphic organizers known as Foldables®. Foldables are used nationally and internationally by parents, teachers, and other professionals in the education field. Zike has developed more than 180 supplemental educational books and materials. Two of her books (*Envelope Graphic Organizers*™ and *Foldables® and VKVs® for Phonics, Spelling, and Vocabulary PreK-3rd)* were each awarded *Learning* Magazine's Teachers' Choice Award for Professional Development in 2014. Two other books (*Notebook Foldables®* and *Foldables®, Notebook Foldables®, and VKV®s for Spelling and Vocabulary 4th–12th)* were each awarded *Learning* Magazine's Teachers' Choice Award in 2011. In 2004, Zike was honored with the CESI Science Advocacy Award. She received her M.Ed. from Texas A&M, College Station, Texas.

Doug Fisher Ph.D. and Nancy Frey Ph.D. are professors in the School of Teacher Education at San Diego State University. Fisher's focus is on literacy and language, with an emphasis on students who are English Learners. Frey's focus is on literacy and learning, with a concentration in how students acquire content knowledge. Both teach elementary and secondary teacher preparation courses, in addition to their work with graduate and doctoral programs. Their shared interests include supporting students with diverse learning needs, instructional design, and curriculum development. Fisher and Frey are coauthors of numerous articles and books, including *Better Learning Through Structured Teaching*, *Checking for Understanding*, *Background Knowledge*, and *Improving Adolescent Literacy*. They are coeditors (with Diane Lapp) of the NCTE journal *Voices From the Middle*.

CONSULTANTS AND REVIEWERS

ACADEMIC CONSULTANTS

David Berger, Ph.D.
Ruth and I. Lewis Gordon
  Professor of Jewish History
Dean, Bernard Revel Graduate
  School
Yeshiva University
New York, New York

Albert S. Broussard, Ph.D.
Professor of History
Texas A & M University
College Station, Texas

Sheilah F. Clarke-Ekong, Ph.D.
Associate Professor, Cultural
  Anthropology
University of Missouri–St. Louis
St. Louis, Missouri

Tom Daccord
Educational Technology
  Specialist
Co-Director, EdTechTeacher
Boston, Massachusetts

Dr. Kenji Oshiro
Professor Emeritus of
  Geography
Wright State University
Dayton, Ohio

Justin Reich
Educational Technology
  Specialist
Co-Director, EdTechTeacher
Boston, Massachusetts

Joseph Rosenbloom, Ph.D.
Adjunct Professor, Jewish
  and Middle East Studies
Washington University
St. Louis, Missouri

TEACHER REVIEWERS

Mary Kathryn Bishop
Fairhope Middle School
Fairhope, Alabama

Janine Brown
Social Studies Department
  Chairperson
Discovery Middle School
Orlando, Florida

Carl M. Brownell
Social Studies Department
  Chairperson
Maine East High School
Park Ridge, Illinois

James Hauf
Berkeley Middle School
St. Louis, Missouri

Amy Kanuck
Morgan Village Middle School
Camden, New Jersey

Kim J. Lapple
Grades 6–12 Social Studies
  Chairperson
H.C. Crittenden Middle School
Armonk, New York

CONTENTS

Norbert Millauer/AFP/Getty Images

CHAPTER 1

What Does a Historian Do? 1

Essential Questions

Why is history important? • How do we learn about the past? • How do you research history?

ZUMA Press Inc/Alamy

CHAPTER 2

Studying Geography, Economics, and Citizenship 25

Essential Questions

How does geography influence the way people live? • Why do people trade? • Why do people form governments?

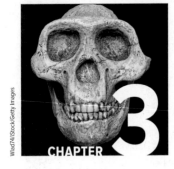

CONTENTS

Lebrecht Music and Arts Photo Library/Alamy

CHAPTER 6

Danita Delimont/Gallo Images/Getty Images

CHAPTER 7

CONTENTS

Danita Delimont/Gallo Images/Getty Images

CHAPTER 8

Dinodia Photo Library/Age fotostock

CHAPTER 9

Apic/Hulton Archives/Getty Images

CHAPTER 10

CONTENTS

CONTENTS

CONTENTS

The British Library Heritage/Age fotostock

CHAPTER 17

Max Paddler/Flickr/Getty Images

CHAPTER 18

CONTENTS

Peter Willi/SuperStock/Getty Images

CHAPTER 19

Erich Lessing/Art Resource, NY

CHAPTER 20

The Granger Collection, NYC All rights reserved Joseph Walter

CHAPTER 21

CONTENTS

CONTENTS

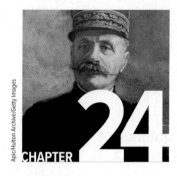

Apic/Hulton Archive/Getty Images

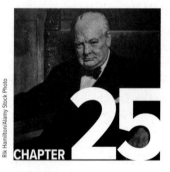

Rik Hamilton/Alamy Stock Photo

CONTENTS

DoD photo by Erin A. Kirk-Cuomo

CHAPTER 26

FEATURES

FEATURES

MAPS, CHARTS, AND GRAPHS

REFERENCE ATLAS MAPS

CHAPTER MAPS

CHAPTER MAPS (CONTINUED)

MAPS, CHARTS, AND GRAPHS

CHARTS, GRAPHS, AND TIME LINES

⌄ Videos

Videos (continued)

Interactive Charts/Graphs

Slide Shows

Interactive Graphic Organizers

Interactive Graphic Organizers (continued)

Maps

All maps that appear in your printed textbook are also available in an interactive format in your Online Student Edition.

TO THE STUDENT

Welcome to McGraw-Hill Education's **Networks** Online Student Learning Center. Here you will access your Online Student Edition, as well as many other learning resources.

(1) LOGGING ON TO THE STUDENT LEARNING CENTER

Using your Internet browser, go to connected.mcgraw-hill.com.

Enter your username and password or create a new account using the redemption code your teacher gave you.

(2) SELECT YOUR PROGRAM

Click your program to launch the home page of your Online Student Learning Center.

HOW TO USE THE ONLINE STUDENT EDITION

Using Your Home Page

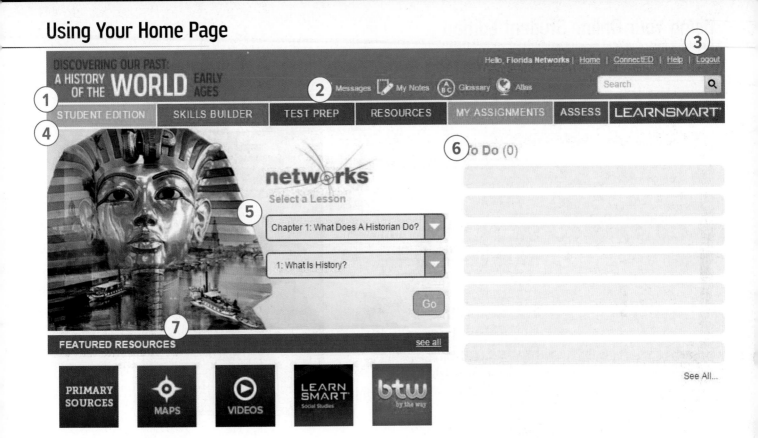

1 HOME PAGE

To return to your home page at any time, click the Networks logo in the top left corner of the page.

2 QUICK LINKS MENU

Use this menu to access:

- Messages
- Notes (your personal notepad)
- The online Glossary
- The online Atlas

3 HELP

For videos and assistance with the various features of the Networks system, click Help.

4 MAIN MENU

Use the menu bar to access:

- The Online Student Edition
- Skills Builder (for activities to improve your skills)
- Test Prep
- Resources
- Assignments
- Assessments
- LearnSmart®

5 ONLINE STUDENT EDITION

Go to your Online Student Edition by selecting the chapter and lesson and then click Go.

6 ASSIGNMENTS

Recent assignments from your teacher will appear here. Click the assignment or click See All to see the details.

7 RESOURCE LIBRARY

Use the carousel to browse the Resource Library.

HOW TO USE THE ONLINE STUDENT EDITION

Using Your Online Student Edition

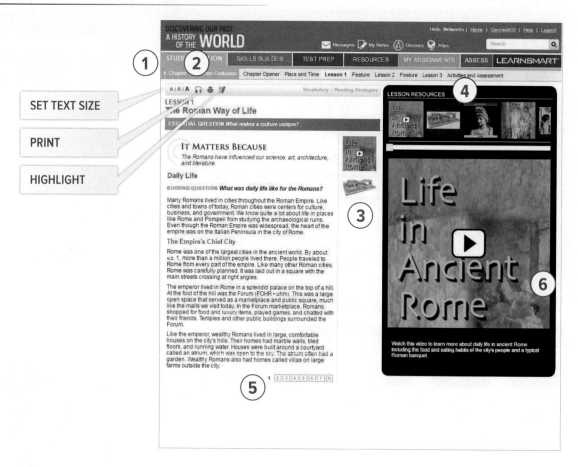

SET TEXT SIZE

PRINT

HIGHLIGHT

---

1 LESSON MENU

- Use the tabs to open the different lessons and special features in a chapter.
- Clicking on the unit or chapter title will open the table of contents.

2 AUDIO EDITION

Click on the headphones symbol to have the page read to you. MP3 files for downloading each lesson are available in the Resource Library.

3 RESOURCES FOR THIS PAGE

Resources appear in the middle column to show that they go with the text on this page. Click the images to open them in the viewer.

4 LESSON RESOURCES

Use the carousel to browse the interactive resources available in this lesson. Click on a resource to open it in the viewer below.

5 CHANGE PAGES

Click here to move to the next page in the lesson.

6 RESOURCE VIEWER

Click on the image that appears in the viewer to launch an interactive resource, including:

- Lesson Videos
- Photos and Slide Shows
- Maps
- Charts and Graphs
- Games
- Lesson Self-Check Quizzes

HOW TO USE THE ONLINE STUDENT EDITION

Reading Support in the Online Student Edition

Your Online Student Edition contains several features to help improve your reading skills and understanding of the content.

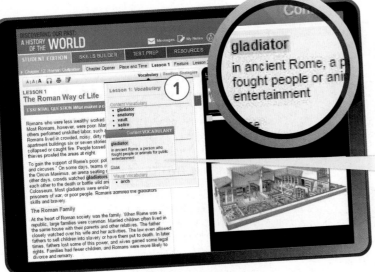

1 LESSON VOCABULARY

Click Vocabulary to bring up a list of terms introduced in this lesson.

VOCABULARY POP-UP

Click on any term highlighted in yellow to open a window with the term's definition.

2 NOTES

Click Notes to open the note-taking tool. You can write and save any notes you want in the Lesson Notes tab.

Click on the Guided Notes tab to view the Guided Reading Questions. Answering these questions will help you build a set of notes about the lesson.

3 GRAPHIC ORGANIZER

Click Reading Strategies to open a note-taking activity using a graphic organizer.

Click the image of the graphic organizer to make it interactive. You can type directly into the graphic organizer and save or print your notes.

HOW TO USE THE ONLINE STUDENT EDITION

Using Interactive Resources in the Online Student Edition

Each lesson of your Online Student Edition contains many resources to help you learn the content and skills you need to know for this subject.

Networks provides many kinds of resources. This symbol shows that the resource is a slide show.

1 **LAUNCHING RESOURCES**

Clicking a resource in the viewer launches an interactive resource.

2 **QUESTIONS AND ACTIVITIES**

When a resource appears in the viewer, one or two questions or activities typically appear beneath it. You can type and save your answers in the answer boxes and submit them to your teacher.

3 **INTERACTIVE MAPS**

When a map appears in the viewer, click on it to launch the interactive map. You can use the drawing tool to mark up the map. You can also zoom in and turn layers on and off to display different information. Many maps have animations and audio as well.

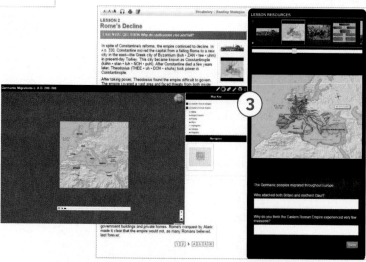

4 **CHAPTER FEATURE**

Each chapter begins with a feature called *Place and Time*. This feature includes a map and time line to help you understand when and where the events in this chapter took place.

The map and time line are both interactive. You can click on the map and the time line to access an interactive version.

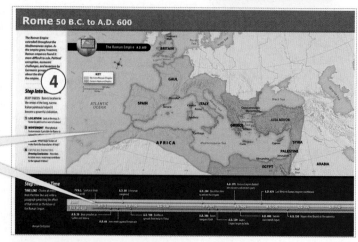

HOW TO USE THE ONLINE STUDENT EDITION

Activities and Assessment

(1) CHAPTER ACTIVITIES AND ASSESSMENT

At the end of each chapter is the Activities and Assessment tab. Here you can test your understanding of what you have learned. You can type and save answers in the answer boxes and submit them to your teacher.

When a question or an activity uses an image, graph, or map, it will appear in the viewer.

Finding Other Resources

There are hundreds of additional resources available in the Resource Library.

(2) RESOURCE LIBRARY

Click the Resources tab to find collections of Primary Sources, Biographies, Skills Activities, and the Reading Essentials and Study Guide.

You can search the Resource Library by lesson or keyword.

Click the star to mark a resource as a favorite.

REFERENCE ATLAS

ATLAS KEY

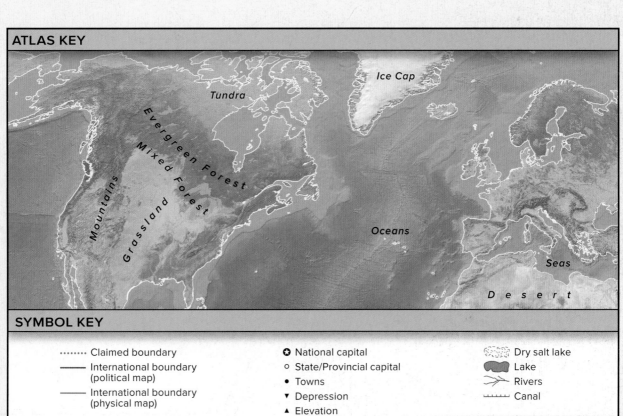

SYMBOL KEY

········· Claimed boundary	✪ National capital	🌫 Dry salt lake
—— International boundary (political map)	○ State/Provincial capital	🟫 Lake
—— International boundary (physical map)	• Towns	⤳ Rivers
	▼ Depression	⊢⊢⊢⊢ Canal
	▲ Elevation	

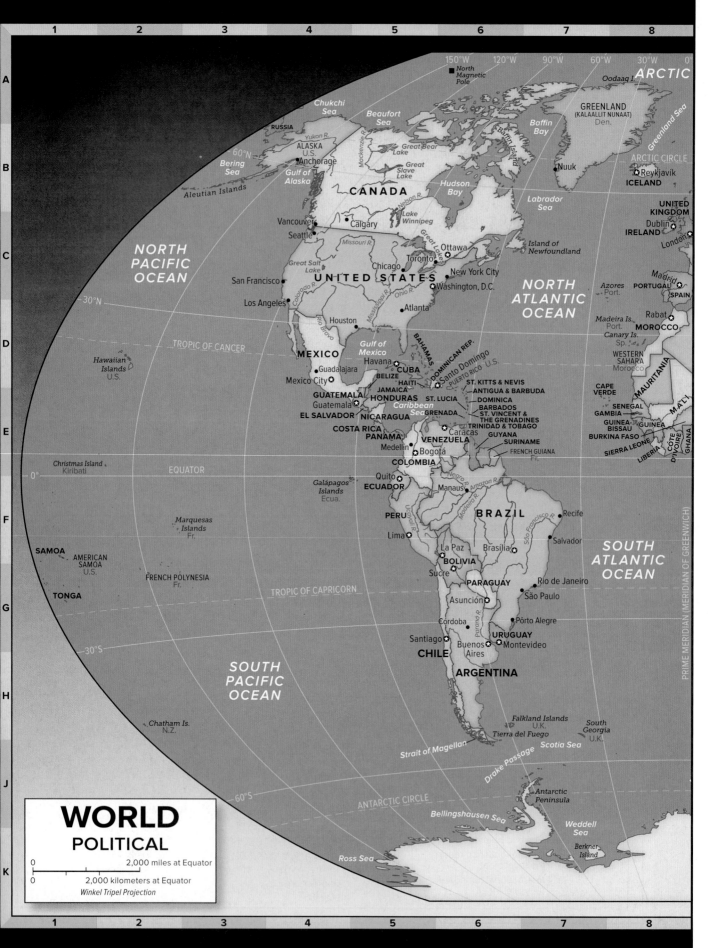

WORLD
POLITICAL

0   2,000 miles at Equator

0   2,000 kilometers at Equator

Winkel Tripel Projection

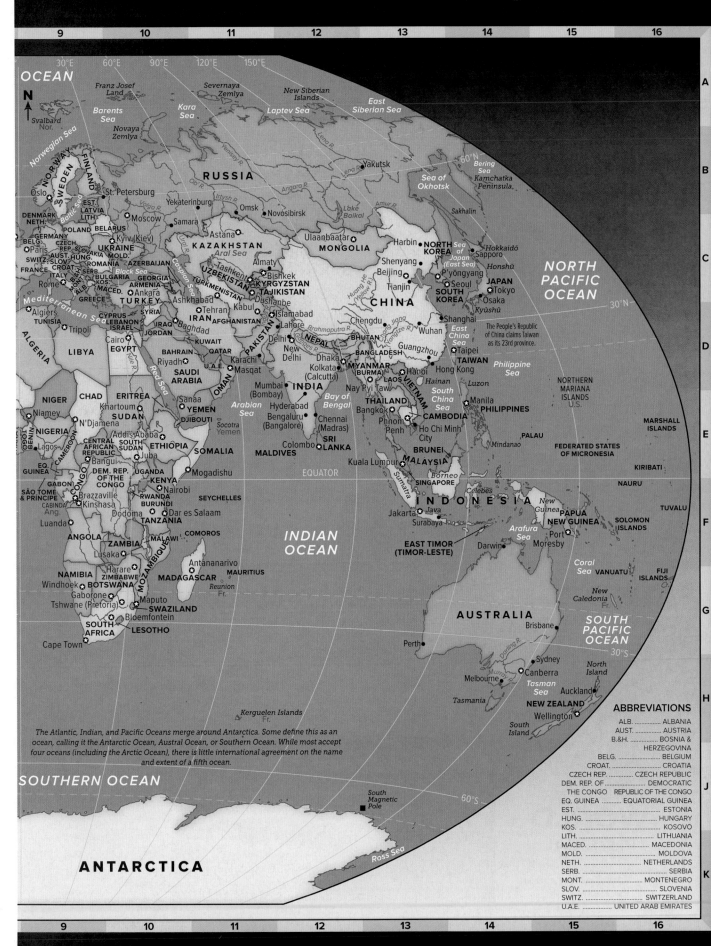

N

OCEAN

30°E 60°E 90°E 120°E 150°E

Franz Josef Land

Severnaya Zemlya

New Siberian Islands

Barents Sea

Novaya Zemlya

Kara Sea

Laptev Sea

East Siberian Sea

Svalbard Nor.

Norwegian Sea

NORWAY

SWEDEN

FINLAND

Oslo

St. Petersburg

Yekaterinburg

Omsk

Novosibirsk

RUSSIA

Lake Baikal

Yakutsk

Lena R.

Amur R.

Sea of Okhotsk

Bering Sea

Kamchatka Peninsula

Sakhalin

Ob' R.

Irtysh R.

Angara R.

Lena R.

60°N

DENMARK
NETH.
BELG.
GERMANY
CZECH REP.
POLAND
SLOVAKIA
AUST. HUNG.
SWITZ. SLOV.
FRANCE CROAT.
SERB.
ITALY MONT.
ALB.
ROMANIA
BULGARIA
MACED.
GREECE

Paris
Rome

EST.
LATVIA
LITH.
BELARUS
UKRAINE
MOLD.

Kyiv (Kiev)

Moscow
Samara

Volga R.

Ural R.

Astana

KAZAKHSTAN
Aral Sea

Almaty

Tashkent
UZBEKISTAN
TURKMENISTAN

Bishkek
KYRGYZSTAN
TAJIKISTAN
Dushanbe

MONGOLIA

Ulaanbaatar

CHINA

Harbin

Shenyang

Beijing

Tianjin

NORTH KOREA

P'yongyang

Seoul
SOUTH KOREA

Sea of Japan (East Sea)

Hokkaidō
Sapporo

Honshū

JAPAN
Tokyo
Osaka

Kyūshū

NORTH PACIFIC OCEAN

30°N

Caspian Sea

Black Sea

TURKEY
CYPRUS
SYRIA
LEBANON
ISRAEL
JORDAN
IRAQ

Ankara

Athens
Algiers
TUNISIA
Tripoli

Mediterranean Sea

GEORGIA
ARMENIA
AZERBAIJAN

Tehran

Baghdad

KUWAIT

Ashkhabad

Kabul
AFGHANISTAN

Islamabad

Lahore

Delhi
New Delhi

Chengdu

Huang He (Yellow R.)

Chang Jiang (Yangtze R.)

Wuhan

Shanghai

Guangzhou

Hong Kong

East China Sea

Taipei
TAIWAN

The People's Republic of China claims Taiwan as its 23rd province.

Philippine Sea

NORTHERN MARIANA ISLANDS U.S.

ALGERIA
LIBYA
EGYPT

Cairo

Nile R.

Red Sea

SAUDI ARABIA

Riyadh

BAHRAIN
QATAR
U.A.E.

Masqat
OMAN

IRAN
PAKISTAN

Karachi

NEPAL
BHUTAN

BANGLADESH
Dhaka

Kolkata (Calcutta)

MYANMAR (BURMA)

Nay Pyi Taw

LAOS
VIETNAM
Hanoi
Hainan

South China Sea

Manila
PHILIPPINES

Luzon

NIGER
CHAD
SUDAN
ERITREA
Khartoum
YEMEN
DJIBOUTI

Sanaa

N'Djamena

Niamey

Brahmaputra R.

Arabian Sea

Mumbai (Bombay)

INDIA

Hyderabad

Bengaluru (Bangalore)

Chennai (Madras)

Bay of Bengal

Socotra Yemen

THAILAND
Bangkok

CAMBODIA
Phnom Penh

Ho Chi Minh City

PALAU

Mindanao

MARSHALL ISLANDS

FEDERATED STATES OF MICRONESIA

NIGERIA
CAMEROON
CENTRAL AFRICAN REPUBLIC
SOUTH SUDAN
ETHIOPIA
SOMALIA

Addis Ababa

BENIN
TOGO
GHANA
Lagos
EQ. GUINEA
GABON
SÃO TOMÉ & PRÍNCIPE
CABINDA Ang.
CONGO

Bangui

Juba

Colombo
SRI LANKA

MALDIVES

BRUNEI

Kuala Lumpur
MALAYSIA

Borneo

KIRIBATI

DEM. REP. OF THE CONGO
UGANDA
KENYA
RWANDA
BURUNDI

Brazzaville

Kinshasa

Nairobi

EQUATOR

SINGAPORE

I N D O N E S I A

New Guinea

PAPUA NEW GUINEA

SOLOMON ISLANDS

NAURU

TUVALU

Luanda
ANGOLA
ZAMBIA

Dodoma
TANZANIA

Dar es Salaam

SEYCHELLES

COMOROS

Jakarta
Java
Surabaya

Celebes

Arafura Sea

Port Moresby

Lusaka

MALAWI
MOZAMBIQUE

Antananarivo
MADAGASCAR

MAURITIUS

Reunion Fr.

INDIAN OCEAN

EAST TIMOR (TIMOR-LESTE)

Darwin

Coral Sea

VANUATU

FIJI ISLANDS

NAMIBIA
ZIMBABWE
BOTSWANA
Harare

Windhoek

Gaborone

New Caledonia Fr.

Tshwane (Pretoria)

Maputo

SWAZILAND

AUSTRALIA

Brisbane

SOUTH PACIFIC OCEAN

30°S

Bloemfontein
SOUTH AFRICA

LESOTHO

Cape Town

Perth

Darling R.

Murray R.

Sydney

Canberra

Melbourne

Tasman Sea

North Island

Auckland

Tasmania

NEW ZEALAND

Wellington

South Island

Kerguelen Islands Fr.

The Atlantic, Indian, and Pacific Oceans merge around Antarctica. Some define this as an ocean, calling it the Antarctic Ocean, Austral Ocean, or Southern Ocean. While most accept four oceans (including the Arctic Ocean), there is little international agreement on the name and extent of a fifth ocean.

SOUTHERN OCEAN

South Magnetic Pole

60°S

ANTARCTICA

Ross Sea

ABBREVIATIONS

ALB.	ALBANIA
AUST.	AUSTRIA
B.&H.	BOSNIA & HERZEGOVINA
BELG.	BELGIUM
CROAT.	CROATIA
CZECH REP.	CZECH REPUBLIC
DEM. REP. OF THE CONGO	DEMOCRATIC REPUBLIC OF THE CONGO
EQ. GUINEA	EQUATORIAL GUINEA
EST.	ESTONIA
HUNG.	HUNGARY
KOS.	KOSOVO
LITH.	LITHUANIA
MACED.	MACEDONIA
MOLD.	MOLDOVA
NETH.	NETHERLANDS
SERB.	SERBIA
MONT.	MONTENEGRO
SLOV.	SLOVENIA
SWITZ.	SWITZERLAND
U.A.E.	UNITED ARAB EMIRATES

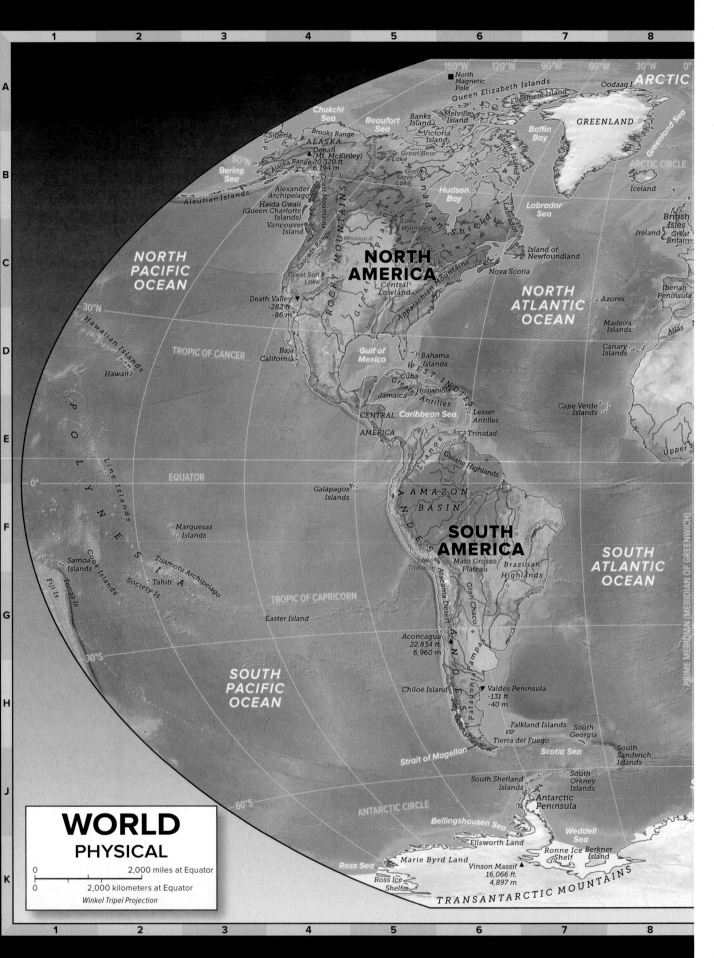

WORLD
PHYSICAL

0 — 2,000 miles at Equator
0 — 2,000 kilometers at Equator
Winkel Tripel Projection

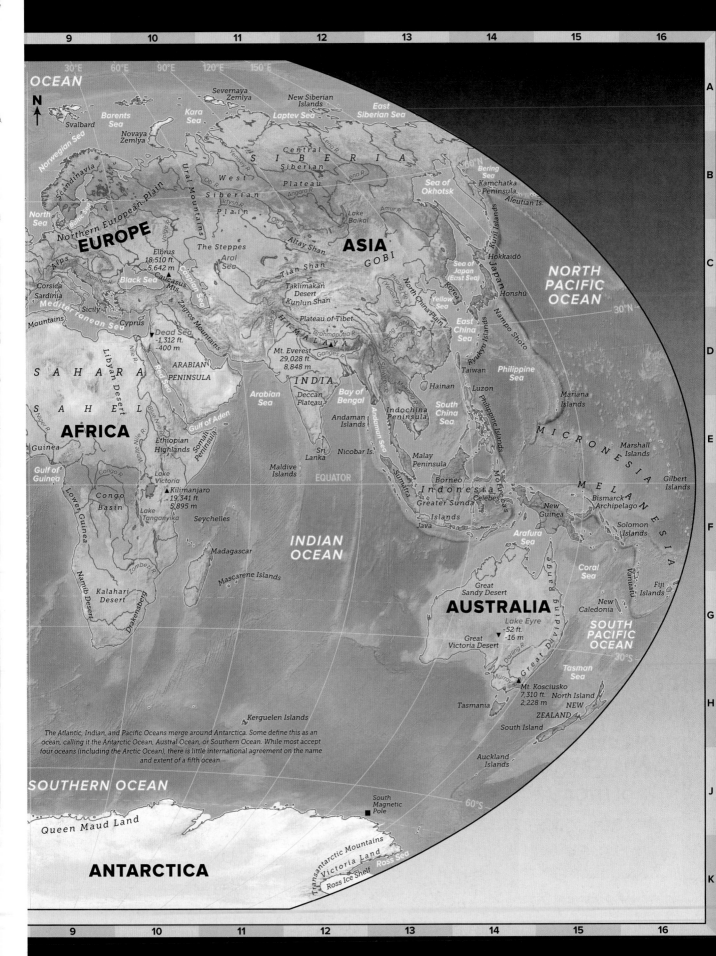

The Atlantic, Indian, and Pacific Oceans merge around Antarctica. Some define this as an ocean, calling it the Antarctic Ocean, Austral Ocean, or Southern Ocean. While most accept four oceans (including the Arctic Ocean), there is little international agreement on the name and extent of a fifth ocean.

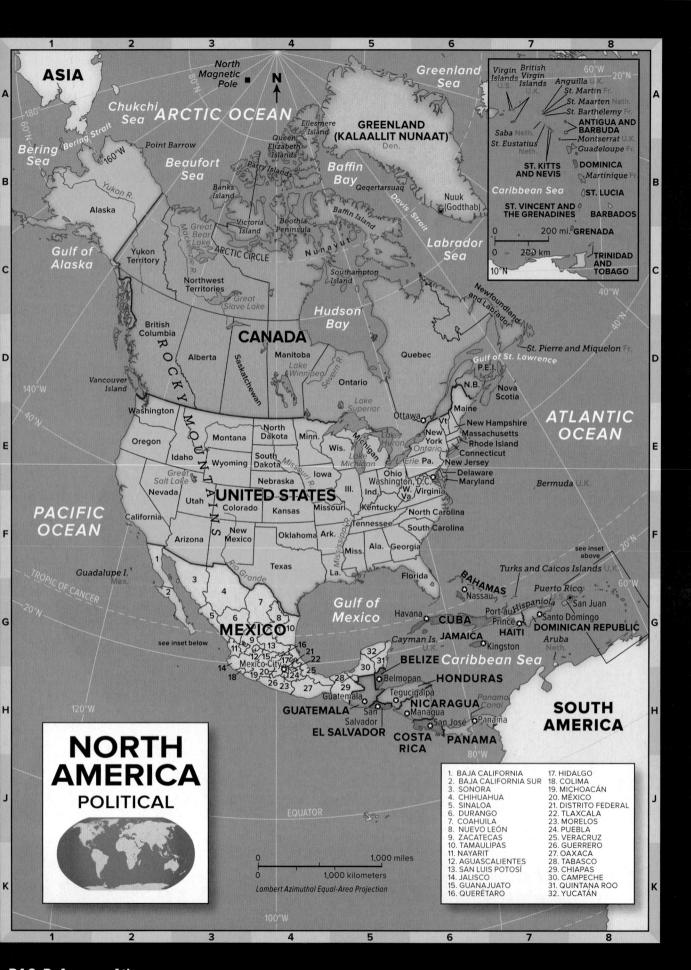

NORTH AMERICA POLITICAL

1. BAJA CALIFORNIA	17. HIDALGO
2. BAJA CALIFORNIA SUR	18. COLIMA
3. SONORA	19. MICHOACÁN
4. CHIHUAHUA	20. MÉXICO
5. SINALOA	21. DISTRITO FEDERAL
6. DURANGO	22. TLAXCALA
7. COAHUILA	23. MORELOS
8. NUEVO LEÓN	24. PUEBLA
9. ZACATECAS	25. VERACRUZ
10. TAMAULIPAS	26. GUERRERO
11. NAYARIT	27. OAXACA
12. AGUASCALIENTES	28. TABASCO
13. SAN LUIS POTOSÍ	29. CHIAPAS
14. JALISCO	30. CAMPECHE
15. GUANAJUATO	31. QUINTANA ROO
16. QUERÉTARO	32. YUCATÁN

0   1,000 miles
0   1,000 kilometers
Lambert Azimuthal Equal-Area Projection

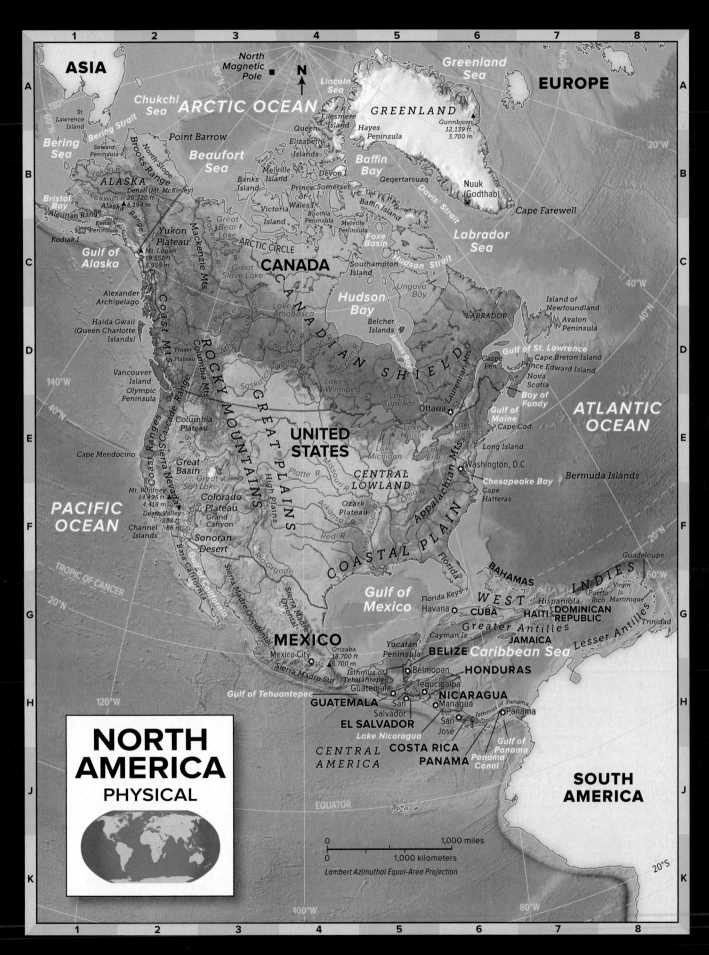

NORTH AMERICA PHYSICAL

1 2 3 4 5 6 7 8

ASIA

North Magnetic Pole ■

N

Lincoln Sea

Greenland Sea

EUROPE

Chukchi Sea

ARCTIC OCEAN

GREENLAND

Gunnbjørn 12,139 ft. 3,700 m

St. Lawrence Island

Bering Strait

Point Barrow

North Slope

Brooks Range

Ellesmere Island

Queen Elizabeth Islands

Hayes Peninsula

Bering Sea

Seward Peninsula

ALASKA

Denali (Mt. McKinley) 20,320 ft. Alaska 6,194 m Range

Yukon R.

Melville Island

Banks Island

Devon I.

Somerset I.

Prince of Wales I.

Baffin Bay

Qeqertarsuaq

Nuuk (Godthåb)

Cape Farewell

Bristol Bay

Aleutian Range

Kuskokwim R.

Victoria Island

Boothia Peninsula

Baffin Island

Davis Strait

Kenai Peninsula

Mackenzie Mts.

Great Bear Lake

Melville Peninsula

Labrador Sea

Kodiak I.

Gulf of Alaska

Mt. Logan 19,551 ft. 5,959 m

ARCTIC CIRCLE

Great Slave Lake

CANADA

Foxe Basin

Southampton Island

Hudson Strait

Island of Newfoundland

Alexander Archipelago

Coast Mts.

Fraser Plateau

Peace

Slave R.

Lake Athabasca

Athabasca R.

CANADIAN

Hudson Bay

Belcher Islands

Ungava Bay

James Bay

LABRADOR

Avalon Peninsula

Haida Gwaii (Queen Charlotte Islands)

Columbia Mts.

Churchill R.

Nelson R.

SHIELD

Gulf of St. Lawrence

Cape Breton Island

Prince Edward Island

Vancouver Island

Olympic Peninsula

Columbia Plateau

ROCKY MOUNTAINS

GREAT PLAINS

Saskatchewan R.

Severn R.

Gaspé Pen.

Laurentian Mts.

Nova Scotia

Bay of Fundy

ATLANTIC OCEAN

Cape Mendocino

Cascade Range

Columbia R.

Snake R.

Lake Winnipeg

Lake Superior

Ottawa

St. Lawrence R.

Gulf of Maine

Coast Ranges

Sierra Nevada

Great Basin

Great Salt Lake

UNITED STATES

Platte R.

Lake Michigan

Lake Huron

Lake Ontario

Lake Erie

Cape Cod

Long Island

Bermuda Islands

Mt. Whitney 14,495 ft. 4,418 m

Death Valley -282 ft. -86 m

Colorado Plateau

Grand Canyon

High Plains

Missouri R.

CENTRAL LOWLAND

Ohio R.

Appalachian Mts.

Washington, D.C.

Chesapeake Bay

Cape Hatteras

PACIFIC OCEAN

Channel Islands

Sonoran Desert

Baja California

Gulf of California

Rio Grande

Sierra Madre Oriental

Ozark Plateau

Arkansas R.

Red R.

Mississippi R.

COASTAL PLAIN

Florida

TROPIC OF CANCER

20°N

Sierra Madre Occidental

Gulf of Mexico

Florida Keys

Havana

BAHAMAS

WEST INDIES

Guadeloupe

MEXICO

Mexico City

Orizaba 18,700 ft. 5,700 m

Yucatán Peninsula

Cayman Is.

CUBA

HAITI

Greater Antilles

Hispaniola

DOMINICAN REPUBLIC

Puerto Rico

Virgin Is.

Martinique

Lesser Antilles

Sierra Madre Sur

Isthmus of Tehuantepec

BELIZE

JAMAICA

Caribbean Sea

Trinidad

Gulf of Tehuantepec

Guatemala

Belmopan

HONDURAS

Tegucigalpa

NICARAGUA

GUATEMALA

San Salvador

EL SALVADOR

San José

Managua

Lake Nicaragua

COSTA RICA

Isthmus of Panama

Panama

Gulf of Panama

Panama Canal

CENTRAL AMERICA

PANAMA

SOUTH AMERICA

EQUATOR

0 1,000 miles
0 1,000 kilometers
Lambert Azimuthal Equal-Area Projection

20°S

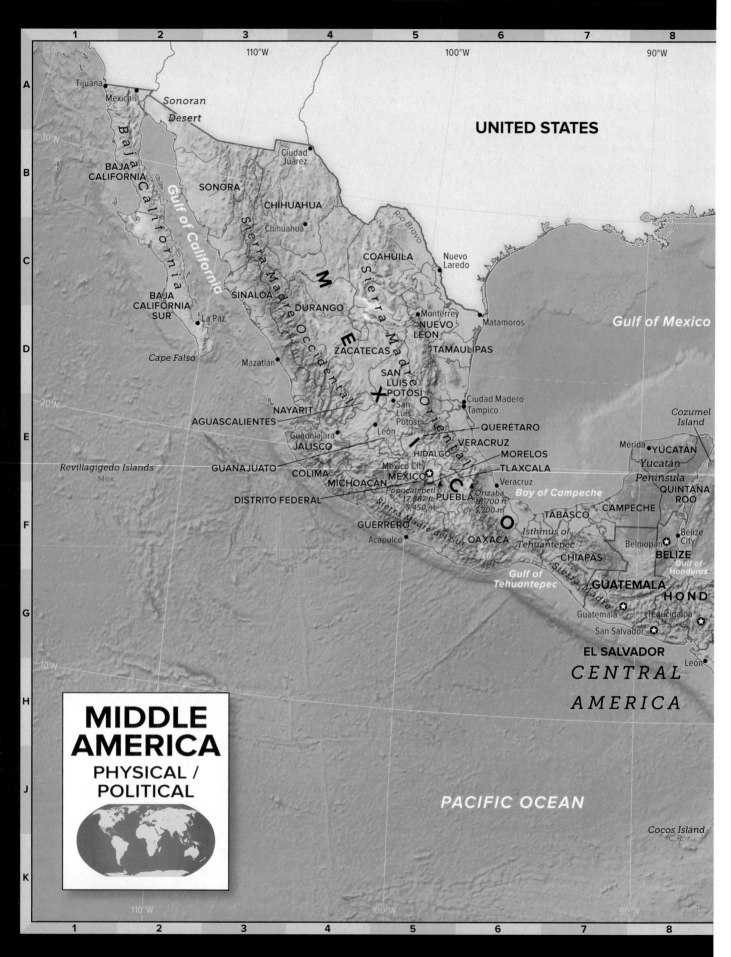

UNITED STATES

1   2   3   4   5   6   7   8

110°W   100°W   90°W

Tijuana

Mexicali

Sonoran Desert

30°N

BAJA CALIFORNIA

SONORA

Ciudad Juárez

CHIHUAHUA

Gulf of California

Chihuahua

COAHUILA

Nuevo Laredo

Sierra Madre Occidental

Baja California

BAJA CALIFORNIA SUR

SINALOA

DURANGO

La Paz

Sierra Madre Oriental

Monterrey

NUEVO LEÓN

Matamoros

Gulf of Mexico

Cape Falso

Mazatlán

ZACATECAS

TAMAULIPAS

20°N

SAN LUIS POTOSÍ

San Luis Potosí

Ciudad Madero
Tampico

Cozumel Island

NAYARIT

AGUASCALIENTES

QUERÉTARO

Mérida •YUCATÁN

Revillagigedo Islands
Mex.

Guadalajara

León

VERACRUZ

Yucatán Peninsula

JALISCO

HIDALGO

MORELOS

QUINTANA ROO

GUANAJUATO

COLIMA

Mexico City

TLAXCALA

Bay of Campeche

MÉXICO

CAMPECHE

MICHOACAN

Popocatepetl
*17,887 ft.
5,450 m*

PUEBLA

Orizaba
*18,700 ft.
5,700 m*

Veracruz

TABASCO

Belize City

DISTRITO FEDERAL

Sierra Madre del Sur

Belmopan

GUERRERO

OAXACA

Isthmus of Tehuantepec

BELIZE

Acapulco

CHIAPAS

Gulf of Honduras

Gulf of Tehuantepec

Sierra Madre

GUATEMALA

HOND

10°N

Guatemala

Tegucigalpa

San Salvador

EL SALVADOR

León

CENTRAL

AMERICA

MIDDLE AMERICA

PHYSICAL / POLITICAL

PACIFIC OCEAN

Cocos Island
C.R.

110°W   100°W   90°W

1   2   3   4   5   6   7   8

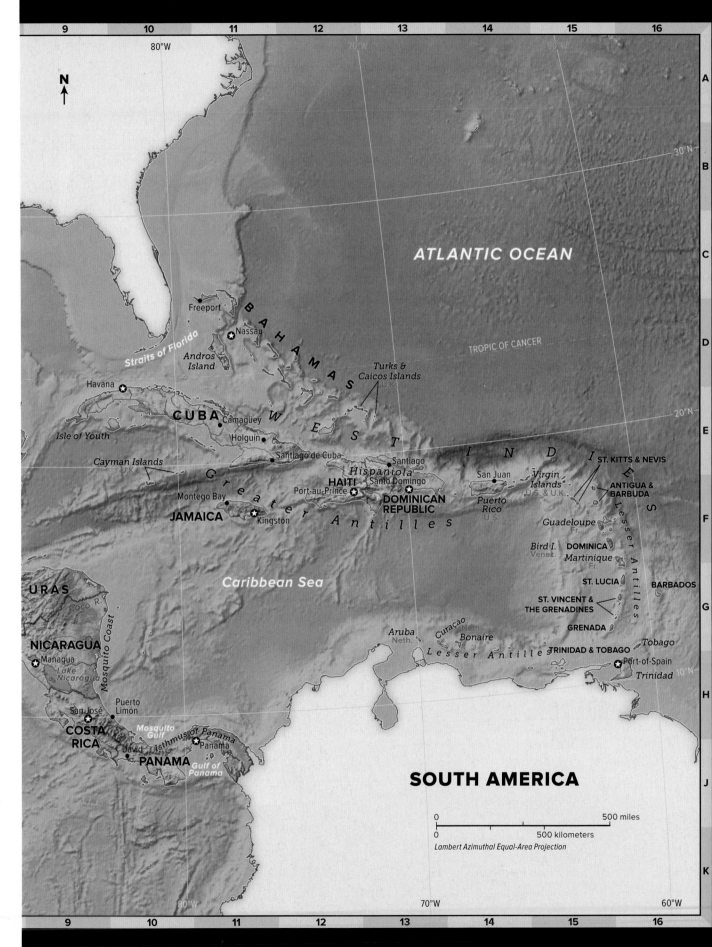

N

80°W

30°N

ATLANTIC OCEAN

TROPIC OF CANCER

20°N

70°W

80°W

Freeport

B A H A M A S

Nassau

Andros Island

Turks & Caicos Islands
U.K.

Straits of Florida

Havana

CUBA Camagüey

W   E   S   T

Isle of Youth

Holguín

Santiago de Cuba

Santiago

San Juan

Virgin Islands
U.S. & U.K.

ST. KITTS & NEVIS

I   N   D   I   E   S

ANTIGUA & BARBUDA

Cayman Islands
U.K.

G r e a t e r   A n t i l l e s

Hispaniola

HAITI

Port-au-Prince

Santo Domingo

DOMINICAN REPUBLIC

Puerto Rico
U.S.

Lesser Antilles

Montego Bay

JAMAICA

Kingston

Guadeloupe
Fr.

Bird I.
Venez.

DOMINICA

Martinique
Fr.

ST. LUCIA

BARBADOS

Caribbean Sea

ST. VINCENT & THE GRENADINES

GRENADA

URAS

Coco R.

Mosquito Coast

Aruba
Neth.

Curaçao
Neth.

Bonaire

Lesser Antilles

TRINIDAD & TOBAGO

Tobago

NICARAGUA

Managua

Lake Nicaragua

Port-of-Spain

Trinidad

10°N

San José

Puerto Limón

COSTA RICA

Mosquito Gulf

Isthmus of Panama

David

Panama

PANAMA

Gulf of Panama

SOUTH AMERICA

0   500 miles

0   500 kilometers

Lambert Azimuthal Equal-Area Projection

70°W   60°W

SOUTH AMERICA POLITICAL

Caribbean Sea

N

0   1,000 miles

0   1,000 kilometers
Lambert Azimuthal Equal-Area Projection

Caracas

VENEZUELA

GUYANA

Lake
Maracaibo

Orinoco R.

Georgetown

SURINAME

Paramaribo

Bogotá

Angel Falls
Total drop
3,212 ft. 979 m

GUIANA   HIGHLANDS

Cayenne

FRENCH GUIANA

Malpelo I.

COLOMBIA

Boundary claimed
by Suriname

Marajó
Island

Quito

Río Negro

EQUATOR

ECUADOR

A M A Z O N

Amazon R.

Marañón R.

Amazon R.

B A S I N

Xingu R.

Tapajós R.

Araguaia R.

São Francisco R.

PERU

S e l v a s

Purus R.

Madeira R.

BRAZIL

Tocantins R.

Lima

A

Machu
Picchu

*MATO GROSSO
PLATEAU*

B R A Z I L I A N

La Paz

Lake
Titicaca

BOLIVIA

Brasília

N

Altiplano

Sucre

H I G H L A N D S

Salar
de Uyuni

G
R
A
N

Paraguay R.

Paraná R.

PARAGUAY

D

C
H
A
C
O

Iguazú
Falls

TROPIC OF CAPRICORN

San Ambrosio I.

E

Asunción

**ATLANTIC
OCEAN**

San Félix I.

S

P
A
M
P
A
S

Paraná R.

Juan Fernández Is.

CHILE

Acóncagua
22,834 ft.
6,960 m

Santiago

Uruguay R.

Buenos Aires

URUGUAY

Montevideo

ARGENTINA

Río de la Plata

**SOUTH
AMERICA**
PHYSICAL

Colorado R.

Negro R.

Chiloé Island

Valdés Peninsula
-131 ft.
-40 m

P
A
T
A
G
O
N
I
A

Gulf of
San Jorge

**PACIFIC
OCEAN**

Taitao
Peninsula

*Falkland Islands
(Islas Malvinas)*

Wellington I.

Laguna
del Carbón
-344 ft.
-105 m

Stanley

Tierra del Fuego

Strait of
Magellan

Cape Horn

South Georgia Island

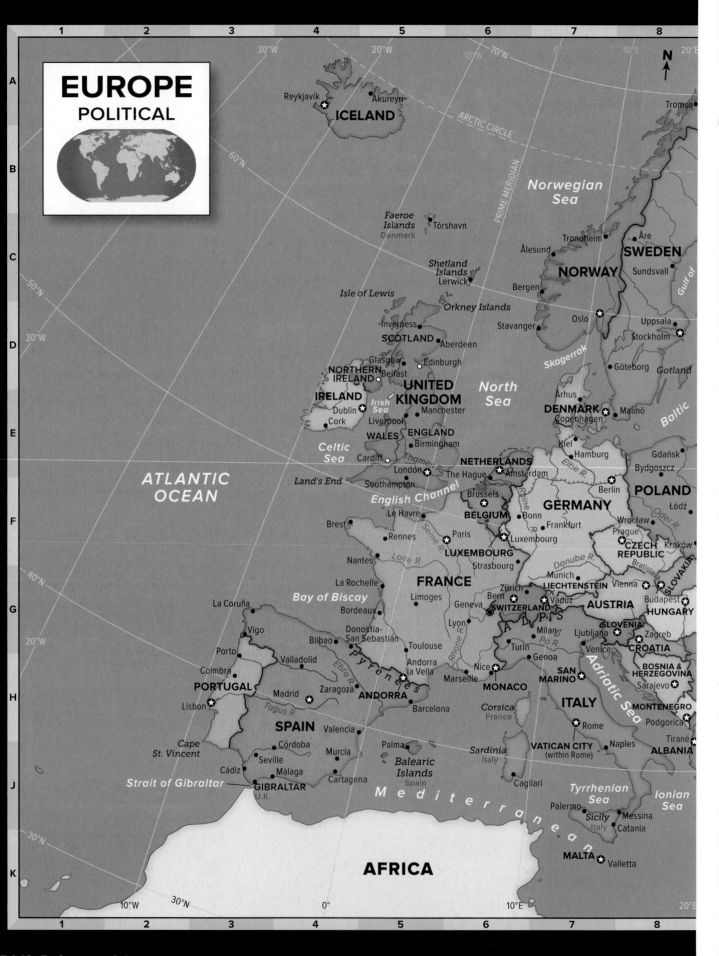

EUROPE
POLITICAL

N

Reykjavík · **Akureyri**
ICELAND
ARCTIC CIRCLE

PRIME MERIDIAN

Faeroe Islands Denmark · **Tórshavn**

Norwegian Sea

Tromsø

Trondheim · **Åre**
Ålesund
SWEDEN
NORWAY **Sundsvall**
Bergen
Oslo · **Uppsala**
Stavanger **Stockholm**

Shetland Islands **Lerwick**

Isle of Lewis
Orkney Islands
Inverness
SCOTLAND **Aberdeen**
Glasgow · **Edinburgh**
NORTHERN IRELAND **Belfast**
IRELAND *Irish Sea*
Dublin **UNITED KINGDOM**
Cork **Liverpool** · **Manchester**
WALES **ENGLAND**
Celtic Sea **Cardiff** · **Birmingham**

Göteborg *Gotland*
Århus
Skagerrak
DENMARK · **Malmö**
Copenhagen
Kiel
Hamburg **Gdańsk**
Bydgoszcz
North Sea

NETHERLANDS
Thames R. **The Hague** · **Amsterdam** *Elbe R.* **Berlin** **POLAND**
London **Brussels** **Łódź**
Southampton **BELGIUM** **Bonn** *Rhine R.* **GERMANY** **Wrocław** *Oder R.*
Land's End *English Channel* **Frankfurt** **Prague**
Le Havre **LUXEMBOURG** **CZECH** **Kraków**
Brest **Paris** **Luxembourg** **REPUBLIC**
ATLANTIC OCEAN **Rennes** *Seine R.* **Strasbourg** *Danube R.* **Bratislava**
Nantes *Loire R.* **Munich** **Vienna** **SLOVAKIA**
FRANCE **LIECHTENSTEIN** **Budapest**
La Rochelle **Zürich** **Vaduz** **AUSTRIA**
Bay of Biscay **Limoges** **Bern** **HUNGARY**
La Coruña **Bordeaux** **Geneva** **SWITZERLAND** **Milan** **SLOVENIA** **Zagreb**
Vigo **Lyon** **Turin** **Ljubljana** **CROATIA**
Porto **Bilbao** **Donostia-San Sebastián** *Po R.* **Venice**
Coimbra **Valladolid** **Andorra la Vella** **Genoa** **BOSNIA & HERZEGOVINA**
PORTUGAL **Zaragoza** **ANDORRA** **Nice** **SAN MARINO** **Sarajevo**
Lisbon **Madrid** **Marseille** **MONACO** **MONTENEGRO**
Barcelona **ITALY** **Podgorica**
Cape St. Vincent **SPAIN** **Valencia** *Corsica* France **Rome** **Tiranë**
Córdoba **Palma** **VATICAN CITY** (within Rome) **Naples** **ALBANIA**
Cádiz **Seville** **Murcia** *Sardinia* Italy
Strait of Gibraltar **Málaga** **Cartagena** *Balearic Islands* Spain
GIBRALTAR U.K. *Mediterranean* **Cagliari** *Tyrrhenian Sea* **Palermo** *Ionian Sea*
Pyrenees *Sicily* Italy **Messina**
Ebro R. **Catania**
Tagus R.
Rhône R.
ALPS
Adriatic Sea

AFRICA

MALTA **Valletta**

10°W 30°N 0° 10°E 20°E

30°W 20°W 10°W 0° 10°E 20°E
70°N
60°N
50°N
40°N
30°N
20°W

Gulf of
Baltic

A commonly accepted division between Asia and Europe—here marked by a gray line—is formed by the Ural Mountains, Ural River, Caspian Sea, Caucasus Mountains, and the Black Sea with its outlets, the Bosporus and the Dardanelles.

Europe/Asia boundary

ASIA

RUSSIA

FINLAND

ESTONIA

LATVIA

LITHUANIA

BELARUS

UKRAINE

MOLDOVA

ROMANIA

SERBIA

KOSOVO

BULGARIA

MACEDONIA

GREECE

KAZAKHSTAN

GEORGIA

AZERBAIJAN

TURKEY

CYPRUS

ASIA

Barents Sea
Kola Peninsula
White Sea
L A P L A N D
Murmansk
Ivalo · Kirovsk
Kiruna
Kemi
Umba
Luleå · Oulu
Umeå
Vaasa
Kuopio
Pori · Tampere
Turku
Helsinki
Tallinn
Riga
Daugavpils
Vilnius
Kaunas
Kaliningrad
Warsaw
Minsk
Homyel'
Vitsyebsk
Smolensk
Novgorod
St. Petersburg
Lake Ladoga
Lake Onega
Northern Dvina R.
Arkhangel'sk
Severodvinsk
Kem'
Tobseda
Pechora
Syktyvkar
U R A L   M O U N T A I N S
Perm'
Kirov
Kazan'
Yaroslavl'
Nizhniy Novgorod
Tver'
Moscow
Ryazan'
Penza
Bryansk
Kursk
Chernihiv
Sumy
Kyiv (Kiev)
L'viv
Vinnytsya
Poltava
Kharkiv
Donets'k
Dnipropetrovs'k
Chişinău
Odessa
Kerch
Crimea
Simferopol'
Sevastopol'
Yalta
Belgrade
Bucharest
Priština
Sofia
Skopje
Thessaloniki
Athens
Peloponnese
Iraklíon
Crete
Greece
Rhodes
Nicosia
Istanbul
Sea of Marmara
Dardanelles
Aegean Sea
Bosporus
Balkan Mts.
Varna
Constanța
Black Sea
Sea of Azov
Rostov
Stavropol'
Grozny
Caucasus   Mountains
Baku
Caspian Sea
Astrakhan
Volgograd
Saratov
Samara
Orenburg
Oral
Ufa
Ural R.
Volga R.
Don R.
Dnieper R.
Dniester R.
Carpathian Mts.
Vistula R.
Bothnia
Sea
 Vaasa

9 10 11 12 13 14 15 16

30°E 40°E 50°E 60°E 70°E 80°E 60°N

50°N 70°E 40°N 60°E 30°N 50°E 40°E

0 ___ 400 miles
0 ___ 400 kilometers
Lambert Azimuthal Equal-Area Projection

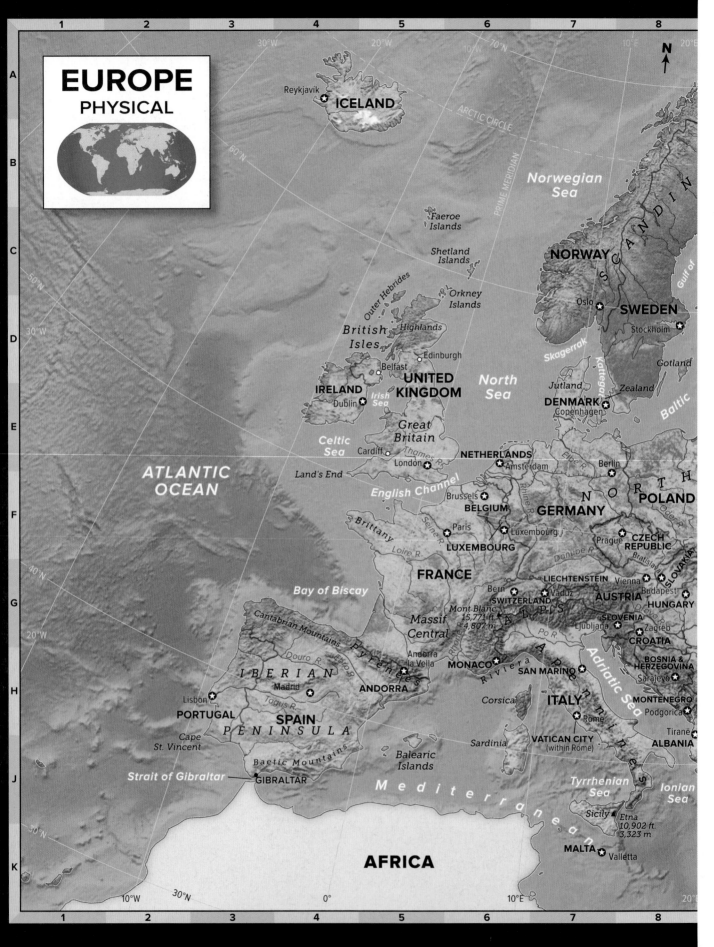

EUROPE
PHYSICAL

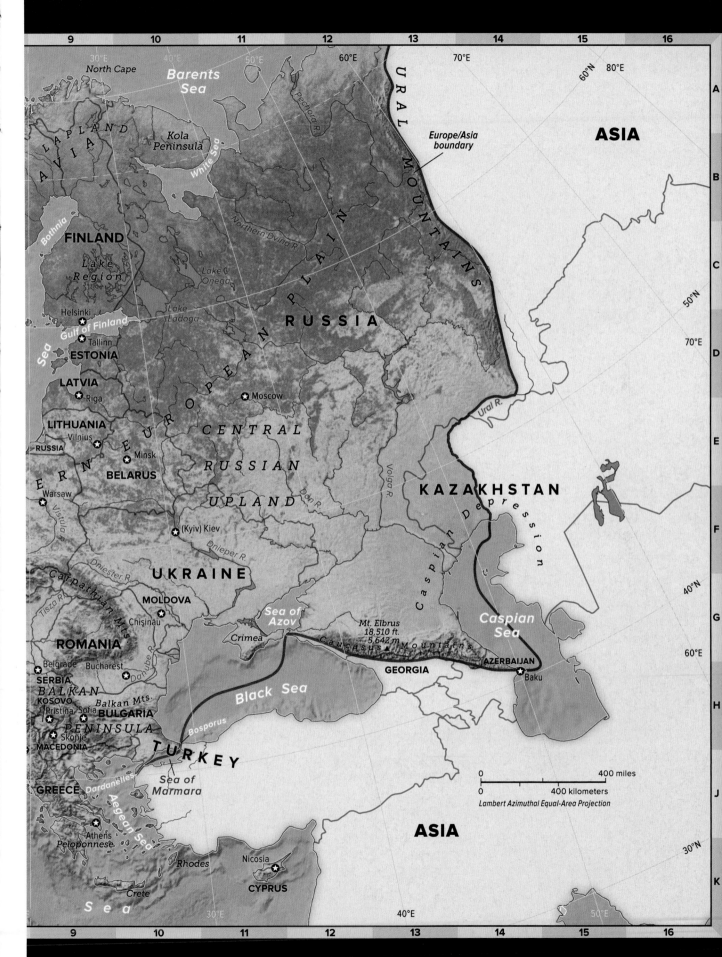

North Cape

Barents Sea

ASIA

LAPLAND

A V I A

Kola Peninsula

White Sea

Pechora R.

U R A L

Europe/Asia boundary

FINLAND

Bothnia

Lake Region

Northern Dvina R.

Lake Onega

M O U N T A I N S

Helsinki

Lake Ladoga

RUSSIA

Gulf of Finland

Tallinn

ESTONIA

E U R O P E A N   P L A I N

Sea

LATVIA

Riga

Moscow

Ural R.

LITHUANIA

Vilnius

C E N T R A L

RUSSIA

Minsk

R U S S I A N

KAZAKHSTAN

BELARUS

Warsaw

U P L A N D

Don R.

Volga R.

Caspian Depression

Vistula R.

(Kyiv) Kiev

Dnieper R.

Dniester R.

UKRAINE

Carpathian Mts.

Tisza R.

MOLDOVA

Chişinău

Sea of Azov

Mt. Elbrus 18,510 ft. 5,642 m

Caspian Sea

Crimea

ROMANIA

Danube R.

C a u c a s u s ▲ M o u n t a i n s

AZERBAIJAN

Belgrade

Bucharest

GEORGIA

Baku

SERBIA

BALKAN

Black Sea

KOSOVO

Balkan Mts.

Pristina

Sofia

BULGARIA

Bosporus

Skopje

PENINSULA

0   400 miles

MACEDONIA

T U R K E Y

0   400 kilometers

Lambert Azimuthal Equal-Area Projection

GREECE

Dardanelles

Sea of Marmara

Aegean Sea

ASIA

Athens

Peloponnese

Rhodes

Nicosia

Sea

Crete

CYPRUS

30°E   40°E   50°E   60°E

60°N   80°E

50°N

70°E

40°N

60°E

30°N

9   10   11   12   13   14   15   16

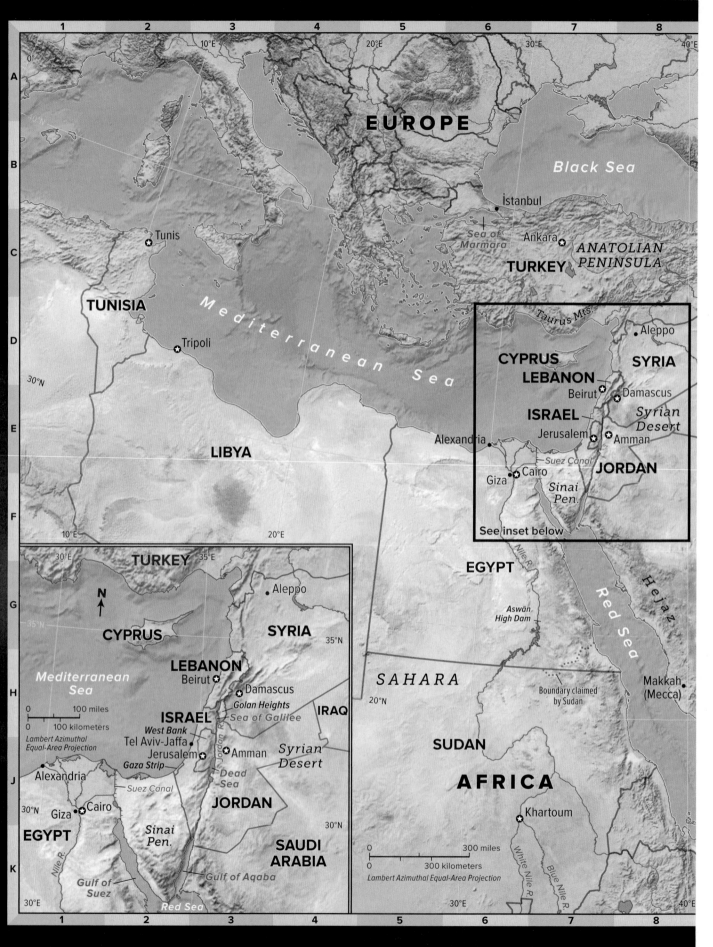

1   **2**   **3**   **4**   **5**   **6**   **7**   **8**

0°

10°E

20°E

30°E

40°E

A

EUROPE

Black Sea

B

İstanbul

C

Tunis

Sea of Marmara

Ankara

ANATOLIAN PENINSULA

TURKEY

TUNISIA

Taurus Mts.

Aleppo

D

Tripoli

M e d i t e r r a n e a n   S e a

CYPRUS

SYRIA

LEBANON

Beirut

Damascus

30°N

ISRAEL

Syrian Desert

E

Alexandria

Jerusalem

Amman

LIBYA

Suez Canal

JORDAN

Giza Cairo

Sinai Pen.

F

10°E

20°E

See inset below

30°E

35°E

EGYPT

TURKEY

Nile R.

Hejaz

G

N

Aleppo

Aswān High Dam

35°N

CYPRUS

SYRIA

35°N

Red Sea

LEBANON

Beirut

Damascus

Makkah (Mecca)

H

Mediterranean Sea

Golan Heights

Sea of Galilee

IRAQ

S A H A R A

Boundary claimed by Sudan

0   100 miles

ISRAEL

20°N

0   100 kilometers

West Bank

Lambert Azimuthal Equal-Area Projection

Tel Aviv-Jaffa

Jordan R.

Syrian Desert

Jerusalem

Amman

SUDAN

J

Alexandria

Gaza Strip

Dead Sea

A F R I C A

30°N

Suez Canal

JORDAN

30°N

Giza Cairo

Khartoum

EGYPT

Sinai Pen.

SAUDI ARABIA

0   300 miles

K

Nile R.

Gulf of Suez

Gulf of Aqaba

0   300 kilometers

White Nile R.

Blue Nile R.

Red Sea

Lambert Azimuthal Equal-Area Projection

30°E

30°E

40°E

1   **2**   **3**   **4**   **5**   **6**   **7**   **8**

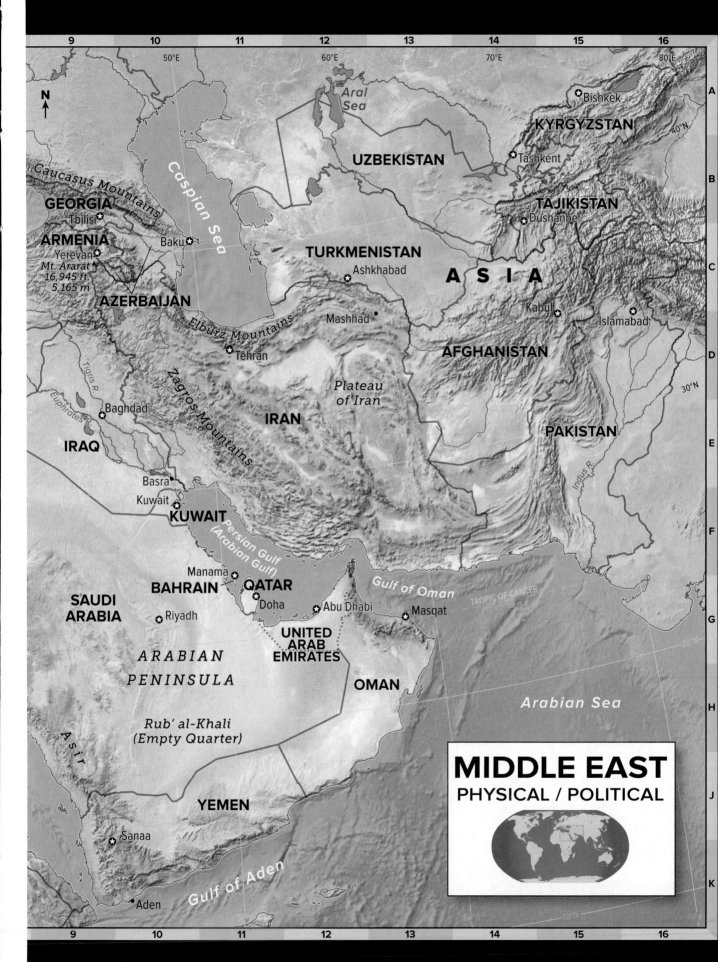

N

50°E   60°E   70°E   80°E

Aral Sea

☆ Bishkek

KYRGYZSTAN

40°N

Caucasus Mountains

UZBEKISTAN

Caspian Sea

☆ Tashkent

GEORGIA
Tbilisi ☆

ARMENIA
Yerevan ☆
Mt. Ararat
16,945 ft.
5,165 m

Baku ☆

TAJIKISTAN
☆ Dushanbe

AZERBAIJAN

TURKMENISTAN

A S I A

Ashkhabad ☆

Elburz Mountains

Mashhad •

Kabul ☆

Islamabad ☆

● Tehran

AFGHANISTAN

Plateau of Iran

30°N

Tigris R.

Zagros Mountains

Baghdad •

IRAN

PAKISTAN

Euphrates

IRAQ

Indus R.

Basra •

Kuwait ☆

KUWAIT

Persian Gulf (Arabian Gulf)

Gulf of Oman

TROPIC OF CANCER

Manama ☆

BAHRAIN   **QATAR**

SAUDI ARABIA

Doha ☆

Abu Dhabi •   ☆ Masqat

● Riyadh

UNITED ARAB EMIRATES

20°N

ARABIAN

OMAN

PENINSULA

Arabian Sea

Rub' al-Khali (Empty Quarter)

Asir

YEMEN

☆ Sanaa

MIDDLE EAST
PHYSICAL / POLITICAL

• Aden

Gulf of Aden

10°N

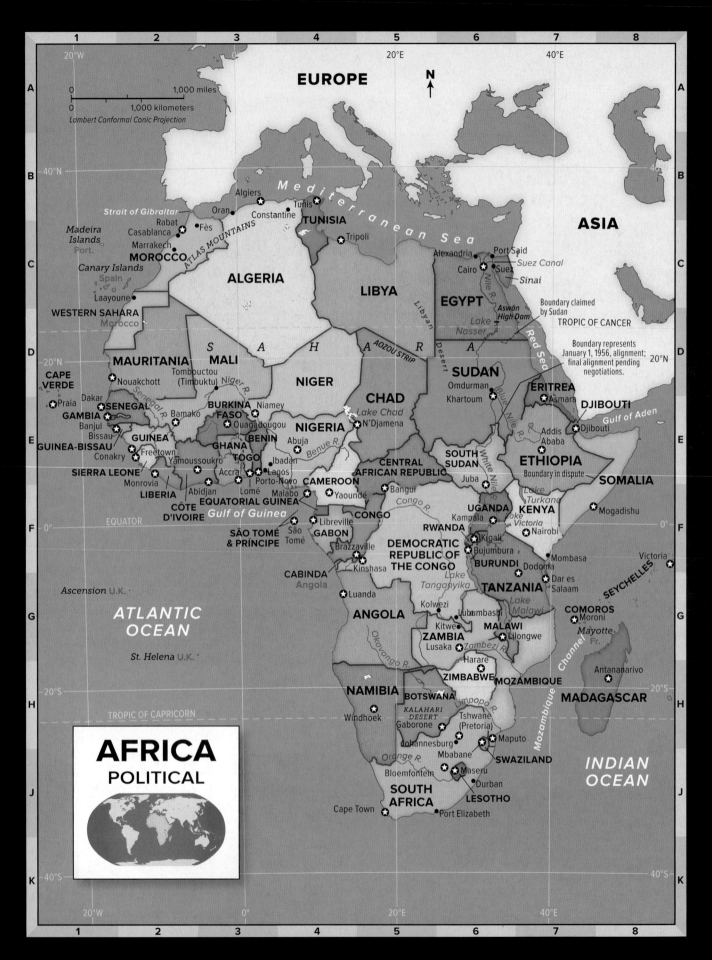

AFRICA
POLITICAL

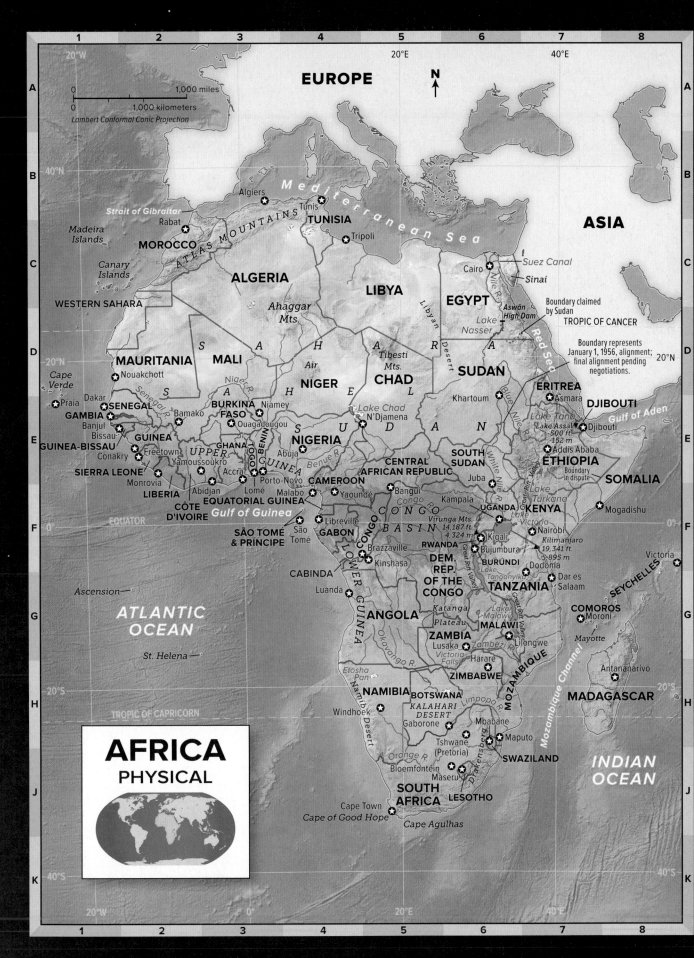

AFRICA
PHYSICAL

EUROPE

N

20°W · 20°E · 40°E

0 1,000 miles
0 1,000 kilometers
Lambert Conformal Conic Projection

ASIA

Mediterranean Sea

Algiers
Strait of Gibraltar
Rabat
Tunis
TUNISIA
Tripoli

Madeira Islands

MOROCCO

Canary Islands

ALGERIA

LIBYA

Cairo
Suez Canal
Sinai

EGYPT

Boundary claimed by Sudan
TROPIC OF CANCER

WESTERN SAHARA

Ahaggar Mts.

Tibesti Mts.

Aswān High Dam
Lake Nasser

Boundary represents January 1, 1956, alignment; final alignment pending negotiations.
20°N

20°N

MAURITANIA
Nouakchott
MALI
NIGER
CHAD

Libyan Desert

SUDAN

Red Sea

ERITREA
Asmara

DJIBOUTI

Cape Verde
Dakar
Praia
SENEGAL
GAMBIA
Banjul
Bissau
GUINEA-BISSAU
Conakry
GUINEA
Freetown
SIERRA LEONE
Monrovia
LIBERIA

Senegal R.
Bamako
Niger R.
Niamey
BURKINA FASO
Ouagadougou
Yamoussoukro
GHANA
Accra
Abidjan
CÔTE D'IVOIRE

Air

S   A   H   A   R   A
S   A   H   E   L

Lake Chad
N'Djamena

Khartoum

Lake Tana
Lake Assal 500 ft. -152 m
Addis Ababa
Djibouti
Gulf of Aden

NIGERIA
Abuja
Benue R.

CENTRAL AFRICAN REPUBLIC
SOUTH SUDAN
Juba

ETHIOPIA

Blue Nile
White Nile
Nile R.

Boundary in dispute
SOMALIA

EQUATOR
0°

Porto-Novo
BENIN
TOGO
Lomé
Malabo
CAMEROON
Yaoundé
EQUATORIAL GUINEA
Gulf of Guinea
SÃO TOMÉ & PRÍNCIPE
São Tomé
Libreville
GABON

UPPER GUINEA
LOWER GUINEA

Bangui
Congo R.
CONGO BASIN

Virunga Mts. 14,187 ft. 4,324 m

Kampala
UGANDA
Kigali
RWANDA
Bujumbura
BURUNDI
Lake Victoria

Nairobi
KENYA
Mogadishu

Kilimanjaro 19,341 ft. 5,895 m

Lake Turkana
Great Rift Valley

Victoria
SEYCHELLES

0°

CABINDA
Brazzaville
Kinshasa
DEM. REP. OF THE CONGO
Luanda

Dodoma
TANZANIA
Dar es Salaam

Lake Tanganyika

ATLANTIC OCEAN

Ascension

St. Helena

ANGOLA
Katanga Plateau
ZAMBIA
Lusaka

Lake Malawi
MALAWI
Lilongwe

COMOROS
Moroni
Mayotte

Okavango R.
Zambezi R.
Victoria Falls
Harare
Great Rift Valley

MOZAMBIQUE

Antananarivo

Etosha Pan

ZIMBABWE

Mozambique Channel

MADAGASCAR

20°S

NAMIBIA
Windhoek
BOTSWANA
Gaborone
KALAHARI DESERT

Namib Desert

Limpopo R.

Mbabane
Maputo
SWAZILAND

INDIAN OCEAN

20°S

TROPIC OF CAPRICORN

Orange R.
Bloemfontein
Maseru
LESOTHO

Tshwane (Pretoria)
Drakensberg

SOUTH AFRICA
Cape Town
Cape of Good Hope
Cape Agulhas

40°S

40°S

20°W · 0° · 20°E · 40°E

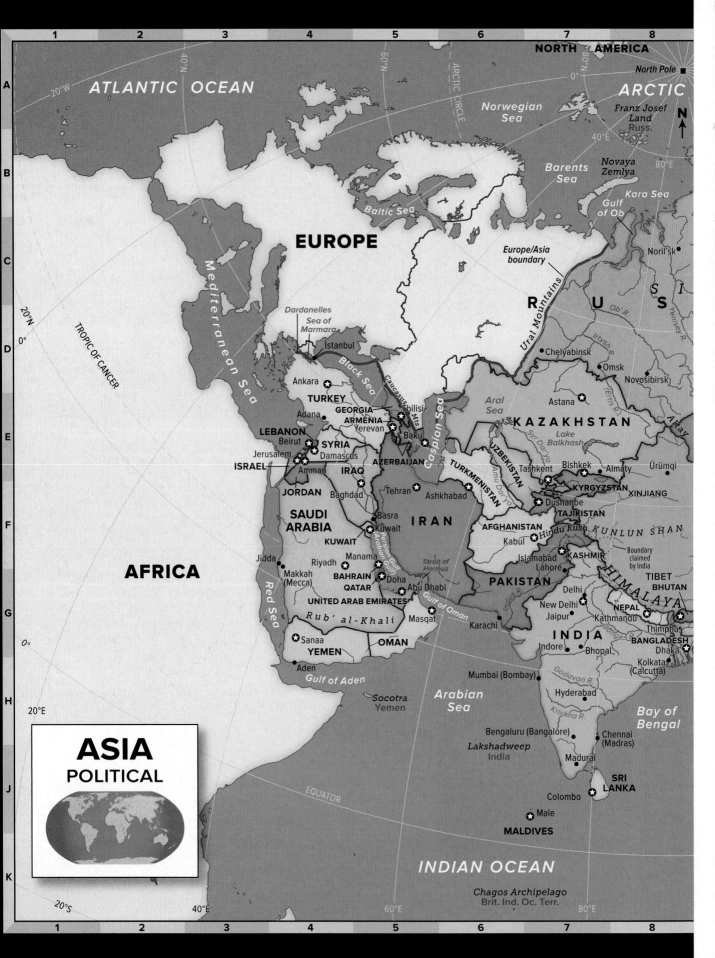

ASIA
POLITICAL

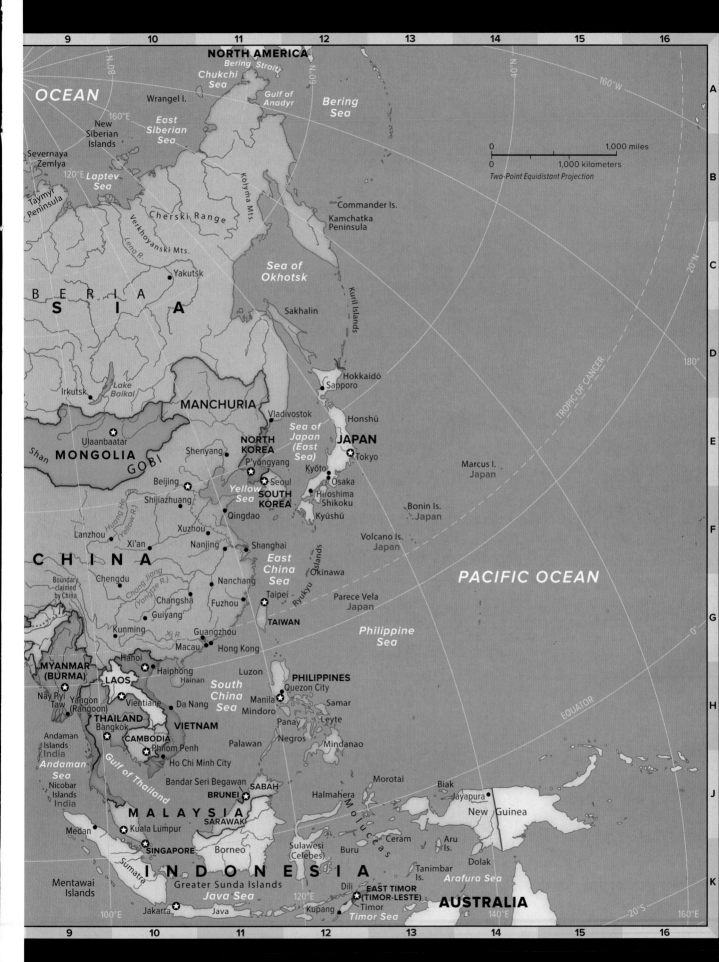

9 10 11 12 13 14 15 16

NORTH AMERICA

OCEAN

Chukchi
Sea

Bering Strait

Wrangel I.

*Gulf of
Anadyr*

Bering
Sea

New
Siberian
Islands

160°E

East
Siberian
Sea

Severnaya
Zemlya

120°E *Laptev
Sea*

Commander Is.

Kamchatka
Peninsula

Taymyr
Peninsula

Cherski Range

Kolyma Mts.

Verkhoyanski Mts.

Lena R.

Sea of
Okhotsk

Kuril Islands

Yakutsk

S I B E R I A

Sakhalin

S I A

Irkutsk

*Lake
Baikal*

MANCHURIA

Vladivostok

Hokkaidō
Sapporo

Honshū

Ulaanbaatar

Shan

MONGOLIA

GOBI

Shenyang

NORTH
KOREA

P'yŏngyang

Sea of
Japan
(East
Sea)

JAPAN
Tokyo

Marcus I.
Japan

Beijing

Huang He
(Yellow R.)

Shijiazhuang

Seoul

SOUTH
KOREA

Kyōto
Ōsaka
Hiroshima
Shikoku
Kyūshū

*Yellow
Sea*

Qingdao

Lanzhou

Xi'an

Xuzhou

Nanjing

Shanghai

Bonin Is.
Japan

C H I N A

Chengdu

Chang Jiang
(Yangtze R.)

Changsha

Nanchang

Fuzhou

East
China
Sea

Okinawa

Ryukyu Islands

Volcano Is.
Japan

PACIFIC OCEAN

Boundary
claimed
by China

Guiyang

Xi R.

Taipei

TAIWAN

Parece Vela
Japan

Kunming

Guangzhou

Macau

Hong Kong

*Philippine
Sea*

Hanoi

Haiphong

Luzon

PHILIPPINES
Quezon City

**MYANMAR
(BURMA)**

LAOS

Hainan

*South
China
Sea*

Manila

Samar

EQUATOR

Nay Pyi
Taw
Yangon
(Rangoon)

Vientiane

Da Nang

Mindoro

Leyte

THAILAND

VIETNAM

Panay

Andaman
Islands
India

Bangkok

CAMBODIA
Phnom Penh

Palawan

Negros

Mindanao

*Andaman
Sea*

Ho Chi Minh City

Morotai

Biak

Nicobar
Islands
India

Bandar Seri Begawan

SABAH

Halmahera

Jayapura

Medan

Gulf of Thailand

BRUNEI

Moluccas

New Guinea

M A L A Y S I A

SARAWAK

Ceram

Aru
Is.

Kuala Lumpur

Borneo

Sulawesi
(Celebes)

Buru

Dolak

Sumatra

SINGAPORE

Tanimbar
Is.

Arafura Sea

Mentawai
Islands

I N D O N E S I A

Greater Sunda Islands

120°E

Dili

**EAST TIMOR
(TIMOR-LESTE)**
Timor

AUSTRALIA

140°E

Java Sea

Jakarta

Java

Kupang

Timor Sea

20°S

160°E

9 10 11 12 13 14 15 16

80°N
60°N
40°N
20°N

160°W
180

TROPIC OF CANCER

0   1,000 miles
0   1,000 kilometers
Two-Point Equidistant Projection

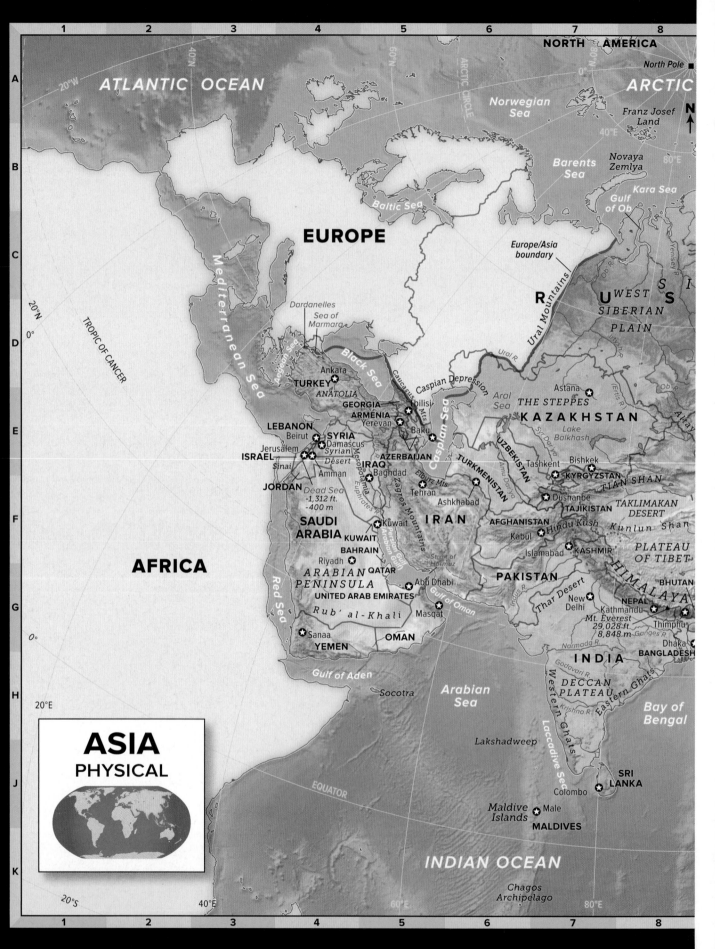

ASIA
PHYSICAL

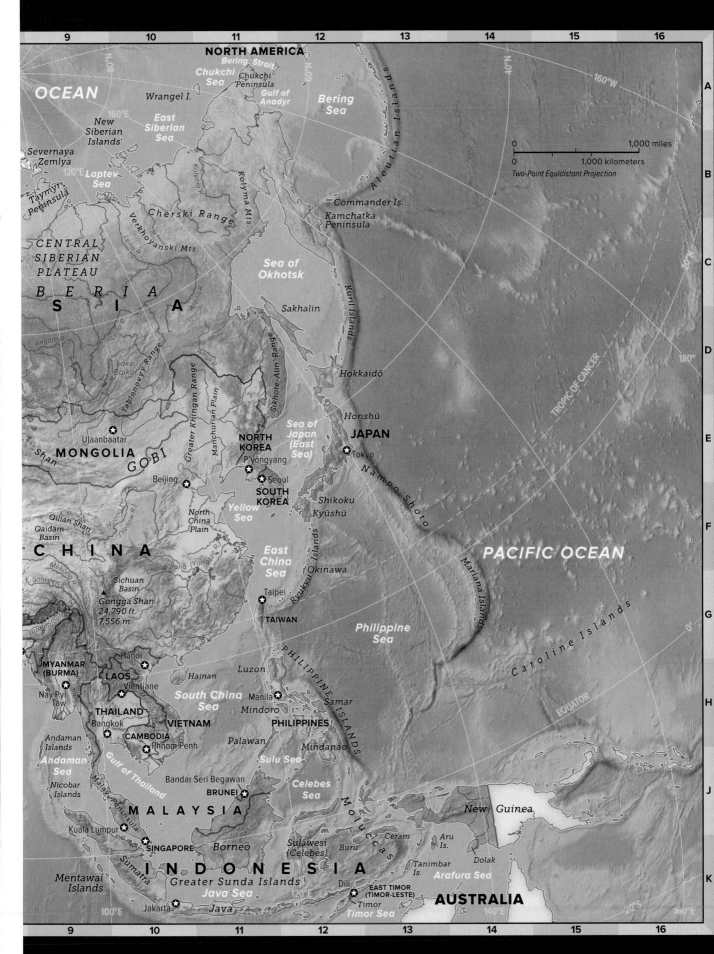

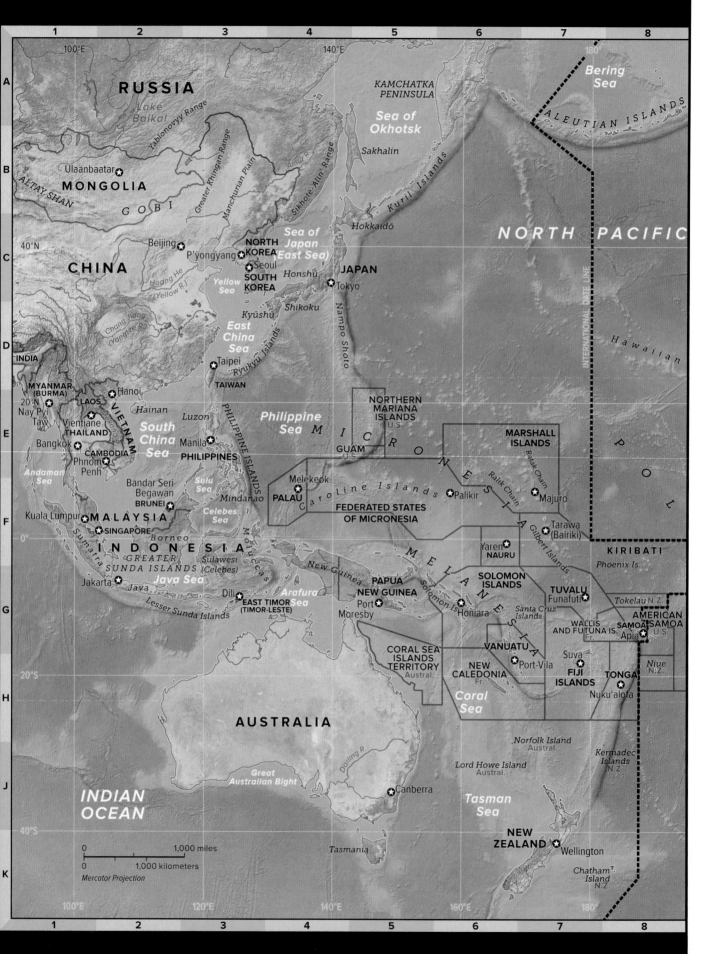

PACIFIC RIM

PHYSICAL / POLITICAL

GEOGRAPHIC DICTIONARY

Archipelago

Ocean

Gulf

Reservoir

Volcano

Isthmus

Plateau

Highlands

Canyon

Cliff

Cape

Bay

Reef

Harbor

Island

Channel

Peninsula

archipelago a group of islands

basin area of land drained by a given river and its branches; area of land surrounded by lands of higher elevations

bay part of a large body of water that extends into a shoreline, generally smaller than a gulf

canyon deep and narrow valley with steep walls

cape point of land that extends into a river, lake, or ocean

channel wide strait or waterway between two landmasses that lie close to each other; deep part of a river or other waterway

cliff steep, high wall of rock, earth, or ice

continent one of the seven large landmasses on the Earth

delta flat, low-lying land built up from soil carried downstream by a river and deposited at its mouth

divide stretch of high land that separates river systems

downstream direction in which a river or stream flows from its source to its mouth

escarpment steep cliff or slope between a higher and lower land surface

glacier large, thick body of slowly moving ice

gulf part of a large body of water that extends into a shoreline, generally larger and more deeply indented than a bay

harbor a sheltered place along a shoreline where ships can anchor safely

highland elevated land area such as a hill, mountain, or plateau

hill elevated land with sloping sides and rounded summit; generally smaller than a mountain

island land area, smaller than a continent, completely surrounded by water

isthmus narrow stretch of land connecting two larger land areas

lake a sizable inland body of water

lowland land, usually level, at a low elevation

mesa broad, flat-topped landform with steep sides; smaller than a plateau

mountain land with steep sides that rises sharply (1,000 feet or more) from surrounding land; generally larger and more rugged than a hill

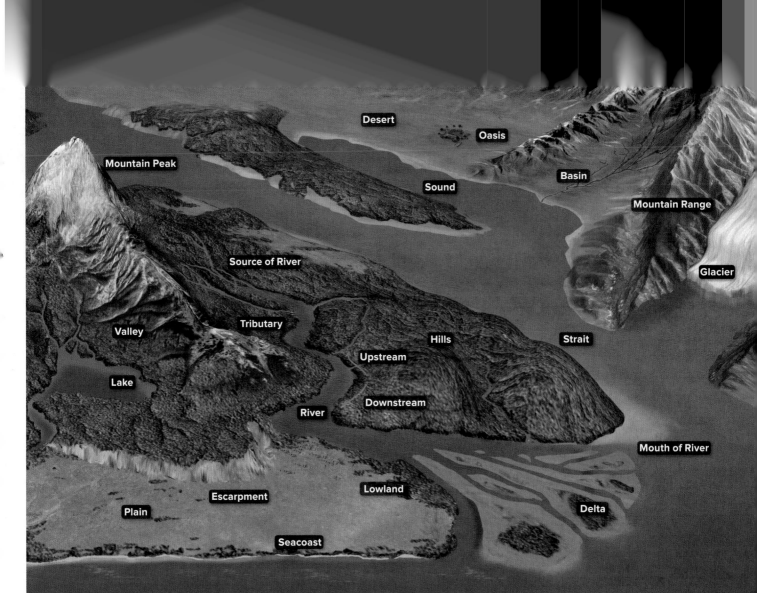

mountain peak pointed top of a mountain

mountain range a series of connected mountains

mouth (of a river) place where a stream or river flows into a larger body of water

oasis small area in a desert where water and vegetation are found

ocean one of the four major bodies of salt water that surround the continents

ocean current stream of either cold or warm water that moves in a definite direction through an ocean

peninsula body of land jutting into a lake or ocean, surrounded on three sides by water

physical feature characteristic of a place occurring naturally, such as a landform, body of water, climate pattern, or resource

plain area of level land, usually at low elevation and often covered with grasses

plateau area of flat or rolling land at a high elevation, about 300 to 3,000 feet (90 to 900 m) high

reef a chain of rocks, coral or sand at or near the

river large natural stream of water that runs through the land

sea large body of water completely or partly surrounded by land

seacoast land lying next to a sea or an ocean

sound broad inland body of water, often between a coastline and one or more islands off the coast

source (of a river) place where a river or stream begins, often in highlands

strait narrow stretch of water joining two larger bodies of water

tributary small river or stream that flows into a large river or stream; a branch of the river

upstream direction opposite the flow of a river; toward the source of a river or stream

valley area of low land usually between hills or mountains

volcano mountain or hill created as liquid rock and ash erupt from inside the Earth

SCAVENGER HUNT

NETWORKS contains a wealth of information. The trick is to know where to look to access all the information in the book. If you complete this scavenger hunt exercise with your teachers or parents, you will see how the textbook is organized and how to get the most out of your reading and studying time. Let's get started!

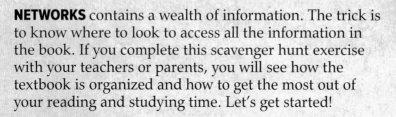

1 How many chapters are in this book?

2 Where in the front of the book can you find page numbers for each lesson?

3 What is the title of Chapter 2?

4 What Essential Questions will you answer in Chapter 5?

5 Who is discussed in the biography feature of Chapter 6, Lesson 1?

6 What is the *Thinking Like a Historian* activity for Chapter 8?

7 What time period does Chapter 11 cover?

8 What is the title of Lesson 2 in Chapter 12?

9 Where in the back of the book can you find the meaning of vocabulary words such as *ephor*?

10 Where in the back of the book can you find page numbers for information about citizenship?

◄ *A museum employee places the head on a statue in the Terra-cotta Warriors exhibit at the Dresden Energy Museum.*

Norbert Millauer/AFP/Getty Images

What Does a Historian Do?

THE STORY MATTERS ...

Hundreds of terra-cotta warriors stood, silent and without expression, in the empty exhibit hall. They were replicas of the original statues found in China in 1974. Since their discovery, the warriors, dating from 210 B.C., have fascinated historians.

The mystery of the warriors captured the imaginations of people all over the world. Museums asked for a chance to show the statues in their cities. Researchers carefully created exact replicas of the statues that would be strong enough to travel around the world. Museum workers assembled heads, arms, and bodies in exactly the correct order. Thousands of visitors came to marvel at the beautiful and mysterious warriors.

ESSENTIAL QUESTIONS

- Why is history important?
- How do we learn about the past?
- How do you research history?

Place & Time: Historians in the 21st Century

Many people are historians. Some study written records of a war that happened decades ago. Some study dinosaur bones and other ancient artifacts from millions of years in the past. Family historians may be the ones you are most familiar with. They are the relatives who remember when everyone's birthday is and can tell you what your great-grandparents did for a living.

Step Into the Place

IMAGE FOCUS There are many ways to study the past. Look at the photos.

1 ANALYZING VISUALS Where do people find information about the past?

2 IDENTIFYING What tools do people use to study the past?

3 CRITICAL THINKING *Making Connections* Where could you go to learn about the history of your community?

Museums display artifacts and other historical information for everyone to see. Archaeologists add to displays as new discoveries are made.

Historians and students use many types of research tools. Computers are valuable resources for locating data.

Step Into the Time

TIME LINE The time line shows different periods in history. What name is given to the first time period in history?

WORLD HISTORY	**Prehistory** up to 3500 B.C.		**Ancient History** 3500 B.C. to A.D. 500	
	B.C. 4000		B.C. 3000	B.C. 2000

Middle Ages
A.D. 500 to A.D. 1400

Modern History
after A.D. 1400 to
present

B.C. 1000   A.D. 1   A.D. 500   A.D. 1000   A.D. 1500

networks
There's More Online!

LESSON 1

What Is History?

ESSENTIAL QUESTION

- Why is history important?

IT MATTERS BECAUSE

Events of the past created the world we live in, and knowing history can help us make decisions about the future.

Why Study History?

GUIDING QUESTION ***What types of things can history reveal about the past?***

History is the study of the people and events of the past. History explores both the way things change and the way things stay the same. History tells the story of the ways that cultures change over time.

People who study history are called historians. A historian's job is to examine the causes, or reasons, that something happened in the past. They also look for the effects, or results, of the event. They ask, "What happened?" and "Why did it happen?" They ask, "How did things change?" and "How has it influenced today?" Sometimes they ask, "What would have happened if . . . ?"

History explains why things are the way they are. The invention of the wheel in prehistoric times paved the way for the use of horse-drawn carts in later time periods. The carts were a step toward the invention of the automobile in modern times. Today, cars are an **integral** part of our culture.

Learning about the past helps us understand the present. It helps us make decisions about the future. Historical instances of conflict and cooperation are examples we can learn from. We can use that knowledge when we face similar choices.

Reading HELPDESK

Taking Notes: *Categorizing*

Use a graphic organizer like the one shown here to list the important details about studying history.

Studying History		
Reasons to Study History	Measuring Historical Time	People Who Study Time

Content Vocabulary

- era
- archaeology
- artifact
- paleontology
- fossil
- anthropology
- species

Studying history helps us understand how we fit into the human story. Some of the clues are the languages we speak, the technologies we use, and the pastimes we enjoy. All these are results of events that happened in the past. History teaches us who we are.

✔ **PROGRESS CHECK**

Explaining Why is it important to understand cause and effect when studying the past?

Measuring Time

GUIDING QUESTION *What are historical periods?*

To study the past, historians must have a way to identify and describe when things happened. They do that by measuring and labeling time in different ways.

Periods of History

One way to measure time is to label groups of years. For example, a group of 10 years is called a **decade**. A group of 100 years is known as a *century*. Centuries are grouped into even longer time periods. Ten centuries grouped together is called a *millennium*, which is a period of 1,000 years.

Historians also divide the past into larger blocks of time known as **eras.** *Prehistory* is the first of these long periods. Prehistory is the time before people developed writing.

©Jean-Pierre Lescourret/Corbis

The ancient Roman Forum has been called the most important meeting place in all of history. Today, it stands next to the buildings of modern Rome. Different historical eras are represented by both ancient and modern buildings.

era a large division of time

Academic Vocabulary

integral essential; necessary

decade a group or set of 10 years

Writing was invented about 5,500 years ago. The period known as *Ancient History* comes next. It ends c. A.D. 500 (c., or circa, means "about"). Historians call the time period between about A.D. 500 and about A.D. 1400 the *Middle Ages,* or the medieval period. *Modern History* begins about A.D. 1400. It continues to the present day.

Calendars

A *calendar* is a system for arranging days in order. Different cultures in the world have developed about 40 different calendars.

Some cultures developed calendars based on nature, such as the cycle of the moon. The Chinese and Jewish calendars base their months on the appearance of the new moon. The ancient Egyptians also based one of their calendars on the moon.

Julian Calendar

The calendar we use today is based in part on a calendar developed by Julius Caesar, a Roman leader. This calendar is called the Julian calendar, and it started counting years at the **founding** of Rome. A year on the Julian calendar was 365¼ days long. The calendar added an extra day every four years. The year with the extra day was called a leap year. However, the Julian calendar was still not **precisely,** or exactly, right. It lost several minutes each year, which added up to about one lost day every 128 years.

The Gregorian calendar is named for its creator, Pope Gregory XIII. Why is it important that most of the world uses a form of the calendar he developed?

Gregorian Calendar

By A.D. 1582, the Julian calendar was losing time—about 10 days. Pope Gregory XIII decided to create a new calendar. First, he started counting from the birth of Jesus. Next, he ordered that the days between October 4th and October 15th of that year be dropped from the calendar. Like the Julian calendar, the Gregorian calendar includes leap years. However, in the Gregorian calendar, no century year will be a leap year unless it is divisible by 400, such as the years 1600 or 2000. That way, it will take thousands of years before there is another lost day.

©Bettmann/Corbis

Not all countries accepted the Gregorian calendar right away. It took more than three centuries for the calendar to be recognized around the world. Today, most of the world uses this calendar. Like the Gregorian calendar, other calendars are also based on events of religious importance. The Jewish calendar begins about 3,760 years before the Gregorian calendar. According to Jewish tradition, that is when the world was created. Muslims date their calendar from the time that Muhammad, their first leader, left the city of Makkah (Mecca) to go to Madinah (Medina). This was the year A.D. 622 in the Gregorian calendar.

This stone calendar was made by the **Minoans**, people who lived on ancient Crete.

Dating Events

In the Gregorian calendar, the years before the birth of Jesus are known as "B.C.," or "before Christ." The years after are called "A.D.," or *anno domini*. This phrase comes from the Latin language and means "in the year of the Lord."

To date events before the birth of Jesus, or "B.C.," historians count backwards from A.D. 1. There is no year "0." The year before A.D. 1 is 1 B.C. (Notice that "A.D." is written before the date and "B.C." is written after the date.) For example, on the time line below, the founder of Buddhism was born about 563 B.C., or 563 years before the birth of Jesus. To date events after the birth of Jesus, or "A.D.," historians count forward, starting at A.D. 1. A date in the first 100 years after the birth of Jesus is between A.D. 1 and A.D. 100. Therefore, on the time line below, Buddhism spread to China in A.D. 100, or 100 years after the birth of Jesus.

To avoid a religious reference in dating, many historians prefer to use the initials B.C.E. ("before the common era") and C.E. ("common era"). These initials do not change the numbering of the years.

Using Time Lines

A time line is another way to track the passage of time. Time lines show the order of events within a period of time. They also show the amount of time between events. Most time lines are divided into even sections of time. Events are placed on a time line at the date when the event occurred.

Nimatallah/Art Resource, NY

INFOGRAPHIC

Time lines can trace the growth and decline of civilizations. This time line tracks the events of ancient India.

1 IDENTIFYING Around what year did the Mauryan Empire's Golden Age begin?

2 CRITICAL THINKING *Analyzing* Which dates and events on this time line give information about the Aryans?

ANCIENT INDIA

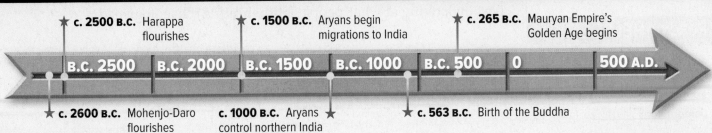

★ **c. 2500 B.C.** Harappa flourishes

★ **c. 1500 B.C.** Aryans begin migrations to India

★ **c. 265 B.C.** Mauryan Empire's Golden Age begins

B.C. 2500   B.C. 2000   B.C. 1500   B.C. 1000   B.C. 500   0   500 A.D.

★ **c. 2600 B.C.** Mohenjo-Daro flourishes

★ **c. 1000 B.C.** Aryans control northern India

★ **c. 563 B.C.** Birth of the Buddha

Heinrich Schliemann
(A.D. 1822–1890)

As a boy, Heinrich Schliemann (SHLEE • MAHN) loved stories about ancient Greece. He dreamed of finding Troy, an ancient city destroyed during the Trojan War.

In 1871, Schliemann began to dig through a human-made mound in Hissarlik (HIH • suhr • LIHK), Turkey. Two years later, he uncovered the remains of a mysterious ancient city in the area where Troy had stood. Some archaeologists believe that Schliemann actually found Troy. Others are unsure. Nevertheless, his work led to the discovery of many ancient Greek treasures. Because of his work, Schliemann is considered the founder of prehistoric Greek archaeology.

▶ **CRITICAL THINKING**
Making Inferences Archaeologists study and catalog evidence they find. What might be the historical value of uncovering evidence of an entire city?

Build Vocabulary: *Word Parts*

The suffix *-ology* means "the study of." The suffix *-ist* means "a person who." For example, *biology* is the study of life. A *biologist* is a person who studies life. What do archaeologists, paleontologists, and anthropologists do?

Usually, the dates on a time line are evenly spaced. Sometimes, however, a time line covers events over too many years to show on one page. In this case, a slanted or jagged line might be placed on the time line. This shows that a certain period of time is omitted from the time line.

Time lines help historians make sense of the flow of events. A time line can be a single line, or it can be two or more lines stacked on top of each other. Stacked time lines are called multilevel time lines.

☑ **PROGRESS CHECK**

Applying When would a historian use a calendar? When would a historian use a time line?

Digging Up the Past

GUIDING QUESTION *What do students of prehistory look for?*

Since the invention of writing, people have recorded important events. These written records give historians a window to the past. Students of prehistory look into an even deeper past, one without writing. They must find a different kind of window.

History and Science

These historians use science to study history. As scientists, they study physical evidence to learn about our ancestors.

Archaeology (ahr•kee•AHL•luh•jee) is the study of the past by looking at what people left behind. Archaeologists dig

Reading**HELP**DESK

archaeology the study of objects to learn about past human life

artifact an object made by people

paleontology the study of fossils

fossil plant or animal remains that have been preserved from an earlier time

anthropology the study of human culture and how it develops over time

species a class of individuals with similar physical characteristics

in the earth for places where people once lived. They never know what they will find. They often discover **artifacts** (AHR·tih·FAKTS)—objects made by people. Common artifacts include tools, pottery, weapons, and jewelry. Archaeologists study artifacts to learn what life was like in the past.

Paleontology (PAY·lee·AHN·TAH·luh·jee) also looks at prehistoric times. Paleontologists study fossils to learn what the world was like long ago. **Fossils** are the remains of plant and animal life that have been preserved from an earlier time.

Anthropology (AN·thruh·PAH·luh·jee) is the study of human culture and how it develops over time. Anthropologists study artifacts and fossils, too. They look for clues about what people valued and believed.

Human Discoveries

In 1974, a team led by paleontologist Donald Johanson made an exciting find in Ethiopia in Africa. They discovered a partial skeleton of a human ancestor who lived more than 3.2 million years ago. Lucy, as she was called, was about three and a half feet tall (1.07 m) and weighed about 60 pounds (27.2 kg). She had long arms and short legs, and she walked upright.

Lucy belonged to the species *Australopithicus afarensis*. A **species** is a class of individuals with similar physical characteristics. Lucy lived long before the species called *Homo sapiens* evolved. All modern human beings belong to this species. The term *Homo sapiens* is Latin for "wise man." Scientists believe that Homo sapiens probably developed about 150,000 to 195,000 years ago.

✓ PROGRESS CHECK

Comparing How are archaeologists, paleontologists, and anthropologists like detectives?

Kevin Fujii/Associated Press

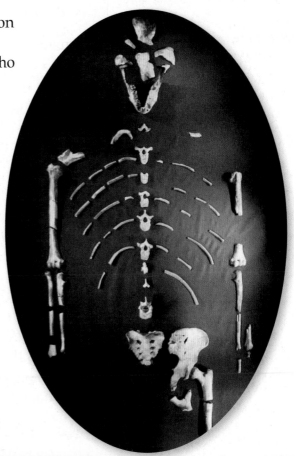

Connections to
TODAY

How Lucy Got Her Name

The night that Lucy was discovered, the team that found her was listening to the song "Lucy in the Sky with Diamonds" by the singing group the Beatles. They nicknamed the skeleton "Lucy," which was more attractive than her official name, AL 288-1.

Scientists have found and pieced together about 40 percent of Lucy's skeleton.

LESSON 1 REVIEW

Review Vocabulary

1. Explain what a historical *era* is.

2. Compare and contrast *artifacts* and *fossils*.

Answer the Guiding Questions

3. *Making Connections* Name one example of how the past influences daily life today.

4. *Listing* Identify different ways that historians measure time.

5. *Describing* How do historians learn about people who lived in the earliest historical eras?

6. **INFORMATIVE/EXPLANATORY** How would a historian describe your life? Write a short essay that identifies the era in which you live and the artifacts that tell about your culture.

How Does a Historian Work?

networks
There's More Online!

ESSENTIAL QUESTION

• How do we learn about the past?

IT MATTERS BECAUSE

Knowing how historians work helps us understand historical information.

What Is the Evidence?

GUIDING QUESTION *What types of evidence do historians use to understand the past?*

Historians ask questions about the information they find from the past. Why did some nations go to war? How were the people affected by that war? How did events of the past change people's lives? These questions help us focus on historical problems.

To learn the answers to the historical questions, historians look for **evidence** (EH·vuh·duhnts). Evidence is something that shows proof or an indication that something is true. Evidence could be in the form of material objects, such as a soldier's uniform or scraps of pottery from an archaeological dig.

Other evidence may appear in documents or written materials that were created during a historical event. Historians use the evidence they read in historical **sources** to interpret what happened in the past.

Primary and Secondary Sources

Historians look for clues about the past in primary and secondary sources. **Primary sources** are firsthand pieces of evidence. They were written or created by the people who saw or experienced an event. Primary sources include letters, diaries, or government records. Literature or artwork from a particular time

Reading**HELP**DESK

Taking Notes: *Sequencing*

As you read, think about the steps in finding and evaluating evidence. Use the sequence chart to note the steps in the process.

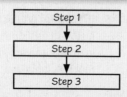

Content Vocabulary

- evidence
- primary source
- secondary source
- point of view
- bias
- conclusion
- scholarly

and place is a primary source. Spoken interviews and objects, such as tools or clothing, are also primary sources. Primary sources help historians learn what people were thinking while the events took place. They use the sources to find evidence that explains historical events.

Historians also use **secondary sources**. Secondary sources are created after an event. They are created by people who were not part of the historical event. The information in secondary sources is often based on primary sources. Examples of secondary sources are biographies, encyclopedias, history books, and textbooks.

A secondary source contains background information. Secondary sources also offer a broad view of an event. However, a historian must use primary sources to find new evidence about a subject.

Reliable Sources

Suppose you were studying the history of England and you wanted to know how ancient people lived. You might look in a book called the *Domesday Book*. This book was created in A.D. 1086 by administrators under William I. The book is a primary source from the period. It contains information about the people of England at the time it was written.

These sculptures of warriors are evidence of life in China during the Qin Dynasty. They give archaeologists and historians information about China's culture and its first emperor.

IMAGEMORE Co. Ltd./Getty Images

evidence something that shows proof that something is true

primary source firsthand evidence of an event in history

secondary source a document or written work created after an event

Academic Vocabulary

source document or reference work

There's More Online! connected.mcgraw-hill.com

Maps can be primary sources. The map on the left was created around A.D. 1500. How does it compare with the modern world map on the right? What can historians learn by comparing these maps?

(l)Digital Vision/Getty Images; (r)Antenna Audio, Inc./Getty Images

The *Domesday Book* is a long list of manors and the names of their owners. It includes details about how many workers worked the land. It lists the number of fishponds, mills, and animals owned by each person. It also estimates the value of each property. The historian's job is to analyze and interpret the information from primary sources. They consider where and when a source was created. They also look for the reasons that the source was created. Was it a secret letter? Was it a document created for the king, such as the *Domesday Book*? Was it written so that all the people in a town or country would read it?

What Is Point of View?

Historians interpret the document and the reasons it was created. Then they form an opinion about whether the source is trustworthy and reliable in its facts. This step is important since each source was written with a particular **point of view** or general attitude about people or life. The authors of primary sources use their points of view to decide what information is important and what to include in the document. Historians evaluate a primary source to find its point of view. They decide if it has a trustworthy viewpoint.

Sometimes a point of view is expressed as a **bias** or an unreasoned, emotional judgment about people and events. Sources with a bias cannot always be trusted.

✓ PROGRESS CHECK

Explaining What is a historian's job when looking at primary sources?

Writing About History

When historians write about an event, they interpret the information from primary sources to draw conclusions and make inferences.

Making an inference means choosing the most likely explanation for the facts at hand. Sometimes the inference is simple. For example, if you see a person who is wearing a raincoat walk into a room with a dripping umbrella, you can infer that it is raining outside. The dripping umbrella and the raincoat are the evidence that combine with your prior knowledge about weather to infer that it is raining.

Making inferences about historical events is more complex. Historians check the evidence in primary sources and compare it to sources already known to be trustworthy. Then, they look at secondary sources that express different points of view about an event. In this way, historians try to get a clear, well-rounded view of what happened. The inference they make is how they explain what happened in the past. This explanation is based on the evidence in primary and secondary sources.

For example, you might read the *Domesday Book* to analyze the types of animals raised in 1086. You could add this knowledge to additional evidence from another source about grain that was planted. Then, you could think about what you know to be true about food. You might use all of this information to make an inference about the types of food people ate in eleventh-century England.

This cave painting was made during the Paleolithic era. It is a primary source.

▶ **CRITICAL THINKING**
Analyzing Primary Sources
What information does the painting give historians?

Yoko Aziz/Age fotostock

Looking at History

Professional historians become experts on their historical subject. Historians gather artifacts and data about a subject and then write what they have learned from the study. Such writing may become an article in a **scholarly** (SKAH·luhr·lee) journal, or magazine. It may become a book on the specific subject.

In most cases, historical books and articles are reviewed by other scholars for accuracy. Experts in the field will review the sources and write their own articles. They evaluate how the historian has interpreted the facts. This study of historical interpretations is called historiography. Historians must keep accurate notes and be careful that their inferences are reasonable.

If you were researching World War I, this photo of American soldiers could help you. Using photos as evidence is a good way to expand information. What do you think these soldiers are waiting for?

Focusing Research

Some historians keep their areas of study very narrow. For example, someone could spend an entire career investigating the events that occurred on a single day, such as the day in the year A.D. 79 that Mount Vesuvius, a volcano in the region that is now Italy, erupted and destroyed the city of Pompeii. This subject is a **finite** place and time. Other historians focus on broader subjects. For example, some historians study the economic history of a period. Others study the political history of a country during a certain period of time. Still others might study military history, the history of medicine, or the history of technology in a certain place.

Drawing Conclusions

A **conclusion** (kuhn·KLOO·zhun) is a final decision that is reached by reasoning. You draw conclusions all the time. For example, you may notice that a friend often wears T-shirts from music concerts that he has attended. You might also remember he can never get together on Thursday nights because he has guitar lessons on Thursdays. Based on these two clues, you could draw the conclusion that your friend is really interested in music. Historians draw conclusions in the same way. They look for facts and evidence in their primary and secondary sources. Then, they use reasoning to make a judgment or draw a conclusion.

Reading HELP DESK

scholarly concerned with academic learning or research

conclusion a decision reached after examining evidence

Academic Vocabulary

finite limited; having boundaries
interpretation an explanation of the meaning of something

Historical Interpretations

Sometimes historians disagree about their **interpretations** of the facts. For example, historians disagree about how to evaluate the historical figure of Genghis Khan. There are historians who argue that Genghis Khan was a fierce and bloodthirsty warrior. Some have expressed horror at the tremendous destruction that Genghis Khan's fierce soldiers brought as they conquered new lands. Yet some historians see Genghis Khan differently. They look at the way Genghis Khan ruled his great Mongol empire. Sources show that this was a time of peace, prosperity, and stability in a huge portion of central and eastern Asia. The people living in the Mongol empire enjoyed a remarkable degree of religious tolerance, higher learning, and consistent laws.

Which conclusion is correct? Was Genghis Khan a ruthless warrior or a strong, intelligent leader of a great land? A historian may rely on evidence to support either position. However, it is the job of the historian to evaluate the primary sources and explain why both interpretations can be argued.

Genghis Khan and his Mongol warriors expanded the Mongol Empire. The violence of their invasions contrasted with the peace inside the empire.

North Wind/North Wind Picture Archives

✓ PROGRESS CHECK

Analyzing Why do historians draw different conclusions about events of the past?

LESSON 2 REVIEW

Review Vocabulary

1. Name one way a *primary source* is different from a *secondary source*.

2. Why does a historian have to understand what *point of view* is?

Answer the Guiding Questions

3. *Drawing Conclusions* Why does drawing a conclusion come at the end of a research process?

4. *Making Generalizations* How does a primary source help a historian understand the past?

5. *Assessing* Explain why some historians differ in their interpretations of historical events.

6. **INFORMATIVE/EXPLANATORY** Think of the reading you do every day. In a short paragraph, give an example of one primary source and one secondary source that you have read recently. Explain why each example fits into the category you have chosen.

What Do You Think?

Should Artifacts Be Returned to Their Countries of Origin?

Imagine you were an archaeologist who found an important ancient artifact in another country. You would want to take that artifact home with you and display it in a museum. The country where you found the artifact might raise a protest. They may want the object to stay in their own country. Many such artifacts are displayed in museums far away from their country of origin. Who has the biggest claim to them? Should artifacts be returned to the countries in which they were found?

TEXT: "Who's Right? Repatriation of Cultural Property," by Malcolm Bell III and James Cuno, Bureau of International Information Programs, U.S. Department of State, November 2, 2010.
PHOTO: Tim Graham/Getty Images

Yes

PRIMARY SOURCE

"The Oxford English Dictionary defines "repatriate" as "to restore (an artifact or other object) to its country of origin." Many artifacts. . . have special cultural value for a particular community or nation. When these works are removed from their original cultural setting, they lose their context and the culture loses a part of its history. A request for repatriation of an artifact. . . usually has a strong legal basis. The antiquity was exported illegally, probably also excavated [dug up] illegally, and most importantly, it is now defined by U.S. courts as stolen property. Even in the United States, where private property rights are greatly respected, the government claims ownership of antiquities from federal lands—and would request their repatriation if they were to be privately excavated and exported."

—Malcolm Bell III, professor emeritus, University of Virginia

The Cairo Museum holds countless artifacts from Egypt's long history. An example is this famous golden burial mask of Pharaoh Tutankhamen.

The Metropolitan Museum of Art in New York is visited by millions of people every year. The museum's collection includes treasures from all over the world, including this sphinx of the Egyptian pharaoh Amenhotep II.

No

❝ History is long and untidy. Territory held today by a given nation-state in the past likely belonged to a different political entity [unit], one with other descendents. Does ancient Hellenistic [Greek] art made and found in Afghanistan, once on the edge of the Greek empire, belong to Greece or to Afghanistan? To which modern nation do they belong? The lines designating [assigning] claims to art and culture are not clear-cut.

I would argue that within the limits of the law, museums, wherever they are, should be encouraged to acquire works of art representative of the world's many and diverse cultures. This can be through purchase or long-term loan and working in collaboration [cooperation] with museums and nations around the world. These collections encourage a cosmopolitan [international] view of the world and promote a historically accurate understanding of the fluidity [constantly changing] of culture. ❞

—James Cuno, president and Eloise W. Martin Director of the Art Institute of Chicago

What Do You Think? DBQ

1. **Identifying** Why is repatriation a legal issue according to Bell?

2. **Contrasting** How do the arguments of Bell and Cuno differ?

CRITICAL THINKING

3. **Problem Solving** Describe a compromise that might solve a conflict over ownership of artifacts.

LESSON 3

Researching History

ESSENTIAL QUESTION
• How do you research history?

IT MATTERS BECAUSE
Knowing where to find information about your subject will make it easier to complete research projects and other schoolwork.

Planning Your Project

GUIDING QUESTION *How do you begin a research project?*

The first step in a history research project is to identify your topic. A topic should not be too broad (The Middle Ages) or too narrow (Middlebury, England, 1535). To test your topic, try looking it up in an encyclopedia. If there is no entry for your topic, it may be too small. If there are many entries, or a very long entry, the topic may be too large. Selecting a topic that is workable is the most important part of the project.

After you choose a topic, you need to decide what you want to learn about it. Create six questions to help you find out *who, what, when, where, why,* and *how.* Then write each question at the top of a note card. These cards will become your research tools. You may need to add additional cards as you research.

Choosing Research Materials

After selecting a topic and creating your question cards, the next step is to gather your research materials. Begin with general reference books, such as encyclopedias and textbooks, or your notes from class. Next, try looking for books about your subject at the library. Your research material must be nonfiction, rather than fiction or persuasive writing.

Reading**HELP**DESK

Taking Notes: *Finding the Main Idea*

As you read, look for the main idea of each section. Use a graphic organizer like this one to write the details that support the main idea.

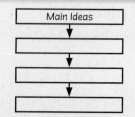

Main Ideas

Content Vocabulary

• **credentials**   • **.edu**
• **URL**   • **.org**
• **.gov**   • **plagiarize**

Distinguishing Fact From Opinion

Scan each possible source to determine if the source is trustworthy. Look for opinion statements in the text. This will give you a clue that a resource could be biased or untrustworthy. Remember, a statement of fact expresses only what can be proven by evidence. A statement of opinion expresses an attitude. It is a conclusion or judgment about something that cannot be proven true or false. Historical research should rely on facts and primary sources rather than opinions.

Making Notes

As you find information, make a note about it on your cards. Your notes should be in your own words and in complete sentences. On the back of each card, make notes about the books in which you found the information.

✓ PROGRESS CHECK

Explaining Why is it important to distinguish fact from opinion in historical writing?

Researching on the Internet

GUIDING QUESTION *How do you safely research on the Internet?*

Looking for information on the Internet is quick and rewarding. However, it can be a challenge to find out if the information you located is true. Good historians follow a few important guidelines as they gather information.

Authorship

Many articles on the Internet are unsigned. A reader has no way of knowing who wrote the content and whether the author is an expert on the subject. However, reliable articles will be signed by well-known experts on the subject. The authors will include details about their **credentials** (kreh·DEN·shulz), or evidence that they are experts.

credentials something that gives confidence that a person is qualified for a task

Web sites such as these may be reliable for certain subjects. There are many clues on a Web site to let you know if it will have reliable information.

There are other ways to decide if an article is worth using for research. You can look at the homepage for the article. If the article is on the site of a university, government office, or museum, it is probably reliable. For example, suppose you find a signed article about the foods eaten by American colonists. You find that the article is published by an academic journal at a university. You can assume that this page is a better source than an unsigned article about the same subject by a blogger on a cooking Web site.

Web URLs

A uniform resource locator, or **URL,** is the address of an online resource. The ending on a URL tells a great deal about the content. A URL that ends in **.gov** is most likely a government entity. This site probably contains accurate **data.** This data is usually as up to date as possible.

A URL that ends in **.edu** is usually a site for an educational institution, such as a college or university. Most .edu sites pride themselves on accuracy. However, it is possible that documents on these sites may contain opinions in addition to facts.

Nonprofit organizations usually use **.org** at the end of their URLs. These sites may be very accurate. However, these groups often gather information to support their cause. Their sites may contain biased information, and they often contain opinions.

You have gathered information and answered the questions on your note cards. Then organize your cards into categories. Once your cards are sorted, you can use them as an outline for writing your research paper.

☑ PROGRESS CHECK

Speculating What are the consequences of using an Internet resource with biased information?

Writing Without Bias

GUIDING QUESTION *How do you interpret historical events accurately?*

You have chosen a good topic. You have created your question cards and used them while reading encyclopedia articles and library books. You have also used your cards while reviewing reliable Internet resources about your topic. You have turned the answers on your question cards into an outline. Now you are ready to write your research report. As you work, be aware of some important guidelines for writing about history.

Plagiarism

To **plagiarize** (PLAY·juh·RYZ) is to present the ideas or words of another person as your own without offering credit to the source. Plagiarism is similar to forgery, or copying something that is not yours. It also **violates** copyright laws. These laws prevent the unauthorized use of a writer's work. If you copy an idea or a written text exactly word-for-word, that is plagiarism. Some scholars have ruined their careers through plagiarism. They used content from books or the Internet without citing the source or giving credit.

To avoid plagiarism, follow these rules:

- Put information in your own words.
- When you restate an opinion from something you read, include a reference to the author: "According to Smith and Jones, . . . "
- Always include a footnote when you use a direct quotation from one of your sources.

"I didn't write the book report. I downloaded and printed it directly from the Internet, but I did collate and staple it myself."

Cartoons can make plagiarism seem humorous, but it is illegal and can lead to serious consequences.

Ancient History and Modern Values

Avoid using modern ideas to evaluate a historical event. For example, a scholar of women's history may want to apply modern ideas to women's rights in historical settings. Ideas have changed over time. Drawing conclusions about women's attitudes in the Middle Ages using modern ideas would be a mistake. Your evaluations of history should be based on the evidence, not on today's understanding of rights and society.

✅ **PROGRESS CHECK**

Listing What is one way to avoid plagiarism when writing about history?

LESSON 3 REVIEW

Review Vocabulary

1. Why is it against the law to *plagiarize*?

2. Which URL ending would identify a Web site for a charity?

   a. .org **b.** .gov **c.** .edu

Answer the Guiding Questions

3. *Assessing* How do you know if a resource in a library book can be trusted?

4. *Listing* Identify the clues you would look for to decide if an online resource is trustworthy.

5. *Determining Cause and Effect* What is one negative effect that can come from applying modern values to a historical event?

6. **ARGUMENT** Your teacher does not want students to use the Internet for research. Write two paragraphs in which you persuade the teacher that the Internet can be a reliable source of information.

Write your answers on a separate piece of paper.

1 **Exploring the Essential Question**

INFORMATIVE/EXPLANATORY Using information you have read in this chapter, give three reasons why we study history.

2 **21st Century Skills**

ANALYZE AND INTERPRET MEDIA Research a historical subject of your choice. Find three reliable sources and at least one source that would not be considered reliable. Write a paragraph that analyzes the online resources you discovered. Describe why each source is reliable or unreliable.

3 **Thinking Like a Historian**

SEQUENCING Create a personal time line using the terms *before my birth* and *after my birth*. Fill in the time line with three key events that happened before and three key events that happened after you were born.

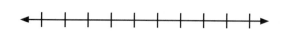

4 **GEOGRAPHY ACTIVITY**

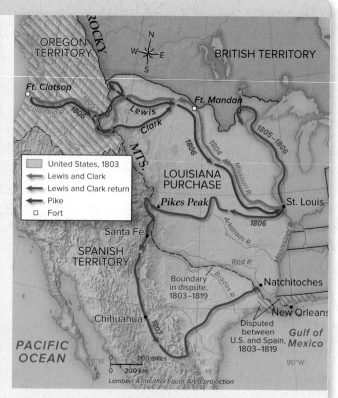

Lewis and Clark expedition journal from the explorations of the Louisiana Territory

Modern map of Lewis and Clark journey, 1803

Comparing Sources

Which map is a primary source? Which is a secondary source? Include definitions of these terms in your answer. Then, explain why each source is useful to a historian.

Directions: Write your answers on a separate piece of paper.

CHECKING FOR UNDERSTANDING

1 Define each of these terms.

A. era

B. artifact

C. fossil

D. evidence

E. primary source

F. secondary source

G. point of view

H. bias

I. conclusion

REVIEW THE GUIDING QUESTIONS

2 *Explaining* What does a historian do?

3 *Identifying* In the Gregorian calendar, what do "B.C." and "A.D." mean? How are they used in dating events?

4 *Defining* What is a primary source? What is a secondary source? Give an example of each.

5 *Listing* List three ways to avoid plagiarism.

6 *Identifying* What is the purpose of a time line? Use the time line about ancient India in this chapter to answer the following questions:

A. What is the earliest event on the time line?

B. In which year did the Aryans bring Hindu ideas to India?

C. Which event occurs between c. 1000 B.C. and c. 265 B.C.?

D. How long was it from when Harappa flourished to when the Aryans controlled northern India?

7 *Describing* How are history and archaeology similar? How are they different?

8 *Discussing* What might you do to help determine whether information you find on the Internet contains reliable information?

9 *Explaining* Why do scholars review historical books and articles?

CRITICAL THINKING

10 *Comparing and Contrasting* Compare and contrast paleontology and anthropology. Provide an example of each.

11 *Formulating Questions* What questions should you ask when you choose an event or time period to study?

12 *Differentiating* How do calendars and time lines differ, even though they might include the same events?

13 *Recognizing Relationships* How are primary sources and secondary sources about the same event related?

14 *Hypothesizing* Why do you think historians have different interpretations of historical facts?

15 *Explaining* How can the study of history help us make decisions about the future?

16 *Sequencing* In researching a protest about a war that occurred fifty years ago, what steps would you follow to find and evaluate evidence?

17 *Assessing* Would you be more likely to use a Web site with a URL that ends in .org or .gov as a source for a research project? Why?

18 *Determining Cause and Effect* Why should you avoid using modern ideas to evaluate a historical event? Give an example.

19 *Distinguishing Fact from Opinion* Decide which of the following statements is an opinion and which is a fact. Explain which statement would be best used for historical research and why.

A. Tutankhamen died after ruling Egypt for nine years.

B. Egyptians were better rulers than the Hyksos.

20 *Reasoning* Why does point of view matter to a historian when interpreting sources?

Need Extra Help?

If You've Missed Question	1	2	3	4	5	6	7	8	9	10	11	12	13	14	15	16	17	18	19	20
Review Lesson	1,2	1	1	2	3	1	1	3	2	1	1	2	1	2	2	1	2	3	3	2

There's More Online! connected.mcgraw-hill.com

DBQ SHORT RESPONSE

"Historians do not perform heart transplants, improve highway design, or arrest criminals. ... History is in fact very useful, actually indispensable [necessary], but the products of historical study are less tangible [physical], sometimes less immediate, than those that stem from some other disciplines."

—Excerpt from "Why Study History?" by Peter N. Stearns

21 Which part of this passage is fact? Which part is opinion?

22 According to Stearns, why is the usefulness of history difficult to identify?

EXTENDED RESPONSE

23 *Narrative* Write two paragraphs that identify primary sources and secondary sources about your life. Would these sources be biased? Explain.

STANDARDIZED TEST PRACTICE

DBQ ANALYZING DOCUMENTS

24 *Identifying* Historian William H. McNeill wrote an essay explaining why people should study history.

"[We] can only know ourselves by knowing how we resemble and how we differ from others. Acquaintance [familiarity] with the human past is the only way to such self knowledge. ...

In [studying history], eternal and unchanging truth does not emerge. Only inspired, informed guesses about what mattered and how things changed through time. ... Not very good, perhaps; simply the best we have in the unending effort to understand ourselves and others ..."

—Excerpt from "Why Study History?" by William H. McNeill

According to McNeill, what do people gain from the study of history?

A. They discover absolute truth.

B. They discover that the past was not very good.

C. They learn more about themselves.

D. They learn to give their best effort in what they do.

25 *Identifying Point of View* With which statement would McNeill agree?

A. Studying history is a waste of time.

B. We have much to learn from history.

C. History has no influence on the present time.

D. We should look to history for the answers to all of our questions.

Need Extra Help?

If You've Missed Question	**21**	**22**	**23**	**24**	**25**
Review Lesson	2	1	3	1	1

The True History of the Conquest of Spain by Bernal Diaz del Castillo. From The Literatures of Colonial America: An Anthology by Susan P. Castillo and Ivy Schweitzer. Copyright © 2001 by Wiley-Blackwell.

◄ *For many people, citizenship comes with being born in a certain country. For others, like this woman, citizenship is a matter of choice.*

Studying Geography, Economics, and Citizenship

ZUMA Press Inc/Alamy

THE STORY MATTERS ...

Why is this woman smiling? She has just become a citizen of the United States. Though she was born in another country, she now enjoys all the rights and responsibilities of U.S. citizenship. Her last step toward gaining citizenship was taking the Oath of Allegiance. In this oath, people swear to "support and defend the Constitution against all enemies, foreign and domestic."

Whether you have taken this oath or not, as a U.S. citizen, you share this duty to defend the laws of your nation. Being a good citizen also means staying informed about the world around you. Understanding history, geography, and economics can help you fulfill this responsibility.

ESSENTIAL QUESTIONS

- How does geography influence the way people live?
- Why do people trade?
- Why do people form governments?

Place & Time: Studying Geography, Economics, and Citizenship

Where in the world are you? How should you spend your money? What are your responsibilities as a citizen? Geography helps us understand the places around us. Economics explores the exchange of goods. Civics explains citizenship. These topics help us understand history.

Step Into the Place

MAP FOCUS Scholars sometimes talk about the natural wonders of the ancient world. These are natural landmarks that helped shape the history around them.

1 **PLACE** Look at the map. Which of the natural wonders shown are mountains?

2 **LOCATION** What natural wonders are located in Asia? In Africa?

3 **CRITICAL THINKING**
Analyzing How do mountains and deserts affect trade and the exchange of ideas?

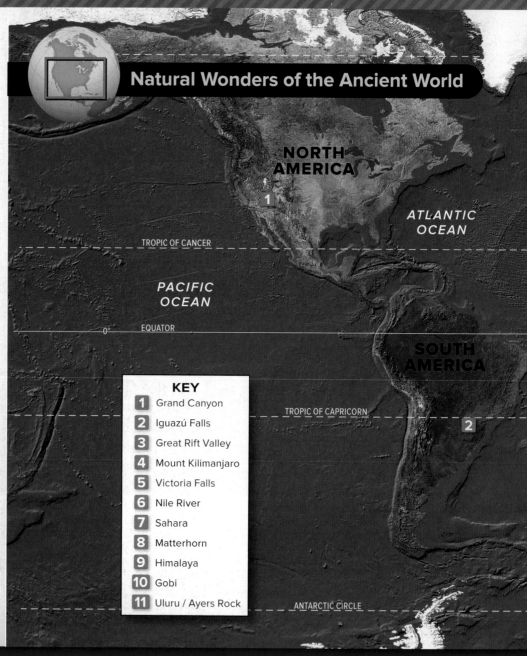

Natural Wonders of the Ancient World

NORTH AMERICA

ATLANTIC OCEAN

TROPIC OF CANCER

PACIFIC OCEAN

0° EQUATOR

SOUTH AMERICA

TROPIC OF CAPRICORN

ANTARCTIC CIRCLE

KEY

1 Grand Canyon
2 Iguazú Falls
3 Great Rift Valley
4 Mount Kilimanjaro
5 Victoria Falls
6 Nile River
7 Sahara
8 Matterhorn
9 Himalaya
10 Gobi
11 Uluru / Ayers Rock

Step Into the Time

TIME LINE Voting is a duty of U.S. citizens. How did the voting rights of U.S. citizens change over time?

KEY DATES IN GEOGRAPHY, ECONOMICS, AND CIVICS

A.D. 150 Ptolemy publishes *Guide to Geography*

A.D. 1000 Chinese invent paper money

A.D. 1522 Spanish explorers sail around world

A.D. 100   A.D. 500   A.D. 1000   A.D. 1500

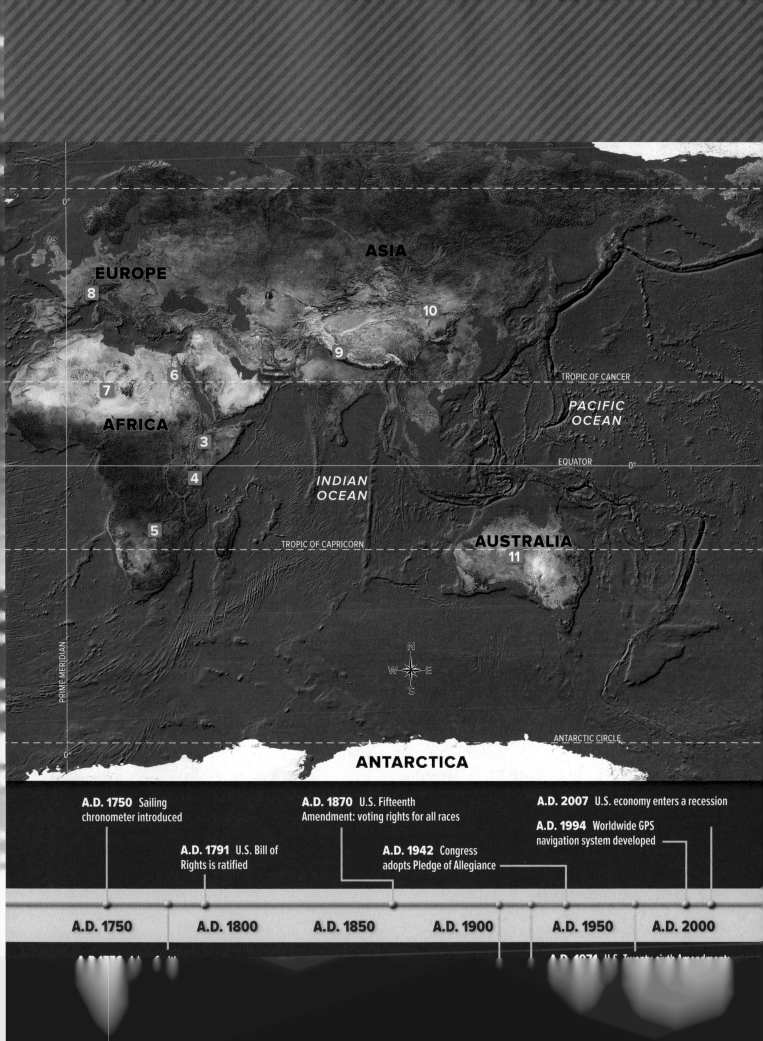

EUROPE

8

ASIA

10

9

6

7

AFRICA

3

4

5

INDIAN
OCEAN

TROPIC OF CANCER

PACIFIC
OCEAN

EQUATOR   0°

TROPIC OF CAPRICORN

AUSTRALIA

11

N
W   E
S

PRIME MERIDIAN

ANTARCTIC CIRCLE

ANTARCTICA

A.D. 1750 Sailing
chronometer introduced

A.D. 1870 U.S. Fifteenth
Amendment: voting rights for all races

A.D. 2007 U.S. economy enters a recession

A.D. 1791 U.S. Bill of
Rights is ratified

A.D. 1942 Congress
adopts Pledge of Allegiance

A.D. 1994 Worldwide GPS
navigation system developed

A.D. 1750   A.D. 1800   A.D. 1850   A.D. 1900   A.D. 1950   A.D. 2000

LESSON 1
Studying Geography

ESSENTIAL QUESTION

• How does geography influence the way people live?

IT MATTERS BECAUSE
Geography helps us understand our place in the world.

Displaying the Earth's Surface

GUIDING QUESTION *What methods do geographers use to show the Earth's surface?*

Hearing reports from explorers who had sailed the oceans, geographers realized the Earth was not flat. A new model for the Earth had to be found. A globe, a spherical scale model of the planet, became the most accurate way to show the Earth. A globe of the Earth best shows the sizes of continents and the shapes of landmasses and bodies of water. Globes also show true distance and direction.

Globes have their limitations. A globe is not as easy to carry as a map. Maps are flat drawings of all or part of the Earth's surface. Maps can show small areas in great detail. Maps can show many things—political borders, population densities, or even voting results. Plus, maps can be folded and carried in a pocket or placed in a car.

Maps, however, cannot show true size, shape, distance, and direction at the same time. The reason for this is they are flat drawings of a round object, the Earth.

Globes and maps have some features in common. Both are marked with imaginary lines that geographers use to locate places on Earth's surface. These lines divide the Earth into halves called hemispheres.

Reading**HELP**DESK

Taking Notes: *Identifying*

Use a diagram like the one shown here to list the Six Essential Elements of Geography.

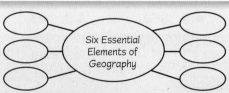

Six Essential Elements of Geography

Content Vocabulary

• **hemisphere**
• **latitude**
• **longitude**

• **projection**
• **physical map**
• **political map**

Hemispheres

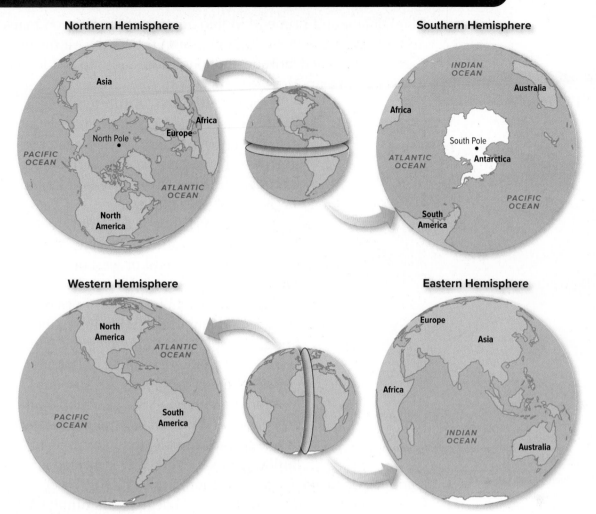

Northern Hemisphere

Asia
Africa
Europe
North Pole
PACIFIC OCEAN
ATLANTIC OCEAN
North America

Southern Hemisphere

INDIAN OCEAN
Australia
Africa
South Pole
Antarctica
ATLANTIC OCEAN
PACIFIC OCEAN
South America

Western Hemisphere

North America
ATLANTIC OCEAN
PACIFIC OCEAN
South America

Eastern Hemisphere

Europe
Asia
Africa
INDIAN OCEAN
Australia

Hemispheres

To find a place on the Earth, geographers use a system of imaginary lines that crisscross the globe. The Equator (ih·KWAY·tuhr) is one of these lines. It circles the middle of the Earth like a belt. It divides the Earth into "half spheres," or **hemispheres** (HEH·muh·sfihrz). Everything north of the Equator is in the Northern Hemisphere. Everything south of the Equator is in the Southern Hemisphere. In which of these hemispheres do you live?

Another imaginary line divides the Earth into Eastern and Western Hemispheres. This line is called the Prime Meridian. Generally, the area east of the Prime Meridian is in the Eastern Hemisphere. Everything west of the Prime Meridian is in the Western Hemisphere.

Dividing the Earth into hemispheres helps geographers locate places on the planet's surface. Which oceans are located in the Western Hemisphere? Which oceans are in the Eastern Hemisphere?

Content Vocabulary

- special-purpose map
- choropleth
- scale
- migration
- cardinal directions
- culture

hemisphere a "half sphere," used to refer to one-half of the globe when divided into North and South or East and West

Finding Places on the Earth

The Equator and Prime Meridian are two of the lines on maps and globes that help you find places on the Earth. All the lines together are called latitude and longitude. Latitude and longitude lines cross one another, forming a pattern called a grid system.

Lines of **latitude** (LA·tuh·tood) circle the Earth parallel to the Equator. They measure distance north or south of the Equator in degrees. The Equator is at 0° (zero degrees) latitude, while the North Pole is at latitude 90° N (90 degrees north).

Lines of **longitude** (LAHN·juh·tood) circle the Earth from Pole to Pole. These lines measure distances east or west of the Prime Meridian, which is at 0° longitude.

The grid system formed by lines of latitude and longitude makes it possible to find the absolute location of a place. This is the exact spot where a line of latitude crosses a line of longitude. An absolute location is written in special symbols called degrees (°) and minutes (′) (points between degrees). For example, the Empire State Building in New York City is located at a latitude of 40° 44′ North and a longitude of 73° 59′ West (40 degrees 44 minutes North and 73 degrees 59 minutes West).

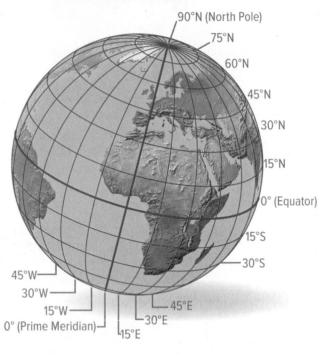

Finding the intersection of latitude and longitude allows geographers to pinpoint absolute location. At what degree point is the Prime Meridian?

Goode's Interrupted Equal-Area Projection

Goode's Interrupted Equal-Area projection shows a realistic representation of continents' sizes and shapes.

ReadingHELPDESK

latitude imaginary lines that circle the Earth parallel to the Equator

longitude imaginary lines that circle the Earth from Pole to Pole, measuring distance east or west of the Prime Meridian

projection a way of showing the round Earth on a flat map

Academic Vocabulary

distort to twist out of shape or change the size of

From Globes to Maps

When the curves of a globe become straight lines on a map, the size, shape, distance, or area can change. Imagine taking an orange peel and trying to flatten it on a table. You would either have to cut it or **distort**, or stretch, parts of it. Mapmakers face a similar problem in showing the surface of the Earth on a map. Using mathematics, they have created different types of map **projections** (pruh·JEK·shuhnz), or ways of showing the Earth on a flat sheet of paper. Each kind of projection shows the Earth's surface in a slightly different way.

Flattening Out the Planet

When you take an image of the Earth and flatten it, big gaps open up. To fill in the gaps, mapmakers stretch parts of the Earth. They show either the correct shapes of places or their correct sizes. It is impossible to show both. As a result, mapmakers use different map projections depending on their goals.

Map Projections

Take another look at that flattened orange peel. You might see something that looks like a map based on Goode's Interrupted Equal-Area projection. A map made using this projection shows continents close to their true shapes and sizes. This projection is helpful for comparing land areas among continents.

The map on the top right was made using the Mercator projection. It shows true direction and land shapes fairly accurately. However, it does not show correct size or distance. Areas located far from the Equator are distorted on this projection. Alaska, for example, appears much larger on a Mercator map than it does on a globe.

A map using the Robinson projection is less distorted. Land on the western and eastern sides of the Robinson map appears much as it does on a globe. Areas near the North and South Poles are distorted the most on this projection.

The Winkel Tripel projection gives a good overall view of the continents' shapes and sizes. You can see that land areas in this projection are not as distorted near the Poles.

✔ PROGRESS CHECK

Analyzing What are an advantage and a disadvantage to using a map rather than a globe to study the Earth's geography?

Mercator Projection

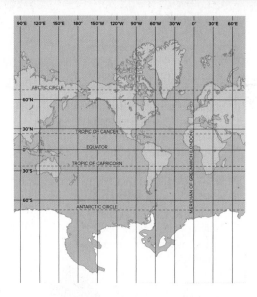

On a Mercator projection, land size and distance appear quite distorted.

Robinson Projection

The Robinson projection shows a truer picture of land size and shape. However, the North and South Poles show a great deal of distortion.

Winkel Tripel Projection

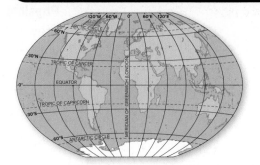

The representation of land areas on the Winkel Tripel projection most closely resembles the globe model.

Technology has changed the way we make maps. Most mapmakers use software programs called geographic information systems (GIS). This software combines information from satellite images, printed text, and statistics. A Global Positioning System (GPS) helps people locate places based on data broadcast by satellites.

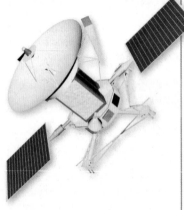

Five Themes and Six Essential Elements of Geography

GUIDING QUESTION *How do geographers use the five themes and six essential elements of geography?*

To understand how our world is connected, some geographers have broken the study of geography into five **themes** or six essential elements.

Five Themes of Geography

The Five Themes of Geography are (1) location, (2) place, (3) human-environment interaction, (4) movement, and (5) regions. You will see these themes highlighted in the geography skills questions throughout the book.

Six Essential Elements

Recently, geographers have begun to divide the study of geography into Six Essential Elements. Understanding these elements will help you build your knowledge of geography.

The World in Spatial Terms What do geographers do when studying a certain place? They first take a look at where the place is located. Location is a useful starting point. By asking "Where is it?" you begin to develop an **awareness** of the world around you.

Places and Regions Place has a special meaning in geography. It refers to more than where a place is. It also describes what a place is like. It might describe physical characteristics such as landforms, climate, and plant or animal life. Or it might describe human characteristics, such as language and way of life.

To help organize their study, geographers often group places into regions. Regions are united by one or more common characteristics.

Physical Systems When geographers study places and regions, they analyze how physical systems—such as hurricanes, volcanoes, and glaciers—shape the Earth's surface. They also look at the communities of livings things. The populations of plants and animals depend upon one another and their surroundings for survival.

Stockbyte/Alamy

Reading**HELP**DESK

Academic Vocabulary

theme a topic that is studied or a special quality that connects ideas

awareness the state of having understanding or knowledge

Human Systems Geographers are interested in human systems. Human systems refer to how people have shaped our world. Geographers look at how borders are decided and why people settle in certain places and not in others. A basic theme in geography is the movement of people, ideas, and goods.

Environment and Society How does the relationship between people and their natural surroundings influence the way we live? The theme of human-environment interaction investigates this. It also shows how people use the environment and how their actions affect the environment.

The Uses of Geography Geography helps us understand the relationships among people, places, and environments. Mastering the tools and technology used for studying geography can also help us in our daily lives.

Central Park in New York covers 843 acres of open land. People use the park for recreation. A yearlong study recorded about 35 million visits by people from the city and from around the world.

✓ **PROGRESS CHECK**

Identifying Which Essential Elements of Geography might be involved in the study of an area's landforms and how they affect people living there?

The 1980 eruption of Mount St. Helens in Washington state removed the top 1,314 feet (400 meters) of the volcano's peak and leveled nearly 230 square miles (595 square km) of surrounding forest. The destruction happened in a matter of minutes.

▶ **CRITICAL THINKING**
Analyzing What does this photo suggest about the wildlife living in the region?

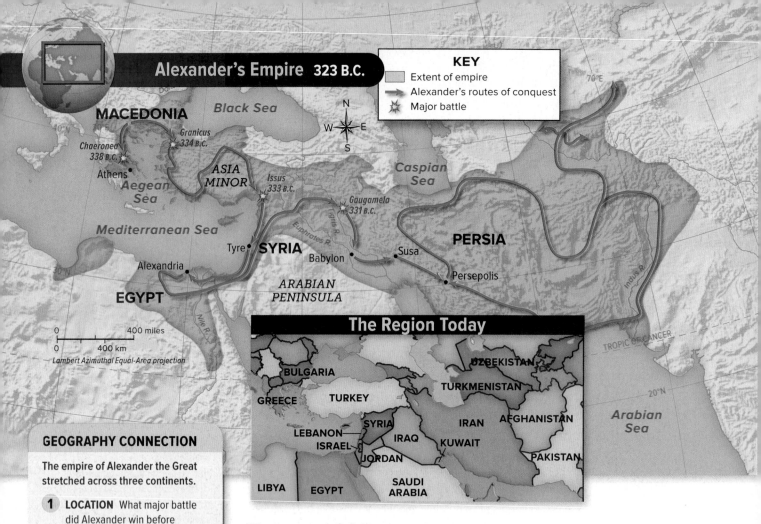

KEY
☐ Extent of empire
➝ Alexander's routes of conquest
✶ Major battle

MACEDONIA

Black Sea

Granicus 334 B.C.

Chaeronea 338 B.C.

Athens

Aegean Sea

ASIA MINOR

Issus 333 B.C.

Caspian Sea

Gaugamela 331 B.C.

Euphrates R.

Tigris R.

PERSIA

Mediterranean Sea

Tyre SYRIA

Babylon

Susa

Alexandria

ARABIAN PENINSULA

Persepolis

Indus R.

EGYPT

Nile R.

0   400 miles
0   400 km
Lambert Azimuthal Equal-Area projection

The Region Today

TROPIC OF CANCER

BULGARIA

UZBEKISTAN

TURKMENISTAN

GREECE TURKEY

20°N

Arabian Sea

LEBANON SYRIA

ISRAEL IRAQ

JORDAN

IRAN AFGHANISTAN

KUWAIT

PAKISTAN

LIBYA EGYPT

SAUDI ARABIA

GEOGRAPHY CONNECTION

The empire of Alexander the Great stretched across three continents.

1 **LOCATION** What major battle did Alexander win before heading to Babylon?

2 **CRITICAL THINKING** *Drawing Conclusions* Why do you think Alexander circled the Mediterranean Sea but did not cross it?

Types of Maps

GUIDING QUESTION *What are some of the key ways that maps are used?*

Geographers use many different types of maps. Maps that show a wide range of information are called general-purpose maps. These maps are often collected into one book called an atlas. An atlas may be a collection of special area maps—such as North America maps—or general maps of the entire world. Two of the most common general-purpose maps found in an atlas are physical and political maps.

Physical maps show land and water features. The colors used on physical maps include brown or green for land and blue for water. Physical maps may also use colors to show elevation. Elevation is the height of an area above sea level. A key explains the meaning of each color. **Political maps** show the names and borders of countries. They also show the location of cities and other human-made features of a place. Often they identify major physical features of a land area.

Reading**HELP**DESK

physical map a map that shows land and water features

political map a map that shows the names and borders of countries

special-purpose map a map that shows themes or patterns such as climate, natural resources, or population

Reading Strategy: *Summarizing*

How do you read a map? Summarize how to read a map by identifying map parts and the information they provide.

Special-Purpose Maps

Some maps show specific kinds of information. These are called **special-purpose maps.** They usually show patterns such as climate, natural resources, or population. A road map is another example of a special-purpose map. Like this map of Alexander's empire, special-purpose maps may also display historical information, such as battles or territorial changes.

Reading Maps

An important step in reading a map is to study the map key. The key explains the lines and colors used on a map. It also explains any **symbols**, or signs and pictures, used on a map. For example, the map of Alexander's empire details the size of the empire, the route of Alexander's conquest, and some important battles. Cities are usually shown as a solid circle (•), like the one for Athens.

The map **scale** is a measuring line that tells you the distances represented on the map. Suppose you wanted to know the approximate distance from Tampa, Florida to New York City. Using the scale bar will help you calculate this distance.

A map has a symbol called a compass rose that tells you the position of the **cardinal directions**—north, south, east, and west. Cardinal directions help you explain the relative location of any place on Earth. Some maps also have a locator map, a small inset map. This shows where the region on the large map is located.

✔ PROGRESS CHECK

Drawing Conclusions Why is reading the map key important when looking at a special-purpose map?

Using Charts, Graphs, and Diagrams

GUIDING QUESTION *What are the uses of charts, graphs, and diagrams?*

Charts, graphs, and diagrams are tools for showing information. The first step to understanding these visual aids is to read the title. This tells you the subject.

Charts show facts in an organized way. They arrange information in rows and columns. To read a chart, look at the labels at the top of each column and on the left side of the chart. The labels explain what the chart is showing.

---

scale a measuring line that shows the distances on a map

cardinal directions north, south, east, and west

Academic Vocabulary

symbol a sign or image that stands for something else

**Gerardus Mercator
(A.D. 1512 to A.D. 1594)**

Gerardus Mercator was a European mapmaker. He is best known for creating the Mercator projection, the first map to show longitude and latitude as straight lines. His map helped sailors navigate at sea. Mercator was also the first person to call a collection of maps an *atlas*. Many people think Mercator was the greatest geographer of the 1500s.

▶ **CRITICAL THINKING**
Speculating Before sailors had a map such as Mercator's, how do you think they were able to find their way on the sea?

Graphs come in different types. Bar graphs use thick, wide lines to compare data. They are useful for comparing amounts. Line graphs show changes over a particular period of time. A climate graph, or climograph (KLY·muh·graf), combines a line graph and a bar graph. It shows the long-term weather patterns in a place.

To read a bar graph, line graph, or climograph, look at the labels along the side and bottom. The vertical line along the left side of the graph is the y-axis. The horizontal line along the bottom is the x-axis. One axis tells you what is being measured. The other axis tells what units of measurement are being used.

Circle graphs show how the whole of something is divided into parts. Each "slice" shows a part or percentage of the whole "circle." The entire circle totals 100 percent.

Diagrams are special drawings. They show steps in a process, point out the parts of an object, or explain how something works. An elevation profile is a diagram that shows a piece of land as if it were sliced open. This shows changes in height.

✔ **PROGRESS CHECK**

Identifying What type of graph shows changes over time?

Population and Culture

GUIDING QUESTION *How do geographers study population and culture?*

Like geographers, historians study population, culture, and the movement of people, ideas, and goods. Historians are interested in how these things change over time.

Population Shifts

Population refers to how many people live in a specific area or place. Geographers study this in great detail. They look at what sorts of people make up a population. They examine how fast a population grows or shrinks over time. They also measure population density. This is the average number of people living in a square mile or square kilometer. A **choropleth** (KAWR·uh·plehth) map uses colors to show population density.

Populations can also change location. The movement of people from one place to settle in another place is called **migration** (my·GRAY·shuhn). Throughout history there have been many migrations of human beings.

choropleth a special-purpose map that uses color to show population density

migration the movement of people from one place to settle in another place

culture the set of beliefs, behaviors, and traits shared by a group of people

UniversalImagesGroup/Getty Images

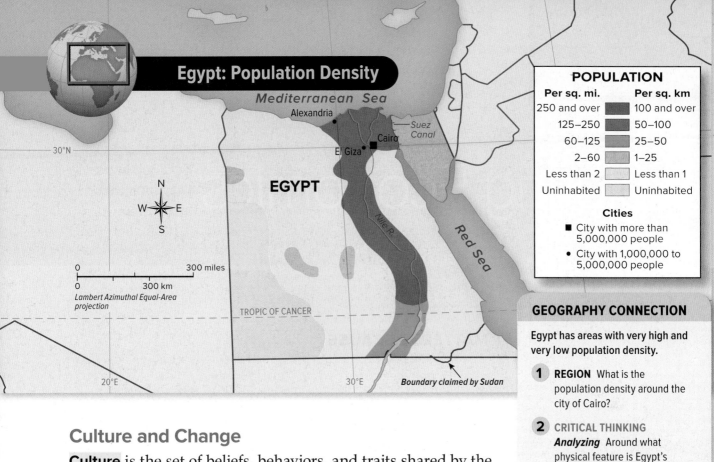

Egypt: Population Density

Mediterranean Sea

POPULATION

Per sq. mi.		Per sq. km
250 and over		100 and over
125–250		50–100
60–125		25–50
2–60		1–25
Less than 2		Less than 1
Uninhabited		Uninhabited

Cities

■ City with more than 5,000,000 people

● City with 1,000,000 to 5,000,000 people

300 miles

300 km

Lambert Azimuthal Equal-Area projection

TROPIC OF CANCER

Boundary claimed by Sudan

GEOGRAPHY CONNECTION

Egypt has areas with very high and very low population density.

1 **REGION** What is the population density around the city of Cairo?

2 **CRITICAL THINKING**
Analyzing Around what physical feature is Egypt's population the densest?

Culture and Change

Culture is the set of beliefs, behaviors, and traits shared by the members of a group. Scholars study cultures by examining the language, religion, government, and customs of different groups.

Throughout history, different peoples have met through exploration, migration, and trade. These meetings often lead to cultural diffusion. In cultural diffusion, each group shares part of its culture with the other. Sometimes a completely new culture is formed. Many historians believe this happened in India as a result of the Aryan migrations.

 **PROGRESS CHECK**

Analyzing Why are geographers interested in contact between cultures?

LESSON 1 REVIEW

Review Vocabulary

1. How do *latitude* and *longitude* help identify your exact location on the Earth?

2. Why would a *scale* be helpful when trying to determine distances on a *physical map*?

Answer the Guiding Questions

3. *Identifying* What type of map would you choose to find the borders between countries? Why?

4. *Finding the Main Idea* Why do mapmakers have to choose between showing the correct land shapes or distances on the Earth?

5. *Contrasting* What is the difference between a chart and a diagram?

6. *Making Inferences* How might migration lead to the spread and mixing of cultures?

7. **INFORMATIVE/EXPLANATORY** Write a paragraph explaining which Essential Elements of Geography you would use to study the weather in an area.

LESSON 2

Exploring Economics

ESSENTIAL QUESTION
• Why do people trade?

IT MATTERS BECAUSE
Most people in our society buy or sell goods and services every day. Trade has also shaped the course of history in major ways.

What Is Economics?

GUIDING QUESTION *What are the basic ideas of economics?*

There are three key questions to ask about any economy: *What* goods and services should we offer? *How* should we create and distribute these goods and services? *Who* will use these goods and services?

Resources and Production

In order to make goods and offer services, people need **resources.** There are four major kinds of resources: land, labor, capital, and entrepreneurship. Land includes the surface of the Earth and its natural resources, such as minerals and water. **Labor** is the ability of people to do work. You need labor to make goods and provide services. **Capital** is money and goods used to help people make or do things. You need capital to run a business. **Entrepreneurship** (ahn·truh·pruh·NUHR·shihp) is the act of running a business and taking on the risks of that business. Entrepreneurship usually describes individual or small businesses. Another kind of resource is **technology**. Technology is using knowledge in a practical way to accomplish a task. Technology can make it easier and cheaper to create goods.

Reading**HELP**DESK

Taking Notes: *Describing*
Use a chart like this one to list these two types of economic systems and their key elements.

Traditional	Command

Content Vocabulary
• capital
• entrepreneurship
• supply
• demand
• scarcity
• opportunity cost
• traditional economy
• command economy
• recession

All of these resources were important to early civilizations. Good land and freshwater were very important to farmers. Early rulers needed many workers for large projects. They gathered capital by collecting taxes. Merchants showed entrepreneurship. They traded goods to earn a profit, or an increase in the value of what they owned.

Supply and Demand

Getting the resources needed to offer a good or service is a first step to providing that good or service. Next, you need to know how much of that good or service to offer. You will also want to decide how much money to charge for the good or service. These choices are affected by the laws of supply and demand.

Supply is the amount of a good or service that a producer wants to sell. The law of supply says that the higher the price you can charge for a good or service, the more of it you will want to sell. **Demand** is the amount of something that a consumer wants to buy. The law of demand says that the lower the price of a good or service, the more of it people will want to buy.

You can see the supply and demand curves in the graph on this page. Look at the supply curve. It shows that people want to make more goods when the price is high. The demand curve shows that buyers want to buy less when the price is high. In a free market, these forces balance each other over time. The seller and buyer will agree on a price and amount that satisfies both.

Academic Vocabulary

resource something that is useful
labor the ability of people to do work
technology the use of advanced methods to solve problems

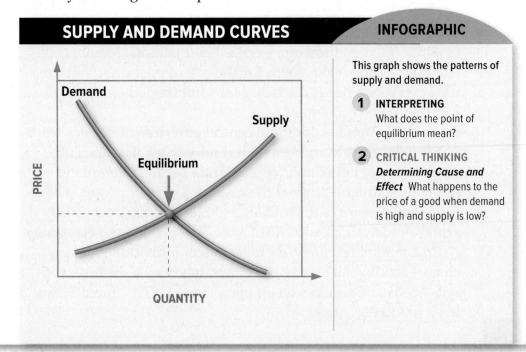

SUPPLY AND DEMAND CURVES   **INFOGRAPHIC**

Demand

Supply

Equilibrium

PRICE

QUANTITY

This graph shows the patterns of supply and demand.

1 **INTERPRETING**
What does the point of equilibrium mean?

2 **CRITICAL THINKING**
Determining Cause and Effect What happens to the price of a good when demand is high and supply is low?

Content Vocabulary

- inflation   - barter
- exports   - globalization
- imports

capital money and goods used to help people make or do things

entrepreneurship the act of running a business and taking on the risks of that business

supply the amount of a good or service that a producer wants to sell

demand the amount of something that a consumer wants to buy

In a hunter-gatherer community, some members might provide food by hunting for meat or gathering vegetables. Others might turn furs into clothing.

There are other factors that affect supply and demand. One is **scarcity** (SKEHR·suh·tee), or lack of a resource. When not much of a needed resource is available, then the demand for it will grow. The higher demand will raise the price. This may force people to seek replacements for that resource.

Another factor is opportunity cost. The **opportunity cost** of something is what you give up to make it or buy it. Suppose you are a farmer. You choose to grow wheat on your land. You spend time and resources to grow the wheat. While you are growing wheat, you cannot use the land to grow beans. You are giving up the chance to grow something else when you grow wheat. The time, resources, and choices that you gave up are all part of the opportunity cost of growing wheat. People are always weighing the opportunity costs of their choices about what to make or buy.

✓ PROGRESS CHECK

Predicting How will the people who make goods and those who buy the goods react if the price goes down?

Managing and Measuring Economies

GUIDING QUESTION *What are the different types of economic systems?*

Dealing with resources, supply, and demand can be very hard. Each society organizes its economy using an economic system.

Economic Systems

A **traditional economy** is based on custom. In such an economy, children often do the same work as their parents. Members of a family or tribe make goods for the rest of their group. In this way, everyone's needs are met. Many hunter-gatherer groups had traditional economies.

In a **command economy,** a central government decides what goods will be made and who will receive them. The ancient civilizations of Egypt and Mesopotamia began as command economies. Rulers gathered the resources of their people. They used these resources to build large projects or raise powerful armies. Today, Cuba and North Korea have command economies.

In a market economy, each person, or **individual,** makes choices about what to make, sell, and buy. He or she buys and sells goods and services on an open market. The United States has a market economy.

scarcity the lack of a resource
opportunity cost what is given up, such as time or money, to make or buy something

traditional economy an economic system in which custom decides what people do, make, buy, and sell

command economy an economic system in which a central government decides what goods will be made and who will receive them

In a mixed economy, the government has some control over what and how much is made. Individuals make the rest of the economic choices. Some countries in Europe are mixed economies.

Measuring Economies

Economies grow and shrink over time. This pattern is called the business cycle. When the economy grows quickly, it is often called a boom. When the economy grows very slowly or shrinks, it is called a **recession** (rih·SEH·shuhn). In a recession, companies often close and people lose their jobs. The United States entered a recession in December 2007.

Governments try to keep their economies growing and avoid recessions. One way they do this is by watching prices. Rising prices are a sign of **inflation** (ihn·FLAY·shuhn). High inflation means that money buys less. This raises the cost of living. Say the yearly rate of inflation is 10 percent. This means that something that cost you $10 last year costs you $11 this year. Sometimes inflation can get very high. In Argentina in the 1980s, the yearly rate of inflation hit 1,000 percent. The same goods and services cost 10 times more than they did the year before.

Governments want to avoid having too much inflation. However, **experts** who study economics disagree about what causes inflation. So finding the right government policies is difficult.

✔ **PROGRESS CHECK**

Identifying In which type of economic system are all decisions made by a central government?

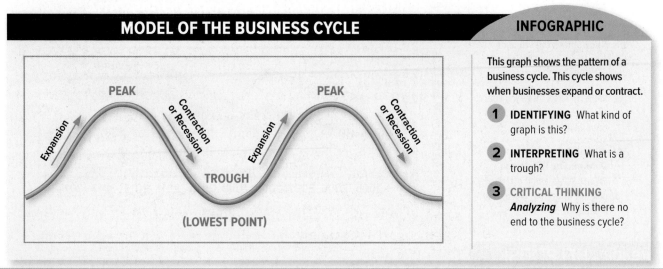

MODEL OF THE BUSINESS CYCLE

INFOGRAPHIC

PEAK
Expansion
Contraction or Recession
PEAK
Expansion
Contraction or Recession
TROUGH
(LOWEST POINT)

This graph shows the pattern of a business cycle. This cycle shows when businesses expand or contract.

1 IDENTIFYING What kind of graph is this?

2 INTERPRETING What is a trough?

3 CRITICAL THINKING
Analyzing Why is there no end to the business cycle?

recession a period of slow economic growth or decline

inflation a continued rise in prices or the supply of money

Academic Vocabulary

individual a single human being

expert a skilled person who has mastered a subject

Trade in World History

GUIDING QUESTION *What are the benefits and disadvantages of trade?*

Trade has been important to many different civilizations. What makes trade between different peoples so common?

Why Do People Trade?

Two countries trade with each other when both sides can gain something from the exchange. **Exports** are goods shipped out of a country and sold somewhere else. **Imports** are the goods and services that a country buys from other countries.

Countries want to export goods of which they have a large supply. They want to import goods that are hard to find in their own lands. For hundreds of years, Europeans traded wool, gold, and silver with Asians for rare goods such as silk and spices.

Early civilizations often traded by bartering. When people **barter,** goods and services are traded for other goods and services. For example, a merchant might trade fish for furs. Eventually, some ancient peoples invented money. Money had a set value, could be traded for anything, and was easier to carry.

Barriers to Trade

Barriers can make international trade difficult. Conflict can stop trade. Geography can make it hard to travel between two places. Sometimes a country chooses to cut off contact with other peoples. In the 1600s, Japan limited trade with European countries. The Japanese wanted to limit European influence on Japanese society.

INFOGRAPHIC

This graph shows the value of U.S. imports and exports over a ten year period.

1 **IDENTIFYING** In which year were U.S. exports at their lowest?

2 **CRITICAL THINKING**
Determining Cause and Effect What is one effect of a country importing more than it exports?

U.S. IMPORTS AND EXPORTS, 2005–2014

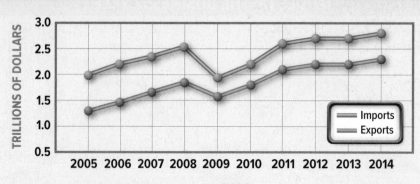

Source: Data for import/export graph comes from U.S. Department of Commerce, Bureau of Economic Analysis, International Economic Accounts, Trade in Goods and Services, 1992–present.

Reading HELP DESK

export a good sent from one country to another in trade

import a good brought into a country from another country

barter to trade by exchanging one good or service for another

globalization the growth in free trade between countries

Finally, nations may try to limit or ban trade that hurts producers in their own country. For example, in the Great Depression, U.S. farmers were worried about food imports from Europe. They feared that European farmers might drive them out of business. So they asked the U.S. government to raise taxes on imported European crops. The government did so to protect American farmers. This led other countries to tax U.S. goods to protect their own farmers and businesses.

Global Trade

Today, most of the world's countries take part in some form of international trade. The process is called **globalization** (gloh·buh·luh·ZAY·shuhn). Countries like the United States have numerous trade partners. Many large companies also have business branches in more than one country.

Much of this growth has come from efforts to increase free trade. The goal of free trade is a world market where people are free to choose what to buy and sell. People who favor free trade say that it boosts trade. It also cuts the prices of goods. These changes help economies grow. Those against free trade say that it makes imports and foreign labor costs too cheap. They fear that a country will lose companies and jobs to other countries.

Globalization has increased the ties among the world's economies. In 2015, the United States had the largest economy in the world. The U.S. economy was bigger than that of the next two leading countries, Japan and China, added together. Every day, Americans buy and use goods made in other countries. At the same time, American goods and services are sold around the world. When the U.S. economy struggles, it affects the entire world. The questions about what to make, how to make it, and who should buy it are no longer just national issues.

Shipping through international ports is an important method of transporting goods. This global trade may help the economies of different countries grow.

▶ **CRITICAL THINKING**
Analyzing Where do you fit into the process of global trade?

 **PROGRESS CHECK**

Finding the Main Idea Why do countries agree to trade with one another?

Ian Murphy/Stone/Getty Images

LESSON 2 REVIEW

Review Vocabulary

1. Why are *capital* and *labor* needed to make goods?

2. How does *demand* relate to buyers of a good?

Answer the Guiding Questions

3. *Explaining* What is opportunity cost?

4. *Contrasting* Describe the differences between a command economy and a traditional economy.

5. *Summarizing* What types of barriers might prevent trade between countries?

6. **INFORMATIVE/EXPLANATORY** Write a paragraph describing how countries decide what goods to export and what goods to import.

LESSON 3
Practicing Citizenship

ESSENTIAL QUESTION

• Why do people form governments?

IT MATTERS BECAUSE
Our system of government needs active citizens who understand their rights and responsibilities.

Principles of Government

GUIDING QUESTION *What are the key principles of the U.S. government?*

The U.S. Constitution is the highest law in the United States. It contains the key ideas of America's government. Many of these ideas came from ancient Greece and Rome. The United States has a **representative government**. This means that citizens vote for officials who serve the will of the people. The government must act in the people's interests and protect their rights.

The Constitution created a **federal system** of government. The central, or federal, government is the highest authority. However, it also shares some powers with the state governments.

The federal government is split into three equal parts, or branches. Each branch has its own specific powers, an idea called **separation of powers**. This concept was adopted so that no one branch could become too powerful. An overly powerful government could harm its citizens. Each branch limits the power of the other branches. The diagram shows this system of **checks and balances**.

What do the three branches of government do? The **legislative** (LEH・juhs・lay・tihv) **branch** is known as the U.S. Congress. It passes laws for the whole country. The **executive branch** includes the office of the U.S. president. The president and other members of the executive branch ensure that the nation's laws are carried out.

Reading**HELP**DESK

Taking Notes: *Summarizing*
Use a graphic organizer like this one to show the rights and responsibilities of citizenship.

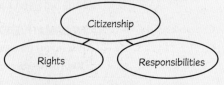

Content Vocabulary

• **representative government**
• **federal system**
• **separation of powers**
• **checks and balances**

Can impeach, or remove, president; Can override veto; Can block appointments; Can refuse to approve treaties

Can impeach, or remove judges; Can block the appointment of judges

Can veto, or block, laws

Can declare acts of Congress to be unconstitutional, or illegal

UNITED STATES CONGRESS

LEGISLATIVE BRANCH

Can appoint, or choose, judges

Can declare presidential actions unconstitutional, or illegal

EXECUTIVE BRANCH

JUDICIAL BRANCH

The presidential veto is one example of checks and balances in action. However, if the president vetoes a bill, Congress can then vote to overturn the veto. This is another example of checks and balances.

1 **IDENTIFYING** How does the legislative branch act as a check on the judicial branch?

2 **CRITICAL THINKING** *Drawing Conclusions* Why did the authors of the Constitution create the system of checks and balances?

The **judicial** (joo·DIH·shuhl) **branch** includes the U.S. Supreme Court and various lesser courts. The judges in the judicial branch use the Constitution to interpret laws. They can strike down laws that violate the Constitution.

legislative branch part of government that passes laws

executive branch part of government that enforces laws

judicial branch part of government that interprets laws

 **PROGRESS CHECK**

Identifying What type of government does the United States have?

What Is Citizenship?

GUIDING QUESTION *What are the civic rights, duties, and responsibilities of U.S. citizens?*

The system of government in the United States provides many freedoms. However, it also needs citizens to carry out certain duties and responsibilities. This idea, called civic participation, comes from ancient Greece and Rome. Good citizenship helps our government and communities work as well as possible.

Rights of Citizenship

All Americans have the right to **seek** life, liberty, and happiness. All Americans have the right to freedom of expression. This means that they can speak and write openly. They can attend peaceful gatherings. They can petition the government to address their needs. The Constitution also protects the right of people to worship as they choose. People who are accused of a crime have the right to receive a fair trial by a **jury** of their peers.

Content Vocabulary

- legislative branch
- executive branch
- judicial branch

representative government government in which citizens elect officials who govern

federal system government which divides power between central and state governments

separation of powers the division of power among the branches of government

checks and balances system in which each branch of government limits the power of another branch

The design of the American flag has changed over the years. However, its red and white stripes still honor the country's thirteen original colonies.

▶ CRITICAL THINKING

Analyzing Like the flags of other countries, the U.S. flag contains symbols. Each of the 50 stars represents a state. If the U.S. wanted a new flag to represent the country today, what symbols would you suggest, and why?

Citizens also have the right to vote for public officials and to serve in public office. The right to vote allows citizens to choose their leaders, while the right to serve lets them represent their fellow citizens in government.

Duties and Responsibilities of Citizenship

By law, citizens must carry out some duties. Obeying all federal, state, and local laws is one of the first duties of citizenship. Citizens also have a duty to pay their taxes to federal, state, and local governments. These taxes pay for the services provided by government to the American people.

Citizens must serve on a jury if the government asks them to. This service is needed in order to honor people's right to a fair trial by jury. Finally, citizens must be ready to defend the United States and the Constitution.

People born in other countries can also become U.S. citizens. First, they must go through naturalization. This is a process of applying for, and being granted, citizenship. To qualify, they have to have lived in the United States for a certain amount of time. They also need to show good moral character. They must be able to use basic English and must know about U.S. history and government. In addition, they must swear to uphold all duties of citizenship.

In addition to their duties, citizens also have responsibilities. Citizens should stay informed about important **issues,** or topics. An awareness of critical issues—such as concern for the global environment—will help them make wise choices when they vote in federal, state, and local elections. Voting is a powerful right and a key responsibility of citizenship. If people do not vote, they give away part of their voice in government.

Citizens should also respect the rights and views of other people. The United States welcomes people of many different backgrounds. They all share the same freedoms. Before you deny a right to someone else, put yourself in that person's place. Think how you would feel if someone tried to take away your rights.

Finally, citizens should take part in their local community. By working with one another, we help make our neighborhoods and towns better places to live. There are different ways to keep our communities strong. We can volunteer our time. We can join neighborhood groups, and we can serve in public office.

✓ PROGRESS CHECK

Summarizing What duties do citizens have?

Reading **HELP**DESK

Academic Vocabulary

seek to look for or try to achieve
jury a group of people sworn to make a decision in a legal case
issue a concern or problem that has not yet been solved

Being a Global Citizen

GUIDING QUESTION *What does it mean to be a global citizen?*

Today the world faces many problems that go beyond the borders of any one country. When sick people travel, disease can spread quickly. In 2014, Ebola, a rare and deadly disease caused by the Ebola virus, spread throughout West Africa. Health agencies from around the world worked to stop the virus. Doctors and nurses provided medical services to people who contracted the disease. Hospital staffs throughout the world were trained on how to treat patients who were infected with the Ebola virus. Many countries also have close economic ties to other nations. Because of these ties, economic problems in one country affect other countries. In addition, the idea is growing around the world that all people should have certain basic human rights. World leaders must often work together to deal with these issues.

Being a global citizen means learning about the different issues that affect the world as a whole. It means taking care of the environment. It also means understanding how people live in other countries. We are all affected by drought and hunger or economic troubles in other countries. Once we understand one another's ways of life, we can work together more easily to solve big problems.

This family is taking the Oath of Allegiance. It is the final step in becoming a U.S. citizen through naturalization.

Being a global citizen does not mean giving up your duties and responsibilities as a citizen of the United States. It means thinking about how you can make the world a better place by your actions. Making the effort to stay informed and to respect the views of others helps all Americans. Through that same effort, you can also help the rest of the world.

Kevork Djansezian/Getty Images News/Getty Images

✔ **PROGRESS CHECK**

Finding the Main Idea What are some of the ways in which you could become a better global citizen?

LESSON 3 REVIEW

Review Vocabulary

1. What is a *federal system* of government?

2. How are *checks and balances* related to the idea of *separation of powers*?

Answer the Guiding Questions

3. ***Finding the Main Idea*** What is the main purpose of a representative government?

4. ***Drawing Conclusions*** Why do citizens have duties and responsibilities as well as rights?

5. ***Summarizing*** How have countries had to work together to stop the spread of disease?

6. **NARRATIVE** Write a paragraph describing how you can fulfill two of the responsibilities of citizenship in your daily life.

Write your answers on a separate piece of paper.

1 **Exploring the Essential Question**

NARRATIVE Think about the role of the Six Essential Elements of Geography in your daily life. How do you affect the environment where you live? How does it affect you? Write a short essay answering these questions. Be sure to include descriptive details.

2 **21st Century Skills**

ANALYZING INFORMATION Imagine that the price of a gallon of gasoline has varied in the following way: January—$2.50, March—$2.45, May—$2.75, July—$3. Create a line graph that shows the rise and fall in gas prices over this period. According to the laws of supply and demand, when would gasoline producers want to sell the most gas?

3 **Thinking Like a Historian**

CITIZENSHIP AND SOCIETY Imagine that you are teaching a class of people seeking citizenship. What are the three topics you would be sure to include in your teaching?

4 **GEOGRAPHY ACTIVITY**

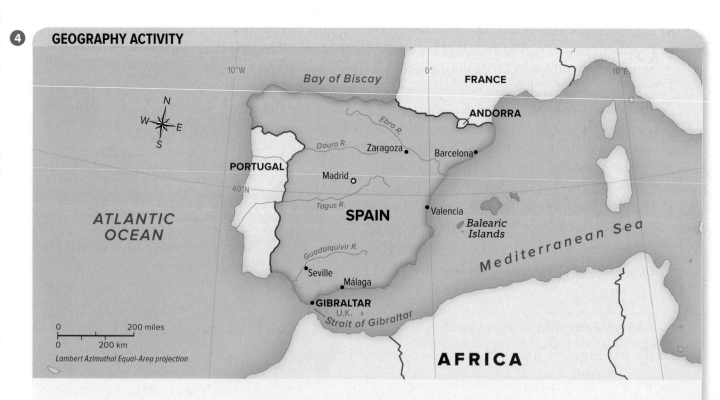

Reading Maps

1. What country lies west of Spain?

2. Spain is located between what two major bodies of water?

3. About how many miles separate Zaragoza and Barcelona?

4. Which city is located along the Prime Meridian?

Directions: Write your answers on a separate piece of paper.

CHECKING FOR UNDERSTANDING

1 Define each of these terms as they relate to geography, economics, or citizenship.

A. political map
B. migration
C. culture
D. supply
E. barter
F. globalization
G. representative government
H. separation of powers
I. executive branch

REVIEW THE GUIDING QUESTIONS

2 *Explaining* What are latitude and longitude, and why are they used by geographers?

3 *Identifying* What does the Essential Element of Geography referred to as Environment and Society investigate?

4 *Explaining* What is technology, and how does it relate to the production of goods?

5 *Listing* List four basic types of economic systems.

6 *Identifying* What is barter, and how is it related to trade?

7 *Specifying* What does the legislative branch of the U.S. federal government do?

8 *Describing* What is civic participation, and where did the idea originate?

9 *Summarizing* Summarize the responsibilities held by citizens.

CRITICAL THINKING

10 *Evaluating* For what purposes is a map using the Mercator projection best suited? Explain.

11 *Recognizing Relationships* According to the Six Essential Elements of Geography, how are the concepts of place and region related?

12 *Differentiating* How do general-purpose and special-purpose maps differ? Provide examples of each type of map in your answer.

13 *Making Generalizations* Study the map showing Egypt's population density in Lesson 1. What generalization can be made about Egypt's population and the country's physical features?

14 *Making Connections* In which type of economic system—a command economy or a market economy—would entrepreneurship play a greater role? Explain.

15 *Assessing* Which of the four major kinds of economic resources—land, labor, capital, and entrepreneurship—do you think might have been most important for the world's earliest civilizations? Explain your answer.

16 *Explaining* Why might a country want to limit or ban trade with other nations?

17 *Determining Cause and Effect* Explain the effects that scarcity of a particular product might have on demand and price for that product.

18 *Analyzing Diagrams* Study the Checks and Balances diagram in Lesson 3. According to the diagram, how does the executive branch check the power of the judicial branch? How does the judicial branch check the power of the executive branch? Why are these powers important to the form of government used in the United States?

19 *Contrasting* How do the tasks of the three branches of U.S. government differ?

20 *Defending* Which of the rights of citizenship discussed in the text do you believe is most important to Americans? Defend your choice in a paragraph.

Need Extra Help?

If You've Missed Question	**1**	**2**	**3**	**4**	**5**	**6**	**7**	**8**	**9**	**10**	**11**	**12**	**13**	**14**	**15**	**16**	**17**	**18**	**19**	**20**
Review Lesson	1,2,3	1	1	2	2	2	3	3	3	1	1	1	1	2	2	2	2	3	3	3

SHORT RESPONSE

"Former Supreme Court Justice Louis Brandeis once said, 'The only title in our democracy superior to that of President [is] the title of citizen.' In the United States, the power of government comes directly from people like you. To protect freedom and liberty, U.S. citizens must participate in the democratic process and in their communities."

—from the *Citizen's Almanac*, U.S. Citizenship and Immigration Services

21 According to the passage, why do citizens need to take part in the democratic process?

22 Why does Brandeis say the title of citizen is greater than the title of President?

EXTENDED RESPONSE

23 *Argument* You are a new American citizen. Write a letter to the editor explaining why citizens must fulfill their duties and responsibilities.

STANDARDIZED TEST PRACTICE

ANALYZING DOCUMENTS

24 *Drawing Conclusions* Adam Smith wrote about reasons people trade in his 1776 economics book, *The Wealth of Nations*:

"Whoever offers to another a bargain of any kind, proposes to do this [trade]. Give me that which I want, and you shall have this which you want, is the meaning of every such offer. … It is not from the benevolence [kindness] of the butcher, the brewer, or the baker that we expect our dinner, but from their regard [attention] to their own interest."

—from *The Wealth of Nations*

According to this passage, why do people trade with each other?

A. to get something illegally

B. to get something that they want

C. to offer gifts

D. to be benevolent

25 *Finding the Main Idea* According to the passage, what convinces the butcher, baker, or brewer to provide food for us?

A. They do it because the government tells them to do it.

B. They do it out of kindness.

C. They do it because it serves their self-interest.

D. They do it because we want the food.

Need Extra Help?

If You've Missed Question	21	22	23	24	25
Review Lesson	3	3	3	2	2

◀ *Ancient human-like fossils tell us about our early ancestors.*

8000 B.C. TO 2000 B.C.

Early Humans and the Agricultural Revolution

THE STORY MATTERS ...

Was eastern Africa the home of the earliest humans? Many scientists believe that is where the first group of human-like beings lived. Some early human skeletons found in Africa are over six million years old. Scientists estimate that this skull may be more than 3.2 million years old. It may have belonged to a three-year-old child who lived in eastern Africa. Fossils like this one tell us a lot about early humans.

Some early people may have begun moving from Africa to other regions about 1.8 million years ago. Over a period of time humans were found in Europe and as far away as China. Everywhere early humans went, they left behind clues about their lives. By studying these clues, scientists can tell us about our past.

ESSENTIAL QUESTION

• How do people adapt to their environment?

Wlad74/iStock/Getty Images

Place & Time: Early Humans
8000 B.C. to 2000 B.C.

During the Paleolithic Age, people began to develop technology, or knowledge that is applied to help people. They created tools that helped them survive in different locations.

Step Into the Place

MAP FOCUS By about 8000 B.C., people in Southwest Asia began to stay in one place and grow crops. They also raised animals for food and clothing.

1 **LOCATION** Look at the map. Near what major body of water are Çatalhüyük and Jericho located?

2 **PLACE** Based on the map, what is the land around both settlements like?

3 **LOCATION** Describe Jericho's location in relation to the three major rivers on the map.

4 **CRITICAL THINKING** *Drawing Conclusions* Why do you think the earliest settlements developed along rivers?

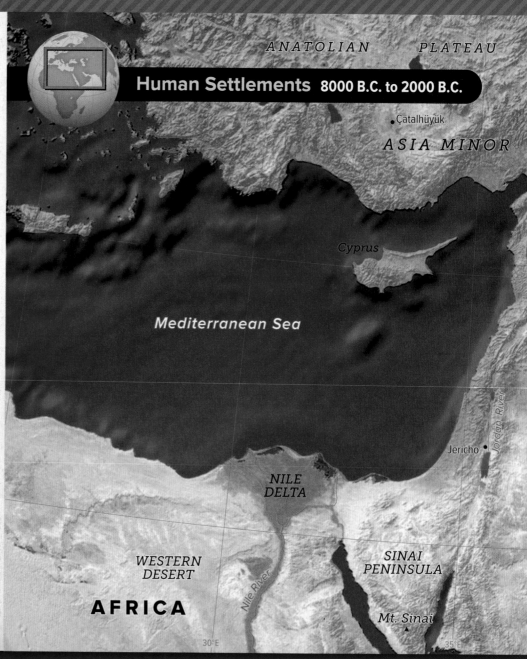

Human Settlements 8000 B.C. to 2000 B.C.

ANATOLIAN PLATEAU

•Çatalhüyük

ASIA MINOR

Cyprus

Mediterranean Sea

Jordan River

Jericho •

NILE DELTA

WESTERN DESERT

AFRICA

SINAI PENINSULA

Nile River

Mt. Sinai

30°E

35°E

Step Into the Time

TIME LINE Choose an event from the Early Settlements time line and write a paragraph predicting the general social or economic effects that event might have had on the world.

EARLY SETTLEMENTS		
THE WORLD	**2.5 MILLION B.C.**	**100,000 B.C.**

c. 2.5 million B.C.
Paleolithic Age begins

c. 100,000 B.C. Last Ice Age begins

Caspian
Sea

M E S O P O T A M I A

Euphrates River

Tigris River

35°N

SYRIAN
DESERT

ASIA

N
W E
S

ARABIAN
DESERT

30°N

0   100 miles
0   100 km
Albers Equal-Area Conic projection

Persian
Gulf

40°E   45°E   50°E

c. 6700 B.C.
Çatalhüyük established

c. 4000 B.C. Farming
established in Europe

c. 8000 B.C. Farming
begins in Southwest Asia

c. 6000 B.C. Farming begins in
Nile Valley in Egypt and in China

c. 3000 B.C. River valley civilizations emerge

8000 B.C. 7000 B.C.   6000 B.C.   5000 B.C.   4000 B.C.   3000 B.C.   2000 B.C.   1000 B.C.

LESSON 1
Hunter-Gatherers

ESSENTIAL QUESTION

• How do people adapt to their environment?

IT MATTERS BECAUSE
Technology led to the expansion and survival of early civilization.

The Paleolithic Age

GUIDING QUESTION *What was life like during the Paleolithic Age?*

Historians call the early period of human history the Stone Age. They do this because it was the time when people used stone to make tools and weapons. The earliest part of this period was the **Paleolithic** (pay·lee·uh·LIH·thick) Age. In Greek, *paleolithic* means "old stone." Therefore, the Paleolithic Age is also called the Old Stone Age. The Paleolithic Age began about 2.5 million years ago and lasted until around 8000 B.C. Remember, that is about 4,500 years earlier than recorded time, which starts about 5,500 years ago.

Surviving in the Paleolithic Age

Try to imagine what life was like during the Paleolithic Age. Think about living in a time long before any roads, farms, or villages existed. Paleolithic people often moved around in search of food. They were **nomads** (NOH·mads), or people who regularly move from place to place to survive. They traveled in groups, or bands, of about 20 or 30 members.

Paleolithic people survived by hunting and gathering. The search for food was their main activity, and it was often difficult. They had to learn which animals to hunt and which plants to eat. Paleolithic people hunted buffalo, bison, wild goats, reindeer,

Reading**HELP**DESK

Taking Notes: *Sequencing*
Use a diagram like the one on the right to list two important inventions of Paleolithic people. Then explain why these inventions were important.

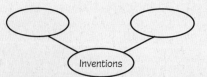

Content Vocabulary
• **Paleolithic**   • **technology**
• **nomads**   • **Ice Age**

54 *Early Humans and the Agricultural Revolution*

and other animals, depending on where they lived. Along coastal areas, they fished. These early people also gathered wild nuts, berries, fruits, wild grains, and green plants.

Finding Food

Paleolithic men and women performed different tasks within the group. Men—not women—hunted large animals. They often had to search far from their camp. Men had to learn how animals behaved and how to hunt them. They had to develop tracking methods. At first, men used clubs or drove the animals off cliffs to kill them. Over time, however, Paleolithic people developed tools and weapons to help them hunt. The traps and spears they made increased their chances of killing their prey.

Women stayed close to the camp, which was often located near a stream or other body of water. They looked after the children and searched nearby woods and meadows for berries, nuts, and grains. Everyone worked to find food, because it was the key to the group's survival.

Paleolithic people traveled in bands to hunt and gather food. Bands lived together in the open, under overhangs such as the one pictured here, or in caves.

▶ **CRITICAL THINKING**
Analyzing Why did these people live together in groups?

Paleolithic relating to the earliest period of the Stone Age

nomads people who move from place to place as a group to find food for themselves

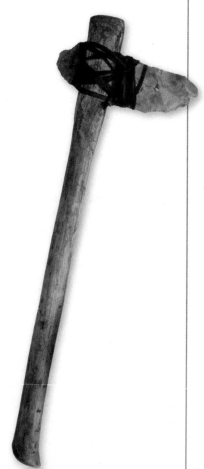

Paleolithic peoples used tools like this for many purposes. Look at this ax and decide what materials it was made of.

▶ CRITICAL THINKING
Predicting What do you think this tool was used for?

Some scientists believe that an equal relationship existed between Paleolithic men and women. It is likely that both made decisions that affected the band or group. Some evidence suggests that some men and women may have hunted in monogamous pairs. This means that a man and a woman worked together to find food for themselves and their children. Such groupings became the first families.

The Invention of Tools

Culture is the way of life for a group of people who share similar beliefs and customs. The **methods** Paleolithic people used to hunt and gather their food were part of their culture, as were the tools they used.

Technology (tehk·NAHL·uh·jee)—tools and methods to perform tasks—was first used by Paleolithic people. Before this time, sticks, stones, and tree branches served as tools. Later, people made devices from a hard stone called flint. Have you ever imagined how difficult it would be to prepare or eat food without a cutting tool? Paleolithic people learned that by hitting flint with another hard stone, the flint would flake into pieces. These pieces had very sharp edges that could be used for cutting. Hand axes, for example, were large pieces of flint tied to wooden poles. Flint technology was a major breakthrough for early peoples.

Over time, early people made better, more complex tools. Spears and bows and arrows made killing large animals easier. Harpoons, or spears with sharp points, and fishhooks increased the number of fish caught. Early humans used sharp-edged tools to cut up plants and dig roots. They used scraping tools to clean animal hides, which they used for clothing and shelter.

By the end of the Paleolithic Age, people were making smaller and sharper tools. They crafted needles from animal bones to make nets and baskets and to sew hides together for clothing. This technology had a far-reaching effect. It drove the development of more advanced farming tools and influenced where people settled.

Changing to Survive

Climate affected how Paleolithic people lived. Some early people lived in cold climates and made clothing from animal skins to stay warm. They sought protection in **available** natural shelters, such as caves and rock overhangs. Remember, there

Dorling Kindersley/Getty Images

technology an ability gained by the practical use of knowledge

Academic Vocabulary

method a way of doing something
available ready to be used
construct to build by putting parts together

were no houses or apartment buildings as we know them in the Paleolithic Age. Gradually, humans learned to make their own shelters. People **constructed** tents and huts of animal skins, brush, and wood. In very cold climates, some people made shelters from ice and snow. In regions where wood was scarce, Paleolithic people used the large bones from dead woolly mammoths, or hairy elephant-like animals, to build frames for shelters. They then covered the bones with animal hides.

People living in warmer climates, on the other hand, needed little clothing or shelter. For the purposes of safety and comfort, however, many lived in caves and huts. These shelters provided protection against attacks by large animals.

Fire Sparks Changes

Life became less difficult for Paleolithic people once they discovered how to make fire. People learned that fire provided warmth in cold caves. It provided light when it was dark and could be used to scare away wild animals. Armed with spears, hunters could also use fire to chase animals from bushes to be killed. Eventually, people gathered around fires to share stories and to cook. Cooked food, they discovered, tasted better and was easier to chew and digest. In addition, meat that was smoked by fire did not have to be eaten right away and could be stored.

How did people learn to use fire? Archaeologists believe early humans produced fire by friction. They learned that by rubbing two pieces of wood together, the wood became heated and charred. When the wood became hot enough, it caught fire. Paleolithic people continued rubbing wood together, eventually developing drill-like wooden tools to start fires. They also discovered that a certain stone, iron pyrite, gave off sparks when struck against another rock. The sparks could then ignite dry grass or leaves— another way to start a fire.

McGraw-Hill Education

Visual Vocabulary

woolly mammoth a large, hairy, extinct animal related to modern-day elephants

Paleolithic art has been found in caves in Argentina. Early people left a message that remains today.

▶ **CRITICAL THINKING**
Identifying What subjects were most common in cave paintings?

Language and Art

Other advancements took place during the Paleolithic Age. One important advancement was the development of spoken language. Up until this time, early people **communicated** through sounds and physical gestures. Then, they began to develop language.

Ancient peoples started to express themselves in words for the same reasons we do. We use language to communicate information and emotions. Language makes it easier for us to work together and to pass on knowledge. We also use words to express our thoughts and feelings. The spoken language of early people was **constantly** growing and changing. New technology and more complicated experiences, for example, required new words.

Early people also expressed themselves through art. Some of this art can still be seen today, even though it is thousands of years old. For example, in 1879 a young girl named Maria de Sautuola wandered into a cave on her grandfather's farm near Altamira, Spain. She was startled by what she discovered on the walls of that cave:

PRIMARY SOURCE

❝ Maria entered the cave … and suddenly reappeared all excited, shouting 'Papa, mira, toros pintados! [Papa, look, painted bulls!]' Maria had discovered one of the most famous animal-art galleries in the world. ❞

—from *Hands: Prehistoric Visiting Cards?* by August Gansser

Eduardo M. Rivero/age fotostock

Reading**HELP**DESK

Academic Vocabulary

communicate to share information with someone
constant always happening

About ten thousand years before Maria's visit, Paleolithic artists had painted mysterious signs, including what looked like a herd of animals—horses, boars, bison, and deer—on the cave's ceiling. In 1940, a cave with similar paintings to those in Spain was discovered near Lascaux (lah•SKOH) in southern France.

Paleolithic cave paintings have been found all around the world. Early artists crushed yellow, black, and red rocks and combined them with animal fat to make their paints. They used twigs and their fingertips to apply these paints to the rock walls. They later used brushes made from animal hair. Early people created scenes of lions, oxen, panthers, and other animals. Few humans, however, appear in these paintings.

Historians are not sure why early artists chose to make cave paintings. Early people may have thought that painting an animal would bring hunters good luck. Some scholars believe, however, that the paintings may have been created to record the group's history. They may have been created simply to be enjoyed.

✔ **PROGRESS CHECK**

Explaining Why was fire important for Paleolithic people?

The paintings in the Lascaux caves are the most famous examples of Paleolithic art. Scientists now believe that such paintings took thousands of years, and hundreds of generations, to produce.

▶ **CRITICAL THINKING**
Speculating Why do you think these paintings lasted so long?

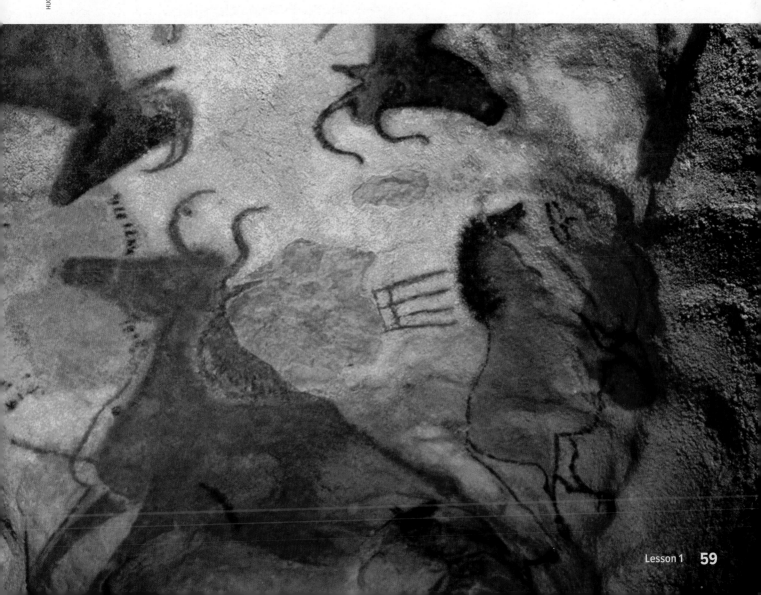

The Ice Ages

GUIDING QUESTION *How did people adapt to survive during the ice ages?*

Tools and fire were two important technological developments of Paleolithic people. Throughout history, people have used new technology to help them survive when the environment changes. The ice ages were major environmental disturbances. The changes they brought about threatened the very survival of humans.

What Changes Came With the Ice Ages?

The **ice ages** were long periods of extreme cold that affected all of Earth. The most recent Ice Age began about 100,000 years ago. Thick sheets of ice moved across large parts of Europe, Asia, and North America. As the ice sheets, or glaciers, grew larger, the water level of the oceans was lowered. The low sea

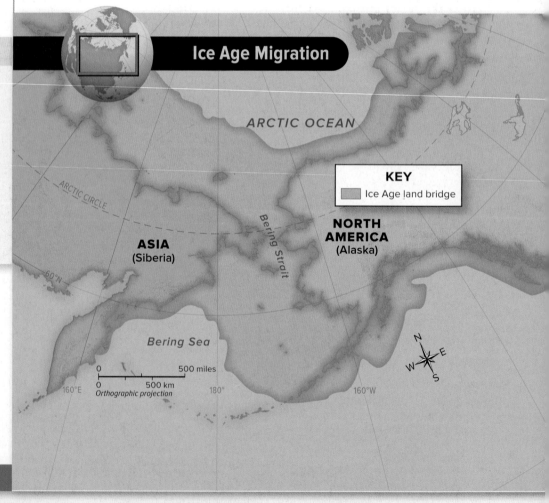

GEOGRAPHY CONNECTION

During the most recent Ice Age, a strip of land connected the continents of Asia and North America.

1 **REGIONS** How did the geography of this region change when the most recent Ice Age ended?

2 **CRITICAL THINKING**
   Analyzing After people arrived in North America, what is a likely reason they moved south rather than staying near the land bridge?

Ice Age Migration

ARCTIC OCEAN

ARCTIC CIRCLE

KEY
Ice Age land bridge

NORTH AMERICA
(Alaska)

ASIA
(Siberia)

Bering Strait

60°N

Bering Sea

0   500 miles
0   500 km
Orthographic projection

160°E   180°   160°W

N
E
W
S

ice age a time when glaciers covered much of the land

levels exposed a strip of dry land connecting the continents of Asia and North America. This strip of land was known as a land bridge. The land bridge acted as a natural highway that allowed people to travel from Asia into North America. From there, Paleolithic peoples moved southward to settle in different regions.

How Did the Ice Ages Affect Humans?

Ice age conditions posed a grave threat to human life. To survive in the cold temperatures, humans had to adapt, or change, many areas of their lives. One way they adapted their diets was by enriching meals with fat. To protect themselves from the harsh environment, they learned to build sturdier shelters. They also learned to make warm clothing using animal furs. Paleolithic people used fire to help them stay warm in this icy environment. The last Ice Age lasted about 90,000 years, ending between about 9000 and 8000 B.C.

✔ PROGRESS CHECK

Explaining How were land bridges formed?

After early people controlled fire, they brought it into their shelters. At the site of some Stone Age huts, scientists have discovered an early form of a fireplace—a shallow hole lined with blackened stones.

LESSON 1 REVIEW

Review Vocabulary

1. What is another name for the *Paleolithic* Age?

Answer the Guiding Questions

2. ***Describing*** By what methods did Paleolithic people get food?

3. ***Summarizing*** How did fire help Paleolithic people survive?

4. ***Determining Cause and Effect*** How did the ice ages affect where people settled in the Americas?

5. ***Making Connections*** How does climate affect the type of house you live in or the clothes you wear?

6. **NARRATIVE** You are a mother or father who lives in the early Paleolithic Age. In a few paragraphs, describe your daily life.

LESSON 2

The Agricultural Revolution

ESSENTIAL QUESTION
• How do people adapt to their environment?

IT MATTERS BECAUSE
The Agricultural Revolution allowed people to set up permanent settlements.

Neolithic Times

GUIDING QUESTION *How did farming change people's lives?*

The earliest people were nomads who moved from place to place to hunt animals and gather plants. After the last Ice Age ended, Earth's temperatures rose. As the climate warmed, many nomads moved into areas with a mild climate and fertile land.

Another historical revolution then occurred. For the first time, people began staying in one place to grow grains and vegetables. Gradually, farming replaced hunting and gathering as the main source of food. At the same time, people began to **domesticate** (duh·MEHS·tih·kayt), or tame, animals for human use. Animals transported goods and provided meat, milk, and wool.

The Neolithic Age

This change in the way people lived marked the beginning of the **Neolithic Age** (nee·uh·LIH·thick). It began about 8000 B.C. and lasted until around 4000 B.C.—about 4,000 years. The word *neolithic* is Greek for "new stone." Calling this time period the New Stone Age, however, is somewhat misleading. Although new stone tools were made, the real change in the Neolithic Age was the shift from hunting and gathering to **systematic agriculture**. This is growing food on a regular basis.

Reading**HELP**DESK

Taking Notes: *Identifying*

Use a diagram like this to identify three advancements made during the Neolithic Age.

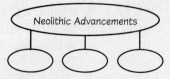
Neolithic Advancements

Content Vocabulary

• **domesticate**
• **Neolithic Age**
• **systematic agriculture**
• **shrine**

• **specialization**
• **Bronze Age**
• **monarchy**

This shift from hunting and gathering to food production, however, did not happen quickly. Even during the Mesolithic Age, or Middle Stone Age, some people continued to hunt and gather, while others began to grow their own food.

Big Changes for Humankind

Historians call this settled farming during the Neolithic Age the Agricultural Revolution. The word *revolution* refers to any change that has an enormous effect on people's ways of life. While hunter-gatherers ate wild grains that they collected, early farmers saved some of the grains to plant. Humans lived differently once they learned how to grow crops and tame animals that produced food. They now could produce a constant food supply. This allowed the population to grow at a faster rate. Nomads gave up their way of life and began living in settled communities. Some historians consider the Agricultural Revolution the most important event in human history.

GEOGRAPHY CONNECTION

Between about 7000 and 2000 B.C., farming developed on different continents.

1 REGIONS What crops were grown south of the Equator?

2 CRITICAL THINKING
Speculating Why do you think so many different crops were grown in Central America?

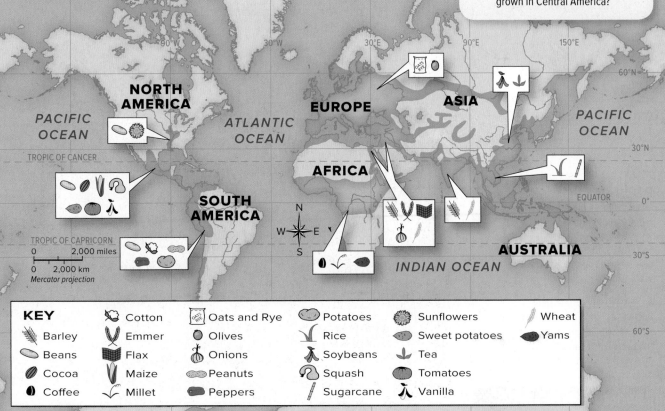

Early Farming

KEY

- 🌸 Cotton
- 📦 Oats and Rye
- 🥔 Potatoes
- 🌻 Sunflowers
- 🌾 Wheat
- 🌾 Barley
- 🌾 Emmer
- 🫒 Olives
- 🌾 Rice
- 🍠 Sweet potatoes
- 🍠 Yams
- 🫘 Beans
- 🧶 Flax
- 🧅 Onions
- 🌿 Soybeans
- 🍃 Tea
- 🍫 Cocoa
- 🌽 Maize
- 🥜 Peanuts
- 🎃 Squash
- 🍅 Tomatoes
- ☕ Coffee
- 🌾 Millet
- 🌶️ Peppers
- 🎋 Sugarcane
- 🌱 Vanilla

domesticate to adapt an animal to living with humans for the advantage of humans

Neolithic Age relating to the latest period of the Stone Age

systematic agriculture the organized growing of food on a regular schedule

Widespread Farming

By 8000 B.C., people in Southwest Asia began growing wheat and barley. They also domesticated pigs, cows, goats, and sheep. From there, farming spread into southeastern Europe. By 4000 B.C., farming was an established **economic** activity in Europe.

At about the same time, around 6000 B.C., people had begun growing wheat and barley in the Nile Valley in Egypt. Farming soon spread along the Nile River and into other regions in Africa. In Central Africa, different types of crops emerged. There, people grew root crops called tubers, which included yams. They also grew fruit crops, such as bananas. Wheat and barley farming moved eastward into India between 8000 and 5000 B.C.

By 6000 B.C., people in northern China were growing a food grain called millet and were domesticating dogs and pigs. By 5000 B.C., farmers in Southeast Asia were growing rice. From there, rice farming spread into southern China.

In the Western Hemisphere, between 7000 and 5000 B.C., people in Mexico and Central America were growing corn, squash, and potatoes. They also domesticated chickens and dogs.

☑ PROGRESS CHECK

Explaining How did the spread of farming change the lives of nomads?

Originally, Neolithic people built large dwelling places that housed a small clan, or family group, along with their cattle and grain stores. Eventually, these were replaced by one- or two-room houses, which were usually clustered in groups.

▶ CRITICAL THINKING
Analyzing Why would construction methods vary depending on geographical location?

Reading**HELP**DESK

Academic Vocabulary

economy the system of economic life in an area or country; an economy deals with the making, buying, and selling of goods or services

► **CRITICAL THINKING**
Analyzing The village of Çatalhüyük grew into a large community. These ruins reveal well thought out construction. *Why do you think some people were happy to settle in villages?*

Life in the Neolithic Age

GUIDING QUESTION *What was life like during the Neolithic Age?*

During the Neolithic Age, people settled in villages where they built permanent homes. They **located** villages near fields so people could plant, grow, and harvest their crops more easily. People also settled near water sources, especially rivers.

Neolithic Communities

Neolithic farming villages developed throughout Europe, India, Egypt, China, and Mexico. The biggest and earliest known communities have been found in Southwest Asia. One of the oldest communities was Jericho (JAIR·ih·koh). This farming village grew in an area between present-day Israel and Jordan called the West Bank. The village of Jericho was well established by about 8000 B.C. It extended across several acres. The area of sun-dried-brick houses was surrounded by walls that were several feet thick.

Academic Vocabulary

locate to set up in a particular place

**Ötzi the Iceman
(c. 3300 B.C.)**

Mystery Man Ötzi was a Neolithic man whose remains were discovered in 1991 in the Austrian Alps. Also called the "Iceman," Ötzi presented a mystery. Did he live where he died? Did he spend his life in another location? What did he do for a living? Scientists found the same form of oxygen in Ötzi's teeth as in the water of the southern Alpine valleys. They have concluded that, even though Ötzi was found in the mountains, he lived most of his life in the valleys south of the Alps. Scientists believe Ötzi was either a shepherd or a hunter who traveled from the valleys to the mountains.

▶ **CRITICAL THINKING**
Analyzing What types of clothing or tools do you think Ötzi used?

Another well-known Neolithic community was Çatalhüyük (chah·tahl·hoo·YOOK) in present-day Turkey. Although little evidence of the community remains, historians know that between 6700 and 5700 B.C., it covered 32 acres and was home to about 6,000 people. The people lived in simple mud-brick houses that were built close together. What if, instead of a front door, your house had a roof door? In Çatalhüyük, the houses did not have front doors. Instead of going through a door in the wall, people entered their homes through holes in the rooftops. They could also walk from house to house across the roofs. People decorated the inside of their homes with wall paintings.

In addition to homes, Çatalhüyük had special buildings that were **shrines** (SHREYENZ), or holy places. These shrines were decorated with images of gods and goddesses. Statues of women giving birth have also been found in the shrines. Both the shrines and the statues show that the role of religion was growing in the lives of Neolithic people.

Farmers grew fruits, nuts, and different grains on land outside Çatalhüyük. People grew their own food and kept it in storerooms within their homes. They raised sheep, goats, and cattle that provided milk and meat. They ate fish and bird eggs from nearby low-lying wetlands called marshes. Scenes drawn on the walls of the city's ruins show that the people of Çatalhüyük also hunted.

What Were the Benefits of a Settled Life?

Neolithic people needed protection from the weather and wild animals. A settled life provided greater security. Steady food supplies created healthier, growing populations. As the population increased, more workers became available. Those individuals could grow more crops. Villagers produced more than they could eat, so they began to trade their food for supplies they could not produce themselves.

Because an abundant amount of food was produced, fewer people were needed in the fields. Neolithic people began to take part in economic activities other than farming. **Specialization** (speh·shuh·leh·ZAY·shun) occurred for the first time. People took up specific jobs as their talents allowed. Some people became artisans, or skilled workers. They made weapons and jewelry that they traded with neighboring communities. People made pottery from clay to store grain and food. They made

Marco Albonico/agefotostock

baskets from plant fibers. They also used plant fibers to weave cloth. Ötzi, the Neolithic Iceman, wore a cape made from woven grass fibers. These craftspeople, like farmers, also exchanged the goods they produced for other things they did not have.

The roles of men and women changed when people moved into settlements. Men worked in the fields to farm and herd animals. They gradually became more responsible for growing food and protecting the village. Men emerged as family and community leaders. Women bore the children and stayed in the villages. They wove cloth, using the wool from their sheep. They also used bone needles to make clothing from cloth and animal skins. In addition, women managed food supplies and performed other tasks.

The growth of communities did not always bring benefits. In some places, such as settlements in present-day Jordan, rapid population growth caused resources such as wood supplies to be used up quickly. On occasion, this loss of forestation caused desert-like conditions to spread. Where this type of ecological damage occurred, many settlements were abandoned.

The End of the Neolithic Age

During the late Neolithic Age, people made more technological advances. Toolmakers created better farming tools as the need for them arose. These included hoes for digging soil, sickles for cutting grain, and millstones for grinding flour. In some regions, people began to work with metals, including copper. Workers heated rocks and discovered melted copper inside them. They then experimented with making the copper into tools and weapons. These proved to be easier to make and use than those made of stone.

Craftspeople in western Asia discovered that mixing copper and tin formed bronze. This was a technological breakthrough because bronze was stronger than copper. Bronze became widely used between 3000 and 1200 B.C. This period is known as the **Bronze Age**. Few people, however, could afford bronze and continued to use tools and weapons made of stone.

✔ **PROGRESS CHECK**

Explaining How did the spread of agriculture affect trade?

Bronze Age the period in ancient human culture when people began to make and use bronze

Making Inferences

In Çatalhüyük the homes were built very close together. Each house had a door in its roof. People climbed into their homes using ladders. Use the Internet to research why the people of Çatalhüyük used this style of building. Then make an inference about the reason for the roof doors and present it to the class. For more information about making inferences, read the chapter *What Does a Historian Do?*

Bronze Age pottery shows fine details. The use of bronze for tools and weapons was another step forward for ancient peoples.

▶ **CRITICAL THINKING**
Analyzing Why do you think bronze tools and weapons would have been an important achievement?

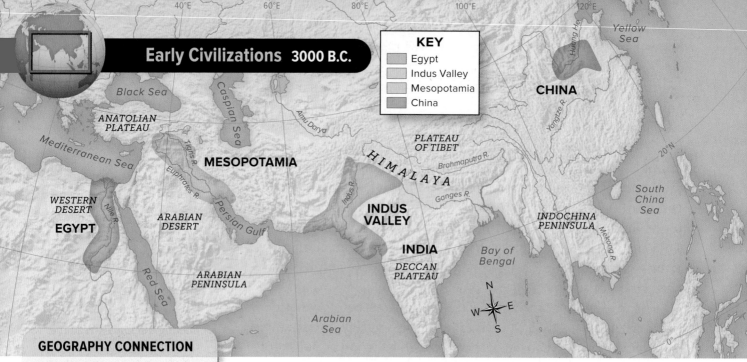

KEY
- Egypt
- Indus Valley
- Mesopotamia
- China

GEOGRAPHY CONNECTION

Civilizations developed in the river valleys of Mesopotamia, Egypt, India, and China.

1 PLACE Along which rivers did the early civilizations of Mesopotamia and Egypt develop?

2 CRITICAL THINKING
Analyzing As these cultures became more complex, what characteristics set some of them apart as civilizations?

Civilizations Emerge

GUIDING QUESTION *What characteristics did early civilizations share?*

Humans continued to develop more complex cultures, or ways of life. By the beginning of the Bronze Age, communities were widespread. More complex cultures called civilizations began to develop in these communities. Four of the great river valley civilizations—Mesopotamia, Egypt, India, and China—emerged around 3000 B.C. All civilizations share similar characteristics.

Cities and Government

One characteristic of these early civilizations was that they developed cities and formed governments. The first civilizations developed in river valleys, where fertile land made it easy to grow crops and feed large numbers of people. The rivers provided fish and water. They also encouraged trade, which allowed the exchange of both goods and ideas. The cities that developed in these valleys became the centers of civilizations.

People formed governments to protect themselves and their food supplies. In these early civilizations, the first governments were monarchies. A **monarchy** is a type of government led by a king or queen. Monarchs created armies to defend against enemies and made laws to keep order. They also appointed government officials who managed food supplies and building projects.

Reading**HELP**DESK

monarchy a government whose ruler, a king or queen, inherits the position from a parent

Religions

Religions emerged in the new civilizations to help people explain their lives. For example, religions helped explain the forces of nature and the role of humans in the world.

Early people believed that gods were responsible for a community's survival. Priests performed religious ceremonies to try to win the support of the gods. Rulers claimed that their own power was based on the approval of the gods.

Social Structure

Early civilizations had social class structures. That is, people in society were organized into groups. These groups were defined by the type of work people did and the amount of wealth or power they had. Generally, rulers and priests, government officials, and warriors made up the highest social class. They set the rules and made the important decisions. Below this class was a large group of free people, including farmers, artisans, and craftspeople. At the bottom of the class structure were enslaved people, most of whom were captured from enemies during war.

Writing and Art

To pass on information, people invented ways of writing. These early systems used symbols in place of letters and words. Writing became an important feature of these new civilizations. People used writing to keep accurate records and to preserve stories.

Civilizations also created art for enjoyment and practical purposes. Artists created paintings and sculptures portraying gods and forces of nature. People designed massive buildings that served as places of worship or burial tombs for kings.

☑ **PROGRESS CHECK**

Speculating Why did early peoples form governments?

LESSON 2 REVIEW

Review Vocabulary

1. What was *systematic agriculture*?

2. How did *specialization* affect the lives of Neolithic peoples?

Answer the Guiding Questions

3. *Stating* What was the Agricultural Revolution?

4. *Identifying Cause and Effect* How did farming lead to new types of economic activities?

5. *Inferring* What are the advantages and disadvantages when a community grows?

6. *Identifying* Which groups made up the largest social class in early civilizations?

7. **ARGUMENT** You are the leader of a band of hunter-gatherers. You have seen other bands settle in river valleys and begin to farm. Write a speech to persuade your own band to settle and begin farming.

Write your answers on a separate piece of paper.

1 Exploring the Essential Question

INFORMATIVE/EXPLANATORY How would you describe the ways people adapted to a colder environment during the Ice Age? Write an essay telling how some changes people made may have led to the development of agriculture when the last Ice Age was over.

2 21st Century Skills

ANALYZING AND MAKING JUDGMENTS Early humans made several technical advancements during the Paleolithic Age. These included the use of fire, flint tools and weapons, spoken language, and tents and wooden structures. Write a paragraph telling which of these helped them most to become more efficient hunters and why.

3 Thinking Like a Historian

COMPARING AND CONTRASTING Create a diagram like the one shown to compare and contrast the technological advancements of the Paleolithic Age with those of the Neolithic Age.

Paleolithic Age Advancements	Neolithic Age Advancements

4

GEOGRAPHY ACTIVITY

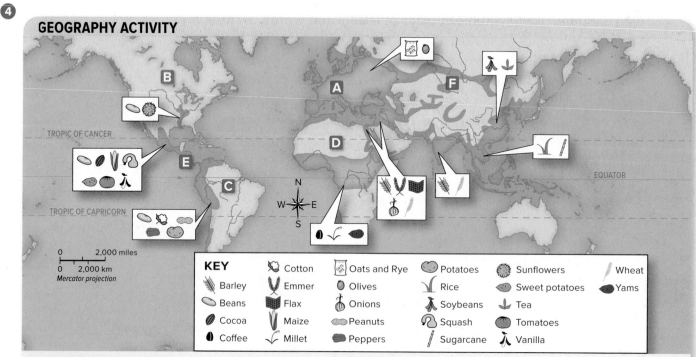

Locating Places

Match the letters on the map to the numbered list of crops grown there.

1. soybeans and tea
2. beans and sunflowers
3. coffee, millet, and yams
4. oats and olives
5. beans, cotton, peanuts, peppers, and potatoes
6. beans, cocoa, corn, squash, tomatoes, sweet potatoes and vanilla

Directions: Write your answers on a separate piece of paper.

CHECKING FOR UNDERSTANDING

1 Define each of these terms as they relate to early humans.

- **A.** nomad
- **B.** technology
- **C.** iron pyrite
- **D.** ice age
- **E.** Neolithic Age
- **F.** Agricultural Revolution
- **G.** shrine
- **H.** Bronze Age
- **I.** monarchy

REVIEW THE GUIDING QUESTIONS

2 *Explaining* Why is the early period of human history called the Stone Age? What is the Paleolithic Age?

3 *Identifying* What was the main activity of Paleolithic people?

4 *Listing* List some of the tools developed by humans during the Paleolithic Age.

5 *Describing* How did early humans adapt to ice age conditions?

6 *Finding the Main Idea* Why is the change from hunting and gathering to farming considered a revolution?

7 *Specifying* Near what types of landforms did Neolithic peoples build their villages? Why?

8 *Identifying* In Neolithic villages, who were artisans, and what types of products did they create?

9 *Finding the Main Idea* Why did the first civilizations develop in river valleys?

10 *Identifying* In general, who belonged to the highest social class in early civilizations?

CRITICAL THINKING

11 *Contrasting* How did the roles of Paleolithic men and women differ within their groups?

12 *Recognizing Relationships* Describe the relationship between the animals hunted by Paleolithic people and how those peoples survived in harsh or difficult climates.

13 *Making Connections* What were the subjects of paintings by Paleolithic people? Why might these paintings have been created?

14 *Determining Central Ideas* Why is the term Neolithic Age a misleading name for the time period?

15 *Comparing and Contrasting* Study the map titled Early Farming in Lesson 2. Then compare and contrast the crops grown in Africa and Southwest Asia to those grown in the rest of Asia.

16 *Contrasting* Contrast the dwellings found in a Neolithic village such as Çatalhüyük with those used by Paleolithic peoples. Discuss layout, building materials, and any other relevant details.

17 *Determining Cause and Effect* How did the switch to a farming lifestyle lead to changes in technology? Describe the new types of tools that were created and the new materials being used.

18 *Evaluating* Were all the effects of the Agricultural Revolution beneficial? Explain.

19 *Explaining* Explain how the Agricultural Revolution is related to the origins of government. Describe the form of government that developed in the first civilizations in your answer.

20 *Analyzing* Consider the characteristics that were shared by early civilizations—cities and government, religion, social structure, and writing and art. Do you think these characteristics are shared by civilizations today? Explain.

Need Extra Help?

If You've Missed Question	**1**	**2**	**3**	**4**	**5**	**6**	**7**	**8**	**9**	**10**	**11**	**12**	**13**	**14**	**15**	**16**	**17**	**18**	**19**	**20**
Review Lesson	1,2	1	1	1	1	2	2	2	2	2	1	1	1	2	2	2	2	2	2	2

DBQ **SHORT RESPONSE**

Write your answers on a separate piece of paper.

"Agriculture developed at different times and in different places. … Over the years, people have domesticated many different plants and animals. Domestication of some species has been abandoned. Following the last Ice Age, people began to cultivate rice, wheat, potatoes, and corn. However, herding of reindeer declined because of the climate changes."

—From "History of Agriculture," *Encyclopaedia Britannica*

21 Was the change from hunting and gathering to agriculture sudden? Explain.

22 What are some possible reasons that people stopped raising some domesticated species?

EXTENDED RESPONSE

Write your answer on a separate piece of paper.

23 *Narrative* You are a member of a Paleolithic group of hunter-gatherers. Write a letter to a friend describing the hunting stories you are recording in cave paintings. Explain how you think your stories might help other hunters improve their skills.

STANDARDIZED TEST PRACTICE

DBQ **ANALYZING DOCUMENTS**

24 *Making Connections* Study this example of one of the oldest Paleolithic cave paintings. What kind of animals does this painting appear to represent?

A. woolly mammoths

B. cattle

C. horses

D. reindeer

25 *Identifying* What type of tools did Paleolithic people use for painting on the cave walls?

A. wood blocks

B. paint rollers

C. pencils

D. twigs

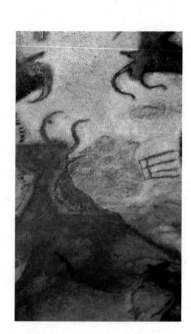

Need Extra Help?

If You've Missed Question	**21**	**22**	**23**	**24**	**25**
Review Lesson	2	2	1	1	1

◄ *Relief sculpture of Ashurnasirpal II, Assyrian king from 883-859 B.C.*

3000 B.C. TO 500 B.C.

Mesopotamia

THE STORY MATTERS ...

Have you ever watched a large subdivision of homes being built? Did you notice solid structures beginning to appear on what was once only flat land? Assyrian King Ashurnasirpal II built such a project during his reign from 883–859 B.C. He took the small town of Nimrud and made it his capital. When he was finished, the city occupied about 900 acres. Around it, Ashurnasirpal II built a wall 120 feet thick, 42 feet high, and 5 miles long. The gates were guarded by two huge human-headed winged bulls. Parts of these gates can be seen in the New York Metropolitan Museum today. When he finished the city, the king held a festival attended by about 70,000 people. Here, he said, were "the happy people of all lands together. ..."

ESSENTIAL QUESTIONS

• How does geography influence the way people live?
• Why does conflict develop?

©Charles & Josette Lenars/Corbis

Mesopotamia
Place & Time: 3000 B.C. to 500 B.C.

Mesopotamia extended from the Tigris River to the Euphrates River. The Sumerians were the first settlers in the region. They are the people who developed the world's first civilization. Soon several civilizations appeared in Mesopotamia. This area was called the Fertile Crescent because of its shape.

Step Into the Place

MAP FOCUS There were many Mesopotamian cities that arose along the Tigris and Euphrates Rivers.

1 PLACE What river flowed through the western side of Mesopotamia?

2 LOCATION What is the approximate distance from Nineveh to Ur?

3 MOVEMENT To what larger body of water did the people living along these rivers sail?

4 CRITICAL THINKING
Making Inferences Why do you think many cities in Mesopotamia developed near rivers?

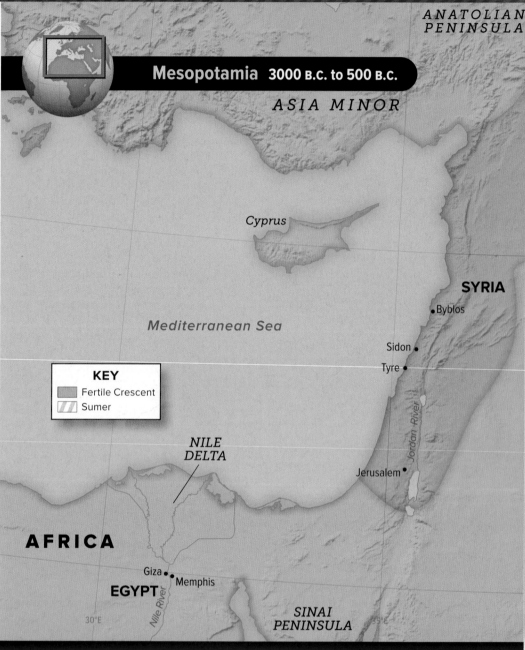

Mesopotamia 3000 B.C. to 500 B.C.

ANATOLIAN PENINSULA

ASIA MINOR

Cyprus

Mediterranean Sea

SYRIA
Byblos
Sidon
Tyre

Jordan River

NILE DELTA

Jerusalem

AFRICA

Giza
Memphis
EGYPT

Nile River

30°E

SINAI PENINSULA

KEY
Fertile Crescent
Sumer

Step Into the Time

TIME LINE Place these events in order, starting with the earliest: Assyrians control Mesopotamia, settlements develop along the Indus River, Sumerians invent cuneiform, and first Olympic Games take place.

c. 3000 B.C. City-states arise in Sumer

c. 3200 B.C. Sumerians invent cuneiform writing system

c. 2340 B.C. Sargon conquers Sumer

c. 1792 B.C. Hammurabi becomes king of Babylonian Empire

MESOPOTAMIA

THE WORLD

3000 B.C.

2000 B.C.

c. 2700 B.C. Chinese master art of silk weaving

c. 2300 B.C. Ceramics are produced in Central America

c. 1800 B.C. Egyptians use mathematics for architecture

c. 2500 B.C. Settlements develop along Indus River

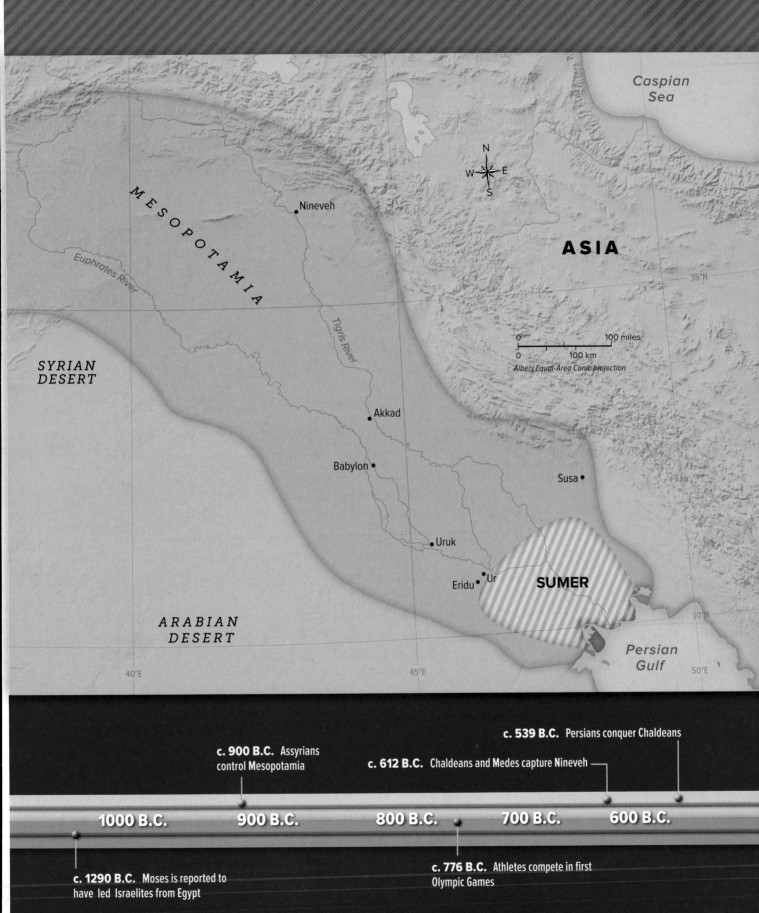

Caspian
Sea

N
W · E
S

MESOPOTAMIA

Euphrates River

• Nineveh

Tigris River

ASIA

35°N

0   100 miles
0   100 km
Albers Equal-Area Conic projection

SYRIAN
DESERT

• Akkad

Babylon •

Susa •

Uruk •

Eridu • • Ur

SUMER

ARABIAN
DESERT

30°N

Persian
Gulf

40°E

45°E

50°E

c. 539 B.C. Persians conquer Chaldeans

c. 900 B.C. Assyrians
control Mesopotamia

c. 612 B.C. Chaldeans and Medes capture Nineveh

1000 B.C.   900 B.C.   800 B.C.   700 B.C.   600 B.C.

c. 1290 B.C. Moses is reported to
have led Israelites from Egypt

c. 776 B.C. Athletes compete in first
Olympic Games

LESSON 1

The Sumerians

• How does geography influence the way people live?

IT MATTERS BECAUSE

The Sumerians made important advances in areas such as farming and writing that laid the foundation for future civilizations.

The First Civilizations in Mesopotamia

GUIDING QUESTION *Why did people settle in Mesopotamia?*

Civilizations first developed about 3000 B.C. in the river valleys of Mesopotamia (MEH·suh·puh·TAY·mee·uh), Egypt, India, and China. Throughout history, the need to have water for drinking and growing crops influenced where people settled. Although there were differences among the early civilizations, they were alike in many ways. As these early civilizations developed, people formed social classes. The social class people belonged to partly depended on their occupations. They did specialized types of work. Using improved technology, they made more and better goods. They set up governments to pass laws, defend their land, and carry out large building projects. The people of these civilizations also developed systems of values and beliefs that gave meaning to their lives.

The Two Rivers

Mesopotamia, the earliest known civilization, developed in what is now southern Iraq (ih·RAHK). Mesopotamia means "the land between the rivers" in Greek. The civilization began on the plain between the Tigris (TY·gruhs) and the Euphrates (yu·FRAY·teez) Rivers.

Reading**HELP**DESK

Taking Notes: *Identifying*

On a diagram like this one, idenify two major inventions of the Sumerians.

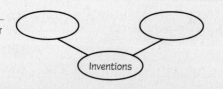
Inventions

Content Vocabulary

- silt
- irrigation
- surplus
- city- state
- polytheism
- ziggurat
- cuneiform
- scribe
- epic

These rivers are nearly **parallel** to each other and flow more than 1,000 miles (1,600 km). They run southeast from the mountains of southeastern Asia to the Persian (PUR·zhuhn) Gulf.

Mesopotamia itself was located in the eastern part of the larger Fertile Crescent. This curving strip of good farmland extends from the Mediterranean (mehd·uh·tuh·RAY·nee·uhn) Sea to the Persian Gulf. The Fertile Crescent includes parts of the modern countries of Turkey, Syria, Iraq, Lebanon, Israel, and Jordan.

Early Valley Dwellers

For thousands of years, clues to Mesopotamia's history lay buried among its ruins and piles of rubble. In the 1800s, archaeologists began to dig up many buildings and artifacts. These finds revealed much about early Mesopotamia.

Historians believe that people first settled Mesopotamia about 7000 B.C. The first settlers were hunters and herders. By about 4000 B.C., some of these groups had moved to the plain of the Tigris-Euphrates valley. They built farming villages along the two rivers.

Taming the Rivers

Early Mesopotamian farmers used water from the Tigris and Euphrates Rivers to water their fields. However, the farmers could not always rely on the rivers for their needs. Little or no rain fell in the summer. As a result, the rivers were often low. The farmers did not have enough water to plant crops in the fall.

Irrigation canals help farmers grow crops in areas that would otherwise be dry and not suitable for farming.

During the spring harvest, rains and melting snow from the northern mountains caused rivers to overflow their banks. This flooded the plains. Sometimes, unexpected and violent floods swept away crops, homes, and livestock.

Yet farmers in Mesopotamia knew that the floods were also helpful. Flooded rivers were filled with **silt**, or small particles of soil. When the floods ended, silt was left on the banks and plains. The silt proved to be a very good soil for farming.

Over time, people in Mesopotamia learned to build dams to control the seasonal floods. They dug canals that let water flow from a water source to their fields. This method of watering crops is called **irrigation** (IHR · uh · GAY · shuhn).

FLPA/Alamy

---

silt fine particles of fertile soil

irrigation a system that supplies dry land with water through ditches, pipes, or streams

Academic Vocabulary

parallel moving or lying in the same direction and the same distance apart

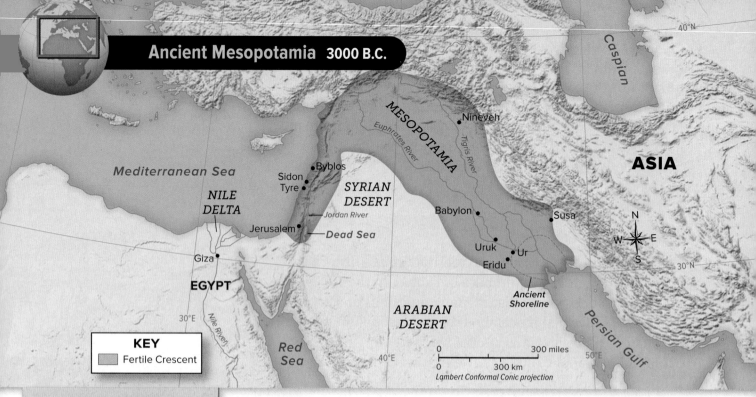

Ancient Mesopotamia 3000 B.C.

Caspian

40°N

MESOPOTAMIA

Nineveh

Euphrates River

Tigris River

ASIA

Mediterranean Sea

Byblos
Sidon
Tyre

SYRIAN
DESERT

Babylon

Susa

N
W   E
S

NILE
DELTA

Jordan River

Jerusalem

Dead Sea

Uruk   Ur

30°N

Giza

Eridu

EGYPT

Ancient
Shoreline

30°E

Nile River

ARABIAN
DESERT

Persian Gulf

KEY

Fertile Crescent

Red
Sea

40°E

0   300 miles
0   300 km
Lambert Conformal Conic projection

50°E

GEOGRAPHY CONNECTION

A number of great civilizations developed in Mesopotamia.

1 LOCATION What city was located in northern Mesopotamia?

2 CRITICAL THINKING
Making Inferences Why do you think Mesopotamia was a good location for the growth of civilization?

Irrigation let these early farmers grow **surpluses** (SUHR·plus· ehz)—or extra amounts—of food. Farmers stored the surpluses for later use.

When food was plentiful, not all people needed to farm. Some became artisans, or skilled workers. They specialized in weaving cloth and making pottery, tools, and weapons.

As artisans made more goods, people's lives changed. People began to live together in places that favored trade. Small farming villages grew into cities. By 3000 B.C., several cities developed in Sumer (SOO·mer), a region in southern Mesopotamia.

✔ **PROGRESS CHECK**

Explaining How did floods sometimes help farmers?

Sumer's Civilization

GUIDING QUESTION *What was life like in Sumer?*

Sumer's people were known as Sumerians. They built the first cities in Southwest Asia, including Ur (uhr), Uruk (OO· rook), and Eridu (ER·i·doo). These cities became centers of civilization that controlled the lower part of the Tigris and Euphrates valleys.

Reading**HELP**DESK

surplus an amount that is left over after a need has been met

city-state a city that governs itself and its surrounding territory

polytheism a belief in more than one god

City-States Arise

Sumer's cities were surrounded by mudflats and patches of scorching desert. The harsh landscape made it hard to travel by land and communicate with other groups. This meant that each city was largely cut off from its neighbors.

As a result, Sumerian cities became independent. The people of each city raised their own crops and made their own goods. As the cities grew, they gained political and economic control over the lands around them. By doing this, they formed **city-states**. Each city-state had its own government and was not part of any larger governing state. The population of the city-states ranged from about 5,000 to 20,000 people.

Historians think that each Sumerian city-state was protected by a large city wall. Ruins and artifacts have been found by archaeologists that support this theory. Because stone and wood were in short supply, the Sumerians used mud from the rivers as their main building material. They mixed mud with crushed reeds, formed bricks, and left them in the sun to dry. The gates of the wall stayed open during the day but were closed at night for protection. The ruler's palace, a large temple, and other public buildings were located in the center of the city.

Often, these city-states went to war with one another over resources and political borders. Sometimes, they fought to win glory or to gain more territory. During times of peace, city-states traded with each other. They also agreed to help each other by forming alliances (uh·LY·uhns·uhs) to protect their common interests.

Gods, Priests, and Kings

The Sumerian people worshipped many gods, a type of belief known as **polytheism** (PAH·lee·thee·ih·zuhm). These multiple gods played different roles in Sumerian life. The Sumerians thought that some gods had power over parts of nature, such as the rain or the wind. They also believed that some gods guided the things that people did, such as plowing or brick-making. They honored whatever god would help their activity.

Although Sumerians honored all the gods, each city-state claimed one as its own.

In areas where there was little rainfall, farmers watered their fields using irrigation channels.

▶ CRITICAL THINKING
Analyzing What other water sources were available in addition to the river?

The ziggurat was built to be visible throughout the city-state. The walls of the ziggurat enclosed the royal warehouses and the city's treasury.

▶ CRITICAL THINKING
Speculating Why do you think the Sumerians would want the ziggurat to be highly visible?

To honor its god, a city-state often included a large temple called a **ziggurat** (ZIG·oo·rat). The word *ziggurat* means "to rise high" in the ancient Akkadian (uh·KAY·dee·uhn) language. The very top of the ziggurat was a holy place. It was the god's home, and only special priests were allowed to go there. In the early days, priests of the ziggurat ruled the city-states. Groups of important men helped them govern. Later, Sumerian city-states became monarchies.

Sumerian kings claimed they received their power to rule from the city's god. The first kings were most likely war heroes. Over time, their rule became hereditary. This meant that after a king died, his son took over. In most cases, the wives of kings did not have political power. However, some controlled their own lands.

Social Groups

People in Sumer were organized into social classes. Generally, people remained in the social class into which they were born. Kings, priests, warriors, and government officials belonged to the upper class. The middle class **consisted** of merchants, farmers, fishers, and artisans. The middle class was Sumer's largest social group. Enslaved people made up Sumer's lowest class. Most of these people had been captured in war. Also, criminals and people who could not pay their debts often were enslaved. Enslaved men and women worked for the upper class.

Women and men had different roles in Sumerian society. The basic unit of society was the family. Men were the head of the home. Boys went to school and were trained for a specific job. Sumerian women ran the home, taught their daughters to do the same, and cared for the children. Women had a few civil rights. Some owned businesses. Sumerian law required parents to care for their children. The law also required adult children to care for their parents if their parents needed help.

Reading**HELP**DESK

ziggurat a pyramid-shaped structure with a temple at the top

Academic Vocabulary

consist to be made up of

Reading Strategy: *Summarizing*

When you summarize, you find the main idea of a passage and restate it in your own words. Read the paragraph under the heading "Social Groups." On a separate sheet of paper, summarize the paragraph in one or two sentences.

Farmers and Traders

If you lived in Sumer, you were most likely a farmer. Each farmer had a plot of land located in the area around a city-state. Dams and waterways ran through this farmland. Wheat, barley, and dates were the major crops. Farmers also raised sheep, goats, and pigs.

Trade was another key part of Sumer's economy. The Sumerians did not have some of the goods that they needed. For example, even though many Sumerians were skilled metalworkers, they had to trade with other peoples to obtain most of their metals. Trade routes linked Sumer to places as far away as India and Egypt.

Sumerian merchants went to other lands. They traded wheat, barley, and tools for timber, minerals, and metals. The minerals and metals were then used to make jewelry or tools. For jewelry making, Sumerians valued a red stone called carnelian from India's Indus Valley. They also searched for a blue stone known as lapis lazuli from what is now Afghanistan. Traders returned with iron and silver from present-day Turkey.

Sumerian artisans produced a variety of goods, including jewelry. This piece is made of gold and lapis lazuli.

▶ **CRITICAL THINKING**
Speculating If you were an artisan in ancient times, what would you produce?

 **PROGRESS CHECK**

Analyzing Why do you think the Sumerians built cities with walls around them?

Sumerian Contributions

GUIDING QUESTION *What ideas and inventions did Sumerians pass on to other civilizations?*

The Sumerians created the first civilization that had a great influence on history. Later civilizations copied and improved many of the ideas and inventions that began in Sumer. As a result, Mesopotamia has been called the "cradle of civilization." It was the beginning of organized human society.

Writing

Of all the contributions made by Sumerians to the world, writing is perhaps the most important. The writing system they developed was the earliest known system in the world.

This Royal Standard of Ur—the royal design—shows scenes of everyday life in Sumer. *Which methods of travel are shown on this standard?*

Sumerians needed materials for building and making tools. They sailed to other lands to trade for wood logs to take home.

Writing was a way for Sumerians to keep records of their lives and their history. Writing was also a way to share information. They could pass on their ideas to later generations.

Sumerians created a way of writing called **cuneiform** (kyoo· NEE·uh·FAWRM). The cuneiform writing system was made up of about 1,200 different characters. Characters represented such things as names, physical objects, and numbers. Cuneiform was written by cutting wedge-shaped marks into damp clay with a sharp reed. The name *cuneiform* comes from a Latin word meaning "wedge." Sumerians wrote on clay because they did not have paper. Archaeologists have found cuneiform tablets that have provided important information about Mesopotamian history.

Only a few people—mostly boys from wealthy families— learned how to read and write cuneiform. After years of training, some students became **scribes** (SKRYBS), or official record keepers. Scribes wrote documents that recorded much of the everyday life in Mesopotamia, including court records, marriage contracts, business dealings, and important events. Some scribes were judges and government officials.

Sumerians told stories orally for centuries. After developing writing, they were able to record these stories. Their tales praised the gods and warriors for doing great deeds. The world's oldest known story is from Sumer. Written more than

©Gianni Dagli Orti/Corbis

Reading**HELP**DESK

cuneiform a system of writing developed by the Sumerians that used wedge-shaped marks made in soft clay

scribe a person who copies or writes out documents; often a record keeper

epic a long poem that records the deeds of a legendary or real hero

4,000 years ago and still studied today, this story is called the *Epic of Gilgamesh* (GIHL·guh·MEHSH). An **epic** is a long poem that tells the story of a hero.

Technology and Mathematics

The people of Mesopotamia also made many useful inventions. For example, the Sumerians were the first people to use the wheel. The earliest wheels were solid wood circles made from carved boards that were clamped together. A Sumerian illustration from about 3500 B.C. shows a wheeled vehicle. They built the first carts, which were pulled by donkeys. They also introduced vehicles into military use with the development of the chariot.

For river travel, Sumerians developed the sailboat. They invented a wooden plow to help them in the fields. Artisans made the potter's wheel, which helped to shape clay into bowls and jars. Sumerians were also the first to make bronze out of copper and tin. They used bronze to craft stronger tools, weapons, and jewelry.

The Sumerians also studied mathematics and astronomy. They used geometry to measure the size of fields and to plan buildings. They created a place-value system of numbers based on 60. They also devised tables for calculating division and multiplication. The 60-minute hour, 60-second minute, and 360-degree circle we use today are ideas that came from the Sumerians. Sumerians watched the positions of the stars. It showed them the best times to plant crops and to hold religious ceremonies. They also made a 12-month calendar based on the cycles of the moon.

✓ **PROGRESS CHECK**

Explaining Why did the Sumerians invent a writing system?

Sumerian writing etched on stone has been found by archaeologists.

The Sumerians invented or improved many items and methods. To classify these, look for topics with broad characteristics, such as *farming* or *communication*. Under each broad classification, you can divide the topic into narrower categories. Under farming, for example, include the category *irrigation*. Create a chart to organize broad topics and categories for the Sumerians' inventions and present your information to the class. For more about classifying and categorizing, read the chapter *What Does a Historian Do?*

Thinking Like a
HISTORIAN

Classifying and Categorizing Information

The Sumerians invented or improved many items and methods. To classify these, look for topics with broad characteristics, such as *farming* or *communication*. Under each broad classification, you can divide the topic into narrower categories. Under farming, for example, include the category *irrigation*. Create a chart to organize broad topics and categories for the Sumerians' inventions and present your information to the class. For more about classifying and categorizing, read the chapter *What Does a Historian Do?*

LESSON 1 REVIEW

Review Vocabulary

1. How were *polytheism* and *ziggurats* related in Sumerian civilization?

Answer the Guiding Questions

2. *Describing* Where is the Fertile Crescent located? Where is Mesopotamia located?

3. *Comparing* How were the social classes of Sumer organized?

4. *Identifying* What was the most common role for women in Sumerian society?

5. *Describing* Why were scribes important in Sumerian society?

6. **ARGUMENT** Sumerians developed many inventions. Choose the invention that you think is the most significant and explain why you made this choice.

There's More Online! connected.mcgraw-hill.com

Epic of Gilgamesh

Gilgamesh ruled Uruk in southern Mesopotamia sometime around 2000 B.C. According to mythology, he was a god and a human. It is believed that Gilgamesh was a harsh ruler until his friendship with Enkidu (EN • kee • doo) taught him to be fair and kind. In this epic poem, Gilgamesh faces many challenges. He suffers many losses and must confront his biggest fear: death. Eventually, Gilgamesh learns he cannot avoid death.

This excerpt tells the story of when Gilgamesh and his friend, Enkidu, decide to become heroes. They set out to kill Humbaba (hum • BAH • bah), a monstrous giant who ruled the cedar forest where gods lived. Humbaba has the face of a lion and his breath ignites fire, while his roar unleashes floods.

Gilgamesh (c. 2000 B.C.)

❝ Don't be afraid, said Gilgamesh. We are together. There is nothing We should fear.❞

—from **Gilgamesh: A Verse Narrative**
tr. Herbert Mason

❝ Enkidu was afraid of the forest of Humbaba
And urged him [Gilgamesh] not to go, but he
Was not as strong as Gilgamesh in argument,
And they were friends:

They had **embraced** and made their vow
To stay together always,
No matter what the **obstacle**.
Enkidu tried to hold his fear …

Don't be afraid, said Gilgamesh.
We are together. There is nothing
We should fear.

I learned, Enkidu said, when I lived
With the animals never to go down
Into that forest. I learned that there is death
In Humbaba. Why do you want
To raise his [Humbaba's] anger? …

After three days they reached the edge
Of the forest where Humbaba's watchman stood.
Suddenly it was Gilgamesh who was afraid,
Enkidu … reminded him to be fearless.
The watchman sounded his warning to Humbaba.
The two friends moved slowly toward the forest gate.

When Enkidu touched the gate his hand felt numb,
He could not move his fingers or his wrist,
His face turned pale like someone's witnessing a death[.]

He tried to ask his friend for help
Whom he had just encouraged to move on,
But he could only **stutter** and hold out
His paralyzed hand. ❞

—from *Gilgamesh: A Verse Narrative*, **tr. Herbert Mason**

The Gilgamesh epic was written on 12 tablets and discovered in Nineveh, in present-day Iraq. The tablets were found in the library of the Assyrian king Ashurbanipal (ah • shur • BAH • nuh • puhl), who reigned 668–627 B.C.

Analyzing Literature DBQ

1. *Identifying* How many times is death mentioned in this excerpt?

2. *Describing* How do you know that Gilgamesh and Enkidu are friends?

3. *Speculating* Enkidu is left in a risky situation. What do you think happens to him?

Vocabulary

embrace to hug with arms around
obstacle something that stands in the way
stutter an uneven repetition of sounds and words

LESSON 2
Mesopotamian Empires

ESSENTIAL QUESTION

• Why does conflict develop?

IT MATTERS BECAUSE
Mesopotamia's empires greatly influenced other civilizations. Hammurabi's Code even influenced the legal codes of Greece and Rome.

The First Empires

GUIDING QUESTION *How did Mesopotamia's first empires develop?*

By 2400 B.C., Sumer's city-states were weakened by conflict. As the strength of Sumer faded, powerful kingdoms arose in northern Mesopotamia and in neighboring Syria. Seeking new lands, rulers of these kingdoms built empires. An **empire** (EHM·PYR) is a group of many different lands under one ruler. Through conquest and trade, these empires spread their cultures over a wide region.

Who Was Sargon?

The kingdom of Akkad (AK·ad) developed in northern Mesopotamia. Sargon (SAHR·GAHN) was an ambitious leader who ruled the people of Akkad, known as Akkadians (uh·KAY·dee·uhnz). About 2340 B.C., Sargon moved his well-trained armies south. He conquered the remaining Sumerian city-states one by one. Sargon united the conquered territory with Akkad and became known as the king of Sumer and Akkad. In doing so, he formed the world's first empire. Eventually, Sargon extended this empire to include all of the peoples of Mesopotamia. His Mesopotamian empire lasted for more than 200 years before invaders conquered it.

Reading**HELP**DESK

Taking Notes: *Identifying*

On a diagram like this one, identify the major Mesopotamian empires from this lesson.

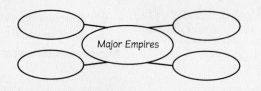

Major Empires

Content Vocabulary

• empire
• tribute
• province
• caravan
• astronomer

Who Was Hammurabi?

A people called the Amorites lived in the region west of Mesopotamia. In the 1800s B.C., they conquered Mesopotamia and built their own cities. Babylon (BA·buh·luhn) was the grandest of these cities. It was located on the eastern bank of the Euphrates River in what is now Iraq. Around 1792 B.C., the Babylonian king, Hammurabi (HA·muh·RAH·bee), began conquering cities controlled by the Amorites to the north and south. By adding these lands, he created the Babylonian Empire. This new empire stretched north from the Persian Gulf through the Tigris-Euphrates valley and west to the Mediterranean Sea.

Hammurabi's Code

Hammurabi was thought to be a just ruler. He is best known for creating a set of laws for his empire. He posted this law **code** for all to read. The code dealt with crimes, farming, business, marriage, and the family—almost every area of life. The code listed a punishment for each crime.

The Code of Hammurabi was stricter than the old Sumerian laws. The code demanded what became known as "an eye for an eye, and a tooth for a tooth." This means that the punishment for a crime should match the seriousness of the crime. It was meant to limit punishment and do away with blood feuds.

The code also protected the less powerful. For example, it protected wives from abuse by their husbands. Hammurabi's Code influenced later law codes, such as those of Greece and Rome.

✔ **PROGRESS CHECK**

Finding the Main Idea Why was Hammurabi's Code important?

The Assyrian Empire

GUIDING QUESTION *How did the Assyrians influence Southwest Asia?*

The Assyrian Empire arose about 1,000 years after the empire of Hammurabi. Assyria (uh·SIHR·ee·uh) was a large empire, extending into four present-day countries: Turkey, Syria, Iran, and Iraq.

The Assyrians built a large and powerful **military** to defend their hills and fertile valleys. Around 900 B.C., their army began taking over the rest of Mesopotamia.

BIOGRAPHY

Sargon (c. 2300 B.C.)

What king created the world's first empire? Sargon united Akkad with Sumer in the region between the Tigris and Euphrates Rivers. Sargon's Akkadian name, Sharrum-kin, means "the true king."

Under Sargon's rule, the cultures of Akkad and Sumer mixed. The people of Mesopotamia spoke the Akkadian language, but they wrote in Sumerian cuneiform. They also worshipped Sumerian gods. Sargon's empire grew wealthy through its many trade routes.

▶ **CRITICAL THINKING**
Identifying Evidence What made Sargon a "true king"?

---

empire a large territory or group of many territories governed by one ruler

Academic Vocabulary

code a set of official laws
military having to do with soldiers, weapons, or war

The Assyrian Army

The army of Assyria was well trained and disciplined. In battle, the troops numbered around 50,000 soldiers. This army was made up of infantry, or foot soldiers; cavalry, or horse soldiers; and charioteers. The Assyrians fought with slingshots, bows and arrows, swords, and spears.

The Assyrians robbed people, set crops on fire, and destroyed towns and dams. They took **tribute**, or forced payments, from conquered people. The Assyrian army also drove people from their homes. Stories of Assyrian brutality spread. Sometimes people were so afraid of the Assyrians that they would surrender to them without a fight.

One of the key factors in the Assyrian successes was iron weapons. The Hittites (HIH·tyts), a people to the north, had mastered iron production, making iron stronger than tin or copper. The Assyrians learned from Hittite technology.

Kings and Government

Assyria extended from the Persian Gulf in the east to the Nile River in the west. The capital was located at Nineveh (NIH· nuh·vuh), along the Tigris River.

Assyrian kings had to be powerful leaders to rule such a large area. They divided their empire into **provinces** (PRAH· vuhn·suhs), or political districts. The government built roads that connected these provinces. The kings chose officials to govern, collect taxes, and carry out the laws in each province. Soldiers stood guard at stations along the roads to protect traders from bandits. Messengers on government business used the stations to rest and change chariot horses.

Life in Assyria

The lives of the Assyrians were built on what they learned from other Mesopotamian peoples. The Assyrians had law codes, but their punishments were harsher. Assyrians based their writing on Babylonian writing. They worshipped many of the same gods.

Assyrians built large temples and palaces filled with wall carvings and statues. They also wrote and collected stories. An ancient Assyrian king named Ashurbanipal (ah·shur·BAH· nuh·puhl) built one of the world's first libraries in Nineveh. It held 25,000 tablets of stories and songs to the gods. Historians have learned much about ancient civilizations from this library.

Hammurabi's Code was carved on stone slabs that were placed where the most people would see them. Sometimes a statue of the king was placed with it.

▶ CRITICAL THINKING
Drawing Conclusions Why was displaying the code important for Babylonians?

(l)Réunion des Musées Nationaux/Art Resource, NY; (r)akg-images

Reading**HELP**DESK

tribute a payment made to a ruler or state as a sign of surrender

province a territory governed as a political district of a country or empire

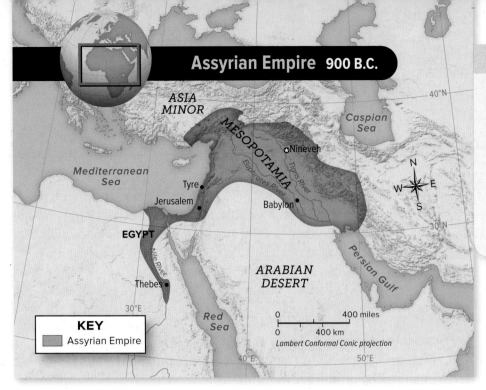

Assyrian Empire 900 B.C.

ASIA MINOR
MESOPOTAMIA
Caspian Sea
40°N
Mediterranean Sea
◊Nineveh
Euphrates River
Tigris River
Tyre •
Jerusalem •
Babylon •
30°N
EGYPT
Nile River
ARABIAN DESERT
Persian Gulf
Thebes •
30°E
Red Sea
0   400 miles
0   400 km
Lambert Conformal Conic projection
40°E   50°E

KEY
▬ Assyrian Empire

GEOGRAPHY CONNECTION

The Assyrians conquered lands from Mesopotamia to Egypt.

1 LOCATION What geographic feature lay to the south of the Assyrian Empire?

2 CRITICAL THINKING
Making Inferences Several major rivers flowed through the Assyrian Empire. Why were these rivers important?

Farming and trade were both important to the Assyrians. They brought in wood and metal from far away to supply their empire with material for building and for making tools and weapons.

✓ PROGRESS CHECK

Summarizing Why was Assyria's army so strong?

The Chaldean Empire

GUIDING QUESTION *Why was Babylon an important city in the ancient world?*

For 300 years, Assyria ruled the area from the Persian Gulf to Egypt. Because they were harsh rulers, people often rebelled. In about 650 B.C., fighting broke out over who would be the next Assyrian ruler. With the Assyrians in turmoil, a group of people called the Chaldeans (kal·DEE·uhns) took power.

A New Empire

Centuries before, about 1000 B.C., the Chaldean people had moved into southern Mesopotamia. At that time, the Assyrians had quickly conquered the Chaldeans' small kingdom. The Chaldeans hated their harsh new rulers and were never completely under Assyrian control.

Connections to
TODAY

Libraries

The United States Library of Congress in Washington, D.C., ranks as the largest library in the world. It holds millions of books, photographs, and other documents.

Visual Vocabulary

slingshot a weapon that is used to throw stones or other objects

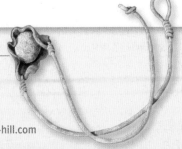

1 LOCATION In which direction would someone travel from Sidon to reach the Persian Gulf?

2 CRITICAL THINKING
Evaluating Why do you think the Chaldeans became traders?

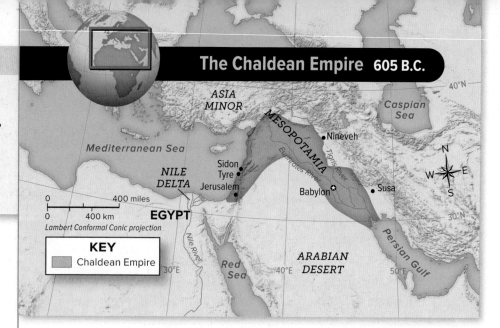

The Chaldean Empire 605 B.C.

Years later, when the Assyrians were fighting each other, the Chaldean king Nabopolassar (NAH·buh·puh·LAH·suhr) decided to reclaim his kingdom.

In 627 B.C., Nabopolassar led a revolt against the Assyrians. Within a year, he had forced the Assyrians out of Uruk and was crowned king of Babylonia. The Medes, another people in the **region** who wanted to break free from Assyrian rule, joined the Chaldeans. Together, they defeated the Assyrian army. In 612 B.C., they captured the Assyrian capital of Nineveh and burned it to the ground. The hated Assyrian Empire quickly crumbled.

Nabopolassar and his son, Nebuchadnezzar (NEH·byuh·kuhd·NEH·zuhr), created a new empire. Most of the Chaldeans were descendants of the Babylonians who made up Hammurabi's empire about 1,200 years earlier. Through conquest, the Chaldeans gained control of almost all of the lands the Assyrians had once ruled. The city of Babylon served as their capital. Because of this, the Chaldean Empire is sometimes called the New Babylonian Empire.

The Greatness of Babylon

King Nebuchadnezzar rebuilt Babylon, making it the largest and richest city in the world. Huge brick walls surrounded the city. Soldiers kept watch in towers that were built into the walls.

Grand palaces and temples were located in the center of Babylon. A huge ziggurat stood more than 300 feet (92 m) tall. When the sun shone, its gold roof could be seen for miles.

Academic Vocabulary

region a geographic area

Academic Vocabulary

complex having many parts, details, or ideas

The richness of the ziggurat was equaled by that of the king's palace. The palace had a giant staircase of greenery known as the Hanging Gardens.

Babylon's Hanging Gardens were considered one of the Seven Wonders of the Ancient World. These terraced gardens—built like huge steps—included large trees, masses of flowering vines, and other beautiful plants. A **complex** irrigation system brought water from the Euphrates River to water the gardens. It is believed that Nebuchadnezzar built the gardens to please his wife. She missed the mountains and plants of her homeland in the northwest.

For his people, Nebuchadnezzar built a beautiful street near the palace that they could visit. It was paved with limestone and marble, and lined with walls of blue glaze tile.

These ruins of the original gardens stand today as a reminder of Babylon's glory.

The grand Hanging Gardens of Babylon were watered from the top down using irrigation. Water flowed from one level to the next.

▶ **CRITICAL THINKING**
Making Generalizations
Why do you think ancient cities had at least one magnificent building?

King Nebuchadnezzar in the Hanging Gardens.

Each spring, thousands of people crowded into Babylon to watch a gold statue of the god Marduk (MAHR·dook) as it was wheeled along the street. Chaldeans believed that the ceremony would bring peace and bigger crops to their empire.

The Babylonians built many new canals, making the land even more fertile. To pay for his building projects and to maintain his army, Nebuchadnezzar had to collect very high taxes and tributes. Because his empire stretched as far as Egypt, it had to have an efficient system of government.

One Greek historian in the 400s B.C. described the beauty of Babylon. He wrote, "In magnificence, there is no other city that approaches it." Outside the center of Babylon stood houses and marketplaces. There artisans made pottery, cloth, and baskets. The major trade route between the Persian Gulf and the Mediterranean Sea passed through Babylon. Merchants came to the city in traveling groups called **caravans** (KAR·uh·VANZ). They bought Babylonian goods—pottery, cloth, baskets, and jewelry. Babylon grew wealthy from this trade; under the Assyrians, the area had been fairly poor.

The people of Babylon also made many scientific advancements. The Chaldeans, like other people in Mesopotamia, believed that the gods showed their plans in the changes in the sky. Chaldean **astronomers** (uh·STRAH·nuh·muhrs)—people who study the heavenly bodies—mapped the stars, the planets, and the phases of the moon as it changed. The Chaldeans invented one of the first sundials to measure time. They also were the first to follow a seven-day week.

The Fall of the Empire

After Nebuchadnezzar died, a series of weak kings ruled the Chaldean Empire. Poor harvests and slow trade further weakened the empire. In 539 B.C., the Persians recognized

©Stapleton Collection/Corbis

Reading**HELP**DESK

caravan a group of merchants traveling together for safety, usually with a large number of camels

astronomer a person who studies planets and stars

Camels have been called the ships of the desert because they can live in extreme conditions. Merchants traveled to Babylon by caravan to buy and sell goods.

Christopher Boisvieux/agefotostock

that the Chaldeans had lost their strength and leadership. The Persians took advantage and captured Babylon and made Mesopotamia part of their empire. However, they allowed their newly captured land to keep its distinct culture. The Persians wisely did not want to destroy all the Chaldeans had accomplished.

✔ PROGRESS CHECK

Identifying Which wonder of the ancient world was located in Babylon?

LESSON 2 REVIEW

Review Vocabulary

1. How could *caravans* passing through Babylon be helped by *astronomers*?

2. How might conquered people feel about paying *tribute* to the Assyrians?

Answer the Guiding Questions

3. *Comparing* How did Hammurabi's Code differ from earlier Sumerian laws?

4. *Describing* How did the Assyrians rule their empire?

5. *Explaining* Why did the Chaldeans overthrow the Assyrians?

6. **ARGUMENT** You live in an area that the Assyrian army is attempting to conquer. Write a speech that you might give to your neighbors to persuade them either to defend themselves or to surrender without a fight.

There's More Online! connected.mcgraw-hill.com

Write your answers on a separate piece of paper.

1 Exploring the Essential Question

INFORMATIVE/EXPLANATORY How would you describe the influence of Mesopotamia's physical geography on the region? Write an expository essay about how geography influenced the way people lived in Mesopotamia. Think about the Tigris River and the Euphrates River and the effect of flooding on the region. Include information about how geography influenced the formation of city-states in your essay.

2 21st Century Skills

CREATING A COMMUNICATIONS PRODUCT Write a script for a documentary about the technological and mathematical contributions made by the Sumerians. Divide your script into two columns. The left column should include the narration for your documentary. The right column should describe the images that will be shown. These images should match with the narration in the left column. Read your script to the class, or, if you have access to a video camera, shoot a short film based on your script.

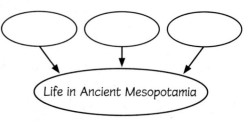

3 Thinking Like a Historian

IDENTIFYING Create a diagram like the one here to identify types of archeological evidence that researchers might search for to learn about ancient Mesopotamia.

4 GEOGRAPHY ACTIVITY

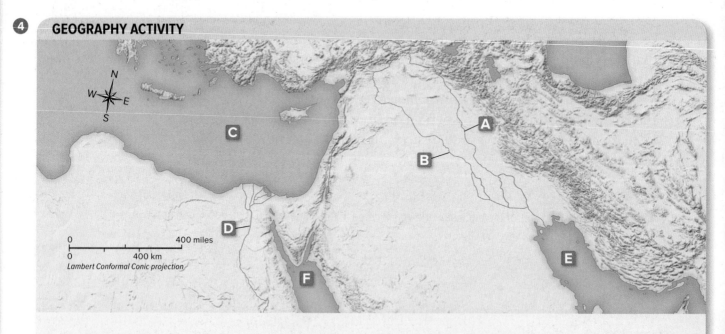

Locating Places
Match the letters on the map with the numbered places listed below.

1. Nile River	**3.** Mediterranean Sea	**5.** Persian Gulf
2. Euphrates River	**4.** Tigris River	**6.** Red Sea

Directions: Write your answers on a separate piece of paper.

CHECKING FOR UNDERSTANDING

1 Define each of these terms as they relate to Mesopotamia.
- **A.** Irrigation
- **B.** city-state
- **C.** scribe
- **D.** epic
- **E.** empire
- **F.** province

REVIEW THE GUIDING QUESTIONS

2 *Explaining* Describe the methods devised by the Mesopotamians to control the flooding of the Tigris and Euphrates Rivers and improve agriculture.

3 *Explaining* Why did the Sumerian civilization develop as a number of independent city-states?

4 *Describing* Describe the role of trade in ancient Sumer, including the products and resources that were part of that trade.

5 *Identifying* Identify one important invention that originated in Sumer and describe its uses and/or value.

6 *Describing* Describe the Code of Hammurabi. With what aspects of life did it deal? How did it treat the less powerful segment of society?

7 *Summarizing* Describe the extent of the Assyrian Empire. How did Assyrian leaders successfully rule such a large area?

8 *Identifying* What scientific advancements were made by the Chaldeans?

CRITICAL THINKING

9 *Determining Cause and Effect* How did the growth of surplus food in Mesopotamia lead to the development of Sumer's first cities?

10 *Making Connections* How were the gods worshipped by Sumerians related to everyday life?

11 *Contrasting* Contrast the social classes that developed in Sumer. What peoples/occupations belonged to each class?

12 *Evaluating* Do you think the development of writing was important to the success of Sumer as a civilization? Explain your answer.

13 *Sequencing* Describe, in order, the series of empires that developed in Mesopotamia following Sumer's fade from power.

14 *Making Generalizations* Aside from their military organization and advanced weapons, what generalization can be made about the reasons for the Assyrian Empire's military successes? Explain the reasoning for your generalization.

15 *Contrasting* During the Chaldean Empire, why did the city of Babylon grow wealthy? Why do you think this differed from when the Assyrians controlled the area?

16 *Assessing* Assess the rule of King Nebuchadnezzar of the Chaldean Empire. What were his accomplishments? Which do you consider most important?

Need Extra Help?

If You've Missed Question	**1**	**2**	**3**	**4**	**5**	**6**	**7**	**8**	**9**	**10**	**11**	**12**	**13**	**14**	**15**	**16**
Review Lesson	1,2	1	1	1	1	2	2	2	1	1	1	1	2	2	2	2

DBQ SHORT RESPONSE

"The vast majority of the inhabitants of Babylonia, Assyria, and other Mesopotamian empires were poor and had no political power. ...Under some circumstances a person could change his or her social status. ... a trader or merchant who was uncommonly diligent or lucky in business might ... be able to afford his own plots of land."

—From *Empires of Mesopotamia* by Don Nardo

17 How might a trader improve his social status?

18 How did a person show their wealth at this time? Do you think people often improved their social status in ancient Mesopotamia? Explain your answer.

EXTENDED RESPONSE

19 *Informative/Explanatory* You are a diplomat from Egypt who is visiting Babylon around 565 B.C. The leader of your country wants information about the city, including the Hanging Gardens. How is the city organized? What do the Hanging Gardens look like? Write a report that describes your opinion about the city.

STANDARDIZED TEST PRACTICE

DBQ ANALYZING DOCUMENTS

This poem was written by an unknown Mesopotamian mother.

Hark the piping!
My heart is piping in the wilderness where the young man once went free.
He is a prisoner now in death's kingdom lies bound where once he lived.
The ewe gives up her lamb and the nanny goat her kid
My heart is piping in the wilderness, an instrument of grief.
    —"The Mesopotamian View of Death," *Poems of Heaven and Hell from Ancient Mesopotamia*, N. K. Sanders, trans

20 **Drawing Conclusions** What has happened to the young man in the poem?

  A. He has died.

  B. He is in prison for life.

  C. He is a successful warrior.

  D. He tends a flock of sheep.

21 **Explaining** How does the mother react to what has happened?

  A. She wants a chance to hug her son again.

  B. She blames the king for what has happened.

  C. She says she should have been tending her sheep.

  D. She believes that her body is acting out her feelings.

Need Extra Help?

If You've Missed Question	**17**	**18**	**19**	**20**	**21**
Review Lesson	1	1	2	2	1,2

◄ *The god Osiris was respected because he represented new life and new crops.*

5000 B.C. TO A.D. 350

Ancient Egypt and Kush

THE STORY MATTERS ...

When you think of the most powerful person in your country, who is it? Is it the president? For ancient Egyptians, one of the most important beings was the god Osiris. Osiris controlled the power of life and death. As the god of agriculture, he controlled the very food Egyptians ate. He allowed the Nile River to flood its banks and bring fertile soil and water to the Egyptian desert. Osiris also knew death. In the underworld, the souls of the dead met the god Osiris. He did not have the power to return the dead to life, but he was a symbol of ongoing life. As you read this chapter, you will learn how the forces of life and death shaped the daily life of the ancient Egyptians and Kushites.

©Corbis

ESSENTIAL QUESTIONS

• How does geography influence the way people live?
• What makes a culture unique?
• Why do civilizations rise and fall?

Place & Time: Ancient Egypt and Kush
5000 B.C. to A.D. 350

The Egyptian Empire covered the northeastern corner of Africa. It centered on the mysterious Nile River valley. Egypt extended from central Africa to coastal areas along the Red and Mediterranean Seas. Despite periods of weakness, the empire expanded over the centuries of the Middle Kingdom and the New Kingdom.

Step Into the Place

MAP FOCUS Egypt's location in a river valley surrounded by deserts helped it become powerful.

1 LOCATION Look at the map. Is Egypt located north or south of the Mediterranean Sea?

2 PLACE What physical features made it possible for Egyptians to travel and trade?

3 LOCATION Describe the location of Egypt using cardinal directions.

4 CRITICAL THINKING
Analyzing How does location near a waterway contribute to the success of a civilization?

The hot, dry climate of Egypt allowed ancient Egyptians to preserve the bodies of their dead as mummies.

These jars were used for storage during the process of making mummies. The tops of the jars show the heads of Egyptian gods.

(t)RABOUAN Jean-Baptiste/Alamy; (b)SSPL/Science Museum/The Image Works

Step Into the Time

TIME LINE What events in the time line suggest that the Egyptians were unified, organized, and determined to build an empire?

ANCIENT EGYPT AND KUSH

THE WORLD

3000 B.C.

c. 3000 B.C. Egyptians develop hieroglyphics

c. 2540 B.C. Great Pyramid built

c. 2600 B.C. Old Kingdom period begins

c. 3100 B.C. Narmer unites Egypt

c. 3000 B.C. India's early civilization begins

c. 2700 B.C. Chinese begin making bronze artifacts

c. 2500 B.C. Mesopotamia sets up world's first libraries

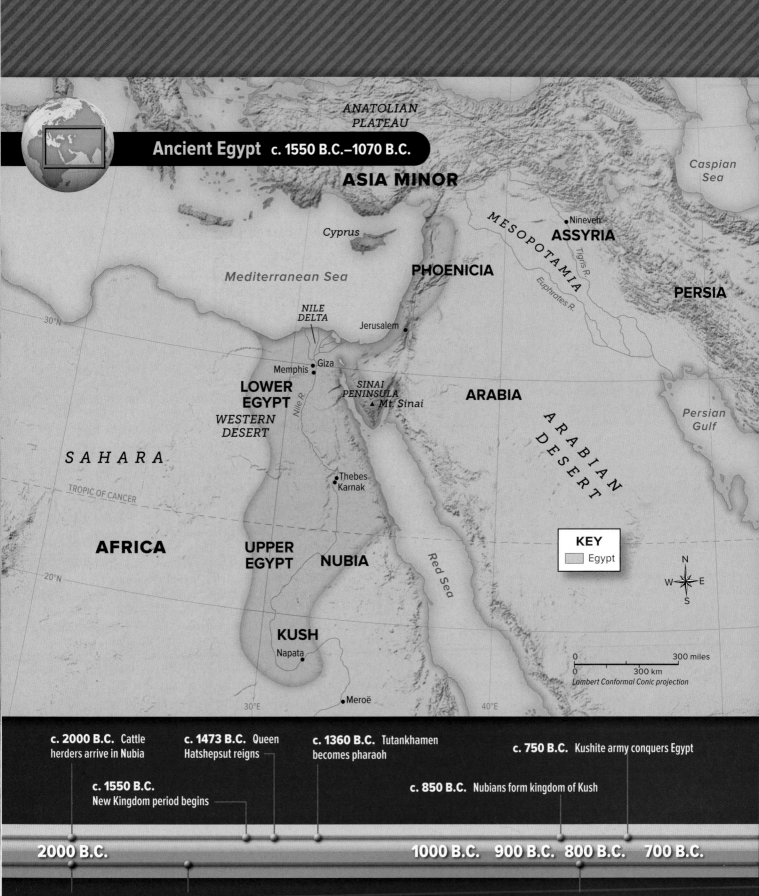

Ancient Egypt c. 1550 B.C.–1070 B.C.

ANATOLIAN PLATEAU

ASIA MINOR

Caspian Sea

Cyprus

Mediterranean Sea

MESOPOTAMIA

Nineveh

ASSYRIA

Tigris R.

Euphrates R.

PHOENICIA

PERSIA

30°N

NILE DELTA

Jerusalem

Memphis   Giza

LOWER EGYPT

WESTERN DESERT

Nile R.

SINAI PENINSULA
▲ Mt. Sinai

ARABIA

Persian Gulf

S A H A R A

TROPIC OF CANCER

A R A B I A N
D E S E R T

AFRICA

UPPER EGYPT   NUBIA

Red Sea

20°N

KEY
☐ Egypt

N
W   E
S

KUSH

Napata

0   300 miles
0   300 km
Lambert Conformal Conic projection

30°E   Meroë   40°E

c. 2000 B.C. Cattle herders arrive in Nubia

c. 1473 B.C. Queen Hatshepsut reigns

c. 1360 B.C. Tutankhamen becomes pharaoh

c. 750 B.C. Kushite army conquers Egypt

c. 1550 B.C. New Kingdom period begins

c. 850 B.C. Nubians form kingdom of Kush

2000 B.C.

1000 B.C.   900 B.C.   800 B.C.   700 B.C.

c. 2000 B.C. First permanent settlements begin in Central Mexico

c. 1700 B.C. Building of stone circle begins at Stonehenge

c. 825 B.C. Trading crossroads established in Syria

LESSON 1
The Nile River

IT MATTERS BECAUSE
The Nile River was the most important factor in the development of ancient Egypt.

The Nile River Valley

GUIDING QUESTION *Why was the Nile River important to the ancient Egyptians?*

While empires flourished and fell in Mesopotamia, two other civilizations developed along the Nile River in northeastern Africa. One of these civilizations was Egypt (EE·jihpt). It developed in the northern part of the Nile River valley. The other civilization, Kush (CUSH), emerged in the far southern part of the Nile River valley. Although Egypt and Kush were **unique** civilizations, they influenced one another throughout their long histories.

Valley Civilization

The Nile River valley was ideal for human settlement because of its fertile land. As early as 5000 B.C., hunters and gatherers from the drier areas of Africa and Southwest Asia began to move into the Nile River valley. Permanent settlements were created by early groups who farmed the land and built villages along the Nile's banks. These people were the earliest Egyptians and Kushites.

The early Egyptians lived in the northern region of the Nile River valley. They called their land *Kemet* (KEH·meht), which means "black land," after the dark, rich soil. Later, this northern Nile area would be called *Egypt*. Of the world's early river valley

Reading**HELP**DESK

Taking Notes: *Identifying*

Use a web diagram like this one to identify three reasons why most ancient Egyptians lived near the Nile River.

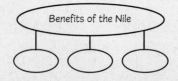
Benefits of the Nile

Content Vocabulary

• **cataract**　　• **papyrus**
• **delta**　　• **hieroglyphics**
• **shadoof**　　• **dynasty**

civilizations, you probably are most familiar with ancient Egypt. People still marvel at its ruins located in present-day Egypt. These ruins include the enormous stone Sphinx that has the body of a lion and a human head. Archaeologists also study the wondrous pyramids and the mummies found buried in tombs once full of riches.

The Gift of the River

Many of ancient Egypt's structures survived because Egypt has a hot, dry climate. Since the region receives little rainfall, ancient Egyptians depended on the Nile for drinking and bathing. The river also supplied water to grow crops. To the Egyptians, the Nile was the "creator of all good." They praised it in a hymn:

PRIMARY SOURCE

❝ You create the grain, you bring forth the barley,
Assuring perpetuity [survival] to the temples.
If you cease your toil and your work,
Then all that exists is in anguish [suffering]. ❞

—from *"Hymn to the Nile"*

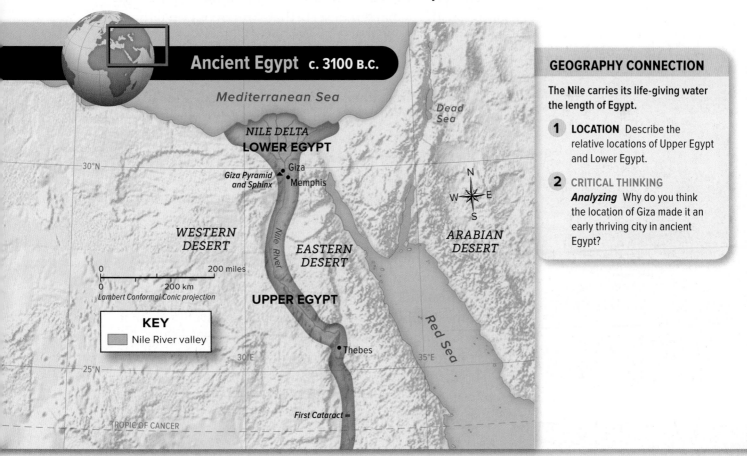

Ancient Egypt c. 3100 B.C.

Mediterranean Sea

NILE DELTA
LOWER EGYPT

Dead Sea

30°N

Giza Pyramid and Sphinx ▲ ● Giza
● Memphis

WESTERN DESERT

Nile River

EASTERN DESERT

ARABIAN DESERT

0   200 miles
0   200 km
Lambert Conformal Conic projection

UPPER EGYPT

Red Sea

KEY
☐ Nile River valley

30°E   ● Thebes   35°E

25°N

First Cataract ◄

TROPIC OF CANCER

GEOGRAPHY CONNECTION

The Nile carries its life-giving water the length of Egypt.

1 LOCATION Describe the relative locations of Upper Egypt and Lower Egypt.

2 CRITICAL THINKING
Analyzing Why do you think the location of Giza made it an early thriving city in ancient Egypt?

Academic Vocabulary

unique one of a kind; different from all others

Narrow cataracts on the Nile limit river travel, especially for larger ships.

Do you know which is the world's longest river? It is the Nile that flows north about 4,000 miles (6,437 km) from central Africa to the Mediterranean Sea. It has been called the "lifeblood" of Egypt.

At its source, the Nile is two separate rivers: the Blue Nile and the White Nile. The Blue Nile begins in the snowy mountains of eastern Africa. The White Nile starts in the tropics of central Africa. The two rivers join just south of Egypt to form the Nile River. There, steep cliffs and large boulders form dangerous, fast-moving waters called **cataracts** (KA·tuh·RAKTS). Cataracts make traveling by ship along the Nile difficult.

A Protected Land

As with many rivers, the Nile's flow throughout the centuries has created a valley. You can see on the map on the previous page that the Nile looks like the long winding root of a plant. Shortly before the Nile reaches the Mediterranean Sea, it splits into many branches that resemble a plant's bloom. These waterways form a fan-shaped area of fertile marshland called a **delta** (DEHL·tuh).

In the Nile River valley, we see the effect that water has on the landscape. The lush, green Nile valley and delta contrast sharply with the barren deserts that stretch out on either side of the river. The change in landscape can be so sudden that a person can stand with one foot in fertile soil and one foot in barren sand.

The Nile borders the largest deserts in the world. To the west of the Nile River is the Libyan Desert, which forms part of the Sahara (suh·HAR·uh). To the river's east lies the Eastern Desert that extends to the Red Sea. The ancient Egyptians called these deserts the "Red Land" because of their scorching heat. These large desert areas were not favorable to humans or animals. They kept Egypt **isolated,** however, from outside invaders.

In addition to the deserts, other physical features protected Egypt. To the far south, the Nile's dangerous cataracts prevented enemy ships from attacking Egypt. In the north, delta marshes stopped invaders who sailed from the Mediterranean Sea. These physical features gave the Egyptians advantages that Mesopotamians lacked. The Egyptians rarely faced the danger of invasion. As a result, Egyptian civilization developed peacefully.

The Egyptians, though isolated, were not completely cut off from other peoples. The Mediterranean Sea to the north and the Red Sea to the east provided routes for trade.

Daniela Dirscherl/WaterFrame/Age fotostock

Reading**HELP**DESK

cataract a waterfall or rapids in a river

delta a fan-shaped area of silt near where a river flows into the sea

Academic Vocabulary

isolate to separate from others

The stark contrast between watered and not watered land can be seen along the banks of the Nile.

Egyptians took advantage of the region's wind patterns so that they could travel and trade. Although the natural flow of the Nile's currents carried boats north, winds from the north pushed sailboats south.

✓ PROGRESS CHECK

Explaining How were the Egyptians protected by their physical environment?

People of the River

GUIDING QUESTION *How did the ancient Egyptians depend on the Nile River to grow their crops?*

We know that the Mesopotamians controlled the floods of the Tigris and Euphrates Rivers to grow crops. They developed the technology to do so, but the unpredictable rivers constantly challenged them. In Egypt, however, the flooding of the Nile River was seasonal and consistent from year to year. So the Egyptians did not face the same challenge.

Predictable Floods

As in Mesopotamia, flooding along the Nile in Egypt was common. The Nile floods, however, were more predictable and less destructive than those of the Tigris and the Euphrates. As a result, the Egyptians were not afraid that heavy floods would destroy their homes and crops. Each year, during late spring, heavy tropical rains in central Africa and melting mountain snow in eastern Africa added water to the Nile. Around the middle of summer, the Nile overflowed its banks and flooded the land. Egyptian farmers were ready to take advantage of this cycle. When the waters returned to their normal level in late fall, thick deposits of fertile soil remained.

©Michel Gounot/Godong/Corbis

Special techniques and tools—such as this shadoof—helped farmers grow crops in the dry season.

How Did Egyptians Farm?

Farmers planted wheat, barley, and flax seeds while the soil was still wet. Over time, they grew enough food to feed themselves and the animals they raised.

During the dry season, Egyptian farmers irrigated their crops. They scooped out basins, or bowl-shaped holes, in the earth to store river water. They then dug canals that extended from the basins to the fields, allowing water to flow to their crops. Raised areas of soil provided support for the basin walls.

In time, Egyptian farmers developed new tools to make their work easier. For example, farmers created a **shadoof** (shuh‑DOOF), which is a bucket attached to a long pole that lifts water from the Nile and empties it into basins. Many Egyptian farmers still use this method today.

Egyptian farmers also needed a way to measure the area of their lands. When floods washed away boundary markers that divided one field from another, farmers used geometry to help them recalculate where one field began and the other ended.

Egyptians gathered **papyrus** (puh‑PY‑ruhs), a reed plant that grew wild along the Nile. They used the long, thin reeds to weave rope, sandals, baskets, and river rafts. Later, they used

We learn about ancient farming methods from Egyptian art murals such as this.

▶ CRITICAL THINKING

Describing What details about ancient farming methods can you find in this painting of farmers?

Reading**HELP**DESK

shadoof a bucket attached to a long pole used to transfer river water to storage basins

VERITABLE EXTRAIT DE VIANDE LIEBIG.

Histoire du papier. 2.
Fabricants de papier égyptiens.

papyrus to make paper. To do this, the Egyptians cut strips from the stalks of the papyrus plant and soaked them in water. Next, the strips were laid side by side and pounded together. They were then set out to dry, forming a large sheet of papyrus on which the Egyptians could write.

How Did the Egyptians Write?

Like the Mesopotamians, the Egyptians developed their own writing system. At first, Egyptian writing was made up of thousands of picture symbols that represented objects and ideas. A house, for example, would be represented by a drawing of a house. Later, Egyptians created symbols that represented sounds, just as the letters of our alphabet do. The combination of pictures and sound symbols created a complex writing system called **hieroglyphics** (hy·ruh·GLIH·fihks).

Few ancient Egyptians could read and write hieroglyphics. Some Egyptian men, however, attended special schools to prepare for careers as scribes in government or business. The Egyptians did not write on clay tablets like the Mesopotamians. For their daily tasks, Egyptian scribes developed a simpler script that they wrote or painted on papyrus. These same scribes carved hieroglyphics onto stone walls and monuments.

Papyrus reeds grow wild along rivers. From harvesting the reeds to final product, the process of making paper from papyrus took many days.

▶ **CRITICAL THINKING**
Predicting If Egyptians had not developed papyrus, what other material could they have used to write on?

✔ **PROGRESS CHECK**

Identifying What kind of writing system did the Egyptians develop?

papyrus a reed plant that grew wild along the Nile

hieroglyphics a writing system made up of a combination of pictures and sound symbols

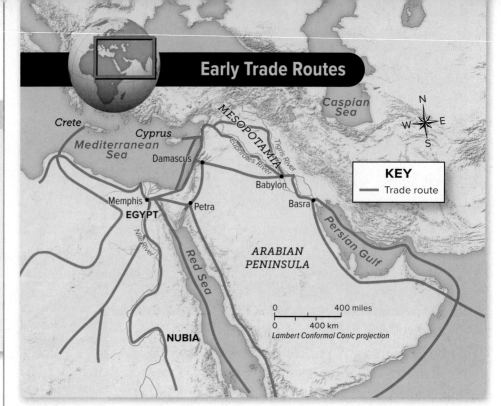

Uniting Egypt

GUIDING QUESTION *How did Egypt become united?*

Protected from outside attacks by desert barriers, Egyptian farmers were able to grow surpluses—extra amounts—of food. In Egypt, as in Mesopotamia, extra food meant that some people could leave farming to work in other occupations. Artisans, merchants, and traders began to play an important role in Egypt's economy. As more goods became available, villages along the Nile traded with one another. Before long, Egyptian caravans were carrying goods to Nubia (NOO·bee·uh) to the south, Mesopotamia to the northeast, and other places outside Egypt's borders. Along with the exchange of goods, Egyptian traders learned about the ways of life and governments of other societies.

Forming Kingdoms

The need for organized government became increasingly important as farming and trade increased. A government was necessary to oversee the construction and repair of irrigation ditches and dams. A government was needed to develop a process for storing and distributing grain during famines. In addition, conflicts over land ownership had to be settled.

Reading**HELP**DESK

dynasty a line of rulers from one family

Academic Vocabulary

unify to unite; to bring together into one unit

Over time, groups of villages merged to form small kingdoms. Each of these kingdoms was ruled by a king. The weaker kingdoms eventually fell under the control of the stronger ones. By 4000 B.C., Egypt was made up of two large kingdoms. One was Upper Egypt, which was located in the south-central part of the Nile River valley. The other was Lower Egypt, which was located along the Nile River's north delta.

Who Was Narmer?

Narmer (NAHR·mer) was a king of Upper Egypt. About 3100 B.C., he led his armies from the valley north into the delta. Narmer conquered Lower Egypt and married one of Lower Egypt's princesses, which **unified** the kingdoms. For the first time, all of Egypt was ruled by one king.

Narmer established a new capital at Memphis, a city on the border between Upper Egypt and Lower Egypt. He governed both parts of Egypt from this city. Memphis began to flourish as a center of government and culture along the Nile.

Narmer's kingdom lasted long after his death. The right to rule was passed from father to son to grandson. Such a line of rulers from one family is called a **dynasty** (DY·nuh·stee). When one dynasty died out, another took its place.

From about 3100 B.C. to 332 B.C., a series of 30 dynasties ruled Egypt. These dynasties are organized into three time periods: the Old Kingdom, the Middle Kingdom, and the New Kingdom. Throughout these three time periods, Egypt was usually united under a single ruler and enjoyed stable government.

✔ PROGRESS CHECK

Explaining How did the separate kingdoms of Egypt unite?

Egyptian art often glorified rulers. The man in the center of this carving is Narmer.

▶ CRITICAL THINKING
Analyzing How does the carving show that Narmer was a powerful leader?

LESSON 1 REVIEW

Review Vocabulary

1. Why did the Egyptians need *hieroglyphics*?

2. How does a *dynasty* work?

Answer the Guiding Questions

3. **Identifying** What physical feature is to the east and west of the Nile River? How did this feature help Egyptians?

4. **Contrasting** How did the flooding of major rivers affect both the Mesopotamians and the Egyptians?

5. **Explaining** What was significant about the joining of the two kingdoms under Narmer?

6. **Analyzing** How did the Nile River help the ancient Egyptians develop as a well-governed civilization?

7. **INFORMATIVE/EXPLANATORY** Why has the Nile River been described as the "lifeblood" of Egypt? Why was the river essential to the Egyptians? Explain your answer in the form of a short essay.

LESSON 2
Life in Ancient Egypt

ESSENTIAL QUESTION

• What makes a culture unique?

IT MATTERS BECAUSE
The Egyptian pharaohs were all-powerful rulers. Egyptians built such gigantic and sturdy pyramids in their honor that the pyramids still stand today.

Egypt's Early Rulers

GUIDING QUESTION *How was ancient Egypt governed?*

Around 2600 B.C., Egyptian civilization entered the period known as the Old Kingdom. The Old Kingdom lasted until about 2200 B.C. During these years, the Egyptians built magnificent cities and increased trade. They also formed a unified government. The Egyptians prized unity. They understood the importance of everyone working and living according to similar principles and beliefs. Therefore, they developed a government under an all-powerful ruler who controlled both religious and political affairs. A government in which the same person is both the political leader and the religious leader is called a **theocracy** (thee·AH·kruh·see).

A Political Leader

At first, the Egyptian ruler was called a king. Later, he was known as **pharaoh** (FEHR·oh). The word *pharaoh* originally meant "great house." It referred to the grand palace in which the king and his family lived.

The Egyptians were fiercely loyal to the pharaoh because they believed that a strong ruler unified their kingdom. The pharaoh held total power. He issued commands that had to

Reading**HELP**DESK

Taking Notes: *Organizing*

Use a diagram like this one to list information about ancient Egypt by adding one or more facts to each of the boxes.

Ancient Egypt		
Ruler	Religion	Social Groups

Content Vocabulary

- **theocracy**
- **pharaoh**
- **bureaucrat**

- **embalming**
- **pyramid**

be obeyed. Egyptians believed that a pharaoh's wise and far-reaching leadership would help their kingdom survive such disasters as war and famine.

The pharaoh appointed **bureaucrats** (BYUR·uh·kratz), or government officials, to carry out his orders. Bureaucrats supervised the construction and repair of dams, irrigation canals, and brick granaries. Granaries (GRAY·nuh·reez) were used to store grain from bountiful harvests so people would not starve during times of poor harvests.

The pharaoh owned all the land in Egypt and could use it as he pleased. The pharaoh's officials collected tax payments of grain from farmers. The pharaoh also **distributed** land to officials, priests, and wealthy Egyptians whom he favored.

A Religious Leader

Egyptians were also loyal to the pharaoh because they thought he was the son of Re (RAY), the Egyptian sun god. They believed their pharaoh was a god on earth who protected Egypt. Whenever the pharaoh appeared in public, people played music on flutes and cymbals and bowed their heads.

The pharaoh (left) had many servants to wait on him and provide him with all his needs.

Explaining What role did the pharaoh play as a political leader?

INTERFOTO/Alamy

theocracy government by religious leaders	**Academic Vocabulary**
pharaoh ruler of ancient Egypt	**distribute** to divide into shares and deliver the shares to different people
bureaucrat a government official	

As Egypt's religious leader, the pharaoh participated in ceremonies to help the kingdom thrive. For example, the pharaoh rode a bull around Memphis because the Egyptians believed that this would help keep the soil fertile. The pharaoh was also the first person to cut the ripened grain at harvest time. Egyptians believed this action would produce abundant crops.

✔ **PROGRESS CHECK**

Analyzing How was the pharaoh a political leader and a religious leader?

Religion in Egypt

GUIDING QUESTION *What kind of religion did the ancient Egyptians practice?*

Religion influenced every aspect of Egyptian life. Like the people of Mesopotamia, ancient Egyptians worshipped many gods and goddesses. The people of Egypt, however, thought their gods were more powerful. The Egyptians believed these deities (DEE·uh·teez) controlled natural forces as well as human activities.

The Egyptians depended on the sun to grow their crops and on the Nile River to make the soil fertile. Thus, two of the most **crucial** gods were the sun god Re and the river god Hapi (HAH·pee). Another important god was Osiris (oh·SY·ruhs). According to legend, Osiris was an early pharaoh who gave the Egyptian people laws and taught them farming. His wife Isis (EYE·suhs) represented the faithful wife and mother. Osiris and Isis together ruled over the world of the dead. Thoth (THOHTH) was the god of learning. He could take human or animal form—or both—as did most gods and goddesses.

The Afterlife

The Egyptians had a positive view of the afterlife. They believed that life after death would be even better than the present life. After a long journey, the dead arrived at a place of peace.

The Egyptians gave offerings to their gods, whom they believed controlled their lives.

▶ **CRITICAL THINKING**
Speculating Why do you think the god being offered a gift has the head of a bird?

©Gianni Dagli Orti/Corbis

Reading Strategy: *Contrasting*

Look for clue words such as *however, but,* and *although.* These words tell you that the author is contrasting two ideas. Which sentence on this page uses a contrasting clue word? What ideas are being contrasted?

Academic Vocabulary

crucial important or significant

One of the most important writings of ancient Egypt was *The Book of the Dead*. Egyptians studied its prayers and magic spells to prepare for the afterlife. They believed that Osiris greeted those who had just died at the gate to the next world. If people had led good lives and knew the spells, Osiris would give them eternal life. This passage from *The Book of the Dead* explains what a person who enters the happy afterlife can expect:

PRIMARY SOURCE

" Wheat and barley ... shall be given unto him therein, and he shall flourish there just as he did upon earth. "

—from *Papyrus of Ani—The Egyptian Book of the Dead*

The earliest Egyptians believed that only the pharaohs could enjoy the afterlife. They thought that the pharaoh's soul **resided** in his body, and that the body had to be protected in order for the soul to complete the journey to the afterlife. There, the pharaoh would continue to protect Egypt. If the pharaoh's body decayed after death, his soul would not have a place to live. The pharaoh would not survive in the afterlife. As the centuries passed, however, Egyptians came to believe that the afterlife was not only for pharaohs. All people—rich and poor—could hope for eternal life with the help of the god Osiris. As a result, the process of **embalming** (ihm·BAHLM·ihng) emerged so that Egyptians could protect bodies for the afterlife.

Before a body was embalmed, priests removed the body's organs. The organs were stored in special jars that were buried with the body. Then the priests covered the body with a salt called natron and stored it for several days. The natron dried up the water in the body, causing it to shrink. The shrunken, dried body was then filled with burial spices and tightly wrapped with long strips of linen. The wrapped body was then known as a mummy (MUH·mee). The mummy was sealed in a coffin and placed in a decorated tomb.

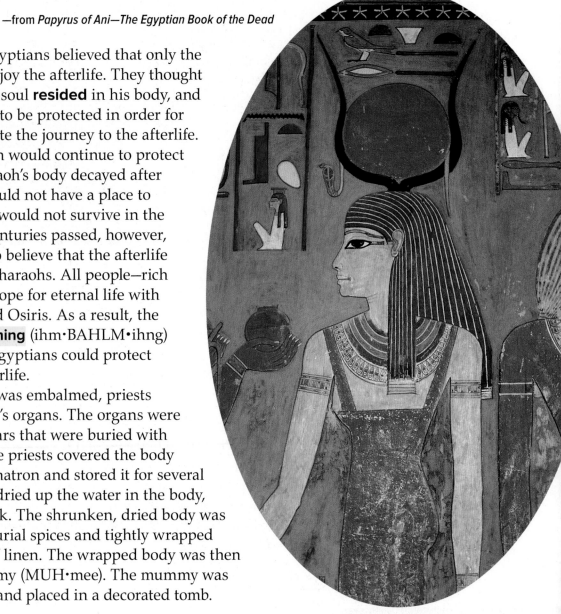

The goddess Isis was the wife of the god Osiris. She was a powerful god respected on her own.

▶ CRITICAL THINKING
Inferring Why do you think the Egyptians worshipped some powerful gods that were men and others that were women?

DEA/G. SIOEN/De Agostini Picture Library/Getty Images

embalming the process of treating a body to keep it from decaying

Academic Vocabulary

reside to be present continuously or have a home in a particular place

Preparing the pharaoh's body for burial involved a mix of science and religion. Special priests performed the process.

Explaining What do you think Egyptians learned about the human body by embalming?

Wealthy people had their mummies placed in coffins and buried in tombs. Poorer people had their mummies buried in caves or in the sand. Even animals were embalmed. Egyptians viewed animals not only as pets, but also as sacred creatures. As a result, they buried the mummies of cats, birds, and other animals at temples honoring their gods and goddesses.

Medical Skills

The Egyptians learned much about the human body from embalming. This knowledge helped them to develop basic medical skills. Egyptian doctors sewed up cuts and set broken bones. They were the first to use splints, bandages, and compresses. Egyptians also wrote down medical information on papyrus scrolls. These records were the world's first medical books.

✔ PROGRESS CHECK

Analyzing Why did Egyptians protect a person's body after death?

WildLife Art, LTD

Reading**HELP**DESK

pyramid great stone tomb built for an Egyptian pharaoh

Academic Vocabulary

labor work

Pyramid Tombs

GUIDING QUESTION *Why and how were pyramids built?*

The Egyptians honored their pharaohs in a special way. They built great tombs called **pyramids** (PIHR·uh·mihds) for the pharaohs. These enormous structures were made of stone and covered the area of several city blocks. Centuries after they were built, these monuments still tower over the desert sands. The pyramids protected the bodies of dead pharaohs from floods, wild animals, and robbers. The Egyptians believed the pharaohs would be happy after death if they had their personal belongings. For that reason, they placed the pharaoh's clothing, weapons, furniture, and jewelry in the pyramids.

The pyramids preserved, or saved, these objects in relatively good condition for centuries. Today, archaeologists are able to study the pyramids and the treasures they hold to learn about life in ancient Egypt.

How Were Pyramids Built?

Thousands of workers spent years of hard **labor** to build the pyramids. Farmers did much of the work during the summer months when the Nile River flooded and they could not farm.

The Sphinx is one of the most famous Egyptian monuments. It was built to honor one of Egypt's pharaohs and stands today among the pyramids at Giza, Egypt.

Sylvain Grandadam/Getty Images

There's More Online! connected.mcgraw-hill.com

INSIDE A PYRAMID

❶ Air Shaft

❷ King's Burial Chamber The king's mummified body was placed in a room at the pyramid's center.

❸ Grand Gallery This tall, sloping hall held large granite blocks that sealed the tomb.

❹ Queen's Burial Chamber This chamber held a statue of the king, not the queen's body.

❺ Entrance

❻ Underground Burial Chamber Sometimes kings were buried here instead.

❼ Queen's Pyramids These smaller pyramids are believed to be tombs for the kings' wives.

❽ Mastaba These tombs surrounding the pyramids held royal family members and other nobles.

❾ Valley Temple This temple may have been used for rituals before the king was buried.

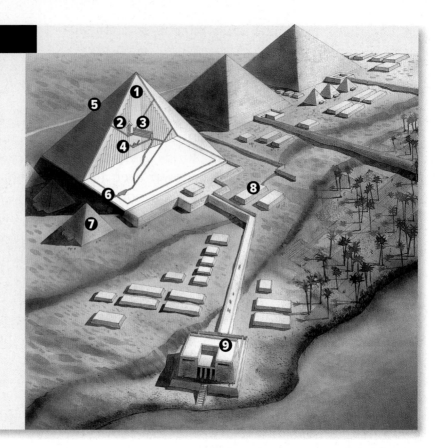

INFOGRAPHIC

The pyramids contained many rooms, each used for a different purpose.

▶ **CRITICAL THINKING**
Speculating Why was the king's burial chamber constructed in the middle of the pyramid and not at the top?

Surveyors, engineers, carpenters, and stonecutters also helped build the pyramids. The first great engineer who built pyramids was Imhotep (ihm·HOH·tehp). He also served as an official for the pharaoh.

Workers searched for stone in places throughout the Nile River valley or in Upper Egypt. After locating the stone, skilled artisans used copper tools to cut the stone into huge blocks. Next, workers used rope to fasten the blocks onto wooden sleds. The sleds were pulled along a path made of logs to the Nile River. There, the stones were moved onto barges that carried them to the building site. Workers unloaded the blocks and dragged or pushed them up ramps to be set in place at each new level of the pyramid.

The Egyptians faced many challenges as they built the pyramids. These challenges, however, led to important discoveries. For example, each pyramid rested on a square-shaped foundation, with an entrance facing north. To find north, the Egyptians studied the skies and developed an understanding of astronomy. With this knowledge, they invented a 365-day calendar with 12 months divided into three seasons. This calendar became the basis for our modern calendar.

Egyptians also made advancements in mathematics. Egypt's pyramid builders had to calculate how much stone was needed to build a pyramid. They had to measure angles in order to **construct** a pyramid's walls. To do this, they invented a system of written numbers based on 10. They also created fractions, using them with whole numbers to add, subtract, and divide.

An Egyptian Wonder

About the mid-2000s B.C., the Egyptians built the biggest and grandest of the pyramids—the Great Pyramid. It lies about 10 miles (16.1 km) from the modern city of Cairo. Built for King Khufu (KOO·foo), the Great Pyramid is one of three pyramids still standing at Giza on the Nile's west bank. It is about the height of a 48-story building, towering nearly 500 feet (153 m) above the desert. It extends over an area equal in size to nine football fields. More than 2 million stone blocks were used in the pyramid's construction, each weighing an average of 2.5 tons (2.3 metric tons). For more than 4,000 years, the Great Pyramid stood as the tallest structure in the world.

In this photo of the Great Pyramid, the pyramid in the center belongs to King Khafre, son of Khufu. Khafre's pyramid has a width (at its base) to height ratio of about 708:471 ft (216:143 m). Khufu's pyramid has a ratio of about 756:481 ft (230:147 m).

▶ CRITICAL THINKING
Comparing Which pyramid is larger?

✔ PROGRESS CHECK

Explaining Why did the Egyptians build the pyramids?

©Free Agents Limited/Corbis

Academic Vocabulary

construct to build

Daily Life

GUIDING QUESTION *How was Egyptian society organized?*

At its peak, ancient Egypt was home to about 5 million people. This would be about equal to the number of people living today in the state of Colorado. Most ancient Egyptians lived in the fertile Nile valley and delta. The delta is found at the mouth of the river. These two areas, which make up only 3 percent of Egypt's land, are densely populated even today.

Egypt's Social Groups

The **roles** of the people in ancient Egypt reflected their social status, or position in society. Look at the diagram of the different social groups, or classes, in ancient Egypt. The king or pharaoh and his family held the highest social position in Egypt, followed by a small upper class of army commanders, nobles, and priests. The priests served as government officials and supervised people who worked as clerks and scribes. A larger group of traders, artisans, and scribes made up the middle class. The lowest but largest groups in Egyptian society

INFOGRAPHIC

SOCIAL STATUS IN ANCIENT EGYPT

People lived according to their social status and occupation. People who were ambitious could improve their status.

Identifying What level of society do you think a teacher would occupy?

- Pharaoh
- Priests and nobles
- Traders, artisans, shopkeepers, and scribes
- Farmers and herders
- Unskilled workers

Reading**HELP**DESK

Academic Vocabulary

role the function or part an individual fills in society

Build Vocabulary: *Word Forms*

As a noun, *official* means "someone who holds an office or who manages the rules of a game." As an adjective, it means "authorized." The verb *officiate* means "to act in an official role."

These ancient Egyptian women are chemists. Women were educated and valued for their special skills.

▶ CRITICAL THINKING
Analyzing What social class would these women belong to?

were made up of farmers and unskilled workers. Even though there were divisions in Egyptian class structures, ambitious people in the lower classes were able to improve their social position.

How People Lived

Egypt's upper class lived in elegant homes and on estates along the Nile River. Their homes were constructed of wood and sun-dried mud bricks, and some were two or three stories tall. Surrounding their homes were lush gardens and pools filled with fish and water lilies. Men and women from the upper class dressed in fashionable white linen clothes and wore dark eye makeup and jewelry. Servants waited on them and performed household tasks.

The middle class of ancient Egyptian society was made up of people who owned businesses and held skilled jobs. These jobs included trading and working as a scribe. Artisans were also important members of the middle class. These craft-makers produced linen cloth, jewelry, pottery, and metal goods. The middle class lived in smaller homes and dressed more simply than the upper class.

©Bettmann/Corbis

Reading Strategy: *Finding the Main Idea*

Remember that each paragraph contains ideas that are related. Usually one sentence summarizes the main idea of a paragraph. Find the main idea in the last paragraph on this page.

The felucca, an ancient Egyptian river craft, sailed the Nile. Sailors today still use the same ship and sail design.

▶ **CRITICAL THINKING**
Analyzing Into what Egyptian social class would fishers fit?

The largest Egyptian social classes included farmers, unskilled workers, and enslaved people. Most farmers worked on land that was owned by wealthy nobles. They paid rent to the landowners, usually with a portion of their crops. Farmers lived in houses that were made of mud brick. The houses generally had only one room and a roof made of palm leaves. Farmers ate a simple diet of bread, vegetables, and fruit.

Unskilled workers performed **manual** labor, such as unloading cargo from boats and transporting it to markets. Some were fishers. Most unskilled workers settled in crowded city neighborhoods. They lived in small mud-brick houses with hard-packed dirt floors. Their houses sometimes included a courtyard. Families often gathered on the flat rooftops to socialize, play games, and sleep. Because of the hot Egyptian climate, they also did their cooking on the rooftop. This helped their homes stay cooler.

Some of these unskilled workers were enslaved people. Many of them had been captured in war, and they could earn their freedom over time. Some of these enslaved people helped build the pyramids.

Egyptian Families

The family was the most important group in ancient Egyptian society. Even the gods and goddesses were arranged in family groupings. The father was the head of the family in ancient Egypt, but women had more rights than women in other early civilizations had. Egyptian women held a legal status similar to that of men. They could own property, buy and sell goods, and **obtain** divorces.

Wealthy women even served as priests, managing temples and performing religious ceremonies. Wives of farmers often worked in the fields with their husbands. Women of the higher social classes were more likely to stay at home while their husbands worked at their jobs.

Image Source/Getty Images

Reading**HELP**DESK

Academic Vocabulary
manual involving physical effort
obtain to gain something through a planned effort

Few Egyptian children attended school. Egyptian children had time for fun, playing with board games, dolls, spinning tops, and stuffed leather balls. As in many other cultures, Egyptian children were expected to respect their parents. Mothers taught their daughters to sew, cook, and run a household. Boys learned farming or other trades from their fathers. Learning their father's trade was important, because very often the oldest son would inherit his father's business.

When boys and girls became teenagers, they were expected to get married and start families of their own. In Egyptian cities and among the upper class, people usually lived in nuclear families. A nuclear family is made up of two parents and their children. Some farm families and others in the lower class lived as extended families. In an extended family, older adults, along with their married children and their families, live together. For farm families, this provided more people to work the fields.

The oldest son, and sometimes the oldest daughter, were also responsible for taking care of their parents when the parents became too old or sick to take care of themselves. This responsibility included making sure the parents were given a proper burial after they died.

Egyptian sons learned their fathers' trades, such as fishing or farming. This ancient art piece shows fishers hauling nets.

✓ PROGRESS CHECK

Identifying What types of people made up Egypt's upper class?

LESSON 2 REVIEW

Review Vocabulary

1. Explain the role a *pharaoh* played in a *theocracy*.

2. What was the social status of a *bureaucrat* in ancient Egypt?

Answer the Guiding Questions

3. *Describing* What kind of religion did the ancient Egyptians practice? Describe at least one way that their religion was tied to agriculture.

4. *Analyzing* What was the most important purpose of the pyramids? Explain your reasoning.

5. *Comparing and Contrasting* How was life for Egyptian children similar to or different from that of children today?

6. *Defending* Why did the Egyptians spend years and many resources to build enormous tombs for their dead pharaohs?

7. **INFORMATIVE/EXPLANATORY** If you could be anyone in ancient Egypt except the pharaoh, who would you choose to be? Explain the reasons for your choice. Make sure to include the advantages and disadvantages of your social position.

There's More Online! connected.mcgraw-hill.com

networks

There's More Online!

LESSON 3

Egypt's Empire

ESSENTIAL QUESTION

- Why do civilizations rise and fall?

IT MATTERS BECAUSE

The leaders during the golden age of Egypt expanded the empire through war and trade. Although Egypt later declined, it greatly influenced other civilizations.

A Golden Age

GUIDING QUESTION *Why was the Middle Kingdom a "golden age" for Egypt?*

Around 2200 B.C., the ruling pharaohs in Memphis began to weaken. Ambitious nobles fought for control of Egypt. For more than 200 years, disorder and violence swept through the region. Finally, a new dynasty of pharaohs came to power. They moved the capital south to a city called Thebes (THEEBZ). These new pharaohs began a period of peace and order called the Middle Kingdom that lasted from about c. 2055 B.C. to c. 1650 B.C.

Conquests

During the Middle Kingdom, Egypt conquered new territories. Egyptian armies gained control of Nubia to the south and expanded northeast into present-day Syria. The Egyptian pharaohs added to their kingdom's wealth. They required tribute, or forced payments, from the peoples their armies had conquered.

Within Egypt, the pharaohs made many improvements. They added thousands of acres to the land already being farmed to increase crop production. They had more irrigation dams and channels built to supply more water to the population. The pharaohs also ordered the construction of a canal between the

Reading HELPDESK

Taking Notes: *Organizing*

As you read this lesson, complete a chart like this one about the Middle Kingdom and the New Kingdom.

	Middle Kingdom	New Kingdom
Date		
Government		
Economy		

Content Vocabulary

- incense
- envoy

Nile River and the Red Sea. As a result, Egyptian traders were able to send goods south by ship through the Red Sea. From there, the ships sailed to ports along the coasts of Arabia and East Africa.

The Arts Flourish

Egyptian arts and architecture thrived during the Middle Kingdom. Painters decorated the walls of tombs and temples with colorful scenes. These tomb paintings illustrated stories about the deities, as well as scenes from everyday life. Sculptors carved hunting, fishing, and battle scenes on large stone walls. They created statues of the pharaohs, showing them as ordinary humans rather than gods.

During the Middle Kingdom, the Egyptians developed a new kind of architecture. Pharaohs no longer had pyramids built. Instead, they had their tombs cut into limestone cliffs west of the Nile River. This area became known as the Valley of the Kings.

The Hyksos

During the 1600s B.C., some Egyptian nobles challenged the power of the pharaohs. Civil war divided Egypt, ending an era of peace and prosperity. As the Middle Kingdom weakened, outsiders invaded Egypt. A people from western Asia known as the Hyksos (HIHK·sahs) swept across the desert into Egypt.

The Hyksos were powerful warriors who used methods of warfare unknown to the Egyptians. The Hyksos rode in horse-drawn chariots and fought with sturdy weapons made of bronze and iron. As a result, they overwhelmed the Egyptian soldiers and took control of the land.

For more than 100 years, Hyksos kings ruled Egypt. The Hyksos borrowed some Egyptian customs but remained separate from the Egyptian people. Meanwhile, most Egyptians hated the Hyksos and planned to overthrow them. The Egyptians learned how to steer horse-drawn chariots and use Hyksos weapons. Around 1550 B.C., an Egyptian prince named Ahmose (AH·mohs) formed an army and drove the Hyksos out of Egypt.

✔ **PROGRESS CHECK**

Analyzing How were the Egyptians able to defeat the Hyksos?

Artisans produced jewels for pharaohs and decorative objects from gold, such as this chair.

▶ **CRITICAL THINKING**
Differentiating What about this chair makes you think it was made for royalty?

The Hyksos introduced chariots to Egypt. Battle scenes show the advantage a soldier on a chariot has over those on foot.

(t)Robert Harding/Robert Harding World Imagery/Getty Images; (b)©Jon Bower/LOOP IMAGES/Corbis

Building an Empire

GUIDING QUESTION *Why was the New Kingdom a unique period in ancient Egypt's history?*

Ahmose founded a new dynasty. It began a period known as the New Kingdom, which lasted from about 1550 B.C. to 1070 B.C. During this time, Egypt prospered through trade, gained more lands through conquest, and reached the height of its power. No longer isolated, Egyptians benefited from the spread of goods, ideas, and cultures within their empire.

A Woman Pharaoh

A queen named Hatshepsut (hat·SHEHP·soot) was one of the few women to rule Egypt. She came to power in about 1473 B.C. and governed with her husband. Then, after his death, she made herself pharaoh and ruled on behalf of her young nephew.

Because the title of pharaoh was usually passed from father to son, Hatshepsut had to prove that she was a good leader. In order for the people to accept her, Hatshepsut dressed in the clothes of a male pharaoh. She even wore the false beard to copy the one worn by male Egyptian kings. She built magnificent temples and restored old monuments. Her tomb in the Valley of the Kings contains large wall carvings that illustrate some of the major events of her reign.

One of the few women to govern Egypt, Hatshepsut ruled with the support of her subjects. This enormous tomb stands today in honor of her reign.

Reading**HELP**DESK

Reading Strategy: *Sequencing*

Key words such as *then*, *later*, and *after* are clues to the order in which events happened. Which of these key words is used on this page?

Growth of Trade

Hatshepsut was more interested in promoting trade than starting wars. She made great efforts to restore trade relations that had been interrupted by the Hyksos invasion.

During the rule of Hatshepsut, Egyptian seafarers sailed to ports in Arabia and East Africa. There, Egyptian traders exchanged beads, metal tools, and weapons for gold, ivory, ebony wood, and **incense** (IN·sens), a material burned for its pleasant smell.

The Egyptians valued wood products because the Nile River valley had few trees. They needed wood to build boats, furniture, and other items. To find wood, Egyptian traders traveled to the east coast of the Mediterranean Sea where the present-day country of Lebanon is located. The people in this region were called the Phoenicians (fih·NEE·shuns). The Phoenicians had a great impact on other cultures in the region. Their invention of an alphabet and a system of writing influenced others. Phoenician trade routes and settlements also encouraged the spread of goods and ideas across a large part of the ancient world.

Trade and Politics

The Egyptians traded wheat, paper, gold, copper, tin and tools to the Phoenicians for purple dye, wood, and furniture. The traders exchanged goods they had for supplies they needed, rather than selling goods for money. The Phoenicians in turn traded Egyptian goods to other people. By trading with the Phoenicians, Egyptians spread their food and goods across Southwest Asia. Trade in the eastern Mediterranean helped make the Egyptian kingdom wealthier. Hatshepsut used some of this wealth to build monuments.

In addition to trade, New Kingdom pharaohs developed political ties between Egypt and nearby kingdoms. For example, the Egyptian dynasty became joined by treaty or marriage with ruling families in the Babylonian Empire in Mesopotamia, the Mittani (mih·TAH·nee) in Syria, and the Hittite Empire in Anatolia (ah·nuh·TOH·lee·uh).

To maintain close ties, pharaohs and the other rulers also exchanged **envoys** (EHN·voyz), or representatives. These actions marked the first time in history that a group of nations tried working together to reach common goals.

BIOGRAPHY

Hatshepsut (reigned 1473–1458 B.C.)

Hatshepsut was one of the most successful rulers of Egypt. Hatshepsut chose people who were loyal to her to serve in government positions. She valued the opinions of common Egyptians and sought their support for decisions she made. After her death, Thutmose III, Hatshepsut's nephew, had her name removed from royal texts and monuments. Historians believe that he did this to show that no female ruler interrupted the royal line of males.

▶ **CRITICAL THINKING**
Drawing Conclusions What actions of hers helped make Hatshepsut a successful ruler?

---

incense a material that produces a pleasant smell when burned

envoy a government representative to another country

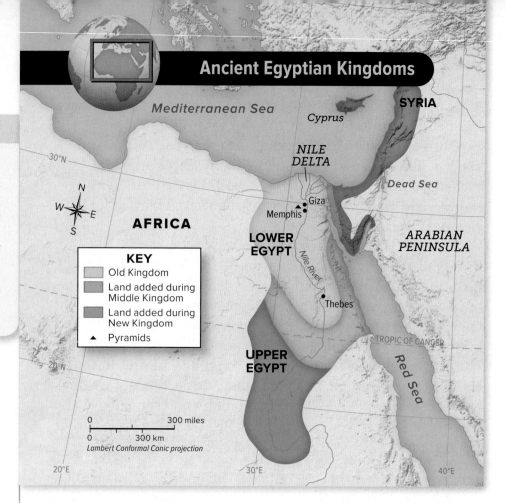

Ancient Egyptian Kingdoms

GEOGRAPHY CONNECTION

During the Middle Kingdom, the capital of Egypt was moved from Memphis to Thebes.

1 LOCATION Identify the relative location of Thebes.

2 PLACE Describe the borders of the New Kingdom.

3 CRITICAL THINKING
Comparing Which kingdom added the most territory?

Mediterranean Sea

SYRIA

Cyprus

NILE DELTA

Dead Sea

30°N

AFRICA

Giza

Memphis

LOWER EGYPT

ARABIAN PENINSULA

Nile River

KEY

Old Kingdom

Land added during Middle Kingdom

Land added during New Kingdom

▲ Pyramids

Thebes

TROPIC OF CANCER

UPPER EGYPT

Red Sea

20°N

0   300 miles
0   300 km
Lambert Conformal Conic projection

20°E   30°E   40°E

Expanding the Empire

When Hatshepsut died, her nephew, Thutmose III (thoot· MOH·suh), became pharaoh. Thutmose was a strong leader and general who expanded Egypt's control north to the Euphrates River in Mesopotamia. His troops also moved south far up the Nile and conquered Nubia, which had once thrown off Egyptian rule. Egyptian armies captured nearly 350 cities during Thutmose's reign.

As Thutmose and his armies conquered more areas, the Egyptian Empire grew wealthy, and slavery became more common. Egypt **acquired** gold, copper, ivory, and other valuable goods from conquered peoples. Egyptians captured and enslaved many prisoners of war. Enslaved people had some rights, however, including the right to own land, marry, and eventually gain their freedom.

✔ PROGRESS CHECK

Explaining Why did the Egyptians want to trade with the Phoenicians?

Two Unusual Pharaohs

GUIDING QUESTION *How did two unusual pharaohs change ancient Egypt?*

During the New Kingdom, two remarkable pharaohs came to power. One pharaoh, Amenhotep IV, tried to make dramatic changes, and one, Tutankhamen, was very young. Their actions set them apart from other rulers in Egypt's long history.

A Religious Founder

A new pharaoh named Amenhotep IV (ah·muhn·HOH·tehp) came to power in about 1370 B.C. Supported by his wife, Nefertiti (nehf·uhr·TEE·tee), Amenhotep tried to change Egypt's religion, which was based on the worship of many deities.

Amenhotep believed that Egypt's priests had grown too powerful and wealthy. He felt threatened by their power. To lessen the priests' **authority**, Amenhotep started a new religion. He introduced the worship of Aton (AHT·n), a sun god, as Egypt's only god. When Egypt's priests opposed this change, Amenhotep removed many of them from their posts, took their lands, and closed temples. He then changed his name to Akhenaton (ahk·NAH·tuhn), meaning "Spirit of Aton." The capital was moved to a new city north of Thebes called Akhetaton (ahk·heh·TAH·tuhn).

These changes unsettled Egypt. Most Egyptians rejected Aton and continued to worship many deities. In addition, the priests of the old religion resisted their loss of power. The discontent with Akhenaton's rule spread to the army leaders. They believed Akhenaton, devoted to his new religion, neglected his duties as pharaoh. Under Akhenaton's weak rule, Egypt lost most of its lands in western Asia to outside invaders.

Who Was "King Tut"?

When Akhenaton died about 1360 B.C., his son, 10-year-old Tutankhamen (too·tang·KAH·muhn), became pharaoh. The young pharaoh relied on advice from priests and officials to rule Egypt. Tutankhamen quickly restored the worship of many deities. Tutankhamen's short rule ended after only nine years, when he died unexpectedly. The cause of his death is still a mystery to historians, and he remains a fascinating figure.

King Tut is shown wearing the false beard worn by all pharaohs. Tut was a child when he became pharaoh. He died at the age of 19.

Egyptian National Museum, Cairo/SuperStock,

Academic Vocabulary

authority the right or power to give orders, make decisions, or control people

Even though "King Tut" played a small role in the history of Egypt, he is the most famous of the pharaohs. British archaeologist Howard Carter attracted public attention when he discovered Tut's tomb in 1922. Carter's find was amazing because most tombs of the pharaohs had been robbed by thieves. Tut's tomb, however, contained the pharaoh's mummy and many treasures, including a brilliant gold mask of the young ruler's face.

✓ **PROGRESS CHECK**

Evaluating Why are Akhenaton and Tutankhamen considered unusual pharaohs?

Recovery and Decline

GUIDING QUESTION *Why did the Egyptian empire decline in the late 1200s B.C.?*

During the 1200s B.C., the pharaohs worked to restore Egypt's greatness. They fought battles for more territory, increased Egypt's wealth through trade, and built large temples and monuments.

Ramses II

The most successful of these pharaohs was Ramses II (RAM·seez), who ruled from 1279 B.C. to 1213 B.C. Ramses conquered the region of Canaan and moved north into Syria. To get this territory, he fought the Hittites, who lived in present-day Turkey. After many battles, Ramses and the Hittite king signed a peace treaty.

Age of Temples

During his 66-year reign, Ramses also devoted himself to peaceful activities. Ramses II and other New Kingdom rulers had many temples built throughout Egypt. One of the most magnificent was Karnak (KAHR·nack) at Thebes. Its huge columned hall still impresses visitors today. A poem celebrating a victory by Ramses is carved in the temple. In part of the poem, Ramses says this to his chariot driver:

❝ Halt! take courage, charioteer, As a sparrow-hawk swoops down upon his prey, So I swoop upon the foe, and I will slay, I will hew [cut] them into pieces, I will dash them into dust. ❞

—from *Pen-ta-tur: The Victory of Ramses II Over the Khita*

Most Egyptians prayed in their homes, so temples were used only for special occasions. Egyptians saw the temples as the

Few rulers reigned as long as Ramses. He reigned three years longer than England's Queen Victoria, who ruled for 63 years. What mathematical expression would tell you the length of Ramses' reign?

©Sandro Vannini/Corbis

Reading**HELP**DESK

Academic Vocabulary

decline to become weaker

Reading Strategy: *Understanding Cause and Effect*

The word *so* indicates the effect of an event. Read the first sentence in the last paragraph above. The *effect* is that temples were used only for special occasions. What is the cause?

Still in use after more than 3,000 years, Karnak remains to honor Ramses' many achievements.

homes of their deities. Priests and priestesses performed daily rituals, washed the statues of the deities, and brought them food.

Temples were important to Egypt's economy. Priests hired people to work in temple workshops and granaries. Temples also served as banks. Egyptians used them to store valuable items, such as gold jewelry, fragrant oils, and finely woven textiles.

Why Did Egypt Decline?

After Ramses II died, Egypt **declined**. Pharaohs fought costly wars. Armies from the eastern Mediterranean attacked Egypt. By 1150 B.C., the Egyptian empire controlled only the Nile delta.

In the 900s B.C., the Libyans conquered Egypt. Then, the people of Kush seized power. Finally, in 670 B.C., Egypt was taken over by the Assyrians from Mesopotamia.

✔ PROGRESS CHECK

Summarizing What were the accomplishments of Ramses II?

LESSON 3 REVIEW

Review Vocabulary

1. Why would someone want to buy *incense*?

2. What might have been the duties of an ancient Egyptian *envoy*?

Answer the Guiding Questions

3. *Describing* Discuss two reasons why the Middle Kingdom period was a "golden age" for Egypt.

4. *Explaining* Why was the New Kingdom a unique period in ancient Egypt's history?

5. *Summarizing* Describe the religious changes brought about by Akhenaton and Tutankhamen.

6. *Analyzing* In what ways were temples important to Egypt's economy?

7. **ARGUMENT** You are a scribe who works for Queen Hatshepsut. Write a brief report that explains why she is a good pharaoh and deserves the support of the people.

There's More Online! connected.mcgraw-hill.com

LESSON 4
The Kingdom of Kush

ESSENTIAL QUESTION
- Why do civilizations rise and fall?

IT MATTERS BECAUSE
The kingdoms of Nubia and Kush were influenced by Egyptian culture, and they continued many Egyptian traditions.

The Nubians

GUIDING QUESTION *How did Nubia and Egypt influence each other?*

In addition to Egypt, other civilizations flourished in Africa. One of these African civilizations was Nubia, later known as Kush. Nubia was located south of Egypt along the Nile River in present-day Sudan.

Cattle herders were the first people to settle in this region, arriving about 2000 B.C. They herded long-horned cattle on the **savannas** (suh·VA·nuhs), or grassy plains, that stretch across Africa south of the Sahara. Later, people settled in farming villages along the Nile River.

Unlike the Egyptians, the Nubians did not **rely** on the Nile floods to create fertile soil. Their land had fertile soil and received rainfall all year long. Nubian villagers grew crops such as beans, yams, rice, and grains. The Nubians also hunted for food. Their hunters and warriors excelled at using the bow and arrow.

The Rise of Kerma

Gradually, the stronger Nubian villages took over the weaker ones and formed the kingdom of Kerma (KAR·muh). The Nubians of Kerma grew wealthy from agriculture and the mining of gold. Their kingdom developed a close relationship

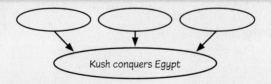

with Egypt in the north. Kerma's central location in the Nile Valley benefited the Nubians. It made Kerma an important trade link between Egypt and the tropical areas of southern Africa. From Kerma, the Egyptians acquired cattle, gold, incense, ivory, giraffes, and leopards. They also obtained enslaved people. They hired Nubians to serve in their armies because of the Nubians' skills in warfare. Kerma's artisans produced fine pottery, jewelry, and metal goods.

Workers built tombs for Kerma's kings, usually on a smaller scale than Egyptian tombs. Like the Egyptian pharaohs, the kings of Kerma were buried with their personal belongings, including valuable gems, gold, jewelry, and pottery. These artifacts were as magnificent as those found in Egypt's royal tombs that were built during the same time period.

Egyptian Invasion

Egyptian armies invaded Nubia in the 1400s B.C. After a 50-year war, the Egyptians conquered the kingdom of Kerma and ruled it for the next 700 years.

As a result of Egyptian rule, the Nubians adopted many of the beliefs and customs of Egyptian culture. For example, the Nubians worshipped Egyptian gods and goddesses along with their own Nubian deities. They learned to use copper and bronze to make tools. The Nubians adapted Egyptian hieroglyphs to fit their own language and created an alphabet.

The savannas of Africa are grassy and dotted with trees and herds of wildlife. The grasses can withstand long, hot periods without rain. These broad plains covered much of Nubia.

✔ PROGRESS CHECK

Analyzing Why did Kerma become an important center for trade?

Mike D. Kock/Gallo Images/Getty Images

savanna a flat grassland, sometimes with scattered trees, in a tropical or subtropical region

Academic Vocabulary

rely to depend on someone or something

The Kushite Kingdom

GUIDING QUESTION *Why did the kingdom of Kush prosper?*

By the end of the Middle Kingdom, Egypt was weak. It could no longer govern its conquered peoples effectively, and the Nubians were able to break away from Egyptian rule.

The Rise of Kush

By 850 B.C., the Nubians had formed an independent kingdom known as Kush. Powerful kings ruled the country from its capital at Napata (NA·puh·tuh).

The city of Napata was located where trade caravans crossed the upper part of the Nile River. Caravans came from central Africa, bringing ivory and other goods. They stopped at Napata for Kushite products and then continued on to Egypt. The Egyptians traded with Kush for goods the Egyptians could not make. Such trade brought wealth to the traders and kings of Kush.

Kush Conquers Egypt

In time, Kush became powerful enough to **challenge** Egypt. About 750 B.C., a Kushite king named Kashta (KAHSH·tuh) invaded Egypt. His soldiers reached the city of Thebes. After Kashta died, his son Piye (PY) became king and completed the conquest of Egypt in 728 B.C. Piye founded the Twenty-fifth Dynasty that governed Egypt and Kush from Napata.

The kings and wealthy people of Kush continued to admire Egyptian culture. Kushites built white sandstone temples and monuments similar to those in Egypt. The Kushites also believed

In this scene, Nubian royalty offer gifts to an Egyptian pharaoh. The procession shows respect for the pharaoh.

©Sandro Vannini/Corbis

Kush Kingdom c. 250 B.C.

Mediterranean Sea

Memphis

EGYPT

Thebes

SAHARA

20°N

Napata

Meroë

0   400 miles

0   400 km
Lambert Conformal Conic projection

10°N   20°E

30°E

ARABIA

Red Sea

Persian Gulf

KEY

☐ Kush

50°E

GEOGRAPHY CONNECTION

Trade caravans crossed the Nile near Napata, which made the city a busy trading center.

1 **LOCATION** In what direction would traders travel to get from Napata to Meroë?

2 **CRITICAL THINKING**
Analyzing How is the Nile different south of Meroë?

Kushite artisans worked in gold, creating objects such as this statue of Amon-Re. They also made fine pottery.

in a close relationship between their rulers and their deities, many of whom were Egyptian. For example, when a king died, Kushite officials met at the temple to ask the Egyptian god Amon-Re to appoint a new leader:

PRIMARY SOURCE

❝ So the commanders of His Majesty and the officials of the palace ... [found] the major priests waiting outside the temple. They said to them, "Pray, may this god, Amon-Re ... give us our lord. ... We cannot do a thing without this god. It is he who guides us. ..." Then the commanders ... and the officials ... entered into the temple and put themselves upon their bellies before this god. They said, "We have come to you, O Amon-Re, ... that you might give to us a lord, to revive us, to build the temples of the gods, ..." ❞

—from *The Selection of Aspalta as King of Kush*

The Kushites also built small, steeply sloped pyramids as tombs for their kings. Some people in Kush, however, adopted customs and styles similar to those worn by southern Africans. This included wearing ankle and ear jewelry. By this time, the people of Kush also had developed their own style of painted pottery. The elephant, a sacred animal in Kush, was used as a theme in sculpture and other arts.

INTERFOTO/Alamy

Reading Strategy: *Reading a Map*

When reading a map, first locate the key. It will help you identify what is being shown on the map. What is the key identifying on the map above?

Using Iron

Kush ruled Egypt for about 60 years. In 671 B.C., the Assyrians invaded Egypt. Armed with iron weapons, the Assyrians defeated the Kushites, who only had bronze weapons, which were not as strong. The Kushites fled Egypt and returned to their homeland in the south.

Despite their defeat in Egypt, the Kushites learned how to make iron from the Assyrians. Farmers in Kush used iron to make their hoes and plows instead of copper or stone. With better tools, they were able to grow more grain and other crops. Kushite warriors also created iron weapons, which boosted their military strength.

The Capital of Meroë

About 540 B.C., Kush's rulers moved their capital to the city of Meroë (MEHR·oh·ee), near one of the Nile's cataracts. This move made them safer from Assyrian attacks. The Nile River continued to provide a means for trade and transportation for the Kushites. Large deposits of iron ore and trees were nearby and were used to fuel furnaces for making iron. As a result, Meroë became a major center for iron production as well as a busy trading city.

Kushite kings modeled the layout and design of Meroë after Egypt's great cities. A temple dedicated to the god Amon-Re stood at the end of a long avenue lined with sculptures of rams. The walls of palaces and houses were decorated with paintings. Small pyramids stood in the royal graveyard, modeled on the larger pyramids of Egypt. Meroë, however, was different from a typical Egyptian city because it contained iron furnaces. Huge columns of smoke poured out of iron furnaces. Heaps of shiny black slag, or waste from iron making, lay around the furnaces.

The Kushites adopted pyramids as tombs. They usually built tombs that were smaller than those of the Egyptians, however.

giovanni mereghetti/Marka/Age fotostock

textile woven cloth

Modeled on Egyptian cities, Meroë had a special purpose. It was an iron-making city with smokestacks and soot.

A Trading Center

Meroë was at the heart of a large web of trade that ran north to Egypt's border and south into central Africa. Kush's merchants received leopard skins and valuable woods from the tropical interior of Africa. They traded these items, along with their own iron products, to places as far away as Arabia, India, China, and Rome. Enslaved people were also traded. In return, they brought back cotton, **textiles** (TEHK·styls), or woven cloth, and other goods. Kush's merchants used their wealth to build fine houses and public baths like ones they had seen in Rome.

Kush remained a great trading kingdom for nearly 600 years. Then, another kingdom called Axum (AHK·soom) emerged near the Red Sea in eastern Africa. Axum is located in the present-day country of Ethiopia. Axum gained its strength from its location on the Red Sea. Goods from Africa flowed into Axum. Over time, it served as a trading center for the ancient Mediterranean and East African worlds. Around A.D. 350, the armies of Axum invaded Kush and destroyed Meroë.

✔ PROGRESS CHECK

Explaining How did the use of iron affect Kush?

LESSON 4 REVIEW

Review Vocabulary

1. What are the characteristics of a *savanna*?

2. What are *textiles* used to make?

Answer the Guiding Questions

3. *Explaining* How did Nubia and Egypt influence each other?

4. *Comparing and Contrasting* How were the cities of Kush similar to and different from those of Egypt?

5. *Drawing Conclusions* How did natural resources help make Meroë a great trading city?

6. **ARGUMENT** Create an advertisement that could have been used in ancient Egypt and Kush to encourage people to use iron.

Write your answers on a separate piece of paper.

1 Exploring the Essential Question

INFORMATIVE/EXPLANATORY Why did the ancient Egyptian civilization fall? Write an essay that explains the events and decisions that led to the end of Egypt's role as a political, economic, and cultural power.

2 21st Century Skills

GIVING A PRESENTATION Prepare a presentation that identifies the key events and achievements of Egypt's Old Kingdom, Middle Kingdom, and New Kingdom. Compare and contrast the developments in each time period. End your presentation with a brief statement about the importance of the Egyptian civilization.

Characteristics of the Nile River	Pros	Cons
Regular flooding		
Cataracts		
Downhill flow		

3 Thinking Like a Historian

UNDERSTANDING PROS AND CONS Create a chart like the one here to identify the pros and cons of living along the Nile River. Then, write a sentence that tells why early Egyptians settled there.

4 **GEOGRAPHY ACTIVITY**

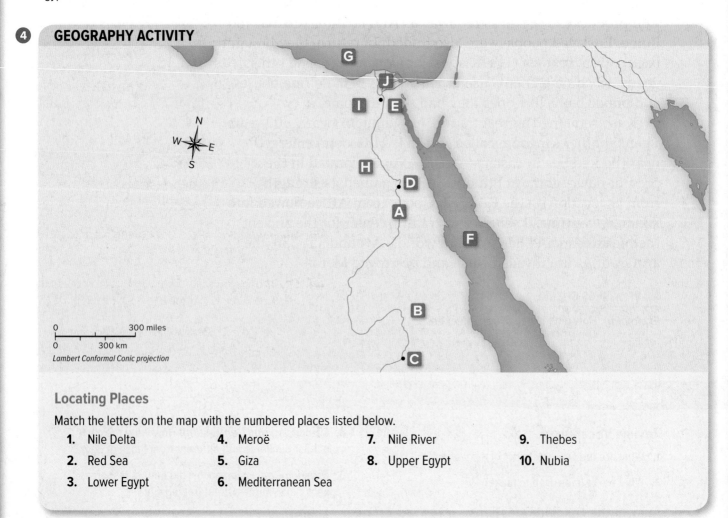

0 | 300 miles
0 | 300 km
Lambert Conformal Conic projection

Locating Places

Match the letters on the map with the numbered places listed below.

1. Nile Delta

2. Red Sea

3. Lower Egypt

4. Meroë

5. Giza

6. Mediterranean Sea

7. Nile River

8. Upper Egypt

9. Thebes

10. Nubia

Directions: Write your answers on a separate piece of paper.

CHECKING FOR UNDERSTANDING

1 Define each of these terms as they relate to ancient Egypt and Kush.

A. delta
B. papyrus
C. Memphis
D. bureaucrat
E. embalming
F. Middle Kingdom
G. Karnak
H. Nubia
I. Napata

REVIEW THE GUIDING QUESTIONS

2 *Identifying* What bodies of water allowed Egypt to remain in contact and trade with the outside world?

3 *Describing* Describe the methods of irrigation used by Egyptian farmers along the Nile River.

4 *Explaining* How did the Egyptian form of writing advance beyond the use of symbols to represent objects and ideas?

5 *Explaining* Did Narmer's kingdom last after his death? Explain.

6 *Specifying* Why were the gods Re and Hapi especially important to the Egyptians?

7 *Identifying* Who was Imhotep, and what was his significance in ancient Egypt?

8 *Listing* List some of the items traded by the Egyptians to the Phoenicians during the New Kingdom.

9 *Explaining* How did Kerma's location benefit that kingdom?

10 *Identifying* What practice did the Kushites adopt from the conquering Assyrians? How did they use this new skill?

CRITICAL THINKING

11 *Determining Cause and Effect* What effect did the landforms surrounding the Nile Valley have on the development of Egyptian civilization?

12 *Identifying Central Issues* Why was an organized government needed in Egypt? Describe the development of government in the Nile Valley through the time of Narmer.

13 *Making Connections* How did the Egyptians' belief of an afterlife contribute to medical advancements? Describe some of those advancements in your answer.

14 *Giving Examples* Provide examples of the scientific and mathematical discoveries made by the Egyptians as they built the pyramids.

15 *Making Inferences* Study the diagram titled Social Status in Ancient Egypt in Lesson 2. What do you think the diagram tells you about relative wealth among the different classes in Egypt? Explain your reasoning.

16 *Assessing* Was the reign of Hatshepsut a successful period for the kingdom of Egypt? Explain your answer.

17 *Evaluating* Is Tutankhamen deserving of his status as the best-known Egyptian ruler? Explain.

18 *Summarizing* Summarize the events in the decline of the Egyptian kingdom.

19 *Contrasting* How did Nubian agriculture and farming practices differ from those of the Egyptians?

20 *Comparing and Contrasting* What differences and similarities existed in the societies of Egypt and Kush?

Need Extra Help?

If You've Missed Question	**1**	**2**	**3**	**4**	**5**	**6**	**7**	**8**	**9**	**10**	**11**	**12**	**13**	**14**	**15**	**16**	**17**	**18**	**19**	**20**
Review Lesson	1,2, 3, 4	1	1	1	1	2	2	3	4	4	1	1	2	2	2	3	3	3	4	4

DBQ SHORT RESPONSE

"To build such monumental structures, the Egyptians needed a highly organized workforce. From tomb inscriptions and from laborers' instructions on walls, [. . .] researchers can now draw something close to a modern personnel chart for the ancient workers. 'Every project like a pyramid had a crew of workers,' explains Ann Roth, an Egyptologist who has studied the groups of workers in detail. 'And each group was responsible for one part of the pyramid complex.'"

— from "The Pyramid Builders," by Virginia Morell

21 How did Egyptian workers cooperate to build the pyramids?

22 Why did workers need to be organized to build the pyramids?

EXTENDED RESPONSE

23 *Narrative* You are an Egyptian trader visiting the Kush city of Meroë. Write a journal entry in which you describe the city, and compare it to your Egyptian home.

STANDARDIZED TEST PRACTICE

DBQ ANALYZING DOCUMENTS

24 *Drawing Conclusions* An epic poem describes the victory of King Ramses II over the Hittites.

"Then the King spake [spoke] to his squire,
Halt! take courage, charioteer,
As a sparrow-hawk swoops down on his prey,
So I swoop upon the foe [enemy], and I will slay.'"

—from *Pen-ta-tur: The Victory of Ramses II Over the Khita*

Which word best describes Ramses as he is depicted in the poem?

A. bird-like   **C.** uncertain

B. innocent   **D.** courageous

25 *Inferring* How might the Egyptians have reacted to this poem?

A. It made them afraid of their king.

B. It made them regret going to war.

C. It made them feel proud to be Egyptian.

D. It made them worry about losing to the enemy.

Need Extra Help?

If You've Missed Question	**21**	**22**	**23**	**24**	**25**
Review Lesson	2	2	4	3	3

◄ *As a young man, David was known for his bravery and his skill in playing the lyre, a type of harp.*

1800 B.C. TO A.D. 70

The Israelites

Lebrecht Music and Arts Photo Library/Alamy

THE STORY MATTERS ...

David is considered to be the greatest Israelite king, yet he was not born into royalty. David, a shepherd, became a leader of the Israelite people. As their king, he united the Israelites and expanded their lands. He was also the author of the Psalms, or poems often used in prayer and song. David stands as the greatest among many important leaders who guided the Israelites throughout their history.

ESSENTIAL QUESTIONS

- How do religions develop?
- What are the characteristics of a leader?
- How does religion shape society?
- Why does conflict develop?

Place & Time: The Israelites 1800 B.C. to A.D. 70

The ancient Israelites struggled for centuries to build a secure homeland. This was difficult because their location in the eastern Mediterranean region was surrounded by more powerful empires. Their religion, Judaism, became a world religion. It would later influence Christianity and Islam.

Step Into the Place

MAP FOCUS The Israelites constructed the city of Jerusalem atop seven hills.

LOCATION Look at the map. Where is Jerusalem located relative to the Mediterranean Sea?

1 **REGIONS** Which geographic features surround Jerusalem?

2 **LOCATION** Where is Jerusalem located relative to Egypt?

3 **CRITICAL THINKING**
Analyzing Why might the Israelites have chosen Jerusalem for their capital city?

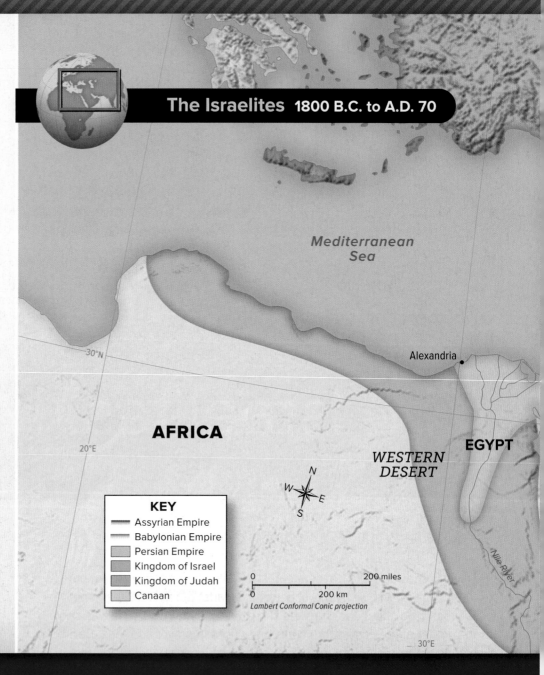

The Israelites 1800 B.C. to A.D. 70

Mediterranean Sea

Alexandria

AFRICA

EGYPT

WESTERN DESERT

Nile River

KEY
- Assyrian Empire
- Babylonian Empire
- Persian Empire
- Kingdom of Israel
- Kingdom of Judah
- Canaan

0   200 miles
0   200 km
Lambert Conformal Conic projection

Step Into the Time

TIME LINE What was happening to new ideas all over the world as Judaism grew?

c. 1290 B.C. According to the Hebrew Bible, Moses leads Israelites from Egypt

c. 1800 B.C. According to the Hebrew Bible, Abraham traveled to Canaan

THE ISRAELITES
THE WORLD   3000 B.C.   2000 B.C.

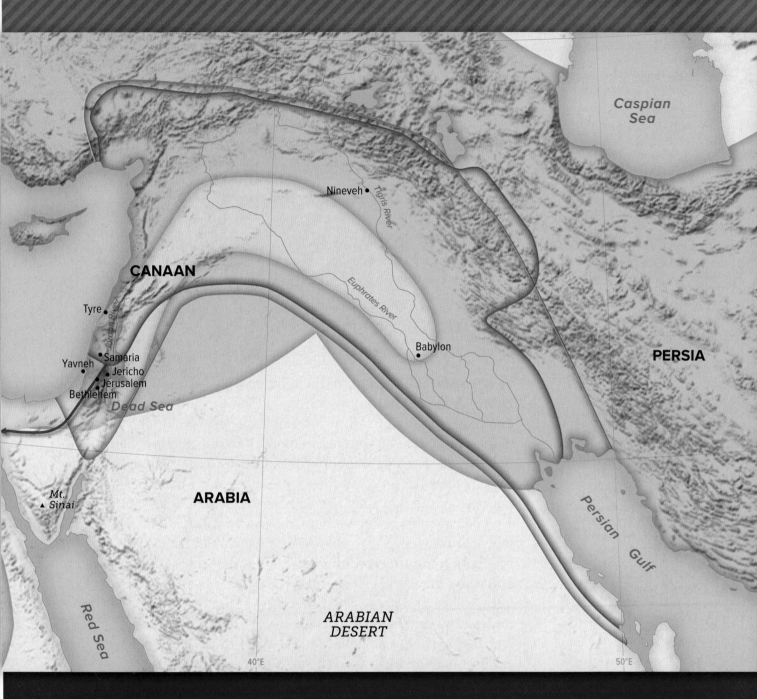

Caspian
Sea

Nineveh •

Tigris River

CANAAN

Tyre •

Jordan River

Yavneh •
• Samaria
• Jericho
• Jerusalem
Bethlehem •

Dead Sea

Euphrates River

Babylon •

PERSIA

Mt.
▲ Sinai

ARABIA

Red Sea

Persian Gulf

*ARABIAN
DESERT*

40°E   50°E

c. 722 B.C. Assyrians invade northern kingdom of Israel

c. A.D. 66 Jews revolt against Rome

c. 1000 B.C. King
David rules in Jerusalem

c. 586 B.C. Chaldeans
destroy Jerusalem

c. 168 B.C.
Maccabean revolt

c. A.D. 70 Romans destroy temple
in Jerusalem

| 1000 B.C. | 750 B.C. | 500 B.C. | 250 B.C. | A.D. 100 | A.D. 1000 |

c. 700 B.C. Homer
writes the *Iliad* and *Odyssey*

c. 530 B.C. Confucius
develops his philosophy in China

c. 330 B.C. Alexander the
Great conquers Persian Empire

c. A.D. 55 Paul preaches
Christianity in Asia Minor

c. 530 B.C. Buddhism arises in India

LESSON 1
Beginnings

IT MATTERS BECAUSE
The beliefs and early leaders of the ancient Israelites represent the foundations of Judaism.

Beginnings

GUIDING QUESTION *What did the ancient Israelites believe?*

You probably have heard of the religion of Judaism (JOO·dee·ih·zuhm). You may not know, however, that it is both an ancient and modern religion. Many ancient societies worshipped many deities, or gods. The worship of more than one god is called polytheism. A group of people in Southwest Asia known as the Israelites (IHZ·ree·ah·lites) were different. Unlike other **cultures** of the day, they worshipped only one God.

The Israelites believed that God sent **prophets** (PRAH·fehts), or messengers, to share God's word with the people. The prophets communicated to the Israelites that their God created and ruled the world. They argued that God is very powerful but also just and good. The prophets wanted the Israelites to understand that God expects goodness from his people.

The prophets also believed that every individual could connect personally to God through prayer, religious study, and good and just acts. The belief in one all-powerful, just, and personal God is called **monotheism** (MAH·nuh·thee·ih·zuhm). The practice of monotheism made Judaism unique among ancient religions.

Reading**HELP**DESK

Taking Notes: *Summarizing*
Use a diagram like this one to list at least two facts about each category.

Hebrew Bible →
Promised Land →
Twelve Tribes →
Ancient Israelites

Content Vocabulary

- • **prophet**
- • **monotheism**
- • **tribe**
- • **Exodus**
- • **covenant**
- • **Torah**
- • **commandment**
- • **alphabet**

The Hebrew Bible

The Israelites recorded their beliefs and history. These writings became known as the Hebrew Bible or Tanakh (TAH·nahk). Through the Hebrew Bible, the beliefs and faith of the ancient Israelites lived on to become the religion of Judaism. The followers of Judaism are today known as Jews.

Although the original Israelite population was small, their influence was great. Judaism played an important part in the development of two other major monotheistic religions—Christianity and Islam. Christians call the Hebrew Bible the Old Testament. Christianity grew directly out of Judaism. Islam also accepted many of Judaism's beliefs and practices. Through the Hebrew Bible, Judaism influenced the values, ethics, and principles of many other societies.

Abraham

Around 1200 B.C. great changes took place in the Mediterranean region. Egypt's empire ended, and new peoples, including the Israelites, created kingdoms in the region. The early Israelites depended on herding and trading to survive. According to the Hebrew Bible, Abraham and his family migrated from Mesopotamia and settled in Canaan (KAY·nuhn) along the Mediterranean Sea. Today, the countries of Lebanon, Israel, and Jordan occupy the land that was once Canaan.

According to Jewish belief, the ancestors of the ancient Israelites were a man named Abraham and his family. The Hebrew Bible gives this account of Abraham's family and the early history of the Israelites. The Hebrew Bible states that God told Abraham to journey to Canaan, which would belong to Abraham and his descendants forever. According to the Hebrew Bible, Abraham, his wife Sarah, and their entire household accepted God's promise and settled in Canaan. The land is often called the Promised Land because of God's promise to Abraham.

The Hebrew Bible says that Abraham led his family to Canaan. In addition to his role in Judaism, Abraham is regarded as an important figure in Christianity and Islam.

Tom Lovell/National Geographic Society Image Collection

prophet a messenger sent by God to share God's word with people

monotheism a belief in one God

Academic Vocabulary

culture the beliefs and behaviors of a group of people

Moses
(c. 14th–13th century B.C.)

According to the Hebrew Bible, Moses was born in Egypt to an Israelite woman enslaved by the pharaoh. After the pharaoh demanded all newborn Israelite boys be killed, Moses's mother hid him in a basket and floated him down the Nile River. The pharaoh's daughter rescued him and adopted him.

▶ **CRITICAL THINKING**
Explaining What important leadership traits did Moses show?

Isaac and Jacob

After Abraham died, his son Isaac and later his grandson Jacob headed the family. According to the Hebrew Bible, an angel gave Jacob the new name of Israel, which means "one who struggles with God." Later Jacob's descendants were called "Israelites." As stated in the Hebrew Bible, Jacob's 12 sons became the leaders of **tribes** (TRYBS), or separate family groups. Jacob's sons were the ancestors of the Twelve Tribes of Israel.

After living in Canaan for many years, Jacob's family left because of a famine. They migrated to Egypt and lived there in peace for several generations. As the Israelite population increased, however, the Egyptian pharaoh grew uneasy. He feared that one day the Israelites would rebel. To prevent this, the Egyptians forced the Israelites into slavery.

Moses and the Exodus

The Israelites were forced to work at hard labor, so they prayed to God to be set free. According to the Hebrew Bible, an Israelite prophet named Moses turned out to be their deliverer. While tending sheep in the wilderness outside Egypt, Moses saw a bush in flames. God called to Moses from the burning bush. He told Moses to tell the pharaoh to let the Israelites go.

Moses went before the pharaoh to demand the release of the Israelites. When the pharaoh refused, the Hebrew Bible says that God sent 10 plagues upon Egypt. These plagues were events that caused problems for the Egyptians, such as **locusts** devouring the fields or outbreaks of disease. The plagues convinced the pharaoh to free the Israelites. After the Israelites left Egypt for Canaan, the pharaoh decided to send his army to pursue them.

When the Israelites reached the Red Sea, there was no way to cross the waters. According to the Hebrew Bible, God parted the Red Sea to let his people cross to the other side. When the pharaoh's army tried to follow, the waters flooded back and drowned them. The departure of the Israelites out of slavery in Egypt is known as the **Exodus** (EHK·suh·duhs). Jews celebrate a holy festival called Passover to remember their freedom from slavery.

The Covenant

On their way from Egypt, according to the Hebrew Bible, the Israelites received a **covenant** (KUHV·uh·nuhnt), or agreement with God. In the agreement, God promised to return the Israelites

Reading**HELP**DESK

tribe a social group made up of families or clans

Exodus the departure of the Israelites out of slavery in Egypt

covenant an agreement with God

Visual Vocabulary

locust a grasshopper that often migrates in large numbers

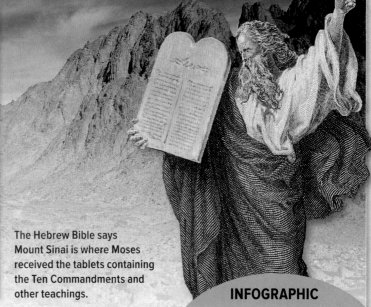

❶ Do not worship any god except me.

❷ Do not... bow down and worship idols.

❸ Do not misuse my name.

❹ Remember the Sabbath Day and keep it holy.

❺ Honor your father and your mother.

❻ Do not murder.

❼ Be faithful in marriage.

❽ Do not steal.

❾ Do not testify falsely [tell lies] about others.

❿ Do not want anything that belongs to someone else.

—**Paraphrased** from Exodus 20:3–17

The Hebrew Bible says Mount Sinai is where Moses received the tablets containing the Ten Commandments and other teachings.

INFOGRAPHIC

1 FINDING THE MAIN IDEA
What is the main idea of the fourth commandment?

2 CRITICAL THINKING
Identifying Which commandments address family relationships?

safely to Canaan and they promised to follow God's teachings. Moses climbed to the top of Mount Sinai (SY·ny). There, as God's chosen leader, he received teachings from God. Known as the **Torah** (TAWR·uh), these teachings later became part of the Hebrew Bible.

The Torah made clear what God considered to be right and wrong. One important part of the Torah is the Ten **Commandments** (kuh·MAND·muhnts).

Loyalty to God is the central idea of the Ten Commandments. The name of God was never to be misused. The Israelites were not to worship any other gods or images. This belief that there is only one God became the basis for both Christianity and Islam.

In addition, the Ten Commandments later helped shape the moral principles of many nations. Think about the laws and rules we have today and how they might relate to these commandments. For example, the principles on which many laws are based, such as rules against stealing or killing, come from the Ten Commandments. The Ten Commandments also promoted social justice and a feeling of community. They contribute to the democratic belief that laws should apply equally to all.

✔ PROGRESS CHECK

Comparing and Contrasting How did the Israelites' beliefs differ from the beliefs of most other ancient peoples?

The Ark of the Covenant was a wooden chest, overlaid in gold, that held the tablets on which the Ten Commandments—part of God's covenant with the Israelites—appeared.

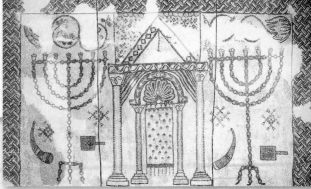

Torah teachings that Moses received from God; later became the first part of the Hebrew Bible

commandment a rule that God wanted the Israelites to follow

The Phoenicians' small, yet durable, ships influenced shipbuilding for centuries. Phoenician sailors also helped advance the use of astronomy in navigation.

▶ **CRITICAL THINKING**
Comparing and Contrasting How do the Phoenician ships appear to be similar to and different from contemporary ships?

The Land of Canaan

GUIDING QUESTION *How did the Israelites settle Canaan?*

The Hebrew Bible states that Moses died before the Israelites reached the land God had promised them. A new leader named Joshua guided the Israelites into Canaan, but they found other people living there. These peoples included the Canaanites (KAY·nuh·NYTS) and—somewhat later—the Philistines (FIH·luh·STEENS). Unlike the Israelites, these people of Canaan worshipped many gods and goddesses. They also had different ways of life.

Who Were the Canaanites?

Nomadic tribes probably settled in Canaan as early as 3000 B.C. At first, most of the people were herders. They journeyed with their flocks of sheep and other animals from pasture to pasture. Later, they settled in villages, farmed the land, and learned to trade.

Many different groups lived in Canaan. One Canaanite group was the Phoenicians (fih·NEE·shuhns). The Phoenicians lived in cities along the Mediterranean Sea in northern Canaan. Located near a major waterway, the Phoenicians were skilled sailors and talented traders. They used the sun and the stars to plot long sea voyages. Well-built Phoenician ships with oars and sails carried trade goods across the Mediterranean Sea to Greece, Spain, and even western Africa. Phoenician sailors may even have traveled as far as the British Isles in northwestern Europe.

Reading**HELP**DESK

alphabet a set of letters or other characters used to write a language

The Phoenicians soon controlled Mediterranean shipping and trade. At various ports, they exchanged cedar logs, glass, and jewelry for tin and other precious metals. One of the most valued Phoenician products was cloth colored with a beautiful purple dye. This dye was **extracted** from shellfish along the Phoenician coast.

As they traded, the Phoenicians founded settlements throughout the Mediterranean world. Carthage, a settlement on the coast of North Africa, in time became the most powerful city in the western Mediterranean.

As a result of these settlements, Phoenician ideas and goods spread to other peoples. Think what your life might be like without written language. One of the Phoenicians' important contributions was an **alphabet** (AL·fuh·beht), or a group of letters that stand for sounds. The letters could be used to spell out the words in their language. The alphabet made writing simpler and helped people keep better records.

Philistines

Another group in Canaan, the Philistines, migrated from near present-day Greece. They were one of the groups known as the "Sea People" who invaded the Mediterranean area about 1200 B.C. The Philistines set up five walled towns in southern Canaan along the Mediterranean coast. They were skilled in making iron tools and weapons, which helped them create the strongest army in Canaan. The Philistines kept their own language and religion. Still, they accepted many ideas and practices from their neighbors in Canaan.

Connections to
TODAY
Alphabets

The Phoenicians began using the alphabet as a way to keep track of trade. Later, the Greeks adapted the Phoenician alphabet. From the Greek alphabet, the Romans created their alphabet. The Roman alphabet is the most widely used writing system in the world today.

EARLY ALPHABETS

INFOGRAPHIC

Modern Characters	Ancient Phoenician	Ancient Hebrew	Ancient Greek	Early Roman
A				
B				
G				
D				
E				
F				
Z				
TH				
I				

The Phoenician alphabet contained 22 letters. Unlike the alphabet, it was written from right to left.

▶ **CRITICAL THINKING**
Making Inferences How would the lack of written language have made trade more difficult for ancient people?

Academic Vocabulary

extract to remove by a physical or chemical process

Reading in the Content Area

Tables organize information in a way that helps you remember it. To read a table, look first at the title and headings. Ask yourself questions such as "How is the information organized? What is the table trying to show me?"

Military Conquest

Because other groups lived in the region, the Israelites faced a challenge establishing Canaan as their new homeland. They believed, however, that it was God's will that they claim the land. Joshua led them in a series of battles to conquer Canaan.

The Hebrew Bible tells about the battle at the city of Jericho. There, Joshua told the Israelites to march around the city walls. For six days, they marched while priests blew their trumpets. On the seventh day, according to the account:

PRIMARY SOURCE

❝ Joshua commanded the people, "Shout, for the LORD has given you the city. … At the sound of the trumpet, when the people gave a loud shout, the wall collapsed. ❞

—from *the Hebrew Bible, the book of Joshua, 6: 16–20*

The Israelites took control of the city after the walls of Jericho crumbled.

According to the Hebrew Bible, Joshua led the Israelites in other battles. Any land they seized was divided among the 12 tribes. After Joshua died, political and military leaders called judges ruled the tribes. The judges settled disputes. They also led troops into battle. The Hebrew Bible tells of a woman judge named Deborah, who was admired for her wisdom and bravery. She told the commander Barak (Buh·RAHK) to attack the army of the Canaanite king Jabin. Deborah went to the battlefield as an adviser. With her help, Barak and 10,000 Israelites destroyed the Canaanite forces.

Jericho is one of the oldest continuously inhabited sites in the world. Here we see an illustration of the Hebrew Bible story of Joshua bringing down the walls of the city.

Mary Evans Picture Library

Life in Canaan

After many battles, the Israelite tribes won control of the hilly region of central Canaan and settled there. Most Israelites farmed and herded animals. The land was rocky and dry, with little water. So during the rainy season, farmers collected the rainwater. They stored it in small caves or under the ground. They used the stored water to irrigate crops such as olives, flax, barley, and grapes.

Imagine a rocky countryside dotted by square white houses. Most Israelites lived in houses with two levels. The walls of the houses were made of mud-brick or stone plastered with mud and white-washed. Floors were made of clay. Wooden beams supported a flat, thatched roof, covered with clay. During the day, people cooked and did household chores in the home's lower level. At night, donkeys and goats bedded down there. The family slept on the upper level.

The Tabernacle

According to the Hebrew Bible, the Israelite tribes worshipped God in a large tent-like structure called the tabernacle (TA·buhr·na·kuhl). The Israelites believed that the tabernacle housed God's presence. This structure was taken down and put away as the Israelites moved from place to place. In Canaan, they erected the tabernacle at a religious center called Shiloh.

The Hebrew Bible says that the tabernacle housed a sacred object called the Ark of the Covenant. The ark, a gold-covered wooden chest, held tablets, or stone slabs. The Israelites believed that the Ten Commandments were written on these tablets. The Israelites believed the ark was a sign of God's presence and that having it with them in battle would **ensure** victory.

The ancient tabernacle was a tent constructed from beautiful tapestries, or woven fabric, that were decorated with angels. It was an elaborate structure, containing a courtyard and two rooms. The measurements of the structure were said to have come directly from God, according to the Hebrew Bible.

 **PROGRESS CHECK**

Identifying Who were the Phoenicians, and what was their major contribution to world civilization?

Dorling Kindersley/Getty Images

LESSON 1 REVIEW

Review Vocabulary

1. Describe the difference between *monotheism* and *polytheism*.

Answer the Guiding Questions

2. *Describing* What subjects are covered in the Hebrew Bible?

3. *Explaining* How did the Israelites settle Canaan?

4. *Summarizing* What is the central theme of the Ten Commandments?

5. *Identifying* Which group living in Canaan included skilled sailors and traders?

6. **INFORMATIVE/EXPLANATORY** Moses was chosen to lead the Israelites out of Egypt. Write a paragraph to explain the qualities you think Moses possessed to undertake this difficult task.

LESSON 2

The Israelite Kingdom

ESSENTIAL QUESTION

• What are the characteristics of a leader?

IT MATTERS BECAUSE

The Israelites were ruled by several important kings. After this time, they were divided into two kingdoms and faced threats from neighboring empires.

Early Kings

GUIDING QUESTION *What was the role of kings in Israelite history?*

By 1100 B.C., the Israelites had settled much of the land of Canaan. They developed a prosperous culture, creating an alphabet and a calendar based on Canaanite ideas. Yet one powerful enemy—the Philistines—remained. When the Philistines moved inland from the Mediterranean Sea, they came into conflict with the Israelites. Many Israelites called for a king to unite the Twelve Tribes and lead them in battle against the Philistines.

Saul: The First King

According to the Hebrew Bible, the Israelites asked the judge Samuel to choose a king. Samuel, though, warned that a king would tax them and enslave them. The Israelites, however, still demanded a king so Samuel chose a young man named Saul (SAWL). Samuel anointed Saul as king, pouring holy oil on him to show that God had blessed him.

Under Saul's leadership, the Israelites won many battles against the Philistines. With each victory, Saul gained greater fame. Later, however, Saul lost the support of the people. According to the Hebrew Bible, Saul disobeyed some of God's commands.

Reading**HELP**DESK

Taking Notes: *Listing*

Use a chart like this one to list the achievements of King David and King Solomon.

King David	King Solomon

Content Vocabulary

• **psalm**   • **exile**
• **proverb**

God then instructed Samuel to choose and anoint another king. Samuel chose a young shepherd named David.

King David

Even before he became Israel's king, David had won praise for his bravery. The Hebrew Bible provides an account of David and his victory over Goliath, a giant Philistine warrior. In a bragging fashion, Goliath dared any Israelite to fight him one-on-one. Young David stepped forward with his shepherd's staff, a slingshot, and five smooth stones. With a heavy spear in hand, Goliath rushed forward. David hurled one stone straight at the giant's forehead. Goliath dropped dead.

Impressed by David's skill, King Saul placed his army under David's command. As David won more and more victories, the women of Israel sang his praises: "Saul has slain his thousands, and David his tens of thousands." Then, seized by jealousy, Saul tried to kill David, but David escaped. When Saul died in battle against the Philistines, David returned and became king.

According to the Hebrew Bible, once David was in power, he united the Israelite tribes. David and his army defeated the Philistines. He then established a capital city for Israel at Jerusalem (juh•ROO•suh•lehm). The Israelites built their capital in the hill country away from the coast. A fine musician and poet, David is believed to have written many of the sacred songs found in the Hebrew Bible's Book of **Psalms** (SALMZ)—also found in the Christian Bible. One of the most famous is Psalm 23, which begins:

The Twelve Tribes of Israel were family groups. According to the Hebrew Bible, each family descended from a son of Jacob. Scholars note that family connections and a common religion bound the tribes together long before they united under David.

According to the Hebrew Bible, David was tending sheep when Samuel arrived to anoint him.

PRIMARY SOURCE

" The LORD is my shepherd, I shall not be in want.
He makes me lie down in green pastures,
  he leads me beside quiet waters,
  he restores my soul.
He guides me in the paths of righteousness [fairness]
  for his name's sake. "

—Psalm: 23:1–3

psalm a sacred song or poem used in worship

Solomon built the First Temple on a site David had selected, the Temple Mount. The spot had religious significance. It was the place, according to the Hebrew Bible, where Abraham had tried to sacrifice Isaac.

Under David's rule, the Israelites enjoyed prosperous times. Farmers cultivated the tough, dry land by building terraces on the steep hillsides. Terraced fields are strips of land cut out of a hillside like stair steps. Terraces prevented soil from washing down the hillside when it rained. After David's death, the Israelites honored him as their greatest king, as do Jews today. King David's son Solomon (SAH·luh·muhn) became the next Israelite king around 970 B.C. Through trade and treaties with other peoples, Solomon brought a long **period** of peace to the region. He constructed many cities and, according to the Hebrew Bible, built the first temple in Jerusalem. Built of fragrant cedar wood and costly stone, Solomon's temple—also called the First Temple—held the Ark of the Covenant and other sacred objects.

King Solomon was also known for his wisdom. He is believed to be the author of **proverbs** (PRAHV·uhrbz), or wise sayings, that are recorded in the Hebrew Bible. Solomon shared his proverbs in hopes of helping his people:

PRIMARY SOURCE

❝ Whoever walks in integrity walks securely,
    but whoever takes crooked paths will be found out. ❞

—Proverbs: 10:9

Despite Solomon's accomplishments, many Israelites turned against him. They did not like working on his building projects or paying the high taxes he demanded. After Solomon's death around 922 B.C., the Israelites entered a troubled period in their history. Deep disagreements split their kingdom. In addition, powerful neighbors threatened their survival.

☑ PROGRESS CHECK

Evaluating Why did the Israelites believe David was their greatest king?

Two Kingdoms

GUIDING QUESTION *How did neighboring empires respond to the Israelites?*

After Solomon's death, the ten northern tribes rebelled against the government in Jerusalem. These tribes **founded** a separate kingdom, Israel. Its capital was Samaria. The two tribes in the south founded the smaller kingdom of Judah (JOO•duh). Judah's capital was Jerusalem. Although split politically, the people of Israel and Judah preserved the Israelite religion.

During this time, large empires formed around Israel and Judah. As you read previously, the Assyrians and the Chaldeans built powerful empires. Their rulers wanted to control the trade routes that ran through the Israelite kingdoms. Small and weak, the kingdoms of Israel and Judah felt threatened by their powerful neighbors.

The Fall of Israel

The Assyrians spread fear throughout the region. They forced conquered peoples to pay tribute. If they did not receive tribute, the Assyrians destroyed towns, burned estates, and carried away all valuable goods. Then they forced the conquered people to move to different areas to start new settlements.

When the kingdom of Israel refused to pay tribute, the Assyrians invaded Israel in 722 B.C. The Assyrians captured major cities, including the capital at Samaria. They wanted absolute control.

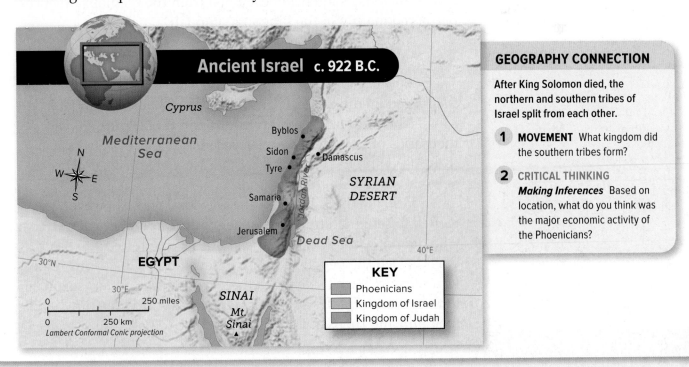

Ancient Israel c. 922 B.C.

Cyprus

Mediterranean Sea

Byblos
Sidon
Tyre
Damascus

Samaria

Jerusalem

SYRIAN DESERT

Dead Sea

EGYPT

SINAI

Mt. Sinai ▲

40°E
30°N
30°E

0   250 miles
0   250 km
Lambert Conformal Conic projection

KEY
- Phoenicians
- Kingdom of Israel
- Kingdom of Judah

GEOGRAPHY CONNECTION

After King Solomon died, the northern and southern tribes of Israel split from each other.

1 **MOVEMENT** What kingdom did the southern tribes form?

2 **CRITICAL THINKING**
Making Inferences Based on location, what do you think was the major economic activity of the Phoenicians?

Academic Vocabulary

found to set up or establish

ISRAELITE PROPHETS

Jeremiah was one of several prophets. The Israelites believed the prophets brought them the word of God.

▶ **CRITICAL THINKING**
Comparing What do the teachings of Hosea and Jeremiah have in common?

Name	Time Periods	Teachings
Elijah	874–840 B.C.	Only God should be worshipped—not idols or false gods.
Amos	780–740 B.C.	The kingdom of King David will be restored and will prosper.
Hosea	750–722 B.C.	God is loving and forgiving.
Isaiah	738–700 B.C.	God wants us to help others and promote justice.
Micah	735–700 B.C.	Both rich and poor have to do what is right and follow God.
Jeremiah	626–586 B.C.	God is just and kind—he rewards as well as punishes.
Ezekiel	597–571 B.C.	Someone who has done wrong can choose to change.

So they forced some of the Israelites to resettle in the Assyrian Empire. Assyrians then brought in people from other parts of their empire to live in Israel. These settlers mixed with the Israelites still living there. A new mingled culture developed. These people became known as Samaritans.

The Samaritans adopted many of the Israelites' religious beliefs. They worshipped the God of Israel, read the Torah, and followed the Israelites' religious laws. The Samaritans, however, adopted religious practices that the Israelites did not accept. In time, the Samaritans and the people of Israel had little in common. Today's Judaism developed from the religious practices preserved mainly in the kingdom of Judah.

The Fall of Judah

The people of Judah **survived** the Assyrian conquests, but their freedom did not last. In 597 B.C., the Chaldeans under King Nebuchadnezzar (NEHB·uh·kuhd·NEHZ·zuhr), forced thousands of people to leave Jerusalem and live in Babylon (BAB·uh·lahn), the Chaldean capital. Nebuchadnezzar chose a new king, a Judean, to rule Judah.

At first, Judah's king did as he was told. Soon, however, he plotted to set Judah free. A prophet named Jeremiah warned that God did not want Judah to rebel, but the king refused to listen. The king led the people of Judah to revolt. The Chaldeans retook Jerusalem in 586 B.C. Nebuchadnezzar then leveled Jerusalem to the ground. He destroyed the temple, captured the king, and took him and thousands of Judah's people to Babylon.

Reading**HELP**DESK

exile a forced absence from one's home or country

Academic Vocabulary

survive to continue to live; to live through a dangerous event

In Jewish history, this time became known as the Babylonian **Exile** (EHG·zyl). When people are exiled, they are forced to leave their home or country. Psalm 137 in the Hebrew Bible describes the sadness many of Judah's people felt in living far away from their homeland:

By the rivers of Babylon we sat and wept. . . .

How can we sing the songs of the LORD while in a foreign land?

If I forget you, O Jerusalem, may my right hand forget its skill.

May my tongue cling to the roof of my mouth if I do not remember you,

if I do not consider Jerusalem my highest joy...

—Psalm 137:1–6

What Was the Prophets' Message?

The prophets had an important role in Judean life. They offered words of hope in times of despair. At other times, the prophets explained that the people were not obeying God. They urged people to change their ways and make the world a better place.

The prophet Amos said, "But let justice roll on like a river, righteousness like a never-failing stream!" This means that all people should work for a just society in which everyone is treated fairly. Dr. Martin Luther King, Jr., quoted the prophet's words in the 20th century in his "I Have a Dream" speech. The goal of a just society later became a primary part of the teachings of Christianity and Islam. Jewish prophets also stressed the importance of leading a moral life and helping others in order to connect with God.

✓ PROGRESS CHECK

Identifying What empires conquered Israel and Judah?

LESSON 2 REVIEW

Review Vocabulary

1. How might reading a series of *proverbs* affect people?

Answer the Guiding Questions

2. *Explaining* Why was it important that King David united the tribes of Israel?

3. *Explaining* How did Solomon's death affect the Israelites?

4. *Identifying* Which group mixed with the Israelites to form the Samaritan culture?

5. *Identifying* What was the Babylonian Exile?

6. **NARRATIVE** The Jews were exiled and forced to spend 70 years in Babylon. If you were forced to live far away from your homeland, how would you react to your situation? Write a journal entry describing your thoughts about being forced to live away from your homeland.

There's More Online! connected.mcgraw-hill.com

The Development of Judaism

ESSENTIAL QUESTION

• How does religion shape society?

IT MATTERS BECAUSE

Religion served as the basis for all daily activities for the ancient Israelites. Many of their religious beliefs and practices continue today.

Return to Judah

GUIDING QUESTION *How did the people of Judah practice their religion while in exile and in their homeland?*

The families of Judeans who were exiled to Babylon spent 70 years away from Judah. During their exile, they became known as the Jews. We call their religion Judaism.

While in Babylon, the Jews no longer had a temple in which to worship God. It is believed that small groups of Jews began to meet at **synagogues** (SIHN·uh·GAHGS), or Jewish houses of worship. They worshipped on the **Sabbath** (SA·buhth). According to **tradition**, the Sabbath lasts from sundown Friday to nightfall Saturday. During this weekly day of worship and rest, Jews prayed and talked about their religion and history. Jews still observe the Sabbath today.

Rebuilding Judah

While some Jews accepted Babylon as their permanent home, others hoped to return to Judah some day. This hope was achieved when a group of people called the Persians swept across Southwest Asia. The Persians defeated the Chaldeans and took over Babylon. In 538 B.C., the Persian king Cyrus II let Jews return to Judah.

Reading**HELP**DESK

Taking Notes: *Identifying the Main Idea*

As you read, complete a graphic organizer like this one to describe the roles of both synagogues and scribes in the survival of Judaism.

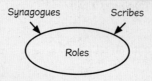
Synagogues   Scribes
Roles

Content Vocabulary

• **synagogue**   • **scroll**
• **Sabbath**   • **kosher**

Some Jews stayed in Babylon, but many returned to Judah. They rebuilt Jerusalem and constructed a new temple to replace the one destroyed by the Chaldeans. This new place of worship became known as the Second Temple.

Meanwhile, the Persians chose officials to rule the country and collect taxes from the people. They did not allow the Jews to have their own government or king. The Jews depended on religious leaders—the temple priests and scribes—to guide their society.

Many priests were religious scholars. These priests had a deep understanding of the Jewish faith. Scribes often lectured in the synagogues and taught in the schools. Led by a scribe named Ezra, the Jews wrote the five books of the Torah on pieces of parchment. They sewed the pieces together to make long **scrolls** (SKROHLZ). The Torah and writings that were added later make up the Hebrew Bible.

What Is In the Hebrew Bible?

Isn't it easier to follow rules when they are clearly explained? That is what the Hebrew Bible provided for the ancient Jews. Three parts—the Torah, the Prophets, and the Writings—make up the Hebrew Bible. It contains a series of 24 books written and collected over many centuries. The Hebrew Bible presents the laws and rules of the Israelites. It also reflects the culture of the people. Jewish history, art, literature, poetry, and proverbs are also part of the Hebrew Bible.

Genesis, the first book of the Torah, presents the Israelite view of human beginnings. It tells how God created the Earth in six days and rested on the seventh day. Genesis also describes how God punished the world for wicked behavior. In this book, God warns a man named Noah that a flood is coming and commands him to build an ark, or large boat. As the rains poured and flood waters rose, Noah, his family, and two of every animal on Earth boarded the ark. The Earth flooded and many perished. Only those on the ark escaped drowning. After the rain stopped, God placed a rainbow in the sky as a sign that the world would never again be destroyed by a flood.

Genesis also explains why the people of the world speak many different languages. It tells how the citizens of the city of Babel tried to build a tower to reach heaven.

In Jewish synagogues, the Torah is read from scrolls kept in a cabinet called the Ark of the Law. These scrolls are handled with great respect and care during worship.

©Richard T. Nowitz/Corbis

synagogue a Jewish house of worship

Sabbath a weekly day of worship and rest

scroll a long document made from pieces of parchment sewn together

Academic Vocabulary

tradition a custom, or way of life, passed down from generation to generation

According to the Hebrew Bible, Daniel's faith in God protected him from the lions. As a result, Daniel became a model of faith and strength to Jews facing difficult challenges.

▶ **CRITICAL THINKING**
Analyzing What lesson does the story of Daniel provide for Jewish people, especially during hard times?

God disapproved and made the people speak in different languages. The people could not **communicate** with one another. As a result, they could not work together to complete the tower. God then scattered the people across the Earth.

Later parts of the Hebrew Bible describe Jewish hopes for the future. The book of Isaiah describes what the Jews believed to be God's plan for a peaceful world. It says that the nations:

PRIMARY SOURCE

〃 [W]ill beat their swords into plowshares and their spears into pruning hooks. Nation will not take up sword against nation, nor will they train for war anymore. 〃

— Isaiah 2:4

The book of Daniel explains that the Jews also believed that evil and suffering would eventually be replaced by goodness. Daniel was a trusted adviser to a Babylonian king. As a Jew, however, he refused to worship Babylonian gods. For punishment, the Chaldeans threw Daniel into a lions' den. God, however, protected Daniel from the wild beasts. The story of Daniel reminds Jews that God will rescue them. Christians and Muslims share with the Jews the hope of a better world in which good triumphs over evil.

☑ **PROGRESS CHECK**

Explaining Why did religious leaders guide Jewish society after the Jews returned from exile?

Reading**HELP**DESK

Academic Vocabulary

communicate to exchange knowledge or information

Jewish Daily Life

GUIDING QUESTION *How did religion shape the Jewish way of life?*

The Torah provides teachings for daily living. These teachings shaped the family life of the early Jews. The teachings gave instructions about what foods to eat and what clothes to wear. They also required Jews to help the poor, deal honestly with their neighbors, and apply laws fairly. Jewish teachings emphasized individual worth and responsibility, as well as self-discipline. It also reminded Jews of their loyalty to God.

The Jewish Family

The ancient Israelites stressed the importance of family life. The Torah identifies specific roles for the father and the mother of the house. If a father died, his sons would take his place to lead the family.

The Jewish family also stressed education—especially for young men. When sons grew old enough, fathers taught them to worship God and to learn a trade. Later, under the guidance of religious teachers, boys learned to read the Torah. Everything the students learned—from the alphabet to Jewish history—they learned from the Torah. Because reading the Torah was central to Jewish life, religious teachers became important **community** leaders.

Daughters, who were educated at home by their mothers, learned to be wives, mothers, and housekeepers. This included learning Jewish teachings about food, the Sabbath, and holidays. They also learned about the women of ancient Israel. Two of these women were Ruth and her mother-in-law, Naomi.

According to the Hebrew Bible, Naomi's husband and her two sons died. One of the sons was married to Ruth. Ruth, who was not a Jew herself, made a difficult decision. To help Naomi, Ruth chose to leave her Moabite homeland. She moved to Bethlehem to be with Naomi. Naomi had urged Ruth to stay with her own people, but Ruth responded:

Richard T. Nowitz/Age fotostock

Stories of brave leaders like Daniel have inspired Jews to maintain their faith during times of trial and trouble. Brainstorm a list of present-day individuals or groups who inspire others with their bravery in the face of great difficulty or danger.

Sabbath comes from the Hebrew word *Shabbat*, which means "cease or desist." The Sabbath is the day of the week when, according to Jewish tradition, people stop working in order to worship. In traditional Jewish homes, the Sabbath begins with a prayer and a family meal.

Academic Vocabulary

community a group of people with common interests living in an area

Because Ruth was Naomi's daughter-in-law, she was accepted with kindness in Bethlehem.

PRIMARY SOURCE

❦ Where you go I will go, and where you stay I will stay. Your people will be my people and your God my God. Where you die I will die, and there I will be buried. ❦

—The Book of Ruth 1:16-17

Ruth's courage and devotion to her family provided an example for Jewish girls to follow.

Dietary Laws

Jewish law tells Jews what they can eat. Ancient Jews could eat the meat of only certain animals. For example, they could eat beef and lamb but not pork. Laws about food are known as *kashrut*, which means "that which is proper." By following laws related to food, Jews believed they were showing obedience to God.

Today, food that is prepared according to Jewish dietary laws is called **kosher** (KOH·shuhr). Many items you see in a grocery store have the symbol for kosher on the label. Animals used for kosher meat must be killed in a certain way. The meat must

This symbol can be found on some food packages. It indicates that foods have been prepared according to Jewish dietary laws.

Reading**HELP**DESK

kosher prepared according to Jewish dietary law

be inspected, salted, and soaked in water. Foods that are not kosher are considered to be unclean. Dietary law prohibits Jews from eating meat and dairy products together. Jews also cannot eat shellfish, such as crab or shrimp.

Specific foods with religious significance are eaten during some meals. For example, the seder (SAY·duhr) is a special meal eaten during the festival of Passover. It is a holiday that celebrates the Exodus of the Jewish people from Egypt. Foods such as lamb, hardboiled eggs, vinegar, salt water, herbs, and flat bread called matzoh, are served at the seder. During the meal, the youngest child at the table asks a series of questions about the food and the meaning of Passover. The adults and older children at the table recite the answer to the question together. For example, they tell how the bitter herbs reflect the bitter experience of the Jews living in exile. The tradition of eating special foods at Passover and reflecting on history is sacred to the Jewish people.

✔ **PROGRESS CHECK**

Evaluating Why did religious teachers become important leaders in Jewish communities?

The foods of the seder are symbolic. For example, the egg is a symbol of God's kindness. Bitter herbs are dipped in fruit juice or honey to symbolize the sweetness and bitterness of life.

Identifying What is a particular food your friends or family include when you have a special dinner?

LESSON 3 REVIEW

Review Vocabulary

1. Use the terms *synagogue*, *Sabbath*, and *kosher* to describe traditional Jewish practices.

Answer the Guiding Questions

2. *Identifying* What are the three parts of the Hebrew Bible?

3. *Explaining* How did the people of Judah practice their religion while in exile?

4. *Comparing* How were Jewish sons and daughters educated differently?

5. *Identifying* What is one type of food that is considered unclean according to Jewish dietary laws?

6. **ARGUMENT** What do you think is the main lesson to be learned from the story of Daniel in the lions' den? Write a paragraph describing your thoughts.

The Jews in the Mediterranean World

ESSENTIAL QUESTION

• Why does conflict develop?

IT MATTERS BECAUSE

The Jews experienced many significant changes under Greek and Roman rule.

The Arrival of Greek Rule

GUIDING QUESTION *What was life like for the Jews in Greek-ruled lands?*

The Jews of Judah remained under Persian rule for nearly 200 years. That is about the same amount of time as the entire history of the United States. Then, in 331 B.C., a king from Macedonia, who had conquered Greece, defeated the Persians. This king was Alexander the Great. Alexander admired Greek ways and wanted to spread them. He introduced the Greek language and culture to Judah. Alexander allowed the Jews to stay in Judah.

How Did Jewish Ideas Spread?

Under Alexander, Judah remained the center of Judaism. Many Jews at that time, however, had long lived outside Judah. Thousands had been exiled to Babylon in 586 B.C. When in 538 B.C. the conquering Persians gave them permission to return to Judah, many chose to stay in Babylon or go to other Mediterranean lands instead. These groups of Jews living outside of the Jewish homeland became known as the **Diaspora** (deye·AS·puh·ruh). *Diaspora* is a Greek word that means "scattered." Where these Jews settled, they practiced their customs, and Jewish ideas spread.

Reading**HELP**DESK

Taking Notes: *Comparing and Contrasting*

As you read, complete a diagram like this one by identifying similarities and differences between Greek rule and Roman rule.

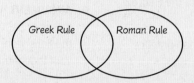

Greek Rule   Roman Rule

Content Vocabulary

• **Diaspora** • **rabbi**

The Jews of the Diaspora remained loyal to Judaism. At the same time, many learned the Greek language and adopted features of Greek culture. A group of Jewish scholars in Egypt copied the Hebrew Bible into Greek. This Greek **version**, called the Septuagint (sehp·TOO·uh·juhnt), helped people who were not Jews to read and understand the Hebrew Bible. As a result, Jewish ideas spread throughout the Mediterranean world.

The Revolt of Maccabeus

After Alexander's death, four of his generals divided his empire into separate kingdoms. One kingdom covered much of Southwest Asia. A family known as the Seleucids (suh·LOO·suhds) ruled this kingdom. By 200 B.C., Judah was under the control of Seleucid kings.

In 176 B.C., Antiochus IV (an·TEE·uh·kuhs) came to power as the Seleucid king. As ruler of Judah, Antiochus required the Jews to worship the many Greek gods and goddesses.

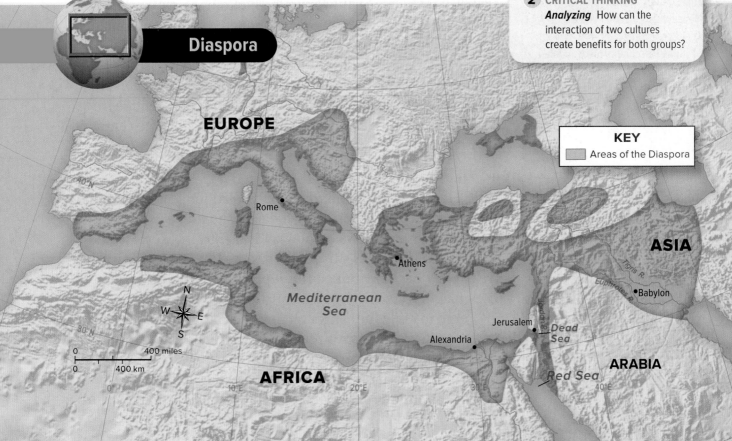

Diaspora

EUROPE

Rome

Athens

Mediterranean Sea

Jerusalem Dead Sea

Alexandria

AFRICA

Red Sea

ASIA

Babylon

Tigris R.

Euphrates R.

ARABIA

N W E S

0 400 miles
0 400 km

KEY
Areas of the Diaspora

GEOGRAPHY CONNECTION

The Diaspora continued throughout Alexander's Greek empire. During the first century A.D., Jews represented about 40 percent of the empire's population.

1 **MOVEMENT** How did the Diaspora help spread Jewish ideas?

2 **CRITICAL THINKING**
Analyzing How can the interaction of two cultures create benefits for both groups?

Diaspora the groups of Jews living outside of the Jewish homeland

Academic Vocabulary

version a different form or edition; a translation of the Bible

**Judas Maccabeus
(c. 190 B.C.–160 B.C.)**

Judas Maccabeus and his followers engaged in guerrilla warfare against the Greek armies. Guerrilla warfare is irregular combat carried out by small groups of independent soldiers. This strategy helped the Maccabees succeed in battle against the Seleucids. The family of Judas Maccabeus ruled Judah and expanded its lands. With more territory surrounding it, Judah was protected and remained free until the Roman conquest.

Explaining Why is Judas Maccabeus considered a hero?

Reading**HELP**DESK

Academic Vocabulary

expand to enlarge

A large number of Jews, however, refused to abandon their religion. In 167 B.C., Judas Maccabeus (JOO·duhs MAK·uh·BEE·uhs), a Jewish priest, led the fight against Seleucid rule. He and his followers fled to the hills. They formed a rebel army known as the Maccabees.

After many battles, the Maccabees succeeded in capturing the Temple. They cleared it of all statues of Greek gods and goddesses. They then rededicated the temple to the worship of God. Each year, Jews recall the cleansing of the Temple when they celebrate the festival of Hanukkah (HAH·nuh·kuh).

✓ PROGRESS CHECK

Analyzing How did Alexander and later the Seleucids affect the people of Judah?

Roman Rule in Judaea

GUIDING QUESTION *How did the Jews react to Roman rule of their homeland?*

By 100 B.C., the Romans controlled much of the eastern Mediterranean lands. The name *Roman* came from Rome, their capital. Rome was located far to the west in what is known today as Italy. Led by powerful generals, the Romans **expanded** their empire. In 63 B.C., Roman forces conquered Judah and renamed it Judaea (joo·DEE·uh).

At first, the Romans chose a follower of the Jewish religion, Herod (HEHR·uhd), to rule as king of Judaea. Herod built many forts and cities in Judaea. The Second Temple in Jerusalem, rebuilt during Herod's reign, served as the center of Jewish worship.

Jewish Groups

After Herod's death, Roman officials ruled Judaea. At that time, disagreement grew about how Judaism should be practiced. Jews also had different views on how to deal with the Romans.

One group of Jews was known as the Pharisees (FEH·ruh·seez). The Pharisees gained the support of the common people. They taught in the synagogues and applied the teachings of the Torah to daily life. Through their teachings, the Pharisees helped to make Judaism a religion of the home and family. The Pharisees wanted to help people obey the Ten Commandments. To do this, they stressed both written and oral law. Oral law is the unwritten interpretations passed down over time by word of mouth.

Hulton Archives/Getty Images

The Pharisees wanted Judaea free of Roman rule. However, they did not urge Jews to fight the Romans. Instead, they told people to resist Roman control. They urged the people to practice the Torah's teachings with greater **devotion**.

Another Jewish group made up of wealthy noble families was the Sadducees (SA·juh·SEEZ). Many of them served as priests and scribes in the Temple. The Sadducees accepted the laws of the Torah. They were more concerned, however, with applying the laws to temple ceremonies. They also did not agree with many of the Pharisees' teachings. For example, the Sadducees emphasized the written law but rejected oral law. The Sadducees favored **cooperation** with the Romans. They wanted to keep peace and order in Judaea.

A third group was called the Essenes (ih·SEENZ). They were priests who broke away from the Temple in Jerusalem. Many Essenes lived at Qumrān, an area in the desert near the Dead Sea. They spent their lives praying and waiting for God to deliver the Jews from Roman rule. The Essenes followed only the written law of the Torah.

Centuries later, in A.D. 1947, ancient scrolls were found in caves at Qumrān. Because the caves were near the Dead Sea, the scrolls became known as the Dead Sea Scrolls. Many of the scrolls were most likely written by Essenes. The scrolls are important to historians because they reveal details of a particular place and time.

Herod was primarily responsible for developing the fortress at Masada. It was the scene of a major Roman and Jewish battle. Visitors may tour its mountainous ruins today.

Francesco Dazzi/Flickr/Getty Images

Academic Vocabulary

devotion dedication, a strong commitment
cooperation working together

There are rocky cliffs along the shores of the Dead Sea. Caves in these cliffs contained the Dead Sea Scrolls.

1 **LOCATION** Describe the location of the Dead Sea in relation to the Mediterranean Sea.

2 **CRITICAL THINKING**
Drawing Conclusions Why would the discovery of the Dead Sea Scrolls be considered so significant?

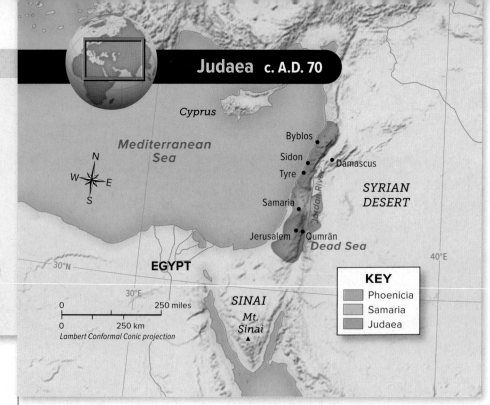

Judaea c. A.D. 70

Cyprus

Mediterranean Sea

Byblos
Sidon
Tyre
Damascus

Samaria

SYRIAN DESERT

Jerusalem
Qumrān
Dead Sea

30°N

30°E

40°E

EGYPT

SINAI
Mt. Sinai ▲

0 — 250 miles
0 — 250 km
Lambert Conformal Conic projection

KEY
Phoenicia
Samaria
Judaea

Locating the Dead Sea Scrolls is considered to be one of the most significant modern archaeological discoveries.

They let historians see that Judaism was not always an established religion. The scrolls show that not all followers practiced Judaism in the same way during Roman times.

Some of the scrolls tell a story about a group of Jews who, in exile, developed their own beliefs about good and evil. They saw themselves as alone in the world, surrounded by enemies. They were waiting for someone to lead them. Some scrolls describe the beliefs, holy days, and practices of other Jewish groups. The variety of the scrolls makes some historians believe that the writings were perhaps the contents of a library. The reasons for hiding the scrolls are unclear. Someone may have wanted to protect them from destruction during times of conflict with the Romans. Since their discovery, however, the scrolls have helped historians understand more about Judaism during Roman times.

A fourth Jewish group, the Zealots, lived in Judaea. They wanted to fight for their freedom against the Romans. During the A.D. 60s, Jewish hatred of Roman rule reached its peak. Hope remained in the Jewish faith, however. Many Jews were waiting for God to send a deliverer to free them from Roman rule. As **tensions** between Romans and Jews in Judaea increased, the Zealots prepared to act.

www.facsimili-editions.com

Reading**HELP**DESK

Academic Vocabulary

tension opposition between individuals or groups; stress

Jewish-Roman Wars

In A.D. 66, the Zealots revolted. They overpowered the small Roman army in Jerusalem. Four years later, Roman forces retook the city. They killed thousands of Jews and forced many others to leave. The Romans also destroyed the Second Temple in Jerusalem. Today the Western Wall still stands in Jerusalem. This structure is all that remains of the Temple complex. It is a long-standing Jewish custom to come to this wall to pray.

After a number of years passed, some Jews rebelled once again. In A.D. 132, a military leader named Simon ben Kosiba, known as Bar Kochba, led the Jews in the battle for freedom. However, three years later, Roman forces crushed the revolt. They killed Bar Kochba and many other Jewish leaders during the fighting.

With the revolt put down, the Romans imposed stricter controls and did not allow Jews to live in or even visit Jerusalem. The Romans renamed Judaea and called it Palestine. This name refers to the Philistines, whom the Israelites had conquered centuries before.

The ancient Western Wall is the only remaining structure of the Temple of Jerusalem. Coming here to pray has been a Jewish custom for hundreds of years. Those who visit the wall often leave prayers on paper stuffed into its cracks.

Explaining Why might people still come to this site to pray?

In A.D. 1947, a shepherd in the Judaean desert entered a cave along the shore of the Dead Sea. There he discovered several large clay jars. Some jars were empty, but in others he found ancient scrolls of leather, papyrus, and copper. These **documents**, written between 200 B.C. and A.D. 68, are called the Dead Sea Scrolls. The scrolls found in several caves in the area include the oldest complete copy of the Book of Isaiah and pieces of many other books of the Hebrew Bible. Among the documents are works in ancient Hebrew, Greek, and Aramaic. Most scholars believe that the scrolls were part of a library that belonged to an early Jewish community.

The Rabbis

Despite losing their struggle for independence, the Jews regrouped with the help of their **rabbis** (RA·byz), or religious leaders. The Jewish people no longer had a temple or priests. Instead, the synagogues and rabbis gained importance. The rabbis taught and explained the Torah. They provided moral guidance—accepted notions of right and wrong—to the people.

One of the most famous rabbis was Yohanan ben Zaccai (YOH·kah·nahn behn zah·KY). Ben Zaccai lived in Judaea when Jerusalem fell to the Romans in A.D. 70. He persuaded the Romans to spare the Jewish city of Yavneh. There, he founded a school to continue teaching the Torah.

Ben Zaccai helped the Judaic spirit survive the destruction of the temple and the loss of Jerusalem. He placed great importance on the study of the Torah. He also stressed acts of loving kindness and community service. Because of ben Zaccai's efforts, the school at Yavneh became a center of Torah studies and a model for other schools. Other rabbis founded Torah schools in places as far away as Babylon and Egypt.

Through the efforts of ben Zaccai and other rabbis, the basic beliefs of Judaism were preserved. Eventually, the rabbis gathered their oral discussions about Jewish law and recorded them in a work known as the Mishnah. Later, the Mishnah was combined with other Jewish legal traditions into an authoritative collection of Jewish tradition known as the Talmud. The word *Talmud* is a Hebrew term that means "instruction." The Talmud became the basis for Jewish teachings throughout the ages.

A part of the Talmud called the Mishnah began as an oral history of Jewish law passed from one generation of rabbis to another.

Godong/Robert Harding World Imagery/Getty Images

Even today, the Talmud remains central to Jewish teaching and is the ultimate authority on Jewish law. A prayer at the end of part of the Talmud reveals the Jewish reverence for the Torah:

Rabbis continue to educate students today. They might also perform charity or social functions for their congregations.

PRIMARY SOURCE

" Make sweet, O Lord, our God, the words of Thy Law in our mouths, and in the mouth of Thy people the house of Israel; and may we, our children, and the children of Thy people the house of Israel, all know Thy Name and learn Thy Law. "

—from *The Babylon Talmud, Book 1: Tract Sabbath*

✓ **PROGRESS CHECK**

Explaining How did the rabbis help Judaism survive after the Roman conquest?

SAFRA Sylvain/Age fotostock

LESSON 4 REVIEW

Review Vocabulary

1. In what way did *rabbis* help the Jews during the period of Roman rule?

Answer the Guiding Questions

2. *Explaining* What was life like for the Jews in Greek-ruled lands?

3. *Identifying* Which group gained control of Judah following Alexander's death?

4. *Explaining* How did the Jews react to Roman rule of their homeland?

5. *Identifying* Who established a school for teaching the Torah at Yavneh?

6. **ARGUMENT** You are living in Judaea during the Roman conquest. Write a letter to a friend describing what action you would like to see taken to make Judaea free again.

CHAPTER 6 Activities

Write your answers on a separate piece of paper.

1 Exploring the Essential Question

INFORMATIVE/EXPLANATORY Write an expository essay about how key leaders influenced the Israelites during the time periods discussed in this chapter. Identify specific leaders who had the most significant effect. Explain how they led during times of conflict.

2 21st Century Skills

CREATING A SLIDE SHOW Create a slide show about an aspect of Jewish culture that you have studied in this chapter. When presenting, briefly introduce each image, and offer a clear interpretation of why it is significant.

3 Thinking Like a Historian

COMPARING AND CONTRASTING Create a diagram like the one shown to compare and contrast the Jewish groups that existed under Roman rule.

4 GEOGRAPHY ACTIVITY

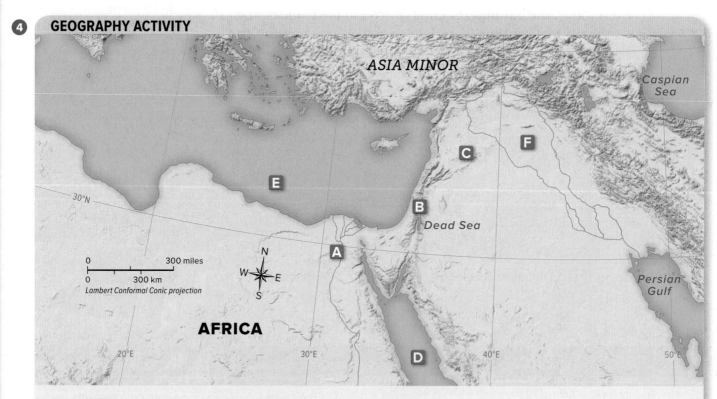

Locating Places

Match the letters on the map with the numbered places listed below.

1. Mesopotamia
2. Mediterranean Sea
3. Red Sea
4. Canaan
5. Israel
6. Egypt

Directions: Write your answers on a separate piece of paper.

CHECKING FOR UNDERSTANDING

1 Define each of these terms.
- **A.** prophet
- **B.** Exodus
- **C.** covenant
- **D.** Torah
- **E.** psalm
- **F.** scroll
- **G.** seder
- **H.** Diaspora
- **I.** Zealots

REVIEW THE GUIDING QUESTIONS

2 *Describing* Based on the teachings of their prophets, what did the Israelites believe about God?

3 *Identifying* Name two other monotheistic religions whose development was influenced by Judaism.

4 *Listing* List the products traded by the Phoenicians in the Mediterranean area.

5 *Finding the Main Idea* Why did the Israelites in 1100 B.C. call for a king? Which of the Israelite kings fulfilled the desires of the people?

6 *Identifying* What events led to the Babylonian Exile?

7 *Explaining* What is the Jewish Sabbath? How is it observed?

8 *Describing* What basic principles about daily living are found in the teachings of the Torah?

9 *Identifying* What event does the Jewish festival of Hanukkah celebrate?

10 *Explaining* What is the Talmud, and why is it significant?

CRITICAL THINKING

11 *Making Connections* How have the Ten Commandments helped shape today's basic moral principles, laws, and democratic beliefs?

12 *Making Inferences* Why might the Ark of the Covenant have been an especially sacred object to the Israelites?

13 *Comparing and Contrasting* Compare and contrast the accomplishments of the first three kings of the Israelites.

14 *Evaluating* Explain the actions taken by the Assyrians after their invasion and conquest of Israel to gain absolute control of the area. Then evaluate the effectiveness of those actions.

15 *Making Generalizations* Study the chart on the Israelite prophets in Lesson 2. Read the teachings of the various prophets and make a generalization about their messages.

16 *Making Connections* Explain the types of information found in the 24 books of the Hebrew Bible and how the contents reflect the culture of the people. Why might such a collection of information be important to a people such as the Jews?

17 *Determining Central Ideas* Why did religious teachers become important community leaders in Jewish society? Include information about the role of religious leaders during the time of Persian control of Judah in your answer.

18 *Making Connections* How did Greek dominance in the Mediterranean help to spread Jewish ideas in that area?

19 *Contrasting* Contrast the views of the four Jewish groups—the Pharisees, Sadducees, Essenes, and Zealots—on how the Jews should deal with Roman control of Judaea.

20 *Determining Cause and Effect* What effect did the actions of the Romans after they put down the revolt of the Zealots have on the Jewish people and religion?

Need Extra Help?

If You've Missed Question	1	2	3	4	5	6	7	8	9	10	11	12	13	14	15	16	17	18	19	20
Review Lesson	1,2, 3, 4	1	1	1	2	2	3	3	4	4	1	1	2	2	2	3	3	4	4	4

DBQ SHORT RESPONSE

"The biblical King Solomon was known for his wisdom, his wealth and his writings. … Solomon's downfall came in his old age. … Within Solomon's kingdom, he placed heavy taxation on the people, who became bitter. He also had the people work as soldiers, chief officers and commanders of his chariots and cavalry. He granted special privileges to the tribes of Judah and this alienated [angered] the northern tribes."

—From *"Solomon"* by Shira Schoenberg

21 What is believed to have weakened Solomon as a king?

22 Why might Solomon granting special privileges to the tribes of Judah have displeased the other tribes?

EXTENDED RESPONSE

23 *Narrative* Write a short essay in which you compare and contrast the daily life of Jews under Greek and Roman rule. Consider how Greek and Roman rule affected the Jewish peoples' ability to practice their religion. Describe how conflicts eventually developed between the Jews and the ruling groups.

STANDARDIZED TEST PRACTICE

DBQ ANALYZING DOCUMENTS

24 *Summarizing* Which of the following best states the main purpose of the Ten Commandments?

- **A.** to suggest ways to observe the Sabbath
- **B.** to describe the qualifications for kings
- **C.** to reveal warnings to Israelites
- **D.** to provide rules for living

25 *Drawing Conclusions* The message found in the Ten Commandments can best be seen today in

- **A.** modern biology.
- **B.** modern geography.
- **C.** modern politics.
- **D.** modern law.

Need Extra Help?

If You've Missed Question	**21**	**22**	**23**	**24**	**25**
Review Lesson	2	2	4	1	1

The Ten Commandments

❶ Do not worship any god except me.

❷ Do not … bow down and worship idols.

❸ Do not misuse my name.

❹ Remember the Sabbath Day and keep it holy.

❺ Honor your father and your mother.

❻ Do not murder.

❼ Be faithful in marriage.

❽ Do not steal.

❾ Do not testify falsely [tell lies] about others.

❿ Do not want anything that belongs to someone else.

—*Paraphrased from Exodus 20:3-17*

◀ *The gods and goddesses of Greek mythology are part of our most enduring literature. As shown here, the goddess Athena is usually depicted with a helmet ready for battle.*

2000 B.C. TO 400 B.C.

The Ancient Greeks

Danita Delimont/Gallo Images/Getty Images

THE STORY MATTERS ...

In ancient times, Greek language, culture, and mythology spread throughout the Mediterranean region. Traditional figures, such as the goddess Athena, were featured in art and on pottery and other household objects.

In time, ancient Greek civilization was absorbed by the more powerful Romans. Because the Romans imitated Greek culture in many ways, the achievements of the Greeks in politics, philosophy, and literature were passed on through the centuries. In this way, the ancient Greeks continue to influence Western civilization.

ESSENTIAL QUESTIONS

- How does geography influence the way people live?
- Why do people form governments?
- Why does conflict develop?
- How do governments change?

Place & Time: Greece 2000 B.C. to 400 B.C.

Greek city-states developed after the civilizations of the Minoans and Mycenaeans. By the 700s B.C., city-states and colonies flourished in the Mediterranean region. The Persian Empire attempted unsuccessfully to invade Greece. By the late 400s, however, all of Greece had been weakened during a bitter war between Athens and Sparta.

Step Into the Place

MAP FOCUS The location of Greece put it at the crossroads of Europe, Africa, and Asia.

1 **LOCATION** Is Greece located east or west of Asia Minor?

2 **PLACE** What influence would the Greeks' location on the Mediterranean Sea have on the way they earned a living and traveled?

3 **PLACE** What type of geographic landform is mainland Greece as a whole?

4 **CRITICAL THINKING**
Analyzing Visuals What makes the area occupied by the ancient Greeks a crossroads between three continents?

The city-state of Sparta was a military society. Spartan boys began training for the military at the age of seven. Between the ages of 20 and 60, Spartan men served as soldiers in the city-state's army. Discipline was strict, and in battle soldiers were expected to win—or die trying. Sparta's differences with Athens made it impossible for ancient Greece to become a politically unified state.

Spartan girls learned sports, such as throwing the javelin, wrestling, and running. Spartan women could own property and enjoyed more freedom than women in other Greek city-states. This statue of a girl exercising is an example of Spartan sculpture. Unlike the Athenians, however, Spartan rulers emphasized war and the military over arts and literature. As a result, today there are a relatively small number of Spartan artifacts.

(t)Foto Marburg/Art Resource, NY; (b)Figurine of a girl running, (bronze), Greek, (6th century BC)/British Museum, London, UK/The Bridgeman Art Library

TIME LINE What events in Greece point out that conflict was often a part of ancient Greek life?

c. 2000 B.C. Minoans control eastern Mediterranean

c. 1450 B.C. Mycenaeans conquer Minoans; control Aegean

c. 1200 B.C. Mycenaean civilization declines

GREECE

2000 B.C.

1000 B.C.

c. 1792 B.C. Hammurabi becomes king of Babylonian Empire

c. 1500 B.C. Queen Hatshepsut reigns in Egypt

c. 1390 B.C. Writing appears in China

c. 1020 B.C. Saul chosen as first king of Israel

Ancient Greece 2000 B.C. TO 400 B.C.

Black Sea

MACEDONIA

Sea of
Marmara

Mt. Olympus ▲

40°N

BALKAN
PENINSULA

• Troy

KEY

Ancient Greece

Ionian
Sea

GREECE

Aegean
Sea

ASIA MINOR

Delphi •

Gulf of Corinth

• Thebes

Corinth •

• Athens

N

Mycenae •

W   E

PELOPONNESUS

• Miletus

S

• Sparta

Mediterranean
Sea

Knossos
•

35°N

Crete

0   100 miles

0   100 km

Lambert Azimuthal Equal-Area projection

20°E   25°E   30°E

c. 650 B.C. Greeks colonize
shores of the Mediterranean

c. 480 B.C. Xerxes invades Greece

499 B.C. Greeks revolt
against Persian rulers

c. 431 B.C. Peloponnesian
War begins

c. 330 B.C. Alexander the Great
conquers Persian Empire

800 B.C.   600 B.C.   400 B.C.   200 B.C.

c. 680 B.C. Iron-making skills
spread in East Africa

486 B.C. Xerxes
becomes king of Persia

c. 241 B.C. Rome defeats
Carthage in First Punic War

LESSON 1

Rise of Greek Civilization

• How does geography influence the way people live?

IT MATTERS BECAUSE
The early Greeks developed important settlements, trade routes, and political ideas in the Mediterranean region.

Mountains and Seas

GUIDING QUESTION *How did physical geography influence the lives of the early Greeks?*

Greece was the first civilization to develop in Europe and the westernmost part of Asia. In other early civilizations, people first settled in river valleys that had rich soil. Greek civilization began in an area **dominated** by mountains and seas.

If you flew over this region today, you would see rugged landscapes and beautiful seas. The Greek mainland is on the southern part of Europe's Balkan Peninsula. A **peninsula** (puh·NIHN·suh·luh) is a body of land with water on three sides. Far to the east of the Greek mainland is another peninsula called Anatolia. It is part of present-day Turkey.

Between these two land areas are the dazzling blue waters of the Aegean Sea. The Aegean Sea is part of the larger Mediterranean Sea. There are hundreds of islands in the Aegean Sea. They look like stepping stones between the Greek mainland and Anatolia.

The Greeks traded goods and ideas between islands and along the area's coastlines. Today many Greeks fish and trade for a living, much as the ancient Greeks did before them. Other ancient Greeks settled in farming **communities**. These settlements began on narrow, fertile plains that ran along the

Reading**HELP**DESK

Taking Notes: *Comparing*
Use a Venn diagram like the one here to compare the Minoans and Mycenaeans.

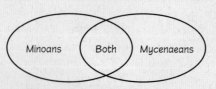

Content Vocabulary
• **peninsula**   • **polis**
• **bard**   • **agora**
• **colony**   • **phalanx**

coast and between the mountains. In the area's mild climate, farmers grew crops, such as wheat, barley, olives, and grapes. They also raised sheep and goats.

Even though some Greek communities were near the sea, others were far from the coast. Inland communities were separated from each other by rugged mountains and deep valleys. As a result, communities in many parts of ancient Greece became fiercely independent. They came to think of their communities almost as small separate countries.

✅ PROGRESS CHECK

Understanding Cause and Effect How did seas influence the way many ancient Greeks lived?

GEOGRAPHY CONNECTION

All parts of ancient Greece were near water.

1 **LOCATION** Which body of water lies east of the Balkan Peninsula?

2 **CRITICAL THINKING**
Making Inferences What type of transportation was probably most useful to the early Greeks?

Ancient Greece c. 2000 B.C.

MACEDONIA

Sea of Marmara

Mt. Olympus ▲

Troy

BALKAN PENINSULA

KEY
Ancient Greece

GREECE

Ionian Sea

Aegean Sea

ASIA MINOR

Delphi

Gulf of Corinth

Thebes

Corinth

Athens

Mycenae

Miletus

PELOPONNESUS

N
W E
S

Sparta

Mediterranean Sea

Knossos

Crete

0   100 miles
0   100 km
Lambert Azimuthal Equal-Area projection

40°N

35°N

20°E   25°E   30°E

peninsula a piece of land nearly surrounded by water

Academic Vocabulary

dominate to control or influence something or someone
community people with common interests living in a particular area; the area itself

An Island Civilization

GUIDING QUESTION *How did the civilization of the Minoans develop?*

Greek myths describe an early civilization that developed on Crete (KREET), an island southeast of the Greek mainland. About A.D. 1900, a British archaeologist named Arthur Evans discovered a site on Crete called Knossos (NAH·suhs). He unearthed the amazing palace of a legendary king named Minos (MY·nuhs).

Evans **concluded** that Minos and his family lived in the palace. The palace had numerous rooms that were connected by twisting passageways. Some of these rooms were used to store oil, wine, and grain. Other rooms were workshops where people made jewelry, vases, and statues. There were even bathrooms in the palace.

An ancient people called the Minoans (muh·NOH·uhnz) built the palace at Knossos. The Minoan civilization was the first to develop in the Aegean region, but they were not Greeks. Their civilization lasted from about 2500 B.C. to 1450 B.C.

Trade was an important **economic** activity for the Minoans. They built ships using the wood from Crete's forests of oak and cedar trees. The Minoans sailed to Egypt and Syria. There they traded pottery and stone vases for ivory and metals. Minoan ships also patrolled the eastern Mediterranean Sea to protect Minoan trade from pirates.

Sometime around 1450 B.C., however, the Minoan civilization collapsed. Historians do not know why this happened. One theory for the collapse is that undersea earthquakes caused huge waves that destroyed Minoan cities. Other historians think that people from the Greek mainland, known as Mycenaeans (my·suh·NEE·uhns), invaded Crete.

✓ PROGRESS CHECK

Explaining What did the discovery at Knossos reveal about the Minoans?

A Mainland Civilization

GUIDING QUESTION *How did the Mycenaeans gain power in the Mediterranean?*

About 2000 B.C., the Mycenaeans left their homeland in central Asia. They moved into mainland Greece. There, they gradually mixed with the local people and set up several kingdoms.

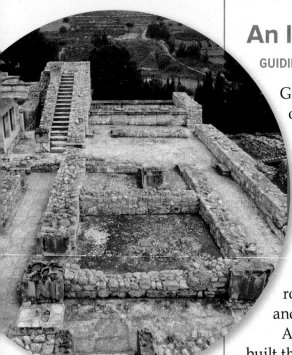

The palace at Knossos included a large outdoor theater. Colorful wall paintings decorated the palace, both inside and outside.

▶ CRITICAL THINKING
Analyzing What kind of activities do the ruins of the palace suggest?

DEA/A. VERGANI/De Agostini Editore/Age fotostock

Reading**HELP**DESK

Academic Vocabulary

conclude to reach an understanding; to make a decision

economic the system in a country that involves making, buying, and selling goods

Mycenaean Kingdom

Little was known about the Mycenaeans until the late 1800s. That was when a German archaeologist named Heinrich Schliemann (HYN·rihk SHLEE·mahn) discovered the ruins of a palace in Mycenae (my·SEE·nee). He named the people of this civilization the Mycenaeans.

Each Mycenaean king lived in a palace built on a hill. Thick stone walls circled the palace and protected the kingdom's people. Nobles lived outside the walls on large farms, called estates. The workers and enslaved people who farmed the land lived in villages on these estates.

Mycenaean palaces were centers of government. Artisans there made leather goods, clothes, and jars for wine and olive oil. Other workers made swords and ox-hide shields. Government officials recorded the wealth of the kingdom's residents. They also collected wheat, livestock, and honey as taxes.

Traders and Warriors

Minoan traders from Crete visited the Greek mainland. Gradually, the Mycenaeans adopted features of Minoan culture. They built ships and worked with bronze. They used the sun and stars to navigate the seas. The Mycenaeans also worshipped the Earth Mother, the Minoans' chief god.

By the mid-1400s B.C., the Mycenaeans had conquered the Minoans and controlled the Aegean area. This brought new wealth to the Mycenaeans, which they used to expand their military strength. The Mycenaeans were proud of their military successes in the Trojan War.

A Dark Age

However, the Mycenaean civilization **declined** over time. Mycenaean kingdoms fought one another, and earthquakes destroyed their palace fortresses. By 1100 B.C., the Mycenaean civilization had crumbled.

About this time, groups of warring peoples moved from place to place throughout the eastern Mediterranean region.

GUIZIOU Franck/Hemis/Age fotostock

Academic Vocabulary

decline to move toward a weaker condition

Analyzing Primary and Secondary Sources

German historian Heinrich Schliemann is considered the modern discoverer of the Mycenaean world. Schliemann (1822–1890) discovered several palaces and the ancient city of Troy. Research a biography or articles about Schliemann to create a short report about the archaeologist. Present your report to the class. For more information about using primary and secondary sources, read the chapter *What Does a Historian Do?*

Mycenaean artisans made golden masks to cover the faces of their dead kings. This is known as the Mask of Agamemnon.

THE GREEK ALPHABET

Greek Letter	Written Name	English Sound
A	alpha	a
B	beta	b
Γ	gamma	g
Δ	delta	d
E	epsilon	e
Z	zeta	z
H	eta	e
Θ	theta	th
I	iota	i
K	kappa	c,k
Λ	lambda	l
M	mu	m
N	nu	n
Ξ	xi	x
O	omicron	o
Π	pi	p
P	rho	r
Σ	sigma	s
T	tau	t
Y	upsilon	y,u
Φ	phi	ph
X	chi	ch
Ψ	psi	ps
Ω	omega	o

One of these groups was a Greek-speaking people known as the Dorians (DOHR·ee·uhns). They invaded the Greek mainland from the north and took control of most of the region.

Historians call the next 300 years of Greek history a Dark Age. During this difficult time, trade slowed down, people made fewer things to sell, and most were very poor. Farmers grew only enough food to feed their families. Many people also stopped writing and keeping records.

In Greece, several positive developments also happened during this time. Dorian warriors introduced iron weapons and the skill of iron making. Iron weapons and farm tools were stronger and cheaper than the bronze ones used by the Mycenaeans. As the Dorians pushed into Greece, thousands of people fled the Greek mainland. They settled on the Aegean islands and the western shore of Anatolia.

The Hellenes

By 750 B.C., many descendants of the people who ran away returned to the Greek mainland. They brought back new ideas, crafts, and skills. Small independent communities developed under local leaders who became kings. These people called themselves Hellenes, or Greeks. Farmers in these communities grew more food than their families could use. The Greeks traded their surplus food with each other and with neighboring peoples, such as the Egyptians and Phoenicians. As trade increased, a new need for writing developed. The Greeks adopted an alphabet from Phoenician traders who sailed from the Mediterranean coast.

The Greek alphabet had 24 letters that represented different sounds. It greatly simplified reading and writing in the Greek language. Record keeping became easier. Soon, people wrote down the tales that had been told by **bards**, or storytellers. Previously, these tales had been passed down from generation to generation orally. Now they could finally be kept in written form.

✓ PROGRESS CHECK

Determining Cause and Effect How did the Dorian invasion help spread Greek culture?

Reading HELP DESK

bard someone who writes or performs epic poems or stories about heroes and their deeds

Build Vocabulary: *Word Origins*

Geographers call the place where a large river divides into smaller rivers near the ocean a *delta*. Deltas often form in the shape of a triangle, like the Greek letter delta. Try writing a word using the Greek alphabet.

Colonies and Trade

GUIDING QUESTION *How did early Greeks spread their culture?*

As Greece recovered from the Dark Age, its population increased rapidly. By 700 B.C., local farmers could not produce enough grain to feed the growing population. To solve this problem, Greek communities began to send people outside the Aegean area to establish **colonies** (KAH·luh·nees). A colony is a settlement in a new territory that has close ties to its homeland.

The Greeks founded many colonies along the coasts of the Mediterranean Sea and the Black Sea between 750 B.C. and 550 B.C. Greek culture spread into new areas, such as southern Italy, Sicily, France, Spain, North Africa, and western Asia.

The colonies traded with their "parent" cities on the Greek mainland. They shipped goods such as grains, metals, fish, and timber, as well as enslaved people to Greece. In return, the Greek mainland sent wine, olive oil, and pottery to the colonies. As the Greeks began to make coins from metal, this **affected** their trade. Trade expanded as merchants traded money for goods rather than bartered for goods. This system increased a colony's wealth. As the demand for goods grew, artisans made more goods to meet the demand. People in different colonies specialized in making certain products. For example, in colonies where farmers raised sheep, people began to make cloth from the sheep's wool.

✔ PROGRESS CHECK

Determining Cause and Effect How did the colonies affect trade and industry in the Greek world?

The Greek City-State

GUIDING QUESTION *How did Greek city-states create the idea of citizenship?*

Mountains and seas separated Greek communities from one another. As a result, people developed a loyalty to the community in which they lived. Communities became fiercely independent. By the end of the Dark Age, nobles who owned large estates had overthrown the Greek kings. Across Greece, nobles ruled numerous city-states.

Georgios Kollidas/Panther Media/Age fotostock

---

colony a group of people living in a new territory who have ties to their homeland; the new territory itself

Academic Vocabulary

affect to influence; to cause a change

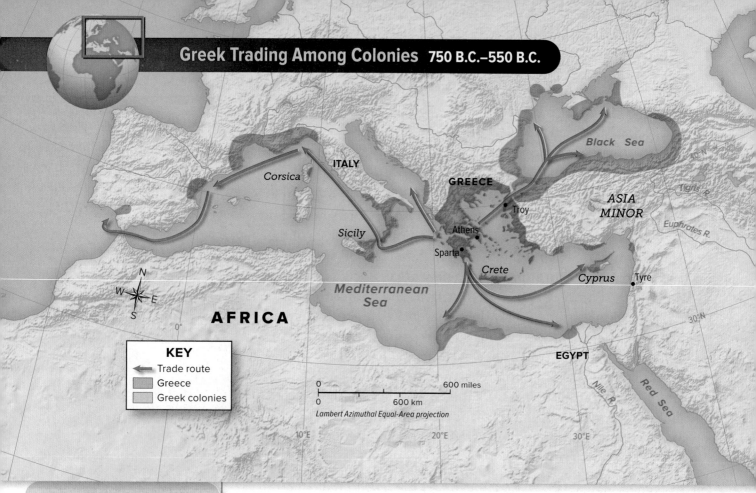

KEY
→ Trade route
Greece
Greek colonies

0 ——————— 600 miles
0 ——————— 600 km
Lambert Azimuthal Equal-Area projection

GEOGRAPHY CONNECTION

Greece set up trading posts and colonies north to the Black Sea.

1 **LOCATION** On which islands were Greek colonies located?

2 **CRITICAL THINKING**
Drawing Conclusions In addition to the buying and selling of goods, what effect would Greece have on the people of its colonies and surrounding lands?

As in Mesopotamia, the Greek city-states were made up of a town or city and the surrounding area. Each city-state or **polis** (PAH·luhs), was like an independent country. Today, English words such as *police* and *politics* come from the Greek word *polis*.

What Did a Polis Look Like?

The polis was the basic political unit of Greek civilization. At the center of each polis was a fort built on a hilltop. The hilltop that a fort stood on was called an acropolis (uh·KRAH·puh·luhs). Local people could take refuge in the acropolis when invaders attacked. The Greeks built temples on the acropolis to honor local gods.

Outside the acropolis was an open area called an **agora** (A·guh·ruh). This space was used as a marketplace. It was also an area where people could gather and debate issues, choose officials, pass laws, and carry out business. City neighborhoods surrounded the agora. Just beyond the city were the villages and farmland that also were part of the polis.

Reading HELP DESK

polis a Greek city-state

agora a gathering place; marketplace in ancient Greece

Because most city-states were surrounded by mountains and seas, they were usually small. Some were only a few square miles in area, while others covered hundreds of square miles. By 500 B.C., nearly 300,000 people lived in the city-state of Athens. Most city-states, however, were much smaller.

What Did Citizenship Mean to the Greeks?

Today, in the United States, a person who is born here is considered a citizen. We owe many of our ideas about citizenship to the ancient Greeks.

Who was a Greek citizen? Citizens were members of a political community with rights and responsibilities. In Greece, male citizens had the right to vote, hold public office, own property, and defend themselves in court. In return, citizens had the responsibility to serve in government and to fight for their polis as citizen soldiers. Ancient Greek citizenship was very different from that of ancient Mesopotamia or Egypt, where most people were subjects. They had no rights, no voice in government, and no choice but to obey their rulers.

In most Greek city-states, only free, land-owning men born in the polis could be citizens. They believed the responsibility to run the city-state was theirs because the polis was made up of their property. Some city-states later ended the requirement of owning land for a person to be a citizen. Women and children might qualify for citizenship, but they had none of the rights that went with it.

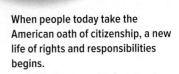

When people today take the American oath of citizenship, a new life of rights and responsibilities begins.

In the agora at Athens, people of different professions met in different parts of the space. Theatrical performances were also held here.

Citizen Soldiers

In Greece, wars were fought by wealthy nobles riding horses and driving chariots. By 700 B.C., citizens called hoplites (HAHP·lyts) made up the city-state armies. The hoplites fought on foot. Each heavily armed soldier carried a round shield, a short sword, and a spear. During battles, rows of hoplites marched forward together, shoulder to shoulder. They raised their shields above them to protect them from the enemy's arrows. This unified formation is called a **phalanx** (FAY·langks).

The success of the hoplites came from their pride in fighting as brave warriors. In Athens, for example, soldiers took this oath:

PRIMARY SOURCE

" I will not disgrace my sacred arms nor desert my comrade, [fellow soldier] wherever I am stationed [located]… And I will observe the established laws and whatever laws in the future may be reasonably established. If any person seek to overturn the laws … I will oppose him. I will honor the religion of my fathers. "

—from *Athenian Ephebic Oath*, tr. Clarence A. Forbes

The polis gave Greek citizens a sense of belonging. This is similar to how people feel about their home states today. The citizens put the needs of the polis above their own. Such strong loyalty to their own city-state divided the Greeks. They were not as unified as a whole country. This lack of unity weakened Greece, making it easier to conquer.

✓ PROGRESS CHECK

Explaining What were the rights and responsibilities of Greek citizens?

The Greek soldiers' round shield was important for survival in battle.

phalanx a group of armed foot soldiers in ancient Greece arranged close together in rows

---

LESSON 1 REVIEW

Review Vocabulary

1. Explain the difference between a *colony* and a *polis*.

Answer the Guiding Questions

2. *Analyzing* What were the ancient Greeks' most important economic activities?

3. *Explaining* How did the Minoans develop wealth?

4. *Summarizing* What happened to Mycenaean civilization during the Dark Age?

5. *Explaining* Why did the Greeks establish colonies?

6. **INFORMATIVE/EXPLANATORY** How did Greek city-states apply democracy? How did they limit democracy? Write a short essay explaining your answers.

Sparta and Athens: City-State Rivals

ESSENTIAL QUESTION

• Why do people form governments?

IT MATTERS BECAUSE
The city-states of Athens and Sparta had two quite different governments. Athenian democracy strongly influenced later forms of democracy.

Political Changes

GUIDING QUESTION *Which types of government did the Greek city-states have?*

As Greek city-states grew, wealthy nobles seized power from kings. They did not rule very long, however. Owners of small farms resented the nobles' power. Many of the farm owners had borrowed money from the nobles to buy land. When the farmers could not repay the loans, the nobles often took their land. The farmers then had to work for the nobles or move to the city to find jobs. In some cases, they even had to sell themselves into slavery.

By 650 B.C., small farmers wanted political change and a greater voice in government. Merchants and artisans also called for reforms. Merchants and artisans had earned a good living in the growing city-states. However, because they did not own land, they were not **considered** citizens. That meant they had no role in ruling the polis.

The growing unrest led to the rise of tyrants. A **tyrant** (TY·ruhnt) is someone who seizes power and rules with total authority. Most tyrants who commanded city-states ruled fairly.

Reading HELPDESK

Taking Notes: *Comparing*

Use a Venn diagram like this one to compare life in Sparta and Athens.

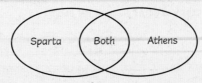

Sparta   Both   Athens

Content Vocabulary

• **tyrant**   • **helot**
• **oligarchy**   • **ephor**
• **democracy**

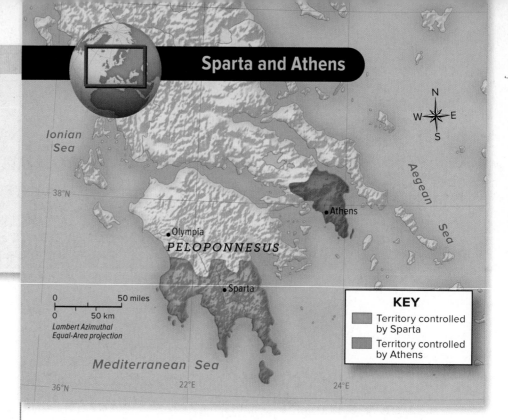

GEOGRAPHY CONNECTION

Sparta and Athens were the dominant city-states in ancient Greece.

1 LOCATION About how many miles apart were Sparta and Athens?

2 CRITICAL THINKING
Analyzing Which city-state's geography might make it more open to attack in a military battle? Explain.

However, the harsh rule of a few tyrants gave the word *tyranny* its current meaning; that is, rule by a cruel and unjust person.

The common people of Greece supported the tyrants when they overthrew the nobles during the 600s B.C. Tyrants also gained support from the hoplites, or citizen soldiers, in the army. Tyrants strengthened their popularity by building new temples, fortresses, and marketplaces. Nevertheless, most Greeks objected to rule by a single person. They wanted a government in which all citizens could participate.

Tyrants ruled many of the Greek city-states until about 500 B.C. From then until 336 B.C., most city-states developed into either oligarchies or democracies. In an **oligarchy** (AH·luh·gahr·kee), a few wealthy people hold power over the larger group of citizens. In a **democracy** (dih·MAH·kruh·see), all citizens share in running the government. Two of the major city-states, Sparta and Athens, were governed differently and created very different societies.

✔ PROGRESS CHECK

Evaluating Why were tyrants able to hold power in various Greek city states?

Reading**HELP**DESK

tyrant an absolute ruler unrestrained by law

oligarchy a government in which a small group has control

democracy a government by the people

Academic Vocabulary

consider to give careful thought

Sparta: A Military Society

GUIDING QUESTION *Why did the Spartans focus on military skills?*

The city-state of Sparta was located on the Peloponnesus (peh·luh·puh·NEE·suhs) Peninsula in southern Greece. The Spartans were descended from the Dorians who invaded Greece in the Dark Age. Like other city-states, Sparta's economy was based on agriculture.

Sparta did not set up overseas colonies. Instead, Sparta invaded neighboring city-states and enslaved the local people. The Spartans called their enslaved laborers **helots** (HEH·luhts), a word that comes from the Greek word for "capture."

A Strong Military

About 650 B.C., the helots revolted against their Spartan masters. The Spartans crushed that uprising. Sparta's leaders wanted to prevent future revolts. They decided to make Sparta a **military** society that stressed discipline. They also believed in simplicity, and strength through self-denial. The leaders thought that a military society created more obedient and loyal citizens.

Sparta's government prepared all boys and men for a life of war. Boys left their homes at age seven to join the military. In military camps, they learned to read, write, and use weapons. They also were treated harshly. The military leaders believed that harsh treatment would turn the young boys into adults who would survive the pain of battle. The Greek historian Plutarch (PLOO·tahrk) described life for Spartan boys:

Spartan warriors depended on their training to help them survive.

▶ **CRITICAL THINKING**
Synthesizing What types of weapons were used in hand-to-hand combat?

PRIMARY SOURCE

❝They were enrolled in certain companies ..., where they all lived under the same order and discipline, doing their exercises and taking play together. Of these he who showed the most conduct and courage was made captain; they ... obeyed his orders and underwent patiently whatsoever punishment he inflicted [delivered]; so that the whole course of their education was one continued exercise of a ready and perfect obedience.❞

—from *Plutarch: The Lives of the Noble Grecians and Romans*

North Wind/North Wind Picture Archives

---

helots enslaved people in ancient Sparta

Academic Vocabulary

military relating to soldiers, arms, or war

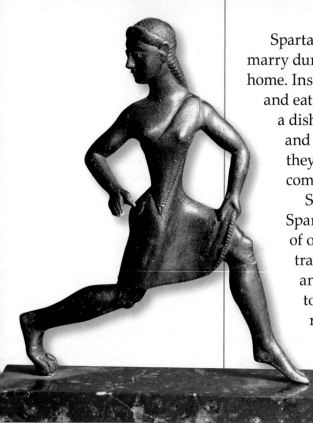

Physical fitness was important for Spartan women. Girls trained in sports to increase their athletic abilities.

Spartan men entered the regular army at age 20. Men could marry during their twenties, but they were not allowed to live at home. Instead, they stayed in military camps, sharing barracks and eating meals with other soldiers. A typical army meal was a dish called black broth—pork boiled in animal blood, salt, and vinegar. Spartan men could live at home again when they reached the age of 30, but they continued to train for combat. They finally retired from the army at age 60.

Since many Spartan men lived away from home, Spartan women enjoyed more freedom than the women of other Greek city-states. They could own property and travel. Girls were trained in sports, such as wrestling and throwing the javelin. They remained physically fit to fulfill their roles as mothers. Their main goal was to raise sons who were brave, strong Spartan soldiers.

Spartan women expected their men to either win or die in battle. Spartan soldiers must never surrender. One Spartan mother ordered her son to "Come home carrying your shield or being carried on it."

How Was Sparta Governed?

Sparta's government was an oligarchy. Two kings ruled jointly, but they had little power. Their only duties were to lead the army and carry out religious ceremonies. In addition to the kings, Sparta had two other governing bodies, the assembly and the council of elders.

The assembly included all male citizens over the age of 30. The assembly made decisions about war and peace. However, the council of elders was the most powerful body in the government. Council members served as judges. They were the only officials who could order executions or exile. Each year, the council elected five people to be **ephors** (EH·fuhrs). The ephors enforced the laws and managed the collection of taxes.

Sparta's strict government brought **stability**. But that stability cost the people of Sparta. Because the government feared losing the helots, it discouraged free thinking and new ideas. Officials believed learning could lead to unrest. As a result, Sparta did not welcome foreign visitors and prevented citizens from traveling outside the city-state except for military reasons. It even discouraged people from studying literature and the arts.

Reading**HELP**DESK

ephor a high-ranked government official in Sparta who was elected by the council of elders

Academic Vocabulary

stability the condition of being steady and unchanging

In addition, Sparta resisted other types of change. For example, Spartans continued to use heavy iron bars for money when other Greeks used coins. This discouraged trade and isolated Sparta from the rest of Greece. While other city-states built up business and trade and improved their standard of living, Sparta remained a poor farming society.

For Sparta's strong, well-trained army, the only important goals were military power and victory. The Spartans **achieved** Greece's greatest military strength and power. Sparta would play a key role in defending Greece against invaders.

✔ PROGRESS CHECK

Determining Cause and Effect Why did Sparta fall behind other Greek city-states in many areas?

Athens: A Young Democracy

GUIDING QUESTION *How did the culture in Athens differ from other Greek city-states?*

The Italian artist Raphael painted this picture, *School of Athens*, in 1510–11. This shows younger students mixing with teachers and older students.

Another great Greek city-state was Athens. It was located northeast of Sparta, about a two-day trip away. Athens was founded by the descendants of the Mycenaeans and differed from Sparta in its ideas about society and government.

An Athenian Education

Athenians received an education far different from that of the Spartans. Athens educated its males, as Sparta did. In Athenian schools, boys studied subjects such as arithmetic, geometry, drawing, music, and public speaking. They also participated in sports. The Athenians believed that this type of education produced young people with strong minds and bodies. At age 18, when boys finished school, they were expected to take an active role in public affairs.

Academic Vocabulary

achieve to succeed; to gain something as the result of work

Solon (c. 630 B.C.–560 B.C.)

The great reformer Solon was the son of a well-to-do family, but he did not live the life of a rich Greek. Solon was a poet and a lawmaker. His goal was to find agreement between nobles and farmers who needed to be able to work together. He improved the economy by requiring all sons to continue in the same job their fathers had. He promoted trade by farmers and rewrote the Athenian constitution.

▶ **CRITICAL THINKING**
Predicting How do you think people today would accept Solon's ruling that sons follow fathers in their life's work?

This clay ballot was used to select jurors for Athenian courts. How different is the ballot voters use today?

Reading HELP DESK

Academic Vocabulary
construct to build

Athenian mothers educated their daughters at home. Girls were taught spinning, weaving, and other household duties. In some wealthy families, they learned to read, write, and play music. Women were expected to marry and care for their children. For the most part, women were not active in business or government in Athens.

Early Reforms

The history of Athens was much like that of the other Greek city-states. By about 600 B.C., most Athenian farmers owed money to the nobles. Some farmers were forced to sell themselves into slavery to repay their debts. Athenians began to rebel. Farmers called for an end to all debts. They also asked that land be distributed to the poor.

To avoid an uprising, the nobles agreed to make some changes. They turned to a respected merchant named Solon (SOH·luhn) for leadership. In 594 B.C., Solon ended the farmers' debts and freed those who were enslaved. He also opened the assembly and the law courts to all male citizens. The assembly was responsible for passing laws written by a council of 400 wealthy citizens.

The common people praised Solon's reforms. Still, many Athenians were unhappy. Wealthy people felt Solon had gone too far, while poor people thought he had not gone far enough. By the time Solon left office, he had lost much of his support.

In 560 B.C., a tyrant named Peisistratus (py·SIHS·truht·uhs) took over the government. A relative of Solon, Peisistratus made reforms that went even further than those that Solon had made. Peisistratus divided large estates among farmers who had no land. He provided loans to help farmers buy equipment to work their farms. He gave citizenship to Athenians who did not own land. He also hired the poor to **construct** temples and other public works. Since religion was important in Athens, Peisistratus built additional shrines to different gods. He also encouraged the worship of the goddess Athena. Under Peisistratus, festivals held to honor Athena were expanded by the addition of athletic contests.

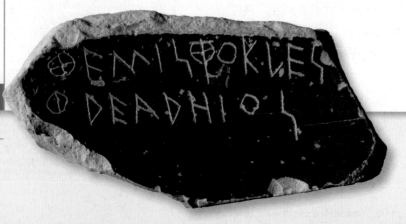

Toward Democracy

After the death of Peisistratus, a noble named Cleisthenes (KLYS·thuh·neez) became the next leader of Athens. Prizing democracy, Cleisthenes made the assembly the city-state's major governing body. As before, all male citizens could participate in the assembly and vote on laws. Assembly members could now discuss issues freely, hear legal cases, and appoint army officials.

Cleisthenes also created a new council of 500 citizens. They were to help the assembly manage daily government affairs. The council introduced laws and controlled the treasury. They also managed relations with other city-states. Each year Athenian citizens held a lottery to choose the council members. Athenians preferred the lottery system over an election. In their view, an election might unfairly favor the rich, who were well-known. Terms on the council were limited to one year, and no one could serve on the council for more than two terms. Thus, every citizen had a chance to be a council member.

While Cleisthenes's reforms made the government of Athens more democratic, many residents were still excluded from the political process. People who were not citizens still could not participate in the government. This group included all Athenian women, foreign-born men, and enslaved people.

☑ **PROGRESS CHECK**

Explaining Why was Solon chosen to be leader of Athens?

Connections to
TODAY

The Olympics

The ancient Olympic Games were held every four years at Olympia, in the western part of Greece, in honor of the god Zeus. The first Olympics were organized in 776 B.C. According to one legend, the founder of the games was the hero Hercules. The modern Olympics began in 1896 in Athens.

In the 500s B.C., Athenian pottery was decorated with dramatic black and red images of heroes and gods.

SuperStock/Getty Images

LESSON 2 REVIEW

Review Vocabulary

1. What might a *tyrant* say to citizens who are asking for democracy?

Answer the Guiding Questions

2. *Explaining* Why were the tyrants able to seize control in Athens?

3. *Determining Cause and Effect* Why did the Spartans emphasize military training?

4. *Describing* How did Athenians feel about the changes Solon put in place?

5. *Identifying* What was a major accomplishment of Cleisthenes?

6. **NARRATIVE** You are a student living in ancient Sparta or Athens. Write a journal entry that describes a day in your life.

There's More Online! connected.mcgraw-hill.com

LESSON 3

Greece and Persia

ESSENTIAL QUESTION

• Why does conflict develop?

IT MATTERS BECAUSE

Although it was large and powerful, the Persian Empire could not defeat the Greeks.

Persia's Empire

GUIDING QUESTION *How did the Persians rule a vast empire?*

About the time that the government in Athens was undergoing political changes, the Persians were building a powerful empire in Southwest Asia. Persia (PUHR·zhuh), the homeland of the Persians, was located in what is today southwestern Iran.

Early Persians were warriors and cattle herders from the grasslands of central Asia. After settling in the highlands of Persia, they came under the control of other peoples. Then a dynasty of kings brought the Persians together into a powerful kingdom. In the 500s B.C., a talented king named Cyrus (SY·ruhs) the Great built a strong Persian army. With that army, he began creating an empire that became the largest in the ancient world.

Creating an Empire

During the 540s B.C., Persian troops swept into neighboring lands. They brought Mesopotamia, Syria, Judah, and the Greek city-states of the area of Anatolia under Persian rule. King Cyrus held his growing empire together by treating conquered peoples fairly. He allowed them to keep their own languages, religions, and laws. In addition, Cyrus decided that the Jews exiled in Babylon would be allowed to return to their homeland.

Reading HELP DESK

Taking Notes: *Identifying*

As you read the lesson, fill in a chart like this one with the names of participants.

Persian Kings Attacking Greece	Greek Defenders

Content Vocabulary

• **satrapy**
• **satrap**
• **Zoroastrianism**

After Cyrus, other Persian rulers continued to expand the empire. Their armies took over Egypt, western India, and lands to the northeast of Greece. From west to east, the Persian Empire stretched a distance of some 3,000 miles (4,800 km). This is about the size of the continental United States today.

To link this large territory, the Persians improved the network of roads begun by the Assyrians. The most important route, the Royal Road, ran more than 1,500 miles (2,400 km) from Persia to Anatolia. Travelers could **obtain** food, water, and fresh horses at roadside stations along the route. Using the Royal Road, messengers could travel from Persia to Anatolia in just seven days. That same journey had taken three months before the road was built.

Persian Government

As the Persian Empire expanded, its increasing size made it more difficult to manage. Darius I (duh·RY·uhs), who ruled Persia from 522 to 486 B.C., reorganized the government to make it more efficient. He divided the empire into provinces called **satrapies** (SAY·truh·peez). Each satrapy was ruled by a governor called a **satrap** (SAY·trap), which means "defender of the kingdom." The satrap collected taxes, judged legal cases, managed the police, and recruited soldiers for the Persian army.

GEOGRAPHY CONNECTION

Persian kings built the Royal Road to connect the areas of their large empire.

1 **MOVEMENT** About how far was the shortest distance from Greece to the western end of the Royal Road?

2 **CRITICAL THINKING**
Making Inferences Based on the map, why might the Persian Empire have posed a danger to Greece?

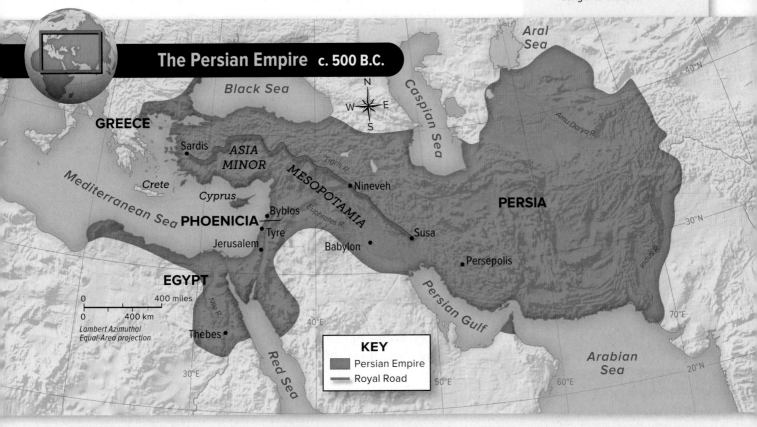

The Persian Empire c. 500 B.C.

Aral Sea
Black Sea
GREECE
Sardis
ASIA MINOR
Crete
Cyprus
Mediterranean Sea
PHOENICIA Byblos
Tyre
Jerusalem
EGYPT
Thebes
Tigris R.
Nineveh
MESOPOTAMIA
Euphrates R.
Babylon
Susa
Persepolis
Caspian Sea
Amu Darya R.
PERSIA
Indus R.
Persian Gulf
Red Sea
Nile R.
Arabian Sea

0   400 miles
0   400 km
Lambert Azimuthal
Equal-Area projection

40°N
30°N
20°N
30°E   40°E   50°E   60°E   70°E

KEY
Persian Empire
Royal Road

satrapy the territory governed by an official known as a satrap

satrap the governor of a province in ancient Persia

Academic Vocabulary

obtain to acquire or receive something

King Darius I of Persia established Persepolis as the center of his government. This sculpture from one of the main buildings in Persepolis shows a line of nobles and dignitaries waiting to speak with the king.

▶ **CRITICAL THINKING**
Speculating The artist shows all of the nobles, except one, facing forward. Why do you think the artist chose to show one person looking back?

This Zoroastrian holy site is in present-day Iran.

(t)DEA /W. BUSS/Getty Images; (b)roberto fumagalli/Age fotostock

Persia maintained a full-time, paid, professional army. In comparison, the Greek army consisted of citizens called to serve only during times of war. The best fighters in the Persian army were the 10,000 soldiers who were trained to guard the king. They were known as the Immortals because when a member died, another soldier immediately took his place.

Who Was Zoroaster?

The Persians at first worshipped many gods. Then, sometime in the 600s B.C., a religious teacher named Zoroaster (ZOHR·uh·WAS·tuhr) preached a new monotheistic religion. Most Persians accepted his religion, which was called **Zoroastrianism** (zohr·uh·WAS·tree·uh·nih·zuhm).

Zoroaster taught that there was one supreme god. This deity was called Ahura Mazda, or "Wise Lord." Ahura Mazda was the creator of all things and the leader of the forces of good. Zoroaster believed that evil existed in the world. People were free to choose between good and evil, but at the end of time, goodness would be victorious. Zoroastrian teachings, prayers, and hymns (sacred songs) were written down in a holy book. Because of Zoroastrianism, the Persians began to view their monarchy as a sacred institution or role.

Reading**HELP**DESK

Zoroastrianism a Persian religion based on the belief of one god

Persian kings believed that they ruled by the power of Ahura Mazda and were responsible to him alone. Darius I had the following statement carved on a cliff:

PRIMARY SOURCE

" For this reason Ahura Mazda [the Zoroastrian god] bore me aid... because I was not an enemy, I was not a deceiver, I was not a wrong-doer, neither I nor my family; according to rectitude [righteousness] I ruled. "

—from Darius I, *Behistun Inscription*, column 4, line 4.13

After Darius's rule ended, the Persians continued to practice Zoroastrianism for centuries. The religion has about 200,000 followers today. Most of them live in South Asia.

 **PROGRESS CHECK**

Explaining How did Persian rulers unite their vast empire?

The Persian Wars

GUIDING QUESTION *How did the Greeks defeat the Persians?*

As the 400s B.C. began, the Persians were ready to expand into Europe. However, they soon clashed with the Greeks, who had colonies in the Mediterranean area. Persia and Greece were very different civilizations. While the Persians obeyed an all-powerful king, many of the Greeks believed that citizens should choose their own rulers and government.

As a result of the conquests made by Cyrus, the Persians already controlled the Greek cities in Anatolia. In 499 B.C., these Greeks revolted against their Persian rulers. The Athenians sent warships to help the rebels, but the Persians crushed the uprising. The Persian king Darius was angry that the Athenians interfered. He decided to punish the mainland Greeks for meddling in his empire.

How Did the Greeks Win at Marathon?

In 490 B.C., Darius sent a fleet of 600 ships and an army to invade Greece. The Persians landed at Marathon (MAR·uh·thahn), which was a plain about 25 miles (40 km) northeast of Athens. The Persians waited there for several days. They expected the Greeks to come there and fight them. However, the Athenians did not come forward. They had only 10,000 troops compared to the Persians' 20,000 soldiers.

King Darius I, shown in this carving, believed that the Zoroastrian god approved of his rule.

Build Vocabulary: *Words With Multiple Meanings*

One word can have many meanings, depending on how the word is used in a sentence. The noun *fleet*, for example, means "a group of vehicles operated under one control." As an adjective, *fleet* means "fast" or "temporary."

©Gianni Dagli Orti/Corbis

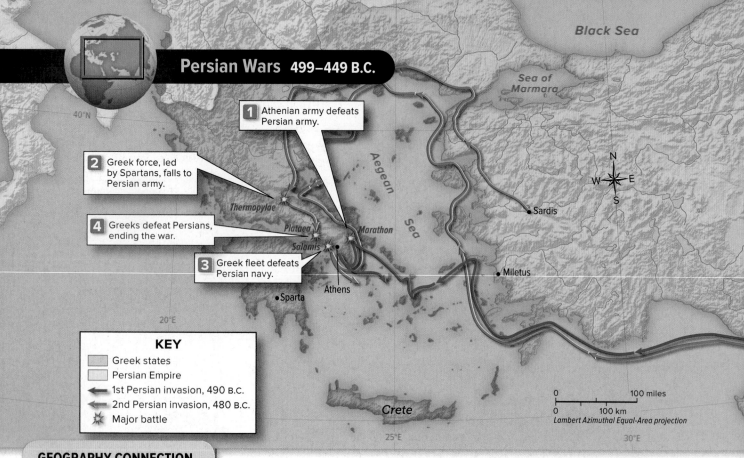

Persian Wars 499–449 B.C.

1 Athenian army defeats Persian army.

2 Greek force, led by Spartans, falls to Persian army.

4 Greeks defeat Persians, ending the war.

3 Greek fleet defeats Persian navy.

Black Sea

Sea of Marmara

Aegean Sea

Sardis

Miletus

Thermopylae

Plataea

Salamis

Marathon

Athens

Sparta

Crete

40°N

20°E

25°E

30°E

KEY

- Greek states
- Persian Empire
- ← 1st Persian invasion, 490 B.C.
- ← 2nd Persian invasion, 480 B.C.
- ✹ Major battle

0 — 100 miles
0 — 100 km
Lambert Azimuthal Equal-Area projection

GEOGRAPHY CONNECTION

The Greek city-states successfully defended their territory against two invasions by the Persian Empire.

1 **LOCATION** Which Greek city-state defeated the Persian army in a major battle?

2 **CRITICAL THINKING** *Speculating* Why might the Greek city-states have had an advantage over the Persians?

When their enemy refused to fight, the Persians decided to sail directly to Athens and attack it by sea. The Persians began loading their ships with their strongest units—the cavalry. As soon as the Persian horsemen were on the ships, the Athenians charged down the hills and onto the plain of Marathon. The Athenians caught the Persian foot soldiers standing in the water, out of formation. They were without any help from their cavalry.

The Persians suffered a terrible defeat. According to Greek legend, a young messenger raced 25 miles from Marathon to Athens with news of the victory. When the runner reached Athens, he cried out "Victory" and then **collapsed** and died from exhaustion. Today's marathon races are named for that famous run and are just over 26 miles (42.2 km) long.

Land and Sea Battles

After the defeat at Marathon, the Persians vowed revenge against the Athenians. In 480 B.C., a new Persian king named Xerxes (ZUHRK·seez) invaded Greece with about 200,000 troops and thousands of warships and supply vessels. The Greek city-states banded together to fight the Persians.

Reading**HELP**DESK

Academic Vocabulary

collapse to break down; to lose effectiveness

Reading Strategies: *Ask Questions*

Asking questions as you read helps you understand what you read. Ask questions with the words *who, what, why, where, when,* and *how.*

King Leonidas (lee·AH·nuh·duhs) of Sparta supplied the most soldiers. Themistocles (thuh·MIHS·tuh·kleez) of Athens directed the Greek naval forces and devised a battle plan.

Persian ships supplied the invaders with food. Themistocles wanted to attack the Persians' ships and cut off the army's supplies. To do this, the Greeks had to stop the Persian army from reaching Athens. Sparta's King Leonidas led 7,000 soldiers into a battle that lasted for three days. The Spartans' bravery at Thermopylae (thur·MAH·puh·lee) was much celebrated.

The Greeks, however, could not stop the Persians at Thermopylae. A traitor showed the Persians a trail leading around the Greek line, allowing them to attack from behind. Realizing that his Greek army would soon be surrounded, Leonidas dismissed most of the troops. He and 300 Spartans remained and fought to the death. The Greek historian Herodotus (hair·RAH·deh·tuhs) gave this description of the battle:

PRIMARY SOURCE

❝ They [the Spartans] defended themselves to the last, those who still had swords using them, and the others resisting with their hands and teeth; till the barbarians [Persians], who in part … had gone round and now encircled them upon every side, overwhelmed and buried the remnant [remainder] which was left beneath showers of missile weapons. ❞

—from *The Histories* by Herodotus

Connections to TODAY

Marathons

The first marathon runner is said to have been a Greek soldier. He is thought to have run from Athens to Sparta.

The first Olympic marathon—which took its name from that battle—was held when the modern games began in 1896. In 1924, the Olympic marathon distance was set at 26 miles and 385 yards (42.195 km).

At the Battle of Salamis, smaller, faster Greek ships defeated the Persian fleet.

▶ **CRITICAL THINKING**
Analyzing Why were the Persians at a disadvantage in the battle?

The Persian king Xerxes watches his fleet battle the Greeks at the Battle of Salamis.

▶ CRITICAL THINKING

Contrasting Xerxes led his armies into battle. How is his role in wartime different from that played by most modern political leaders?

The Spartans' heroic stand gave Themistocles time to carry out his plan to attack Persia's ships. The Athenian fleet of ships lured the Persian fleet into the strait of Salamis (SA·luh·muhs), near Athens. A strait is a narrow **channel** of water between two pieces of land. The Greeks hoped this move would give them an advantage in battle. Themistocles believed that the heavy Persian ships would crowd together in the strait, making them difficult to move. His assumption proved to be correct. Vigorous fighting

©National Geographic Society/Corbis

took place between the two navies. The Greeks had fewer ships, but their boats were smaller and faster, and could outmaneuver the Persian ships. The plan worked. The Greeks sank about 300 Persian ships and lost only about 40 ships of their own. The Persian fleet was almost entirely destroyed. Still, the Persian foot soldiers marched on to Athens. Finding the city almost deserted, the Persians set it on fire.

The combined forces of the Greek city-states in 479 B.C. formed their largest army yet. They had improved their fighting forces with better armor and weapons. At Plataea (pluh·TEE· uh), northwest of Athens, the Greek army again faced the Persians. In numbers, the two sides were evenly matched. Each fielded a force of about 100,000 men. This time, however, the Greeks defeated the Persian army. Fighting continued as the Greeks went on the defensive to free the city-states in Anatolia from Persian rule. Peace between the Greek allies and the Persians did not come until 449 B.C.

Decline of Persia

After its losses in Greece, Persia faced many challenges. The Persian army was no longer strong enough to defend the entire empire. Also, the Persian people grew unhappy with their government. The kings taxed the people heavily to pay for magnificent palaces and other luxuries. Members of the royal family disagreed about who should rule.

As Persia weakened, it became open to outside attacks. In the 300s B.C., Persia could not resist the invasion of an army led by a young and powerful ruler named Alexander. The Persian Empire ended, and a new Greek empire emerged that extended beyond even Persia's boundaries.

☑ **PROGRESS CHECK**

Explaining After the losses in Greece, why did the Persians grow unhappy with their government?

LESSON 3 REVIEW

Review Vocabulary

1. What were the responsibilities of the *satrap*?

Answer the Guiding Questions

2. *Explaining* Why did Darius I create satrapies?

3. *Determining Cause and Effect* What brought Sparta and Athens together as allies?

4. *Analyzing* Why did Persia invade Greece?

5. *Differentiating* Which Persian leader do you think made the biggest contribution? Why?

6. **ARGUMENT** You are an officer in the Athenian army. The Persians have just landed at Marathon to invade Greece. Write a letter to a friend explaining why the Athenian army did not go out to fight the Persians when they arrived at Marathon.

LESSON 4

Glory, War, and Decline

ESSENTIAL QUESTION

- How do governments change?

IT MATTERS BECAUSE

The Peloponnesian War had a decisive effect on Greece. Greek culture declined after the Athenian loss to Sparta.

The Rule of Pericles

GUIDING QUESTION *How did Pericles influence government and culture in Athens?*

As the Persian Wars ended, Athens became a powerful and self-confident city-state. From 461 B.C. to 429 B.C., the Athenians, under their new leader Pericles (PEHR•uh•kleez), enjoyed a golden age of prosperity and achievement. Their city-state became the economic and cultural center of Greece. Athens also practiced democratic government.

Democracy in Athens

Athenians took great pride in their democratic system. The form of government practiced by the Athenians is called **direct democracy** (dih•MAH•kruh•see). In a direct democracy, all citizens meet to debate and vote on government matters. In a **representative democracy**, such as the one we have in the United States today, citizens elect a smaller group of people. This group represents them, makes laws, and governs on their behalf.

In ancient Athens, direct democracy worked because of its relatively small number of citizens. The assembly consisted of some 43,000 male citizens over the age of 18. Often, however, fewer than 6,000 participated in the meetings, which were held

Reading HELPDESK

Taking Notes: ***Identifying***

Use a chart like this one to list the accomplishments during the age of Pericles.

Age of Pericles

Content Vocabulary

- **direct democracy**
- **representative democracy**
- **philosopher**

every 10 days. At those meetings, participating citizens passed laws, elected officials, and made policy on war and foreign affairs. The ten top officials, elected each year, were known as generals.

Pericles in Charge

After the Persian Wars, the most important general in Athenian government was Pericles. His wise rule guided the city-state for more than 30 years.

Pericles made Athens a more democratic city-state. He appointed people to positions because of their abilities, not because they were members of a certain social class. Pericles brought more ordinary Athenians into government. As a result, even shopkeepers and laborers could, for the first time, share in the government along with nobles and farmers.

Under Pericles's rule, Athens became a center of learning and the arts. The Persians had burned much of the city during the Persian Wars. Under Pericles, Athens was rebuilt. He erected new temples, monuments, and statues throughout the city.

Pericles also supported writers, artists, teachers, sculptors, and architects. **Philosophers** (fuh·LAH·suh·fuhrs) also flourished during the rule of Pericles. Philosophers are thinkers who reflect on the meaning of life. Athens became a great center for knowledge. Pericles called the city "the school of Greece."

✓ PROGRESS CHECK

Explaining How was Athens able to become a direct democracy?

Political discussion was highly popular in Athens.

▶ CRITICAL THINKING
Speculating Citizens in Athens would meet on a hill in the city set aside for political discussion. What issues do you think Athenian citizens might have debated there?

©National Geographic Society/Corbis

direct democracy a form of democracy in which all citizens can participate firsthand in the decision-making process

representative democracy a form of democracy in which citizens elect officials to govern on their behalf

philosopher a person who searches for wisdom or enlightenment

Athens was able to have a direct democracy because it had a low number of citizens.

1 **IDENTIFYING** In Athens, what involvement could citizens have in the passage of laws?

2 **CRITICAL THINKING** *Analyzing* Under which government does a broader segment of the population have the right to vote?

	Athenian Democracy	American Democracy
Type of Democracy	Direct	Representative
Right to Vote	Only adult males born in Athens	All citizens, male and female age 18 or over
Laws	Proposed by the council and approved by a majority in the assembly	Approved by both houses of Congress and signed by the president
Citizen Involvement	Citizens with voting rights can vote for or against any law	Citizens with voting rights can vote for or against the officials who make the laws

Athenian Life

GUIDING QUESTION *What was life like for Athenians under the rule of Pericles?*

At its height in the 400s B.C., Athens was the largest Greek city-state. Its population numbered about 285,000. Of this number, about 150,000 were citizens. Only 43,000 of these citizens, however, were males who had political rights. Athens was home to about 35,000 foreigners and 100,000 enslaved people.

Athenian Men and Women

Athenian men worked as farmers, artisans, and merchants. They often finished their daily work in the morning. They spent afternoons exercising at the gymnasium. In the evening, upper-class men enjoyed all-male gatherings where they ate, drank, and discussed philosophy or politics.

Athenian women focused on their homes and families. Girls married at a young age, often in their mid-teens. Their duties centered on having children and taking care of their households. Women of poor families helped with the farm work or sold goods in the local marketplace. Most upper-class women rarely left their houses except to attend funerals and festivals. Even then, they had to be **accompanied** by a male relative. Upper-class women generally supervised the servants and spun, dyed, or wove cloth.

Athenian women could not attend school, but many learned to read and to play music. However, Athenian society did not consider educated women as equal to men. Women could not participate in political activities or own property. Greek women were always under the care of a male family member. Husbands were responsible for their wives and unmarried daughters. Sons looked after their widowed mothers.

A few women had more freedom, especially foreigners, who were regarded differently than Athenian-born women. One well-regarded woman was Aspasia (as·PAY·zhuh). She was known for her intelligence and charm. Aspasia taught public speaking, and her ideas were popular among Athenians. Both Plato (PLAY·toh), the famous Greek philosopher, and Pericles were influenced by her.

What Was the Role of Slavery in Athens?

Slavery was common in ancient civilizations. It was often considered to be a normal part of life, even by enslaved people themselves. Even in a democracy like Athens, slavery was common. Most Athenian households had at least one enslaved person. Wealthy Athenian families often had several.

Many enslaved people were prisoners who had been captured in battle. These included both Greeks and non-Greeks. Enslaved men worked on farms, in the shops of artisans, or at hard labor. Enslaved women were cooks and servants in wealthy homes and sometimes taught upper-class children. The treatment of enslaved people varied. Those who labored in mines often died very young. Slaves who worked as craftspeople had easier lives. Sometimes, enslaved people could earn money and, in rare cases, buy their freedom. Slavery might have helped Athens develop its prosperous economy.

BIOGRAPHY

Aspasia (c. 470–400 B.C.)

Aspasia originally came from the Greek-speaking city of Miletus in Asia Minor. Her beauty and intellect made her a democratic symbol to many Greeks who treated her like a modern rock star.

She aggressively entered into the male-dominated society and government of Greece. She was one of the first women to encourage other females to participate in government and demand their rights.

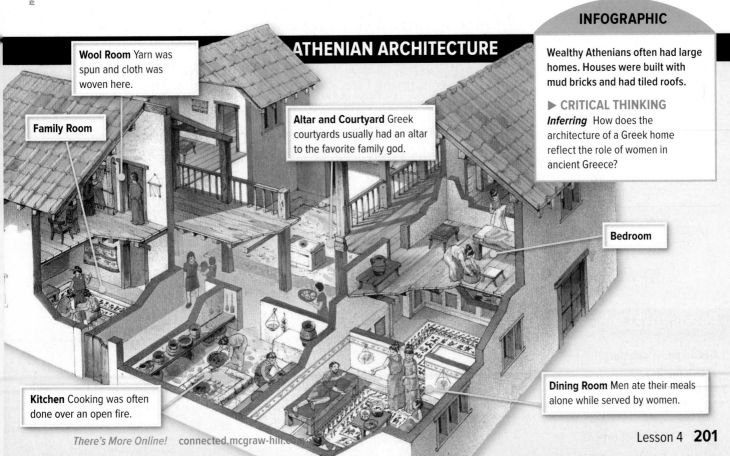

ATHENIAN ARCHITECTURE

Wool Room Yarn was spun and cloth was woven here.

Family Room

Altar and Courtyard Greek courtyards usually had an altar to the favorite family god.

Bedroom

Kitchen Cooking was often done over an open fire.

Dining Room Men ate their meals alone while served by women.

INFOGRAPHIC

Wealthy Athenians often had large homes. Houses were built with mud bricks and had tiled roofs.

▶ **CRITICAL THINKING**
Inferring How does the architecture of a Greek home reflect the role of women in ancient Greece?

There's More Online! connected.mcgraw-hill.c

Marble lions like this one guarded the way from the harbor to the temples in Delos.

The Athenian Economy

Farming was a common occupation among Athenians. Local farmers grew grains, vegetables, and fruits, including grapes and olives to make wine and olive oil for shipment to foreign markets.

Athenian farms lacked **sufficient** land to grow enough food to support the city-state. Although Athenians grew some grain, they had to import more from other places. Athens built a large fleet of ships to trade with colonies and other city-states in the Mediterranean world. During the 400s B.C., Athens led the Greek world in trade. Important goods made and traded in Athens included pottery and leather products.

✔ **PROGRESS CHECK**

Comparing and Contrasting How did the roles of Athenian men and women differ?

War Between Athens and Sparta

GUIDING QUESTION *How did the Peloponnesian War affect the Greek city-states?*

As time passed, the Greek city-states learned that their survival depended on cooperation. Even after the Persian Wars ended, the Persian threat against Greece remained. In 478 B.C., Athens joined with other city-states to form a defensive league, or protective group, to defend its members against the Persians. Because the league at first had its headquarters on the island of Delos (DEE·LAHS), it became known as the Delian League.

Athens provided the Delian League with most of its sailors and soldiers, while the other city-states supplied money and ships. During the next several **decades**, the league drove Persia out of the remaining Greek territories in Anatolia. Free of Persian domination, Greece grew richer through increased overseas trade.

The Athenian Empire

In spite of its successes, the Delian League failed. Athens was the strongest city-state, and the league's officials and commanders and most of the troops were Athenian. Over time, Athens began to use its influence to control the other member city-states. The league was no longer an alliance of equal city-states fighting Persia. It had become a group of city-states controlled by Athens.

Christian Handl/imagebroker/Age fotostock

Pericles's leadership helped Athens dominate the Delian League. He treated the other city-states like subjects, demanding strict loyalty and regular payments from them. He even insisted that they use Athenian coins and measures. In 454 B.C., the Athenians moved the Delian League's treasury from Delos to Athens. They also sent troops to other Greek city-states to help the common people rebel against the nobles in power.

War Breaks Out

As the economic and political power of Athens grew, other city-states, especially Sparta, became alarmed. Politically and socially, Sparta and Athens were quite different. Neither trusted the other. Both wanted to be the major power in the Greek world.

Sparta became the leader of an alliance of city-states opposed to Athens. In 433 B.C., Athens began interfering with some of Sparta's allies. These allies pressured Sparta to attack Athens. War broke out in 431 B.C. and continued until 404 B.C. The possibility of future cooperation among the Greek city-states disappeared as a result of this war. Historians call this **conflict** the Peloponnesian War because Sparta was located in the Peloponnesus.

Pericles's Funeral Oration

During the war's first winter, Athens held a public funeral to honor soldiers who had died in battle. Afterward, the Athenian families gathered to mourn their losses. In a famous speech, called the *Funeral Oration*, Pericles talked about the greatness of Athens and reminded the people that they made their government strong. He reminded them that citizens had to obey the rules in their constitution—their framework of government. They accepted certain duties, such as paying taxes and defending the city. They were also awarded certain rights, such as the ability to vote and run for office.

PRIMARY SOURCE

" Our constitution is called a democracy because power is in the hands not of a minority but of the whole people. When it is a question of settling private disputes, everyone is equal before the law. ... "

—Pericles, *Funeral Oration*, quoted in *History of the Peloponnesian War*

In his speech, Pericles **emphasized** that the democratic way of life is worth protecting. He urged his listeners to have the courage to continue fighting. The ideas Pericles expressed are still valued by citizens of democratic countries today.

The historian Thucydides described Pericles as "the first citizen" of Athens.

▶ **CRITICAL THINKING**
Evaluating Pericles was not an emperor, a king, or even a president, yet he was able to lead Athens to the greatest glories the city would ever know. How do you think he was able to accomplish what he did?

César Crespo/Age fotostock

Academic Vocabulary

conflict a battle or war
emphasize to attach a sense of importance to something; to express the importance of something

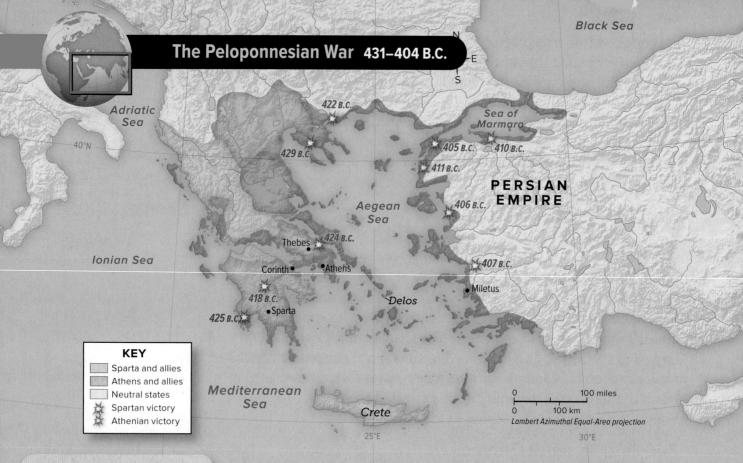

The Peloponnesian War 431–404 B.C.

Black Sea

Adriatic Sea

40°N

422 B.C.

429 B.C.

Sea of Marmara

405 B.C.   410 B.C.

411 B.C.

PERSIAN EMPIRE

Aegean Sea

406 B.C.

Thebes 424 B.C.

Ionian Sea

Corinth   Athens

407 B.C.

418 B.C.

Miletus

425 B.C.   Sparta

Delos

KEY

- Sparta and allies
- Athens and allies
- Neutral states
- ✶ Spartan victory
- ✶ Athenian victory

Mediterranean Sea

Crete

25°E

0   100 miles

0   100 km

Lambert Azimuthal Equal-Area projection

30°E

GEOGRAPHY CONNECTION

The Peloponnesian War between Sparta and Athens lasted for 27 years.

1 PLACE In what year was the final battle of the war? In whose territory was it fought?

2 CRITICAL THINKING
Speculating Which cities were on the side of Athens? Why do you think having those allies was not enough help for Athens to win the war?

Why Did Athens Lose the War?

In a battle soon after the war started, Sparta and its allies surrounded Athens. They knew that, in an open battle, they could easily defeat the Athenian army. Pericles understood the weakness of the Athenian troops. He chose to keep his army and the people within the walls of the surrounded city. The powerful Athenian navy would bring supplies to the city from its colonies and allies. Sparta lacked a navy and could not stop the Athenian ships.

For almost two years, Athens remained safe. Then a deadly disease broke out within the overcrowded city's population. More than a third of the people died, including Pericles. During the next 25 years, each side won some victories but was unable to defeat its opponent.

Finally, Sparta made a deal with the Persian Empire. The Spartans agreed to give the Persians some Greek territory in Anatolia. In return, Sparta received enough Persian gold to build its own navy.

Reading HELP DESK

Reading Strategy: *Rereading*

When a paragraph is difficult to understand, try reading it again. Read it once to understand the main idea. Read it again to understand the details.

As the war dragged on, Athens fell into a state of unrest. The democracy had been overthrown. The government that replaced it was then overthrown. By the end of 411 B.C., democracy had been restored. The war, however, continued. In 405 B.C., Sparta's newly built navy destroyed the Athenian fleet. Sparta then placed a blockade around Athens, preventing food and other supplies from entering the city. Starving, the Athenians finally surrendered a year later. The Spartans and their allies then knocked down the city walls. The Athenian empire collapsed.

The Effects of the War

The Peloponnesian War brought disaster to the Greek city-states. The governments were left divided and weak. Many people had died in battle or from disease. Fighting had destroyed farms and left many people with no way to earn a living. As a result, thousands of young Greeks left Greece to join the Persian army.

After the conflict, Sparta ruled its newly acquired empire, much as Athens had ruled its empire before. This harsh treatment angered Sparta's former allies. An uneasy political situation developed. During the next 30 years, Sparta tried to put down rebellions and fought Persia again. Finally, in 371 B.C., the city-state of Thebes seized Sparta and ended the Spartan empire. About 10 years later, Thebes also collapsed.

As the city-states fought, they failed to notice the growing threat from the kingdom of Macedonia to the north. Macedonia's strength and desire for expansion would eventually cost the Greek city-states their independence.

☑ PROGRESS CHECK

Explaining Why was Sparta's deal with Persia so important in the war against Athens?

LESSON 4 REVIEW

Review Vocabulary

1. Explain why a group taking a vote on something is an example of a *direct democracy*.

Answer the Guiding Questions

2. *Describing* How did Pericles choose people for positions in the government in Athens?

3. *Explaining* What jobs did enslaved people in Athens do?

4. *Determining Cause and Effect* Why did the Delian League break apart?

5. *Identifying* What was the most important accomplishment of Pericles?

6. **ARGUMENT** Ancient Athens was a direct democracy. The United States Constitution provides for a representative democracy. Do you think the United States should change to a direct democracy? Why or why not?

Write your answers on a separate piece of paper.

1 **Exploring the Essential Question**

INFORMATIVE/EXPLANATORY Why does conflict develop? Write an essay describing the ways that conflict played an important role in the lives of the ancient Greeks. In your writing, discuss such examples as Mycenaeans versus Minoans, Persia versus Greece, and Athens versus Sparta.

2 **21st Century Skills**

ANALYZING AND MAKING JUDGMENTS Which of these experiences would help you to better understand the meaning of *democracy*?

- **A.** running for class president
- **B.** trading games with your friend
- **C.** picking up litter in your neighborhood
- **D.** checking out a book at a library

3 **Thinking Like a Historian**

COMPARING AND CONTRASTING Create a diagram like the one below to compare and contrast the causes and effects of the Persian Wars with those of the Peloponnesian War.

Persian Wars	Peloponnesian War

4 **GEOGRAPHY ACTIVITY**

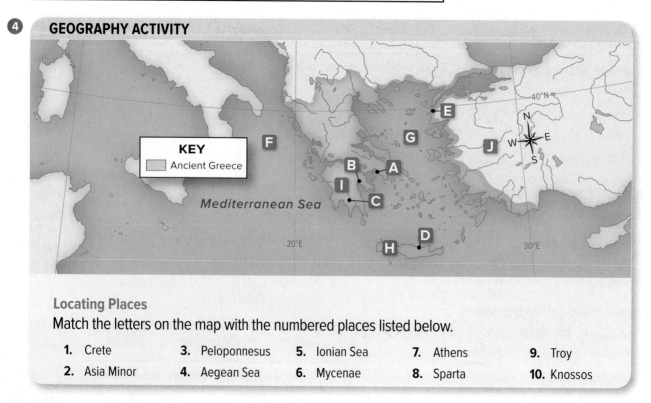

Locating Places

Match the letters on the map with the numbered places listed below.

1. Crete
2. Asia Minor
3. Peloponnesus
4. Aegean Sea
5. Ionian Sea
6. Mycenae
7. Athens
8. Sparta
9. Troy
10. Knossos

Directions: Write your answers on a separate piece of paper.

CHECKING FOR UNDERSTANDING

1 Identify the meaning of the following words.

A. peninsula	**J.** helot
B. bard	**K.** ephor
C. colony	**L.** satrapy
D. polis	**M.** satrap
E. agora	**N.** Zoroastrianism
F. phalanx	**O.** direct democracy
G. tyrant	**P.** representative democracy
H. oligarchy	**Q.** philosopher
I. democracy	

REVIEW THE GUIDING QUESTIONS

2 *Explaining* How did the mountains of Greece affect the development of ancient Greek communities?

3 *Identifying* Who were important trading partners of the Minoans? What goods did the Minoans trade?

4 *Listing* List the major factors that contributed to the decline of the Mycenaeans.

5 *Describing* What effect did Greek colonization have on the Mediterranean and Black Sea regions?

6 *Stating* How did ancient Greek citizenship differ from that of most other ancient civilizations?

7 *Identifying* What were the two main forms of government in Greek city-states?

8 *Summarizing* How did the Spartans' emphasis on military discipline affect the citizens of Sparta?

9 *Contrasting* How was the education Athenian boys received different from that of boys in Sparta?

10 *Listing* What were the main duties of the satraps?

11 *Determining Cause and Effect* What was the consequence of the Battle of Salamis?

12 *Identifying* Who was Pericles, and how did he influence life in Athens?

13 *Explaining* How did the Peloponnesian War weaken Greek city-states?

CRITICAL THINKING

14 *Evaluating* Which event of the Dark Age of Greek history do you consider the most significant? Explain.

15 *Identifying Evidence* Which democratic concepts developed in ancient Greece served as a foundation for American constitutional democracy? How are these concepts applied in the United States today?

16 *Speculating* Why do you think Cleisthenes created a council of citizens to help the assembly manage Athenian government?

17 *Assessing* Which form of government was superior: Spartan or Athenian? Support your response.

18 *Analyzing Maps* Study the Persian Wars map found in Lesson 3. Where were the major battles of the Persian Wars fought? How did this impact the Greek city-states during and after the wars?

19 *Drawing Conclusions* Why is the Age of Pericles sometimes referred to as the "Golden Age" of Athens?

20 *Compare and Contrast* How is the role of women in modern American society different from that of women in ancient Athens? How is it similar?

Need Extra Help?

If You've Missed Question	**1**	**2**	**3**	**4**	**5**	**6**	**7**	**8**	**9**	**10**	**11**	**12**	**13**	**14**	**15**	**16**	**17**	**18**	**19**	**20**
Review Lesson	1,2, 3,4	1	1	1	1	1	2	2	2	3	3	4	4	1	1	2	2	3,4	4	4

DBQ SHORT RESPONSE

"Further, we [Athenians] provide plenty of means [ways] for the mind to refresh itself from business. We celebrate games and sacrifices all the year round, and the elegance of our private establishments forms a daily source of pleasure ... while the magnitude [large size] of our city draws the produce of the world into our harbor."

—from Pericles' Funeral Oration, quoted in
The Complete Writings of Thucydides

21 How did Athenians live a more varied lifestyle than Spartans?

22 In what ways might a modern city want to imitate ancient Athens?

EXTENDED RESPONSE

23 *Informative/Explanatory* The lives of Athenian girls were very different from the lives of girls today. Write a brief essay that explains the differences, giving real-life examples.

STANDARDIZED TEST PRACTICE

DBQ ANALYZING DOCUMENTS

Greek historian Plutarch describes the state-run education of boys in Sparta:

"Reading and writing they gave them, just enough to serve their turn; their chief care was to make them good subjects, and to teach them to endure pain and conquer in battle."

—from Plutarch, *The Lives of the Noble Grecians and Romans*

24 *Identifying* Spartans were educated and trained to be

A. lawyers.

B. politicians.

C. soldiers.

D. doctors.

25 *Drawing Conclusions* According to Plutarch, what Spartan educators most wanted from students was for them to

A. write epics.

B. win wars.

C. reject discipline.

D. serve in the assembly.

Need Extra Help?

If You've Missed Question	**21**	**22**	**23**	**24**	**25**
Review Lesson	2,4	2,4	2	2	2

◀ *This marble bust of Alexander the Great, carved in 330 B.C., is in the Louvre, a famous museum located in Paris, France.*

700 B.C. TO 212 B.C.

Greek Civilization

THE STORY MATTERS ...

Alexander became king of Macedonia when he was only 20 years old. Before his death at age 32, he built the largest empire the world had known. His strong will and personality enabled him to lead armies to victory. He is considered one of the greatest generals who ever lived.

Alexander's childhood tutor was the Greek philosopher Aristotle, who encouraged Alexander's interest in philosophy, medicine, and science. As an adult, Alexander spread Greek art, ideas, language, and architecture into all the lands he conquered. The impact of his rule lasted for centuries.

ESSENTIAL QUESTIONS

- What makes a culture unique?
- How do new ideas change the way people live?
- What are the characteristics of a leader?

Danita Delimont/Gallo Images/Getty Images

Place & Time: Greek Civilization 700 B.C. to 212 B.C.

The Greeks are remembered for their advances in the study of science, philosophy, mathematics, and the arts. When Alexander the Great conquered the Persian Empire, he spread Greek culture and ideas throughout southwest Asia and the Mediterranean world.

Step Into the Place

MAP FOCUS By 100 B.C., Alexandria was the largest city in the Mediterranean world. Alexandria included two excellent harbors, a towering lighthouse, and a library with the largest collection of writings in ancient times.

1 **LOCATION** Look at the map. On which continent is Alexandria located?

2 **PLACE** What happened at Chaeronea?

3 **CRITICAL THINKING**
Analyzing How might the region's physical features allow Greek culture to spread to other areas?

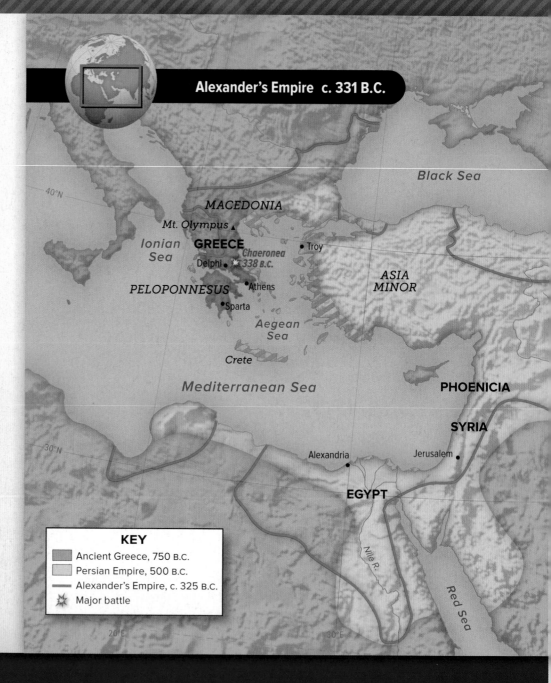

Alexander's Empire c. 331 B.C.

KEY
- Ancient Greece, 750 B.C.
- Persian Empire, 500 B.C.
- Alexander's Empire, c. 325 B.C.
- ✷ Major battle

Step Into the Time

TIME LINE Choose an event from the time line and write a paragraph predicting the general social, political, or economic consequences that event might have on the world

c. 700s B.C. Homer writes the *Iliad* and the *Odyssey*

776 B.C. First Olympic Games

ANCIENT GREECE
THE WORLD

800 B.C.   650 B.C.

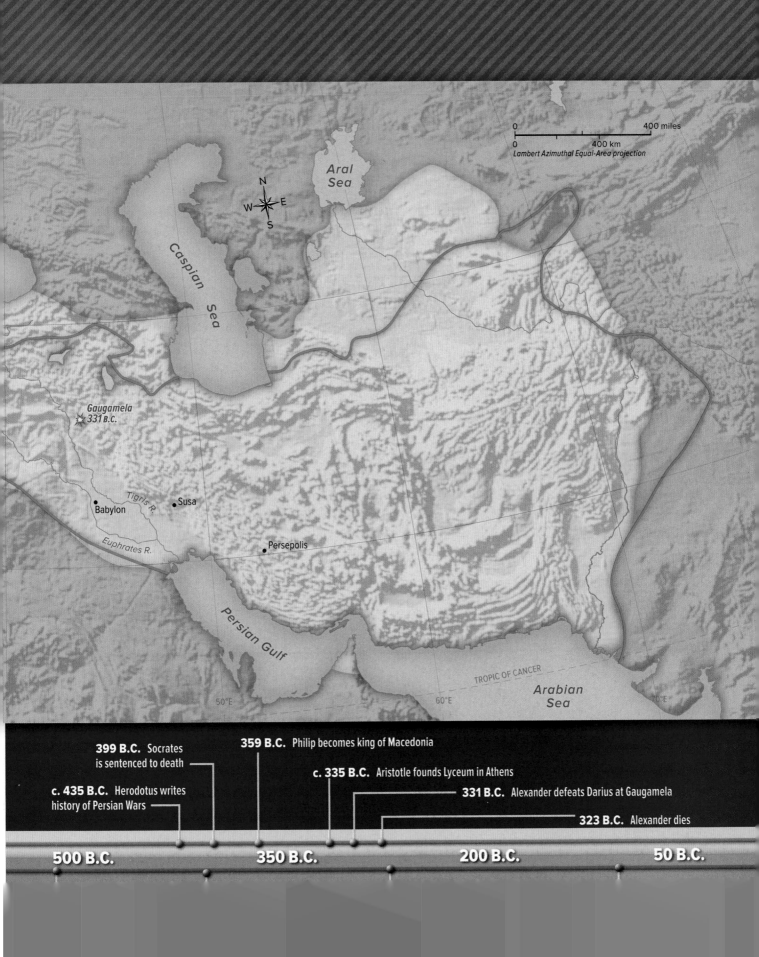

Aral Sea

Caspian Sea

Gaugamela
331 B.C.

Tigris R.
Babylon
Susa
Euphrates R.
Persepolis

Persian Gulf

TROPIC OF CANCER

Arabian Sea

50°E   60°E   70°E

0   400 miles
0   400 km
Lambert Azimuthal Equal-Area projection

399 B.C. Socrates
is sentenced to death

359 B.C. Philip becomes king of Macedonia

c. 335 B.C. Aristotle founds Lyceum in Athens

c. 435 B.C. Herodotus writes
history of Persian Wars

331 B.C. Alexander defeats Darius at Gaugamela

323 B.C. Alexander dies

500 B.C.   350 B.C.   200 B.C.   50 B.C.

LESSON 1

Greek Culture

• What makes a culture unique?

IT MATTERS BECAUSE
The Greeks made many advancements that continue to shape our world.

Greek Beliefs

GUIDING QUESTION *How did the ancient Greeks honor their gods?*

You have learned that the ancient Greeks formed city-states. These are independent states made up of a city and the land that surrounds it. Although city-states separated Greece politically, the Greek people were united by a common culture. They spoke the Greek language. They shared many beliefs and customs. The Greek people also believed many of the same **myths**, or traditional stories about gods and heroes. Greek myths expressed the religious beliefs of the ancient Greeks.

Who Were the Greek Gods?

Like other people of the ancient world, the Greeks believed in gods and goddesses. The Greeks, however, did not think of their gods as all-powerful beings. In Greek myths, the gods have great powers, but they look and act like human beings. In Greek mythology, they marry and have children. At times, they act like children, playing tricks on each other. Because the gods showed human qualities, the Greek people did not fear them. Greeks believed that the 12 most important gods and goddesses lived on Mount Olympus (uh·LIHM·puhs), Greece's highest mountain.

Reading**HELP**DESK

Taking Notes: *Summarizing*
Use a diagram like this one to identify three ways Greek culture influences our world today.

Greek Influences

Content Vocabulary

• **myth**   • **fable**   • **tragedy**
• **ritual** • **oral tradition** • **comedy**
• **oracle** • **drama**

GREEK GODS AND GODDESSES

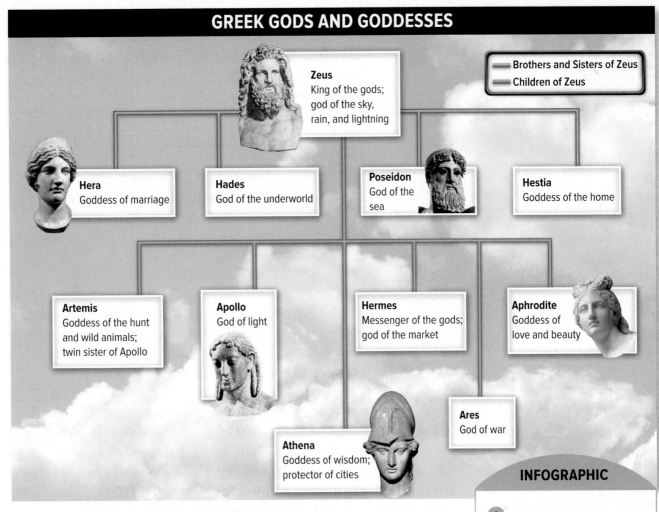

Brothers and Sisters of Zeus
Children of Zeus

Zeus
King of the gods; god of the sky, rain, and lightning

Hera
Goddess of marriage

Hades
God of the underworld

Poseidon
God of the sea

Hestia
Goddess of the home

Artemis
Goddess of the hunt and wild animals; twin sister of Apollo

Apollo
God of light

Hermes
Messenger of the gods; god of the market

Aphrodite
Goddess of love and beauty

Athena
Goddess of wisdom; protector of cities

Ares
God of war

(tl)DEA/G. DAGLI ORTI/Getty Images; (tcl)©Bettmann/Corbis; (tr)DEA/G. NIMATALLAH/Getty Images; (bl)SuperStock/Getty Images; (bc)Danita Delimont/Gallo Images/Getty Images; (br)Buena Vista Images/Getty Images; (bkgd) Don Farrall/Photodisc/Getty Images

A gate of clouds protected Olympus. The gods could come and go as they pleased, but humans were stopped from entering through the gate of clouds.

Zeus was the king of the Olympian gods, while Athena was the goddess of wisdom and crafts. Apollo was worshipped as the god of the sun and poetry. People looked up to Aphrodite, the goddess of love. Two fierce gods were Ares, the god of war, and Poseidon, the god of the seas and earthquakes.

All Greeks worshipped Zeus as their chief god. Each city-state also chose one god or goddess as its protector. To win the favor of their god, the people of the city-state performed rituals. A **ritual** (RIH·chuh·wuhl) is an action that is part of a religious ceremony. The people worshipped the god in temples and at home. They prayed and offered gifts to the god. Through these rituals, the Greeks hoped the god would reward them.

INFOGRAPHIC

1 **IDENTIFYING** Which god or goddess protected the city of Athens?

2 **CRITICAL THINKING**
Analyzing How were Athena and Hera related?

---

myth a traditional story that explains the practices or beliefs of a people, or something in the natural world

ritual words or actions that are part of a religious ceremony

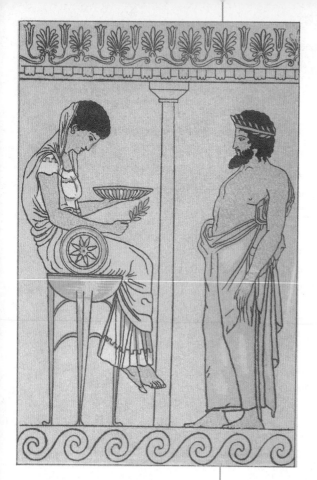

Greeks visited oracles for predictions and advice about their futures.

▶ CRITICAL THINKING

Analyzing Why do you think people sometimes misunderstood the oracles' predictions?

Festivals honoring the gods and goddesses were an important part of Greek life. Each city-state scheduled public feasts and sacrifices. Every four years, Greek athletes took part in athletic competitions. These games were "for the greater glory of Zeus." They were held at the city of Olympia and were called the Olympic Games. Beginning in 776 B.C., the ancient Olympic Games took place for more than 1,000 years. The first modern Olympics were held in 1896 in Athens.

The Greeks believed their gods would be pleased if people showed skill in the arts, in athletic games, or in thinking.

Greek Oracles

The Greeks believed that each person had a fate or destiny. Certain events were going to happen no matter what they did. They also believed in prophecy, or a prediction about the future. The Greeks believed that the gods gave prophecies to warn people about the future in time to change it.

To find out about the future, many Greeks visited an **oracle** (AWR·uh·kuhl). This was a sacred shrine where a priest or priestess spoke for a god. The most famous was the oracle at the Temple of Apollo at Delphi (DEHL·fy). The oracle chamber was deep inside the temple. The room had an opening in the floor where volcanic smoke hissed from a crack in the earth.

There a priestess sat on a stool and listened to questions. The priests translated her answers. State leaders or their messengers traveled to Delphi to ask advice from the Oracle of Apollo.

☑ PROGRESS CHECK

Explaining Why did the ancient Greeks seek advice from oracles?

Epics and Fables

GUIDING QUESTION *Why were epics and fables important to the ancient Greeks?*

Greek poems and stories are some of the oldest literature in Western civilization. For hundreds of years, Europeans and Americans used ancient Greek works as models for writing their own literature. England's William Shakespeare is an example.

Mary Evans Picture Library

Reading**HELP**DESK

oracle a sacred shrine where a priest or priestess spoke for a god or goddess

Academic Vocabulary

construct to build

He borrowed Greek plots and settings for his many dramas. He also organized his plays similarly to the way Greek dramas were organized.

The first Greek stories were epics. Two great epics of ancient Greece were the *Iliad* and the *Odyssey*. The poet Homer (HOH·muhr) composed them during the 700s B.C. Homer based these epics on stories about a war between Greece and the city of Troy. Troy once existed in the area that is today northwestern Turkey.

The Trojan Horse

In the *Iliad*, a prince of Troy falls in love with Helen, the wife of a Greek king, and kidnaps her. The kidnapping angers the Greeks, who attack Troy in revenge. The Greeks, however, cannot break through the thick walls surrounding the city. In order to get into the city, the Greeks trick the Trojans and **construct** a huge, hollow wooden horse. The finest Greek soldiers hide inside the horse. All the other Greek soldiers board ships and sail away.

The Trojans think they have won the war and that the horse is a victory prize from the Greeks. The Trojans roll the giant horse into the city. That night, the Greeks creep out of the horse and open the city gates. They allow the rest of the Greek army, who have sailed back to Troy after dark, to enter the city. The Greeks then capture the city, rescue Helen, and take her home.

The *Odyssey* tells the story of Odysseus (oh·DYS·ee·uhs), a Greek hero of the Trojan War. It describes his long trip home after the fall of Troy. He faces storms, monsters, and witches along the way. Odysseus finally returns to his wife. According to the poem, it takes Odysseus 10 years to accomplish his arrival in Greece. Today, people use the word *odyssey*—a word taken from his name—to describe a long, exciting journey.

The epic the *Iliad* tells how the Greeks built the Trojan Horse as a way to get a small group of soldiers into Troy. The term "Trojan Horse" is still used today to mean the use of deception.

The Greek soldiers hid in the belly of the horse.

Troops left the horse through a trapdoor.

The wooden horse was placed on a platform with wheels.

Greeks believed the *Iliad* and the *Odyssey* were more than stories. They looked on the epics as real history. These poems gave the Greeks an ideal past with a cast of heroes. One Athenian wrote, "My father, in his pains to make me a good man, compelled me to learn the whole of Homer's poems."

Homer's stories taught courage and honor. They also taught that it was important to be loyal to your friends and to value the relationship between husband and wife. The stories showed heroes striving to be the best they could be. Heroes fought to protect their own honor and their family's honor. Homer's heroes became role models for Greek boys.

PRIMARY SOURCE

❝ O friends, be men; so act that none may feel
Ashamed to meet the eyes of other men.
Think each one of his children and his wife,
His home, his parents, living yet or dead. ❞

— from *The Iliad* by Homer,

Aesop's Fables

Have you heard the stories "The Fox and the Grapes" or "The Boy Who Cried Wolf"? These stories have traditionally been credited to a man named Aesop (EE·sahp). He is supposed to have lived and told his stories around 550 B.C. Historians now know that Aesop probably never existed. However, the stories he is supposed to have told certainly do exist. They are known as Aesop's fables. A **fable** (FAY·buhl) is a short tale that teaches a lesson. In most of Aesop's fables, animals speak and act like people. These stories are often funny and show human weaknesses and strengths. Each fable ends with a moral, or useful truth.

One of Aesop's popular fables is "The Hare and the Tortoise." In this fable, a slow-moving tortoise, or turtle, and a speedy hare, or rabbit, race each other. Soon, the hare is far ahead. Sure of victory, the hare stops to take a nap. Meanwhile, the tortoise keeps slowly moving. He passes the sleeping rabbit and wins the race.

The moral of the story is "slow and steady wins the race." Many phrases from Aesop's fables are still in use, including: "It is easy to dislike something you cannot have," and "Appearances can be deceiving."

Aesop's fables teach moral lessons in an entertaining way.

▶ **CRITICAL THINKING**
Theorizing Why might Aesop have used animal characters to tell his fables?

Alinari/Art Resource, NY

ReadingHELPDESK

fable a story meant to teach a lesson

oral tradition the custom of passing along stories by speech

Aesop's fables were told during the time that is known as the Golden Age of Greece. During this period, art, philosophy, architecture, and literature flourished.

For 200 years, Aesop's fables were a part of Greek **oral tradition**. This means that the stories were passed from generation to generation by word of mouth. It took many years before these tales were written down. Since then, Aesop's fables have been translated into many languages. They are still read by people around the world today.

✓ PROGRESS CHECK

Describing How do fables usually end?

The Impact of Greek Drama

GUIDING QUESTION *How did Greek dramas develop?*

The ancient Greeks created and performed the first dramas (DRAH·muhs). A **drama** is a story told mainly through the words and actions of a cast of characters. A drama is performed by actors. In ancient Greece, they were performed on stage. Many of today's movies, plays, and television shows are dramas.

Think about your favorite movie. How would you describe it? Is it humorous? Is it a serious story? Greek drama can be divided into two categories: tragedy and comedy. In a **tragedy** (TRA·juh·dee), the main character struggles to overcome hardships but does not succeed. As a result, the story has a tragic, or unhappy, ending. The earliest Greek plays were tragedies. Later, the Greeks also wrote comedies. In a **comedy** (KAH·muh·dee), the story ends happily. Today, the word *comedy* means a story filled with humor.

During the fifth century B.C., four writers emerged as the greatest Greek dramatists, or writers: Aeschylus, Sophocles, Euripides, and Aristophanes. These four dramatists wrote their plays during the Golden Age of Greece, which was from about 500 to 350 B.C.

Aeschylus (EHS·kuh·luhs) was the earliest Greek dramatist. One of his dramas is a set of three plays called the *Oresteia* (ohr·eh·STY·uh). This drama tells about a Greek king's return from the Trojan War and the troubles that strike his family. The Oresteia is a story about revenge and murder. It shows how one evil action can lead to another. Although the play ends tragically, good triumphs over evil in the end.

Then

Theaters in ancient Greece were often located outside. Plays took place in a level semicircle partially surrounded by stepped seating.

Today, most plays are performed in enclosed theaters like the one below. However, you can still attend plays at outdoor theaters in Greece and in other parts of the world.

Now

▶ CRITICAL THINKING
Speculating Why do you think Greek plays were performed outside?

(t)Gaetano Barone/SuperStock,(b)©Eric Robert/Corbis

---

drama a story written in the form of a play

tragedy a play or film in which characters fail to overcome serious problems

comedy a play or film that tells a humorous story

Athena
The statue of Athena, covered in ivory and gold, was about 43 feet high.

Treasure Room
Held the city's gold.

Greek architects used these three styles of columns

Doric   Ionic   Corinthian

Festival
Athenians came to honor Athena every four years.

INFOGRAPHIC

The Greeks built the Parthenon to honor Athena.

1 **DESCRIBING** What features of the temple tell you that it was built by the Greeks?

2 **CRITICAL THINKING**
Drawing Conclusions Why were temples the most important buildings in Greek city-states?

Sophocles (SAH·fuh·kleez) was a great Athenian writer. In his plays, Sophocles accepted suffering as a real part of life. He also stressed courage and understanding. In his play *Antigone* (an·TIH·guh·nee), Sophocles questions whether it is better to obey orders or to do what one believes to be right.

Another leading Greek dramatist was Euripides (yuh·RIH·puh·deez). Unlike Aeschylus and Sophocles, Euripides wrote about ordinary human beings in realistic situations. His plays often show the suffering caused by war.

In theaters today, the actors include men, women, and children. In ancient Greece, however, only men could be actors. Even female characters were played by male actors. The most famous writer of Greek comedies was Aristophanes (ar·uh·STAH·fuh·neez). His works poked fun at the leaders and issues of his day. He encouraged people to think and laugh. Many of Aristophanes' comedies included jokes, just as television comedy shows do today.

Reading**HELP**DESK

Academic Vocabulary

conflict a fight or disagreement
style a distinctive form or type of something

How Greek Drama Developed

Drama was more than entertainment for the people of ancient Greece. It was part of religious festivals and a way to show loyalty to their city-state.

In early Greek dramas, a group of performers, called the chorus, presented the story through singing and dancing. Later, dramas used several actors on stage. Then, stories were created using action and **conflicts** among the characters.

✓ PROGRESS CHECK

Determining Cause and Effect How did Greek drama influence how people are entertained today?

Greek Art and Architecture

GUIDING QUESTION *What ideas did the Greeks express in their art and architecture?*

The ancient Greeks excelled in the arts and architecture. They created works that expressed the ideals of reason, balance, and harmony. The characteristics of Greek art became the artistic **style** that we now call classical. Classical Greek art set standards of beauty that people still admire today.

The Greeks constructed beautiful buildings. Every Greek city-state had a temple dedicated to a god or goddess. Temples such as the Parthenon included a central room that housed statues of the gods. Large, graceful columns supported many Greek buildings. Some famous buildings in Washington, D.C., such as the White House and the Capitol, have Greek columns.

Sculpture decorated many Greek temples. The human body was the favorite subject of Greek artists. Greek sculptors tried to show ideal beauty in perfect human forms.

The design of the Lincoln Memorial in Washington, D.C., is similar to the Parthenon. Its 36 columns represent the number of states in the union at the time President Lincoln died.

✓ PROGRESS CHECK

Explaining How did the Greeks design their buildings?

Brand X Pictures/PunchStock

LESSON 1 REVIEW

Review Vocabulary

1. How is a *fable* part of an *oral tradition*?

Answer the Guiding Questions

2. *Explaining* Why was Mount Olympus important to the Greeks?

3. *Identifying* What epic included the story of the Trojan horse?

4. *Comparing* What two types of drama did the Greeks create? How do they differ?

5. *Inferring* Why are some computer viruses called Trojan horses?

6. **INFORMATIVE/EXPLANATORY** Compare Greek theater actors to modern theater actors. How are they alike and different? Write a paragraph or two that compares these types of actors.

LESSON 2
The Greek Mind

ESSENTIAL QUESTION

• How do new ideas change the way people live?

IT MATTERS BECAUSE

Greek thinkers developed ideas that shaped their world as well as ours today. The Greeks created the study of history, political science, biology, and logic.

Greek Thinkers

GUIDING QUESTION *What ideas did the Greeks develop to explain the world around them?*

The Greeks believed the human mind was capable of great understanding. During the Golden Age of Greece, from approximately 500 B.C. to 350 B.C., art, architecture, and literature all flourished. This was also a very fertile time for the life of the mind. Most of the thinkers discussed in this chapter were part of that exciting time. They were pondering deep questions about truth and also developing the study of science and mathematics. Greek thinkers produced some of the most remarkable ideas the world has ever known.

One type of thinker was involved in creating a new body of knowledge. These thinkers were known as philosophers. The body of knowledge they created is called philosophy (fih·LAH·suh·fee). Philosophy is a Greek word that means "love of wisdom." Through philosophy, Greek philosophers helped develop the study of many subjects, including history, political science, biology, and logic, or the study of reasoning.

Reading**HELP**DESK

Taking Notes: *Identifying*

Use a diagram like the one here to list the Greek thinkers you read about in this lesson. With each name you list, write down one thing the person is known for.

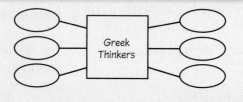

Greek Thinkers

Content Vocabulary

• **Sophists**
• **rhetoric**
• **Socratic method**
• **Hippocratic Oath**

The Sophists

Many Greek philosophers were teachers. A group of philosophers known as the **Sophists** (SAH·fihsts) traveled from polis to polis. They made a living by teaching. The Sophists taught many subjects, including mathematics, science, and history. However, they were best known for teaching **rhetoric**, or the art of public speaking and debate.

Sophists did not believe that the gods influenced human actions. They also **rejected** the idea of absolute right or wrong. For the Sophists, a way of life that was right for one person might be wrong for another.

The Sophists not only challenged Greek traditions, but they also accepted money for their teaching. Other Greek philosophers did not approve of this practice. Many Greeks also thought that the Sophists lacked ideals and values. Critics claimed the Sophists taught students to win arguments rather than seek truths.

Who Was Socrates?

Although a sculptor by training, Socrates (SAH·kruh·teez) loved philosophy. He lived in Athens and spent most of his time teaching. Socrates did not leave a written record of his beliefs. Information about him is found in his students' writings. These writings **reveal** that Socrates was a harsh critic of the Sophists.

Unlike the Sophists, Socrates believed in absolute truth and that all real knowledge was within each person. In his search for truth, Socrates created a new way of questioning called the **Socratic** (suh·KRA·tihk) **method**. Today, many university professors use the Socratic Method when they teach. Socrates did not lecture. Instead, he asked pointed questions and waited for his students to respond. He wanted students to find the answers for themselves and form their own opinions.

Some Athenian leaders believed that the Socratic method was dangerous. At one time, Athens had allowed its people to speak freely. They could publicly question their leaders. However, when Athens lost the Peloponnesian War, its new rulers limited this freedom. The Athenians no longer trusted open debate. This method of discussion, however, was exactly what Socrates thought was necessary. He continued to teach his students.

Socrates believed that obeying the law was more important than his own life. Rather than leave Athens, he accepted a sentence of death.

rhetoric the art of public speaking and debate
Sophists Greek teachers of philosophy, reasoning, and public speaking
Socratic method philosophical method of questioning to gain truth

Academic Vocabulary

reject to refuse to accept or consider
reveal to make information public; to tell a secret

There's More Online! connected.mcgraw-hill.com

©Araldo de Luca/Corbis

Plato (c. 428–347 B.C.)

Plato had planned a career in government. However, he was horrified by the death of his teacher, Socrates. As a result, Plato left politics and spent many years traveling and writing. When Plato returned to Athens in 387 B.C., he started the Academy, which was a school where students learned using Socrates' method of questioning. His academy attracted young people from Athens and other Greek city-states. He believed that by training the mind, people could discover truth. Plato's teachings and writings would influence the Western world for centuries.

▶ **CRITICAL THINKING**
Speculating Why do you think Plato felt he could not have a career in government?

In 399 B.C., city leaders—fearing his influence—arrested Socrates. They charged that he had urged young people to rebel against the government. A jury found Socrates guilty and sentenced him to death.

Following the verdict of the court, Socrates was given the opportunity to leave Athens and live. Instead, he stayed. Surrounded by his students and friends, Socrates gave his last speech.

He said that he was living under the city's laws. As a result, he stated, he was committed to obeying them. Socrates then drank poison to carry out the jury's sentence, and died.

Plato's Ideas

The two Greek philosophers you may have heard of are Plato and Aristotle. The philosopher Plato (PLAY·toh) was one of Socrates' students. Plato became a teacher and founded a school in Athens called the Academy. Unlike Socrates, Plato recorded his ideas in writing. One work Plato wrote was *The Republic*. It presented his plan for an ideal society and government.

In *The Republic*, Plato organized society into three groups. At the top were philosopher kings. They ruled through logic and wisdom. Warriors, the second group, defended society from attack, using force. The third group included the rest of the people. Their role was to produce society's food, clothing, and shelter. They lacked the wisdom of the kings and the courage of the warriors.

Plato believed that an ideal society must have a just and reasonable government. In *The Republic*, Plato noted his dislike of Athenian democracy. He wrote that the common people did not think for themselves and that they could be easily influenced into making foolish decisions. Plato believed that "philosopher kings" were intelligent and well-educated. He felt these kings would place the needs of the community ahead of their own needs. Plato wanted only these philosopher kings to govern the citizens of Greece.

Despite his distrust of the common people, Plato was willing to grant more rights to women. He believed that women should have the same opportunities for education and jobs that men have.

SEF/Art Resource, NY

Reading**HELP**DESK

Academic Vocabulary

despite in spite of, regardless of

Before starting his own school, the Lyceum, Aristotle taught at Plato's Academy. Here he tutors a young man who soon would be called Alexander the Great.

Who Was Aristotle?

Another great thinker of ancient Greece was Aristotle (AR·uh·stah·tuhl). He wrote more than 200 works on topics such as government, astronomy, and political science. In 335 B.C., Aristotle started a school called the Lyceum. At this school, he taught his students the "golden mean." The mean is the middle position between two extremes. The idea of the golden mean is that people should live moderately. For example, **individuals** should not eat too little or too much. Instead, they should eat just enough to stay well.

Aristotle had many interests, including science. He studied the stars, plants, and animals and carefully recorded what he observed. Aristotle classified living things according to their similarities and differences. Aristotle's methods were an important step in the development of modern science.

Like Plato, Aristotle also wrote about government. He studied and compared the governments of different city-states and hoped to find the best political system. In his book *Politics*, Aristotle divided governments into three types.

Academic Vocabulary

individuals human beings, persons

GREEK PHILOSOPHERS

Thinker Or Group	Sophists	Socrates	Plato	Aristotle
Main Idea	Sophists like Libanius (above) thought that people should use knowledge to improve themselves. They believed that there is no absolute right or wrong.	Socrates was a critic of the Sophists. He believed that there was an absolute truth.	Plato rejected the idea of democracy as a form of government. He believed that philosopher-kings should rule society.	Aristotle taught the idea of the "golden mean." He believed observation and comparison were necessary to gain knowledge.
Important Contribution	They developed the art of public speaking and debate.	He created the Socratic method of teaching.	He described his vision of the ideal government in his work the *Republic*.	He wrote over 200 books on philosophy and science. He divided all governments into three basic types.
Influence on Today	The importance of public speaking can be seen in political debates between candidates.	His methods influenced the way teachers interact with their students.	He introduced the idea that government should be fair and just.	His political ideas still shape political ideas today.

INFOGRAPHIC

The influence of Greek thinkers is felt today in education and politics.

1 **IDENTIFYING** What did the Sophists believe?

2 **CRITICAL THINKING**
Analyzing Would Plato approve or disapprove of the American system of government? Why?

The first was monarchy, or rule by one person. The second was oligarchy (OHL·uh·gahr·kee), which is rule by a few people. The third type was democracy, or rule by many.

Aristotle believed the best government had features of all three. A chief executive would serve as head of state. A council or legislature would assist this leader and be supported by the people.

Aristotle's ideas influenced the way Europeans and Americans thought about government. The authors of the United States Constitution, like Aristotle, believed that no one person or group should have too much power.

✓ PROGRESS CHECK

Explaining Why did Plato dislike Athenian democracy?

Reading**HELP**DESK

Academic Vocabulary

investigate to observe or study by examining closely and questioning systematically

New History and Science Ideas

GUIDING QUESTION *What did the Greeks believe about history and science?*

The Greeks used their thinking skills to write history. They also **investigated** the natural world. They developed new ways of studying science and history.

The Greeks and History

In many ways, the ancient Greeks were like most people living at that time. They believed that legends and myths were true. People did not analyze events in order to explain the past. Then, in 435 B.C., the Greek thinker Herodotus (hih·RAH·duh·tuhs) wrote a history of the Persian Wars. Herodotus wrote that the gods played a role in historical events. However, he made a great effort to separate fact from fiction. Like a news reporter, he questioned many people to get information, but then he investigated the truthfulness of these sources. Because of Herodotus's careful research, many European and American historians consider him "the father of history."

Another famous historian of ancient Greece was Thucydides (thoo·SIH·duh·deez). He was a general in the Peloponnesian War. The two great Greek city-states of Athens and Sparta fought in this conflict, which lasted nearly 30 years. Thucydides considered this war to be a major event in world history. After the war, he wrote *The History of the Peloponnesian War.*

Herodotus was careful about any information he recorded. He wanted to be sure of the accuracy of what he wrote.

Unlike Herodotus, Thucydides rejected the idea that the gods affected human history. Thucydides believed that only people made history. In his writing, Thucydides tried hard to be accurate and impartial. Thucydides acted like a modern roving reporter. He visited battle sites, and he also carefully examined documents. In addition, he accepted only actual eyewitness reports of events.

Michele Falzone/Agency Jon Arnold Images/age fotostock

Thales was one of the first scientists to explain the physical world using examples from nature. He is pictured here with some of the tools he used to develop his theories.

Thucydides did not just state the facts. He also explored the causes and effects of events. He believed that future generations could learn from the past. Moreover, as a historian, he wanted to leave behind ideas and commentary so that others could learn.

For example, in *The History of the Peloponnesian War*, Thucydides wrote of a warning to Sparta:

PRIMARY SOURCE

❝ And yet, [Sparta], you still delay. You fail to see that peace stays longest with those who … show their determination not to submit to injustice. … Your habits are old-fashioned as compared with [those of Athens]. It is the law as in art, so in politics, that improvements [will win out]. … Athens has [made greater progress] than you on the path of innovation. ❞

— from *The History of the Peloponnesian War*, by Thucydides, c. 431 B.C.

The First Scientists

The ancient Greeks developed many scientific ideas. These ideas have influenced scientific thinking for centuries. In ancient times, most people thought that their gods controlled nature. Early Greek scientists had a different idea. They thought that natural events could be explained logically and that people could discover the causes of these events by using reason.

The first important Greek scientist was Thales (THAY·leez) of Miletus. Born in the mid-600s B.C., Thales studied astronomy and mathematics. He did not have telescopes and other instruments that scientists use today. Thales made discoveries and developed theories by observing and thinking.

Another Greek scientist, Pythagoras (puh·THA·guh·ruhs), taught his pupils that the universe followed the same laws that governed music and numbers. He believed that all relationships could be expressed in numbers. As a result, he developed many new ideas about mathematics. Most people know his name because of the Pythagorean Theorem that is still used in geometry today. It is a way to determine the length of the sides of a triangle.

Hulton Archive/Getty Images

ReadingHELPDESK

Hippocratic Oath a set of promises about patient care that new doctors make when they start practicing medicine

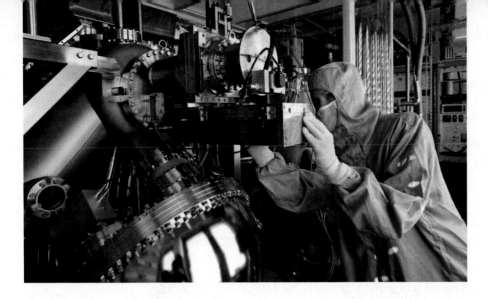

Today's scientists have the use of many tools that were not available to Thales and other ancient Greeks.

▶ **CRITICAL THINKING**
Analyzing What might Thales have discovered about water if he had been able to use a modern microscope?

Ancient Greek Medicine

Greek scientists also studied medicine, or the science of treating diseases. Hippocrates (hih·PAH·kruh·TEEZ) was a physician in ancient Greece who is regarded as the "father of medicine." He believed diseases came from natural causes. Most people at that time thought evil spirits caused diseases. Hippocrates traveled all over Greece to help the sick. He used his new ideas to diagnose different illnesses. He also discovered his own treatments to help cure sick people.

Hippocrates created a list of rules about how doctors should use their skills to help patients. His rules are listed in the **Hippocratic Oath** (HIH·puh·KRAT·ihk). The oath says that doctors should do their best to help the patient. It also says that they should protect the patient's privacy. Today, doctors around the world still promise to honor the Hippocratic Oath.

☑ **PROGRESS CHECK**

Explaining Why is Herodotus called "the father of history"?

LESSON 2 REVIEW

Review Vocabulary

1. How would someone use *rhetoric* in everyday life?

Answer the Guiding Questions

2. ***Comparing and Contrasting*** What was one important similarity between Plato and Aristotle? What was one major difference?

3. ***Describing*** What is the Hippocratic Oath?

4. ***Explaining*** Who are the three most important and famous philosophers from ancient Greece? Explain the teacher-student relationships among the three of them. What do all three have in common?

5. **ARGUMENT** Think about the people you read about in this lesson. Whose ideas are still important to us today? Why? Express your opinion in a one-page paper.

What Do You Think?

Did Socrates Commit Treason?

After Athens lost the Peloponnesian War, there was a period of political disorder in the city-state. Athenian leaders restricted free speech to help keep peace and order in Athens.

Socrates was critical of the decision to limit free speech. He taught his students to question everything and to think for themselves. The Athenian leaders felt his criticisms were a threat. They thought that his influence with the young people was dangerous. They accused Socrates of misleading students by teaching them to question authority. Following a trial, Socrates was found guilty of treason and sentenced to death.

Yes

PRIMARY SOURCE

❦ Socrates is guilty of … corrupting [misguiding] the young. Did not Socrates cause his associates to despise the established laws. … [His] [w]ords … tended to incite the young to contemn [to treat with scorn] the established constitution, rendering them violent and headstrong. … Socrates taught sons to pour contumely [harsh criticism] upon their fathers by persuading his young friends that he could make them wiser than their sires [fathers], or by pointing out that the law allowed a son to sue his father for aberration [unsoundness] of mind, and to imprison him. **❦**

—Socrates' accusers, Meletus, Anytus, and Lycon, quoted in *The Memorabilia: Recollections of Socrates* by Xenophon (translated by Henry Graham Daykns)

Freedom of speech was not guaranteed in ancient Greece. Citizens gathered daily to discuss current issues.

North Wind/North Wind Picture Archives

This famous painting, *The Death of Socrates*, shows Socrates speaking to his followers as he is given a cup of poison hemlock. At his death, Socrates was still committed to reason.

No

" Men of Athens, I honor and love you; but I shall obey God rather than you, and while I have life and strength I shall never cease from the practice and teaching of philosophy, exhorting [urging] anyone ... I meet ... saying: my friend—a citizen of the great and mighty and wise city of Athens,—are you not ashamed of heaping up [so much] money and honor and reputation, and caring so little about wisdom and truth and the greatest improvement of the soul, which you never regard or heed [pay attention to] at all? ... For I do nothing but go about persuading you all, old and young alike, not to take thought for your persons and your properties, but ... to care about the greatest improvement of the soul. ... This is my teaching, and if this is the doctrine which corrupts the youth, I am a mischievous person. But if any one says that this is not my teaching, he is speaking an untruth. Wherefore, O men of Athens, I say to you ... whichever you do, understand that I shall never alter my ways, not even if I have to die many times. "

–Socrates, as quoted in *Apology*, by Plato (translated by Benjamin Jowett)

The Print Collector/Heritage/Age fotostock

What Do You Think? DBQ

1 **Explaining** Socrates' accusers claim that he is teaching young people to question their constitution. Why do the accusers say this is an example of Socrates being a bad influence on the young?

2 **Describing** What does Socrates say is the main idea he teaches?

3 **Evaluating** Who do you think makes the stronger argument, Socrates or his accusers?

LESSON 3
Alexander's Empire

ESSENTIAL QUESTION
- What are the characteristics of a leader?

IT MATTERS BECAUSE
Strong leaders can bring change to society. Philip II and Alexander the Great, as strong leaders, spread many Greek ideas to conquered lands.

Philip II of Macedonia

GUIDING QUESTION *Why did Macedonia become powerful?*

As you learned earlier, the Persians set out to conquer the Greek city-states but failed. The Macedonians (ma·suh·DOH·nee·uhnz) were people who lived north of Greece. In the 300s B.C., they conquered Greece.

Conquering Greece

The Macedonians were farmers. They raised sheep and horses and grew crops in their river valleys. For much of its history, Macedonia was not a very strong kingdom. Under King Philip II, however, Macedonia became a superpower in the ancient world.

As a young man, Philip had lived in Greece. He came to admire Greek culture and military skill. Philip became king of Macedonia in 359 B.C. He **created** a strong army. Philip planned to unite the Greek city-states under his rule and destroy the mighty Persian Empire. Philip trained a vast army of foot soldiers to fight like the Greeks. At this time, the Greek city-states were weak. They had been divided by the Peloponnesian War. As a result, they could not defend themselves against Philip's powerful army.

Reading**HELP**DESK

Taking Notes: *Summarizing*
Use a diagram like this one to describe how Philip II and Alexander changed Greece.

How Alexander and Philip II Changed Greece

Content Vocabulary
- **cavalry**
- **Hellenistic Era**

Philip took control of the city-states one by one. He defeated some city-states in battle, and he bribed the leaders of others to surrender. A few city-states **voluntarily** agreed to join with Macedonia.

Many Greeks worried about Philip's plans. Demosthenes (dih·MAHS·thuh·neez) was an Athenian who opposed Philip. He was a lawyer and one of Athens's great public speakers. Demosthenes warned the Athenians that Philip was a threat to Greek freedom. He urged all the city-states to join together to fight the Macedonians:

PRIMARY SOURCE

❝ Remember only that Philip is our enemy, that he has long been robbing and insulting us ... that the future depends on ourselves, and that unless we are willing to fight him there we shall perhaps be forced to fight here. ... You need not speculate [guess] about the future except to assure yourselves that it will be disastrous unless you face the facts and are willing to do your duty. ❞

—Demosthenes, "The First Philippic" in *Orations of Demosthenes*

By the time the Greeks tried to unite, it was too late. The Athenians joined with Thebes and a few other free city-states. They battled Philip's army, but they could not stop his invasion. In 338 B.C., the Greeks and the Macedonians fought one last major battle. At the Battle of Chaeronea (kehr·uh·NEE·uh), Philip's army crushed the Greeks. Philip now ruled most of Greece.

✔ PROGRESS CHECK

Summarizing How was Philip II able to gain control over most of Greece?

Alexander Takes Over

GUIDING QUESTION *What were Alexander's goals as a ruler?*

After conquering Greece, Philip hoped to lead the Greeks and Macedonians to war against the Persian Empire. Before Philip could carry out his plans, however, he was killed. His son Alexander became king.

Alexander was only 20 when he became ruler of Macedonia and Greece, but Philip had carefully prepared his son for the job. By age 16, Alexander was serving as a commander in the Macedonian army. He quickly won the respect of his soldiers.

Thinking Like a HISTORIAN

Researching on the Internet

Philip II of Macedonia admired the art and ideas of the Greeks—and their armies. Philip set out to take over the Greek city-states. Why do you think Philip wanted to conquer the Greeks rather than be allies with them? Use the Internet to find reliable sources about Philip's goals. Then present them to your class. For more information about using the Internet for research, read *What Does a Historian Do?*

▶ CRITICAL THINKING
Finding the Main Idea Demosthenes spoke out against Philip. Why was Demosthenes opposed to Philip's plans?

Academic Vocabulary

create to make or produce something; to bring something into existence

voluntarily by choice or free will; willingly

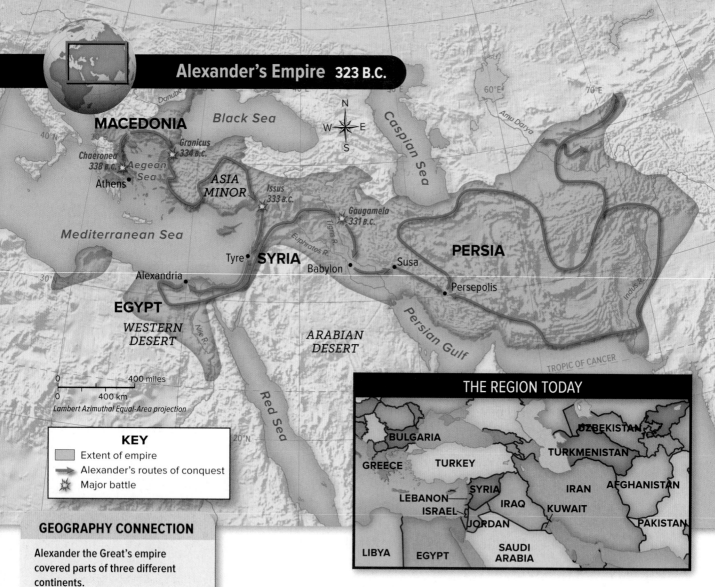

Alexander's Empire 323 B.C.

MACEDONIA

Black Sea

Danube

Granicus
334 B.C.

Chaeronea
338 B.C.

Aegean
Sea

Athens

ASIA
MINOR

Issus
333 B.C.

Caspian
Sea

Amu Darya

Gaugamela
331 B.C.

Mediterranean Sea

Tyre

SYRIA

Euphrates R.

Tigris R.

Babylon

Susa

PERSIA

Persepolis

Indus R.

Alexandria

EGYPT

WESTERN
DESERT

Nile R.

ARABIAN
DESERT

Persian Gulf

TROPIC OF CANCER

Red Sea

0   400 miles
0   400 km
Lambert Azimuthal Equal-Area projection

KEY
Extent of empire
Alexander's routes of conquest
Major battle

THE REGION TODAY

BULGARIA

UZBEKISTAN

GREECE

TURKEY

TURKMENISTAN

LEBANON
ISRAEL

SYRIA

IRAQ

IRAN

KUWAIT

AFGHANISTAN

PAKISTAN

JORDAN

LIBYA

EGYPT

SAUDI
ARABIA

GEOGRAPHY CONNECTION

Alexander the Great's empire
covered parts of three different
continents.

1 PLACE In what place today
are the people known as
Persians living?

2 CRITICAL THINKING
Analyzing Visuals Why did
Alexander go primarily east and
south from Macedonia and
Greece in his conquests?

They admired him for his bravery and military skill. After
Philip's death, Alexander was ready to fulfill his father's dream.
He prepared to invade the Persian Empire.

War with Persia

In the spring of 334 B.C., Alexander led about 40,000 Macedonian
and Greek soldiers into Asia Minor. Their goal was to defeat one
of the strongest armies in the world—the Persians. Alexander's
cavalry (KAV·uhl·ree), or soldiers on horseback, proved to be a
stronger force. They fought a battle at Granicus, in what is today
northwestern Turkey. In that battle, Alexander's cavalry crushed
the Persian forces. Alexander's forces continued to march across
Asia Minor. They freed Greek city-states that had been under
Persian rule.

Reading**HELP**DESK

cavalry part of an army in which the soldiers
ride horses

Academic Vocabulary

pursue to follow in order to capture or defeat

A year and a half later, in November 333 B.C., Alexander fought the next major battle against the Persians at Issus (IH·suhs), in Syria. Once again, Alexander's military skills resulted in a victory. The Persian king Darius III was forced to flee from Issus.

Alexander and his troops did not **pursue** Darius, though. Instead, they moved south along the Mediterranean coast. In early 331 B.C., they conquered Egypt. Alexander built a new city in Egypt and named it Alexandria (a·lihg·ZAN·dree·uh) after himself. As a center of business and trade, Alexandria became one of the most important cities of the ancient world. It remains a vital city in the Mediterranean region today.

In late 331 B.C., Alexander's army headed back north. He turned eastward and invaded Mesopotamia, now ruled by the Persians. Alexander's army smashed Darius's forces at Gaugamela (gaw·guh·MEE·luh), near the Tigris River. After this victory, Alexander's army took over the rest of the Persian Empire.

After he conquered Persia, Alexander did not stop. In 327 B.C., he marched his army into northwestern India. There he fought a number of bloody battles. His soldiers were tired of constant fighting and refused to go farther. Alexander agreed to lead them home.

On the return march, the troops crossed a desert in what is now southern Iran. Heat and thirst killed thousands of soldiers. At one point, a group of soldiers found a little water and scooped it up in a helmet. They offered the water to Alexander. According to a Greek historian:

PRIMARY SOURCE

" Alexander, with a word of thanks for the gift, took the helmet, and, in full view of his troops, poured the water on the ground. So extraordinary was the effect of this action that the water wasted by Alexander was as good as a drink for every man in the army. "

—*The Campaigns of Alexander* by Arrian, tr. by Aubrey De Sélincourt

At the far left of this battle scene is Alexander the Great, who fought alongside his soldiers.

▶ CRITICAL THINKING
Hypothesizing What was Alexander trying to show when he threw water on the ground in front of his thirsty soldiers?

©David Lees/Corbis

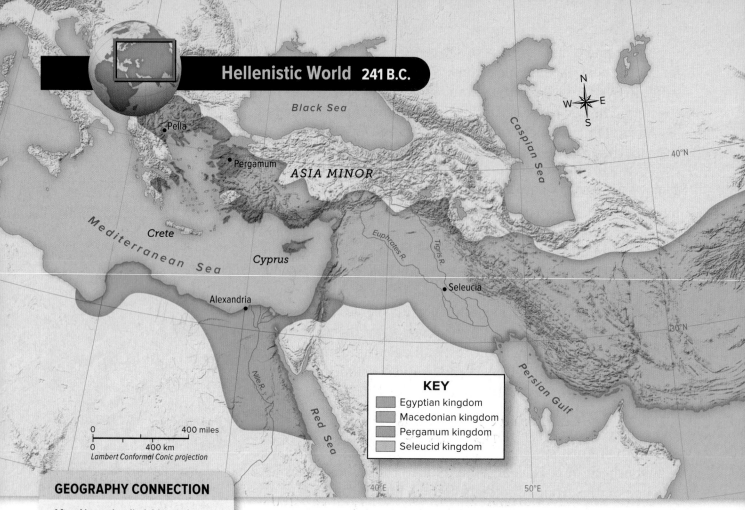

Black Sea

Pella

Pergamum

ASIA MINOR

Caspian Sea

40°N

Mediterranean Sea

Crete

Cyprus

Euphrates R.

Tigris R.

Seleucia

Alexandria

30°N

Nile R.

Red Sea

Persian Gulf

KEY
- Egyptian kingdom
- Macedonian kingdom
- Pergamum kingdom
- Seleucid kingdom

0   400 miles
0   400 km
Lambert Conformal Conic projection

40°E   50°E

GEOGRAPHY CONNECTION

After Alexander died, his empire was divided up into four separate kingdoms, which were all part of the Hellenistic World.

1 **LOCATION** In which kingdom was Greece mostly located?

2 **CRITICAL THINKING**
Analyzing Visuals How many different continents was Alexander's empire on, and which continents were they?

In 323 B.C., Alexander returned to Babylon, one of the Persian cities now under his control. The hardships of the journey had wrecked his health. Suffering from wounds and worn out by fever, Alexander died. He was only 32 years old.

✓ **PROGRESS CHECK**

Explaining Why was the Battle of Gaugamela so important to Alexander?

Alexander's Legacy

GUIDING QUESTION *How successful was Alexander in achieving his goals?*

Alexander was a great general who feared nothing. He rode into battle ahead of his soldiers and marched into unknown lands. The key to Alexander's courage may have been his early education. As a boy, Alexander read the Greek epics. His role model was Homer's warrior-hero Achilles. Today, Alexander is called Alexander the Great.

Reading HELP DESK

Hellenistic Era the time period following the death of Alexander during which Greek culture spread through the known world

Reading Strategy: *Summarizing*

When you finish reading a section of text about an important person or event in history, write a paragraph that tells what the person did or what happened. Use your own words. Then compare your summary to the text and check any facts.

Alexander's armies extended Greek rule over a vast region. They spread Greek language, ideas, art, and architecture throughout Southwest Asia and Egypt. Alexander's successes marked the beginning of the **Hellenistic Era** (heh·luh·NIHS·tihk EHR·uh). *Hellenistic* means "like the Greeks." The Hellenistic Era refers to when Greek culture spread to the non-Greek peoples that Alexander had conquered.

A Divided Empire

Alexander planned to unite Macedonians, Greeks, Egyptians, and Asians in his new empire. His dream of creating one great empire, however, didn't last. After Alexander died, his generals divided the empire into four separate kingdoms. These kingdoms were Macedonia, Pergamum (PUHR·guh·muhm), Egypt, and the Seleucid (suh·LOO·suhd) Empire.

The Hellenistic Kings

People who served in the governments of the Hellenistic kings had to speak Greek. The Hellenistic kings preferred to give jobs to Greeks and Macedonians. In this way, they were able to keep control of the governments.

By 100 B.C., Alexandria, in Egypt, was the largest city in the Mediterranean world. It included two excellent harbors and a towering lighthouse. The lighthouse stood on a harbor island with a burning flame at its top. The library at Alexandria had the largest collection of writings in ancient times.

The Hellenistic kings also created new cities and military posts. These new Greek communities needed architects, artists, engineers, and philosophers. Hellenistic rulers encouraged Greeks and Macedonians to settle in the conquered lands. These colonies spread Greek culture widely—into Egypt and India.

The lighthouse at Alexandria was one of the Seven Wonders of the Ancient World. It was completed about 280 B.C. and stood on an island in the harbor.

▶ CRITICAL THINKING
Analyzing Why was a fire kept burning on top of the lighthouse at night?

✓ PROGRESS CHECK

Explaining What happened to Alexander's empire after he died?

LESSON 3 REVIEW

Review Vocabulary

1. Why was the *cavalry* an important part of Alexander's army?

Answer the Guiding Questions

2. *Summarizing* What did Demosthenes want the Greek city-states to do about the Macedonians? Did they follow his advice?

3. *Describing* What is the Hellenistic Era?

4. *Identifying* What were some of the policies of Alexander and the Hellenistic kings that helped to spread Greek culture throughout the empire?

5. **ARGUMENT** Alexander admired the heroes of the Trojan War so much that he traveled with a copy of Homer's *Iliad*. What book would you carry if you traveled as Alexander did? Write a description of your choice and explain your reasons for it.

LESSON 4
Hellenistic Culture

• How do new ideas change the way people live?

IT MATTERS BECAUSE
Hellenistic cities became centers of learning and culture. Philosophy and the arts flourished, and new discoveries that were made are still important to us today.

Hellenistic Arts

GUIDING QUESTION *How did Greek culture spread during the Hellenistic Era?*

During the Hellenistic Era, philosophers, scientists, poets, and writers moved to the new Greek cities of Southwest Asia and Egypt. Alexandria, for example, served as the Greek capital of Egypt and was a major center of learning. Many scholars were attracted to Alexandria's library. It contained more than 500,000 scrolls. Alexandria also had a museum that attracted scholars to do research. The city's reputation as a place of learning and its location on the Mediterranean Sea contributed to Alexandria's economic growth. Today, Alexandria remains a vital city in Egypt where nearly 4 million people live and work.

Buildings and Statues

Greek architects served an important role in expanding Alexander's empire. They planned public building projects for new cities that were being founded and for old cities that were being rebuilt. Hellenistic kings wanted these cities to be like Athens and other cultural centers in Greece. They were willing to spend huge amounts of money to make this happen.

Reading **HELP**DESK

Taking Notes: *Describing*
Use a chart like this one to describe the achievements of the Greek scientists.

Greek Scientist	Achievements
Eratosthenes	
Euclid	
Archimedes	

Content Vocabulary

• Epicureanism
• Stoicism
• circumference

• plane geometry
• solid geometry

These kings wanted to line the streets with Greek temples, theaters, and baths.

Hellenistic kings and other wealthy citizens hired Greek sculptors, who created thousands of statues for towns and cities. Hellenistic sculptors proved to be as talented as the sculptors of Greece's Golden Age. These sculptors, however, developed new styles. They did not carve ideal figures to reflect beauty and harmony. Instead, they showed people in a more realistic style. They even created statues that looked angry or sad.

Hellenistic Writers

Hellenistic rulers also supported talented writers. As a result, poets and writers produced a large amount of literature during the Hellenistic Era. Very little of this writing has survived today.

One work that we do know about is an epic poem called *Argonautica*. Written by Appolonius (a·puh·LOH·nee·uhs) of Rhodes (ROHDZ), the poem tells the story of Jason and his band of heroes. You may have read or seen a modern version of this poem, often called *Jason and the Argonauts*. Jason and his band sail the seas **seeking** a ram with a golden fleece. Along the way, they have many adventures. Another poet, Theocritus (thee·AH·kruh·tuhs), wrote short poems about the beauty of nature.

Athens remained the center for Greek theater. There, writers of plays produced comedies, not tragedies. These comedies are known as Greek New Comedy. However, the comedies of the Hellenistic Era were not like the comedies of Greece's Golden Age. Those of the Hellenistic Era did not poke fun at political leaders. Instead, the plays told stories about love and relationships of ordinary people. One of the best known of the new playwrights was Menander (muh·NAN·duhr). He lived from 343 B.C. to 291 B.C. and is considered the most important poet of Greek New Comedy. The temple of Apollo at Delphi had an inscription that read "Know thyself." Making a humorous comment on that inscription, Menander said "This 'Know Yourself' is a silly proverb in some ways; To know the man next door is a much more useful rule." His works were later adapted by Roman writers. Through his works, Menander influenced the development of European comedy during the Renaissance (reh·nuh·ZAHNTS) and even comedy today.

✔ PROGRESS CHECK

Explaining How did Greek sculpture and drama change during the Hellenistic Era?

Hellenistic artists were masters at capturing movement and emotion. This statue, *Winged Victory*, seems to be walking forcefully forward.

▶ CRITICAL THINKING
Drawing Conclusions Washington D.C.'s buildings showcase many statues in the Greek style. Why do you think so many of them are in this style?

©Carl & Ann Purcell/Corbis

Academic Vocabulary

seek to search for

Thinkers and Scientists

GUIDING QUESTION *What ideas and discoveries emerged during the Hellenistic Era?*

During the Hellenistic Era, Athens continued to support Greek philosophers. These philosophers tried to answer questions such as, "What is a good life?" and "How can people find peace of mind in a troubled world?" The two most important Hellenistic philosophers were Epicurus and Zeno.

Who Was Epicurus?

Epicurus founded a philosophy known as **Epicureanism** (eh·pih·kyu·REE·uh·nih·zuhm). He taught his students that finding happiness was the goal of life. He believed that the way to be happy was to avoid pain.

Today the word *epicurean* means the love of physical pleasure, such as good food or comfortable surroundings. For Epicurus, however, pleasure meant spending time with friends. It meant learning not to be upset about problems in life. Epicureans avoided worry. They limited their wants and lived simply.

The Stoics

A Phoenician thinker named Zeno developed a philosophy called **Stoicism** (STOH·uh·sih·zuhm). Zeno did not have the money to rent a lecture hall in which to teach. Instead, he taught at a building called the "painted porch". The Greek word for *porch* was *stoa*. The term "Stoicism" thus comes from the Greek word *stoa*. The Stoics claimed that people who were guided by their emotions lived unhappy lives. They believed that happiness resulted from using reason. Sound thinking, they thought, should guide decisions. Today, the word *stoic* is used to describe someone who seems not affected by joy or sadness. Unlike Epicureans, Stoics thought people had a duty to serve their **community**. The ideas of the Stoics would later influence Roman thinkers.

Science and Mathematics

Science also flourished during the Hellenistic Era. Even though Hellenistic scientists used simple instruments, they performed many experiments and developed new theories.

Other astronomers would not believe Aristarchus when he stated that the solar system moved around the sun. This diagram shows his idea.

MODEL OF SOLAR SYSTEM BY ARISTARCHUS

Moon

Sun

90°

X°

Earth

Reading**HELP**DESK

Epicureanism the philosophy of Epicurus, stating that the purpose of life is to look for happiness and peace

Stoicism the philosophy of the Stoics who believed that people should not try to feel joy or sadness

Academic Vocabulary

community a group of various kinds of people living in a particular area or a common location

Aristarchus (ar·uh·STAHR·kuhs) claimed that the sun was at the center of the universe. He said that Earth circled the sun. At the time, other astronomers rejected his ideas. They thought that Earth was the center of the universe. Euclid taught others his theories about geometry. If you study geometry today, you will be learning about the same topics studied by ancient Greeks.

Another scientist, Eratosthenes (ehr·uh·TAHS·thuh·neez), was the chief librarian at the library at Alexandria. After study and research, Eratosthenes concluded that Earth was round. He then used his knowledge to measure Earth's **circumference** (suhr·KUHM·fuhr·ens)—the distance around Earth.

In order to measure the Earth's circumference, Eratosthenes put two sticks in the ground far apart from each other. When the sun was directly over one stick, he measured its shadow. By measuring the shadows, he was able to calculate the curve of Earth's surface.

Using his measurements, Eratosthenes tried to figure the distance around Earth. Remarkably, his estimate was within 185 miles (298 km) of the actual distance. Using similar **methods**, he tried to determine how far it was to the sun and to the moon. Although his measurements were not **accurate**, he concluded that the sun was much larger than Earth and the moon.

The Modern age owes a great debt to the Hellenistic thinkers. Many scientists and mathematicians are portrayed in "The School of Athens," a painting by sixteenth-century artist Raphael. The work can be viewed today at the Vatican in Rome.

GREEK SCIENTISTS AND THEIR CONTRIBUTIONS

CHART

Scientists	Scientific "Firsts"
Archimedes	Established the science of physics Explained the lever and compound pulley
Aristarchus	Established that Earth revolves around the sun
Eratosthenes	Figured out that Earth is round
Euclid	Wrote a book that organized information about geometry
Hipparchus	Created a system to explain how planets and stars move
Hippocrates	Known as the "Father of Medicine" First to write a medical code of good behavior
Hypatia	Expanded knowledge of mathematics and astronomy
Pythagoras	First to establish the principles of geometry

The ancient Greeks made advances in science.

1 **IDENTIFYING** How was Euclid's achievement important for the study of geometry?

2 **CRITICAL THINKING** *Analyzing* Why did Aristarchus's ideas upset some people?

Photos.com/Getty Images

circumference the outer border of a circle; the measurement of that border

Academic Vocabulary

method a procedure or process; a way of doing something

accurate free from error; in agreement with truth

Constant *pi*

Astronomers in the Hellenistic Era made amazing discoveries. Many of the measurements they made were very accurate. Even though scientists today can measure more accurately, no one has ever been able to improve on Archimedes' calculation of *pi*. The number *pi* (π) is a ratio. When the circumference of a circle is divided by its diameter, you get *pi*. Pi is always the same for every circle—about 3.1416.

Archimedes' calculation of *pi* is used daily in mathematics, more than 2,000 years after he made it.

Euclid (YOO·kluhd) of Alexandria advanced the field of mathematics. His best-known book, *Elements,* describes plane geometry. **Plane geometry** is one branch of mathematics. It shows how points, lines, angles, and surfaces relate to one another. Around 300 B.C., Egypt's King Ptolemy I (TAH·luh·mee) asked Euclid if he knew a faster way to learn geometry. Euclid answered that "there is no royal way" to learn geometry. In other words, if the king wanted to understand Euclid's ideas, he would have to study. Euclid's theories still influence mathematicians today.

The most famous scientist of the Hellenistic Era was Archimedes (ahr·kuh·MEE·deez). Archimedes worked on **solid geometry.** He studied ball-like shapes, called spheres, and tube-like shapes, called cylinders. He also figured out the value of *pi.* This number is used to measure the area of circles. It is represented by the Greek symbol π.

Archimedes was also an inventor. He developed machinery and weapons of war. Archimedes was known as a modest man. According to one story, however, he boasted, "Give me a lever and a place to stand on . . . and I will move the earth."

The king of Syracuse heard of Archimedes' boast. He asked Archimedes to build a machine to defend the city, so Archimedes designed catapults. These machines could throw rocks, arrows, and spears over long distances.

When the Romans attacked Syracuse in 212 B.C., the catapults drove them back. It took the Romans three years to capture the city. During the massacre that followed, Archimedes was killed.

Hellenistic thought and culture had long-lasting effects. The mathematician Hypatia (hy·PAY·shuh) lived in Alexandria in Egypt around A.D. 400, more than 700 years after the Hellenistic Era. She kept up the Greek tradition of studying philosophy and mathematics. Like the great Greek thinkers of the past, Hypatia also championed the use of reason over superstition:

PRIMARY SOURCE

❞ To teach superstitions as truth is a most terrible thing. ❞
❞ Reserve your right to think, for even to think wrongly is better than not to think at all. ❞

—**from Hypatia,** *Encyclopaedia Britannica Profiles, 300 Women Who Changed the World*

✔ **PROGRESS CHECK**

Comparing and Contrasting How were Epicureanism and Stoicism similar? How were they different?

TEXT: "Hypatia." Reprinted with permission from Encyclopaedia Britannica, Inc. © 2011 by Encyclopaedia Britannica, Inc.
PHOTO: North Wind Picture Archives

Reading **HELP**DESK

plane geometry a branch of mathematics centered around measurement and relationships of points, lines, angles, and surfaces of figures on a plane

solid geometry a branch of mathematics about measurement and relationships of points, lines, angles, surfaces, and solids in three-dimensional space

Greece and Rome

GUIDING QUESTION *How did Greece fall under Roman rule?*

The four kingdoms that formed from Alexander's empire shared Hellenistic culture. Despite their common culture, the kingdoms were unable to work together. They often fought wars with one another.

Macedonia held power over Greece for a time. It could not keep the Greek city-states permanently under control, though. Sparta and some other city-states regained their independence. These city-states had Hellenistic cultures, but they did not have strong armies. They remained free for only a short time.

Rome was a city-state in central Italy. In the late 200s B.C., Rome conquered the entire Italian Peninsula. Greece lost its lands in southern Italy. The Greeks now feared that Rome would take control of Greece.

The Greeks tried to stop Rome's growing power, but failed. They began supporting Rome's enemies in various wars. The Romans won these conflicts, however. Gradually, Rome gained control of the Greek mainland.

Sicily is a beautiful island in the Mediterranean. Ruled by ancient Greeks and then the Romans, it is the home today of many historic ruins of both cultures.

✔ **PROGRESS CHECK**

Explaining How did the Greek city-states react to Rome's growing power?

Author's Image/Punchstock

LESSON 4 REVIEW

Review Vocabulary

1. Why did Greek scientists study the *circumference* of Earth?

Answer the Guiding Questions

2. ***Explaining*** Why did Alexandria become a major center of learning?

3. ***Describing*** What contributions did Archimedes make to science?

4. ***Explaining*** How did the Greeks attempt to stop Rome's invasion of Greece?

5. ***Drawing Conclusions*** What beliefs about Earth and the heavens were proved by the discoveries of Aristarchus and Eratosthenes?

6. **ARGUMENT** Compare the Stoic and Epicurean views about life. Which of these views appeals to you? Write a paragraph that explains the reasons for your choice.

Write your answers on a separate piece of paper.

1 **Exploring the Essential Question**

INFORMATIVE/EXPLANATORY Write an expository essay about what made the Greek people and their culture unique. Think of the new ideas they developed in philosophy and the sciences. Think of the new forms of art and architecture that they created. Include in your essay a discussion of the lasting influences that Greece has had on the world.

2 **21st Century Skills**

APPLY TECHNOLOGY EFFECTIVELY Create a blog entry to compare and contrast the sculpture and architecture of the Hellenistic Era with that of the modern world. Choose photos that show the general differences and details. Write copy that analyzes the styles and points out the differences. Include your personal opinions of the two styles.

3 **Thinking Like a Historian**

COMPARING AND CONTRASTING Select one of the historical maps from the chapter. Then search the Internet for maps of the same area today. Write one or two paragraphs explaining how the area has changed or remained the same between the time of ancient Greece and now.

4

GEOGRAPHY ACTIVITY

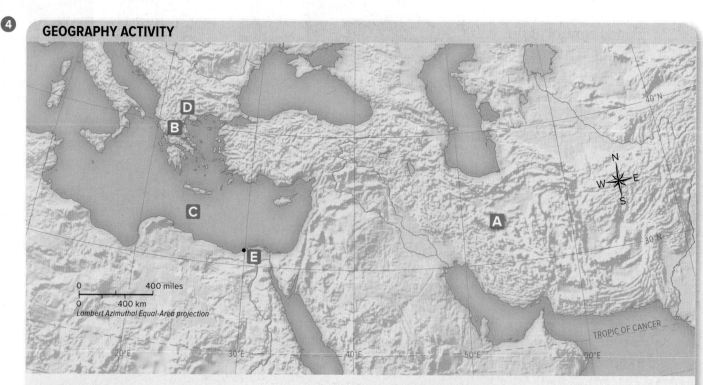

Locating Places
On a separate sheet of paper, match the letters on the map with the numbered places listed here.

1. Greece
2. Africa
3. Alexandria
4. Persia
5. Mediterranean Sea

Directions: Write your answers on a separate piece of paper.

CHECKING FOR UNDERSTANDING

1 Describe each of the following terms.

A. myth	**K.** Socratic method
B. ritual	**L.** Hippocratic Oath
C. oracle	**M.** cavalry
D. fable	**N.** Hellenistic Era
E. oral tradition	**O.** Epicureanism
F. drama	**P.** Stoicism
G. tragedy	**Q.** circumference
H. comedy	**R.** plane geometry
I. Sophist	**S.** solid geometry
J. rhetoric	

REVIEW THE GUIDING QUESTIONS

2 *Identifying* What were two types of events that the Greeks held to honor their gods?

3 *Paraphrasing* Use your own words to explain why Homer's epics were important to the ancient Greeks.

4 *Summarizing* Summarize how drama developed in ancient Greece.

5 *Describing* According to Aristotle, what are the three types of government in the world? Describe each one.

6 *Discussing* What did the early Greek scientists, such as Thales, believe about science?

7 *Explaining* How did King Philip II help Macedonia become powerful?

8 *Discussing* How was Greek culture able to spread so quickly during the Hellenistic Era?

9 *Stating* What idea did Aristarchus develop based on his studies of the universe?

10 *Summarizing* Summarize the goals of Alexander as ruler of his empire.

CRITICAL THINKING

11 *Recognizing Relationships* How were oracles related to the religious beliefs of the ancient Greeks?

12 *Drawing Conclusions* Why did Athenians limit free speech after the Peloponnesian War?

13 *Contrasting* How was Herodotus's approach to history different from that of earlier Greeks?

14 *Determining Central Ideas* What do you think is the main idea that Homer wanted readers to understand about the Trojan horse? Explain.

15 *Analyzing Visuals* Study the map of the Hellenistic World in Lesson 3. Why do you think Alexandria became the main center of learning for the Hellenistic world, rather than another city, such as Persepolis?

16 *Comparing and Contrasting* How were Stoics similar to and different from Epicureans?

17 *Applying* Assume that you need to raise a small building two feet higher than its current position. What advice might Archimedes give you? Explain.

18 *Giving Examples* How might you use the Socratic method to teach sixth-graders the advantages of living in a democracy? Give at least one specific example.

19 *Defending* Your city is building a new courthouse. Many people think the building should have a modern design, but you think it should have a classical Greek design. Write a paragraph defending your position.

20 *Speculating* If Alexander had not read the Greek epics as a boy, do you think he still would have become a great warrior and leader? Explain your answer.

Need Extra Help?

If You've Missed Question	**1**	**2**	**3**	**4**	**5**	**6**	**7**	**8**	**9**	**10**	**11**	**12**	**13**	**14**	**15**	**16**	**17**	**18**	**19**	**20**
Review Lesson	1,2, 3,4	1	1	1	2	2	3	4	4	3	1	2	2	1	3	4	4	2	1	3

DBQ SHORT RESPONSE

"The choice of the site ... was determined by the abundance of water from [the lake] ... and by the good anchorage [harbor]. ... Alexandria became, within a century of its founding, one of the Mediterranean's largest cities and a centre of Greek scholarship and science."

—From *Encyclopaedia Britannica Online*, "Alexandria."

21 How did Alexandria's physical features help make it a great city?

22 Why do you think the city flourished, even after the death of Alexander?

EXTENDED RESPONSE

23 *Narrative* You are a citizen in a new city of the Hellenistic Era. Write a description of the ideal Hellenistic city.

STANDARDIZED TEST PRACTICE

DBQ ANALYZING DOCUMENTS

24 *Inferring* This excerpt is from a speech by Demosthenes. He spoke to the people of Athens about Philip II of Macedonia.

"Remember only that Philip is our enemy, that he has long been robbing and insulting us, ... that the future depends on ourselves, and that unless we are willing to fight him there we shall perhaps be forced to fight here [our homeland]. ... You need not speculate [guess] about the future except to assure yourselves that it will be disastrous unless you face the facts and are willing to do your duty."

—From "The First Philippic," *Orations of Demosthenes*

Demosthenes says the Athenians must "do their duty." What is their duty?
- **A.** to fight Philip when he comes to Athens
- **B.** to speculate about what will happen in the future
- **C.** to go fight Philip now
- **D.** to seek aid from other city-states

25 *Predicting* What does Demosthenes predict?
- **A.** If the Athenians are not good to Philip, he will rob them.
- **B.** It is still possible to make peace with Philip.
- **C.** There are others who will help the Athenians fight Philip.
- **D.** If the Athenians ignore Philip, there will be disaster.

Need Extra Help?

If You've Missed Question	**21**	**22**	**23**	**24**	**25**
Review Lesson	1	2	2	3	4

"Alexandria." Reprinted with permission from Encyclopaedia Britannica, © 2011 by Encyclopaedia Britannica, Inc.

This picture of Radha emphasizes her eternal beauty. The ornate jewelry is typical of ancient Indian art.

C. 3000 B.C. TO A.D. 500

Ancient India

Dinodia Photo Library/Age fotostock

THE STORY MATTERS ...

Have you ever read a love story? Some of the earliest immortal love stories are found in ancient Indian writing. Radha is the supreme deity featured in many of these stories. She is the Hindu deity with a special companion—Krishna. Together they appear in many tales with happy events and beautiful descriptions. Radha and Krishna represent examples of true love, beauty, loyalty, and devotion. The early Hindu culture honored these qualities as necessary for a good life. The love of Radha and Krishna is said to go on for eternity.

ESSENTIAL QUESTIONS

- How does geography influence the way people live?
- How do religions develop?
- What makes a culture unique?

Place & Time: Ancient India 3000 B.C. to A.D. 500

The first civilizations of ancient India developed in the Indus Valley. The arrival of the Aryans brought great changes to India, including the social system and beliefs that would become Hinduism. By the rise of the Mauryan and Gupta Empires, Buddhism had joined Hinduism as a major world religion that began in ancient India.

Step Into the Place

MAP FOCUS The history of India has been affected greatly by the Himalaya mountain ranges.

1 **LOCATION** Look at the map. Where are the Himalaya located?

2 **REGION** What rivers shown on the map flow from the Himalaya?

3 **PLACE** How tall is Mount Everest?

4 **CRITICAL THINKING**
Making Inferences How would the Himalaya have affected the settlement of India or its trade with other countries?

One of the most honored deities by Hindus is Gnesha. Representing education, wisdom, and wealth, Gnesha is called upon in many Hindu ceremonies. His popularity also stems from the belief that he can solve problems for his worshippers.

Indian emperor Ashoka (c. 273–233 B.C.) was a powerful ruler and Buddhist. He believed humans and animals should be treated with compassion. This carving of lions sits atop a pillar built by Ashoka. The sides of the pillar are covered with Buddhist teachings and Ashoka's laws.

(l)Ancient Art & Architecture Collection
(r)©Philippe Lissac/Godong/Corbis

Step Into the Time

TIME LINE Which event occurred first—the Buddha was born or athletes competed in the first Olympic Games?

c. 2600 B.C. Mohenjo-Daro flourishes

c. 2500 B.C. Harappa flourishes

ANCIENT INDIA

THE WORLD

3000 B.C.

2000 B.C.

c. 2055 B.C. Egypt's Middle Kingdom begins

c. 1790 B.C. Hammurabi's code of laws introduced

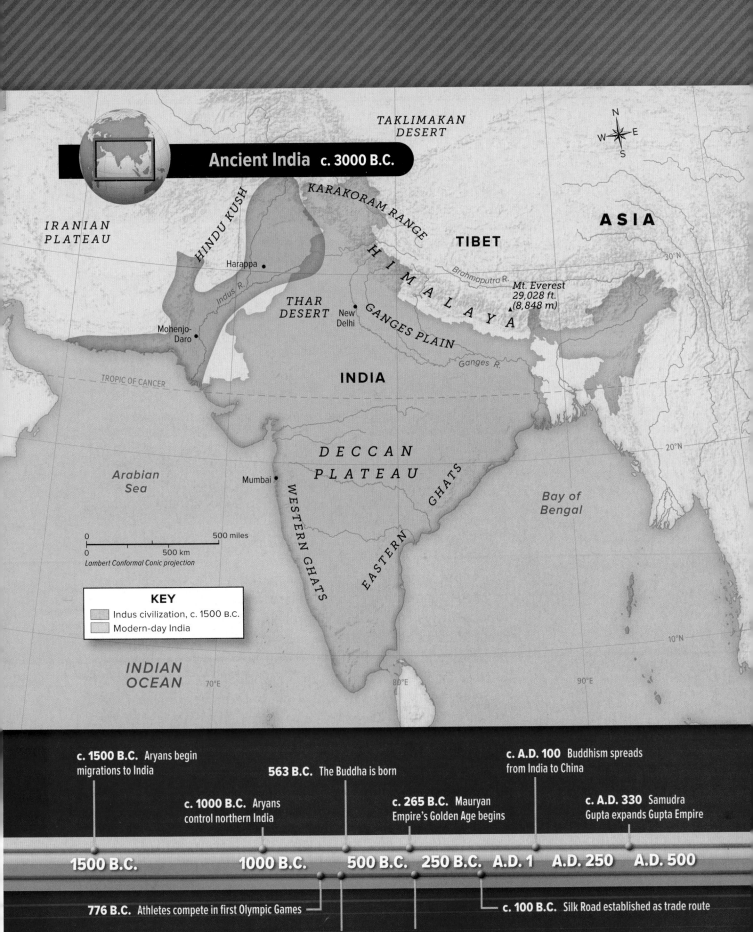

Ancient India c. 3000 B.C.

TAKLIMAKAN DESERT

IRANIAN PLATEAU

ASIA

HINDU KUSH

KARAKORAM RANGE

TIBET

HIMALAYA

Brahmaputra R.

Mt. Everest
29,028 ft.
(8,848 m)

Harappa

Indus R.

THAR DESERT

New Delhi

GANGES PLAIN

Ganges R.

Mohenjo-Daro

INDIA

TROPIC OF CANCER

30°N

Arabian Sea

DECCAN PLATEAU

WESTERN GHATS

EASTERN GHATS

Mumbai

20°N

Bay of Bengal

0   500 miles
0   500 km
Lambert Conformal Conic projection

KEY
Indus civilization, c. 1500 B.C.
Modern-day India

INDIAN OCEAN

70°E   80°E   90°E

10°N

c. 1500 B.C. Aryans begin migrations to India

563 B.C. The Buddha is born

c. A.D. 100 Buddhism spreads from India to China

c. 1000 B.C. Aryans control northern India

c. 265 B.C. Mauryan Empire's Golden Age begins

c. A.D. 330 Samudra Gupta expands Gupta Empire

1500 B.C.   1000 B.C.   500 B.C.   250 B.C.   A.D. 1   A.D. 250   A.D. 500

776 B.C. Athletes compete in first Olympic Games

c. 100 B.C. Silk Road established as trade route

597 B.C. Nebuchadnezzar II captures Jerusalem

c. 330 B.C. Greek philosopher Aristotle writes *Politics*

247

LESSON 1

Early Civilizations

• How does geography influence the way people live?

IT MATTERS BECAUSE

India's geography shaped the rise of the first civilizations in the Indus Valley.

The Geography of India

GUIDING QUESTION *How did physical geography and climate influence the development of civilization in India?*

India and several other modern-day countries make up the **subcontinent** of India. A subcontinent is a large landmass that is smaller than a continent. The Indian subcontinent is part of the continent of Asia.

Mountains, Plains, and Rivers

On its northern border, India is separated from the rest of Asia by rugged mountain systems. The Himalaya are one of these mountain systems. You have probably heard of Mount Everest, the highest peak in the Himalaya. Mount Everest is 28,028 feet tall. That is nearly 5.5 miles (8.8 km), which makes Mount Everest the tallest mountain in the world.

Wide fertile plains lie at the foot of India's extensive mountain ranges. The plains owe their rich soil to the three great rivers that flow through the region. These rivers are the Indus (IHN·duhs), the Ganges (GAN·jeez), and the Brahmaputra (BRAHM·uh·POO·truh). India's people rely on these rivers for farming, transportation, and trade.

Reading**HELP**DESK

Taking Notes: *Summarizing*

Using a diagram like this one, describe three ways the Aryans changed India.

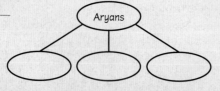

Content Vocabulary

- **subcontinent**
- **monsoon**
- **language family**
- **raja**
- **Sanskrit**
- **Vedas**
- **guru**

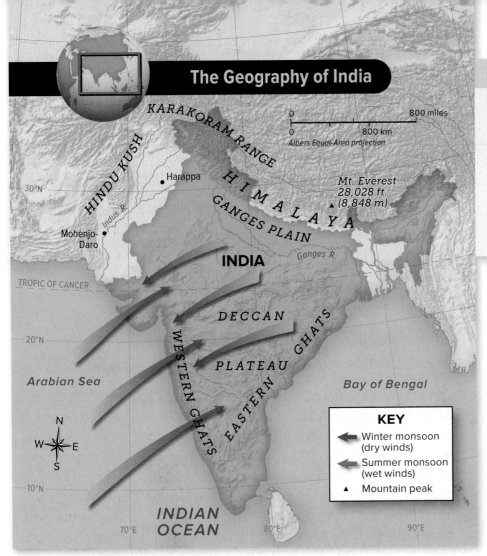

The Geography of India

KARAKORAM RANGE

HINDU KUSH

HIMALAYA

• Harappa

Indus R.

Mohenjo-
Daro •

30°N

GANGES PLAIN

INDIA

Ganges R.

Mt. Everest
28,028 ft.
▲ (8,848 m)

800 miles

0   800 km
Albers Equal-Area projection

TROPIC OF CANCER

DECCAN

20°N

PLATEAU

WESTERN GHATS

EASTERN GHATS

Arabian Sea

Bay of Bengal

N
W   E
S

10°N

**INDIAN
OCEAN**

70°E   80°E   90°E

KEY
← Winter monsoon
   (dry winds)
← Summer monsoon
   (wet winds)
▲ Mountain peak

Philippe Michel/Age fotostock

GEOGRAPHY CONNECTION

The mighty Himalaya and major
bodies of water border the Indian
subcontinent.

1 PLACE Which two rivers are
found in northern India?

2 CRITICAL THINKING
Predicting What might happen
to India's farmers if the summer
monsoons did not occur?

The landforms in central and southern India are much
different from the landforms in the north. Along the west and
east coasts of the subcontinent are lush fertile lands. Farther
inland, there are two chains of mountains that have worn down
over time. As the mountains eroded, they left areas of rugged
hills. Between the mountains is a dry highland known as the
Deccan Plateau (DEH·kuhn pla·TOH). The southern two-thirds
of India is part of this huge **plateau.**

India's civilization has been shaped by its climate as well
as by its physical landscape. Seasonal winds called **monsoons**
(mahn·SOONZ) have a large influence on India's climate.

During winter, monsoon winds blow cold, dry air from the
Himalaya east to west across India. During summer, warmer
land temperatures cause the winds to change direction. Summer
monsoon winds blow west to east from the Arabian Sea. They
bring warm, wet air and pouring rains.

---

subcontinent a large landmass that is
smaller than a continent

monsoon seasonal wind, especially in the
Indian Ocean and southern Asia

Visual Vocabulary

plateau a broad flat area of
high land

The summer rains bring farmers water that they need for their crops. With good rainfall, farmers can grow large amounts of food. Because of this, people celebrate the arrival of the monsoon rains. However, monsoon rains can also cause damage. Very heavy rains sometimes cause floods that destroy crops. Floods can even kill people and animals.

Too little rain can also be a problem. If the rains come late, there may be a long dry period called a drought. A serious drought can bring disaster to farmers. If lots of farm crops are ruined, many people may go hungry or starve.

✓ PROGRESS CHECK

Explaining How do monsoon winds affect life in India?

The Indus Valley Civilization

GUIDING QUESTION *How did the people of the Indus River Valley build cities?*

Thousands of years ago, India's first civilization began in the valley around the Indus River. The Indus Valley civilization is called the cradle of ancient India. Like the early civilizations in Mesopotamia and Egypt, the Indus Valley civilization developed near a great river system.

About 5,000 years ago, nomads settled in valleys along the Indus River in an area that is now Pakistan. The first settlements were built on the shores of the river. The soil was rich there, and farmers grew large crops of wheat, barley, and beans.

Archaeologists have studied the ruins of Mohenjo-Daro (below) and found many artifacts. These include statues of priest-kings, jewelry, and pottery.

(l)©Corbis Art/Corbis; (b)Borromeo/Art Resource, NY

Build Vocabulary: *Word Forms*

The word *celebrate* exists in several forms. The verb form means "to honor a person or a holiday with festivities." The noun *celebration* means "an event held to honor a holiday or person." The adjective used to describe a celebration is *celebratory*.

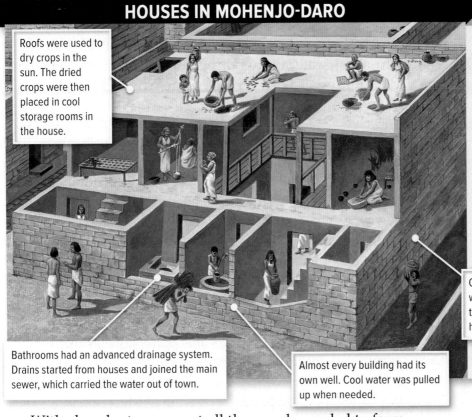

Roofs were used to dry crops in the sun. The dried crops were then placed in cool storage rooms in the house.

Bathrooms had an advanced drainage system. Drains started from houses and joined the main sewer, which carried the water out of town.

Almost every building had its own well. Cool water was pulled up when needed.

Outer walls of buildings had no windows. This helped prevent the hot summer sun from heating the insides of the house.

Houses in Mohenjo-Daro were built around central courtyards.

1 **EXPLAINING** Why were buildings constructed without windows in the outside walls?

2 **CRITICAL THINKING**
Making Inferences What was a benefit of having a well in every house?

With abundant crops, not all the people needed to farm. Many people made tools and constructed houses. Some supported themselves by trading extra food and goods. The Indus people prospered and built cities. The Indus civilization spread over much of western India and Pakistan.

Mohenjo-Daro and Harappa

The Indus culture flourished between 2600 B.C. and 1900 B.C. We know about the Indus culture from studying the ruins of two major cities, Mohenjo-Daro (moh·HEHN·joh DAHR·oh) and Harappa (huh·RA·puh).

At their peak, both Mohenjo-Daro and Harappa had more than 35,000 residents. The cities were designed almost exactly alike. Each city had dozens of streets. Larger streets were paved with tan-colored bricks. The smaller streets that crossed them were often left unpaved. At the west end of each city stood a fortress built on a brick platform and surrounded by strong, thick walls.

The Indus Valley people used oven-baked bricks to build their homes. Most houses had flat wooden roofs. The houses had enclosed courtyards, and some were several stories tall.

Ancient Indian art portrays daily life, such as driving this ox cart.

Harappan National Museum of Karachi, Karachi, Pakistan/Bridgeman Art Library

Historians have found many clay seals and stamps in Harappa. These objects are covered in writing and pictures. Historians have not determined the meaning of these writings. Use the Internet to find images of some of these seals. Create a list of what you think each might mean. Then discuss your theories with your class. For more information about using the Internet for research, read the chapter *What Does a Historian Do?*

The civilization's engineers and builders were highly skilled. Large buildings stored grain for the entire population. Wells supplied water, and every house had at least one indoor bathroom. Wastewater flowed through pipes to pits outside the city walls. Houses also had garbage chutes connected to bins in the streets.

What was life like?

Archaeologists have learned much about Indus Valley culture by studying its city ruins. For example, the ruins show that cities' royal palaces and temples may have been enclosed in a fortress. This shows the importance of both religion and government in the settlements of the Indus Valley.

Most Indus Valley people **resided** in farming villages surrounding the cities. They grew rice, barley, wheat, peas, and cotton. City residents were merchants, shopkeepers, and artisans. They made and sold copper and bronze tools, clay pottery, and cotton cloth. Artisans also made jewelry from shells, ivory, and gold. Archaeologists have even found toys among the ruins.

Indus Valley merchants traveled as far as Mesopotamia to trade. Some traders made the difficult trip through the mountains to Mesopotamia. Others probably sailed to Mesopotamia along the southern coast of Asia.

☑ PROGRESS CHECK

Describing How did most Indus Valley people earn a living?

Aryan Migrations and Settlements

GUIDING QUESTION *How did the Aryans influence early India?*

Sometime around 1900 B.C., the people of the Indus Valley began to **abandon** their cities and villages. Why did the people leave? Archaeologists have found several possible causes. There was a severe drought that lasted for hundreds of years. It destroyed crops and caused people to starve. Earthquakes and floods killed many more people and changed the course of the Indus River. Meanwhile, groups of people called the Aryans (AR·ee·uhnz) **migrated** to India. Soon a new civilization **emerged**.

CM Dixon/Heritage-I/Age fotostock

Reading**HELP**DESK

Academic Vocabulary

reside to live
abandon to leave and not return

migrate to move from one place to another
emerge to come into being or become known

252 *Ancient India*

The Indo-Europeans

The Aryans were not a race or ethnic group. Many historians believe that the Aryan people's language was part of a large language family known as Indo-European. A **language family** is a group of similar languages. Many modern Indian languages, like Hindi, are part of the Indo-European family. So are many European languages, including English. The Aryans were speakers of Indo-European languages.

Indo-European people lived in central Asia but began migrating to other places. Some moved west to Europe or south to Iran. The Aryans went to India. Like most Indo-Europeans, the Aryans raised cattle for meat, milk, and butter. They moved from place to place to find pastures and water for their cattle. The Aryans were expert horse riders and hunters, as well as fierce warriors. As they moved about, the Aryans sometimes raided nearby villages for food.

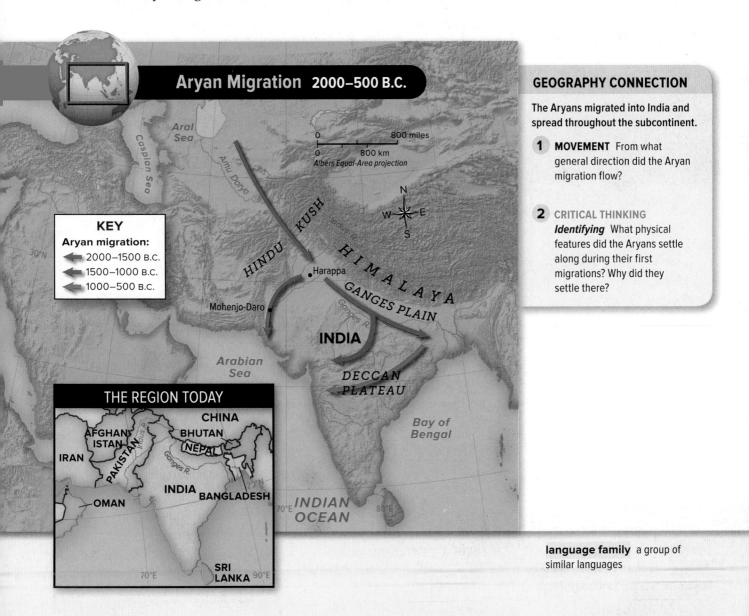

Aryan Migration 2000–500 B.C.

KEY
Aryan migration:
- 2000–1500 B.C.
- 1500–1000 B.C.
- 1000–500 B.C.

800 miles
800 km
Albers Equal-Area projection

Aral Sea
Caspian Sea
Amu Darya
HINDU KUSH
HIMALAYA
Harappa
GANGES PLAIN
Mohenjo-Daro
INDIA
Arabian Sea
DECCAN PLATEAU
Bay of Bengal
INDIAN OCEAN

THE REGION TODAY
CHINA
AFGHANISTAN
BHUTAN
NEPAL
IRAN
PAKISTAN
Indus R.
Ganges R.
INDIA
BANGLADESH
OMAN
SRI LANKA
70°E
90°E

GEOGRAPHY CONNECTION

The Aryans migrated into India and spread throughout the subcontinent.

1. **MOVEMENT** From what general direction did the Aryan migration flow?

2. **CRITICAL THINKING**
   Identifying What physical features did the Aryans settle along during their first migrations? Why did they settle there?

language family a group of similar languages

Hindi, India's national language, developed over time from ancient Sanskrit. The Aryans used Sanskrit to record many things.

▶ CRITICAL THINKING
Drawing Conclusions Why did early people develop a system of writing once they settled in groups?

From about 1500 to 1000 B.C., bands of Aryans moved throughout India. These groups mixed with the descendants of the Indus Valley people. Together, they created a new culture. Over time, the Aryans in India adopted a new way of life. They settled down in one place and became farmers, though they still raised cattle. Eventually, the Aryans saw their herds as sacred and banned the use of cattle as food.

The Aryans began to make iron tools to clear forests so they could farm the land. They also built irrigation systems. Gradually, they turned the Ganges River valley into productive farmland. In the north, farmers grew grains such as wheat, millet, and barley. Millet is a grain that is still an important food in many parts of the world. Farmers planted rice in the fertile river valleys. In the south, farmers grew crops such as cotton, vegetables, pepper, ginger, and cinnamon.

The Aryans lived in tribes. Each tribe was led by a **raja** (RAH·jah), or prince. The rajas created their own small kingdoms, which often fought each other over cattle, treasure, and land.

Like most nomadic people, the early Aryans had no written language. After they settled in villages, they developed a written language called **Sanskrit** (SAN·skriht). Sanskrit gave people a way to record sales, trade, and land ownership. Eventually, Aryan hymns, stories, poems, and prayers were also written in Sanskrit. Later, they were recorded and collected into sacred **texts** known as the **Vedas** (VAY·duhs). Examples of the Vedas remain today. This prayer in the Vedas asks for divine help in offering sacrifices:

PRIMARY SOURCE

❝ Let us invoke [call upon] today, to aid our labour, the Lord of Speech, … May he hear kindly all our invocations [prayers] who gives all bliss for aid, whose works are righteous. ❞

—from Visvakarman," *Rig-Veda*, Book 10, Hymn LXXXI

✔ PROGRESS CHECK

Identifying How did the Aryans change their way of life after they settled in India?

Egmont Stringl/Imagebroker RF/Age fotostock

Reading**HELP**DESK

raja an Indian prince
Sanskrit the first written language of India
Vedas ancient sacred writings of India

guru a teacher

Academic Vocabulary

text words written down in a particular form, such as a book
manual work done by hand

Ancient Indian Society

GUIDING QUESTION *How was society in ancient India organized?*

As the Aryans settled into India, people set up towns along India's Ganges River. Most people still farmed for a living. Some workers specialized in crafts such as carpentry or weaving. Others took part in trade. As India's economy grew, a system of social classes gradually developed.

What were the *Varnas*?

The four social classes of ancient India are called *varnas* (VUR·nehs). People were considered members of the *varna* into which they were born. The most powerful *varnas* were the Brahmins (BRAH·mihns) and Kshatriyas (KSHA·tree·uhs). The Brahmins were the priests—the people who performed religious ceremonies. The Kshatriyas were warriors who ran the government and army.

Craftspeople in India belonged to the Vaisyas *varna*.

There's More Online! connected.mcgraw-hill.com

Next were the Vaisyas (VYSH·yuhs), or commoners. Vaisyas were usually farmers, craftspeople, and merchants. Below the Vaisyas came the Sudras (SOO·druhs). Sudras were **manual** workers and servants who had few rights. Most Indians were in the Sudra *varna*. The four *varna* gradually divided into thousands of smaller groups known as *jati* (JAH·tee). Many *jati* were based on the type of work a person did. These *jati* had their own strict rules for diet, marriage, and social customs.

Scholars refer to the *jati* system as a caste (KAST) system. In such a system, people remain in the same social group for life. People's *jati* determine the jobs they may take. *Jati* also affects people's choice of marriage partners.

At the lowest level of society were the Untouchables. The Untouchables were not part of the *jati* system. They did work that *jati* Indians would not do, such as collecting trash, skinning animals, and carrying dead bodies.

In ancient India, the family was the center of life. Grandparents, parents, and children lived together in an extended family. Elder family members were respected. The oldest male in the family was in charge of the entire household.

Indian men had more rights than women. Males inherited property, unless there were no sons in the family. Men attended school or became priests, while women were educated at home.

In India's leading families, a boy had a **guru** (GUR·oo), or teacher, until he attended school in the city. Young men from these families could marry only after finishing 12 years of education.

In India, parents arranged marriages for their children. Even today, many marriages are arranged. In early India, boys and girls often married in their teens. People could not get divorced.

✔ **PROGRESS CHECK**

Explaining What was family life like in ancient India?

LESSON 1 REVIEW

Review Vocabulary

1. Why was the development of *Sanskrit* important to making the *Vedas* last?

Answer the Guiding Questions

2. *Explaining* Although the monsoons may bring severe storms, they are considered necessary in India. Why?

3. *Summarizing* What characteristics did the Indus Valley cities have in common?

4. *Describing* How did the Aryans interact with the Indus Valley people?

5. *Categorizing* What are the four major social groups in the *varna* system?

6. **ARGUMENT** What is the most important way the Aryans affected India? Write a brief essay that summarizes your ideas about their impact.

LESSON 2
Religions of Ancient India

ESSENTIAL QUESTION

• How do religions develop?

IT MATTERS BECAUSE
Millions of people around the world today follow the beliefs of religions that began in ancient India.

Origins of Hinduism

GUIDING QUESTION *What are the basic beliefs of Hinduism? How did Hinduism develop?*

Hinduism (HIHN·doo·ih·zuhm) is one of the world's oldest religions. It is also the third largest religion, after Christianity and Islam. Hinduism has no one founder and no one holy book. Hindus usually pay respect to the Vedas. They also take part in religious rituals, either at home or in a local temple.

At first, the Vedas had to be memorized by Brahmin priests and spoken out loud. Much later, they were written down in Sanskrit. Over time, the Brahmin religion blended with the ideas of other people of India. This mix of beliefs eventually became known as Hinduism.

What is Hinduism?

Hinduism includes many beliefs and practices. A core belief of Hinduism is that there is one universal spirit called **Brahman** (BRAH·muhn).

Ancient texts known as the Upanishads (oo·PAH·nih·SHADZ) describe the search for Brahman. These writings say that every living thing has a soul that is part of Brahman. The body is part of life on Earth. At death, the soul leaves the body and joins with Brahman.

ReadingHELPDESK

Taking Notes: *Describing*

Use a diagram like this one to identify three important facts about the religions of ancient India.

| Hinduism | Buddhism |

| Jainism |

Content Vocabulary

- **Hinduism**
- **Brahman**
- **reincarnation**
- karma
- **dharma**
- **Buddhism**
- **nirvana**
- **Jainism**

The Upanishads (upper right) present basic Hindu views about the universe. Many Hindus regard the deity Brahma as the creator of the universe. Images of Brahma show him with four heads. Each head is believed to have delivered one of the four Vedas, or early sacred texts.

The Upanishads say that a soul that becomes one with Brahman is like a lump of salt thrown into water. The lump of salt is gone, but the water tastes salty. The salt has become part of the water.

Most ancient Indians, however, could not easily understand the idea of Brahman. They believed in many different deities that were more like people. Hindus built temples and statues and held ceremonies for these deities. Eventually, three deities became the most important: *Brahma* the Creator, *Vishnu* the Preserver, and *Shiva* the Destroyer. Over time, many Hindus came to think of all the deities as different parts of Brahman, the one universal spirit.

Another part of Hinduism is the belief in **reincarnation** (REE·ihn·kahr·NAY·shuhn), or the rebirth of the soul. Hindus strive for *moksha*, the ultimate peace. Hindus believe that most souls do not reunite with Brahman immediately after death. Instead, each soul must first pass through many lives. The Upanishads describe reincarnation as a process in this way:

PRIMARY SOURCE

❝ As a caterpillar, having reached the end of a blade of grass, takes hold of another blade, then draws its body from the first, so the Self having reached the end of his body, takes hold of another body, then draws itself from the first. ❞

—from *Brihadaranyaka Upanishad, Fourth Brahmana*, line 3

Reading HELPDESK

Hinduism a major religion that developed in ancient India

Brahman the universal spirit worshipped by Hindus

reincarnation the rebirth of the soul

karma a force that decides the form that people will be reborn into in their next lives

dharma a person's personal duty, based on the individual's place in society

Academic Vocabulary

status a person's rank compared to others

In Hinduism, the idea of reincarnation is closely related to another idea known as **karma** (KAHR·muh). According to karma, people's **status** in life is not an accident. It is based on what they did in past lives. In addition, the things people do in this life decide how they will be reborn. If someone leads a bad life, that person is reborn into a lower form of life. When good people die, their souls are reborn into a higher form of life.

Hindus believe they have to earn a better existence in the next life. To do that, they must follow **dharma** (DAHR·muh), or their personal duty. People's duties are different, depending on their place in society. A farmer has different duties than a priest. Men have different duties than women.

How did Hindu beliefs shape the way of life in ancient India? For one thing, Indians accepted the Hindu idea that all life is sacred. Animals as well as people were treated with kindness and respect.

Beliefs such as reincarnation also made many Indians more accepting of the *jati* system. A devout Hindu believed that the people in a higher *jati* were superior and deserved their status. At the same time, the belief in reincarnation gave hope to people from every walk of life. A person who leads a good life is reborn into a higher *jati*.

✓ PROGRESS CHECK

Understanding Cause and Effect How did Hinduism affect the way ancient Indians lived day to day?

There's More Online! connected.mcgraw-hill.com

Hindu Beliefs

Many Hindus today believe that a man should go through four stages in his life: a student (preparing to live in the world), a married man (accepting worldly responsibilities), a forest dweller (retirement from the world), and finally, a wandering monk (completely renouncing the world).

Indian Hindus believe the Ganges River is sacred. They believe that the river is the physical form of a female deity, and they bathe in the river to purify themselves. What tells you this photo shows Hindus in modern times?

MIXA Co. Ltd./Getty Images

**The Buddha
(c. 563 B.C.–c. 483 B.C.)**

In his search for wisdom, Siddhartha Gautama lived a very simple life. He lived apart from people and slept on the ground. To clear his mind, he stopped eating for a time.

Still, after years, he felt he was no closer to the truth. One day he sat down in the shade of a tree to meditate. At last, Buddhist texts say, he learned the truth he had been seeking. Once he began teaching, he became known to his followers as the Buddha, or "Enlightened One."

▶ **CRITICAL THINKING**
Speculating Why do you think Siddhartha Gautama sought wisdom by living in such a simple way?

Rise of Buddhism

GUIDING QUESTION *Why did Buddhism appeal to many people in various parts of Asia?*

During the 500s B.C., some Indians felt unhappy with the many ceremonies of the Hindu religion. They wanted a simpler, more spiritual faith. They left their homes and looked for peace in the hills and forests. Many trained their minds to **focus** and think in positive ways. This training was called meditation. Some seekers developed new ideas and became religious teachers.

One of these teachers was Siddhartha Gautama (sih·DAHR·tuh GOW·tah·muh). He became known as the Buddha (BOO·dah). He founded a new religion called **Buddhism** (BOO·dih·zuhm).

The Buddha

Today, Buddhism is one of the major world religions. Most Buddhists live in Southeast Asia and East Asia. Only a few live in India, Buddhism's birthplace.

Siddhartha Gautama was born around the year 563 B.C. The exact date of his birth is not known. He grew up as a prince in a small kingdom near the Himalaya. Today, this area is in southern Nepal (nuh·PAWL).

As a young man, Siddhartha seemed to have everything. He was rich, handsome, and happily married with a newborn son. Then one day he left his palace to explore the life of ordinary people in the kingdom. As he traveled, Siddhartha was shocked at the misery and poverty around him. He saw beggars, people who were sick, and aged people with nowhere to live. For the first time, he understood that the world was filled with suffering.

Siddhartha gave up all he had and became a monk. Saying good-bye to his wife and son, he began his journey to find the meaning of life. Dressed in a yellow robe, he traveled the country, stopping to **meditate**, or think deeply. As he preached his message to people, he gathered followers. His teachings became known as Buddhism.

What Did the Buddha Teach?

Some of the Buddha's ideas were not new to India. He followed some Hindu ideas and changed others. Like Hindus, the Buddha believed that the world of the spirit was more important than the everyday world. He felt that one reason people suffered in life was that they cared too much about the wrong things. These included fame, money, and personal possessions. Wanting such

---

Reading**HELP**DESK

Buddhism a religion founded in ancient India by the religious teacher the Buddha

Academic Vocabulary

focus to place all of one's attention on something
meditate to focus one's thoughts to gain a higher level of spiritual awareness

things could fill people with bad emotions like greed or anger. But seeking spiritual truth, he believed, led to inner peace.

The Buddha taught his followers the Four Noble Truths. He believed these would help people seek spiritual truth.

The Four Noble Truths:

1. Life is full of suffering.
2. People suffer because they desire worldly things and want to satisfy themselves.
3. The way to end suffering is to stop desiring things.
4. The only way to stop desiring things is to follow the Eightfold Path.

The Buddha's fourth truth says that people can end suffering by following eight steps.

The Eightfold Path:

1. Know and understand the Four Noble Truths.
2. Give up worldly things and do not harm others.
3. Tell the truth, do not gossip, and do not speak badly of others.
4. Do not **commit** evil acts, such as killing, stealing, or living an unclean life.
5. Do rewarding work.
6. Work for good and oppose evil.
7. Make sure your mind keeps your senses under control.
8. Practice meditation to see the world in a new way.

When people were finally free from all earthly concerns, they would reach **nirvana** (nihr·VAH· nuh). According to Buddhist teaching, nirvana is not a physical place. It is an emotional or spiritual state, a feeling of perfect peace and happiness.

Buddhism spread because it welcomed people from all walks of life. The Buddha placed little importance on the *jati* system. He believed people's place in life did not depend on the *jati* into which they were born. The Buddha explained that the success of life depended on peoples' behavior now.

Like Hindus, the Buddha believed in reincarnation, but in a different way. He taught that people could end the cycle of rebirth by following the Eightfold Path rather than their dharma.

Buddhist monks devote their lives to honoring the Buddha through prayer and gifts. Monks are considered to be on a higher spiritual level than other people, and they serve as spiritual teachers.

Martin Puddy/Corbis

nirvana a state of perfect happiness and peace

Academic Vocabulary

commit to carry out or do

Many people accepted the Buddha's message, especially Untouchables and Indians in the lower *jati*. For the first time, these groups heard that they, too, could reach enlightenment.

For more than 40 years, the Buddha taught his ideas. After his death, Buddha's followers disagreed over the meaning of the Buddha's ideas. Eventually, the Buddhists divided into two groups: Theravada (ther·uh·VAH·duh) Buddhists and Mahayana (mah·huh·YAH·nuh) Buddhists.

Theravada Buddhism

Theravada means "teachings of the elders." Followers of Theravada view the Buddha as a great teacher, but not a god. Theravada Buddhism is the major religion of the modern-day country of Sri Lanka (sree LAHN·kuh). Buddhist teachers spread the ideas of Theravada to Myanmar (MEEAHN·mahr), Thailand (TEYE·land), Cambodia (kam·BOH·dee·uh), and Laos (LAH·ohs).

Mahayana Buddhism

Mahayana Buddhism teaches that the Buddha is a god. Followers of Mahayana Buddhism believe that the Eightfold Path is too difficult for most people. By worshipping the Buddha, people will go to a heaven after they die. There, they can follow the Eightfold Path and reach nirvana.

Bodhisattvas (BOH·dih·SUHT·vuhz) hold a special place in Mahayana Buddhism. Bodhisattvas are enlightened people who do not enter heaven. Instead, they stay on Earth to do good deeds and help others on the path to nirvana.

Mahayana Buddhism spread northward into China and from there to Korea and Japan. A special kind of Mahayana Buddhism arose in the central Asian country of Tibet (tih·BEHT).

Buddhist leaders called lamas led the government of Tibet. The Dalai Lama (DAH·ly LAH·muh) led Tibet's government, and the Panchen Lama led the religion. Tibetans considered both leaders to be reincarnations of the Buddha.

Today, few Buddhists live in India where the Buddha first preached. Buddhism, however, is widely practiced in Southeast Asia and East Asia. There are an **estimated** 376 million Buddhists in the world today.

 PROGRESS CHECK

Identifying Where is Buddhism practiced today and in what forms?

It is a tradition for Buddhist monks in Tibet to create geometric patterns using brightly colored powders, stones, or pieces of metal. The shapes in the patterns represent the cosmos, or universe, and are believed to have special powers.

Jainism

GUIDING QUESTION *What are the teachings of Jainism?*

Along with Hinduism and Buddhism, another Indian faith known as **Jainism** (JEYE·nih·zihm) arose about 500 B.C. Today, there are 6 million followers of Jainism. Most of them live in India.

Who is Mahavira?

The exact origins of Jainism are unknown. Its current form was developed by a religious leader named Mahavira. Mahavira lived in India at about the same time as Siddhartha Gautama.

Like Siddhartha, Mahavira came from a wealthy royal family in northern India. After his parents died, Mahavira gave up his wealth and property. He owned nothing and begged for his food.

Mahavira became known as the Jina, or the conqueror. His followers came to be known as Jains. Many of Mahavira's teachings were like those of the Buddha. Both taught that people needed to stop wanting worldly things. Only by doing so could they escape the cycle of rebirth and reach nirvana. The Jains practiced strict poverty.

Jainism a religion of ancient India that does not believe in a supreme being. It emphasizes nonviolence and respect for all living things.

Gandhi (center) used nonviolence as an effective protest tool. He often protested by fasting, or not eating, to show support for a cause.

What is *Ahimsa*?

The key value of Jainism is *ahimsa* (ah·HIM·sah). This means practicing nonviolence toward all living things. Believing that all life is sacred, Mahavira's followers tried to avoid harming any living creature. For example, they used brooms to sweep away insects so that they would not step on them. Jains did not farm because they were afraid of plowing under worms and other living things in the soil.

The idea of *ahimsa* has long influenced India's culture and politics. In the 1900s, the Indian leader Mohandas Gandhi (MOE·han·dahs GANH·dee) wanted to free India from Great Britain. He led a nonviolent struggle against British rule. Thousands would come to hear Gandhi speak or to simply sit with him while he prayed. At the time, Indians refused to pay taxes or buy British goods as a show of protest. Many protesters were jailed, but India eventually gained its independence. Gandhi himself was jailed many times.

Gandhi's method of nonviolent resistance influenced many others. In the United States, Dr. Martin Luther King, Jr., led nonviolent protests to gain rights for African Americans. Like Gandhi, Dr. King was able to use nonviolence to bring about great change in his country.

✓ PROGRESS CHECK

Identifying What is the belief of *ahimsa*?

LESSON 2 REVIEW

Review Vocabulary

1. What do the ideas of *reincarnation* and *karma* have in common?

2. How would practicing *Buddhism* affect people's daily lives?

Answer the Guiding Questions

3. *Explaining* What do Hindus believe about Brahman?

4. *Drawing Conclusions* How did the Buddha say people should live?

5. *Comparing* What beliefs do Buddhism and Jainism share?

6. **INFORMATIVE/EXPLANATORY** Write a paragraph comparing Hindu and Buddhist beliefs about reincarnation and how one should live.

LESSON 3
The Mauryan Empire

• What makes a culture unique?

IT MATTERS BECAUSE
The Mauryan and Gupta dynasties formed the first great Indian empires. Their cultures were the basis for civilizations that followed.

Origin of an Empire

GUIDING QUESTION *How did religion affect the development of the Mauryan Empire?*

By the 500s B.C., India was divided into many small kingdoms. Conflict over land and trade weakened the kingdoms, leaving them open to foreign invasion. Persian armies conquered the Indus Valley in the 500s B.C. and made it part of the Persian Empire. The Greeks, under Alexander the Great, then defeated the Persians. Alexander entered India but turned back in 325 B.C., when his homesick troops threatened to rebel.

India's First Empire

After Alexander left India, an Indian military officer named Chandra Gupta Maurya (CHUHN·druh GUP·tuh MAH· oor·yuh) built a strong army. He knew that only a large and powerful empire could defend India against invasion. In 321 B.C., Chandra Gupta set out to conquer northern India and unify the region under his rule.

Chandra Gupta was the first ruler of the Mauryan dynasty. He was a skilled administrator. He set up a well-run government in his capital city of Pataliputra (PAH·tah·lih·POO·truh). One of his major achievements was an efficient postal system. The system improved communications throughout his empire.

Reading**HELP**DESK

Taking Notes: *Identifying*

Use a chart like this one to identify important information about the Mauryan and Gupta Empires.

Mauryan	Gupta

Content Vocabulary

• stupa   • *Bhagavad Gita*
• pilgrim

CONNECTION

The Mauryan dynasty built the first great Indian empire.

1 REGION Which part of India was not in the Mauryan Empire?

2 CRITICAL THINKING
Analyzing What does the map key tell you about the religion of the Mauryan Empire?

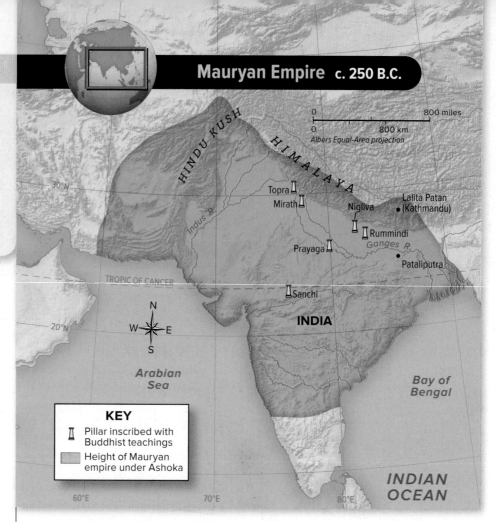

Mauryan Empire c. 250 B.C.

KEY

- Pillar inscribed with Buddhist teachings
- Height of Mauryan empire under Ashoka

Chandra Gupta's powerful army crushed any resistance to his rule. He also used spies to report any disloyalty among his subjects. While he was a strong ruler, Chandra Gupta was very cautious. He was afraid of being poisoned, so he had servants taste his food before he ate it. He was so concerned about being attacked that he never slept two nights in a row in the same bed.

What Did Ashoka Accomplish?

The Mauryan Empire reached the height of its glory under Chandra Gupta's grandson Ashoka (uh·SOH·kuh). Ashoka governed most of northern and central India from about 273 B.C. to 232 B.C.

Ashoka was an unusual king. Like many rulers, Ashoka began his rule with fierce wars of conquest. **Eventually**, he came to hate killing. After one battle, he looked at the fields covered with dead and wounded soldiers. He was horrified by what he saw. He decided that he would follow Buddhist teachings and become a man of peace.

Reading**HELP**DESK

stupa a Buddhist shrine, usually dome-shaped

Academic Vocabulary

eventual taking place at an unnamed later time
promote to encourage the doing of something

Ashoka kept his promise. During the rest of his life, he tried to improve the lives of his people. Ashoka made laws that encouraged people to do good deeds, practice nonviolence, and respect others. He created hospitals for people and for animals. He built fine roads, with rest houses and shade trees for the travelers' comfort.

Ashoka was the first ruler to **promote** Buddhism. He sent teachers to spread the religion throughout India and other parts of Asia. Buddhist teachings and the laws of Ashoka were carved on rocks and tall stone pillars for all the people to read. Carved on one rock is the idea that:

PRIMARY SOURCE

" Father and mother must be hearkened [listened to]; similarly, respect for living creatures must be firmly established; truth must be spoken. These are the virtues of the Law of Piety [devotion] which must be practiced. "

—from "Summary of the Law of Piety," The Edicts of Ashoka

Ashoka also had thousands of **stupas** (stoo•puhs) built throughout India. Stupas are Buddhist shrines shaped like a dome or burial mound. The stupas contained religious objects and served as places of worship. Although he was a devout Buddhist, Ashoka was tolerant of all beliefs and allowed his Hindu subjects to practice their religion.

Ashoka's able leadership helped the Mauryan Empire prosper. India's good roads helped it become the center of a large trade network that stretched to the Mediterranean Sea.

Ashoka—shown here—made regular visits to rural people of his empire to spread Buddhist ideas and learn about their needs. He also had this "Great Stupa" built in honor of Buddha.

▶ **CRITICAL THINKING**
Speculating Why do you think Ashoka had so many stupas built?

The End of the Mauryan Empire

After Ashoka died in 232 B.C., the Mauryan Empire **declined**. The kings who came after Ashoka lacked his kindness and skills. The new rulers made merchants pay heavy taxes and took lands from the peasants. The Indian people rebelled against the harsh treatment. In 183 B.C., the last Mauryan king was murdered by one of his own generals. The land of the Mauryan Empire split into many small warring kingdoms.

✅ **PROGRESS CHECK**

Explaining What caused Ashoka to denounce violence? What was the result?

The Gupta Empire

GUIDING QUESTION *Why did the Gupta Empire become powerful?*

For 500 years, the small warring kingdoms fought one another for control of India. Then, in A.D. 320, the Gupta dynasty came to power in the Ganges River valley. The city of Pataliputra had been the capital of the old Mauryan Empire. It now became the capital of the Gupta Empire. Chandra Gupta I, the first Gupta ruler, had the same name as the first ruler of the Mauryan dynasty.

Chandra Gupta I ruled for 10 years. He chose his son, Samudra Gupta (suh·MOO·druh GUP·tuh), to rule after him. Samudra Gupta expanded the Gupta Empire in northern India. He was a great military leader and a patron of arts and literature. Under Samudra Gupta, India entered a golden age.

Gupta rulers practiced the Hindu religion like many of their subjects did. They donated money to support Hindu scholars and build Hindu temples. Many temples had brightly painted sculptures of deities and images from Hindu sacred writings.

Trade helped the Gupta Empire thrive. Salt, cloth, and iron were common goods traded in India. Indian merchants also traded with China and with lands in Southeast Asia and the Mediterranean area. The Gupta rulers benefited from their control of much of the trade. They owned silver and gold mines and large estates.

Cities arose along trade routes. People called **pilgrims** (PIHL·gruhms) used the trade routes to journey to holy sites. Cities with famous temples grew wealthy from visiting pilgrims.

✅ **PROGRESS CHECK**

Explaining How did the Gupta Empire profit from trade routes?

Reading**HELP**DESK

pilgrim a person who travels to holy sites

Academic Vocabulary

decline to become smaller or weaker

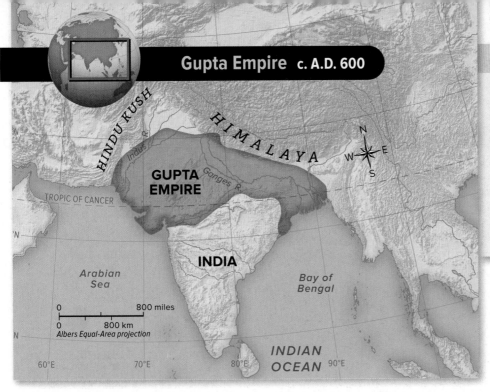

Gupta Empire c. A.D. 600

GEOGRAPHY CONNECTION

The Gupta dynasty founded the second great Indian empire.

1 LOCATION Where was the Gupta Empire located? Around what river valleys was it formed?

2 CRITICAL THINKING
Analyzing What does this map suggest about the power of the Gupta Empire?

Culture in Ancient India

GUIDING QUESTION *What were the cultural contributions of the Mauryan and Gupta Empires?*

Ancient India produced a brilliant culture. Artists, builders, writers, and scientists made many **contributions** while the Mauryan and Gupta kings ruled.

The Literature of India

The Vedas were among the first works written in the Sanskrit language. The literature of ancient India also includes epics. Hindus consider their epics to be sacred texts that teach important moral lessons. The people could learn the correct and acceptable behavior through interesting stories.

The *Mahabharata* (muh·HAH·BAH·ruh·tuh) is an ancient religious epic. It is also the longest poem in any written language, with about 90,000 verses. The *Mahabharata* describes a struggle for control of an Indian kingdom that took place about 1100 B.C. Its exciting stories about great heroes influenced Hindus then and now.

The best-known section of the *Mahabharata* is the **Bhagavad Gita** (BAH·guh·VAHD GEE·tuh), or "Song of the Lord." In it, the deity Krishna goes with a prince into battle. The prince does not want to fight because members of his family are on the other side.

Bhagavad Gita a section of the Indian epic the *Mahabharata*

Academic Vocabulary

contribute to give or donate something

Hindu artists tried to depict the deities. This picture shows Krishna (left) and Prince Arjuna (right).

Krishna reminds the prince to obey his duty as a warrior. The prince makes the painful choice to fight his family.

A second epic, the *Ramayana* (rah·mah·YAH·nah), is a poem that grew to about 25,000 verses before it was written down. It tells the story of Rama, the perfect king, and Sita, his faithful wife. When Sita is kidnapped by an evil king, Rama rushes to her rescue with the help of friends.

The Arts and Architecture

The ancient Hindus believed that music was a gift from the gods. Many sacred texts, such as the Bhagavad Gita, were probably sung. At yearly festivals, people danced, sang, and played music. Musical instruments included tambourines, flutes, drums, and lutes.

Much of early India's art was created on fragile materials, such as paper, and has not survived. What is left today is mostly religious art—elaborate sculptures carved in stone. Sculptors carved images of the Buddha as early as the A.D. 100s.

The most important **structures** in early India were the rulers' palaces and the temples used for religious worship. During Ashoka's reign, many stone pillars carved with Buddhist messages were placed alongside roads.

Mathematics

Indian mathematicians of the Gupta period made important contributions. Aryabhata (AHR·yuh·BUHT·uh) was one of the first scientists known to have used algebra. Indian mathematicians explained the idea of infinity—something without an end. They also invented the symbol "0" and connected it with the idea of nothing. The Indians' invention of zero affected the study of mathematics and science. Modern technology, such as computers, would not be possible without the concept of zero.

Soltan Frédéric/Corbis Documentary/Getty Images

Academic Vocabulary

structure a building or other built object

Gupta mathematicians developed symbols for the numbers 1 to 9 that we use today. In the A.D. 700s, Arab traders adopted these number symbols, or numerals. European traders later borrowed them from the Arabs. In the A.D. 1200s, use of these numbers spread though Europe and replaced Roman numerals. Today, this system of number symbols is known as the Indian-Arabic numerical system.

Advances in Science

Scientists and scholars in ancient India also made important advances in astronomy and technology. Indian astronomers mapped the movements of planets and stars. They proposed the theory that the Earth was round and revolved around the sun. During the Gupta period, scientists advanced metalworking. Among their most impressive constructions is the pillar of iron of Delhi, dating from around A.D. 400. It is still standing, and, in spite of its age, it has hardly rusted.

Advances in Medicine

Can you imagine doctors performing dental surgery 1600 years ago? Indian doctors treated dental problems using tools such as the bow drill. The doctors used this tool, which was usually used to make fire, to drill teeth.

Doctors during the Gupta era were advanced for their time. They could set broken bones, sew wounds, and perform complicated surgeries. They also were skilled in making medical instruments, such as scalpels and needles.

A doctor named Shushruta (shoosh·ROO·tah) repaired damaged noses in an early type of plastic surgery. Indian doctors used herbs to cure illnesses. They also believed in healing the causes of a disease, not just treating the disease itself.

✅ **PROGRESS CHECK**

Analyzing What lasting achievement did Indian mathematicians make?

Connections to TODAY

Math Poems

Some writings about mathematics from the Gupta dynasty have survived. The math formulas are written as poems. Scholars had to find ways to fit numbers into the poems so that they would sound correct. Imagine having to turn in your math homework in the form of a poem.

Ancient Indian contributions to mathematics made much of today's math-based technology possible.

LESSON 3 REVIEW

Review Vocabulary

1. How would a *pilgrim* in ancient India use a *stupa*?

2. What is the *Bhagavad Gita*?

Answer the Guiding Questions

3. *Determining Cause and Effect* How did religion influence the Mauryan Empire?

4. *Describing* How did the Gupta Empire grow powerful?

5. *Identifying* What were the written epics of the Mauryan and Gupta period?

6. **NARRATIVE** You are living in India during the rule of Ashoka. Write a letter to a friend describing the things Ashoka is doing as a leader. In your letter, explain whether you think Ashoka is a great ruler.

Write your answers on a separate piece of paper.

1 **Exploring the Essential Question**

NARRATIVE You are a scholar living in India among the descendants of the Aryans. One day you stumble across a great mural that shows what life was like in the city of Mohenjo-Daro at its height. Write a description to your friends of what the art shows about people and daily life in the city. How does it compare to your life?

2 **21st Century Skills**

MANAGE INFORMATION Create a poster that displays what you have learned about the Hindu religion. Include the concepts of karma and dharma, with pictures and captions that help show the meaning of each.

3 **Thinking Like a Historian**

GEOGRAPHY AND CIVILIZATION Use a graphic organizer like the one shown here to show why river valleys were the best locations for early civilizations. Write "River" in the center circle and the advantages of living by a river in the surrounding circles. Refer back to the way the citizens of Harappa and Mohenjo-Daro—and later the Aryans—used the river in their daily lives.

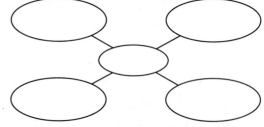

4 **GEOGRAPHY ACTIVITY**

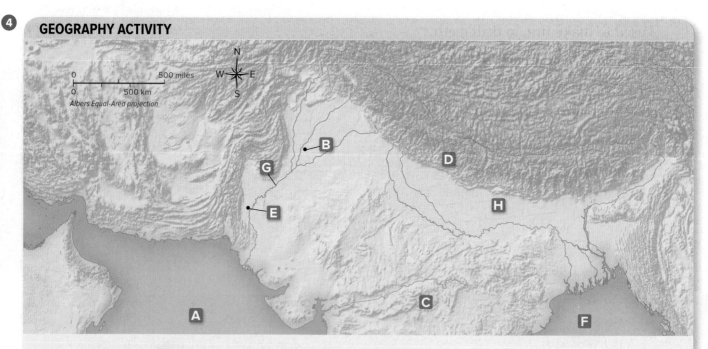

Locating Places

Match the letters on the map with the numbered places listed below.

1. Himalaya
2. Arabian Sea
3. Ganges River
4. Harappa
5. Bay of Bengal
6. Deccan Plateau
7. Mohenjo-Daro
8. Indus River

Directions: Write your answers on a separate piece of paper.

CHECKING FOR UNDERSTANDING

1 Match each of the terms with its definition.

1. guru
2. nirvana
3. Buddhism
4. pilgrim
5. reincarnation
6. monsoon
7. subcontinent
8. Hinduism

A. a religion founded in ancient India by the Buddha
B. a large landmass that is smaller than a continent
C. seasonal wind in the Indian Ocean and south Asia
D. a major religion that developed in ancient India
E. a teacher
F. the rebirth of the soul
G. a state of perfect happiness and peace
H. a person who travels to holy sites

REVIEW THE GUIDING QUESTIONS

2 *Explaining* How did natural forces and the geography of India affect the development of civilization there?

3 *Locating* Where did the Indus Valley civilization begin?

4 *Identifying* How did the creation of iron tools affect the Aryans' lifestyle?

5 *Listing* List the four main social classes of ancient India, in order from most to least powerful.

6 *Sequencing* How did the two main traditions of Buddhism spread through Asia?

7 *Explaining* Why would people in the lower *jati* be especially attracted to Buddhism?

8 *Summarizing* What are the main tenets of Jainism?

9 *Describing* How did Ashoka's commitment to Buddhism impact the Mauryan Empire?

10 *Explaining* What were the reasons behind the economic prosperity of the Gupta Empire?

11 *Specifying* How have the achievements of Indian mathematicians affected the modern world?

CRITICAL THINKING

12 *Analyzing* How did the physical geography of India protect the Indus Valley civilization?

13 *Speculating* What evidence exists to suggest that the Indus Valley civilization was a central government rather than a group of autonomous city-states?

14 *Determining Cause and Effect* What impact did the the Aryans have on the Indus Valley civilization?

15 *Comparing and Contrasting* In what ways does the social structure of the United States resemble ancient India? In what ways is it different?

16 *Interpreting* Why do Hindus believe that most people are reincarnated after death?

17 *Making Inferences* How might the ideas about karma and *jati* influence the way a Hindu lives his or her life?

18 *Assessing* What was the greatest achievement of the Mauryan Empire?

19 *Evaluating* Do you think epics such as the *Mahabharata* and the *Ramayana* are effective ways to teach people how to live? Why or why not?

20 *Constructing an Argument* Do you think the Gupta period was a "golden age" of ancient India? Explain.

Need Extra Help?

If You've Missed Question	**1**	**2**	**3**	**4**	**5**	**6**	**7**	**8**	**9**	**10**	**11**	**12**	**13**	**14**	**15**	**16**	**17**	**18**	**19**	**20**
Review Lesson	1,2,3	1	1	1	1	2	2	2	3	3	3	1	1	1	1	2	2	3	3	3

DBQ SHORT RESPONSE

"There were a number of similarities [between Buddhism and Jainism]. Religious rituals were essentially congregational [performed in groups]. [M]onasteries [groups of men—monks—who center their lives entirely on religion] [were] organized on democratic lines, and initially accepting persons from all strata [walks] of life. Such monasteries were dependent on their neighborhoods for material support. Some of the monasteries developed into centres of education. The functioning of monks in society was greater, however, among the Buddhist orders. Wandering monks, preaching and seeking alms, gave the religions a missionary flavour. The recruitment of nuns signified a special concern for the status of women."

— Encyclopaedia Britannica Online

21 Buddhism and Jainism both established monasteries. Why were these groups called monasteries and how did they choose their members?

22 What purpose did a monk serve in the Buddhist religion and in the Jain religion?

EXTENDED RESPONSE

23 *Informative/Explanatory* Describe how the changes made by Ashoka during his reign reflected Buddhist teachings.

STANDARDIZED TEST PRACTICE

DBQ ANALYZING DOCUMENTS

24 *Drawing Conclusions* This passage is from the text *The Word of the Buddha*:

"He avoids the killing of living beings. ... He avoids stealing and abstains from [avoids] taking what is not given to him. Only what is given to him he takes, waiting till it is given; and he lives with a heart honest and pure."

According to the passage, what is the correct way to obtain something?

A. by taking whatever one needs   **C.** by demanding what one wants

B. by giving something in return   **D.** by waiting for it to be given

25 *Comparing and Contrasting* The first line of the passage expresses a view similar to what belief?

A. ahimsa   **C.** varna

B. karma   **D.** jati

Need Extra Help?

If You've Missed Question	21	22	23	24	25
Review Lesson	1	1	2	2	2

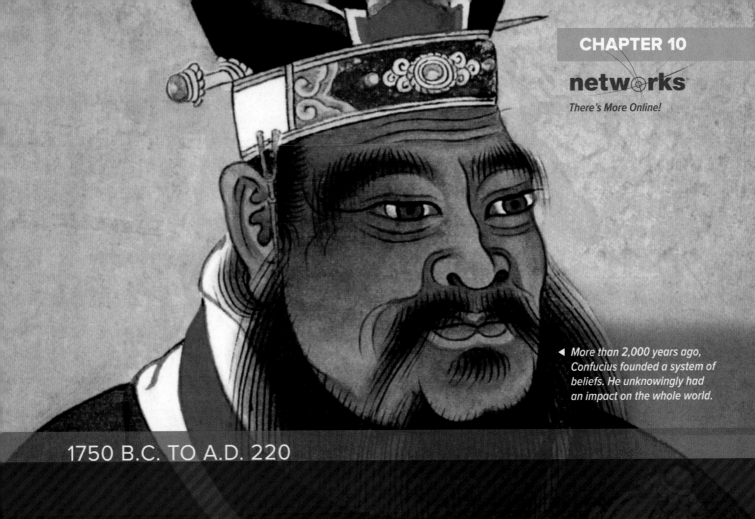

◀ *More than 2,000 years ago, Confucius founded a system of beliefs. He unknowingly had an impact on the whole world.*

1750 B.C. TO A.D. 220

Early China

Apic/Hulton Archives/Getty Images

THE STORY MATTERS ...

Confucius is considered to be one of early China's great teachers. Thousands of years after his death, his teachings are still followed. During his lifetime, Confucius taught people there was a way to build a better life for themselves and for society. To do that, he said, people must put the needs of their families and community above their own wants. He urged people to honor traditions and seek knowledge.

The teachings of Confucius spread throughout China. His legacy includes a respect for education and the importance of fulfilling all duties toward one's parents and community. That philosophy influences many Asian countries today.

ESSENTIAL QUESTIONS

- What makes a culture unique?
- How do new ideas change the way people live? • How do governments change?

Place & Time: Early China 1750 B.C. to A.D. 220

How and where did civilization begin in China? Artifacts that archaeologists have found in the Huang He Valley show that this valley is the first center of Chinese civilization. Historians believe that the valley's rich soil encouraged people to settle there to farm and eventually to build towns.

Step Into the Place

MAP FOCUS The borders of a country are rarely permanent. The land that makes up China has changed over the years.

1 **LOCATION** What bodies of water border Chinese lands to the east?

2 **MOVEMENT** In which direction did most of the Han Empire expansion take place?

3 **REGIONS** How does the area of modern China compare to the land controlled by early Chinese dynasties?

4 **CRITICAL THINKING**
Analyzing What causes the borders of a country to change?

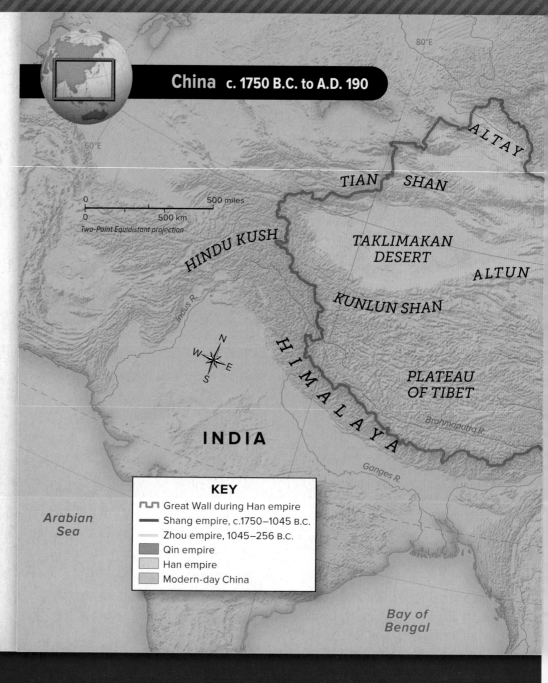

China c. 1750 B.C. to A.D. 190

KEY
- Great Wall during Han empire
- Shang empire, c.1750–1045 B.C.
- Zhou empire, 1045–256 B.C.
- Qin empire
- Han empire
- Modern-day China

500 miles
500 km
Two-Point Equidistant projection

ALTAY
TIAN SHAN
TAKLIMAKAN DESERT
ALTUN
HINDU KUSH
KUNLUN SHAN
Indus R.
HIMALAYA
PLATEAU OF TIBET
Brahmaputra R.
INDIA
Ganges R.
Arabian Sea
Bay of Bengal

Step Into the Time

TIME LINE Choose an event from the time line and write a paragraph predicting the general social, political, or economic consequences that event might have for the world.

c. 1750 B.C. Shang dynasty begins

EARLY CHINA			
THE WORLD	2000 B.C.	1750 B.C.	1500 B.C.

c. 2540 B.C. Great Pyramid built in Giza

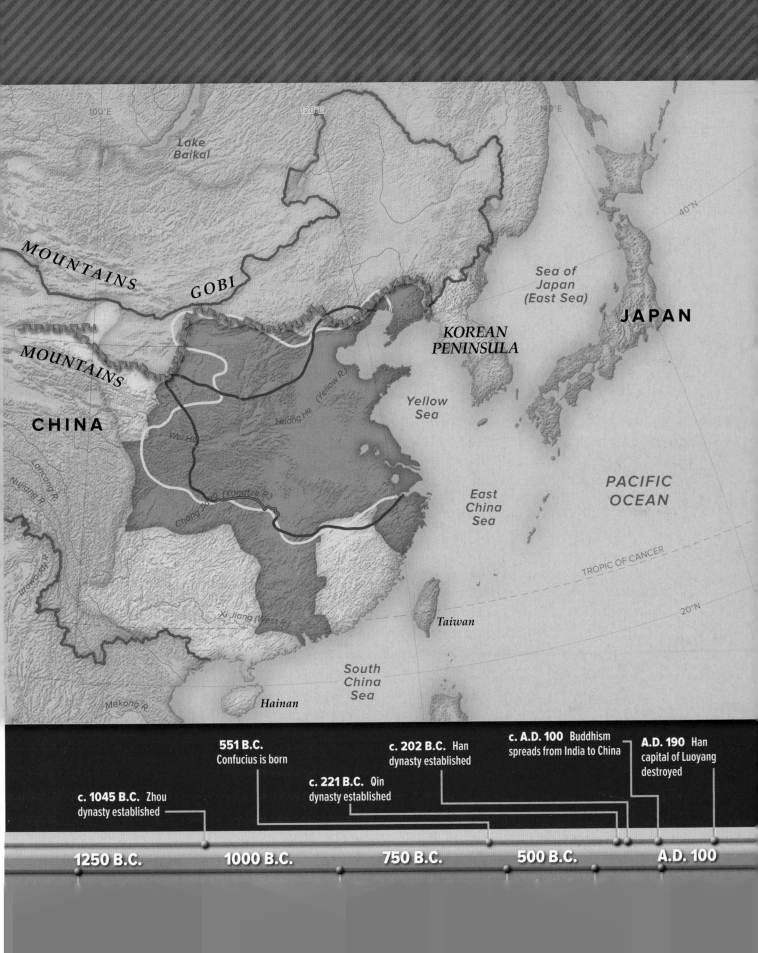

MOUNTAINS

GOBI

MOUNTAINS

CHINA

Lake
Baikal

100°E

120°E

120°E

40°N

Sea of
Japan
(East Sea)

JAPAN

KOREAN
PENINSULA

Yellow
Sea

Huang He (Yellow R.)

Wei He

Chang Jiang (Yangtze R.)

Lancang R.

Nujiang R.

Irrawaddy R.

Xi Jiang (West R.)

Mekong R.

Hainan

South
China
Sea

Taiwan

East
China
Sea

PACIFIC
OCEAN

TROPIC OF CANCER

20°N

551 B.C.
Confucius is born

c. 202 B.C. Han
dynasty established

c. A.D. 100 Buddhism
spreads from India to China

A.D. 190 Han
capital of Luoyang
destroyed

c. 221 B.C. Qin
dynasty established

c. 1045 B.C. Zhou
dynasty established

1250 B.C.   **1000 B.C.**   **750 B.C.**   **500 B.C.**   **A.D. 100**

The Birth of Chinese Civilization

There's More Online!

• What makes a culture unique?

IT MATTERS BECAUSE
Today, China is one of the world's most powerful countries.

The Land of China

GUIDING QUESTION *How have rivers, mountains, and deserts shaped the development of China's civilization?*

The ancient civilizations of Egypt, Mesopotamia, and India developed along large rivers. Hundreds of years later in East Asia, another civilization began along the Huang He (HWANG HUH). In Chinese, Huang He means "yellow river." This civilization was China. China has gone through many changes over the centuries, but it is still a strong and growing civilization today.

Powerful Rivers

The Huang He stretches east across China for more than 2,900 miles (4,666 km). It begins in China's western mountains and flows to the Pacific Ocean. On its way, the Huang He cuts through thick layers of rich, yellow soil. This soil is called loess (LEHS). The river carries away large amounts of loess and spreads it farther downstream. The yellow color of the soil in the Huang He gives the river its name.

The rich soil helps farmers grow large amounts of food on small plots of land. As a result, the Huang He valley **emerged** as one of the great wheat-producing areas of the ancient world.

The Huang He has benefited the people of the Huang He valley. The river has also brought great misfortune. The Huang He often overflows its banks, causing enormous floods. Since

Reading**HELP**DESK

Taking Notes: *Analyzing*

Use a web diagram like this one to identify three ways the lives of the Chinese people changed under Shang rule.

How Life Changed Under Shang Rule

Content Vocabulary

• warlord
• aristocrat
• ancestor

• pictograph
• ideograph
• bureaucracy

600 B.C., the Chinese have recorded more than 1,500 floods of the Huang He. These floods have taken millions of lives. The Chinese call the Huang He "China's Sorrow" in honor of the people killed by the floods.

Over time, the people of China moved south and settled near another great river, the Chang Jiang (CHAHNG JYAHNG), or the Yangtze River. The Chang Jiang flows from west to east across central China. It flows through spectacular canyons and broad plains on its way to the East China Sea. The Chang Jiang is about 3,915 miles (6,300 km) long. Only the Amazon in South America and the Nile in Africa are longer.

Like the Huang He, the Chang Jiang provides rich soil for farming. Early farmers grew rice along the river's shores. The Chang Jiang was also an important waterway for trade and transportation.

Mountains and Desert

China has fertile river valleys, but only about one-tenth of its land can be farmed. Mountains and desert cover much of the country's land. To the southwest, the towering Himalaya separate China from South Asia. The Kunlun Shan and Tian Shan mountain ranges slice through western China. East of the Tian Shan is a vast, rocky desert known as the Gobi.

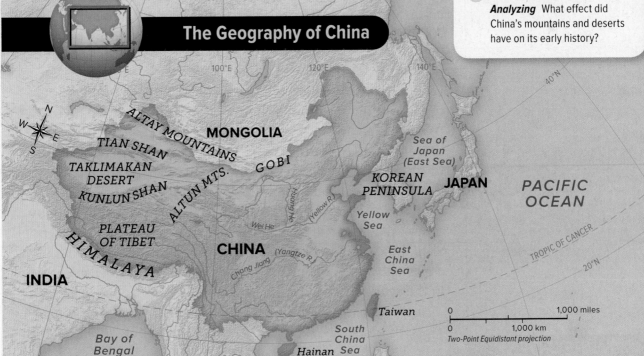

The Geography of China

Academic Vocabulary

emerge to become known

- **hereditary**
- **Mandate of Heaven**
- **Dao**

For centuries, these rugged mountains and the barren desert acted like walls around the country. These barriers limited contacts between China and other civilizations. The Chinese developed a unique culture and a strong sense of independence. They called their land "the Middle Kingdom." To them, it was the center of the world.

☑ **PROGRESS CHECK**

Identifying How did rivers help civilization develop in China?

Terraced farming, shown here, helps overcome the difficult landscape in China. Farmers plant every strip of land they can, even in the mountains.

The First Chinese Dynasty

GUIDING QUESTION *Why did China's Shang rulers become powerful?*

What we know about the early people of China comes from the things they left behind. Archaeologists have unearthed clay pots and cups in the Huang He valley that date back thousands of years. These artifacts show that the Huang He valley was the birthplace of Chinese civilization.

Archaeologists think that people settled in the valley because of its rich soil. Early settlers farmed the land. As in other early civilizations, people here also used the river for travel and trade. As the population grew, the Chinese began building towns.

Myths and Legends

Like other early peoples, the ancient Chinese created myths to explain the creation of their world. Many Chinese myths celebrate the deeds of great heroes. Yü the Great was one of these heroes. According to myths, Yü dug the first **channels** to control the floodwaters of the Huang He. Yü chased away the dragon that caused the floods. Then, he started digging the channels. According to the myth, Yü was aided in his task by other dragons. One dragon used its tail to help dig the channels. Still, it took 13 long years to complete the work. After the channels were finished, the flood waters could flow safely away to the sea.

Legend has it that Yü founded China's first dynasty. That dynasty, named the Xia (SHYAH), began about 2000 B.C.

Reading HELP DESK

Academic Vocabulary

channel a canal; a narrow body of water between two landmasses

Archaeologists, however, have not found any historical evidence of the Xia. Based on written records, China's first dynasty is the Shang. Shang kings ruled China from about 1750 B.C. to 1045 B.C.

Who Were the Shang?

Archaeologists have unearthed long-buried walls and buildings. These ruins show that the Shang built the first cities in China. Among these cities was the royal capital of Anyang (AHN·YAHNG). A palace and temple stood at the center of the city. Public buildings and the homes of government officials circled this central area. Beyond the city's center stood workshops and other homes.

The king was the most powerful person, serving as the political, religious, and military leader of Shang China. At first, Shang kings controlled only a small area of northern China. In time, the Shang conquered neighboring areas. They ruled over most of the people of the Huang He valley.

As the Shang kingdom grew, kings sent out large armies to defend the kingdom's borders. They appointed people called warlords to govern local territories. **Warlords** are **military** leaders who lead their own armies. Shang kings **relied** on the warlords to stay in power.

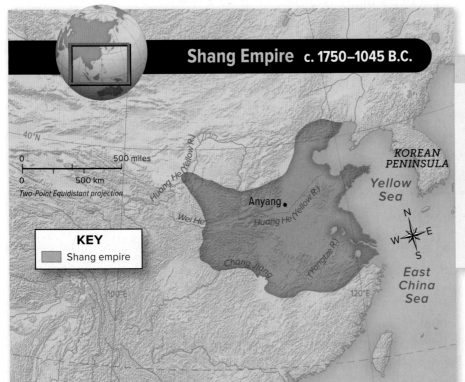

Shang Empire c. 1750–1045 B.C.

KOREAN PENINSULA

Yellow Sea

Anyang

Huang He (Yellow R.)

Wei He

Huang He (Yellow R.)

(Yangtze R.)

Chang Jiang

East China Sea

KEY

Shang empire

40°N

0   500 miles
0   500 km
Two-Point Equidistant projection

100°E

120°E

GEOGRAPHY CONNECTION

The Shang are thought to have built the first Chinese cities.

1 LOCATION What rivers were found within the borders of the Shang dynasty?

2 CRITICAL THINKING
Analyzing Anyang is the only Chinese city shown on the map. Where would you expect other Chinese cities to be located?

warlord a military commander exercising civil power by force, usually in a limited area

Academic Vocabulary

military related to soldiers, arms, or war
rely to be dependent

Analyzing Sources

Archaeologists study what ancient societies have left behind. Some of what we know about early China and Chinese writing comes from the study of oracle bones. They are a primary source. Suppose you were an archaeologist who dug up a collection of oracle bones. You would want to analyze them. Use the library to find secondary sources about oracle bones. Write a brief report summarizing your findings and present it to the class. For more information about analyzing sources, read the chapter *What Does a Historian Do?*

Messages written on animal bones show that the Chinese language originated with pictures representing words.

Under the king, warlords and other royal officials formed the upper class. They were **aristocrats** (uh·RIHS·tuh·krats), people of noble birth whose wealth came from the land they owned. Aristocrats passed their land and power to their children or to younger family members.

Most people of Shang China were farmers. There were much smaller groups of merchants, artisans, and slaves. The farmers lived in rural villages and worked the land that belonged to the aristocrats. They raised cattle, sheep, and chickens and grew grains, such as millet, wheat, and rice.

People in Shang China worshipped many gods. The god Shang Ti ruled as supreme god over the lesser gods. According to legend, the gods lived in the mountains, rivers, and seas.

The early Chinese both admired and feared the gods. They believed the gods could bring good or bad fortune. They attempted to please the gods by offering gifts of food and other goods.

The Chinese also honored their **ancestors**, or long-dead family members. They made offerings to their ancestors. They hoped that their ancestors would bring good luck and help in difficult times. Today, many Chinese still pay respect to their ancestors by going to temples and burning small paper copies of food, clothing, and other items. These copies represent things that departed relatives need in the afterlife.

Seeking Guidance from Ancestors

Shang kings believed that they received their power to rule from the gods and their wisdom from their ancestors. For this reason, religion and government were closely linked. For the kings, an important duty was to contact the gods and the ancestors before making important decisions.

The kings asked for help by using oracle (AWR·uh·kuhl) bones. They instructed priests to scratch questions on the bones, such as "Will I win the battle?" or "Will there be an abundant harvest?" Priests heated the oracle bones over a fire until they cracked. The pattern of cracks provided answers from the gods and ancestors to the king's questions.

The ancient Chinese wrote in pictographs and ideographs. **Pictographs** (PIKH·tuh·grafs) are characters that represent objects. For example, the Chinese characters for the sun and the moon are pictographs. **Ideographs** (IH·dee·uh·grafs) are another kind of character used in Chinese writing. They link

Reading HELP DESK

aristocrat a member of an upper class of society, usually made up of hereditary nobility

ancestor a person that someone is descended from

pictograph a symbol in a writing system based on pictures

ideograph a symbol in a writing system that represents a thing or an idea

two or more pictographs to express an idea. For example, the ideograph that stands for "forest" combines three pictographs of the word "tree."

Unlike the Chinese language, English and many other languages have writing systems based on an alphabet. An alphabet uses characters that represent sounds. Most characters in the Chinese language represent entire words.

Shang Arts

During the Shang dynasty, the Chinese created objects made of bronze. These works of art are some of the finest bronzes ever made. To make bronze objects, artisans made clay molds in several parts. Then they carved designs into the clay. Finally, they joined the parts of the mold together and poured in melted bronze. When the bronze cooled, the artisans removed the mold. The finished object was a beautifully decorated work of art.

Shang bronze objects included sculptures, daggers, vases, cups, and urns—or large ceremonial containers. The Shang used bronze urns to prepare and serve food for ceremonies to honor their ancestors.

Chinese artists and artisans made many other important advances. Farmers raised silk worms that produced silk. Weavers then made the silk into colorful clothing for wealthy people. Artisans crafted vases and dishes from kaolin (KAY·eh·lehn), a fine, white clay. They also carved statues from ivory and a green stone called jade.

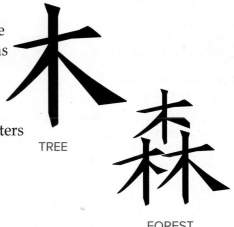

TREE

FOREST

Chinese ideographs combine the pictographs of single items to form a more complex word.

▶ **CRITICAL THINKING**
Speculating Why do you think many Chinese today practice the ancient craft of pictographs?

✔ **PROGRESS CHECK**

Explaining Why did Shang kings have questions scratched on oracle bones?

The Zhou: China's Longest Dynasty

GUIDING QUESTION *How did the Zhou claim the right to rule China?*

According to legend, the last of the Shang rulers was a wicked tyrant. Many Chinese turned against him. In 1045 B.C., rebels led by an aristocrat named Wu Wang (WOO WAHNG) overthrew the Shang government. When his victory was complete, Wu declared a new dynasty called the Zhou (JOH). The Zhou ruled China for more than 800 years—longer than any other dynasty in Chinese history.

The Chinese made bronze objects for many uses. What do you think this elephant might have been used for?

©Asian Art & Archaeology, Inc./Corbis

GEOGRAPHY CONNECTION

Zhou rulers maintained the longest lasting dynasty in Chinese history.

1 LOCATION What body of water made up the eastern border of Zhou territory?

2 ANALYZING Why did the Zhou divide their kingdom into smaller territories?

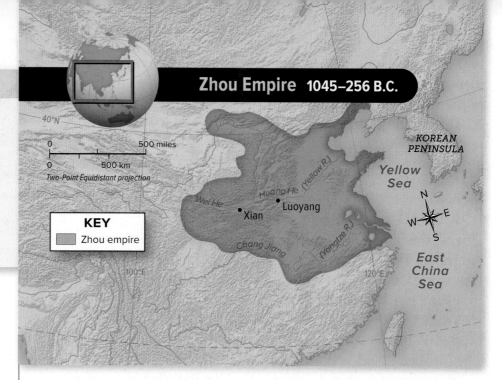

Zhou Empire 1045–256 B.C.

KOREAN PENINSULA

Yellow Sea

40°N

0   500 miles
0   500 km
Two-Point Equidistant projection

Huang He (Yellow R.)

Wei He

• Xian   • Luoyang

KEY
Zhou empire

Chang Jiang

(Yangtze R.)

100°E

120°E

East China Sea

How did the Zhou Rule China?

Zhou kings governed China much as Shang rulers had. The king led the government, ruling with the help of a bureaucracy (byu·RAH·kruh·see). A **bureaucracy** is made up of officials who carry out the tasks of government. The king also put together a strong army to bring weaker kingdoms under Zhou rule.

Soon the Zhou kingdom was larger than that of the Shang. To govern effectively, the king divided the kingdom into territories. He assigned loyal aristocrats to govern each of the territories. The positions the aristocrats held were **hereditary**. This meant that when an aristocrat died, a son or another member of his family governed the territory.

The Chinese believed their king represented them before the gods. The king's chief duty was to carry out religious ceremonies to please the gods. Zhou kings claimed that kings ruled China because they had the Mandate of Heaven.

The Right to Rule

The **Mandate of Heaven** is the belief that the Chinese king's right to rule came from the gods. The Mandate stated the idea that the gods chose a wise and good person to rule. The person chosen by the gods would govern honestly and well.

The Mandate of Heaven changed what the Zhou people expected from their king. The king must rule by the proper

bureaucracy a group of non-elected government officials

hereditary having title or possession by reason of birth

Mandate of Heaven the belief that the Chinese king's right to rule came from the gods

Dao Chinese system of beliefs which describes the way a king must rule

"Way," known as the **Dao** (DOW). His duty was to honor and please the gods. If there was a natural disaster or a bad harvest, that meant the king had failed and he could be replaced.

Technology and Trade

For many centuries, Chinese farmers had to depend on rain to water their crops. Under Zhou kings, the Chinese developed new systems to irrigate the land. With a better water supply, farmers were able to grow more crops than ever before.

China's trade also expanded. Archaeologists have found pieces of Chinese silk in central Asia and as far away as Greece.

War Between the States

Over time, the aristocrats who ruled the territories of the Zhou kingdom grew more powerful. They ignored the king's commands and took control of their own territory. The aristocrats began to fight one another for power. These wars began in the 400s B.C. and went on for nearly 200 years. Because each aristocrat formed his own state, this time in China's history is called the "Period of the Warring States."

To fill the ranks of their armies, the aristocrats forced farmers to serve as soldiers. Chinese soldiers were armed with swords, spears, and crossbows. As the fighting continued through the years, warriors began using horses. The Chinese developed the saddle and stirrup. Now soldiers could ride around the battlefield while throwing spears or shooting crossbows. The wars fought at this time would result in a new dynasty.

This dragon is an example of bronze work from the Zhou dynasty.

✔ **PROGRESS CHECK**

Identifying What technology was developed in China during the Zhou dynasty?

©Burstein Collection/Corbis

LESSON 1 REVIEW

Review Vocabulary

1. How did a *pictograph* differ from an *ideograph*?

Answer the Guiding Questions

2. ***Describing*** What geographic features isolated ancient China from other civilizations?

3. ***Explaining*** How did Shang rulers gain power?

4. ***Identifying*** What was the chief duty of Zhou kings?

5. ***Describing*** Describe the biggest change for the Chinese people during the Zhou dynasty.

6. **INFORMATIVE/EXPLANATORY** China's geographic features separated it from other civilizations. Write a paragraph explaining the advantages and disadvantages of isolation.

7. **INFORMATIVE/EXPLANATORY** Write a paragraph that explains why "China's Sorrow" is an appropriate description of the Huang He.

Society and Culture in Ancient China

networks
There's More Online!

• How do new ideas change the way people live?

IT MATTERS BECAUSE
Ideas that started in early China continue to influence today's world.

Chinese Philosophies

GUIDING QUESTION *How did Chinese thinkers influence society and government?*

During the Period of the Warring States, rulers of rival states fought each other. Armies wiped out entire villages of men, women, and children. Many Chinese looked for ways to stop the killing. They wanted to bring order to society.

Between 500 B.C. and 200 B.C., Chinese thinkers developed three major **philosophies**. They were Confucianism, Daoism, and legalism. These philosophies were different from one another. However, the philosophies had the same goal. Each philosophy aimed to create a well-run and peaceful society. After decades of war, Chinese people welcomed these new ideas.

What Ideas Did Confucius Teach?

Confucianism (kuhn·FYOO·shuh·nih·zuhm) was based on the teachings of a man named Confucius (kuhn·FYOO·shuhs). Born about 550 B.C. to a farming family, Confucius lived when rival kings fought each other for power. Confucius criticized the misrule of these kings. He urged the people to follow the beliefs of their ancestors. If people would do that, Confucius believed, it would bring peace and harmony to China.

Reading**HELP**DESK

Taking Notes: *Identifying*

Use a graphic organizer like the one shown here to identify the three Chinese philosophies that emerged after the fall of the Zhou dynasty.

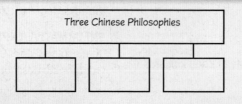

Three Chinese Philosophies

Content Vocabulary

• **Confucianism**   • **legalism**

• **Daoism**   • **filial piety**

Duty is a central idea of Confucianism. Duty means that a person places the needs of family and community above his or her own needs. Each **individual** has certain duties to fulfill. It is the duty of parents to love their children, and it is the children's duty to respect their parents. Husbands should support their wives, and wives should obey their husbands. Above all, a ruler had a duty to rule justly and to set an example of right living. In return, subjects should be loyal and obey the law.

Confucius believed that if each individual carried out his or her duties, society would do well. He urged people to be good. This meant behaving moderately, keeping one's promises, honoring traditions, and respecting the elderly. Confucius also advised people to seek knowledge:

PRIMARY SOURCE

" By extensively . . . studying all learning, and keeping himself under the restraint [control] of the rules of propriety [correct behavior], one may thus likewise not err . . . from what is right. **"**

— Confucius, *Analects*, XII, 15

To Confucius, the right way to live was **similar** to the idea known as the Golden Rule: "Do unto others as you would have others do unto you."

The Influence of Confucius

Confucius believed that government service should be open to all men of ability and merit and not limited to those of noble birth. The aristocrats did not want to open government to more people. They did not want to lose their power. However, over time Chinese emperors developed the practice of choosing government officials through civil service tests.

Many people honored Confucius as a great teacher. His followers wrote down his sayings and collected them in a work called the *Analects*. After Confucius died in 479 B.C., his teachings spread throughout China. Confucianism continued to shape Chinese society and government until the early A.D. 1900s.

Connections to TODAY

Confucianism in Asia

Confucianism still has millions of followers today. Most of these followers are in China. Over the centuries, however, the basic teachings of Confucius spread across Asia. The concepts he handed down—a belief in duty and correct behavior and respect for education—are a part of the culture in many Asian countries today.

The Chinese philosopher Confucius taught that people should do their duty and keep promises.

Confucianism a system of beliefs based on the teachings of Confucius

Academic Vocabulary

philosophy the study of the basic ideas about society, education, and right and wrong

individual a single human being as contrasted with a group

similar having things in common

CHINESE PHILOSOPHERS

1 **IDENTIFYING** Which philosophy encourages followers to concentrate on duty and humanity?

2 **CRITICAL THINKING**
Analyzing Which of these philosophies do you think would be most popular in the world today? Explain.

	Confucianism	Daoism	Legalism
Founder	Confucius	Laozi	Hanfeizi
Main Ideas	People should put the needs of their family and community first.	People should give up worldly desires in favor of nature and the Dao.	Society needs a system of harsh laws and strict punishment.
Influence on Modern Life	Many Chinese today accept his idea of duty to family. His ideas helped open up government jobs to people with talent.	Daoism teaches the importance of nature and encourages people to treat nature with respect and reverence.	Legalists developed laws that became an important part of Chinese history.

The Philosophy of Daoism

Another Chinese philosophy, known as **Daoism** (DOW·ih·zuhm) also promoted a peaceful society. The word *Dao* means "path" and is often translated as "the Way." Daoism began with the ideas of Laozi (LOW·DZUH). Laozi is believed to have lived during the same time as Confucius.

Like Confucianism, Daoism teaches people how to live a good life. Daoists believed that people should free themselves from worldly desires and live simply. They should turn to nature and the Dao—the spiritual force that guides all things. In this way, they would enjoy a happy life.

Daoism is different from Confucianism in some ways. Followers of Confucius taught that people should work hard to make the world better. Daoism taught people to turn away from worldly affairs and live in harmony with nature. Many Chinese followed both Confucianism and Daoism. They believed that the two philosophies supported each other.

Reading**HELP**DESK

Daoism a Chinese philosophy concerned with obtaining long life and living in harmony with nature

Legalism

A third philosophy stressed the importance of a system of laws. This philosophy became known as **legalism** (lee·guh·lih·zuhm), or the "School of Law."

A thinker named Hanfeizi (HAN·fay·DZOO) introduced the ideas of legalism during the 200s B.C. Unlike Confucius or Laozi, Hanfeizi believed that humans are naturally evil. Strict laws and harsh punishments were necessary to force people to do their duty.

Many aristocrats supported legalism because it emphasized force. Legalism did not require rulers to consider the needs or wishes of their people. Its ideas led to cruel punishments for even the smallest crimes.

✓ PROGRESS CHECK

Comparing and Contrasting How are the ideas of Confucius and Laozi similar? How are they different?

Chinese Life

GUIDING QUESTION *How was early Chinese society organized?*

Early Chinese society was made up of four social classes. A **social class** includes people who have the same economic and social position. In ancient China, these social classes were land-owning aristocrats, farmers, artisans, and merchants.

Lives of the Aristocrats

China's aristocratic families were wealthy. They owned large estates and lived in tile-roofed houses with courtyards and gardens. Walls surrounded their homes as protection against bandits. Inside, fine furniture and carpets filled the rooms.

Aristocratic families owned large plots of land. After the father died, a family's land was divided equally among all of the male heirs. As a result, sons and grandsons owned much less land than their fathers and grandfathers owned.

Lives of the Farmers

About nine out of ten Chinese farmed for a living. The farmers lived in rural villages surrounded by mud walls. Beyond the village walls were fields owned by the aristocrats. The farmers rented the fields by turning over part of their crops to the owners.

The ideas of Laozi became popular in China between around 500 B.C. and 300 B.C. Here he is shown riding a water buffalo into the desert.

Giraudon/Art Resource, NY

---

legalism a Chinese philosophy that stressed the importance of laws

Academic Vocabulary

social class a group of people who are at a similar cultural, economic, or educational level

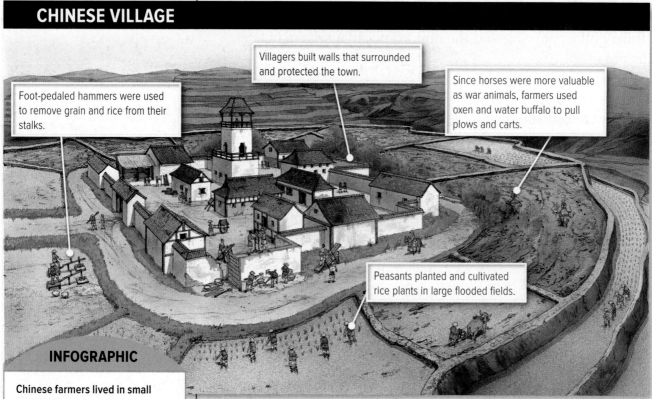

Villagers built walls that surrounded and protected the town.

Foot-pedaled hammers were used to remove grain and rice from their stalks.

Since horses were more valuable as war animals, farmers used oxen and water buffalo to pull plows and carts.

Peasants planted and cultivated rice plants in large flooded fields.

INFOGRAPHIC

Chinese farmers lived in small villages made up of several families. They farmed fields outside the village walls.

▶ CRITICAL THINKING
Analyzing What are some possible disadvantages for farmers of working on land they do not own?

In northern China, farmers grew wheat and a grain called millet. In the south, where the climate was warmer and wetter, they grew rice. Most farmers also owned a small plot of land where they grew food for their own use.

The government required farmers to pay taxes and to work one month each year on projects such as building roads. In wartime, farmers were forced to serve as soldiers. In addition, farmers had to face constant threats from famine and floods.

Lives of the Artisans and Merchants

Artisans are skilled workers who make useful objects. The artisans of Zhou China crafted iron tools and weapons, silk cloth, and vessels made of bronze or jade. Many were architects, artists, and woodworkers. Most artisans learned their skills from their fathers and, in turn, passed them along to their sons.

Shopkeepers, traders, and bankers made up the merchant class. Merchants lived in towns and provided goods and services to the aristocrats.

Some merchants became wealthy, but they were not respected members of society. People believed that merchants worked only for their own gain, not for the good of society.

Reading**HELP**DESK

filial piety the responsibility children have to respect, obey, and care for their parents

While artisans made useful goods and farmers grew food for all, merchants made money for themselves. Merchants were also barred from government jobs.

What Were Chinese Families Like?

The family was at the center of early Chinese society. Farming in ancient China required many workers, so parents had many children to help them with the work. Even young children worked in the fields. Chinese families took care of those members in need—the aged, the young, and the sick.

Chinese families practiced **filial piety** (FIH·lee·uhl PY·uh·tee). Filial refers to a son or daughter. Piety refers to duty or devotion. Therefore, *filial piety* refers to people's responsibility to respect and obey their parents.

It also requires people to take care of their parents as they grow older. Family members placed the needs of the head of the family before their own. The head of the family was the oldest male, usually the father. Respect for parents and the elderly were central to the teachings of Confucius. Even today, filial piety is an important part of Chinese culture.

Roles of Men and Women

Men and women had very different roles in early China. Men were respected because of the jobs they did—growing crops, attending school, running the government, and fighting wars. The Chinese considered these jobs more important than the work carried out by women. Most women raised children and saw to their education. They also managed the household and family finances.

✔ PROGRESS CHECK

Explaining Why were merchants not respected in ancient China?

The man and woman here are shown in brightly colored dress. The colors on these ancient Chinese figures have lasted thousands of years. Why do you think there is such attention to detail?

(l & r)Best View Stock/Age fotostock

LESSON 2 REVIEW

Review Vocabulary

1. Describe a situation in which you might show *filial piety*.

Answer the Guiding Questions

2. *Explaining* Why did many aristocrats support legalism?

3. *Identifying* What were the main social classes of early China?

4. *Assessing* Which philosophy do you most strongly agree with—Confucianism, Daoism, or legalism? Why?

5. *Paraphrasing* Read the following quotation by Laozi. Then restate the quotation in your own words: "A journey of a thousand miles begins with a single step."

6. **ARGUMENT** Which system of belief—Confucianism, Daoism, or legalism—would lead to the best government? Write a paragraph expressing your opinion in order to convince others.

The Qin and the Han Dynasties

• How do governments change?

IT MATTERS BECAUSE
Stable government builds solid growth and strength in a civilization.

The Qin Emperor

GUIDING QUESTION *How did the Qin Emperor unite China?*

You have read about the fighting in China from about 400 B.C. to 200 B.C. During the Period of the Warring States, the strong rulers of local states fought one another and ignored the weak Zhou kings. One of these states was called Qin (CHIHN). In 221 B.C., the ruler of Qin sent a large cavalry force to defeat the other states and end the Zhou dynasty. The Qin then controlled China from the Huang He to the Chang Jiang.

To mark a new beginning for China, the Qin ruler declared himself Qin Shihuangdi (CHIHN SHEE·hwahng·dee), which means "the First Qin Emperor." Qin brought changes to Chinese government that would last for many centuries.

How Did Qin Change China?

Qin wanted to strengthen and **unify** China. To do that, he took direct control of China's provinces. Under the Zhou rulers, the governors of the provinces had passed on their positions to sons or relatives. Now, only Qin had the power to appoint the governors.

Qin ruled China with absolute control and swift, harsh punishment. Anyone who disagreed with him was punished or killed. Writings that displeased Qin were burned.

Reading HELP DESK

Taking Notes: *Comparing*

Use a Venn diagram like the one shown here to compare and contrast the Qin and Han dynasties.

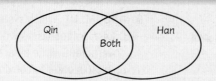
Qin   Han
Both

Content Vocabulary

• censor
• currency
• civil service
• tenant farmer
• acupuncture

Qin also increased the power of his government by appointing officers known as **censors**. The censors' job was to make sure government workers did their work.

Qin developed other policies and projects to unify the empire. He created a **currency**, or type of money, that everyone had to use. He hired scholars to simplify and set rules for the Chinese writing system. Qin also undertook building projects, including the construction of his own tomb. Qin's tomb was so large that it housed an army of life-sized clay soldiers and horses. Qin also ordered tens of thousands of farmers to build palaces, roads, dams, and a huge canal. The canal connected the Chang Jiang in central China to what is today the city of Guangzhou (GWAHNG·JOH) in southern China. The government transported supplies on the canal to soldiers in distant territories.

Why Was the Great Wall Built?

Qin united the different parts of China into one empire. He wanted to keep the empire safe from invasion. A vast desert known as the Gobi was on the edge of China's northern border. Nomads, people who move from place to place with herds of animals, lived in the Gobi. The Chinese knew them as the Xiongnu (SYEHN·NOO). The Xiongnu were skilled warriors who fought on horseback and often attacked Chinese settlements. Earlier Chinese rulers had constructed separate walls in the north to keep out the Xiongnu. Qin planned to have the walls joined and strengthened.

The End of Qin Rule

In 221 B.C., Qin boasted that his dynasty would rule China forever. The Qin dynasty actually ended soon after Qin's death in 210 B.C. Both aristocrats and farmers revolted against the harsh Qin rule. Fighting erupted throughout China. By 206 B.C. the Qin dynasty was over and a new dynasty arose.

☑ **PROGRESS CHECK**

Explaining How would you describe Qin as a ruler?

ImageMore/Age fotostock

Connections to
TODAY

The Great Wall

Many things get built and rebuilt over time. Building the Great Wall in China took several years. Qin forced hundreds of thousands of farmers to leave their fields to work on the wall. Thousands of laborers died before the project was completed. The finished wall, the Great Wall of China, was built mainly on the northern slopes of mountains, using stone, sand, and rubble. However, Qin did not build the wall that stands today. The Great Wall today consists of a series of walls and towers built during the Ming dynasty beginning in the late 1400s.

Qin Shihuangdi had a large goal: to organize and strengthen the country.

---

censor an official who watches others for correct behavior

currency something, such as coins or paper money, that is used as a medium of exchange

Academic Vocabulary

unify to make into a single unit

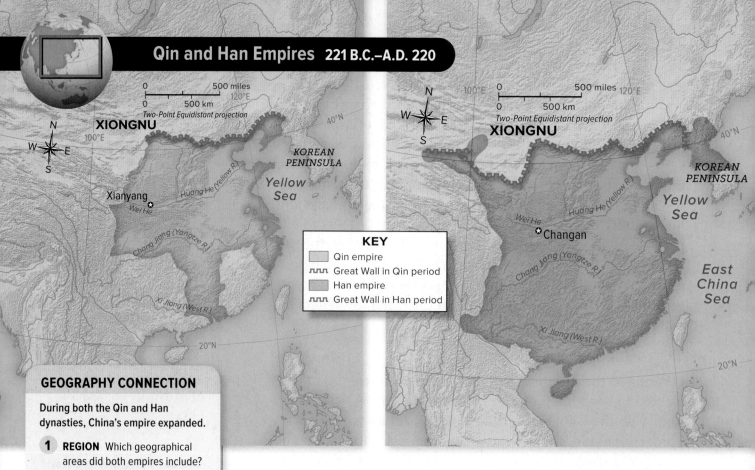

KEY

- Qin empire
- ⌐⌐ Great Wall in Qin period
- Han empire
- ⌐⌐ Great Wall in Han period

GEOGRAPHY CONNECTION

During both the Qin and Han dynasties, China's empire expanded.

1 REGION Which geographical areas did both empires include?

2 CRITICAL THINKING
Drawing Conclusions Why do you think the Han empire was able to expand farther west than the Qin?

Han Rulers

GUIDING QUESTION *What improvements did the Chinese make under Han rulers?*

In 202 B.C., a new dynasty known as the Han dynasty came to power in China. Its founder was Liu Bang (LYOO BAHNG), a farmer turned soldier. His family began the powerful Han dynasty that would rule China for more than 400 years.

Han Wudi

The first strong emperor of the Han dynasty was Han Wudi (HAHN WOO·DEE), who ruled from 141 B.C. to 87 B.C. Han Wudi took important steps to improve China's government. Earlier emperors chose family members and loyal aristocrats to help them run the government. Han Wudi wanted to end this practice. He recruited dedicated and talented people for **civil service**, government workers who were chosen on the basis of competitive tests.

First, scholars and officials recommended qualified candidates. Then, the candidates took long, difficult written examinations. Finally, officials graded the tests, and the emperor reviewed the results. The candidates with the highest scores got the jobs.

ReadingHELPDESK

civil service the administrative service of a government

Although this system of selecting government officials raised the quality of government, the system also had its faults. Supposedly, government work was open to anyone with talent and ability. Realistically, the system actually favored the rich. Only wealthy families could afford to educate their sons for the difficult civil service tests.

Education

The Han government created schools to prepare students for civil service. Students prepared for the exams by studying law, history, and the ideas of Confucius. After many years of schooling, the students took the civil service examinations. If they passed, they earned jobs as government workers or teachers. They also won great respect in society because they were well educated.

The Empire Expands

During the years of Han rule, China's population rose to about 60 million. To meet the needs of China's growing population, farmers needed to produce more food. However, China's farmers faced special challenges in doing so.

When farmers died, their land was divided among their sons. Gradually, over several **generations**, the amount of land farmed by a family became smaller and smaller. By the middle of the Han dynasty, the average farmer owned only about one acre of land.

Farmers could not raise enough food to feed their families on such small plots of land. They had no choice but to sell their land and work as tenant farmers. **Tenant farmers** work land owned by someone else. Eventually, wealthy landlords owned thousands of acres. The tenant farmers remained very poor.

As China's population grew, the Han Empire took in new territory. Han armies conquered lands to the north, including Korea. They moved south into Southeast Asia and west as far as northern India. After Han Wudi's armies pushed back the Xiongnu—the nomads to the north—the Chinese lived in peace for almost 150 years.

Han Culture

During this era of peace, literature and the arts blossomed. Writers wrote about current events. They made copies of old historical works. In the arts, painters and sculptors reached out to new audiences.

BIOGRAPHY

Ban Zhao (c. A.D. 45–A.D. 116)

Ban Zhao was the first female Chinese historian. She served as the imperial historian during the Han dynasty. Along with her historical pieces, she wrote poems and essays. One well-known work is a guide for women titled *Nu Jie (Lessons for Women)*. It details how women should behave and encourages education for females. The Chinese followed her teachings for hundreds of years, though her emphasis on education was largely ignored.

▶ **CRITICAL THINKING**
ANALYZING Why do you think Ban Zhao emphasized education for women?

---

tenant farmer a farmer who works land owned by someone else and pays rent in cash or as a share of the crop

Academic Vocabulary

generation a group of individuals born and living at the same time

In early China, people made paper one sheet at a time from hemp or rag pulp. This modern artist (above) makes paper the ancient way. Today's paper mills (below) manufacture huge rolls of paper on machines like this one.

▶ **CRITICAL THINKING**

Analyzing What would be the effect on today's publishing industry if all paper were once again made by hand?

Visual Vocabulary

waterwheel a wheel made to turn by the water flowing against it

In earlier times, artists had created religious works for rulers and aristocrats. Now, under Han rule, artists created beautiful works of art for less prominent families.

Under the Han, the ideas of Confucius gained influence. The idea of filial piety became very strong. The stability of the government also helped strengthen family ties. The new class of scholarly civil servants greatly influenced government, but other social classes in China remained the same. Daily life also was very similar to what it had been before.

Chinese Inventions

During the Han dynasty, new technology helped Chinese farmers and workers produce more than ever before. One major development was the cast-iron plow, which could break up the soil more easily than wooden plows could. New iron tools and techniques were used to drain swamps and direct water to parched fields. As a result, land that was once unfit for farming now produced food and other crops.

Improvements took place in areas besides farming. Millers invented **waterwheels** to grind more grain, and miners fashioned iron drill bits to mine more salt. Another Chinese invention, the wheelbarrow, was first used to carry heavy material on building sites. Artisans developed silk manufacturing and invented paper. Used first for wrapping, paper became an ideal writing material. Like Egyptian papyrus, paper provided a way to keep written records.

Two remarkable achievements of Han inventors were the rudder and a new way to move the sails of ships. With these inventions, ships could sail against the wind for the first time. They could also travel farther than ever before. As a result, China's merchants shipped their goods to areas as far away as India and the Red Sea.

Medical Advances

Chinese medicine advanced under the Han. Doctors discovered that certain foods prevented disease. They used a variety of herbs to treat illnesses. Doctors also relieved pain by piercing patients' skin at vital points with thin needles. This treatment is known as **acupuncture** (A·kyuh·puhngk·chuhr). Acupuncture renews the body by increasing the flow of energy.

✓ **PROGRESS CHECK**

Explaining Why did Han rulers create civil service examinations?

(t)Marco Cristofori/Age fotostock; (c)©Dean Conger/Corbis; (b)BambooSil/Purestock/SuperStock

On the Silk Road

GUIDING QUESTION *How did the Silk Road benefit China and the rest of the world?*

During the Han period, Chinese traders grew rich by sending expensive goods to other parts of the world. Over time, both sea and land trade routes led to an exchange of many different goods and ideas between China and other areas.

New Contacts With the West

China's trade increased in part as a result of Chinese exploration. In 139 B.C., the emperor Han Wudi sent out a general named Zhang Qian (JAHNG CHYEHN) to explore areas west of China. Zhang's mission was to recruit allies to help China fight against its enemies, especially the Xiongnu to the north.

Thirteen years later, Zhang returned to China. He had failed to find allies. He had learned, however, about the people, geography, and culture of the areas west of China. He also visited a kingdom far to the west, probably in the area of present-day Kazakhstan. There, he saw horses of great strength and size.

Emperor Han Wudi was delighted to hear this report. He wanted horses for his soldiers, so he encouraged trade between China and western regions.

In exchange for the horses, Chinese merchants traded silk, spices, and other luxury goods. The trade route to the west was later called the Silk Road in honor of China's most famous export.

Trade Expands

The Silk Road was not just one road. It was a **network** of trade routes. When the road was completed in the A.D. 100s, it was 4,000 miles (6,436 km) long and stretched from western China to the Mediterranean. The distance, rough terrain, and bandits along the road made travel difficult and dangerous.

Over the years, merchants traded many items in addition to luxury goods. These included fruits, vegetables, flowers, and grains. For example, China sent peaches and pears to India, while India sent cotton and spinach to China. In time, Chinese inventions, such as paper, would also travel to other regions along the Silk Road.

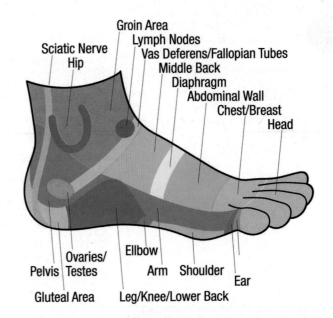

Acupuncture is based on finding pressure spots in the human body to help ease pain. Chinese doctors detected certain places on the body that correspond to spots on the foot. Needles can be applied to these spots to help relieve the pain.

Groin Area
Lymph Nodes
Sciatic Nerve
Hip
Vas Deferens/Fallopian Tubes
Middle Back
Diaphragm
Abdominal Wall
Chest/Breast
Head
Ovaries/
Pelvis | Testes
Gluteal Area
Elbow
Arm   Shoulder
Ear
Leg/Knee/Lower Back

PeterHermesFuran/iStock/Getty Images

acupuncture originally, a Chinese practice of inserting fine needles through the skin at specific points to treat disease or relieve pain

Academic Vocabulary

network a connected group or system

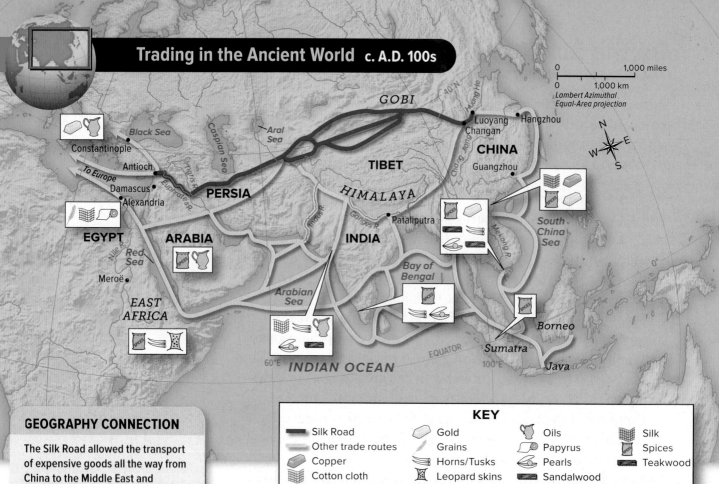

Trading in the Ancient World c. A.D. 100s

KEY

- Silk Road
- Other trade routes
- Copper
- Cotton cloth
- Gold
- Grains
- Horns/Tusks
- Leopard skins
- Oils
- Papyrus
- Pearls
- Sandalwood
- Silk
- Spices
- Teakwood

GEOGRAPHY CONNECTION

The Silk Road allowed the transport of expensive goods all the way from China to the Middle East and beyond.

1 **REGIONS** What regions were near or along the route of the Silk Road?

2 **CRITICAL THINKING**
Analyzing Visuals Chinese merchants sold many products along the Silk Road. What products do you think Chinese merchants bought as they traveled and traded?

Through trade, China encountered other civilizations. A huge variety of items awaited the ancient traders. Chinese writers described a mighty empire to the far west:

PRIMARY SOURCE

❝ It has more than four hundred walled towns. ... The walls of the towns are made of stone. ... The common people are farmers. ... The country produces plenty of gold, silver, and precious jewels. ... They make gold and silver coins. ... ❞

—from *Hou Hanshu* 88, Second Edition

The Chinese writers were describing the Roman Empire. For more than 1,000 years, the Silk Road was the main trade **link** between Asia and Europe.

☑ **PROGRESS CHECK**

Identifying Cause and Effect What developments led to the creation of the Silk Road?

Academic Vocabulary

link a connecting element or factor

Buddhism Reaches China

GUIDING QUESTION *Why did Buddhism become a popular religion in China?*

The Silk Road served as a way to spread knowledge, culture, and religions. Buddhism, in particular, spread across the Silk Road from India to China. Buddhism won few followers in China at first. The fall of the Han dynasty and the long period of unrest that followed, however, spurred the spread of Buddhism.

Why Did the Han Dynasty Collapse?

Many of the emperors who succeeded Han Wudi were weak and dishonest. Corrupt officials and greedy aristocrats took over more of the land, forcing many farmers to give up their property. People began to rise up and rebel against the Han rulers.

Rebel armies destroyed the Han capital, Luoyang (LWAW·YAHNG) in A.D. 190. By A.D. 220, civil war divided China. For the next 400 years, China remained divided into many small kingdoms.

Buddhism Wins Followers

The fall of the Han dynasty and the long years of civil war frightened many Chinese. Feeling anxious, fearful, and unsafe, many people turned to Buddhist ideas. Followers of Confucius and Daoists also admired Buddhist ideas, which influenced their own religious rituals and moral ideas. By the A.D. 400s, Buddhism had become one of China's major religions.

✔ PROGRESS CHECK

Determining Cause and Effect Why did the fall of the Han dynasty help Buddhism spread in China?

LESSON 3 REVIEW

Review Vocabulary

1. What are the advantages of having a *civil service* system to select government workers?

Answer the Guiding Questions

2. *Describing* How did Qin rulers unite China?

3. *Explaining* How did the civil service system change China's government?

4. *Determining Cause and Effect* What was one result of the building of the Great Wall?

5. *Explaining* What caused the downfall of the Han dynasty?

6. *Analyzing Visuals* What was one fact that you put in the "Both" part of the Venn diagram comparing the Qin and Han?

7. **INFORMATIVE/EXPLANATORY** How do you think early China's history would be different if the Silk Road had never developed? Write a paragraph expressing your view.

Write your answers on a separate sheet of paper.

1 **Exploring the Essential Question**

INFORMATIVE/EXPLANATORY How would you compare the culture of China to other ancient cultures you have read about? Write an essay explaining how the culture of ancient China is different from these other civilizations. What factors led to the development of a unique culture in China?

2 **21st Century Skills**

ANALYZING NEWS MEDIA Work with a partner. Find an article from the business section of a newspaper or magazine about China and trade. What does the article tell you about trade and China today? What goods does China trade today? With whom does China trade? Present your article and your findings to the class. In your presentation, discuss how trade today between China and her trading partners is different from trade in the time of the Han dynasty.

3 **Thinking Like a Historian**

UNDERSTANDING RELATIONSHIPS A pyramid diagram can be used to show relationships. In a pyramid diagram, the group with the most members goes on the bottom. Create a pyramid diagram like the one on the right showing the social classes in ancient China from most powerful (top) to least powerful (bottom).

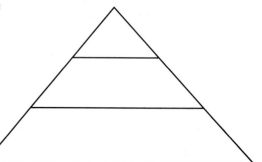

4 **GEOGRAPHY ACTIVITY**

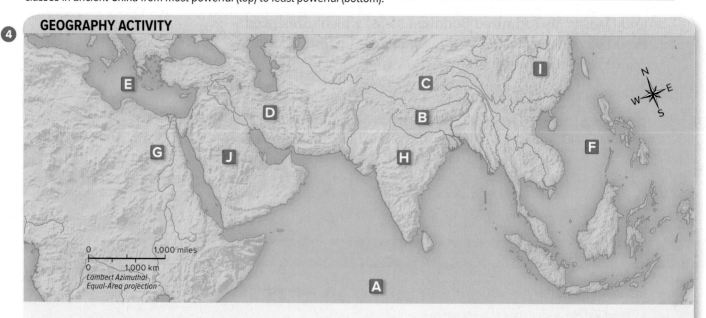

Locating Places

Match the letters on the map with the numbered places listed below.

1. Egypt
2. Arabia
3. Persia
4. India
5. Tibet
6. China
7. Indian Ocean
8. South China Sea
9. Himalaya
10. Mediterranean Sea

CHAPTER 10 Assessment

Directions: Write your answers on a separate piece of paper.

CHECKING FOR UNDERSTANDING

1 Define each of the following terms.

- **A.** warlord
- **B.** aristocrat
- **C.** bureaucracy
- **D.** Mandate of Heaven
- **E.** Dao
- **F.** Confucianism
- **G.** Daoism
- **H.** legalism
- **I.** censor
- **J.** currency
- **K.** civil service
- **L.** acupuncture

REVIEW THE GUIDING QUESTIONS

2 *Identifying* What natural features isolated China from other regions and cultures?

3 *Naming* Along which rivers did Chinese civilization first develop? Why did this occur?

4 *Describing* How did Shang kings rule over their large kingdoms?

5 *Paraphrasing* What was the Mandate of Heaven?

6 *Contrasting* What is one way Confucianism differs from Daoism?

7 *Naming* Which was the largest social class of ancient China?

8 *Identifying* Who was Qin Shihuangdi and why was he important?

9 *Listing* What were the main medical and technological advancements of the Han dynasty?

10 *Summarizing* How did trade along the Silk Road impact China?

11 *Explaining* How did Buddhist ideas spread to China?

CRITICAL THINKING

12 *Identifying Central Issues* How do you think ancient China's geographic isolation from other cultures affected the Chinese view of themselves and the world? Explain.

13 *Analyzing* What do oracle bones tell us about the development of the Chinese language?

14 *Making Inferences* How might the Chinese have used the Mandate of Heaven to justify rebellions against their rulers?

15 *Evaluating* What are the advantages and disadvantages of organizing a society around the ideas of Hanfeizi?

16 *Recognizing Relationships* How does the concept of filial piety relate to the teachings of Confucius about how society should function?

17 *Drawing Conclusions* Why was the Qin dynasty so short-lived?

18 *Assessing* Did the civil service examination system implemented by Han Wudi result in better governance of China? Why or why not?

19 *Classifying* What do you believe was the most important achievement of Han inventors? Explain.

20 *Speculating* Why were Buddhist ideas appealing to people after the fall of the Han dynasty?

Need Extra Help?

If you've missed question	**1**	**2**	**3**	**4**	**5**	**6**	**7**	**8**	**9**	**10**	**11**	**12**	**13**	**14**	**15**	**16**	**17**	**18**	**19**	**20**
Review Lesson	1, 2, 3	1	1	1	1	2	2	3	3	3	3	1	1	1	2	2	3	3	3	3

There's More Online! connected.mcgraw-hill.com

DBQ SHORT RESPONSE

"A hundred years ago the Shang (SHAHNG) dynasty was ... lost ... existing only in historical texts. ... But over the course of the 20th century, the Shang steadily reappeared, the myths replaced by tangible [easily seen] artifacts: massive bronzes, eloquent oracle bones, burial complexes."

—Peter Hessler, "The New Story of China's Past,"
National Geographic, (July 2003)

21 How would your study of early China have been different if you were studying 100 years ago?

22 What might "tangible artifacts" tell us about the Shang?

EXTENDED RESPONSE

23 *Informative/Explanatory* Write a brief report that compares and contrasts the characteristics of the four ancient Chinese dynasties you have read about.

STANDARDIZED TEST PRACTICE

DBQ ANALYZING DOCUMENTS

24 *Assessing* The main ideas of Daoism are explained in a book titled *Dao De Jing* (*The Way of the Dao*).

"When leading by the way of the Tao [Dao], abominate [hate] the use of force, for it causes resistance, and loss of strength. ...

The wise leader achieves results, but does not glory in them ... and does not boast of them.

—"A Caveat Against Violence," The *Tao Te Ching*, Stan Rosenthal, trans.

According to Daoist thought, what is the result of using force or violence?

A. It causes resistance and loss of strength.

B. It builds strength and breaks down resistance.

C. It causes resistance without an effect on strength.

D. It builds strength and resistance.

25 *Analyzing* What do you think this statement means? "The wise leader achieves results, but does not glory in them."

A The wise leader finishes projects but is not pleased with them.

B. The wise leader reaches goals but does not notice them.

C. The wise leader is effective but not proud.

D. The wise leader is efficient and is boastful.

Need Extra Help?

If You've Missed Question	**21**	**22**	**23**	**24**	**25**
Review Lesson	1	1	1, 3	2	2

(t)TAO TE CHING, Stanley Rosenthal (Shi-ten Roshi) previously British School of Zen Taoism Cardiff, September 1984. stan@stanrosenthal.com; (b)The New Story of China's Ancient Past by Peter Hessler. National Geographic Magazine July 2003. Copyright © 2003. National Geographic Society

Goddesses were depicted in Roman mosaics, but this woman was most likely a wealthy woman of Pompeii.

500 B.C. TO A.D. 180

Rome: Republic to Empire

©Araldo de Luca/Corbis

THE STORY MATTERS ...

When the volcano Vesuvius erupted in A.D. 79, it covered the Roman city of Pompeii with a thick layer of burning ash. As many as 20,000 people were killed, and the buried city was lost for centuries. When explorers dug into its remains in the early 1700s, they discovered a time capsule of Roman times, with buildings, art, and everyday objects all perfectly preserved.

This mosaic, which is an image of a woman created out of small stones and glass, was discovered in one of the homes of Pompeii. Historians have learned much about the daily life of Romans from artifacts unearthed at Pompeii and other archaeological sites.

ESSENTIAL QUESTIONS

- How does geography influence the way people live?
- How do governments change? • Why does conflict develop?
- What are the characteristics of a leader?

Place & Time: Rome 500 B.C. to 180 A.D.

Rome grew from a small farming village into one of the world's greatest empires. The factors that linked the empire together—a common language, a common money, and massive public works projects—influence Western civilization even today.

Step Into the Place

MAP FOCUS In 500 B.C., Rome was just a small city on the Italian peninsula's Tiber River. By A.D. 200, the Roman Empire had conquered an area roughly the size of the continental United States.

1 LOCATION Using cardinal directions, compare and contrast the boundaries of Rome in 500 B.C. with the boundaries in A.D. 200.

2 PLACE Look at the map. What body of water might have aided the growth of Rome?

3 CRITICAL THINKING
Analyzing Why do you think Romans desired to expand their territory?

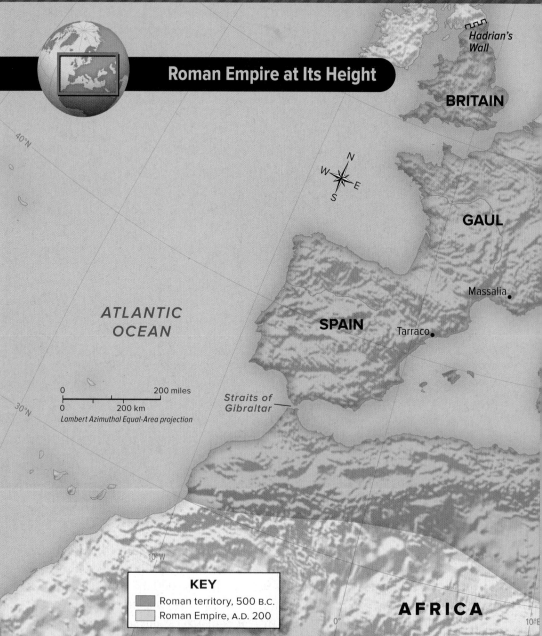

Roman Empire at Its Height

Hadrian's Wall

BRITAIN

GAUL

Massalia

SPAIN

Tarraco

ATLANTIC OCEAN

Straits of Gibraltar

AFRICA

0 ——— 200 miles
0 ——— 200 km
Lambert Azimuthal Equal-Area projection

KEY
Roman territory, 500 B.C.
Roman Empire, A.D. 200

Step Into the Time

TIME LINE Rome changed greatly during the years shown on the time line. About how many years passed between the Republic being established and Rome having its first emperor?

509 B.C. Rome becomes a republic

c. 451 B.C. Romans adopt Twelve Tables

ROME
THE WORLD

500 B.CRE. | **400 B.C.** | **300 B.C.**

c. 490 B.C. Greeks at war with Persians

323 B.C. Alexander the Great dies

c. 321 B.C. Mauryan Dynasty begins in India

North Sea

Rhine R.

Danube R.

ASIA

Caspian Sea

ITALY

Adriatic Sea

Black Sea

Corsica

Rome

Ostia

Puteoli

Sardinia

Byzantium

ASIA MINOR

GREECE

Athens

Tigris R.

SYRIA

Sicily

Carthage

Crete

Cyprus

Sidon

PALESTINE

Mediterranean Sea

Jerusalem

Euphrates R.

Alexandria

EGYPT

ARABIA

10°E   20°E   30°E   40°E

c. 267 B.C. Rome controls most of Italy

27 B.C. Octavian becomes Rome's first emperor

264 B.C. Punic Wars begin

A.D. 66 Jews revolt against Romans

A.D. 96 Rule of Good Emperors begins

c. A.D. 180 *Pax Romana* ends

200 B.C.   100 B.C.   A.D. 1   A.D. 100   A.D. 200

c. 221 B.C. Qin Dynasty begins in China

c. A.D. 200 Kush Kingdom begins decline

c. A.D. 100 Silk Road is established

LESSON 1

The Founding of Rome

ESSENTIAL QUESTION

• How does geography influence the way people live?

IT MATTERS BECAUSE
Rome's location, especially its nearby farmlands and easy access to the Mediterranean Sea, enabled it to grow and influence the world.

The Beginning of Rome

GUIDING QUESTION *What effect did geography have on the rise of Roman civilization?*

Greek culture did not die when Greece's power declined. Parts of it were adapted and used by the Romans. The Romans had been mostly isolated from the great civilizations of the eastern Mediterranean region. Over time, however, they learned from these civilizations and used their new knowledge to build a vast and powerful empire. Roman rule extended throughout much of present-day Europe, Africa, and Asia.

The Settling of Italy

Italy's location has attracted people for thousands of years. Italy is centrally located in the Mediterranean region. People can easily travel to it from Africa, Asia, and Europe. In addition, people and goods moved with little difficulty through passes in Italy's rugged mountains. These mountain passes also linked settlements together.

There is another key reason why Italy has attracted settlers. Italy has a sunny, mild climate and fertile farmland. Its mountain slopes level off to large flat plains that are ideal for growing crops. With the ability to grow plenty of food, Italy could support a large population.

Reading**HELP**DESK

Taking Notes: *Creating a Time Line*

Use a time line like this one to order events from the founding of Rome through the Roman Republic's conquest of most of Italy.

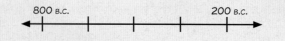

800 B.C.   200 B.C.

Content Vocabulary

• **republic**
• **legion**

Rome's Location

The Romans made their home on the Italian Peninsula. This long, thin peninsula juts out from central Europe into the Mediterranean Sea. On a map, Italy looks like a high-heeled boot. The boot's heel points to Greece. The toe points to the island of Sicily (SIH·suh·lee). The Alps are like shoelaces that are strung across the top of the boot. These rugged mountains separate Italy from northern Europe. Another mountain range in Italy is the Apennines (A·puh·NYNZ). These mountains extend from north to south. Volcanoes dot southern Italy's landscape. Italy has long been affected by volcanic eruptions and earthquakes.

Physical features influenced Rome's development. Rome was **founded** about 15 miles (24 km) up the Tiber (TY·buhr) River from the Mediterranean Sea. People used the river to move goods easily between northern and southern Italy. Merchants could also ship their goods out to the Mediterranean Sea using the river. In addition, Rome was far enough up the Tiber River to escape raids by sea-going pirates. Rome's location across seven steep hills made it easy to defend against enemy attacks.

Roman Origins

Several different legends describe how Rome began. One legend about the founding of Rome is contained in the *Aeneid* (ih·NEE·ihd), written by the Roman poet Virgil. He described what took place after the Greeks captured the city of Troy. First, the Trojan Aeneas (ih·NEE·uhs) and his soldiers escaped from Troy to find a new homeland. The Trojans settled in Italy and waged war. Then Aeneas married a local king's daughter. Their marriage united the Trojans with a group of Latin-speaking people who lived in this region. Because of this, Aeneas is known as the "father" of the Romans.

Another legend describes the founding of Rome much differently. This tale **involves** twin brothers, Romulus (RAHM·yuh·luhs) and Remus (REE·muhs). After they were born, they were left beside the Tiber River. A female wolf discovered the boys and cared for them. A shepherd and his wife found and raised the twins.

According to legend, Romulus and Remus were the sons of the Roman war god Mars. The historian Livy tells of the brothers' argument about how to build Rome's first walls. As depicted here, Romulus killed Remus in the conflict.

Mary Evans Picture Library/Alamy Stock Photo

Academic Vocabulary

found to establish or create
involve to include

The Roman historian Livy wrote about the history of Rome. What were his sources? What other sources about these events do we have that are as reliable as Livy's? For example, is a fresco a historical source? If so, is it a primary or secondary source? Which type of source is more trustworthy? Write a brief explanation of how you would compare sources if sources were reliable, such as Livy's writing and images painted on a wall. For more information about analyzing primary and secondary sources, read the chapter *What Does a Historian Do?*

When the brothers grew up, they planned to build a city along the Tiber River. However, the two boys argued about the construction of the city. Remus made fun of the walls that Romulus built. The Roman historian Livy (LIH·vee) tells what happened next:

PRIMARY SOURCE

❝ Then followed an angry altercation [argument]; heated passions [emotions] led to bloodshed; in the tumult [uproar] Remus was killed. The more common report is that Remus contemptuously [spitefully] jumped over the newly raised walls and was forthwith killed by the enraged Romulus, . . . Romulus thus became sole ruler, and the city [Rome] was called after him, its founder. ❞

—from *History of Rome*, by Livy

Historically, little is known about the first people to settle in Italy. Archaeological artifacts (AHR·tih·fakts) suggest that Neolithic people might have settled in Italy as early as 5000 B.C. These early groups built farming villages but moved after they had used up the nutrients in the soil. Between 2000 B.C. and 1000 B.C., other groups of people settled permanently in the hills and on the plains. Latin-speaking people, called Latins, settled on the plain of Latium (LAY·shee·uhm) in central Italy.

One group of Latins built straw-roofed huts on Rome's hills. They tended animals and grew crops. This settlement, which **occurred** (uh·KUHRD) between 800 B.C. and 700 B.C., marks the birth of Rome. The people living there became known as Romans.

Influences of Greeks and Etruscans

After 800 B.C., other groups moved into the region where the Romans lived. Two of these groups, the Greeks and the Etruscans (ih·TRUHS·kuhnz), would greatly influence Roman civilization.

From about 750 B.C. to 500 B.C., Greeks settled in farming villages in southern Italy. The Greeks introduced grape and olive farming to the region. The Greeks also passed on the Greek alphabet to the Romans. Later, the Romans would model their buildings, sculpture, and literature after those of the Greeks.

The Etruscans had an even greater influence on Roman civilization. The Etruscans settled north of Rome in Etruria (ih·TROOR·ee·uh). After 650 B.C., they moved south. The Etruscans **eventually** (ee·VEN·choo·uh·lee) took control of Rome and its surrounding area.

Etruscan wall paintings were frescoes, meaning they were painted on wet plaster. Many Etruscan frescoes show people enjoying music or dance.

▶ CRITICAL THINKING:
Analyzing What does the image suggest about how the Etruscans lived?

The Etruscans were ruled by nobles, who grew wealthy from trade and mining. Other Etruscans **devoted** themselves to the study of the arts. Skilled Etruscan artisans worked with copper, iron, lead, and tin. They turned these metals into weapons, tools, and jewelry. Etruscan artists covered the walls of tombs with colorful paintings. They painted men and women feasting, dancing, and playing music. Some wall paintings also displayed violent battle scenes. These images showed that the Etruscans were proud of their powerful army.

The Etruscans taught the Romans to build with brick and to roof their homes with tiles. They drained the water from marshes that lay between Rome's hills. They laid out city streets. The Etruscans built temples, passing on their religious rituals to the Romans. They even influenced the style of clothing that the Romans wore. Roman men adopted the Etruscan fashion of wearing short cloaks and togas. Finally, the Etruscan army served as the model for the mighty army that the Romans would later create.

✓ **PROGRESS CHECK**

Explaining How did the Etruscans influence early Rome?

Academic Vocabulary

devote to give one's time, effort, or attention earnestly

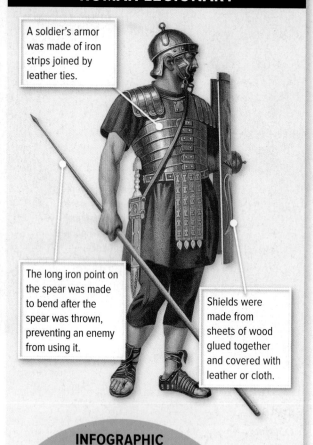

A soldier's armor was made of iron strips joined by leather ties.

The long iron point on the spear was made to bend after the spear was thrown, preventing an enemy from using it.

Shields were made from sheets of wood glued together and covered with leather or cloth.

INFOGRAPHIC

Originally the soldiers in the Roman army were untrained citizens. Through harsh training, the Roman army became known as one of the world's best.

▶ **CRITICAL THINKING**
Analyzing Why was it an advantage to Rome to have a professional army?

Becoming a Republic

GUIDING QUESTION *How did Rome become a great power?*

The Romans greatly **benefited** from the contributions of the Etruscans. However, they grew weary of Etruscan rulers. According to Roman tradition, in 509 B.C., the Romans overthrew Tarquin the Proud, the Etruscan king, and established a **republic** (rih·PUH·blihk). A republic is a form of government in which citizens elect their leaders. The creation of a republic began a new era in Rome's history. When Rome became a republic, it was still a small city. It was also still surrounded by different groups of people. These groups included Etruscans, Greeks, and other Latins. Over the next 200 years, the Romans fought many wars against these neighbors. By 267 B.C., Rome controlled almost all of Italy. The Roman Republic was able to **acquire** land because of its strong army. During the early years of the republic, every male citizen who owned land had to serve in the army. Roman soldiers were well trained, and deserters were punished by death. This strict discipline ensured soldiers stayed loyal to Rome.

The Romans also developed new battle strategies. In the early days of the republic, the Romans fought like the Greeks. Rows of soldiers moved in a single large group. They attacked from only one direction. Roman generals realized that this way of fighting was slow and hard to control. They reorganized their soldiers into smaller groups, called **legions** (LEE·juhnz). Each legion had about 6,000 men. A legion was further divided into groups of 60 to 120 soldiers. These smaller groups could move quickly around the battlefield to wherever they were most needed.

Roman soldiers were also well armed. Most soldiers carried a short, double-edged iron sword called a *gladius* (GLAY·dee·uhs) and an iron spear called a *pilum* (PY·luhm). Each of the small groups in a legion carried its own standard into battle. The standard was a tall pole topped with a symbol, such as an eagle.

Reading**HELP**DESK

republic a form of government in which citizens elect their leaders
legions large groups of Roman soldiers

Academic Vocabulary

benefit to receive help; to gain
acquire to get as one's own

Because the standard could be seen above the action, it showed soldiers where they were supposed to be on the battlefield.

Who Ruled Rome?

In addition to having a strong army, the Romans ruled effectively. After they conquered a region, they built permanent military outposts to protect it. These settlements were built at strategic locations, such as on a high hill or at a river crossing. They also built roads between settlements. As a result, troops and supplies could move quickly within the conquered lands.

The Romans stressed the need to treat conquered people fairly. If conquered people were treated well, the Romans believed, the people would become loyal subjects. To encourage fair treatment, the Romans created the Roman Confederation. This system gave some conquered peoples, especially other Latins, full Roman citizenship. They could vote and serve in the government of Rome. They were treated the same as other citizens under the law.

Other conquered peoples became allies, or friends, of Rome. As allies, they paid Roman taxes. In addition, they were required to supply soldiers to fight for Rome. Allies, however, were free to manage their own local affairs.

With these policies, the Romans hoped to maintain the peace in their conquered lands. If conquered peoples turned against Rome, its rulers were ready to crush any revolts. Rome's generosity paid off. The republic grew stronger and more unified.

The Roman soldiers, called legionaries, were disciplined and well trained. In groups called legions, they developed new battle strategies.

PROGRESS CHECK

Analyzing Why were the Romans able to expand their control of Italy?

SuperStock/SuperStock

LESSON 1 REVIEW

Review Vocabulary

1. How was the growth of the *republic* aided by the Roman army's use of *legions* in warfare?

Answer the Guiding Questions

2. ***Explaining*** How did Rome's location affect its development?

3. ***Summarizing*** How did the Roman government maintain control over conquered territories?

4. ***Differentiating*** How did the attitude of Romans toward the Etruscans change over time?

5. **ARGUMENT** You are a Roman living about 650 B.C. The Etruscans have taken over, and your friends are worried about the new rulers. Write a persuasive speech in which you encourage them to adopt Etruscan ways. Tell what Romans may learn from the Etruscans and why they should not turn against the new rulers.

There's More Online! connected.mcgraw-hill.com

LESSON 2

Rome As a Republic

ESSENTIAL QUESTION

• How do governments change?

IT MATTERS BECAUSE
Rome's ideas about democracy would greatly influence the people who founded the United States many centuries later.

Governing Rome

GUIDING QUESTION *How did conflict between classes change Rome's government?*

Not everyone was treated fairly in the Roman Republic. Rome's government reflected divisions within its society.

Early Romans were divided into two classes: patricians and plebeians. The **patricians** (puh·TRIH·shuhnz) were Rome's ruling class. Patricians were wealthy landowners. They came from Rome's oldest and most prominent families. Most Romans, however, were **plebeians** (plih·BEE·uhnz). Plebeians were not as wealthy as the patricians. In some cases, they were very poor. Plebeians included artisans, shopkeepers, and owners of small farms.

Patrician and plebeian men were Roman citizens and had the right to vote. Both groups were required to pay taxes and serve in the army. Plebeians, however, had a lower social position than the patricians. For example, it was illegal for a patrician and a plebeian to marry each other. Plebeians also lacked important basic rights. They could not hold public office or lead the public ceremonies that honored the gods of Rome. Rome's republic would be shaped by a struggle between the patricians and the plebeians over the right to govern.

Reading **HELP**DESK

Taking Notes: *Categorizing Information*
Use a web diagram like the one here to list facts about patricians and plebeians and their roles in the government of Rome.

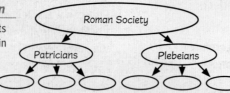

Content Vocabulary
• **patrician** • **veto** • **dictator**
• **plebeian** • **praetor** • **civic duty**
• **consul** • **tribune**

Government of the Republic

The government of the Roman Republic was organized into three branches. One branch made laws; another ran the daily affairs of government; a third branch acted as judges. The republic had a system of checks and balances. This system was designed to prevent one branch from becoming too strong. It did not separate powers like the United States government does today, however. Judges helped run the government and could lead armies. Some leaders who ran the government also helped make laws.

Two patrician **consuls** (CAHN·suhlz) headed the government. The consuls were administrators and army leaders. Each consul served one year in office. Their terms of office were short so that they would not become too powerful. Each consul could **veto** (VEE·toh), or reject, the other's decision. The word veto is Latin for "I forbid." Rome also had other major government officials called **praetors** (PREE·tuhrz). They interpreted the law and served as judges in court. They could also lead armies.

The Senate was Rome's **legislature.** The Senate was a group of 300 patrician men. These senators served the republic for life. During the early republic, the Senate only advised the consuls. By the 200s B.C., however, senators debated foreign policy, proposed laws, and approved the construction of roads and temples.

The Assembly of Centuries was another legislative body in Rome. It elected consuls and praetors and passed laws. The Assembly of Centuries was, like the Senate, controlled by patricians.

Conflict Between Classes

As time passed, the plebeians grew frustrated. They had to serve in the army and pay taxes, yet they had no power in the government.

In 494 B.C., many plebeians went on strike, refusing to fight in the army. They even left Rome to create a government of their own. The patricians feared that the republic was in danger of collapsing, so they agreed to share power with the plebeians.

The patricians allowed the plebeians to have their own body of representatives, called the Council of the Plebs. The Council of the Plebs elected officials called **tribunes** (TRIH·byoonz). Tribunes voiced plebeian concerns to the government.

This plebeian strike to gain a voice in government turned violent. The Roman plebeians went on at least five strikes in order to establish their rights.

patricians the ruling class

plebeians ordinary citizens

consul head of government, usually with a limited term in office

veto to reject

praetors government officials who interpret the law and serve as judges

tribune an elected official who protects the rights of ordinary citizens

Academic Vocabulary

legislature a group of people who make the laws

There's More Online! connected.mcgraw-hill.com

ALPS

PYRENEES

Po R.

APPENNINES

Tiber R.

Danube R.

40°N

SPAIN

10°W

New Carthage

Corsica

0°

Sardinia

Rome

ITALY

Adriatic Sea

Black Sea

MACEDONIA

GREECE

ASIA MINOR

10°E

Carthage

Sicily

Corinth

Rhodes

SYRIA

AFRICA

Mediterranean Sea

Crete

Cyprus

20°E

30°E

0   500 miles
0   500 km
Lambert Azimuthal Equal-Area projection

KEY
- Rome, 500 B.C.
- Territory added by 264 B.C.
- Territory added by 146 B.C.

GEOGRAPHY CONNECTION

Within 350 years, the Roman Republic conquered territory along much of the Mediterranean Sea's northern coast.

1 **PLACE** What major islands did Rome conquer?

2 **CRITICAL THINKING**
Making Inferences Why do you think Rome did not expand farther north?

Tribunes could also veto government decisions. Later, plebeians were even allowed to become consuls, and marriages between plebeians and patricians were made legal.

In 287 B.C., the plebeians won another important political victory. The Council of the Plebs was given the right to pass laws for all Romans. Politically, all male citizens were now considered equal. In practice, however, a few wealthy patrician families still held most of the power. Women did not have any political rights. The Roman Republic had become more representative, but it was still not democratic.

Cincinnatus and Civic Duty

The Romans believed that there were times when the republic needed a strong leader. To lead Rome, the Romans created the office of **dictator** (DIHK·tay·tuhr). Today, this word is used to describe an oppressive ruler who has total control over a country. In the Roman Republic, however, the consuls resigned during difficult or dangerous times, and the senate appointed a dictator to lead the republic. During a crisis, the dictator had complete control over Rome. After the crisis was over, the dictator was expected to give up his power, and the regular government's power would then be restored.

One of the most famous Roman dictators was Cincinnatus (SIHN·suh·NA·tuhs). Cincinnatus had been a respected Roman consul who was known for his loyalty to Rome. In

Reading HELPDESK

dictator a person granted absolute power

458 B.C., a powerful enemy of Rome threatened to destroy the Roman army. The Senate appointed Cincinnatus as dictator to handle this emergency. Messengers were sent to his farm to tell him about his appointment. They found him plowing his fields. Cincinnatus accepted the role of dictator, and he immediately created an army. Then, he led it into battle, easily defeating the enemy. Next, Cincinnatus marched his army back to Rome and resigned as dictator. Just 16 days after taking control of the republic, Cincinnatus returned to his farm.

Cincinnatus was widely admired because he fulfilled his **civic duty**. Civic duty is the idea that citizens have a responsibility to help their country. This idea was important to the Romans and has been valued by other people as well. George Washington, for example, was inspired by Cincinnatus. Like Cincinnatus, Washington was a farmer who was asked to lead an army: the Continental Army in the American War for Independence. After leading the Americans to victory, Washington returned to his farm in Virginia. Later, he **reluctantly** agreed to become the first president of the United States.

When called to serve, Cincinnatus willingly left his farm to fulfill his civic duty.

▶ **CRITICAL THINKING**

Analyzing What role did Cincinnatus play in government to fulfill his civic duty?

Rome's System of Law

One of Rome's greatest contributions to later civilizations was its system of law. Roman law has influenced the legal systems of the United States and other countries.

At first, Roman laws were not written down. This sparked criticism from the plebeians. They believed that patrician judges would always rule in favor of the upper classes if there were no written laws. The plebeians demanded that laws be put into writing. Thus, the judges would have to refer to the laws when they made a legal decision. The patricians eventually agreed.

In 451 B.C., Rome adopted its first written code of laws known as the Twelve Tables. The laws were carved on twelve bronze tablets and placed in Rome's marketplace, called the Forum (FOHR·uhm). These laws served as the foundation for all future Roman laws. The Twelve Tables supported the ideal that all free citizens—patrician and plebeian alike—had the right to be treated equally in the Roman legal system.

These bundles of rods and axes, called fasces, were carried by Roman officials as a symbol of legal authority.

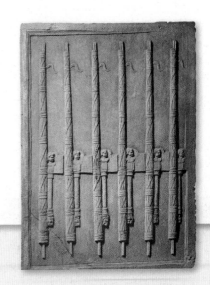

civic duty the idea that citizens have a responsibility to help their country

Academic Vocabulary

reluctantly hesitantly or unwillingly

(t)North Wind/North Wind Picture Archives; (b)Alinari/Art Resource, NY

The Roman court system shared many similarities with the legal system in the United States today. Judges heard cases before an audience of citizens.

As the Romans conquered more people, they expanded their system of laws. They created laws that would apply to people who were not Roman citizens. These new laws were known as the Law of Nations. The Law of Nations identified the laws and rights that applied to all people everywhere in the Roman lands.

Roman Justice

The ideas found in Roman laws are woven throughout the American legal system today. For example, the American legal system, like the Roman legal system, **assumes** that a person is innocent until proven guilty. People accused of crimes have the right to defend themselves before a judge. Judges must carefully consider all the evidence in a case before making a decision.

The *rule of law* is one of the key ideas that the Romans passed on to the world. The rule of law means that laws apply to everyone equally. It also means that the legal system should treat everyone the same way. Before the Romans, the rule of law was unfamiliar to people.

In many regions, people of the upper classes enjoyed special privileges. They often had different laws and courts from the lower classes. People in the lower classes, however, had few legal rights or none at all. The Romans extended the idea of the rule of law to all their lands. Today, the rule of law is the guiding principle of the American legal system.

☑ PROGRESS CHECK

Explaining What was the emergency that caused Cincinnatus to be appointed dictator?

The Punic Wars

GUIDING QUESTION *How did Rome conquer the Mediterranean region?*

Rome continued to grow as a republic. Its power, however, was threatened by another civilization in the Mediterranean region. Carthage (KAHR·thihj) was a powerful trading empire based along the north African coast. Carthage traced its beginnings to the Phoenicians, who created a trading colony there about 800 B.C. Carthage became the largest and wealthiest city in the western Mediterranean area because of trade. Its territory included parts of northern Africa and southern Europe.

©National Geographic Society/Corbis

Academic Vocabulary

assume to take for granted to be true
intensify to become stronger
innovation the introduction of something new

Carthage became Rome's main rival. Each wanted to control the entire Mediterranean world. In 264 B.C., their rivalry **intensified**. It grew into a series of wars that took place over a period of nearly 120 years.

The Punic Wars Begin

War between the Romans and the Carthaginians, or the people of Carthage, erupted in 264 B.C. The original conflict is known as the First Punic War. The First Punic War began when Rome sought control of the fertile island of Sicily. The Carthaginians had already established colonies on the island. So they were determined to stop the Roman invasion.

Carthage used its strong navy to protect its trading empire. Although Rome had a powerful army, it did not have a navy. It was forced to build a fleet quickly in order to fight Carthage. The Romans modeled their new warships after those of Carthage. They made one key **innovation**. They built a small moveable bridge on the front of each ship. This bridge allowed Roman soldiers to board a Carthaginian ship and fight hand-to-hand on its decks. In a way, it changed a sea war into a land war.

For more than 20 years, the Romans and Carthaginians fought each other at sea. Finally, in 241 B.C., a Roman fleet badly defeated Carthage's navy off the coast of Sicily. Carthage was forced to give up Sicily and pay a huge fine to the Romans. Rome then took control of the island.

GEOGRAPHY CONNECTION

After defeating Carthage in the Second Punic War, Rome was the strongest power in the Mediterranean region.

1 LOCATION From what direction did Hannibal of Carthage attack Rome?

2 CRITICAL THINKING
Analyzing Why did Hannibal take the route he did instead of sailing directly to Rome?

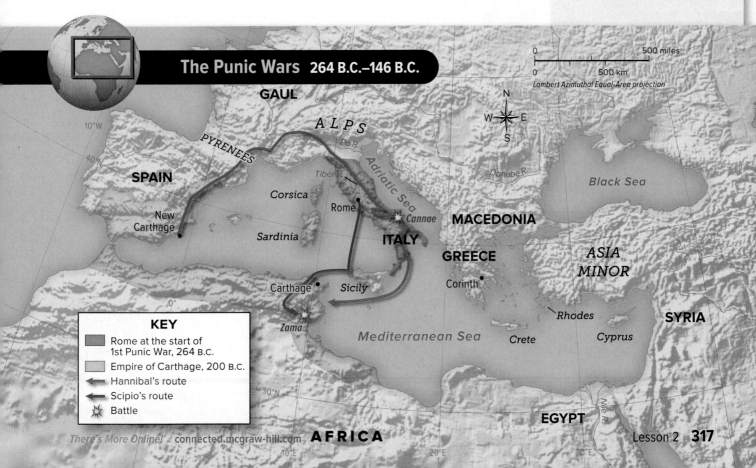

The Punic Wars 264 B.C.–146 B.C.

GAUL

ALPS

PYRENEES

SPAIN

New Carthage

Corsica

Sardinia

Tiber R.

Rome

Po R.

Adriatic Sea

Cannae

ITALY

Carthage

Sicily

Zama

MACEDONIA

GREECE

Corinth

Danube R.

Black Sea

ASIA MINOR

Rhodes

Crete

Cyprus

SYRIA

Mediterranean Sea

EGYPT

Nile R.

AFRICA

0   500 miles
0   500 km
Lambert Azimuthal Equal-Area projection

KEY
- Rome at the start of 1st Punic War, 264 B.C.
- Empire of Carthage, 200 B.C.
- Hannibal's route
- Scipio's route
- Battle

Hannibal Attacks: The Second Punic War

After losing Sicily, Carthage tried to expand its empire into Spain. They wanted to make up for the losses caused by Rome taking over Sicily. Spain had valuable resources of silver, copper, gold, lead, and iron.

The Romans bitterly opposed Carthage's attempt to establish territory so near to Rome. So the Romans encouraged the Spanish to rebel against Carthage. In response, Carthage sent its greatest general, Hannibal (HA·nuh·buhl), to attack Rome. This event, in 218 B.C., started the Second Punic War.

Hannibal planned to fight the Romans in Italy. To do this he gathered an army of about 46,000 men and 37 elephants. He sailed from Carthage to Spain. Then, his soldiers marched through southern Gaul, or present-day France.

Next, they crossed the Alps into Italy. The Carthaginians crossed the Alps with their elephants, hoping to overpower the Roman army. Instead, the bitter cold and attacks by mountain tribes killed almost half of the Carthaginian soldiers and most of the elephants. The remaining army, however, was still a powerful fighting force when it reached Italy.

In December 218 B.C., the Carthaginian forces defeated the Romans in northern Italy. Hannibal made good use of his elephants in the attack. Unfortunately, most of the animals died after the conflict.

▶ **CRITICAL THINKING**
Analyzing Why was this battle important?

As Hannibal and his army grew closer and closer to Italy and the Roman forces, Roman military leaders looked to the Senate for advice.

" They [the Roman commanders] therefore sent frequent messages to Rome asking for instructions, . . .in view of the fact that the country was being plundered, . . . The Senate passed a resolution . . .give the enemy battle. "

—from *The Histories of Polybius*, by Polybius

In 216 B.C., Hannibal defeated the Romans at the Battle of Cannae (KA·nee) in southern Italy. Following the battle, Hannibal's army raided the country. In response, the Romans assembled another army to stop the Carthaginians. In 206 B.C. Roman forces, led by Scipio (SIH·pee·oh), captured Spain and then attacked the city of Carthage. Hannibal returned home to North Africa to defend his people. Scipio's troops defeated the Carthaginians in 202 B.C. at the Battle of Zama (ZAY·muh). Carthage was forced to give up its navy and pay Rome a large sum of money. It also had to give its Spanish territory to Rome. As a result, Rome became the supreme power in the western Mediterranean.

The Third Punic War

Rome still considered Carthage a military threat. In 146 B.C., Rome finally destroyed it in the Third Punic War. At the same time, Rome also waged war against other states in the eastern Mediterranean region. In the 140s B.C., all of Greece fell under Roman rule. About twenty years later, Rome acquired its first province in Asia.

☑ **PROGRESS CHECK**

Describing How did Hannibal lose the Second Punic War?

Connections to TODAY

Hannibal's Elephants

Historians have wondered how Hannibal obtained elephants for his march. Were they Indian or African elephants? Indian elephants are easier to train. In fact, most circus elephants today are Indian elephants. However, it would have been very difficult for Hannibal to obtain elephants from India. Even African elephants are not native to North Africa, where Hannibal started his march. Historians continue to question which type of elephant Hannibal used—or how he obtained them.

LESSON 2 REVIEW

Review Vocabulary

1. Why were Roman *consuls* awarded the power of the *veto*?

Answer the Guiding Questions

2. *Explaining* How did plebeians gain power in the republic? For what changes were they responsible?

3. *Distinguishing Fact from Opinion* Identify whether the following statement is a fact or an opinion: "At first, patricians had more rights than plebeians."

4. *Summarizing* Describe how Rome defeated Carthage to become the ruler of the Mediterranean region.

5. **INFORMATIVE/EXPLANATORY** In an essay, describe what the idea of "rule of law" meant to the average Roman.

LESSON 3

The End of the Republic

ESSENTIAL QUESTION

• Why does conflict develop?

IT MATTERS BECAUSE

Without a strong system of checks and balances, a powerful individual or group can easily take control of a representative government.

Problems in the Republic

GUIDING QUESTION *What factors led to the decline of the Roman Republic?*

The Roman army won victories abroad, but the republic faced mounting economic troubles at home. The gap between the rich and the poor grew wider. Many farmers faced financial ruin. The cities of the republic were becoming overcrowded and dangerous.

Romans—Rich and Poor

Most Romans were plebeians who farmed small plots of land. The plebeians had made some political gains in the Roman Republic, but they lacked real power. Power was still held by the patricians. The upper class still made up most of the Senate and served in key government positions. They also managed Rome's finances and directed its wars.

In the 100s B.C., farmers began to fall into poverty and debt. Why? Many small farmers had neglected their fields while fighting in Roman wars. Others had their farms destroyed by the Carthaginians. Now, the farmers did not have crops to harvest. As a result, they could not pay back loans they owed.

Reading**HELP**DESK

Taking Notes: *Sequencing*

Complete a diagram like this one to identify the events that led to the fall of the Roman Republic. You may add more boxes if necessary.

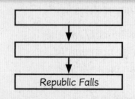

Content Vocabulary

• **latifundia**
• **triumvirate**

In addition, small farmers could not compete with wealthy Romans, who owned **latifundia** (la·tuh·FUHN·dee·uh), or large farming estates. Farmers could not even find jobs on these huge farms. Those jobs went to a new source of labor—the thousands of prisoners captured in the Roman wars. Wealthy landowners did not have to pay wages to enslaved workers. Instead, they bought more land for their latifundia. Small farms were pushed out of business.

As small farms shut down, thousands of poor unemployed people left the countryside. They poured into Rome's cities looking for jobs. Even in the cities, however, enslaved people did most of the work. Paying jobs were hard to find. If free people could find a paying job, it was generally for a low wage.

Desperate economic conditions created mounting anger among the poor. Roman leaders worried about a rebellion. To prevent a revolt, Roman leaders began offering cheap food and free entertainment to the poor. Numerous Roman rulers used this policy of "bread and circuses" to acquire or stay in power.

Roman Reformers

Not all wealthy Romans ignored the problems of the poor. Two government officials, who were also brothers, worked for reforms. Tiberius and Gaius Gracchus (GRA·kuhs) thought that Rome's problems were caused by the actions of wealthy landowners. The brothers wanted to stop the wealthy from taking over small farms to create their latifundia. They urged the Senate to take some land from the latifundia and return it to the poor.

Stone carvings such as this show that artists felt farming was an important topic to include. Oxen did the heavy work for farmers.

▶ **CRITICAL THINKING**

Analyzing How did the reforms of the Gracchus brothers affect Roman farmers?

The Art Archive/Archeological Museum Aquileia/Dagli Orti

latifundia large farming estates

The Gracchus brothers tried to help the poor farmers who had lost their land to latifundia.

▶ **CRITICAL THINKING**
Analyzing What does the murder of these brothers tell us about the Roman government at this time?

The Senate was made up of wealthy Romans, some of whom owned the latifundia. They fought the Gracchus brothers' proposals. A group of senators even killed Tiberius in 133 B.C. Gaius was also murdered 12 years later. Dark days had fallen on the Roman Republic. The people charged with making and upholding the laws repeatedly broke them.

Roman Politics and the Army

The republic soon faced more challenges. Rome's military leaders began to seek political power. In 107 B.C., a general named Marius (MARE•ee•uhs) became consul. Marius, the son of a worker, was not a patrician.

Marius believed that he could solve Rome's economic problems. He **transformed** the army in order to provide opportunities for the poor. Until then, only property owners served in the military. Marius, however, recruited soldiers from the landless poor. In return for their service, he paid them wages—and promised them land. The Roman army was no longer a force of citizen volunteers. It was now a force of **professional** soldiers.

The plan that Marius put into action provided work for many jobless, landless Romans. However, it also weakened the republican form of government. Soldiers felt more loyalty to the general who hired and paid them than to the republic. As a result, military generals grew enormously powerful. Some generals sought political office. This allowed them to pass laws that gave land to their soldiers—and increased their power.

The creation of a professional army led to new power struggles. Marius was soon opposed by another general, named Sulla (SUH•luh), who commanded his own army. In 82 B.C., Sulla drove his enemies out of Rome and named himself dictator. It marked the first time a Roman general had led his army into the capital.

Over the next three years, Sulla made changes to the government. He reduced the power of the tribunes and gave the senators more responsibilities. Sulla then stepped down as dictator. Sulla hoped that his reforms would restore the Roman Republic to its earlier days of glory. Instead, Rome plunged into conflict that lasted for the next 50 years. Some Romans took notice of how Sulla had used an army to achieve his goals. Those who were eager for power decided that they would do the same thing.

 **PROGRESS CHECK**

Analyzing What was the purpose of "bread and circuses"?

ReadingHELPDESK

Academic Vocabulary

transform to change the structure of
professional relating to a type of job that usually requires training and practice

The Rise of Julius Caesar

GUIDING QUESTION *How did Julius Caesar rise to power in Rome?*

After Sulla left office, different Roman leaders fought among themselves for power. Many of them were military officials who relied on their loyal armies to support them. In 60 B.C., three men ruled the Roman Republic: Crassus, Pompey (PAHM·pee), and Julius Caesar (JOOL·yuhs SEE·zuhr). Crassus was a general and one of Rome's wealthiest men. Pompey and Caesar were also rich and known for their military accomplishments. These three men formed the First Triumvirate to rule Rome. A **triumvirate** (try·UHM·vuh·ruht) is a political group of three people who share equal power.

Caesar's Conquests

Each Triumvirate member commanded a military post in an outlying area of the Roman Republic. Pompey led in Spain, Crassus in Syria, and Caesar in Gaul. Gaul was made up mostly of what are now France and Belgium. While serving in Gaul, Caesar fought the Celts and invaded Britain. He won the admiration and support of the poorer classes. Roman senators grew uneasy with Caesar, however. They feared that he was becoming too popular and would seek power as Sulla had.

By 50 B.C., the First Triumvirate no longer existed. Crassus had died in battle, and Pompey emerged as Caesar's main rival. In 49 B.C., the Senate gave its support to Pompey. It ordered Caesar to give up his army and return to Rome. Caesar, however, refused. He knew that if he returned to Rome, he might be imprisoned or killed by his rivals. Caesar gathered his loyal troops and crossed the Rubicon (ROO·bih·KAHN) River.

Julius Caesar made himself Rome's first dictator for life in 44 B.C. As dictator, Caesar was greatly admired by the poor for his reforms. But he was hated by his enemies for his ambition.

©Bettmann/Corbis

triumvirate three rulers who share equal political power

Crossing the Rubicon

Caesar crossed the Rubicon at great risk. Even today, the phrase "crossing the Rubicon" is used when a person makes a decision that cannot be undone.

Caesar crossed the Rubicon even though he knew it would lead to civil war.

▶ **CRITICAL THINKING**

Predicting What might have happened if Caesar had not decided to cross the Rubicon?

This small river separated Caesar's military command area from Roman Italy. According to legend, Caesar saw a vision that inspired him to cross the Rubicon. He exclaimed to his troops:

PRIMARY SOURCE

❝ Even yet we may draw back; but once cross yon little bridge, and the whole issue is with the sword. . . . Take we the course which the signs of the gods and false dealing of our foes point out. The die is cast. ❞

—from *Life of Julius Caesar* by Suetonius

Caesar had refused to obey the Senate and was now marching on Rome. He realized that he was starting a **civil** war. His decision, however, could not be reversed.

Caesar and his soldiers swiftly captured all of Italy. They drove Pompey's forces out of the country. The fighting then spread eastward, with Caesar finally crushing Pompey's army in Greece in 48 B.C.

SuperStock

Reading**HELP**DESK

Academic Vocabulary

civil of or relating to citizens

Caesar Takes Power

In 44 B.C., Caesar took over the Roman government. He ended the practice of dictators serving in office for short terms by declaring himself dictator for life. To strengthen his power, Caesar appointed people to the Senate who supported him.

Meanwhile, Caesar introduced reforms that made him popular with Romans, especially the poor. He gave citizenship to many people living in Roman territories. He created jobs for the unemployed. In the countryside, he organized new settlements for landless laborers. He ordered landowners using slave labor to hire more free workers.

One of the most famous reforms that Caesar introduced was the creation of a new calendar. It had 12 months, 365 days, and a leap year. Known as the Julian calendar, it was used throughout Europe until A.D. 1582. Then it was changed slightly to become the Gregorian calendar. The Gregorian calendar is based on the date of the birth of Jesus. This calendar is still used by most countries in the world today.

Caesar developed the new calendar with the help of the astronomer Sosigenes (soh • SIHJ • ee • neez). It has movable pegs to allow for changing days.

Many Romans praised Caesar as a wise ruler because he brought peace and good government to Rome. Others, however, hated him. They believed that he wanted to be a king. Caesar's enemies, led by the senators Brutus and Cassius, plotted to kill him. In 44 B.C., Caesar's opponents gathered around him as he entered the Senate and stabbed him to death. Caesar was killed on March 15, also known as the "Ides of March" in the Julian calendar. His murder was made famous in the play *Julius Caesar*, by William Shakespeare. In the play, Caesar was warned to "Beware the Ides of March."

☑ PROGRESS CHECK

Explaining Why did some Romans oppose Caesar?

Build Vocabulary: *Words With Multiple Meanings*

plot: a secret plan
plot: (verb) to plan; to locate; to invent a story line

**Mark Antony
(83 B.C. – 30 B.C.)**

Mark Antony, a Roman, supported Caesar during the civil war between Caesar and Pompey. Antony was known as a wise politician. He was also a talented orator, meaning he was an effective public speaker. Antony was married twice before he fell in love with the Egyptian queen Cleopatra. He first met her around 40 B.C., when he accused her of assisting his enemies. Soon after, they formed a romantic and military partnership that lasted until their famous deaths.

**Cleopatra
(69 B.C. – 30 B.C.)**

Cleopatra was the daughter of an Egyptian king. When her father died in 51 B.C., Cleopatra took the throne with her brother. They soon became rivals. To hold on to the throne, Cleopatra formed an alliance with Julius Caesar. After Caesar died, Cleopatra allied herself with Mark Antony. When they fled to Egypt, Antony, it is said, heard a false report that Cleopatra had died. Deeply saddened, he killed himself. After Cleopatra buried him, she then took her own life.

▶ **CRITICAL THINKING**
Explaining Why did Mark Antony and Octavian first join forces? Why did Mark Antony and Octavian become divided?

From Republic to Empire

GUIDING QUESTION *How did Rome become an empire?*

After Caesar's death, civil war broke out. Caesar's 18-year-old grandnephew Octavian (ahk·TAY·vee·uhn) joined two of Caesar's top generals, Mark Antony (AN·tuh·nee) and Marcus Lepidus (LEH·puh·duhs). The three leaders' forces defeated those who killed Caesar. In 43 B.C., they formed the Second Triumvirate. Next, they divided the Roman Empire among themselves. Octavian took command of Italy and the west. Antony ruled in Greece and the east. Lepidus took charge in North Africa.

Antony and Cleopatra

The Second Triumvirate, however, did not last long. Lepidus retired from politics. Soon Octavian and Antony became rivals. Antony fell in love with the Egyptian queen Cleopatra. Together, they formed an alliance. Octavian accused Antony and Cleopatra of plotting against Rome. According to Octavian, Antony planned to make himself the sole ruler of the republic with Cleopatra's help. Many Romans grew alarmed at this news. Their support **enabled** Octavian to declare war on Antony.

In 31 B.C., Octavian and Antony's navies clashed off the coast of Greece. At the Battle of Actium (AK·shee·uhm), Octavian's forces defeated those of Antony and Cleopatra. After Octavian,

Roger-Viollet/The Image Works

Reading**HELP**DESK

Academic Vocabulary

enable to make possible

captured Alexandria, Antony heard false news that Cleopatra had died, and he killed himself. Cleopatra killed herself in response to Antony's death. Octavian became the supreme ruler of Rome. The civil wars had ended and so, too, did the Roman Republic.

Octavian—a New Direction

Octavian could have made himself a life-long dictator. However, he knew that many Romans favored a republic. These Romans were influenced by Cicero (SIH·suh·ROH) who was a well-known political leader and writer in Rome. Cicero strongly supported the representative, republican government. Cicero also did not trust dictators.

Throughout Rome's civil wars, Cicero had argued that a representative government should be restored to Rome. He died before Octavian rose to power. Cicero's ideas, however, would influence the writers of the United States Constitution centuries later.

Publicly, Octavian voiced his support for a republic. Privately, however, Octavian felt differently. He believed that a republican government was too weak to solve Rome's problems. Octavian felt that Rome needed a strong leader. With a strong and loyal army supporting Octavian, the senate consented to his wishes. It declared Octavian consul, tribune, and commander-in-chief for life in 27 B.C. Octavian, however, took the title *Augustus* (aw·GUHS·tuhs), or "the majestic one." Caesar Augustus, as Octavian was now called, became Rome's first emperor, or all-powerful ruler.

Octavian overcame many obstacles to become emperor of Rome.

▶ **CRITICAL THINKING**
Contrasting How did Octavian's leadership differ from Caesar's?

Robert Emmett Bright/Photo Researchers

☑ **PROGRESS CHECK**

Predicting How do you think Cicero might have reacted when the senate named Octavian the first emperor of Rome?

LESSON 3 REVIEW

Review Vocabulary

1. Why did the creation of *latifundia* cause poor people to move to cities?

Answer the Guiding Questions

2. *Understanding Cause and Effect* How did the election of Marius as consul reflect a change in Rome's government?

3. *Summarizing* What changes did Julius Caesar bring about as ruler of Rome?

4. *Explaining* How did Octavian's rule serve as a transition from a Roman republic to an empire?

5. *Identifying* Who was Caesar Augustus?

6. **NARRATIVE** You own a small Roman farm in the 100s B.C. Write a letter to a friend describing the changes you have witnessed in agriculture and the Roman government. Describe how those changes have affected you personally.

There's More Online!

LESSON 4

Rome Builds an Empire

ESSENTIAL QUESTION

- What are the characteristics of a leader?

IT MATTERS BECAUSE
The achievements of the Roman Empire influenced the Western world for centuries and continued to affect the modern world today.

The Rule of Augustus

GUIDING QUESTION *How did Augustus create a new age of prosperity for Rome?*

The rule of Caesar Augustus (formerly called Octavian) marked the beginning of a new era. For nearly two hundred years, the Roman world enjoyed peace and prosperity. This time period lasted until about A.D. 180. It is known as the **Pax Romana** (PAHKS roh·MAH·nah), or "Roman Peace." During this time, Rome reached the height of its power.

What Reforms Did Augustus Make?

As emperor, Augustus was determined to protect the empire. To do this, he created a permanent professional army. About 150,000 soldiers—all Roman citizens—made up this powerful military force. In addition, Augustus created a special unit known as the Praetorian Guard. The 9,000 men in this select unit guarded the emperor.

Augustus thought that Rome's borders should be easier to defend. He established the empire's boundaries along natural physical features. These included the Rhine (RYN) River and Danube (DAN·yoob) River to the north, the Atlantic Ocean to the west, the Sahara to the south, and near the Euphrates River to the east. Troops were stationed along these frontier areas to protect the empire from invaders.

Reading**HELP**DESK

Taking Notes: *Identifying*

Use a web diagram like this one to identify the important achievements of Emperor Augustus.

Achievements of Emperor Augustus

Content Vocabulary
- *Pax Romana*
- proconsul

328 *Rome: Republic to Empire*

In addition to protecting the empire, Augustus wanted to display the power of Rome. Augustus had many public buildings, fountains, and palaces rebuilt to reflect the greatness of Rome. "I found Rome a city of brick," he boasted, "and left it a city of marble."

Augustus also worked to improve Rome's government. During his reign, more than 50 million people lived within the empire's borders. This is slightly fewer than the number of people living in Italy today. To maintain control over his empire, Augustus named an official called a **proconsul** (PROH·KAHN·suhl), or governor, to oversee each of Rome's provinces. These new local officials replaced the politicians who had been appointed by the Senate. Augustus himself often visited the provinces to **inspect** the work of the proconsuls.

With new leaders in place, Augustus changed the empire's tax system. Before Augustus, tax collectors paid the government for the right to collect taxes. Tax collectors could keep some of what they collected from the people. Many tax collectors, however, were dishonest and took too much from the people. To solve this problem, Augustus made tax collectors permanent government officials and paid them regular wages.

Augustus also changed Rome's legal system. He created a code of laws for people living in the provinces who were not Roman citizens. As time passed, most of these people became citizens, so eventually, the laws were applied to everyone. However, the legal system often favored the authority of the empire over individual citizens' rights.

Augustus rebuilt many of Rome's buildings in marble to reflect the city's grandeur.

Victoria & Albert Museum, London/Bridgeman Art Library

Pax Romana Roman peace
proconsul governor

Academic Vocabulary

inspect to look over carefully

Natural disasters can shape people's interactions with their environment. In August A.D. 79 the volcano Mt. Vesuvius erupted and destroyed the city of Pompeii, in what is now Italy. Several thousand people escaped, while thousands more died. Today, about 600,000 people live near the volcano, although scientists warn it may be due to erupt again soon.

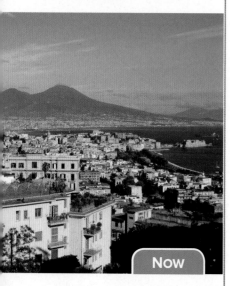

Now

▶ **CRITICAL THINKING**
Analyzing Why might people live in an area where a natural disaster has happened?

Reading**HELP**DESK

Academic Vocabulary

distribute to give or deliver to members of a group
contrast the act of comparing by looking at differences

Despite all of his reforms, Augustus feared that people might still be unhappy with his leadership. To preserve his rule and the empire, Augustus imported grain from Africa and **distributed** it to the poor. Augustus believed that a well-fed population would be less likely to revolt against him.

Emperors After Augustus

Augustus ruled Rome for almost 40 years. After Augustus died in A.D. 14, his adopted son, Tiberius, became emperor. After Tiberius, three other emperors from Augustus's family ruled Rome—Caligula (kuh·LIH·gyuh·luh), Claudius, and Nero (NEE·roh). They are known as the Julio-Claudian emperors. Tiberius and Claudius governed the empire effectively. In **contrast**, Caligula and Nero proved to be cruel rulers.

Caligula murdered many people and spent money recklessly. He even appointed his favorite horse as consul. The Praetorian Guard murdered him and made Claudius emperor.

Nero was also a brutal emperor who killed many people. Among his victims were his mother and two wives. Nero committed suicide after the Senate had sentenced him to death for treason.

☑ PROGRESS CHECK

Explaining How did Augustus protect Rome's borders?

The Roman Peace

GUIDING QUESTION *How did the Roman Empire become rich and prosperous?*

After Nero died, violence erupted throughout the Roman Empire. Then, in A.D. 69, a general named Vespasian (veh·SPAY·zhee·uhn), became emperor. Vespasian restored order, but he treated harshly anyone who opposed Roman rule. Vespasian crushed several uprisings throughout the empire. One such uprising was the Jewish revolt in the eastern province of Judaea. Vespasian's son, Titus, commanded troops that defeated the Jewish rebels. Roman soldiers also destroyed the Jewish temple in Jerusalem in A.D. 70.

Vespasian began the construction of the Colosseum, the huge amphitheater located in central Rome. After Vespasian died, his sons Titus and Domitian each governed Rome. While Titus was emperor, two disasters struck the empire. In A.D. 79, the volcano Mount Vesuvius erupted, destroying the city of Pompeii. A year later, a great fire badly damaged Rome. Both sons, however, ruled during an era of relative growth and prosperity.

THE "GOOD EMPERORS" OF THE *PAX ROMANA*

Nerva
A.D. 96–A.D. 98
Revised taxes; land reforms helped the poor

Trajan
A.D. 98–A.D. 117
Greatly expanded the empire; gave money for education

Hadrian
A.D. 117–A.D. 138
Made Roman law easier to understand and apply

Antoninus Pius
A.D. 138–A.D. 161
Enacted laws that assisted orphans

Marcus Aurelius
A.D. 161–A.D. 180
Reformed Roman law; assisted in uniting empire's economy

INFOGRAPHIC

These emperors, who earned the title the Five Good Emperors, together ruled for almost 75 years.

1 **IDENTIFYING** Under which emperor did the empire grow significantly?

2 **CRITICAL THINKING** *Analyzing* How would the contributions of Hadrian and Marcus Aurelius affect the empire's legal system?

Five Good Emperors

During the early A.D. 100s, several emperors who were not related to Augustus or Vespasian ruled the empire. Nerva, Trajan, Hadrian, Antoninus Pius, and Marcus Aurelius are known as the "good emperors." The five "good emperors" did not abuse their power. They were among the most **capable** rulers in Rome's history.

The five emperors governed during a time of economic growth. Agriculture and trade flourished during this period, which lasted from A.D. 96 to A.D. 180. Tertullian, a Roman writer, described this time:

PRIMARY SOURCE

❝ All places are now accessible [easy to reach], all are well known, all open to commerce ... cultivated fields have subdued [tamed] forests ... marshes are drained; and where once were ... solitary cottages, there are now large cities... everywhere are houses, and inhabitants, and settled government, and civilized life. *❞*

—from *Treatise on the Soul* by Tertullian

The five emperors introduced programs to help the empire's people. For example, Trajan made money available so that poor children could receive an education. Hadrian made Roman laws easier for ordinary citizens to understand.

Academic Vocabulary

capable able, competent

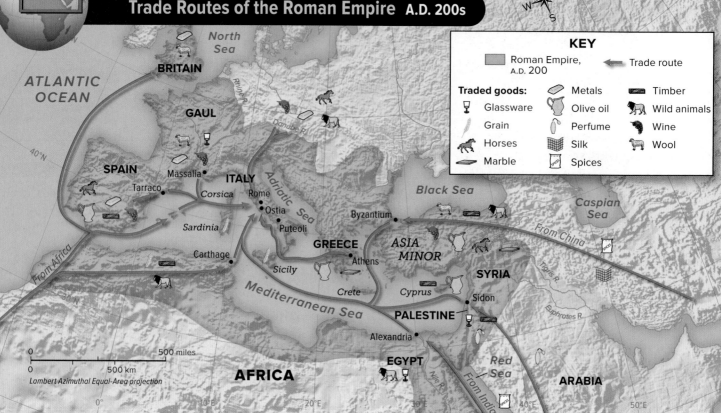

Trade Routes of the Roman Empire A.D. 200s

KEY

Roman Empire, A.D. 200

Trade route

Traded goods:
- Glassware
- Grain
- Horses
- Marble
- Metals
- Olive oil
- Perfume
- Silk
- Spices
- Timber
- Wild animals
- Wine
- Wool

ATLANTIC OCEAN

North Sea

BRITAIN

GAUL

SPAIN

Massalia

Tarraco

ITALY

Corsica

Rome

Ostia

Puteoli

Sardinia

Carthage

Sicily

GREECE

Athens

Crete

Black Sea

Caspian Sea

Byzantium

ASIA MINOR

Cyprus

SYRIA

Sidon

PALESTINE

Alexandria

From China

Tigris R.

Euphrates R.

Mediterranean Sea

Adriatic Sea

AFRICA

From Africa

EGYPT

Nile R.

From India

Red Sea

ARABIA

0   500 miles

0   500 km

Lambert Azimuthal Equal-Area projection

40°N

30°N

0°   10°E   20°E   30°E   40°E   50°E

GEOGRAPHY CONNECTION

Trade goods flowed to Rome and kept the city well supplied.

1 **PLACE** Which areas of the empire shipped timber to Rome?

2 **CRITICAL THINKING**
   Drawing Conclusions Why do you think Romans traded for horses and wild animals?

The five emperors also improved Roman cities. They spent tax money to build arches and monuments, bridges, roads, and harbors. They also built extensive **aqueducts** (A·kwuh·duhkts) to bring water from the country to the city.

A United Empire

The Emperor Trajan expanded the Roman Empire to its maximum size. The empire's borders extended to Britain in the northwest and Mesopotamia in the east.

Trajan's **successors** believed that the empire had become too large to rule effectively. They withdrew Roman forces from regions they could not defend and reinforced areas that were easier to protect. Hadrian pulled troops from Mesopotamia but strengthened defenses at the Rhine and Danube rivers.

By the A.D. 100s, the Roman Empire was one of the largest empires in history. Its land area was about 3.5 million square miles (9.1 million square km), almost the size of the United States.

Imagesource/PictureQuest

Reading HELP DESK

Academic Vocabulary

successor one that comes after

Visual Vocabulary

aqueduct a human-made channel that carries water long distances

Many groups of people lived in the Roman Empire. Roman law, Roman rule, and a shared Roman identity united them all. By A.D. 212, every free person within the empire was considered a Roman citizen. All citizens were treated equally under Roman laws.

The Empire's Economy

Agriculture remained the most important economic activity in the Roman Empire. Most people were farmers. Farmers in northern Italy and in the provinces of Gaul and Spain grew grapes to make wine and olives to make olive oil. Grain from Britain, Sicily, and Egypt supplied Rome's people with food.

Industry thrived in the cities. Potters, weavers, and jewelers produced pottery, cloth, and jewelry. Other artisans made glass, bronze, and brass. These goods were exported throughout the Mediterranean region.

Trade flourished. By A.D. 100, a common Roman system of money was used within the empire. Merchants used the same money in Gaul, Greece, or Egypt as they did in Rome. People also used a standard system of weights and measurements.

A network of paved roads extended throughout the empire. The roads allowed the Romans to communicate and move armies and goods easily. The Roman navy eliminated piracy on the Mediterranean Sea and other waterways. As a result, goods could be shipped safely to and from the empire's ports.

Traders from all over the empire arrived in Rome's port cities. Traders sold luxury goods to wealthy Romans. The Romans also imported raw materials, such as British tin and Spanish silver and lead. Roman workshops turned them into different goods.

Trade made many people wealthy. The wealth, however, did not extend to all Romans. Most city dwellers and farmers remained poor, and many other people remained enslaved.

✔ PROGRESS CHECK

Analyzing Why were five of Rome's rulers known as the "good emperors"?

LESSON 4 REVIEW

Review Vocabulary

1. What was the role of a *proconsul* under Augustus?

Answer the Guiding Questions

2. *Explaining* How did the changes that Augustus made to the Roman tax system reduce government corruption?

3. *Analyzing* How did roads contribute to the empire's success?

4. *Drawing Conclusions* What do you think was the greatest achievement of Augustus?

5. **INFORMATIVE/EXPLANATORY** You are a Roman living around A.D. 215. Write an essay about how the Roman Empire has changed since the reign of Trajan. As an ordinary citizen, which change affects you most?

Write your answers on a separate piece of paper.

1 Exploring the Essential Question

ARGUMENT Suppose you support the efforts of Tiberius and Gaius Gracchus to reform Rome. Write a letter or speech to other Romans that explains why reform is needed and what types of reforms should occur.

2 21st Century Skills

COLLABORATE WITH OTHERS Use the Internet and your local library to research the Twelve Tables of Rome. Work with your classmates to design a similar series of laws that are needed in society today. Record them, using modern language. How is your law code similar to and different from the Twelve Tables?

3 Thinking Like a Historian

PROBLEM SOLVING Roman leaders faced many problems and obstacles in expanding the empire and creating a peaceful society. Using a chart like this one, list some of the major problems they faced and how they solved these problems

Problem	Solution

4 GEOGRAPHY ACTIVITY

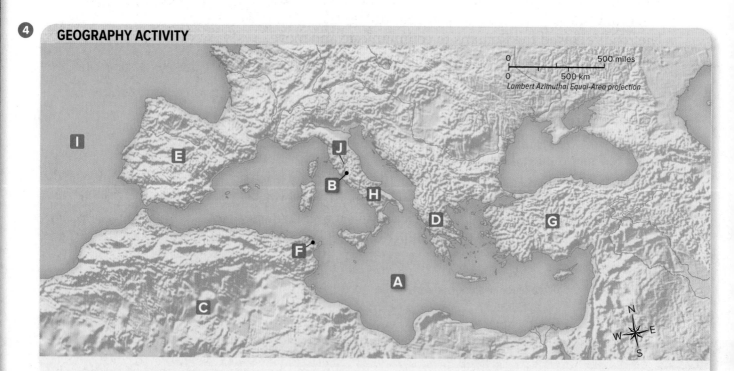

Locating Places

Match the letters on the map with the numbered places listed below.

1. Rome
2. Spain
3. Tiber River
4. Africa
5. Mediterranean Sea
6. Carthage
7. Asia Minor
8. Italy
9. Atlantic Ocean
10. Greece

Directions: Write your answers on a separate piece of paper.

CHECKING FOR UNDERSTANDING

1 Define each of these terms as they relate to the Roman Republic and the Roman Empire.

A. republic
B. legion
C. patrician
D. plebeian
E. consul
F. veto
G. dictator
H. civic duty
I. latifundia
J. *Pax Romana*

REVIEW THE GUIDING QUESTIONS

2 *Identifying* What are three ways that physical geography affected the rise of Roman civilization?

3 *Explaining* How did Rome's army make Rome a great Mediterranean power?

4 *Naming* What two groups had the right to vote in the Roman Republic? What two groups did not have this right?

5 *Summarizing* Summarize how the Punic Wars helped Rome conquer the Mediterranean region.

6 *Describing* What were some of the reasons that the Roman Republic began to decline?

7 *Paraphrasing* Use your own words to briefly explain how Julius Caesar became Rome's sole ruler.

8 *Explaining* How did Octavian become Rome's first emperor?

9 *Listing* List at least three actions that Augustus took that led to Rome reaching a new age of prosperity.

10 *Discussing* What were some ways that the five "good emperors" helped Rome to become rich and prosperous?

CRITICAL THINKING

11 *Analyzing Visuals* Study the illustration of the Roman legionary in Lesson 1. What conclusions can you draw concerning these soldiers based on the illustration?

12 *Comparing and Contrasting* How was the separation of powers in the Roman Republic similar to that in the United States? How was it different?

13 *Differentiating* How were the lives of patricians and plebeians different during the Roman Republic?

14 *Determining Central Ideas* Why was the idea of civic duty so important in the Roman Republic?

15 *Drawing Conclusions* Why was it important to the growth of the Roman Empire that the navy was able to eliminate piracy on the Mediterranean Sea?

16 *Determining Cause and Effect* What do you think was a major cause for the decline of the Roman Empire after the Pax Romana?

17 *Defending* If you lived in ancient Rome, would you have been for or against Julius Caesar declaring himself dictator for life? Defend your position.

18 *Predicting Consequences* How do you think the Mediterranean region would have been different by 140 B.C. if Carthage had won the Punic wars?

19 *Problem Solving* If you were a Roman Senator in the 100s B.C., how might you solve the problems of small farmers? Be specific in your answer.

20 *Speculating* During the Roman Empire, a standard system of weights and measurements was used. What problems might have occurred if the Empire did not have this standard system for weighing and measuring goods?

Need Extra Help?

If you've missed question	**1**	**2**	**3**	**4**	**5**	**6**	**7**	**8**	**9**	**10**	**11**	**12**	**13**	**14**	**15**	**16**	**17**	**18**	**19**	**20**
Review Lesson	1, 2, 3, 4	1	1	2	2	3	3	3	4	4	1	2	2	2	4	4	3	2	3	4

DBQ SHORT RESPONSE

The historian Plutarch wrote of Julius Caesar's leadership:

"He was so much master of the good-will and hearty service of his soldiers that those who in other expeditions [special trips] were but ordinary men displayed a courage past defeating ... when they went upon any danger where Caesar's glory was concerned. ... there was no danger to which he [a soldier] did not willingly expose himself, no labour from which he pleaded an exemption [asked to be excused]."

—From *Caesar* by Plutarch

21 How did Caesar's soldiers perform under his leadership?

22 What aspect of Caesar's leadership inspired his soldiers' actions?

EXTENDED RESPONSE

23 *Argument* Who do you think was the greatest leader of Rome? Write a persuasive essay in support of your candidate.

STANDARDIZED TEST PRACTICE

DBQ ANALYZING DOCUMENTS

24 *Drawing Conclusions* Augustus wrote a historical document describing his accomplishments. This passage is about his military leadership:

"About 500,000 Roman citizens were under military oath to me. Of these, when their terms of service were ended, I settled in colonies . . . and to all these I allotted lands or granted money as rewards for military service."

—Augustus, *Res Gestae*, from *Aspects of Western Civilization, Vol. I*

Why would Roman citizens have wanted to serve in Augustus's army?
A. for the opportunity to travel and see new places
B. for the chance to show off Rome's military strength
C. for the honor of serving under a great military leader
D. for the benefits of land and money after serving

25 *Summarizing* How did rewarding retired soldiers benefit Augustus?
A. It made the soldiers want to hurry through their time in service.
B. It caused the soldiers to become ambitious and daring.
C. It ensured the soldiers would always remain loyal to Augustus.
D. It improved Augustus's reputation as a kind-hearted leader.

Need Extra Help?

If You've Missed Question	**21**	**22**	**23**	**24**	**25**
Review Lesson	3	3	3, 4	4	4

◄ *This mosaic depicts Emperor Constantine I. Mosaics like this one can be seen covering the inside walls of Hagia Sophia, a mosque in the present-day city of Istanbul.*

50 B.C. TO A.D. 600

Roman Civilization

THE STORY MATTERS ...

When Constantine defeated his brother-in-law in battle, he became emperor of the Western Roman Empire. At that time, Christians were persecuted in Rome, but Constantine thanked "the God of the Christians" for his victory.

This mosaic shows more than just how Constantine looked. The crown on his head represents his power. This reminds us that Constantine granted religious freedom to Christians and made it possible for Christianity to become widespread in the Roman Empire.

Constantine's influence was so great that 10 other Roman emperors were named after him.

LESSON 1
The Roman Way of Life

LESSON 2
Rome's Decline

LESSON 3
The Byzantine Empire

ESSENTIAL QUESTIONS
- What makes a culture unique?
- Why do civilizations rise and fall?
- How does geography influence the way people live?

Place & Time: Roman Civilization
50 B.C. to A.D. 600

The Roman Empire extended throughout the Mediterranean region. As the empire grew, however, Roman emperors found it more difficult to rule. Political corruption, economic challenges, and invasions by Germanic groups brought about the division of the empire.

Step Into the Place

MAP FOCUS Rome's location in the center of the long, narrow Italian Peninsula helped it become a powerful civilization.

1 LOCATION Look at the map. Is Rome located east or west of Greece?

2 MOVEMENT What physical feature made it possible for Rome to extend its influence to Africa?

3 PLACE What major bodies of water form the boundaries of Italy?

4 CRITICAL THINKING
Drawing Conclusions How does location near a waterway contribute to the spread of ideas?

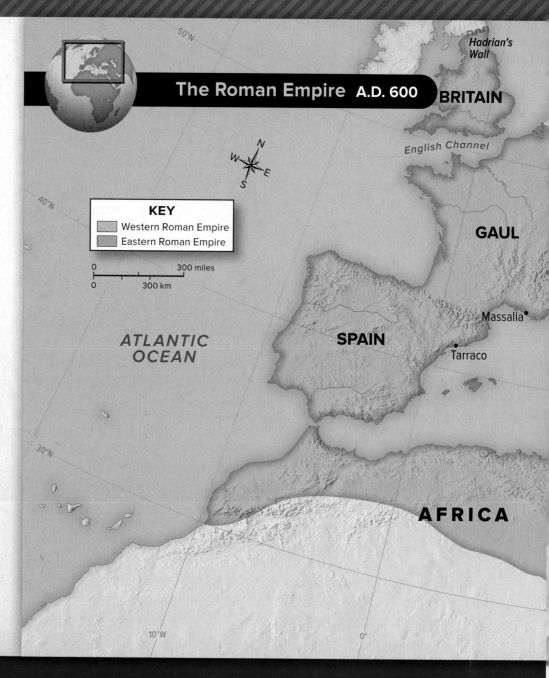

The Roman Empire A.D. 600

KEY
Western Roman Empire
Eastern Roman Empire

0   300 miles
0   300 km

ATLANTIC OCEAN

BRITAIN
Hadrian's Wall
English Channel
GAUL
SPAIN
Massalia
Tarraco
AFRICA

Step Into the Time

TIME LINE Choose an event from the time line and write a paragraph predicting the effect of that event on the future of the Roman Empire.

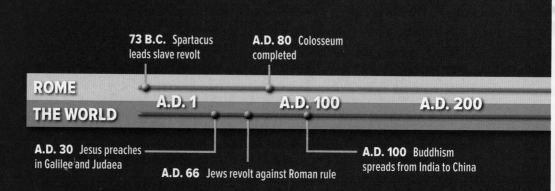

73 B.C. Spartacus leads slave revolt

A.D. 80 Colosseum completed

ROME

THE WORLD

A.D. 1   A.D. 100   A.D. 200

A.D. 30 Jesus preaches in Galilee and Judaea

A.D. 66 Jews revolt against Roman rule

A.D. 100 Buddhism spreads from India to China

North Sea

Baltic Sea

Rhine R.

Danube R.

Corsica

ITALY

Adriatic Sea

Rome

Sardinia

Carthage

Mediterranean Sea

Black Sea

Constantinople (Byzantium)

Aegean Sea

GREECE

Athens

Crete

ASIA MINOR

Caspian Sea

Tigris R.

Euphrates R.

Cyprus

SYRIA

PALESTINE

Jerusalem

Alexandria

EGYPT

Nile R.

Red Sea

ARABIA

10°E   20°E   30°E   40°E

A.D. 395 Roman Empire divided into eastern and western parts

A.D. 476 Last Western Roman emperor overthrown

A.D. 284 Diocletian tries to reform the empire

A.D. 527 Byzantine Justian begins rule

A.D. 537 The *Hagia Sophia* completed

A.D. 300   **A.D. 400**   **A.D. 500**   **A.D. 600**   **A.D. 700**

The Roman Way of Life

• What makes a culture unique?

IT MATTERS BECAUSE
The Romans have influenced our science, art, architecture, and literature.

Daily Life

GUIDING QUESTION *What was daily life like for the Romans?*

Many Romans lived in cities throughout the Roman Empire. Like cities and towns of today, Roman cities were centers for culture, business, and government. We know quite a lot about life in places like Rome and Pompeii from studying the archaeological ruins. Even though the Roman Empire was widespread, the heart of the empire was on the Italian Peninsula in the city of Rome.

The Empire's Chief City

Rome was one of the largest cities in the ancient world. By about A.D. 1, more than a million people lived there. People traveled to Rome from every part of the empire. Like many other Roman cities, Rome was carefully planned. It was laid out in a square with the main streets crossing at right angles.

The emperor lived in Rome in a splendid palace on the top of a hill. At the foot of the hill was the Forum (FOHR·uhm). This was a large open space that served as a marketplace and public square, much like the malls we visit today. In the Forum marketplace, Romans shopped for food and luxury items, played games, and chatted with their friends. Temples and other public buildings surrounded the Forum.

ReadingHELPDESK

Taking Notes: *Identifying*
Use a table like the one here to list the ideas the Romans borrowed from the Greeks to create their own culture.

The Greeks and the Romans

Greeks	Romans

Content Vocabulary
• **gladiator**   • **satire**
• **anatomy**   • **ode**
• **vault**

Like the emperor, wealthy Romans lived in large, comfortable houses on the city's hills. Their homes had marble walls, tiled floors, and running water. Houses were built around a courtyard called an atrium, which was open to the sky. The atrium often had a garden. Wealthy Romans also had homes called villas on large farms outside the city.

Romans who were less wealthy worked as shopkeepers or artisans. Most Romans, however, were poor. Many did not have jobs, while others performed unskilled labor, such as delivering goods. Poor Romans lived in crowded, noisy, dirty neighborhoods in wooden apartment buildings six or seven stories tall. These buildings often collapsed or caught fire. People tossed garbage into the streets, and thieves prowled the areas at night.

To gain the support of Rome's poor, political leaders offered "bread and circuses." On some days, teams of chariot racers competed in the Circus Maximus, an arena seating more than 150,000 people. On other days, crowds watched **gladiators** (GLA·dee·ay·tuhrz) fight each other to the death or battle wild animals in stadiums such as the Colosseum. Most gladiators were enslaved people, criminals, prisoners of war, or poor people. Romans admired the gladiators' skills and bravery.

INFOGRAPHIC

Many wealthy Romans lived in homes built around courtyards.

1 **IDENTIFYING** In which part of the home did Romans entertain guests?

2 **CRITICAL THINKING** *Comparing and Contrasting* How is a Roman home similar to homes in your neighborhood? How is it different?

ROMAN HOME

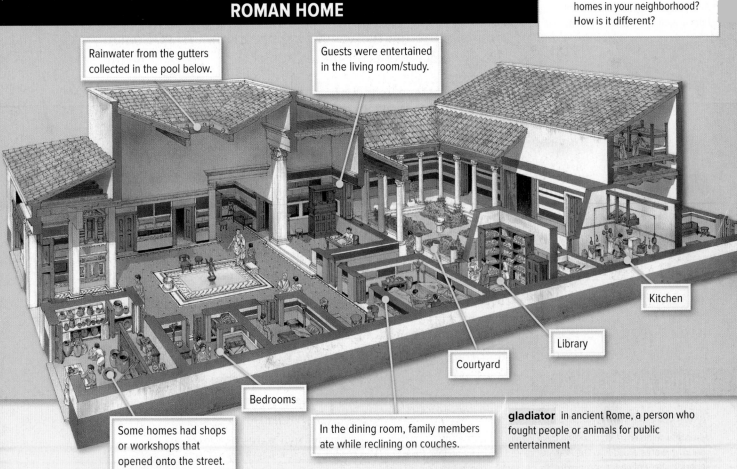

Rainwater from the gutters collected in the pool below.

Guests were entertained in the living room/study.

Kitchen

Library

Courtyard

Bedrooms

Some homes had shops or workshops that opened onto the street.

In the dining room, family members ate while reclining on couches.

gladiator in ancient Rome, a person who fought people or animals for public entertainment

Spartacus—a gladiator—has been portrayed as a hero in literature and in the movies. Use the Internet to find reliable sources about what his life was like and what he tried to accomplish. Identify three facts that you discover from your research and present them to the class. For more about using the Internet for research, read *What Does a Historian Do?*

Upper-class Roman women were often educated and expected to teach their children about Roman culture.

▶ **CRITICAL THINKING**
Analyzing How were the roles of Roman men and women different?

The Roman Family

At the heart of Roman society was the family. When Rome was a republic, large families were common. Married children often lived in the same house with their parents and other relatives. The father closely watched over his wife and her activities. The law even allowed fathers to sell children into slavery or have them put to death. In later times, fathers lost some of this power, and wives gained some legal rights. Families had fewer children, and Romans were more likely to divorce and remarry.

Fathers in upper-class families were responsible for the education of their children. When they were young, wealthy boys and girls learned from private lessons at home. As they grew older, boys from wealthy families went to schools where they studied reading, writing, arithmetic, and rhetoric, or public speaking. Older girls continued to study at home. Poorer Romans could not afford to go to school, but some of them learned enough reading, writing, and arithmetic to help them conduct business.

At about the age of 15, a Roman boy celebrated becoming an adult. He would burn his toys as offerings to the household gods. Then he would put on a white toga, a loose-fitting robe that Roman men wore. Once he became an adult, a man might work at his family's business, join the army, or get a job in the government. Men tended to marry later, but women usually married around the age of 14. Once they married, Roman women were considered adults.

What Was Life Like for Roman Women?

Women in early Rome were not full citizens and had few rights. They had a strong influence on their families, however, and often advised their husbands in private. When Rome was an empire, the wives of emperors began to exercise more power. For example, while the emperor Septimius fought rebels in distant parts of the empire, the empress Julia Domna **administered,** or was in charge of, political affairs in Rome.

The freedoms a Roman woman enjoyed depended on her husband's wealth and position. By the A.D. 100s, wealthy women had more independence.

DEA/G. DAGLI ORTI/De Agostini/Getty Images

Reading**HELP**DESK

Reading Strategy: *Summarizing*

When you summarize, you find the main idea of a passage and restate it in your own words. Read how the Romans treated enslaved people. On a separate sheet of paper, summarize the passage in one or two sentences.

Academic Vocabulary

administer to be lawfully in charge of
protect to defend from trouble or harm

They could own land, run businesses, and sell property. They managed the household while enslaved people did the housework. This left women free to study literature, art, and fashion. Outside the home, they could go to the theater or attend races and fights, but they had to sit in areas separate from men.

Women with less money had less freedom. They spent their time doing housework or helping their husbands in family-run shops. They were allowed to leave home to shop, visit friends, worship at temples, or go to the baths. A few women worked independently outside the home. Some served as priestesses, carrying out religious rituals in temples, while others worked as hairdressers and even doctors.

Rome and Slavery

Slavery was a part of Roman life from early times. The use of slave labor grew, however, as Rome acquired more territory. Roman soldiers took conquered peoples as prisoners. These captives were brought to Rome and sold into slavery. By 100 B.C., about 40 percent of the people in Italy were enslaved.

Enslaved people performed many different jobs. They worked in homes and harvested crops. They mined ore and helped build roads, bridges, and aqueducts throughout the empire. Many enslaved Greeks, though, were well educated. They served as teachers, doctors, and artisans.

For most enslaved people, life was miserable. They were often forced to work long hours and could be sold at any time. They were punished severely for poor work or for running away. To escape their hardships, enslaved people often rebelled.

In 73 B.C., a gladiator named Spartacus (SPAHR·tuh·kuhs) led a slave rebellion. As Spartacus and his forces moved through Italy, their numbers swelled to 70,000. Spartacus planned to reach the Alps. From there, the enslaved people could return to their homelands. The Roman army, however, crushed the revolt. Spartacus was killed in battle and 6,000 of his followers were crucified, or put to death by being nailed to a cross.

Religion and Philosophy

Romans believed that gods controlled all parts of life. Household spirits protected the home and family. Gods **protected** the entire empire. Greek gods and goddesses were given Roman names. For example, Zeus became Jupiter, the sky god, and Aphrodite became Venus, the goddess of love and beauty. Beginning with Augustus, emperors were officially made gods by the Roman Senate.

Romans worshipped their gods and goddesses by praying and offering food to them. Every Roman home included an altar for its household gods. At altars, the head of the family made offerings of incense, wine, honey, and the family meal.

DEA/S.VANNINI/Getty Images

BIOGRAPHY

Livia (58 B.C.–A.D. 29)

Livia Augustus, as she was later called, stood out among Roman women. As the wife of Caesar Augustus for 52 years, she was a symbol of Roman marriage and family. She was also seen as a model of Roman morality. When her grandson, Claudius, became emperor, she took the title of Augustus and held a position of high honor.

▶ **CRITICAL THINKING**
Making Inferences What does the honoring of Livia tell us about the beliefs of the Roman people?

Government officials made offerings in temples where important gods and goddesses of Rome were honored. Temples were open to all people.

The Romans also adapted ideas from Greek **philosophy,** such as the philosophy of Stoicism. For the Greeks, Stoicism was about finding happiness through reason. Romans, however, believed Stoicism was about learning to live in a practical way. Stoic philosophers urged people to participate in public affairs, to do their civic duty, and to treat conquered peoples well.

As the empire grew, Romans came into **contact** with people who practiced different religions. Rome allowed these people to practice their religions if they did not threaten the government.

✔ **PROGRESS CHECK**

Explaining Why was the family important in Roman society?

Science and Art

GUIDING QUESTION *How did the Greeks influence Roman culture?*

As a republic and later as an empire, Rome was influenced by Greek civilization. The Romans admired and studied Greek art, architecture, and philosophy. They copied the Greeks in many ways but changed, or adapted, what they borrowed to match their own needs.

Science

The Romans learned from Greek science. A Greek doctor named Galen introduced many **medical** ideas to Rome. He emphasized the importance of **anatomy** (uh·NA·tuh·mee), the study of body structure. To learn about inner organs, Galen cut open dead animals and recorded his findings. Doctors in the Western world studied Galen's work for more than 1,500 years.

An important scientist of the Roman Empire was Ptolemy (TAH·luh·mee). Ptolemy lived in the city of Alexandria, in Egypt. He studied the sky and carefully mapped over 1,000 different stars. He studied the motion of planets and stars and created rules to explain their movements. Educated people in Europe accepted his ideas for centuries.

The Romans developed practical engineering skills. They built roads that connected Rome to every part of the empire. The first major Roman road, the Appian Way, linked Rome to southeastern Italy. The roads allowed Roman soldiers to travel quickly to different regions. Merchants used the roads, to trade their goods in different regions throughout the empire.

This urn is an example of the glass objects that were made and traded throughout the Roman Empire. Just as people recycle glass today, so did ancient Roman glass workers.

DEA/A.DAGLI ORTI/De Agostini Picture Library/Getty Images

anatomy the study of the body's structure

Academic Vocabulary

philosophy basic beliefs, concepts, and attitudes
contact communication or connection
medical relating to the practice of medicine

Roman engineers supplied cities with fresh water using aqueducts. They built aqueducts to bring water from the hills into the cities. Aqueducts were long troughs supported by rows of high **arches.** Aqueducts carried water over long distances. One Roman-built aqueduct in Segovia, Spain, is still used today—nearly 1,900 years after it was completed.

The Roman system of numbers, also called numerals, helped business people with their accounting. The system used letter-like symbols borrowed from the Greeks and the Etruscans. We still use Roman numerals to show dates on buildings, to create outlines, and to count items in a series, like Super Bowl games.

Art and Architecture

The Romans also adopted many features of Greek art and architecture. Roman artists, however, developed their own styles. The Greeks made statues that showed perfect-looking people with beautiful bodies. Roman statues were more realistic and included wrinkles, warts, and other less attractive features.

Roman builders also introduced their own features to Greek ideas. They used arches in bridges, aqueducts, and buildings. Rows of arches were often built against one another to form a **vault,** or curved ceiling. Using this method, the Romans were able to create domes from many rings of shaped stone.

The Romans were the first people to master the use of concrete, a mixture of volcanic ash, lime, and water. When it dried, this mix was as hard as rock. The Romans used concrete, domes, and arches to build many different structures. One of the most famous Roman structures is the Colosseum, a huge arena completed about A.D. 80. Another example is the Pantheon (PAN·thee·AHN), a temple built to honor Rome's gods. The Pantheon's domed roof was the largest of its time. Today, it is one of the oldest undamaged buildings in the world.

Literature

Like the Greeks, Romans respected writers and philosophers. The Romans were also idealists searching for the meaning of life. Roman writers, however, went beyond the Greek myths and plays to create their own style. They honored their gods but also wrote comedies about them. The Romans praised military successes but also wrote about failures in battle.

THEN

The Greeks and Romans used medical tools they designed themselves. Greek physicians passed medical knowledge to the Romans, who advanced it further. The Romans then passed along medical techniques that the world still uses today.

Now

▶ **CRITICAL THINKING**
Making Connections What are some of the medical ideas the Romans learned from the Greeks? How are these ideas in use today?

vault a curved ceiling made of arches

Visual Vocabulary

arch a curved part of a structure that serves as a support

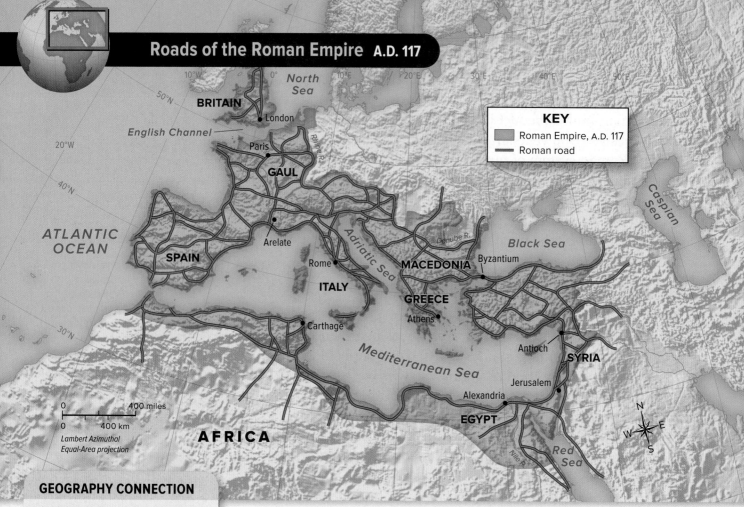

Roads of the Roman Empire A.D. 117

KEY
Roman Empire, A.D. 117
Roman road

GEOGRAPHY CONNECTION

Before the Romans built a system of roads, much long-distance travel and trade was done by water. Roads reached areas that ships could not, so trade and travel improved.

1 **LOCATION** In relation to the rest of the empire, where is Rome located?

2 **CRITICAL THINKING**
Drawing Conclusions Why were so many Roman roads built along waterways?

The Greeks presented inspirational plays ending with a moral. The Romans did the same but also added a touch of reality. Sometimes situations did not work out well for their characters. The Romans added a twist to their writing, revealing a more human side to people. They were not afraid to poke fun at the gods, political leaders, and heroes.

The Roman poet Virgil (VUHR·juhl) drew ideas from the *Odyssey,* an epic poem by a Greek writer named Homer. Virgil's epic poem, the *Aeneid* (uh·NEE·uhd), tells the story of the founding of Rome. In the *Aeneid,* Virgil expresses the values that he believed should guide Rome:

PRIMARY SOURCE

" But you, remember, are to be a Roman. ... Your task is to impose peace by law and order: to protect the downtrodden, and to crush the arrogant [very proud] in war. "

—from the *Aeneid,* Book VI. 1151–1154, by Virgil

Reading**HELP**DESK

satire verse or prose that pokes fun at human weaknesses

ode a lyric poem that expresses strong emotions about life

Using Greek models, the Roman poet Horace (HAWR·uhs) wrote **satires** (SA·tyrs). These works poked fun at human weaknesses, much like comedians do today. Horace also wrote **odes,** or poems that express strong emotions about life.

Inspired by the Greek historian Herodotus (hih·RAH·duh·tuhs), Livy and Tacitus (TA·suh·tuhs) wrote about Roman history. In his *History of Rome*, Livy describes Rome's rise to power. He said that history had moral lessons to teach people.

While Livy celebrated Rome's greatness, Tacitus took a more critical view. He believed that Rome's emperors had taken away people's freedom. Tacitus also thought Romans were losing the values that made them strong. He accused them of wasting time on sports and other pleasures.

Theater and Language

One of the most popular pastimes in Rome was attending plays. Roman plays were staged as part of religious celebrations or national festivals. The actors wore masks to represent the characters. Masks allowed actors to play different roles. For most of Rome's history, men and boys played all the roles in a play. Women were allowed to act only in comedy plays called mimes.

Latin, the language of the Romans, had an even bigger impact than Roman writings. Latin became Europe's language for government, trade, and learning until about A.D. 1500. Latin is the basis of many modern European languages, such as Italian, French, and Spanish. It shaped several others as well. Some of the English words we use today come from Latin.

Romans attending the theater sat in stadiums much like those in sports arenas today.

©Richard Hamilton Smmith/Corbis

✔ **PROGRESS CHECK**

Explaining Describe Roman improvements to Greek architecture.

LESSON 1 REVIEW

Review Vocabulary

1. What is the difference between a *satire* and an *ode*?

2. Why would a doctor today need to study *anatomy*?

Answer the Guiding Questions

3. *Identifying* What were the different roles a father played in the Roman family?

4. *Describing* What was daily life like for Roman women? Describe two differences that existed between women who were wealthy and those who were poor.

5. *Contrasting* How did the Romans differ from the Greeks in their art that shows the human body?

6. *Differentiating* How did the Greeks influence Roman writers?

7. **INFORMATIVE/EXPLANATORY** Why do civilizations borrow elements from earlier civilizations? Think of two elements of American culture that have been borrowed from ancient Roman cultures. Explain what they are in a short essay.

Aeneid

by Virgil (70 B.C. –19 B.C.)

Virgil (70 B.C.–19 B.C.), the author of the epic *Aeneid*

Virgil is one of ancient Rome's greatest poets. He grew up on a farm and spent much of his life away from Rome. Virgil also served as a member in the court of Emperor Augustus.

After Emperor Augustus defeated his rivals and took power, he asked the poet Virgil to write a poem to honor Rome. Virgil wrote the *Aeneid*. It is an epic that retells the Greek legend of the battle of Troy from a Roman point of view.

In writing the *Aeneid*, Virgil did what many Roman artists did—he modeled his work on the earlier works of the Greeks. In the *Aeneid*, Virgil echoed the words of the Greek poet Homer.

In this excerpt, Aeneas (ih • NEE • uhs) is visiting the Underworld, the mythical world of the Dead, where he finds his father, Anchises (an • KEE • seez). There, Anchises explains some of the mysteries of the Underworld and predicts that future members of Aeneas's family will found Rome.

" But you, *remember, are to be a Roman. . . . Your task is to impose peace by law and order: to protect the downtrodden, and to crush the arrogant in war. "*

—from *Aeneid*, Book VI, by Virgil

Aeneas carries Anchises—his father—from burning Troy.

// Now: I will describe to you the glory that will come upon the future generations of Trojans. I will tell you who our Italian **descendants** (dih • SEHN • duhnts) will be, and what distinction they will bring to our name. Do you see that young man leaning on a simple spear? He . . . will be the first to have in his veins a mixture of Trojan and Italian blood. He will be your son, Silvius. His mother will be called Lavinia. … She will bring him up in the woods to be a king and the father of kings. … And there are his glorious successors, next to him. Look especially at Silvius Aeneas, who will share your name: if ever he comes to the throne, he will be remembered equally for his devotion to the gods and for his courage in war. What excellent young men they are—don't you think?

"Next comes Romulus: he will be the son of Mars and Rhea Silvia, herself descended from my grandfather. Do you see the double **plume** (PLOOM) on the crest of his helmet? And how he is marked out by his father to be a god himself? He will be the founder of Rome—a wall will enclose her seven hills, but her empire will reach to the farthest edges of the world, her fame to the heights of Olympus. She will be fortunate in the race that she will nurture [care for]. …

"To sum up: there are some places where **smiths** and sculptors will shape bronze more subtly, or carve more lifelike portraits out of marble; in others, **orators** (AWR • uh • tuhrs) will argue more persuasively, and astronomers will observe more accurately the motion of the heavenly bodies and predict the rising stars. But you, remember, are to be a Roman, and the Romans' art is to be art of a different kind: the art of government, of ruling nations. Your task is to impose peace by law and order: to protect the **downtrodden**, and to crush the arrogant in war." //

—from Vergil's* *Aeneid: Hero, War, Humanity*. tr. G.B. Cobbold.

*Vergil is an alternate spelling of Virgil

NIK keevil/Alamy

Vocabulary

descendant
future member of a family

smith
craftsperson who works with metal

orator
public speaker

downtrodden
people who are poor or suffering

Visual Vocabulary

A **plume** is a group of feathers or horse hair often worn on the top of a headpiece.

Analyzing Literature DBQ

1 *Analyzing* What is the purpose of Anchises's speech to Aeneas? What parts of the passage show that purpose?

2 *Interpreting* What does Anchises describe as the "Romans' art"?

LESSON 2

Rome's Decline

ESSENTIAL QUESTION
• Why do civilizations rise and fall?

IT MATTERS BECAUSE

The fall of Rome resulted from political uproar, distant wars, and economic crises.

A Troubled Empire

GUIDING QUESTION *What problems led to Rome's decline?*

Marcus Aurelius was the last of five emperors who reigned during the *Pax Romana*, a time of peace and progress. Nearly a century of confusion and violence followed.

Political Confusion

During this time, Rome's government grew weak, while the army became very powerful. To stay in office, an emperor had to pay increasingly higher wages to the soldiers who supported him. When these payments could not be made, soldiers would turn against the emperor. Then civil wars broke out, as legion fought legion to put a new emperor on the throne. In a span of about 50 years, ending in A.D. 284, Rome had 22 different emperors. Most were murdered by the army or by their bodyguards.

Roman society also suffered during this period. Many Romans no longer honored the traditional values of duty, courage, and honesty. Dishonest government officials took bribes, and few talented citizens wanted to hold government office. Interest and support for education declined, and many wealthy Romans simply stopped paying taxes. Enslaved laborers now made up a large part of the empire's population.

Reading**HELP**DESK

Taking Notes: *Organizing*
Use a graphic organizer like the one shown here to identify reasons the Roman Empire collapsed.

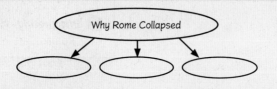
Why Rome Collapsed

Content Vocabulary
• reforms

Economic Weaknesses

Rome's weakened government led to a weakened economy during the A.D. 200s. Roman soldiers and foreign invaders attacked farms and disrupted trade. These attacks led to food shortages, and food prices soared. People had less money to spend, so they bought fewer goods. The price of wheat from Egypt rose from seven or eight drachmae (DRAYK·muh) per unit to 120,000. Merchants saw their profits decline, forcing many out of business. Many workers lost their jobs.

To stop this economic decline, the government produced more coins. The government, however, did not have a large supply of gold and silver. As a result, the new coins had less of these precious metals in them, which reduced their value. In order to get the same profit for their goods, farmers and merchants continued to raise their prices. These actions led to inflation, or a steep rise in prices with a matching decline in the value of money. As the value of Roman coins decreased, people began to barter, or to exchange goods instead of money.

Invasions

While Rome continued to struggle, Germanic tribes raided the western empire, and Persian armies invaded in the east. People living in cities built protective walls around them. With less money to use, the government started to hire Germanic soldiers. Germanic soldiers, however, had no loyalty to the empire.

When Roman coins were made, they were imprinted with the image of the ruling emperor.

These well-preserved walls were built by the Romans in the late A.D. 200s to protect the town of Lugo, Spain.

▶ **CRITICAL THINKING**
Drawing Conclusions Why did Roman towns require protection in the A.D. 200s?

Who Was Diocletian?

A general named Diocletian (DY·uh·KLEE·shuhn) became emperor in A.D. 284. He introduced **reforms,** or political changes to make things better. To defend the empire against invasions, Diocletian built forts along its frontiers. To rule the large empire more efficiently, he divided it into four parts, each with its own ruler. He held ultimate authority over all of them.

Diocletian also tried to strengthen the economy. He set maximum prices for wages and goods in order to prevent prices from rising further. To improve productivity, he ordered workers to remain at the same jobs until they died. Diocletian also made local officials personally responsible for the taxes their communities had to pay. Despite these efforts, Diocletian's reforms did not succeed. People ignored his rules, and Diocletian was not a strong enough emperor to enforce them.

☑ **PROGRESS CHECK**

Explaining How did Diocletian try to improve Rome's economy?

The Fall of Rome

GUIDING QUESTION *What effect did Germanic invaders have on the Roman Empire?*

When Diocletian left office in A.D. 305, conflict again broke out in the empire. Fighting continued until another general named Constantine (KAHN·stuhn·TEEN) became emperor in A.D. 312.

Constantine's Rule

To improve the economy, Constantine issued several orders to **reinforce** the rules of Diocletian. Constantine also wanted a stable workforce and military. For example, the sons of workers had to follow their fathers' trades. The sons of farmers had to work their fathers' lands. The sons of soldiers served in the army.

In spite of Constantine's reforms, the empire continued to decline. In A.D. 330, Constantine moved the capital from a failing Rome to a new city in the east—the Greek city of Byzantium (buh·ZAN·tee·uhm) in present-day Turkey. This city became known as Constantinople (kahn·stan·tuh·NOH·puhl). After Constantine died a few years later, Theodosius (THEE·uh·DOH·shuhs) took power in Constantinople.

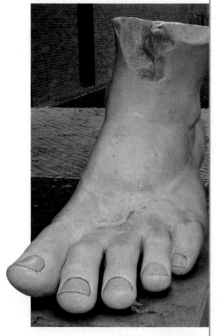

A giant's foot? No, it is actually a replica of a foot from a statue of the Roman Emperor Constantine. This 30-foot (9.1-m) statue once stood in a public building in the Roman Forum.

▶ **CRITICAL THINKING**
Hypothesizing Why do you think Constantine's reforms did not end Rome's decline?

---

reforms changes to bring about improvement

Academic Vocabulary

reinforce to strengthen
expand to spread out

After taking power, Theodosius found the empire difficult to govern. The empire covered a vast area and faced threats from both inside and outside its borders. Theodosius realized the empire had become too large to control from one seat of government. Theodosius decided that—when he died—the eastern and western parts should become separate empires. This division took place in A.D. 395. One empire was the Western Roman Empire, with its capital remaining at Rome. The other was the Eastern Roman Empire, with its capital city at Constantinople.

Following their rebellion and victory at Adrianople, the Visigoths invaded Rome.

Germanic Invaders

During the late A.D. 300s and 400s, many Germanic tribes migrated from northern Europe and fought to **expand** their hold over Roman territory. Some were looking for better land for raising livestock and farming. Many, however, were fleeing the Huns, a fierce group of warriors from Mongolia in Asia.

In the late A.D. 300s, the Huns entered Eastern Europe. Fearing a Hun attack, one Germanic tribe, the Visigoths (VIH·zuh·gahths), asked the Roman government for protection. The Romans let them settle just inside the empire's border. Here they were under the protection of the Roman army. In return, the Visigoths promised to be loyal to the empire. They promised not to attack the empire from the inside.

The Romans, however, treated the Visigoths badly. They charged them high prices for food and enslaved some of their people. Tired of Roman demands, the Visigoths finally rebelled. In A.D. 378, they fought and defeated the Roman legions at Adrianople (AY·dree·uh·NOH·puhl).

The modern city of Istanbul was known as Byzantium during the last days of the Western Roman Empire. When Emperor Constantine moved the capital of the empire there from Rome, Byzantium became Constantinople.

▶ CRITICAL THINKING
Analyzing Why did Constantine move the capital to Byzantium?

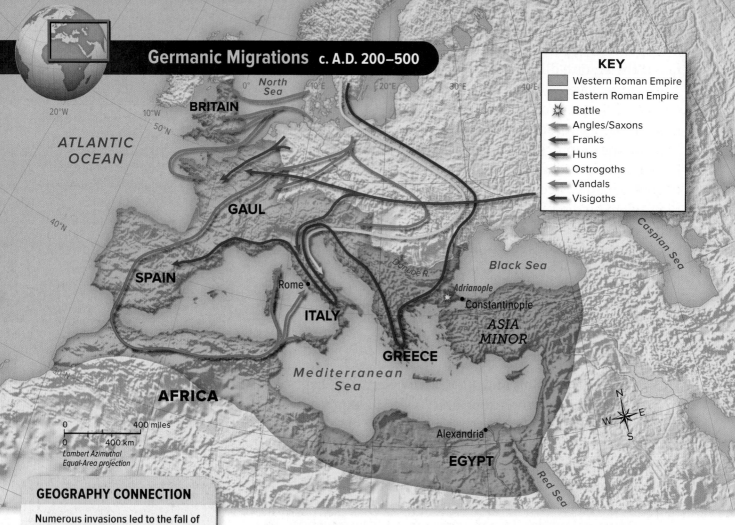

Germanic Migrations c. A.D. 200–500

KEY
- Western Roman Empire
- Eastern Roman Empire
- ✶ Battle
- ⬅ Angles/Saxons
- ⬅ Franks
- ⬅ Huns
- ⬅ Ostrogoths
- ⬅ Vandals
- ⬅ Visigoths

ATLANTIC OCEAN

BRITAIN

North Sea

GAUL

SPAIN

Rome •

ITALY

GREECE

Danube R.

Adrianople

• Constantinople

ASIA MINOR

Black Sea

Caspian Sea

Mediterranean Sea

AFRICA

Alexandria •

EGYPT

Red Sea

0   400 miles
0   400 km
Lambert Azimuthal
Equal-Area projection

GEOGRAPHY CONNECTION

Numerous invasions led to the fall of the Roman Empire.

1 MOVEMENT Who attacked both Britain and northern Gaul?

2 CRITICAL THINKING
Drawing Conclusions Why do you think the Eastern Roman Empire experienced very few invasions?

The Visigoths' victory brought more attacks on Roman territory. Soon, Germanic tribes invaded Gaul, which is today France. Then, in A.D. 410, the Visigoth leader Alaric (A·luh·rihk) led his people into Italy and captured Rome itself. The Visigoths looted the city's government buildings and private homes. Rome's conquest by Alaric made it clear that the empire would not, as many Romans believed, last forever.

The Vandals, another Germanic group, attacked Roman lands in Spain and northern Africa. Then they sailed to Italy, and in A.D. 455, entered Rome. They were able to overcome the Romans living there. The Vandals spent almost two weeks seizing valuables and burning buildings. The English word *vandalism*, meaning "the willful destruction of property," comes from the actions of the Vandals.

The Germanic people had entered every part of Rome's organization. By the mid-A.D. 400s, Germanic soldiers had been working for the Roman government for centuries.

Reading HELP DESK

Reading in the Content Area: *Charts*

Flowcharts can show a chain of events. To read a flowchart, follow the arrows. Ask yourself questions such as, "What are the steps in this event? How does one event lead to another?"

Roman Emperor Forced Out

As a result, several Germanic leaders held high posts in Rome's government and army. In A.D. 476, the Germanic general named Odoacer (OH·duh·WAY·suhr) had enough support from soldiers that he was able to take control. Odoacer overthrew the western emperor, a 14-year-old boy named Romulus Augustulus (RAHM·yuh·luhs aw·GUHS·chah·luhs).

After Odoacer seized control, no Roman emperor ever again ruled from Rome. From then on, foreign powers ruled what had been the Roman Empire. Historians often use this event to mark the end of the Western Roman Empire. It was a major turning point in history.

Odoacer controlled Rome for almost 15 years. The Germanic peoples, however, continued to fight amongst themselves. During Odoacer's rule, a group of Visigoths attacked the city of Rome. After much fighting, they seized the city and killed Odoacer. They set up their new kingdom in Italy under their leader, Theodoric (thee·AH·duh·rihk). Elsewhere in Europe, other Germanic kingdoms arose and came to power.

The Western Roman Empire ceased to exist. Pope Gregory I wrote about the fall of Rome and how it affected people who had lived within its borders.

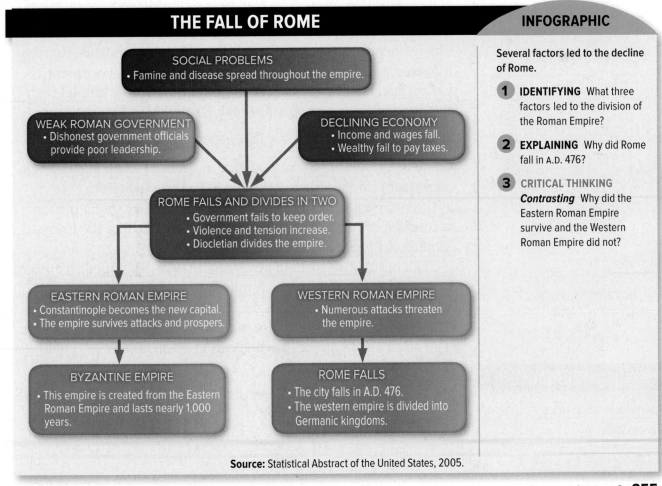

THE FALL OF ROME

INFOGRAPHIC

SOCIAL PROBLEMS
• Famine and disease spread throughout the empire.

WEAK ROMAN GOVERNMENT
• Dishonest government officials provide poor leadership.

DECLINING ECONOMY
• Income and wages fall.
• Wealthy fail to pay taxes.

ROME FAILS AND DIVIDES IN TWO
• Government fails to keep order.
• Violence and tension increase.
• Diocletian divides the empire.

EASTERN ROMAN EMPIRE
• Constantinople becomes the new capital.
• The empire survives attacks and prospers.

WESTERN ROMAN EMPIRE
• Numerous attacks threaten the empire.

BYZANTINE EMPIRE
• This empire is created from the Eastern Roman Empire and lasts nearly 1,000 years.

ROME FALLS
• The city falls in A.D. 476.
• The western empire is divided into Germanic kingdoms.

Several factors led to the decline of Rome.

1 **IDENTIFYING** What three factors led to the division of the Roman Empire?

2 **EXPLAINING** Why did Rome fall in A.D. 476?

3 **CRITICAL THINKING** *Contrasting* Why did the Eastern Roman Empire survive and the Western Roman Empire did not?

Source: Statistical Abstract of the United States, 2005.

"We see on all sides sorrows; We hear on all sides groans. Cities are destroyed, fortifications razed [forts destroyed] to the ground, fields devastated [left in ruin], land reduced to solitude. No husbandman [farmer] is left in the fields, few inhabitants remain in the cities. … What Rome herself, once deemed [regarded as] the Mistress of the World, has now become, we see—wasted away with … the loss of citizens, the assaults of enemies, the frequent fall of ruined buildings. "

—from *Homiliarum in Ezechielem*, by Pope Gregory I

By A.D. 550, a group of Germanic-ruled territories had replaced the Western Roman Empire, yet Roman culture did not completely disappear. Western Europe's new Germanic rulers adopted the Latin language, Roman laws, and Christianity. In the eastern Mediterranean, the Eastern Roman Empire thrived. It became known as the Byzantine Empire and lasted nearly 1,000 more years.

✔ PROGRESS CHECK

Identifying Why do historians consider A.D. 476 an important date?

Rome's Legacies

GUIDING QUESTION *What are the key achievements and contributions of Roman civilization?*

The influence of the ancient Romans still surrounds us. Roman achievements live on in our system of laws and government today. The peace and order created by Roman rule helped with the rapid growth and spread of the Christian religion.

Rome's Influence on Law and Government

Many beliefs about law and justice in the American legal system come from Roman ideas. Like the Romans, we believe that everyone is equal under the law. We also believe that a person is considered innocent until proven guilty. We, like the Romans, require our judges to decide cases fairly.

The republican form of government was developed in ancient Rome. Certain citizens in a republic elected their leaders. The United States and a number of other countries today are democratic republics. We also believe that a republic works best if all adult citizens vote, **participate** in government, and help to improve their communities.

ReadingHELPDESK

Academic Vocabulary

participate to take part

Rome's Cultural Impact

Many Western countries use the Latin alphabet, which has expanded from 22 to 26 letters. The Italian, French, Spanish, Portuguese, and Romanian languages are derived from Latin—the language of the Romans. Many English words have Latin roots. Latin phrases are part of the vocabulary of scientists, doctors, and lawyers. The Romans continue to influence the literature we read and enjoy. The great Roman writers such as Virgil, Horace, Livy, and Tacitus are still admired and studied. Architecture and construction also owe much to the ancient Romans. Government buildings in Washington, D.C., and the capital cities of many states often use domes and arches inspired by Roman architecture. Concrete, a Roman development, remains a major building material today.

Ancient Rome and Christianity

Christianity is a major world religion. It began in the eastern part of the Roman Empire and was adopted by Rome's emperors in the A.D. 300s. Those emperors helped the new religion grow and spread.

The Roman road system allowed the early Christians to travel throughout the empire safely and quickly. As a result, Christian ideas were easily shared with other groups of people. After the fall of the Western Roman Empire, Christianity continued to attract new believers.

The Roman arch can support large domes. The design of our U.S. Capitol building was influenced by the Romans. The image behind the building shows what the U.S. Capitol dome looks like from the interior.

☑ **PROGRESS CHECK**

Comparing What Roman contributions still influence our lives today?

LESSON 2 REVIEW

Review Vocabulary

1. Why were Diocletian's *reforms* unsuccessful?

Answer the Guiding Questions

2. *Describing* Discuss two problems that led to Rome's decline.

3. *Explaining* How did the division of the Roman Empire make it easy for people to invade it?

4. *Summarizing* Describe how Rome contributed to the development of world languages.

5. **ARGUMENT** What do you think was the greatest accomplishment of Roman civilization? Write a one-page essay that describes the accomplishment and why you feel it was the civilization's greatest.

What Do You Think?

Did People Benefit from Roman Rule?

Throughout their vast empire, the Romans built roads, bridges, and irrigation systems. These improvements allowed trade and agriculture to flourish. To accomplish these changes, however, the Romans had to sail to other lands to obtain materials. With the traders came Roman soldiers.

Some people, however, did not want to be ruled by the Romans. Many died fighting against the Roman invaders.

Mosaic of Romans unloading a boat

Yes

❝ From neighboring continents far and wide a ceaseless [endless] flow of goods pours into Rome. From every land and every sea come each season's crops, the produce of countryside, rivers, and lakes, and articles skillfully made by Greeks and foreigners.

… So many merchants arrive from all points of the compass with their cargoes throughout the year, and with each return of harvest, that the city is like the common warehouse of the world … clothing from Babylonia, luxuries from barbarian lands beyond. … Egypt, Sicily and Africa are your farms. … Everything converges [comes together] here—trade, shipping, agriculture, metallurgy [making products from metals], all the skills that exist and have existed, everything that is bred or grown. Anything that cannot be seen in Rome does not exist. ❞

—**Aelius Aristides,**
To Rome

TEXT: From Roman Civilization: Selected Readings, Volume 1, by Naphtali Lewis and Meyer Reinhold. Copyright © 1990 Columbia University Press. Reprinted with permission of the publisher.
PHOTO: t)DEA PICTURE LIBRARY/Getty Images; (b)Michele Falzone/Photographers Choice/Getty Images

The Destruction of the Temple in Jerusalem by the Emperor Titus, a painting by Nicolas Poussin

No

PRIMARY SOURCE

❝ As the legions [soldiers] charged in, neither persuasion nor threat could check [stop] their impetuosity [impulsive behavior]: passion [frenzy] alone was in command. ... Most of the victims were peaceful citizens, weak and unarmed, butchered [killed] wherever they were caught. While the Sanctuary [Temple] was burning, looting went on right and left and all who were caught were put to the sword. There was no pity for age, no regard for rank; little children and old men, laymen and priests alike were butchered; every class was held in the iron embrace of war, whether they defended themselves or cried for mercy ... They also burnt the treasuries which housed huge sums of money, huge quantities of clothing, and other precious things. ❞

—(Flavius) Josephus describing the destruction of the Jewish temple by the Romans in A.D. 70, *The Jewish War*

What Do You Think? DBQ

❶ *Identifying* Which person has a favorable view of Rome?

❷ *Describing* Does (Flavius) Josephus believe the Romans were merciful when they conquered people? How does he try to persuade the reader to support his belief?

❸ *Making Inferences* What do you think Aristides meant when he said, "Anything that cannot be seen in Rome does not exist"?

LESSON 3

The Byzantine Empire

ESSENTIAL QUESTION

• How does geography influence the way people live?

IT MATTERS BECAUSE

At the height of its power, the Byzantine Empire united people on three continents. Its system of laws and its strong leadership helped the empire flourish.

The New Rome

GUIDING QUESTION *How did the Byzantine Empire become rich and powerful?*

After the Roman Empire was divided in A.D. 395, the eastern half eventually became known as the Byzantine Empire. At the height of its power in the A.D. 500s, the Byzantine territory extended west to Italy, south to Egypt, and east to the Arabian border. A variety of peoples lived within the empire's borders. Greeks made up the largest population. Egyptians, Syrians, Arabs, Armenians, Jews, Persians, Slavs, and Turks also lived in the empire. Under Emperor Justinian, the laws improved, the arts flourished, and the empire grew dramatically.

Constantinople

Constantine moved the capital of the Roman Empire from Rome to the Greek city of Byzantium and renamed the city Constantinople. The new capital thrived. By the A.D. 500s, multicultural Constantinople had become one of the world's most advanced cities.

Constantinople's location was a major factor in the city's success. Located on a peninsula between the Black Sea and the Aegean Sea, the city's excellent harbors attracted fishing

Reading**HELP**DESK

Taking Notes: *Listing*

Use a graphic organizer like this one to list reasons why the Byzantine Empire thrived.

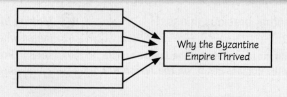

Why the Byzantine Empire Thrived

Content Vocabulary

• mosaics • saints

boats, trading ships, and warships. Because of its location at the crossroads of trade routes between Europe and Asia, Constantinople became the wealthiest part of the Roman Empire.

Constantinople was also easy to defend. Lying on a peninsula, the city was protected on three sides by the sea, and a large wall protected it on the fourth side. Later, a huge chain was strung across the city's harbor for greater protection. Surprise attacks were not easily carried out on Constantinople.

What Cultural Influences Shaped the Byzantines?

Constantinople at first resembled other cities in the Roman Empire. The "New Rome," as it was called, had government buildings and palaces built in the Roman style. The city also had an oval arena called the Hippodrome (HIHP·uh·drohm) where chariot races and other events were held.

Rome influenced the political and social life of the Byzantine Empire. Emperors spoke Latin and enforced Roman laws. Many wealthy Roman families traveled east to the Byzantine Empire and lived in towns or on large farming estates. Similarly to how things were done in Rome, the government gave the empire's poor people free bread and entertainment shows.

Over time, the Roman influence on the Byzantine Empire faded, while Greek influence in the area increased. Most Byzantines spoke Greek, and Byzantine emperors and officials also began to speak Greek instead of Latin. The ideas of non-Greek peoples, like the Egyptians and the Slavs, also shaped Byzantine life. Still other customs came from Persia to the east. All of these cultures blended together to form the Byzantine civilization.

Between A.D. 500 and A.D. 1200, the Byzantines developed one of the world's most advanced civilizations. They preserved and passed on Greek culture and Roman law to other peoples. As you will learn, they also brought Christianity to people in Eastern Europe.

✔ **PROGRESS CHECK**

Explaining Why was Constantinople important to the Byzantine Empire?

Sculptures of horses, such as the one above, greeted people who enjoyed chariot races at the Hippodrome.

▶ CRITICAL THINKING
Making Connections Why did Greek culture gradually influence the Byzantine Empire more than Roman culture?

Build Vocabulary: *Word Origins*

The word *hippodrome* comes from the Greek words *hippos*, meaning "horse," and *dromos*, meaning "race" or "course."

Justinian I (A.D. 483–565)

Justinian's uncle, Justin, provided Justinian with an excellent education at a school in Byzantium. When Justin became emperor, he adopted Justinian and made him his chief advisor and, later, co-ruler. In A.D. 527, Justin died, and Justinian became emperor.

Empress Theodora (A.D. 500–548)

Theodora was a member of a lower social class. Justinian could not marry her: it was illegal for people of lower classes to marry nobles. Justinian's uncle Justin, who was the emperor, changed the law so that the couple could marry.

▶ CRITICAL THINKING
Making Inferences Why do you think there were laws preventing people from the lower classes from marrying nobles?

Reading HELP DESK

Academic Vocabulary

legal of or relating to the law
restore to bring back to an original state

Justinian's Rule

GUIDING QUESTION *How did Emperor Justinian and Empress Theodora strengthen the Byzantine Empire?*

Justinian (juh·STIH·nee·uhn) ruled the Byzantine Empire at the height of its power. A skilled general and a strong leader, Justinian ruled from A.D. 527 until A.D. 565. He governed with supreme power and controlled the military and all of the **legal** decisions made within the empire. Many historians view Justinian as the greatest Byzantine emperor.

Who Was Theodora?

Justinian's wife, the empress Theodora (THEE·uh·DOHR·uh), was a beautiful, intelligent, and ambitious woman. She participated actively in government and helped Justinian choose government officials. Theodora helped Byzantine women win more legal rights. At her urging, Justinian changed Byzantine law so that a wife could own land. If a woman became a widow, her land would provide the income she needed to take care of her children.

Theodora showed her political wisdom during a crisis in A.D. 532. When angry taxpayers in Constantinople threatened the government, Justinian's advisers urged Justinian to flee the city. Theodora, however, told her husband to stay and fight. According to one Byzantine historian, Theodora told Justinian that she would rather die as an empress than escape and live as an outlaw:

PRIMARY SOURCE

❞ May I never be separated from this purple [royal color], and may I not live that day on which those who meet me shall not address me as mistress. If, now, it is your wish to save yourself, O Emperor, there is no difficulty. For we have much money, and there is the sea, here the boats. However consider whether it will not come about after you have been saved that you would gladly exchange that safety for death. For as for myself, I approve a certain ancient saying that royalty is a good burial-shroud. ❞

—from "The Nika Riot," by Procopius

Taking Theodora's advice, Justinian stayed in the city and fought back. His army crushed the rebels. By doing this, Justinian was able to **restore** order and strengthen his power as emperor.

Reading Strategy: *Listing*

Listing information you have read about helps you remember it. Create a bulleted list that shows the ways Theodora influenced or helped the Byzantine Empire.

Justinian's Legal Reforms

One of Justinian's lasting contributions to future civilizations was in the area of law. Shortly after he became emperor, Justinian realized that the empire's laws were disorganized and confusing. He ordered a group of legal scholars headed by Tribonian (truh·BOH·nee·uhn) to create a simpler and better code of laws.

The group's new legal code became known as the Justinian Code. The code helped officials and businesspeople better understand the empire's laws. Throughout the centuries, the Justinian Code has been the basis for the legal systems of almost every country in the Western world.

Byzantine Arts

Justinian, along with other Byzantine emperors, was interested in arts and architecture. The emperors ordered the construction of churches, forts, and government buildings throughout the Byzantine Empire. Among the hundreds of beautiful churches and palaces in Constantinople was the church called Hagia Sophia (HAH·jee·uh soh·FEE·uh), or "Holy Wisdom."

The dome of the Hagia Sophia towers more than 180 feet above the ground. For more than 1,000 years, the Hagia Sophia was the largest cathedral in the world. When the Ottoman Turks conquered Constantinople in A.D. 1453, the cathedral was converted to a mosque. Today, Hagia Sophia is a museum.

R. Matina/Age fotostock

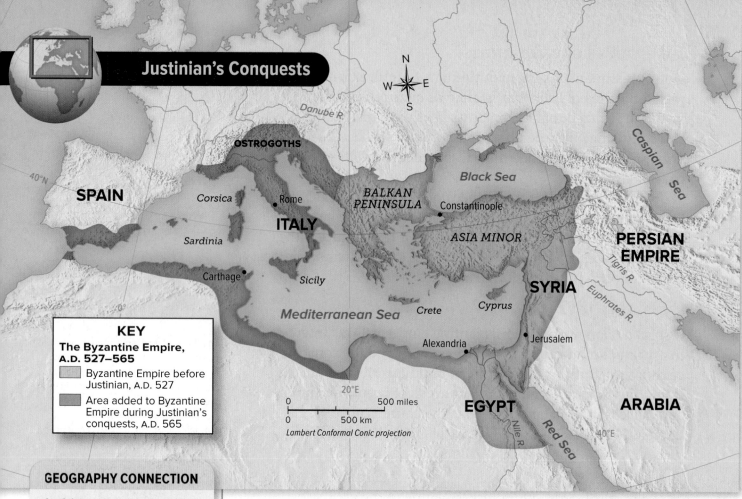

Justinian's Conquests

KEY

The Byzantine Empire, A.D. 527–565

Byzantine Empire before Justinian, A.D. 527

Area added to Byzantine Empire during Justinian's conquests, A.D. 565

0   500 miles
0   500 km
Lambert Conformal Conic projection

GEOGRAPHY CONNECTION

Justinian extended the Byzantine Empire's borders but was unable to maintain them.

1 **PLACE** How far west did the empire extend after Justinian's conquests?

2 **CRITICAL THINKING**
Inferring Why might a cavalry be useful for defending this large empire?

Under Justinian's orders, nearly 10,000 workers labored in shifts to build the church. Upon its completion in A.D. 537, the domed church became the religious center of the Byzantine Empire. The interior of Hagia Sophia contains walls of polished marble and beautiful gold and silver ornaments. This unique building still stands in Istanbul today.

Numerous mosaics also decorated the interior walls of Hagia Sophia. **Mosaics** (moh·ZAY·ihks) are patterns or pictures made from small pieces of colored glass or stone. Popular in the Byzantine Empire, most mosaics showed figures of **saints**, or Christian holy people. Other mosaics, such as the one at the beginning of the chapter, honored Byzantine emperors.

In addition to the arts and architecture, Emperor Justinian was concerned about education. Learning was highly respected in the Byzantine culture. In Byzantine schools, boys studied religion, medicine, law, arithmetic, grammar, and other subjects. Some were schooled by private tutors. Girls did not generally attend schools and received any teaching at home.

Reading**HELP**DESK

mosaics motifs or images created by an arrangement of colored glass or stone

saints people considered holy by followers of the Christian faith

Military Conquests

Justinian wanted to restore the Roman Empire and bring back the glory of Rome. Led by a general named Belisarius (BEH·luh·SAR·ee·uhs), the Byzantine army was strengthened and reorganized. Instead of relying on foot soldiers, the new army used cavalry—soldiers mounted on horses. Byzantine cavalry wore armor and carried bows and lances, which were long spears.

Between A.D. 533 and A.D. 555, the Byzantine military conquered territories that were once part of the great Roman Empire. These territories included Italy and parts of Spain and northern Africa. They also defeated the Persians, which increased the security of the eastern borders of the empire. However, the conquests of Justinian's army were short-lived. During the mid-500s, a deadly disease known to historians as "Justinian's Plague" swept through Asia and Europe. The plague killed millions of people, including many men in Justinian's army. The loss of so many soldiers severely weakened the Byzantine Empire's ability to fight wars.

In addition, the Byzantines did not have the money to support an army large enough to defend against the Persians in the east and protect the lands in the west. Most of the western territories that Justinian conquered were lost after his death.

☑ **PROGRESS CHECK**

Understanding Cause and Effect What effect did Theodora have on Justinian's rule?

In addition to body armor such as this, Byzantine cavalry soldiers also wore plumed helmets. Cavalry made the Byzantine army a formidable fighting force.

EXPLAINING How did Belisarius strengthen the army of the Byzantine Empire?

LESSON 3 REVIEW

Review Vocabulary

1. How were *saints* shown in *mosaics*?

Answer the Guiding Questions

2. ***Explaining*** How did Constantinople's location help it become a wealthy city?

3. ***Describing*** How did the advancements made by Greek and Roman civilizations influence the Byzantine Empire?

4. ***Identifying Cause and Effect*** What effect did the Justinian Code have on the Byzantine Empire?

5. ***Drawing Conclusions*** Why did the Byzantine military grow weaker?

6. **ARGUMENT** Write a speech that Theodora might have given to Justinian to convince him to stay in Constantinople during the rebellion in A.D. 532.

There's More Online! connected.mcgraw-hill.com

Write your answers on a separate piece of paper.

1 Exploring the Essential Question

INFORMATIVE/EXPLANATORY How would you describe the Romans compared to people who lived before them? Write a summary of what made the Romans a unique people. Think of the many ways they were different from the Greeks and other people who lived before them. Include what you think their strongest characteristic was and why.

2 21st Century Skills

DETERMINING CAUSE AND EFFECT Create a poster or other visual aid about the division of the Roman Empire in A.D. 395. Identify two causes and two effects of the split.

3 Thinking Like a Historian

DISTINGUISHING FACT FROM OPINION Review the primary source in Lesson 2, *Homiliarum in Ezechielem*, by Pope Gregory I. Decide which statements in the source are facts and which statements are opinions. List the statements of fact and the statements of opinion from the source in a chart like this one.

FACT	OPINION

4 GEOGRAPHY ACTIVITY

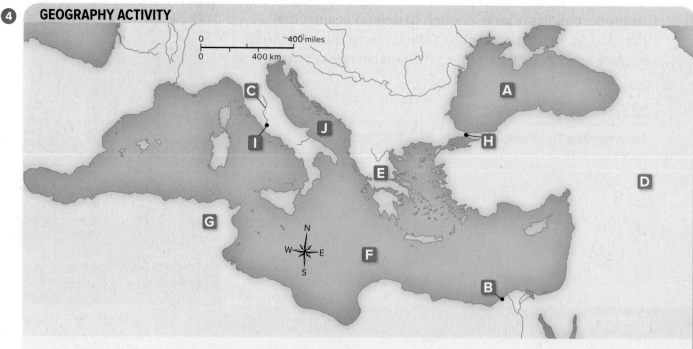

Locating Places

Match the letters on the map with the numbered places listed below.

1. Alexandria
2. North Africa
3. Mediterranean Sea
4. Constantinople
5. Black Sea
6. Greece
7. Adriatic Sea
8. Rome
9. Tiber River
10. Persia

Directions: Write your answers on a separate piece of paper.

CHECKING FOR UNDERSTANDING

1 Define each of these terms.

A. gladiator   E. ode

B. anatomy   F. reforms

C. vault   G. mosaics

D. satire   H. saints

REVIEW THE GUIDING QUESTIONS

2 *Contrasting* How were living conditions different for rich and poor Romans?

3 *Explaining* In what ways did the Romans adapt forms of Greek literature?

4 *Listing* What problems challenged Rome in the A.D. 200s?

5 *Stating* Why did Diocletian strengthen the Roman army?

6 *Identifying* To what city did Constantine move the capital of the Roman Empire? Why?

7 *Naming* Which groups invaded the Western Roman Empire?

8 *Explaining* How does the Latin language impact life in the United States?

9 *Summarizing* What did Justinian hope to accomplish by creating a new code of laws?

10 *Identifying* Which cultures most influenced life in the Byzantine Empire? Which ultimately became most important?

CRITICAL THINKING

11 *Analyzing* In what respects was ancient Roman society patriarchal?

12 *Drawing Conclusions* How did spectacles such as chariot races and gladiator fights support the political purposes of Rome's rulers?

13 *Contrasting* How did the Roman approach to art and knowledge differ from the Greek approach? Give examples.

14 *Determining Cause and Effect* What caused inflation in Rome in the A.D. 200s? What were some consequences of this inflation?

15 *Making Connections* What is a vandal? Why does the word *vandal* have this meaning?

16 *Predicting Consequences* How might Rome's history have been different had the Romans treated the Visigoths fairly?

17 *Defending* Defend or refute the following statement: Foreign invasion was the main reason for the fall of the Roman Empire.

18 *Identifying Evidence* What principles from ancient Rome are reflected in the modern American legal and political systems?

19 *Speculating* Justinian's achievements did not last long after his death. What might he have done differently to ensure that his accomplishments lasted longer than they did?

20 *Drawing Conclusions* What does Byzantine art tell us about the role of religion in the Byzantine Empire?

Need Extra Help?

If you've missed question	1	2	3	4	5	6	7	8	9	10	11	12	13	14	15	16	17	18	19	20
Review Lesson	1, 2, 3	1	1	2	2	2	2	2	3	3	1	1	1	2	2	2	2	2	3	3

DBQ SHORT RESPONSE

"[The] Romans were proud of making their roads go straight even when this meant constructing long bridges over deep valleys or tunneling through solid rock mountains. ... As the Roman Empire expanded ... [t]hey helped the Romans ... by enabling troops to be rushed to trouble spots ... facilitated [made easier] long-distance trade and ... sped up communication among the different regions."

—from *Daily Life in the Roman City* by Gregory Aldrete

21 What advantages did the system of roads provide to Romans?

22 What obstacles to building the network of roads did the Romans face?

EXTENDED RESPONSE

23 *Narrative* You are a citizen of Athens, Greece, who recently moved to Rome. Write a letter to a friend in Athens about your new home. Explain the differences and similarities between the two cities and cultures.

STANDARDIZED TEST PRACTICE

DBQ ANALYZING DOCUMENTS

Christian leader Jerome wrote this in a letter about attacks on Rome:

"Who would believe that Rome, victor over all the world would fall, that she would be to her people both the tomb [grave] and the womb [birthplace]."

—from The Epistles of St. Jerome, trans. Roland Bainton

24 *Drawing Conclusions* Which statement best summarizes what Jerome thinks about Rome before its fall?
- **A.** Jerome sees Rome as strong.
- **B.** Jerome sees a bright future for Rome.
- **C.** Jerome sees Rome as weak.
- **D.** Jerome sees that Rome is in danger.

25 *Comparing* Why does Jerome compare Rome to a womb [birthplace] and a tomb [grave] for its people?
- **A.** He has seen Rome on the decline from its beginning.
- **B.** There have been many births and deaths in Rome.
- **C.** The birth of Rome has meant the death of her people.
- **D.** The words *womb* and *tomb* represent a beginning and an end.

Need Extra Help?

If You've Missed Question	**21**	**22**	**23**	**24**	**25**
Review Lesson	1	1	1	2	2

TEXT: "News of the Attacks" is from Jerome, Epistles, 123, 15 in The Medieval Church, ed. Roland H. Bainton (Princeton: D. Van Nostrand, 1962), pp. 89-90. Copyright © 1962 by Roland H. Bainton.

This image of Peter was painted by the Greek artist El Greco around 1600. St. Peter's Basilica, or church, in the city of Rome, Italy, is named in his honor.

A.D. 30 TO A.D. 600

The Rise of Christianity

Scala/Art Resource, NY

THE STORY MATTERS ...

One of the chosen apostles of Jesus, Simon Peter of Galilee, was called "the rock "of the Christian church. He brought many followers to the Christian faith.

Soon after the death of Jesus, Peter, as he was called, became a leader of the early Christian church. He played an important role in spreading the teachings of Jesus and in contributing to the rise of Christianity. This painting imagines Peter as an older man.

ESSENTIAL QUESTIONS
- What are the characteristics of a leader?
- How do religions develop?
- How do new ideas change the way people live?

Place & Time: The Rise of Christianity
A.D. 30 to A.D. 600

As Jesus gained followers, he alarmed Rome's rulers. They feared his growing influence and eventually executed him. Jesus' followers carried his message to many lands, and what began as a Jewish group developed into a separate religion.

Step Into the Place

MAP FOCUS Christianity began in Judaea, an area that was part of the Roman Empire. From Judaea, Christianity spread through the Mediterranean region and beyond.

1 LOCATION Look at the map. Is Rome located northwest or southeast of Jerusalem?

2 MOVEMENT To which other parts of Europe would you expect Christianity to spread most quickly?

3 CRITICAL THINKING
Analyzing How did the Mediterranean Sea make it easier for Christianity to spread?

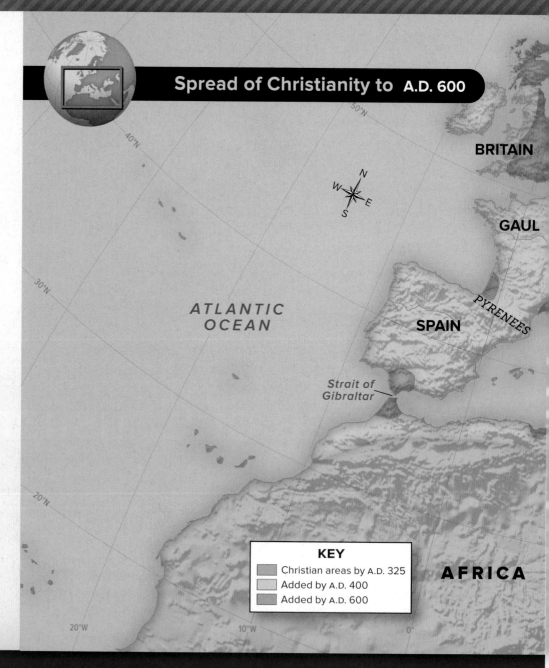

Spread of Christianity to A.D. 600

BRITAIN

GAUL

PYRENEES

SPAIN

ATLANTIC OCEAN

Strait of Gibraltar

AFRICA

KEY
- Christian areas by A.D. 325
- Added by A.D. 400
- Added by A.D. 600

Step Into the Time

TIME LINE Choose an event from the time line and write two or three sentences explaining how the ancient Romans dealt with Christianity during that time.

c. A.D. 30 Jesus begins his preaching

c. A.D. 6 Augustus makes Judaea a Roman province

c. A.D. 33 Romans execute Jesus

c. A.D. 64 Romans outlaw Christianity

c. A.D. 135 Romans force Jews out of Jerusalem

EARLY CHRISTIANITY
THE WORLD

A.D. 1   A.D. 50   A.D. 200

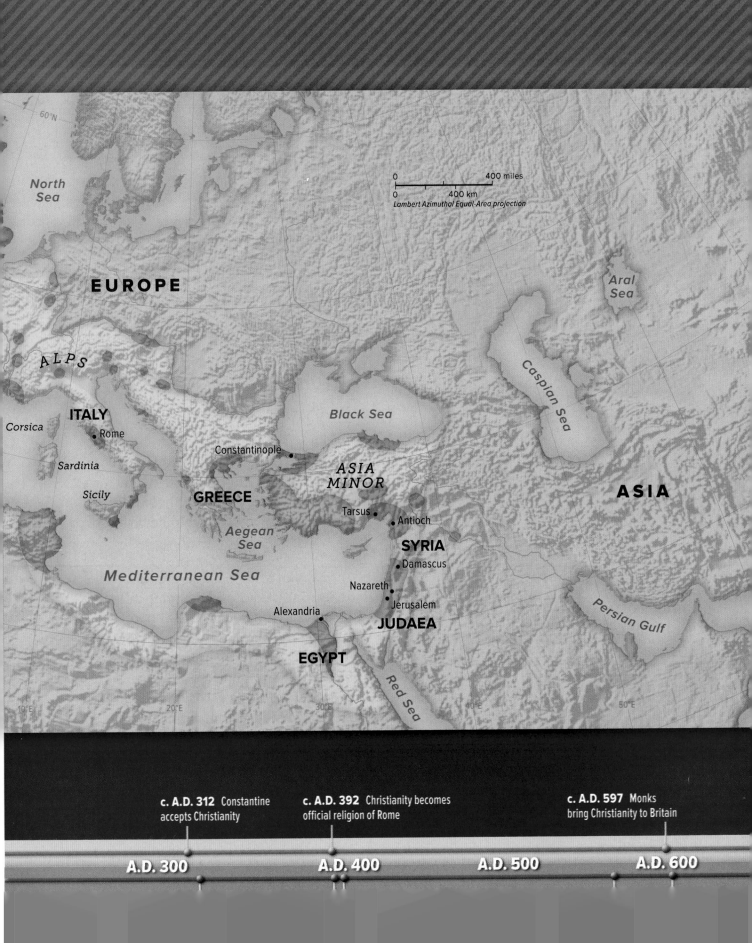

North
Sea

60°N

EUROPE

ALPS

ITALY

Corsica

Rome

Sardinia

Sicily

GREECE

Mediterranean Sea

Aegean
Sea

Black Sea

Constantinople

ASIA
MINOR

Tarsus

Antioch

SYRIA

Damascus

Nazareth

Jerusalem

JUDAEA

Alexandria

EGYPT

Red Sea

Caspian Sea

Aral
Sea

ASIA

Persian Gulf

0   400 miles
0   400 km
Lambert Azimuthal Equal-Area projection

10°E   20°E   30°E   40°E   50°E

c. A.D. 312 Constantine
accepts Christianity

c. A.D. 392 Christianity becomes
official religion of Rome

c. A.D. 597 Monks
bring Christianity to Britain

A.D. 300   A.D. 400   A.D. 500   A.D. 600

LESSON 1
Early Christianity

• What are the characteristics of a leader?

IT MATTERS BECAUSE
Christianity is one of the world's major religions and continues to influence people around the globe.

Judaism and Rome

GUIDING QUESTION *How did the Jews respond to Roman rule?*

The Romans allowed Judaism (JOO·dee·IH·zuhm) to be practiced throughout the empire. In Judaea and Galilee, however, Romans ruled the Jews with an iron hand. Many Jews hoped that God would send a deliverer to rescue them from Roman rule. They wanted the kingdom of Israel to be restored.

Control by Romans

The Romans had taken over Judah in 63 B.C., but they allowed Jewish kings to rule it. In A.D. 6, Augustus made Judah a Roman province and called it by the Roman name of Judaea (joo·DEE· uh). Augustus replaced the Jewish ruler with a Roman governor, called a procurator (PRAH·kyuh·RAY·tuhr). Judaea was now more tightly controlled by the Roman Empire.

The Jews disagreed among themselves over how to deal with the Romans. Some Jews wanted to avoid conflict with their rulers. They preferred to cooperate with them. Others limited their contact with Roman officials and continued to practice Jewish traditions. Some Jews completely ignored the Romans. They established communities in remote places, away from Roman rule. Jerusalem, however, remained their holy city.

Reading**HELP**DESK

Taking Notes: *Identifying*
On a graphic organizer like this one, list three things we know about the life of Jesus.

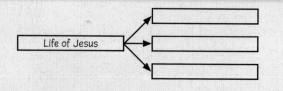

Life of Jesus

Content Vocabulary
• **parable**   • **apostle**
• **resurrection** • **salvation**

Jewish Revolts

One group of Jews believed that they should fight the Romans for their freedom. These people, called Zealots (ZEH·luhtz), rebelled against Roman rule in A.D. 66. The Romans, however, brutally crushed the uprising. They destroyed the Jewish temple in Jerusalem and killed thousands of Jews.

The ruins of an ancient Jewish fortress called Masada (muh·SAH·duh) stand on a mountaintop in southeastern Israel. After Jerusalem fell to the Romans in A.D. 70, about 1,000 Jewish defenders overtook the Masada fortress. For almost two years, these defenders held off an army of 15,000 Roman soldiers.

In A.D. 73, the Romans broke through the walls of the fortress but found only a few Jewish survivors—two women and five children. The others had taken their own lives rather than surrender to the Romans. The fortress is now recognized as a symbol of Jewish heroism.

The Jews organized another unsuccessful rebellion in A.D. 132. In response, the Romans forced all Jews to leave Jerusalem. The Romans then declared that no Jews could ever return to the city. Many Jews, mourning the loss of their city, established communities elsewhere.

By A.D. 700, the Jews had settled in regions as far west as Spain and as far east as Central Asia. In later centuries, they settled throughout Europe and the Americas.

An armed group of Jews captured this mountain fortress of Masada from the Romans. They defended it against a Roman army that outnumbered them 15 to one.

▶ CRITICAL THINKING
Drawing Conclusions Why do you think the Jews wanted to control Masada?

(t & b)Duby Tal/Albatross/Age fotostock

There's More Online

Peter

Most of what we know about the disciple Peter comes from the Christian Bible. According to tradition, Peter deserted Jesus when Jesus was arrested in the garden outside Jerusalem. Later, Peter felt ashamed and regretted his lack of courage. In the years following the death of Jesus, Peter emerged as a respected leader of the earliest Christian community.

▶ **CRITICAL THINKING**
Drawing Conclusions Why do you think Peter deserted Jesus when Jesus was arrested?

Although the Jews were scattered around the world, they kept their faith alive. They did this by studying and following their religious laws and traditions.

✓ **PROGRESS CHECK**

Identifying Cause and Effect How did the A.D. 132 revolt affect the Jews of Judaea?

Jesus of Nazareth

GUIDING QUESTION *Why were the life and death of Jesus of Nazareth important to his followers?*

A few decades before the first Jewish revolt, a Jew named Jesus (JEE·zuhs) grew up in a small town called Nazareth (NA·zuh·ruhth) in Galilee (GA·luh·LEE), the region just north of Judaea. In about A.D. 30, Jesus began to travel throughout Galilee and Judaea, preaching to people about his ideas. A group of 12 close followers called disciples (dih·SY·puhlz) traveled with Jesus.

What Was the Message of Jesus?

According to the Christian Bible, Jesus preached that God was coming soon to rule the world. Jesus urged people to turn from their selfish ways and welcome the kingdom of heaven. In the excerpt below, Jesus calls on his followers to joyfully accept God's coming as a precious gift:

PRIMARY SOURCE

❞ The kingdom of heaven is like a treasure buried in a field, which a person finds and hides again, and out of joy goes and sells all that he has and buys that field. ❞

—Matthew 13:54, *New American Bible*

Jesus preached that God **created** all people and loved them the way a father loves his children. Therefore, people should love God and one another. In this way, they would be obeying God.

The message of Jesus reinforced the Jewish teachings: "Love the Lord your God with all your heart and with all your soul and with all your mind and with all your strength" and "Love your neighbor as yourself."

The teachings of Jesus are summarized in his Sermon on the Mount. Jesus preached on a mountainside to a crowd of thousands.

Reading**HELP**DESK

Academic Vocabulary

create to bring into existence; to produce by a course of action

Alan Spencer/Age fotostock

In it Jesus gave the people simple rules to live by called "The Beatitudes." He told people that it was not enough to follow religious laws. People had to love God and forgive others from the heart.

Jesus spoke using everyday language. He often preached using **parables** (PA·ruh·buhlz). These were stories about things his listeners could understand, using events from everyday life. They helped people **interpret**, or explain, the ideas Jesus taught.

In one parable, Jesus told of a Samaritan man who saw an injured traveler by the side of the road. Even though the injured man was not a Samaritan, the passerby helped him. In another parable, Jesus told the story of a father who forgave his son's mistakes. He welcomed his prodigal—or wasteful—son back into the family. Both parables taught that God is like the concerned Samaritan or the forgiving father. He loves people who have erred and will forgive them if they trust in him.

How Did Christianity Begin?

Jesus and his message sparked strong reactions from people. His followers spoke of times in which he healed the sick and performed other miracles. Stories about him were widely told.

INFOGRAPHIC　　　　**THE BEATITUDES**

The *Beatitudes* are sayings or teachings intended to guide people. They are part of Jesus' Sermon on the Mount. The Sermon includes the Lord's Prayer and nine Beatitudes for leading a better life.

1 **DOCUMENT-BASED QUESTION** Jesus says the meek—or humble—shall inherit the Earth. What do you think he meant by this?

2 **CRITICAL THINKING** *Making Generalizations* Based on what Jesus says in the Beatitudes, what kind of people is he speaking to in his sermon?

A few selected Beatitudes from the Sermon on the Mount in Matthew 5: 3-12.

"Blessed are the poor in spirit, for theirs is the kingdom of heaven.

Blessed are those who mourn, for they will be comforted.

Blessed are the meek, for they will inherit the Earth.

Blessed are those who hunger and thirst for righteousness, for they will be filled.

Blessed are the merciful, for they will be shown mercy.

Blessed are the pure in heart, for they will see God.

Blessed are the peacemakers, for they will be called sons of God."

---

parable a short story that teaches a principle about what is good behavior

Academic Vocabulary

interpret to explain the meaning of

The parables of the Good Samaritan (left) and the Prodigal Son (right) are shown here. In each case, one person is helping another.

▶ CRITICAL THINKING

Synthesizing What do you think of today when you hear that someone is a "good samaritan"?

Many believed he was the promised deliverer. Some Jews felt Jesus was deceiving people and opposed him. Roman rulers feared his preaching and growing influence and popularity. They viewed Jesus as a threat to law and order.

At the time of the Jewish holy days of Passover, there was growing tension between the Romans and the Jews. The Romans brought statues of the emperor into Jerusalem, the holy city of the Jews. Many Jews saw these statues as false idols and objected to their presence. The Jews had also grown weary of Roman rule and high taxes. Many Romans were angry because the Jews refused to worship statues of the Roman emperor.

In about A.D. 33, Jesus traveled to Jerusalem with his 12 disciples to celebrate the Jewish holy days of Passover. When he arrived in the city, an enthusiastic crowd greeted him as their promised deliverer. In an event known as the Last Supper, Jesus celebrated the Passover meal with his disciples.

(l)Tate Gallery, London/Art Resource, NY; (r)Erich Lessing/Art Resource, NY

Reading HELP DESK

Reading Strategy: *Paraphrasing*

Paraphrasing is restating what you read using your own words. Paraphrasing is a good way to check that you really understood what you read. As you finish reading a paragraph or a passage, ask yourself, "What is the main idea?" Then try to restate the main idea using your own words.

Betrayal of Jesus

After the meal, however, one of Jesus' closest followers betrayed him. Leaders in Jerusalem arrested Jesus to prevent trouble from erupting in the city. They may have charged Jesus with treason, or disloyalty to the government. He was questioned by the Roman governor and sentenced to death.

According to the Christian Bible, Jesus was crucified, or hung from a wooden cross, and died. Romans regularly crucified criminals and political rebels. The followers of Jesus were greatly saddened by his death. According to Christian belief, Jesus rose from the dead three days after his death and appeared to some of his disciples.

Early Christian writings state that Mary Magdalene, one of Jesus' followers, was the first to see him alive again. The message of Jesus' **resurrection** (REH·zuh·REHK·shuhn), or rising from the dead, led to the birth of Christianity. During this very early period, Christians were still one of the many groups that made up Judaism.

☑ **PROGRESS CHECK**

Explaining How did Jesus reinforce traditional Jewish teachings?

Who Were the Apostles?

GUIDING QUESTION *How did early Christianity spread throughout the Roman Empire?*

The early Christian leaders who spread the message of Jesus were called **apostles** (uh·PAH·suhlz). The apostles first spoke to the Jews in Judaea and Galilee. The apostles then traveled to other parts of the Mediterranean region. Small groups of Jews and non-Jews in the Greek-speaking cities of the eastern Mediterranean believed the message about Jesus.

Those who accepted Jesus and his teachings became known as "Christians" and referred to Jesus as "Jesus Christ." The word *Christ* comes from *Christos*, which is a Greek term that means "the anointed one."

The first Christians formed churches, or local groups for worship and teaching. Early Christians met in homes of men and women. At these gatherings, Christians prayed and studied the Hebrew Bible and early Christian writings. They also ate a meal similar to the Last Supper to remember the death and resurrection of Jesus.

BIOGRAPHY

Mary Magdalene

A practical, down-to-earth woman, Mary Magdalene went with Jesus during his travels throughout Galilee. Biblical accounts of the life of Jesus maintain that she was present during his crucifixion and burial. These accounts also say she and two other women went to his tomb a few days after he was placed there. Finding it empty, Mary hurried to tell the other followers. She then returned to the tomb with Peter, also a follower of Jesus.

▶ **CRITICAL THINKING**
Analyzing What risks did Mary Magdalene face by being loyal to Jesus?

resurrection the act of rising from the dead

apostle Christian leader chosen by Jesus to spread his message

Leonardo da Vinci/The Bridgeman Art Library/Getty Images

At the end of the 1400s, the Italian artist Leonardo da Vinci created this famous painting of Jesus. Called *The Last Supper*, it was painted on a wall in Milan, Italy.

▶ CRITICAL THINKING
Analyzing What do you think is happening in this illustration of Jesus and his followers?

Early Christian Leaders

Apostles played an important part in the growth of Christianity. Peter and Paul were two important apostles in the early Christian church. Peter was a Jewish fisher from Galilee. He had known Jesus while he was alive and had been one of the 12 disciples Jesus had chosen to preach his message. According to Christian tradition, Peter helped set up a Christian church in Rome after the death of Jesus. Today, the center of the Catholic branch of Christianity is still located there.

Paul of Tarsus was another important Christian apostle. He was a well-educated Jew and a Roman citizen. He was raised as a loyal Roman who, as an adult, distrusted the Christians. Saul—his Hebrew name—at first tried to stop Christian ideas from spreading in Judaea and Galilee. The chief Jewish priest in Jerusalem then sent him to Damascus, a city in neighboring Syria. There, he was supposed to stop Christians in the city from spreading their ideas.

According to Christian belief, while he was traveling to Damascus in Syria, Paul saw a great light and heard the voice of Jesus. As a result of this encounter, Paul soon became a Christian and devoted his life to spreading the message of Jesus.

salvation the act of being saved from the effects of sin

Paul traveled throughout the eastern Mediterranean region and founded numerous Christian churches. Many of his important letters to churches in Rome, Greece, and Asia Minor are found in the Christian Bible.

What Are Basic Christian Beliefs?

The early Christians believed in one God, not the many gods of Rome. They believed that Jesus was the Son of God. They believed he had come to save people. By becoming Christians and by accepting Jesus and his teachings, people could gain **salvation** (sal·VAY·shuhn). They would be saved from their sins, or wrongdoings, and allowed to enter heaven. Like Jesus, people would be resurrected after death and join God in everlasting life.

Because of their faith in Jesus, Christians began to believe in God in a new way. Like the Jews, Christians believed in the God of Israel and studied the Hebrew Bible. However, they also believed in the Christian Trinity, which comes from a word meaning "three." In Christian belief, the Trinity refers to the three persons of God: the Father, Son, and Holy Spirit. These teachings became the basis of the Christian faith.

During the 100 years after Jesus' death, Christianity won followers throughout the world. The peace and order established by the Roman Empire gave people the ability to spread the Christian religion.

Before becoming an apostle, Paul of Tarsus tried to stop the spread of Christian ideas. After he came to believe in Jesus, Paul became one of the most influential leaders of the early Christian movement.

▶ CRITICAL THINKING
Speculating Why do you think Paul at first tried to stop the spread of the message of Jesus?

 PROGRESS CHECK

Identifying Why were the apostles important to early Christianity?

LESSON 1 REVIEW

Review Vocabulary

1. Why did Jesus preach using *parables*?

2. How did the *apostles* spread the message of Jesus?

Answer the Guiding Questions

3. *Explaining* How did Jewish traditions survive after A.D. 132?

4. *Describing* When Jesus said "love your neighbor as yourself," what was his message?

5. *Contrasting* How did some Jews differ in their beliefs about Jesus?

6. *Explaining* Why did Jesus have disciples?

7. **INFORMATIVE/EXPLANATORY** In a paragraph, explain why there were growing tensions between the Romans and the early Christians.

There's More Online! connected.mcgraw-hill.com

LESSON 2
The Early Church

ESSENTIAL QUESTION
• How do religions develop?

IT MATTERS BECAUSE
The Roman Empire's system of roads, shared languages, and stability made it easier for Christianity to spread.

Christianity and the Empire

GUIDING QUESTION *How did Christianity change over time?*

As the apostles spread the message of Jesus, many people in the Mediterranean world became Christians. The Roman Empire contributed to this growth.

Christianity Spreads

Several factors helped Christianity spread throughout the empire. Areas controlled by the Romans were generally peaceful. Well-constructed roads meant Christians could easily travel from one **region** to another. Most people in the empire spoke Latin or Greek. This allowed Christians to communicate with them about the message of Jesus.

Another reason Christianity spread throughout the empire was that it had an attractive message. The official religion of Rome required people to honor the emperor and the state. This religion did not offer help to people when they experienced personal or economic problems. Christianity, however, provided comfort to people during difficult times. Christianity gave people hope that even if life was bad on Earth, there was the promise of a better afterlife.

Reading**HELP**DESK

Taking Notes: *Listing*

Use a graphic organizer like this one to list the major reasons that Christianity spread.

Reasons Christianity Spread
•
•
•
•

Content Vocabulary

- martyr
- hierarchy
- clergy
- doctrine
- gospel
- pope
- laity

Christianity also spread quickly throughout the empire because it provided its followers with security. Christians lived in **communities** where each member was responsible for taking care of the needs of others.

Why Did Romans Mistreat Christians?

As the number of Christians grew, some Romans believed that they were dangerous. They thought Christians were a threat to the empire. Romans expected everyone to worship the emperor as a god. The Christians, like the Jews, however, believed that only God could be worshipped. Christians criticized popular Roman festivals that honored the numerous Roman gods. Also, Christians did not support warfare as a way to resolve problems. As a result, they refused to serve in the Roman army. Furthermore, Christians buried their dead outside Rome in catacombs, or underground burial places. Christians could also meet there to hold memorial services.

GEOGRAPHY CONNECTION

Even though the Romans persecuted the Christians, the Christian religion continued to grow and spread its influence.

1 **LOCATION** What areas did Paul visit during his second journey?

2 **CRITICAL THINKING**
Speculating What might have prevented Christianity from spreading to more places during its first three centuries?

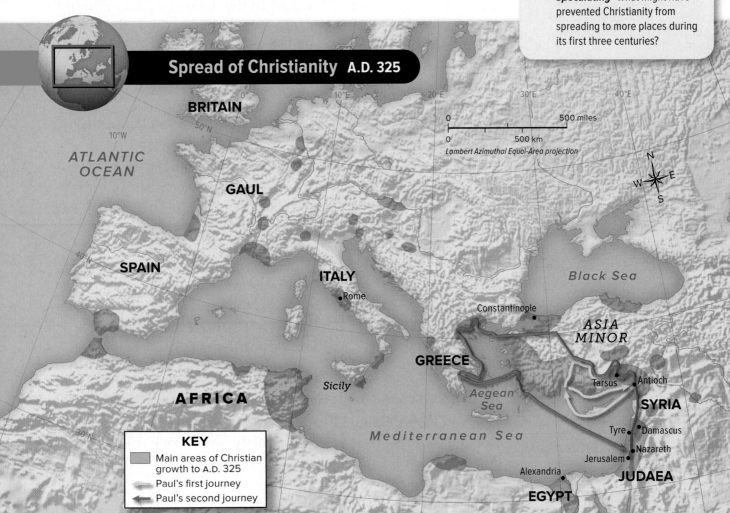

Spread of Christianity A.D. 325

BRITAIN

ATLANTIC OCEAN

GAUL

SPAIN

ITALY
•Rome

Constantinople•

Black Sea

ASIA MINOR

GREECE

Sicily

Aegean Sea

Tarsus• •Antioch

SYRIA

AFRICA

Mediterranean Sea

Tyre• •Damascus

•Nazareth

Jerusalem•

Alexandria•

JUDAEA

EGYPT

KEY
☐ Main areas of Christian growth to A.D. 325
→ Paul's first journey
← Paul's second journey

500 miles
500 km
Lambert Azimuthal Equal-Area projection

10°W · 50°N · 40°N · 30°N · 0° · 10°E · 20°E · 30°E · 40°E

Academic Vocabulary

region a broad geographic area
community people living in a particular area; the area itself

During the early centuries of Christianity, the Roman Catacombs were used for burials and funeral meals. Today, cemeteries are still places where we go to honor our families, experience shared history, and reflect on the sacrifices of others.

Now

▶ **CRITICAL THINKING**
Analyzing Why do you think early Christians buried their dead in hidden catacombs?

People who thought the Christians were dangerous believed that they should be punished. Some Romans blamed Christians for causing natural disasters. In A.D. 64, the emperor Nero falsely accused Christians of starting a fire that burned most of Rome. As a result, Christianity was outlawed.

Christians were often mistreated. They were arrested and beaten. Some Christians became **martyrs** (MAHR·tuhrz), or people who were willing to die rather than give up their beliefs. Despite the mistreatment, Christianity continued to flourish.

The Empire Accepts Christianity

In the early A.D. 300s, the emperor Diocletian carried out the last great persecution of Christians. But his attempt failed. Christianity had grown too strong to be destroyed by force.

In A.D. 312, the Roman emperor Constantine (KAHN·stuhn·TEEN) prepared to lead his **military** forces into battle. According to some early Christian writers, Constantine had a remarkable dream the night before the battle. In the dream he saw a flaming cross in the sky. Written beneath the cross were the Latin words that meant "In this sign you will conquer."

The next day, Constantine ordered his soldiers to paint the Christian cross on their battle shields. Constantine won the battle and believed the Christian God had helped him.

Constantine became a strong supporter of Christianity. In A.D. 313, he issued the Edict of Milan. This decree allowed all religious groups in the empire, including Christians, to practice their religions freely. Constantine attended religious meetings of Christian leaders and gave government aid to Christians. With the help of his mother, Helena (HEH·luh·nuh), he built Christian churches in Rome and Jerusalem. Christians were allowed to serve in government and were excused from paying taxes. They started to serve in the army.

One of Constantine's successors, the emperor Theodosius (THEE·uh·DOH·shuhs), banned Greek and Roman religions. In A.D. 392, he made Christianity the official religion of the Roman Empire.

Axum and Kush

At about the same time Christianity was flourishing in the Roman Empire, great trading kingdoms were rising in East Africa. The empire of Ethiopia, also known as Abyssinia, was powerful.

martyr a person who is willing to die for his or her beliefs

Academic Vocabulary

military relating to armed forces

Its city-state of Axum served as a trading center for Mediterranean and East Asian worlds sending goods into and out of Africa. Around A.D. 300, Axum defeated neighboring Kush, another city-state. In A.D. 334, King Ezana (ah·ZAH·nah) of Axum made Christianity the official religion of Axum.

✔ PROGRESS CHECK

Evaluating How did Constantine support Christianity?

Organizing the Church

GUIDING QUESTION *How did early Christians organize their church and explain their beliefs?*

As the number of Christians grew, the church had to become more organized to unite its followers. In addition, separate Christian communities began to practice Christianity differently. The early Christian leaders had to clarify and write down their beliefs.

Church Leadership

Early Christians were familiar with how the Roman Empire was ruled. They used the empire as their model for organizing the church. Like the empire, the church came to be ruled by a **hierarchy** (HY·uh·RAHR·kee). A hierarchy is an organization with different levels of authority.

Constantine led his troops to victory at the Battle of Milvian Bridge near Rome. This triumph led Constantine to convert to Christianity.

▶ CRITICAL THINKING
Analyzing Do you think the Romans could have destroyed Christianity if Constantine hadn't been converted? Explain.

hierarchy an organization with different levels of authority

Richard Bonson/Wildlife Art, LTD

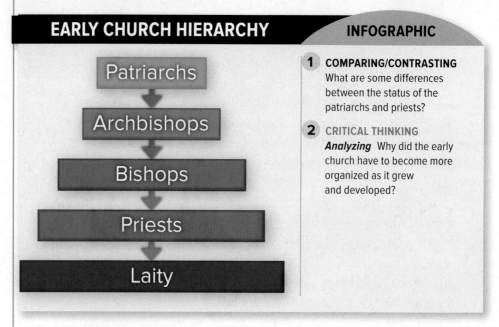

EARLY CHURCH HIERARCHY   **INFOGRAPHIC**

Patriarchs

Archbishops

Bishops

Priests

Laity

1 **COMPARING/CONTRASTING**
What are some differences between the status of the patriarchs and priests?

2 **CRITICAL THINKING**
Analyzing Why did the early church have to become more organized as it grew and developed?

The **clergy** (KLUHR·jee), or church officials, were the leaders of the church. The role of the clergy was different from that of the **laity** (LAY·uh·tee), or regular church members. Although women were not allowed to serve in the clergy, they were members of the church. Women cared for sick and needy church members.

By A.D. 300, individual churches were headed by clergy called priests. Priests led worship services and managed local church activities. Clergy called bishops supervised the dioceses (DY·uh·suh·suhz), or several churches grouped together. Bishops explained Christian beliefs and managed regional church affairs. A bishop in charge of an entire region was called an archbishop. The five leading archbishops—in charge of the cities of Rome, Constantinople, Alexandria, Antioch, and Jerusalem—were known as patriarchs (PAY·tree·AHRKS).

The bishops met in councils to define the teachings of the Church. They wanted to make sure that Christians practiced the same beliefs. The decisions they reached at these councils were accepted as **doctrine** (DAHK·truhn), or official church teaching. The ideas that the bishops rejected were heresies (HER·uh·seez), or teachings that did not support the Christian faith.

What Writings Shaped Christianity?

Church leaders also preserved stories about Jesus and the writings of the apostles. Jesus did not write down what he said or did. His followers, however, passed on what they remembered about him.

Reading HELP DESK

clergy church officials
laity regular church members
doctrine official church teaching

gospel the accounts that apostles wrote of Jesus' life

pope the title given to the Bishop of Rome

By A.D. 300, four accounts of the life and teachings of Jesus were widely known. Christians believed that four apostles of Jesus—Matthew, Mark, Luke, and John—wrote these accounts.

Each account was called a **gospel** (GAHS·puhl), which means "good news." Christians later included the four gospels with the writings of Paul and other early Christian leaders. Together, these works became known as the New Testament. The New Testament was added to the Greek version of the Jewish sacred writings, which Christians called the Old Testament. Together, these works formed the Christian Bible.

Other writings influenced the early church. Christian thinkers who explained church teachings became known as the Church Fathers. One of the most important Church Fathers was Augustine, a bishop in North Africa. In his writings, Augustine defended Christianity against its critics. Augustine wrote *The City of God*. This was one of the first history books written from the viewpoint of a Christian.

The Bishop of Rome

As the church grew, the bishop of Rome claimed power over the other bishops. He believed that he had received the authority from the apostle Peter. Also, his diocese was in Rome, the capital of the Roman Empire. By A.D. 600, the bishop of Rome was called by a special title—**pope** (POHP). The title is from a Latin word, *papa*, related to the word *pater*, meaning "father." Latin-speaking Christians in the western part of the empire accepted the pope as head of all the churches. The Latin churches as a group became known as the Roman Catholic Church. Greek-speaking Christians, however, would not accept the authority of the pope over them. Also claiming a link to the apostles, their churches became known as the Eastern Orthodox Church.

Augustine was one of the most important writers and thinkers in the history of Christianity. Even today, his books continue to inform and inspire.

▶ CRITICAL THINKING
Making Inferences Why do you think Augustine is remembered as one of the Church Fathers?

 **PROGRESS CHECK**

Identifying What writings are included in the New Testament?

Scala/Art Resource, NY

LESSON 2 REVIEW

Review Vocabulary

1. How did church *doctrine* help to unify early Christians?

2. How is the *pope* similar to and different from other bishops?

Answer the Guiding Questions

3. *Identifying* What were two main reasons Christianity spread during Roman times?

4. *Describing* Why were early Christians considered traitors to the Roman Empire?

5. *Comparing* Compare the responsibilities of a priest and a bishop in the early Christian church.

6. *Making Inferences* Why did bishops meet in councils?

7. **NARRATIVE** Write a journal entry that Constantine might have written after the battle he believed God helped him win.

LESSON 3

A Christian Europe

ESSENTIAL QUESTION

• How do new ideas change the way people live?

IT MATTERS BECAUSE

Christianity divided into the Roman Catholic and the Eastern Orthodox branches. Despite this division, all Christians share core beliefs that go back to Jesus of Nazareth.

Two Christian Churches

GUIDING QUESTION *What issues divided the western and eastern Christian churches?*

The Roman Catholic Church was based in Rome, the capital of the Western Roman Empire. The church was led by the very powerful pope. As the Western Roman Empire declined, the Christian church of Rome survived. At the same time, the Roman Empire in the east, which soon became known as the Byzantine Empire, thrived. The Byzantines developed their own Christian church. Their church reflected their Greek heritage. This church became known as the Eastern Orthodox Church.

Byzantine Government and Religion

The emperor of the Byzantine Empire and the officials of the Eastern Orthodox Church worked closely together. The Byzantines believed their emperor was God's representative on Earth. Beginning in the A.D. 400s, emperors were crowned in a religious ceremony. They also took an oath to defend Eastern Orthodox Christianity. They believed it was their duty to unite the empire under one Christian faith. Thus, the emperors controlled the Eastern Orthodox Church. Emperors appointed church leaders and defined how people would worship. They also controlled the wealth of the church and helped settle disputes about church beliefs.

Reading**HELP**DESK

Taking Notes: *Describing*

Create a diagram like this one, and describe how the western and eastern Christian churches viewed the authority of the pope.

Authority of the Pope	
Western Church	Eastern Church

Content Vocabulary

- **icon**
- **iconoclast**
- **excommunicate**
- **schism**
- **monastery**

What Are Icons?

Both Byzantine clergy and the Byzantine people discussed and often argued about religious matters. These arguments frequently became political issues and led to fights and riots.

In the A.D. 700s, a heated dispute about **icons** (EYE·KAWNZ) divided the Eastern Orthodox Church. Icons are paintings of Jesus, Mary (the mother of Jesus), and the saints, or Christian holy people. Many Byzantines **displayed** icons in their homes. They also covered the walls of their churches with them.

People who displayed icons claimed that these images symbolized the presence of God in their lives. They also believed that the images helped people understand Christian teachings. The thinker John of Damascus was the leading defender of icons.

Some Byzantines, however, did not approve of the use of icons. They thought it was a form of idol worship forbidden by God. In A.D. 726, Emperor Leo III ordered that all icons be removed from the churches. Government officials who carried out his orders were called **iconoclasts** (eye·KAH· nuh·KLASTS), or image breakers. Today, this word refers to someone who criticizes traditional beliefs or practices.

Most Byzantines, many church leaders, and even the pope in Rome disapproved of Emperor Leo's actions. The dispute over icons severely damaged the relationship between the Roman Catholic Church and the Eastern Orthodox Church. Over the next century, the argument became less heated, and icons were used once again. They are still important today.

The Great Split

Icons were only one of the issues that divided the eastern and western Christian churches. The most serious disagreement was about church authority. The pope claimed to be head of all Christian churches. He believed he was a successor, or person who follows another person, to Peter, disciple of Jesus. Peter was the first bishop of Rome. The Byzantines **rejected** the claim of the pope. They believed the patriarch of Constantinople and other bishops were equal to the pope.

This icon painted on wood shows the angel Gabriel. According to the Christian Bible, Gabriel was a messenger sent from God.

▶ **CRITICAL THINKING**
Explaining Why do you think some Byzantine people were against the use of icons?

Scala/Art Resource, NY

---

icon a representation of an object of worship

iconoclast *originally:* a person who destroys icons; *today:* a person who criticizes traditional beliefs

Academic Vocabulary

display to place an object where people can view it

reject to refuse to accept

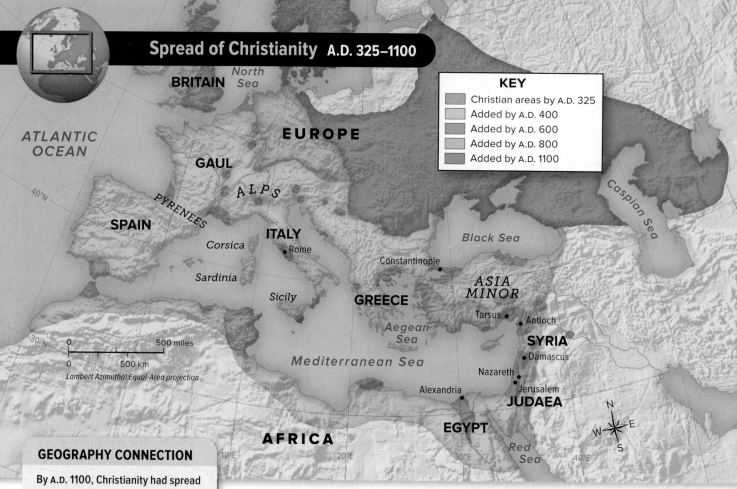

KEY

- Christian areas by A.D. 325
- Added by A.D. 400
- Added by A.D. 600
- Added by A.D. 800
- Added by A.D. 1100

ATLANTIC OCEAN

BRITAIN
North Sea
EUROPE
GAUL
ALPS
PYRENEES
SPAIN
Corsica
ITALY
Rome
Sardinia
Sicily
GREECE
Aegean Sea
Mediterranean Sea
Black Sea
Constantinople
ASIA MINOR
Tarsus
Antioch
SYRIA
Damascus
Nazareth
Alexandria
Jerusalem
JUDAEA
EGYPT
Red Sea
AFRICA
Caspian Sea

40°N
30°N
10°E
20°E
30°E
40°E

0   500 miles
0   500 km
Lambert Azimuthal Equal-Area projection

GEOGRAPHY CONNECTION

By A.D. 1100, Christianity had spread throughout Western and Eastern Europe and into far northern lands.

1. **UNDERSTANDING A MAP KEY** Which of these two areas became Christian first: Britain or Syria?

2. **CRITICAL THINKING**
   Analyzing Why do you think some areas took longer to convert to Christianity than others?

Military events also damaged the relationship between the pope and the patriarch of Constantinople. In the late A.D. 700s, Italy was invaded. The pope appealed to the Byzantine emperor for help, but the emperor refused. The pope then asked the Franks to help defend Rome. The Franks were a Germanic people that supported the pope as head of the Christian church.

The Franks successfully defended Italy against the invaders. To show his gratitude, the pope crowned the Frankish king, Charlemagne (SHAHR·luh·MAYN), emperor in A.D. 800. The pope's actions upset the Byzantines. They believed their ruler was the only Roman emperor.

The eastern and western churches also viewed their roles in government differently. In the Byzantine Empire, the emperor controlled both church and government. Byzantine church leaders supported the decisions of the emperor. In the West, the pope claimed he had religious and political authority over all of Europe. He often quarreled with kings about church and government affairs.

Reading HELP DESK

Finally, in A.D. 1054, after centuries of bitterness, the patriarch of Constantinople and the pope **excommunicated** (EHK·skuh·MYOO·nuh·KAY·tuhd) each other. To excommunicate means to declare that a person or group no longer belongs to the church. This created a **schism** (SIH·zuhm), or separation, between the two major churches of Christianity. The split between the Eastern Orthodox Church and the Roman Catholic Church still exists today.

✅ **PROGRESS CHECK**

Identifying What issues divided the eastern and western Christian churches?

The Spread of Christianity

GUIDING QUESTION *How did Christianity spread across Europe?*

After the fall of the Western Roman Empire, people in many parts of Europe faced disorder and violence. Many looked to the Christian church for help. They hoped that Christianity would bring peace, order, and unity.

New Christian Communities

During the A.D. 300s, devout Christians in the Eastern Roman Empire formed religious communities called **monasteries** (MAH·nuh·STEHR·eez). In the monasteries, men called monks lived apart from the world. At the same time, they performed good deeds and modeled how Christians should live.

Christian women established religious communities of their own. These women were called nuns, and they lived in convents. During this time, one of the best known nuns was a Roman widow named Paula. In the early A.D. 400s, Paula helped a scholar named Jerome translate the Christian Bible into Latin.

The Greek bishop Basil (BAY·zuhl) created a list of rules for monks and nuns. Known as the Basilian (buh·ZIH·lee·uhn) Rule, this list told people how to live and pray in Eastern Orthodox monasteries and convents.

In the West, religious communities followed another set of regulations called the Benedictine Rule. An Italian monk named Benedict (BEH·nuh·DIHKT) wrote these rules about A.D. 529. Benedictines gave up material goods. They devoted their days to work and prayer. One of their major duties was to serve as missionaries. Missionaries teach their religion to those who are not followers.

Charlemagne believed his authority to rule came from God. Inspired by the teachings of St. Augustine, he considered both the spiritual and material needs of his subjects.

▶ **CRITICAL THINKING**
Explaining Why do you think Charlemagne, a Frankish king, defended Rome?

Popperfoto/Getty Images

excommunicate to declare that a person or group is no longer a member of the church

schism a separation or division from a church

monastery a religious community

THE CYRILLIC ALPHABET

Cyrillic Letter	Written Name	English Sound
Б	beh	B
Г	gey	G
Ж	zheh	ZH
М	em	M
П	pey	P
С	ess	S
Ф	ef	F
Ч	cheh	CH

Cyril and Methodius quarreled with German church leaders who opposed the use of Slavic languages for preaching and worship. The Germans wanted only Latin to be used.

INFOGRAPHIC

Cyril, a Byzantine missionary, developed the Cyrillic alphabet, part of which is shown here. The original alphabet, based on Greek, had 43 letters.

1 **IDENTIFYING** Which Cyrillic letters make the same sounds as the letters "p" and "f" in the English alphabet?

2 **CRITICAL THINKING**
Applying Why did Cyril create a new alphabet for people who spoke Slavic languages?

In addition, the Rule stated that monks were to welcome outsiders who were in need of food and shelter:

TEXT: Chapter 53: The Reception of Guests. From Rule of Saint Benedict in English, edited by Timothy Fry. Copyright © 1981 by The Order of St. Benedict, Inc.; PHOTO: ©José F. Poblete/Corbis

PRIMARY SOURCE

" All guests who present themselves are to be welcomed as Christ, for he himself will say: I was a stranger and you welcomed me. … Once a guest has been announced, the superior and the brothers are to meet him with all the courtesy of love. … All humility [being humble] should be shown in addressing a guest on arrival or departure. "

—**Benedictine Rule, Chapter 53: The Reception of Guests**

Monks and nuns had important roles in Christian Europe. They helped the poor and ran hospitals and schools. They also helped preserve ancient Greek and Roman writings.

Christianity and the Slavs

The Byzantines wanted to bring their religion and culture to groups who lived north of their empire. Two brothers, Cyril (SIHR·uhl) and Methodius, were among the most dedicated Byzantine missionaries. Their mission was to deliver the Christian message to the Slavs, a people in Eastern Europe.

Cyril and Methodius believed that the Slavs would be more interested in Christianity if they heard about it in their own languages. About A.D. 863, Cyril invented an alphabet for the Slavic languages. It is known today as the Cyrillic (suh·RIH·lihk)

Reading HELP DESK

Build Vocabulary: *Word Origins*

The English word *slave* comes from the word *Slav*. In the early Middle Ages, so many Slavic people were taken into slavery that their name came to be used for anyone who was treated as the property of another and forced to work.

alphabet in honor of its inventor. The Cyrillic alphabet was based on Greek letters. It is still used today by Russians, Ukrainians, Serbs, and Bulgarians.

Christianity in Western Europe

In Western Europe, Christian missionaries sought to convert the peoples of Britain and Ireland to Christianity. Roman soldiers were stationed there also. In the A.D. 300s, Roman soldiers left Britain to defend the empire against Germanic invaders.

Beginning in the A.D. 400s, Germanic tribes from present-day Germany and Denmark invaded much of Britain. Over time, these groups united to become known as the Anglo-Saxons. They built farming villages and founded several small kingdoms. Southern Britain soon became known as Angleland, or England. The people became known as the English.

In Britain, the Anglo-Saxons pushed aside the Celts (KEHLTS), the people already living there. Some Celts fled to remote, mountainous areas of Britain. Others crossed the sea to Ireland. In the A.D. 400s, a priest named Patrick brought Christianity to Ireland. He set up churches and monasteries where monks helped preserve Christian and Roman learning.

In A.D. 597, Pope Gregory I sent about 40 monks from Rome to bring Christianity to the Anglo-Saxons of Britain. They converted King Ethelbert of Kent to Christianity. Ethelbert allowed the missionaries to build a church in his capital city of Canterbury. In about 100 years, most of England had accepted the Christian faith. Monasteries were built throughout England. As in Ireland, they became centers of religion and culture.

Pope Gregory I is also known as Gregory the Great. A former monk, he was an excellent administrator. As pope, he continued to live as a monk and tried to bring about reforms in the church.

▶ CRITICAL THINKING
Analyzing How might Pope Gregory's background have affected the spread of Christianity?

✓ PROGRESS CHECK

Analyzing Why were monasteries and convents important in Christian Europe?

LESSON 3 REVIEW

Review Vocabulary

1. Is an *iconoclast* someone who believes in using icons in worship or someone who opposes this practice?

2. When the early church underwent a *schism*, does that mean it changed its most important doctrines?

Answer the Guiding Questions

3. *Comparing and Contrasting* What different views of the role of the church in government did the Eastern and Western churches have?

4. *Making Inferences* Why do you think the Byzantine emperor refused to help the pope defend Rome from invaders?

5. *Explaining* What were monasteries and what purpose did they serve?

6. *Identifying Cause and Effect* How did the Cyrillic alphabet help the spread of Christianity?

7. **INFORMATIVE/EXPLANATORY** Write a paragraph to describe what happened to Ireland once Patrick brought Christianity to its lands.

Giraudon/Art Resource, NY

Write your answers on a separate piece of paper.

1 **Exploring the Essential Question**

NARRATIVE Imagine you are Paul of Tarsus. You want to write your thoughts about how Christianity has developed and spread. You decide to do this in the form of a letter to church leaders. What part did you play in helping Christianity develop? What challenges did you personally face? Which accomplishments are you most proud of?

2 **21st Century Skills**

RESEARCH ON THE INTERNET Find the Gospels of Luke and Matthew in an online version of the New Testament. Compare and contrast the different ways Luke and Matthew tell the story of the birth of Jesus. (In Luke, read Chapter 2, verses 1–20. In Matthew, read Chapter 1, verses 18–25 and Chapter 2, verses 1–15.) Write a report explaining the results of your research.

3 **Thinking Like a Historian**

UNDERSTANDING CAUSE AND EFFECT Create a cause-and-effect diagram like the one shown here. Fill it in with the results or effects of Emperor Constantine's conversion to Christianity.

4 **GEOGRAPHY ACTIVITY**

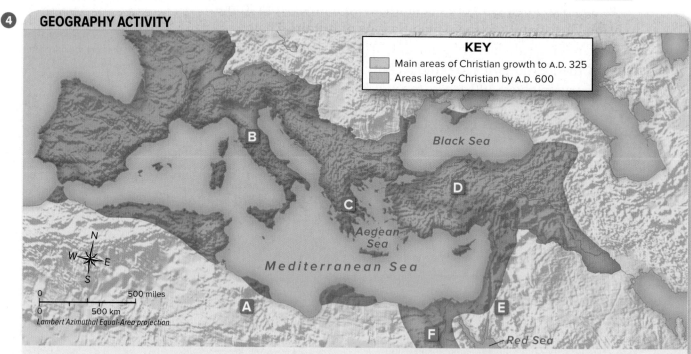

Locating Places

By A.D. 600, Christianity had spread to many parts of the known world as shown on the map. Match the letters on the map with the numbered places listed below.

1. North Africa
2. Judaea
3. Asia Minor
4. Italy
5. Egypt
6. Greece

Directions: Write your answers on a separate piece of paper.

CHECKING FOR UNDERSTANDING

1 Define each of these terms as they relate to the rise of Christianity.

A. parable	**G.** laity
B. resurrection	**H.** doctrine
C. apostle	**I.** pope
D. salvation	**J.** icon
E. hierarchy	**K.** schism
F. clergy	**L.** monastery

REVIEW THE GUIDING QUESTIONS

2 *Identifying* Who were the Zealots?

3 *Stating* What did Jesus's followers believe happened to him after he died?

4 *Explaining* How did the Roman Empire contribute to the spread of Christianity?

5 *Recognizing Relationships* What is the relationship between Constantine and the spread of Christianity throughout the Roman Empire?

6 *Listing* List the hierarchy of the early Christian church in order from most to least authority.

7 *Describing* Name and describe the writings that comprise the Christian Bible.

8 *Explaining* Why did iconoclasts disapprove of the use of icons?

9 *Summarizing* How do the Eastern Orthodox Church and the Roman Catholic Church view the pope's power?

10 *Describing* How did Christianity come to England?

CRITICAL THINKING

11 *Making Generalizations* How did the Jewish people react to Roman rule?

12 *Determining Cause and Effect* What were the effects of the Zealots' rebellion against Roman rule of Judea?

13 *Giving Examples* How does Jesus's parable of the Good Samaritan reinforce his teachings?

14 *Evaluating* Who was more important in the spread and development of early Christianity: Peter or Paul? Explain your answer.

15 *Comparing and Contrasting* How was the Christian understanding of God similar to Judaism? How was it different?

16 *Predicting Consequences* How might the development of Christianity have differed if Constantine had not become a Christian himself?

17 *Identifying Central Issues* On what basis did the bishop of Rome claim authority over other bishops?

18 *Speculating* Why was early Christianity able to attract so many followers despite the threat of persecution?

19 *Making Inferences* How did the dispute over the use of icons reflect a larger issue in the early Christian church?

20 *Making Generalizations* What contributions did monks and nuns make to medieval Europe?

Need Extra Help?

If You've Missed Question	**1**	**2**	**3**	**4**	**5**	**6**	**7**	**8**	**9**	**10**	**11**	**12**	**13**	**14**	**15**	**16**	**17**	**18**	**19**	**20**
Review Lesson	1, 2,3	1	1	1, 2	2	2	2	3	3	3	1	1	1	1	1	2	2	2	3	3

TEXT: "Zealot." Reprinted with permission from Encyclopaedia Britannica, © 2011 by Encyclopaedia Britannica, Inc.

DBQ SHORT RESPONSE

"Extremists among the Zealots turned to terrorism and assassination. … They frequented [went to] public places with hidden daggers to strike down persons friendly to Rome. … [A]t Masada in [A.D. 73] they committed suicide rather than surrender the fortress."

—Encyclopaedia Britannica, "Zealot," 2011

21 Why do you think the Zealots were so against Roman rule?

22 What effect do you think Zealot tactics had on other Jews and Romans?

EXTENDED RESPONSE

23 *Narrative* You are a young person who lives in Judaea during the time of Jesus' ministry. You have attended his Sermon on the Mount. Write a letter to your grandparents telling them about it.

STANDARDIZED TEST PRACTICE

DBQ ANALYZING DOCUMENTS

Drawing Conclusions Before becoming pope, Gregory I wrote this account of a monk who had not shared three gold coins with his fellow monks:

"When he was dead his body was not placed with the bodies of the brethren, but a grave was dug in the dung pit, and his body was flung down into it, and the three pieces of gold he had left were cast upon him, while all together cried, 'Thy money perish with thee!'"

—"Life in a Christian Monastery, ca. 585"

24 Which statement best captures the attitude of Gregory toward monks who hold on to personal property?

   A. They should be pitied for their selfishness.

   B. They deserve to die alone, with no one to comfort them.

   C. They must be treated with scorn, even when they are dead.

   D. Their sins must be punished severely to keep others from sinning.

25 *Inferring* What does Gregory's way of treating the dead monk reveal about life in an early Christian monastery?

   A. Monks were expected to be cruel and hard-hearted.

   B. Money was thought of as sinful and wicked.

   C. Life was lived in common; all personal wealth was to be shared.

   D. Monks paid a high price if they broke the rules.

Need Extra Help?

If You've Missed Question	21	22	23	24	25
Review Lesson	1	1	1	3	3

◄ *Portrait paintings of leaders such as Suleiman II are important historical artifacts that tell us about the cultures in which the leaders lived.*

A.D. 600 TO A.D. 1629

Islamic Civilization

THE STORY MATTERS ...

In the 1300s, in the area now known as Turkey, a Muslim tribal chieftain named Osman gained power. He gradually took control of more lands and established the Ottoman Empire. The Ottoman Empire lasted for nearly six centuries and was ruled by Muslim leaders called sultans.

This painting of Suleiman II, sultan of the Ottoman Empire from 1687–1691, shows the elegant clothes worn by a sultan. The large turban, or headdress, indicates his status and position. For centuries, turbans were a part of dress throughout the Islamic world. An elaborate turban and richly decorated robes showed a person's high rank in society.

ESSENTIAL QUESTIONS

- How do religions develop?
- How does religion shape society?
- How do new ideas change the way people live?

Italian School/The Bridgeman Art Library/Getty Images

Islamic Civilization
Place & Time: A.D. 600 to A.D. 1629

Islamic civilization extended across Southwest Asia, North Africa, and parts of Europe. It later spread into India and Southeast Asia. Over time, Islamic rule was challenged by rivalries within Islam and by invasions of outside groups. A series of Islamic empires ruled until the early 1900s.

Step Into the Place

MAP FOCUS Arabia was a crossroads of trade and culture between East and West in the first century A.D.

1 LOCATION Look at the map. Is Arabia east or west of India?

2 MOVEMENT How did Arabia's location make it a trading crossroads between the East and the West?

3 REGIONS Describe all of the boundaries of Arabia.

4 CRITICAL THINKING
Determining Cause and Effect
How does a trading center contribute to the spread of culture and ideas?

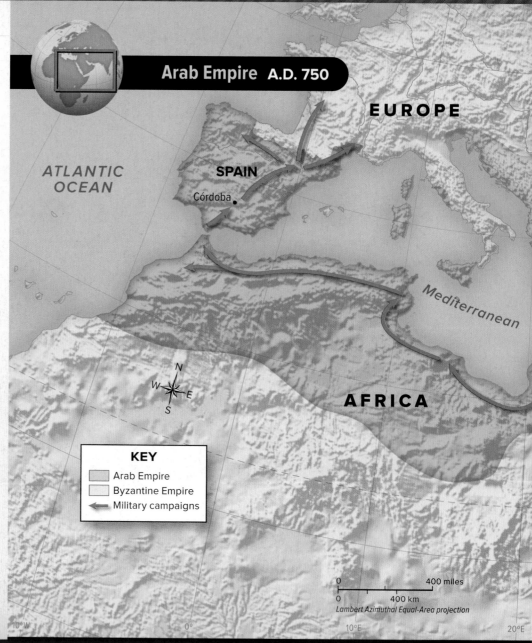

Arab Empire A.D. 750

EUROPE

ATLANTIC OCEAN

SPAIN

Córdoba

Mediterranean

AFRICA

KEY
- Arab Empire
- Byzantine Empire
- → Military campaigns

0 400 miles
0 400 km
Lambert Azimuthal Equal-Area projection

10°W 0° 10°E 20°E

Step Into the Time

TIME LINE Choose an event from the time line and write a paragraph predicting the consequences that event might have for the world.

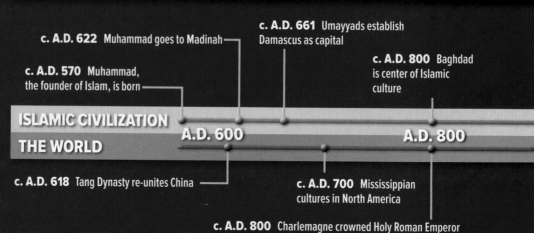

c. A.D. 622 Muhammad goes to Madinah

c. A.D. 661 Umayyads establish Damascus as capital

c. A.D. 570 Muhammad, the founder of Islam, is born

c. A.D. 800 Baghdad is center of Islamic culture

ISLAMIC CIVILIZATION

A.D. 600

A.D. 800

THE WORLD

c. A.D. 618 Tang Dynasty re-unites China

c. A.D. 700 Mississippian cultures in North America

c. A.D. 800 Charlemagne crowned Holy Roman Emperor

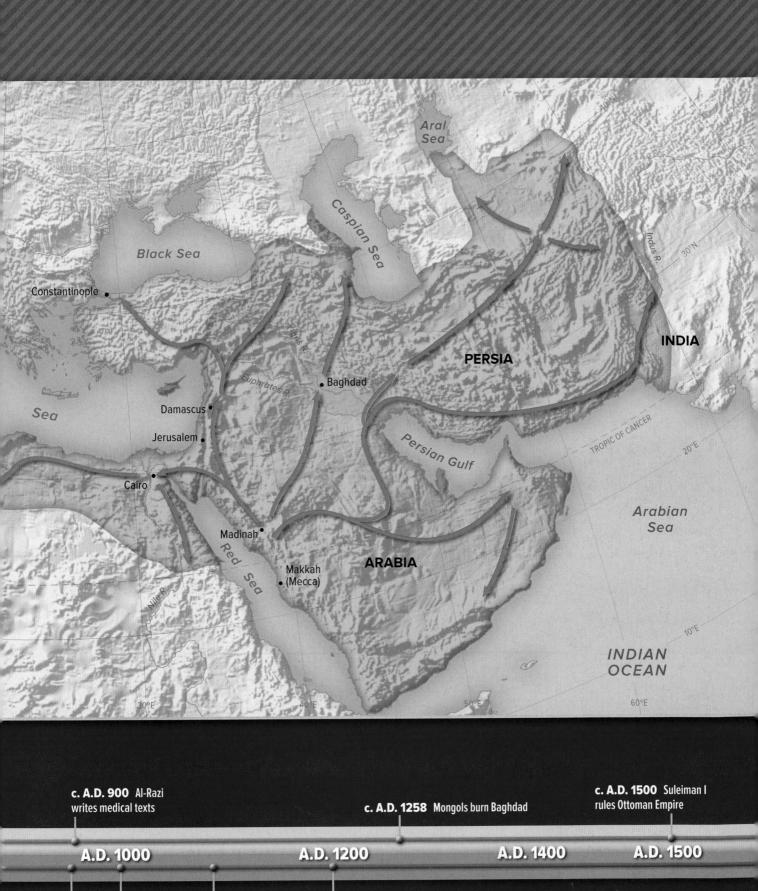

Aral Sea

Black Sea

Caspian Sea

Constantinople

PERSIA

INDIA

Baghdad

Damascus

Jerusalem

Sea

Cairo

Persian Gulf

TROPIC OF CANCER

Madinah

Red Sea

Arabian Sea

Makkah (Mecca)

ARABIA

Nile R.

INDIAN OCEAN

c. A.D. 900 Al-Razi writes medical texts

c. A.D. 1258 Mongols burn Baghdad

c. A.D. 1500 Suleiman I rules Ottoman Empire

A.D. 1000

A.D. 1200

A.D. 1400

A.D. 1500

c. A.D. 1000 Vikings reach North America

c. A.D. 1200 Mayapán is ruling Mayan city-state in the Yucatán

c. A.D. 1095 Pope Urban II calls for first Crusade

c. A.D. 868 China uses woodblock printing

LESSON 1
A New Faith

ESSENTIAL QUESTION

• How do religions develop?

IT MATTERS BECAUSE
Islam is one of the most widely practiced religions in the world today. Approximately 25 percent of the people in the world are Muslim.

Arab Life

GUIDING QUESTION *How did physical geography influence the Arab way of life?*

Beginning in the A.D. 630s, people called Arabs created a new empire in Southwest Asia. The driving force behind their empire was the religion of **Islam** (IS·lahm). Within a century, Islam spread throughout parts of Asia, northern Africa, and Europe.

The Land of Arabia

The Arabian Peninsula, also called Arabia, is the homeland of the Arab people. It is also the center of Islam. Arabia is a huge wedge of land between the Red Sea and the Persian Gulf. Very dry plains and deserts cover most of the land. The desert heat can be intense. Summer temperatures can rise above 122° F (50° C). Water is available only at scattered springs and water holes. Such a spot is called an **oasis** (oh·AY·suhs). At an oasis, trees and other plants grow. Not all of Arabia is desert, however. There are mountains and valleys in the southwestern region. Enough rain falls in these locations for juniper and olive trees to grow.

In ancient times, the Arabian Peninsula was surrounded by many different civilizations. At various times, the Egyptian civilization was to the west, the Mesopotamian and Persian

ReadingHELPDESK

Taking Notes: *Describing*

On a chart like this one, describe the importance of these places to the development of the religion of Islam.

The Development of Islam

Place	Importance
Arabia	
Makkah	
Madinah	

Content Vocabulary

• **Islam**   • **caravan**
• **oasis**   • **Quran**
• **sheikh**   • *shari'ah*

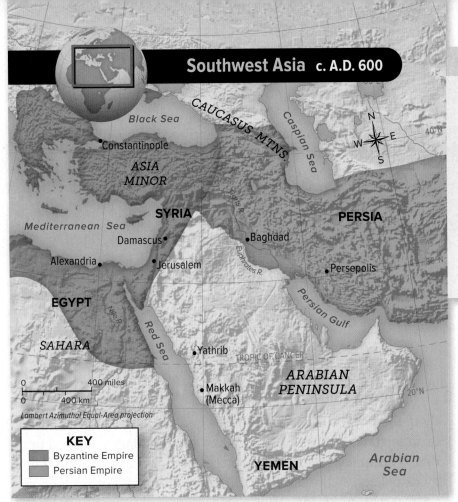

Southwest Asia c. A.D. 600

Black Sea
Constantinople
CAUCASUS MTNS
Caspian Sea
ASIA MINOR
Mediterranean Sea
SYRIA
Damascus
Baghdad
PERSIA
Alexandria
Jerusalem
Persepolis
Tigris R.
Euphrates R.
EGYPT
Nile R.
Red Sea
Persian Gulf
SAHARA
Yathrib
TROPIC OF CANCER
ARABIAN PENINSULA
0 400 miles
0 400 km
Makkah (Mecca)
Lambert Azimuthal Equal-Area projection
YEMEN
Arabian Sea

KEY
- Byzantine Empire
- Persian Empire

GEOGRAPHY CONNECTION

The prophet Muhammad brought the message of Islam to the people of Arabia.

1 REGIONS Which empire was located north and west of the Arabian Peninsula?

2 PLACE About how far is it from Makkah to Yathrib?

3 CRITICAL THINKING
Analyzing How did Makkah's location make it a center for trade?

civilizations were to the north and east, and farther north were the civilizations of the Israelites, Greeks, and Romans. Long distances and the severe Arabian climate had kept these civilizations from invading the peninsula. This **isolation,** however, was not absolute, as trade brought some outside ideas and practices to the Arab civilization.

Life in the Desert

Long ago, many Arabs were nomads who herded animals and lived in tents. These nomads are called bedouin. The bedouin raised camels, goats, and sheep and traveled from oasis to oasis. The bedouin ate mainly fresh or dried dates and drank milk. On very special occasions they ate goat or sheep meat.

To survive the harsh desert climate, early Arabs formed tribes whose members were loyal to one another. The leader of each tribe was called a **sheikh** (SHAYK). Arab tribes raided other tribes to take camels and horses. Rival tribes battled one another over land and water.

Islam a religion based on the teachings of Muhammad

oasis a green area in a desert fed by underground water

sheikh the leader of an Arab tribe

Academic Vocabulary

isolation separation from other populated areas

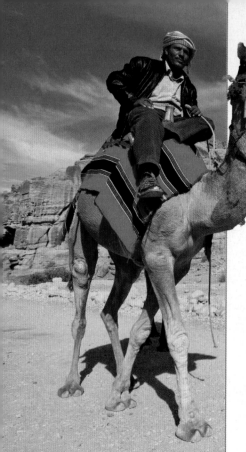

Bedouins value the camel as a reliable carrier. Their wide, flat feet allow the camel to move very quickly across the dunes.

Can you imagine what a camel race might be like? The bedouin enjoyed camel and horse races and other games that improved their battle skills. In the evenings, they told stories around campfires. Poets wrote and recited poems about battles, camels, horses, and love. The lines below are about an Arab warrior and a battle he must fight. He describes his reliable camel.

" My riding-camels are tractable [obedient],
they go wherever I wish;
while my intellect is my helper,
and I drive it forward with a firm order. "

—from *The Poem of Antar*

Life in Towns

By the A.D. 500s, many Arab tribes had settled around oases or in fertile mountain valleys. They set up villages, farmed or raised animals, and traded goods. Merchants carried goods by camel across the desert to different markets. For protection against bedouin raids, some made journeys in **caravans** (KEHR· uh·vanz), or groups of traveling merchants and animals.

As trade grew, Arab merchants built towns along the trade routes in Arabia. The most important town was Makkah (MAH·kuh), also known as Mecca. Makkah was located about 50 miles (80 kilometers) inland from the Red Sea. The town became a crossroads of trade. Large caravans from southwestern Arabia passed through Makkah on their way to Syria and Mesopotamia. Some caravans traveled as far away as China.

Makkah was also an important religious site. In the center of the city was the Kaaba (KAH·buh). This was a low, block-like building surrounded by statues of Arabian gods and goddesses. The people of Arabia worshipped many deities, but the most important was Allah. They believed that Allah was the creator. Arabs believed that a large stone inside the Kaaba came from heaven. Many pilgrims, people who travel to a holy place, visited the Kaaba.

✓ PROGRESS CHECK

Contrasting How did the lives of desert Arabs and town Arabs differ?

Michael Runkel/Robert Harding World Imagery/Getty Images

Reading Strategy: *Formulating Questions*

Asking questions can help you understand and remember what you read. Read about the life of Muhammad. On a separate sheet of paper, write down two or three questions that you would like answered.

Academic Vocabulary

authority power over thoughts, opinions, and behavior

Muhammad and His Message

GUIDING QUESTION *What message did Muhammad preach to the people of Arabia?*

Trade increased the contact between Arabs and other civilizations. Life in Arabia changed as people were exposed to new ideas. Arabs searched for ways to deal with these new challenges. Their search paved the way for the rise of Islam.

Who Was Muhammad?

The religion of Islam arose in the Arabian Peninsula in the A.D. 600s. Islam grew from the preachings of a man named Muhammad (moh·HAH·muhd). Muhammad was born into a merchant family in Makkah in A.D. 570. He was orphaned at the age of five or six. As a teenager, Muhammad worked as a caravan leader and eventually became a merchant.

Despite his success, Muhammad was troubled by many things he saw around him, including the greed of Makkah's wealthy citizens. He despised their dishonesty, neglect of the poor, and disregard for family life. Seeking guidance, he spent time alone praying in a cave outside the city.

Muslim tradition says that in A.D. 610, Muhammad had a vision in which a voice called him to preach Islam. Islam means "surrendering [to the will of Allah]." In the Arabic language, Allah is the word for "God." Three times the voice said, "Recite!" When Muhammad asked what he should recite, the voice said:

PRIMARY SOURCE

" Recite in the name of your Lord Who created, created man from a clot of congealed [thickened] blood. Recite: and your Lord is Most Generous, Who taught by the pen, taught man what he did not know. "

—*Quran*, Surah 96:1-5

Muhammad returned to Makkah and began preaching. He told people that there was only Allah to worship, the one true God. He said they must destroy their statues of fake gods.

Muhammad also preached that people were equal in God's sight, and the rich should share their wealth with the poor. Everywhere he went, Muhammad preached that God valued good deeds. Muhammad urged people to prepare for the Day of Judgment, when God would punish evildoers and reward the just.

Muhammad's Opponents

The first people to become Muslims, or followers of Islam, were Muhammad's family members. Slowly, Muhammad won the support of the poor, who were attracted to his message of sharing. Most wealthy merchants and religious leaders, however, thought Muhammad was trying to destroy their **authority.**

There's More Online! connected.mcgraw-hill.com

BIOGRAPHY

Muhammad (A.D. 570–632)

The tomb of the prophet Muhammad is a holy place to Muslims. During Muhammad's lifetime, he was well known for fairly resolving disputes among his followers. According to Islamic tradition, when Muhammad was asked to resolve which tribe would have the honor to place the holy black stone in the corner of the rebuilt Kaaba, Muhammad put his cloak on the ground with the stone in the center and had each tribe lift a corner to bring the stone to the correct height to be placed in the Kaaba. Muhammad's legacy has made a major impact on the world.

▶ **CRITICAL THINKING**
Drawing Conclusions Why do you think Muhammad had each tribe carry his cloak with the holy black stone?

Thousands of Muslim pilgrims surround the Kaaba in Makkah. A call to worship on special days draws thousands of people.

▶ **CRITICAL THINKING**
Making Inferences Why do you think the Muslim calendar begins with the year of the Hijrah?

In A.D. 622, Muhammad and his followers believed Makkah had become too dangerous. They moved to Yathrib (YA·thruhb). Muhammad's departure to Yathrib became known as the Hijrah (HIHJ·ruh). This Arabic word means "breaking off relationships." The year of the Hijrah later became the first year of the Muslim calendar. The people of Yathrib accepted Muhammad as God's prophet and their ruler. They renamed their city Madinah (mah·DEE·nah), which means "the city of the prophet."

The Islamic State

Muhammad was a skilled political and religious leader. He applied the laws he believed God had given him to all areas of life. He used these laws to settle disputes among the people. Muhammad also established the foundation for an Islamic state. The government of the state used its political power to uphold Islam. Muhammad required all Muslims to place loyalty to the Islamic state above loyalty to their tribes.

Muhammad formed an army to protect his new state. In a series of battles, Muhammad's soldiers regained Makkah and made it a holy city of Islam. The Muslims then began to expand into new areas. When Muhammad died in A.D. 632, the entire Arabian Peninsula was part of the Islamic state.

☑ **PROGRESS CHECK**

Analyzing Why did Makkah's merchants and religious leaders oppose Muhammad and his message?

Reading**HELP**DESK

Quran the holy book of Islam
shari'ah Islamic code of law

Beliefs and Practices of Islam

GUIDING QUESTION *How does Islam provide guidance to its followers?*

Islam shares some beliefs with Judaism and Christianity. Like Jews and Christians, Muslims are monotheists. Muslims believe in one all-powerful God who created the universe. They believe that God decides what is right and wrong.

Like Jews and Christians, Muslims believe that God spoke to people through prophets. For Muslims, these prophets include Adam, Abraham, Moses, Jesus, and Muhammad. In Islam, Muhammad is seen as the last and the greatest of the prophets.

The Quran

According to Muslim belief, Muhammad received messages from Allah for more than 20 years. These messages were not gathered into a written collection until after Muhammad died. This collection became the **Quran** (kuh·RAN), or holy book of Islam. Muslims believe the Quran is the written word of God. It contains accounts of events, teachings, and instructions.

For Muslims, the Quran provides guidelines for how to live. For example, the Quran instructs Muslims to be honest and treat others fairly. Muslims must respect their parents and be kind to their neighbors. The Quran forbids murder, lying, and stealing.

Islam stresses the need to obey the will of Allah. This means practicing acts of worship known as the Five Pillars of Islam. The Five Pillars are belief, prayer, charity, fasting, and pilgrimage.

Over centuries, Islamic scholars created a code of law called the **shari'ah** (shuh·REE·uh). *Shari'ah* is based on the Quran. According to *shari'ah*, Muslims may not gamble, eat pork, or drink alcoholic beverages. The *sunna* also guides Muslims. It is a set of customs based on Muhammad's words and deeds.

☑ **PROGRESS CHECK**

Evaluating Why is the Quran important in the daily life of Muslims?

Thinking Like a
HISTORIAN

Using a Time Line

Many important events led Muhammad to establish Islam. Select three events from his life that you consider important to his founding of Islam. Sequence them on a time line, and present your time line to the class. Be sure to explain your choices in your presentation. For more information about time lines, read *What Does a Historian Do?*

LESSON 1 REVIEW

Review Vocabulary

1. Why would the people in a *caravan* be glad to see an *oasis*?

Answer the Guiding Questions

2. *Determining Cause and Effect* How did physical geography shape life in Arabia?

3. *Explaining* Why did Muhammad and his followers move to Madinah?

4. *Describing* What is the *shari'ah* and what is it based on?

5. *NARRATIVE* Imagine that you are a bedouin. Write a letter to a friend who lives in Makkah describing a day in your life.

LESSON 2

The Spread of Islam

ESSENTIAL QUESTION

• How does religion shape society?

IT MATTERS BECAUSE

The religion of Islam continues to influence modern politics and society.

Founding an Empire

GUIDING QUESTION *How did the Arabs spread Islam and create an empire?*

When Muhammad died in A.D. 632, he left no instructions about who should be the next leader of Islam. Muslims knew that no person could take Muhammad's role as a prophet. They realized, however, that the Islamic state needed a strong leader to keep it united. A group of Muslim leaders chose a new type of leader called the **caliph** (KAY·luhf), or "successor."

The First Caliphs

The first four caliphs were close friends or relatives of Muhammad. The goal of the caliphs was to protect and spread Islam. Their military forces carried Islam beyond the Arabian Peninsula. Because the Muslim conquerors were Arab, the territory became known as the Arab Empire. By the 660s, the Arab Empire included all of southwest Asia and northeast Africa.

The Umayyads

Expansion continued under new caliphs known as the Umayyads (oo·MY·uhds). The Umayyads governed the Arab Empire from the city of Damascus (duh·MAS·kuhs) in Syria. They ruled from 661 to 750. Under the Umayyads, Muslim rule extended farther into Asia and Africa.

Reading**HELP**DESK

Taking Notes: *Summarizing*

On a diagram like this one, describe the ways in which the religion of Islam spread.

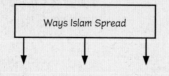

Ways Islam Spread

Content Vocabulary

• **caliph**   • **Sunni**   • **Shia**   • **sultan**

caliph a Muslim leader

A century after the death of Muhammad, Muslims had created a large and powerful empire. Arab soldiers were experienced horse riders and warriors, having raided rival tribes in the past. Now they used those same skills to fight large armies. In addition, Arab soldiers believed they had a religious duty to spread Islam.

The policies of their opponents also helped the Muslims. Byzantine and Persian rulers had tried to unite their peoples under an official religion. They often mistreated those who practiced other faiths. When Muslim armies attacked, many of these people were willing to accept Muslim rule.

After the Arabs gained control, they usually let conquered peoples practice their own religions. Islam teaches that Christians and Jews are "People of the Book," people who believe in one God and follow sacred writings. Therefore, many Muslims respect their beliefs and practices. As time passed, many of the conquered peoples in the Arab Empire became Muslims and learned the Arab language. The customs of the conquered peoples also influenced the Arab rulers. Eventually, the term *Arab* meant a speaker of Arabic, not a resident of Arabia.

Islamic Spain

Muslim warriors entered Spain from North Africa in the early 700s. They brought their religion, customs, and traditions. Spanish Muslims made the city of Córdoba a center of Islam.

Spain was home to many of Islam's greatest thinkers. Ibn Rushd (IH·buhn RUHSHT), also known as Averroës (uh·VEHR·uh·weez), practiced law and medicine in Córdoba.

GEOGRAPHY CONNECTION

After Muhammad's death, the territory of the Arab Empire expanded.

1 **MOVEMENT** What area of Europe came under Muslim control?

2 **PLACE** Describe the territories conquered by the Arabs by the year A.D. 661.

3 **CRITICAL THINKING**
Making Connections Why do you think Muslim armies entered Europe from North Africa and not through Asia Minor?

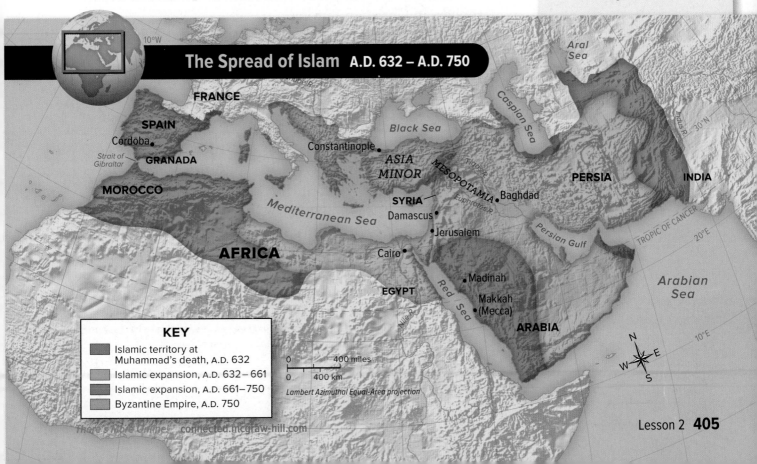

The Spread of Islam A.D. 632 – A.D. 750

KEY
- Islamic territory at Muhammad's death, A.D. 632
- Islamic expansion, A.D. 632–661
- Islamic expansion, A.D. 661–750
- Byzantine Empire, A.D. 750

0   400 miles
0   400 km
Lambert Azimuthal Equal-Area projection

FRANCE, SPAIN, Córdoba, Strait of Gibraltar, GRANADA, MOROCCO, AFRICA, Mediterranean Sea, Constantinople, Black Sea, ASIA MINOR, MESOPOTAMIA, SYRIA, Damascus, Jerusalem, Cairo, EGYPT, Red Sea, Madinah, Makkah (Mecca), ARABIA, Caspian Sea, Baghdad, Euphrates R., Tigris R., Persian Gulf, PERSIA, INDIA, Indus R., Aral Sea, Arabian Sea, TROPIC OF CANCER

There's More Online! connected.mcgraw-hill.com

THE FIRST FOUR CALIPHS

	Abu Bakr	Umar	Uthman	Ali
Relationship to Muhammad	father-in-law	friend	son-in-law, member of the Umayyad family	first cousin, son-in-law
Career	merchant	merchant	merchant	soldier, writer
Years as Caliph	A.D. 632–634	A.D. 634–644	A.D. 644–656	A.D. 656–661
Achievements as Caliph	spread Islam to all of Arabia; restored peace after death of Muhammad; created code of conduct in war; compiled Quran verses	spread Islam to Syria, Egypt, and Persia; redesigned government; paid soldiers; held a census; made taxes more fair; built roads and canals; aided poor	spread Islam into Afghanistan and eastern Mediterranean; organized a navy; improved the government; built more roads, bridges, and canals; distributed text of the Quran	reformed tax collection and other government systems; spent most of caliphate battling Muawiya, the governor of Syria

CHART

1 **IDENTIFYING** Which caliph ruled the longest? Whose rule was the shortest?

2 **CRITICAL THINKING** *Contrasting* How was Ali different from the other caliphs?

He is best known for his writings based on the works of the Greek philosopher Aristotle. Ibn Rushd's work influenced Christian and Jewish thinkers in Europe during the Middle Ages.

Muslims in Spain were generally tolerant, or accepting, of other cultures. In some schools, Muslims, Jews, and Christians studied medicine and philosophy together. In particular, the Jewish community in Córdoba flourished.

A Jewish scholar in Spain, Solomon ben Gabirol, wrote philosophy and poetry. His most famous book of philosophy, *The Well of Life*, shows the influence of the Greek philosophers. The book was translated from Arabic into Latin and influenced many philosophers in Christian Europe.

Another Jewish thinker called Moses Maimonides (my·MAHN·ih·deez) had to leave Spain at a very young age because it was conquered by a Muslim group that was not as accepting of other cultures. He later became a physician in the Muslim royal court in Egypt and wrote philosophy as well as a collection of Jewish laws.

Preachers and Traders

Muslim armies were not the only ones who spread Islam. Some Muslims used preaching to win followers to their religion. A group called Sufis (SOO·feez) won followers by teaching Islam.

Muslim merchants built trading posts throughout Southeast Asia and taught Islam to the people there. Today, the country of Indonesia (ihn·duh·NEE·zhuh) has more Muslims than any other nation in the world.

Some Muslim merchants crossed the Sahara to trade with powerful kingdoms in West Africa. In the 1300s, the West African city of Timbuktu (tihm·buhk·TOO) became a leading center of Muslim culture and learning.

☑ **PROGRESS CHECK**

Explaining Why was the Arab military successful?

Division and Growth

GUIDING QUESTION *How did the Arab Empire change after the Umayyads?*

While Arab Muslims created an empire, rival groups within Islam argued about who had the right to succeed Muhammad as caliph. Muslims divided into two groups, the **Sunni** (SU·nee) and the **Shia** (SHEE·ah). This split still divides Muslims today. Most Muslims are Sunni. Shia Muslims, however, make up most of the populations in present-day Iran and Iraq.

The Shia believed that Ali, Muhammad's son-in-law, was his rightful heir. They also believed that all future caliphs had to be Ali's descendants. According to the Shia, the Umayyad caliphs in Damascus had no right to rule. The Sunni, who outnumbered the Shia, disagreed. They recognized the Umayyad caliphs as rightful rulers, though they did not always agree with their actions.

The Shia and the Sunni agreed on the major **principles** of Islam. They both believed that there was only one God. They also believed in the Quran as Islam's holy book and the Five Pillars of Islam. In other ways, the two groups developed different religious practices and customs.

A New Dynasty

During the 700s, opposition to the Umayyad caliphs grew. Many non-Arab Muslims were angry that Arab Muslims had the best jobs and paid lower taxes. Discontent was especially strong in Mesopotamia and Persia, where Shia Islam was popular.

About 750, the Shia Muslims rebelled and won support from other Muslims throughout the empire. They overthrew the Umayyads, and the Abbasid (uh·BA·suhd) dynasty came to power. Abbasid caliphs ruled the Arab Empire until 1258.

Muslim architecture can still be found in many parts of Spain today. The high interior arches, decorative columns, and bright colors are all details of Muslim design.

▶ **CRITICAL THINKING**
Drawing Conclusions Why was Spain home to many of Islam's great thinkers?

Sunni group of Muslims who accepted the rule of the Umayyad caliphs

Shia group of Muslims who believed the descendants of Ali should rule

Academic Vocabulary

principle an important law or belief

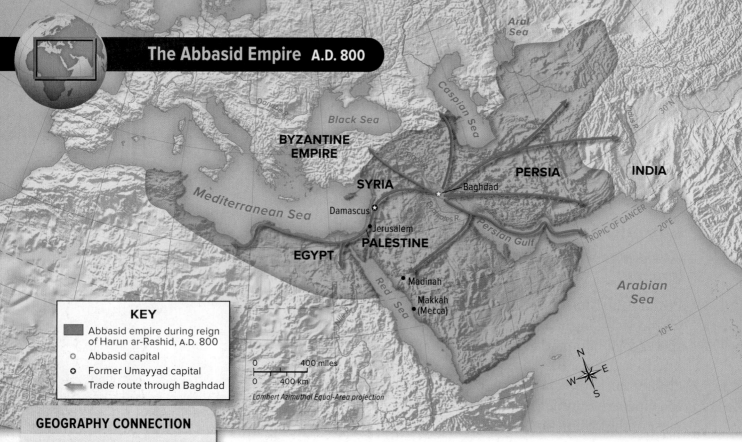

The Abbasid Empire A.D. 800

KEY

- Abbasid empire during reign of Harun ar-Rashid, A.D. 800
- ⊙ Abbasid capital
- ⊘ Former Umayyad capital
- ← Trade route through Baghdad

0   400 miles
0   400 km
Lambert Azimuthal Equal-Area projection

GEOGRAPHY CONNECTION

Baghdad became the capital of the Abbasid empire and an important center for trade.

1 REGIONS What blocked Abbasid expansion to the northwest?

2 CRITICAL THINKING
Evaluating Does Baghdad appear to be well located for trade? Explain.

The Abbasids focused on improving trade and **culture.** They made Baghdad (BAG·dad) their capital city. Baghdad's location along the Tigris River was on trade routes that connected the Mediterranean Sea to East Asia. By the 900s, Baghdad was one of the world's most beautiful and prosperous cities.

Under Abbasid rule, the Arab Empire enjoyed a golden age. The Abbasids appreciated Persian culture and brought many Persian influences into the Arab Empire.

Who are the Seljuk Turks?

The Abbasids developed a rich culture, but they could not hold their empire together. Over time, many territories broke free from Abbasid rule. In Egypt and Spain, the Muslims set up their own caliphs. Rival rulers took over much of Persia. By the 1000s, the Abbasids ruled little more than the area around Baghdad.

Around this time, the Seljuk Turks of central Asia began moving into Abbasid territory. The Seljuk Turks were nomads and great warriors. In 1055, the Seljuks seized Baghdad. They took control of the government and army but allowed the Abbasid caliph to manage religious matters. The Seljuk ruler called himself **sultan** (SUHL·tuhn), or "holder of power."

For 200 years, Seljuk sultans ruled with the Abbasid caliphs. Then, in the 1200s, people from central Asia known as the Mongols, swept into the empire. In 1258 they stormed into Baghdad. There, the Mongols burned buildings and killed more than 50,000 people. This fierce attack brought an end to the Arab Empire.

✔ PROGRESS CHECK

Comparing and Contrasting How did the Sunni and Shia differ? What beliefs did they share?

Three Muslim Empires

GUIDING QUESTION *How did the Turks, Safavids, and Moguls rule their empires?*

After the Arab Empire ended, other Muslim groups created their own empires. These empires included the Ottoman Empire based in what is now Turkey, the Safavid (sah·FAH·weed) Empire in Persia, and the Mogul Empire in India.

The Ottomans

During the late 1200s, Turkish clans settled part of Asia Minor. They called themselves Ottoman Turks, after their leader named Osman. The Ottomans conquered much of the Byzantine Empire. In 1453, the Ottoman ruler Mehmet II, known as "the Conqueror," seized the Byzantine capital, Constantinople. The Ottomans renamed the city Istanbul and made it their capital.

The Ottomans then pushed into southeastern Europe, Southwest Asia, and North Africa. The Ottomans controlled much of the Mediterranean region until the late 1500s.

The Ottoman leader was called a sultan, like the leader of the Seljuks. The most famous Ottoman sultan was Suleiman I (SOO·luh·mahn). He ruled during the 1500s. He was called "The Lawgiver" because he organized Ottoman laws. Suleiman also built many schools and mosques throughout the empire.

The Shah Mosque in Isafahan, Iran, shows traditional Muslim architecture. It is known for its interior design featuring mosaic tiles.

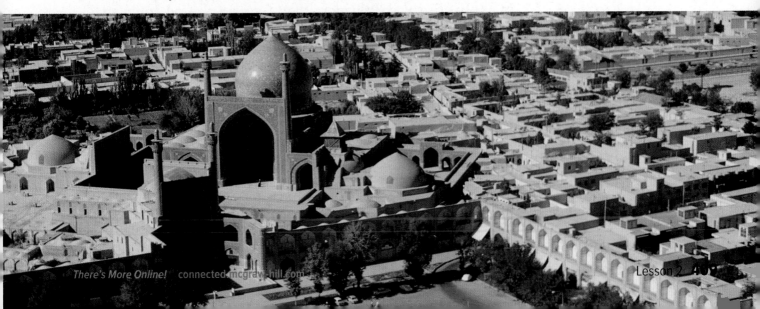

Suleiman I (1494–1566)

In 1520, at the age of 26, Suleiman I became the sultan of the Ottoman Empire. His reign is known as the Golden Age of the Ottoman Empire. He is often referred to as "Suleiman the Magnificent" or "The Lawgiver." He achieved many military successes and expanded the territory of the empire. Suleiman was responsible for the empire's greatest achievements in law, art, architecture, and literature.

▶ **CRITICAL THINKING**
Defending Why was Suleiman "magnificent"?

How Did the Ottomans Rule?

Because their empire was so large, the Ottomans ruled many peoples who practiced many religions. Islam was the empire's official religion, and Muslims enjoyed special privileges. The government passed different laws for non-Muslims. For example, non-Muslims had to pay a special tax. In return, they were free to practice their religion.

After Suleiman, the Ottoman Empire began to break down. It lost lands to the Europeans. Local rulers and conquered people broke away. The empire finally crumbled in the early 1900s.

The Safavids

In 1501, a Shia leader named Ismail proclaimed himself shah, or king, of Persia. Ismail founded the Safavid dynasty, which ruled Persia until the 1700s. During this period, Persian spread as a language of culture and trade. Urdu, a language spoken in Pakistan today, is partly based on Persian.

India's Mogul Empire

During the 1500s, the Moguls (MO·guhlz) set up a Muslim empire in India. Under Akbar (AHK·bar), the Mogul empire prospered. He allowed people to practice their religions. Later Mogul rulers, however, persecuted Hindus and Sikhs (SEEKS).

Sikhs practice the religion of Sikhism, which arose in the 1500s. The Sikhs believe in one God. They rely on one holy book, the *Adigranth*, and honor a line of teachers descending from Guru Nanak, their founder. Today, Sikhism is the world's fifth largest religion.

☑ **PROGRESS CHECK**

Identifying What is Urdu?

LESSON 2 REVIEW

Review Vocabulary

1. How did the *Sunni* feel about the Umayyad *caliphs*?

2. In addition to the Seljuks, who else used the title *sultan*?

Answer the Guiding Questions

3. *Identifying* What area of Europe came under Muslim control at this time?

4. *Describing* What changes did Abbasid rulers bring to the world of Islam?

5. *Determining Cause and Effect* What effect did the burning of Baghdad in 1258 have on the Islamic Empire?

6. *Explaining* What led to the downfall of the Ottoman Empire?

7. **INFORMATIVE/EXPLANATORY** Write a paragraph that compares how the Ottomans and Moguls each treated non-Muslims.

LESSON 3
Life in the Islamic World

ESSENTIAL QUESTION

• How do ideas change the way people live?

IT MATTERS BECAUSE

Muslim advances in mathematics, business, science, architecture, and the arts helped to create our modern society.

Daily Life and Trade

GUIDING QUESTION *How did people live and trade in the Islamic world?*

Muslim merchants controlled trade in much of Asia and Africa from the A.D. 700s until the 1400s. Their caravans traveled from Egypt and Mesopotamia to China. Their ships sailed the Indian Ocean to East Africa, India, and Southeast Asia. Muslim traders set out on their journeys with spices, cloth, glass, and carpets from their homelands. They traded these items for rubies from India, silk from China, and spices from Southeast Asia. They also traded for gold, ivory, and enslaved people from Africa. In addition, Muslim merchants sold crops such as sugar, rice, oranges, cherries, and cotton.

Why Were Muslim Traders Successful?

Muslim trade flourished for several reasons. Muslims spread the religion of Islam along with the Arabic language. As a result, Arabic became the language of business and trade in much of Asia and Africa. Muslim rulers also helped traders by providing them with coins to use for buying and selling goods. This was an easier trading method than bartering for goods.

Muslim merchants kept detailed records of their business dealings and their earnings. In time, these practices created a new industry—banking. Muslims respected merchants for their business skills and the wealth they created.

Reading**HELP**DESK

Taking Notes: *Organizing*

Draw a diagram like this one. Fill in details about Muslim contributions in the field of science.

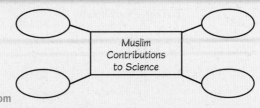

Muslim Contributions to Science

Content Vocabulary

• **mosque** • **astrolabe**
• **bazaar** • **minaret**

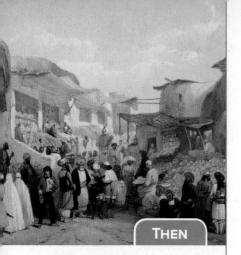

THEN

The word "bazaar" is Persian and refers to the public market district in a town. These ancient markets with many stalls and shops sold both local and imported goods from all over the world. They were the forerunners of modern shopping centers that we know today.

Now

▶ CRITICAL THINKING

Evaluating What are the advantages of having a central marketplace?

Reading**HELP**DESK

mosque a Muslim house of worship

Muslim Cities and Farms

Increased trade led to the growth of cities throughout the Islamic world. Makkah, Baghdad, Cairo (KY·roh), and Damascus were located on major trade routes. Muslim cities, however, were more than places of trade. They also became centers of government, education, and culture.

Muslim cities generally had narrow streets separating closely packed buildings. The main buildings were mosques and palaces. **Mosques** (MAHSKS) are Muslim houses of worship. They also served as schools, courts, and centers of learning.

Another important feature of every Muslim city was the **bazaar** (buh·ZAHR), or marketplace. Like shopping malls today, bazaars were full of shops and stalls where goods were sold. They were often covered to protect merchants and customers from the scorching sun. Nearby inns provided travelers a place to eat and rest.

Despite the importance of cities, most Muslims, however, lived in villages and farmed the land. The dry climate and the lack of rainfall, however, made farming difficult. Muslim farmers relied on irrigation to water their crops. They raised wheat, rice, beans, cucumbers, and melons in their fields. They planted orchards that provided almonds, apricots, figs, and olives. Farmers also grew flowers for use in perfume.

Some Muslim villagers owned small farms. Most of the productive land, however, was owned by wealthy landowners. They had large estates and hired farmers from nearby villages or used enslaved people to farm the land.

How was Muslim Society Organized?

People in the Muslim world were divided into social groups based on their power and wealth. Government leaders, landowners, and wealthy merchants held the greatest power. Below them were artisans, farmers, and workers. Enslaved people held no power.

As in other civilizations, slavery was common in Muslim lands. Many enslaved people were prisoners of war. Although they faced hardships, enslaved people had some rights under Islamic law. For example, mothers and young children could not be separated, and enslaved people could buy their freedom.

Men and women had separate roles in the Muslim world. Men were in charge of government, society, and business. Women managed their families and households.

bazaar a marketplace

(t)Image Asset Management/World History Archive/Age fotostock; (b)©Atlantide Phototravel/Corbiws

Women were also allowed to own property, invest in trade, and inherit wealth. Some upper-class women received an education and contributed to the arts.

✓ **PROGRESS CHECK**

Explaining Why were Muslim merchants successful?

Muslim Contributions

GUIDING QUESTION *What were Muslim contributions in mathematics, science, and the arts?*

Arabic was the most widely spoken language in the Muslim world. The use of Arabic helped with the exchange of goods and ideas among the different Islamic peoples. For example, in A.D. 830 the Abbasid caliph Mamun (mah·MOON) founded the House of Wisdom in Baghdad. At this research center, Muslim, Jewish, and Christian thinkers translated Greek, Persian, and Indian works into Arabic.

From the 700s to the 1400s, scholars in Muslim lands preserved learning of the ancient world. Europeans had lost many ancient Greek writings. In Spain, however, Jewish and Muslim scholars translated some Greek writings into Arabic. When these Arabic translations were translated into Latin, western Europeans learned about ancient Greek thinkers.

Science and Mathematics

At the Baghdad observatory founded by Mamun, Muslim astronomers studied the skies. These studies helped them create mathematical models of the universe. They correctly described the sun's eclipses and proved that the moon affects ocean tides. They gave many stars names that are still used today.

Muslim astronomers improved the Greek **astrolabe** (AS • truh • layb). Sailors used this tool to determine their location at sea. Muslim scientists used the astrolabe to measure the distance around the Earth. Based on their measurements, they **confirmed** that the Earth is round.

Other Muslim scientists experimented with metals. As a result, Muslims are considered the founders of chemistry. One of the most famous Muslim chemists was al-Razi (ahl-RAH·zee). Al-Razi was the first scientist to label substances as animal, vegetable, or mineral. This type of labeling is still used today.

astrolabe a tool that helps sailors navigate by the positions of the stars

Academic Vocabulary

confirm to prove that something is true; to remove doubt

— Connections to —
TODAY

Becoming a Doctor

Ancient Arab doctors had to attend medical school and pass a test before they could practice medicine. Today, doctors in the United States have similar requirements. To become a doctor, students must pass an exam to get into medical school and then complete four years of medical school. After completing those four years, medical students must pass another test to earn a license, or permit, to practice medicine. Without that license, they cannot be doctors.

Islamic civilization made important contributions to science, learning, and philosophy. This astrolabe advanced the Greek invention.

Omar Khayyam—known for his poetry—was also a mathematician, philosopher, and astronomer.

Muslims also made contributions in mathematics. The Persian scholar al-Khawarizmi (ahl-khwa·RIHZ·meh) invented algebra. He and the Arab scholar al-Kindi borrowed the symbols 0 through 9 from Hindu scholars. These numbers were passed on to Europeans. Today, they are known as "Arabic numerals."

Medicine

Muslims made important medical discoveries too. Arab doctors discovered that blood circulates, or moves, to and from the heart. They also diagnosed certain diseases. Al-Razi wrote a book identifying the differences between smallpox and measles.

Muslim doctors shared their knowledge by **publishing** their findings. The Persian doctor Ibn Sina (ih·buhn SEE·nuh) produced the *Canon of Medicine*, which described how diseases spread and analyzed hundreds of different medicines.

Unlike doctors in most other places, Arab doctors had to pass a test before they could practice medicine. The Arabs created the first medical schools and pharmacies. They also built medical clinics that gave care and medicine to the sick.

Literature

Muslims wrote non-religious literature. One of the best known works is *The Thousand and One Nights*, also called *The Arabian Nights*. It includes tales from India, Persia, and Arabia. Aladdin is one of the work's well-known characters.

Another Muslim, the Persian poet Omar Khayyam (OH·MAHR ky·YAHM), wrote the *Rubaiyat* (ROO·bee·aht). Many consider it one of the finest poems ever written. In a section of the poem, Khayyam describes the human being as a mystery:

PRIMARY SOURCE

❞ Man is a cup, his soul the wine therein,
Flesh is a pipe, spirit [give life to] the voice within;
O Khayyam, have you fathomed [figured out] what man is?
A magic lantern with a light therein! ❞

—from *The Rubaiyat* by Omar Khayyam, tr. E.H. Whinfield

©Bettmann/Corbis

Reading HELP DESK

minaret the tower of a mosque from which Muslims are called to prayer

Academic Vocabulary

publish to produce the work of an author, usually in print

Muslim scholars studied history. During the late 1300s, the Muslim historian Ibn Khaldun (IH·buhn KAL·DOON) looked for cause-and-effect relationships to explain historical events. He was one of the first historians to study how geography and climate shape human activities.

Art and Architecture

Muslims developed forms of art based on Islam and the different cultures of the Muslim world. Opposed to idol worship, Muslim leaders discouraged artists from creating images of living creatures. Instead, Muslim art included designs entwined with flowers, leaves, stars, and beautiful writing.

Muslim cities were known for their beautiful buildings. Mosques dominated the skylines of Baghdad, Damascus, Cairo, and Istanbul. The most prominent features of a mosque are its **minarets** (mih·nuh·REHTS). These are towers from which an announcer calls Muslims to prayer five times each day.

Islamic rulers lived in large palaces with central courtyards. To cool the courtyards, architects added porches, fountains, and pools. To provide protection, they surrounded the palaces with walls. One famous example of a Muslim palace is the Alhambra (al·HAM·bruh) in Granada (gruh·NAH·duh), Spain.

Another famous Muslim building is the Taj Mahal in Agra (AH·gruh), India. The Mogul ruler Shah Jahan built it as a tomb for his wife. The Taj Mahal is made of marble and precious stones and is considered one of the world's most beautiful buildings.

It took Shah Jahan's workers and craftspeople more than 20 years to build the Taj Mahal.

▶ CRITICAL THINKING

Making Inferences What does the size and beauty of the Taj Mahal say about Shah Jahan's feelings for his wife?

©Renaud Visage/age fotostock

✔ **PROGRESS CHECK**

Listing What achievements were made by Muslims in medicine?

LESSON 3 REVIEW

Review Vocabulary

1. Why is a *minaret* an important feature of a *mosque*?

Answer the Guiding Questions

2. ***Identifying*** What groups held the greatest power in Muslim society?

3. ***Explaining*** What did Muslim scientists discover once they improved the astrolabe?

4. ***Describing*** What are the defining features of Muslim art?

5. ***Summarizing*** Summarize the contributions that Muslim doctors made in the field of medicine.

6. **ARGUMENT** What Islamic invention or development do you think has had the greatest effect on our world today? Explain your choice.

Write your answers on a separate piece of paper.

1 Exploring the Essential Question

INFORMATIVE/EXPLANATORY How does the spread of a religion change the way people live? Write an essay that discusses how the influence of Islam changed the way people lived throughout the Islamic Empire. Include the influence of Islam in daily life as well as in trade, government, and culture.

2 21st Century Skills

RECOGNIZE QUALITY SOURCES Using a computer word processing program, create a five-page report on the range of Islamic arts. Include arts that flourished in the Ottoman Empire during the reign of Suleiman I. Use primary source photos and information from reliable Internet sources such as the Metropolitan Museum of Art and national Turkish museums. Include secondary source information from encyclopedias.

3 Thinking Like a Historian

SEQUENCING EVENTS Create a time line. Place these four events in the correct order on the time line:

- Mongols burn Baghdad
- Abbasids replace the Umayyads
- Muhammad begins preaching
- Suleiman I rules the Ottoman Empire

4 GEOGRAPHY ACTIVITY

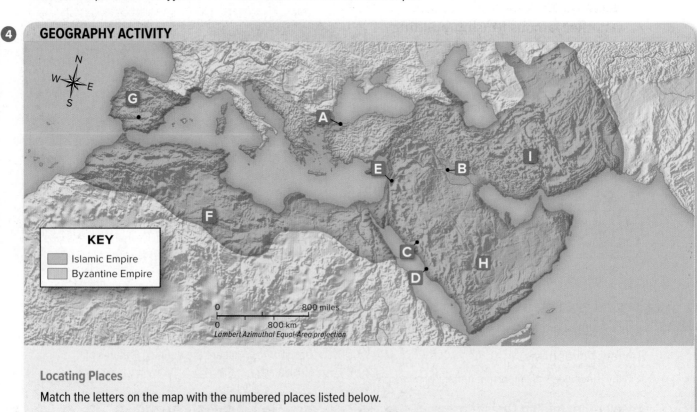

KEY
Islamic Empire
Byzantine Empire

0 — 800 miles
0 — 800 km
Lambert Azimuthal Equal-Area projection

Locating Places

Match the letters on the map with the numbered places listed below.

1. Africa
2. Arabia
3. Spain
4. Persia
5. Makkah
6. Baghdad
7. Constantinople
8. Damascus
9. Madinah

Directions: Write your answers on a separate piece of paper.

CHECKING FOR UNDERSTANDING

1 Define each of these terms as they relate to Islam.

A. oasis	**G.** Sunni
B. sheikh	**H.** Shia
C. caravan	**I.** mosque
D. Quran	**J.** bazaar
E. *shari'ah*	**K.** astrolabe
F. caliph	**L.** minaret

REVIEW THE GUIDING QUESTIONS

2 *Explaining* How did the geography of the Arabian Peninsula affect the lives of the people who lived there?

3 *Identifying* What was Muhammad's message to the people of Arabia?

4 *Listing* What are two ways that Islam provides guidance to its followers?

5 *Summarizing* Summarize how the Arabs were able to create an empire.

6 *Describing* What happened to the Arab Empire after the Umayyad caliphs?

7 *Discussing* How did the Ottoman Turks rule their empire?

8 *Identifying* When Muslim traders went to places like India, China, and Southeast Asia, what kinds of goods might they take? What might they bring back?

9 *Naming* What were three Muslim contributions to science? Use clear and coherent language when writing your answer.

10 *Specifying* What were some of the contributions that Muslims made to the arts and architecture? Use clear and coherent language when writing your answer.

CRITICAL THINKING

11 *Drawing Conclusions* Study the map of the Arab Empire in A.D. 750 at the beginning of this chapter. Why do you think the empire spread to Spain rather than to other parts of Europe, such as France and Germany?

12 *Making Connections* Why was a member's loyalty to his or her tribe extremely important to life in the desert?

13 *Making Connections* In Islam, how is the *shari'ah* related to the Quran?

14 *Analyzing Primary Sources* Study the image of Suleiman I in Lesson 2. What does the size of his turban tell you about his status and position?

15 *Comparing and Contrasting* How is a bazaar similar to a mosque? How is it different?

16 *Determining Cause and Effect* What factors led to trading becoming so important and widespread in the Islamic world? Use clear and coherent language in your explanation.

17 *Analyzing* Why do mosques typically contain designs such as flowers and stars rather than illustrations of people and animals?

18 *Making Decisions* If you were a merchant crossing the desert in A.D. 500, would you rather travel with one or two close friends or with a caravan of several hundred people? Explain your answer.

19 *Defending* When the Muslims conquered a new territory, they usually let the people continue to practice their own religion. Do you think this was a good idea or a bad idea? Defend your choice.

20 *Speculating* What might have happened to Greek knowledge if Jewish and Muslim scholars had not translated some Greek writings into Arabic between 700 and 1400?

Need Extra Help?

If You've Missed Question	**1**	**2**	**3**	**4**	**5**	**6**	**7**	**8**	**9**	**10**	**11**	**12**	**13**	**14**	**15**	**16**	**17**	**18**	**19**	**20**
Review Lesson	1, 2, 3	1	1	1	2	2	2	3	3	3	Opener	1	1	2	3	3	3	1	2	3

TEXT: "Persia." Student Encyclopaedia. Britannica Online for Kids. Encyclopaedia Britannica, 2011. Web. 4 Jan. 2011.

DBQ SHORT RESPONSE

*"In the 7th century [600s] Persia fell to the conquering armies of Islam. **Islamic** rule, under the **empire** of the caliphate, persisted for the next seven centuries. … Although Islam gave the Persians a wholly new religion and altered their way of living, Persian culture remained intact [unchanged]."*

—from "Islamic Dynasties" in *Encyclopedia Britannica Kids*

21 How did Islamic rule affect the Persians?

22 How did allowing Persian culture to remain unchanged strengthen the Islamic Empire?

EXTENDED RESPONSE

23 *Narrative* You are a merchant during the era of the Umayyads. You travel the empire buying and selling goods. Write a diary entry describing one of your travels.

STANDARDIZED TEST PRACTICE

DBQ ANALYZING DOCUMENTS

Baghdad became a center of political and cultural power. A visitor, Yakut, describes the city after visiting it in A.D. 800.

"Baghdad formed two vast semi-circles on the right and left banks of the Tigris. … Baghdad was a veritable [true] City of Palaces, not made of stucco and mortar, but of [precious] marble."

—from *Readings in Ancient History,* edited by William Stearns Davis

24 *Summarizing* Which statement best summarizes Yakut's opinion about Baghdad?
   A. Yakut is critical of Baghdad.
   B. Yakut describes Baghdad as a small city on the Tigris River.
   C. Yakut sees Baghdad as a poor city.
   D. Yakut's description paints Baghdad as a splendid city of fine buildings.

25 *Comparing and Contrasting* Why does Yakut mention building materials?
   A. All these materials were scarce throughout the Islamic Empire.
   B. The building materials show how magnificent Baghdad was.
   C. Stucco and mortar were unusual building materials.
   D. Marble was a common building material throughout the Islamic Empire.

Need Extra Help?

If You've Missed Question	**21**	**22**	**23**	**24**	**25**
Review Lesson	2	2	2	2	2

◄ *The African kingdom of Benin became well known for the detailed works of its artists, such as this ivory carving.*

400 B.C. TO A.D. 1500

African Civilizations

Peter Horree/Alamy

THE STORY MATTERS ...

Around A.D. 1400 the steamy rain forests of Africa were home to the kingdom of Benin. The region's steamy climate and fertile soil allowed farmers to grow surpluses of crops. Over time, communities and societies developed.

As a result, arts became very important in Benin. The kingdom became well known for the ivory and wood carvings its artists produced. An example is this rare pendant carved in ivory in honor of Queen Idia. Other artists worked with metals to produce realistic-looking masks. Today, this surviving art allows historians to learn more about the rich history and culture of early African civilizations.

ESSENTIAL QUESTIONS

- Why do people trade?
- How does religion shape society?
- How do religions develop?

Place & Time: AFRICA 400 B.C. to A.D. 1500

The earliest civilizations in Africa emerged about five thousand years ago. These early kingdoms developed rich cultures that excelled at many art forms. Later African empires were affected by the arrival of Islam and then Europeans. All had an impact creating the Africa we know today.

Step Into the Place

MAP FOCUS The vast and varied landscape of Africa influenced the development of civilizations on the continent.

1 **REGION** In which part of Africa would you find the most land that is difficult to farm?

2 **PLACE** What climate region runs along the Equator in Africa?

3 **LOCATION** Describe the location of the Mediterranean climate in Africa.

4 **CRITICAL THINKING**
Human-Environment Interaction
What impact do you think the Great Rift Valley might have had on where people settled?

The geography of Africa has determined where people settle. This aerial photo of Cape Town, South Africa, shows a coastal city. The Table Bay Harbour is visible in the foreground. Near it stands the Greenpoint Stadium, home of the 2010 men's soccer World Cup.

Wildlife abounds in Africa. Individual countries now have laws protecting their wildlife. These elephants, living near Kilimanjaro, are a protected species. Environmentalists are concerned about other types of wildlife. All over the continent, animal life is recognized as one of Africa's most valuable resources.

(t)Eric Nathan/Photographer's Choice/Getty Images; (b)©DLILLC/Corbis

Step Into the Time

TIME LINE A variety of climates are found in Africa. According to the time line, where and in what climate zone did the earliest kingdoms appear?

c. 250 B.C. Mali is West Africa's largest trading center

c. A.D. 250 Bantu peoples settle south of Sahara

AFRICAN CIVILIZATIONS

THE WORLD

500 B.C.   A.D. 1   A.D. 500

c. 312 B.C. Romans build Appian Way

c. 44 B.C. Julius Caesar killed

c. A.D. 400 Yamato control Japan

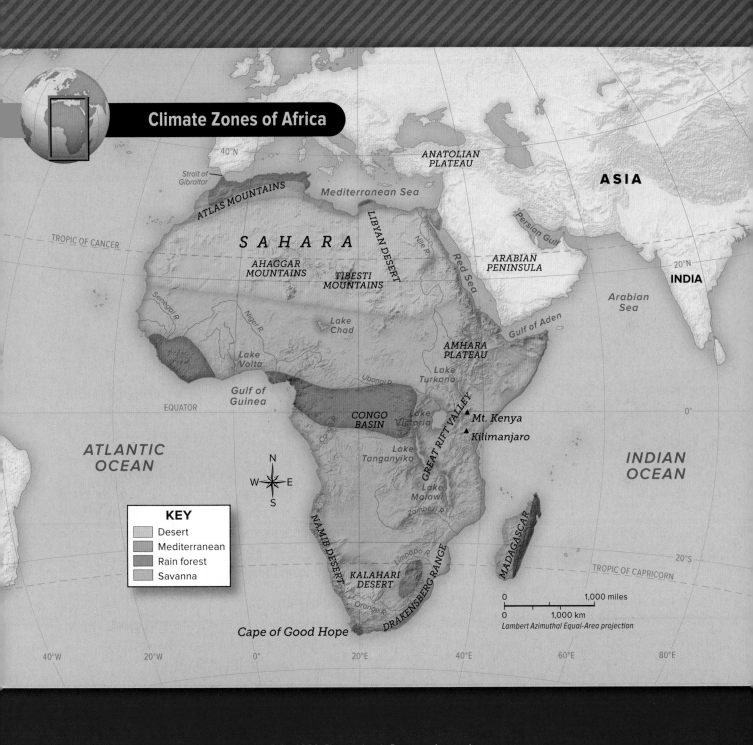

Climate Zones of Africa

40°N

Strait of Gibraltar

ATLAS MOUNTAINS

Mediterranean Sea

ANATOLIAN PLATEAU

ASIA

TROPIC OF CANCER

S A H A R A

LIBYAN DESERT

AHAGGAR MOUNTAINS

TIBESTI MOUNTAINS

Nile R.

Red Sea

Persian Gulf

ARABIAN PENINSULA

20°N

INDIA

Senegal R.

Niger R.

Lake Chad

Gulf of Aden

Arabian Sea

Lake Volta

AMHARA PLATEAU

Lake Turkana

EQUATOR

Gulf of Guinea

Ubangi R.

CONGO BASIN

Congo R.

Lake Victoria

GREAT RIFT VALLEY

▲ Mt. Kenya

▲ Kilimanjaro

0°

ATLANTIC OCEAN

N
W   E
S

Lake Tanganyika

INDIAN OCEAN

Lake Malawi

Zambezi R.

KEY
- Desert
- Mediterranean
- Rain forest
- Savanna

NAMIB DESERT

KALAHARI DESERT

Limpopo R.

DRAKENSBERG RANGE

MADAGASCAR

20°S

TROPIC OF CAPRICORN

Orange R.

Cape of Good Hope

0   1,000 miles
0   1,000 km
Lambert Azimuthal Equal-Area projection

40°W   20°W   0°   20°E   40°E   60°E   80°E

c. A.D. 1441 First captives in European slave trade

c. A.D. 800s–900s Ghana is trading empire

c. A.D. 1352 Ibn Battuta reaches West Africa

c. A.D. 1493 Muhammad Ture rules Songhai

A.D. 1000   **A.D. 1100**   **A.D. 1200**   **A.D. 1300**   **A.D. 1400**   **A.D. 1500**

The Rise of African Civilizations

ESSENTIAL QUESTION
• Why do people trade?

IT MATTERS BECAUSE
The geography of Africa affected the development and interaction of civilizations all over the huge continent.

African Beginnings

GUIDING QUESTION *How did early peoples settle Africa?*

People have lived in Africa for a very long time. Scientists believe that the first humans appeared in eastern and southern Africa between 150,000 and 200,000 years ago. Early human groups in Africa lived as hunters and gatherers. These early peoples moved from place to place to hunt and gather food.

About seven or eight thousand years ago, hunters and gatherers in Africa began to settle in villages. They learned to tame animals and grow crops. Around 3000 B.C., as farming villages became more widespread and organized, Africa's first civilizations developed. These early civilizations were Egypt and Kush.

A Vast and Varied Landscape

The people of Africa found opportunities and challenges in the geography of the continent. First of all, Africa is very large in size. After Asia, Africa is the world's largest continent.

Most of Africa lies in the Tropics. However, this enormous continent is made up of four distinct geographic zones.

Rain forests stretch along the Equator, which slices through the middle of the continent. These forests make up about 10 percent of Africa's land **area**. The rain forest zone gets heavy rainfall, and it is warm there all year long. The dense growth of

---

Reading **HELP**DESK

Taking Notes: *Identifying*

On a chart like this one, list the three major West African trading kingdoms. Then add one product that each kingdom traded.

West African Kingdom	Product

Content Vocabulary

• **savanna**   • **griot**
• **plateau**   • **dhow**

Geography and Climate Zones in Africa

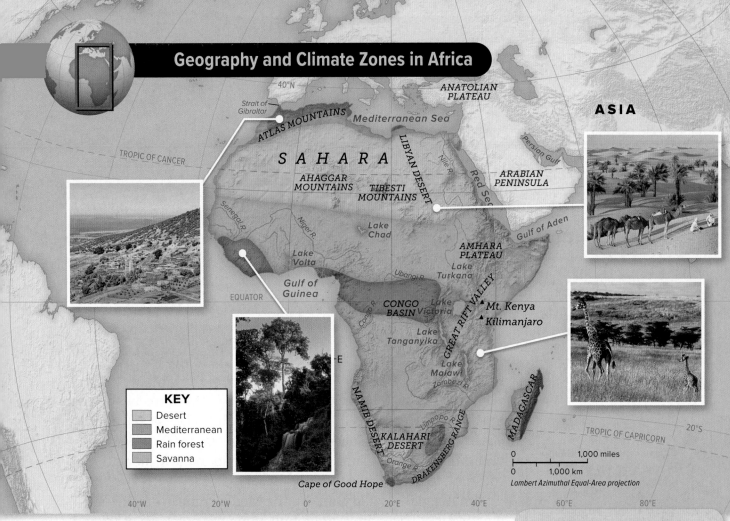

KEY
- Desert
- Mediterranean
- Rain forest
- Savanna

0 — 1,000 miles
0 — 1,000 km
Lambert Azimuthal Equal-Area projection

trees and plants in the rain forest can make farming difficult. Farmers, however, clear some of the forestland to grow root crops, such as yams.

Grasslands and Deserts

Vast grasslands make up the second zone. They stretch north and south of the rain forest. **Savannas** (suh·VAN·uhs) are tropical grasslands dotted with small trees and shrubs. These flat or rolling plains cover about 40 percent of Africa's land area. The savannas have high temperatures and uneven rains. However, they get enough rainfall for farming and herding. Farmers grow grains, such as millet and sorghum (SAWR·guhm). Herders raise cattle and other animals.

In northern Africa, the savannas connect with an area of even drier grasslands known as the Sahel (SA·hil). Plants that grow there provide barely enough food for people and animals. The people of the Sahel were traditionally hunters and herders.

GEOGRAPHY CONNECTION

Differences in geographic features, such as climate, have had a strong influence on life in Africa's geographic zones.

1 **LOCATION** Which geographic feature covers most of East Africa?

2 **CRITICAL THINKING**
Making Inferences How might the geographic zones of Africa have affected interaction between people from the northeastern and northwestern parts of the continent?

---

savanna tropical grasslands dotted with small trees and shrubs

Academic Vocabulary

area the land included within a set of boundaries

Reading Strategy: *Contrasting*

When you contrast two things, you determine how they are different from each other. Read the information about savannas and the Sahel. On a separate sheet of paper, explain how these two areas differ.

There's More Online! connected.mcgraw-hill.com

	Africa	United States
Size	11,667,159 square miles (30,217,894 sq. km)	3,794,085 square miles (9,826,680 sq. km)
Population Today	about 1.03 billion people	about 308 million people
Longest River	Nile River 4,160 miles (6,693 km)	Missouri River 2,565 miles (4,130 km)
Largest Desert	Sahara 3,500,000 square miles (9,065,000 sq. km)	Mojave 15,000 square miles (38,850 sq. km)

UNITED STATES

AFRICA

Encyclopaedia Britannica OnLine s.v., "Africa," http://www.britannica.com/EBchecked/topic/7924/Africa

INFOGRAPHIC

Many areas of Africa remain mostly unpopulated. Africa's population represents only about 10 percent of the world's total population.

1 IDENTIFYING What are the longest rivers in Africa and the United States?

2 CRITICAL THINKING
Comparing and Contrasting
How do Africa and the United States compare in size and population?

Deserts are Africa's third zone. They are found north and south of the grasslands. About 40 percent of the land in Africa is desert. The world's largest desert—the Sahara—stretches across much of North Africa. The Kalahari (KA·luh·HAHR·ee), another desert region, lies in southwestern Africa. For many years, the deserts limited travel and trade. People had to move along the coastline to avoid these vast seas of sand.

Small areas of mild climate—the Mediterranean—make up the fourth zone. These areas are found along the northern coast and southern tip of Africa. In these areas, **adequate** rainfall, warm temperatures, and fertile land produce abundant crops. This food surplus can support large populations.

Africa's Landforms and Rivers

Most of Africa is covered by a series of plateaus. A **plateau** (pla· TOH) is an area of high and mostly flat land. In East Africa, mountains, valleys, and lakes cross the plateau. Millions of years ago, movements of the Earth's crust created deep cuts in the surface of the plateau. This activity created the Great Rift Valley. In recent years, scientists have found some of the earliest human fossils in the Great Rift Valley.

Many large river systems are found in Africa. The civilizations of Egypt and Kush flourished along the banks of the Nile River in North Africa. The major river system in West Africa is found along the Niger (NY·juhr) River. Trade and farming led to the growth of villages and towns throughout the Niger River area.

Reading**HELP**DESK

plateau an area of high and mostly flat land

Academic Vocabulary

adequate enough to satisfy a need
transport to transfer or carry from one place to another

People living south of the Sahara also learned to make iron. This skill spread from East and Central Africa to West Africa. By 250 B.C., Djenné-jeno (jeh·NAY-JEH·noh) emerged as the largest trading center in West Africa. Its artisans produced iron tools, gold jewelry, copper goods, and pottery.

 PROGRESS CHECK

Determining Cause and Effect How did Africa's climate zones affect people's ability to raise crops?

This photo shows the Great Rift Valley, a deep crack in Earth's crust that is 6,000 miles (9,659 km) long. The valley began forming 20 million years ago.

Trading Empires in Africa

GUIDING QUESTION *How did trade develop in Africa?*

For thousands of years, the hot, dry Sahara isolated North Africa from the rest of the continent. Then, about 400 B.C., the Berber people of North Africa found ways to cross the Sahara to West Africa. Trade soon opened between the two regions.

How Did the Sahara Trade Develop?

For hundreds of years, the Berbers carried goods across the Sahara on donkeys and horses. The animals often did not survive the desert heat. The Romans introduced the central Asian camel in A.D. 200. The use of camels greatly changed trade in Africa. Camels are well suited for the desert. Their humps store fat for food, and they can travel for many days without water. The Berbers quickly adopted camels, both as a source of food and as a way to travel.

Berber traders formed caravans of many camels. These caravans crossed the Sahara between North Africa and West Africa. West African merchants sent gold mined in their region to towns bordering the Sahara. From there, caravans carried the gold northward. Some of this African gold reached Europe and Asia. Christian and Muslim rulers in these areas valued African gold.

Caravans from West Africa also carried ivory, spices, leather, and ostrich feathers. In addition, they **transported** enslaved people captured in wars. Merchants sent these captives to the Mediterranean area and Southwest Asia where they were forced to serve as soldiers or servants.

 PROGRESS CHECK

Explaining Why were camels essential for the Sahara trade?

West African Kingdoms

GUIDING QUESTION *Why did West African trading empires rise and fall?*

Caravans also headed from North Africa to West Africa. They transported cloth, weapons, horses, paper, and books. Once in West Africa, they traded for salt from mines in the Sahara.

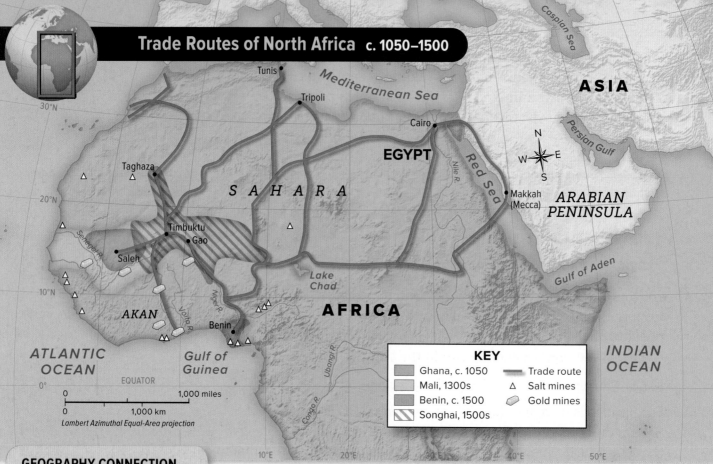

Trade Routes of North Africa c. 1050–1500

Tunis

Mediterranean Sea

Tripoli

ASIA

Cairo

EGYPT

S A H A R A

Taghaza

Timbuktu
Gao

Saleh

AKAN

Benin

Lake
Chad

A F R I C A

Red Sea

Nile R.

Makkah
(Mecca)

ARABIAN
PENINSULA

Gulf of Aden

Caspian Sea

Persian Gulf

Senegal R.

Niger R.

Volta R.

ATLANTIC
OCEAN

Gulf of
Guinea

EQUATOR

Ubangi R.

Congo R.

INDIAN
OCEAN

0   1,000 miles

0   1,000 km

Lambert Azimuthal Equal-Area projection

30°N

20°N

10°N

0°

10°E   20°E   30°E   40°E   50°E

KEY

▨	Ghana, c. 1050	▬	Trade route
▨	Mali, 1300s	△	Salt mines
▨	Benin, c. 1500	⬭	Gold mines
▨	Songhai, 1500s		

GEOGRAPHY CONNECTION

The opening of trade routes allowed
the people of North Africa and West
Africa to exchange products, such as
gold and salt.

1 LOCATION What resource was
found in the kingdom of Benin?

2 CRITICAL THINKING
Calculating Use the map's scale
to determine how many miles a
caravan might travel along a route
from Tunis to Benin.

During the A.D. 700s, Berber and Arab traders brought Islam to
West Africa. They established ties with West African merchants,
many of whom became Muslims.

The Saharan trade brought prosperity to West Africa. As a
result of trade, the population grew, and powerful city-states
emerged in the region. Eventually, rulers of these city-states
began to build empires. From the A.D. 500s to the A.D. 1300s, these
African empires were bigger than most European kingdoms in
wealth and size.

How Did Ghana Begin?

Ghana (GAH·nuh) was the first great trading empire in West
Africa. It rose to power during the A.D. 400s. The kingdom of
Ghana was located in the Sudan. This area was mostly grassland,
stretching across north central Africa. Fertile soil and iron tools
helped the farmers of Ghana produce enough food.

Ghana was located between the Sahara salt mines and
gold mines near the West African coastal rain forests. As a
result, Ghana became an important crossroads of trade. From
Ghana, trade routes extended into North Africa to the Niger River.

Reading HELP DESK

Reading in the Content Area

When reading primary source quotes, note any words or phrases
in brackets. The use of brackets provides you with additional
words that help clarify the meaning of the quote.

griot traditional storytellers

They also linked to kingdoms in the Central African rain forest. Some routes reached all the way to Africa's eastern coast.

Traders interested in salt or gold had to pass through Ghana, which came at a price. Traders had no choice but to pay taxes to Ghana's kings. First, Ghana had iron ore and knew how to make iron weapons. Although Ghana owned no gold mines, it controlled the West Africans who did. Second, Ghana's kings had a well-trained army to enforce their wishes. Third, people were willing to pay any price for salt, a highly desired item used to flavor and preserve food. Berber traders wanted gold so they could buy goods from Arab countries and from Europe.

Abdullah Abu-Ubayd Al-Bakri (ehl·BEHK·ree), an Arab travelling writer in about A.D. 1067, described the way Ghana taxed merchants:

PRIMARY SOURCE

❝ The king [of Ghana] exacts the right of one dinar [of gold] on each donkey-load of salt that enters his country, and two dinars of gold on each load of salt that goes out. ❞

—from *Ghana* in 1067

Ghana reached the height of its trading power in the A.D. 800s and 900s. Muslim Arabs and Berbers involved in the salt and gold trade brought Islam to Ghana.

Rise of Mali

During the A.D. 1100s, invaders from North Africa disrupted Ghana's trade, and the empire fell. As Ghana weakened, local groups separated to form new trading states in West Africa.

In the A.D. 1200s, a small state named Mali (MAH·lee) conquered Ghana. Mali created a new empire. West African **griots** (GREE·ohz), or storytellers, credit a great king for Mali's rise. His name was Sundiata Keita (sun·dee·AH·tuh KY·tuh)—the "Lion Prince." Sundiata ruled from 1230 to 1255. He united the people of Mali.

Sundiata conquered territory extending from the Atlantic coast inland to the trading city of Timbuktu (TIHM·BUHK·TOO). His conquests put Mali in control of the gold mines in West Africa. As a result, Mali built its wealth and power on the gold and salt trade.

How Did Songhai Begin?

Mali weakened after the death of king Mansa Musa (MAHN·sah moo·SAH) in 1337. One of the states that eventually broke away from Mali's control was Songhai (SAWNG·eye). In 1464, Sunni Ali (sun·EE ah·LEE) became the ruler of Songhai. He seized control of Timbuktu. Sunni Ali used Songhai's location along the Niger River to extend his territory.

There's More Online! connected.mcgraw-hill.com

This West African sculpture is of the Queen Mother of Benin. Benin had great rulers. By the mid-1500s, the kingdom of Benin stretched from the Niger River delta to what is now Lagos.

AFRICAN TRADING EMPIRES A.D. 100–1600

	East Africa	West Africa	West Africa	West Africa	SE Africa
Location	AXUM Adulis	GHANA Saleh	MALI Timbuktu	SONGHAI Gao	ZIMBABWE Great Zimbabwe
Time Period	c. 100–1400	c. 400–1200	c. 1200–1450	c. 1000–1600	c. 700–1450
What Was Traded	ivory, frankincense, myrrh, enslaved people	iron products, animal products, salt, gold	salt, gold	salt, gold	gold, copper, ivory
Key Facts	King Ezana converted to Christianity; made it the official religion.	Taxes from traders passing through made Ghana rich.	King Mansa Musa built mosques and libraries.	Songhai gained control of West African trade by conquering Timbuktu.	Kings Mutota and Matope built huge empires.

INFOGRAPHIC

West African empires controlled trade for more than 1,000 years.

1 **IDENTIFYING** How long after the decline of Ghana did the Songhai Empire come to an end?

2 **CRITICAL THINKING** *Comparing and Contrasting* How were the goods traded by Ghana and Mali alike and different?

He took control of the river and then seized the salt mines. Songhai soon controlled the trade in salt from the Sahara and gold. By 1492, Songhai was the largest empire in West Africa. Invaders from North Africa ended the empire by A.D. 1600.

The West African kingdoms ruled the savannas. The rain forest, near the Equator, also had its own kingdoms. They included Benin, which arose in the Niger delta, and Kongo, which formed in the Congo River basin.

✓ **PROGRESS CHECK**

Identifying What were two valuable products traded through Ghana?

East African Kingdoms

GUIDING QUESTION *How did trade affect the development of East African kingdoms?*

In ancient times, powerful kingdoms also arose in East Africa. The kingdom of Kush thrived on the Nile River for hundreds of years. One of Kush's neighbors was the kingdom of Axum (AHK·SOOM) on the Red Sea.

Axum benefited from its location on the Red Sea. It was an important stop on the trade route linking Africa, the Mediterranean, and India. Axum exported ivory, incense, and enslaved people. It imported cloth, metal goods, and olive oil.

Reading**HELP**DESK

dhow sailboat using wind-catching, triangular sails

Axum fought Kush for control of trade routes to inland Africa. Around A.D. 300, King Ezana (ay·ZAHN·uh) conquered Kush. In A.D. 334, Ezana made Christianity the official religion of Axum. Islam was introduced to Axum later. Both religions had a major impact on Axum and other trading states.

Coastal States

In the early A.D. 600s, Arab traders from the Arabian Peninsula had reached East Africa. They sailed to Africa in boats called **dhows** (dowz). In the A.D. 700s, many Arab Muslim traders settled along the Indian Ocean in East Africa. They shared goods and ideas with Africans living there. By the 1300s, a string of key trading ports extended down the East African coast. They included Mogadishu (MAH·guh·DIH·shoo), Kilwa, Mombasa (mahm·BAH·suh), and Zanzibar (ZAN·zuh·BAHR).

The Rise of Zimbabwe

The Indian Ocean trade reached far inland and led to the rise of wealthy states in Central and Southern Africa. These inland territories mined rich deposits of copper and gold. During the A.D. 900s, traders from the coastal cities of Africa began to trade with the inland states. The coastal traders brought silk, glass beads, carpets, and pottery. They traded for minerals, ivory, and coconut oil. They also bought enslaved Africans for export to countries overseas.

An important trading state known as Zimbabwe (zihm·BAH·bway) arose in southeastern Africa. During the 1400s, this large empire reached from south of the Zambezi (zam·BEE·zee) River to the Indian Ocean.

A dhow usually had one or two sails. The bow, or front, of a dhow pointed sharply upward.

▶ CRITICAL THINKING
Making Inferences How do you think an invention such as the sails used on dhows might have benefited the Arab traders?

✓ **PROGRESS CHECK**

Explaining Why did Axum become a prosperous trading center?

Mary Evans Picture Library

LESSON 1 REVIEW

Review Vocabulary

1. How is a *savanna* different from a *plateau*?

Answer the Guiding Questions

2. *Explaining* What are the four main geographic zones of Africa?

3. *Identifying* What role did the cities of Mogadishu and Mombasa play in the economic life of East Africa?

4. *Naming* What products did West Africans trade?

5. *Describing* What unique factors allowed the East African trading kingdoms to expand their trade?

6. **NARRATIVE** You live in ancient West Africa. Your family is traveling to East Africa. In a personal journal, describe what you might experience when you arrive in East Africa. Tell about the people, land, and weather.

Africa's Governments and Religions

• How does religion shape society?

IT MATTERS BECAUSE

Ancient African societies showed the effects of government disputes, traditional religious beliefs, and Islam.

African Rulers and Society

GUIDING QUESTION *How did African rulers govern their territories?*

In most ancient societies, rulers were isolated from their subjects. In Africa south of the Sahara, the distance between kings and the common people was not as great. Often, African rulers would hold meetings to let their people voice complaints. In Ghana, drums called the people to the king. Anybody with a concern could address him. Before talking, subjects demonstrated their respect. They poured dust over their heads or fell to the ground. Next, they bowed and stated their business. Then they waited for their king's reply.

Kings and the People

Africans developed different ways to rule their territories. Powerful states, such as Ghana and Mali, favored strong central governments. Power rested with the rulers. They settled disputes, controlled trade, and defended the empire. They expected total loyalty from their people. Everyone benefited from the relationship. Merchants received favors from kings and paid the kings taxes in return. Local rulers held some power and gave the kings their support. This system allowed kingdoms to grow rich, control their lands, and keep the peace.

Reading**HELP**DESK

Taking Notes: *Organizing*

In a graphic organizer like this one, record at least one accomplishment of each of the leaders listed.

Leader	Accomplishments
Mansa Musa	
Muhammad Ture	
Askia Muhammad	

Content Vocabulary

• clan   • Swahili

What Was Ghana's Government Like?

The kings of Ghana were strong rulers who played active roles in running the kingdom with the help of ministers and advisors. As the empire grew, the kings divided their territory into provinces. Lesser kings often governed the provinces, which were made up of districts and governed by district chiefs. Each district was composed of villages belonging to the chief's **clan**. A clan is a group of people descended from the same ancestor.

Ghana's government had a **unique** method of transferring power from one ruler to another. "This is their custom and their habit," stated an Arab writer, "that the kingdom is inherited only by the son of the king's sister." In Arab lands, property was inherited by a man's sons. In Ghana, leadership passed to the king's nephew.

The Government of Mali

Mali had a government like that of Ghana, but on a grander scale. Mali had more territory, more people, and more trade. As a result, royal officials had more responsibilities.

Mali's kings controlled a strong central government. The empire was divided into provinces, like those of Ghana. However, the kings put generals in charge of these areas. Many people supported the generals because the generals protected Mali from invaders. Also, the generals often came from the provinces they ruled.

Mansa Musa, Mali's most powerful king, won the loyalty of his subjects by giving them gold, property, and horses. He gave military heroes the "National Honor of the Trousers." As one Arab writer said:

This king of Benin was treated with respect by his subjects. This carving shows a public gathering.

▶ CRITICAL THINKING
Analyzing How does this carving show us that the people honored their king?

PRIMARY SOURCE

❝ Whenever a hero adds to the lists of his exploits [adventures], the king gives him a pair of wide trousers. ... [T]he greater the number of the knight's [soldier's] exploits, the bigger the size of his trousers. ❞
—from *Medieval West Africa: Views from Arab Scholars and Merchants*, excerpt by Ibn Fadl Allah al-'Umari

In Mali, only the king and his family could wear clothing that was sewn, like the clothes we wear today. Other people wore pieces of cloth wrapped around their bodies to form clothing. The trousers awarded to military heroes were truly a great honor.

Werner Forman/Art Resource, NY

clan a group of people descended from the same ancestor

Academic Vocabulary

unique one of a kind

The kings of Ghana taxed gold. This tax helped to control the amount of gold produced.

Government in Songhai

Songhai built on the political traditions of Ghana and Mali. It reached the height of its power under Muhammad Ture. A general and a devout Muslim, Muhammad Ture seized power in 1493 and created a new dynasty. He was a capable administrator who divided Songhai into provinces. A governor, a tax collector, a court of judges, and a trade inspector ran each province. Muhammad Ture **maintained** the peace and security of his empire with a navy and soldiers on horseback.

☑ PROGRESS CHECK

Describing Why did many people in Mali support the generals who ruled the provinces?

Traditional African Religions

GUIDING QUESTION *How did traditional religions influence African life?*

Most African societies shared some common religious beliefs. One of these was a belief in a single creator god. Many groups, however, carried out their own religious practices. These practices differed from place to place. For example, the Yoruba lived in West Africa. They believed that their chief god sent his son from heaven in a canoe. The son then created the first humans. This religion was practiced by many of the enslaved people brought by Europeans to the Americas.

In some religions, the creator god was linked to a group of lesser gods. The Ashanti people of Ghana believed in a supreme god whose sons were lesser gods. Others held that the creator god had once lived on Earth but left in anger at human behavior. This god, however, was forgiving if people corrected their ways.

Even though Africans practiced different religions in different places, their beliefs served similar purposes. They provided rules for living and helped people honor their history and ancestors. Africans also relied on religion to protect them from harm and to **guarantee** success in life. A special group of people, called diviners, were believed to have the power to predict events. Kings often hired diviners to guarantee good harvests and protect their kingdoms.

☑ PROGRESS CHECK

Explaining What was the role of diviners in African religion?

Photodisc/Getty Images

Reading**HELP**DESK

Academic Vocabulary

maintain to keep in the same state
guarantee to promise

challenge to present with difficulties
convert to accept a new belief

Reading in the Content Area

When you interpret a circle graph, remember that each slice or wedge represents a part of the whole. That is, a slice may stand for a fraction or a percentage—a smaller part of the whole.

Islam Arrives in Africa

GUIDING QUESTION *How did Islam spread in Africa?*

Beginning in the A.D. 700s, traditional African religions were **challenged** by the arrival of Islam. Through trade, Berber and Arab merchants eventually introduced Muslim beliefs to West Africa. African rulers welcomed Muslim traders and allowed their people to **convert** to Islam. The rulers did not become Muslims themselves until the A.D. 1000s. By the end of the 1400s, much of the population south of the Sahara had converted to Islam.

Who Was Ibn Battuta?

Ibn Battuta (IH·buhn bat·TOO·tah) was a young Arab lawyer from Morocco. In 1325, he set out to see the Muslim world. He reached West Africa in 1352. There, he found that people had been following Islam for centuries. Yet not all West Africans were Muslims. People in rural areas still followed traditional African religions. Some rulers and traders accepted Islam only because it helped them trade with Muslim Arabs.

Ibn Battuta described in detail the people and places of West Africa. Some things amazed him. He was surprised that women did not cover their faces with a veil, as was the Muslim custom.

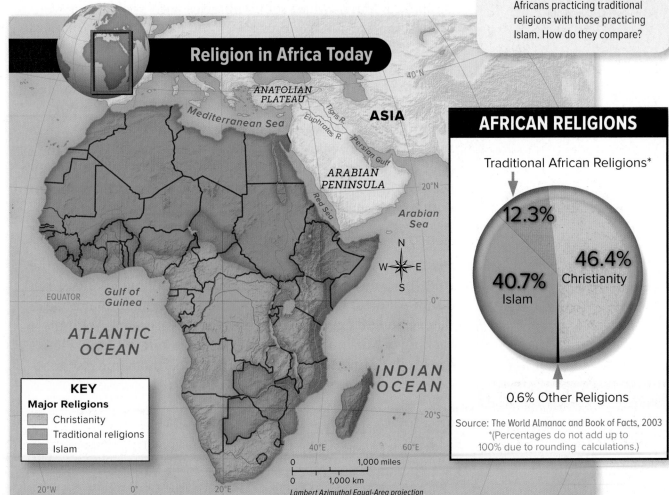

Religion in Africa Today

ANATOLIAN PLATEAU

Mediterranean Sea

Tigris R.
Euphrates R.
Persian Gulf

ASIA

ARABIAN PENINSULA

Red Sea

Arabian Sea

40°N

20°N

N
W E
S

ATLANTIC OCEAN

EQUATOR   Gulf of Guinea

0°

INDIAN OCEAN

20°S

KEY
Major Religions
- Christianity
- Traditional religions
- Islam

40°E   60°E

0   1,000 miles

0   1,000 km

Lambert Azimuthal Equal-Area projection

20°W   0°   20°E

AFRICAN RELIGIONS

Traditional African Religions*

12.3%

46.4%
Christianity

40.7%
Islam

0.6% Other Religions

Source: The World Almanac and Book of Facts, 2003
*(Percentages do not add up to 100% due to rounding calculations.)

Muslim architecture, such as this mosque, demonstrates the lasting influence of Islam in Africa.

However, he did find that West African Muslims "zealously [eagerly] learned the Quran by heart" and faithfully performed their religious duties:

❝ On Fridays, if a man does not go early to the mosque [a Muslim place of worship], he cannot
find a corner to pray in, on account of the crowd.
It is a custom of theirs to send each man his boy
[to the mosque] with his prayer-mat; the boy spreads
it out for his master in a place befitting him [and remains on it]
until he comes to the mosque. Their prayer-mats are made of
the leaves of a tree resembling a date-palm, but without fruit. ❞

—from Travels in Asia and Africa, by Ibn Battuta

The Journey of Mansa Musa

Ibn Battuta was impressed by Mansa Musa, Mali's most famous ruler. Mansa Musa let his subjects practice different religions. However, he was devoted to spreading Islam. Mansa Musa used his empire's wealth to build more mosques. In Timbuktu, Mansa Musa set up libraries with books from around the Muslim world.

In 1324, Mansa Musa increased the fame of Mali during a journey to Makkah (MAH·kuh). All Muslims are expected to travel to the Muslim holy city of Makkah. Mansa Musa made certain that people knew he was the ruler of a great empire.

Mansa Musa traveled in grand style. Eighty camels carried two tons of gold. Mansa Musa gave away so much gold to the poor on his journey that the price of gold fell. While in Makkah, Mansa Musa met scholars of Islam. He convinced them to return with him to Mali. They helped spread Islam in West Africa.

Islam in Songhai

Islam won followers among the Songhai people. Sunni Ali, the ruler, became a Muslim to keep the loyalty of merchants. After Sunni Ali died, his son refused to accept Islam. Muhammad Ture, a Songhai general, took over the government. With the backing of Muslim townspeople, he made himself king. He drove out Sunni Ali's family. He then took the name Askia.

Sylvain Grandadam/age fotostock

ReadingHELPDESK

Swahili the unique culture of Africa's East Coast and the language spoken there

Academic Vocabulary

survive to continue to function or prosper

Under Askia Muhammad (moo·HAH·muhd), the Songhai created the largest empire in West Africa's history. He ordered local courts to follow Muslim laws. He also made Timbuktu an important center of Islamic learning. Askia Muhammad set up a famous university and opened schools to teach the Quran.

The Songhai Empire **survived** disputes among royal family members. It did not, however, survive the guns of Moroccan invaders. This invasion in 1591 brought down the empire.

How Did Islam Develop in East Africa?

Islam spread slowly in East Africa. Islam arrived in the A.D. 700s, but the religion did not gain many followers until the 1100s and 1200s. A new society arose known as **Swahili** (swah·HEE·lee). It was based on a blend of African and Muslim cultures. The word *Swahili* comes from an Arabic word meaning "people of the coast." By 1331, however, it referred to the culture of East Africa's coast and the language spoken there.

The African influences on the Swahili culture came from the cultures of Africa's interior. Muslim influences came from Arab and Persian settlers. The Swahili culture and language still thrive in Africa.

Islam's Effect on Africa

Islam had a far-reaching effect on much of Africa. Africans who accepted Islam adopted Islamic laws and ideas. They also were influenced by Islamic learning. Muslim schools introduced the Arabic language to their students. In addition, Islam influenced African art and its buildings. Muslim architects built beautiful mosques and palaces in Timbuktu and other cities.

✔ PROGRESS CHECK

Determining Cause and Effect What caused a unique brand of Islam to develop in Africa?

BIOGRAPHY

**Mansa Musa
(ruled 1312–1337)**

Mansa Musa attracted the attention of many nations with his famous pilgrimage, or trip, to Makkah (Mecca). Countries in Europe, as well as kingdoms in North Africa and Southwest Asia, took notice. These nations hoped to trade with Mali and gain some of its wealth. Mansa Musa expanded his empire by capturing the cities of Gao (GAH • oh) and Timbuktu. During his reign, Mali was one of the world's largest empires. Mansa Musa once boasted that traveling from the empire's northern border to its southern border would take a year.

▶ CRITICAL THINKING
Identifying Cause and Effect How did Mansa Musa's pilgrimage to Makkah benefit the kingdom of Mali?

LESSON 2 REVIEW

Review Vocabulary

1. What two meanings developed for the word *Swahili*?

Answer the Guiding Questions

2. *Comparing* What did all the early governments of African kingdoms have in common?

3. *Explaining* How did the leaders of Mali manage the grand scale of their government?

4. *Describing* What similar purposes did traditional African religions share?

5. *Summarizing* What did Ibn Battuta observe about the different religious groups in West Africa?

6. **INFORMATIVE/EXPLANATORY** Write a brief paragraph in which you explain how Mansa Musa worked to spread Islam in West Africa.

African Society and Culture

ESSENTIAL QUESTION

• How do religions develop?

IT MATTERS BECAUSE

The people of early Africa formed complex societies with many common characteristics. They created artistic works that reflected their beliefs and built economies.

African Society

GUIDING QUESTION *Why do people in different parts of Africa have similar traditions and cultures?*

In early Africa, most people lived in rural villages. Their homes consisted of small, round dwellings made of packed mud. Villagers generally were farmers. Africa's urban areas often began as villages with protective walls. These villages grew into larger **communities**. African towns and cities were centers of government and trade. Traders and artisans thrived in these communities. Artisans were skilled in metalworking, woodworking, pottery making, and other crafts.

Family Ties

The family formed the basis of African society. People often lived in **extended families**, or families made up of several generations. Extended families included parents, children, grandparents, and other relatives. These families ranged in size from a few individuals to hundreds of members.

Extended families were part of larger social groups known as lineage groups. Members of a lineage group could trace their family histories to a common ancestor. As in many other ancient

Reading**HELP**DESK

Taking Notes: *Finding the Main Idea*

Use a chart like this one to record and organize important ideas about the different elements of African culture.

Cultural Element	Main Idea
Art	
Music and Dance	
Storytelling	

Content Vocabulary

• **extended family**
• **matrilineal**
• **oral history**
• **sugarcane**
• **spiritual**

436 *African Civilizations*

societies, older members had more power than younger people. Members of a lineage group were expected to support and care for each other.

Bantu Migrations

Many of Africa's social practices are a result of migrations that began in West Africa about 3000 B.C. and lasted hundreds of years. The migrants, known as the Bantu (BAN · too), shared similar languages, cultures, and technologies. The Bantu migrated from West Africa to the south and east. They spread their farming and iron-working skills, along with their languages. Today, about 220 million Africans speak hundreds of Bantu languages.

Bantu villages were also **matrilineal** (ma·truh·LIH·nee·uhl). They traced their descent, or ancestry, through mothers, not fathers. When a woman married, however, she joined her husband's family. To make up for the loss, her family received presents from the husband's family. These gifts might include cattle, goats, cloth, or metal tools.

How Did African Children Learn?

In Africa's villages, education was the duty of both the family and other villagers. Children learned the history of their people and the basic skills they would need as adults.

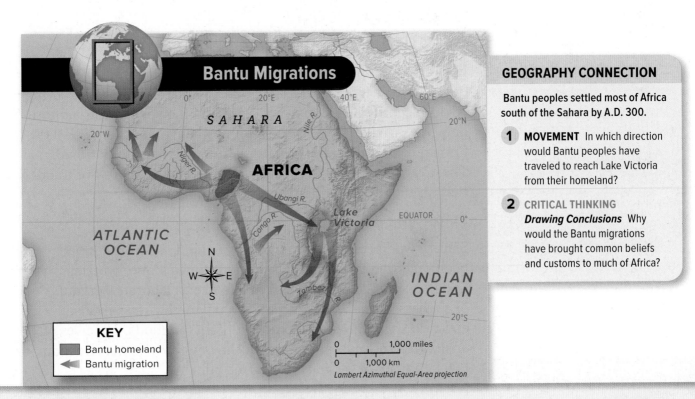

Bantu Migrations

KEY
- Bantu homeland
- Bantu migration

1,000 miles
1,000 km
Lambert Azimuthal Equal-Area projection

GEOGRAPHY CONNECTION

Bantu peoples settled most of Africa south of the Sahara by A.D. 300.

1 **MOVEMENT** In which direction would Bantu peoples have traveled to reach Lake Victoria from their homeland?

2 **CRITICAL THINKING** *Drawing Conclusions* Why would the Bantu migrations have brought common beliefs and customs to much of Africa?

---

extended family a family made up of several generations

matrilineal tracing family descent through mothers rather than fathers

Academic Vocabulary

community a large group with common values living in an area

Some women in early Africa served as soldiers and political leaders. Queen Nzinga ruled in southern Africa.

▶ **CRITICAL THINKING**
Making Connections Why might European explorers have been surprised to observe women serving in these roles?

In West Africa, griots helped to teach the children. They vividly told their village's oral history . These stories were told and retold, and people passed them down from generation to generation. Many stories included a lesson about life. Lessons also were given through short proverbs. One Bantu proverb stated, "Patience is the mother of a beautiful child."

African Women

As in most other early societies, women in Africa acted mostly as wives and mothers. Men had more rights and supervised much of what women did. Visitors to Africa, however, noticed some exceptions. European explorers were amazed to learn that women served as soldiers in some African armies.

African women also served as rulers. In the A.D. 600s, Queen Dahia al-Kahina (dah·HEE·uh ahl·kah·HEE·nah) led an army against Arab invaders, who attacked her kingdom. Another woman ruler was Queen Nzinga (ehn·ZIHN·gah), who governed lands in southwestern Africa. She spent almost 30 years fighting Portuguese invaders and resisting the slave trade.

☑ **PROGRESS CHECK**

Describing What were families like in early Africa?

The Slave Trade

GUIDING QUESTION *How did the slave trade affect Africans?*

In 1441, a ship from the European nation of Portugal sailed down Africa's western coast. The ship captain's plan was to bring African captives back to Europe. During the voyage, the captain and crew seized 12 Africans—men, women, and boys. With its human cargo on board, the ship then sailed back to Portugal. These captives were the first Africans to be part of a slave trade that would involve millions of people.

How Was African Slavery Practiced?

Slavery was a common practice throughout the world. It had been practiced in Africa since ancient times. Bantu warriors raided nearby villages for captives to use as laborers, servants, or soldiers. Some were set free for a payment. Africans also enslaved their enemies and traded them for goods. The lives of enslaved Africans were hard, but they might win their freedom through work or by marrying a free person.

Mary Evans Picture Library

oral history stories passed down from generation to generation

sugarcane a grassy plant that is a natural source of sugar

Academic Vocabulary

contact interaction with other people
major great in rank or importance

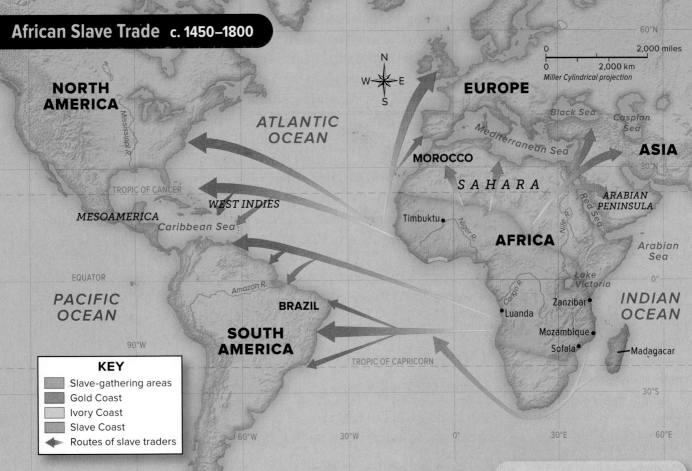

African Slave Trade c. 1450–1800

NORTH AMERICA

ATLANTIC OCEAN

EUROPE

60°N

Black Sea

Caspian Sea

2,000 miles

2,000 km

Miller Cylindrical projection

30°N

MOROCCO

ASIA

S A H A R A

ARABIAN PENINSULA

TROPIC OF CANCER

WEST INDIES

MESOAMERICA

Caribbean Sea

Timbuktu

Niger R.

AFRICA

Red Sea

Nile R.

Arabian Sea

EQUATOR

PACIFIC OCEAN

Amazon R.

BRAZIL

SOUTH AMERICA

Lake Victoria

0°

Congo R.

Luanda

Zanzibar

INDIAN OCEAN

90°W

Mozambique

TROPIC OF CAPRICORN

Sofala

Madagacar

30°S

60°W

30°W

0°

30°E

60°E

KEY
- Slave-gathering areas
- Gold Coast
- Ivory Coast
- Slave Coast
- Routes of slave traders

The trade in humans grew as Africa's **contact** with the Muslim world increased. The Quran banned the enslavement of Muslims. Muslims, however, could enslave non-Muslims. Arab Muslim merchants, therefore, began to trade cotton and other goods for enslaved non-Muslim Africans.

When Europeans arrived in West Africa, a new market for enslaved Africans opened. Africans armed with European guns began raiding villages to seize captives to sell.

The European Slave Trade

In 1444, a Portuguese ship brought 235 enslaved Africans to a dock in Portugal. An official of the royal court saw the Africans being taken off the vessel. He was moved to ask:

PRIMARY SOURCE

" What heart could be so hard as not to [be] pierced with ... feeling ...? For some kept their heads low, and their faces bathed in tears. ... Others stood groaning ... crying out loudly, as if asking [for] help. ... others struck their faces. ... But to increase their sufferings still more, ... was it then needful to part fathers from sons, husbands from wives, brothers from brothers? "

—from Gomes Eannes de Zurara, as quoted in *The Slave Trade* by Hugh Thomas

GEOGRAPHY CONNECTION

The slave trade carried enslaved Africans to different parts of the world.

1 **MOVEMENT** By what route is it likely a slave trader would have traveled from Mozambique to Brazil?

2 **CRITICAL THINKING** *Speculating* What developments in world history might have caused the slave trade to grow during the time period shown here?

This colorful blanket is made from Kente cloth. Its name comes from an African word that means "basket."

Griots, such as this woman, often accompany themselves on a stringed instrument called a kora.

▶ **CRITICAL THINKING**
Evaluating How might the tradition of oral storytelling have affected African stories over time?

Portuguese merchants now sold humans. At first, most enslaved Africans were forced to work in Portugal. Later, they were sent to the Atlantic islands of Madeira, the Azores, and Cape Verde. The Portuguese had settled these islands. The mild climate was ideal for growing **sugarcane** on plantations, or huge farms.

Harvesting sugarcane was hard work. Plantation owners could not pay high wages. Instead, they used enslaved Africans. Enslaved people received no wages. By 1500, Portugal had become the world's **major** supplier of sugar.

In the late 1400s, Europeans arrived in the Americas. They forcibly transported enslaved Africans across the Atlantic Ocean to grow sugar, tobacco, rice, and cotton.

✔ PROGRESS CHECK

Analyzing How did increased contact with other parts of the world affect the slave trade in Africa?

Culture in Africa

GUIDING QUESTION *Why were art forms important to Africans?*

Africans excelled in many art forms, including painting, weaving, woodcarving, poetry, dancing, and metalworking. These arts served a religious purpose. They also taught people the history of their communities.

Art in Africa

The earliest art forms in Africa were rock paintings. These paintings show the life of people in the area as they hunted animals, danced, and carried out everyday tasks.

African woodcarvers made masks and statues for religious ceremonies and teaching purposes. People believed the masks held spiritual powers. Clay and metal figures served **similar** purposes. Metalworkers in the West African region of Benin made beautiful bronze and iron statues of people and animals.

Reading**HELP**DESK

spiritual a gospel song

Academic Vocabulary

similar having characteristics in common

Reading Strategy: *Listing*

Making a list helps you organize facts presented while reading a passage. Make a list of the different types of art produced in early Africa.

Early African Music and Dance

Music and dance were connected to everyday African life. People used these arts to express their religious feelings. They also used the arts to help ease an everyday task, such as planting a field. Music and dance also had a vital role in community activities.

African music included group singing. In many African songs, a singer calls out a line, then other singers repeat it. Musical instruments, such as drums, whistles, horns, flutes, or banjos, were used to keep the beat in early African music.

Enslaved Africans relied on music to remind them of their homeland. In America, songs of hardship eventually developed into a type of music called the blues. Songs of religious faith and hopes for freedom became **spirituals**, or gospel songs. Over time, other forms of African-based music developed, such as ragtime, jazz, rock and roll, and, more recently, rap.

For many Africans, dance was a way to communicate with the spirits and express the life of a community. Lines of dancers swayed and clapped their hands. In the background, drummers sounded out the rhythm. Many African peoples had dance rituals that marked particular stages of life, such as when young boys or girls became adults.

African Storytelling

In addition to music and dance, Africans also kept alive their storytelling tradition. A few enslaved Africans escaped and shared their stories. Those who heard these stories retold them. They also retold popular stories that focused on the deeds of famous heroes.

✔ PROGRESS CHECK

Explaining What role did music and dance play in the everyday lives of early Africans?

©Erika Goldring/Retna Ltd./Corbis

LESSON 3 REVIEW

Review Vocabulary

1. What made a Bantu village *matrilineal*?

Answer the Guiding Questions

2. *Explaining* How did the Bantu spread their language, culture, and technology throughout Africa?

3. *Describing* What roles did women play in early African society?

4. *Identifying* Which European nation established the slave trade between Africa and Europe?

5. *Sequencing* How did art in Africa change over time?

6. **INFORMATIVE/EXPLANATORY** Describe your extended family. How might your extended family be similar to or different from extended families in early Africa?

There's More Online! connected.mcgraw-hill.com

What Do You Think?

Africa's Water Resources: Should Private Companies Control Them?

In ancient Africa, and today, the most precious natural resource is water. People worry about its availability. Many people cannot easily get clean water for daily use. Efforts are now underway to set up reliable water systems in Africa. Some local governments create their own water systems. Citizens are taxed according to their water use. Other governments cannot supply water. Then private companies agree to provide water to citizens for a fee. This system is known as *privatization*. Should control of water be left to governments or should private companies be allowed to control water?

Yes

PRIMARY SOURCE

❰❰ During the 1990s, it also became apparent [clear] that private participation could bring better oversight and management. The most detailed studies ... concluded [found] that well designed private schemes [systems] have brought clear benefits—but not perfection. For example, in water, the most difficult sector, in cities as diverse as ... Abidjan and Conakry service coverage has increased significantly.... Extended coverage tends to bring the biggest benefits to households with lower incomes, as they previously had to pay much more for the service by small informal vendors. ❱❱

—Klein, Michael. "Where Do We Stand Today with Private Infrastructure?" Development Outreach. March 2003. Washington, D.C.: World Bank.

During the dry seasons, some areas of Africa are completely without natural water.

Image Source/Getty Image

African governments are trying to find ways to provide clean drinking water for their people.

No

PRIMARY SOURCE

❚❚ Water is about life. The saying that 'water is life' cannot be more appropriate. Privatizing water is putting the lives of citizens in the hands of a corporate entity [business structure] that is accountable [responsible] only to its shareholders. Secondly, water is a human right and this means that any philosophy, scheme, or contract that has the potential to exclude [leave out] sections of the population from accessing water is not acceptable both in principal and in law. Privatization has that potential because the privateers are not charities: they are in for the profit. Price therefore becomes an important barrier to access by poor people. Water is the collective heritage of humanity and nature. . . . Water must remain a public good for the public interest. *❚❚*

—Interview with Rudolf Amenga–Etego. "The rains do not fall on one person's roof. . ." *Pambazuka News.* 26 August 2004. Issue 171. *http://pambazuka.org/en/category/features/24190*

LYNN JOHNSON/National Geographic Stock

What Do You Think? DBQ

❶ *Describing* What is privatization?

❷ *Identifying* According to Michael Klein, where have private companies been most successful at providing water?

Critical Thinking

❸ *Analyzing* What about Michael Klein's background would cause him to believe that privatization is the best solution?

❹ *Analyzing Information* Why does Amenga-Etego mean when he says that "water is a human right. . ."?

Read to Write

❺ *Narrative* Write a paragraph describing your feelings about whether private companies have the right to make a profit by providing water to citizens.

CHAPTER 15 Activities

Write your answers on a separate piece of paper.

1 Exploring the Essential Question

INFORMATIVE/EXPLANATORY How would you explain the ways in which trade affected the history of early African civilizations? Write a short essay in which you consider the parts of these civilizations that were affected by trade. You may choose to focus on topics such as the civilizations' growth, government, religion, or culture. Ask an adult to help you plan, revise, edit, and rewrite your essay so that it addresses the question and focuses on a unique topic.

2 21st Century Skills

SUMMARIZING Write a paragraph summarizing what you have learned about one of the African civilizations discussed in this chapter. Your paragraph should describe why the civilization you chose is important in African and world history. It should also include significant events, people, and accomplishments related to this civilization.

3 Thinking Like a Historian

GEOGRAPHY AND CIVILIZATION Create a graphic organizer that lists at least three geographic features of Africa and explains their impact on the growth of civilizations there. For instance, you might write "Sahara" on the left side of your organizer. Then, on the opposite side, you could explain that for many years the Sahara limited travel and trade in Africa.

> Feature → Impact on African Civilization

4 **GEOGRAPHY ACTIVITY**

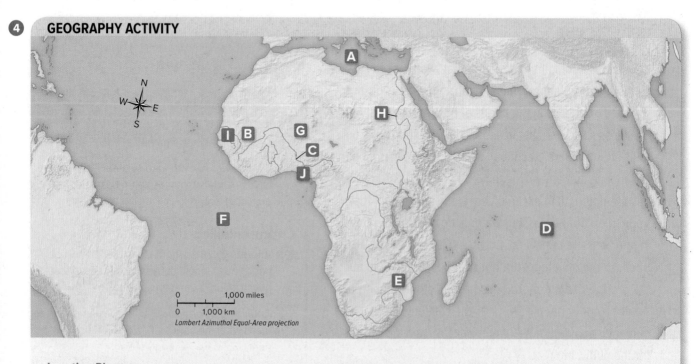

```
0        1,000 miles
0    1,000 km
Lambert Azimuthal Equal-Area projection
```

Locating Places

Match the letters on the map with the numbered places listed below.

1. Zimbabwe
2. Benin
3. Ghana
4. Mali
5. Songhai
6. Mediterranean Sea
7. Atlantic Ocean
8. Indian Ocean
9. Nile River
10. Niger River

Directions: Write your answers on a separate piece of paper.

CHECKING FOR UNDERSTANDING

1 Define each of these terms.

A. savanna	**F.** Swahili
B. plateau	**G.** extended family
C. griot	**H.** matrilineal
D. dhow	**I.** oral history
E. clan	**J.** spiritual

REVIEW THE GUIDING QUESTIONS

2 *Describing* What challenges does the environment of Africa pose to settlement there?

3 *Identifying* What natural barrier limited trade between North Africa and other parts of the continent?

4 *Explaining* How did Ghana's location help it become a great trading kingdom?

5 *Naming* What products were traded from Africa's inland territories?

6 *Identifying* Which two religions had major impacts on the development of Axum and other East African trading states?

7 *Making Comparisons* In what ways were the governments of Ghana and Mali similar?

8 *Summarizing* How was Islam introduced into West Africa?

9 *Defining* What role did griots play in early African cultures?

10 *Locating* From which part of Africa did most enslaved Africans originate?

11 *Listing* What social and cultural traditions did many African societies have in common?

CRITICAL THINKING

12 *Determining Cause and Effect* Why might raising livestock have developed in some parts of Africa before agriculture?

13 *Assessing* Which region in Africa is most suited for permanent human settlement? Explain your answer.

14 *Defending* Which African trading empire was the greatest? Explain your answer.

15 *Making Connections* In what ways did lineage groups relate to traditional African religions?

16 *Predicting Consequences* How might the pilgrimage of Mansa Musa ultimately have led to the downfall of Mali?

17 *Analyzing* Discuss the relationship between the spread of Islam and the growth of trade between Africa and Muslim traders to the east.

18 *Determining Cause and Effect* What were the most important effects of the Bantu migration?

19 *Making Generalizations* Describe the role of family in African societies.

20 *Determining Central Ideas* Explain why music, art, and dance were integral to African society.

Need Extra Help?

If You've Missed Question	**1**	**2**	**3**	**4**	**5**	**6**	**7**	**8**	**9**	**10**	**11**	**12**	**13**	**14**	**15**	**16**	**17**	**18**	**19**	**20**
Review Lesson	1,2, 3	1	1	1	1	1	2	2	3	3	3	1	1	1, 2	2, 3	2	2	3	3	3

DBQ SHORT RESPONSE

"Mansa Musa was a skilled organizer and administrator who built Mali into one of the world's largest empires of the time. The empire was significant in both size and wealth. Mansa Musa encouraged the growth of trade in the empire. He also strongly supported the arts and education in Mali. He ordered the construction of mosques [Islamic temples] and established a university for Islamic studies."

—EncyclopediaBritannica Online, "Musa."
http://www.britannica.com/EBchecked/topic/398420/Musa

21 How did Mansa Musa show his support for education in Mali?

22 What traits do you think made Mansa Musa a successful ruler?

EXTENDED RESPONSE

23 *Informative/Explanatory* Write an essay in which you seek to explain the importance of the arts to early African society. What purposes did African art play in people's lives? How is the influence of early African art forms still felt today? Use details from the chapter to support your explanation.

STANDARDIZED TEST PRACTICE

DBQ ANALYZING DOCUMENTS

Ibn Battuta wrote during his travels in Mali that

"[The people of Mali] are careful to observe the hours of prayer, and assiduous [always dutiful] in attending them in congregations, and in bringing up their children to them."

—from *Travels in Asia and Africa, 1325–1354*

24 *Drawing Conclusions* Which statement best describes Ibn Battuta's impressions of the people of Mali?

A. He praises their system for educating children.

B. He criticizes the policies of the leaders of Mali.

C. He criticizes the system of government used in Mali.

D. He praises their devotion to their religious beliefs.

25 *Making Inferences* From the passage, you can infer that Ibn Battuta likely views the people of Mali with

A. wonder. **C.** respect.

B. confusion. **D.** jealousy.

Need Extra Help?

If You've Missed Question	21	22	23	24	25
Review Lesson	2	2	2	2	3

◀ *Xiuhtecuhtli was also known as "The Turquoise Lord." This mask is made of wood and covered with turquoise mosaic. The teeth are made from shells.*

1500 B.C. TO A.D. 1600

The Americas

Werner Forman/Art Resource, NY

THE STORY MATTERS ...

Why do the seasons change? What causes thunder? Today, we look to science to answer these questions. Ancient people told stories.

The native people of Central America told a story to explain the origin of the sun. According to the legend, Nanahuatzin (nah • nah • WAHT • zeen), an Aztec god, had warts, or bumps, all over his face. At the time the world was created, Nanahuatzin threw himself into a great fire. Rather than dying in the flames, Nanahuatzin arose and became the sun.

This mask was made in Mexico about 600 years ago. Some historians believe it is a mask of Nanahuatzin. Other historians believe this represents Xiuhtecuhtli (zhee • ooh • tay • COOT • lee), the Aztec god of fire.

ESSENTIAL QUESTIONS

- How does geography affect the way people live?
- What makes a culture unique?

Place & Time: The Americas
1500 B.C. to A.D. 1600

Early people in the Americas depended on natural resources to survive. The development of farming and trade allowed them to build complex cultures. The Maya, Inca, and Aztec Empires ruled over large parts of Mesoamerica and South America.

Early American mountain dwellers lived on wide plateaus such as this, found in mountain ranges. The level areas provided land for settlements and farming.

Step into the Place

MAP FOCUS The geography and climates in North and South America influenced early people who lived there and caused them to develop different cultures.

1 **LOCATION** Look at the map. Is Cahokia located north or south of the Amazon River?

2 **PLACE** How did the location of Tenochtitlán affect Aztec trade?

3 **LOCATION** Use cardinal directions to locate Cuzco compared to Cahokia.

4 **CRITICAL THINKING**
   Analyzing How does location affect the strength of an empire?

The Navajo are known for their complex religious ceremonies. Many of these ceremonies take place within buildings that are constructed so that the entrance faces east—toward the rising sun. When a fire is built inside the building, the opening at the top allows smoke to escape.

(t)Judith Lienert/Shutterstock.com; (b)Robert F. Sisson/National Geographic/Getty Images

Step Into the Time

TIME LINE Choose an event from the time line and write a paragraph predicting the general social, political, or economic consequence that event might have for the world.

c. A.D. 500 Maya cities flourish in Mesoamerica

THE AMERICAS				
THE WORLD				
A.D. 500	A.D. 600	A.D. 700	A.D. 800	A.D. 900

c. A.D. 800 Pope crowns Charlemagne emperor

c. A.D. 830 Baghdad is center of Islamic learning

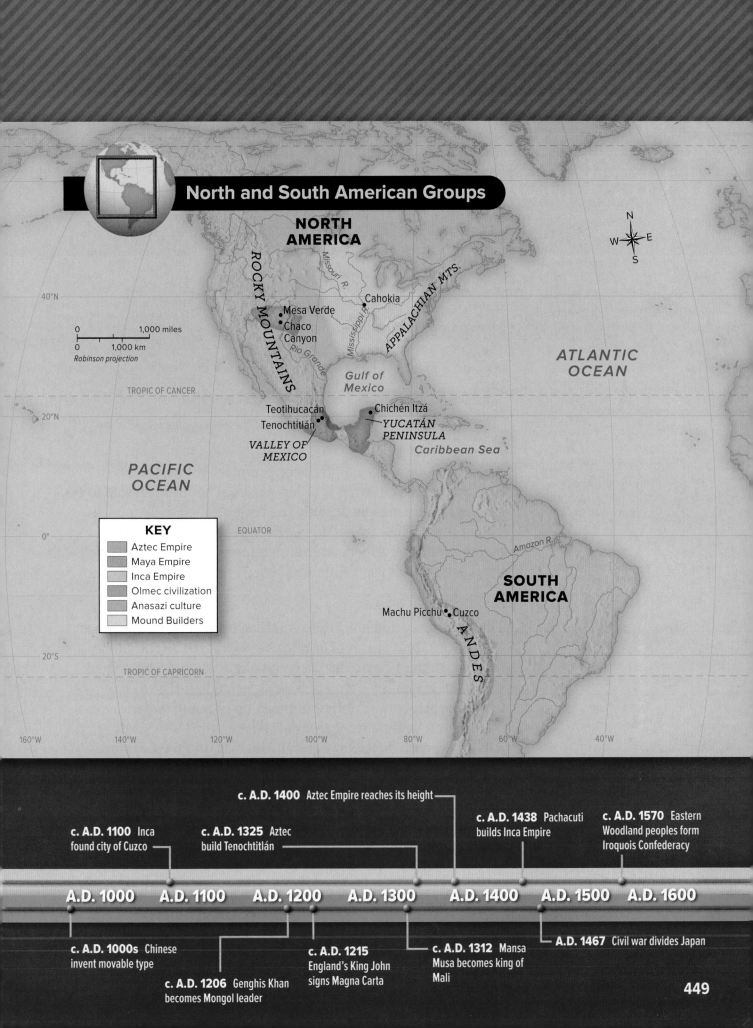

North and South American Groups

NORTH AMERICA

ROCKY MOUNTAINS

Missouri R.

APPALACHIAN MTS.

Mississippi R.

Rio Grande

Cahokia

Mesa Verde

Chaco Canyon

Gulf of Mexico

TROPIC OF CANCER

40°N

20°N

Teotihuacán

Tenochtitlán

VALLEY OF MEXICO

Chichén Itzá

YUCATÁN PENINSULA

Caribbean Sea

PACIFIC OCEAN

ATLANTIC OCEAN

EQUATOR

0°

Amazon R.

SOUTH AMERICA

Machu Picchu • Cuzco

ANDES

20°S

TROPIC OF CAPRICORN

160°W 140°W 120°W 100°W 80°W 60°W 40°W

KEY
- Aztec Empire
- Maya Empire
- Inca Empire
- Olmec civilization
- Anasazi culture
- Mound Builders

0   1,000 miles
0   1,000 km
Robinson projection

c. A.D. 1400 Aztec Empire reaches its height

c. A.D. 1100 Inca found city of Cuzco

c. A.D. 1325 Aztec build Tenochtitlán

c. A.D. 1438 Pachacuti builds Inca Empire

c. A.D. 1570 Eastern Woodland peoples form Iroquois Confederacy

A.D. 1000   A.D. 1100   A.D. 1200   A.D. 1300   A.D. 1400   A.D. 1500   A.D. 1600

c. A.D. 1000s Chinese invent movable type

c. A.D. 1206 Genghis Khan becomes Mongol leader

c. A.D. 1215 England's King John signs Magna Carta

c. A.D. 1312 Mansa Musa becomes king of Mali

A.D. 1467 Civil war divides Japan

LESSON 1

The First Americans

ESSENTIAL QUESTION

• How does geography affect the way people live?

IT MATTERS BECAUSE
Early people in the Americas built the beginnings of several civilizations.

Geography of the Americas

GUIDING QUESTION *How did geography shape the ways people settled in the Americas?*

About 15,000 years ago, prehistoric hunters left northeastern Asia and arrived in what is today Alaska. They are believed to be among the first people to settle the region called the Americas. Their descendants are called Native Americans. Over the centuries, Native American groups adopted different ways of life. Each group's way of life was based on local resources.

A Diverse Region

The Americas stretch north to south nearly 11,000 miles (almost 18,000 km). This vast region begins north at the Arctic Circle. It reaches south to Tierra del Fuego (tee•EHR•eh del FWAY•goh). Tierra del Fuego is a group of islands located off the coast of Chile and Argentina, at the southern tip of South America.

The four geographical areas of the Americas are North America, South America, Central America, and the Caribbean. North America and South America are both continents and make up most of the Americas. Central America is an **isthmus** (IHS•muhs), a narrow piece of land that connects two larger areas of land. East of Central America is the Caribbean Sea, where the Caribbean islands spread across to the Atlantic Ocean.

Reading**HELP**DESK

Taking Notes: *Summarizing*

Use a chart like the one here to record the climates and mountain ranges of the four main areas of the Americas.

	Climate	Mountains
North America		
South America		
Central America		
Caribbean		

Content Vocabulary

• **isthmus**   • **maize**

isthmus a narrow piece of land linking two larger areas of land

Within the vast expanse of the Americas you can find many different geographic features and climates. North America lies north of the Equator and has climates that range from cold to tropical.

Central America and the Caribbean islands are also north of the Equator. South America extends both north and south of the Equator. Most of these areas have a warm, rainy climate. A broad range of plants grows in the three areas.

Towering Mountains

In the west, rugged mountain chains run nearly the entire length of the Americas. They separate coastal plains near the Pacific Ocean from broad eastern plains that sweep toward the Atlantic Ocean.

The Rocky Mountains and the Pacific coastal ranges are in western North America. These mountains contain passes, or low areas. Even with these passes, overland travel across the mountains could be difficult.

In eastern North America, a range of mountains—the Appalachians—runs near the Atlantic coast. The Appalachians are lower than the Rockies and Pacific coastal ranges. Early Americans had no difficulty traveling over the Appalachians.

The Andes are the world's longest mountain system. These mountains stretch along the Pacific coast of South America. Valleys and plateaus (plah·TOES) lie between the mountain chains. Plateaus are large areas of raised land that have a flat surface.

Denali (Mount McKinley) is the tallest mountain in North America. It stands in Denali National Park, Alaska.

MIMOTITO/Getty Images

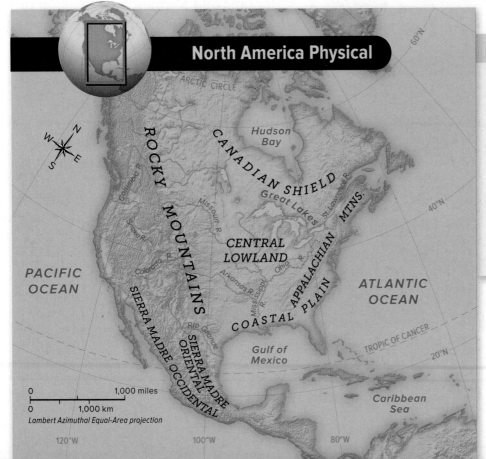

North America Physical

GEOGRAPHY CONNECTION

North America is the third-largest continent on Earth. It is mostly surrounded by water. Mountain ranges take up more than one-third of the total land area.

1 PLACE Which mountain range is closest to where you live?

2 CRITICAL THINKING
Analyzing What would have made travel across North America difficult for early Americans?

Rolling Plains

North America has many coastal and inland plains. The rolling grasslands of central North America are known as the Great Plains. The Great Plains have fertile soil for farming and raising cattle.

South America also has large areas of plains. In the northeast, the tropical Amazon Basin covers about 2.7 million square miles (7.0 million sq km). It is home to the world's largest rain forest.

Additional lowland plains are located north and south of the Amazon Basin. Tropical grasslands stretch across the northwest. Another area of plains called the Pampas lies in the south. The mild climate of the Pampas makes them a good place for growing grains. Many ranchers herd cattle there as well.

Rushing Rivers

Large river systems drain the Americas. They begin in the mountain ranges and flow through interior plains to the oceans. Today, the many waterways of the Americas transport people, goods, and ideas.

In North America, the largest river system is the Mississippi. It flows 2,350 miles (3,782 km), from present-day Montana and Minnesota to the Gulf of Mexico. The Mississippi is the major waterway for the central part of North America.

The Amazon is South America's largest river system. It starts in the Andes and flows about 4,000 miles (6,437 km) to the Atlantic Ocean. The Amazon carries the highest **volume** of water of any river on Earth.

✓ **PROGRESS CHECK**

Describing Which four separate areas make up the Americas?

The land surrounding the Amazon is home to the greatest variety of plants on Earth. As many as 250 species of trees may grow in one acre of the Amazon River basin.

▶ CRITICAL THINKING
Analyzing How might early Americans have used the Amazon River?

Reading**HELP**DESK

Academic Vocabulary

volume amount included within limits
link to connect

Settling the Americas

GUIDING QUESTION *How did prehistoric people reach the Americas and form settlements?*

How did prehistoric people come to the Americas? Today, the Americas are not **linked** to the world's other landmasses, but they were long ago.

Reaching the Americas

Some scientists think that people walked across a land bridge from Asia into the Americas during the last Ice Age. Evidence of ancient tools and other artifacts reveals that these first Americans were hunters following herds of animals.

Other scientists argue that the first Americans arrived by boat. They passed by Alaska and sailed south along the Americas' Pacific coast. The travelers first explored coastal areas. They then journeyed inland where they set up campsites.

Once they arrived, the first Americans did not stay in one place. They moved south and east. They travelled in boats to islands in the Caribbean. In time, there were people living in different groups in North, Central, and South America.

Hunters and Gatherers

How did the first Americans survive? Historians believe it is likely that the first people in the Americas lived in small groups. These early Americans moved from place to place to find food.

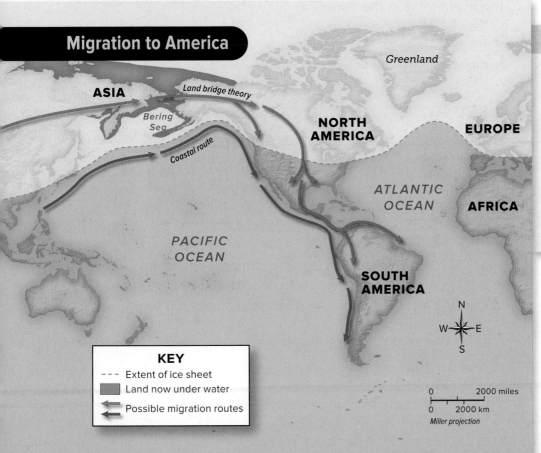

Migration to America

KEY
- - - Extent of ice sheet
- Land now under water
- Possible migration routes

0 — 2000 miles
0 — 2000 km
Miller projection

GEOGRAPHY CONNECTION

Over thousands of years, prehistoric people migrated southward through the Americas.

1 MOVEMENT How do scientists think prehistoric people got to North America from Asia?

2 CRITICAL THINKING
Analyzing Why do you think prehistoric people moved from one place in the Americas to another?

Early Americans used corn in many forms. The corn grinding stone like this Anasazi tool developed out of necessity.

▶ CRITICAL THINKING
Predicting How do you think early Americans used ground corn?

Archaeologists have unearthed evidence of early American ways of life. This evidence includes heaps of shells, rounded grinding stones, and bone fishhooks.

Hunter-gatherers in the Americas used natural resources for food, clothing, and shelter. People living along seacoasts collected shellfish and snails. People who lived inland fished in rivers and gathered roots, nuts, and fruits in forests. Early Americans also hunted large animals, which provided meat, hides for clothing, and bones for tools.

The Beginnings of Agriculture

As the last Ice Age ended, the climate grew warmer. People in the Americas learned to plant the seeds of grains and other plants. The seeds would grow into crops that could be eaten. This activity became the start of farming in the Americas.

Farming began in Mesoamerica (meh·zoh·uh·MEHR·ih·kuh) 9,000 to 10,000 years ago. *Meso* comes from the Greek word for "middle." This region includes lands stretching from central Mexico to Costa Rica in Central America.

The geography of Mesoamerica was suited for farming. Much of the area had rich, volcanic soil and a mild climate. The first crops that early Americans grew included peppers, pumpkins, squash, gourds, beans, and potatoes. Corn, also known as **maize** (mayz), took longer to develop. However, it became the most important food in the Americas.

☑ PROGRESS CHECK

Describing What were the first crops grown in the Americas?

First American Societies

GUIDING QUESTION *How did farming make civilization possible in the Americas?*

Growing and trading crops helped early Americans form more **complex** societies. The first American cultures emerged in Mesoamerica and along the western coast of South America.

Olmec Culture

About 1200 B.C., a people called the Olmec (OHL·mehk) built what may be the oldest culture in Mesoamerica. Based on farming and trade, the Olmecs lasted about 800 years.

Harald Sund/Riser/Getty Images

ReadingHELPDESK

maize corn

Academic Vocabulary

complex made up of many related parts

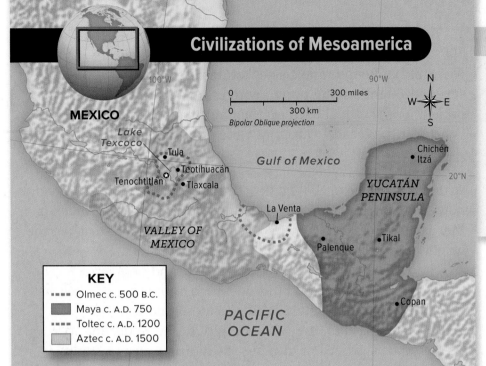

Civilizations of Mesoamerica

MEXICO

Lake Texcoco

Tula

Teotihuacán

Tenochtitlán

Tlaxcala

VALLEY OF MEXICO

La Venta

Gulf of Mexico

Chichén Itzá

YUCATÁN PENINSULA

20°N

Palenque

Tikal

Copán

PACIFIC OCEAN

100°W

90°W

0   300 miles
0   300 km
Bipolar Oblique projection

N W E S

KEY
- Olmec c. 500 B.C.
- Maya c. A.D. 750
- Toltec c. A.D. 1200
- Aztec c. A.D. 1500

GEOGRAPHY CONNECTION

Mesoamerican societies developed in Mexico and Central America.

1 PLACE Which culture occupied the Yucatán Peninsula?

2 CRITICAL THINKING
Making Inferences The Olmec built a pyramid of clay and sand at La Venta. Why do you think they did not use stone?

The Olmec set up farms in the tropical lowlands along the Gulf of Mexico. They grew beans and produced salt. The Olmec traded with people living inland. They exchanged salt and beans for jade and obsidian, or volcanic glass. Olmec artisans used the jade for jewelry. They made sharp knives from the obsidian.

The Olmec created centers for religious ceremonies. In these areas, they built pyramids and other stone monuments.

First Planned Cities

About 400 B.C., the Olmec culture collapsed. A group of inland peoples rose to power in central Mexico. This group built one of the first planned cities in the Americas, Teotihuacán (tay•oh•tee•wuh•KAHN), or "Place of the Gods." It lasted from about A.D. 250 to A.D. 800. Around 120,000 to 200,000 people lived in Teotihuacán. Temples and palaces lined its main street, which led to the Pyramid of the Sun.

A people called the Zapotec (ZAH•poh•tehk) built farms and cities in south central Mexico. Their magnificent capital, Monte Albán (MON•teh AL•bahn), had a main square surrounded by stone temples, monuments, and tombs. In addition to farming, the Zapotec created pottery and traded with Teotihuacán and other places in Mesoamerica. The Zapotec developed a writing system based on hieroglyphs (HIGH•roh•glifz).

Another people called the Maya (MY•uh) prospered in the steamy rain forests of the Yucatán Peninsula (yoo•kuh•TAN). Like the Zapotec, the Maya traded throughout Mesoamerica. From their central location, the Maya spread into southern Mexico and Central America.

One of the things the Olmecs are most famous for is colossal heads made out of rock. Some were more than seven feet high. How they managed to get them to the sites where they remain to this day is unknown.

De Agostini/Getty Images

Teotihuacán and the Zapotec flourished between the A.D. 300s and A.D. 500s. Then, they declined. Historians are not sure why this happened. The causes for decline might have been a severe drought—a long period with little rainfall—or revolts by populations that had used up the natural resources of the area. Whatever the reason, the cities were **abandoned**.

Who Were the Toltec?

After the collapse of these cities, the Toltec (TOHL·tehk) rose to power in central Mexico. The warlike Toltec conquered much of Mexico and northern Central America. Their empire reached the height of its power between A.D. 950 and A.D. 1150.

The Toltec grew crops of beans, maize, and pepper in irrigated fields. They also built pyramids and palaces. Toltec artisans introduced metalworking to Mesoamerica.

Around A.D. 1125, the Toltec Empire began to decline. Within a few decades, groups of invaders, including Aztec (AZ·tek) people, attacked and burned the Toltec city of Tollan (toh·lahn). For nearly 200 years, there was no ruling group in central Mexico.

Early Cultures in South America

In South America, several different early civilizations thrived along the Pacific coast. About 900 B.C., the Chavín developed a civilization in the coastal areas of present-day Peru and Ecuador. They built a large temple with stones from nearby hills. Part of a ceremonial center, the temple was surrounded by pyramids and stone figures of different deities, or gods. For unknown reasons, they declined around 200 B.C. The Moche (MOH·cheh), developed around A.D. 100 in the dry coastal desert of Peru. The Moche built canals to bring water from rivers in the Andes foothills to their desert homeland to grow food. Much about Moche culture is known from their arts and crafts.

In spite of everything they **achieved**, the Chavín and the Moche did not build empires. The first empire in South America was built by another people called the Inca (IHNG·kuh).

The story of the Moche culture is told through their artwork, such as this pottery figure of an alpaca.

▶ **CRITICAL THINKING**
Analyzing Visuals What can you tell about the Moche based on this example of art?

✓ **PROGRESS CHECK**

Explaining Why did early American cultures decline?

©Nathan Benn/Corbis

Reading**HELP**DESK

Academic Vocabulary

abandon to leave, often because of danger
achieve to successfully complete a task; to gain something by working for it

456 *The Americas*

Pueblo Bonito, located in present-day New Mexico, was a four-story sandstone village.

▶ CRITICAL THINKING
Analyzing How did the location near cliffs help people living in Pueblo Bonito survive?

Early Cultures in North America

GUIDING QUESTION *Why did a large number of societies develop in North America?*

North of Mesoamerica, other early Americans developed their own ways of living. Despite their cultural differences, many of these groups learned the same farming methods as their Mesoamerican neighbors. Farming spread to the American Southwest and then along the coasts and up the Mississippi, Missouri, and Ohio Rivers. As farming developed in these areas, so did new cultures.

Peoples of the Southwest

The scorching desert of what is now Arizona was home to the Hohokam (hoh·hoh·KAHM). About A.D. 300, the Hohokam planted gardens on lands between the Salt and Gila rivers. They dug hundreds of miles of irrigation canals to carry river water to their fields. They grew corn, cotton, beans, and squash. The Hohokam also made pottery, carved stone, and etched shells.

Another group called the Anasazi (ah·nuh·SAH·zee) lived about the same time as the Hohokam. The Anasazi settled in the canyons and cliffs of the Southwest. Like the Hohokam, they practiced farming. To water their crops, they gathered the water that ran off cliffs and sent it through canals to their fields.

The Anasazi were skilled at making pottery and jewelry.

The Anasazi built large stone dwellings that the Spanish explorers later called pueblos (PWEH·blohs). They also built dwellings in the walls of steep cliffs. Cliff dwellings were easy to defend and offered protection from winter weather.

The Anasazi and the Hohokam both prospered until the early A.D. 1000s. At that time, they faced droughts that killed their crops. The two groups eventually abandoned their settlements.

(t)Martin Gray/Getty Images; (b)©Dewitt Jones/Corbis

Build Vocabulary: *Prefixes*

Meso is a prefix that means "middle." Another, more common prefix meaning middle is "mid." *Midterm* is the middle of the school term. *Midway* is halfway between two places. What other words with the prefix *mid* can you think of?

The Mound Builders

East of the Mississippi River, another early American civilization arose. It began about 1000 B.C. and lasted until about A.D. 400. Its founders built huge mounds of earth that were used as tombs or for ceremonies. These constructions gave these people their name—Mound Builders.

The Mound Builders were mostly hunters and gatherers, but they began to practice farming. Two major groups made up the culture—the Adena people and the Hopewell. Scientists believe that the Mound Builders domesticated many wild plants, such as sunflowers, gourds, and barley. Corn became another popular crop after it was introduced to the region about A.D. 100.

The Great Serpent Mound, made by the Mound Builders, still exists in southern Ohio. This mound may have been used in religious ceremonies.

▶ CRITICAL THINKING

Analyzing Why do you think the Great Serpent Mound has maintained its shape?

©Richard A. Cooke/Corbis

Who Were the Mississippians?

By A.D. 700, a new people known as the Mississippians arose. Their name came from their location in the Mississippi River Valley. The Mississippians were able to produce enough corn, squash, and beans to become full-time farmers. They also built mounds and lived in cities.

Their largest city was Cahokia (kuh•HOH•kee•uh). It may have had 16,000 to 30,000 residents. Mississippian government was centered there between A.D. 850 and 1150. Cahokia was the site of the largest Mississippian mound. Cahokia and the Mississippian society collapsed during the A.D. 1200s.

✔ PROGRESS CHECK

Explaining How were early Americans able to grow crops in desert areas of the Southwest?

LESSON 1 REVIEW

Review Vocabulary

1. Which main area of the Americas is an *isthmus*?

2. How did *maize* help early people in the Americas?

Answer the Guiding Questions

3. *Explaining* How did mountain ranges affect the way people lived in the Americas?

4. *Summarizing* How did prehistoric people reach the Americas?

5. *Comparing* In what ways did early civilizations in North America produce food?

6. **INFORMATIVE/EXPLANATORY** Write a two-paragraph essay that describes the ways of life of the Olmec and the Zapotec.

LESSON 2
Life in the Americas

ESSENTIAL QUESTION
• What makes a culture unique?

IT MATTERS BECAUSE
Long before the arrival of Europeans, people in the Americas created complex societies.

The Maya

GUIDING QUESTION *How did the Maya live in the rain forests of Mesoamerica?*

In A.D. 1839, archaeologists John Lloyd Stephens and Frederick Catherwood discovered an ancient city, hidden for centuries by vines and trees. The people who had built the city were called the Maya. These early Americans were the ancestors of the millions of Maya who live in present-day Mexico, Guatemala, Honduras, El Salvador, and Belize.

Maya Communities

About A.D. 300, the Maya developed a complex culture in parts of southern Mexico and Central America. The ancient Maya faced many challenges in the area that they settled, which was called Petén (peh·TEHN). Thick forests nearly blocked out sunlight. Stinging insects filled the air. Yet, the ancient Maya prospered.

Swamps and sinkholes gave the Maya a year-round source of water. A **sinkhole** is an area where the soil has collapsed into a hollow or depression. Sinkholes gave the Maya access to a network of underground rivers and streams.

The Maya began to develop a society. They worked together to clear forested areas. They planted fields of corn and other crops and built cities under government direction.

Reading HELPDESK

Taking Notes: *Organizing*
Use a pyramid like the one here to place the Aztec social classes in order. Begin at the top level of the pyramid and list classes from highest to lowest.

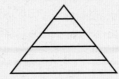

Content Vocabulary
• sinkhole   • hogan

Connections to TODAY

The Maya Today

Modern-day descendants of the Maya speak about 70 different languages. They typically live on farms and grow corn, beans, and squash. As weaving and spinning have become less common, most present-day Maya, especially women, wear traditional clothing made of cloth produced in a factory.

Maya artists often portrayed Chac seated, waiting to receive the arrival of captives.

The Maya set up more than 50 independent city-states. The Maya city-states were connected by culture, political ties, and trade. However, they often fought each other for control of territory.

What Was Maya Society Like?

Each Maya city-state was ruled by a king, who claimed he was descended from the sun god. As god-kings, Maya rulers expected people to serve them. The greatest Maya king was Pacal II. He ruled the city-state of Palenque (puh•LENGH•KAY) for 67 years in the A.D. 600s. Pacal II built many structures considered to be some of the best examples of Maya architecture.

The Maya city-states had a strict class system. Nobles and priests assisted kings in governing the city-states. Below them were farmers, artisans, and hunters. People of this class paid taxes and worked on large building projects.

The Maya believed that the gods controlled everything that happened on Earth. Priests performed ceremonies to please the gods. These ceremonies sometimes included human sacrifice.

When the Maya fought battles, they wanted captives and they wanted land. When drought came and threatened their crops, Maya priests tried to please Chac (CHOCK), the god of rain, by offering the lives of their captives.

Women played a significant role in the Maya city-states. In the city-state of Calakmul (kah•lahk•MOOL), at least two women served as ruling queens. One of them may have helped to found the city.

Royal Maya women often married into royal families in other Maya city-states. This practice increased trade. It also helped form alliances—political agreements between people or states to work together.

Maya Achievements

Maya rulers turned to priests for advice. The priests thought the gods revealed their plans through movements of the sun, moon, and stars. By watching the sky, the priests learned about astronomy. They developed calendar systems to **predict** eclipses and to schedule religious festivals.

Reading**HELP**DESK

sinkhole a depression or hollow where soil has collapsed

Academic Vocabulary

predict to describe something that will happen in the future

They also used calendars to decide when to plant and harvest crops. The Maya had two major calendars. They used a 260-day calendar for religious events. They used a 365-day calendar for events related to the seasons and agriculture.

The Maya developed a system of mathematics. They invented a method of counting based on 20, and they used the concept of zero. They also developed a written language to record numbers and dates. Like the Zapotec, they used hieroglyphics. They carved hieroglyphics on stone monuments and used them in books.

About A.D. 900, the Maya civilization collapsed. Historians do not know why this happened. Some evidence shows that conflict and warfare increased among city-states. Also, erosion and overuse of the soil may have caused a drop in food production. Too little food would have led to illnesses and starvation.

In Maya society, a birth in the royal family called for a musical celebration, such as the one depicted above.

▶ **CRITICAL THINKING**
Drawing Conclusions Why do you think most early people developed music?

☑ **PROGRESS CHECK**

Explaining How were the Maya governed?

The Aztec

GUIDING QUESTION *How did the Aztec establish their society in central Mexico?*

The Aztec came to power in Mesoamerica during the A.D. 1300s. The early Aztec were hunters and warriors. About A.D. 1200, they moved into central Mexico.

Rise of the Aztec

For many years, the Aztec had been searching for a home they believed had been promised to them by their sun god—the feathered serpent Quetzalcoatl (KWEHT·suhl·kuh·WAH·tuhl). In A.D. 1325, the Aztec took refuge on a swampy island in Lake Texcoco (tehs·KOH·koh). Although the land was hardly welcoming, the Aztec chose this site to be their new home.

This shield made of feathers most likely belonged to an Aztec emperor.

▶ CRITICAL THINKING
Analyzing What do you think the animal represented here is holding in its mouth?

Aztec priests declared that the gods demanded they build a great city upon this spot. Laborers worked around the clock. They built bridges to the mainland with soil dug from the lake bottom. Floating gardens dotted the surface of the lake. The wondrous city they built was Tenochtitlán (tay•nawch•teet•LAHN).

For the next 100 years, Aztec workers built temples, palaces, and homes in Tenochtitlán. The city eventually became the largest city in Mesoamerica. It was the center of a web of trade routes that reached throughout Mexico.

The Aztec **relied** on strong kings, or emperors, who claimed to be descended from the gods. A council of priests, nobles, and warriors usually named a new emperor from the ruling family. Council members wanted someone skilled in warfare who could lead troops into battle.

Montezuma I (MAHN•tuh•ZOO•muh) was perhaps the most powerful Aztec ruler. He governed from A.D. 1440 to A.D. 1469. Montezuma used his armies to expand the empire to the Gulf of Mexico. He also built temples, aqueducts, and roads.

By A.D. 1500, Aztec armies had conquered much of what is today Mexico. The new empire was a collection of partly independent territories governed by local leaders. The Aztec ruler supported these leaders in return for tribute—goods or money paid by conquered peoples to their conquerors.

Aztec Life

The emperor was at the top of Aztec society. There were four classes of people under the emperor. These were nobles, commoners, unskilled workers, and enslaved people. Most of the Aztec were commoners, who worked as farmers, artisans, or merchants.

From an early age, boys in Aztec society were taught to be warriors. Girls were trained to work at home, weave cloth, and prepare for motherhood. Although not equal to men, Aztec women could own and inherit property.

Priests played an important role in Aztec society. Some sacrificed captives to please the gods. Death was considered honorable. The Aztec believed that those sacrificed would be rewarded in the afterlife.

Aztec priests also worked to preserve the religion, history, and literature of their people. Priests recorded these in books that historians still refer to today. Like the Maya, the Aztec

INTERFOTO/Alamy Stock Photo

Academic Vocabulary

rely to depend on

developed two different calendars. They used a religious calendar with 260 days to keep track of important ceremonies and festivals. They also had a 365-day calendar for everyday use and for marking the time for planting and harvesting crops.

Much of Mexico was not suited for farming. The Aztec overcame this difficulty by irrigating and fertilizing the land. Aztec crafts, as well as fruit, vegetables, and grain from Aztec farms, passed through markets and along trade routes. The trade in these goods and the tribute from conquered peoples helped make the Aztec Empire wealthy.

☑ PROGRESS CHECK

Explaining Why did the Aztec develop two different calendars?

The Inca

GUIDING QUESTION *How did the Inca organize their government and society?*

In the late A.D. 1300s, the Inca were only one of many groups that fought over scarce fertile land in the valleys of the Andes Mountains. From their capital of Cuzco, the Inca raided nearby groups and seized territory. Within 100 years, the Inca had created a powerful empire.

Inca Rulers

A series of strong emperors helped build the Inca Empire. Pachacuti (PAH•chah•KOO•tee) was the first of these rulers. In the A.D. 1430s, he launched a campaign of conquest. The two emperors who followed continued this expansion, building the largest empire in the Americas.

According to Aztec legend, in 1325 an eagle was seen atop a cactus with a snake in its mouth. This event fulfilled an Aztec prediction. As a result, this location became the capital of the Aztec Empire, Tenochtitlán.

**Pachacuti
(ruled A.D. 1438–1471)**

As emperor, Pachacuti concentrated on expanding the Inca Empire. When he wanted to conquer a kingdom, he first sent messengers to tell the local rulers all the benefits of being part of the Inca Empire. Pachacuti then asked the other rulers to join his empire. If they accepted willingly, they were treated with respect and given some rights. If they refused, the Inca attacked with brutal force.

▶ **CRITICAL THINKING**
Analyzing What do you think would be the advantages and disadvantages of joining the Inca Empire?

To hold the empire together, Inca rulers created a strong central government. They set up tax bureaus, legal courts, military posts, and other government offices. Inca emperors required people to learn Quechua (KEH•chuh•wuh), the language spoken by the Inca. People also had to work for the government for several weeks each year.

Inca Projects

The Inca had people work on projects such as a system of roads. When finished, these roads connected all parts of the empire. This large network helped the Inca overcome geographic barriers. The roads helped move soldiers, goods, and information quickly over the coastal deserts and high mountains.

The Inca also used irrigation and fertilizers to improve the soil. Inca engineers developed terrace farming. Terrace farming uses a series of wide steps built into a mountainside. Each step creates level farmland. Inca farmers grew potatoes and quinoa, a protein-rich grain. Government officials stored food when there were good harvests and **distributed** it when harvests were poor.

How Was Inca Society Organized?

The Inca believed their rulers had the protection of the sun god Inti (IHN•tee). As divine rulers, Inca emperors controlled the lives of their subjects. They owned all the land and set rules for growing crops and distributing food.

Below the emperor and his family were the head priest and the leading commander of the army. Next came regional army leaders. Below them were temple priests, local army commanders, and skilled workers. At the bottom were farmers, herders, and ordinary soldiers.

Like the Aztec Empire, the Inca Empire was built on war. All young men were required to serve in the army, which made it the largest and best armed military force in the region.

Culture of the Inca

The Inca believed in many gods. Unlike the Aztec, the Inca rarely sacrificed humans to honor their gods. They did, however, build large stone structures to please these dieties. They had no system of writing, no wheels, and no iron tools. Yet they built places like Machu Picchu (mah•choo PEE•choo), a retreat for Inca emperors. Constructed of white granite and thousands of feet high, Machu Picchu was located in the Andes.

Oscar Garces/Photo Stock/Agefotostock

Building enormous structures like Machu Picchu required the Inca to develop a method for doing mathematics. The Inca used a **quipu** (KEE•poo), a rope with knotted cords of different lengths and colors. This was a useful tool for both mathematics and for record keeping.

The Inca were also skilled engineers. Inca workers fit stones so tightly together that they needed no mortar. Because the stone blocks could slide up and down during earthquakes, many Inca structures have survived.

✔ **PROGRESS CHECK**

Describing What building projects did the Inca carry out?

North American Peoples

GUIDING QUESTION *What were the societies of North American peoples like?*

By A.D. 1500, many different groups of Native Americans lived north of Mesoamerica. They spoke about 300 languages and called themselves by thousands of different names. As they spread across North America, these peoples adapted to the different environments.

How Did People Live in the Far North?

The first people to reach the far northern areas of North America called themselves the Inuit (IH•new•weht), which means "the people." The Inuit settled along the coasts of the tundra (TUN•drah) region, the treeless land south of the Arctic.

The Inuit adapted well to their cold environment. They used dogsleds on land and seal-skin kayaks (KEYE•ackz) at sea. In winter, they built homes from stone and blocks of earth. When they traveled, they built igloos, **temporary** homes made from cut blocks of hard-packed snow.

The Inuit were skilled hunters. They used spears made from animal antlers or tusks to hunt seals, walruses, caribou, and polar bears. Blubber, or fat, from seals and whales was a food that provided needed calories and furnished oil for lamps.

The ruins of Machu Picchu draw thousands of visitors. Research suggests that this monument was used as a home for the royal family and as a center for celebrations.

(t)Jeremy Horner/Getty Images; (b)Werner Forman/Art Resource, NY

Academic Vocabulary

temporary not permanent; lasting for a limited period

Visual Vocabulary

quipu a tool used in mathematics and as a system of historical record keeping. The quipu used knots to represent numbers and items.

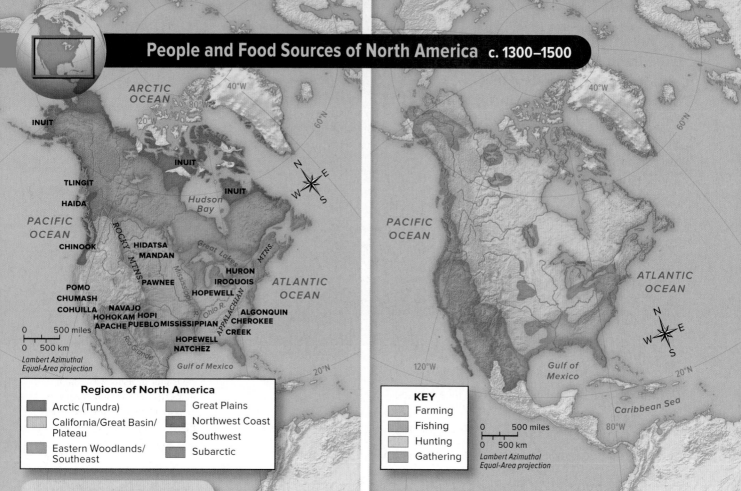

Regions of North America

- Arctic (Tundra)
- California/Great Basin/Plateau
- Eastern Woodlands/Southeast
- Great Plains
- Northwest Coast
- Southwest
- Subarctic

0   500 miles
0   500 km
Lambert Azimuthal Equal-Area projection

KEY

- Farming
- Fishing
- Hunting
- Gathering

0   500 miles
0   500 km
Lambert Azimuthal Equal-Area projection

GEOGRAPHY CONNECTION

Certain groups lived in different North American regions. Depending on the geography of their region, North Americans found food in different ways.

1. **PLACE** What was the most common method for obtaining food on the Atlantic coast?

2. **CRITICAL THINKING**
   Analyzing Why do you think fishing was more common along the Gulf of Mexico and Florida than along the northern Atlantic coast?

West Coast Life

The Pacific coast of North America had a mild climate and reliable food sources. As a result, this was the most heavily populated region north of Mesoamerica.

In the Pacific Northwest, peoples such as the Tlingit (TLIHNG·kuht), Haida (HEYE·deh), and Chinook (shuh·NOOK) used cedar trees to build wooden houses and canoes. They hunted and fished for otters, seals, whales, and their main food—salmon.

More than 500 early American cultures thrived in the area that is now California, including the Chumash (choo·MASH), the Cahuilla (kuh·WEE·uh), and the Pomo (POH·moh).

In the Southwest, the Hopi (HOH·pee), the Acoma (AHK·eh·meh), and the Zuni (ZOO·nee) built apartment-like homes from sun-dried mud bricks called adobe (uh·DOH·bee). The Southwest peoples dug irrigation canals to bring water to their fields. Their major crops were corn, beans, squash, and melons. They developed a trade network that spread into Mesoamerica.

Reading HELPDESK

hogan a square wooden home

In the A.D. 1500s, two new groups—the Apache (uh·PAH·chee) and the Navajo (NAH·vah·hoe)—settled in the Southwest. The Apache and Navajo were hunters and gatherers. In time, the Navajo became farmers and settled in villages made up of square wooden homes called **hogans** (HOH·gahns). The Apache, however, remained hunters.

Life on the Great Plains

Native Americans living on the Great Plains were nomads. They set up temporary villages that lasted for only one or two growing seasons. Their homes were cone-shaped skin tents called tepees. Farming on the Great Plains was not easy. Peoples like the Mandan (MAHN·dahn) and Pawnee (paw·NEE), however, planted gardens in the fertile soil along rivers.

Plains women grew beans, corn, and squash. Before the arrival of the horse, men hunted by driving herds of antelope, deer, and bison over cliffs to their deaths. Plains peoples had many uses for the bison. They ate the meat, used the skins for clothing and tepees, and made tools from the bones.

How Did People Live in the Eastern Woodlands?

The land east of the Mississippi River was known as the Eastern Woodlands because of its dense forests. Farming was widely practiced in the southeast. The most important crops were corn, beans, and squash. In the cooler northeast, people depended more on hunting animals, such as deer, bear, rabbits, and beaver.

The people of the Eastern Woodlands formed complex societies with different kinds of governments. One plan was formed in the 1500s to end fighting among five groups. The Iroquois (IHR·uh·kwoy) Confederacy created the first constitution, or plan of government, in what is now the United States.

✔ PROGRESS CHECK

Explaining Why did the Iroquois form a confederacy?

Thinking Like a HISTORIAN

Comparing and Contrasting

Early Americans adapted to the environments in which they settled. As a result, many different cultures and ways of life developed. As you read, note the similarities and differences among Native Americans living in the far north, the Pacific Coast, the Southwest, the Great Plains, and the Eastern Woodlands. Share your findings with the class. For more information on comparing and contrasting, read the chapter *What Does a Historian Do?*

LESSON 2 REVIEW

Review Vocabulary

1. How did *sinkholes* help the Maya?

2. How did a *hogan* differ from a tepee?

Answer the Guiding Questions

3. *Evaluating* What were the advantages and disadvantages for the Maya of living in the rain forest?

4. *Contrasting* How did Native American groups on the Pacific Coast differ from those in the Southwest?

5. *Drawing Conclusions* How did establishing a confederacy benefit Woodlands Native Americans?

6. **NARRATIVE** Describe daily life in a Maya city-state from the point of view of a Maya priest.

Write your answers on a separate piece of paper.

1 **Exploring the Essential Question**

INFORMATIVE/EXPLANATORY How did geography affect the societies and cultures that developed in the early Americas? Choose two early civilizations or cultures that developed in different parts of the Americas. Write an essay describing how each adapted to its environment. Describe their food, shelter, government, and religion.

2 **21st Century Skills**

DEBATING Which civilization that you read about in this chapter do you think had the greatest achievements? Choose a civilization and list its achievements as well as the reasons those achievements are important. Then, debate the issue with a fellow classmate who chose a different civilization.

3 **Thinking Like a Historian**

SEQUENCING Create a time line like the one shown. Fill in significant dates and events in the history of the Maya Empire.

A.D. 300
Maya develop civilization in southern Mexico and Central America

4 **GEOGRAPHY ACTIVITY**

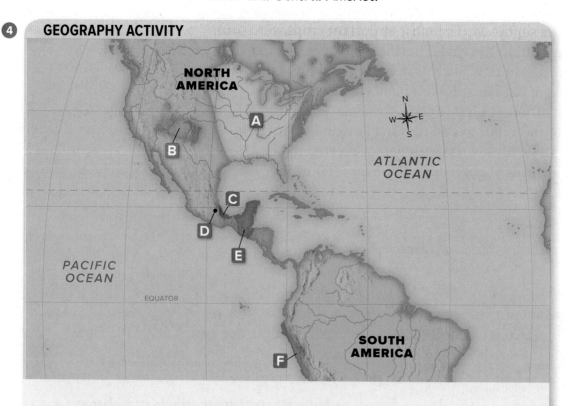

Locating Places

Match the letters on the map with the numbered groups listed below.

1. Anasazi
2. Aztec
3. Chavín
4. Maya
5. Mound Builders
6. Olmec

CHAPTER 16 Assessment

Directions: Write your answers on a separate piece of paper.

CHECKING FOR UNDERSTANDING

1 Match the following terms with their descriptions.
1. isthmus
2. maize
3. sinkhole
4. hogan

A. corn
B. a narrow piece of land that connects two larger areas of land
C. a square wooden home
D. an area where the soil has collapsed into a hollow or depression

REVIEW THE GUIDING QUESTIONS

2 *Identifying* Based on the geography of the Great Plains, what advantages did people settling in that area have?

3 *Describing* In what two ways do scientists think prehistoric people reached the Americas?

4 *Explaining* Why was it necessary for people to become farmers in order for civilization to begin?

5 *Summarizing* Use your own words to summarize why so many different societies developed in North America.

6 *Specifying* What steps did the Maya take to make the rain forests livable?

7 *Paraphrasing* Use your own words to describe how the Aztec established their society in central Mexico.

8 *Listing* What were the different levels of Inca society?

9 *Discussing* What kind of society did the Inuit create?

CRITICAL THINKING

10 *Analyzing* Why were bison important to Native Americans living on the Great Plains?

11 *Speculating* Why do you think the first planned cities were built in areas such as central Mexico rather than in areas such as the northeast region of North America?

12 *Contrasting* How was farming in Costa Rica different from farming in North America's Southwest?

13 *Drawing Conclusions* Why do you think the Maya had two types of calendars? Give specific reasons for your answer.

14 *Giving Examples* What are two examples of how the people of the Pacific Northwest adapted to their environment?

15 *Integrating Visual Information* Study the image of the mask on the first page of this chapter. Based on this mask and what you have learned about the Aztec's religion, what conclusions can you draw about the mask?

16 *Determining Cause and Effect* What were two reasons that the Anasazi built their homes in the walls of steep cliffs?

17 *Predicting Consequences* What do you think might have happened if the Inca had not had a complex system of roads?

18 *Reasoning* Why do you think salt was an important item that the Olmec traded with people living inland?

19 *Recognizing Relationships* How was the location of Tenochtitlán related to the Aztec religion?

20 *Defending* Do you think it is more likely that the first people who came to the Americas from Asia arrived by boat or walked across a land bridge to Alaska? Give reasons for your opinion.

Need Extra Help?

If You've Missed Question	1	2	3	4	5	6	7	8	9	10	11	12	13	14	15	16	17	18	19	20
Review Lesson	1,2	1	1	1	1	2	2	2	2	2	1	1,2	2	2	2	1	2	1	2	1

DBQ SHORT RESPONSE

"Recently, archaeologists have studied the Maya in many new ways . . . A big breakthrough was learning to read Maya writing.

"Archaeologists also look at layers of dirt in lake bottoms to see how the land has changed. . . . They even dig through the Maya's trash.

"All this work has given scientists new ideas . . . A big one was that the Maya world probably had too many people . . . ."

—Guy Gugliotta, "Maya Mystery," *National Geographic* 2007

21 Why do you think archaeologists think it is important to know about rain?

22 What does it mean, "the Maya world probably had too many people"?

EXTENDED RESPONSE

23 ***Narrative*** You are an early American. Write a journal entry describing an encounter with a Native American people in one of the regions described in the chapter. Describe their daily life. Focus on the unique characteristics of their culture.

STANDARDIZED TEST PRACTICE

DBQ ANALYZING DOCUMENTS

The author of the following creation myth of the Inca is unknown:

"Thus our imperial city . . . was divided into two halves: . . . [Upper] Cuzco was founded by our king and . . . [Lower] Cuzco by our queen . . . There existed only one single difference between them, . . . that the inhabitants of Upper-Cuzco were to be considered as the elders . . . [they] had been brought together by the male, and those below by the female element."

24 ***Analyzing*** Which statement best describes how the imperial city was separated?
A. The citizens in Upper-Cuzco chose to be independent.
B. A council of elders decided to divide the city into four kingdoms.
C. Invaders captured the lower half of the city.
D. The king founded one half of the city and the queen founded the other.

25 ***Evaluating*** Why were the inhabitants of Upper-Cuzco considered to be elders?
A. They were located to the north.
B. They had founded their city first.
C. Their city was founded by a male.
D. They had defeated the citizens of Lower-Cuzco.

Need Extra Help?

If You've Missed Question	**21**	**22**	**23**	**24**	**25**
Review Lesson	2	2	1, 2	2	2

◄ *Empress Wu showed no mercy to her enemies and demanded absolute acceptance of her rulings.*

A.D. 600 TO 1644

Imperial China

The British Library/Heritage/Age fotostock

THE STORY MATTERS ...

The year is A.D. 683, and the Chinese Emperor Gaozong (GOW • ZUNG) has died from a crippling stroke. Who will rule China? His empress steps in and takes control of the government. Empress Wu at first places her sons on the throne, although she holds the real power. Then, in 690, she seized the throne for herself. Wu would be the only woman ever to rule China as emperor. She governed China using ruthless methods. Yet she is remembered for achieving prosperity, being fair to the people, and improving government services. Her long career outlasted many government officials who criticized her. Wu ruled China until her death at age 80.

ESSENTIAL QUESTIONS

• How does geography influence the way people live?
• How do new ideas change the way people live?
• What are the characteristics of a leader?

Place & Time: Imperial China A.D. 600 to 1644

In the late 1200s, the Mongol Empire stretched from Eastern Europe to the Pacific Ocean. China's borders expanded and contracted under Mongol rulers. For centuries, Mongols and other dynasties in China seized power, extended the territory, and developed trade routes. Eventually, they would collapse or be overthrown.

Step Into the Place

PLACE In A.D. 1200s, the Mongols conquered China. They set up a new dynasty and extended the empire south and west.

1 PLACE What challenges did the geography of the Mongol empire present for travelers?

2 REGIONS Describe the extent of the Silk Road. What were its farthest boundaries at either end?

3 CRITICAL THINKING
Analyzing Identify two advantages and disadvantages of building and maintaining an enormous empire.

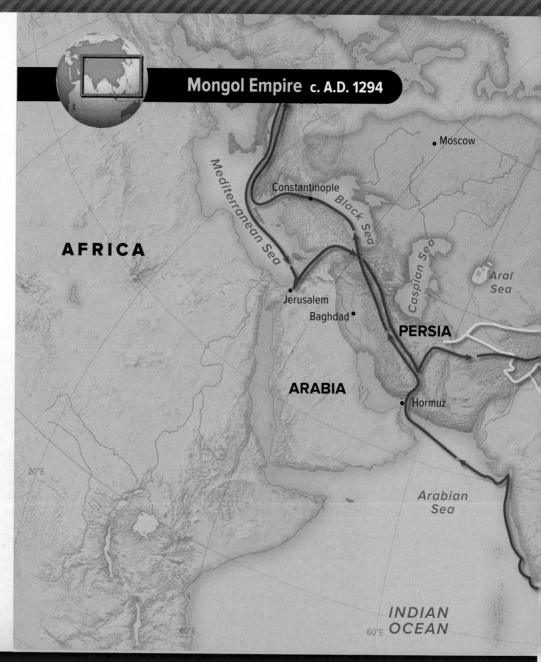

Mongol Empire c. A.D. 1294

Moscow

Mediterranean Sea

Constantinople

Black Sea

Caspian Sea

Aral Sea

AFRICA

Jerusalem

Baghdad

PERSIA

ARABIA

Hormuz

20°E

40°E

60°E

Arabian Sea

INDIAN OCEAN

Step Into the Time

TIME LINE Choose an event from the time line and write a paragraph predicting the general social, political, or economic consequence that event might have for the

c. A.D. 590 Grand Canal links northern and southern China

A.D. 690 Empress Wu begins rule

A.D. 898 Earliest known book printed

IMPERIAL CHINA

THE WORLD

A.D. 450   A.D. 600   A.D. 750   A.D. 900

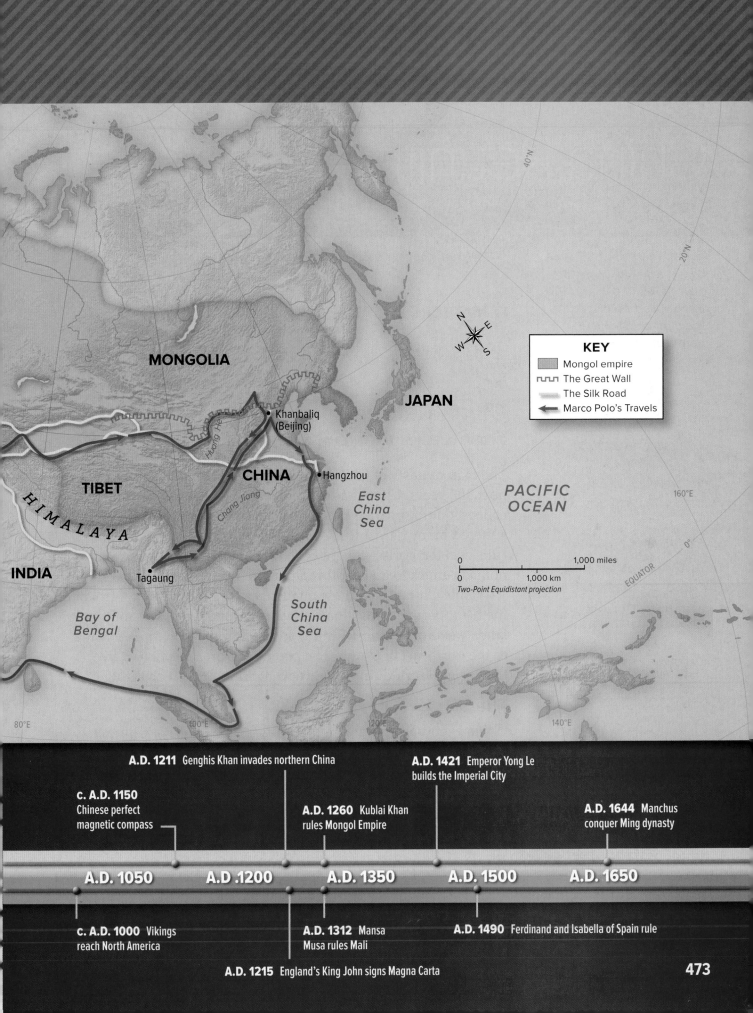

MONGOLIA

JAPAN

Khanbaliq
(Beijing)

CHINA

Hangzhou

TIBET

Chang Jiang

East
China
Sea

PACIFIC
OCEAN

HIMALAYA

INDIA

Tagaung

Bay of
Bengal

South
China
Sea

KEY
Mongol empire
The Great Wall
The Silk Road
Marco Polo's Travels

0   1,000 miles
0   1,000 km
Two-Point Equidistant projection

A.D. 1211 Genghis Khan invades northern China

A.D. 1421 Emperor Yong Le
builds the Imperial City

c. A.D. 1150
Chinese perfect
magnetic compass

A.D. 1260 Kublai Khan
rules Mongol Empire

A.D. 1644 Manchus
conquer Ming dynasty

A.D. 1050   **A.D .1200**   **A.D. 1350**   **A.D. 1500**   **A.D. 1650**

c. A.D. 1000 Vikings
reach North America

A.D. 1312 Mansa
Musa rules Mali

A.D. 1490 Ferdinand and Isabella of Spain rule

A.D. 1215 England's King John signs Magna Carta

LESSON 1

China Reunites

ESSENTIAL QUESTION

• How does geography influence the way people live?

IT MATTERS BECAUSE

Ideas and innovations introduced during the Sui,. Tang, and Song dynasties united China after centuries of chaos and helped it become a powerful empire.

China Rebuilds Its Empire

GUIDING QUESTION *How did China rebuild its empire after years of war?*

The Han dynasty of China came to an end in A.D. 220. For the next 300 years, China had no central government. The country collapsed into separate kingdoms, and the Chinese people suffered many hardships. Warlords—military leaders who rule local territories—fought each other. Meanwhile, groups of nomads attacked and captured parts of northern China.

While China faced these challenges at home, it lost control of the neighboring lands it had previously conquered. One of these lands was Korea (kuh·REE·uh), located on the Korean Peninsula to the northeast of China. The people of Korea decided to free themselves from Chinese rule and build their own civilization.

The Sui

China eventually became more unified. In A.D. 581, a Chinese general named Wendi (WHEHN·dee) declared himself emperor. He won many battles and set up a new dynasty called the Sui (SWAY). The Sui dynasty again unified China under the rule of emperors.

Reading**HELP**DESK

Taking Notes: *Identifying*

Use a chart like this one to list important events and accomplishments during each Chinese dynasty.

Sui	Tang	Song

Content Vocabulary

• **neo-Confucianism**

After Wendi died, his son Yangdi (YAHNG·dee) became emperor. Yangdi wanted to expand China's territory. He tried to regain lost lands. His army fought the Koreans, but it was badly defeated.

Within China, Yangdi had more success at expanding his dynasty. He wanted to bring back the glory of the Han dynasty. Yangdi repaired the Great Wall, which had fallen into ruins. He also rebuilt the magnificent Han capital city of Changan (CHAHNG·AHN).

Yangdi's most ambitious project was building the Grand Canal. This system of waterways connected China's two great rivers, the Huang He (HWAHNG HUH) (Yellow River) and the Chang Jiang (CHAHNG JYAHNG) (Yangtze River). The two rivers flowed east to west and were connected by the Grand Canal, which was built north to south. The Grand Canal made it easier to ship rice and other products between northern and southern China and united China's economy.

To rebuild China, Yangdi required help from the Chinese people. Farmers were forced to work on the Great Wall and the Grand Canal. They had to pay higher taxes to support these projects. Their taxes also paid for the emperor's luxurious way of life, which made the farmers angry. The farmers revolted and Yangdi was killed, bringing an end to the Sui dynasty.

GEOGRAPHY CONNECTION

The Tang dynasty lasted about 300 years.

1. **PLACE** What two cities were connected by the Grand Canal?

2. **CRITICAL THINKING** *Determining Cause and Effect* How might these cities have been affected by the building of the Grand Canal?

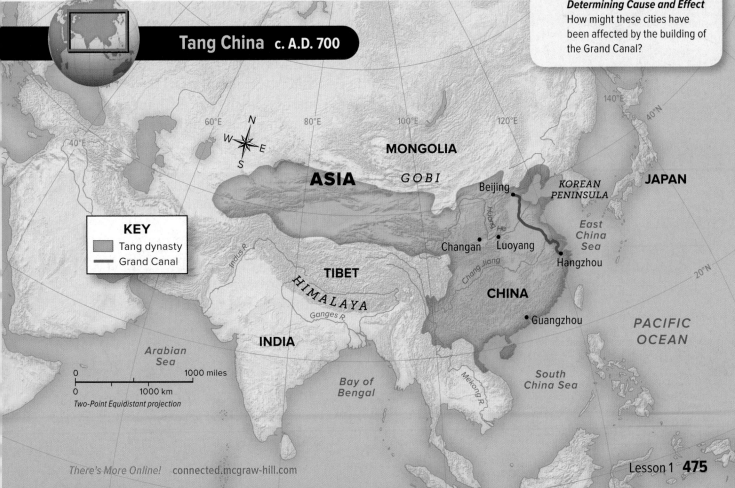

Tang China c. A.D. 700

KEY
- Tang dynasty
- Grand Canal

Empress Wu (A.D. 624–705)

Chinese ruler Empress Wu did not come from an upper-class family. As a young woman, she joined the emperor's court, where she used her intelligence to influence important people. Emperor Gaozong (GOW • ZUNG) declared her his empress, and she ruled China in his name during his many illnesses. After the death of Emperor Gaozong, Empress Wu's sons were rulers. In A.D. 690, Empress Wu overthrew her second son. Wu won the respect of the people because of her ability to rule and her determination to make China stronger.

Explaining How did Empress Wu gain a great deal of support from the people?

The Tang Dynasty

In A.D. 618, one of Yangdi's generals took over China. He made himself emperor and founded a new dynasty called the Tang (TAHNG). Unlike the short-lived Sui, the Tang dynasty lasted for nearly 300 years—from A.D. 618 to A.D. 907.

Tang rulers worked to **restore** a strong central government in China. They made many reforms, or changes, to improve the government. The most powerful Tang emperor was named Taizong (TY•DZUNG). He brought back the system of **civil** service examinations. Once again, government officials were selected based on how well they did on exams rather than on their family connections. Taizong also gave land to farmers and brought peace and order to the countryside.

During the late A.D. 600s, Empress Wu (WOO) ruled China. She was the only woman in Chinese history to rule the country on her own. Empress Wu was a powerful leader who added more officials to the government and strengthened the military.

Growth and Trade

Tang rulers worked to restore China's power in Asia. They expanded their rule westward to Tibet (tuh•BEHT), an area north of the Himalaya (HIH•muh•LAY•uh). The Chinese also took control of the Silk Road and northern Vietnam. They increased trade with other parts of Asia and forced neighboring states, such as Korea, to pay them tribute.

As trade increased, Chinese cities became wealthy. Changan, the Tang capital, grew to be the world's largest city. About one million people lived there. Visitors were impressed by its wide avenues and large market squares. Merchants in Changan sold goods from places as far away as India and Southwest Asia.

By the mid-A.D. 700s, however, the Tang faced growing challenges to their rule. Turkish nomads drove Tang armies out of central Asia and won control of the Silk Road. Because Chinese merchants could not use the Silk Road safely, trade and the economy suffered.

Revolts by Chinese farmers further weakened the Tang. In response, the Tang rulers hired Uighurs (WEE•GURZ), a Turkish-speaking people in the northwest, to fight for them. However, it was too late. Continued unrest led to the fall of the Tang rule in A.D. 907.

Time & Life Pictures/Getty Images

Reading**HELP**DESK

Academic Vocabulary

restore to bring something back to an earlier or better condition
civil relating to the state or government

CITY LIFE IN TANG CHINA

Musicians and dancers

Farmers selling goods

Civil service examinations

Print Shop

Making pottery

The Song Dynasty

After the fall of the Tang, military leaders ruled China. Then in A.D. 960, one of the generals became emperor and founded the Song (SUNG) dynasty. The Song governed from A.D. 960 to A.D. 1279. During this time, the Chinese enjoyed economic prosperity and made many cultural achievements.

From the beginning, the Song emperors faced many challenges. They did not have enough military forces to protect their entire empire. In the north, groups of nomads took over parts of the country. For protection, the Song rulers moved their government south to the city of Hangzhou (HAHNG·JOH). Hangzhou was on the coast near the Chang Jiang delta.

✓ PROGRESS CHECK

Explaining How did the Grand Canal help China's economy?

INFOGRAPHIC

Under the Tang, China grew wealthy. Its growing cities contained many shops and temples.

1 **DESCRIBING** What activities took place in the cities of Tang China?

2 **CRITICAL THINKING** *Explaining* How does producing a variety of goods make a country stronger?

Song China c. A.D. 1200

GOBI
40°N
100°E
Beijing
120°E
KOREAN PENINSULA
Changan
Luoyang
Huang He
East China Sea
CHINA
Hangzhou
Chang Jiang

KEY
Song empire
Grand Canal

0 ____ 500 miles
0 ____ 500 km
Two-Point Equidistant projection

N W E S

Guangzhou

20°N

Bay of Bengal

Mekong R.

South China Sea

GEOGRAPHY CONNECTION

The Song dynasty moved the capital city from Changan to Hangzhou.

1 **LOCATION** About how far is the Korean Peninsula from the Song capital city of Hangzhou?

2 **CRITICAL THINKING** *Comparing* How did the size of Song China compare with the size of Tang China?

Buddhism in China

GUIDING QUESTION *Why did Buddhism become popular in Tang China?*

Traders and missionaries from India brought Buddhism to China during the A.D. 100s. At the time, the Han dynasty was in decline, and civil war soon broke out in China. Many people died from the fighting, hunger, and lack of shelter. Buddhism taught that people could escape suffering by following its teachings. As a result, many Chinese seeking peace and comfort became Buddhists.

How Did Tang Rulers View Buddhism?

Early Tang rulers did not practice Buddhism, but they did not interfere with its following in China. They approved the building of new Buddhist temples and shrines.

Many Chinese Buddhists joined religious communities called monasteries, where they lived, worked, and worshipped. The men in these communities were monks, and the women were nuns. Buddhist monks and nuns helped local people by running schools and providing food and shelter for travelers. Monks also served as bankers and provided medical care.

Although numerous Chinese became Buddhists, a large part of the population opposed the religion. Many believed that Buddhist temples and monasteries had grown too wealthy because of the donations they received. Others believed that monks and nuns weakened respect for family life because they were not allowed to marry.

Tang officials feared Buddhism's growing influence. They saw Buddhism as an enemy of China's Confucian (kuhn·FYOO·shuhn) traditions. Confucian traditions are customs related to the teachings of Confucius. In A.D. 845, the Tang government destroyed many Buddhist monasteries and temples. Buddhism in China never fully recovered from these attacks.

Buddhism in Korea

Korea broke free of Chinese rule when the Han dynasty fell in A.D. 220. For several hundred years afterward, Korea was divided into three distinct kingdoms.

In the A.D. 300s, Chinese Buddhists brought their religion to Korea. About A.D. 660, the three Korean kingdoms united to form one country. Because the new Korean government favored Buddhism, the religion attracted a large number of followers throughout Korea.

Reading**HELP**DESK

Reading Strategy: *Summarizing*

When you summarize, you restate important ideas in your own words. Read about how Tang rulers viewed Buddhism. On a separate sheet of paper, summarize what you read in one or two sentences.

Buddhism later spread from Korea to the nearby islands of Japan. In A.D. 552, a Korean king sent missionaries to the emperor of Japan. The missionaries brought Buddhist writings and a statue of the Buddha. They also brought a letter from the king meant to influence the emperor of Japan. As time passed, many people in Japan became Buddhists.

In a letter to the emperor, the Korean king wrote about Buddhism and its teachings:

PRIMARY SOURCE

❝ This religion is the most excellent of all teachings. . . . It brings endless and immeasurable [countless] blessings . . . , even the attainment [achieving] of supreme enlightenment. . . . Moreover, the religion has come over to Korea far from India, and the peoples (in the countries between these two) are now ardent [eager] followers of its teaching. ❞

—from *Nihonji* (Chronicles of Japan)

✔ **PROGRESS CHECK**

Describing How did Buddhist monks and nuns help the Chinese?

This towering monument to the Buddha was carved in about A.D. 460 in the Yuan Kang caves of China.

▶ **CRITICAL THINKING**
Identifying Points of View Why might Buddhism appeal to people who had just experienced a civil war?

Revival of Confucian Ideas

GUIDING QUESTION *How did Confucian ideas shape China's government?*

Confucius believed that a good government depended on having wise leaders. The civil service examinations begun by Han rulers were based on Confucian **principles.** The exams helped provide China's government with well-educated, talented officials.

After the fall of the Han dynasty, China had no central government to give civil service examinations. Confucianism went into decline, and Buddhism won many followers with its message of escape from suffering. Tang and Song rulers worked to return Confucianism to the respected position it had held previously in Chinese society.

Confucius wrote about ethical and moral behavior, both by governments and individuals.

Neo-Confucianism

The Tang and Song dynasties backed a new understanding of Confucianism called **neo-Confucianism** (NEE·oh-kuhn·FYOO·shuhn·ih·zuhm). One reason this new Confucianism was created was to stop the growing influence of Buddhism. Neo-Confucianism taught that people should be concerned about this world as well as the afterlife. Followers were expected to be active in society and to help others. A Confucian thinker named Han Yü (HAHN YOO) lived from A.D. 768 to A.D. 824. He encouraged the Chinese to remain faithful to the Confucian teachings of their ancestors:

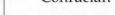
PRIMARY SOURCE

" What were the teachings of our ancient kings? Universal love is called humanity. To practice this in the proper manner is called righteousness. To proceed according to these is called the Way. ... They [ancestors] offered sacrifices to Heaven and the gods came to receive them. ... What Way is this? I say: This is what I call the Way, and not what the Taoists [Daoists] and the Buddhists called the Way. "

—from *An Inquiry on The Way*, by Han Yü

This new form of Confucianism also included some Buddhist and Daoist beliefs. Chinese culture was developing and changing at this time. For many Chinese, Confucianism became more than a set of rules for good behavior. It became

Panorama Media/Panorama Stock RF/Photolibrary

Reading **HELP**DESK

neo-Confucianism a new form of the ideas of the philosopher Confucius; included Buddhist and Daoist beliefs

Academic Vocabulary

principle a basic truth or belief

a religious tradition with beliefs about the spiritual world. Confucian thinkers taught that people would find peace of mind if they followed the teachings of Confucius.

The Civil Service

Tang and Song rulers saw neo-Confucianism and civil service examinations as a way to strengthen the government. They believed that a government run by educated people was less likely to become corrupt or weak.

The examinations tested candidates on their knowledge of Confucian writings. Only men were allowed to take the tests, and the examination system favored the rich. Few poor families could pay tutors to help their sons qualify for the tests.

Preparing for the tests was very difficult. At the age of four, boys began learning to write the characters of the Chinese language. Later, students had to memorize all the writings of Confucius. They had to recite the writings aloud. After years of preparing, the boys took the exams. Despite all the hard work, only one in five boys passed the tests. Those who did not pass usually found jobs teaching or helping government workers, but they were never given a government job.

Over the years, the examination system created a new class of leaders in China. This group was made up of scholar-officials. Strict rules set the scholar-officials apart from the rest of society. One rule was that the scholar-officials could not perform any job that required physical work. These scholar-officials influenced Chinese thought and government well into modern times.

☑ PROGRESS CHECK

Determining Cause and Effect How did the civil service examinations affect Chinese society?

Connections to
TODAY

Civil Service Examinations

As in imperial China, most people who apply for government jobs in the United States must take a civil service examination. Before the late 1800s, most government posts in the U.S. were appointed. Many people were placed in important jobs because of their political connections.

LESSON 1 REVIEW

Review Vocabulary

1. How was *neo-Confucianism* different from Confucianism?

Answer the Guiding Questions

2. *Identifying* How did the emperor Yangdi change China?

3. *Describing* How did access to the Silk Road affect China's economy?

4. *Explaining* Why did Buddhism become widely adopted in China?

5. *Comparaing and Contrasting* How is Buddhism different from neo-Confucianism?

6. **ARGUMENT** You have just passed the civil service examination in Song China. You will be given a government job. What opinion are you likely to have about neo-Confucianism? Write a short persuasive letter in which you explain how neo-Confucianism will help or hurt your career.

LESSON 2
Chinese Society

ESSENTIAL QUESTION

• How do new ideas change the way people live?

IT MATTERS BECAUSE

During the Tang and Song dynasties, the economy of China grew through trade and improvements in technology.

Economic Growth

GUIDING QUESTION *How did China's economy change under the Tang and Song dynasties?*

The fall of the Han dynasty in the A.D. 200s crippled the economy of China. Widespread fighting destroyed farms and cities. Farmers faced poor harvests. Artisans made fewer products, and merchants had fewer goods to trade. Under the Tang dynasty, China's economy recovered and even prospered.

Farming Improvements

After taking power in A.D. 618, the Tang gave more land to farmers. Farmers made many advances in farming these large land plots. They improved irrigation methods, which increased the growth of their crops. They developed new kinds of rice that grew well in poor soil. The new varieties of rice produced more rice per acre and resisted disease. Farmers also began to grow tea, which became a popular drink.

Because more food was available, China's population increased as well. People began to settle in new areas, which then developed into cities. Groups of farmers moved from the north to southern China. They grew abundant amounts of rice in the Chang Jiang valley.

Reading**HELP**DESK

Taking Notes: *Categorizing*

Use a graphic organizer like the one here to identify Chinese advancements in the economy, technology, and the arts.

Economy   Technology   The Arts

Chinese Advancements

Content Vocabulary

• **porcelain**   • **calligraphy**

Why Did China's Trade Grow?

Tang rulers built roads and waterways. As a result, travel within and outside of China became much easier. Chinese merchants increased trade with people in other parts of the world. After years of decline, the Silk Road reopened and thrived. Caravans traveled along it, carrying goods from China to other parts of Asia.

Silk fabric was one of the goods traded by the Chinese. Silk was in high demand in areas west of China. In addition, China traded other products, such as tea, steel, paper, and porcelain. **Porcelain** (POHR·suh·luhn) is made of fine clay that is baked at high temperatures. It is used to make dishes, vases, and other items. In return for Chinese products, countries sent goods such as gold, silver, precious stones, and fine woods to China.

Other trade routes were also opened. Roads connected China to other parts of Asia. In addition, the Tang opened new seaports along China's coast to increase trade.

✔ PROGRESS CHECK

Determining Cause and Effect How did advancements in farming affect China's population?

Technological Advances

GUIDING QUESTION *How did new inventions change China's society?*

During the Tang and Song dynasties, new discoveries and inventions brought change to Chinese society. In time, these technological advancements spread to other parts of the world.

Coal and Steel

Important changes took place in the use of fuels and metals. For most of their history, the Chinese burned wood to heat their homes and cook their food. By the A.D. 600s, less wood was available in China. The Chinese, however, discovered that coal could be used as a fuel. This discovery led to the development of a coal-mining industry.

Silk worms spin cocoons made of raw silk thread. Workers then collect and unravel the valuable cocoons by hand.

▶ **CRITICAL THINKING**
Making Inferences Why do you think silk is still expensive today?

porcelain a ceramic made of fine clay baked at very high temperatures

(t)David R. Frazier/The Image Works; (b)fotohunter/iStock/Getty Images

The Chinese used coal to heat furnaces to high temperatures. This process led to another discovery. When iron was produced in coal-heated furnaces, the melted iron mixed with carbon from the coal. This mixing created a new, stronger metal known today as steel.

The Chinese used steel to make many different products. They made armor, swords, and helmets for their armies. They also produced stoves, farm tools, and drills. Nails and sewing needles were made from steel as well.

The Invention of Printing

Paper had been invented during the time of the Han dynasty. Under the Tang, paper was produced in large amounts.

The manufacture of paper led to another important Chinese invention: a **method** for printing books. Before printing, books were copied by hand and were very expensive.

Chinese Buddhist monks began woodblock printing in the A.D. 600s. In woodblock printing, printers used a wooden block for each page they needed to print. They carved the page's Chinese characters into the block. Then they put ink on the block and pressed a piece of paper onto it. The printers rubbed the sheet of paper to **transfer** the Chinese characters onto the page. Each wooden block could be used to make thousands of copies.

The earliest known printed book dates from about A.D. 868. It is a Buddhist book called the *Diamond Sutra*. Even though woodblock printing was a major advancement, changes could not be made to a page once the wooden block was carved.

In the A.D. 1000s, a Chinese printer named Pi Sheng (PEE SHUHNG) solved this printing problem by inventing movable type. With movable type, each character is an individual piece. The pieces can be arranged to form sentences and used again and again. Pi Sheng made his pieces from clay and put them together to make book pages.

The Chinese invented movable type. It was necessary to carve individual symbols that could be moved and set into a printing press. Printing presses still use techniques pioneered by the Chinese.

▶ **CRITICAL THINKING**
Speculating What physical skill would a block printer need to have?

AFP/Getty Images

Reading**HELP**DESK

Academic Vocabulary

method a way of doing something
transfer to copy from one surface to another by contact

Reading Strategy: *Using Context Clues*

Context clues are not always in the same sentence as the unfamiliar word. Which sentence contains a context clue about the meaning of the word *transfer*?

Printing also led to the invention of paper currency. During the Tang dynasty, both rice production and trade greatly increased. Chinese traders needed more money to carry out business. The Chinese already produced copper coins, but they could not make enough coins to support the empire's economy.

In A.D. 1024, during the Song dynasty, the Chinese began to print the world's first paper money as a way to benefit traders. It still had the value of coin money, and it was lighter to carry. The use of paper money helped both the economy and cities to grow.

Gunpowder and Ships

Gunpowder was another Chinese invention created during the Tang dynasty. Gunpowder was used in explosives and weapons, such as the fire lance. This invention worked somewhat like a gun. It could shoot a mix of flames and objects a distance of 40 yards (36.6 m). The fire lance helped make China's army a powerful fighting force. The Chinese also used gunpowder to make fireworks.

Different Chinese inventions helped increase long-distance trade. The Chinese built large ships with rudders and sails, which helped with steering. About A.D. 1150, Chinese inventors perfected the magnetic compass. This compass helped Chinese sailors navigate their ships' locations and sail farther from land. As a result of these inventions, the Chinese were able to sail to Southeast Asia, India, and other places to the west.

The Tang capital city of Changan had a population of about one million people at its peak. The royal palace, shown below, was surrounded by park lands. It is thought to be one of the largest palaces ever built.

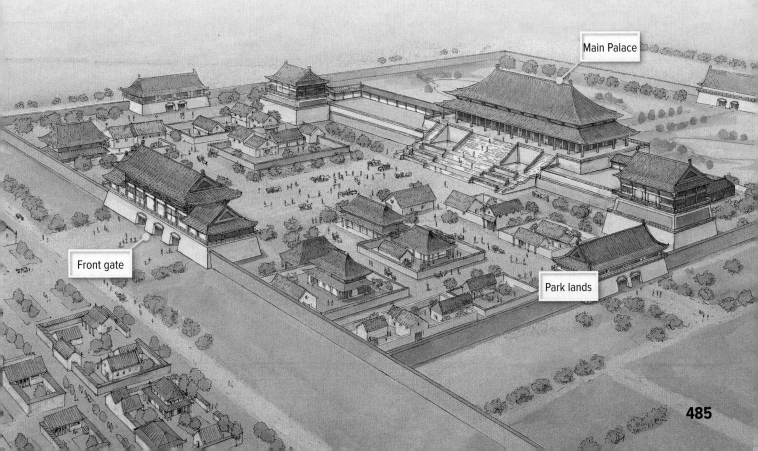

Main Palace

Front gate

Park lands

In time, many of these Chinese inventions would have a great effect on Europe. For example, printing made it possible to publish books in large quantities. Gunpowder changed how wars were fought. The magnetic compass enabled Europeans to explore the world.

✓ **PROGRESS CHECK**

Analyzing Why was the Chinese invention of printing important?

Literature and the Arts

GUIDING QUESTION *Why were the Tang and Song dynasties a golden age of literature and the arts?*

The Tang and Song dynasties were a golden age of Chinese culture. The invention of woodblock printing helped make literature more available and popular. Art, especially landscape painting, flourished during this period. Chinese rulers supported artists and writers. They invited them to live and work in the capital city of Changan.

An Age of Poetry

The Tang dynasty is regarded as the great age of poetry in China. The best known Chinese writers of this time are poets. Chinese poets often expressed a Daoist appreciation of the world. They wrote about the beauty of nature, the changes of the seasons, and the joys of friendship. They also expressed sadness at the shortness of life.

Li Bo (LEE BWAW) was one of the most popular poets of the Tang dynasty. Known for leading a carefree life, Li Bo wrote poems about nature. His poem below is one of the best-known poems in China. For years, the Chinese have memorized it. Its title is "Alone Looking at the Mountain."

According to legend, Li Bo drowned after reaching for the moon's reflection in the water beside his boat. He most likely died, poor and out of favor, in eastern China.

PRIMARY SOURCE

❝ All the birds have flown up and gone;
A lonely cloud floats leisurely by.
We never tire of looking at each other—
Only the mountain and I. ❞

—from "Alone Looking at the Mountain," by Li Bo

Another favorite Tang poet was Du Fu (DOO FOO). He was a poor civil servant who faced many hardships. During Du Fu's lifetime, civil war raged throughout China. Food was scarce, and Du Fu nearly died of starvation. As a result, Du Fu often wrote about issues such as the problems of the poor, the unfairness of life, and the wastefulness of war. Du Fu wrote the poem below after an uprising left the capital city in ruins.

PRIMARY SOURCE

" Behind those red gates
meat and wine are left to spoil
outside lie the bones
of people who starved and froze. "

—from "Five Hundred Words About My Journey to Fengxian," by Du Fu

Landscape Painting

During the Song dynasty, many Chinese artists painted landscapes. However, they did not try to show the exact appearance of places. Instead they tried to portray the "idea" of mountains, lakes, and other scenes. They left empty spaces in their paintings on purpose. This style reflects the Daoist belief that a person cannot know the whole truth about something. Daoism is the belief that people should turn to nature and give up their worldly concerns.

This landscape (left)—painted in the 1100s—shows the Daoist love of nature. The lettering of the Chinese poems (right) is as delicate as the images in the art.

Daoism also influenced the way people are portrayed in landscape paintings. Humans are shown as very small figures in a natural landscape. The paintings express the idea that people are part of nature but do not control it. People are only one part of a much larger natural setting.

Chinese painters often wrote poems on their works. They used a brush and ink to write beautiful characters called **calligraphy** (kuh·LIH·gruh·fee).

Porcelain

During the Tang dynasty, Chinese artisans became skilled in making porcelain. As you may recall, porcelain is a ceramic made of fine clay baked at very high temperatures. Because porcelain later came from China to the West, people today sometimes call porcelain "china."

Porcelain can be made into figurines, vases, cups, and plates. An Arab traveler in A.D. 851 described Chinese porcelain:

PRIMARY SOURCE

❝ There is in China a very fine clay from which are made vases having the transparency [clearness] of glass bottles; water in these vases is visible through them, and yet they are made of clay. ❞

—from *Account of Voyages Made by Arabs and Persians in India and China*

Methods for making porcelain spread to other parts of the world. They finally reached Europe in the A.D. 1700s.

✓ PROGRESS CHECK

Identifying What themes did Chinese poets often write about?

This bowl is Chinese porcelain. The word porcelain comes from French and Italian words for "shell," which the pottery resembles.

Henry Gan/Photodisc/Getty Images

LESSON 2 REVIEW

Review Vocabulary

1. What natural material do you need in order to make *porcelain*?

2. How is *calligraphy* similar to painting?

Answer the Guiding Questions

3. *Describing* How did the reopening of the Silk Road affect the economy and culture of China?

4. *Explaining* How did the printing of paper money help the economy of China?

5. *Speculating* Why did the rulers of the Tang and Song dynasties support the arts and literature?

6. *Analyzing* Which technological development had a greater impact on the Chinese empire—printing or gunpowder? Explain why.

7. **INFORMATIVE/EXPLANATORY** You are an imperial scholar-official. Your job is to report to the emperor about changes taking place. Which technological, economic, or cultural development do you think the emperor should know about? Write a short report that describes an important development. Support your ideas with at least two reasons.

LESSON 3
The Mongols in China

ESSENTIAL QUESTION

• What are the characteristics of a leader?

IT MATTERS BECAUSE
In the 1200s, Mongols led by Genghis Khan conquered northern China and regions to the west, creating the world's largest land empire.

Mongol Expansion

GUIDING QUESTION *Why were the Mongols able to build a vast empire so quickly?*

By the A.D. 1200s, Chinese civilization had made many achievements in government, technology, and the arts. However, enemies to the north were preparing to invade China. These people were the Mongols (MAHNG·guhlz), the dominant nomadic group in central Asia. They became the first non-Chinese people to rule all of China.

Who Were the Mongols?

The Mongols came from an area north of China called Mongolia (mahn·GOHL·yuh). The Mongols lived in movable tents called yurts and raised horses, sheep, and yaks, or long-haired oxen. Mongols were made up of clans, or groups of related families, that were loosely joined together. They followed their herds as the animals grazed the large **steppes** (STEHPS) of Mongolia. The steppes are wide, grassy plains that stretch from the Black Sea to northern China.

Early in their history, the Mongols developed skills that were necessary for nomadic living. The Mongols were excellent horseback riders. Their children learned to ride a horse at ages four or five and then they spent much of their lives on horseback.

Reading**HELP**DESK

Taking Notes: *Sequencing*
Use a graphic organizer like the one here to sequence the events that led to Mongol control of China.

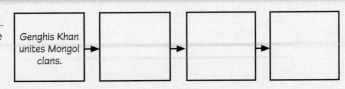

Genghis Khan unites Mongol clans. → □ → □ → □

Content Vocabulary
• **steppe** • **terror**

During the reign of Genghis Khan, the Mongols conquered many kingdoms in central Asia.

1 MOVEMENT In what direction did Genghis Khan launch his first campaign? What was the year?

2 CRITICAL THINKING
Contrasting How would you describe the difference in size between Genghis Khan's empire and the Mongol homeland?

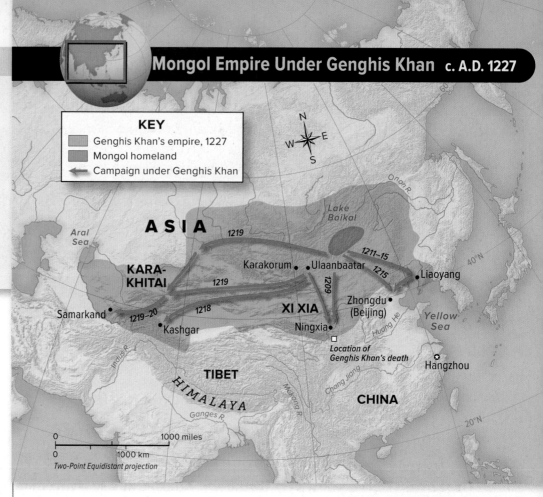

Mongol Empire Under Genghis Khan c. A.D. 1227

KEY
- Genghis Khan's empire, 1227
- Mongol homeland
- Campaign under Genghis Khan

ASIA

Aral Sea

KARA-KHITAI

Samarkand

Kashgar

TIBET

HIMALAYA

Ganges R.

Lake Baikal

Onon R.

1219

1219

1218

1219-20

1211-15

Karakorum   Ulaanbaatar   1215

1209

XI XIA

Ningxia

Zhongdu (Beijing)

Location of Genghis Khan's death

CHINA

Hangzhou

Liaoyang

Yellow Sea

Huang He

Chang Jiang

Mekong R.

Indus R.

0   1000 miles
0   1000 km
Two-Point Equidistant projection

The Mongols also developed their fighting skills. Riding on their horses toward an enemy, the Mongols could accurately shoot arrows from far distances. As they got closer to their enemy, the Mongols attacked them with swords and spears.

Genghis Khan

In A.D. 1206, a meeting of Mongol leaders took place in the Gobi (GOH·BEE). This is a vast desert that covers parts of Mongolia and China. At that meeting, a warrior named Temujin (the· MOO·juhn) was elected Genghis Khan (jehng·guhs KAHN), which means "strong ruler."

Genghis Khan set out to **unify** the Mongol clans. He organized Mongol laws to create a new legal code. He also formed a group of clan chiefs to help him plan military campaigns. From the time of his election until the end of his life, Genghis Khan fought to conquer lands beyond Mongolia.

Genghis Khan created an army of more than 100,000 trained warriors. The soldiers were placed in groups called units. The units were then placed under the command of skilled officers.

Reading **HELP**DESK

steppe flat, dry grassland
terror violent acts that are meant to cause fear in people

Academic Vocabulary

unify to bring together as one

The army officers were chosen for their abilities rather than their social position. These changes made the Mongols the most skilled fighting force in the world at that time.

Under Genghis Khan, Mongol forces first conquered other people of the steppes. These victories brought tribute money to the Mongol treasury. The victories also attracted new recruits to the army. Soon the Mongols were powerful enough to attack major civilizations. In A.D. 1211, thousands of Mongols on horseback invaded China. Within three years, they had taken control of all of northern China. They then turned west and invaded the kingdoms that controlled parts of the Silk Road.

Genghis Khan and his Mongol warriors became known for their cruel fighting and use of **terror**. Terror refers to violent acts that are meant to cause fear. Mongol soldiers attacked, looted, and burned cities. Within a short time, many people began surrendering to the Mongols without even fighting them.

Empire Builders

After Genghis Khan died in A.D. 1227, his vast territory was divided into several areas. Each area was ruled by one of his sons.

Despite these divisions of troops, Mongol conquests continued. The warriors swept into parts of eastern and central Europe. They also conquered Persia located in Southwest Asia.

GEOGRAPHY CONNECTION

In less than 100 years, the Mongols created the largest land empire in the history of the world.

1 **REGIONS** What country to the east was attacked but not conquered by 1294?

2 **CRITICAL THINKING**
Speculating What physical feature might have prevented the Mongols from conquering India?

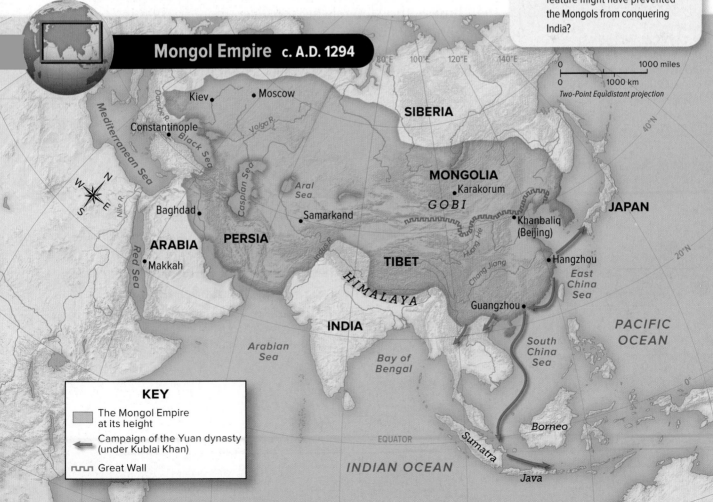

Mongol Empire c. A.D. 1294

KEY
- The Mongol Empire at its height
- Campaign of the Yuan dynasty (under Kublai Khan)
- Great Wall

**Genghis Khan
(c. A.D. 1167–1227)**

Genghis Khan's father, the Mongol chief Yisugei, named his son Temujin. According to folklore, Temujin had a large blood clot in his right hand, which meant he was destined to become a great warrior. In 1206, 40-year-old Temujin successfully took command of the Mongol forces in the Gobi. It is believed that he was inspired to rule because he grew up extremely poor, and his father was murdered by his enemies.

▶ **CRITICAL THINKING**
Determining Cause and Effect What about the personal life of Genghis Khan would have led him to want to rule?

In A.D. 1258, the Mongols captured the Muslim city of Baghdad. The Mongols then moved into Syria and Palestine to Egypt. The Muslim leaders of Egypt stopped the Mongol's advance in A.D. 1260.

All of these different areas formed the vast Mongol Empire. Mongol rule stretched from the Pacific Ocean in the east to eastern Europe in the west and from Siberia in the north to the Himalaya in the south. The Mongols created the largest land empire in history.

The Mongols caused a great amount of damage to the lands they conquered, but they also brought stability. This stability encouraged trade and closer contact between Asia and Europe. Many of the great trade routes between Asia and Europe crossed Mongol lands. The Mongols grew wealthy because they taxed the products that were traded along these roads.

The Mongols admired the cultures they conquered, and sometimes they adopted their beliefs and customs. For example, the Mongols in Southwest Asia accepted Islam and adopted Arab, Persian, and Turkish ways.

The Mongols also learned from the Chinese. As they fought Chinese troops, the Mongols learned about gunpowder and its use as an explosive. They saw the Chinese use the fire lance, a weapon that the Chinese later developed into the gun and cannon. Adopting gunpowder and the fire lance from the Chinese, the Mongols became even more frightening to their opponents.

☑ **PROGRESS CHECK**

Determining Cause and Effect How were the Mongols influenced by their opponents?

Mongol Conquest of China

GUIDING QUESTION *How did the Mongols rule the Chinese?*

In A.D. 1260, the grandson of Genghis Khan, Kublai, became the new Mongol ruler. Kublai Khan (KOO·BLUH KAHN) continued the conquest of China that his grandfather had begun. In A.D. 1264, Kublai established his capital at Khanbaliq—the city of the khan—in northern China. Today, the modern city of Beijing (BAY·JIHNG) is located on the site of the former Mongol capital.

Reading HELP DESK

Academic Vocabulary

regime rulers during a given period of time

The Mongols invaded other areas after conquering China. Despite a fleet of warships built by the Koreans, the planned Mongol invasion of Japan ended in failure.

Mary Evans Picture Library

Mongols and Chinese

In 1271, Kublai Khan decided he would control all of China. By A.D. 1279, Kublai Khan finished conquering southern China. He brought an end to the Song dynasty and declared himself emperor. Kublai Khan started the Yuan (YWAN) dynasty. The term *Yuan* means "beginning." The Yuan dynasty would last only about 100 years. Kublai Khan would rule for 30 of those years, until his death in A.D. 1294.

To keep tight control of these new lands, Kublai appointed Mongol leaders to top jobs in China. He also kept some Chinese officials in positions of power.

The Mongol culture was quite different from the Chinese culture. The Mongols had their own language, laws, and customs. These characteristics separated them from the Chinese people they ruled. Mongols lived apart from the Chinese and did not mix with them socially.

Government and Religion

In government affairs, the Yuan **regime** did not use civil service examinations as was previously done in China. Government jobs were open to non-Chinese people, including Mongols and Turks. However, the Yuan rulers respected Confucian writings and allowed Chinese scholar-officials to keep their posts.

This colored lithograph was taken from a manuscript that described Marco Polo's journeys. It shows him leaving Venice in 1338.

▶ **CRITICAL THINKING**
Explaining Why were Marco Polo's travels important to Europeans?

Like many Chinese, the Mongols in China practiced Buddhism, but they were respectful of other religions. For example, Kublai Khan encouraged Christians, Muslims, and Hindus from outside China to practice their faiths.

Under Mongol rule, China reached the height of its wealth and power. Foreigners were drawn to its capital city. Although they were foreigners, the Mongols gradually won the support of many Chinese people. Some Chinese appreciated the order and prosperity that the Mongols brought to the country. Foreign visitors were attracted to China and reached it by traveling along the Silk Road.

Marco Polo

One of the most famous European travelers to reach China was Marco Polo. He came from the city of Venice in Italy. Polo lived in the capital of Khanbaliq during the reign of Kublai Khan. He wrote his impressions of the magnificent appearance of this city:

North Wind/North Wind Picture Archives

❛❛ The streets are so straight and wide that you can see right along them from end to end and from one gate to the other. And up and down the city there are beautiful palaces, and many great and fine hostelries [inns], and fine houses in great numbers. ❜❜

—from "Concerning the City of Cambaluc [Khanbaliq]," by Marco Polo

Kublai was fascinated by Marco Polo's stories about his journeys. For about 16 years, Polo was a privileged resident of China. Kublai sent him on trips all over the region to gather information and carry out business. For some of those years, Polo ruled the Chinese city of Yangzhou. When Polo returned to Italy, he wrote a book about his adventures.

Trade and Empire

The Mongol Empire stretched from China to eastern Europe. As a result, Mongol China prospered from increased overland trade with many parts of the world. The Yuan dynasty also built ships and expanded seagoing trade. China traded tea, silk, and porcelain in exchange for goods such as silver, carpets, cotton, and spices. Muslims and Europeans also took Chinese discoveries back to their homelands.

Mongol armies advanced into Vietnam and northern Korea. The rulers of Korea, called the Koryo (koh·RY·oh), remained in power because they agreed to Mongol control. The Mongols forced thousands of Koreans to build warships. The Mongols used these ships in two attempts to invade Japan. Both voyages ended in failure when huge storms destroyed much of the fleet.

☑ PROGRESS CHECK

Describing What was Marco Polo's reaction to seeing China's cities?

LESSON 3 REVIEW

Review Vocabulary

1. If you were to visit the Mongolian *steppes*, what would you likely see?

Answer the Guiding Questions

2. *Identifying* Why did trading improve under Mongolian rule? Give examples of goods that were traded and how they were traded.

3. *Analyzing* How did the Mongols use terror in their conquests?

4. *Summarizing* How did China benefit from being ruled by the Mongols?

5. *Evaluating* Make a list of the leadership qualities of Genghis Khan and evaluate him as a leader.

6. **NARRATIVE** As Genghis Khan, you are concerned about how your empire will be ruled after your death. Write a journal entry in which you record advice that you want your family members to follow.

Monkey

by Wu Cheng'en (c. A.D. 1505–1580)

Wu Cheng'en was a writer during the Ming Dynasty. He wrote stories in a language that most Chinese could read. His Monkey King stories are his most popular works. These stories describe Monkey King's encounters with gods, demons, fairies, and masters during his travels.

The Monkey King stories are allegories. They have a hidden meaning, such as a moral or a lesson. The characters, setting, and plot in an allegory are often symbols. As you read the excerpt, think about what Monkey symbolizes.

In the excerpt, the clever Monkey has been crowned king, but he is unhappy. He travels in search of someone who can teach him about the meaning of life. Monkey comes upon a teacher, the **Patriarch** (PAY • tree • AHRK), and his students. The Patriarch teaches Monkey some magical skills but warns Monkey to keep them secret. Later, Monkey joins the other students.

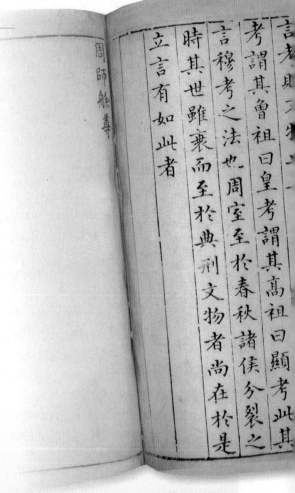

Chinese writing

" If you saw someone turn into a tree, wouldn't you at once ask how it was done? "

—from *Monkey: Folk Novel of China* by Wu Cheng'en

An actor playing the Monkey King searching for truth

(l)The British Library/Heritage/Age fotostock; (b)China Images/Alamy

The **disciples** (dih • SY • puhls) clapped and burst into loud applause. "Bravo, Monkey, bravo," they cried. There was such a **din** that the **Patriarch** came running out. … "Who's making all this noise?" he asked. … Monkey changed himself back into his true form and slipped in among the crowd, saying, "Reverend Master, we are doing lessons out here. I assure you there was no noise in particular." "You were all bawling," said the Patriarch angrily. "It didn't sound in the least like people studying. I want to know what you were doing here, shouting and laughing." "To tell the truth," said someone, "Monkey was showing us a **transformation** (TRANS • fuhr • MAY • SHUHN) just for fun. We told him to change into a pine tree, and he did it so well that we were all applauding him." … "Go away, all of you!" the Patriarch shouted. "And you, Monkey, come here! … Did you think I taught you [magic] in order that you might show off in front of other people? If you saw someone turn into a tree, wouldn't you at once ask how it was done? If others see you doing it, aren't they certain to ask you? If you are frightened to refuse, you will give the secret away; and if you refuse, you're very likely to be roughly handled. You're putting yourself in grave danger." "I'm terribly sorry," said Monkey. "I won't punish you," said the Patriarch, "but you can't stay here." Monkey burst into tears. "Where am I to go to?"

—From *Monkey: Folk Novel of China* by Wu Cheng'en

The mask of the adventurous Monkey King

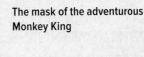

Vocabulary

disciples
students

din
loud noise

patriarch
an older male figure of authority, often within a religious community

transformation
a complete change

Analyzing Literature DBQ

1 **Describing** What does Monkey do in front of the disciples?

2 **Identifying Points of View** Why is the Patriarch angry at Monkey after discovering what Monkey has done?

3 **Synthesizing** Do you agree with the Patriarch that showing off can lead to great danger? Why or why not?

LESSON 4

The Ming Dynasty

ESSENTIAL QUESTION

• How do new ideas change the way people live?

IT MATTERS BECAUSE

The Ming dynasty's early emperors wanted to spread China's influence. By the late 1500s, however, China had limited its contact with the rest of the world.

The Ming Dynasty

GUIDING QUESTION *How did Ming rulers bring peace and prosperity to China?*

After Kublai Khan died in A.D. 1294, a series of weak emperors came to the throne. Mongol power in China began to decline, and problems increased for the Yuan dynasty. The government spent too many resources on foreign conquests. At the same time, many officials stole from the treasury and grew wealthy. Yuan rulers lost the respect of the people. As a result, many Chinese resented Mongol controls.

The Rise of the Ming

Unrest swept through China and finally ended Mongol rule. In A.D. 1368, a military officer named Zhu Yuanzhang (JOO YWAHN·JAHNG) became emperor. Zhu reunited the country and then set up his capital at Nanjing (NAN·JIHNG) in southern China. There, he founded the Ming, or "Brilliant," dynasty. The Ming dynasty would rule China for the next 300 years.

As emperor, Zhu took the name Hong Wu (HAHNG WOO), or the "Military Emperor." He brought peace and order, but he was also a harsh leader. Hong Wu trusted few people and punished officials that he suspected of treason, or disloyalty to

Reading**HELP**DESK

Taking Notes: *Identifying Cause and Effect*

Use this graphic organizer to note the causes and effects of the voyages of Zheng He.

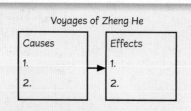

Voyages of Zheng He

Causes
1.
2.

Effects
1.
2.

Content Vocabulary

• **census**
• **novel**
• **barbarian**

the government. After Hong Wu died in A.D. 1398, his son became emperor and took the name of Yong Le (YUNG LEE).

Yong Le was determined to be a powerful ruler. In A.D. 1421, he moved the capital north to Beijing. There, he built the Imperial City, a large area of palaces and government buildings. The center of this area, known as the Forbidden City, was where the emperor and his family lived. Only top government officials were allowed to enter the Forbidden City.

The Forbidden City had beautiful gardens and palaces with thousands of rooms. China's emperor and court lived there in luxury for more than 500 years. The buildings of the Forbidden City still stand. You can visit them if you travel to China today.

How Did the Ming Change China?

Ming emperors needed government officials to carry out their decisions. To make sure that officials took their jobs seriously, the emperors brought back the civil service examinations. As during the Tang and Song dynasties, the tests were extremely difficult and required years of preparation.

One responsibility of officials was to carry out a **census** (SEHN·suhs), or a count of the number of people in China. The census helped officials identify the people who owed taxes.

GEOGRAPHY CONNECTION

During the Ming dynasty, emperor Yong Le moved the capital to Beijing.

1 **PLACE** What feature forms the northern border of Ming China?

2 **LOCATION** Along what river is the city of Nanjing?

3 **CRITICAL THINKING**
Speculating Why might Yong Le have moved the capital to Beijing?

Ming China 1368–1644

MONGOLIA

GOBI

Great Wall

Beijing

Huang He (Yellow R.)

Yellow Sea

Nanjing

Chang Jiang (Yangtze R.)

CHINA

Quanzhou

Guangzhou

Bay of Bengal

South China Sea

KEY
Ming dynasty
Great Wall

0 ___ 500 miles
0 ___ 500 km
Two-Point Equidistant projection

The strong government of the early Ming emperors provided peace and security. As a result, the Chinese economy began to grow. Hong Wu rebuilt many canals and farms. He also ordered that new roads be paved and new forests planted. Agriculture thrived as farmers worked on the new lands and grew more crops.

Ming rulers also repaired and expanded the Grand Canal. This allowed merchants to ship rice and other products between southern and northern China. Chinese traders introduced new types of rice from Southeast Asia that grew faster. More food was available to the growing number of people living in cities.

The Ming also supported the silk industry. They encouraged farmers to start growing cotton and weaving cloth. For the first time, cotton became the cloth worn by most Chinese.

Arts and Literature

The arts flourished during the Ming dynasty. Newly wealthy merchants and artisans wanted entertainment and could afford to pay for printed books and trips to the theater. During the Ming period, Chinese writers produced **novels,** or long fictional stories. One of the most popular was *The Romance of the Three Kingdoms*. It described military rivalries at the end of the Han period. Many novels of the time were written in vernacular, or everyday language. Writers avoided formal language to tell their tales. Instead they tried to make their stories sound as if they had been told aloud by storytellers. Traditional Chinese dramas had been banned during the years of Mongol rule, but under the Ming they were restored to the stage. Actors in costumes performed stories of the day using words, music, dance, and symbolic gestures.

 PROGRESS CHECK

Explaining What was the purpose of the Imperial City?

Chinese Exploration

GUIDING QUESTION *How did Chinese contact with the outside world change during the Ming dynasty?*

Early Ming emperors wanted to know more about the world outside of China and to expand Chinese influence abroad. Ming emperors built a large fleet of ships to sail to other countries. The ships, known as junks, usually traveled along the coast of

This painting from a Ming vase shows Chinese farm workers collecting tea.

Reading**HELP**DESK

census a count of the number of people in a country

novel a long fictional story

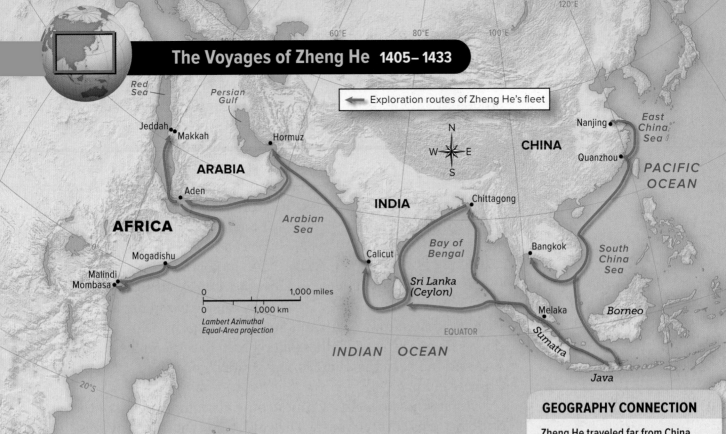

The Voyages of Zheng He 1405–1433

← Exploration routes of Zheng He's fleet

Lambert Azimuthal
Equal-Area projection

GEOGRAPHY CONNECTION

Zheng He traveled far from China and brought back many exotic items. He also spread Chinese culture.

1 **REGIONS** About how far is Nanjing from Chittagong?

2 **PLACE** Jeddah is on the coast of what body of water?

3 **CRITICAL THINKING** *Making Connections* Why were Zheng He's voyages important to the Chinese and other parts of the world?

China. They could also sail on the open sea. Between A.D. 1405 and A.D. 1433, Ming emperors sent the Chinese fleet on seven overseas voyages. They wanted to trade with other kingdoms and demonstrate Chinese power. They also wanted to demand that weaker kingdoms pay tribute to China.

The leader of these journeys was a Chinese Muslim and court official named Zheng He (JUNG HUH), or Chengho as he was also called. The voyages of Zheng He were quite impressive. On the first voyage, nearly 28,000 men sailed on 62 large ships and 250 smaller ships. The largest ship was over 440 feet (134 m) long. That was more than five times as long as the Santa María that Christopher Columbus sailed almost 90 years later.

The Travels of Zheng He

Zheng He took his first fleet to Southeast Asia. In later voyages, he reached the western coast of India and the city-states of East Africa. Zheng He wrote about his travels:

PRIMARY SOURCE

❝ We have traversed [traveled] more than 100,000 li [30,000 mi. or 50,000 km] of immense water spaces and have beheld in the ocean huge waves like mountains rising sky-high, … and we have set eyes on barbarian [foreign] regions far away, hidden in a blue transparency of light vapours, [fog] while our sails, loftily unfurled like clouds, day and night continued their course, rapid like that of a star, traversing [crossing] those savage waves. ❞

—from tablet erected in Fujian, China, by Zheng He

The Jesuits tried to convert the Chinese to Christianity. This image shows a Jesuit convent in China.

At the different ports he visited, Zheng He traded Chinese goods, such as silk, paper, and porcelain. He returned with items unknown in China. For example, Zheng He brought giraffes and other animals from Africa, which fascinated Emperor Yong Le. Yong Le placed them in his imperial zoo in Beijing. Zheng He also brought back visitors from the outside world, including representatives from South and Southeast Asia. The voyages of Zheng He encouraged Chinese merchants to settle in Southeast Asia and India. In these places, they traded goods and spread Chinese culture.

Despite these benefits, Chinese officials complained that the **ongoing** trips cost too much. They also said that these voyages would introduce unwanted foreign ideas. Some officials also believed that being a merchant was an unworthy and selfish occupation. A Confucian teaching said that people should place loyalty to society ahead of their own desires.

After Zheng He died in A.D. 1433, Confucian officials convinced the emperor to end the voyages. The fleet's ships were taken apart, and the construction of seagoing vessels was stopped. As a result, China's trade with other countries sharply declined. Within 50 years, the Chinese shipbuilding technology became outdated.

Arrival of Europeans

Ming China was not able to cut off all contacts with the rest of the world. In A.D. 1514, ships from the European country of Portugal (POHR·chih·GUHL) arrived off the coast of southern China. It was the first direct contact between China and Europe since the journeys of Marco Polo.

The Portuguese wanted to trade with China and **convert** the Chinese to Christianity. At the time, the Ming government paid little attention to the arrival of the Portuguese. China was a powerful civilization and did not feel threatened by outsiders. To the Chinese, the Europeans were **barbarians** (bahr·BEHR·ee·uhnz), or uncivilized people.

©Bettmann/Corbis

At first, local officials refused to trade with the Portuguese. The Chinese hoped the foreigners would give up and go home. By A.D. 1600, however, the Portuguese had built a trading post at the port of Macao (muh·KAU) in southern China. Portuguese ships carried goods between China and Japan. Trade between Europe and China, however, remained limited.

Despite limited contact, European ideas did reach China. Christian missionaries made the voyage to China on European merchant ships. Many of these missionaries were Jesuits, a group of Roman Catholic priests. The Jesuits were highly educated and hoped to establish Christian schools in China. Their knowledge of science impressed Chinese officials. However, the Jesuits did not convince many Chinese to accept Christianity.

The Fall of the Ming

After a long period of growth, the Ming dynasty began to weaken. Dishonest officials took over the country. They placed heavy taxes on farmers. The farmers objected to the taxes and began to revolt.

As law and order collapsed, a people from the north, the Manchus, prepared to invade a weakened China. Like the Chinese, the Manchus had been conquered by the Mongols. They had retreated to an area northeast of China's Great Wall, known today as Manchuria. The Manchus defeated the Chinese armies and captured Beijing. In A.D. 1644, they set up a new dynasty called the Qing (CHEENG) dynasty.

✓ **PROGRESS CHECK**

Analyzing Why did Chinese officials oppose overseas voyages?

LESSON 4 REVIEW

Review Vocabulary

1. How would officials have taken a *census* of China's population?

2. Why did the Chinese consider Europeans to be *barbarians*?

Answer the Guiding Questions

3. *Describing* Describe the Imperial City and the Forbidden City.

4. *Identifying* How did the Ming dynasty change China?

5. *Explaining* Why did China's officials discourage the voyages of Zheng He?

6. *Summarizing* What effect did the arrival of the Jesuits have on the Chinese?

7. **ARGUMENT** You are Zheng He, and government officials have threatened to stop supporting your voyages. Write a letter to persuade officials to let you continue traveling. Give at least three reasons why you should be allowed to continue.

Write your answers on a separate piece of paper.

1 Exploring the Essential Question

INFORMATIVE/EXPLANATORY How would you describe imperial China's relations with other cultures through trade, travel, and war? Write an essay that summarizes how and why imperial China came into contact with groups outside its borders.

2 21st Century Skills

SEQUENCE EVENTS Review the chapter and identify at least 10 important events that took place during imperial China. Try to vary the types of events, including military as well as cultural and civic developments. Then create a time line that shows the sequence of the events or developments and explains their importance. Use presentation software or art supplies to create a time line that includes images and text. Present your work to the class.

3 Thinking Like a Historian

DRAWING CONCLUSIONS Think about the effects that an invention such as gunpowder had on imperial China. Then create a diagram like the one shown here. In the diagram, draw a conclusion about how that invention might have affected China.

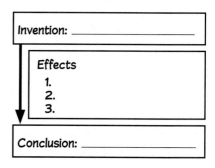

Invention: _____

Effects
1.
2.
3.

Conclusion: _____

4 GEOGRAPHY ACTIVITY

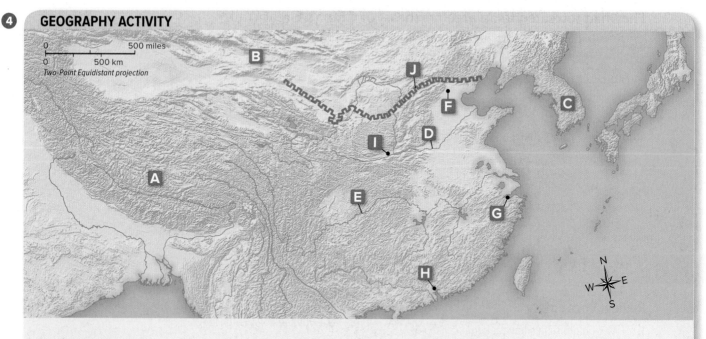

0   500 miles
0   500 km
Two-Point Equidistant projection

Locating Places

Match the letters on the map with the numbered places listed below.

1. Beijing
2. Hangzhou
3. Guangzhou
4. Changan
5. Great Wall
6. Tibet
7. Mongolia
8. Korean Peninsula
9. Huang He (Yellow River)
10. Chang Jiang (Yangtze River)

Directions: Write your answers on a separate piece of paper.

CHECKING FOR UNDERSTANDING

1 Identify the vocabulary word with its description.

   A. a new form of the ideas of the philosopher Confucius; included Buddhist and Daoist beliefs

   B. a ceramic made of fine clay baked at very high temperatures

   C. artistic handwriting

   D. flat, dry grassland

   E. violent acts that are meant to cause fear in people

   F. a count of the number of people in a country

   G. a long fictional story

   H. an uncivilized person

REVIEW THE GUIDING QUESTIONS

2 *Explaining* What are some ways Sui and Tang rulers rebuilt China?

3 *Summarizing* Why did Buddhism eventually lose favor with Tang rulers?

4 *Naming* Which philosophy had the official support of the Tang and Song dynasties? Why?

5 *Identifying* What factors helped the economy of Tang China flourish?

6 *Listing* What products did the Chinese make from steel?

7 *Specifying* Which forms of literature and art were especially popular during the Tang and Song dynasties?

8 *Stating* What methods did Genghis Khan and the Mongols use to create their empire?

9 *Explaining* How were the Mongols able to rule China successfully under Kublai Kahn?

10 *Identifying* Who were Hong Wu and Yong Le and how did they impact China?

11 *Naming* Traders from which European nation unsuccessfully attempted to establish trade relations with Ming China?

CRITICAL THINKING

12 *Assessing* What was the greatest accomplishment of the Sui dynasty? Explain.

13 *Comparing and Contrasting* How was the rule of Taizong similar to that of Yangdi? How was it different?

14 *Speculating* Why did Buddhism become popular among the Chinese as the Han dynasty was in decline?

15 *Theorizing* What opinion do you think most Chinese had toward the scholar-officials of Tang and Song China? Explain.

16 *Defending* Which innovation of the Tang or Song dynasty do you believe has had the greatest impact on world history? Explain.

17 *Evaluating* How did the changes to the Mongol system instituted by Genghis Khan make it easier for the Mongols to build their empire?

18 *Assessing* Do you believe Kublai Kahn was an effective ruler? Why or why not?

19 *Analyzing* How did the exploits of Zheng He (or Chengho) demonstrate Chinese power and wealth?

20 *Drawing Conclusions* How did cultural differences between China and Europe affect Ming China?

Need Extra Help?

If You've Missed Question	**1**	**2**	**3**	**4**	**5**	**6**	**7**	**8**	**9**	**10**	**11**	**12**	**13**	**14**	**15**	**16**	**17**	**18**	**19**	**20**
Review Lesson	1,2, 3,4	1	1	1	2	2	2	3	3	4	4	1	1	1	1	2	3	3	4	4

DBQ SHORT RESPONSE

"[Empress Wu] continued to eliminate [get rid of] potential rivals, even when these were her own relatives, but she governed the empire with great efficiency, ... Her great ability as an administrator, her courage, decisive [able to make judgments quickly] character, and readiness to use ruthless [unforgiving] means ... won her the respect, if not the love, of the court."

—From "Wuhou," *Encyclopedia Britannica*

21 According to the reading, how did Empress Wu treat her opponents?

22 Why did the empress win the respect of the court?

EXTENDED RESPONSE

23 ***Informative/Explanatory*** You are studying for the civil service examination during the Tang dynasty. Write an essay to explain the examination and how it helps China. Tell why the examination is important to you and your family.

STANDARDIZED TEST PRACTICE

DBQ ANALYZING DOCUMENTS

John of Plano Carpini explained why the Mongols were skilled warriors.

"Their children begin as soon as they are two or three years old to ride and manage horses and to gallop on them, and they are given bows to suit their stature [size] and are taught to shoot; they are extremely agile [able to move quickly] and also intrepid [fearless]."

—from *History of the Mongols*, by John of Plano Carpini

24 ***Drawing Conclusions*** Which statement best summarizes why the Mongols were skilled soldiers?

A. They believed that children should be free to play.

B. They made children fight their battles for them.

C. They taught their children to hate other people.

D. They were trained to ride horses and fight at a young age.

25 ***Inferring*** What can you infer about the author's experiences with the Mongols?

A. He read about them in a book.

B. He was captured by the Mongols.

C. He was a visitor to the Mongol empire.

D. He was a Mongol fighter.

Need Extra Help?

If You've Missed Question	21	22	23	24	25
Review Lesson	1	1	1	3	3

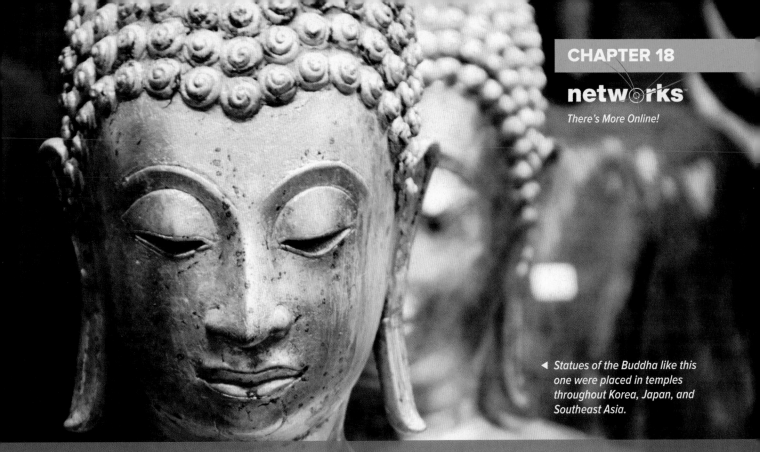

◀ *Statues of the Buddha like this one were placed in temples throughout Korea, Japan, and Southeast Asia.*

A.D. 300 TO A.D. 1300s

Civilizations of Korea, Japan, and Southeast Asia

THE STORY MATTERS ...

Buddhism began in India. By the A.D. 1200s, it was almost extinct there. The followers of the Buddha, however, carried his teachings to new lands. In time, Buddhism took firm root in Southeast Asia, China, Korea, and Japan. As Buddhism spread, it took on new forms and influenced the cultures of many nations in Asia.

Buddhism became more popular in countries outside of Asia in the second half of the twentieth century. Today, more than 375 million people around the world practice some form of Buddhism.

ESSENTIAL QUESTIONS

- Why do people form governments?
- How does geography influence the way people live?
- How do new ideas change the way people live?
- What makes a culture unique?

Max Paddler/Flickr/GettyImages

Place & Time: Korea, Japan, and Southeast Asia A.D. 300 to A.D. 1300s

Korea, Japan, and Southeast Asia were greatly affected by China and India, their neighbors to the north and west. These influences first began between about 150 B.C. and A.D. 150. They lasted for almost a thousand years and greatly changed the regions.

Step Into the Place

MAP FOCUS Large bodies of water separate Korea, Japan, and Southeast Asia. As trade grew, however, those bodies of water formed a link between these regions and the outside world.

1 PLACE What are the largest two empires shown on the map?

2 LOCATION Between which two empires is Korea located?

3 LOCATION Which major bodies of water surround Japan?

4 CRITICAL THINKING
   Making Predictions How would ideas spread from China to Japan and Southeast Asia?

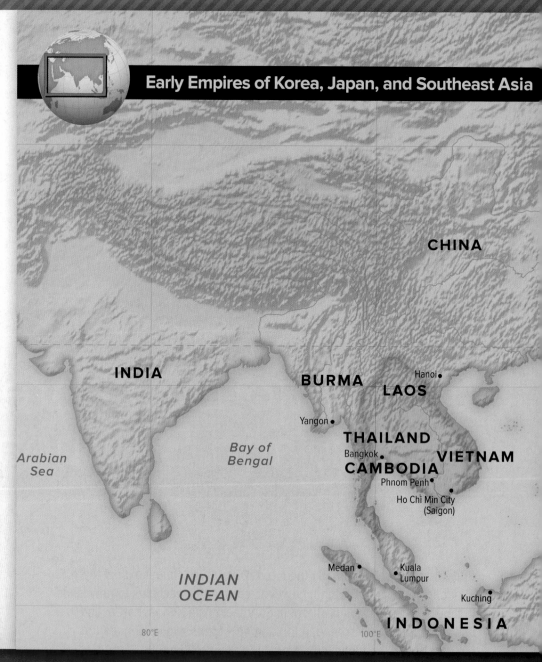

Early Empires of Korea, Japan, and Southeast Asia

CHINA

INDIA

BURMA

LAOS

Hanoi

Yangon

THAILAND

Bangkok

CAMBODIA

VIETNAM

Phnom Penh

Ho Chi Min City (Saigon)

Arabian Sea

Bay of Bengal

Medan

Kuala Lumpur

INDIAN OCEAN

Kuching

INDONESIA

80°E   100°E

Step Into the Time

TIME LINE Choose an event from the time line that happened in one region and write a paragraph predicting the effect of that event on the surrounding regions.

c. A.D. 604 Prince Shotoku writes Japanese constitution

c. A.D. 300 Yayoi people organize in Japan

c. A.D. 400 Yamato control Japan

c. A.D. 631 Taika reforms in Japan

CIVILIZATIONS OF KOREA, JAPAN, AND SOUTHEAST ASIA

THE WORLD   **A.D. 300**   **A.D. 500**   **A.D. 700**

c. A.D. 590 Grand Canal links northern and southern China

c. A.D. 610 Muhammad preaches Islam

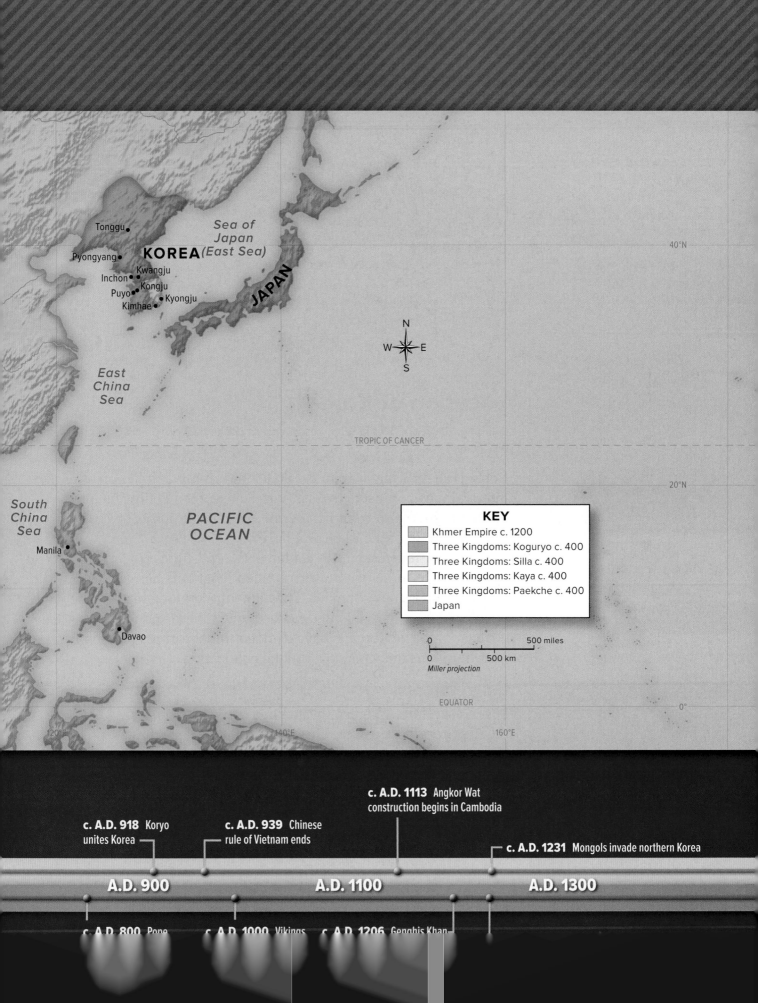

Tonggu

Sea of Japan (East Sea)

Pyongyang

KOREA

Inchon Kwangju
Kongju
Puyo
Kimhae Kyongju

JAPAN

East China Sea

40°N

N
W—E
S

TROPIC OF CANCER

20°N

South China Sea

PACIFIC OCEAN

Manila

KEY

	Khmer Empire c. 1200
	Three Kingdoms: Koguryo c. 400
	Three Kingdoms: Silla c. 400
	Three Kingdoms: Kaya c. 400
	Three Kingdoms: Paekche c. 400
	Japan

Davao

0   500 miles
0   500 km
Miller projection

EQUATOR

0°

120°E   140°E   160°E

c. A.D. 1113 Angkor Wat
construction begins in Cambodia

c. A.D. 918 Koryo
unites Korea

c. A.D. 939 Chinese
rule of Vietnam ends

c. A.D. 1231 Mongols invade northern Korea

A.D. 900   **A.D. 1100**   **A.D. 1300**

c. A.D. 800 Pope   c. A.D. 1000 Vikings   c. A.D. 1206 Genghis Khan

LESSON 1

Korea: History and Culture

ESSENTIAL QUESTION

• Why do people form governments?

IT MATTERS BECAUSE
Located between two powerful civilizations—Japan and China—Korea has forged its own cultural identity over the centuries.

Location of Korea

GUIDING QUESTION *Why is Korea described as a bridge between China and Japan?*

Korea is slightly larger than the state of Minnesota. It lies on a mountainous peninsula in East Asia. The Korean Peninsula juts out to the southeast from northeastern China. It points toward the western tip of the islands of Japan.

Korea has been seen as a bridge between China and Japan. Being close to these two powerful Asian neighbors has greatly affected Korea's development. Throughout their long history, the people of Korea have adopted features of Chinese and Japanese civilizations. The Koreans have blended these features with their own traditions and created a unique civilization.

Early Koreans

Legend says that Tangun, the son of a bear and a god, founded the first Korean kingdom. Historians today believe that the first Koreans were nomads. They came to the peninsula from northern or central Asia. These groups were organized into tribes. The early Koreans lived in scattered villages with no central government. They grew rice and made tools and weapons of bronze. Later, they used iron to make these items.

Reading**HELP**DESK

Taking Notes: *Identifying*
Use a graphic organizer like this one to list details about the Silla kingdom and the two dynasties that followed it.

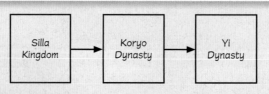

Silla Kingdom → Koryo Dynasty → Yi Dynasty

Content Vocabulary
• **shamanism**
• **tribute**

Early Koreans believed in **shamanism** (SHAH·muh·nih· zuhm). They thought that certain people could communicate with spirits. These people, known as shamans, acted as a connection between humans and spirits. Many shamans were women. They carried out rituals—songs, dances, and chants—to convince the spirits to help people. Shamans were thought to have the ability to cure illnesses.

The Three Kingdoms

According to tradition, the earliest kingdom in Korea was founded in 2333 B.C. Historians know that the Chinese took over the northern part of the Korean Peninsula in 109 B.C. The Koreans drove them out in the A.D. 200s. Eventually, three kingdoms emerged: Koguryŏ (koh·goo·ryeoh) in the north, Paekche (payk·cheh) in the southwest, and Silla (sheel·lah) in the southeast. Historians call the years from about A.D. 300 to A.D. 700 the Three Kingdoms period.

Chinese culture spread from Koguryŏ to the other Korean kingdoms. The people of all three kingdoms used the Chinese writing system and adopted Buddhism and Confucianism.

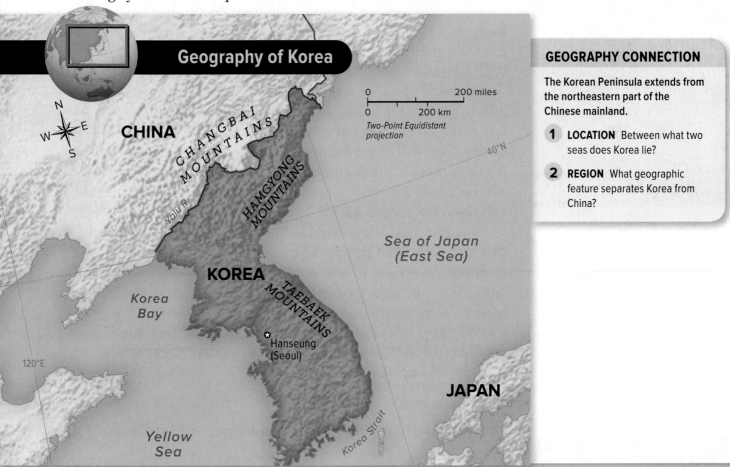

Geography of Korea

0 — 200 miles
0 — 200 km
Two-Point Equidistant projection

CHINA

CHANGBAI MOUNTAINS

HAMGYONG MOUNTAINS

Yalu R.

40°N

Sea of Japan (East Sea)

KOREA

TAEBAEK MOUNTAINS

Korea Bay

★ Hanseung (Seoul)

120°E

JAPAN

Yellow Sea

Korea Strait

GEOGRAPHY CONNECTION

The Korean Peninsula extends from the northeastern part of the Chinese mainland.

1 **LOCATION** Between what two seas does Korea lie?

2 **REGION** What geographic feature separates Korea from China?

shamanism belief in gods and spirits

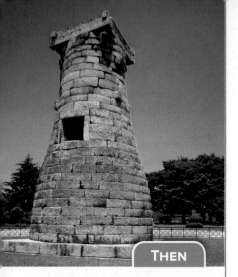

The early Koreans built this astronomical observatory during the Silla era. Today, observatories around the world use high-powered telescopes to give scientists the best view of stars, planets, and even faraway galaxies.

▶ **CRITICAL THINKING**

Speculating How would ancient astronomers from Silla have observed the movement of stars and other objects compared to astronomers today?

Reading**HELP**DESK

Academic Vocabulary

achievement something gained by working for it

They began using Buddhist sacred writings in Chinese translation. They applied Confucian principles to political life. Each Korean kingdom modeled its government on China's government. In addition, each kingdom was ruled by a powerful monarch with the help of scholarly officials and noble families.

During the Three Kingdoms period, influences from Japan also reached the Korean Peninsula. Paekche in the southwest was located closer to Japan than the other two Korean kingdoms. As a result, it developed trade with the Japanese. Japanese merchants, artisans, and scholars settled in Paekche and introduced elements of Japanese culture there.

Although the Koreans adapted many outside ideas and practices, they also made their own unique contributions. For example, in the A.D. 300s, Koguryŏ artists created enormous cave art paintings. In Silla, a queen built an astronomical observatory that still stands today. This stone structure is considered the oldest observatory in Asia.

The Silla Kingdom

Despite their close cultural ties, the three Korean kingdoms were hostile to one another. In the A.D. 500s and 600s, they fought wars for control of the Korean Peninsula. In one conflict during the A.D. 660s, the Tang dynasty of China sided with the Silla kingdom. With Chinese help, Silla conquered Paekche and Koguryŏ.

The rise of Silla brought a time of peace to Koreans as the Silla kings tried to create an ideal Buddhist kingdom. Society was made up of a few nobles at the top and a large group of farmers below. The government made some vital improvements. It gave land to farmers and helped build irrigation systems for rice fields. As a result, more food was produced, trade increased, and the economy prospered.

Silla kings also supported cultural advances. They wanted to employ educated people. To make that easier, they used an examination system to hire government officials. They also encouraged the arts, especially the building of many Buddhist temples. One temple was a nine-story wooden tower. This was perhaps the tallest structure in East Asia at the time. The printing of Buddhist sacred texts with wooden blocks was another Silla **achievement**.

 **PROGRESS CHECK**

Determining Cause and Effect How did outside influences affect early Korea?

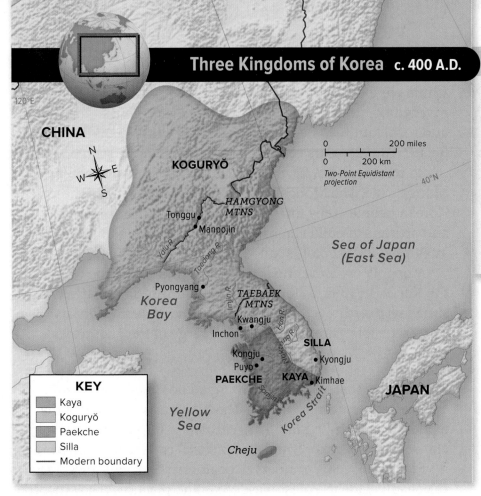

Three Kingdoms of Korea c. 400 A.D.

CHINA

KOGURYŎ

HAMGYONG MTNS

Tonggu
Manpojin

Yalu R.

Taedong R.

Pyongyang

Korea Bay

Imjin R.

TAEBAEK MTNS

Kwangju

Inchon

Han R.

SILLA

Kongju
Puyo

Kyongju

PAEKCHE

KAYA
Kimhae

Naktong R.

Somjin R.

Yellow Sea

Korea Strait

JAPAN

Cheju

Sea of Japan (East Sea)

40°N

120°E

200 miles
200 km
Two-Point Equidistant projection

KEY
- Kaya
- Koguryŏ
- Paekche
- Silla
- Modern boundary

GEOGRAPHY CONNECTION

During the Three Kingdoms period (c. 400 A.D.), Koguryŏ, Paekche, and Silla were the three main powers.

1 REGION Which kingdom was the smallest?

2 CRITICAL THINKING
Analyzing Why might Buddhism and Confucianism have reached Koguryŏ before they reached the other Korean kingdoms?

Korean Civilization

GUIDING QUESTION *How did Korea build a civilization?*

After years of conflict, the Silla kingdom finally collapsed. Nobles in the north fought one another for power. By A.D. 935, a general named Wang Kon (wahng·keon) had won out over these rivals. He became the first Korean ruler to unite the entire Korean Peninsula. Wang Kon also founded a new dynasty known as Koryo (KAW·ree·oh). The English word "Korea" comes from the term *Koryo*.

The Koryo Kingdom

Rulers of the Koryo kingdom followed the Chinese model of government that Silla had used. They were able to keep their territory united, and they remained in power for 400 years.

The Koryo rulers set up a code of laws. They also established a civil service system based on examinations. Under this leadership, Buddhism continued to grow and spread throughout the peninsula. Artisans developed movable metal type and produced the world's oldest book printed by this method.

Korean artisans also perfected the making of celadon pottery. This type of pottery is known for its green color and elegant shapes.

There's More Online! connected.mcgraw-hill.com

Over many centuries, as the people of Korea struggled to unite and defeat foreign invasions, several strong Korean military leaders arose. Admiral Yi Sun-shin, shown here, was a Korean hero who helped defeat Japanese invaders in the 1500s.

©Bohemian Nomad Picturemakers/Corbis

Like other Korean kingdoms before it, Koryo faced internal disorders and outside threats. The Mongols who had taken over China were the main outside danger. In A.D. 1231, the Mongols invaded the northern part of Korea. They forced the Koryo king and royal family to flee to an island near the present-day city of Seoul. After 25 years of struggle, the royal family surrendered.

To remain in power, the Koryo dynasty agreed to accept Mongol rule. The Mongols brought much suffering to the Korean people. They forced thousands of Korean peasants and artisans to build ships for the Mongol ruler Kublai Khan's attempted invasion of Japan.

Mongol power eventually declined, and so did the rule of the Koryo. In 1392, a Korean general named Yi Song-gye (YEE sung·jay) overthrew the Koryo and founded a new dynasty. The Korean people were once again in charge of their country.

The Yi Dynasty

The dynasty that Yi Song-gye founded became known as the Yi. It lasted for over 500 years. The Yi dynasty was one of the world's longest ruling families. Yi rulers set up their capital at Hanseong, the site of Seoul, the modern capital of South Korea.

From Hanseong, Yi rulers strengthened their rule of Korea. Yi rulers still made use of Chinese ideas and practices. They named neo-Confucianism the state philosophy. They opened schools to teach Chinese classics to civil service candidates. However, at the same time, they refused to support Buddhism. The religion declined during this period. Despite the influences from China, the Koreans kept their own traditions and unique identity.

One of the greatest Yi kings was Sejong. He ruled from 1394 to 1450. Sejong was interested in science and technology. He used bronze to invent the first instruments for measuring rain. As a result, Korea has the world's oldest record of rainfall. Sejong was also involved in producing water clocks, sundials, and globes. These globes showed the position and motion of planets in the solar system.

Sejong and his advisers worked to spread literacy, or the ability to read, among the Korean people. They made a great contribution by creating an alphabet called *hangul*. Chinese and Japanese use thousands of characters. Hangul is based on symbols that represent sounds.

In the popular Korean fan dance, dancers in traditional robes hold brightly colored fans. They open and close and move the fans to make shapes of butterflies, flowers, and waves.

▶ **CRITICAL THINKING**
Drawing Conclusions Where do you think you would be most likely to see a traditional fan dance performance?

©Ludovic Maisant/Documentary/Corbis

Reading**HELP**DESK

tribute payment to a ruler as a sign of submission or for protection

It uses one letter for each sound, similar to the English alphabet. Hangul is still the standard writing system in present-day Korea.

War and Technology

In 1592, Japanese forces attacked Korea. Their goal was to cross the Korean Peninsula and conquer China. With Chinese help, the Koreans stopped the Japanese attack on land. In the war at sea, the Koreans developed a unique and powerful new ship to defeat the Japanese navy.

Before fighting the Japanese, a Korean admiral named Yi Sun-shin and a team of workers had produced several ships. The vessels were known as turtle ships. The plates that covered the entire top of the ship looked like a turtle shell. They had cannons on all sides and rows of spikes to keep attackers from boarding. These well-protected ships had strong firepower. The general used them to carry out fierce attacks on the Japanese fleet and they were the clear winners.

Korean Struggles

Although the Koreans were able to defeat the Japanese, their victory came at a high price. The fighting on land had destroyed Korean farms, villages, and towns. The Japanese had killed or kidnapped many Korean farmers and workers.

In the early 1600s, while still recovering from Japan's invasion, the Koreans were attacked by the Chinese. China at this time was ruled by a foreign dynasty known as the Manchus. The Yi dynasty was forced to surrender. They had to pay **tribute** to China's Manchu rulers. Korea's relations with its powerful neighbor remained tense for many centuries.

The dragon's head at the bow of the turtle ships might have 'breathed' smoke to cover the movements of the ship, or had a cannon rigged to shoot through the open mouth.

▶ CRITICAL THINKING
Explaining How did technology change warfare?

 PROGRESS CHECK

Explaining How did the building of turtle ships help the Koreans?

LESSON 1 REVIEW

Review Vocabulary

1. How was *shamanism* important to the Koreans?

Answer the Guiding Questions

2. *Identifying* What is the physical location of Korea, and how did its location affect China and Japan?

3. *Summarizing* What did the first Koryo rulers do to establish a lasting civilization?

4. *Explaining* Why was the period of Silla rule considered a time of peace?

5. *Describing* Describe the achievements of Sejong that led him to be called one of the greatest Yi kings.

6. **NARRATIVE** Review the description of the Korean turtle ships. Write a letter to a friend describing the ships.

LESSON 2
Early Japan

ESSENTIAL QUESTION

• How does geography influence the way people live?

IT MATTERS BECAUSE
Many of the characteristics of modern Japanese culture can be traced back to Shinto and to the samurai.

Geography and Settlement

GUIDING QUESTION *How did geography shape Japan's early society?*

Japan (juh·PAN) lies to the east of Korea and China. Japan is an **archipelago** (ahr·kuh·PEH·luh·goh), or a chain of islands, that runs north to south in the Pacific Ocean. For centuries, most Japanese have lived on the four largest islands: Hokkaido (haw·KY·doh), Honshu (HAHN·shoo), Shikoku (shee·KOH·koo), and Kyushu (KYOO·shoo).

The islands of Japan are actually the tops of mountains that rise from the ocean floor. Earthquakes occur in Japan due to its position along an unstable part of the earth's crust. Because of the mountains, only a small amount of Japan's land can be farmed. Local armies have fought over this limited land for centuries.

Many Japanese turned to the sea to make a living. They built villages along the coast and fished. The Japanese also traveled by ship among their many islands. Still, the seas around Japan kept the Japanese **isolated**, or separated, from the rest of Asia. As a result, Japan developed a strongly independent civilization.

The First Settlers

The first people to settle in Japan probably came from northeastern Asia around 20,000 years ago. About 300 B.C., a new group of people, the Yayoi (YAH·yoy), brought farming to Japan

Reading HELP DESK

Taking Notes: *Identifying*
Use a graphic organizer like the one here to show how Chinese culture influenced the early Japanese.

Chinese Culture

Content Vocabulary

• archipelago
• animism
• constitution

516 *Civilizations of Korea, Japan, and Southeast Asia*

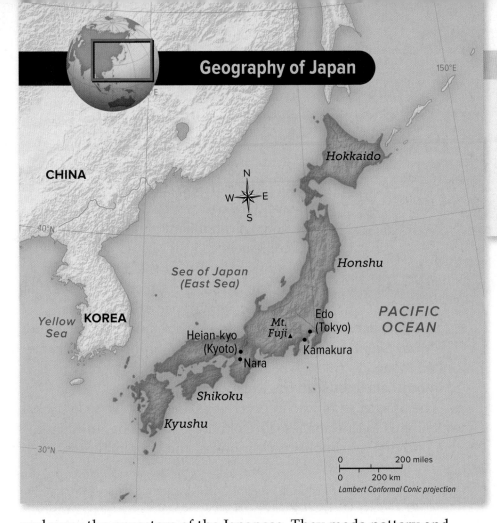

Geography of Japan

150°E

GEOGRAPHY CONNECTION

Japan lies just 110 miles (204 km) east of Korea.

1 **LOCATION** Between what two bodies of water does Japan lie?

2 **CRITICAL THINKING**
Analyzing How did Japan's geography affect its relationships with its neighbors?

CHINA

Hokkaido

N
W · E
S

40°N

Sea of Japan
(East Sea)

Honshu

Yellow   **KOREA**
Sea

PACIFIC
OCEAN

Mt.   Edo
Fuji▲   (Tokyo)
Heian-kyo ·
(Kyoto) ·   · Kamakura
     · Nara

Shikoku

Kyushu

30°N

0   200 miles
0   200 km
Lambert Conformal Conic projection

and were the ancestors of the Japanese. They made pottery and grew rice and were skilled metalworkers. By A.D. 300, the Yayoi had organized themselves into clans, each headed by warrior chiefs. The clan's warrior chiefs protected the people.

The Yamato

During the A.D. 500s, a clan called the Yamato (YAH·mah·taw) ruled most of Japan. Other clans had to give their loyalty to the Yamato chief. Yamato chiefs claimed that they were descended from a sun goddess who sent her grandson to rule over the people of Japan. Japanese legend states that a Yamato leader named Jimmu (jeem·moo) was the great-grandson of this goddess. This gave him the right to rule Japan. Jimmu took the title "emperor of heaven" and became the first emperor of Japan.

The skillfulness of the Yayoi people can be seen in their metalwork, such as this bronze bell.

✓ **PROGRESS CHECK**

Identifying What skills did the Yayoi bring to Japan?

DEA/L. DE MASI/De Agostini/Getty Images

archipelago an expanse of water with many scattered islands

Academic Vocabulary

isolate to set apart from others

Many Japanese still follow Shinto today and visit shrines such as the Kanda Myojin shrine in Tokyo. The design of this temple is similar to the temple built by Prince Shotoku hundreds of years before.

▶ **CRITICAL THINKING**
Explaining What about Shinto beliefs do you think appeals to modern people?

Shinto: Way of the Spirits

GUIDING QUESTION *Why did the early Japanese believe that nature was important?*

The early Japanese believed that humans, animals, plants, rocks, and rivers all have their own spirits. This idea is known as **animism** (A·nuh·mih·zuhm). People believed they could call on the *kami* (KAH·mih), or the nature spirits for help. To show respect to the *kami*, the Japanese worshipped at holy places.

Early Japanese beliefs developed into a religion called Shinto. The word *Shinto* means "way of the spirits." Shinto later became linked to Japan's rulers. Their duties included taking part in Shinto rituals to **ensure** the well-being of Japan.

The practice of Shinto affects the Japanese people today. It has contributed to the Japanese love of nature. It also has influenced their striving for simplicity, cleanliness, and good manners.

☑ PROGRESS CHECK

Explaining How did the Japanese show respect to the *kami*?

Prince Shotoku

GUIDING QUESTION *How did Prince Shotoku reform Japan's government?*

About A.D. 600, a Yamato prince named Shotoku (shoh·TOH·koo) ruled Japan on **behalf** of his aunt. He wanted to give Japan a strong, well-organized government, so Shotoku created a **constitution** (kahn·stuh·TOO·shuhn), or a plan of government. Shotoku's constitution stated that the emperor was an all-powerful ruler. The Japanese were expected to obey him. Specific rules in the constitution, based on the ideas of Confucius, stated how they should perform their duties.

Shotoku admired Chinese civilization and wanted the Japanese to learn from it. Officials and students studied Buddhism, as well as Chinese art, philosophy, and medicine.

After Shotoku's death, officials continued to use China as a model for Japan. In A.D. 646, the Yamato began the Taika (ty·kuh), or Great Change. Japan was divided into districts ruled by officials

P. Narayan/Age fotostock

Reading**HELP**DESK

animism belief in spirits that are outside of the body
constitution basic laws of a state that define the role of government and guarantee its obligation to the people

Academic Vocabulary

ensure to make sure; guarantee
behalf representing; in the place of

who reported to the emperor. All farmland was placed under the emperor's control. Clan leaders could oversee the farmers' work, but government officials now collected taxes. The Taika reforms created Japan's first strong central government.

✔ PROGRESS CHECK

Describing What was the goal of Shotoku's constitution?

The Nara Period

GUIDING QUESTION *How did Chinese ways influence Japan during the Nara period?*

In the early A.D. 700s, Japanese emperors built a new capital city called Nara. It had broad streets, large public squares, Buddhist temples, and Shinto shrines. Nobles' families lived in large, Chinese-style homes. During the Nara period, the Japanese emperors ranked government officials into a hierarchy. However, they did not follow the Chinese practice of using examinations to hire officials. Instead, the emperor gave positions to nobles from powerful families. In return for their services, these officials received large farms. The emperor's control of the land gave him great power.

Buddhist teachings had reached Japan from Korea in the A.D. 500s. During the Nara period, Buddhism became powerful in Japan. In A.D. 770, a Buddhist monk tried to seize the throne. Shaken, the emperor decided to leave Nara for a new capital.

✔ PROGRESS CHECK

Explaining What was Nara?

This grand statue of the Buddha stands in the Todaiji temple, which is one of the world's largest wooden buildings. This temple served as the major temple for Buddhism in Japan.

yannick luthy/Alamy

LESSON 2 REVIEW

Review Vocabulary

1. How does a *constitution* benefit society?

Answer the Guiding Questions

2. *Explaining* Why was early society in Japan isolated?

3. *Drawing Conclusions* How did animism affect people's views about nature?

4. *Identifying* What was Prince Shotoku's main reform in government?

5. *Contrasting* How did the Japanese way of hiring officials during the Nara period differ from that of the Chinese?

6. **ARGUMENT** You are a Japanese worker under Prince Shotoku's rule. Write a persuasive plea to Prince Shotoku asking him to change his new constitution to give workers more rights.

There's More Online! connected.mcgraw-hill.com

LESSON 3
Medieval Japan

ESSENTIAL QUESTION
• How do new ideas change the way people live?

IT MATTERS BECAUSE
Japanese society was transformed under the shoguns. The cultural influences from this time period still influence Japan and the world.

Samurai and Shoguns

GUIDING QUESTION *Why did military leaders rise to power in Japan?*

In A.D. 794, the emperor of Japan moved the capital from Nara to a new city called Heian-kyo (HAY·ahn kyoh). This city later became known as Kyoto (KYOH·toh). The city of Heian-kyo looked much like a major Chinese city.

Nobles Rise to Power

During the A.D. 800s, emperors continued to rule Japan, but their power greatly weakened. Why did this happen? After a period of strong emperors, a number of weak emperors came to the throne. Court officials known as regents governed for them. A regent is a person who rules for an emperor who is too young or too sick to govern.

The regents handled the city's day-to-day government, leaving the Japanese emperors to turn to learning and the arts. Emperors studied Buddhism or wrote poetry in their palace at Heian-kyo.

At the same time, other nobles took control in the outlying provinces of Japan. The government gave these nobles land in return for their support. It also let them stop paying taxes. It made the nobles responsible for governing the lands under their control. To pay for the local government, the nobles increased the taxes on the farmers working the land.

Reading**HELP**DESK

Taking Notes: *Showing Relationships*

Use a graphic organizer like the one here to show the relationship between daimyo and samurai.

Content Vocabulary

• samurai	• feudalism	• martial arts
• shogun	• guild	• meditation
• vassal	• sect	

The Samurai and Their Code

The nobles gave land to warriors who agreed to fight for them. These warriors became known as **samurai** (SA·muh·ry). In battle, samurai fought on horseback with swords, daggers, and bows and arrows. They wore armor made of leather or steel scales and helmets with horns or crests.

A few Japanese women were outstanding warriors. Perhaps the most famous was Tomoe. She fought in the A.D. 1100s during a time of civil war in Japan. One account from the A.D. 1200s describes her:

The samurai were warriors in Japan who followed a very strict code of behavior known as Bushido.

▶ CRITICAL THINKING
Explaining Why did samurai agree to fight for a noble?

PRIMARY SOURCE

❝ [S]he was a fearless rider whom neither the fiercest horse nor the roughest ground could dismay, and so dexterously [skillfully] did she handle sword and bow that she was a match for a thousand warriors and fit to meet either god or devil. … and so in this last fight, when all the others had been slain or had fled, among the last seven there rode Tomoe. ❞

—from *Heike Monogatori (The Tale of Heike)*

The word *samurai* means "to serve." The samurai lived by a strict code of conduct. This code was called Bushido (BU·shih·doh), or "the way of the warrior." It demanded that a samurai be loyal to his master. The samurai must also be brave and honorable. Samurai were not supposed to be concerned about riches. They viewed merchants as lacking in honor.

Bound to these principles, a samurai would rather die in battle than betray his master. He also did not want to suffer the disgrace of being captured in battle. The sense of loyalty that set apart the samurai lasted into modern times. During World War II, many Japanese soldiers fought to the death rather than accept defeat or capture. The Japanese have since turned away from the beliefs of the samurai.

Shoguns Assume Power

By the early 1100s, a period similar to the Middle Ages in Europe, noble families of Japan used their samurai armies to fight one another. They fought over land and to gain control of the emperor. In 1180, a civil war broke out between the two most powerful families: the Taira and the Minamoto. In a sea battle in 1185, the Taira were defeated. The commander of the Minamoto forces was Minamoto Yoritomo (mee·nah·MOH·toh yoh·ree·TOH·moh).

De Agostin Picture Library/Getty Images

samurai a warrior who served a Japanese lord and lived by a strict code of loyalty

Minamoto Yoritomo became the first shogun to rule Japan in 1185. One of his favorite pastimes was to release wild cranes on the beach near his castle. By this he believed he gained Buddhist merit.

▶ **CRITICAL THINKING**
Analyzing How did Minamoto Yoritomo come to power?

After Yoritomo won the civil war, the emperor feared that the Minamoto family would take the throne. To avoid this, he decided to reward Yoritomo to keep him loyal. In 1192, he gave Yoritomo the title of **shogun** (SHOH·guhn), or commander of the military forces.

This created two governments in Japan. The emperor remained in his palace at Heian-kyo with his advisers. He was Japan's official leader. Meanwhile, the shogun set up his own government in the small seaside town of Kamakura (kah·MAH·kuh·rah). This military government was known as a shogunate. For about the next 700 years, shoguns ran Japan's government.

Mongol Attacks

In the late 1200s, Japan was twice invaded by China's Mongol emperor. During both attempts, violent storms called typhoons destroyed many ships. The Mongols who made it to shore were defeated by the Japanese.

The victorious Japanese named the typhoons *kamikaze* (kah·mih·KAH·zee), or "divine wind," in honor of the spirits they believed had saved their islands. During World War II, Japanese pilots deliberately crashed their planes into enemy ships. They were named kamikaze pilots after the typhoons of the 1200s.

✅ **PROGRESS CHECK**

Identifying What is Bushido, and why was it important to the samurai?

A Divided Japan

GUIDING QUESTION *Why did Japan experience disunity from the 1300s to the 1500s?*

The Kamakura shogunate ruled Japan until 1333. At that time, a general named Ashikaga (ah·shee·KAH·gah) resisted the emperor and made himself shogun. A new government, the Ashikaga shogunate, began.

©Asian Art & Archaeology, Inc./Corbis

ReadingHELPDESK

shogun a military governor who ruled Japan

Academic Vocabulary

labor work; the tasks that workers perform for pay

Reading Strategy: *Explaining*

Explaining means you give all the details of something. Why did the emperor make Minamoto Yoritomo shogun?

The Ashikaga shoguns turned out to be weak leaders. Uprisings swept Japan. The country soon divided into a number of small territories. These areas were headed by powerful military lords known as daimyo (DY·mee·oh).

The daimyo pledged to obey the emperor and the shogun. Still, they governed their lands as if they were independent states. To guard their lands, the daimyo used samurai warriors. They formed their own local armies.

Many samurai became **vassals** (VA·suhlz) of a daimyo. These samurai gave an oath of loyalty to their daimyo and pledged to serve him in battle. In return, each daimyo gave land to his samurai. This bond of loyalty between a lord and a vassal is known as **feudalism** (FYOO·duh·lih·zuhm). A similar form of feudalism existed in Europe between the fall of the Western Roman Empire and the early modern period.

With the collapse of central government, warriors battled one another throughout Japan. The violence finally ended the Ashikaga shogunate in 1567. By that time, only a few powerful daimyo were left. Each of these daimyo was eager to conquer his rivals—and rule all of Japan.

✓ **PROGRESS CHECK**

Analyzing Why did feudalism develop in Japan?

Society Under the Shoguns

GUIDING QUESTION *How were the Japanese affected by their country's growing wealth?*

Under the shoguns, Japan produced more goods and grew richer. However, only the emperor and his family, noble families of the emperor's court, and leading military officials enjoyed this wealth. A small but growing class of merchants and traders also benefited from Japan's prosperity. Most Japanese, however, were farmers who remained poor.

Farmers, Artisans, and Trade

For the most part, Japan's wealth came from the hard **labor** of its farmers. Some farmed their own land, but most lived and worked on the estates of the daimyo. Rice, wheat, millet, and barley were their chief crops. Life improved for Japan's farmers during the 1100s, despite their many hardships.

vassal a person under the protection of a lord to whom he has vowed loyalty

feudalism the system of service between a lord and the vassals who have sworn loyalty to the lord

The collapse of a shogunate often led to a period of civil war. This daimyo is one of the powerful military lords that took control and governed.

▶ CRITICAL THINKING
Contrasting What was the difference between the shoguns and the daimyo?

Culver Pictures Inc./SuperStock

In this painting, Japanese farmers are shown working their rice paddies.

Explaining How did improved irrigation practices help farmers?

A better irrigation process enabled them to plant more crops. This meant they could sell more food to the markets that were forming in the towns.

On the daimyo estates, other Japanese were producing a greater number of goods. Artisans made armor, weapons, and tools. These goods were sold by merchants in town markets throughout Japan. As trade increased, each region began to make certain goods that they were best at producing. These goods included pottery, paper, textiles, and lacquered ware.

Heian-kyo, now called Kyoto, developed into a major center of production. It also benefited from trade with Korea, China, and Southeast Asia. Japanese merchants traded wooden goods, sword blades, and copper for silk, dyes, pepper, books, and porcelain. More and more artisans and merchants began to live in Kyoto. They set up groups called **guilds** (GIHLDZ), or *za* in Japanese, to protect their jobs and increase their earnings.

Women in Shogun Japan

During the time of the shoguns, the typical Japanese family included grandparents, parents, and children in the same household. A man was head of the family. He had complete control over family members.

At the time of Prince Shotoku, wealthy Japanese women enjoyed a high standing in society. Several women were empresses, and women could own property. Wives who were abandoned could divorce and remarry. When Japan became a warrior society, upper-class women lost these freedoms.

In farming families, women had a greater say in choosing their husbands. However, they worked long hours in the fields. They also cooked, spun and wove cloth, and cared for their children. In the towns, the wives of artisans and merchants helped run the family businesses.

Despite the lack of freedom, some women were able to contribute to Japanese culture. These talented women gained fame as artists, writers, and entertainers.

✓ **PROGRESS CHECK**

Explaining Why did Japan's wealth increase under the rule of the shoguns?

Erich Lessing/Art Resource, NY

Reading**HELP**DESK

guild a group of merchants or craftspeople during medieval times

sect a religious group

martial arts sports that involve combat and self-defense

Religion and the Arts

GUIDING QUESTION *How did religion and the arts relate to each other under the shoguns?*

During the time of the shoguns, religion and the arts flourished in Japan. Many Japanese monks, artists, scribes, and traders visited China. This led to a borrowing of ideas and practices. Much of this borrowing from the Chinese affected Japan in the areas of government and philosophy. Chinese culture also influenced Japan's art, literature, science, and religion.

The Religions of Japan

Under the shoguns, religion influenced every part of daily life in Japan. Most Japanese came to believe in both Shinto and Buddhism. They worshipped at Shinto shrines and at Buddhist temples. To them, each religion met different needs. Shinto was concerned with daily life. It linked the Japanese to nature and their homeland. Buddhism promised spiritual rewards to the good. It prepared people for the life to come. In shogun Japan, religious ideas inspired many Japanese to write poems and plays and produce paintings. They also built shrines and temples.

Mahayana Buddhism, which teaches that the Buddha is a god, began in India and spread to China and Korea. By the time Buddhism reached Japan, it had formed into many different **sects** (SEHKTS), or small groups. One of the major sects in Japan was Zen. Buddhist monks brought Zen to Japan from China during the 1100s. Zen taught that people could find inner peace through self-control and a simple way of life. Followers of Zen disciplined their bodies through **martial arts** (MAHR· shuhl), or sports that involved combat and self-defense.

Zen Buddhists also practiced **meditation** (meh·duh· TAY·shuhn). A person who meditated sat cross-legged and motionless. The person tried to clear the mind of all worldly thoughts and desires. Meditation was considered a way for people to relax and find inner peace.

The Phoenix Hall was originally a single noble's home but was converted to a Buddhist temple in 1053.

©B.S.P.I/Corbis

There's More Online!

**Murasaki Shikibu
(c. A.D. 978–1014)**

In addition to *The Tale of Genji*, Lady Murasaki Shikibu wrote a diary and more than 120 poems. Her father was a scholar and a governor, and he broke with tradition by educating his daughter Murasaki in Chinese language and literature. Her family was noble but not rich. While serving as a lady-in-waiting in the royal court, Murasaki began writing her novel based on observations of life around her.

▶ **CRITICAL THINKING**

Explaining How did Murasaki herself break from tradition?

Visual Vocabulary

meditation mental exercise to reach a greater spiritual awareness

Writing and Literature

During the A.D. 500s, the Japanese adopted China's writing system. They used Chinese picture characters that represented whole words. The Japanese and Chinese languages were very different, so the Japanese found it difficult to use these characters. Then, in the A.D. 800s, they added symbols that stood for sounds, much like the letters of an alphabet. Reading and writing became much easier.

The Japanese greatly admired calligraphy, or the art of writing beautifully. Every well-educated person was expected to practice it. Handwriting was believed to reveal much about a person's education, social standing, and character.

Under the shoguns, the Japanese wrote poems, stories, and plays. By the 1600s, a form of poetry called *haiku* (HY·koo) had emerged. A haiku consists of 3 lines of words with a total of 17 syllables. Haiku usually expresses a mood or feeling. The most noted writer of haiku was a man of samurai descent. Below are two of his most famous haiku.

PRIMARY SOURCE

First snow
falling
on the half-finished bridge.

A field of cotton—
As if the moon
had flowered.

—tr. by Robert Hass

Japan's first great prose literature was written around A.D. 1000 by women at the emperor's palace at Heian-kyo. Lady Murasaki Shikibu (mur·uh·SAH·kee shee·KEE·boo) wrote *The Tale of Genji*. This work describes the romances and adventures of a Japanese prince. Some people believe the work is the world's first novel, or long fictional story.

The Japanese also wrote plays. The oldest type of play is called Noh. Created during the 1300s, Noh plays developed out of religious dances and were used to teach Buddhist ideas. Many Noh plays are still performed in Japan today.

Architecture and Art

During the time of the shoguns, the Japanese adopted building and artistic ideas from China and Korea. They went on to develop their own styles. The architecture and art of Japan revealed the Japanese love of simplicity and beauty.

Shinto shrines were built in the Japanese style, usually as a simple wooden building, with one room and a rice straw roof. Often they were built near a sacred tree or rock.

Unlike Shinto shrines, Buddhist temples were built in the Chinese style. They had massive tiled roofs held up by thick, wooden pillars. Inside, the temples were richly decorated. They had many altars, paintings, and statues.

Around buildings, the Japanese created gardens that copied nature on a small scale. Carefully placed large rocks served as symbols of mountains, while raked sand gave the sense of water flowing. They might contain only a few plants. The gardens were built this way to create a feeling of peace and calmness.

Creative Artisans

To create beauty inside buildings, Japan's artisans made wooden statues, furniture, and household items. They used a shiny black or red coating called lacquer on many decorative and functional objects. Other Japanese artists learned to do landscape painting from the Chinese. Using ink or watercolors, they painted scenes of nature or battles on paper scrolls or on silk. Japanese nobles at the emperor's palace learned to fold paper to make decorative objects. This art of folding paper is called origami. Buddhist monks and the samurai turned tea drinking into a beautiful ceremony.

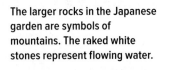

The larger rocks in the Japanese garden are symbols of mountains. The raked white stones represent flowing water.

©Craig Tuttle/Corbis

✔ PROGRESS CHECK

Analyzing How did meditation play a part in Buddhism?

LESSON 3 REVIEW

Review Vocabulary

1. How did the *samurai* advisers serve the *shoguns*?

Answer the Guiding Questions

2. *Determining Cause and Effect* How did regents affect the rise to power of military leaders in Japan?

3. *Determining Cause and Effect* What caused Japanese disunity from the 1300s to the 1500s?

4. *Identifying* What groups of Japanese benefited the most from the increasing wealth in Japan?

5. *Analyzing* What effect did religion have on the arts during the time of the shoguns?

6. **NARRATIVE** Write a narrative in which you describe an encounter with a samurai in the 1300s. This samurai tells you about the code of Bushido. Be sure to include how the samurai dresses and acts.

Southeast Asia: History and Culture

- What makes a culture unique?

IT MATTERS BECAUSE

The varied cultures of Southeast Asia have been shaped by outside influences and, in turn, have shaped other cultures.

Early Civilization

GUIDING QUESTION *How did geography affect settlement and early ways of life in Southeast Asia?*

China, Korea, and Japan were not alone in developing civilizations along Asia's Pacific coast. Farther south, other civilizations arose in a region known today as Southeast Asia. Southeast Asians developed their own traditions, though they were influenced by India, China, and Islam.

The Geography of Southeast Asia

Southeast Asia has two major parts. One is a mainland area made up of long, winding peninsulas. The other is a large archipelago, or chain of islands.

Mountain ranges cross mainland Southeast Asia, running north to south. Between the ranges are narrow river valleys and broad coastal deltas. These lowlands are rich in fertile soil. They became prosperous farming and trading centers and home to most mainland Southeast Asians.

South and east of the region's mainland are thousands of mountainous islands. Part of a geographical area known for being unstable, these islands hold many active **volcanoes**. These

Reading**HELP**DESK

Taking Notes: *Identifying*

Use a graphic organizer like this one to show what purposes the temple of Angkor Wat served.

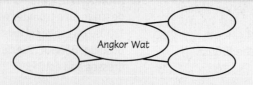

Angkor Wat

Content Vocabulary

- **volcano**
- **tsunami**
- **maritime**

KEY
— Modern boundary

CHINA

INDIA

MYANMAR

BANGLADESH

LAOS

THAILAND

CAMBODIA

VIETNAM

Bay of
Bengal

Andaman
Sea

Gulf of
Thailand

South
China
Sea

PHILIPPINES

PACIFIC
OCEAN

TROPIC OF CANCER

30°N

20°N

10°N

Strait of Malacca

BRUNEI

MALAYSIA

SINGAPORE

INDIAN
OCEAN

INDONESIA

EQUATOR

0°

N
W E
S

0   600 miles
0   600 km
Miller projection
90°E   100°E   110°E   120°E

GEOGRAPHY CONNECTION

Southeast Asia is made up of long
peninsulas and a large archipelago,
or chain of islands.

1 **LOCATION** Between which
   five countries is Laos located?

2 **CRITICAL THINKING**
   Drawing Conclusions Looking
   at the map, why do you think a
   tsunami would be especially
   dangerous in this region?

volcanoes provide rich soil for farming. Earthquakes affect the
island peoples of Southeast Asia. One particular danger comes
from **tsunamis** (soo·NAH·meez). A tsunami is a huge ocean
wave caused by an underwater earthquake. Tsunamis usually
strike coastal lowlands, killing many people and destroying
buildings. This happened in Japan in 2011.

Sea trade and inland mountain barriers shaped Southeast
Asia into a region of many ethnic groups, languages, and
religions. As a result, Southeast Asia was never united under a
single government. Instead, it was an area of separate territories.

Early Years

Early peoples in Southeast Asia grew rice, raised cattle and pigs,
and made metal goods. These early people believed in animism,
the idea that spirits exist in living and nonliving things. They
practiced different rituals to honor their ancestors as well as
animal and nature spirits.

volcano a mountain that may release hot or
melted rocks from inside the Earth

tsunami a huge ocean wave caused by an
undersea earthquake

Musicians from Vietnam perform traditional music using string and wind instruments.

Southeast Asians also developed their own forms of art. Artisans made a cloth of detailed patterns later called batik (buh·TEEK). Musicians played instruments including the *dan bau* (similar to a xylophone), the *dan day* (a type of guitar), and the *rammana* (a type of drum). Artists created a type of theater that used shadow puppets to tell stories. Performers holding long rods controlled the puppets behind a white screen, while audiences on the other side could see the puppets' moving shadows.

Outside Contacts

During the A.D. 100s, Hindu traders from India reached coastal areas of Southeast Asia. They set up a trading **network** that exchanged goods and ideas among the peoples of Southeast Asia, India, and the Middle East. As these contacts increased, the cultures of other civilizations spread throughout Southeast Asia. Over time, the people of the region blended Hindu and Chinese ways with their own traditions.

✓ **PROGRESS CHECK**

Analyzing Why did outside influences have a powerful effect on early Southeast Asia?

Kingdoms and Empires

GUIDING QUESTION *Why did powerful kingdoms and empires develop in Southeast Asia?*

From A.D. 500 to 1500, many kingdoms and empires thrived in Southeast Asia. States covering fertile inland areas drew their wealth from the land. States on the coast became **maritime** (MEHR·uh·tym), or seafaring, powers that controlled shipping.

Vietnam

Along the coast of the Indochinese Peninsula lies the present-day country of Vietnam. The ancient Viet were one of the first people in Southeast Asia to develop their own state and culture. During the 200s B.C., the Viet people ruled most of the Indochinese Peninsula.

During the early A.D. 900s, the Viet rebelled against China's weakened Tang dynasty. In A.D. 938, the Viet forces defeated a fleet of Chinese warships in the Battle of the Bach Dang River. The Viet had finally won independence.

©STR/epa/Corbis

maritime related to the sea or seafaring

Academic Vocabulary

network a system in which all parts are connected
style a distinctive form or type of something

The new state was modeled on the government of China and was known as Dai Viet, or Great Viet. Confucianism became its official religion. Viet emperors adopted Chinese court ceremonies. Just as in China, Viet government officials were selected through civil service examinations.

The Khmer Empire

West of Vietnam is the present-day country of Cambodia (kam·BOH·dee·uh). In ancient times, this region was the home of the Khmer (kuh·MEHR) people. During the A.D. 1100s, the Khmer founded an empire that covered much of mainland Southeast Asia. They became wealthy from growing rice.

Khmer kings based their rule on Hindu and Buddhist ideas from India. They increased their power by presenting themselves as god-kings to their people. A Chinese traveler once described the splendor, in dress and manner, of a Khmer king in about 1297:

PRIMARY SOURCE

His crown of gold is high and pointed like those on the heads of the mighty gods. . . . His neck is hung with ropes of huge pearls; . . . his wrists and ankles are loaded with bracelets and on his fingers are rings of gold. . . . He goes barefoot—the soles of his feet, like the palms of his hands, are rouged [colored] with a red stuff. When he appears in public, he carries the Golden Sword.

—from *A Record of Cambodia: The Land and Its People*, by Zhou Daguan, tr. by Peter Harris

Supported by Khmer kings, architects created a new **style** of building based on Indian and local designs. The most magnificent structure was Angkor Wat. It served as a religious temple, a royal tomb, and an astronomical observatory. Angkor Wat still stands today and attracts many visitors.

By the 1440s, building costs, high taxes, and internal revolts had weakened the Khmer Empire. In A.D. 1432, the Thai (TY), a neighboring Southeast Asian people, captured the capital city of Angkor. With this attack, the Khmer Empire faded into history.

There's More Online connected.mcgraw-hill.com

Saving Angkor Wat

Angkor Wat was overgrown by thick tropical plants and trees after its capture by the Thai in A.D. 1432. During the late 1900's the site was further damaged during various wars. Mostly, however, it suffered from neglect. In 1992, Angkor was named a UNESCO World Heritage site, a major step in protecting it for generations to come.

Angkor Wat, the largest religious structure in the world, is a temple complex built in Cambodia. Built in the 1100s, it took nearly 40 years to complete.

▶ **CRITICAL THINKING**
Making Inferences Why do you think it took so long to build Angkor Wat?

Buddhist monks dress in robes to symbolize simple living and a rejection of material goods.

▶ CRITICAL THINKING

Drawing Conclusions How did Buddhist monks from India influence the Thai people?

The Thai

The earliest Thai settlements arose along the border of China. Between A.D. 700 and 1100, Thai groups moved southward. They set up a kingdom at Sukhothai (SOO·kah·TY) in what is today north central Thailand.

The Thai developed a writing system and made the kingdom a center of learning and the arts. Artisans from China taught the making of porcelain. Buddhist monks from India converted many Thai to Buddhism. The Thai were influenced by Hinduism in their political practices, dance, and literature.

About A.D. 1350 a new Thai kingdom known as Ayutthaya (ah·yoo·TY·uh) arose. Its capital city was located where the city of Bangkok, the present Thai capital, stands today.

The Ayutthaya kingdom lasted for about 400 years. At its height, it held control over large areas of Southeast Asia. The Thai region was an important center of Buddhist learning and culture. Its merchants traded in teak wood, salt, spices, and hides with China and neighboring Asian kingdoms.

Burma

West of the Thai kingdom, a people known as the Burmese developed a civilization. In A.D. 849, they set up a capital city called Pagan (pah·GAHN). During the next 200 years, Pagan became a major influence in the western part of Southeast Asia.

Melba Photo Agency/Alamy

Reading**HELP**DESK

Academic Vocabulary

institution a custom or practice that many people accept and use

The city eventually became a center of Buddhist learning and culture. Like the Thai, the Burmese adopted Buddhism, as well as Indian political **institutions** and culture.

Attacks by the Mongols in the late 1200s weakened Pagan. To escape Mongol rule, many people in Burma moved south and built fortified towns along the rivers. Burmese culture was preserved, but the kingdom did not arise again until the 1500s.

The Malay States

On the Malay Peninsula and the islands of Indonesia, independent states developed around seaport cities. They traded porcelain, textiles, and silk, as well as Southeast Asian spices and wood.

Most of the people living on Southeast Asian islands were Malays. Despite common cultural ties, the Malays were divided into many separate communities by distance and trade rivalries. However, in the A.D. 700s, a Malay state arose on the islands of Java and Sumatra in present-day Indonesia. This state controlled the trade route passing through the Strait of Malacca.

Many Southeast Asian states continue to share common farming and trade ideas and practices.

Islam in Southeast Asia

Muslim Arab traders and missionaries settled coastal areas of Southeast Asia during the A.D. 800s. Eventually, many people in these places converted to Islam. The first major Islamic center was Melaka, a trading port on the Malay Peninsula.

From Melaka, Islam spread throughout the Indonesian islands. Bali was the only island to remain outside of Muslim influence. Even today, Bali keeps its Hindu religion and culture.

✔ **PROGRESS CHECK**

Summarizing How did the culture of China affect Southeast Asian states?

Juliet Coombe/Lonely Planet Images/Getty Images

LESSON 4 REVIEW

Review Vocabulary

1. Why do *maritime* workers live along a seacoast?

Answer the Guiding Questions

2. *Identifying* What separated early Southeast Asians?

3. *Listing* What were the most powerful kingdoms to develop on mainland Southeast Asia by A.D. 1500?

4. *Contrasting* Why did some Southeast Asian states rely mostly on trading while others relied on farming?

5. *Explaining* Why was Angkor Wat significant to the Khmer?

6. **INFORMATIVE/EXPLANATORY** Look at the photograph of Angkor Wat. Then write a paragraph describing its appearance to someone who has never seen it before.

Write your answers on a separate sheet of paper.

1 **Exploring the Essential Question**

INFORMATIVE/EXPLANATORY Review the section about the first settlers in Japan. Then write a paragraph in which you discuss the Yayoi. How did they live? How were they organized? What kind of government did they have?

2 **21st Century Skills**

USING LATITUDE AND LONGITUDE Many Southeast Asian countries are linked by water. Notice where the Equator falls in the region on the map below. Do research to find out what effect living on the Equator can have on the lives of the people of Southeast Asia. How might this latitude influence their economies and lifestyle? Share your finding with the class, using the map as part of your presentation.

3 **Thinking Like a Historian**

UNDERSTANDING CAUSE AND EFFECT Create a diagram like the one to the right to identify what events caused shoguns to rise to power in Japan.

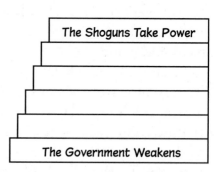

4 **GEOGRAPHY ACTIVITY**

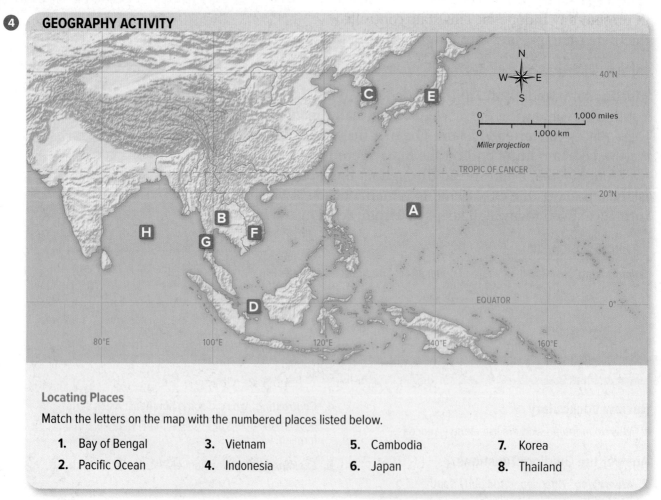

Locating Places

Match the letters on the map with the numbered places listed below.

1. Bay of Bengal
2. Pacific Ocean
3. Vietnam
4. Indonesia
5. Cambodia
6. Japan
7. Korea
8. Thailand

Directions: Write your answers on a separate piece of paper.

CHECKING FOR UNDERSTANDING

1 Define each of these terms as they relate to Korea, Japan, and Southeast Asia.

A. archipelago

B. samurai

C. shogun

D. vassal

E. feudalism

F. guild

G. volcano

H. tsunami

REVIEW THE GUIDING QUESTIONS

2 *Explaining* How did the geography of Korea affect its early settlement?

3 *Summarizing* Summarize how the Koryo rulers built a civilization on the Korean Peninsula.

4 *Finding the Main Idea* How was Japan's early society shaped by geography?

5 *Paraphrasing* Use your own words to explain how Prince Shotoku reformed Japan's government.

6 *Stating* What is one way the Chinese influenced Japan during the Nara period?

7 *Identifying* What events led to military leaders becoming increasingly powerful in Japan?

8 *Discussing* Why was there no central government in Japan from the 1300s to the 1500s?

9 *Describing* How did Japan's growing wealth affect its people?

10 *Naming* What two factors of Southeast Asia's geography led to it having many different ethnic groups?

11 *Explaining* Why were the kingdoms of Southeast Asia able to become wealthy and powerful?

CRITICAL THINKING

12 *Comparing and Contrasting* How was the constitution that Shotoku wrote similar to the Constitution of the United States? How was it different?

13 *Analyzing* Why was nature important to the early Japanese?

14 *Determining Cause and Effect* Why did the Koryo king and his family have to leave the mainland of Korea and flee to an island around A.D. 1231?

15 *Recognizing Relationships* How were religion and the arts related to each other under the shoguns?

16 *Making Connections* How did the fact that Southeast Asia has a great deal of coastal land lead to Islam being widely adopted in that region?

17 *Analyzing Maps* Study the map titled "Geography of Korea" in Lesson 1. Do you think the development of the Korean Peninsula might have been different if there were no mountains where the peninsula connects to the mainland? Explain your answer.

18 *Problem-Solving* As a Khmer king during the early 1400s, when the Khmer Empire was weakening, what might you do to make your kingdom stronger? Use clear and concise language when explaining your ideas.

19 *Predicting Consequences* During the Nara period, the Japanese were influenced by the Chinese in many ways. However, the Japanese did not adopt the Chinese civil service system. How do you think this might have affected the type of people who worked for the government? Give reasons for your answer.

20 *Making Decisions* You are a farmer in Southeast Asia. In what part of Southeast Asia would you want to live? Give two specific reasons.

Need Extra Help?

If You've Missed Question	1	2	3	4	5	6	7	8	9	10	11	12	13	14	15	16	17	18	19	20
Review Lesson	1,2, 3,4	1	1	2	2	2	3	3	3	4	4	2	2	1	3	4	1	4	2	4

DBQ SHORT RESPONSE

"During the Three Kingdoms , . . . power in all three of the kingdoms was held by those who lived in the capital and by the aristocratic families who dominated a very rigid and hereditary social status system. Members of the upper and lower classes were differentiated in almost every aspect of their lives, including clothing, food, housing, and occupation. . . . The lifestyle of the aristocracy was supported by slaves, who led miserable lives."

—May Connor, editor, *The Koreas*

21 What factors differentiated members of the upper and lower classes?

22 What privileges did aristocrats have that the lower class didn't have?

EXTENDED RESPONSE

23 *Informative/Explanatory* Write a short essay in which you explain the concept of animism and its influence on the culture of the Japanese.

STANDARDIZED TEST PRACTICE

DBQ ANALYZING DOCUMENTS

A great Noh actor, explained how acting is mastered.

"As long as an actor is trying to imitate his teacher, he is still without mastery. ... An actor may be said to be a master when, by means of his artistic powers, he quickly perfects the skills he has won through study and practice, and thus becomes one with the art itself."

—*The Book of the Way of the Highest Flower (Shikadō-Sho)*
by Seami Jūokubushū Hyōshaku

24 *Analyzing* Which of the following best summarizes when actors become "masters"?

A. when they can imitate the teacher

B. when they begin to study and practice acting

C. when they learn artistic skills

D. when they become part of the art of acting

25 *Comparing and Contrasting* What might a master actor and a samurai have in common?

A. Both were well paid.

C. Both owned land.

B. Both worked for shoguns.

D. Both practiced their skills to perfection.

Need Extra Help?

If You've Missed Question	**21**	**22**	**23**	**24**	**25**
Review Lesson	4	4	4	3	2, 3

◄ *As a teenage girl in battle armor, Joan of Arc inspired the French army to defeat the English and rescue the French city of Orleans.*

A.D. 500 TO 1475

Medieval Europe

THE STORY MATTERS ...

Who would have predicted that a devout peasant girl, born in France in 1412, could help a prince become king? Yet Joan of Arc, shown in this painting, accomplished that for King Charles VII of France. She also helped defeat the English, whose armies occupied her native land.

The story of Joan of Arc reflects the history of medieval Europe in many ways. The Middle Ages were a time of struggle and conflict. They were also a period when the Catholic Church influenced almost every aspect of people's lives.

ESSENTIAL QUESTIONS

- Why does conflict develop?
- What is the role of religion in government?
- What are the characteristics that define a culture?
- How do governments change?

Peter Willi/SuperStock/Getty Images

Place & Time: Medieval Europe A.D. 500 to 1475

During the Middle Ages, Europeans lived in an ordered society of monarchs, nobles, and peasants. As trade and cities grew, the number of merchants and laborers rose. The Catholic Church greatly influenced all of these groups.

Step into the Place

MAP FOCUS Rivers, seas, and mountains provided both natural barriers and trade opportunities for medieval Europeans.

1 REGION Look at the map. Which countries border the Atlantic Ocean?

2 LOCATION What is the only inland country without a coastal area link to a sea?

3 PLACE What major rivers flowed through the Holy Roman Empire?

4 CRITICAL THINKING
Drawing Conclusions How does a location near a waterway contribute to the growth of trade?

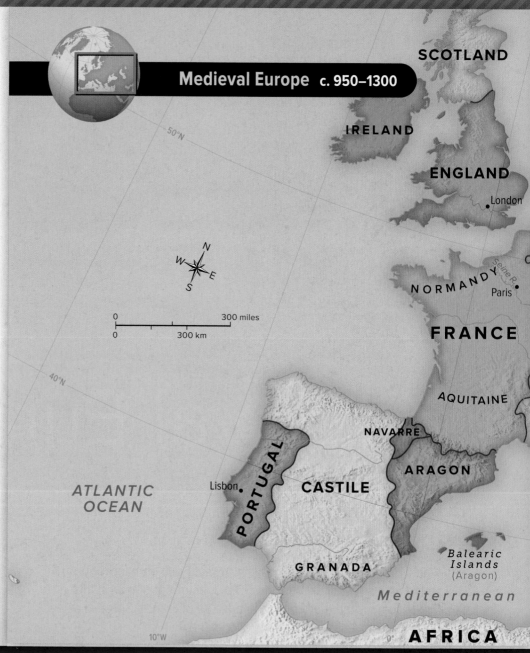

Medieval Europe c. 950–1300

Step Into the Time

TIME LINE Choose an event from the time line and write a paragraph about the role religion played in that event.

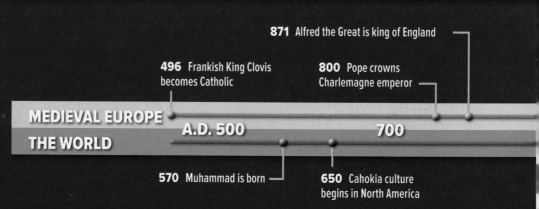

871 Alfred the Great is king of England

496 Frankish King Clovis becomes Catholic

800 Pope crowns Charlemagne emperor

MEDIEVAL EUROPE

THE WORLD

A.D. 500

700

570 Muhammad is born

650 Cahokia culture begins in North America

NORWAY

SWEDEN

North
Sea

DENMARK

Baltic Sea

Oder R.

POLAND

Vistula R.

HOLY

Rhine R.

ROMAN

Danube R.

EMPIRE

Vienna

• Budapest

HUNGARY

ASIA

Volga R.

• Milan

Po R.

• Venice

Genoa •

• Bologna

Marseilles •

• Florence

Corsica
(Genoa)

PAPAL
STATES

Adriatic Sea

SERBIA

BULGARIA

Black Sea

• Rome

Sardinia
(Aragon)

KINGDOM OF

• Naples

SICILY

BYZANTINE   EMPIRE

Sea

Sicily

10°E

20°E

30°E

1492   Spanish conquer last Muslim kingdom in Spain

1429   Joan of Arc inspires French

1209   Francis of Assisi founds Franciscan Order

1346   The Black Death
arrives in Europe

1095   First Crusade begins

900   1100   1300   1500

900s Maya
classic period ends
in Mesoamerica

1140 Temple
complex of Angkor
Wat built in Cambodia

1223 Genghis Khan leads
Mongolian invasion of Russia

1498 Vasco da Gama
travels to India by sea

539

LESSON 1
The Early Middle Ages

ESSENTIAL QUESTION

• Why does conflict develop?

IT MATTERS BECAUSE
Medieval European governments, religions, languages, and culture still influence the modern world.

Geography of Europe

GUIDING QUESTION *How did geography shape life in Europe after the fall of Rome?*

During the 400s, Germanic groups invaded the Western Roman Empire. In A.D. 476, these groups overthrew the last emperor in Rome and brought the Empire to an end. Europe then entered a new era called the Middle Ages, or medieval times. This was a 1,000-year period between ancient and modern times. During the Middle Ages, Western Europe was divided into many kingdoms, and Catholic Christianity strongly influenced society.

Physical geography shaped Europe's development. The continent of Europe is a huge peninsula, with many smaller peninsulas branching out from it. As a result, most land in Europe lies within 300 miles (483 km) of a seacoast. This encouraged trade and helped the European economy to grow.

Rivers and Seas

Rivers also played an important **role** in Europe's growth. Major rivers, such as the Rhine, Danube, Seine, and Po, flow from inland mountains into the oceans and seas surrounding the continent. These rivers are navigable, or wide and deep enough for ships to use. People and goods can sail easily from inland areas to the open sea and, from there, to other parts of the world.

Reading**HELP**DESK

Taking Notes: *Identifying*

Choose four European leaders from this lesson. Use a diagram like this one to identify the achievements of each leader.

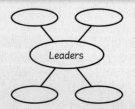

Leaders

Content Vocabulary

• **fjord**   • **concordat**

• **missionary**

Europe's seas and rivers provided protection as well as possibilities for trade. The English Channel, for example, separated the islands of Britain and Ireland from the rest of Europe. As a result, these people were far enough away to be largely safe from the many wars fought on Europe's mainland. They were able to develop their own governments and societies. In mainland Europe, wide rivers like the Rhine also kept groups of people separated. Because of this separation and isolation, many different cultures developed.

Europe also has many mountain ranges. In the southwest, the Pyrenees isolated what is now Spain and Portugal from the rest of Europe. In the middle of the continent, the Alps separated Italy from central Europe. The Carpathians cut off what is now Ukraine and Russia from southeast Europe. The mountains, like the rivers, made it difficult for one group to control all of Europe and encouraged the growth of independent territories.

✓ PROGRESS CHECK

Explaining Why were rivers important to the peoples of Europe?

GEOGRAPHY CONNECTION

After the Western Roman Empire came to an end, many different peoples lived throughout Europe.

1 LOCATION Where did the Celtic peoples live?

2 CRITICAL THINKING
Speculating Why do you think there are no national boundaries on this map?

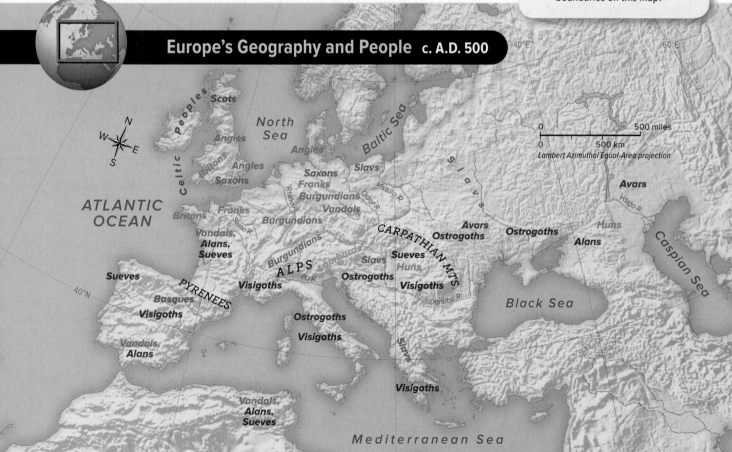

Europe's Geography and People c. A.D. 500

Academic Vocabulary

role something that plays a part in a process

Kingdoms in Western Europe

GUIDING QUESTION *How did Germanic groups build kingdoms in Western Europe?*

By A.D. 500, Western Europe had divided into many Germanic kingdoms. Germanic people in Italy and Spain adopted many Roman ways. People farther from Rome held on to more of their Germanic traditions.

Roman influence was even weaker in Britain. After Roman armies abandoned the area that is today England, Germanic groups known as Angles and Saxons settled there. In time, they became the Anglo-Saxons.

The Anglo-Saxons pushed aside earlier settlers known as the Celts (KEHLTS). Some Celts fled north and west, while others crossed the sea to Ireland. The Scottish, Welsh, and Irish peoples today are largely descended from the Celts.

The Franks in Europe

The Franks were the strongest Germanic group. They settled what is now France and western Germany. In 481, Clovis (KLOH·vuhs) became king of the Franks. Fifteen years later, he became the first Germanic ruler to accept Catholic Christianity. Before long, nearly all of the Franks became Catholic.

After Clovis died, Frankish kings lost much of their power. By 700, power had passed from kings to government officials known as mayors of the palace.

In 714, Charles Martel (mahr·TEHL), or "Charles the Hammer," became mayor of the palace. The pope, who was the head of the Catholic Church, gave Martel his support. Martel and the pope wanted to restore order and strengthen Catholic Christianity in the lands of the old Western Roman Empire.

Martel's first move was to halt the spread of Islam into Europe. By the early 700s, Muslims from North Africa had conquered Spain and entered France. In 732, Charles Martel defeated the Muslims at the Battle of Tours. This battle stopped the advance of Islam into Western Europe. It also ensured that Christianity would remain Western Europe's major religion.

After Charles Martel died, his son Pepin (PEH· puhn) became mayor of the palace. With the support and blessing of the pope, Pepin became king of the Franks. In return, Pepin was expected to help the

King Clovis won the support of Romans living in his kingdom when he accepted Christianity.

▶ **CRITICAL THINKING**
Speculating Why might the Romans in the kingdom have accepted Clovis more after he became a Christian?

Florent Lamontagne/Age fotostock

Florent Lamontagne/Age fotostock

Reading**HELP**DESK

Reading Strategy: *Analyzing Primary Sources*

Why might Einhard—in his quote on the next page—have described Charlemagne's appearance in such positive terms?

pope. In 754, Pepin forced a Germanic group called the Lombards to leave Rome. He then gave the pope a large strip of Lombard land in Italy. These lands became known as the Papal States.

The Emperor Charlemagne

After Pepin died in 768, his son Charles became king of the Franks. In the years that followed, Charles sent his armies into neighboring lands. He nearly doubled the size of his kingdom to include what is today Germany, France, northern Spain, and most of Italy.

By 800, Charles's kingdom had grown into an empire. For the first time since the fall of Rome, most Western Europeans were ruled by one government. His conquests won Charles the name of Charlemagne (SHAHR·luh·MAYN), or Charles the Great. A monk named Einhard described Charlemagne this way:

Pope Leo III crowned Charlemagne "Emperor of the Romans."

▶ **CRITICAL THINKING**
Making Inferences Why was it important that the pope led the crowning ceremony?

PRIMARY SOURCE

❝ Charles was large and strong, and of lofty stature [height] . . . [his] nose a little long, hair fair, and face laughing and merry. . . . He used to wear the . . . Frankish dress—next [to] his skin a linen shirt and linen breeches [pants], and above these a tunic fringed with silk. . . . Over all he flung a blue cloak, and he always had a sword girt [fastened] about him. ❞

—from *The Life of Charlemagne*, by Einhard

In 800, Charlemagne came to Rome and defended the pope against unruly Roman nobles. On Christmas day, Charlemagne was worshipping at the church of St. Peter in Rome. After the service, the pope placed a crown on Charlemagne's head and declared him the new Roman emperor. Charlemagne was pleased but also concerned. He did not want people to think the pope had the power to choose who was emperor.

Despite this concern, Charlemagne accepted his duties as emperor and worked to strengthen the empire. The central government, located in the capital of Aachen (AH·kuhn), was small. As a result, Charlemagne relied on local officials called counts to help him govern. The counts ran local affairs and raised armies for Charlemagne. Royal messengers went on inspections and told the emperor how the counts were doing.

Charlemagne wanted to advance learning in his kingdom. He had tried late in life to learn to write and wanted his people to be educated too. He **established** a school for the children of government officials. Students at the school studied religion, Latin, music, literature, and arithmetic.

Waves of Invaders

More than anything else, Charlemagne's forceful personality held the empire together. After Charlemagne died in 814, his empire did not last long. It was soon divided into three kingdoms.

These Frankish kingdoms were prey to outside attacks. In the 800s and 900s, waves of invaders swept across Europe. Muslims from North Africa raided France and Italy. Fierce nomads called Magyars from Hungary invaded eastern parts of France and Italy. Vikings launched raids from their homeland in Scandinavia (SKAN·duh·NAY·vee·uh).

Scandinavia is in northern Europe. Norway, Sweden, and Denmark are all part of modern Scandinavia. Much of Scandinavia has a long, jagged coastline. It has many **fjords** (fee·AWRDS), or narrow inlets of the sea. The fjords, surrounded by steep cliffs or slopes, were carved by glaciers long ago. The Viking people, known as Norsemen or "north men," lived in villages near the fjords.

Scandinavia has little farmland, so the Vikings had to depend on the sea for food and trade. They became skilled sailors and traveled in sturdy longboats. These boats could survive the rough Atlantic and also navigate shallow rivers.

Vikings sailed the northern seas in boats powered by oars and the wind. This longship is a replica of a Viking ship that carried explorers.

Reading**HELP**DESK

fjord a narrow inlet of the sea between cliffs or steep slopes

Academic Vocabulary

establish to start; to bring into existence

In the 700s and 800s, the Vikings left their crowded homeland and carried out raids along Europe's coasts. The word *viking* comes from their word for raiding. The Vikings attacked villages and churches, seizing grain, animals, and other valuable items. They burned whatever they could not steal.

The Vikings were more than just raiders. They were also explorers and settlers. They sailed across the Atlantic, settled the islands of Greenland and Iceland, and even landed in North America. For a short time, Viking groups also lived in England. They founded the territory of Normandy in northwestern France and settled in parts of what are now Russia and Ukraine.

Formation of the Holy Roman Empire

Muslim, Magyar, and Viking invaders brought much suffering to Europe's people. Their attacks also weakened the Frankish kingdoms. By the 900s, the eastern Frankish kingdom, known as Germany, became a collection of small territories ruled by nobles. In 911, a group of these nobles sought to unite Germany by electing a king.

In 936, Duke Otto of Saxony was elected king of Germany. Otto became a powerful ruler. Germanic forces defeated the Magyars and freed the pope from the control of Roman nobles. To reward Otto, the pope crowned him emperor of the Romans in 962. Otto's territory became known as the Holy Roman Empire. It included most of present-day Germany and northern Italy.

GEOGRAPHY CONNECTION

During the Early Middle Ages, several different groups invaded and settled in Europe.

1 **MOVEMENT** Which groups of invaders traveled by sea?

2 **CRITICAL THINKING**
Speculating Why might an army have found it more difficult to invade Italy than Hungary?

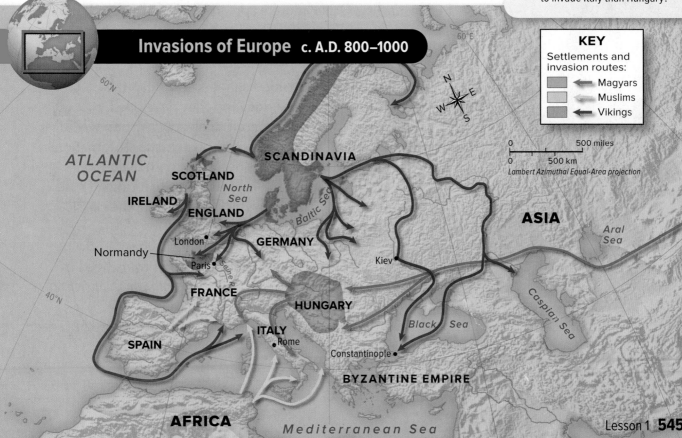

Invasions of Europe c. A.D. 800–1000

KEY
Settlements and invasion routes:
- Magyars
- Muslims
- Vikings

0   500 miles
0   500 km
Lambert Azimuthal Equal-Area projection

ATLANTIC OCEAN

SCANDINAVIA

SCOTLAND

IRELAND

North Sea

ENGLAND

Baltic Sea

London

GERMANY

Normandy

Paris

Seine R.

FRANCE

Kiev

ASIA

Aral Sea

HUNGARY

Caspian Sea

SPAIN

ITALY

Rome

Black Sea

Constantinople

BYZANTINE EMPIRE

AFRICA

Mediterranean Sea

After Otto, two important emperors, Frederick I and Frederick II, tried to bring Germany and Italy under a strong central government during the 1100s and 1200s. The popes did not want the emperor to control them. They joined with Italy's cities to resist the emperors' forces. Ongoing conflict kept Germany and Italy from becoming united countries until the 1800s.

☑ PROGRESS CHECK

Explaining What impact did the Battle of Tours have on European history?

The Church and Its Influence

GUIDING QUESTION *How did the Catholic Church influence life in early medieval Europe?*

The Roman Catholic Church played an important role in the growth of a new civilization in medieval Western Europe.

Christianity in Europe

At the time of Rome's fall, large areas of northwestern Europe practiced a variety of non-Christian religions. Ireland was different. In the 400s, a Christian priest named Patrick traveled to Ireland. There, Patrick spread Christianity and founded churches and monasteries, or religious houses.

Patrick inspired Pope Gregory I, or Gregory the Great, to spread Christianity. Gregory asked monks to become **missionaries** (MIH·shuh·NEHR·eez)—people who are sent out to teach their religion. In 597, Gregory sent 40 monks to Britain to teach Christianity. Other monks spread Christianity, so that by 1050, most Western Europeans had become Catholic Christians.

The Contributions of Monks and Nuns

Monks and monasteries provided schools and hospitals. They taught carpentry and weaving, and they developed improvements in farming. Many monks copied Christian writings as well as Roman and Greek works. They also made illuminations, which are manuscripts decorated with beautiful lettering and miniature religious paintings. These monks helped preserve knowledge of the classical and early Christian worlds.

Monks lived in communities headed by abbots (A·buhtz). Women called nuns lived in their own monasteries called convents. Convents were headed by abbesses (A·buhs·ihs).

This image shows Pope Gregory VII wearing his official vestments as head of the Church.

▶ CRITICAL THINKING
Drawing Conclusions Why do you think Pope Gregory VII wanted to stop kings from choosing Church officials?

©Elio Ciol/Corbis

Reading**HELP**DESK

missionaries people who are sent by a religious organization to spread the faith

concordat agreement between the pope and the ruler of a country

Church Authority

Many monasteries became wealthy. As their influence increased, abbots became active in political affairs. This caused disagreements. Kings wanted Church leaders to obey them. Popes, however, believed kings should obey the Church.

Elected pope in 1073, Gregory VII declared that only the pope had the power to appoint high-ranking Church officials. Pope Gregory's order angered Henry IV, the Holy Roman emperor. For many years, the Holy Roman emperor had chosen bishops in Germany. Henry insisted on naming his own bishops. Gregory then declared that Henry was no longer emperor and excommunicated him. This meant that he no longer had the rights of church membership and could not go to heaven.

When the German nobles supported the pope, Henry changed his mind. He traveled to Italy and begged the pope for forgiveness. Gregory forgave Henry, but the German nobles chose a new emperor. When Gregory accepted the new emperor, Henry seized Rome and named a new pope.

The struggle continued until 1122, when a new German king and a new pope agreed that only the pope could choose bishops, but only the king or emperor could give them government posts. This agreement, called the *Concordat of Worms*, was signed in the German city of Worms. A **concordat** (kuhn·KAWR·DAT) is an agreement between the pope and the ruler of a country.

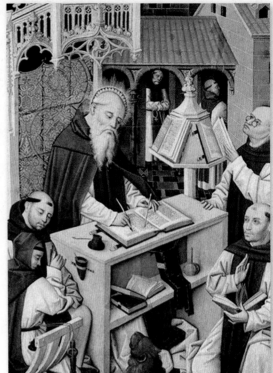

In the days before printing presses, monks helped preserve knowledge by copying classical Greek and Roman writings as well as the Bible and other early Christian writings.

☑ PROGRESS CHECK

Describing What major issue did kings and popes disagree on?

©The Gallery Collection/Corbis

LESSON 1 REVIEW

Review Vocabulary

1. What is a *missionary* meant to do?

2. What natural process created the *fjords*?

Answer the Guiding Questions

3. *Summarizing* How did mountains and rivers make it difficult for one group to control all of Europe?

4. *Explaining* What happened in Britain after Roman armies abandoned the area during the 400s?

5. *Identifying* In what modern countries did the Franks settle?

6. *Analyzing* What did Charlemagne do to advance education?

7. *Analyzing* What role did monasteries play in medieval Europe?

8. **INFORMATIVE/EXPLANATORY** Henry IV begged for the pope's forgiveness. If you were going to interview King Henry about this incident, what three questions would you ask him? Write your answer in a paragraph.

Feudalism and the Rise of Towns

ESSENTIAL QUESTION

• What are the characteristics that define a culture?

IT MATTERS BECAUSE

The organization of society in medieval Europe affected nearly every aspect of people's lives.

The Feudal Order

GUIDING QUESTION *How did Europeans try to bring order to their society after the fall of Charlemagne's empire?*

After the fall of Charlemagne's empire, strong governments collapsed in Western Europe. Kings lost much of their power. Local land-owning nobles became increasingly important in political affairs. They raised armies. They also collected taxes and imposed laws on the people living on their lands.

When invaders swept through Europe, people turned to the nobles for protection. Nobles governed and protected the people in return for services, such as fighting in a noble's army or farming the land. This led to a new political and social order known as **feudalism** (FYOO·duh·LIH·zuhm).

By 1000, Europe's kingdoms were divided into hundreds of feudal territories. Most of these territories were small. A noble's castle was the center of each territory.

Lords, Vassals, and Knights

Feudalism was based on ties of loyalty and duty among members of the nobility. Nobles were both lords and vassals. A lord was a high-ranking noble who had power over others. A **vassal** (VA·suhl) was a lower-ranking noble who served a lord. In return, the lord protected the vassal.

Reading**HELP**DESK

Taking Notes: *Summarizing*

Use a cluster diagram like the one shown here to list important features of feudalism as a social system during the Middle Ages.

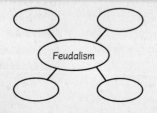

Feudalism

Content Vocabulary

- feudalism
- vassal
- fief
- knight
- serf
- guild
- chivalry

The tie binding a lord and his vassal was declared in a public ceremony. The vassal took an oath and placed his hands between those of his lord. Then the vassal swore:

PRIMARY SOURCE

❝ Sir, I enter your homage [service] and faith and become your man by mouth and hands [that is, by taking the oath and placing his hands between those of the lord], and I swear and promise to keep faith and loyalty to you against all others. ❞

—from *A Source Book for Medieval History*, 1905

A vassal helped his lord in battle. In exchange for the vassal's **military** service, a lord gave his vassal land. The property granted to a vassal was known as a **fief** (FEEF).

Many lower-ranking vassals were known as **knights** (NYTS). They were armed warriors who fought on horseback. In early medieval times, warriors in Western Europe mostly fought on foot. In the 700s, knights began to use a foot piece called a stirrup. Stirrups allowed a knight to sit on a horse and attack.

Nobles and Knights in Medieval Society

During the Middle Ages, nobles were the most powerful people in Europe. Great lords had more land and wealth than ordinary knights. Yet, a shared belief in the feudal order united lords and knights in defending their society.

Knights followed the code of **chivalry** (SHIH·vuhl·ree). These rules stated that a knight was to be brave and obey his lord. A knight was also required to respect women of noble birth, honor the Church, and help people. Many of today's ideas about manners come from the **code** of chivalry.

Kings and queens

Lords and ladies

Knights

Peasants and serfs

---

feudalism political order; under feudalism, nobles governed and protected people in return for services

vassal a low-ranking noble under the protection of a feudal lord

fief a feudal estate belonging to a vassal

knight a mounted man-at-arms serving a lord

Academic Vocabulary

military relating to soldiers, arms, or war

code a system of rules

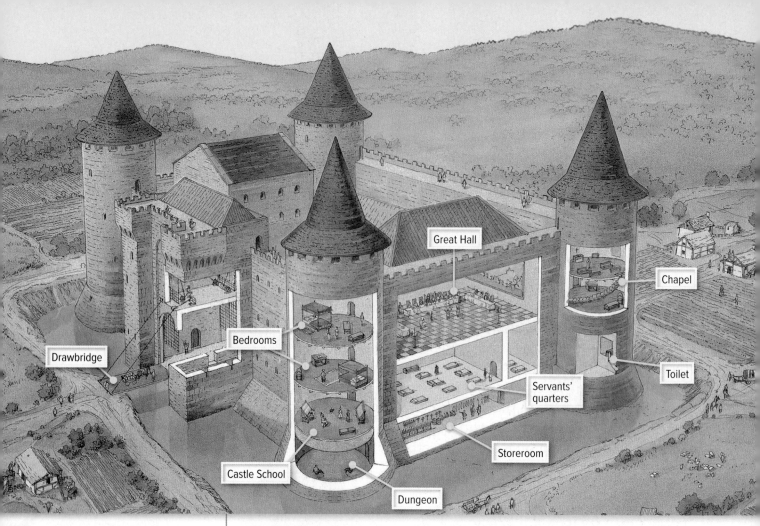

Drawbridge

Bedrooms

Great Hall

Chapel

Toilet

Servants' quarters

Storeroom

Castle School

Dungeon

Castles in the Middle Ages were designed to provide good defenses for their owners. For example, castles often occupied high ground. High towers at each corner gave soldiers the chance to drive attackers away.

Knights trained for war by fighting one another in tournaments, or special contests. The most popular event was the joust. Two knights on horseback carrying lances, or spears, galloped toward each other and tried to knock each other off.

Nobles were often at war and away from their castles. In their absence, their wives or daughters ran the estates.

The castle was at the center of the estate. Every castle had two parts. The first was a motte (MAHT), or steep-sided hill. The second part was the bailey, an open space next to the motte. Both parts were encircled by high walls. The castle keep, its central building, was constructed on the motte.

In the basement of the keep, tools and food were stored. On the ground floor were kitchens and stables. Above these was a great hall. The lord held court and met visitors here.

✔ PROGRESS CHECK

Identifying What were the rules of behavior that knights followed?

Reading**HELP**DESK

chivalry the system, spirit, or customs of medieval knighthood

serf a member of the peasant class tied to the land and subject to the will of the landowner

The Medieval Manor

GUIDING QUESTION *How did most Europeans live and work during the Middle Ages?*

Nobles, knights, and peasants (or farmers) depended on the land for everything they needed. The lands of a fief consisted of manors. A manor was a farming community that a noble ran and peasants worked. It usually consisted of the noble's castle, the surrounding fields, and a peasant village.

Two Groups of Peasants

During the Middle Ages, the vast number of Europeans were peasants living and working on manors. There were two groups of peasants—freemen and serfs. Freemen paid the noble for the right to farm the land. They worked only on their own land and had rights under the law. They moved wherever and whenever they wished.

Most peasants, however, were **serfs** (SUHRFS). Serfs and their descendants were tied to the manor. They could not own property, move to another area, or marry without the noble's permission. Serfs were not enslaved, however. Nobles could not sell them or take away the land they farmed to support themselves. Nobles were also expected to protect their serfs.

Serfs worked long hours in the fields and did many services for the nobles. They spent three days of the week working the noble's land and the rest of the week farming their own. However, they had to give part of their own crops to the noble. They also had to pay him for the use of the village's mill, bread oven, and winepress.

It was not easy for serfs to gain their freedom. One way was to escape to the towns. If a serf was not caught and remained in a town for more than a year, he or she was considered free. By the end of the Middle Ages, serfs in many areas were allowed to buy their freedom.

The Lives of the Peasants

Peasants—both freemen and serfs—lived in villages clustered around an open area called a village green. Their homes were simple cottages. The poorest peasants lived in a single room.

Peasants worked year round. In late winter and spring, they planted crops of beans, peas, barley, and oats. In early summer, they weeded fields and sheared sheep. In late summer, they harvested grain. They also slaughtered livestock.

Serfs had a busy life working in the fields growing the lord's crops and their own.

▶ CRITICAL THINKING
Differentiating What happened to the crops that serfs grew on their own land?

Buyenlarge/Archive Photos/Getty Images

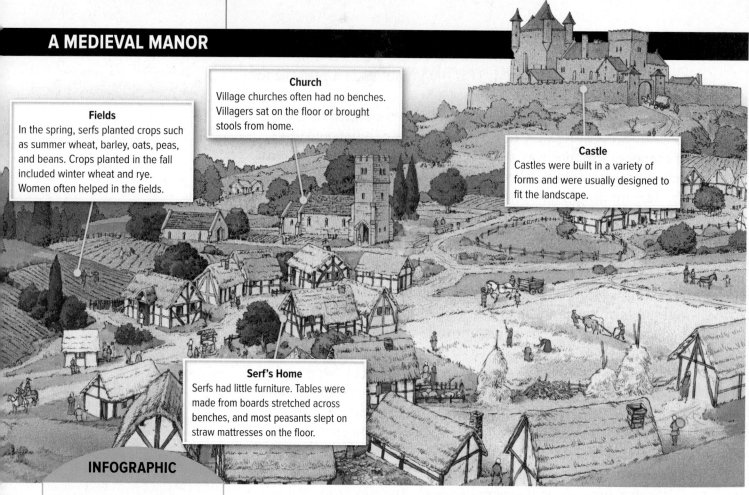

Fields
In the spring, serfs planted crops such as summer wheat, barley, oats, peas, and beans. Crops planted in the fall included winter wheat and rye. Women often helped in the fields.

Church
Village churches often had no benches. Villagers sat on the floor or brought stools from home.

Castle
Castles were built in a variety of forms and were usually designed to fit the landscape.

Serf's Home
Serfs had little furniture. Tables were made from boards stretched across benches, and most peasants slept on straw mattresses on the floor.

INFOGRAPHIC

A medieval manor had several parts. At the center was the lord's castle or fortified manor house. Peasants usually lived in a small village nearby. The village contained cottages, huts, barns, gardens, and perhaps a small church. The peasants grew crops in the fields around the village. Manors were found not only in western Europe, but were also common in Russia and Japan.

Explaining What were the four areas of a medieval manor?

During times of leisure, peasant life centered on the church and the village green. Peasants took a break from work and went to church on Sunday and Catholic feast days. Certain feast days were celebrated with singing and dancing on the green. Peasant men took part in sports such as wrestling and archery.

Besides working in the fields, peasant women raised children and prepared the family's food. They made dark, heavy bread, which peasants ate with vegetables, milk, nuts, and fruits. They also ate eggs and meat, washed down with ale.

Improvements in Farming

Manors usually produced only enough food to support the peasants and the lord's household. However, over time, Europeans developed new ways to increase the number of crops they could grow, as well as how much the crops produced.

One major improvement was a heavy wheeled plow with an iron blade. The new plow made deeper cuts in the dense clay soil. The heavier plow meant peasant farmers spent less time

Reading HELPDESK

Reading Strategy: *Analyzing*

When you analyze a passage you have read, you think about how the facts lead to main conclusions. Reread the section about the medieval manor looking for facts. Then analyze how the manor was beneficial to peasants.

in the fields. The horse collar was another important invention. The collar enabled a horse to pull a plow. Horses could pull plows faster than oxen could. This invention made it possible for peasants to produce more food.

Water and wind power also became important during the Middle Ages. Europe's rivers provided power for water mills to grind grain into flour. In places without rivers, windmills could be used for grinding grain, pumping water, and sawing wood.

Another improvement in agriculture was crop rotation. Peasants used three fields rather than two to keep the soil fertile. One field was planted in the fall, a second one in springtime, and the third field was left unplanted. With this system, only one-third of the land was left unused at a time, rather than one-half. More crops could be grown as a result. As food production increased, the population of Europe grew.

☑ **PROGRESS CHECK**

Comparing and Contrasting How did the lives of freemen and serfs differ?

The Growth of Towns and Cities

GUIDING QUESTION *How did increased trade change life in medieval Europe?*

When the Roman Empire collapsed, trade throughout Europe sharply declined. Bridges and roads fell into ruin. Law and order largely disappeared. Most people spent their entire lives in the farming villages where they were born. They knew very little about the rest of the world.

By 1100, feudalism had made Europe safer. Nobles repaired roads, arrested bandits, and enforced the law. Meanwhile, new technology enabled people to produce more food and goods. Europe's population grew for the first time since the fall of Rome.

Peasants began to make cloth and metal products. Nobles also sought luxury items, such as sugar, spices, silks, and dyes. These goods came from the East.

Wealthy Trading Centers

As Europe's trade increased, towns grew larger. Several cities became wealthy from trade. The cities of Venice (VEH·nuhs), Pisa, and Genoa in Italy built fleets of trading ships. They became major trading centers. By 1200, these Italian cities controlled the profitable Mediterranean trade with the Byzantine Empire.

As Europe became more feudalistic, towns and cities grew. Tall stone buildings lining narrow streets were similar in England and France. This street is still in use in Blesle, France.

©Robert Landau/Corbis

Trade was lively in medieval marketplaces with a variety of products for sale.

▶ CRITICAL THINKING
Analyzing Visuals What kinds of goods appear to be available at this market?

Meanwhile, Flanders—a region that is today part of Belgium—became a center of trade on Europe's northern coast. Towns in Flanders, such as Bruges and Ghent, were known for wool. Merchants from all over Western Europe traveled to these towns to trade their goods for woolen cloth.

Trade fairs were established in northern France. At these fairs, northern European merchants bartered their products. They traded furs, tin, honey, and wool for swords and cloth from northern Italy and silks, sugar, and spices from Asia.

As trade increased, merchants demanded payment in gold and silver coins. People again began using money to buy goods. Some merchants set up banks.

Government in Cities

The rise of trade and cities created a new middle class in medieval Europe. People in the middle class had some wealth as a result of their roles as merchants, bankers, or artisans. They became important leaders in the cities.

Eventually, medieval towns began to set up their own governments. Only males were considered citizens. In many cities, the citizens elected the members of a city council. These elected officials served as lawmakers and judges.

Under the feudal system, towns were often part of the territory belonging to a noble. As a result, nobles tried to control town affairs. Townspeople, however, disliked owing taxes and services to nobles. They wanted freedom to make their own

Scala/Art Resource, NY

Reading**HELP**DESK

guild a group of merchants or craftspeople

laws. As their wealth increased, townspeople forced nobles to grant them basic rights. These included the right to buy and sell property and the freedom from having to serve in the army.

What Did Guilds Do?

Trade encouraged townspeople to produce many different kinds of products. Craftspeople organized **guilds**, or business groups. Each craft had its own guild.

Guilds controlled business and trade in a town. The guild set the price for a product or service. Guilds also set and enforced standards of quality for products.

In addition, guilds decided who could join a trade. An apprentice, or trainee, learned a trade from a master artisan who provided room and board but no wages. After completing this training, the apprentice became a journeyman who worked under a master for a daily wage.

Life in a Medieval City

Medieval cities were surrounded by stone walls. Inside the walls, stone public buildings and wooden houses were jammed close together. Candles and fireplaces were used for light and heat.

Towns could be unhealthy places. Wood and coal fires in people's homes and shops filled the air with ashes and smoke. Sewers were open, and there was little concern for cleanliness.

City women kept house, cared for children, and managed the family's money. Wives often helped their husbands in their trade, sometimes carrying on the trade after their husbands' deaths.

✔ **PROGRESS CHECK**

Analyzing How did guilds affect the way medieval townspeople made a living?

Thinking Like a HISTORIAN

Researching Using Internet Resources

One of England's earliest historians was Bede. Bede (A.D. 673–735) was an educated monk who lived in northern England. He wrote the *Ecclesiastical History of the English People*, using the Latin language. Use the Internet to find reliable copies or selections from Bede's history. Choose three facts you discover about English history and present them to your class. For more information about using sources, review *What Does a Historian Do?*

LESSON 2 REVIEW

Review Vocabulary

1. What was a *fief*?

Answer the Guiding Questions

2. *Describing* Draw a chart to show the major parts of a medieval manor.

3. *Summarizing* What impact did the code of chivalry have on knights during the Middle Ages?

4. *Identifying Cause and Effect* What explains the development of cities and towns during the Middle Ages?

5. *Drawing Conclusions* If you were a person in business in medieval Europe, why would membership in a guild be important to you?

6. **INFORMATIVE/EXPLANATORY** What new inventions allowed people in Western Europe to grow more food during the Middle Ages? What was the result of this increase in food production?

LESSON 3

Kingdoms and Crusades

ESSENTIAL QUESTION

• How do governments change?

IT MATTERS BECAUSE

The development of law and government during the Middle Ages in Europe still affects us today.

Royal Power in England

GUIDING QUESTION *How was the king's power strengthened and then limited in medieval England?*

In the late 800s, Vikings from Scandinavia attacked Britain, where the Anglo-Saxons had founded many small kingdoms. King Alfred of Wessex, later known as Alfred the Great, united the Anglo-Saxons and halted the Viking advance. The kingdom that Alfred united became known as "Angleland," or England.

Alfred ruled England from A.D. 871 to 899. Unfortunately for England, the Anglo-Saxon kings who followed Alfred were generally weak rulers.

William the Conqueror

In 1066, the last Anglo-Saxon king of England died without an heir. A noble named Harold Godwinson claimed the English throne. In France, a relative of the Anglo-Saxon kings, William, Duke of Normandy (NAWR·muhn·dee), said that he, not Harold, was the rightful king of England.

In the fall of 1066, William and his army of Norman knights landed in England. They defeated Harold and his foot soldiers at the Battle of Hastings. William was crowned king of England and became known as William the Conqueror.

Reading**HELP**DESK

Taking Notes: *Sequencing*

Complete a sequence diagram like this one to show the causes and effects of the Crusades.

Content Vocabulary

• **grand jury**   • **trial jury**

At first, the Anglo-Saxons resisted William's rule. To stop the Anglo-Saxon revolts, William seized the land of Anglo-Saxon nobles and divided it among his Norman knights.

William wanted to learn as much as possible about his new kingdom. To decide taxes, he carried out the first census since Roman times. Every person and farm animal in England was counted and recorded in the *Domesday Book*.

The Normans who ruled England kept many Anglo-Saxon laws and practices. However, they also brought many customs from mainland Europe. Under William's rule, officials and nobles in England spoke French, the language of Normandy. They built castles, cathedrals, and monasteries in the Norman style. Anglo-Saxons learned new skills from Norman weavers and artisans. Yet, they still spoke their own Anglo-Saxon language, which later became English. As more and more Normans and Anglo-Saxons married, their customs merged into a new English culture.

Henry II

After the death of William, English kings further strengthened their power. From 1154 to 1189, King Henry II ruled England as well as most of Wales, and Ireland. He was also a feudal lord in France and Scotland. Some of the French lands belonged to his wife, Queen Eleanor of Aquitaine.

Henry set up a central royal court with lawyers and judges. Circuit judges, who traveled across the country to hear cases, brought the king's law to all parts of England.

At the Battle of Hastings, William the Conqueror led Norman knights on horseback as well as infantry to attack the English foot soldiers.

▶ CRITICAL THINKING
Identifying Points of View Why did William believe that he was the rightful king of England?

The courts created a body of common law, or law that was the same throughout the whole kingdom. Common law helped unite England by replacing laws that differed from place to place.

Henry also set up juries of citizens to settle disputes. Traveling circuit judges met with a **grand jury.** It decided if people should be accused of a crime. Next came a **trial jury** to decide whether a person was innocent or guilty.

The Magna Carta and Parliament

Henry's son John became king of England in 1199. King John increased taxes in England and punished his enemies without trials. English nobles began to rebel.

In 1215, the nobles met with King John at Runnymede, a nearby meadow. There they forced John to put his seal on a **document** called the Magna Carta, or the Great Charter. The Magna Carta placed limits on the king's power. The king could collect taxes only if a group of nobles called the Great Council agreed.

The Magna Carta also forced the king to uphold the rights of freemen, including the right to fair trials by jury:

“ No free man shall be taken, imprisoned, disseised [seized], outlawed, banished [sent away], or in any way destroyed, nor will We proceed against or prosecute him, except by the lawful judgment of his peers [equals] and by the law of the land. ”

—from the *Magna Carta*, 1215

King John signed the Magna Carta, a document that brought significant change to England.

The Magna Carta relied on the feudal idea that the king and his noble vassals both had certain rights and duties. Over time, the Magna Carta helped strengthen the idea that all people have rights, and the power of government should be limited.

Edward I, king of England in the late 1200s, increased the authority of his council. This group of lords, church leaders, knights, and townspeople became known as Parliament (PAHR· luh·muhnt). Parliament came to be divided into two groups— an upper house and lower house. This growth of Parliament marked an important step toward representative government.

✓ PROGRESS CHECK

Explaining How did the common law help unite England?

Reading**HELP**DESK

grand jury a group of citizens that meets to decide whether people should be accused of a crime

trial jury a group of citizens that decides whether an accused person is innocent or guilty

Academic Vocabulary

document an original or official paper used as the basis or proof of something

Building Vocabulary: *Word Origins*

The English word *Parliament* comes from the French word *parler*, meaning to talk or converse. Parliament was where people could talk about problems or concerns facing the kingdom.

Monarchy in France

GUIDING QUESTION *How did the kings of France increase their power?*

In 843, Charlemagne's empire was split into three parts. The western part became the kingdom of France. In 987, the west Frankish nobles made Hugh Capet their king. Hugh began the Capetian (kuh·PEE·shuhn) dynasty of French kings. Capetian kings controlled only the area around Paris, the capital. Many French nobles had more power than the kings did. This began to change when Philip II became the king of France in 1180.

Philip worked to expand the French monarchy's wealth and power. At the beginning of Philip's reign, the king of England ruled feudal lands in western France. Philip fought wars against the English and gained some of these territories.

Philip IV wanted to raise taxes to pay for his wars. In 1302, he gained approval for this plan from representatives of the three estates, or classes, of French society. The first estate was the clergy, or priests. Nobles made up the second estate, and townspeople and peasants were the third estate. This meeting began the Estates-General, France's first parliament. The Estates-General never became as powerful as Parliament in England.

☑ PROGRESS CHECK

Comparing and Contrasting How was the Estates-General of France different from England's Parliament?

GEOGRAPHY CONNECTION

In 1160, Europe was divided into many small kingdoms and states.

1 **LOCATION** Which empire bordered Hungary to the south?

2 **CRITICAL THINKING**
Analyzing What was the effect of having many small states ruled by French nobles?

European Kingdoms c. 1160

Eastern States of the Slavs

GUIDING QUESTION *How did the cities of Kiev and Moscow become centers of powerful Slavic states?*

In Eastern Europe, people called the Slavs established villages and towns along the rivers of that region. The Slavs consisted of three important groups: the southern Slavs, the western Slavs, and the eastern Slavs.

The Rise of Kiev

In the 800s, the eastern Slavs began to expand the city of Kiev (KEE·EHF). The medieval state of Kievan Rus grew wealthy from its river trade with Scandinavia and the Byzantine Empire.

In 988, the Rus ruler, Vladimir, married the sister of the Byzantine emperor. Vladimir became an Eastern Orthodox Christian. Soon, priests from Constantinople came to teach the people of Kievan Rus religious rituals and the art of painting icons.

Mongol Invaders

About 1240, Mongol warriors from Central Asia conquered Kievan Rus. The Slavic city of Novgorod was the only major city to be spared attack by the Mongols. However, Novgorod's rulers had to pay tribute to the khan, the Mongol leader, and accept the Mongols as their rulers.

Although the Mongols spared Novgorod, the city faced attacks from the west by Germans and Swedes. In 1240, Novgorod forces led by a prince named Alexander Nevsky (NEHV·skee) defeated these invaders.

Mongol warriors attacked towns and cities on horseback and had a reputation for being more hostile than previous invaders. The image below is from a film that recreated the Mongol invasions.

ANDREEVSKY FLAG FILM CO/KINOFABRIKA/KINOKOMPANIYA CTB/X-FILME CREATIVE POOL/Ronald Grant Arc/Mary Evans Picture Library

Reading**HELP**DESK

Academic Vocabulary

cooperate to work together with

Reading Strategy: *Making Connections*

As you read, try to link new information in your reading to what you already know.

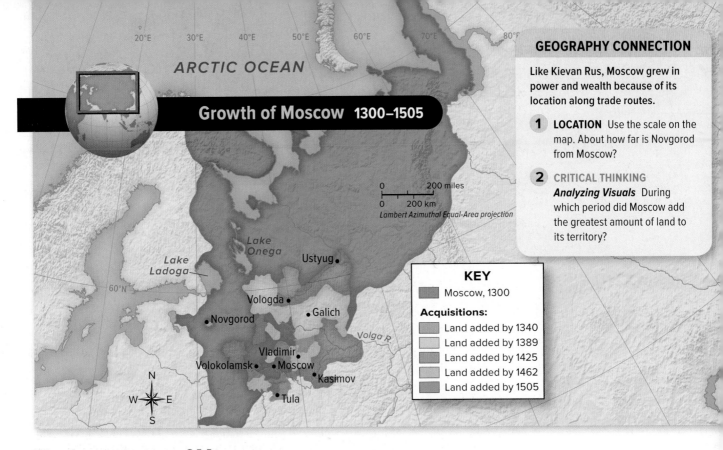

Growth of Moscow 1300–1505

ARCTIC OCEAN

Lake Onega
Lake Ladoga
Ustyug
Vologda
Novgorod
Galich
Volga R.
Vladimir
Volokolamsk
Moscow
Kasimov
Tula

0   200 miles
0   200 km
Lambert Azimuthal Equal-Area projection

KEY

Moscow, 1300

Acquisitions:
Land added by 1340
Land added by 1389
Land added by 1425
Land added by 1462
Land added by 1505

GEOGRAPHY CONNECTION

Like Kievan Rus, Moscow grew in power and wealth because of its location along trade routes.

1 **LOCATION** Use the scale on the map. About how far is Novgorod from Moscow?

2 **CRITICAL THINKING**
Analyzing Visuals During which period did Moscow add the greatest amount of land to its territory?

The Importance of Moscow

During the period of Mongol rule, many Slavs moved north from Kiev and built settlements in the area that is now Russia. One new settlement was Moscow (MAHS·KOH). Moscow became a large city that prospered because it was at the crossroads of several major trade routes.

The rulers of Moscow learned to **cooperate** with the Mongols. In return, the Mongols gave them the right to collect taxes from other Slav territories. If a territory could not provide soldiers or tax money, Moscow's rulers took control of it. In this way, Moscow was able to gradually expand its territory.

Ivan III Becomes Czar

Ivan III became the ruler of Moscow in 1462. He married Sophia, a niece of the Byzantine emperor. Ivan adopted the lavish style of Byzantine rulers and was referred to as czar. The Russian word czar, like Caesar in Latin, means "emperor."

By 1480, Ivan III had finally driven the Mongols from Moscow and Russian territory. He turned next to the north and west to add territory. By then, the people of Moscow, now known as Russians, had made great strides toward establishing a huge empire.

✓ PROGRESS CHECK

Determining Cause and Effect Why did the rulers of Moscow work with the Mongols?

Ivan III's reign focused on expanding the Russian empire. During his rule, the Russian territory tripled in size.

Hulton Archive/Getty Images

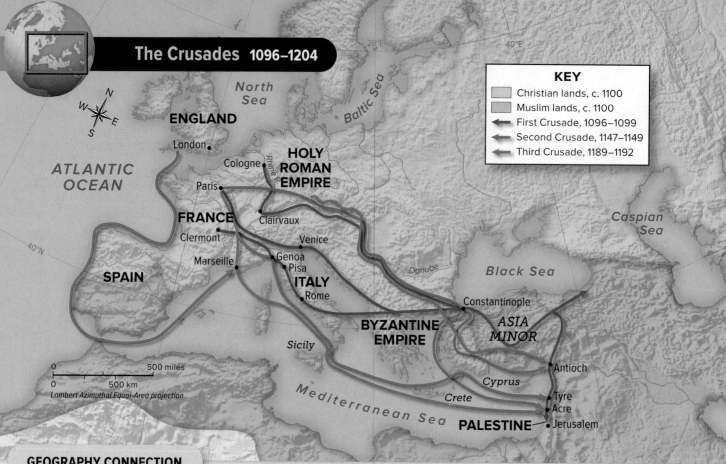

The Crusades 1096–1204

KEY
- Christian lands, c. 1100
- Muslim lands, c. 1100
- → First Crusade, 1096–1099
- → Second Crusade, 1147–1149
- → Third Crusade, 1189–1192

North Sea
Baltic Sea
ENGLAND
London
ATLANTIC OCEAN
Cologne
HOLY ROMAN EMPIRE
Paris
FRANCE
Clairvaux
Clermont
Venice
Marseille
Genoa
Pisa
SPAIN
ITALY
Rome
Caspian Sea
Danube
Black Sea
Constantinople
ASIA MINOR
BYZANTINE EMPIRE
Sicily
Cyprus
Antioch
Crete
Tyre
Mediterranean Sea
Acre
PALESTINE
Jerusalem

0 — 500 miles
0 — 500 km
Lambert Azimuthal Equal-Area projection

GEOGRAPHY CONNECTION

This map shows that the crusaders came from all over Europe. It also shows the land and sea routes that they took to the Holy Land.

1 MOVEMENT On the First Crusade, how did the crusaders from Cologne reach the Holy Land? In what direction did they travel?

2 CRITICAL THINKING **Comparing** Which crusade involved the most travel: the First, the Second, or the Third?

European Crusaders

GUIDING QUESTION *Why did Western Europeans go on crusades?*

During the 1000s, the Byzantine Empire in the east came under attack. In 1071, an army of Muslim Turks defeated the Byzantines and seized control of most of the Byzantine lands in Asia Minor.

The Byzantine emperor asked Pope Urban II for military aid to save his Christian empire from Muslim forces. The pope agreed to help the Byzantines. He hoped that, in return, the Eastern Orthodox Church would again unite with the Roman Catholic Church and accept him as its religious leader.

In 1095, the pope asked Europe's nobles to begin a crusade, or holy war, against the Muslim Turks. He urged them to capture Jerusalem and free the Holy Land, where Jesus had lived, from the Muslims.

The Crusades Begin

Thousands of European soldiers on horseback and on foot headed east on the First Crusade. They reached Jerusalem in 1099. In a fierce battle with Muslims, they stormed the city.

Reading HELP DESK

Academic Vocabulary

accurate correct and free from errors

The crusaders conquered several regions. They set up four states controlled by Europe: the Kingdom of Jerusalem in the Holy Land, Edessa and Antioch in Asia Minor, and Tripoli in what is now Lebanon. These states were surrounded by Muslim territory. They depended on supplies from the Italian cities of Genoa, Pisa, and Venice.

Continued Conflicts

After Muslim forces retook Edessa, the Second Crusade began. This time, the Muslims easily defeated the Europeans. In 1174, led by a brilliant general named Saladin (SA·luh·DEEN), Muslims recaptured Jerusalem.

This action triggered the Third Crusade, which was also a failure. Throughout the 1200s, Europeans continued to organize crusades. They made few gains. By the end of the century, the Muslims had regained all the land conquered by the crusaders.

The Effects of the Crusades

The Crusades brought Western Europeans into contact with Byzantines and Muslims. As a result, Western Europeans gained new knowledge. In architecture, they learned how to build domes and create mosaics. They discovered how to build better ships and make more **accurate** maps. They also learned how to use the compass to tell direction. Wealthy people in Western Europe began to demand eastern goods such as spices, sugar, lemons, and silk.

The Crusades, however, weakened feudalism. Nobles who joined the Crusades sold their lands and freed their serfs. This reduced their power. Kings were able to build stronger central governments.

The Crusades lasted over a period of more than 200 years. They caused bitter feelings between Christian Western Europe and the Islamic world.

Many crusaders wore red crosses on their tunics to show they were risking their lives in support of Christianity and the pope.

©The Print Collector/Corbis

 PROGRESS CHECK

Determining Cause and Effect What was one way the Crusades changed Christian Europe?

LESSON 3 REVIEW

Review Vocabulary

1. How is a *grand jury* different from a *trial jury*?

Answer the Guiding Questions

2. *Explaining* How did the Magna Carta limit the power of the king of England?

3. *Describing* How did royal power in England progress from William, to Henry II, to John, to Edward I?

4. *Describing* How did the cities of Kiev and Moscow become centers of powerful Slavic states?

5. *Identifying Cause and Effect* Why did Western Europeans go on the Crusades?

6. **INFORMATIVE/EXPLANATORY** Write a paragraph discussing how the Crusades affected feudalism.

LESSON 4

Culture and the Church

ESSENTIAL QUESTION

• What is the role of religion in government?

IT MATTERS BECAUSE

Architecture, education, literature, and religion played very important roles in medieval life.

European Culture in the Middle Ages

GUIDING QUESTION *What types of learning and art developed during the Middle Ages?*

By the 1100s, the Crusades and the rise of strong governments made medieval Europeans more confident and **secure**. As a result, trade, banking, and businesses thrived. A better economy meant more money to spend on building and learning.

Styles in Architecture

In the 1000s and 1100s, Europeans began to construct many buildings. Because medieval society valued religion, many of the new buildings were churches and monasteries. Church leaders, wealthy merchants, and nobles supported the building of large churches called cathedrals. Soaring above the rooftops of medieval towns, cathedrals were built in either Romanesque (ROH·muh·NEHSK) or Gothic styles.

Early medieval churches were Romanesque, a style that combined the features of Roman and Byzantine buildings. Romanesque churches were rectangular buildings with long, rounded ceilings called barrel vaults. These ceilings were supported by heavy walls and thick pillars set close together. The churches' small windows let in little light.

About 1150, builders began to construct churches in the Gothic style. They replaced Romanesque heavy walls with flying buttresses. These stone arches extended off the outside walls of the church and supported the weight of the building. They made it possible to build churches with thinner walls and large stained glass windows. Gothic churches were taller and had more space than Romanesque churches.

Colorful stained glass windows often presented scenes from the life and teachings of Jesus. They also let in sunlight, which symbolized the divine light of God.

Development of Universities

The universities of today trace their origins to the Middle Ages. Two of the first medieval universities were in Bologna (buh·LOH·nyuh), Italy, and Paris, France. Universities also were founded in England at Oxford and Cambridge. By 1500, Europe had 80 universities.

Groups of students and teachers created the first universities to educate scholars. Medieval university students studied grammar, public speaking, logic, arithmetic, geometry, music, and astronomy. Teachers read from a text and discussed it, while students took notes on small, portable chalkboards called slates. Students did not have books because books were rare before the European printing press was created in the 1400s.

To get a degree, students took oral exams after four to six years. They could earn a bachelor of arts and later a master of arts. In about ten more years, a student could earn a doctor's degree in law, medicine, or **theology** (thee·AH·luh·jee)—the study of religion and God. People with doctor's degrees were officially able to teach but could also pursue other careers. For example, the monk Roger Bacon turned from teaching theology to studying the natural world. His interest in using experiments to test ideas helped pave the way for the rise of modern science.

What is Scholasticism?

By 1100, a new way of thinking called **scholasticism** (skuh·LAS·tuh·SIH·zuhm) was changing the study of theology. Its followers wanted to show that ideas accepted on faith did not have to contradict ideas developed by reason. The first scholastic thinker was Anselm, who served as archbishop of Canterbury in England from 1093 to 1109. Anselm became known for his reasoning about the existence of God.

THEN

Advances in architecture enabled the French to build the great Gothic cathedral at Chartres. The Gothic style was revived in the 1700s. Today, architects still use this distinctive style of architecture. An example is this 1920s building in Hamburg, Germany.

NOW

▶ CRITICAL THINKING
Speculating Why do you think elements of the Gothic style might still be in use today?

theology the study of religious faith, practice, and experience

scholasticism a way of thinking that combined faith and reason

Academic Vocabulary

secure free from danger

There's More Online! connected.mcgraw-hill.com

Thomas Aquinas became one of the best-known scholars in the history of the Catholic Church.

▶ **CRITICAL THINKING**
Analyzing Visuals Why do you think Thomas Aquinas is shown with a church in one hand and a book in the other?

During the 1100s, the ideas of the ancient Greek philosopher Aristotle had a major influence on Europe. After the fall of Rome in the late 400s, Aristotle had been almost forgotten in Europe. Muslim libraries, however, had preserved copies of his books. In the 1100s, Muslim and Jewish scholars reintroduced Aristotle to Europe. The ancient philosopher's ideas disturbed some Christian thinkers. Aristotle used reason, rather than faith, to reach his conclusions.

In the 1200s, an Italian Dominican friar named Thomas Aquinas (uh·KWY·nuhs) became scholasticism's greatest thinker. His **goal** was to find agreement between Aristotle's teachings and Christian teachings. Aquinas taught that truths arrived at through reason could not conflict with truths arrived at through faith. Reason, unaided by faith, could discover truths about the physical universe but not spiritual truths.

Aquinas's major work was *Summa Theologica*, or a summary of knowledge on theology. In this book, Aquinas followed a logical order of scholarly investigation. First, he asked a question such as, "Does God exist?" Next, he quoted sources that offered opposing opinions and presented ways of reconciling these views. Finally, he drew his own conclusions.

In his writings about government, Thomas Aquinas stressed the concept of natural law. According to this idea, some laws have authority from human nature. Such laws do not have to be made by governments. Aquinas taught that natural law gives people certain basic rights. These include the right to live, to learn, to worship, and to marry. The ideas of Aquinas continue to influence human societies to the present day.

Language and Literature

In medieval times, Latin was the language of educated people, both for speaking and writing. Latin was also the language of the Church and of university teachers and scholars.

Besides Latin, each region in Europe had its own local language. People used this language, called the **vernacular** (vuhr·NA·kyuh·luhr), in everyday life. Early English, Italian, Spanish, French, and German were vernacular languages.

Starting in the 1100s, writers created much new literature in the vernacular. Educated people became interested in this literature. One popular type of vernacular literature was troubadour (TROO·buh·DAWR) poetry. Troubadour poets often sang love poems, especially about the love of a knight for a lady.

INTERFOTO/Alamy

ReadingHELPDESK

vernacular the everyday spoken language of a region

Academic Vocabulary

goal something that a person works to achieve; aim

A second important type of vernacular literature was the heroic epic. Epics often tell the story of bold knights fighting in the service of kings and lords. *The Song of Roland* is an epic that was written in France about 1100. In this tale, a brave knight named Roland fights in the service of Charlemagne against the Muslims.

At a moment of crisis in the battle, Roland sounds his horn for Charlemagne to help him. For many the battle was over:

" Roland looks up on the mountains and slopes,
sees the French dead, so many good men fallen,
and weeps for them, as a great warrior weeps:

Barons, my lords, may God give you his grace,
may he grant Paradise [heaven] to all your souls,
make them lie down among the holy flowers.
I never saw better vassals than you.
All the years you've served me, and all the times,
the mighty lands you conquered for Charles our King! "

—from *The Song of Roland*

In this illustration from *The Song of Roland*, Roland is sounding his horn for Charlemagne to help him.

✔ PROGRESS CHECK

Explaining Why was it important that literature was written in everyday language?

Religion Affected Society

GUIDING QUESTION *How did the Catholic Church affect the lives of medieval Europeans?*

During the Middle Ages, the Catholic Church became rich and powerful. Beginning in the 1000s, many Western Europeans became worried about the direction in which the Church was headed. They set out to return the Church to Christian ideals. They built more monasteries and formed new religious orders, or groups of priests, monks, and nuns.

New Religious Orders

One of the most important new orders was the Cistercian (sihs· TUHR·shuhn) order. It was founded in 1098 by monks who were unhappy with wealthy monasteries and wanted a simpler, more spiritual way of life. Cistercian monks worshipped, prayed, and farmed the land. They developed new farming methods. Bernard of Clairvaux (klehr·VOH) was a famous Cistercian monk.

Hildegard of Bingen composed music for the Catholic Church at a time when most church music was written by men.

▶ **CRITICAL THINKING**

Making Inferences What advantages would medieval nuns have had over other women that would have enabled them to create music, literature, or art?

Bernard supported the Second Crusade, advised the pope, and took the side of the poor against the rich.

Between A.D. 1000 and 1200, many women joined female religious orders. Most of these women, called nuns, came from wealthy noble families. One famous nun of this period was Hildegard of Bingen. She was the abbess, or leader, of a convent in Germany and wrote music for the church. Most composers of church music at that time were men.

The Mission of Friars

Until the 1200s, most people in religious orders spent their time inside their monasteries in prayer or at work. They lived a simple life separate from the world. In the 1200s, several new religious orders were created. The men in these religious orders were called friars.

Friars were different from other monks. They left their monasteries and took Christianity to people in the towns. Friars preached, served as missionaries, and aided the poor. Friars could not own property or keep any personal wealth.

Two well-known orders of friars were the Franciscans (fran‧SIHS‧kuhns) and the Dominicans (duh‧MIH‧nih‧kuhns). The Franciscan order was founded in 1209 by Francis of Assisi (uh‧SIH‧see). Franciscans were known for their cheerfulness and deep love of nature.

A Spanish monk named Dominic de Guzmán (DAH‧muh‧NIHK deh gooz‧MAHN) started the Dominican order in 1216. Like the Franciscans, the Dominicans lived a life of poverty. Their chief goal was to defend the teachings of the Church.

The Role of Religion in Everyday Life

In medieval times, the Catholic Church affected almost every part of people's lives. On Sundays and holy days, most medieval Europeans gathered to attend **mass**, the Catholic worship service.

Medieval Christians also took part in church rituals called sacraments. The most important sacrament was Holy Communion during mass. People received bread and wine to remind them of the death of Jesus. Only clergy could give people the sacraments.

Saints also played an important role in the lives of medieval

Franz Waldhäusl/Age fotostock

Reading**HELP**DESK

mass religious worship service for Catholic Christians

heresy ideas that go against church teachings

anti-Semitism hostility toward or discrimination against Jews

Christians. People prayed to the saints to ask for God's favor. Mary, the mother of Jesus, was the most honored of all the saints.

The Challenge of Heresy

Despite its power, the Church had to deal with **heresy** (HEHR·uh·see), or ideas that conflicted with Church teaching. In the Middle Ages, heresy was regarded as a serious crime against the Church. In 1233, the pope set up a Church court called the Inquisition (IHN·kwuh·ZIH·shuhn). The Inquisition's task was to question and deal with people accused of heresy.

People who were found guilty by the Inquisition were allowed to confess their heresy and ask for forgiveness. Those who refused were excommunicated and punished. Punishment could mean going to prison, losing property, or being executed.

Anti-Semitism in the Middle Ages

In medieval Europe, Jews became scapegoats, or people blamed for other people's problems. Jews were often accused in times of trouble, such as famine, plague, or economic decline. Hostility toward Jews is called **anti-Semitism** (AN·tee·SEH·muh·TIH·zuhm).

In troubled times during the Middle Ages, anti-Semitism flared up. In towns and villages, Christians often discriminated against and even killed Jews. As a minority, Jews were often forced to live in separate neighborhoods called ghettos. Often, Jews were forbidden to own land and to practice certain trades.

Beginning in the 1100s, rulers in England, France, and central Europe even drove out their Jewish subjects. Many of these Jews settled in Eastern Europe, especially Poland. Over the centuries, the Jews of Eastern Europe developed thriving communities.

✔ PROGRESS CHECK

Explaining Why did Church officials set up the Inquisition?

LESSON 4 REVIEW

Review Vocabulary

1. What is *heresy*?

Answer the Guiding Questions

2. *Contrasting* Contrast the chief characteristics of Romanesque and Gothic architecture.

3. *Identifying* During the Middle Ages, what were two popular types of vernacular literature? Briefly describe each type.

4. *Analyzing* Why did the writings and ideas of Aristotle disturb some medieval Christians?

5. *Comparing and Contrasting* How were monks and friars similar? How did they differ from each other?

6. **INFORMATIVE/EXPLANATORY** Write a brief announcement to attract students to a medieval university. In your announcement, include the location of the university, the subjects that students may study, and the degrees they can earn.

LESSON 5

The Late Middle Ages

ESSENTIAL QUESTION

• How do governments change?

IT MATTERS BECAUSE

During the Late Middle Ages, Europe experienced serious economic, political, and religious conflicts.

Famine and Plague

GUIDING QUESTION *How did the Black Death affect Europe during the Late Middle Ages?*

Medieval Europe enjoyed prosperity and growth during the 1200s. Then, early in the next century, disaster struck. Extremely cold winters and rainy summers created miserable conditions. Crops rotted in the fields, and herds of livestock died from diseases. Soon, there was not enough food for Europe's growing population. The result was a great famine in northern Europe that lasted from about 1315 to 1322. During this time, many people died from starvation and epidemics.

The Plague Comes to Europe

The great famine was only the beginning of troubles. During the 1300s, a **plague** (PLAYG) spread from Asia across Europe. A plague is a disease that spreads quickly and kills large numbers of people. The Black Death, as the disease was known, was probably bubonic plague. This illness is caused by a type of bacteria spread by fleas. Rats carry the fleas. The Black Death probably began in central Asia and spread to other places through trade. It first broke out in China in the 1330s. Between 40 and 60 million people eventually died, nearly half of the Chinese population.

Reading**HELP**DESK

Taking Notes: *Summarizing*

Use a pie chart like the one shown to summarize the effects of the Black Death in Europe in the mid-1300s.

Content Vocabulary

• **plague**   • **Reconquista**

Trade between China, India, the Middle East, and Europe was greatly encouraged by the Mongols. Merchants used the Silk Road and other trade routes. Expanded trade also made it possible for the Black Death to spread quickly. More and more traders used the Silk Road and other routes linking Asia and Europe. As a result, rat-infested caravans and ships carried the disease from region to region. The plague then traveled to India and spread to Muslim territories.

In 1346, the Black Death reached the trading city of Caffa on the Black Sea. Italian ships carried the plague to the island of Sicily. From there, it spread to the Italian mainland and onto the continent of Europe. By the end of the 1340s, it had surfaced in France, Germany, and England. By 1351, the plague had reached Scandinavia, Eastern Europe, and Russia. Estimates of the dead in Europe between 1347 and 1351 range from 19 to 38 million people—nearly one out of every two Europeans.

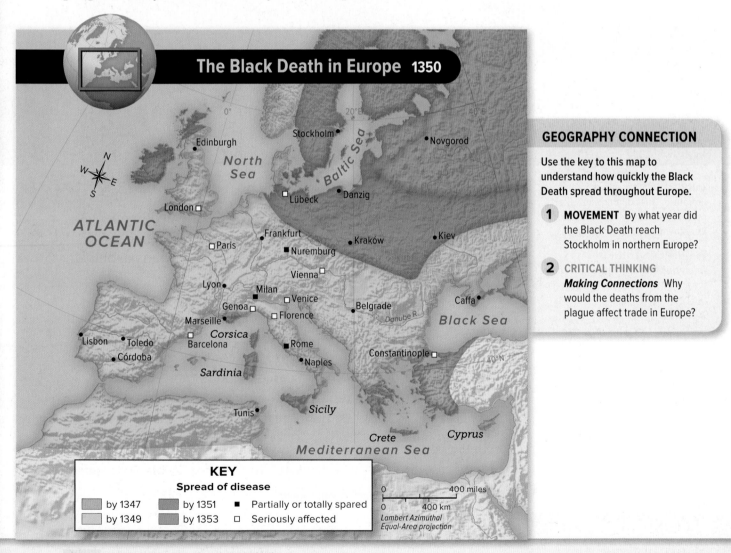

The Black Death in Europe 1350

KEY
Spread of disease

by 1347	by 1351 ■ Partially or totally spared
by 1349	by 1353 □ Seriously affected

0 — 400 miles
0 — 400 km
Lambert Azimuthal Equal-Area projection

GEOGRAPHY CONNECTION

Use the key to this map to understand how quickly the Black Death spread throughout Europe.

1 **MOVEMENT** By what year did the Black Death reach Stockholm in northern Europe?

2 **CRITICAL THINKING**
Making Connections Why would the deaths from the plague affect trade in Europe?

plague a disease that spreads quickly and kills many people

The Black Death inspired art and literature. This painting shows carts picking up those who had died to bury them quickly in mass graves.

▶ **CRITICAL THINKING**
Analyzing Visuals Why do you think the artist portrayed skeletons collecting the bodies of the dead?

The Effects of the Plague

People at the time did not know why the plague had happened. Some people thought God was punishing them for their sins. Others blamed the Jews. For this reason, the Germans expelled many Jews from some of their cities.

The plague had an enormous effect on the **economy** of Europe. With so many deaths, trade declined. Wages rose steeply because of a high demand for workers. Fewer people, though, meant less demand for food, so food prices fell sharply.

Landlords now had to pay scarce workers more. Some peasants began to pay rent instead of providing services. Serfs gained more rights. Like the Crusades, the Black Death weakened feudalism.

 **PROGRESS CHECK**

Explaining How did the Black Death spread?

Reading**HELP**DESK

Academic Vocabulary

economy a country's system for the making, selling, and buying of goods and services

authority the power to influence or command thought, opinion, or behavior

Divisions in Religion and Politics

GUIDING QUESTION *How did disputes and wars change societies in Europe during the Late Middle Ages?*

In addition to the bubonic plague, conflict swept through Europe during the Late Middle Ages. Disputes in the Church reduced its **authority**. English and French kings battled over territory in the Hundred Years' War. Christians in the Iberian Peninsula fought to drive out the Muslims who had conquered land there.

Conflict in the Church

From 1378 to 1417, a dispute called the Great Schism (SIH·zuhm) deeply divided the Church. During this time, two and even three church leaders claimed to be the rightful pope. This caused great confusion and doubt throughout Western Europe. In 1417, a council of bishops met at the German city of Constance. It finally ended the Great Schism with the election of a pope that all church members could accept.

The Great Schism was only one challenge the Church faced during the Late Middle Ages. Powerful European kings questioned the authority of popes. The kings of England and France would soon go to war. Many people criticized the growing wealth and corruption of the clergy. Reform leaders emerged who called on church leaders to return to a more spiritual form of Christianity. These reformers included John Wycliffe in England and Jan Hus in the Holy Roman Empire.

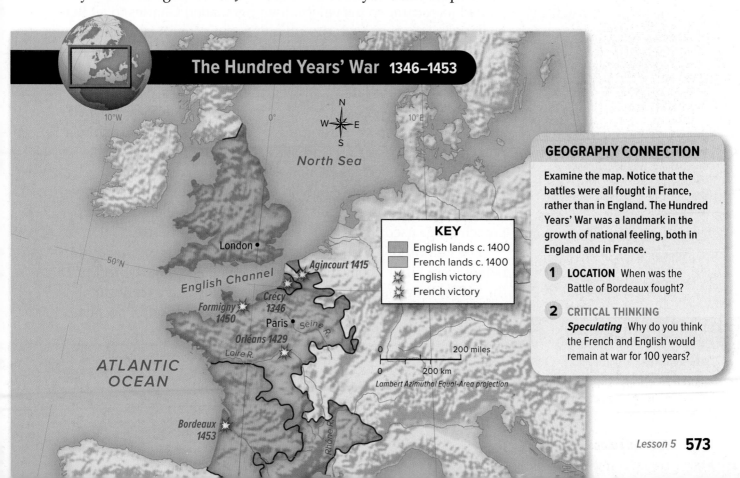

The Hundred Years' War 1346–1453

North Sea

London

English Channel

Agincourt 1415

Formigny 1450

Crécy 1346

Paris

Seine R.

Orléans 1429

Loire R.

ATLANTIC OCEAN

Bordeaux 1453

Rhône R.

KEY
- English lands c. 1400
- French lands c. 1400
- ★ English victory
- ★ French victory

0   200 miles

0   200 km

Lambert Azimuthal Equal-Area projection

GEOGRAPHY CONNECTION

Examine the map. Notice that the battles were all fought in France, rather than in England. The Hundred Years' War was a landmark in the growth of national feeling, both in England and in France.

1 LOCATION When was the Battle of Bordeaux fought?

2 CRITICAL THINKING
Speculating Why do you think the French and English would remain at war for 100 years?

Joan of Arc (1412–1431)

Joan of Arc was born in the village of Domrémy in eastern France. She was the daughter of a tenant farmer. In her teens, Joan felt herself guided by the voices of three saints. Joan traveled from her native village in France to ask to fight for Charles, the crown prince. She faced examination by church authorities about her faith and the voices she heard. Convinced, they allowed Joan to take part in a battle against the English at the town of Orléans. The French victory there unified France and led to the coronation of Charles as king. However, Joan was captured later by the English, tried for heresy, and executed.

▶ **CRITICAL THINKING**
Speculating Why do you think a teenage girl like Joan of Arc was able to inspire the French troops and lead them into battle?

The Hundred Years' War

Western Europe at this time was torn apart by political as well as religious disputes. For centuries, England's monarchs had ruled areas of France. France's kings, however, wanted to unite these lands with their kingdom. Then King Edward III of England declared himself king of France and invaded that country. The conflict that followed lasted over 100 years.

At first, the English were victorious—at Crécy (kray·SEE) in 1346 and Agincourt in 1415. The English had superior weapons: a longbow and an early form of the cannon. The longbow shot arrows that were able to pierce heavy armor at 300 yards (274 km). A French medieval writer described the effects of the longbow at Crécy:

PRIMARY SOURCE

❝ Then the English archers stept forth one pace and let fly their arrows so wholly [together] and so thick, that it seemed snow. When the [French soldiers] felt the arrows piercing through heads, arms, and breasts, many of them cast down their cross-bows and did cut their strings and [retreated]. ❞

—from *The Chronicles of Froissart*, by Jean Froissart

Joan of Arc Aids the French

The French prince Charles wanted to take back French lands held by the English. In 1429, a 17-year-old French peasant girl named Joan came to his palace. Joan persuaded Charles to let her go with a French army to the city of Orléans. Joan's faith stirred the French soldiers. They defeated the English and freed the city.

Shortly after, with Joan at his side, Charles was crowned king. A few months later, however, the English army captured Joan. The English accused her of being a witch. Joan was burned at the stake for heresy. Later known as Joan of Arc, she became a French national hero and Catholic saint.

Joan's courage led the French to rally around their king. By 1453, French armies had driven the English out of most of France. Victory gave the French a new sense of loyalty to their country. French kings used that loyalty to strengthen their power.

The Hundred Years' War also affected the English. England's nobles were bitter about the loss of French lands. For the rest of the 1400s, they fought over who should be king in a civil war known as the Wars of Roses. The winner, Henry Tudor, became King Henry VII of England.

©Stapleton Collection/Corbis

Jews and Muslims in Spain

During the Middle Ages, Muslims ruled much of the Iberian Peninsula. Today, the Iberian Peninsula is made up of Spain and Portugal. Medieval Muslims in this area developed a rich culture. They set up schools and built beautiful mosques and palaces, such as the Alhambra in Granada.

The Christians drove out the Muslims in a struggle called the **Reconquista** (ray·kohn·KEES·tuh), or "reconquest." By 1250, there were three Christian kingdoms: Portugal, Castile, and Aragon. The only remaining Muslim kingdom was Granada. In 1469, Prince Ferdinand of Aragon married Princess Isabella of Castile. They united their kingdoms into one Catholic country called Spain.

Under Muslim rule, Iberian Jews had lived freely for the most part. As Christians gained control, they sometimes mistreated the Jews. In order to avoid persecution by Christians, many Jews became Christian. Ferdinand and Isabella, however, believed that some of the Jews secretly practiced Judaism. To force obedience to the Catholic Church, the rulers put the Spanish Inquisition into place.

The Spanish Inquisition tried and tortured thousands of people who were accused of being disloyal to the Catholic Church in Spain. In 1492, Ferdinand and Isabella ordered Jews to convert or leave Spain. Most Jews left to avoid the charge of heresy. After Spain conquered Granada in 1492, Muslims were given the same choice. Rather than convert to Catholicism, most Muslims left for North Africa.

✔ **PROGRESS CHECK**

Determining Cause and Effect How did Ferdinand and Isabella treat those of Muslim and Jewish faiths?

LESSON 5 REVIEW

Review Vocabulary

1. What is a *plague*?

Answer the Guiding Questions

2. *Explaining* How did the Black Death spread from continent to continent?

3. *Analyzing* What was the major cause of the Hundred Years' War?

4. *Identifying* After the Battle of Orléans, what happened to Joan of Arc?

5. *Explaining* In what ways did the Muslims develop a rich culture in Spain and Portugal before they were forced out of those lands?

6. **INFORMATIVE/EXPLANATORY** You are the ruler of France. A young girl, Joan of Arc, has told you she believes the saints want her to help save France. Write three questions you might ask Joan of Arc to determine if she is fit for battle.

Write your answers on a separate piece of paper.

1 **Exploring the Essential Question**

INFORMATIVE/EXPLANATORY How would you describe the influence of religion on life in medieval Europe? In a summary essay, identify and evaluate the relationships between the Church and the government, as well as the ways in which religion influenced everyday life.

2 **21st Century Skills**

EVALUATING Consider the medieval order of feudalism. What strengths and weaknesses can you identify in feudalism? Do you think feudalism would work in modern society? Write your answer in a paragraph or two.

3 **Thinking Like a Historian**

COMPARING Describe the equipment that students in present-day universities might use and compare it to the equipment available to students in medieval universities. In particular, compare the role of books in university education then and now.

4 **GEOGRAPHY ACTIVITY**

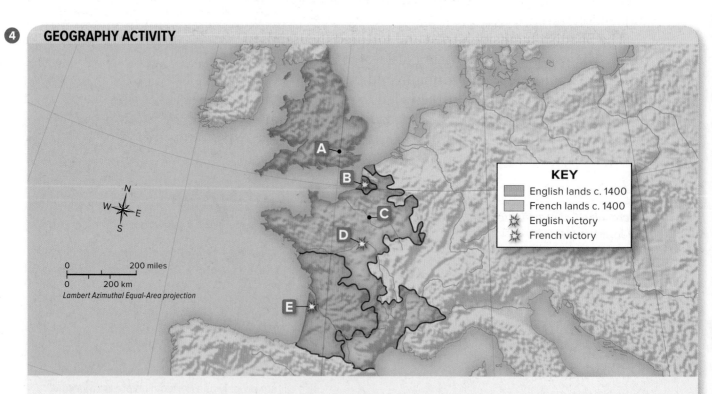

KEY
- English lands c. 1400
- French lands c. 1400
- English victory
- French victory

N W E S

0 — 200 miles
0 — 200 km
Lambert Azimuthal Equal-Area projection

Locating Places

Match the letters on the map with the numbered places listed below.

1. Paris
2. Bordeaux
3. Orléans
4. London
5. Crécy

Directions: Write your answers on a separate piece of paper.

CHECKING FOR UNDERSTANDING

1 Identify the vocabulary words with their descriptions as they relate to medieval Europe.

  A. ideas that go against church teachings
  B. religious worship service for Catholic Christians
  C. a way of thinking that combined faith and reason
  D. the everyday spoken language of a region
  E. hostility toward or discrimination against Jews
  F. a narrow inlet of the sea between cliffs or steep slopes
  G. a feudal estate belonging to a vassal
  H. a member of the peasant class tied to the land and subject to the will of the landowner
  I. a group of citizens that decides whether an accused person is innocent or guilty
  J. the study of religious faith, practice, and experience
  K. the system, spirit, or customs of medieval knighthood
  L. a low-ranking noble under the protection of a feudal lord
  M. people who are sent by a religious organization to spread the faith
  N. a mounted man-at-arms serving a lord

REVIEW THE GUIDING QUESTIONS

2 *Finding the Main Idea* How did the English Channel impact the development of culture in Britain and Ireland?

3 *Explaining* What environmental conditions led to Viking raids on other countries?

4 *Identifying* What two leadership roles did the pope play in medieval Europe?

5 *Summarizing* What were a lord's duties to his vassals? What were a vassal's duties to his lord?

6 *Describing* How did peasants and lords benefit from the manorial system?

7 *Explaining* How did trade slowly help win some political freedoms for medieval townspeople?

8 *Naming* What document limited the power of the English monarch?

9 *Stating* How did Philip II increase the power of the French monarchy? How did Ivan III achieve the same in Russia?

10 *Specifying* What were some popular subjects of medieval writers?

11 *Defining* What is heresy and how did the medieval church deal with it?

12 *Stating* About what percentage of Europe's population died as a result of the Black Death?

13 *Explaining* How did the Reconquista change the political landscape of Europe?

CRITICAL THINKING

14 *Analyzing* Why was it significant that the pope crowned Charlemagne emperor?

15 *Hypothesizing* Why did both kings and popes want the right to select bishops?

16 *Drawing Conclusions* How can feudalism be considered a political system?

17 *Comparing and Contrasting* How was a medieval manor much like a medieval town? How was it different?

18 *Determining Cause and Effect* Explain the causes and effects of the Crusades.

19 *Assessing* How did the Franciscans and Dominicans likely impact life in medieval Europe?

20 *Evaluating* How did the Black Death cause the collapse of the manorial system in medieval Europe?

Need Extra Help?

If You've Missed Question	**1**	**2**	**3**	**4**	**5**	**6**	**7**	**8**	**9**	**10**	**11**	**12**	**13**	**14**	**15**	**16**	**17**	**18**	**19**	**20**
Review Lesson	1,2,3 4,5	1	1	1	2	2	2	3	3	4	4	5	5	1	1	2	2	3	4	5

DBQ SHORT RESPONSE

"A more lasting and serious consequence [of the plague] was the drastic reduction of the amount of land under cultivation [able to be farmed] due to the deaths of so many labourers. ... The psychological effects of the Black Death were reflected . ... by a preoccupation with death and the afterlife evinced [displayed] in poetry, sculpture, and painting."

—"Black Death," Encyclopaedia Britannica

21 According to the passage, what was one effect of the plague?

22 Why did the lack of labor have a negative effect on Europe?

EXTENDED RESPONSE

23 *Informative/Explanatory* You have been asked to contribute to a reference article about the Middle Ages. You are responsible for these areas of medieval culture: architecture, literature, and education. Write an outline showing the specific facts and details you plan to cover in your article.

STANDARDIZED TEST PRACTICE

DBQ ANALYZING DOCUMENTS

SUMMARIZING King Louis IX asked the following of his vassals:

"All vassals of the king are bound to appear before him when he shall summon [call] them, and to serve him at their own expense for forty days and forty nights, with as many knights as each one owes."

—King Louis IX, "Legal Rules for Military Service"

24 Which of the following best describes the obligations of the king's vassals?
- **A.** manorial system
- **B.** scholasticism
- **C.** feudalism
- **D.** guild system

25 *Making Inferences* Based on what you have learned about medieval Europe, which of the following best describes what would happen if the king needed vassals and knights for more than 40 days and nights?
- **A.** The vassals and knights would overthrow the king.
- **B.** The knights would rebel against the vassals.
- **C.** The vassals and knights would continue serving at the king's expense.
- **D.** The vassals and knights would withdraw to the manor.

Need Extra Help?

If You've Missed Question	**21**	**22**	**23**	**24**	**25**
Review Lesson	2	2	3	5	5

◄ *Benozzo Gozzoli painted* The Procession of the Magi *(1459) for the Medici family.*

1350 TO 1650

Renaissance and Reformation

THE STORY MATTERS ...

The Renaissance was a brilliant flowering of European culture from the 1300s to 1600s. During this time, the city-state of Florence in Italy became the center of business, art, and learning. It attracted many artists who are still famous today, including Michelangelo and Leonardo da Vinci.

This image is from a Renaissance painting of the three wise men traveling to see the baby Jesus. The painting was made to decorate the palace of the powerful Medici family. The Medicis ruled Florence during the Renaissance. Lorenzo de' Medici was the model for the wise man shown here.

ESSENTIAL QUESTIONS

- Why do people make economic choices?
- How do new ideas change the way people live?
- How do religions develop?
- Why does conflict develop?

Erich Lessing/Art Resource, NY

During the Renaissance, wealthy Italian states developed new ideas about art and learning. Meanwhile, a movement to reform the Church began in the Holy Roman Empire. As this Reformation spread, new Protestant churches arose in northern Europe. Southern Europe, however, remained Catholic.

Step Into the Place

MAP FOCUS The states of the Italian peninsula became the center of the Renaissance.

1 REGIONS Look at the map. What territories are found on the Italian peninsula?

2 PLACE What physical features would make the cities of Venice and Naples important trade centers?

3 CRITICAL THINKING
Contrasting Why might new ideas spread differently in the Italian region than in countries such as Austria and Bohemia?

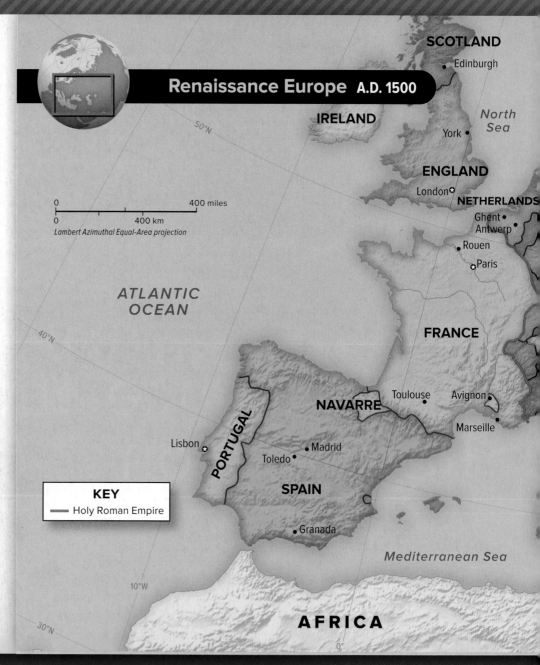

Renaissance Europe A.D. 1500

400 miles
400 km
Lambert Azimuthal Equal-Area projection

SCOTLAND
Edinburgh
IRELAND
North Sea
York
ENGLAND
London
NETHERLANDS
Ghent
Antwerp
Rouen
Paris
ATLANTIC OCEAN
50°N
40°N
FRANCE
Toulouse
Avignon
NAVARRE
Marseille
Lisbon
PORTUGAL
Madrid
Toledo
SPAIN
Granada
Mediterranean Sea
10°W
30°N
AFRICA
0°

KEY
— Holy Roman Empire

Step Into the Time

TIME LINE Choose an event from the time line and write a paragraph predicting the religious, social, or political consequences that event might have for Europe.

1440 Gutenberg prints with movable type

EUROPE
THE WORLD

A.D. 1350   A.D. 1400   A.D. 1450

c. 1400 Aztec Empire reaches its height

NORWAY

SWEDEN

TEUTONIC
ORDER

MUSCOVY

DENMARK

Baltic Sea

Wittenberg

LITHUANIA

HOLY ROMAN
EMPIRE

POLAND

BOHEMIA

Salzburg

Vienna

ASIA

AUSTRIA

HUNGARY

MOLDAVIA

Milan

Venice

Bologna

Black Sea

Florence

PAPAL
STATES

Adriatic Sea

Rome

O T T O M A N

E M P I R E

NAPLES AND SICILY

Palermo

10°E   20°E   30°E   40°E

1517 Martin Luther writes Ninety-Five Theses

1508 Michelangelo
begins painting Sistine
Chapel

1543 Copernicus presents
view of universe

1555 Peace of Augsburg
divides Germany

1593 Henry of Navarre
becomes Catholic

1648 Thirty
Years' War ends

A.D. 1500   A.D. 1550   A.D. 1600   A.D. 1650

LESSON 1
The Renaissance Begins

ESSENTIAL QUESTION
• Why do people make economic choices?

IT MATTERS BECAUSE
Renaissance developments helped shape today's arts, architecture, literature, and science.

The Renaissance in Italy

GUIDING QUESTION *Why did the states of Italy become leading centers of culture during the Renaissance?*

Between 1350 and 1650, ways of thinking changed greatly in Europe. As the Black Death eased, people became more confident about the future. Their interest in learning and the arts was renewed. This new interest in culture is called the **Renaissance** (reh·nuh·SAHNTZ), from the French word for "rebirth."

Rebirth of the Classics

The Renaissance sparked a renewed interest in ancient Greeks and Romans. European scholars improved their understanding of Greek and Latin languages, which they used to study ancient Greek and Roman writings.

Europeans also adopted many Greek and Roman ideas. They began to see that individual people could make a difference. They began to believe that people could change the world for the better.

During the Renaissance, most Europeans were still religious. However, they also began to value human efforts outside religion. As a result, people became more **secular** (SEH·kyuh·luhr). That is, they became more interested in worldly ideas and events, not just religious ones.

Reading**HELP**DESK

Taking Notes: *Identifying*

Use a chart like this one to show the reasons Italian states grew wealthy.

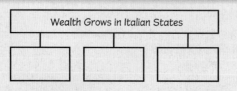

Wealth Grows in Italian States

Content Vocabulary

• **Renaissance**   • **mercenary**
• **secular**   • **diplomacy**
• **urban**

The Renaissance is Born

The birthplace of the Renaissance was Italy, the heart of the old Roman Empire. The ruins and statues were familiar to Italians. Because of this, Italians readily turned to ancient examples to inspire them in their own artistic efforts.

Art also flourished because by the 1300s, Italian cities had become very wealthy. Their leading citizens could pay painters, sculptors, and architects to produce many new works.

The powerful states of Italy encouraged the Renaissance. The population of Italy was becoming more **urban** (UHR·buhn). That is, more people were living in cities than in the country. In other parts of Europe, most people still lived in rural areas, including the nobles who owned estates.

As a result of its city life, Italy began to develop a different society. Large city populations meant more discussion among people. Strong economies developed. It also meant more customers for artists and more money for a new kind of art.

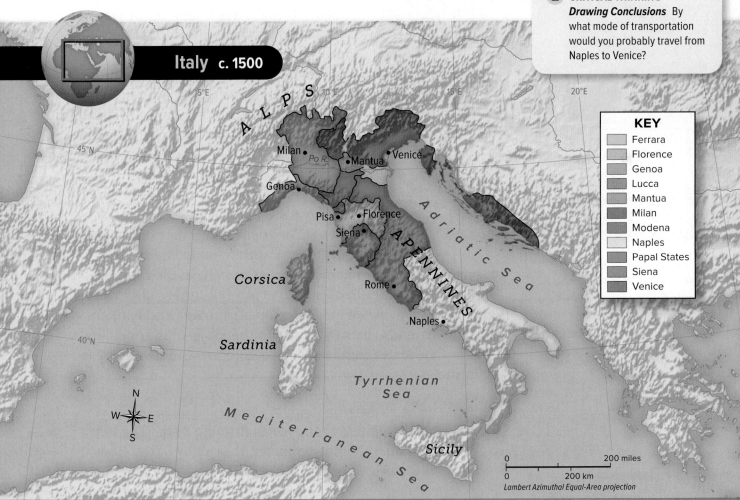

Italy c. 1500

KEY
- Ferrara
- Florence
- Genoa
- Lucca
- Mantua
- Milan
- Modena
- Naples
- Papal States
- Siena
- Venice

0   200 miles
0   200 km
Lambert Azimuthal Equal-Area projection

GEOGRAPHY CONNECTION

Many Italian states prospered during the Renaissance.

1 LOCATION In which territory was Rome located?

2 CRITICAL THINKING
Drawing Conclusions By what mode of transportation would you probably travel from Naples to Venice?

Renaissance a renewal or rebirth of interest in Greek and Roman arts

secular related to worldly things

urban having to do with a town or city

Like the city-states of ancient Greece, Renaissance Italy's urban society and scholars produced many great works of art and literature.

✔ **PROGRESS CHECK**

Explaining Why did wealthy Italians support artists during the Renaissance?

The States of Italy

GUIDING QUESTION *How did Italy's states become wealthy and powerful?*

During the Middle Ages, Italy remained a collection of states, many of which were independent city-states. There were several reasons for this. The states of Italy did not want emperors and kings to rule them. In addition, the Catholic Church did not want a united Italy. It did not want a powerful emperor or king to control the pope.

The independent states in Italy were equally strong. They fought many wars and often took land from each other. However, no state was able to rule the others. Florence (FLAWR·uhntz), Venice (VEH·nuhs), Genoa (JEH·nuh·wuh), Milan (mih·LAN), and Rome were some of the most important cities of the Italian Renaissance. The Renaissance began in Italy because city life was stronger than in other parts of Europe.

Above all, Italy's states were independent because of their riches. They used their wealth to build large fleets of ships. They also hired mercenaries to fight in their armies. A **mercenary** (MUHR·suh·nehr·ee) is a full-time soldier who fights in an army for money. Wealthy merchants and bankers in Italy's states also loaned money to the kings of Europe. The kings left the states alone so they could borrow more money in the future.

Riches from Trade

The Italian states gained their wealth through trade. The long stretch of the Italian peninsula meant that many of the cities were port cities located on the coast.

The Gonzaga family ruled the Italian city-state of Mantua during the 1400s.

▶ **CRITICAL THINKING**
Explaining Why was it possible for one family to become so powerful in Italy at this time?

Fratelli Alinari IDEA S.p.A./Corbis Historical/Getty Images

mercenary a soldier who fights for money rather than loyalty to a country

The Italian peninsula was in the center of the Mediterranean world. The Byzantine and Ottoman Empires lay to the east, and Spain and France lay to the west. North Africa was only a short distance to the south. Italy's location made trade with these regions easier.

In eastern ports like Constantinople, Italian merchants bought Chinese silk and Indian spices from Byzantine, Turkish, and Arab merchants. The Italians sold these goods in Italy and Western Europe for very high prices. Italian merchants bought wool, wine, and glass in Europe and sold them in the Middle East. Italian artisans bought raw materials and made goods to sell abroad for high prices.

In addition to geography, two important events helped the Italians succeed in trade. One event was the Crusades. These conflicts brought Italian merchants into contact with Arab merchants in the Middle East. The second event was the Mongol conquests, which united much of Asia into one large trading network.

The Mongols protected trade along the Silk Road. This made it easier and cheaper for caravans to carry goods between China and the Middle East. As more silk and spices were sent from Asia, the price of these goods fell. More Europeans could pay for the luxuries, and demand for the goods increased.

An illustrated book written by a Florence merchant named Marco Polo made many Europeans excited about Asia and its wealth. He wrote about the riches he found there.

Who Was Marco Polo?

In the 1270s, the merchant Marco Polo, his father, and his uncle left Venice and traveled to China. Their goal was to meet Kublai Khan (KUH·bluh KAHN), the Mongol emperor of China.

When the Polo family reached the Khan's court, the emperor was amazed by the stories that Marco Polo told of his travels. Kublai sent Marco Polo on fact-finding trips all over China. Polo learned more about Asia than any other European. After returning to Europe, Polo wrote a book about his adventures. His stories about life in China amazed Europeans, who then wanted to buy Chinese goods.

Florence: A Renaissance City

The city of Florence was the first major center of the Renaissance. Its wealth and central location attracted many artists, sculptors, writers, and architects. Florence lay on the banks of the Arno River in central Italy. The city was surrounded by walls with tall towers for defense. Soaring above the city was the dome of its cathedral. A local architect, Filippo Brunelleschi (fih·LEEP·oh broon·ehl·EHS·kee), completed the dome in 1436. It is considered to be the greatest engineering achievement of the time.

FLORENCE CATHEDRAL

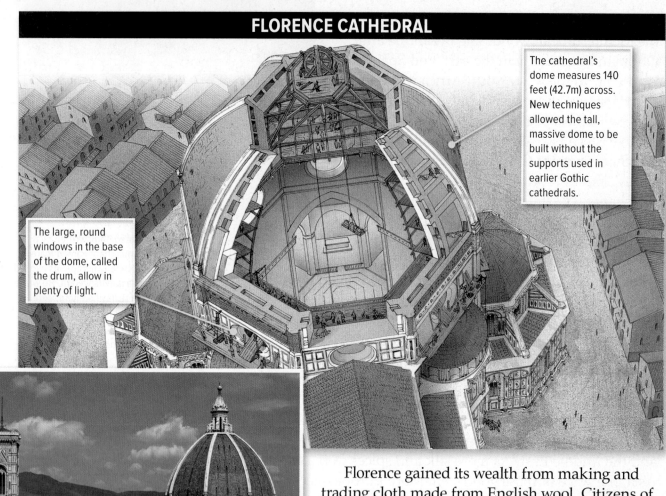

The cathedral's dome measures 140 feet (42.7m) across. New techniques allowed the tall, massive dome to be built without the supports used in earlier Gothic cathedrals.

The large, round windows in the base of the dome, called the drum, allow in plenty of light.

The dome of the cathedral in Florence, Italy, became a symbol of the city. It was considered a great architectural design of its time.

▶ **CRITICAL THINKING**
Making Connections What earlier civilization was known for building domes?

Florence gained its wealth from making and trading cloth made from English wool. Citizens of Florence also made money from banking, which included lending money and charging interest. As goods poured into Italy from abroad, merchants had to determine the value of **currency,** or money, from different countries. Florentine bankers used the florin, the gold coin of Florence, to measure the value of other money. The city's wealthiest family, the Medici (MEH·duh·chee), owned the largest bank in Europe during the 1400s. The Medici had branch banks, or other offices, as far away as Flanders.

Venice: A City of Canals

Another leading Renaissance city was Venice. Located on the northern coast of the Adriatic Sea in eastern Italy, Venice was built on many small islands. Venetians drove long wooden poles into mud to support their buildings. Instead of paving roads, the Venetians built canals and used boats for transportation around the city. Even today, Venice's canals and waterways serve as streets.

Reading**HELP**DESK

diplomacy the practice of conducting negotiations between countries

Academic Vocabulary

currency money, in the form of coins or paper
complex complicated

akg-images/Rabatti · Domingie

During the Renaissance, Venice became an important link between Europe and Asia. Venetian merchants, such as Marco Polo, traveled abroad and made contacts with eastern civilizations. The city also was known as a major shipbuilding center. In a part of the city called the Arsenal, teams of workers built wooden ships and also made sails and oars.

✅ **PROGRESS CHECK**

Determining Cause and Effect How did the travels of Marco Polo affect Europeans?

A New Ruling Class

GUIDING QUESTION *Who controlled the states of Italy?*

Wealthy merchants and bankers in the Italian city-states formed a new kind of leadership. Before the Renaissance, nobles in Europe gained their wealth from land, not trade.

In Italy, old noble families moved from the country to the cities. They became urban nobles. They formed ties of business and friendship with wealthy merchants.

Meanwhile, merchants began to adopt the customs of the nobles. Soon, the sons and daughters of nobles and rich merchants were marrying each other. These new families became the upper class of the city-states.

Who Ruled Italian City-States?

Many Italian city-states began as republics. A republic is a government in which power comes from its citizens. However, not all people in an Italian city-state were citizens. Citizenship belonged only to merchants and artisans.

In ancient Rome, power was often given to a dictator during a war or revolt. A dictator was a ruler who had absolute power. In many cases, the Italian city-states relied on a single powerful individual to run the government. Some of these leaders ruled harshly, using force to keep control. Others used a more gentle approach. To win support, these rulers improved city services.

In Venice, the ruler was the duke, or doge (DOHJ). He officially ran the city, but a council of wealthy merchants held the real power. This council passed laws and elected the doge.

In Florence, the powerful Medici family controlled the government for many years. Lorenzo de' Medici governed Florence from 1469 to 1492. He used his wealth to support artists, architects, and writers. As a result of Florence's prosperity and fame, Lorenzo was known as "the Magnificent."

Philippe Michel/Age fotostock

Thinking Like a HISTORIAN

Drawing Conclusions

During the Renaissance, Venice's canals were avenues of transportation. The famous Grand Canal formed a large "S" shape winding through the city. Lining the canal were the homes of wealthy merchants. Many of these still stand today. Compare Venice with other Italian Renaissance cities. Then draw a conclusion about Renaissance Italy. For more information about drawing conclusions, read the chapter *What Does a Historian Do?*

The Venetians cut canals through the swampy land around the city's original islands. Today, gondolas— long, narrow boats—still carry people along these canals.

Keeping the Peace

Political affairs in Italy were **complex,** or complicated. Within each state, rulers had to put down revolts by the poor. They also had to prevent other wealthy people and city leaders from seizing control. At the same time, the rulers had to keep good relations with bordering states.

To deal with the neighboring states, the Italians developed **diplomacy** (duh·PLOH·muh·see). Diplomacy is the art of making agreements with other countries. Italians worked to be sure that no single state had enough power to threaten the others.

How could a ruler keep his hold on power in the Italian states? Niccolò Machiavelli (nee·koh·LOH mah·kee·uh·VEH·lee), a diplomat in Florence, tried to answer this question. In 1513, he wrote *The Prince*, a book that took a critical look at politics in Renaissance Italy. In this work, Machiavelli stated that rulers should do whatever was necessary to keep power and protect their city, even if they had to lie and kill. Machiavelli gave leaders the following advice:

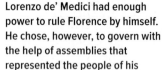

Lorenzo de' Medici had enough power to rule Florence by himself. He chose, however, to govern with the help of assemblies that represented the people of his city-state.

▶ **CRITICAL THINKING**
Theorizing Through what means do you think de' Medici would settle a dispute between nobles?

PRIMARY SOURCE

❞ Upon this a question arises: whether it is better to be loved than feared or feared than loved? It may be answered that one should wish to be both, but, because it is difficult to unite them in one person, it is much safer to be feared than loved. ❞

—from *The Prince*, by Niccolò Machiavelli

Today when we say someone is being "Machiavellian," we mean that person is cunning or acting without a conscience.

✓ **PROGRESS CHECK**

Analyzing Why did the Italian states develop diplomacy?

LESSON 1 REVIEW

Review Vocabulary

1. What elements of Renaissance culture show *secular* ideas?

2. How could a focus on *diplomacy* have helped the states of Italy?

Answer the Guiding Questions

3. ***Explaining*** Why would ideas about art and culture develop faster in the city than in the countryside?

4. ***Identifying*** What was one reason Italian trade grew during the Renaissance?

5. ***Differentiating*** How were urban nobles different from nobles who lived in the country?

6. **INFORMATIVE/EXPLANATORY** Why did Renaissance ideas arise in the 1300s? Explain your answer in the form of a short essay.

LESSON 2
New Ideas and Art

ESSENTIAL QUESTION
• How do new ideas change the way people live?

IT MATTERS BECAUSE
Renaissance artists, scientists, and scholars helped shape the way we see our world.

Renaissance Humanism

GUIDING QUESTION *How did Renaissance writers rely on the past to develop new ideas?*

In the 1300s and 1400s, European scholars developed a new way of understanding the world called **humanism.** It was based on ancient Greek and Roman ideas. Humanists, as these scholars were called, gave importance to the individual and to human society. They wanted to gain knowledge through reason, not just through religious faith. Humanism encouraged people to be active in their cities and to develop their talents.

Discovering Ancient Works

In the 1300s, Italian scholars began to study ancient Roman and Greek works. For most of the Middle Ages, Western Europeans knew little about these writings. During the Crusades, however, they came into contact with the Middle East. Arab Muslim scholars there and in Spain knew the classic Greek and Roman writings. They passed on their knowledge to the Western Europeans. Byzantine scholars also brought classical works to Italy.

One famous humanist scholar was Petrarch (PEE·trahrk). Francesco Petrarch lived in Italy during the 1300s. He studied Roman writers such as Cicero (SIH·suh·roh) and wrote biographies of famous Romans.

Reading **HELP**DESK

Taking Notes: *Describing*
Create a word web to list examples of Renaissance art. For each type of art, describe how it reflects Renaissance ideas.

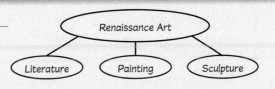

Content Vocabulary
• **humanism**

Petrarch traveled to different monasteries to find old Latin manuscripts. Scholars throughout Europe followed Petrarch's example. In time, new libraries were built to hold the newly found manuscripts. The largest of these libraries was at the Vatican, the home of the pope in Rome.

Italians also began to value the ancient buildings and statues all around them. Throughout Rome, workers removed dirt and rubble from damaged columns and statues. Artists then eagerly studied the proportion of ancient works. For example, artists compared the length of a statue's arms to its height. They believed this comparison could tell them why the statue looked perfect.

A New Literature

In addition to studying the classics, humanists in Italy and other parts of Europe made important achievements of their own. One of their contributions was new forms of literature.

During the Renaissance, educated Europeans wrote in the classical Latin used in ancient Rome. However, they also began writing in the vernacular, the everyday language people spoke in a region. Vernacular languages included Italian, French, and German. For example, Petrarch used Italian to write sonnets, or short poems, which expressed his love for a woman who died from the Black Death. Many more people could read works written in the vernacular instead of in Latin.

In the early 1300s, a poet from Florence named Dante Alighieri (DAHN·tay ah·lee·GYEHR·ee) wrote *The Divine Comedy*. It is known as one of the world's greatest poems. Written in the vernacular, it tells of a person's journey from hell to heaven. The poem describes the horrible punishments for different sins.

The English writer Geoffrey Chaucer (CHAW·suhr) also wrote popular vernacular literature. Chaucer wrote his famous work *The Canterbury* (KAN·tuhr·behr·ree) *Tales* in English. *The Canterbury Tales* is a collection of stories told by pilgrims on a religious journey to the town of Canterbury, England. In this work, Chaucer portrayed the entire **range** of English society. His work shows both nobles at the top of society and the poor at the bottom. The English we speak today comes from the form of English that Chaucer used in his writing.

Petrarch has been called the father of Italian Renaissance humanism.

Reading HELPDESK

humanism belief in the worth of the individual and that reason is a path to knowledge

Academic Vocabulary

range the limits between which something can change or differ

Gutenberg's Printing Press

The printing press helped spread humanist ideas throughout Europe. In the early 1450s, a German printer named Johannes Gutenberg (yoh·HAHN·uhs GOO·tuhn·buhrg) developed a printing press that used movable metal type. This new press held individual carved letters that could be arranged to form words and then could be used again. As a result, books could be quickly printed by machine rather than slowly written by hand.

The Chinese had already invented movable type. However, their written language had so many characters that the movable type system did not work well. For Europeans, the printing press was a great advance. It was easy to use with linen paper, another invention from China.

Gutenberg's printing press made many more books available to people. Its invention came at a time when many townspeople were learning to read and think for themselves. Scholars could read each other's works and discuss their ideas, often in letters. Ideas developed and spread more quickly than ever before in Europe.

In 1455, Gutenberg produced the first European printed book, the Christian Bible, on the new press. Soon, many books became available in Europe. In fact, more books were printed in the first 50 years of printing than were written by hand in the entire history of the world up to 1450. Half of the 40,000 books published by the year 1500 were religious works such as the Christian Bible or prayer books.

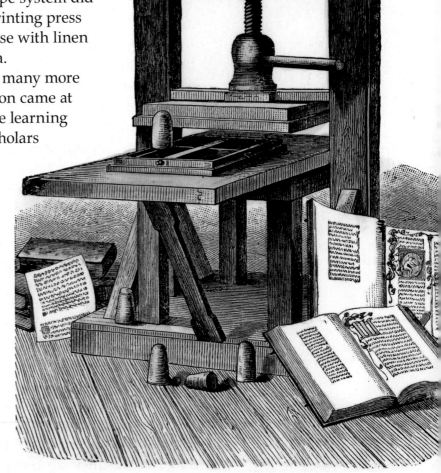

Gutenberg produced bibles on this printing press. Today, there are five complete, original Gutenberg Bibles in the United States.

What Effect Did Humanism Have on Society?

Humanist scholars were curious about such subjects as biology, medicine, and astronomy. Scholars' study of mathematics helped them in many areas of knowledge.

One of the leading Renaissance scientists was also a great artist, Leonardo da Vinci (lee·uh·NAHR·doh duh VIHN·chee). Da Vinci cut open dead bodies to learn more about the human body. He studied fossils to understand Earth's early history. Da Vinci was also an inventor and an engineer.

There's More Online!   connected.mcgraw-hill.com

The *Mona Lisa* by Leonardo da Vinci is one of the most famous paintings from the Renaissance. It hangs today in the *Louvre*, a museum in Paris.

▶ **CRITICAL THINKING**
Speculating Why do you think people have been so fascinated by Mona Lisa's smile?

Most of what we know about da Vinci comes from his notebooks. Da Vinci filled the pages of his notebooks with notes and sketches of his scientific and artistic projects. These drawings often pictured parachutes, flying machines, and other mechanical inventions far ahead of his time.

✓ **PROGRESS CHECK**

Explaining How did Gutenberg's printing press bring change to Europe?

Italy's Renaissance Artists

GUIDING QUESTION *How did Renaissance artists learn to make their art look natural and real?*

In Renaissance Italy, wealthy families and church leaders appreciated beautiful buildings and works of art. They hired talented people to construct beautiful buildings and to fill them with artwork. The pope funded works of art to decorate the Vatican, his headquarters in Rome.

Renaissance builders and artists carefully studied ancient Greek and Roman art, science, and mathematics. They also expressed the new humanist ideas. As one artist declared, human beings were "the center and measure of all things."

What New Styles Did Artists Develop?

Renaissance art was very different from medieval art. Artistic works of the Renaissance tried to show what people really looked like. They also tried to reveal people's feelings. An artist from Florence named Giotto (JAH·toh) was the first to show this change in the early 1300s. His series of wall paintings showed the life of Francis of Assisi. The paintings used gestures and facial expressions to reveal people's emotions.

Renaissance painters also used new methods that brought life, color, and action to their works. The most important was **perspective** (puhr·SPEHK·tihv), a way of showing people and things as they appear at different distances. Artists in the past had tried to use perspective, but Renaissance artists such as Leonardo da Vinci perfected it. Perspective, as used by these artists, gave paintings a realistic, three-dimensional look.

Renaissance artists studied the human body to learn how to draw it accurately. They began to experiment with light, color, and shade. To make their paintings more realistic, artists used

Musee du Louvre, Paris/Giraudon, Paris/SuperStock

Reading**HELP**DESK

Academic Vocabulary

perspective a way of drawing to show the relationship of objects in a drawing to give the look of depth or distance

a technique called chiaroscuro (kee·ahr·uh·SKYUR· oh). Chiaroscuro used light and shadows instead of stiff outlines to separate objects. In Italian, *chiaro* means "clear or light," and *oscuro* means "dark." Chiaroscuro created drama and emotion in paintings.

Many Renaissance artists painted on fresh wet plaster with watercolor paint. A painting done this way is called a fresco (FREHS·koh), which means "fresh" in Italian. Frescoes were painted in churches all over Italy.

Da Vinci was a great innovator. His drawing of a helicopter was very advanced for his time, and he is credited with having the first idea for a vehicle that could fly vertically.

Who Were Leading Renaissance Artists?

The period between 1490 and 1520 was the golden age of Italian Renaissance painting. Three of the most famous artists were Leonardo da Vinci, Michelangelo Buonarroti (MY·kuh·LAN· juh·loh bwah·nah·RAH·tee) and Raphael Sanzio (rah·feye·EHL SAHN·zee·oh).

Leonardo da Vinci was born in Florence. He is known for the *Mona Lisa*, a portrait of a young noblewoman. He gave her a smile that makes the viewer wonder what she is thinking. Da Vinci also painted *The Last Supper*, a wall painting of Jesus and his disciples. In this work, da Vinci showed emotion through the way the apostles hold their heads or sit in relation to Jesus.

Another great Renaissance artist was Michelangelo. He began his career as a sculptor in Florence. In 1508, Pope Julius II hired Michelangelo to work at the Vatican. There, Michelangelo painted the ceiling of the Sistine Chapel with scenes from the Bible. These paintings are still famous today. A noted Renaissance biographer praised Michelangelo:

PRIMARY SOURCE

The work [Sistine Chapel ceiling] has been, indeed, a light of our art, illuminating the world which had been so many centuries in darkness. Oh, truly happy age, and oh, blessed artists, who at such a fountain can purge [remove] away the dark films from your eyes. Give thanks to Heaven, and imitate Michael Angelo [Michelangelo] in all things.

—from *Lives of the Artists* by Giorgio Vasari

All of Michelangelo's painted figures were like sculptures. They had muscular bodies that showed life and power. This scene of the creation of Adam appears on the ceiling of the Sistine Chapel in Rome.

Michelangelo Buonarroti (1475–1564)

As a young artist, Michelangelo received support from Lorenzo de' Medici, the ruler of Florence. When he saw the young man's talent, de' Medici let Michelangelo study his art collection of ancient Roman statues. One of Michelangelo's first large sculptures was inspired by these statues. Michelangelo's most famous works, however, were based on Bible stories such as "David and Goliath." He made his 13-foot-tall marble statue of David seem calm, yet ready for action. Most of Michelangelo's sculptures suggested strong but controlled emotions.

▶ **CRITICAL THINKING**
Assessing How important was the de' Medici family to Michelangelo?

Like Michelangelo, the artist Raphael worked at the Vatican. He painted many frescoes for the palace of the pope. Perhaps his best-known fresco, the *School of Athens,* shows Greek philosophers. People also admired his paintings of Mary, the mother of Jesus. These works were done in bright colors and showed the Renaissance ideals of grace and beauty.

Renaissance women had few roles independent of men. Some women, though, contributed to the arts. These women were either the daughters of artists or the children of nobles. The most celebrated female artist was Artemisia Gentileschi (ahr· teh·MIHZ·ee·uh jehn·tih·LEHS·kee). She was one of the first women to paint major historical and religious scenes.

✔ **PROGRESS CHECK**

Describing What is the technique of chiaroscuro?

The Northern Renaissance

GUIDING QUESTION *How did the Renaissance change as it moved from Italy into northern Europe?*

During the late 1400s, the Renaissance spread from Italy to northern Europe. War, trade, travel, and the printing press all spread humanist ideas. The people of northern Europe eagerly accepted Italian Renaissance style but changed it to suit their own tastes and needs.

Northern European Painters

The term "Northern Renaissance" refers to the cultural changes in what is today Belgium, the Netherlands, Luxembourg, and Germany. Like Italian artists, northern artists wanted more realism in their works. However, they used different methods to achieve it.

Northern artists began painting in oils rather than using water-based paints. Oils provided richer colors and allowed changes to be made on the painted canvas. Artists also used oils to show small surface details, such as the gold trim on a robe.

The Flemish painter Jan van Eyck (YAHN van EYEK) was skilled in using oils. One of his best-known paintings is *The Arnolfini* (ahr·nuhl·FEE·nee) *Portrait.* It shows a newly married couple standing together in a formal room. Van Eyck showed every fold in their richly colored clothes and every detail of the ceiling lamp above them.

©Bettmann/Corbis

Reading**HELP**DESK

Reading Strategy: *Finding the Main Idea*

Finding the main idea of a passage will help you understand what the passage is about. Read about the northern European painters. On a separate sheet of paper, write the main idea of that passage in your own words.

Albrecht Dürer (AHL·brehkt DYUR·uhr) of Germany was another important artist of the Northern Renaissance. His work blended Italian Renaissance methods and medieval German traditions. Dürer was skilled in showing perspective and fine detail. He is best known for his engravings. An engraving is produced from an image carved on metal, wood, or stone. Ink is placed on the surface, and then the image is printed on paper.

Dürer's *Four Horsemen of the Apocalypse* (uh·PAH·kuh·lihpz) is an outstanding example of a woodcut, a print made from carved wood. His work shows four fierce riders who announce the end of the world.

England's Theaters

The Renaissance reached its height in England during the rule of Elizabeth I in the late 1500s. The people of Renaissance England were especially fond of plays. About 1580, the first theaters in England were built. Their stages stood in the open air. Some wealthy people sat under a roof or covering. Admission was only one or two cents, so even the poor could attend. The poor stood in a large open area.

English playwrights, or authors of plays, wrote about people's strengths, weaknesses, and emotions. The greatest English playwright of that time was William Shakespeare (SHAYK·spihr). Shakespeare wrote all kinds of plays: histories, comedies, and tragedies. He drew ideas for his plays from the histories of England and ancient Rome. His plays often included Italian scenes, characters, and plots. Many of his plays were about loyalty, family, friendship, or justice. Some of Shakespeare's most famous works are *Hamlet, Macbeth, Romeo and Juliet*, and *Henry V*.

The richly detailed objects in this van Eyck painting reflect the lives of the people portrayed, a merchant and his wife.

▶ **CRITICAL THINKING**
Analyzing Visuals What does this painting tell you about the lives of the people in it?

✔ PROGRESS CHECK

Comparing and Contrasting How did northern Renaissance painters differ from Italian Renaissance painters?

InterfotoScans/Age fotostock

LESSON 2 REVIEW

Review Vocabulary

1. How could *humanism* help people solve problems?

Answer the Guiding Questions

2. *Explaining* How were Renaissance scholars able to study ancient texts?

3. *Determining Cause and Effect* How did Gutenberg's printing press contribute to the spread of the ideas of Renaissance scholars?

4. *Making Inferences* How might scientific advances made during the Renaissance have helped artists create more realistic art?

5. *Contrasting* How did Renaissance ideas influence northern and southern European art differently?

6. **INFORMATIVE/EXPLANATORY** How do you think ancient Greek and Roman ideas have affected the way people learn, relate to, or think about their place in the world? Explain your answer in a short paragraph.

There's More Online! connected.mcgraw-hill.com   Lesson 2 **595**

Henry V

by William Shakespeare

William Shakespeare

William Shakespeare, the greatest English playwright, was enormously successful. His theater company, the King's Men, employed London's best actor and playwright— Shakespeare himself.

Shakespeare's plays included histories of several British kings. In writing *Henry V*, Shakespeare drew on histories of the real King Henry V, who invaded France in 1415. The play tells how a small English army faces a much larger French force. Against all odds, the outnumbered English army wins.

Henry V is most famous for the king's uplifting speech to his men. Tired and outnumbered, the soldiers think they will be defeated in the next day's battle. Henry encourages them by describing their bravery, and how they will be remembered.

Henry V:
"We few, we happy few, we band of brothers;
For he to-day that sheds his blood with me
Shall be my brother."

—from *Henry V*, Act IV, Scene iii, by William Shakespeare

The Globe theater was home to Shakespeare's acting troupe and was where Shakespeare's plays were presented. The theater could hold about 3,000 people, either standing or sitting. The flag on its roof signaled the type of play being presented: black for tragedies, white for comedies, and red for history plays.

© Heritage Images/Corbis

Henry V:

❚❚ This day is called the feast of Crispian:
He that outlives this day, and comes safe home,
Will stand a tip-toe when the day is named,
And **rouse** him at the name of Crispian.

He that shall live this day, and see old age,
Will yearly on the **vigil** feast his neighbors,
And say 'To-morrow is Saint Crispian:'
Then will he strip his sleeve and show his scars.
And say 'These wounds I had on Crispin's day.'

Old men forget: yet all shall be forgot,
But he'll remember with advantages
What **feats** he did that day: then shall our names.
Familiar in his mouth as household words
Harry the king, Bedford and Exeter,
Warwick and Talbot, Salisbury and Gloucester,[1]
Be in their flowing cups freshly remember'd.

This story shall the good man teach his son;
And Crispin Crispian shall ne'er go by,
From this day to the ending of the world,
But we in it shall be remember'd;
We few, we happy few, we band of brothers;
For he to-day that sheds his blood with me
Shall be my brother; be he ne'er so **vile,**
This day shall gentle his condition:
And gentlemen in England now a-bed
Shall think themselves **accursed** they were not here,
And hold their manhoods cheap whiles any speaks
That fought with us upon Saint Crispin's day. "❚❚

—From William *Shakespeare's Henry V*, **Act IV, Scene iii**

[1] Bedford, Exeter, Warwick, Talbot, Salisbury, and Gloucester were noblemen in Henry's army.

Vocabulary

rouse to stir up or excite
vigil the night before a religious feast
feats achievements, successes
vile morally low
accursed doomed, miserable

Analyzing Literature DBQ

❶ *Analyzing* What is the purpose of King Henry's speech to his soldiers? What words show this purpose?

❷ *Interpreting* What does the king mean when he says, "For he to-day that sheds his blood with me / Shall be my brother; …"?

❸ *Assessing* Would the king's speech persuade men to face death in battle? Why or why not?

LESSON 3

The Reformation Begins

ESSENTIAL QUESTION

• How do religions develop?

IT MATTERS BECAUSE

Events during the Reformation led to the development of new Christian churches that still exist today.

Early Calls for Reform

GUIDING QUESTION *Why was the Church under pressure to reform itself?*

Many educated Europeans were influenced by Renaissance humanism. They began to criticize the wealth and power of the Catholic Church. In 1517, a German monk named Martin Luther questioned the authority of the Church.

At first, Luther only wanted to reform the Catholic Church. This is why these events are called the **Reformation** (reh·fuhr·MAY·shuhn). The Reformation, however, produced a new form of Christianity called Protestantism (PRAH·tuhs·tuhnt·ih·zuhm). By 1600, many Protestant churches had risen in Europe.

John Wycliffe Speaks Out

As early as the 1300s, many Europeans recognized problems within the Catholic Church. Church officials had grown wealthy by collecting taxes. Some bishops acted like kings by building palaces and providing jobs for their relatives. Yet, in many villages, priests could barely read. In addition, churches began offering indulgences. An **indulgence** (ihn·DUHL·juhntz) was a certificate issued by the Church. The certificate granted a pardon for a person's sins. Church members who performed "good works," such as giving money to build a church, could receive this pardon.

Reading **HELP**DESK

Taking Notes: *Determining Cause and Effect*

Use a diagram like this one to list some of the reasons for the Reformation.

Reasons for the Reformation

Content Vocabulary

• **Reformation**   • **annul**
• **indulgence**
• **predestination**

People were angry about the Church's focus on money. They also began to question the authority of the Church. Many years before, disputes within the Catholic Church had led to more than one leader claiming to be the rightful pope. Since then, respect for the pope had declined. In the 1370s, an English priest named John Wycliffe (WIH·klihf) preached that Christians needed only to recognize Jesus as head of the Church, not the pope.

Wycliffe also claimed that all religious truth came from the Christian Bible. He wanted everyone to read the Bible, so he translated many passages from Latin into English for his followers to use. After Wycliffe died, his followers finished the translation, creating the first Christian Bible in English.

Who Was Erasmus?

Renaissance humanism led to a new movement called Christian humanism. Christian humanists were loyal Catholics who wanted to restore the simple faith of the early Church. They believed that humanist learning and Bible study were the best ways to improve the Church.

The best known Christian humanist was Desiderius Erasmus (DEHS·ih·DIHR·ee·uhs ih·RAZ·muhs). Erasmus believed that people should use their reason to become better Christians. He said that it was not enough to participate in religious activities like going to church on Sunday. He believed it was more important that Christians be good in their everyday lives. By improving themselves, they would be able to reform the Church and society.

In 1509, Erasmus wrote a book called *Praise of Folly*. In this work, he used humor to criticize Church corruption. He especially attacked the wealth of Renaissance popes. He said the popes were so concerned with luxury and pleasure that they no longer practiced Christianity.

Erasmus entered a monastery early in his life. His studies led him to criticize the wealth and power of Church leaders.

✔ PROGRESS CHECK

Explaining What were the goals of the Christian humanists?

Reformation a religious movement that produced a new form of Christianity known as Protestantism

indulgence a pardon, or forgiveness, of a sin

Luther's Reformation

Martin Luther's family wanted him to become a lawyer, but he decided on a career in the church.

GUIDING QUESTION *How did Luther's reforms lead to a new form of Christianity?*

During the early 1500s, Martin Luther supported the cause of Church reform. Opposed by the pope, Luther broke away from many Catholic teachings. His rebellion led to a religious revolution that changed Europe.

Who Was Martin Luther?

Born in 1483, Martin Luther became a monk and faithfully followed Church teachings and practices. However, he still worried about the fate of his soul. His concern about reaching heaven was not surprising. He had seen epidemics, famine, and war.

Luther's doubts grew after he visited Rome. He was shocked to find that priests there made fun of Catholic rituals. They disobeyed Church rules. Some of them could not read the Bible. How could these disrespectful priests help people get to heaven?

Back in Wittenberg (VIH·tuhn·buhrg), Germany, Luther searched for answers. The Church taught that a person needed both faith and good works to go to heaven. His experiences in Rome caused Luther to question Church policy.

In 1517, Luther became even angrier at Church leaders. Pope Leo X needed money to rebuild St. Peter's Basilica, a large church in Rome, so he sent monks out to sell indulgences. Local Church leaders had offered and sold indulgences for many years. Now the pope was selling them, too. How could Church leaders put a price on God's forgiveness? Luther thought the Church had moved too far away from the Bible in what it was teaching.

Luther made a list of 95 arguments against indulgences. He sent the list to his bishop. Some accounts say that Luther also nailed the list to the door of Wittenberg Cathedral. The list became known as the Ninety-Five Theses. Thousands of copies were printed and read all across Germany.

A New Church

Luther began to openly attack Catholic beliefs. He argued that the only true guide to religious truth was the Bible, which all Christians had a right to read. He said that Christians could confess their sins directly to God without the help of priests.

Reading HELPDESK

Reading Strategy: *Activating Prior Knowledge*

Martin Luther was concerned with salvation. You learned about the idea of salvation in an earlier chapter. What does the word *salvation* mean?

Pope Leo X believed that Luther was dangerous. In 1521, he excommunicated Luther. A person who is excommunicated can no longer belong to the church. Then, a diet, or council, of German princes met in the city of Worms. The princes wanted Luther to change his ideas. Luther refused:

PRIMARY SOURCE

❝ Unless I am convinced by Scripture and plain reason—I do not accept the authority of the popes and councils, for they have contradicted [spoken against] each other—my conscience is captive [loyal] to the Word of God. I cannot and will not recant [take back] anything for to go against conscience is neither right nor safe. God help me. Amen. ❞

—from Martin Luther's speech at the Diet of Worms, 1521

Luther's ideas eventually led to the creation of the first Protestant church, known as Lutheranism (LOO•thuh•ruhn•ihzm). The new church was based on three main ideas. The first idea is that faith in Jesus, not good works, brings someone a place in heaven. The second is that the Bible is the final source for truth about God. Finally, Lutheranism said that the church is made up of all its believers, not just the clergy.

Revolts in Germany

Lutheranism gave rural peasants in Germany hope for a better life. During the 1520s, the peasants suffered as a result of poor crops and high taxes they were forced to pay to noble landowners. The peasants thought that if Luther could rebel against the pope, then they could stand up to greedy nobles.

Huge revolts swept Germany. The peasants looked to Luther for support. At first, Luther agreed with their cause. In his sermons, Luther criticized nobles for their mistreatment of the peasants. However, Luther also feared violence. He told the peasants that God had set the government above them and they must obey it. The nobles soon defeated the peasants.

Rulers and Lutheranism

In the past, the Catholic Church could stop the spread of ideas that it opposed. Why was it unable to stop Protestantism in the 1500s? One reason is that Protestantism had the support of some European rulers. These rulers believed that they could increase their power by supporting Protestantism against the Catholic Church. The Lutheran movement became closely tied to politics.

There's More Online!   connected.mcgraw-hill.com

In this painting, indulgences are being sold at a village market.

Michael Hampshire/National Geographic Society Image Collection

In 1520, the Holy Roman Emperor ruled over a large part of Europe.

1 REGIONS What are some of the areas that made up the Holy Roman Empire?

2 CRITICAL THINKING
Drawing Conclusions Why would it have been difficult for one ruler to control the Holy Roman Empire?

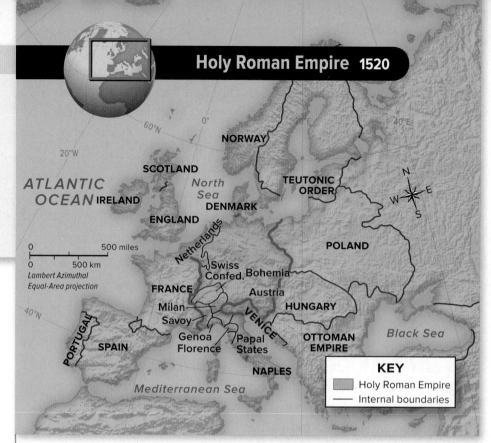

Holy Roman Empire 1520

The Holy Roman Empire was Catholic and covered much of central Europe. It included about 300 German states. In 1519, Charles V became the Holy Roman Emperor. He also ruled Spain, the Netherlands, parts of Italy, and territories in the Americas.

Local German rulers worried about the growing power of Charles V. They wanted to keep their independence. Many of these leaders became Lutherans. By doing so, their states also became Lutheran. After breaking with the Catholic Church, these rulers took over Catholic lands within their territories. Now they, and not the Catholic Church, would earn income from those lands.

When rulers adopted Lutheranism, taxes no longer flowed to the pope in Rome. Rulers could **impose** their own church taxes and keep the money for themselves. This made Lutheran rulers stronger and the Catholic Church weaker.

In order to regain control of these lands, Charles V went to war with the Lutheran rulers. However, he was not able to defeat them. In 1555, an agreement known as the Peace of Augsburg (AUGHZ·buhrg) ended the fighting. Under its terms, each German ruler—whether Catholic or Lutheran—could decide

Reading HELPDESK

predestination a religious belief that God has already decided who will go to heaven and who will not

Academic Vocabulary

impose to establish by force or authority

the religion of his people. The Peace of Augsburg allowed the division of Germany into a Protestant north and a Catholic south. This division remains to this day.

✓ **PROGRESS CHECK**

Determining Cause and Effect How did the Ninety-Five Theses affect the Catholic Church in Germany?

The Reformation Spreads

GUIDING QUESTION *How did the teachings of Protestant reformers shape the western world?*

As the Reformation spread, different forms of Protestantism developed. Soon after Lutheranism began in Germany, many people in nearby Switzerland accepted Protestant ideas. They set up new reformed churches.

Who Was John Calvin?

John Calvin was born in France in 1509. Known for his sharp mind, Calvin studied law, humanism, and religion in Paris. He was especially interested in religion. He got up early and stayed up late to read books about it. The more Calvin read, the more he was convinced that Luther was right.

Eventually, Calvin fled from Paris because it became too dangerous to talk about Protestantism. He finally found safety in Geneva (juh·NEE·vuh), Switzerland. There, his powerful preaching convinced many people to follow him.

What Is Calvinism?

As he studied the Bible, Calvin developed his own ideas. He agreed with Luther that faith alone brought salvation, but he added other ideas. Calvin's main idea was that God decides the final outcome of all events in the universe. Therefore, God has already chosen who will go to heaven and who will not. This belief is called **predestination** (pree·dehs·tuh·NAY·shuhn).

Most of Calvin's followers believed that they were among the people who would be saved. To prove it, they worked hard, behaved well, and obeyed the laws of their towns. In this way, Calvinism became a powerful tool in society. It encouraged people to work hard at their business and watch their behavior.

Another idea of Calvinism is that church members, not kings or bishops, should choose the clergy. This idea influenced people in England, Scotland, and the Netherlands. Because of Calvinism, people began to think that they could elect government leaders.

✓ **PROGRESS CHECK**

Analyzing How did Calvinism influence ideas about government?

There's More Online! connected.mcgraw-hill.com

The writings of John Calvin helped Europeans accept Protestantism.

▶ **CRITICAL THINKING**
Explaining Why would followers of Calvin work to live a good life, even though they believed that God had already decided their fate?

The Reformation in England

Henry VIII challenged the Church to solve his own problems in England.

▶ CRITICAL THINKING
Explaining Why did the Pope refuse Henry's request to undo his marriage to Catherine?

GUIDING QUESTION *How did the Reformation shape England and later its American colonies?*

The Reformation reached England about 10 years after it began in central Europe. In England, religious change at first did not come from church officials or the people. It started as a political quarrel between the king and the pope. Religious beliefs did not play a part until much later.

The Break with Rome

Henry VIII ruled England from 1509 to 1547. He belonged to the Tudor family. Henry wanted to keep the Tudors on the throne. However, he had no son to follow him. Catherine, the first of Henry's six wives, had children. Only one of her children, Mary, survived.

As Catherine grew older, Henry feared she could not have any more children. At the same time, he had fallen in love with Anne Boleyn (buh·LIHN), a young noblewoman. Henry asked the pope to **annul,** or declare invalid, his marriage to Catherine so that he could marry Anne. The Catholic Church did not allow divorce. If the pope granted an annulment, it would be as if Henry and Catherine had never married.

The pope refused Henry's request. Catherine was the daughter of King Ferdinand and Queen Isabella of Spain. Her nephew was Charles V, the Holy Roman Emperor. The pope did not want to anger Catherine's important family.

Henry had the Archbishop of Canterbury—the highest church official in England—end his marriage to Catherine. Henry then married Anne Boleyn. In response, the pope excommunicated Henry. Henry fought back. In 1534, he had Parliament pass the Act of Supremacy. The act made the king head of the new Church of England.

Henry ordered all bishops and priests in England to accept the Act of Supremacy. Some who refused were killed. Henry seized the land of the Catholic Church in England and gave some of it to his nobles. Giving the nobles this property made sure they remained loyal to Henry and his church.

©The Print Collector/Corbis

Who Was Bloody Mary?

The Church of England became known as the Anglican (AYN·glih·kuhn) Church. After Henry's death, the Anglican Church accepted some Protestant ideas, but it kept most Catholic rituals. Many English Catholics wanted more. They supported Henry's Catholic daughter Mary when she became queen.

As queen, Mary **restored** the Catholic Church in England and arrested Protestants who opposed her. More than 300 Protestants were burned at the stake. The English were horrified and turned against their queen, calling her "Bloody Mary."

Mary died in 1558. Her half-sister Elizabeth, the Protestant daughter of Henry VIII and Anne Boleyn, took the throne as Queen Elizabeth I. She restored the Anglican Church. Elizabeth became one of the greatest rulers in English history.

Calvinism in England

Most English people were pleased with the Anglican Church. Some Protestants, however, had become Calvinists. These people became known as Puritans because they wanted to purify, or cleanse, the Anglican Church of Catholic ways. Puritan groups often refused to accept the authority of Anglican bishops.

Queen Elizabeth I tolerated the Puritans. When James I became king in 1603, however, the Puritans faced opposition. James believed that the Puritans threatened his power. He and later his son, King Charles I, closed Puritan churches and imprisoned Puritan leaders. Many Puritans left England and settled in North America to practice their religion freely.

Elizabeth I succeeded her half-sister Mary as queen and halted the persecution of English Protestants.

✔ PROGRESS CHECK

Explaining Why did Henry VIII seize Catholic Church lands in England?

LESSON 3 REVIEW

Review Vocabulary

1. Why did Martin Luther want the *Reformation* of the Catholic Church?

2. Why did the pope want to sell *indulgences*?

Answer the Guiding Questions

3. *Identifying* Why did many Europeans criticize the Catholic Church at the time of the Reformation?

4. *Generalizing* What three types of reforms did Luther want for the Catholic Church?

5. *Making Inferences* Why was Germany's split between Protestants in the north and Catholics in the south important?

6. *Determining Cause and Effect* How did John Calvin's ideas take root in the American colonies?

7. **ARGUMENT** Which argument for religious reform might be convincing to a priest, pope, or king? Choose one idea for reform and support it with evidence. Write a letter to one of these people in the form of a persuasive paragraph that defends your idea.

LESSON 4

Catholics and Protestants

ESSENTIAL QUESTION

• Why does conflict develop?

IT MATTERS BECAUSE

The struggle between Catholics and Protestants during the Reformation shaped the churches that we know today.

The Catholic Reformation

GUIDING QUESTION *How did the Catholic Church respond to the spread of Protestantism?*

In the 1500s and 1600s, Catholics set out to improve their Church and to stop the spread of Protestant ideas. This effort was known as the Catholic Reformation. It helped the Church regain some of the areas in Europe it had lost to Protestantism.

Catholic Reforms

Catholics wanted to fight Protestantism and reform their Church. Pope Paul III called a council of bishops. The council met at different times between 1545 and 1563 at Trent, Italy.

The Council of Trent supported Catholic beliefs that had been challenged by the Protestants. However, it ended many Church abuses, such as the sale of indulgences. The Council ordered bishops and priests to follow strict rules of behavior. The Church set up seminaries. A **seminary** (SEH·muh·nehr·ee) is a special school for training and educating priests.

The Church also set out to win followers and to strengthen the spiritual life of Catholics. In 1540, Pope Paul III recognized a new order of priests, the Society of Jesus, known as the Jesuits. They preached to bring Protestants back to the Catholic faith.

Reading**HELP**DESK

Taking Notes: *Determining Cause and Effect*

Use a diagram like this one to show the results of the Catholic Church's attempts at reform.

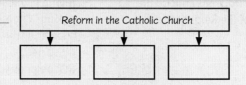
Reform in the Catholic Church

Content Vocabulary

• seminary   • heresy

The man who founded the Jesuits was a Spanish noble, Ignatius (ihg·NAY·shuhs) of Loyola (loy·OH·luh). He was a soldier whose life changed when he was wounded in battle. While recovering, he read about the lives of the saints. Ignatius decided he would be a soldier for Jesus and the Church.

The Spanish nun Teresa of Avila (AH·vih·luh) was another reformer. Teresa founded an order of nuns and opened new convents throughout Spain. Teresa became known for her spiritual writings that rank among the classics of Christian writing.

Ferdinand and Isabella united the separate kingdoms of Aragon and Castile into the country of Spain.

Catholic Spain

Protestant ideas never became very popular in Spain. Still, when religious conflict began to divide Europe, Spain was affected. Spanish rulers distrusted Protestant countries and their own Protestant citizens.

When Luther called for reform in 1517, Spain was a united country. King Ferdinand of Aragon and Queen Isabella of Castile had married and joined their two kingdoms in 1469. They wanted to unite Spain and make all of their subjects be Catholic.

In the late 1400s, many Muslims lived in Spain. Muslims had ruled much of Spain during the Middle Ages. Under Muslim rule, Christians and Jews paid special taxes and had limited rights, but they were able to practice their religions. Muslims and non-Muslims lived in relative peace. This time period was a golden age for Jews in Spain.

This age of religious harmony ended under Ferdinand and Isabella. Spain's rulers pressured Jews and Muslims to convert to Catholicism. But even those who converted were not safe. Spanish officials suspected them of secretly practicing their old religions. To ensure that their orders were being carried out, Ferdinand and Isabella began the Spanish Inquisition.

The Council of Trent is considered one of the most important councils in the history of the Catholic Church.

▶ **CRITICAL THINKING**
Identifying What do you think was the most important decision of the Council?

Spanish Inquisition

The Spanish Inquisition was a religious court. It was similar to the one that the Catholic Church had set up earlier in Europe to root out **heresy** (HEHR·uh·see), or beliefs that opposed Church teaching.

seminary a school for religious training

heresy a religious belief that contradicts what the church says is true

(t)©Corbis; (b)Giraudon/Art Resource, NY

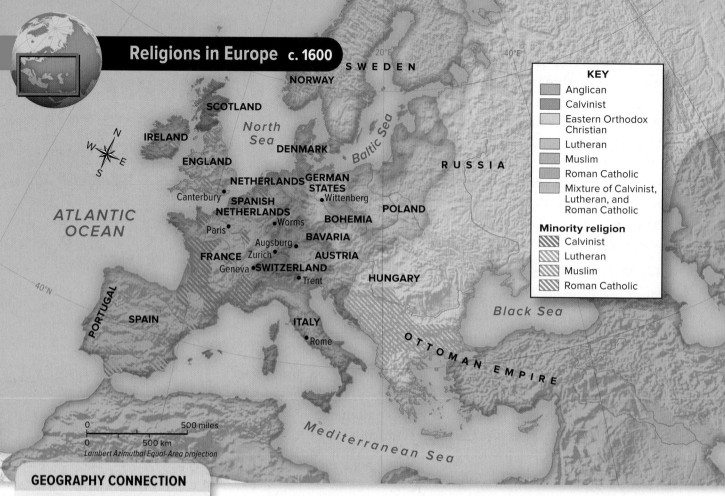

Religions in Europe c. 1600

KEY
- Anglican
- Calvinist
- Eastern Orthodox Christian
- Lutheran
- Muslim
- Roman Catholic
- Mixture of Calvinist, Lutheran, and Roman Catholic

Minority religion
- Calvinist
- Lutheran
- Muslim
- Roman Catholic

0 — 500 miles
0 — 500 km
Lambert Azimuthal Equal-Area projection

GEOGRAPHY CONNECTION

By the late 1500s, many northern Europeans had become Protestants, and most southern Europeans had remained Catholic.

1 PLACE Which areas of Europe became mostly Calvinist?

2 CRITICAL THINKING
Making Inferences Where in Europe was religious conflict most likely to take place?

The purpose of the Spanish Inquisition was to find and punish those guilty of heresy. Torture was used to force people to confess their guilt. The head of the Spanish Inquisition was Tomás de Torquemada (tawr·kay·MAH·duh). Even the pope could not stop him from eventually executing about 2,000 Spaniards.

In 1492, the Spanish monarchs ordered all Jews to become Catholic or leave the country. Ten years later, they gave Muslims the same order. Many people left in response to these orders.

Despite strong Church and government controls, literature and the arts flourished in Catholic Spain. The writer Miguel de Cervantes (mih·GEHL day suhr·VAHN·tehz) wrote the novel *Don Quixote* (dahn kee·HOH·tee), about a comical knight and his peasant servant. A Greek artist whom the Spanish called El Greco (ehl GREH·koh) painted religious figures with very long bodies, parts of which stretched beyond normal size.

☑ PROGRESS CHECK

Explaining What was the goal of the Spanish Inquisition?

Reading HELPDESK

Academic Vocabulary

unify to join; to make into one group

Religious Wars

GUIDING QUESTION *How did wars of religion affect Europe?*

By the mid-1500s, most northern Europeans were Protestant, and most southern Europeans were Catholic. European monarchs had used religion to help **unify,** or unite, their people and to build powerful nations. The kings and queens of Europe expected their subjects to practice the religion of their ruler. People who did not join the churches of their monarchs were persecuted, or treated cruelly and unjustly. This led to bitterness among people of different faiths. Differences in religion led to wars between countries. Toward the end of the 1500s, Europe entered a period of religious wars that lasted until about 1650.

The Spanish Armada

Under the rule of Queen Elizabeth I, England became the leading Protestant power in Europe. At that time, Spain was the leading Catholic power. The Spanish king was Philip II, the son of Charles V and the great-grandson of Ferdinand and Isabella. King Philip at first supported Elizabeth as England's queen, against the wishes of the pope. However, during the 1560s, the Protestant Dutch rebelled against Spanish rule. Elizabeth helped the Dutch by letting Englishmen attack Spanish ships. Philip decided to get revenge against Elizabeth by invading England.

A combination of bad decisions by the Spanish, faster English ships, and stormy weather sank the Spanish Armada.

In 1588, Philip sent a huge fleet known as the Spanish Armada (ahr·MAH·duh) to England. To block the invasion, the English knew they had to make the Spanish ships break their formation. Their chance came when the Spanish fleet entered the English Channel, the narrow body of water between England and Europe. The huge Spanish ships had many guns, but they were hard to steer. The smaller English ships moved much more quickly in the tight channel. Their attacks forced the Armada to retreat. A great storm later broke up the mighty Spanish navy. The English throne was saved, and the English celebrated their victory.

Although Spain was still a powerful nation, England had shown that it could defend itself. The English gained respect throughout Europe as defenders of the Protestant faith.

**Catherine de' Medici
(1519–1589)**

The powerful de' Medici family was led by strong Italian men and women. Catherine de' Medici was a firm supporter of the arts. She promoted Renaissance ideas when she wed Prince Henry of France. She took Italian artists, dancers, musicians, and writers with her to the French court. Catherine supported the arts in France, also. She added to the royal library and sponsored a dance and theater presentation that is thought to be the first ballet performance.

▶ **CRITICAL THINKING**
Speculating How might the French people have felt about having Catherine de' Medici as their queen?

Religious Conflict in France

While England and Spain became rivals, a religious conflict divided France. During the 1500s, most people in France were Catholic. However, many wealthy people in France became Protestants. These Protestants, who were called Huguenots (HYU·guh·nahtz), followed the teachings of John Calvin.

Many French nobles wanted to weaken the king, Henry II. The Huguenot nobles especially wanted the king weak so they could practice their religion freely. At the same time, Henry II wanted to build a strong central government.

Henry died in 1559, and his son Francis II died the next year. As a result, Charles, the younger brother of Francis, became king of France at the age of 10. Because Charles was too young to rule, his mother, Catherine de' Medici, ruled for him. She was the daughter of Lorenzo de' Medici, the powerful Italian leader of Florence.

Influential Rulers

Catherine was determined to keep the French kingdom strong for her son. When a civil war broke out, Catherine tried to keep the peace by supporting both Huguenots and Catholics. But in 1572, she allowed Catholic nobles to kill the leading Huguenots in Paris. Catholics in other parts of France also revolted. They formed mobs that killed Protestants and burned their homes. Many Protestants fled the country. The few who stayed were led by the Huguenot prince, Henry of Navarre (nuh·VAHR). Henry was a member of the powerful Bourbon family. He was in line for the throne of France.

In 1589, Henry of Navarre became King Henry IV of France. He wanted to gain the loyalty of the people. Because most French people were still Catholic, Henry decided to convert to Catholicism. According to tradition, he said that Paris, the French capital, was "worth a [Catholic] mass." Henry meant that being king of France was more important than being Protestant.

As king, Henry worked to end the fighting between Catholics and Protestants in France. In 1598, he issued an edict, or order, while visiting the city of Nantes. The Edict of Nantes said Catholicism was the official religion of France. However, it also allowed Huguenots to worship freely.

Victoria & Albert Museum, London/Art Resource, NY

The Thirty Years' War

The most violent religious war of the Reformation period was fought in the Holy Roman Empire in the early 1600s. The war began in Bohemia, today known as the Czech Republic. Protestant nobles in Bohemia rebelled against their Catholic king. When other Protestant rulers in Germany joined the rebels, the war spread across the empire.

The conflict grew into the Thirty Years' War that lasted from 1618 to 1648. Sweden and Denmark sent troops to help the Protestants. Spain and the Holy Roman Emperor supported the Catholics. Although France was Catholic, it wanted to gain power over neighboring states, so it entered the war on the Protestant side. As France fought against other Catholic countries, the war became a struggle for territory and wealth, not just religion.

The German people suffered great hardships during the war. A city official described the effects of the fighting on the German city of Magdeburg (MAHG·duh·burk):

The Thirty Years' War began when Protestant nobles threw two government officials out a window. The officials represented the Catholic Holy Roman Emperor.

PRIMARY SOURCE

❞ Thus in a single day this noble and famous city, the pride of the whole country, went up in fire and smoke; and the remnant [remainder] of its citizens, with their wives and children, were taken prisoners and driven away by the enemy with a noise of weeping and wailing that could be heard from afar. ❞

—Otto von Guericke, from "Destruction of Magdeburg in 1631"

Finally, in 1643, the Holy Roman Emperor asked for peace. In 1648, the warring nations signed the Peace of Westphalia (wehst·FAYL·yuh). This treaty ended the conflict. The war had weakened Spain and the Holy Roman Empire, while France emerged as a stronger nation.

☑ PROGRESS CHECK

Analyzing Why was the Edict of Nantes important in the history of France?

LESSON 4 REVIEW

Review Vocabulary

1. What kind of training might a priest receive in a *seminary*?

Answer the Guiding Questions

2. *Identifying* Who were the Jesuits?

3. *Making Inferences* How did the spread of Protestantism in Europe threaten the Catholic Church?

4. *Explaining* Why did France fight against Catholic countries in the Thirty Years' War?

5. **NARRATIVE** You are visiting France and have friends who are both Catholic and Huguenot. Write a letter to a friend explaining the difficulties between the two religions and how the Edict of Nantes changes the situation.

There's More Online! connected.mcgraw-hill.com

Write your answers on a separate piece of paper.

1 **Exploring the Essential Question**

INFORMATIVE/EXPLANATORY How would you describe Renaissance ideas about humanism to a medieval person who knows nothing about them? Write a descriptive essay to explain humanism to a medieval person. Describe how these ideas will change this person's life.

2 **21st Century Skills**

ANALYZING IMAGES Create a PowerPoint™ presentation that highlights art of the Renaissance. Use photos of the artwork from important artists such as Michelangelo and Leonardo da Vinci and point out important details in the artwork. Share your presentation with the class.

3 **Thinking Like a Historian**

SEQUENCING The Reformation of the Catholic Church was an important development in Europe's history. Create a time line that shows important events that led to the Reformation of the Catholic Church.

4 **GEOGRAPHY ACTIVITY**

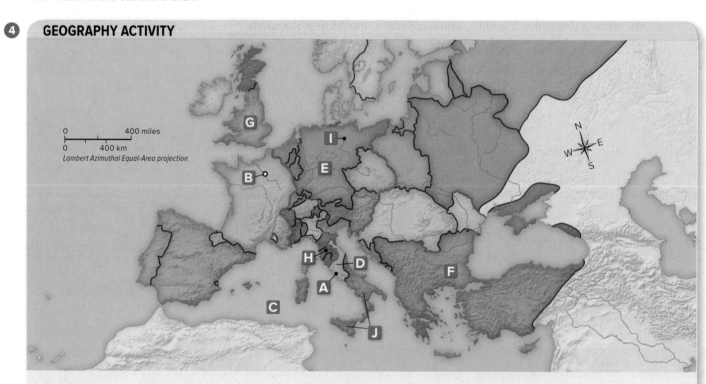

Locating Places

Match the letters on the map with the numbered places listed below.

1. Wittenberg
2. Kingdom of the Two Sicilies
3. Papal States
4. Holy Roman Empire
5. Rome
6. Paris
7. England
8. Florence
9. Mediterranean Sea
10. Ottoman Empire

Directions: Write your answers on a separate piece of paper.

CHECKING FOR UNDERSTANDING

1 Identify the vocabulary words with their descriptions.
- **A.** related to worldly things
- **B.** a renewal or rebirth of interest in Greek and Roman arts
- **C.** a school for religious training
- **D.** a soldier who fights for money rather than loyalty to a country
- **E.** belief in the worth of the individual and that reason is a path to knowledge
- **F.** a religious movement that produced a new form of Christianity known as Protestantism
- **G.** a pardon, or forgiveness, of a sin
- **H.** a religious belief that God has already decided who will go to heaven and who will not

REVIEW THE GUIDING QUESTIONS

2 *Citing Text Evidence* Why did Italy's states become important cultural centers during the Renaissance?

3 *Stating* Why did the Italian states become wealthy?

4 *Identifying* Who made up the new ruling class in the Italian states?

5 *Finding the Main Idea* How did Renaissance writers depend on the past to help them develop new ideas?

6 *Specifying* What methods did Renaissance artists learn to use to make their art look natural?

7 *Describing* How did the Renaissance change as it spread to northern Europe?

8 *Discussing* Why was the Catholic Church pressured into reforming?

9 *Paraphrasing* Use your own words to explain how the changes Martin Luther made resulted in a new form of Christianity. Make certain that your writing is clear and coherent.

10 *Explaining* How did the Catholic Church react to the spread of Protestantism in Europe?

11 *Describing* How did the Thirty Year's War affect Europe?

CRITICAL THINKING

12 *Defending* Which factor most contributed to the development of the Renaissance in Italy? Defend your answer with logical reasoning.

13 *Making Inferences* Why do you think the florin, the gold coin of Florence, helped to make the city a center for trade?

14 *Contrasting* Contrast Martin Luther's view of indulgences with the view of the Catholic Church.

15 *Determining Cause and Effect* What effect did Luther's rebellion against the Pope have on German peasants? What was the end result?

16 *Sequencing* How did King Ferdinand and Queen Isabella respond to those people in Spain who were not Catholic? List in sequence the steps they took against these non-Catholics.

17 *Drawing Conclusions* What effect did the Reformation have on the development of the American colonies?

18 *Speculating* Gutenberg first printed with moveable type in 1440, which was early in the Renaissance. Do you think the Renaissance might have developed differently if moveable type had not been used until the 1550s? Give reasons for your answer.

19 *Making Decisions* You are a writer during the Renaissance. Would you choose to write in classical Latin or in the vernacular? Explain your answer.

20 *Making Generalizations* If you lived in southern France in the mid-1500s, what religion would you most likely follow? Explain your answer.

Need Extra Help?

If You've Missed Question	**1**	**2**	**3**	**4**	**5**	**6**	**7**	**8**	**9**	**10**	**11**	**12**	**13**	**14**	**15**	**16**	**17**	**18**	**19**	**20**
Review Lesson	1,2, 3,4	1	1	1	2	2	2	3	3	4	4	1	1	3	3	4	3	2	2	4

DBQ SHORT RESPONSE

" '*I would not believe a land could have been so despoiled [looted] had I not seen it with my own eyes,' reported the Swedish general Mortaigne ... Marburg, which had been occupied 11 times, had lost half its population by 1648. When ... imperial troops finally sacked [raided] ... Magdeburg in 1631, it is estimated that only 5,000 of its 30,000 inhabitants survived ...*"

—from *Europe's Tragedy: A History of the Thirty Years' War*, by Peter H. Wilson

21 How did the Thirty Years' War affect the people of Marburg?

22 What does the statement from the Swedish general add to the description?

EXTENDED RESPONSE

23 *Narrative* You live in a village where people oppose the sale of indulgences. Write a letter to a friend in Rome and describe how people in your village feel about indulgences.

STANDARDIZED TEST PRACTICE

DBQ ANALYZING DOCUMENTS

24 *Summarizing* Martin Luther's Ninety-Five Theses included the following:

21. *Therefore those [supporters] of indulgences are in error, who say that by the pope's indulgences a man is freed from every penalty, ...*

36. *Every truly repentant Christian has a right to full remission of penalty [forgiveness] and guilt, even without letters of pardon.*

—from "Disputation of Doctor Martin Luther on the Power and Efficacy of Indulgences," by Martin Luther, 1517

Which statement best summarizes Martin Luther's opinion?

A. Christians can be forgiven without indulgences.

B. Letters of pardon may be given by mistake.

C. All true Christians may receive letters of pardon.

D. Only the pope's indulgences are effective.

25 *Making Inferences* What do Luther's statements imply about forgiveness?

A. A pope can forgive only certain sins.

B. Forgiveness is available to all sinners.

C. Sinners should ask a priest for forgiveness.

D. All sinners will receive letters of pardon if they ask.

Need Extra Help?

If You've Missed Question	**21**	**22**	**23**	**24**	**25**
Review Lesson	4	4	3, 4	3	3

◀ *The first voyage of Columbus in 1492 resulted in dramatic changes throughout the Americas, Europe, and the world.*

1400 TO 1700

Age of Exploration and Trade

THE STORY MATTERS ...

Christopher Columbus lived in Genoa, Italy. He joined the Portuguese merchant marine and became a sailor. On trading voyages to Africa, he learned about navigation and wind currents. Columbus believed that if he sailed west, he would eventually reach Asia. He tried to convince various European rulers to help him test his idea.

Finally, Queen Isabella of Spain decided that Columbus could win glory and wealth for Spain. She and her husband, Ferdinand, supplied money for his voyage. When Columbus reached the Americas in 1492, he believed he had reached Asia. Instead, Columbus had opened up the Americas to Europeans.

ESSENTIAL QUESTIONS

- How does technology change the way people live?
- Why do civilizations rise and fall?
- Why do people make economic choices?

Place & Time: Age of Exploration and Trade
1400 to 1700

In order to have direct access to Asia, Europeans wanted to find a water route that would bypass the Middle East. Using the new technology of the time, they searched for a southern route around Africa. In time, Europeans sailed across the Atlantic Ocean and encountered the Americas.

Step Into the Place

MAP FOCUS While searching for a new trade route to East Asia, Europeans came upon other parts of the world.

1 LOCATION In which directions did Europeans explore?

2 PLACE Why did European explorers find the Americas first instead of Asia?

3 MOVEMENT What did Magellan's crew achieve, according to the map? What did that show to others about the world?

4 CRITICAL THINKING
Drawing Conclusions How did the search for a new trade route to Asia affect the exploration of the Americas?

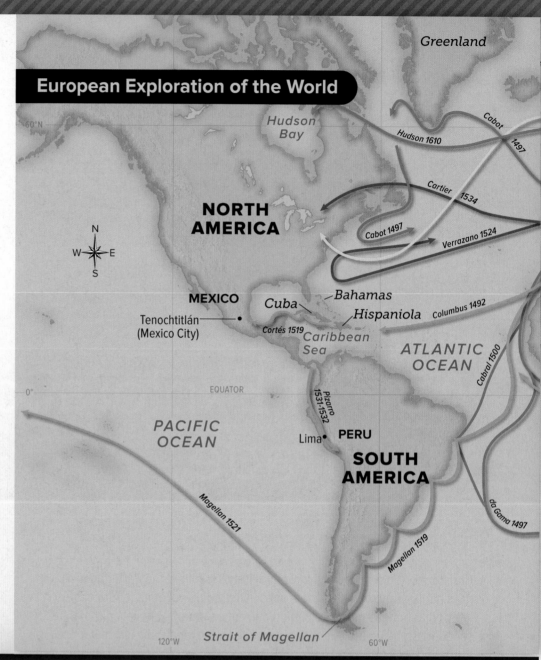

European Exploration of the World

Step Into the Time

TIME LINE Choose two events from the time line. Write a paragraph that explains the gap in time between related events.

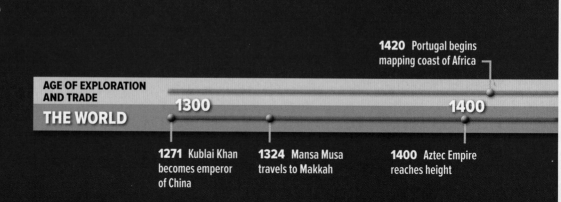

1420 Portugal begins mapping coast of Africa

AGE OF EXPLORATION AND TRADE

THE WORLD

1300

1400

1271 Kublai Khan becomes emperor of China

1324 Mansa Musa travels to Makkah

1400 Aztec Empire reaches height

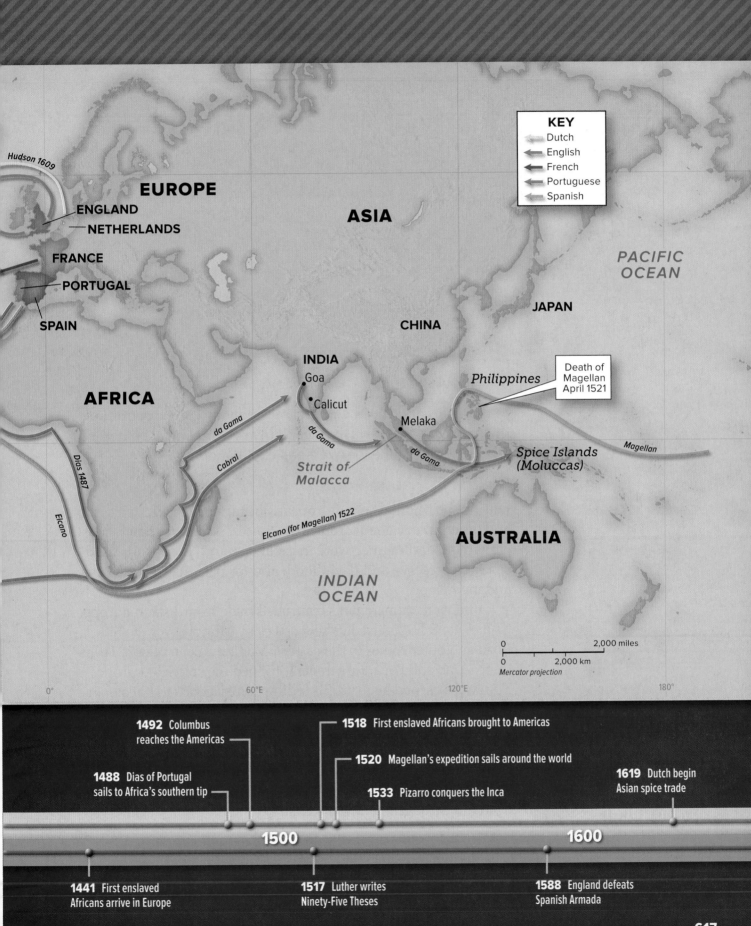

KEY
- Dutch
- English
- French
- Portuguese
- Spanish

Hudson 1609

EUROPE
— ENGLAND
— NETHERLANDS
FRANCE
— PORTUGAL
SPAIN

ASIA

PACIFIC OCEAN

JAPAN

CHINA

INDIA
Goa
• Calicut

AFRICA

da Gama

da Gama

Cabral

Melaka

da Gama

Philippines

Death of Magellan April 1521

Spice Islands (Moluccas)

Magellan

Dias 1487

Strait of Malacca

Elcano

Elcano (for Magellan) 1522

AUSTRALIA

INDIAN OCEAN

0   2,000 miles
0   2,000 km
Mercator projection

0°   60°E   120°E   180°

1492 Columbus reaches the Americas

1518 First enslaved Africans brought to Americas

1520 Magellan's expedition sails around the world

1488 Dias of Portugal sails to Africa's southern tip

1533 Pizarro conquers the Inca

1619 Dutch begin Asian spice trade

1500

1600

1441 First enslaved Africans arrive in Europe

1517 Luther writes Ninety-Five Theses

1588 England defeats Spanish Armada

LESSON 1
The Age of Exploration

• How does technology change the way people live?

IT MATTERS BECAUSE
The demand for goods from Asia as well as advances in technology helped start Europe's age of exploration.

Europe Gets Ready to Explore

GUIDING QUESTION *Why did Europeans begin to explore the world?*

In the 1400s and 1500s, Europeans gradually gained control of the Americas and parts of Asia. Many events came together to create the right time for **overseas** exploration.

Search for Trade Routes

During the Middle Ages, Europeans began to buy silks, spices, and other luxury goods from Asia. Spices, such as pepper, cinnamon, and nutmeg were in great demand. Europeans used spices to preserve and flavor food, and for perfumes, cosmetics, and medicine.

A network of merchants controlled trade from Asia to Europe. Chinese and Indian traders sent spices by caravan over the Silk Road and other routes to the eastern Mediterranean region. From there, Arab and Byzantine traders shipped the spices to Europe. The Arabs earned huge profits selling luxury goods to Italian merchants. The Italians then sold the products to other Europeans.

Political changes eventually disrupted this trading network. However, merchants knew that if they could get goods directly and cheaply, they could make more profits. Also, if Europeans could reach Asia by sea, then they would not have to travel overland through the Middle East.

Reading**HELP**DESK

Taking Notes: *Identifying*
Use a diagram like the one shown here to list the different Europeans who explored Asia and the Americas.

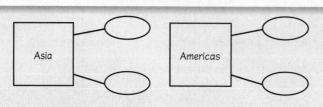

Content Vocabulary
• **circumnavigate**
• **conquistadors**

Technology and Exploration

By the 1400s, a number of technological inventions became available to European explorers. These inventions helped them navigate vast oceans. Europeans learned about the astrolabe (AS·truh·layb) and the compass from the Arabs. The astrolabe was an ancient Greek instrument that was used to find latitude. Sailors used the compass to help determine the direction in which they were sailing.

European mapmakers also improved their skills. During the late Middle Ages, most educated Europeans were aware that the earth was round. The only maps that were available, however, were of Europe and the Mediterranean region. That changed during the Renaissance when people began to study ancient maps and books.

Europeans rediscovered the work of Ptolemy (TAH·luh·mee), a Greek geographer. Ptolemy had drawn maps of the world for his book, *Geography*. He recorded the latitude and longitude of over 8,000 locations. With the invention of the printing press, accurate maps became readily available to sailors and explorers.

European mapmakers also learned about the Indian Ocean by studying the works of the Arab geographer al-Idrisi (ehl-ah·DREE·see). Many Europeans concluded that sailing around Africa was the best way to get to Asia.

In addition, shipbuilders improved ships by using triangular sails developed by Arab traders. With these sails and other improvements, ships could now go in nearly every direction no matter where the wind blew.

Rise of Strong Kingdoms

Even with new sailing skills and tools, exploration was still expensive and dangerous. But by the 1400s, the rise of towns and trade had strengthened Europe's governments. By the end of the 1400s, four strong kingdoms had emerged in Europe: Portugal, Spain, France, and England. All of these kingdoms had ports on the Atlantic Ocean—and all were eager to find a sea route to Asia.

✔ **PROGRESS CHECK**

Explaining How did new technology make it possible for Europeans to make long ocean voyages?

THEN

An astrolabe was made of brass or iron. It had discs with star maps and coordinate lines that rotated around a pin. The pin was in the position of the North Star. Today, navigation systems still look to the heavens. Computers use the positions of satellites in space to help drivers, pilots, sailors, and hikers know exactly where on Earth they are.

Now

▶ **CRITICAL THINKING**
Contrasting What do you think are some of the differences between using an astrolabe and using a computerized system?

(t)Hemera Technologies/Alamy; (b)©Charlie Nucci/Corbis

Academic Vocabulary

overseas across the ocean or sea

Vasco da Gama followed the coastline of Africa to reach India.

1 **LOCATION** What is the southernmost point that da Gama reached?

2 **CRITICAL THINKING**
Cause and Effect Why would sailors take a longer route along the coastline instead of the shortest distance between two points?

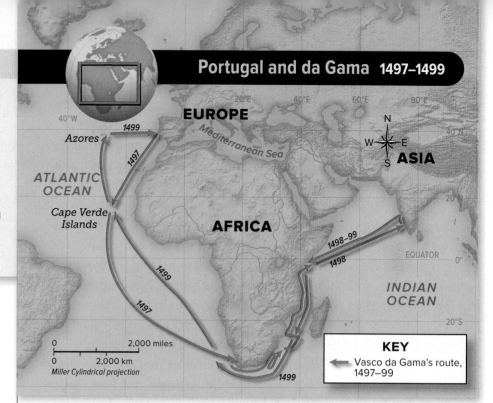

Portugal and da Gama 1497–1499

KEY
← Vasco da Gama's route, 1497–99

During Prince Henry's lifetime, Portuguese sailors explored only about half of the west coast of Africa. Through Henry's efforts, other rulers knew that trade—and gold—could finance further exploration.

► **CRITICAL THINKING**
Drawing Conclusions How did Prince Henry contribute to European exploration?

Early Voyages of Discovery

GUIDING QUESTION *Which leaders were responsible for European exploration of the world?*

During the early 1400s, England and France were still at war with each other, and Spain was still fighting the Muslims. This let Portugal take the lead in exploring new trade routes to Asia.

Portugal Leads the Way

Prince Henry of Portugal became known as "Henry the Navigator," even though he had never made an ocean voyage. Henry was eager for Portugal to explore the world, and he paid for many voyages of exploration. About 1420, Henry's adventurers sailed along Africa's west coast, mapping its features. They **obtained** gold from trade with African kingdoms. The explorers also traveled west into the Atlantic Ocean, where they seized the Azores (AY·zawrz), Madeira (muh·DIHR·uh), and Cape Verde (VUHRD) islands.

In 1488, the Portuguese explorer Bartolomeu Dias (bahr·tuh·luh·MEH·uh DEE·ahsh) sailed to the southern tip of Africa. Nine years later, Vasco da Gama (VAHS·koh dah GAM·uh) rounded the tip of Africa and landed on India's southwest coast. Europeans had at last found a water route to Asia.

©Bettmann/Corbis

ReadingHELPDESK

Academic Vocabulary

obtain to take possession of

The First Voyage of Columbus

While the Portuguese explored Africa's western coast, an Italian navigator named Christopher Columbus formed a bold plan to reach Asia. He would sail west across the Atlantic Ocean.

For years, Columbus had tried to convince various European rulers to pay for a voyage of exploration. Finally, in 1492, Ferdinand and Isabella of Spain agreed to support him. Earlier that year, the Spanish monarchs had defeated the Muslims in Spain. They were now able to pay for voyages seeking new trade routes.

In August 1492, Columbus sailed west from Spain with three ships: the Santa María, the Niña, and the Pinta. As the weeks passed without sight of land, the sailors grew frightened. They wanted Columbus to sail back to Europe. Finally, the expedition sighted land. Columbus and his crew went ashore on San Salvador (sahn SAHL·vuh·dawr), an island in the Caribbean Sea.

Columbus claimed the island of San Salvador for Spain. He then traveled farther west in the Caribbean Sea. Eventually, his ships reached and explored the islands of Cuba and Hispaniola (hihs·puh·NYOH·luh). Today, the countries of Haiti and the Dominican Republic are located on the island of Hispaniola. Columbus began trading with the Taino (TEYE·noh) people.

INFOGRAPHIC

Columbus's flagship, the Santa María, was larger and slower than the other two ships on the voyage

1 TIME What do the details of the ship reveal about the skills sailors at this time would need?

2 CRITICAL THINKING
Making Generalizations
Make a generalization about the hardships the crew probably faced on the long journey.

THE SANTA MARÍA

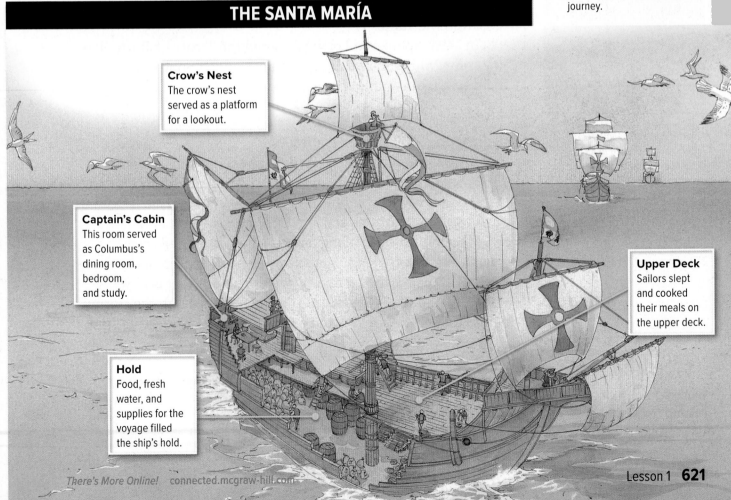

Crow's Nest
The crow's nest served as a platform for a lookout.

Captain's Cabin
This room served as Columbus's dining room, bedroom, and study.

Upper Deck
Sailors slept and cooked their meals on the upper deck.

Hold
Food, fresh water, and supplies for the voyage filled the ship's hold.

The Taino were the island's Native American people. Columbus returned to Spain with colorful parrots, some gold and spices, and several Taino people as proof of his discovery.

Columbus, however, believed that he had been exploring the coast of Asia. He never realized that he had actually arrived in the Americas. It was not until 1502 that another Italian explorer, Amerigo Vespucci (ahm·uh·REE·goh veh·SPOO·chee), became convinced that Columbus had discovered a "new world." In 1507, early map makers labeled what is now the South American continent with the name *America*. Later, the name was applied to North America as well.

Spanish Conquerors

Columbus's success pleased the Spanish monarchs. Eager investors urgently, or quickly, organized a second return voyage. Columbus set out again in 1493. On this voyage, he took soldiers with him to conquer the people of these new lands. In November, the Spanish landed on Hispaniola.

For the first time, the Taino saw the **conquistadors** (kahn·KEES·tuh·dawrz), the soldier-explorers that Spain sent to the Americas. The Taino became frightened by what they witnessed. Men in armor rode on powerful horses, with snarling dogs running alongside them. In a display of might, the soldiers fired guns that shot out flames and lead balls. The conquistadors claimed Hispaniola for Spain, and then they enslaved the Taino.

In 1494, Spain and Portugal signed the Treaty of Tordesillas (tawr·day·SEE·yahs). This agreement divided South America between Spain and Portugal.

Voyage of Magellan

During the 1500s, Spain continued to explore the Americas, but it was still interested in finding a western route to Asia. In 1518, Spain hired Ferdinand Magellan (muh·JEH·luhn) for an exploration voyage. Sailing west from Spain, Magellan's **primary** goal was to sail around the Americas and then on to Asia.

Magellan traveled along South America's eastern coast, searching for a route to Asia. Near the southern tip of the continent, he reached a narrow water passage that is now called the Strait of Magellan. After passing through the stormy strait, the expedition entered a vast sea. It was so peaceful that Magellan named the sea the Pacific Ocean.

Amerigo Vespucci, explorer of the Americas, is believed to have influenced the naming of these lands.

©Stefano Bianchetti/Corbis

ReadingHELPDESK

conquistadors Spanish soldiers who conquered people in other lands
circumnavigate to go completely around something, such as the world

Academic Vocabulary

primary most important; first

Magellan then sailed west. Water and food ran out, and the crew had to eat leather, sawdust, and rats. Some sailors died. Finally, after four months at sea, the expedition reached the present-day Philippines. There, Magellan was killed in a battle between local groups. The remaining crew members continued west across the Indian Ocean, around Africa, and back to Spain. They became the first known people to **circumnavigate** (suhr·kuhm·NAV·uh·GAYT), or sail around, the world.

Early French and English Explorers

The Portuguese successes led England and France to begin their own overseas exploration. In 1497, Englishman John Cabot (KA·buht) explored the North American coasts of Newfoundland and Nova Scotia. He was unsuccessful in finding a waterway to Asia.

In 1524, France sent Giovanni da Verrazano (joh·VAH·nee dah ver·uh·ZAH·noh) to find a northern route to Asia. Verrazano explored and mapped much of the eastern coast of North America, but he did not find a route to Asia. In 1534, the French navigator Jacques Cartier (ZHAHK kahr·TYAY) sailed inland along the St. Lawrence River to present-day Montreal. Cartier claimed much of eastern Canada for France.

After these early expeditions, France and England had to focus their attention on religious conflicts and civil wars in their own countries. By the early 1600s, these countries renewed their overseas explorations. This time, the French and English began to establish their own settlements in the Americas. Since most of Spain and Portugal's territories were in South America, Mexico, and the Caribbean, France and England began to establish colonies in North America.

✔ **PROGRESS CHECK**

Sequencing Why was it important for the explorers of the Americas to use information they learned from earlier explorers?

Thinking Like a
HISTORIAN

Predicting Consequences

Columbus was almost out of supplies when he reached land. Research how Columbus planned for his trip. What supplies did he take, and why? Then think about how his trip would be different today. What supplies would he take with him on a modern first voyage? Use library and Internet resources for your research. Then report your findings and predictions to your class. For more information about making predictions, read the chapter *What Does a Historian Do?*

Magellan, sailing for Spain, did not live to complete his voyage around the world.

LESSON 1 REVIEW

Review Vocabulary

1. How might sailors *circumnavigate* an island?

Answer the Guiding Questions

2. *Explaining* What prevented Europeans from exploring the world sooner, during the Middle Ages?

3. *Differentiating* Why did Portugal begin exploring before France, England, or Spain did?

4. *Identifying* Which European leaders most encouraged exploration of the world?

5. *Contrasting* How did the second voyage of Columbus differ from the first?

6. **NARRATIVE** The crew of Magellan's voyage became the first people to sail all the way around the world. You are a crew member. Write a diary entry expressing your feelings after sailing around the world.

LESSON 2

Spain's Conquests in the Americas

ESSENTIAL QUESTION

• Why do civilizations rise and fall?

IT MATTERS BECAUSE

The Spanish conquest of Central and South America remains a dominant influence in the cultures and customs of these areas.

The Spanish Conquer Mexico

GUIDING QUESTION *How did Spain conquer Mexico?*

The voyages of Christopher Columbus inspired many poor Spanish nobles to become conquistadors. Their goal was to travel to the Americas and seek wealth. Nineteen-year-old Hernán Cortés (ehr·NAHN kawr·TEHZ) was one of these nobles. In 1504, he sailed to Hispaniola. Eleven years later, he took part in Spain's invasion of Cuba.

Cortés Arrives in Mexico

While Cortés was in Cuba, he heard stories of Mexico's riches and the powerful Aztec Empire. In 1519, Cortés traveled to Mexico in search of gold and glory. He arrived near present-day Veracruz (vehr·uh·KROOZ) with about 508 soldiers, 100 sailors, 16 horses, and 14 cannons. How could such a small army expect to defeat the mighty Aztec?

Cortés used his army's guns and horses to frighten Native Americans. In a display of power, he forced thousands of them to surrender. Cortés also **relied** on a Maya woman named Malintzin (mah·LIHNT·suhn) for information about the Aztec.

Reading**HELP**DESK

Taking Notes: *Summarizing*

Use a chart like this one to describe the methods used by Hernán Cortés and Francisco Pizarro to conquer the people of Central and South America.

Hernán Cortés	Francisco Pizarro

Content Vocabulary

• **allies**   • **ambush**
• **smallpox**   • **hostage**

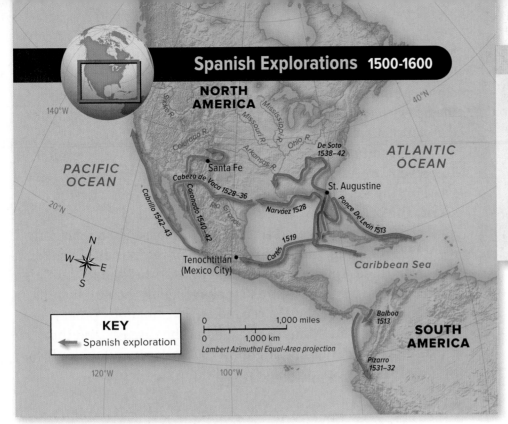

Spanish Explorations 1500-1600

NORTH AMERICA

PACIFIC OCEAN

ATLANTIC OCEAN

Santa Fe

Shake R.

Missouri R.

Colorado R.

Arkansas R.

Ohio R.

Mississippi R.

De Soto 1538–42

Cabeza de Vaca 1528–36

Coronado 1540–42

Rio Grande

Cabrillo 1542–43

Narváez 1528

Ponce De León 1513

St. Augustine

1519

Cortés

Tenochtitlán (Mexico City)

Caribbean Sea

Balboa 1513

SOUTH AMERICA

Pizarro 1531–32

140°W 120°W 100°W 20°N 40°N

KEY

⬅ Spanish exploration

0 _____ 1,000 miles
0 _____ 1,000 km
Lambert Azimuthal Equal-Area projection

GEOGRAPHY CONNECTION

Spanish conquistadors explored during the 1500s.

1 **LOCATION** What is the northernmost point the Spanish explorers reached?

2 **CRITICAL THINKING** *Cause and Effect* What part of the world was affected by the Spanish conquests the most?

Malintzin spoke with Cortés through a Spanish translator who knew Mayan. She told Cortés that many people in her land resented the Aztec rulers. One reason for their anger was the Aztec practice of human sacrifices. Most often to please their gods, the Aztec killed people whom they had captured in war. Malintzin believed that people who were conquered by the Aztec would help Cortés. Malintzin helped Cortés find **allies** (AL·leyes), or other groups willing to battle the Aztec.

Finally, another factor that helped Cortés defeat the Aztec was an invisible ally—germs that carried diseases such as the measles and **smallpox**. These diseases would eventually kill more Aztec people than Spanish weapons would.

Cortés Defeats the Aztec

The Spanish traveled hundreds of miles inland to reach Tenochtitlán (TAY·NAWCH·teet·LAHN), the Aztec capital. Messengers reported their every move to the Aztec ruler, Montezuma II (MAHN·tuh·ZOO·muh). The Aztec believed in a light-skinned god named Quetzalcoatl (KWEHT·zuhl·kuh·WAH·tuhl). According to Aztec legend, this god, who opposed the practice of human sacrifice, had sailed away long ago but had promised to return someday to reclaim his land.

Montezuma II was the ninth Aztec emperor to rule the region of present-day Mexico.

©The Art Archive/Corbis

allies those who support each other for some common purpose

smallpox a disease that causes a high fever and often death

Academic Vocabulary

rely to depend on; to count on for help

Hernán Cortés (1485–1547)

Assigned to lead troops in Mexico, Hernán Cortés forced his men to exercise and be disciplined. His well-trained forces acted quickly allowing Cortés to use their small numbers to outmaneuver a much larger Aztec force. He had also burned his ships so his men knew they had only one option—victory. After conquering Mexico, Cortés left in 1524 to explore Honduras. His two-year absence led to chaos in Mexico and ruined his reputation in Spain. He died in 1540, in debt and haunted by scandals.

▶ **CRITICAL THINKING**
Making Inferences What does it tell you about Cortés that he continued exploring even though he had conquered a great nation?

Montezuma was afraid Cortés was this god returning home. He was afraid to attack the Spanish right away. As Cortés marched closer, Montezuma changed his mind and decided to ambush the Spanish troops. Cortés, however, had already learned about the planned **ambush**.

In November 1519, Cortés took control of the Aztec capital. To prevent an Aztec uprising, Cortés took Montezuma **hostage** (HAHS·tihj), or prisoner. He then ordered the Aztec to stop sacrificing people.

Cortés's orders angered the Aztec, who planned a rebellion. Fighting broke out, and the Spanish killed thousands of Aztec. However, there were far more Aztec, and Cortés had to fight his way out of the city. The Spanish took refuge in the nearby hills.

While Cortés prepared a second attack, smallpox broke out in Tenochtitlán. Many Aztec died of the disease, and the remaining Aztec could not fight off the Spanish and their allies. In June 1521, the Spanish destroyed the Aztec capital.

✔ PROGRESS CHECK

Explaining Why did the Aztec allow Cortés to remain in their lands?

Spain Conquers Peru

GUIDING QUESTION *How did Spanish conquistadors conquer the Inca?*

Like Cortés, Vasco Núñez de Balboa (VAHS·koh NOON·yays day bal·BOH·uh) also sailed to the Americas. In 1513, he led a band of soldiers across the mountains of present-day Panama to look for a golden empire.

Balboa found a sea, known today as the Pacific Ocean, but he never found the golden empire he was looking for. A jealous Spanish official in Panama falsely charged Balboa with treason and had him beheaded.

Francisco Pizarro (fruhn·SIHS·koh puh·ZAHR·oh) had served as one of Balboa's soldiers. After Balboa was executed, Pizarro continued the search for gold. Even though Pizarro could not even write his own name, he knew how to fight. He longed to find the empire that Balboa had sought.

Pizarro Meets the Inca

The Inca ruled the empire that Balboa and Pizarro wanted to conquer. By the 1530s, the powerful Inca Empire had become **considerably** weaker. Despite their weaknesses, the Inca did

---

Reading HELP DESK

ambush a surprise attack

hostage someone held against his or her will in exchange for something

Academic Vocabulary

considerable large in size, quantity, or quality
global involving the entire Earth

not fear Pizarro and his troops. Pizarro had only 168 soldiers, one cannon, and 27 horses compared to the Inca army's 30,000 warriors. Still, Pizarro and his small army moved to attack the Inca homeland. In late 1532, Pizarro decided on a bold plan.

The Inca Fall

Spanish messengers invited the Inca ruler Atahualpa (ah•tuh•WAHL•puh) to meet with Pizarro. Atahualpa agreed and came to the meeting with just 4,000 unarmed bodyguards. At their meeting, Pizarro demanded that Atahualpa give up his gods. The emperor laughed at this, and Pizarro ordered an attack. The Spanish fired into the unarmed Inca crowd. Pizarro dragged Atahualpa from the battlefield.

Atahualpa tried to buy his freedom. He offered Pizarro an entire room full of gold and silver. Pizarro immediately accepted Atahualpa's offer. Atahualpa had his people bring Pizarro the precious metals. Pizarro, however, did not set Atahualpa free. Instead, he charged the emperor with plotting a rebellion, worshipping false gods, and other crimes. In 1533, a military court found the emperor guilty and sentenced him to death.

Pizarro betrayed Atahualpa. He set his soldiers to attack the Inca bodyguards.

The Spanish king rewarded Pizarro by making him governor of Peru. Pizarro chose a new emperor for the Inca, who had to follow Pizarro's orders. Still, the Spanish could not gain complete control of the Inca Empire. Even after Pizarro died in 1541, the Spanish were still fighting Inca rebels. Nonetheless, the conquest of Peru opened most of South America to Spanish rule. Spain would create the world's first **global** empire.

✓ PROGRESS CHECK

Evaluating How successful were the efforts of Atahualpa to free himself from Pizarro?

LESSON 2 REVIEW

Review Vocabulary

1. How did Pizarro's act of taking Atahualpa *hostage* force the Inca to do what Pizarro wanted?

Answer the Guiding Questions

2. *Describing* Describe the troops and weapons that Hernán Cortés brought to Mexico.

3. *Explaining* What factors helped Cortés defeat the Aztec?

4. *Inferring* Why might Núñez de Balboa have believed that his expedition in Panama was a failure?

5. *Differentiating* How were the methods used by Cortés and Pizarro to conquer Native Americans different?

6. **INFORMATIVE/EXPLANATORY** Why do you think the Spanish conquered the Aztec and the Inca instead of trading with them for gold and other resources? Write a paragraph that explains your reasons.

Exploration and Worldwide Trade

• Why do people make economic choices?

IT MATTERS BECAUSE

European nations established colonies that produced great wealth, changing the Americas and other conquered lands forever.

Settling the Americas

GUIDING QUESTION *How did European nations build empires in the Americas?*

The Treaty of Tordesillas divided the Americas between Spain and Portugal. Other nations, however, did not accept this treaty. The Netherlands, France, and England soon joined Spain and Portugal in a race to gain wealth in new lands and to spread Christianity.

The Americas were the primary region where Europeans explored and established settlements. In the 1500s, the Spanish and the Portuguese had built empires in the Americas. Beginning in the 1600s, the French, English, and Dutch also began to establish their own settlements.

Spain's American Empire

By the 1600s, Spain's empire in the Americas had grown to include parts of North America and much of South America. The islands in the Caribbean Sea were also a part of this empire. Spanish rulers sent royal officials called viceroys to govern local areas. Councils of Spanish settlers also advised the viceroys.

The Spanish rulers set two goals for the colonists of their American empire: to bring wealth back to Spain and to convert Native Americans to Christianity. Spanish settlers grew crops of sugarcane on large farms known as **plantations** (plan·TAY·shuns).

Landowners also operated gold and silver mines. At the same time, Spanish priests established missions, or religious communities, to teach Christianity to the Native Americans.

Spain permitted its settlers to use Native American labor to work the plantations. The Spanish, however, enslaved and mistreated the Native Americans. Also, the Spanish settlers unknowingly brought contagious diseases with them. Millions of Native Americans died from illness during the first 50 years of the arrival of Europeans. As the number of Native Americans declined, more laborers were needed. To solve this problem, the Spanish brought over enslaved Africans to work on the plantations and in the mines. In time, this mingling of Europeans, Native Americans, and Africans gave rise to a new **culture**.

Portuguese Brazil

In 1500, the Portuguese explorer Pedro Álvares Cabral (PAY·droh AHL·vahr·ihs kuh·BRAHL) arrived in the region of South America that is now Brazil. He claimed this territory for Portugal. Settlers in Brazil grew **cash crops** such as sugarcane, tobacco, coffee, and cotton. A cash crop is a crop that is grown in large quantities to be sold for profit. With the help of enslaved Africans, Brazil became one of Portugal's most profitable overseas territories.

The French in North America

The fur trade was one of the main reasons the French settled in North America. By the 1600s, beaver fur was very popular in Europe. The French hoped they would become wealthy if they set up fur trading posts in North America. In 1608, French merchants hired explorer Samuel de Champlain (sham·PLAYN) to help them obtain furs in New France, which today is much of Eastern Canada. Champlain set up a trading post named Quebec (kwih·BEHK). Quebec became the capital of New France.

Sugarcane is a tall grassy plant. Its pulpy fibers are processed to create sugar as a final product.

plantation a large estate or farm that used enslaved people or hired workers to grow and harvest crops

cash crops crops grown in large amounts to be sold for profit

Academic Vocabulary

culture the customs, learning, and art of a civilization

IMPORTANT EUROPEAN EXPLORERS

Christopher Columbus	Vasco da Gama	Ferdinand Magellan	Jacques Cartier	Henry Hudson
Voyages: 1492, 1493, 1498, 1502	**Voyage:** 1497–1499	**Voyage:** 1519–1522	**Voyages:** 1534, 1535, 1541	**Voyages:** 1607, 1608, 1609, 1610
First European to sail west searching for a water route to Asia	First European to sail around the south of Africa and reach India	Led the first expedition to sail completely around the world	Explored the St. Lawrence River	Explored the Hudson River and Hudson Bay

INFOGRAPHIC

For more than a hundred years, explorers searched for new trade routes.

1 **TIME** Who was the earliest European explorer?

2 **CRITICAL THINKING** *Cause and Effect* Which explorer gave his name to an important American river?

During the 1660s, the French king began sending political and military officials to rule New France. Jesuit and other Catholic missionaries also arrived. They taught Christianity to the Native Americans. The Native Americans called the Jesuits "Black Robes" because of the black clothes they wore.

From Quebec, French explorers, fur trappers, and missionaries spread out into the central part of New France. In 1673, the explorers Jacques Marquette (mar·KET) and Louis Joliet (joh·lee·EHT) reached the Mississippi River. Just nine years later, the French explorer La Salle (luh SAL) traveled south along the Mississippi to the Gulf of Mexico. He named the region Louisiana in honor of King Louis XIV. Like the Portuguese settlers, the French used enslaved Africans to work the fields.

England's Colonies in North America

During the early 1600s, England started to establish its own settlements in North America. The English government was interested in the natural **resources** from overseas territories.

English settlers sailed to North America for many reasons. Groups of merchants created settlements for trade. Others fled to North America to find religious freedom. Economic troubles in England also helped speed the growth of English settlements.

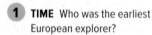

ReadingHELPDESK

Academic Vocabulary

resource a ready supply of something valuable

Reading Strategy: *Identifying Cause and Effect*

As you read, look for key words to help you identify cause and effect, such as "because" and "since." Read about the English colonies in North America. What were the conditions—causes—that sent settlers to the New World?

In 1606, a group of English merchants and nobles formed the Virginia Company. North America's first permanent English settlement was founded with the Virginia Company's support in 1607. The founders named it Jamestown after King James I. It was the first settlement in the new territory called Virginia.

At first, the early settlers in Virginia could barely find enough food to survive. During the winters, many of them starved to death. Others were killed in clashes with Native Americans.

In the early years, the merchants and nobles who invested in the settlement did not make any money. Jamestown needed to develop an economic activity in order to become profitable. Settlers discovered that tobacco grew well in Virginia.

Crops to Sell

Tobacco was very popular in Europe in the 1600s. Soon, the English settlers were producing and shipping it back to England in large amounts. Tobacco became the first cash crop of the English settlements. Eventually, it was grown on large plantations that needed many workers. Once again, enslaved Africans were brought in to work the land.

Encouraged by its success in Virginia, England continued to establish settlements in North America that produced cash crops. South Carolina, for example, began growing rice and indigo, a dye-producing plant. The English established sugarcane plantations on Caribbean islands, such as Jamaica. Enslaved African people worked the lands on English plantations, as they did on French and Portuguese plantations.

Dutch Traders

Another European country, the Netherlands, was interested in overseas exploration and settlement. The Netherlands won its independence from Spain in the late 1500s. Its people, known as the Dutch, believed that trade was key to their survival.

The 1600s were a golden age for the Netherlands. Dutch ships were efficient. Compared with ships from other European countries, Dutch ships could transport more goods and be operated by smaller crews.

Dutch trading ships sailed to the southern tip of Africa to the islands of Southeast Asia and soon set out for North America. An English navigator named Henry Hudson claimed land for the Dutch along the Atlantic coast of North America. In 1621, Dutch traders established settlements in the Americas, including one on Manhattan Island that they called New Amsterdam. Today, this region is part of New York City.

✔ **PROGRESS CHECK**

Summarizing Why did European colonists bring enslaved Africans to their plantations in the Americas?

There's More Online! connected.mcgraw-hill.com

> ### Connections to
> # TODAY
> **Blending Languages**
>
> Spanish and Portuguese settlers brought their languages to the Americas. Over time, Native Americans combined elements of Spanish and Portuguese with their own languages. Native American words such as "chocolate" and "coyote—words that we still use today—migrated into Spanish and later English. Another term—Hispanic—was originally used to describe a Spanish person in the Americas.

King James I (top) approved the creation of the Virginia Company. In 1619, the company created the House of Burgesses, America's first legislature. This seal is the king's official stamp put on important documents.

European Trade in Asia c. 1700

KEY
Port city controlled by:
● England   ● Portugal
● France   ● Spain
● Netherlands

GEOGRAPHY CONNECTION

Sailing east from India, European sailors pushed into other areas of Asia.

1 **PLACE** Which countries had trading posts on the South China Sea?

2 **CRITICAL THINKING** *Cause and Effect* Why would the port cities shown on this map develop differently over time as compared to other cities in Asia?

World Trade Changes

GUIDING QUESTION *How did Europe's merchants change the world trade system?*

As Europeans created empires, profitable trade developed between their homelands and their overseas settlements. As a result, Europe's economy expanded. By the 1600s, European nations were competing for markets and trade goods.

What Is Mercantilism?

Spain and Portugal took advantage of the gold and silver they gained from their empires. Other European countries wanted to do the same. This led to the theory of **mercantilism** (MUHR· kuhn·TEE·lih·zuhm). The key idea of mercantilism is that a country's power depends on its wealth. Countries can increase their wealth by owning more gold and silver. What is the best way for a country to get more gold and silver? According to mercantilism, a country must export, or sell to other countries, more goods than it imports, or buys from other countries.

According to mercantilism, countries should establish colonies. A colony is a settlement of people living in a territory controlled by their home country. Colonists provide raw materials that are not found or made in the home country.

Reading**HELP**DESK

mercantilism an economic theory that depends on a greater amount of exports than imports in order to increase a country's supply of gold and silver

These materials are then shipped to the home country. In the home country, the raw materials are used to manufacture goods so that the home country does not have to buy these goods from other countries.

Europeans established trading posts and colonies in Asia and North America. By the end of the 1500s, Spain had a colony in the Philippines. In the 1600s, English and French merchants arrived in India. They began trading with the people there. In 1619, the Dutch built a fort on the island of Java, in what is now Indonesia. The Dutch became so powerful that they pushed the Portuguese out of the spice trade.

Guns and powerful ships helped Europeans defeat Arab fleets and Indian armies. Across Asia, Europeans forced local rulers to open their lands to trade. The arrival of the Europeans in Japan caused a dramatic change in that society. A new Japanese shogun used European-made guns and cannons to dominate his enemies. He was finally able to defeat the feudal lords and the daimyo and reunite Japan.

Creating Joint-Stock Companies

Europeans found that paying for overseas trading voyages was expensive. In the 1600s, however, Europeans developed new business **methods**. Historians call this the Commercial Revolution. **Commerce** (KAH·muhrs) is the buying and selling of goods in large amounts over long distances.

This type of commerce needed large amounts of money in order to be profitable. So, a new type of businessperson called an **entrepreneur** (AHN·truh·pruh·NUHR) emerged. Entrepreneurs **invest**, or put money into a project. Their goal is to make money from the success of the project.

As overseas trade increased in the 1600s, many projects were too large for one entrepreneur to pay for. If a voyage failed, for example, that individual would lose everything. As a result, groups of entrepreneurs began to form joint-stock companies. A joint-stock company is a business in which many people can invest. Groups or individuals, called investors, buy shares in the company. These shares are called stocks. By owning stock, investors would share the expenses, the risks—and the profits.

Henry Hudson lands in North America ready to establish trade with Native Americans. He was sent by the Netherlands to find a Northwest Passage to Asia.

▶ CRITICAL THINKING
Speculating What do you think Native Americans thought of Hudson and his crew?

©Bettmann/Corbis

---

commerce an exchange of goods; business
entrepreneur one who organizes, pays for, and takes on the risk of setting up a business

Academic Vocabulary
method a way of doing something; a process or procedure
invest to give money to a company in exchange for a return, or profit, on the money

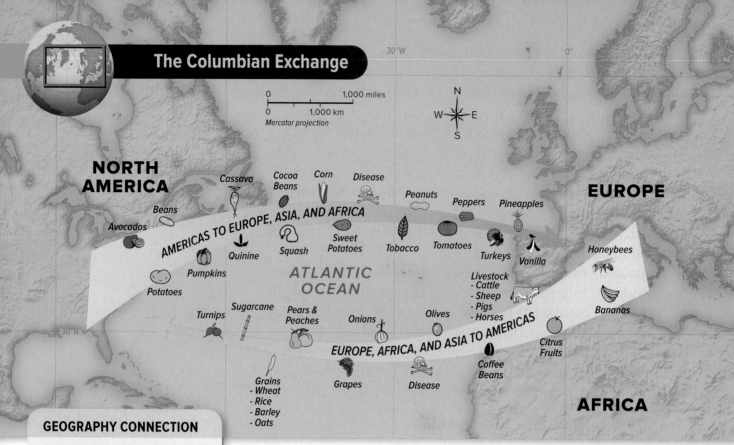

The Columbian Exchange

NORTH AMERICA

EUROPE

AFRICA

AMERICAS TO EUROPE, ASIA, AND AFRICA

EUROPE, AFRICA, AND ASIA TO AMERICAS

ATLANTIC OCEAN

0   1,000 miles
0   1,000 km
Mercator projection

Cassava
Cocoa Beans
Corn
Disease
Peanuts
Peppers
Pineapples
Beans
Avocados
Quinine
Squash
Sweet Potatoes
Tobacco
Tomatoes
Turkeys
Vanilla
Honeybees
Pumpkins
Livestock
- Cattle
- Sheep
- Pigs
- Horses
Potatoes
Bananas
Turnips
Sugarcane
Pears & Peaches
Onions
Olives
Citrus Fruits
Grains
- Wheat
- Rice
- Barley
- Oats
Grapes
Disease
Coffee Beans

GEOGRAPHY CONNECTION

Food items were exchanged between the Americas and Europe, Africa, and Asia.

1 IDENTIFY Where did sugarcane originate, and where was it sent?

2 CRITICAL THINKING
Cause and Effect Why were foods part of the exchange?

What Is a Cottage Industry?

By the 1600s, merchants began to believe that artisans and guilds charged too much for their goods. In addition, the merchants thought that these skilled workers did not make goods fast enough. To solve these problems, merchants began hiring peasants to make goods, especially wool cloth in their homes. This system became known as the **cottage industry** because the small houses where peasants lived and worked were called cottages.

✔ PROGRESS CHECK

Identifying Why did Europeans in the 1600s create joint-stock companies?

A Global Exchange

GUIDING QUESTION *How did trade change the world?*

As Europe's trade expanded, a global exchange of people, goods, technology, ideas—and even diseases—began. Historians call this transfer the Columbian Exchange, after Christopher Columbus. The Columbian Exchange **transformed** the economies of Europe, Africa, Asia, and the Americas.

cottage industry a system for making goods in workers' homes

Academic Vocabulary

transform to bring about a large and widespread change

Merchants introduced foods from the Americas to Europeans. Two of the most important crops were corn and potatoes. In Europe, these crops became essential to daily life. Corn was used to feed livestock, producing larger, healthier animals. This resulted in more meat, leather, and wool. Potatoes helped Europeans feed more people from their land.

Europeans acquired other foods from Native Americans, such as squash, beans, and tomatoes. Tomatoes greatly changed cooking in Italy, where tomato sauces became widely used. Chocolate was a popular food from Central America. By mixing chocolate with milk and sugar, Europeans made candy.

American settlers planted many European and Asian grains, such as wheat, oats, barley, rye, and rice. Coffee and tropical fruits, such as bananas, were brought to the Americas as well. Eventually, coffee and banana farms employed thousands of workers in Central America and South America.

Explorers and settlers also brought pigs, sheep, cattle, chickens, and horses to the Americas. Raising chickens changed the diet of many people in Central and South America.

The lives of Native Americans on the Great Plains changed when they acquired horses. Horses provided a faster way to travel. As a result, Native Americans became more efficient at hunting bison for food and at fighting enemies.

Europeans obtained sugarcane from Asia and began growing it in the Caribbean. This caused a migration, or movement of people. To plant and harvest the sugarcane, over time Europeans enslaved millions of Africans and moved them to the Americas.

The Columbian Exchange also spread diseases from one area to another. When Europeans arrived in America, they were carrying viruses that were new to Native Americans. These diseases were deadly and eventually killed millions.

Bananas—a huge cash crop—grow on plantations in tropical locations such as Central America.

☑ **PROGRESS CHECK**

Evaluating Was the Columbian Exchange a benefit or a problem for the Americas?

LESSON 3 REVIEW

Review Vocabulary

1. How does *mercantilism* benefit the homeland more than the colony?

Answer the Guiding Questions

2. *Explaining* Why was growing tobacco an important boost to help colonists trade?

3. *Describing* Why did the English establish settlements in North America?

4. *Explaining* Who receives the benefits and profits from a joint-stock company?

5. *Identifying* What was the Columbian Exchange?

6. **NARRATIVE** Write a paragraph describing how either Europeans or Native Americans might have reacted when they first tasted foods from another continent. Consider how chocolate, tomatoes, peanuts, and bananas must have puzzled people who were eating it for the first time.

Write your answers on a separate piece of paper.

1 **Exploring the Essential Question**

INFORMATIVE/EXPLANATORY When different cultures share technologies, the interchange can affect the lives of people on different continents. Write an expository essay about how sailing technologies led to changes in Europe and in the Americas.

2 **21st Century Skills**

CREATING A BLOG Create a blog to share your thoughts on exploration. Discuss your observations about the positive and negative effects of the first encounters between Europeans and Native Americans. To encourage an exchange of ideas with other bloggers, ask discussion questions about how these two civilizations saw their contact in very different ways. Your questions should require bloggers to support their opinions with examples.

3 **Thinking Like a Historian**

MAKING CONNECTIONS Create a diagram like the one shown here that traces the progress of European explorations. Start with the first attempts to seek a route to Asia by going around Africa to eventually sailing around the world.

Portuguese Begin Exploring African Coast

4 **GEOGRAPHY ACTIVITY**

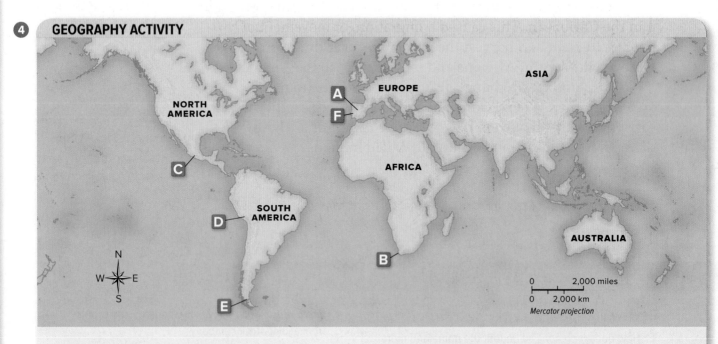

Locating Places

Match the letters on the map with the numbered places listed below.

1. Portugal
2. Aztec Empire
3. Inca Empire
4. Spain
5. Cape of Good Hope
6. Strait of Magellan

Directions: Write your answers on a separate piece of paper.

CHECKING FOR UNDERSTANDING

1 Define each of these terms as they relate to the Age of Exploration and Trade.

A. conquistadors
B. circumnavigate
C. plantation
D. cash crops
E. mercantilism
F. commerce
G. entrepreneur
H. cottage industry

REVIEW THE GUIDING QUESTIONS

2 *Explaining* How did the work of Arab scholars and inventors promote European exploration in the 1400s and 1500s?

3 *Naming* Which European country was the first to launch large-scale voyages of exploration?

4 *Summarizing* What common goals did Spanish, French, and English explorers share?

5 *Identifying* Which Native American empire was conquered by Francisco Pizarro?

6 *Describing* What advantages did Hernán Cortés use to help him defeat the Aztec?

7 *Stating* How did the Treaty of Tordesillas divide the Americas?

8 *Listing* Which cash crops did European settlers produce?

9 *Defining* What was mercantilism? What was the relationship between mercantilism and European colonization of the Americas?

10 *Explaining* Why did merchants form joint-stock companies and use cottage industries?

11 *Summarizing* What was the Columbian Exchange?

CRITICAL THINKING

12 *Speculating* What do you believe was the main motivation of overseas exploration in the 1400s and 1500s? Explain.

13 *Drawing Conclusions* Why did early European mapmakers name the New World after Amerigo Vespucci and not Christopher Columbus?

14 *Making Inferences* Why do you think Malintzin agreed to work with Hernán Cortés?

15 *Hypothesizing* How might the histories of Mexico and South America have been different had Native Americans been resistant to smallpox and other similar diseases?

16 *Speculating* Unlike the Spanish and Portuguese, the French did not enslave Native Americans. Speculate on some reasons why they did not.

17 *Defending* In your opinion, which country's colonization efforts most impacted Native Americans? Explain your answer.

18 *Theorizing* Why might colonists have disliked the economic theory of mercantilism?

19 *Evaluating* How did foods brought from the Americas through the Columbian Exchange benefit Europe? Which provided the greatest benefit? Explain.

20 *Making Generalizations* Why would a strong military benefit a country that supported a mercantilist economic policy?

Need Extra Help?

If You've Missed Question	**1**	**2**	**3**	**4**	**5**	**6**	**7**	**8**	**9**	**10**	**11**	**12**	**13**	**14**	**15**	**16**	**17**	**18**	**19**	**20**
Review Lesson	1, 2, 3	1	1	1	2	2	3	3	3	3	3	1	1	2	2	3	2,3	3	3	3

DBQ SHORT RESPONSE

Write your answers on a separate piece of paper.

"There are all kinds of green vegetables, ... fruits, ... honey and wax from bees ... .Different kinds of cotton thread of all colors in skeins [loose balls] are exposed for sale in one quarter of the market, which has the appearance of the silk-market at Granada; ... everything that can be found throughout the whole country is sold in the markets."

—from *The Second Letter to Charles V, 1520*, by Hernan Cortés

21 What can you tell about the economy of the Aztec empire from this description by Cortés?

22 What comparison does Cortés make to Granada, Spain?

EXTENDED RESPONSE

23 *Informative/Explanatory* Write a paragraph about how the Columbian Exchange presented advantages and disadvantages for Native Americans and Europeans.

STANDARDIZED TEST PRACTICE

DBQ ANALYZING DOCUMENTS

Drawing Conclusions Columbus wrote about meeting Native Americans:

"Thus they bartered [traded], like idiots, cotton and gold for fragments of bows, glasses, bottles, and jars; which I forbad[e] as being unjust, and myself gave them many beautiful ... articles which I had brought with me, taking nothing from them in return; I did this in order that ... I might induce [persuade] them to take an interest in ... delivering to us such things as they possessed in abundance, but which we greatly needed."

—Christopher Columbus, letter to Raphael Sanchez, March 14, 1493

24 Why did Columbus prevent his soldiers from trading items of little value with Native Americans?

A. to get more gold for himself

B. to encourage open and fair trading

C. to prevent any interchange between them

D. to avoid wasting their valuables on useless things

25 *Making Inferences* What were the "things as they possessed in abundance" which Columbus mentions?

A. bows and glasses

B. beautiful articles Columbus had brought

C. fragments of bottles and jars

D. gold and cotton

Need Extra Help?

If You've Missed Question	21	22	23	24	25
Review Lesson	2	2	3	1	1

◄ *Catherine II of Russia became known as Catherine the Great because she expanded her country's borders. This portrait hangs in the Museum of History in Moscow, Russia.*

1500 TO 1800

The Scientific Revolution and the Enlightenment

©The Art Archive/Corbis

THE STORY MATTERS ...

Catherine the Great ruled Russia from 1762 to 1796. Catherine was born a German princess, but at the age of fifteen she married Russian Grand Duke Peter. Soon her husband became the emperor of Russia. Peter, however, was a weak leader. In contrast, Catherine was intelligent and also ambitious. She wanted to rule Russia herself. She used military support to remove her husband from the throne. Soon afterward, he was assassinated.

As empress, Catherine the Great made Russia into a world power. She could be a harsh ruler, especially toward the peasants whom she made serfs. However, she also supported advances in the sciences and culture. Indeed, new ideas were sweeping across most of Europe. Many of them, however, challenged the idea of monarchy.

ESSENTIAL QUESTIONS

- How do new ideas change the way people live?
- How do governments change?

LESSON 1
The Scientific Revolution

LESSON 2
The Enlightenment

The Scientific Revolution and the Enlightenment began in Europe. Thinkers from various countries developed ideas about the world based on reason. These ideas gradually spread throughout Europe and beyond.

Step Into the Place

MAP FOCUS Some cities in Europe were centers for Enlightenment ideas. Many of these cities were national capitals. Monarchs ruled them and supported these ideas.

1 **LOCATION** What was the Enlightenment center of France?

2 **REGION** How many Enlightenment centers were located along a river or coast?

3 **MOVEMENT** Which Enlightenment center was the farthest away from central Europe?

4 **CRITICAL THINKING**
Analyzing Do you think the location of Enlightenment centers helped the spread of ideas? Explain.

Centers of Enlightenment 1785

IRELAND

North Sea

GREAT BRITAIN

NETHERLANDS

London

Amsterdam

ATLANTIC OCEAN

Paris

FRANCE

SWITZ

PORTUGAL

SPAIN

Mediterranean Sea

Step Into the Time

TIME LINE Choose an event from the time line for Europe, and write a paragraph that predicts the results of the event.

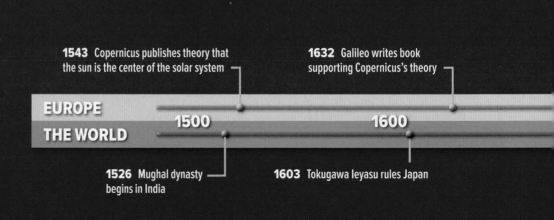

1543 Copernicus publishes theory that the sun is the center of the solar system

1632 Galileo writes book supporting Copernicus's theory

EUROPE

THE WORLD

1500

1600

1526 Mughal dynasty begins in India

1603 Tokugawa Ieyasu rules Japan

KEY

☆ Enlightenment Center

— Holy Roman Empire

0 — 250 miles
0 — 250 km

Lambert Conformal Conic projection

NORWAY

☆ Stockholm

SWEDEN

DENMARK

☆ Copenhagen

Baltic Sea

PRUSSIA

Berlin ☆

GERMAN STATES

☆ St. Petersburg

RUSSIA

POLAND-LITHUANIA

Vienna ☆

AUSTRIA

PAPAL STATES

SERBIA

OTTOMAN EMPIRE

Black Sea

1687 Newton publishes theory of gravity

1690 Locke writes that people have natural rights

1762 Rousseau claims people's will should govern

1785 Lavoisier proves that materials need oxygen to burn

1792 Wollstonecraft writes about equal rights for women

1700

1800

1644 Manchus invade China and establish Qing Dynasty

1722 Chinese emperor Kangxi dies after a 61-year reign

1754 French and Indian War begins

1776 American colonies declare independence

LESSON 1

The Scientific Revolution

ESSENTIAL QUESTION

• How do new ideas change the way people live?

IT MATTERS BECAUSE
The advances made during the Scientific Revolution laid the groundwork for modern science.

Early Science

GUIDING QUESTION *How were the scientific ideas of early thinkers passed on to later generations?*

During the Renaissance and the Age of Exploration, people developed new ways to learn about nature. However, humans have always shown an interest in the world around them. Thousands of years ago, people began watching plants and animals grow. Activities such as these represented the beginnings of science. Science is any organized study of the physical world. Scientists study the physical world to determine how things work.

The First Scientists

The people of ancient civilizations developed science to solve problems. They used mathematics to keep records. People who studied the movement of the stars developed astronomy. This science helped people keep time and decide when to plant crops.

The ancient Greeks developed a large amount of scientific information. They believed that reason was a way to analyze nature. Their studies helped them develop theories. A **theory** is an explanation for how or why something happens. Theories are based on what people can observe about a thing or event.

Reading**HELP**DESK

Taking Notes: *Categorizing*

Use a chart like this one to categorize the main advances of the Scientific Revolution concerning the universe or the human body.

Scientific Advances

Universe	Human Body

Content Vocabulary

• **geocentric**
• **Scientific Revolution**
• **heliocentric**

The ancient Greeks and Romans made many scientific advances. The Greek philosopher Aristotle (A • ruh • STAH • tuhl), for example, gathered facts about plants and animals. He then classified living things by arranging them into groups based on their similarities and differences. However, classical thinkers did not conduct scientific experiments. That means they did not test new ideas to find out whether they were true. Instead, they based their conclusions on "common sense," which led to many false beliefs. For instance, during Roman times, the Egyptian-born astronomer Ptolemy (TAH • luh • mee) stated that the sun and the planets moved around the Earth. His **geocentric** (JEE • oh • SEHN • trihk), or Earth-centered, theory was accepted in Europe for more than 1,400 years.

Medieval Science

During the Middle Ages, most Europeans were interested in religious ideas. Few people were interested in studying nature. Their ideas about science were based mostly on ancient classical writings. They did not think it was necessary to research the facts and draw their own conclusions. Many of the classical writings were poorly preserved. As people wrote out copies of the old texts, they sometimes made errors that changed the information.

At the same time, Arabs and Jews in the Islamic empire preserved Greek and Roman science. They copied many Greek and Roman works into Arabic. They also came into contact with the Indian system of numbers that is used today. This system of numbers is now called Indian-Arabic.

Arab and Jewish scientists made their own advances in mathematics, astronomy, and medicine. Even with these achievements, scientists in the Islamic world did not conduct experiments.

During the 1100s, European thinkers began to have more contact with Islamic peoples. As a result, they gained a renewed interest in science. Europeans began to read copies of Islamic works in Latin. After the Indian-Arabic system of numbers reached Europe, people adopted it in place of Roman numerals.

Thinkstock/JupiterImages

In today's world, we use Indian-Arabic numbers. However, during the Middle Ages in Europe, Roman numerals were more common. The chart at the bottom of this page compares the two number systems.

▶ CRITICAL THINKING

Making Inferences How would the number 17 be written using Roman numerals?

Indian-Arabic Numbers	Roman Numerals
1	I
2	II
3	III
4	IV
5	V
6	VI
7	VII
8	VIII
9	IX
10	X
50	L
100	C
1,000	M

Content Vocabulary

- ellipses
- gravity
- elements
- rationalism
- scientific method

geocentric an earth-centered theory; having or relating to the earth as the center

Academic Vocabulary

theory an explanation for how or why something happens

Thomas Aquinas (uh·KWY·nuhs) and other Christian thinkers showed that Christianity and reason could work together. Also, Europeans began building new universities. In these schools, teachers and students helped the growth of science.

Beginning in the 1400s, voyages of exploration added to scientific knowledge in Europe. Europeans began to create better charts and maps. These tools helped explorers reach different parts of the world. As more of the world was explored, people learned new information about the size of oceans and continents. Scientists gathered data about diseases, animals, and plants and organized the new information.

Gradually, scientific knowledge **expanded** in Europe. As this happened, a new understanding of the natural world developed.

✓ PROGRESS CHECK

Describing How was science practiced in ancient and medieval times?

New Ideas About the Universe

GUIDING QUESTION *Why did European ideas about the universe change during the 1500s and 1600s?*

In the 1500s, Europeans began to think differently about science. They began to realize that scientists had to use mathematics and experiments to make advances. This new way of thinking led to the **Scientific Revolution.** This revolution changed how Europeans understood science and how they searched for knowledge. The Scientific Revolution first affected astronomy, the science that studies the planets and stars of the universe. New discoveries in this field began to change European thinking about the universe. They challenged the traditional idea that God had made the Earth as the center of the universe.

Copernicus and Ptolemy

Nicolaus Copernicus (koh·PUHR·nih·kuhs) was a Polish astronomer. In 1491, he began his career at a university in Poland. A year later, Columbus reached the Americas. Like Columbus, Copernicus challenged old beliefs held by Europeans.

In 1543, Copernicus wrote a book called *On the Revolutions of the Heavenly Spheres.* He disagreed with Ptolemy's theory that the Earth was the center of the universe. Copernicus developed a **heliocentric** (HEE·lee·oh·SEHN·trihk), or sun-centered,

Reading **HELP**DESK

Scientific Revolution a period from the 1500s to the 1700s in which many scientific advances changed people's traditional beliefs

heliocentric having or relating to the sun as the center

ellipses oval shapes

Academic Vocabulary

expand to increase in number, volume, or scope

A NEW VIEW OF THE UNIVERSE

Ptolemaic Universe

Ptolemy, a Greek astronomer of Egyptian descent, claimed that the planets and the sun revolved around Earth. His theory was accepted for more than a thousand years.

Fixed Stars
Prime Mover
Saturn
Jupiter
Mars
Sun
Venus
Mercury
Earth
Moon

The theory of Copernicus gave a new perspective on the universe. He believed that the Earth and other planets orbit the sun. He also stated that Earth rotates daily on its axis. This new theory proved accurate in many ways.

Copernican Universe

Fixed Stars
Saturn
Jupiter
Moon
Mars
Earth
Venus
Sun
Mercury

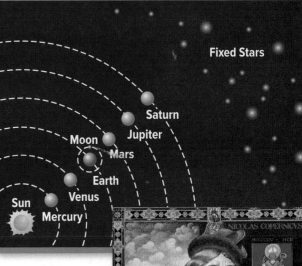

theory of the universe. Copernicus believed that the sun was the center of the universe. Earth and the other planets followed a circular path around the sun.

Copernicus's theory disagreed with church teachings. As a result, publication of his book was delayed. He reportedly did not receive the first copy until he was dying.

Kepler's Ideas About Planets

A German astronomer named Johannes Kepler (KEH·pluhr) made more advances. He used mathematics to support Copernicus's theory that the planets revolve around the sun. His findings also made corrections to the theory. Kepler added the idea that the planets move in oval paths called **ellipses** (ih· LIHP·seez) instead of the circular paths in Copernicus's theory.

Also, Kepler stated that planets do not always travel at the same speed. Instead, they move faster as they approach the sun and slower as they move away from it. Kepler's theory provided a simpler explanation for the movements of the planets. In addition, it marked the beginning of modern astronomy.

▶ **CRITICAL THINKING**
Analyzing Study the diagrams. How did the theory of Copernicus differ from the theory of Ptolemy?

(t)Joos van Gent/The Bridgeman Art Library/Getty Images; (b)©Bettmann/Corbis

Galileo (1564–1642)

In 1632, Galileo, an Italian, published his ideas. Soon afterward, Catholic Church officials banned his book. They believed that the Christian Bible taught that the Earth was the center of the universe. Galileo's theory disagreed and stated the Earth revolved around the sun. Because of this, Galileo was ordered to stand trial for heresy. He was also forced to withdraw many of his statements.

▶ **CRITICAL THINKING**
Explaining Why did the Catholic Church want to stop the spread of Galileo's ideas?

Galileo's Achievements

An Italian scientist named Galileo Galilei (GA·luh·LEE·oh GA·luh·LY) made the next great discovery in the Scientific Revolution. He believed that conducting experiments was the correct way to achieve new scientific knowledge. His studies caused him to disagree with some long-held ideas. For example, Aristotle had thought that heavy objects fall to the ground faster than objects that weigh less. Galileo's experiments proved that was not correct. Objects fall at the same speed no matter what they weigh.

Galileo also believed that scientific instruments could help people better explore the natural world. He heard about an early telescope and designed one of his own. With the telescope, Galileo found evidence that supported Copernicus's theory that Earth revolves around the sun.

Galileo also improved the making of clocks. One day, Galileo was watching an overhead lamp swing back and forth from a cathedral ceiling. He timed each swing and discovered that all of the swings took the same amount of time. Galileo used this idea to make a clock that had a swinging pendulum. The pendulum made the clock more accurate.

Galileo also developed new scientific instruments. In 1593, he invented a water thermometer. People could now measure changes in temperature. An assistant of Galileo then built the first barometer, an instrument that measures air pressure.

✓ **PROGRESS CHECK**

Explaining   How did Galileo go about making scientific discoveries?

New Scientific Advances

GUIDING QUESTION *Which discoveries did scientists make during the 1600s and 1700s?*

During the 1600s and 1700s, scientists built on the advances of Copernicus, Kepler, and Galileo. These scientists made advances in medicine, astronomy, and physics.

Newton's Universe

Isaac Newton was an English mathematician. According to tradition, Newton was sitting in his garden one day when he saw an apple fall to the ground. The apple's fall led him to the

ReadingHELPDESK

gravity the attraction that the Earth has on an object on or near its surface

Stock Montage/Archive Photos/Getty Images

idea of **gravity**. Gravity is the pull of the Earth (or other bodies in space) on objects that are on or near the planet.

In 1687, Newton published a book called *Principia.* This was one of the most important books in the history of modern science. In *Principia,* Newton gave his laws, or well-tested theories, about the motion of objects on Earth and in space. The most important was the law of gravitation. It states that the force of gravity holds the solar system together. It does this by keeping the sun and the planets in their orbits. Newton's ideas greatly influenced the thinking of other scientists.

Studying the Human Body

Many changes were made in medicine during the 1500s and 1600s. Since ancient times, the teachings of the Greek physician Galen had influenced European doctors. Galen wanted to study the human body, but he was not allowed to dissect, or cut open, dead human bodies. So, he dissected animals instead.

In the 1500s, the Flemish doctor Andreas Vesalius (vuh·SAY·lee·uhs) advanced medical research. He began dissecting dead human bodies. In 1543, he published *On the Structure of the Human Body.* In it, Vesalius described the internal structure of the human body. His account challenged many of Galen's ideas.

Isaac Newton analyzed rays of light. His experiments showed that light is made up of a wide band of colors called a spectrum.

▶ **CRITICAL THINKING**
Speculating Do you think Aristotle's scientific method could have been used to discover the spectrum? Explain your answer.

| THE SCIENTIFIC REVOLUTION | | | INFOGRAPHIC |

Scientist	Nation	Discoveries
Nicolaus Copernicus (1473–1543)	Poland	Earth orbits the sun; Earth rotates on its axis
Galileo Galilei (1564–1642)	Italy	other planets have moons
Johannes Kepler (1571–1630)	Germany	planets have elliptical orbits
William Harvey (1578–1657)	England	heart pumps blood
Robert Hooke (1635–1703)	England	cells
Robert Boyle (1627–1691)	Ireland	matter is made up of elements
Isaac Newton (1642–1727)	England	gravity; laws of motion; calculus
Antoine Lavoisier (1743–1794)	France	how materials burn

During the Scientific Revolution, scientists made discoveries in many fields, such as astronomy and medicine. For example, William Harvey discovered that the heart pumps blood.

CRITICAL THINKING
Comparing What other scientists worked with the same subject matter as Galileo?

North Wind Picture Archives

Other advances in medicine took place. In the early 1600s, an English scientist named Robert Hooke began using a microscope. He soon discovered cells, which are the smallest units of living matter. Then the Dutch merchant Antonie van Leeuwenhoek (LAY·vuhn·huk) improved the microscope by using more powerful lenses. He used this microscope to discover tiny organisms later called bacteria (bak·TIHR·ee·uh).

In the mid-1600s, the Irish scientist Robert Boyle proved that all matter is made up of **elements**. Elements are basic materials that cannot be broken down into simpler parts.

During the 1700s, European scientists discovered gases such as hydrogen, carbon dioxide, and oxygen. By 1783, Antoine Lavoisier (AN·twahn luh·WAH·zee·AY) of France proved that materials need oxygen in order to burn. Marie Lavoisier, also a scientist, made contributions to her husband's work.

Early microscopes (left) were used to discover information about items too small to see, like bacteria and cells. Early telescopes (below) were used to learn about larger things in space, like planets and stars.

✓ PROGRESS CHECK

Identifying According to Newton, how are the planets held in orbit?

The Triumph of Reason

GUIDING QUESTION *How did Europeans of the 1600s and 1700s develop new ways of gaining knowledge?*

European thinkers soon began to apply the ideas of science to human society. These thinkers believed science revealed the natural laws of the universe. By using reason, people could study these laws and use them to solve many human problems.

Descartes and Pascal

France became a major center of scientific thought. In 1637, the French thinker René Descartes (reh·NAY day·KAHRT) wrote a book called *Discourse on Method*. In this book, Descartes studied the problem of knowing what is true. To find truth, he decided to ignore everything he had learned and start over. However, one fact seemed to be beyond doubt. This fact was his own existence. To summarize this idea, Descartes wrote the phrase, "I think, therefore I am."

In his work, Descartes claimed that mathematics is the source of scientific truth. In mathematics, he said, the answers are always true. His reasoning was that mathematics begins with

Reading**HELP**DESK

element a substance that consists of atoms of only one kind

rationalism the belief that reason and experience must be present for the solution of problems

scientific method the steps for an orderly search for knowledge

Academic Vocabulary

generation the time span between the birth of parents and the birth of their children

simple principles. It then uses logic, or reason, to move to more complex truths. Descartes is viewed as the founder of modern **rationalism** (RASH·uh·nuh·LIH·zuhm). This is the belief that reason is the main source of knowledge.

During the 1600s, another French thinker, Blaise Pascal (blehz pa·SKAL), studied science. At the age of 19, he invented a calculating machine. Pascal believed that reason and scientific ideas based on experiments could solve many practical problems. However, Pascal was also a religious man. He believed that the solutions to moral problems and spiritual truth could come only from faith in Christian teachings.

What Is the Scientific Method?

In the 1600s, the English thinker Francis Bacon influenced scientific thought. He believed that unproven ideas from earlier **generations** should be put aside. Bacon believed that to find the truth, you had to first find and examine the facts.

He developed the scientific method. This method is an orderly way of collecting and analyzing evidence. Its basic principles are still used in scientific research today.

The **scientific method** consists of several steps. First, scientists observe facts. Then, they try to find a hypothesis (hy·PAH·thuh·suhs), or an explanation of the facts. Scientists conduct experiments to test the hypothesis. These tests are done under all types of conditions. Repeated experiments may show that the hypothesis is true. Then it is considered a scientific law.

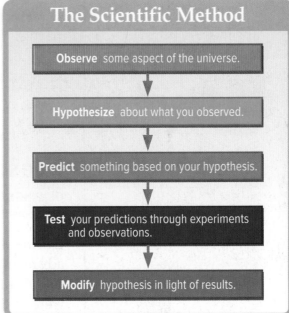

The Scientific Method

Observe some aspect of the universe.

Hypothesize about what you observed.

Predict something based on your hypothesis.

Test your predictions through experiments and observations.

Modify hypothesis in light of results.

The scientific method involves five steps. These steps build on each other.

▶ CRITICAL THINKING
Conjecturing Do you think scientists often have to do the fifth step? Explain.

☑ **PROGRESS CHECK**

Explaining Why did Descartes believe that mathematics is the source of scientific truth?

LESSON 1 REVIEW

Review Vocabulary

1. How is *rationalism* used in the *scientific method*?

Answer the Guiding Questions

2. *Identifying* What was the heliocentric theory and who developed it?

3. *Summarizing* How did the ancient Greeks study nature?

4. *Explaining* What instrument made the discovery of bacteria possible? Explain.

5. *Defining* What is the scientific method?

6. **ARGUMENT** During the Scientific Revolution, advances were made in many scientific fields. Choose the step forward that you think is the most significant and explain your choice.

LESSON 2

The Enlightenment

ESSENTIAL QUESTION

• How do governments change?

IT MATTERS BECAUSE
The ideas of the Enlightenment have strongly influenced the government and society of the United States and many other nations.

Reason and Politics

GUIDING QUESTION *How did European thinkers apply scientific ideas to government?*

During the 1700s, European thinkers were impressed by advances in science. They believed that reason could discover the scientific laws that shaped human behavior. Once these laws were understood, thinkers believed, people could use the laws to improve society.

The Scientific Revolution stressed the use of reason to solve problems. Before this period, people often relied on faith or tradition as guides. However, in the 1700s, many educated Europeans began to break away from tradition. They viewed reason as a "light" that uncovered error and showed the path to truth. As a result, the 1700s became known as the **Age of Enlightenment**.

During the Enlightenment, political thinkers tried to use reason to improve government. They claimed that there was a natural law, or a law that applied to everyone and could be understood by reason. This natural law was the key to making government work properly. As early as the 1600s, two English thinkers used natural law to develop very different ideas about government. The two men were Thomas Hobbes and John Locke.

Reading**HELP**DESK

Taking Notes: *Identifying*

On a chart like this one, list the main thinkers of the Enlightenment and a major idea for each one.

Thinker	Idea

Content Vocabulary

• **Age of Enlightenment**
• **absolutism**
• **Glorious Revolution**
• **constitutional monarchy**
• **social contract**
• **separation of powers**

Who Was Thomas Hobbes?

English writer Thomas Hobbes wrote about England's government and society. At the time, England was torn apart by conflict. King Charles I wanted absolute power. Parliament, however, demanded a greater role in governing. The king's supporters fought those who supported Parliament.

Parliament already had some control over the king. In the 1620s, Parliament had forced Charles to sign the Petition of Right. It said the king could not tax the people without Parliament's approval. Also, he could not imprison anyone without a just reason. The Petition also stated that the king could not declare a state of emergency unless the country was at war.

Charles, however, ignored the Petition. His differences with Parliament led to civil war. The fighting finally forced Parliament's supporters to execute Charles. This event shocked Thomas Hobbes, who supported the monarchy.

Hobbes's Beliefs

In 1651, Hobbes wrote a book called *Leviathan*. In this work, Hobbes argued that natural law made absolute monarchy the best form of government. According to Hobbes, humans were naturally violent and selfish. They could not be trusted to make wise decisions on their own. Left to themselves, people would make life "nasty, brutish, and short."

Therefore, Hobbes said, people needed to obey a government that had the power of a leviathan (luh·VY·uh·thuhn), or sea monster. To Hobbes, this meant the rule of a powerful king, because only a strong ruler could give people direction. Under this ruler, people had to remain loyal. This political theory of Hobbes became known as **absolutism** (AB·suh·LOO·tih·zuhm), since it supported a ruler with absolute, or total, power.

In Hobbes's *Leviathan*, a sea serpent like the one below represents the powerful ruler necessary to running the most effective type of government—an absolute monarchy.

▶ **CRITICAL THINKING**
Analyzing How does the image of a serpent help make Hobbes's point about government?

Age of Enlightenment the time period in the 1700s during which many Europeans began to break away from tradition and rethink political and social norms

absolutism political system in which a ruler has total power

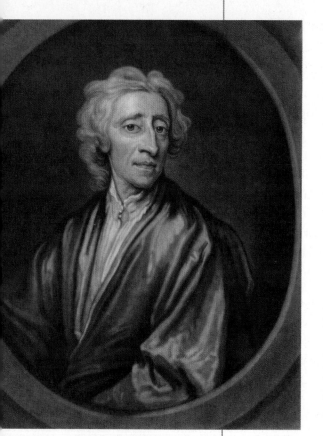

John Locke wrote about many subjects, including education and religion. His ideas contributed to the U.S. Declaration of Independence.

▶ **CRITICAL THINKING**

Making Inferences Would Locke have supported freedom of religion? Explain.

Locke and the Glorious Revolution

Another English thinker, John Locke, believed differently. He used natural law to support citizens' rights. He said the government had to answer to the people. During Locke's life, another English king, James II, wanted to be a strong ruler. Parliament again was opposed to the king's wishes. When civil war threatened in 1688, James fled the country. Parliament then asked Mary, the king's daughter, and her husband, William, to take the throne. This event became known as the "**Glorious Revolution.**"

The Glorious Revolution eventually turned England into a **constitutional monarchy.** This is a form of government in which written laws limit the powers of the monarch. In return for the English throne, William and Mary agreed to a Bill of Rights. This document required William and Mary to obey Parliament's laws. The Bill of Rights also **guaranteed** all English people basic rights. For example, people had the right to a fair trial by jury and the right to freedom from cruel punishment.

In 1690, John Locke wrote a book called Two *Treatises of Government.* His book explained many of the ideas of the Glorious Revolution. Locke stated that government should be based on natural law and natural rights. These rights included the right to life, the right to liberty, and the right to own property.

Locke believed that the purpose of government was to protect people's rights. He said that all governments were based on a **social contract.** This is an agreement between the people and their leaders. If rulers took away people's natural rights, the people had a right to rebel and set up a new government.

Montesquieu and Government

After the Glorious Revolution, many thinkers in France admired the government of England. They liked it better than the absolute monarchy that ruled France. In 1748, a French thinker, Baron Montesquieu (mahn·tuhs·KYOO), published a book called *The Spirit of the Laws,* that stated that England had the best government. He liked English government because it had a **separation of powers**. This means power should be equally divided among the branches of government: legislative,

Reading**HELP**DESK

Glorious Revolution the overthrow of King James II of England

constitutional monarchy a political system in which a king or queen rules according to a constitution

social contract an agreement between the people and their government

executive, and judicial. The legislative branch makes the laws. The executive branch enforces the laws. The judicial branch interprets the laws and makes judgments when the laws are broken. By separating these powers, government could not become too powerful and threaten people's rights. As Montesquieu explained in the case of judges:

❝ Again, there is no liberty, if the power of judging be not separated from the legislative and executive powers. Were it joined with the legislative, the life and liberty of the subject would be exposed to arbitrary [unreasonable] control, for the judge would be then the legislator. Were it joined to the executive power, the judge might behave with all the violence of an oppressor [cruel dictator]. ❞

—from *The Spirit of the Laws, by Baron Montesquieu* 1748

Montesquieu believed in the rights of individuals. His work influenced the writing of the constitutions of many countries, including the United States Constitution.

✓ PROGRESS CHECK

Comparing and Contrasting How did Hobbes and Locke differ in their ideas about government and the people?

The Philosophes of France

GUIDING QUESTION *How did French thinkers influence Europe during the Enlightenment?*

During the 1700s, France became the most active center of the Enlightenment. Thinkers in France and elsewhere became known by the French name *philosophe* (FEE·luh·ZAWF), which means "philosopher." Most philosophes were writers, teachers, and journalists who often discussed and debated new ideas at gatherings. These gatherings were held in the homes of wealthy citizens.

Philosophes wanted to use reason to improve society. They attacked superstition, or unreasoned beliefs, and disagreed with religious leaders who opposed new scientific discoveries. Philosophes believed in freedom of speech and claimed that each person had the right to liberty. Their ideas spread across Europe.

Baron Montesquieu traveled through Europe and compared governments. He wrote his conclusions in *The Spirit of the Laws.*

▶ CRITICAL THINKING
Drawing Conclusions Why did so many scholars respect Montesquieu's ideas?

©Stefano Bianchetti/Corbis

separation of powers a government structure that has three distinct branches: legislative, executive, and judicial

Academic Vocabulary

guarantee to make sure or certain; promise

Who Was Voltaire?

In 1694, François-Marie Arouet (ahr·WEH) was born to a middle-class family in France. He became one of the greatest thinkers of the Enlightenment. Called just Voltaire (vohl·TAR), he wrote novels, plays, and essays that brought him wealth and fame.

Voltaire opposed the government's favoring one religion and forbidding others. He thought people should be free to choose their own beliefs. He often criticized the Roman Catholic Church for keeping knowledge from people in order to maintain the Church's power.

Voltaire was a supporter of deism (DEE·ih·zuhm), a religious belief based on reason. Followers of deism believed that God created the universe and set it in motion. God then allowed the universe to run itself by natural law.

Voltaire had opinions that caused a large amount of controversy. He was jailed for his viewpoints in France's Bastille prison.

During the Enlightenment, wealthy people held gatherings to discuss the ideas of the day. Here a group reads and discusses the works of Voltaire.

Diderot's *Encyclopedia*

The French thinker Denis Diderot (duh·NEE dee·DROH) was also committed to spreading Enlightenment ideas. In the late 1700s, he produced a large, 28-volume encyclopedia that took him about 20 years to complete. The *Encyclopedia* covered a wide range of topics including religion, government,

(t)Bridgeman-Giraudon/Art Resource, NY; (b)Reunion des Musees Nationaux/Art Resource, NY

Reading Strategy: *Analyzing Primary Sources*

How does Mary Wollstonecraft believe women can achieve their potential and fulfill their "specific duties"? What part of the quote on the next page supports your answer?

the sciences, history, and the arts. The philosophes used it as a weapon in their fight against traditional ways. Many articles supported freedom of religion and called for changes to society.

Women and the Enlightenment

Prior to the Enlightenment, women did not have equal rights with men. By the 1700s, a small number of women began to call for such rights. In 1792, the English writer Mary Wollstonecraft (WUL·stuhn·KRAFT) wrote a book called *A Vindication of the Rights of Woman*. In it, she states that women should have the same rights as men. Many consider Wollstonecraft to be the founder of the women's movement.

PRIMARY SOURCE

❝ In short, . . . reason and experience convince me that the only method of leading women to fulfil their peculiar [specific] duties, is to free them from all restraint [control] by allowing them to participate in the inherent [basic] rights of mankind. ❞

—from *A Vindication of the Rights of Woman*, by Mary Wollstonecraft, 1792

Who was Rousseau?

A Swiss thinker named Jean-Jacques Rousseau (roo·SOH) questioned Enlightenment ideas. In 1762 he published a book of political ideas called *The Social Contract*. This book states that government rests on the will of the people and is based on a social contract. This is an agreement in which what society, as a whole, wants should be law.

✔ **PROGRESS CHECK**

Describing What was Diderot's *Encyclopedia*?

Absolute Monarchs

GUIDING QUESTION *How did European monarchs model their countries on Enlightenment ideas?*

During the Enlightenment, thinkers called for controls on government. However, most of Europe was ruled by kings and queens who claimed to rule by divine right, or the will of God. Some absolute rulers used Enlightenment ideas to improve their societies—but they refused to give up any of their powers.

Who was France's Sun King?

During the 1600s and 1700s, France was one of Europe's most powerful nations. In 1643, Louis XIV, called the Sun King, came to the throne. He built the grand Versailles (vuhr·SY) palace. There, he staged large ceremonies to celebrate his power.

Connections to
TODAY

Women's Rights Around the World

Mary Wollstonecraft published *A Vindication of the Rights of Woman* in 1792. Today, many organizations still work to advance and protect the social and political equality of women. In 2010, the United Nations voted unanimously to set up UN Women, an organization to promote gender equality around the world. UN Women is based in New York City.

Mary Wollstonecraft thought that women should have equal rights in education, the workplace, and political life.

▶ CRITICAL THINKING
Explaining How did Mary Wollstonecraft support her argument for women's equality?

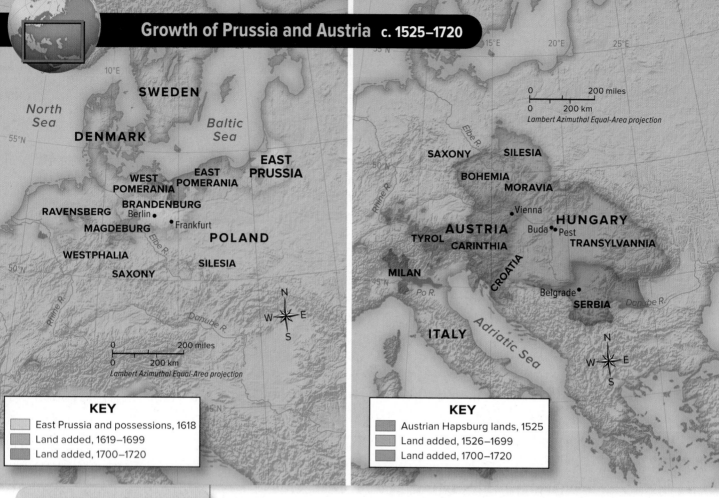

KEY
- East Prussia and possessions, 1618
- Land added, 1619–1699
- Land added, 1700–1720

KEY
- Austrian Hapsburg lands, 1525
- Land added, 1526–1699
- Land added, 1700–1720

GEOGRAPHY CONNECTION

The areas of Prussia and Austria gradually increased from the early 1500s to the early 1700s.

1 **REGION** During which time period did Austria add the most territory?

2 **LOCATION** Which state had better access to the sea—Prussia or Austria? Explain.

Louis held all political authority in France. He is said to have boasted, "I am the State." Louis's army won wars that expanded the area of France. These conflicts, though, cost the country a large amount of money and soldiers. The king's constant wars and spending weakened France and the monarchy.

German Rulers

Germany consisted of many territories during the 1600s and 1700s. The two most powerful German states were Prussia and Austria. The most famous Prussian ruler was Frederick II, also called Frederick the Great. He ruled Prussia from 1740 to 1786. Frederick strengthened the army and fought wars to gain new lands for Prussia.

Although Frederick was an absolute monarch, he saw himself as "first servant of the state." He therefore dedicated himself to the good of his people. Frederick permitted more freedom of speech and religious tolerance.

Reading**HELP**DESK

Academic Vocabulary

military relating to the armed forces, such as the army, navy, and the air force

The other German state, Austria, was ruled by the Hapsburg family. In 1740, a Hapsburg princess named Maria Theresa became the ruler of Austria. She introduced reforms. She set up schools and tried to improve the living conditions of the serfs, people who worked under the harsh rule of landowners.

After Maria Theresa died in 1780, her son, Joseph II, became ruler. He carried her reforms even further. He freed the serfs and made land taxes equal for nobles and farmers. The nobles opposed his reforms. As a result, Joseph was forced to back down.

Russia's Reforming Czars

East of Austria, the vast empire of Russia was ruled by czars. One of the most powerful czars was Peter I, also known as Peter the Great. Peter tried to make Russia a strong European power. He began reforms to help the government run more smoothly. Peter also improved Russia's **military** and created a navy.

Peter wanted Russia to have access to the Baltic Sea, but Sweden controlled the land. Peter went to war with Sweden in a conflict lasting 21 years. Russia won in 1721. Just three years after the war started, Peter founded the city of St. Petersburg (PEE·tuhrz·BUHRG). By 1712, this city was the Russian capital.

After Peter died, a series of weak monarchs governed Russia. Then, in 1762, a German princess named Catherine came to the throne. Catherine II expanded Russia's territory and became known as Catherine the Great. She supported the ideas of the Enlightenment and wanted to free the serfs. However, a serf revolt changed her mind. In the end, Catherine allowed the nobles to treat the serfs as they pleased.

✓ **PROGRESS CHECK**

Explaining How was Frederick the Great influenced by the Enlightenment?

In 1787, Catherine the Great and Joseph II traveled together through Southern Russia. An artist commemorated their trip with this oil painting.

▶ **CRITICAL THINKING**
Comparing What social reforms did both Joseph II and Catherine II seek for their countries?

©Heritage Images/Corbis

LESSON 2 REVIEW

Review Vocabulary

1. How did the *Glorious Revolution* lead to a *constitutional monarchy* in England?

Answer the Guiding Questions

2. *Identifying* Which monarch freed the serfs?

3. *Summarizing* What did the *Encyclopedia* created by Diderot contain?

4. *Describing* What type of government did John Locke support?

5. *Explaining* Why did Voltaire criticize the Roman Catholic Church?

6. **ARGUMENT** You are an Enlightenment thinker who opposes the views of Thomas Hobbes. Write a short letter to Hobbes that explains to him why you disagree with his ideas about government.

Write your answers on a separate piece of paper.

1 **Exploring the Essential Questions**

INFORMATIVE/EXPLANATORY How did governments in Europe change during the 1600s and 1700s? Write a summary essay about how they changed during this period. Think about various Enlightenment ideas that influenced the formation of governments. Include the effects these ideas had on government structure and on rulers.

2 **21st Century Skills**

COMMUNICATION Create a presentation that explains the contributions of Galileo to the world of science. What do you think was his most important new idea? Do further research on the Internet. Write a short summary of Galileo's most important contribution to science. Include any diagrams or charts that will help support your argument. In your presentation, have the class ask you questions that require you to defend your opinion about Galileo.

3 **Thinking Like a Historian**

COMPARING AND CONTRASTING Create a diagram like the one on the right to compare and contrast the ideas and lives of Thomas Hobbes and John Locke.

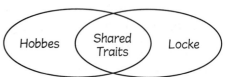

Hobbes · Shared Traits · Locke

4 **GEOGRAPHY ACTIVITY**

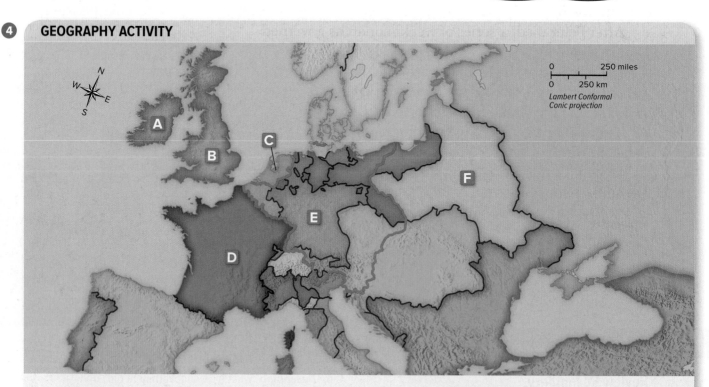

250 miles
250 km
Lambert Conformal Conic projection

LOCATING PEOPLE

Match the scientists and thinkers listed below with their countries.

1. Voltaire
2. Copernicus
3. Locke
4. Kepler
5. Leeuwenhoek
6. Boyle

Directions: Write your answers on a separate piece of paper.

CHECKING FOR UNDERSTANDING

1 Define each term as it relates to the Scientific Revolution and Enlightenment.

A. Scientific Revolution
B. heliocentric
C. ellipses
D. gravity
E. social contract
F. geocentric
G. element

H. rationalism
I. scientific method
J. Age of Enlightenment
K. absolutism
L. Glorious Revolution
M. constitutional monarchy
N. separation of powers

REVIEW THE GUIDING QUESTIONS

2 *Describing* How did thinkers in ancient Greece and Rome pass on scientific ideas to later generations?

3 *Paraphrasing* Use your own words to explain what caused Europeans to change their ideas about the universe during the 1500s and 1600s.

4 *Stating* State two discoveries that scientists made during the 1600s and 1700s.

5 *Discussing* What new way of gaining knowledge did René Descartes develop?

6 *Finding the Main Idea* How did European thinkers apply scientific ideas to government?

7 *Explaining* How did the French thinker Denis Diderot influence Europe during the Enlightenment?

8 *Summarizing* Summarize the ways in which European monarchs used Enlightenment ideas to shape their countries.

CRITICAL THINKING

9 *Recognizing Relationships* Why do you think astronomy was important to the well-being of ancient civilizations?

10 *Contrasting* How did the ancient Greeks try to learn about the world? How was this different from the way in which scientists such as Galileo tried to learn about the world?

11 *Sequencing* Place in proper sequence the steps in the scientific method.

12 *Making Comparisons* Why was Flemish doctor Andreas Vesalius able to learn more about the human body than the Greek physician Galen?

13 *Determining Cause and Effect* What effect did the Enlightenment have on women?

14 *Analyzing* Why do you think separating government into executive, legislative, and judicial branches helps keep the government from becoming overly powerful?

15 *Recognizing Relationships* How is the Age of Enlightenment related to the Scientific Revolution?

16 *Identifying Central Issues* What do you think is an advantage of having a social contract between people in their government? What might be a disadvantage?

17 *Speculating* What do you think would have happened to the serfs under Catherine the Great of Russia if they had not revolted?

18 *Identifying Points of View* How was Thomas Hobbes' point of view on the way in which people should be governed different from Rousseau's point of view?

19 *Speculating* Why do you think the Catholic Church objected to Copernicus's theory that the sun was at the center of the universe?

20 *Defending* If you were an absolute monarch during the Enlightenment, would you rule like Louis XIV of France or like Frederick II of Prussia?

Need Extra Help?

If You've Missed Question	1	2	3	4	5	6	7	8	9	10	11	12	13	14	15	16	17	18	19	20
Review Lesson	1, 2	1	1	1	1	1	2	2	2	1	1	1	1	2	2	2	2	2	1	2

DBQ SHORT RESPONSE

"A sovereign [ruler] is not elevated to his high position ... that he may live in lazy luxury. ... The sovereign is the first servant of the state. He is well paid in order that he may sustain the dignity of his office, but one demands that he work efficiently for the good of the state,..."

—from the *Political Testament*, by Frederick II (the Great) of Prussia

21 What does Frederick mean when he says a ruler should be "the first servant of the state?"

22 What would Frederick think of a king who acted foolish in public?

EXTENDED RESPONSE

23 *Narrative* Write a description of a meeting in which Voltaire, Jean-Jacques Rousseau, and Mary Wollstonecraft discuss and argue their viewpoints. Include dialogue.

STANDARDIZED TEST PRACTICE

DBQ ANALYZING DOCUMENTS

Drawing Conclusions This excerpt was published by John Locke in 1690.

"To understand political power aright ... we must consider what estate all [people] are naturally in, and that is, a state of perfect freedom ..., within the bounds of the law of Nature. ...

A state also of equality, wherein all the power and jurisdiction [enforcement of laws] is reciprocal [shared], no one having more than another."

—from *The Second Treatise of Government*, by John Locke

24 Which statement do you think Locke would agree with?
- **A.** All people have freedom to do what they want.
- **B.** All people should enforce laws.
- **C.** All people should have equal wealth.
- **D.** All people should have few possessions.

25 *Finding the Main Idea* Which of the following is the main idea of the excerpt?
- **A.** People will naturally form democracies.
- **B.** People must obey the laws of nature.
- **C.** People are in a natural state of freedom and equality.
- **D.** People have the freedom to learn about nature.

Need Extra Help?

If You've Missed Question	21	22	23	24	25
Review Lesson	4	1	1	3	3

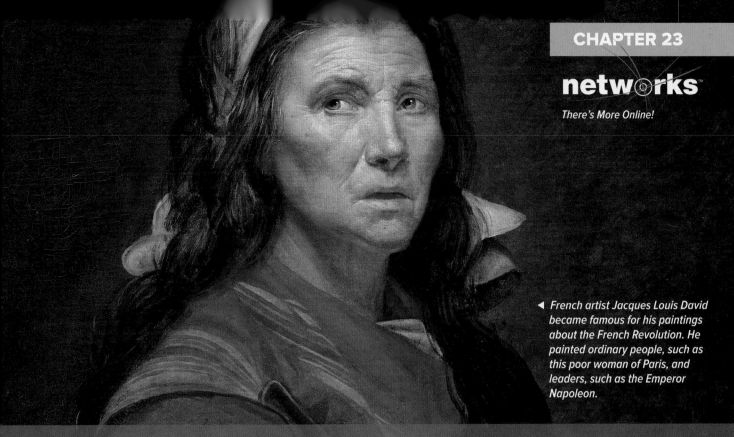

◄ *French artist Jacques Louis David became famous for his paintings about the French Revolution. He painted ordinary people, such as this poor woman of Paris, and leaders, such as the Emperor Napoleon.*

1775 TO 1850

Political and Industrial Revolutions

Josse Christophel/Alamy Stock Photo

THE STORY MATTERS ...

The people of France have risen up. They have stormed prisons, seized property, and set nobles on the run. In Paris, the capital, crowds fill the streets, thrilled with their power. Yet, problems remain. The poor are hungrier than ever. It may be a long time before there will be work to do or safe places to set up markets. As you read this chapter, note how revolution can lead to great joy and great tragedy.

ESSENTIAL QUESTIONS

- Why does conflict develop?
- Why is history important?
- How do governments change?
- How does technology change the way people live?
- How do new ideas change the way people live?

Place & Time: Europe and the Americas 1775 to 1850

Between 1775 and 1815, conflict erupted throughout Europe and the Americas. New ideas led to the overthrow of kings and nobles. New governments favoring citizens' rights were created. Revolutions in one country spread to other countries. At the same time, revolutions in politics were accompanied by advances in economics and technology. Everything seemed to be changing.

Step Into the Place

MAP FOCUS Between 1775 and 1815, political revolutions took place in Europe and the Americas.

1 REGIONS How many revolutions occurred between 1775 and 1815?

2 PLACE Where did revolution happen first?

3 CRITICAL THINKING
Predicting Make a prediction about how these revolutions might influence the rest of the world.

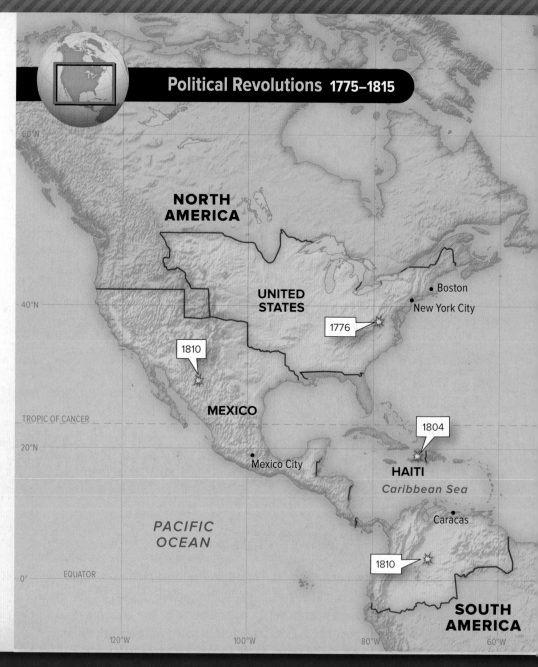

Political Revolutions 1775–1815

NORTH AMERICA

UNITED STATES

1776

Boston
New York City

1810

MEXICO

Mexico City

1804

HAITI
Caribbean Sea

Caracas

1810

PACIFIC OCEAN

SOUTH AMERICA

60°N
40°N
TROPIC OF CANCER
20°N
EQUATOR 0°

120°W   100°W   80°W   60°W

Step Into the Time

TIME LINE Choose an event from the time line and use this information to make a generalization about world events during this time period.

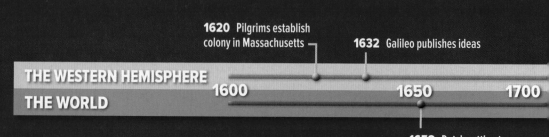

1620 Pilgrims establish colony in Massachusetts

1632 Galileo publishes ideas

THE WESTERN HEMISPHERE

THE WORLD

1600   1650   1700

1652 Dutch settle at Cape Town in South Africa

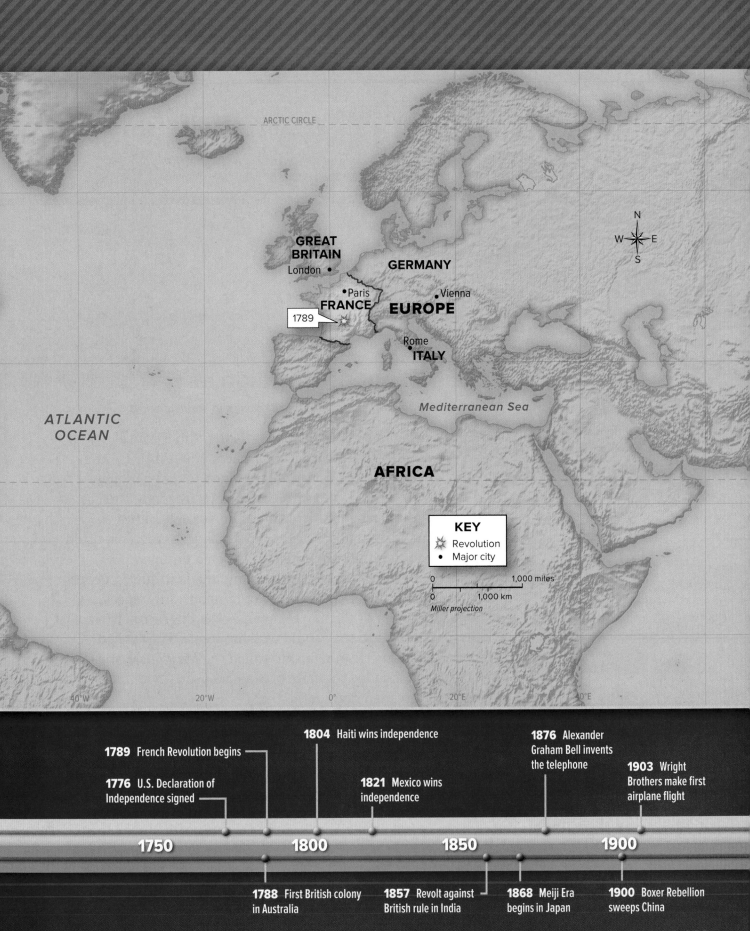

ARCTIC CIRCLE

GREAT
BRITAIN
London •

GERMANY

• Paris
FRANCE

• Vienna

EUROPE

1789

Rome
• ITALY

Mediterranean Sea

ATLANTIC
OCEAN

AFRICA

N
W E
S

KEY
☀ Revolution
• Major city

0   1,000 miles
0   1,000 km
Miller projection

40°W   20°W   0°   20°E   40°E

1804 Haiti wins independence

1876 Alexander
Graham Bell invents
the telephone

1789 French Revolution begins

1903 Wright
Brothers make first
airplane flight

1776 U.S. Declaration of
Independence signed

1821 Mexico wins
independence

1750   1800   1850   1900

1788 First British colony
in Australia

1857 Revolt against
British rule in India

1868 Meiji Era
begins in Japan

1900 Boxer Rebellion
sweeps China

LESSON 1
The American Revolution

ESSENTIAL QUESTION

• Why does conflict develop?

IT MATTERS BECAUSE

The American Revolution guaranteed the freedoms we still have in America today. When we learn about the difficult struggle to gain independence, we value and protect our freedoms.

Britain's American Colonies

GUIDING QUESTION *Why did England found colonies in North America?*

The first permanent English colony in North America was set up by the Virginia Company in the area that is now Virginia. The company owners wanted riches and planned to make money from the colony. People who wanted religious freedom, such as the Puritans, established other colonies in North America.

During the early 1600s, Puritans in England were **persecuted** (PUR·seh·kyoo·tehd) for their beliefs. When a group is persecuted, its members are punished and made to suffer. People sometimes persecute others because of religious differences.

In 1620, a group of Puritans known as the Pilgrims left Britain for America so they could worship freely. They sailed across the Atlantic Ocean in a ship called the *Mayflower* and landed in what is today the state of Massachusetts. Their settlement was called Plymouth.

Founding Colonies

The success of Plymouth may have influenced other Puritans to come to America. In 1630, about 1,000 Puritans founded the Massachusetts Bay Colony. Others soon followed. By the mid-1640s, more than 20,000 Puritans had settled in America.

Reading**HELP**DESK

Taking Notes: *Cause and Effect*

As you read, keep track of the events on a cause-and-effect chart. For each event, note what happened as a result of the event.

The American Revolution

Cause		Effect
Puritans were persecuted.	→	
The Stamp Act	→	
The Articles of Confederation	→	

Other people seeking religious freedom set up colonies elsewhere along the Atlantic coast. For example, English Catholics founded Maryland in 1634. The Quakers, a religious group that had also been persecuted in England, established Pennsylvania in 1680.

When the first English settlers arrived in North America, they came into contact with Native Americans. At first the two groups lived peacefully. The English learned Native American farming skills. Settlers began eating local foods, such as corn and beans. As more English settlers arrived, however, the relationship worsened. Native Americans often died of diseases brought by the English or in battles with the settlers over land.

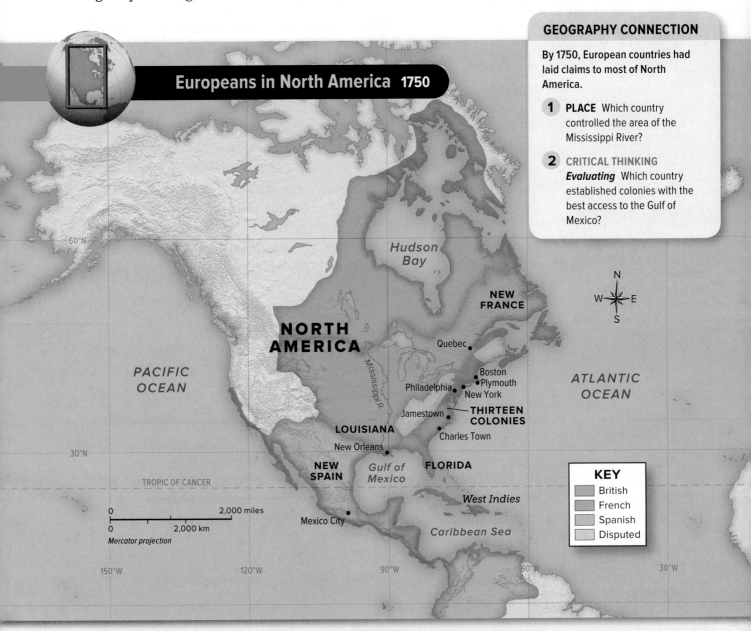

Europeans in North America 1750

GEOGRAPHY CONNECTION

By 1750, European countries had laid claims to most of North America.

1 PLACE Which country controlled the area of the Mississippi River?

2 CRITICAL THINKING *Evaluating* Which country established colonies with the best access to the Gulf of Mexico?

KEY
- British
- French
- Spanish
- Disputed

Content Vocabulary

- persecute
- constitution
- boycott
- popular sovereignty
- limited government

persecute to treat a group of people cruelly or unfairly

By the early 1700s, the English had thirteen colonies along the Atlantic coast of North America. Settlers in northern colonies found a cool or moderate climate and rocky soil. The land was more suitable for smaller farms than the warmer, more fertile southern colonies. In the South, large plantations worked by enslaved African people grew crops for export.

In 1620, before stepping off the *Mayflower*, the Pilgrims signed the Mayflower Compact. The Mayflower Compact was a document that called for the signers to follow any laws that would be established.

Self-Government in the Colonies

Self-government began early in England's American colonies. To attract more settlers, the Virginia Company let colonists in Virginia elect burgesses, or representatives. In 1619 the burgesses formed the first House of Burgesses, which was modeled on England's Parliament.

The House of Burgesses set an example of representative government, or a government in which people elect representatives to make laws. Other colonies soon set up their own legislatures.

The Puritans in Massachusetts also wanted to govern themselves. Before leaving the *Mayflower*, they signed an agreement called the Mayflower Compact. They pledged to choose their own leaders and make their own laws:

PRIMARY SOURCE

We, whose names are underwritten ...Having undertaken for the glory of God, and Advancement of the Christian Faith ... a Voyage to plant [a] colony ... do ... enact, constitute, and frame, such just and equal Laws ... as shall be thought most meet [acceptable] and convenient for the general good of the Colony ... .

—from the *Mayflower Compact*

In time, most of the English colonies developed **constitutions,** or written plans of government. These **documents** let the colonists elect assemblies and protected their rights.

✓ PROGRESS CHECK

Explaining What steps did the colonists take to govern themselves?

Reading**HELP**DESK

constitution a document that describes how a country will be governed and guarantees people certain rights

Academic Vocabulary
document a piece of writing

boycott to protest by refusing to do something

SuperStock/Getty Images

Road to Revolt

GUIDING QUESTION *How did conflict develop between Britain and its American colonies?*

During the 1700s, many changes came to England and its colonies. In 1707, England united with Scotland to form Britain. The term *British* came to mean both the English and the Scots. The colonies came to depend on Britain for trade and defense.

Trade and the Colonies

The American colonies shipped their raw materials to Britain. In return, they received British manufactured products as well as tea and spices from Asia. To control this trade, Britain passed the Navigation Acts. Under these laws, the colonists had to sell their products to Britain even if they could get a better price elsewhere. Any goods bought from other countries had to go to Britain first and be taxed before going to the Americas.

The colonists at first accepted the trade laws because Britain was a guaranteed buyer of their raw materials. Later, as the colonies grew, colonists wanted to produce their own manufactured goods. They also wanted to sell their products elsewhere if they could get higher prices. Many colonial merchants began smuggling goods in and out of the colonies. Smuggling is shipping products without paying taxes or getting government permission.

Britain Tightens Its Controls

Between 1756 and 1763, Britain and France fought a war for control of North America. When Britain won, it gained nearly all of France's North American empire. The conflict, however, left Britain deeply in debt. Desperate for money, the British made plans to tax the American colonists and tighten trade rules.

In 1765, Parliament passed the Stamp Act, which taxed newspapers and other printed material. These items had to bear a stamp showing that the tax was paid. The colonists were outraged. They responded by boycotting British goods. **Boycotting** is refusing to buy specific products in protest.

Finally, nine colonies sent delegates to a Stamp Act Congress in New York City. The Congress declared that Parliament could not tax the colonies because the colonies did not have representatives in Parliament. The colonists united under the slogan, "No taxation without representation!" They believed that only colonial legislatures had the right to tax them. Britain backed down for a while, but it still needed money. In 1767, Parliament put taxes on glass, lead, paper, paint, and tea.

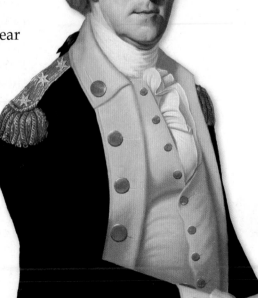

George Washington at first tried to peacefully settle the Americans' differences with Britain. What do you think changed his mind about going to war?

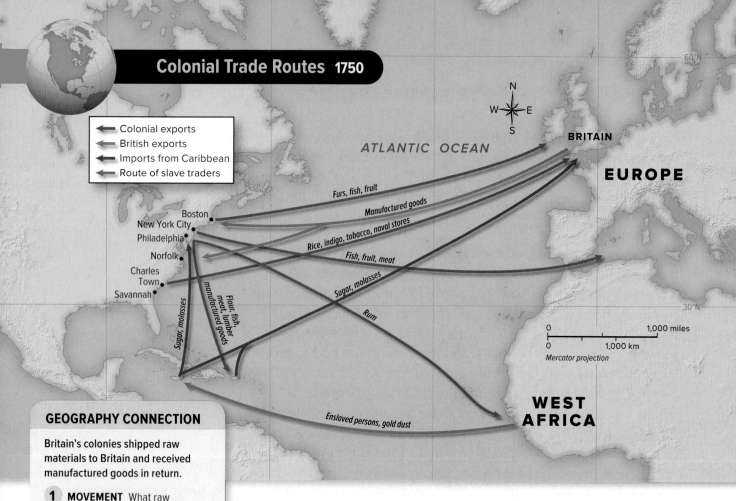

Colonial Trade Routes 1750

Legend:
- Colonial exports
- British exports
- Imports from Caribbean
- Route of slave traders

ATLANTIC OCEAN

BRITAIN

EUROPE

Boston
New York City
Philadelphia
Norfolk
Charles Town
Savannah

Furs, fish, fruit
Manufactured goods
Rice, indigo, tobacco, naval stores
Fish, fruit, meat
Sugar, molasses
Rum
Sugar, molasses
Flour, fish, meat, lumber, manufactured goods
Enslaved persons, gold dust

WEST AFRICA

0   1,000 miles
0   1,000 km
Mercator projection

GEOGRAPHY CONNECTION

Britain's colonies shipped raw materials to Britain and received manufactured goods in return.

1 MOVEMENT What raw materials were shipped from Charles Town?

2 CRITICAL THINKING
Explaining Why were exports from the Southern islands so valuable?

Unrest in Massachusetts

The Americans hated the new taxes. Mobs attacked royal tax collectors, and writers made fun of Britain's king. Worried, the British sent troops to Boston, Massachusetts, where the strongest protests had taken place.

In March 1770, British troops and American colonists clashed. A Boston crowd threw snowballs at British soldiers. The soldiers fired their weapons. Five people were killed. The event became known as the Boston Massacre. In response, Parliament repealed, or canceled, all of the taxes except the one on tea.

In 1773, Parliament passed the Tea Act. It allowed the British East India Company to ship tea to the colonies without paying the tax that American tea merchants had to pay. This allowed the company to sell its tea very cheaply and threatened to drive the American tea merchants out of business.

In Boston, angry colonists decided to take action. A group of protesters disguised themselves as Native Americans. They boarded British ships in Boston Harbor and dumped their tea into the water. This event is known as the Boston Tea Party.

Reading**HELP**DESK

To punish the colonists, Parliament passed laws that shut down Boston Harbor and placed Massachusetts under military control. It also required colonists to house and feed British soldiers. The colonists called these laws the Intolerable Acts, or laws they could not accept. The Acts made the colonies realize that they had to work together to defend their liberties. In September 1774, delegates from twelve colonies met in Philadelphia at the First Continental Congress. They demanded that the Intolerable Acts be repealed. Colonial leaders, however, could not agree about what to do. Some, such as George Washington of Virginia, hoped to settle the dispute with Britain. Others, like Samuel Adams of Massachusetts and Patrick Henry of Virginia, wanted the colonies to declare independence.

✔ PROGRESS CHECK

Identifying Cause and Effect What were the Intolerable Acts? How did the colonists respond to them?

A War for Independence

GUIDING QUESTION *How did war between Britain and the American colonies lead to the rise of a new nation—the United States of America?*

While colonial leaders debated, fighting began in Massachusetts. British soldiers set out to destroy colonial weapons being stored in the town of Concord. On April 19, 1775, they met armed colonists at Lexington and fought the first battle of the American Revolution.

News of the conflict spread throughout the colonies. In May 1775, the Second Continental Congress met in Philadelphia. It created an army with George Washington as commander. The Congress, however, tried one last time to settle differences with the British. Members sent an appeal to King George III, but he refused to listen.

Over 100 people, mostly young artisans and laborers, took part in the Boston Tea Party. Nearly 45 tons of tea—about equal in value to a million dollars today—were tossed into Boston Harbor.

▶ CRITICAL THINKING
Explaining Why did the protesters dress up as Native Americans?

Benjamin Franklin, John Adams, and Thomas Jefferson worked together to write the Declaration of Independence.

▶ CRITICAL THINKING
Speculating Why do you think Americans needed an official document to declare independence?

More and more Americans began to think that independence was the only answer. In January 1776, in a pamphlet called *Common Sense*, writer Thomas Paine called on the colonists to break away from Britain.

The Declaration of Independence

On July 4, 1776, the Congress issued the Declaration of Independence. Written by Thomas Jefferson of Virginia, the Declaration stated that the colonies were separating from Britain and forming a new nation—the United States of America.

In the Declaration, Jefferson explained why the Americans were creating a new nation. He referred to John Locke's idea that people can overthrow a government that ignores their rights. The Declaration stated that "all men are created equal" and have certain God-given rights. King George III had violated colonists' rights, and so the colonists had the right to rebel.

An American Victory

The Declaration turned the conflict into a war for independence. The struggle was long and bitter. The American Continental Army had fewer and less-disciplined soldiers than the British. However, they had a skilled general in Washington. The British had the disadvantage of trying to fight a war a long way from home. Also, they had to conquer the whole country to win. The Americans only had to hold out until the British accepted defeat.

The turning point came in October 1777 when the Americans won the Battle of Saratoga in New York. France, Britain's old enemy, realized that the colonists might win and agreed to help the Americans.

The final victory came in 1781 at the Battle of Yorktown in Virginia. American and French forces surrounded and trapped the British. The British surrendered. Peace talks began, and two years later, the Treaty of Paris ended the war. Britain finally accepted American independence.

The United States Constitution

The United States at first was a confederation, or a loose union of independent states. Its plan of government was called the Articles of Confederation. The Articles created a national government,

Virginia Historical Society/The Bridgeman Art Library

but the states held most powers. It soon became clear that the Articles were too weak to deal with the new nation's problems.

To change the Articles, 55 delegates met in Philadelphia in 1787. They decided instead to write a constitution for an entirely new national government. The new United States Constitution set up a **federal** system, which divided powers between the national government and the states. The delegates divided power in the national government between executive, legislative, and judicial branches. A system called checks and balances enabled each branch to limit the powers of the other branches.

The American leaders who met in Philadelphia in 1787 and wrote the U.S. Constitution were some of the nation's best political minds. What sort of government did the Constitution create?

The Constitution made the United States a republic with an elected president. In 1789, George Washington was elected the first president of the United States. That same year, a Bill of Rights was added to the Constitution. The Bill of Rights guaranteed certain rights to citizens that the government could not violate. These rights included freedom of religion, speech, and press, and the right to trial by jury.

The U.S. Constitution was shaped by Enlightenment principles. One of these is **popular sovereignty**, or the idea that government receives its powers from the people. Another principle is **limited government**, or the idea that a government may use only those powers given to it by the people.

 **PROGRESS CHECK**

Explaining What kind of government did the Americans set up after the American Revolution?

LESSON 1 REVIEW

Review Vocabulary

1. Use the words *persecute* and *boycott* in a sentence about the American colonies.

2. What is meant by *popular sovereignty* and why was it important?

Answer the Guiding Questions

3. *Evaluating* Why did the success of the Pilgrims influence others to settle in the Americas?

4. *Making Connections* What types of British laws did American colonists protest the most?

5. *Drawing Conclusions* Why do you think it was important for the authors of the Constitution to create a Bill of Rights?

6. **ARGUMENT** Write a short essay from the viewpoint of Thomas Paine in which you try to persuade American colonists to declare independence from Britain.

The French Revolution and Napoleon

IT MATTERS BECAUSE

The French Revolution drew on some of the ideas of the American Revolution.

The Revolution Begins

GUIDING QUESTION *Why did revolution break out in France?*

The American Revolution had an immediate effect on many people in France. They also wanted political changes based on the ideas of freedom and equality. The French Revolution began in 1789. It dramatically changed France and all of Europe.

The Causes of the French Revolution

In the 1700s, France was one of the most powerful countries in Europe. French kings ruled with absolute power. Nobles lived in great wealth and enjoyed many privileges. Most of France's people, however, were poor. They had little education and struggled to make a living.

The French people were divided into three **estates,** or classes. This system determined a person's legal rights and social standing. It also created great inequality in French society.

The First Estate was the Catholic clergy, or church officials. They did not pay taxes, and they received money from church lands. The Second Estate was the nobles. They held the highest posts in the military and in government. Like the clergy, the nobles paid no taxes. They lived in luxury at the king's court or in their country houses surrounded by large areas of land.

Taking Notes: *Sequencing*

As you read, use a time line to keep track of when events happened. Note the date and a word or two about the event.

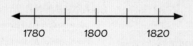

Content Vocabulary

• estate
• bourgeoisie
• coup d'etat

Everyone else in France belonged to the Third Estate. At the top of this group were members of the middle class, known as the **bourgeoisie** (burzh • wah • ZEE). Merchants, bankers, doctors, lawyers, and teachers were members of the bourgeoisie. Next were the city workers—artisans, day laborers, and servants. At the bottom were the peasants, who made up more than 80 percent of the French people. Although the members of the Third Estate paid taxes to the king, they had no voice in governing the country.

As the middle class learned more about Enlightenment ideas, they began to resent the privileges of the nobles and clergy. An Englishman traveling in France discovered how **widespread** the unrest had become:

PRIMARY SOURCE

❚❚ Walking up a long hill . . . I was joined by a poor woman who complained of the times, and that it was a sad country; . . . she said her husband had but a morsel [small piece] of land, one cow, and a poor little horse, yet they had [42 lbs.] of wheat and three chickens to pay as rent to one [lord], and [4 lbs.] of oats, one chicken, and 1s. [a coin] to pay to another, besides very heavy tallies [land taxes] and other taxes. ❚❚

—from *Travels*, by Arthur Young, 1789

The National Assembly

In 1788, food shortages and rising prices caused great discontent throughout France. At the same time, the French government was almost bankrupt because of costly wars and rising expenses for the court of King Louis XVI (LOO•ee). French banks became reluctant to lend money to the government. The king, desperate for funds, asked the nobles and clergy to pay taxes. When these groups refused, Louis called a meeting of the country's legislature, the Estates-General. This group was made up of representatives from all three estates. If the Estates-General agreed, Louis could impose new taxes.

In the Estates-General, the nobles and clergy refused to give up their privileges, including not paying taxes. Frustrated, the delegates of the Third Estate decided to meet separately. They formed a new group—the National Assembly—and agreed not to break up until they wrote a constitution for France.

The people of Paris celebrated this victory, but they worried that the king's troops would shut down the National Assembly. They got ready to fight. On July 14, 1789, a large crowd stormed a prison called the Bastille (ba•STEEL).

THE THREE ESTATES IN PREREVOLUTIONARY FRANCE

Population

98.0%
Third Estate: Commoners

0.5%
First Estate: Clergy

1.5%
Second Estate: Nobility

Land Ownership

65%
Third Estate: Commoners

10%
First Estate: Clergy

25%
Second Estate: Nobility

Taxation

100%
Third Estate: Commoners

Ninety-eight of every 100 people in France were members of the Third Estate.

▶ **CRITICAL THINKING**
Drawing Conclusions Upon which estate in France did the government depend for its income?

---

estate a social class in France before the French Revolution

bourgeoisie the middle class in France

Academic Vocabulary

widespread frequent in many places; common

Connections to TODAY

Political Left and Right

When the National Assembly met in 1789, those who supported far-reaching political changes sat on the left side of the meeting room. The people who favored little or no change sat on the right side. Today we still use the terms *left* and *right* to describe these two political viewpoints.

News of the fall of the Bastille spread to the countryside, where the peasants rose up against the nobles. To satisfy the people, the National Assembly ended the privileges of the clergy and nobles. It also issued the Declaration of the Rights of Man and the Citizen. Based on Enlightenment ideas, the declaration stated that the government's powers came from the people, not the king. All people, it said, were equal under the law.

In 1791, the National Assembly made France a constitutional monarchy. France was to be ruled by an elected legislature. Louis, however, refused to accept these changes and tried to flee Paris. As Europe's kings threatened to crush France's revolution, some leaders in Paris pushed for greater change. In 1792, they set up a new government called the National Convention.

✓ **PROGRESS CHECK**

Identifying What political reforms did the National Assembly adopt?

A Republic in France

GUIDING QUESTION *How did supporters of France's revolution enforce their reforms?*

The National Convention ended the monarchy and made France a republic. It wrote a new constitution giving the vote to every man, whether or not he owned property. Meanwhile, two

The people of Paris demonstrated against the king by violently attacking the hated Bastille prison. Today, the French celebrate the day of attack—July 14—as Bastille Day, their national holiday. Why do you think the French celebrate a day of violence?

Reading HELP DESK

Academic Vocabulary

radical extreme or far-reaching

groups fought for control of the Convention. One group, called Girondists, believed the revolution had gone far enough. The other group, known as Jacobins, favored more **radical** change. The Jacobins finally won and took power.

Toward the Future

In late 1792, the National Convention put King Louis XVI on trial and found him guilty of aiding France's enemies. A month later, Louis was beheaded on the guillotine (GEE·oh·teen)—a new machine designed to quickly execute people.

Louis's execution alarmed Europe's ruling monarchs. The rulers of Austria and Prussia were already at war with France. In early 1793, Britain, Spain, the Netherlands, and Sardinia joined them in battle against France's revolutionary army.

As the threat of foreign invasions rose, many French people rushed to defend the revolution. The people of Paris were dedicated supporters, shopkeepers, artisans, and workers who saw themselves as heroes and heroines and demanded respect from the upper classes. They addressed each other as "citizen" or "citizeness" rather than "mister" or "madame."

The Reign of Terror

Despite widespread support, the revolution had many enemies within France. To deal with growing unrest, the National Convention set up the Committee of Public Safety to run the country. The Committee took harsh steps against anyone they felt opposed the revolution. Revolutionary courts sentenced to death by guillotine anyone believed to be disloyal. This included Girondists, clergy, nobles, and even women and children. To blend in, wealthy people adopted the simple clothing of the lower classes. About 40,000 people died, including Queen Marie Antoinette. This period, from July 1793 to July 1794, became known as the Reign of Terror.

During this time, the Committee came under the control of a lawyer named Maximilien Robespierre (mak·see·meel·ya ROHBZ·pyehr). Robespierre wanted to create a "Republic of Virtue." By this he meant a democratic society made up of good citizens. Under Robespierre's lead, the Committee opened new schools, taught the peasants new farming skills, and worked to keep prices under control. Robespierre even created a new national religion that worshipped a "Supreme Being." This attempt to replace France's traditional Catholic faith, however, did not last.

With France facing pressure from foreign invasions, the Committee decided to raise a new army. All single men between the ages of 18 and 25 were required to join this new army.

BIOGRAPHY

Marie Antoinette (1755–1793)

As the wife of King Louis XVI, Queen Marie Antoinette ruled over a court of luxury. Her many expenses were partly to blame for France's large debt. As problems and debts mounted, many French people turned against her. Public anger rose when the queen was claimed to have said, "Let them eat cake!" in response to the cry that the peasants had no bread. Later, during the Revolution, Louis and Marie Antoinette tried to flee to Austria, where the queen's brother ruled. They did not get far. Soldiers arrested the royal couple and returned them to Paris. In August 1792, the queen was held in prison until she was executed more than a year later.

▶ **CRITICAL THINKING**
Speculating Would Marie Antoinette have been treated differently if she had not fled Paris?

With this new force of almost a million soldiers, France halted the threat from abroad. Revolutionary generals gained confidence from their military victories. They soon became important in French politics.

With the republic out of danger, people in France wanted to end the Reign of Terror. Robespierre lost his influence, and his enemies ordered him to be executed without trial. Wealthy middle-class leaders then came to power.

France's new leaders tried to follow more moderate policies. They wrote a new constitution that allowed only men with property to vote. In 1795, a five-man council known as the Directory was created to run the country. The Directory, however, was unable to handle food shortages, rising prices, government bankruptcy, and attacks by other countries. By 1799, the Directory had lost much support. The French people began to look for a strong leader who could restore order.

☑ **PROGRESS CHECK**

Identifying What was the Reign of Terror?

Napoleon Leads France

GUIDING QUESTION *How was Napoleon able to take over France's government?*

As the Directory weakened at home, the French army won victories in the war with Europe's monarchies. One battle front was in Italy, where the French were fighting against Austrian troops. In those battles, a young French general captured public attention. His name was Napoleon Bonaparte (nuh·POH·lee·uhn BOH·nuh·pahrt).

Born on the Mediterranean island of Corsica in 1769, Napoleon Bonaparte went to military school and became an officer. He supported the revolution. His great talent for military work helped him rise to the rank of general by the time he was 24 years old. After his successes in Italy, Napoleon attacked the British in Egypt in 1799. While in Egypt, he heard of the political troubles back home. He immediately returned to France. There, he opposed the Directory and took part in a **coup d'état** (koo day·TAH). This is when a group seeking power uses force to suddenly replace top government officials.

Napoleon took the title of First Consul and became the strong leader many French people believed they needed.

The guillotine was designed by Dr. Joseph Guillotine to make executions quick and more humane. Instead, the guillotine came to represent harshness and fear during the French Revolution.

Fotosearch

Reading**HELP**DESK

coup d'état a change of government in which a new group of leaders seize power by force

Napoleon quickly reorganized the government to strengthen his control. He changed France's finances and tax system. He appointed local officials and created many new schools. In addition, he created a new legal system known as the Napoleonic Code. This code of laws was based on Enlightenment ideas. Finally, Napoleon established a more peaceful relationship with the Catholic Church, which had opposed the revolution.

Napoleon did not carry out all of the French Revolution's ideas. People were equal under the law, but freedom of speech and the press were restricted. A new class of nobles was created, based on ability rather than wealth or family. Then, in 1804, Napoleon crowned himself emperor, and France became an empire. Now his dream could be fulfilled.

✔ **PROGRESS CHECK**

Explaining How did Napoleon strengthen his control after becoming First Consul?

The Creation of an Empire

GUIDING QUESTION *How did Napoleon build and then lose an empire?*

Napoleon wanted to do more than govern France. He wanted to build a great empire. Beginning in 1803, Napoleon won a number of military battles that helped him reach his goal. By 1807, Napoleon controlled an empire that stretched across Europe from the Atlantic Ocean to Russia.

Many different territories were part of Napoleon's empire. Napoleon directly ruled France and parts of Germany and Italy. He named relatives to govern other lands in his empire, such as Spain and the Netherlands. Outside the empire, independent countries, such as Prussia, Austria, and Sweden, were forced to ally with France.

Two forces, however, helped to bring Napoleon's empire to an end. One was nationalism, or the desire of a people for self-rule. The nations conquered by Napoleon's army rejected his rule and the French practices forced on them. The other force was the combined strength of Britain and Russia working against him.

Napoleon Meets Defeat

Napoleon hoped to cross the English Channel and invade Britain. He never achieved this goal. A major French defeat took place off the coast of Spain. There, in 1805, the British admiral Lord Horatio Nelson defeated the French navy in the Battle of Trafalgar.

This famous portrait of Napoleon shows him riding to battle. It was painted by Jacques-Louis David.

▶ **CRITICAL THINKING**
Analyzing How did the artist show that Napoleon was a powerful leader?

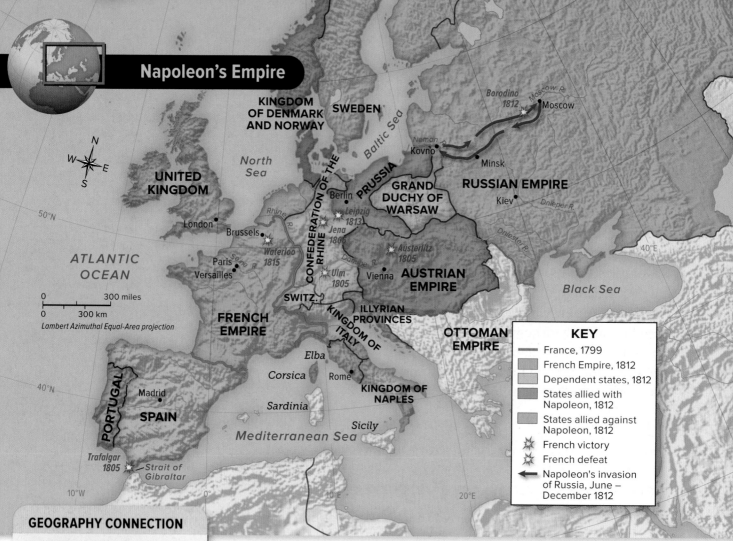

Napoleon's Empire

KINGDOM OF DENMARK AND NORWAY

SWEDEN

UNITED KINGDOM

North Sea

Baltic Sea

CONFEDERATION OF THE RHINE

PRUSSIA

Neman R.

Kovno • Minsk •

Borodino 1812 Moscow ★ *Moscow R.*

Berlin •

GRAND DUCHY OF WARSAW

RUSSIAN EMPIRE

Kiev •

Dnieper R.

London •

Leipzig 1813

Brussels •

Rhine R.

Jena 1806

Seine R.

Waterloo 1815

Paris •
Versailles •

ATLANTIC OCEAN

50°N

Austerlitz 1805

Ulm 1805

Vienna •

AUSTRIAN EMPIRE

Danube R.

Dniester R.

40°E

Black Sea

SWITZ.

FRENCH EMPIRE

KINGDOM OF ITALY

ILLYRIAN PROVINCES

OTTOMAN EMPIRE

Elba

Corsica

Rome •

KINGDOM OF NAPLES

40°N

Madrid •

PORTUGAL

SPAIN

Sardinia

Sicily

Mediterranean Sea

Trafalgar 1805 Strait of Gibraltar

10°W   0°   10°E   20°E

0 — 300 miles
0 — 300 km
Lambert Azimuthal Equal-Area projection

KEY
— France, 1799
� French Empire, 1812
▢ Dependent states, 1812
▢ States allied with Napoleon, 1812
▢ States allied against Napoleon, 1812
★ French victory
✸ French defeat
← Napoleon's invasion of Russia, June – December 1812

GEOGRAPHY CONNECTION

From 1807 to 1812, Napoleon controlled a large part of Europe.

1. **PLACE** About how far south did Napoleon's empire extend by 1812?

2. **CRITICAL THINKING**
   Theorizing What geographic feature of Britain might explain why the British navy was able to defeat Napoleon's attempts at invasion?

After Trafalgar, Napoleon decided to strike at Britain's economic lifeline—trade. In a plan called the Continental System, Napoleon forbade the countries in his empire to trade with Britain. However, the Continental System was difficult to enforce and finally proved unsuccessful.

Napoleon next decided to invade Russia. He organized the Grand Army, a force of about 600,000 soldiers from all over Europe. Napoleon led the Grand Army into Russia in the summer of 1812. Except for one battle, the Russians refused to fight. Instead, they drew Napoleon's army deeper into Russia. When the harsh Russian winter arrived, Napoleon's soldiers were unprepared, helpless, and far from home. Their retreat proved to be a disaster. Fewer than 100,000 soldiers returned alive.

France's enemies then captured Napoleon and exiled him to Elba, an island off the coast of Italy. Napoleon escaped and returned to France in the spring of 1815. He easily won public

Reading**HELP**DESK

Academic Vocabulary

overseas across an ocean

support and assembled his old army. At Waterloo in Belgium, an international force led by Britain's Duke of Wellington finally defeated Napoleon. This time, Napoleon was sent to the island of St. Helena in the southern Atlantic Ocean, where he died in 1821.

What Was the Congress of Vienna?

In September 1814, European leaders gathered in Vienna, Austria. Their goal was to return peace and stability to Europe. This meeting, called the Congress of Vienna, was led by Austria's foreign minister, Klemens von Metternich (MEH·tuhr·nihk).

Metternich and the other leaders were conservative. That is, they opposed changes that threatened traditional ways. Today, conservatives in the U.S. believe in traditional ways but also support self-rule. European conservatives of the early 1800s supported powerful monarchies. They opposed individual liberties and the right of self-rule. Hoping to crush revolutionary ideas, the conservative leaders at the Congress restored the royal families who had ruled in Europe before Napoleon.

European leaders at Vienna also redrew Europe's borders. France lost the lands won by Napoleon. It also had to pay other countries for war damages. At the same time, Russia, Prussia, Austria, and Great Britain expanded in size. Russia increased its share of Poland, Prussia gained more German lands, and Austria acquired territory in Italy. Adding to its **overseas** empire, Britain won colonies in Asia, Africa, and the Caribbean.

The Congress above all wanted to create a balance of power, or equal strength among their countries. They hoped that such a balance would prevent any one nation from controlling Europe. To keep the peace, the leaders agreed to meet from time to time. These meetings were called the Concert of Europe.

Austria's foreign minister Klemens Von Metternich led the Congress of Vienna. This was a gathering of European leaders who shared the goal of returning Europe to a time of unity and stability.

☑ **PROGRESS CHECK**

Analyzing Why did the Congress of Vienna support rule by powerful monarchs?

LESSON 2 REVIEW

Review Vocabulary

1. Use the word *bourgeoisie* in a sentence about the Third Estate in French society.

2. Explain how a *coup d'etat* is different from an election.

Answer the Guiding Questions

3. *Differentiating* What were the three estates in France before the revolution, and how were their tax responsibilities different?

4. *Assessing* What was the result of Napoleon's invasion of Russia in 1812?

5. *Evaluating* What happened at the Battle of Trafalgar, and why was it significant?

6. **INFORMATIVE/EXPLANATORY** Explain the results of the Congress of Vienna in a short paragraph.

What Do You Think?

Did the French People Have Cause to Rebel Against Their Monarchy?

Before the French Revolution, France's peasants, workers, and shopkeepers expressed anger about their lack of political and social rights. The officials of King Louis XVI believed that the lower classes neglected their duties and were disloyal to the government that protected them.

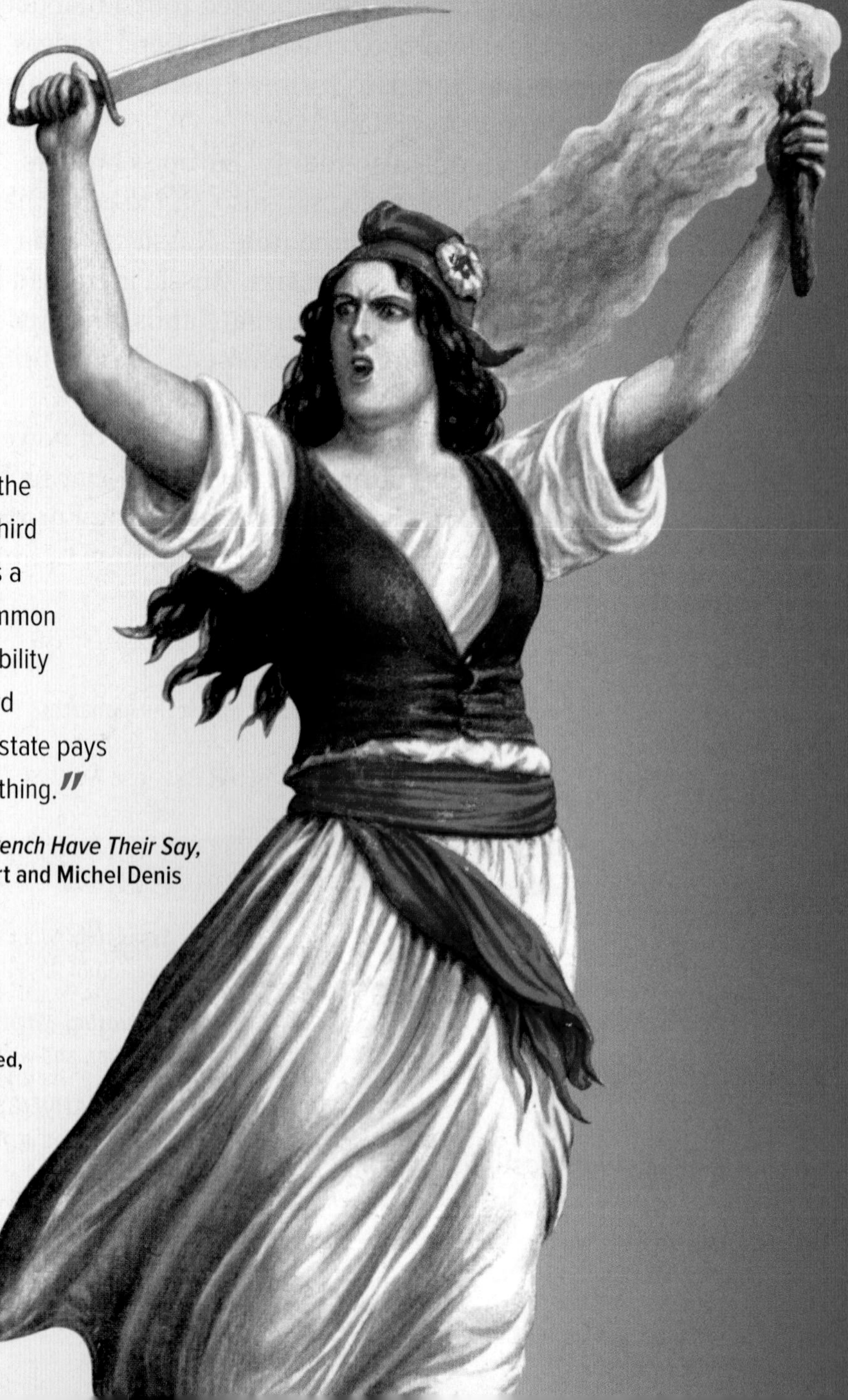

The woman in the painting represents the Third Estate. She wears the colors of the Revolution—red, white, and blue—and carries a torch of freedom.

Hulton Archive/Getty Images

Yes

PRIMARY SOURCE

"The nobility enjoys and owns everything, and would like to free itself from everything. However, if the nobility commands the army, the Third Estate makes it up. If nobility pours a drop of blood, the Third Estate [common people] spreads rivers of it. The nobility empties the royal treasury, the Third Estate fills it up. Finally, the Third Estate pays everything and does not enjoy anything."

—from *1789: The French Have Their Say,* by Pierre Goubert and Michel Denis

Marie Antoinette

King Louis XVI

No

PRIMARY SOURCE

❚❚ [The] districts [of the country] are made up of a certain number of towns and villages, which are in turn inhabited by families. To them belong the lands which yield products, provide for the livelihood of the inhabitants, and furnish the revenues [money] from which salaries are paid to those without land and taxes are levied to meet public expenditures . . . .

Families themselves scarcely know that they depend on this state, of which they form a part: . . . They consider the … taxes required for the maintenance of public order as nothing but the law of the strongest; and they see no other reason to obey than their powerlessness to resist. As a result, everyone seeks to cheat the authorities and to pass social obligations on to his neighbors. ❚❚

—from *The Works of Turgot*, ed. by Gustave Schelle

What Do You Think? DBQ

1. **Explaining** What were conditions like for the Third Estate in France before the Revolution?

2. **Identifying Central Issues** What was the position of the ruling class on taxes? Do you think its attitude was fair or unfair? Why?

3. **Making Inferences** Who does the Third Estate think enjoys the benefits from government money? Why?

(l)UniversalImagesGroup/Getty Images, (r)Imagno/Hulton Archive/Getty Images

Nationalism and Nation-States

ESSENTIAL QUESTION

• How do governments change?

IT MATTERS BECAUSE

The demands of peasants and workers can make changes in a nation's government.

Nationalism and Reform

GUIDING QUESTION *What political ideas shaped Europe during the 1800s and early 1900s?*

Nationalism means the desire of people with the same history, language, and customs for self-rule. During the 1800s, nationalism, along with demands for political reform, led to dramatic and far-reaching changes in Europe and the Americas.

Political Reform in Britain

While war and revolution raged in most of Europe, change came peacefully to Britain. In the early 1800s, nobles ran Britain's government, and the middle and working classes could not vote. Groups having no voice in government began demanding change. In 1832, the British government passed a law that gave voting rights to most middle-class men. New and growing cities gained more seats in Parliament.

As industry continued to grow, dissatisfied workers began to speak out and protest for additional rights. Workers still did not have the right to vote and felt they were being unfairly represented by the government. In 1838, supporters of the working class, known as Chartists, demanded a fully democratic Parliament and reforms, including the vote for all men. They sent a petition to Parliament, stating:

ReadingHELPDESK

Taking Notes: *Organizing*

As you read about the uprisings in each country, keep a list of the nations and the events of each revolt. Write down the outcome in each case.

Country	Uprising and Its Outcome

Content Vocabulary

• **nationalism**
• **guerrilla warfare**
• **kaiser**
• **abolitionism**

" May it please your Honourable House ... to use your utmost endeavors [efforts] ... to have a law passed, granting to every male of lawful age, sane mind, and unconvicted of crime, the right of voting for members of Parliament; and directing all future elections ... to be in the way of secret ballot; ... . "

—from *The Life and Struggles of William Lovett*

The government would not accept the Chartists' demands. By the late 1800s, however, Britain's leaders were willing to make some changes. William Gladstone led the Liberal Party, which was supported by many middle-class voters. After Gladstone became prime minister in 1868, he had Parliament grant the vote to many rural workers and reorganize districts to give more equal representation.

Benjamin Disraeli, the leader of the Conservative Party, was Gladstone's main rival. Disraeli worked to maintain British traditions but cautiously adopted reforms. In 1867, Disraeli's Conservative government gave the vote to many urban workers.

In 1900, a new political group—the Labour Party—formed. It claimed to represent the working class. Labour Party supporters backed a Liberal government elected in 1906. Liberal and Labour members of Parliament tried to improve workers' lives. They passed laws that provided workers with retirement pensions, a minimum wage, unemployment aid, and health insurance.

In the early 1900s, British women known as suffragettes pushed for women to have the right to vote. They marched in protest and went on hunger strikes. In 1918, Parliament gave women over the age of 30 the right to vote. Ten years later, it gave the vote to all women over age 21.

The Palace at Westminster, which includes London's famous Big Ben clock tower also houses the British Parliament. In 1870, the two houses of Parliament—House of Lords and House of Commons—established headquarters there.

Irish Demands for Self-Rule

During the 1800s, Britain had difficulty ruling its neighbor, Ireland. British and Irish Protestants owned most of Ireland's wealth. Yet, most Irish people were Catholic and poor. By 1830, their protests had won them the right to vote and to sit in Britain's Parliament. Still, British leaders refused to grant the Irish their main goal—self-rule.

©Matt Leete/SuperStock/Corbis

---

nationalism the desire of people with the same customs and beliefs for self-rule

Build Vocabulary: *The Suffix –ism*

Throughout this chapter, you will read many words with the suffix *–ism*. The suffix *–ism* means "belief in." *Nationalism*, for example, can mean "belief in nations."

Irish hatred of British rule increased when a severe famine hit Ireland in the 1840s. The British government did not send enough aid. At least one million Irish died of starvation and disease. Millions more left for the United States and other lands.

After this tragedy, pressure rose for Irish home rule, or Ireland's right to its own legislature to handle Irish affairs. Gladstone tried to pass home rule, but Parliament did not support him. Many British and Irish Protestants opposed home rule, fearing it would lead to Irish independence.

Political Changes in France

In 1848, nationalist and reforming revolts swept Europe. Most of them failed, but revolution was somewhat successful in France. There, King Louis-Philippe was overthrown and a republic declared. Louis Napoleon, nephew of Napoleon Bonaparte, soon was elected president and later emperor. Under Napoleon III, France enjoyed prosperity, but its government was not democratic.

In 1870, Napoleon III declared war on Prussia, the most powerful German state. Prussia won, and Napoleon's government fell. France faced civil war when workers took control of Paris. The upper-class government sent troops to crush the workers. By 1875, France was again a republic. However, distrust between upper classes and workers remained strong.

Monarchies in Austria and Russia

During the late 1800s, monarchs in Austria and Russia tried to block reform. However, bitter defeats in war forced both empires to make some changes.

In 1867, Austria made a deal with the Hungarians, who were part of the Austrian Empire. Hungary became a separate kingdom linked to Austria, called Austria-Hungary. The Hungarians were satisfied, but other national groups were not. Their demands for self-rule increased.

In Russia, defeat in war made Czar Alexander II realize that his country was far behind other European powers. He decided to build factories and improve farming. In 1861, Alexander freed the serfs—peasants tied to the land, which they farmed for landlords. The peasants did not get enough land, however, and they remained discontented.

✔ **PROGRESS CHECK**

Inferring Why might the people of France have voted for Louis Napoleon?

After defeat in the Austro-Prussian War, Russian ruler Czar Alexander II introduced reforms in hopes of making Russia the strongest country in Europe.

©Chris Hellier/Corbis

New Nations in Europe

GUIDING QUESTION *Why did new nations arise in Europe during the mid-1800s?*

In the early 1800s, Germany and Italy as we know them today did not exist. They were made up of many territories. After 1850, their peoples began to form united countries.

How Did Italy Unite?

In 1848, Austria controlled most of Italy's small territories. In the north, the kingdom of Piedmont was independent. Piedmont's rulers were King Victor Emmanuel and the prime minister, Camillo di Cavour (kah·MEEL·loh dee kuh·VUR). Both leaders wanted to unite all of Italy into one nation.

In 1854, Piedmont sided with Britain and France in a war with Russia. In return for Piedmont's support, France helped Piedmont drive Austria out of Italy in 1859. Piedmont's victory was the first step toward uniting Italy. Soon, other parts of northern Italy overthrew their rulers and united with Piedmont.

At the same time, nationalist leader Giuseppe Garibaldi (joo·ZEHP·pay gar·uh·BAWL·dee) led uprisings in southern Italy. In 1860, his forces gained control of the island of Sicily. Garibaldi was skilled in **guerrilla warfare** (guh·RIH·luh WAWR·fehr), a type of fighting in which soldiers make surprise attacks on the enemy. Garibaldi's army won Italy's mainland. People in the south then voted to join a united Italy.

GEOGRAPHY CONNECTION

Both Italy and Germany unified their nations in the mid-1800s.

1 **PLACE** What was the effect of adding the North German Confederation to Prussia?

2 **CRITICAL THINKING**
Drawing Conclusions How did nationalism influence the rise of Italy?

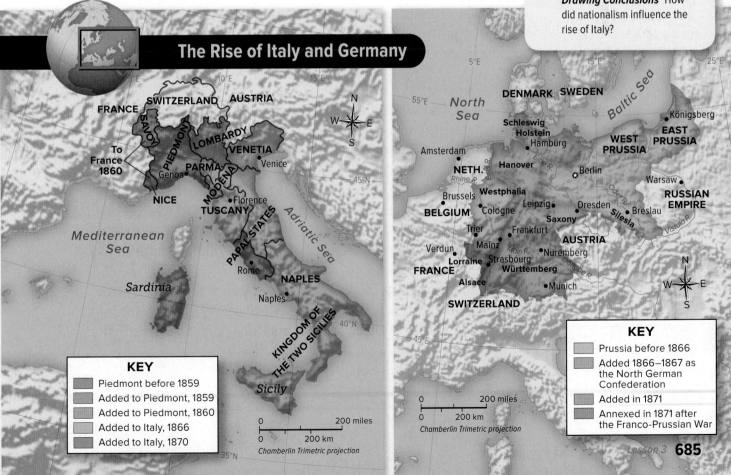

The Rise of Italy and Germany

KEY
- Piedmont before 1859
- Added to Piedmont, 1859
- Added to Piedmont, 1860
- Added to Italy, 1866
- Added to Italy, 1870

0 ___ 200 miles
0 ___ 200 km
Chamberlin Trimetric projection

KEY
- Prussia before 1866
- Added 1866–1867 as the North German Confederation
- Added in 1871
- Annexed in 1871 after the Franco-Prussian War

0 ___ 200 miles
0 ___ 200 km
Chamberlin Trimetric projection

Otto von Bismarck was a firm leader. He decided to govern with an iron fist rather than win people over with speeches.

▶ CRITICAL THINKING
Analyzing How did Bismarck's "iron fist" make him a successful prime minister?

In 1861, Italy became a constitutional monarchy. Two areas remained outside the new kingdom. One was Rome, and the other was Venice. By 1870, wars had brought both areas into Italy.

A New German Empire

During the mid-1800s, nationalism grew stronger in the German states. Many people wanted a united Germany under a strong monarchy. They gained Prussia's support. In 1862, Prussia's King William I named Otto von Bismarck (AHT·oh fawn BIHZ·mahrk) as his prime minister.

Bismarck was a deeply conservative Junker (YUN·kuhr), or wealthy landowner. He vowed to govern Prussia by "blood and iron" rather than by votes and speeches. Bismarck quickly strengthened Prussia's army. He used the army to defeat Denmark, Austria, and France. As a result of Bismarck's victories, other German states agreed to unite with Prussia. On January 18, 1871, William was proclaimed **kaiser** (KY·zuhr), or emperor, of a united Germany.

☑ PROGRESS CHECK

Explaining What role did Bismarck play in uniting Germany?

Growth of the United States

GUIDING QUESTION *How did the United States change during the 1800s?*

Nationalism helped shape the United States during the 1800s. The country's size steadily grew. Many Americans believed that their nation was destined to be rich and powerful.

Westward Expansion

During the 1800s, the United States pushed westward. Many Americans came to believe in "Manifest Destiny," the idea that their country should stretch from the Atlantic Ocean to the Pacific Ocean.

In 1845, the United States annexed Texas, which had declared independence from Mexico. This led to war between the United States and Mexico. The United States won in 1848 and gained the area that today includes California and several other western states.

Settlers set up farms, **founded** communities, and created states in the new lands. The westward drive, however, brought suffering—loss of land, culture, and life—to Native Americans.

Imagno/Hulton Archive/Getty Images

Reading HELP DESK

kaiser emperor of Germany

abolitionism movement to end slavery

Academic Vocabulary

found to establish; to bring into being

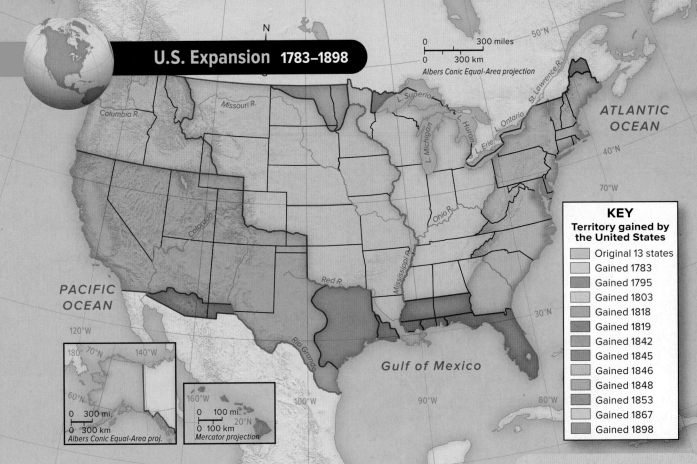

U.S. Expansion 1783–1898

0 —— 300 miles
0 —— 300 km
Albers Conic Equal-Area projection

ATLANTIC OCEAN

PACIFIC OCEAN

Gulf of Mexico

KEY
Territory gained by the United States

	Original 13 states
	Gained 1783
	Gained 1795
	Gained 1803
	Gained 1818
	Gained 1819
	Gained 1842
	Gained 1845
	Gained 1846
	Gained 1848
	Gained 1853
	Gained 1867
	Gained 1898

0 300 mi.
0 300 km
Albers Conic Equal-Area proj.

0 100 mi.
0 100 km
Mercator projection

The American Civil War

Over time, the Northern and Southern states developed different ways of life. The South had an agricultural economy based on raising cotton. Cotton growing depended on the labor of enslaved African Americans. In the North, industries created a manufacturing economy. Some Northerners believed in **abolitionism** (a·buh·LIH·shuhn·ih·zuhm), a movement to end slavery.

The disagreement over slavery grew more heated. In 1860, Abraham Lincoln, an opponent of slavery, was elected president. Southern states feared that he would end slavery. Eleven states seceded, or left, the United States. They formed the Confederate States of America. Fighting erupted between this group and the United States in April 1861. The American Civil War had begun.

The North had more people and more industries than the South. In spite of this, skilled military leaders such as Robert E. Lee led Confederate forces to many early victories. Later, the North threw all of its resources against the South. The conflict ended in a Northern victory. More than 600,000 Americans died in the war.

The North's victory reunited the country. Millions of African Americans were freed from slavery and became citizens. Factories, railroads, and cities were built at increasing speeds. Millions of immigrants from Europe and Asia contributed to the country's growth during the late 1800s.

GEOGRAPHY CONNECTION

Because of continued expansion, the United States reached across the middle of the North American continent by 1848.

1 LOCATION What present-day state was gained in 1819?

2 CRITICAL THINKING
Theorizing Why might Americans have wanted the country to expand all the way to the Pacific Coast?

America Rebounds

During the 1800s, the United States became more democratic. President Andrew Jackson's election in 1828 was called a victory for the "common people." It was made possible by the spread of voting rights to almost all adult white men.

In the 1800s, women also began to demand equality. Women suffragists fought hard for the right to vote. Finally, in 1920, the Nineteenth Amendment to the Constitution was ratified, or approved. This guaranteed women in all states the right to vote.

☑ **PROGRESS CHECK**

Comparing and Contrasting How were the economies of the North and the South different before the American Civil War?

Women suffragists marched in Washington, D.C., the day before President Woodrow Wilson's inauguration in 1913. Though Wilson did not support woman suffrage at first, in the years following he helped pass the Nineteenth Amendment, which gave all women the right to vote.

Independence in Latin America

GUIDING QUESTION *How did the countries of Latin America win independence?*

During the 1700s, Spain and Portugal did not face serious challenges to their rule in Latin America. In the early 1800s, the situation changed. Latin Americans, inspired by the American and French revolutions, wanted independence.

Winning Independence

The first successful revolt against European rule took place in Haiti, an island territory in the Caribbean Sea. There, Toussaint L'Ouverture (TOO·sahn LOO·vehr·toor) led enslaved Africans in a revolt that **eventually** threw off French rule in 1804.

People in the Spanish colonies of Latin America were also ready to revolt. In Mexico in 1810, two Catholic priests, Miguel Hidalgo and José María Morelos, urged Mexican peasants to fight for freedom. Mexico finally won its independence in 1821.

North Wind/North Wind Picture Archives

In 1823, Central America declared its independence from Mexico. During the next decade, it divided into the republics of Guatemala, Honduras, Nicaragua, El Salvador, and Costa Rica.

In the northern part of South America, a wealthy military leader named Simón Bolívar (see·MAWN boh·LEE·vahr) started a revolt in 1810. Bolívar's forces finally crushed the Spanish at the 1819 Battle of Boyacá in Colombia. It took another 20 years, but Bolívar won freedom for the present-day countries of Venezuela, Colombia, Bolivia, Ecuador, Peru, and Panama.

As Bolívar fought in the north, a soldier named José de San Martín (hoh·SAY day san mahr·TEEN) led the struggle in the south. In 1817, San Martín led his army from Argentina across the Andes Mountains into Chile. The crossing was difficult, but San Martín took the Spanish by surprise. A few years later, San Martín and Bolívar together defeated the Spanish in Peru.

Many places have been named after Simón Bolívar to honor his revolutionary spirit, including the South American nation of Bolivia.

Challenges to Growth

Latin Americans wanted their new countries to become stable and prosperous. Their hopes, however, were not realized and these new countries faced many challenges. Political parties quarreled over the role of the Catholic Church. Border disagreements led to wars between countries. Tensions developed between rich and poor.

 **PROGRESS CHECK**

Contrasting How did Haiti's revolution differ from those of other Latin American countries?

LESSON 3 REVIEW

Review Vocabulary

1. Use the term *nationalism* in a sentence about how it relates to revolutions in South America.

Answer the Guiding Questions

2. *Comparing* How were the political reforms that took place in Britain similar to the reforms that took place in France?

3. *Evaluating* How did nationalism play a part in the rise of Italy and Germany?

4. *Determining Cause and Effect* How did the expansion of settlers in the United States affect Native Americans?

5. *Identifying Points of View* Why were Americans divided over abolitionism?

6. *Assessing* What factors led to continued discontent after Latin American countries had won their freedom?

7. **INFORMATIVE/EXPLANATORY** Write a short essay in which you explain how José de San Martín and Simón Bolívar changed life in South America.

©Christie's Images/Corbis

LESSON 4

The Industrial Revolution

ESSENTIAL QUESTION

• How does technology change the way people live?

IT MATTERS BECAUSE
Small steps in industrial development led to big changes over time.

Birth of Industry

GUIDING QUESTION *Why did the Industrial Revolution begin in Britain?*

While political change affected much of Europe and the Americas, a new economic system known as **industrialism** began in Britain. There, people began to use machines to do work that had been performed by animals or humans. Over the next 200 years, industrialism affected life so dramatically that historians call the changes it brought the Industrial Revolution.

Before the rise of industrialism, most people lived in small farming villages. Cloth was made by village people working in their homes. Merchants went from cottage to cottage, bringing the workers raw wool and cotton. The workers used hand-powered wheels to spin the wool and cotton into thread. They worked on looms to weave the thread into cloth. The merchants then sold the finished cloth for the highest possible price.

The Industrial Revolution began in the woven cloth, or textile, industry. Merchants could make a great deal of money from textiles, so they began to look for ways to produce cloth better and faster. By the 1700s, changes in Britain made this possible.

What Caused the Industrial Revolution?

Britain led the way in the Industrial Revolution for many reasons. One important reason was a change in the way British landowners used their land. For hundreds of years, landowners

---

Reading HELPDESK

Taking Notes: *Sequencing*
Use a diagram like the one shown here to list events that led to the Industrial Revolution.

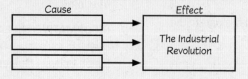

Content Vocabulary

• **industrialism**

• **corporation**

rented land to villagers, who divided it into strips. Different families worked different strips of land. In addition, villagers could keep livestock on public lands.

In the 1700s, new enclosure laws allowed landowners to combine and fence off the strips and public lands. This created large farms where the same crop could be grown on large areas. This meant larger harvests and greater profits. Often the landowners used the land as pasture for sheep. The landowners could then sell wool to the textile industry.

Successful farming provided landowners with more money to spend. Many chose to invest, or put money into new businesses. Money invested in businesses is called capital. A growing middle class of merchants and shopkeepers also began to invest capital in new industries.

GEOGRAPHY CONNECTION

The Industrial Revolution spread throughout Europe in the 1800s.

1 **HUMAN-ENVIRONMENT INTERACTION** In what areas do most of the coal mining and ironworking symbols appear?

2 **CRITICAL THINKING**
Making Generalizations
What generalization can you make about the location of railroads and manufacturing and industrial areas?

Industrial Revolution 1870

0   400 miles
0   400 km
Chamberlain Trimetric projection

KEY

Manufacturing and industrial area

• Major industrial center

⊢⊢⊢ Major railways by 1870

Industry:

🪨 Coal mining

Ⅎ Ironworking

🧵 Textile production

industrialism an economic system where machines do work that was once performed by animals or humans

Increased Population

Still another cause of the Industrial Revolution was the growing workforce. Britain's population grew rapidly in the 1700s. People now had more and better food. They were healthier, lived longer, and had larger families. At the same time, changes in farming helped increase the supply of industrial workers. New machines, such as the steel plow, meant that farms needed fewer workers. Workers forced off the land often went to work in new industries.

Britain's rich supply of natural resources also helped in the rise of industry. The country had fine harbors and a large network of rivers that flowed year-round. Britain's earliest cotton mills were powered by the flow of river water. Britain also had large supplies of coal and iron. Coal, which replaced wood as a fuel, helped to run machines. Iron was used to build machinery.

Inventors Make Advances

In the late 1700s, cloth merchants were looking for new ways to increase production. A textile weaver named James Hargreaves (HAHR·greevz) invented a machine called a spinning jenny that could spin cotton into thread very quickly. Richard Arkwright developed a way to power a spinning machine with water. Edmund Cartwright created a new powered loom. This machine could weave the thread into cloth as fast as the spinning machines produced it.

As industry developed, machines required more power than water could provide. Steam power answered this need. In 1769, the Scottish mathematician James Watt **designed** a steam engine that could power the new machines. Steam soon replaced water as the major source of power.

As the need for machines grew, iron was needed to make machine parts. In 1753, Henry Cort discovered a way to use coal to turn iron ore into pure iron. As a result, iron production grew. Coal mining became a major industry. In 1856, Henry Bessemer, an engineer, invented a less costly way to make large amounts of iron into steel. Steel was excellent for making machinery, because it was stronger than iron. Soon mining towns and steel centers grew in areas with supplies of iron ore and coal.

Henry Bessemer invented the first method of mass-producing steel. This process revolutionized the development of industry and machinery.

Stock Montage/Archive Photos/Getty Images

Reading **HELP**DESK

Academic Vocabulary

design to skillfully plan or create something

A LOCOMOTIVE

1. Water compartment
2. Coal bunker
3. Coal conveyer
4. Throttle lever
5. Firebox
6. Boiler tubes
7. Smokebox
8. Blast pipe
9. Steam chest
10. Cylinder
11. Piston

INFOGRAPHIC

The steam-powered locomotive made trains the fastest way to travel during much of the 1800s.

1. **IDENTIFYING** What natural resource was used to power the locomotive?

2. **CRITICAL THINKING**
   Assessing In addition to speed, what other advantages did a locomotive provide?

Factories and Railroads

Faster modes of transportation and new business successes fueled enormous economic growth. In 1807, Robert Fulton, an American inventor, developed a boat powered by a steam engine.

Then came the railroad—the biggest improvement in land transportation. By the mid-1800s, trains pulled by steam-powered locomotives were faster and cheaper than any other kind of transportation. Railroads soon connected major cities all across Europe. They completely changed the amount of time and money spent on the transport of goods to market. Trains carried raw materials, finished goods, and passengers faster than horses.

Ambitious entrepreneurs, or people who took risks to start businesses, set up and ran Britain's growing industries. They created industries by bringing together capital, labor, and new industrial inventions. Their efforts led to the building of factories, the major centers of the Industrial Revolution.

Why did factories develop? Machines became too large and expensive for home use. Workers and machines were brought together in one place in factories, working under managers. Workers could share skills. Factories provided a better organized and less costly way to produce large amounts of goods.

One British writer described the changes brought by factory organization, especially in weaving cloth:

In 1818, there were in Manchester, Stockport, Middleton, . . . and their vicinities, fourteen factories, containing about two thousand Looms. In 1821, there were in the same neighbourhoods thirty-two factories, containing five thousand seven hundred and thirty-two Looms. Since 1821, their number has still farther increased, and there are at present not less than ten thousand Steam Looms at work in Great Britain.

—from *Compendious History of the Cotton Manufacture* by Richard Guest

Edison's electric lightbulb took about two years to develop and allowed people to use electric lighting in their homes and businesses. How would nighttime be different in your city without this invention?

As the Industrial Revolution developed, entrepreneurs looked for different ways to raise money. One way was to form a partnership in which two or more people owned the business and pooled their own money. Another way was to create a **corporation** (kor·puh·RAY·shuhn). A corporation raises money by selling shares, or partial ownership, in the company to investors. Creating a corporation allowed entrepreneurs to have the capital to build large factories with hundreds of workers.

✓ **PROGRESS CHECK**

Understanding Cause and Effect How did successful farming and a growing population influence the Industrial Revolution in Britain?

Growth of Industry

GUIDING QUESTION *How did new inventions help advance the growth of industry?*

Britain's early start in the Industrial Revolution made it the richest and most productive country in the world. To protect this dominant position, Parliament passed laws restricting the flow of ideas, machines, and skilled workers out of the country. Despite these laws, many inventors and entrepreneurs left Britain. They carried their industrial knowledge with them. As a result, the Industrial Revolution soon spread to other areas.

Reading**HELP**DESK

corporation a type of company that sells shares in the company to investors

Reading Strategy: *Comparing and Contrasting*

When you compare and contrast, you look for similarities and differences between two things as you read. Read the section about the growth of industry in Britain and America. Note one or two similarities between the two countries. Then identify one difference.

Industry Grows in Europe and America

The Industrial Revolution spread from Britain to other European countries. European governments helped build factories, railroads, canals, and roads. The Industrial Revolution also took hold in the United States. British investors and American engineers built factories and ironworks in New England.

Like Britain, the United States had many natural resources. Americans quickly built roads and canals across the vast nation. Fulton's steamboats provided transportation on inland waterways. Railroads soon crisscrossed the country.

New Scientific Advances

During the 1800s, inventors found many ways to use electricity. In the 1830s, Samuel Morse developed the telegraph. It sent coded messages through wires. Soon telegraph lines linked most European and North American cities.

Alexander Graham Bell developed the telephone in 1876. The telephone used tiny electrical wires to carry sound. For the first time, telephones allowed people to speak to each other over long distances. Finally, in 1895, Guglielmo Marconi put together a wireless telegraph, which was later developed into the radio.

Inventors found more ways to use electric power. In 1877, Thomas Edison developed the lightbulb. As demand for electricity rose, investors in Europe and the United States funded the first power plants. These were powered by coal or oil.

Major breakthroughs also took place in transportation. In the 1880s, Rudolf Diesel and Gottlieb Daimler invented internal combustion engines. These engines produced power in autos by burning oil-based fuels. In 1903, Orville and Wilbur Wright successfully tested the world's first airplane.

✔ **PROGRESS CHECK**

Identifying How did electricity change communications?

**The Wright Brothers
(Wilbur Wright 1867–1912;
Orville Wright 1871–1948)**

The brothers Orville and Wilbur Wright were bicycle mechanics. They also were fascinated with the idea of human flight. It took them years of study to develop a flying machine. In their local library, they researched everything they could find on the subject of flight. Finally, when they could learn no more from other experts, they began experimenting with their own airplane models. The brothers eventually built a flying machine that would support a human being. Their research and experiments formed the basis of the modern airplane industry.

▶ **CRITICAL THINKING**
Theorizing How would the Wright Brothers' knowledge of bicycles have helped them build an airplane?

LESSON 4 REVIEW

Review Vocabulary

1. How does a *corporation* raise money?

2. Write a sentence to explain how *industrialism* changed the lives of workers.

Answering the Guiding Questions

3. *Finding the Main Idea* Why do historians consider this time of industrial development a revolution?

4. *Determining Cause and Effect* What inventions had an effect on the textile industry?

5. *Analyzing* Why were the telegraph and telephone important inventions at this time?

6. **INFORMATIVE/EXPLANATORY** Explain how the Industrial Revolution spread from Britain to other places in the world.

LESSON 5

Society and Industry

IT MATTERS BECAUSE
Today's society is largely driven by powerful industry and the movement of goods around the world.

A New Society

GUIDING QUESTION *How did industry change society in Europe and North America during the 1800s and early 1900s?*

By the 1860s, the Industrial Revolution brought sweeping changes to Europe and North America. During the next 100 years, industrialism also changed other regions of the world.

The Growth of Cities

One important change was the rapid growth in the population of cities. **Urbanization** (uhr·buh·nuh·ZAY·shuhn) is the movement of people from the countryside to cities. A nation is urbanized when many of its people live in cities.

Why did cities grow so rapidly? Farms were using more machines. This meant there were fewer jobs for farm workers. To find employment, many rural workers headed to nearby cities. They hoped to find jobs in the new factories.

A New Industrial Society

Before the rise of industry, there were fewer job opportunities. The Industrial Age, however, brought new jobs and a new way of life. The middle class grew as more people took advantage of these new opportunities.

Reading**HELP**DESK

Taking Notes: *Explaining*
Use a web diagram like this one to list ways that the Industrial Revolution affected society.

Social Advances during the Industrial Revolution

Content Vocabulary
• **urbanization**
• **liberalism**
• **utilitarianism**
• **socialism**
• **proletariat**
• **labor union**

Industrial growth expanded not just the size of the middle class, but also its power and wealth. The middle class had once been made up of a small number of bankers, lawyers, doctors, and merchants. Now it included the successful owners of factories, mines, and railroads. Professional workers such as clerks, managers, and teachers added to the growing number.

Industrial growth also created a much larger working class. The members of this group were people who labored in the factories and mines. Their lives were often hard, and they had few of the luxuries enjoyed by the new middle class.

Working-Class Families

Entire working-class families—children as well as adults—had to work to make enough money to live. Working conditions ranged from barely acceptable to dreadful. Workers did the same tasks over and over again. People worked up to 16 hours a day, 6 days a week. Factories and mines were hot and dirty. Diseases spread quickly. The machinery often was unsafe. As a result, many workers lost fingers, limbs, or even their lives.

Living conditions in the cities were often miserable. However, rural workers continued to look for urban factory jobs. Despite low pay and long hours, most city workers had more money than when they lived in the country. Cities also offered many leisure-time opportunities. These included parks, sports, libraries, and education.

As time passed, working conditions improved. Workers organized to demand changes. Middle-class reformers tried to better the lives of workers. As a result, factories were made safer. Working hours for women and children were reduced. New laws were passed that reduced pollution and unclean food and water in the cities.

Women's Lives

During the 1800s, women of all classes had fewer legal rights than men. It was believed that a woman's place was in the home. At this time, women worked to improve their position and find new roles. Women found jobs in businesses and in government service. There were also more opportunities for education.

City life was often hard, but it was usually better than life as a farm worker. Often several families lived together and shared what they had.

▶ **CRITICAL THINKING**
Analyzing Why did people living in cities face hardships?

National Media Museum/SSPL/The Image Works

urbanization the increase in the proportion of people living in cities rather than rural areas

For its time, New Lanark, Scotland, was a socially progressive industrial community. Workers here enjoyed better than average conditions.

▶ **CRITICAL THINKING**
Explaining How did industrialization improve the lives of the working class?

Women began to demand equal rights with men. In the United States, Britain, and other countries, women challenged the long-standing idea that politics was a man's world. They demanded the rights to vote and to hold public office.

✔ **PROGRESS CHECK**

Describing What were working conditions like for early industrial workers?

Industrialization Changes Political Ideas

GUIDING QUESTION *What new political ideas arose as a result of industrial society?*

The Industrial Revolution brought many changes, both good and bad. Starting in the early 1800s, people looked for ways to solve the problems that industry had created. They developed different ideas to address these concerns.

What Is Liberalism?

One of these new ideas was **liberalism.** Liberalism is a political philosophy based on the ideas of the Enlightenment and the French Revolution.

Liberals in the 1800s believed that all people have individual rights. These include equality under the law and freedom of speech and the press. Liberals also believed that government power should be limited by written constitutions. They felt that elected legislatures should make the laws. Most liberals believed that only men who owned property should be allowed to vote.

Reading**HELP**DESK

liberalism a political philosophy based on the Enlightenment ideas of equality and individual rights

utilitarianism the idea that society should promote the greatest happiness for the largest number of people

socialism the idea that the means of production should be owned and controlled by the people, through their government

Academic Vocabulary

cooperate to work together for the good of all

The new middle class adopted liberalism. Middle class businesspeople believed that government should not interfere with business or society. British economist Adam Smith supported this idea. In a book called *The Wealth of Nations*, Smith wrote that government should stay out of the economy and let businesses compete. This idea was known as "laissez-faire," a French word meaning "to let be."

Two other liberal thinkers in Britain, however, believed that government should step in to make society better. Jeremy Bentham (BEHN·thuhm) and John Stuart Mill promoted an idea known as **utilitarianism** (yoo·tih·luh·TEHR·ee·uh·nih·zuhm). As utilitarians, Bentham and Mill believed society should promote the greatest happiness for the most people. They supported ideas like full rights for women and improved health services. They also promoted better education.

What Is Socialism?

Not all thinkers in the 1800s agreed with the ideas of liberalism. Some supported an idea known as **socialism.** Socialists believed that the people should own and control all factories, land, capital, and raw materials. They believed that the government should manage these means of production for the people. In this way, wealth could be distributed equally among all citizens.

Some early socialists set up communities where workers could share equally in the profits. Robert Owen, a wealthy British factory owner, was one of these socialists. Owen believed that if people **cooperated,** they could create a better society.

In 1800, Owen made the Scottish mill town of New Lanark into a model industrial community. He did not turn the mill over to the workers. However, he did greatly improve living and working conditions.

The Socialism of Karl Marx

Other socialists thought Owen's work was impractical. They believed it would do little to change society. One of these socialists was Karl Marx.

Marx believed that history was a continual struggle between social classes. According to Marx, the ruling class controlled production. They also held on to most of the wealth. The working class were the actual makers of goods, therefore they should share in the profits. However, they were not paid enough.

Karl Marx believed in equality and a classless society. He also supported a government controlled by the workers. Why might Marx have been thought of as a rebel?

Marx stated that eventually the working class, which he called the **proletariat** (proh·luh·TEHR·ee·uht), would revolt and create a communist society. Under communism, social classes would end. People would be equal and share the wealth.

Marx's ideas, later called Marxism, were very influential. His ideas were the basic principles of socialist political parties in Germany, Britain, and other countries. These socialist parties encouraged government control of industry. However, instead of calling for revolution, many of these parties adopted the democratic process. Their supporters elected representatives to national legislatures, where they worked to pass laws that helped workers.

The growth of labor unions was another response to the horrors of factory life. A **labor union** is an organization of workers who unite to improve working conditions. Union leaders used strikes, or work stoppages, to force owners to bargain with the unions. One woman who worked in a textile mill wrote about a strike led by factory women in the 1830s:

PRIMARY SOURCE

❝ The mills were shut down, and the girls … listened to incendiary [angry] speeches from some early labor reformers. One of the girls stood on a pump, and gave vent [release] to the feelings of her companions in a neat speech, declaring that it was their duty to resist all attempts at cutting down wages. … [The] event caused … consternation [dismay]. ❞

—from "Early Factory Labor in New England" by Harriet H. Robinson

✔ **PROGRESS CHECK**

Describing What did Adam Smith believe about government and business?

Revolution in the Arts

GUIDING QUESTION *How did artists and writers describe the new industrial society?*

The growth of industry also sparked new movements in art, literature, and music. The often ugly appearance of industrial society caused some artists to turn away from it. Others, however, chose to portray it.

The realistic characters in Charles Dickens's novels such as *Oliver Twist* and *Great Expectations* were the everyday people of England. This painting shows a scene from Dickens's *A Christmas Carol*.

Culture Club/Hulton Archive/Getty Images

proletariat the working class

labor union an organization of those employed who work together to improve wages and working conditions

Academic Vocabulary

symbol something that stands for or suggests something else

What Is Romanticism?

By the late 1700s, artists and writers known as the romantics began to react against the Enlightenment's stress on order and reason. Their movement, called romanticism, valued feelings and the imagination as the best way to find the truth.

Poets, such as Britain's William Wordsworth and Germany's Johann von Goethe (yoh·HAHN fawn GUH·tuh), chose nature, the past, and the unusual as their subjects. They wrote poems to express their inner feelings. Romantic painters, such as Eugène Delacroix (yoo·JEEN deh·luh·KWAH) of France, chose historical or legendary subjects. Their paintings were meant to stir the emotions. The first great romantic musician was Ludwig van Beethoven (LOOD·wihg vahn BAY·toh·vuhn). This German composer's music expressed strong emotions.

Beethoven remains one of Germany's most famous composers. At age 49, Beethoven was completely deaf but continued to compose music. This sculpture stands in his honor in Bonn, Germany.

What is Realism?

By the mid-1800s, some artists and writers began to reject the romantic emphasis on feelings. Known as the realists, they wanted to portray life as it actually was.

Novelists like Britain's Charles Dickens, France's Honoré de Balzac (AHN·uh·ray day BAWL·zak), and Russia's Leo Tolstoy focused on ordinary people in everyday settings. Painters like France's Gustave Courbet (GUS·tahv kur·BAY) and Honoré Daumier (AHN·uh·ray doh·MYAY) also portrayed life in the city and countryside.

The soft sunlight sparkles off the water in Claude Monet's impressionist painting.

Dawn of Modernism

The late 1800s saw the rise of modernism. Modernist artists and writers experimented with new subjects and styles. One group of modernists studied social problems of the day.

Novelists such as Émile Zola of France and American Theodore Dreiser explored issues such as crime, alcoholism, and women's rights. Norwegian Henrik Ibsen also dealt with social issues in his plays. Another modernist group took a different approach. Symbolist artists and writers believed that the outer world was a reflection of an individual's inner reality. They studied dreams and **symbols** and used them in their works.

There's More Online! connected.mcgraw-hill.com

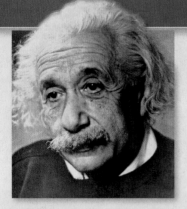

Albert Einstein (1879–1955)

Albert Einstein was born in Germany in 1879. He struggled to do well at school and had trouble finding work after graduation. After attending technical school, Einstein worked as a clerk in a government office. The job was simple for him, and it left him plenty of time to pursue his interest in physics. Einstein's research earned him a job as a professor at a university. When Hitler came to power in Germany, Einstein moved to the United States and continued his work in physics. His ideas about the physical universe eventually led to the development of the atomic bomb and the nuclear reactor.

▶ **CRITICAL THINKING**
Making Inferences Why might Einstein have struggled to find work after graduation?

During the 1870s, a group of artists developed a style called impressionism. The impressionists were interested in color and the effects of light on outdoor subjects. The French impressionists included Claude Monet (moh·NAY),Pierre-Auguste Renoir (REN·wahr), and Edgar Degas (duh·GAH). Mary Cassatt of the United States was also a famous impressionist painter. Composers, led by France's Claude Debussy, created impressionist music. They layered sound upon sound to create a dreamy, shimmering effect.

✓ **PROGRESS CHECK**

Describing What did the romantics emphasize in their works?

The New Science

GUIDING QUESTION *What advances made in science in the mid-1800s have transformed life today?*

During the 1800s, scientists expanded knowledge about life and the universe. Their work also led to medical advances that cured deadly diseases and lengthened life spans.

The Diversity of Life

During the 1800s, many people wondered why the world has so many kinds of plants and animals. Charles Darwin set out to find an answer. His research led him to develop a theory of evolution: plants and animals change very slowly over time.

In a book called *On the Origin of Species,* Darwin stated that plant and animal populations increase faster than the food supply. As a result, they are constantly struggling to survive. Those that survive are better adapted to their environment. They produce offspring that have the same successful characteristics.

Darwin believed that humans evolved, or developed, from animal species. His ideas were controversial. Some people believed that his theory contradicted the biblical story of creation. Others believed it opened the door to a world without moral values. Many people, however, accepted Darwin's theory.

In the 1860s, Gregor Mendel discovered how characteristics were passed to the next generation. From his studies of pea plants, Mendel concluded that offspring receive their traits from their parents. He developed rules to explain what traits parents pass on. Today, Mendel is known as the father of genetics.

Reading**HELP**DESK

Reading Strategy: *Making Inferences*

As you read, you can put together clues to gain information the author doesn't tell you directly. This is called making inferences. Read about Jenner and Pasteur. Make an inference about what it would have been like for someone who became sick in the early 1800s.

What Did Pasteur Discover?

During the 1800s, scientists made advances that gave people longer, healthier lives. One of the first breakthroughs was the discovery of vaccines. In 1796, Edward Jenner noticed that workers who caught a disease called cowpox never caught the deadly smallpox. Jenner found that vaccinating people with cowpox made them immune, or resistant, to smallpox.

About 50 years later, Louis Pasteur learned why Jenner's vaccination worked. In the 1850s, Pasteur discovered that bacteria can cause infectious diseases. Pasteur also showed that killing bacteria prevented many diseases. Pasteur was able to make this discovery thanks to Leeuwenhoek's improvement of the microscope and discovery of bacteria.

The discovery of anesthesia, or pain-deadening drugs, was another great step forward. It enabled patients to sleep through their operations. British surgeon Joseph Lister provided another advance. He developed ways to sterilize medical instruments. Before Lister, many patients died after surgery due to infection.

Einstein and Physics

New ideas also changed the way people understood the world. Expanding the work of Galileo and Newton, scientists developed the atomic theory. This is the idea that all matter is made up of tiny particles called atoms.

Albert Einstein then overturned long-held ideas about the universe. His theory of relativity stated that space and time could not be measured in an absolute sense. Instead, they depended on the relative motion of bodies in space. For example, the speed of two trains appears differently to people on the station platform than it does to passengers on the train.

Darwin's observations led him to develop his theory of natural selection. This is the idea that the animals best adapted to their environment would multiply. Poorly adapted members of a species would die off.

✔ **PROGRESS CHECK**

Explaining How did Louis Pasteur extend the work of Edward Jenner?

LESSON 5 REVIEW

Review Vocabulary

1. Use the word *socialism* in a sentence about working conditions in the Industrial Revolution.

2. Explain the significance of *urbanization* in the context of the Industrial Revolution.

Answer the Guiding Questions

3. *Determining Cause and Effect* How did the lives of women change during the Industrial Revolution?

4. *Analyzing* What effect did labor unions have on the working conditions in factories?

5. *Contrasting* How were the realists different from the romantics?

6. *Assessing* What was the importance of Gregor Mendel's work?

7. **ARGUMENT** Choose a style of art from the lesson. In a paragraph, describe your personal reaction to that style.

CHAPTER 23 Activities

Write your answers on a separate piece of paper.

1 Exploring the Essential Question

INFORMATIVE/EXPLANATORY How do new ideas change the way people live? Write an essay that explains how inventions in the textile industry led to changes in the way British people lived in the nineteenth century.

2 21st Century Skills

BUILD A WEB SITE Plan a Web site with a home page and three linking pages on either the French Revolution or the American Revolution. On the page, identify the important events you will include, the documents you will link to, and the images that will help tell the story. On your home page, set up a logical list of categories to help a visitor navigate your pages.

3 Thinking Like a Historian

IDENTIFYING POINTS OF VIEW Think about the views of a nineteenth century person who believed in liberalism and one who believed in socialism. Using a Venn diagram, compare and contrast the viewpoints of these two belief systems.

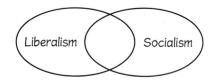

4 GEOGRAPHY ACTIVITY

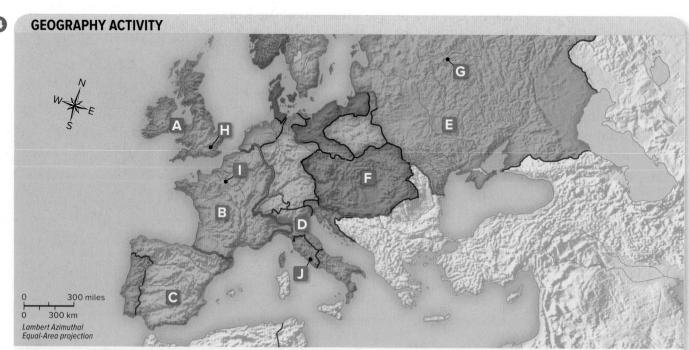

Locating Places

Match the letters on the map with the numbered places listed below.

1. Britain
2. France
3. Spain
4. Kingdom of Italy
5. Russian Empire
6. Austrian Empire
7. Moscow
8. London
9. Paris
10. Rome

Directions: Write your answers on a separate piece of paper.

CHECKING FOR UNDERSTANDING

1 Define each of these terms as they relate to political and industrial revolutions.

A. persecute
B. constitution
C. boycott
D. popular sovereignty
E. limited government
F. estate
G. bourgeoisie
H. coup d'état
I. nationalism
J. guerrilla warfare
K. kaiser
L. abolitionism
M. industrialism
N. corporation
O. urbanization
P. liberalism
Q. utilitarianism
R. socialism
S. proletariat
T. labor union

REVIEW THE GUIDING QUESTIONS

2 *Stating* Why did England found colonies in Virginia? In New England?

3 *Summarizing* What was the main point of contention between Britain and its American colonies?

4 *Naming* Which two Enlightenment principles guided the creation of the U.S. Constitution?

5 *Listing* What were the main causes of the French Revolution?

6 *Identifying* Which groups were most at risk for execution during the Reign of Terror?

7 *Describing* What was the Napoleonic Code?

8 *Explaining* What did Europe's leaders hope to accomplish at the Congress of Vienna?

9 *Identifying* Give one example in which nationalism led to a unified nation-state. Give another example in which nationalism created division.

10 *Naming* Who led the independence movement in Mexico?

11 *Explaining* How did Britain try to maintain its position of economic superiority at the beginning of the Industrial Revolution?

12 *Summarizing* What did Karl Marx believe would happen to the industrialized economic system of the late 19th and early 20th centuries?

13 *Finding the Main Idea* Why were the ideas of Charles Darwin controversial?

CRITICAL THINKING

14 *Contrasting* How did the U.S. Constitution differ from the Articles of Confederation?

15 *Evaluating* Do you believe King Louis XVI did everything he could to avoid revolution in France? Explain your answer.

16 *Making Inferences* Was Maximilien Robespierre a Girondist or a Jacobin? Explain your answer.

17 *Hypothesizing* How did Britain escape the war and revolution that plagued most of Europe during the 1800s?

18 *Identifying Central Issues* Why did the Industrial Revolution begin in Great Britain?

19 *Making Connections* What role did the steam engine play in the development and location of factories in Great Britain?

20 *Reasoning* What is utilitarianism? Identify one potential strength and one potential weakness of this philosophy.

Need Extra Help?

If You've Missed Question	1	2	3	4	5	6	7	8	9	10	11	12	13	14	15	16	17	18	19	20
Review Lesson	1, 2, 3	1	1	1	2	2	2	2	3	3	4	5	5	1	2	2	3	4	4	5

DBQ SHORT RESPONSE

21 In one or two sentences, describe the working conditions shown in the image of the textile factory in England during the Industrial Revolution.

22 Explain what Karl Marx would say about these conditions.

EXTENDED RESPONSE

23 *Argument* You have read Thomas Paine's *Common Sense* and you know American colonists who object to the Intolerable Acts. But the choice to declare independence from England will mean bitter war. Write a letter to the editor in which you take a position on whether the American colonies should declare their independence from England.

STANDARDIZED TEST PRACTICE

DBQ ANALYZING DOCUMENTS

Drawing Conclusions Charles Darwin sums up his research on how animals in nature survive.

"It is not the strongest of the species [group] that survives, nor the most intelligent that survives. It is the one that is the most adaptable to change."

—from *Psyography: Charles Darwin* by Shayla Porter

24 According to Darwin's theory, which species are the most likely to survive?
 A. the strongest
 B. the most intelligent
 C. the least intelligent
 D. the most adaptable to change

25 *Analyzing* According to Darwin, which of the following is correct?
 A. The ability to change is not as important as being strong.
 B. The ability to change is not as important as being intelligent.
 C. The ability to change is as important as being strong and intelligent.
 D. The ability to change is more important than being strong or intelligent.

Need Extra Help?

If You've Missed Question	**21**	**22**	**23**	**24**	**25**
Review Lesson	4	5	1	5	5

◄ *When World War I broke out, Ferdinand Foch received a command at the Western Front. In March 1918, he was given overall control of the Allied forces.*

1850 TO 1920

Imperialism and World War I

THE STORY MATTERS ...

French general Ferdinand Foch (1851–1929) was supreme commander of the Allied Forces in World War I. Born in 1851, Foch wanted to be a soldier when he was a boy. In 1871, he joined the French army. For many years, Foch taught military strategy at the French army college. Under Foch's direction, Allied forces stopped the advance of German troops in early 1918. He then led the counterattack that turned the tide of the war in the Allies' favor. Foch accepted the surrender of Germany's forces in November 1918. After the war, Foch was an important military adviser at the Paris Peace Conference.

ESSENTIAL QUESTIONS

- Why do people trade?
- Why does conflict develop?
- Why is history important?
- How do governments change?

Apic/Hulton Archive/Getty Images

Place & Time: Europe 1854 to 1921

In the late 1800s and early 1900s, several European powers, the United States, and Japan competed to spread their influence abroad. By 1914, they had established large colonial empires in much of the world.

Step Into the Place

MAP FOCUS Long after the countries of the Americas had gained their independence, leading European nations were gaining new colonies in other parts of the world.

1 PLACE Which is the only Asian country to have a colonial empire?

2 PLACE What two regions claimed almost all of North America?

3 REGIONS A writer once observed that "the sun never sets on the British Empire." How does the map illustrate this idea?

4 CRITICAL THINKING
Making Inferences How might the distribution of colonies lead to war?

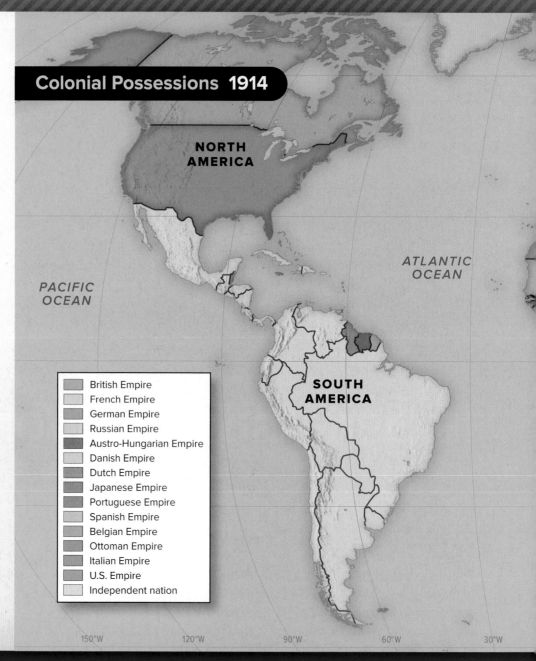

Colonial Possessions 1914

NORTH AMERICA

PACIFIC OCEAN

ATLANTIC OCEAN

SOUTH AMERICA

- British Empire
- French Empire
- German Empire
- Russian Empire
- Austro-Hungarian Empire
- Danish Empire
- Dutch Empire
- Japanese Empire
- Portuguese Empire
- Spanish Empire
- Belgian Empire
- Ottoman Empire
- Italian Empire
- U.S. Empire
- Independent nation

150°W   120°W   90°W   60°W   30°W

Step Into the Time

TIME LINE Choose one event from the time line and write a paragraph that predicts the general social, political, or economic consequences that event might have for the world

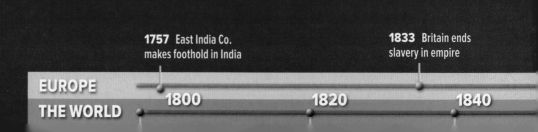

1757 East India Co. makes foothold in India

1833 Britain ends slavery in empire

EUROPE
THE WORLD

1800   1820   1840

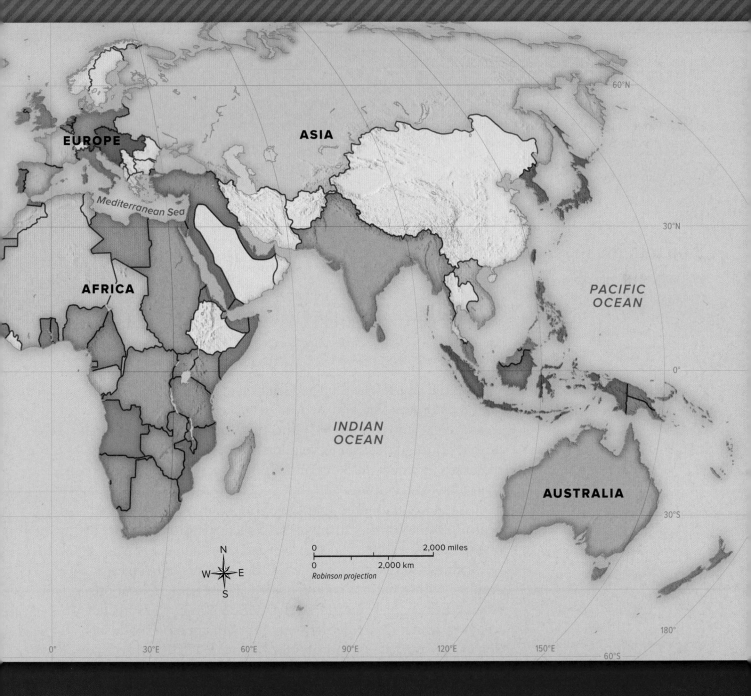

EUROPE

ASIA

Mediterranean Sea

AFRICA

PACIFIC
OCEAN

INDIAN
OCEAN

AUSTRALIA

60°N

30°N

0°

30°S

180°

60°S

0°   30°E   60°E   90°E   120°E   150°E

N
W   E
S

0   2,000 miles
0   2,000 km
Robinson projection

1853 Crimean War begins

1858 Britain takes direct control of India

1869 Suez Canal opens

1914 Archduke Franz Ferdinand is assassinated

1912 Balkan League is formed

1908 Austria-Hungary takes over Bosnia

1917 U.S. declares
war against Germany

1860   **1880**   **1900**   **1920**

LESSON 1

The New Imperialism

ESSENTIAL QUESTION

• Why do people trade?

IT MATTERS BECAUSE
When we realize how imperialism controlled people's lives, we are able to appreciate the desire for freedom that later spread throughout the world.

The Rise of Imperialism

GUIDING QUESTION *Why did Europeans expand their empires at the end of the 1800s?*

During the late 1800s, Europe's leading countries rushed to gain territory in Asia and Africa. Three key factors sparked this race for land overseas: (1) European nations wanted more power; (2) the Industrial Revolution created a demand for raw materials and new markets; and (3) Europeans wanted to impose their ideas and cultures on other peoples. As a result, in the late 1800s, the world entered the Age of Imperialism. **Imperialism** (ihm·PIHR·ee·uh·lih·zuhm) is the direct or indirect control of one nation by another nation.

Britain and France were the leading builders of overseas empires. Other nations soon followed. These imperial nations ruled other peoples in different ways. Sometimes they created a colony, which they ruled directly through appointed officials. Sometimes they set up a **protectorate** (pruh·TEHK·tuh·ruht). There the local people had their own government, but the imperial government controlled the military and could tell the local rulers what to do. In other cases they set up a **sphere of influence**—a region where only one imperial power has the right to invest or to trade.

Reading**HELP**DESK

Taking Notes: *Determining Cause and Effect*

As you read, look for the consequences of the race for colonies. List those effects in a chart like this one.

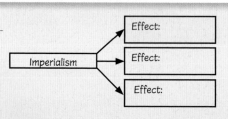

Content Vocabulary
• **imperialism**
• **protectorate**
• **sphere of influence**

Europeans in Southeast Asia

When the Age of Imperialism began, many European nations already held lands in Southeast Asia. As early as the 1500s, Europeans had traveled to the region for its spices. The Dutch occupied the East Indies, while the Spanish controlled the Philippines.

During the 1800s, the British moved into the mainland of Southeast Asia. In 1819, a British government official founded a British colony that became an important port. Located on a small island off the Malay Peninsula, the colony was called Singapore (SIHNG·uh·pohr), or "the city of the lion."

The French followed the British to mainland Southeast Asia and competed for territory. Burma—present-day Myanmar—and the entire Malay Peninsula came under British control. Meanwhile, French missionaries entered nearby Vietnam, making it a protectorate in 1883. Siam—present-day Thailand—was the only Southeast Asian country to keep its freedom.

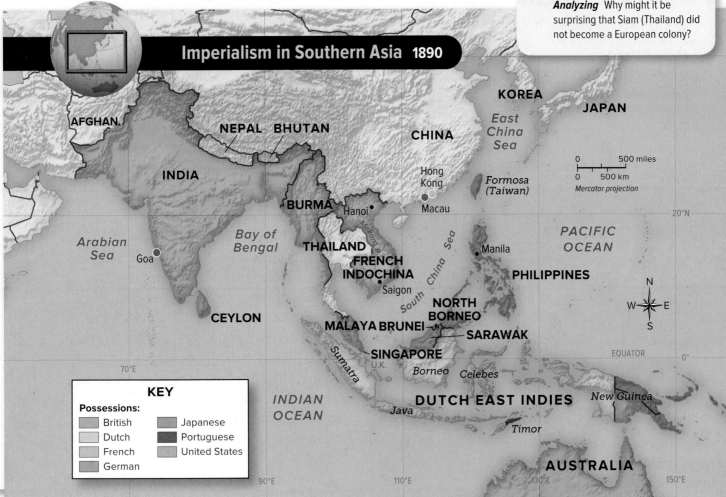

Imperialism in Southern Asia 1890

GEOGRAPHY CONNECTION

By the late 1800s, many of the lands in southern Asia were governed by European nations.

1 PLACE Which European nations controlled New Guinea?

2 CRITICAL THINKING
Analyzing Why might it be surprising that Siam (Thailand) did not become a European colony?

---

imperialism policy of one nation directly or indirectly controlling another

protectorate a nation has its own government, but its military is controlled by another government

sphere of influence a region where only one imperial power had the right to invest or trade

Tea is still an important crop in southern Asia. It is harvested as it has been for centuries.

▶ CRITICAL THINKING
Drawing Conclusions Why wasn't tea grown in Europe?

During the late 1800s and early 1900s, Europeans made enormous profits from their Southeast Asian holdings. However, the riches were earned at the expense of the local people.

European officials, traders, and landowners forced Southeast Asians to grow coffee, tea, and other crops for export. Southeast Asian workers also mined or harvested the area's raw materials—petroleum, rubber, tin, and valuable woods.

✔ PROGRESS CHECK

Describing How did Europeans rule their overseas territories?

The British in India

GUIDING QUESTION *What were the effects of British rule in India?*

India was another Asian land that came under European rule. Europeans were trading in India as early as 1600. At this time, a Muslim group called the Moguls ruled India. During the next 100 years, Mogul power weakened. Mogul rulers taxed people heavily and wasted money on wars and palaces. Some of them also tried to force Hindus—most of India's people—to accept Islam. Growing discontent made it easy for Europeans to take over India.

Struggle for India

In the 1600s and 1700s, British traders from the East India Company extended their control in India. They built trading posts in **strategic** places along India's coast. They set up their own army and supported local Indian rulers who agreed to work with them. Meanwhile, traders from France used the same methods and challenged Britain for control of India's trade.

Robert Clive, an East India Company official, led British and Indian soldiers against French forts. In 1757, Clive's force defeated the French and their Indian allies. The conflict left the French with only one fort and a few coastal holdings.

During the next 100 years, Britain's East India Company took over much of India. Company officials prospered. They also introduced European ideas to India's people. Many Indians, however, felt that the British were trying to change their culture.

©Hans Georg Roth/Corbis

Reading**HELP**DESK

Academic Vocabulary

strategy a careful plan to achieve a goal

By the mid-1800s, Indian discontent with the East India Company had increased. In 1857, sepoys (SEE·poyz), or Indian soldiers in the company's army, revolted against their British officers. In some places, the revolt resulted in massacres of British citizens. British troops arrived in India and crushed the rebellion. As revenge for the massacres, the British killed thousands of Indians. The revolt left bitterness on both sides. It caused the British to tighten their control of India.

What Is the Raj?

In 1858, Britain took direct control of India from the East India Company. British India's government was known as the Raj (rahj), which is from the Sanskrit word for "ruler." The Raj was headed by a British official called a viceroy. *Viceroy* refers to a high official who stands in for the British monarch.

The British did bring order and unity to India. They provided good administration and a well-run government. Under the Raj, communication and education improved. The British introduced railroads, the telegraph, and a postal service to India.

British rule, however, also introduced great hardships. Cheap British fabrics flooded India and destroyed the local textile industry. The British also forced many Indian farmers to grow cotton instead of wheat. Soon India was not growing enough food to feed its people. In the 1800s, millions of Indians died of starvation.

Sepoys serving with the British East India Company were angry about the British lack of respect for their beliefs. They began an armed rebellion against the British.

Indian National Congress

Many Indians were angry about the policies of the Raj. They wanted to move India toward self-rule. In 1885, Indian business and professional leaders formed a political group called the Indian National Congress. Many members of the Congress had been educated in British-style schools. At first, the Congress worked for gradual change. They hoped to gain some level of self-rule over time. When this effort failed, the Congress began a campaign for full independence.

☑ PROGRESS CHECK

Explaining How did British rule of India change in 1858?

The British Library/Heritage/Age fotostock

European Rule in Africa

GUIDING QUESTION *Why did Europeans compete to take over Africa?*

Africa was the last populated continent to be colonized by Europeans. In the 1500s, European traders arrived on Africa's west coast. In the mid-1800s, explorers, like Scottish doctor-missionary David Livingstone, opened up the African interior. During the late 1800s, European powers scrambled to gain control of as much of Africa's rich resources as they could.

North Africa

In the early 1800s, French armies captured Algeria in North Africa. The French later seized Tunisia and claimed Morocco. In 1904, France divided Morocco with Spain.

Meanwhile, European businesses developed in Egypt. The Europeans and Egyptians **constructed** the Suez Canal, which opened in 1869. The canal linked the Mediterranean and Red Seas. Britain took control of the canal in 1875 and eventually made Egypt a protectorate.

West Africa

The Europeans turned next to West Africa. European merchants had been involved for centuries in the trading of enslaved West Africans. In 1833, however, Britain ended slavery in its empire. Other European countries soon followed.

Europeans then sought out West Africa's gold, timber, hides, and palm oil. Britain, France, and Germany took over Africa's Atlantic coast. Eventually, they moved inland. Soon, the only place in West Africa not controlled by Europeans was Liberia. It was founded in 1847 by freed African Americans.

European expansion, however, was challenged. In the 1890s, West African rulers led armies against the Europeans. Well-armed European armies, however, defeated the West Africans.

Central and East Africa

European control of Central Africa began when King Leopold II of Belgium claimed much of the Congo region. Under his rule, the Congolese people were forced to work on rubber plantations.

European imperialists came to Africa to take advantage of the continent's rich natural resources. They also sought the global power that owning colonies brought to them.

©Stefano Bianchetti/Corbis

Reading**HELP**DESK

Academic Vocabulary

construct to build or assemble

Reading Strategy: *Accessing Prior Knowledge*

Remembering what you have already learned can help you understand the context of what you are reading now. For example, the section above headed *West Africa* mentions the slave trade. Think about what facts you previously learned about the slave trade. Put that together with new knowledge.

Complaints from missionaries and other Europeans forced the king to turn over the Congo to the Belgian government. The government finally ended the forced labor system.

Leopold's move into the Congo spurred other European powers into action. They divided the rest of Africa among themselves, with two exceptions. In East Africa, the Italians tried but failed to conquer Ethiopia. Ethiopia, like Liberia in West Africa, remained independent.

South Africa and the Boer War

In South Africa, the European push to acquire new colonies led to the Boer War. In the 1600s, Dutch settlers founded Cape Town on the southwestern coast. These settlers became known as Boers, the Dutch word for "farmers." In the early 1800s, Britain seized the Dutch territory and renamed it Cape Colony. To escape British rule, the Boers moved inland. They named their new settlements the Orange Free State and the Transvaal.

Britain's Cape Colony was governed by Cecil Rhodes, the owner of many gold and diamond companies. When British settlers discovered gold and diamonds in the Transvaal, Rhodes decided to take the territory from the Boers. War erupted in 1899 and ended with the defeat of the Boers three years later.

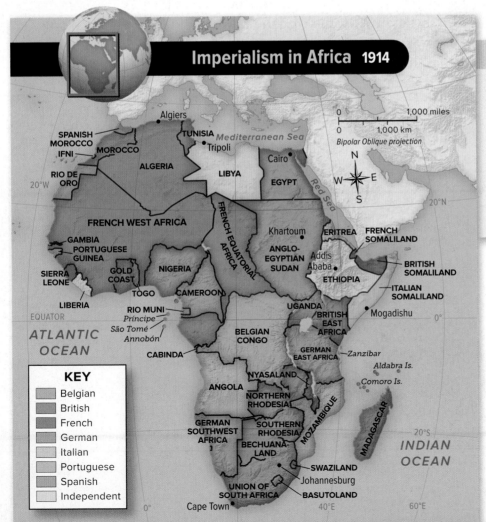

Imperialism in Africa 1914

GEOGRAPHY CONNECTION

European nations controlled almost all of Africa by the early 1900s.

1 **PLACE** Which two African nations remained independent?

2 **CRITICAL THINKING**
Analyzing Britain controlled the Suez Canal. How did that control help Britain govern its other African territories?

KEY
- Belgian
- British
- French
- German
- Italian
- Portuguese
- Spanish
- Independent

Historians make inferences about what they read. Read the paragraph beginning, "In 1910, Britain formed the Union of South Africa." It says that the African National Congress was created, but not why. The reason must be inferred by the reader. Make an inference based on the details in the reading. Tell what you can infer about the living conditions for black South Africans. Write your inference in a sentence or two. For more information about making inferences, read the chapter *What Does a Historian Do?*

In 1910, Britain formed the Union of South Africa. Boer and British settlers ran this new country. They did not allow the much larger nonwhite population to have a role in the government. As a result, black South Africans founded the African National Congress to fight for black rights.

How Did Imperialism Affect Africans?

Europeans greatly affected the lives of Africans. Europeans grew wealthy from mines and plantations. African workers received low wages and had to pay taxes in cash. European schools taught Africans that European ways were best. In some places, African traditions declined as a result of European influences.

By the early 1900s, a small group of European-educated Africans had emerged in many African colonies. These Africans condemned colonial rule as contrary to European ideals of liberty and equality. They founded nationalist groups to push for self-rule.

✓ **PROGRESS CHECK**

Explaining Why were Europeans drawn to Africa in the 1800s?

America's Quest for Empire

GUIDING QUESTION *How did the United States build an overseas empire?*

In the late 1800s, the United States joined the race for colonies. Many American government and business leaders believed that they needed raw materials and new markets to keep the U.S. economy growing.

In February 1898, the U.S. battleship *Maine* exploded and sank in the Havana harbor. The loss of the ship and its 260 crew prompted the Spanish-American War.

North Wind Picture Archives

The Spanish-American War

In the late 1800s the United States gained territory in Latin America and the Pacific. At that time, Spain still ruled the Caribbean islands of Puerto Rico and Cuba. However, in 1895 the Cubans began a revolt against Spanish rule.

In 1898, President William McKinley sent the U.S. battleship *Maine* to protect Americans living in Cuba. While anchored in the harbor of Havana, Cuba's capital, the ship exploded.

Many Americans blamed Spain and called for action. In April 1898, President McKinley asked Congress to declare war. The Spanish-American War lasted only four months, ending with an American victory. Cuba became a republic under American protection. The U.S. also gained Puerto Rico and the Pacific islands of Guam and the Philippines (fih·luh·peenz).

In 1898, the Pacific islands of Hawaii came under American control. Five years earlier, American settlers had overthrown the Hawaiian queen Liliuokalani (lih·lee·uh·woh·kuh·LAH·nee). However, Congress did not approve American control of Hawaii until after the end of the Spanish-American War.

The United States in Latin America

Following the Spanish-American War, U.S. President Theodore Roosevelt pushed to build a canal across Panama (pa·nuh·mah) to connect the Atlantic and Pacific Oceans.

At that time, Panama was part of Colombia. The Colombians refused to give up land needed for the canal. In 1903, Americans helped the people of Panama revolt. Once Panama won its independence, it let the U.S. build the canal. Construction began in 1904 and took 10 years to complete.

The Granger Collection, NYC

✔ **PROGRESS CHECK**

Analyzing How did the United States gain the rights to build the Panama Canal?

LESSON 1 REVIEW

Review Vocabulary

1. Give an example of *imperialism* in Asia.

2. Explain how a *protectorate* is different from the direct rule of a country by an imperialist power.

Answer the Guiding Questions

3. *Determining Cause and Effect* How did the Industrial Revolution help lead to imperialism?

4. *Evaluating* How did the Suez Canal help Europeans?

5. *Making Connections* How was the Indian National Congress similar to the African National Congress?

6. *Analyzing* What were the outcomes of the Spanish-American War?

7. **INFORMATIVE/EXPLANATORY** Explain how imperialist rule affected the majority of Africans.

Shooting an Elephant

by George Orwell (1903–1950)

The essay "Shooting an Elephant" describes the experiences of a British official in Burma. He is called to a poor area of the country and finds that a tame elephant has trampled a man. When the official sends for an elephant rifle, crowds of local people begin to gather around him. They are eager to watch him shoot the elephant that is now munching grass in a nearby field. Even though the official does not want to shoot the animal, he feels pressured by the crowd to appear strong and very sure of himself. Orwell's story shows an example of how British officials struggled to appear in command. The story is considered to be Orwell's criticism of British imperialism.

George Orwell

❝ And it was at this moment, as I stood there with the rifle in my hands, that I first grasped the hollowness, the futility [uselessness] of the white man's dominion [rule] in the East. ❞

In carrying out colonial rule, British officials believed they had to present a strong and forceful manner, even if it went against their personal beliefs.

I had halted on the road. As soon as I saw the elephant I knew with perfect certainty that I ought not to shoot him. It is a serious matter to shoot a working elephant—it is comparable to destroying a huge and costly piece of machinery—and obviously one ought not to do it if it can possibly be avoided. . . . Moreover, I did not in the least want to shoot him. I decided that I would watch him for a little while to make sure that he did not turn savage again, and then go home.

*But at that moment I glanced round at the crowd that had followed me. It was an immense crowd, two thousand at the least and growing every minute. It blocked the road for a long distance on either side. . . . faces all happy and excited over this bit of fun, all certain that the elephant was going to be shot. They were watching me as they would watch a [magician] about to perform a trick. They did not like me, but with the magical rifle in my hands I was momentarily worth watching. And suddenly I realized that I should have to shoot the elephant after all. The people expected it of me and I had got to do it; I could feel their two thousand wills pressing me forward, irresistibly. And it was at this moment, as I stood there with the rifle in my hands, that I first grasped the hollowness, the futility of the white man's **dominion** in the East. Here was I, the white man with his gun, standing in front of the unarmed native crowd—seemingly the leading actor of the piece; but in reality I was only an absurd puppet . . .*

*I perceived in this moment that when the white man turns **tyrant** it is his own freedom that he destroys. He becomes a sort of hollow, posing dummy, the . . . figure of a **sahib**. For it is the condition of his rule that he shall spend his life in trying to impress the "natives," and so in every crisis he has got to do what the "natives" expect of him. He wears a mask, and his face grows to fit it. I had got to shoot the elephant. I had committed myself to doing it when I sent for the rifle. A sahib has got to act like a sahib; he has got to appear resolute, to know his own mind and do definite things. To come all that way, rifle in hand, with two thousand people marching at my heels, and then to trail feebly away, having done nothing—no, that was impossible. The crowd would laugh at me. And my whole life, every white man's life in the East, was one long struggle not to be laughed at.*

—From "Shooting an Elephant" by George Orwell

"Shooting an Elephant" from SHOOTING AN ELEPHANT AND OTHER ESSAYS by George Orwell. (Copyright © George Orwell, 1936 by permission of Bill Hamilton as the Literacy Executor of the Estate of the Late Sonia Brownell Orwell and Seker & Warburg Ltd

Vocabulary

dominion
rule, control

tyrant
harsh ruler

sahib
title meaning "sir" or "master"

Analyzing Literature DBQ

1. ***Determining Cause and Effect*** Why doesn't the official want to shoot the elephant?

2. ***Analyzing*** What makes the official feel that he has to shoot the elephant?

3. ***Evaluating*** How does the official's being British play a part in the story?

Nationalism in China and Japan

ESSENTIAL QUESTION

• Why does conflict develop?

IT MATTERS BECAUSE

European and American economic success greatly influenced trade and society in China and Japan.

China Faces the West

GUIDING QUESTION *How did the arrival of Europeans change Chinese society?*

During the 1800s, China was ruled by the Qing dynasty. Qing rulers wanted the Chinese to hold on to traditional ways. However, Europeans stirred by the Industrial Revolution demanded more contact and trade with China.

Why Were the Opium Wars Fought?

During the early 1800s, the Chinese had very little interest in European products and trade with the West. The British, however, had a great demand for Chinese tea, silk, and porcelain. To get these products, British merchants had to trade valuable goods, such as silver.

The British then found a way to increase their trade with China. They began selling opium from India to the Chinese. Opium is an addictive drug, and soon the demand for it greatly increased in southern China.

China's emperor warned the British to stop the opium trade. The British refused and fought the Chinese in two wars—the First Opium War (1839 to 1842) and the Second Opium War (1856 to 1860). Lacking modern weapons, the Chinese were forced to surrender to European forces in both conflicts.

Reading **HELP**DESK

Taking Notes: *Listing*

As you read, use a graphic organizer like this one to list important events in China and Japan.

China and Japan	
China	Japan
•	•
•	•
•	•
•	•
•	•

Content Vocabulary

• **extraterritoriality**

As a result of these wars, China gave the island of Hong Kong to the British. Furthermore, Europeans in China won the right to bypass Chinese laws and live under their own laws. This legal practice is called **extraterritoriality** (EHK·struh·TEHR·uh·TOHR·ee·A·luh·tee).

Revolt Sweeps China

During the 1850s, severe weather and high taxes caused suffering for China's peasants. Crops failed, leading to food shortages. As a result, peasant unrest spread across China.

In 1851, a religious leader named Hong Xiuquan (HAHNG SHOO·KWAHN) organized an uprising called the Tai Ping Rebellion. The rebels' goal was to overthrow the Qing emperor. Europeans helped the emperor destroy the rebel army.

Chinese officials realized that reforms were needed. They convinced the emperor that Western technology could help end revolts and foreign takeovers. As a result, the Chinese began building railroads, shipyards, and weapons factories. The Qing dynasty's power continued to **decline,** however.

European Spheres of Influence

After the Tai Ping Rebellion, local leaders in China allowed Europeans to trade, mine, and build in their regions. In this way, Europe's powers came to control different parts of China as spheres of influence. The United States did not claim a sphere of influence. Instead, it proposed an Open Door policy that would open China to trade with all countries. Other nations **reluctantly** agreed to this policy in 1899.

By the late 1890s, hatred of foreigners had risen in China. Many Chinese organized secret societies to drive out foreigners. One group, the Righteous and Harmonious Fists, were nicknamed "Boxers" by Westerners. In 1900 the Boxers attacked foreigners and Chinese Christians. In response, foreign powers sent in troops and crushed the Boxer Rebellion.

✔ PROGRESS CHECK

Describing What was the goal of the Tai Ping Rebellion?

extraterritoriality legal practice of foreigners living in a country but not being subject to the laws of that country

Through the strength of its military power, Britain forced China to open its ports to trade.

▶ **CRITICAL THINKING**
Analyzing Why was Britain so interested in opening trade with China?

National Maritime Museum, Greenwich, UK

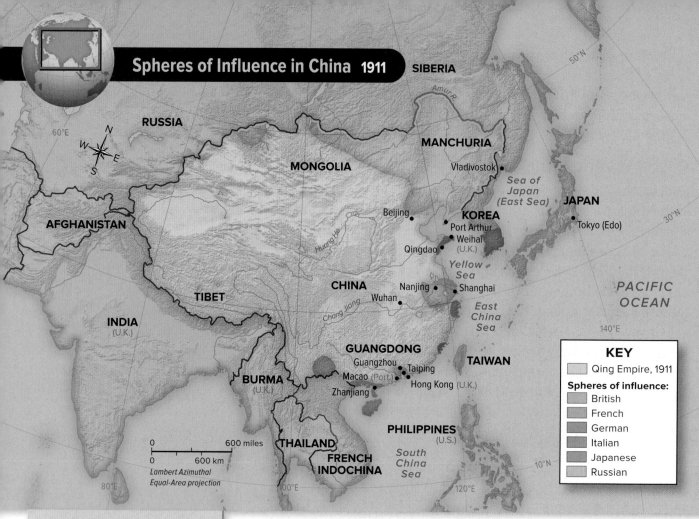

SIBERIA

50°N

RUSSIA

60°E

Amur R.

MANCHURIA

MONGOLIA

Vladivostok

Sea of
Japan
(East Sea)

JAPAN

AFGHANISTAN

Beijing

KOREA

Port Arthur

Weihai

Qingdao

(U.K.)

Tokyo (Edo)

30°N

Huang He

Yellow
Sea

TIBET

CHINA

Nanjing

Shanghai

Wuhan

PACIFIC
OCEAN

INDIA
(U.K.)

Chang Jiang

East
China
Sea

140°E

GUANGDONG

Guangzhou

Taiping

TAIWAN

Macao (Port.)

Hong Kong (U.K.)

BURMA
(U.K.)

Zhanjiang

PHILIPPINES
(U.S.)

South
China
Sea

10°N

THAILAND

FRENCH
INDOCHINA

0   600 miles

0   600 km

Lambert Azimuthal
Equal-Area projection

80°E

100°E

120°E

KEY

☐ Qing Empire, 1911

Spheres of influence:
- British
- French
- German
- Italian
- Japanese
- Russian

GEOGRAPHY CONNECTION

Many European countries established spheres of influence in China during the late 1800s.

1 **PLACE** Which country's sphere of influence reached farthest north?

2 **CRITICAL THINKING**
Analyzing What trading advantage did Britain's sphere of influence have? Explain.

China's 1911 Revolution

GUIDING QUESTION *How did revolution in 1911 bring changes to China?*

During the early 1900s, Chinese officials eager to keep their power tried to make more changes. They set up European-style schools and reorganized the government. Many middle-class Chinese, however, believed that these reforms were too little, too late.

In 1905, a young medical doctor named Sun Yat-sen (SUHN YAHT·SEHN) founded a movement that became known as the Nationalist Party. Its members wanted to remove the Qing dynasty and unite China under a strong government. Sun developed a three-step plan: (1) take over China's government, (2) prepare the people for self-rule, and (3) create a constitution and a democracy.

In 1911, revolution swept China, and the Qing dynasty collapsed. Nationalists proclaimed China a republic. However, they did not have the military or political support to form a

Reading**HELP**DESK

Academic Vocabulary

decline decrease in importance
reluctance resistance, unwillingness

Build Vocabulary: *Multiple Meaning Words*

The word *revolution* has several meanings. It means the orbit of a moon or planet. It also means the turning of a planet on its axis. Revolution may also mean "a sudden or complete change," or "a basic change in a political organization." Which meaning is used on these pages?

government. As a result, they turned to the head of the Chinese army, General Yuan Shikai (YWAN SHIH·ky).

General Yuan agreed to serve as president of a new Chinese republic. However, he understood little about democracy and freedom. Instead, he ruled in a traditional way. When Yuan put an end to the new parliament, the Nationalist Party launched a revolt. The rebellion failed, and Sun Yat-sen fled to Japan.

After Yuan died in 1916, China slipped into chaos. Warlords, or local military leaders, seized power in local areas and fought one another. In 1917, Sun Yat-sen returned to China and worked to rebuild the Nationalist Party. He formed an army with the help of a young officer, Chiang Kai-shek (JYAHNG KY·SHEHK). Sun died in 1925, but three years later, Chiang defeated the warlords and set up a Nationalist government.

Schooled in Hawaii as a teenager, Sun Yat-sen studied European and American political ideas. He became convinced that China needed a revolution. In China, he became a leader in the Nationalist Party.

☑ **PROGRESS CHECK**

Identifying What kind of government did Sun Yat-sen want to establish in China?

The Rise of Modern Japan

GUIDING QUESTION *How did the Japanese reorganize their society and economy as a result of Western influences?*

Like China, Japan in the 1800s faced growing pressures from Europe and the United States. For many centuries, Japan had been isolated from the rest of the world. At the end of the 1400s, the shogun, Japan's military ruler, lost control of the country. The heads of the country's noble families, called daimyo (DY·mee·oh), ruled their own lands and warred with their neighbors.

Military leaders returned strong central government to Japan in the 1500s. The last, and most important of these leaders, Tokugawa Ieyasu, established the Tokugawa shogunate, which governed Japan from 1603 to 1868.

The Opening of Japan

Meanwhile, Europeans were starting to trade with Japan. Jesuit missionaries arrived soon after the traders. They converted thousands of Japanese to Christianity by the late 1500s. The Tokugawa shoguns feared that Christianity and other European ideas would destroy traditional Japanese culture. That concern led them to **prohibit** contact with foreigners.

©Bettmann/Corbis

In the 1850s, however, Japan was finally opened to the outside world. In 1853, Commodore Matthew Perry sailed into Edo Bay (now Tokyo Bay). Perry gave the shogun a letter from U.S. President Millard Fillmore. In his letter, the president called for Japan to trade with the United States.

Perry returned to Japan six months later. Fearing attack by the American fleet, the Japanese shogun agreed to open ports to U.S. trade and to exchange ambassadors. Japan then reached similar agreements with European nations.

Many Japanese people disliked the treaties. They feared the agreements would keep Japan weak. In 1868, a group of samurai overthrew the shogun and took power in the emperor's name.

The Meiji Reforms

At the time of the shogun's overthrow, Emperor Mutsuhito (moot·suh·HEE·toh) was known as the Meiji, or "Enlightened," emperor. Thus, the late 1800s and early 1900s became known as the Meiji era. During this time, the samurai were loyal to the emperor, but the emperor largely obeyed their wishes.

The Meiji leaders wanted to make Japan a modern nation. First, they ended the power of the daimyo. Then they created a constitutional monarchy in 1889, but retained the real power for themselves. Acting on the emperor's behalf, they named the prime minister and his advisers.

Japan's new government set up a modern army and navy. Meiji leaders also made major changes in Japan's society. They improved public schools and required everyone to be educated.

The most important Meiji goal was to build industries that would boost the economy. To raise money for investment, the Meiji improved the tax system. This reform helped them build factories and improvements to roads, railroads, and ports.

By 1914, Japan had become a leading industrial country. Japan's working class, however, did not benefit from the nation's new status. Factory workers were paid little and worked long hours. Miners who refused to work in extreme heat were shot.

Commodore Matthew Perry delivered a letter from U.S. President Fillmore inviting Japan to trade with the United States. The warships accompanying Perry convinced the Japanese that they had to accept the offer.

Courtesy of the United States Naval Academy Museum

Reading**HELP**DESK

Academic Vocabulary

prohibit to forbid something

Japan's Empire

As Meiji leaders watched Europe and the United States grow wealthy and powerful, they wanted Japan to become a world power as well. They believed strength depended on having an overseas empire. The Meiji believed that colonies would be able to supply Japan with natural resources, cheap labor, and markets for manufactured goods.

The first colony Japan wanted was Korea. China had controlled Korea for many years. It did not want a Japanese presence in the country. In 1894, war broke out between Japan and China. Japan easily defeated the Chinese military.

After the war, China agreed to give Taiwan to Japan and independence to Korea. Japan gained some control of Korea's trade, and its influence in the country increased.

Japan and Russia

Japan faced a growing challenge from Russia. Both countries wanted trade with Korea and control of neighboring Manchuria. The Russians already held the Port Arthur naval base in Manchuria. In 1904, Japan attacked Port Arthur. Japanese forces then landed in Korea and marched into Manchuria. Russian troops could not stop the Japanese advance.

Meanwhile, Russia sent its main fleet to attack Japan. However, Japan's new modern navy sank most of the Russian ships. In 1905, Russia agreed to give up Port Arthur and part of Sakhalin (SA·kuh·leen), an island north of Japan. Japan was recognized worldwide as a major power.

✔ **PROGRESS CHECK**

Explaining What changes did the Meiji rulers bring to Japan?

THEN

Following a huge fire in 1872, many wooden buildings in Tokyo's Ginza shopping district were rebuilt with brick. It was a new type of construction in Japan. Today, Ginza is Tokyo's best known shopping area. Modern architecture has replaced the brick buildings of the Meiji period.

NOW

▶ CRITICAL THINKING
Analyzing Why do you think districts develop with many stores and shops all together?

(t)Archive Photos/Getty Images; (b)Radius/SuperStock

LESSON 2 REVIEW

Review Vocabulary

1. Who were the people affected by the policies of *extraterritoriality*?

2. Explain how a *shogun* is similar to a general in the army.

Answer the Guiding Questions

3. ***Assessing*** How was the Open Door Policy good for all the European powers?

4. ***Identifying*** What were the three parts of Sun Yat-sen's plan to change China?

5. ***Explaining*** Why did the Japanese leaders agree to Commodore Matthew Perry's request to trade with the United States?

6. ***Determining Cause and Effect*** According to the Meiji leaders, what benefit would adding colonies bring to the Japanese Empire?

7. **ARGUMENT** Suppose you were President Millard Fillmore. Write a letter to the Japanese shogun to persuade him to begin diplomatic relations with the United States.

There's More Online! connected.mcgraw-hill.com

LESSON 3

World War I Begins

ESSENTIAL QUESTION

• Why is history important?

IT MATTERS BECAUSE

The events of World War I were a social, economic, technological, and political turning point for many nations in the modern era.

Causes of Conflict

GUIDING QUESTION *What factors threatened the peace in Europe after 1900?*

Following Napoleon's defeat, Europeans enjoyed a long period of peace. In the early 1900s, however, tensions increased among the European powers. What factors caused these tensions?

Nationalism

Many of the tensions in Europe were the result of nationalism. Nationalism is a strong feeling of loyalty to one's country. Nationalism had earlier united Italy and Germany into strong nations. There was also a surge of nationalism in France and Britain. Meanwhile, the spread of nationalism threatened to tear apart other European territories, such as Austria-Hungary.

Empire Building

Tensions in Europe also came from the desire to build empires. Britain—also known as the United Kingdom—had issues to face. During the 1800s several European nations had competed to set up colonies in Africa, Asia, and other parts of the world.

Britain and France held the largest overseas empires and wanted to further enlarge them. Germany and Italy also wanted to add to their territories. By 1900, after decades of imperialism,

Reading**HELP**DESK

Taking Notes: *Sequencing*

As you read, use a time line like this one to keep track of the events of World War I. Note the date and a word or two about the event.

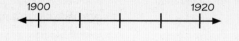
1900   1920

Content Vocabulary

- **militarism**   • **mobilization**
- **conscription**   • **propaganda**
- **entente**   • **blockade**

much of the world's land area was already under the control of European powers. Consequently, European nations often came into conflict with one another as they tried to expand.

Military Increases

As European nations built their empires, they strengthened their military forces. If one nation increased the size of its military, its rivals increased their own forces. As a result, a spirit of **militarism** (MIH·luh·tuh·rih·zuhm) spread throughout Europe. This term refers to a high regard for military might.

Leaders in Germany, France, and Russia formed enormous armies. They used conscription to increase the size of their forces. **Conscription** (kuhn·SKRIHP·shuhn) means that a government requires citizens to serve in the military for a certain period of time. Conscription is also called a "draft."

Britain had the world's largest and most powerful navy. In the early 1900s, Germany set out to expand its naval forces. The British viewed this as a threat and began building even more warships. A rivalry soon grew between Britain and Germany.

GEOGRAPHY CONNECTION

Rivalries among European countries, especially in the Balkan Peninsula, set the stage for World War I.

1 LOCATION What role might Switzerland play if Germany and Italy went to war?

2 CRITICAL THINKING
Analyzing Why might the rise of Germany as a new nation, along with its strong nationalism, make France and Britain feel threatened?

Europe Before WWI 1914

militarism a support for in war and military power

conscription citizens required to serve in the military of their country

The Balkan Wars set the stage for the conflict that became known as World War I. Disputes in the Balkans remained unsettled after the fighting stopped.

▶ **CRITICAL THINKING**
Determining Cause and Effect
How did the Balkan Wars lead to World War I?

Creating Military Alliances

As spending for arms rose, European powers made alliances, or agreements to help one another in the event of war. By 1914 two major alliances had been created. The Triple Alliance was made up of Germany, Austria-Hungary, and Italy. Then Britain, France, and Russia joined in the Triple Entente. An **entente** (ahn· TAHNT) is an understanding among nations.

The purpose of the alliances was to keep peace by creating a balance of power. A balance of power prevents any one country from **dominating** the others. Yet Europe's alliances actually created a great danger. An attack on one nation could easily start a war involving many countries.

Trouble in the Balkans

In the early 1900s, the Balkan Peninsula in southeastern Europe was aflame with nationalist rivalries. The Balkans (BAWL·kuhnz) had long been under the rule of the Ottoman and Austro-Hungarian Empires. As nationalism spread, ethnic groups within both empires demanded self-rule.

The South Slavs were one of these groups. They included the Serbs, Bosnians, Croats, and Slovenes. The first to win freedom were the Serbs. They formed a state called Serbia (SUHR·bee·uh) and united the South Slavs.

The leaders of Austria-Hungary feared that the idea of a South Slav kingdom would harm their empire. As a result, they tried to limit Serbia's expansion. In 1908, Austria-Hungary took over Serbia's neighbor, Bosnia. The Serbs were furious.

With Russian support, the Serbs prepared for war. Then Emperor William II of Germany demanded that Russia accept Austria-Hungary's takeover of Bosnia or face war with Germany. Russia backed down. However, it was determined not to be humiliated by Germany again.

In 1912, the Balkan League—Bulgaria, Greece, Montenegro, and Serbia—declared war on the Ottoman Empire. As a result, the Turks lost nearly all their European territory. The Balkan League, however, soon fell apart.

Mary Evans/Grenville Collins Postcard Collection

Reading**HELP**DESK

entente a formal agreement between two nations to cooperate for specific purposes

mobilization the process of assembling armed forces into readiness for a conflict

Academic Vocabulary

dominate to rule over, govern, or control
neutral not taking sides or not getting involved

Greeks and Serbs demanded land that Bulgaria had won in the war, so Bulgaria attacked the Greeks and Serbs. The Turks saw their chance to win back land and attacked Bulgaria. The Treaty of Bucharest resulted in an uneasy peace.

✅ **PROGRESS CHECK**

Explaining Why did European countries form alliances?

War Breaks Out in Europe

GUIDING QUESTION *Why did war break out in Europe in 1914?*

In June 1914, in Sarajevo, (sar·uh·YAY·voh), a small town in Bosnia, crowds gathered to see Archduke Franz Ferdinand (FRANZ FUHR·duhn·and), heir to the throne of Austria-Hungary. While driving through the streets of Sarajevo, the Archduke and his wife were shot and killed.

A young Bosnian Serb named Gavrilo Princip had pulled the trigger. He belonged to a Serb nationalist group called the Black Hand. This group wanted the Bosnian Serbs, ruled by Austria-Hungary, to be part of a South Slav state headed by Serbia. Austria-Hungary blamed the Serb government for the murder. On July 28, 1914, Austria-Hungary declared war on Serbia.

The Conflict Spreads

Europe's alliance system caused the war to spread quickly. Russia, Serbia's ally, began **mobilization**, or the gathering and movement of troops. Germany aided its ally Austria-Hungary and declared war on Russia on August 1. It then declared war on France, Russia's ally.

In order to attack France, Germany's soldiers had to advance through Belgium. On August 4, German forces invaded Belgium, breaking a treaty that had guaranteed Belgium's **neutrality**. Britain, honoring a promise to protect Belgium, declared war on Germany.

The Great War, as World War I was later called, had begun. On one side were the Allies: France, Russia, Britain, and Italy. On the other side, the Central Powers: Germany, Austria-Hungary, the Ottoman Empire, and Bulgaria.

Archduke Franz Ferdinand was the inspector general of Austria-Hungary's army. As heir to the throne he often made trips throughout the empire. Here he greeted the people of Sarajevo on the day he was attacked and killed.

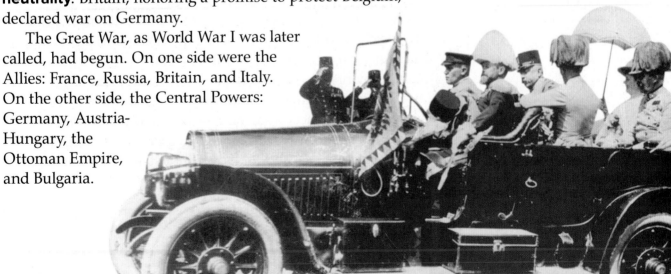

©Bettmann/Corbis

There's More Online! connected.mcgraw-hill.com

This French soldier stands in the trenches, or dugouts, of World War I around 1916. His helmet protects him from shell fire and bullets.

What Was the Western Front?

The Western Front was the battle zone between France and Germany where much of the fighting took place. In September 1914, the French and British stopped the German advance on the Western Front. However, it soon became clear that neither side was going to win the war quickly or easily.

The fighting reached a standoff. For the next three years, the opposing armies became involved in trench warfare. On each side, troops dug themselves into the ground in trenches protected by barbed wire. Trenches along the front lines provided protection and those behind the lines served as medical stations, headquarters, and storage areas.

To break the standoff, soldiers climbed out of the trenches and crossed over open ground while enemy soldiers fired machine guns at them. Neither side made significant military advances and thousands of soldiers were killed or wounded.

War and Technology

World War I was different from earlier conflicts. New technology introduced more powerful weapons. Machine guns fired bullets rapidly. Improved cannons and other artillery fired larger shells at greater distances. Newly developed submarines attacked ships at sea. Early versions of airplanes battled each other with machine guns. They also bombed enemy towns. Tanks, flamethrowers, and poison gases were also introduced.

What is a Total War?

As the war dragged on, it became a total war. This means that entire societies, not just armies, became involved in fighting. World War I affected the lives of all citizens.

Governments on both sides trained and supplied large armies. They raised taxes and borrowed vast sums of money. They rationed, or placed limits on, civilians' use of food and materials needed for the war. Governments also set wages and prices, banned strikes, and took over industries and railroads.

Paul Thompson/FPG/Stringer/Archive Photos/Getty Images

Reading**HELP**DESK

propaganda biased information used to influence public opinion

Government officials also tried to shape public opinion. They used **propaganda**—biased, government-controlled information—to control citizens' thinking about the war.

Total war required many new civilian workers to help in producing war goods. As millions of young men went to the battlefields, women took their places in factories. Women's contributions during the war aided women's rights. By war's end, many countries were ready to give the vote to women.

✓ **PROGRESS CHECK**

Defining What is a total war?

A Global War

GUIDING QUESTION *How did World War I affect the world outside of Europe?*

World War I reached beyond Western Europe to other parts of the world. European nations received badly needed resources from their empires. They also drafted soldiers from their overseas colonies to serve on the Western Front.

Eastern Front

While the war on the Western Front dragged on, Russia battled Germany and Austria-Hungary on the Eastern Front, the battle zone in Eastern Europe. Unlike armies in the west, armies in the east covered a lot of territory. However, neither side was able to win a complete victory.

Germany and Austria-Hungary were determined to remove Russia from the war. Russia was the least industrialized of the European powers and did not have the resources to fight a modern war. Even though the Russians suffered severe losses, they managed to stay in the war.

Gas masks issued to troops in World War I protected against the effects of poisonous gases used as chemical weapons. Different gases could cause blindness, severe lung damage, and death.

TRENCHES OF WW I

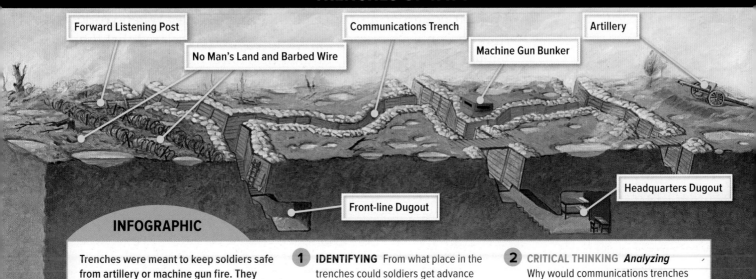

Forward Listening Post

No Man's Land and Barbed Wire

Communications Trench

Machine Gun Bunker

Artillery

Front-line Dugout

Headquarters Dugout

INFOGRAPHIC

Trenches were meant to keep soldiers safe from artillery or machine gun fire. They presented soldiers with other dangers, however, such as mud, rats, and disease.

1 IDENTIFYING From what place in the trenches could soldiers get advance warning of an enemy attack?

2 CRITICAL THINKING *Analyzing* Why would communications trenches be important for protecting soldiers?

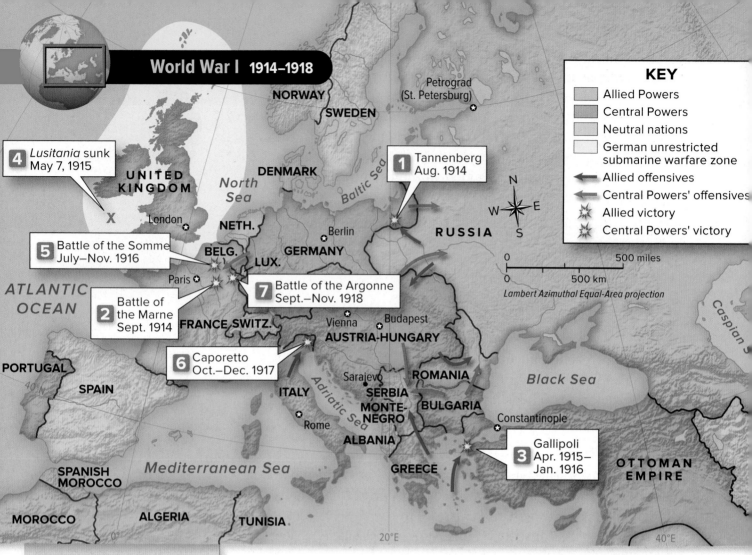

World War I 1914–1918

KEY
- Allied Powers
- Central Powers
- Neutral nations
- German unrestricted submarine warfare zone
- ← Allied offensives
- ← Central Powers' offensives
- ✦ Allied victory
- ✦ Central Powers' victory

4 *Lusitania* sunk May 7, 1915

5 Battle of the Somme July–Nov. 1916

2 Battle of the Marne Sept. 1914

1 Tannenberg Aug. 1914

7 Battle of the Argonne Sept.–Nov. 1918

6 Caporetto Oct.–Dec. 1917

3 Gallipoli Apr. 1915–Jan. 1916

500 miles
500 km
Lambert Azimuthal Equal-Area projection

GEOGRAPHY CONNECTION

World War I battles took place from France to Russia to the Middle East.

1 PLACE Around which country was the unrestricted submarine warfare zone?

2 CRITICAL THINKING
Analyzing What geographic advantage would the Allies seem to have over the Central Powers?

Russia's efforts helped the Allies on the Western Front. To drive back the Russians, Germany had to move some of its Western Front divisions to the Eastern Front. This move brought success in the east, but it weakened Germany's position along the Western Front.

America Supports the Allies

The war in Europe also affected the United States. When World War I began, U.S. president Woodrow Wilson declared that the United States would be neutral in the conflict. Many Americans, however, did take sides.

Many of the president's advisers supported the Allies. They argued that if the Allies won it would strengthen democracy and maintain a balance of power in the world. In addition, the United States had more financial and economic ties to the Allies than they did to the Central Powers.

Reading HELP DESK

blockade the closing off of a port or harbor to prevent entrance or exit

Build Vocabulary: *Word Origins*

The word *U-boat* comes from the German word *unterseeboot*, which means undersea boat.

Controlling the seas, the British navy placed a **blockade** on Germany. That is, British naval ships prevented goods from leaving or entering German ports. To wear down British sea power, the Germans began using submarines, called U-boats. In February 1915, the Germans warned that they would sink any ship entering British waters.

The British passenger liner *Lusitania* ignored the warning and sailed into the war zone. A German submarine torpedoed the ship, killing more than 1,100 passengers—including 128 Americans. President Wilson threatened to end diplomatic ties if Germany did not stop its sea attacks. In response, the Germans stopped unlimited submarine warfare for a while.

America Enters the War

In January 1917, German Foreign Secretary Arthur Zimmermann sent a telegram to the German ambassador in Mexico. Zimmermann suggested that Mexico should ally itself with Germany. In return, Mexico could reclaim "lost territory in Texas, New Mexico, and Arizona." American newspapers printed the telegram and outraged Americans began demanding war with Germany. They realized Germany was trying to control their nearest neighbor.

Also in January, Germany announced that it would sink on sight all merchant vessels sailing to Allied ports. An angry President Wilson broke off relations with Germany. After Germany sank four American merchant ships, President Wilson asked Congress for a declaration of war. On April 6, 1917, the United States entered World War I.

American soldiers helped turn the tide of the war against Germany.

▶ **CRITICAL THINKING**
Assessing What advantages could Americans entering the war provide to the war effort?

©Bettmann/Corbis

✓ **PROGRESS CHECK**

Explaining Why did the U.S. favor the Allies in World War I?

LESSON 3 REVIEW

Review Vocabulary

1. Why would the vocabulary words *militarism*, and *mobilization* be included in a description of WWI?

Answer the Guiding Questions

2. *Predicting* Why might the formation of military alliances make a country more likely to go to war?

3. *Explaining* Why was the Western Front an important location in the war?

4. *Making Inferences* How did new technologies influence the war?

5. *Evaluating* How did World War I change the role of women?

6. **NARRATIVE** Describe life in the trenches from the viewpoint of a soldier. Use vivid word images to make your description come alive. Tell not only what the trenches are like, but also how it feels to live in them.

World War I Brings Change

networks™
There's More Online!

ESSENTIAL QUESTION

• How do governments change?

IT MATTERS BECAUSE

The agreement that ended World War I sowed the seeds for unrest. Post-war countries faced major changes within their own governments.

Peace at Last

GUIDING QUESTION *What changes came to Europe and the Middle East after World War I?*

In late 1917, the Allies were in great need of American help. Years of trench warfare had worn out their armies. When American soldiers began arriving in Europe, Allied hopes soared.

About the time the United States entered the war, Russia pulled out. As a result, German troops on the Eastern Front were moved west and a larger German army advanced on Paris in 1918. On June 1, American and French troops stopped the Germans' advance. In late September the Americans began their own massive attack and broke through the enemy lines.

Meanwhile, Austria-Hungary was close to **collapse**, and the Ottoman Turks surrendered. Revolt in Germany forced the emperor to step down. On November 11, 1918, Germany signed an **armistice** (AHR•muh•stuhs), or cease-fire, ending the war.

Effects of the War

World War I had many destructive effects. Towns and farms were destroyed. Nearly 9 million soldiers had been killed, and another 21 million wounded. About 13 million civilians had died from starvation or disease.

Reading HELP DESK

Taking Notes: *Sequencing*

As you read, list the events that changed Russia. Write your notes in a flowchart like the one shown here.

1905: Russia loses war with Japan
↓
↓
↓

Content Vocabulary

• armistice   • mandate
• genocide   • soviet
• reparations

Europe After World War I 1919

NORWAY
SWEDEN
FINLAND
ESTONIA
LATVIA
LITHUANIA
EAST PRUSSIA (Ger.)
IRELAND
Independent from 1921
UNITED KINGDOM
DENMARK
NETHER-LANDS
GERMANY
POLAND
SOVIET UNION
BELGIUM
Versailles
LUX.
CZECHOSLOVAKIA
FRANCE
SWITZ.
AUSTRIA
HUNGARY
ROMANIA
PORTUGAL
SPAIN
ITALY
YUGOSLAVIA
BULGARIA
SPANISH MOROCCO
ALBANIA
GREECE
TURKEY
MOROCCO
ALGERIA
TUNISIA
LIBYA

ATLANTIC OCEAN
North Sea
Baltic Sea
Caspian Sea
Black Sea
Mediterranean Sea

0   500 miles
0   500 km
Lambert Azimuthal Equal-Area projection

20°W   60°N   60°E   40°N   0°   20°E

GEOGRAPHY CONNECTION

The map of Europe changed greatly following World War I.

1 PLACE Compare this map with the map of Europe before World War I. Which countries appear to have lost the most land following the war?

2 CRITICAL THINKING
Analyzing Describe how the German people may have felt about their territory following World War I.

Some civilians were killed deliberately. During the war, Ottoman officials were furious at what they believed was Armenian support for the Allies. Their anger led them to kill hundreds of thousands of Armenians in a terrible **genocide**. Genocide is the deliberate killing of an ethnic group.

Peace Talks

In January 1919, peace talks began at the Palace of Versailles (vuhr·SY) outside Paris. The major figures at the talks were U.S. president Woodrow Wilson, British prime minister David Lloyd George, French premier Georges Clemenceau (zhawrzh kleh·muhn·SOH), and Italian prime minister Vittorio Orlando (veet·TAWR·yoh awr·LAN·doh).

Wilson presented a plan called the Fourteen Points. It stated that national groups in Europe should form their own countries. It also called for a League of Nations, an organization in which member nations would work to prevent future wars.

armistice a truce or temporary stop in fighting; a cease-fire

genocide the deliberate killing of an ethnic group

Academic Vocabulary

collapse complete failure; breakdown

The major leaders—Georges Clemenceau, Woodrow Wilson, and David Lloyd George—leave the Palace of Versailles after signing the treaty ending World War I.

The Treaty of Versailles focused on the Germans. Under the treaty's terms, Germany owed the Allies billions of dollars in **reparations** (reh·puh·RAY·shuhnz), or payments for war damages. Germany had to give up some territory in Europe as well as its overseas colonies. The treaty greatly reduced Germany's armed forces. The treaty also called for the creation of a League of Nations.

President Wilson tried to win support at home for the treaty and the League. He failed, however, to get the U.S. Senate to approve the treaty. Many senators feared the League might force the country to fight in more foreign wars. As a result, the U.S. did not join the League of Nations.

How Was Europe's Map Redrawn?

The Allies signed separate peace treaties with the other Central Powers. The war and the treaties that followed changed Europe's political borders. The German and Russian empires lost territory, and the Austro-Hungarian Empire disappeared completely. The lands from these three empires became new nation-states or parts of existing ones.

The idea of self-government influenced many decisions at the Paris peace talks. However, the treaties were not able to draw national borders neatly so that all people of a single ethnic group could be within one country. As a result, almost every new country in Eastern Europe had a dominant group and many smaller groups. As time passed, disputes between the different groups made these countries very unstable.

The Ottoman Breakup

In making peace, the Allies broke up the Ottoman Empire. Only the area of present-day Turkey was left to the Ottomans. In 1919, Greece invaded Turkey. Turkish armies led by General Mustafa Kemal drove out the Greeks and overthrew the Ottoman sultan. Turkey became a republic in 1923.

Kemal was soon called Atatürk (AT·uh·tuhrk), or "Father of the Turks." As Turkey's first president, Atatürk worked to make Turkey a modern country. He reformed the legal code and reduced the influence of Islamic religion on government.

Connections to TODAY

Veterans' Day

World War I ended on November 11, 1918. The following year, President Wilson declared November 11 a national holiday called Armistice Day. Other nations soon followed Wilson's lead. In 1954, in the United States, Armistice Day was renamed Veterans' Day, to honor those who served and fought in World War I, World War II, and the Korean War. Today, we still honor veterans of all our armed forces on Veterans' Day.

Reading**HELP**DESK

reparations payments for war damages made to winning countries by defeated ones

mandate a territory that is officially controlled by the League of Nations but is governed by a member nation

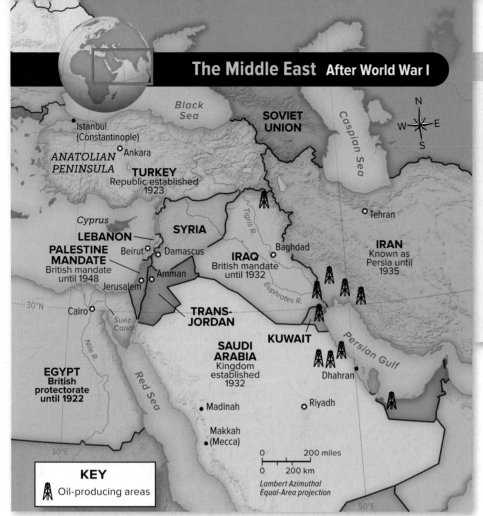

The Middle East After World War I

Black Sea

Istanbul (Constantinople)

ANATOLIAN PENINSULA

Ankara

TURKEY
Republic established 1923

SOVIET UNION

Caspian Sea

Cyprus

Tehran

LEBANON

SYRIA

PALESTINE MANDATE
British mandate until 1948

Beirut

Damascus

IRAQ
British mandate until 1932

Baghdad

IRAN
Known as Persia until 1935

Jerusalem

Amman

Tigris R.

Euphrates R.

30°N

Cairo

TRANS-JORDAN

Suez Canal

KUWAIT

Nile R.

Persian Gulf

EGYPT
British protectorate until 1922

Red Sea

SAUDI ARABIA
Kingdom established 1932

Dhahran

Madinah

Riyadh

30°E

Makkah (Mecca)

0   200 miles
0   200 km

Lambert Azimuthal Equal-Area projection

50°E

KEY

Oil-producing areas

GEOGRAPHY CONNECTION

Following World War I, a number of countries in the Middle East were created from the lands of the Ottoman Empire.

1 PLACE Where does the map show the greatest concentration of oil-producing areas in the Middle East?

2 CRITICAL THINKING
Drawing Conclusions How might the people of Saudi Arabia think about the importance of their country's natural resources to themselves and to the world?

A New Middle East

The Allies divided up the Ottoman Arab lands. France took Syria and Lebanon. Britain gained Iraq, Palestine, and Jordan. These new territories were called **mandates** (MAN·daytz). The League of Nations held each mandate but allowed a member nation to run it. The Arabs felt no loyalty to the foreign-ruled mandates. They did, however, have a strong sense of Arab nationalism.

In the 1920s, the leader Ibn Saud united most of the Arabian Peninsula. In 1932, he founded the kingdom of Saudi Arabia. The new nation at first was very poor. Then U.S. businesses struck oil along the Persian Gulf, and Saudi Arabia grew wealthy.

Meanwhile, in the Palestine Mandate, Jews and Arabs came into conflict. In the late 1800s, Jewish nationalists called Zionists settled in the region. They wanted to build a homeland where the ancient Israelites had formed a kingdom many centuries earlier. In 1917, Britain issued the Balfour Declaration. It promised Jews a homeland in the Palestine Mandate. Arabs, who made up most of the Mandate's people, were outraged. To satisfy the Arabs, the British limited entry of Jewish settlers to the Palestine Mandate.

✔ **PROGRESS CHECK**

Determining Cause and Effect What effects did the Treaty of Versailles have on Europe's population?

Revolution in Russia

GUIDING QUESTION *Why did revolution break out in Russia during World War I?*

During World War I, Russia was an ally of Britain and France. However, the war worsened problems inside of Russia. Russia's ruler, Czar Nicholas II, was unable to deal with these problems. As a result, the Russian people turned against his rigid rule.

Unrest in Russia

During the early 1900s, many Russians were discontented. Peasants had little land but paid high taxes. Groups such as the Jews and the Poles were often mistreated. In 1905, Russia lost a war with Japan. The conflict cost Russia land and money. The czar was blamed for these losses. Following a workers' uprising in 1905, the czar allowed a duma, or parliament, to meet. The duma, however, had only limited powers. The czar shut down the duma when it tried to act independently.

Poverty and scarcity of food were common among Russian peasants after the war. They often stood in long lines just to buy food.

Fall of the Czar

Russia had fewer industries than the other powers in World War I. As a result, its military did not have enough supplies and suffered high casualties. Civilians also faced food and fuel shortages.

In March 1917, striking workers demanding peace and bread flooded the streets of St. Petersburg. Soldiers in the city refused to fire on the protestors calling for the czar's removal. Finally, the czar gave up his throne. He and his family were later executed.

Members of the duma then set up a temporary government, focused mainly on the war effort. As a result, it did not carry out reforms at home and lost the support of many Russians.

Who Was Lenin?

Many Russian workers felt that the government favored the middle class, or those with wealth. They set up committees, called **soviets** (SOH·vee·ehts), to represent their concerns. Soon

©Bettmann/Corbis

Reading**HELP**DESK

soviet a committee to represent the concerns of the Russian people

Academic Vocabulary

radical extreme; in favor of making wide-ranging changes

the soviets and the government began competing for control of the country.

The soviets were made up of workers and peasants from different socialist groups. As socialists, they wanted workers to create a society based on equality for all. The most **radical** group was the Bolsheviks. The Bolsheviks believed that they could use force to bring about this ideal society. Their leader was Vladimir Lenin (VLAD·uh·mihr LEH·nuhn). The Bolsheviks vowed to take Russia out of the war, give all land to the peasants, and put the soviets in charge of the government.

In October 1917, the soviets in Russia's two largest cities, St. Petersburg and Moscow, were under Bolshevik control. As a result, the Bolsheviks were in a position to seize the government.

In November 1917, the Bolsheviks captured St. Petersburg's Winter Palace, which was the location of the temporary government. The government fell with little bloodshed. Lenin became the head of a new government.

Russia's Civil War

In early 1918, Lenin made peace with Germany and gave up large areas of Russia's empire. Meanwhile, Russia slipped into a civil war between the Bolsheviks—now called Communists (the Reds)—and their political opponents (the Whites). Communist leader Leon Trotsky organized the Red Army to defend the Communist government.

The Whites promised to defeat the Reds and bring Russia back into World War I. As a result, the Allies sent them aid. This aid did little to help the Whites. Instead, it stirred Russian patriotic support for the Communists.

During the three-year conflict, both the Reds and the Whites burned villages and killed civilians. In 1921, the Whites gave up. Lenin and the Communists now controlled all of Russia.

©Bettmann/Corbis

✓ **PROGRESS CHECK**

Explaining What role did the soviets play in the Russian Revolution?

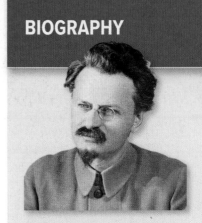
LESSON 4 REVIEW

Review Vocabulary

1. What is one synonym and one antonym for *armistice*?

2. How is *genocide* different from outright war?

Answer the Guiding Questions

3. *Evaluating* What terms did the Treaty of Versailles place on Germany?

4. *Analyzing* What was the Balfour Declaration, and how did it affect Jews?

5. *Making Connections* What conditions did the Russian people face that led to revolution?

6. *Determining Cause and Effect* What events led Nicholas II to give up his throne?

7. **INFORMATIVE/EXPLANATORY** Explain how the Russians felt about the results of World War I.

Write your answers on a separate sheet of paper.

① Exploring the Essential Question

INFORMATIVE/EXPLANATORY How do governments change? Write an essay that explains how the events of World War I led to the end of the czar's rule in Russia.

② 21st Century Skills

WRITE A CASE STUDY Choose a nation that was ruled as a colony in the 1800s or 1900s. Research the conditions of the nation and write a case study telling what foreign rule was like in that country. Include details about wars, conflicts, or political struggles that ended colonial rule of the nation.

③ Thinking Like a Historian

DETERMINING CAUSE AND EFFECT Reread the passage about the assassination of Archduke Franz Ferdinand. Think about how the death of this one person led to a costly world war. Fill in a chart like the one shown listing the cause—the assassination—and some major effects from it in Eastern Europe.

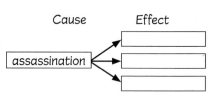

④ **GEOGRAPHY ACTIVITY**

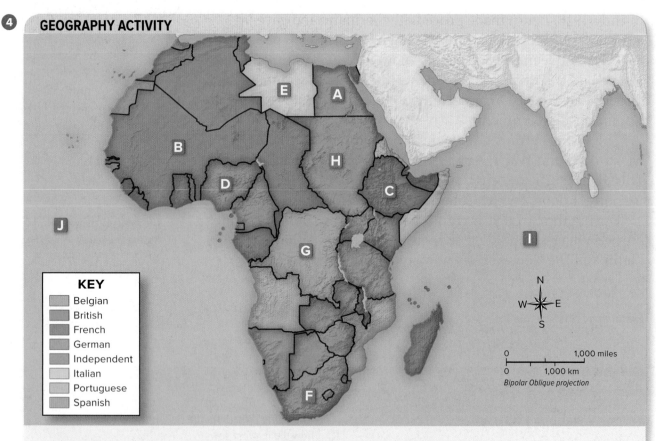

KEY
- Belgian
- British
- French
- German
- Independent
- Italian
- Portuguese
- Spanish

Locating Places

Match the letters on the map with the numbered places listed below.

1. Atlantic Ocean
2. Belgian Congo
3. Egypt
4. Ethiopia
5. French West Africa
6. Indian Ocean
7. Libya
8. Nigeria
9. Sudan
10. Union of South Africa

CHAPTER 24 Assessment

Directions: Write your answers on a separate piece of paper.

CHECKING FOR UNDERSTANDING

1 Define the vocabulary words as they relate to imperialism and World War I.

- **A.** soviet
- **B.** protectorate
- **C.** imperialism
- **D.** genocide
- **E.** sphere of influence
- **F.** propaganda
- **G.** militarism
- **H.** conscription
- **I.** mandate
- **J.** armistice
- **K.** entente
- **L.** blockade
- **M.** extraterritoriality
- **N.** reparations

REVIEW THE GUIDING QUESTIONS

2 *Describing* What were three main motivations for European expansionism at the end of the 1800s?

3 *Identifying* Who were the sepoys?

4 *Locating* Which parts of Africa were claimed by Britain? Which were claimed by Belgium?

5 *Naming* What new territories came under the control of the United States as a result of the Spanish-American War?

6 *Explaining* What did the Chinese Boxers hope to accomplish?

7 *Summarizing* What was the main goal of Sun Yat-sen?

8 *Stating* Why did the United States want to "open" Japan?

9 *Explaining* What led to the buildup of European armies in the late 19th and early 20th centuries?

10 *Determining Cause and Effect* Why did Britain declare war on Germany?

11 *Describing* What was the Zimmerman note and how did it impact American public opinion about World War I?

12 *Explaining* What was the purpose of the League of Nations?

13 *Summarizing* What did the Bolsheviks want to do?

CRITICAL THINKING

14 *Comparing and Contrasting* What were the different ways imperial nations organized and governed their territories?

15 *Evaluating* Did British rule bring more positive or more negative consequences to India? Explain your answer.

16 *Analyzing* How did the Tai Ping Rebellion ultimately help bring down the Qing dynasty?

17 *Identifying Central Issues* How did Japan's response to the Western powers differ from China's? How did this response benefit Japan? Explain.

18 *Defending* Which do you believe was most responsible for World War I—growing militarism or the alliance system? Defend your answer.

19 *Predicting Consequences* How was Europe's map redrawn in Eastern Europe after World War I? How do you believe these new national borders will affect Europe in the years that follow?

20 *Speculating* Which effect of World War I do you believe has had the greatest impact on world history?

Need Extra Help?

If you've missed question	**1**	**2**	**3**	**4**	**5**	**6**	**7**	**8**	**9**	**10**	**11**	**12**	**13**	**14**	**15**	**16**	**17**	**18**	**19**	**20**
Review Lesson	1, 2, 3, 4	1	1	1	1	2	2	2	3	3	3	4	4	1	1	2	2	3	4	4

DBQ SHORT RESPONSE

"In the days of a great struggle against a foreign enemy who has been endeavouring [trying] for three years to enslave our country, it pleased God to send Russia a further painful trial. … The cruel enemy is making his last efforts and the moment is near when our valiant Army, in concert with our glorious Allies, will finally overthrow the enemy.

—Nicholas II, Czar of Russia, March 15, 1917

21 What are the "great struggle" and "foreign enemy" to which Nicholas refers?

22 Is Nicholas correct when he predicts that the Russian army will "overthrow the enemy"? Why or why not?

EXTENDED RESPONSE

23 *Informative/Explanatory* Write a paragraph explaining the pros and cons of imperialism. Tell how the relationship between the ruling country and the colony could have both positive and negative effects on the colony.

STANDARDIZED TEST PRACTICE

DBQ ANALYZING DOCUMENTS

Edward D. Swinton, an official in the British army, describes his difficult experience fighting in the trenches during World War I.

"The offensive against one or two points was renewed at dusk, with no greater success … In spite of the fact that they have been drenched [soaked] to the skin for some days and their trenches have been deep in mud and water … and the almost continuous bombardment [attack] to which they have been subjected, they have … been ready for the enemy's infantry."

—Col. Edward D. Swinton, "Trench Warfare Begins on the Aisne"

24 **Finding the Main Idea** According to the account, what did the soldiers face in the trenches?

A. poison gas and terrible odors

C. illness and terror

B. rats and fleas

D. mud and continuous attack

25 *Analyzing* What feelings does Swinton seem to hold for his fellow soldiers?

A. He admires them for continuing to fight despite difficult conditions.

B. He scorns them for fighting for a useless cause.

C. He is frightened by them and fears that they will attack him.

D. He is sad for them because they have been unsuccessful.

Need Extra Help?

If You've Missed Question	21	22	23	24	25
Review Lesson	4	1	1	3	3

◄ *Winston Churchill was a strong leader. The British people looked to him to help guide them out of World War II.*

1920 TO 1990

World War II and the Cold War

THE STORY MATTERS ...

In the 1930s, British leader Winston Churchill warned about the dangers of Germany's rearming. Overall, Western democracies were slow to listen. They did not want to consider the possibility of another war so soon after World War I.

Churchill was prime minister of Britain through the difficult years of World War II. His frequent radio addresses encouraged the British people to be confident in their fight to defeat the Nazis and preserve democracy.

ESSENTIAL QUESTIONS

- What are the characteristics of a leader?
- How does conflict develop?
- Why is history important?
- How do governments change?
- How do new ideas change the way people live?

Rik Hamilton/Alamy Stock Photo

Place & Time: World War II

After World War I, dictators rose to power in parts of Europe and Asia. Their policies of expansion led to World War II. After this second global conflict, the United States and the Soviet Union competed in a new type of global struggle called the Cold War.

Step Into the Place

MAP FOCUS Nations on every continent except Antarctica fought in World War II. Battles were fought in Asia, Europe, and North Africa.

1 LOCATION Were all the countries bordering the Mediterranean Sea involved in World War II? Explain.

2 PLACE Which continents had areas under Axis control?

3 CRITICAL THINKING
Comparing and Contrasting
From their locations on the map, how similar or different do you think the World War II experience would be for Britain and the United States?

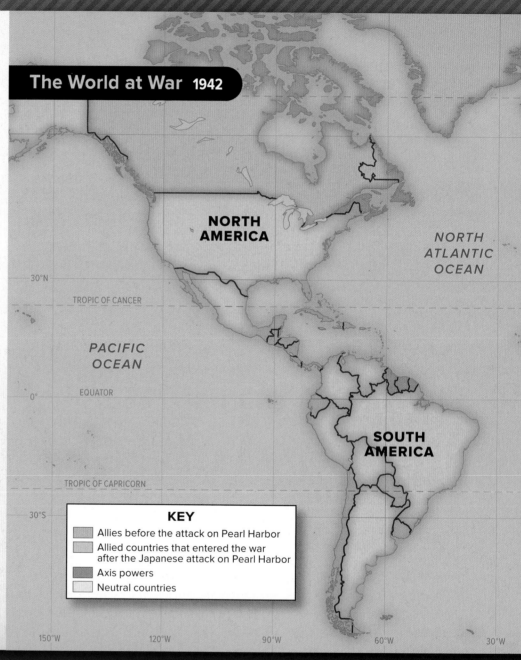

The World at War 1942

NORTH AMERICA

NORTH ATLANTIC OCEAN

30°N

TROPIC OF CANCER

PACIFIC OCEAN

EQUATOR

0°

SOUTH AMERICA

TROPIC OF CAPRICORN

30°S

KEY
- Allies before the attack on Pearl Harbor
- Allied countries that entered the war after the Japanese attack on Pearl Harbor
- Axis powers
- Neutral countries

150°W   120°W   90°W   60°W   30°W

Step Into the Time

TIME LINE Choose a time line event from The World Before and During World War II. Write a paragraph that predicts the results of the event.

1929 The Great Depression begins

1928 Stalin introduces his first 5-Year Plan

1922 Fascist Benito Mussolini becomes leader of Italy

1920 Women gain right to vote in the U.S.

THE WORLD BEFORE AND DURING WORLD WAR II	1920		1930

THE WORLD AFTER WORLD WAR II	1940		1950

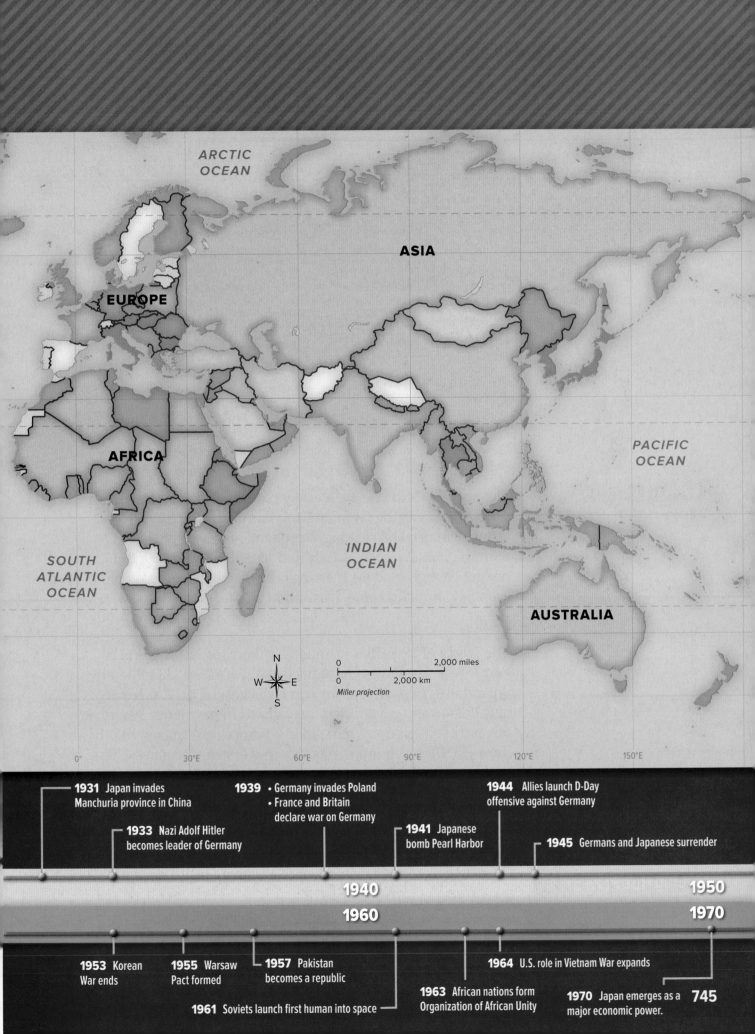

ARCTIC
OCEAN

ASIA

EUROPE

PACIFIC
OCEAN

AFRICA

SOUTH
ATLANTIC
OCEAN

INDIAN
OCEAN

AUSTRALIA

N
W E
S

0   2,000 miles
0   2,000 km
Miller projection

0°   30°E   60°E   90°E   120°E   150°E

1931 Japan invades
Manchuria province in China

1939 • Germany invades Poland
• France and Britain
declare war on Germany

1944 Allies launch D-Day
offensive against Germany

1933 Nazi Adolf Hitler
becomes leader of Germany

1941 Japanese
bomb Pearl Harbor

1945 Germans and Japanese surrender

1940   **1950**

1960   **1970**

1953 Korean
War ends

1955 Warsaw
Pact formed

1957 Pakistan
becomes a republic

1964 U.S. role in Vietnam War expands

1963 African nations form
Organization of African Unity

1961 Soviets launch first human into space

1970 Japan emerges as a
major economic power.   **745**

LESSON 1
The Rise of Dictators

ESSENTIAL QUESTION
• What are the characteristics of a leader?

IT MATTERS BECAUSE
Economic troubles caused by World War I and the ambitions of dictators led to World War II.

Economic Troubles

GUIDING QUESTION *How did the world's industrialized countries respond to economic troubles after World War I?*

The end of World War I left many nations unhappy. Defeated peoples, such as the Germans, felt humiliated. They resented losing territory and making war payments. Even people in winning nations, such as Italy and Japan, felt that they did not get enough land for the sacrifices they had made. When economic troubles came, frustration and fear added to this anger.

Postwar Germany

The Treaty of Versailles blamed Germany for causing World War I. As a result, the Germans owed the Allies $33 billion in reparations, or payments for war damages. In 1922, Germany's new democratic government fell behind in payments. Angry at not getting its share of reparations, France sent troops into the Ruhr (RUR), a rich industrial area in western Germany. The French wanted to make up for unpaid reparations by claiming the wealth of the Ruhr's mines and factories.

Resisting the Ruhr takeover, German workers went on strike. When France took over Ruhr steel mills and coal mines, Germany lost a major source of income. To pay the strikers' wages, the German government printed more and more paper money.

Reading**HELP**DESK

Taking Notes: *Listing*

In a chart like this one, list the events in Germany, Italy, and Japan that led to
World War II.

Events Leading to War

Country	Events
Germany	
Italy	
Japan	

Content Vocabulary

• **depression**
• **totalitarian state**
• **collectivization**

When a country prints too much money, the currency loses value. This causes inflation as businesses raise prices. Germany's currency lost so much value it became nearly worthless.

To help **ensure** Germany's recovery, the U.S. and European nations created the Dawes Plan in 1924. Developed by American banker Charles Dawes, the plan reduced the amount of reparations Germany owed and set payments that Germany could handle. The plan also arranged for American investors to lend $200 million to Germany. The economic situation improved in Germany, but this did not last long.

Causes of the Great Depression

During the 1930s, an economic depression struck the world's industrialized countries. A **depression** is a time of reduced economic activity during which businesses often fail and many people lose their jobs. The economic crisis of the 1930s was so severe it became known as the Great Depression.

In the 1920s, American companies were producing much of the world's manufactured goods. Many people bought stock in these companies with the hope of making a profit. The stock market boomed in the 1920s.

Despite the stock market boom, the U.S. economy had problems. Farm prices were falling. Wages were not rising as fast as the production of goods, so people bought fewer goods. This mix of overproduction and falling demand created an economic crisis. Factories slowed production and cut the number of workers they employed.

By October 1929, fears about the economy grew. The investors who had borrowed to buy stocks were pressured to pay back their loans. When they failed to pay, panic struck. Stock prices fell drastically, and people found their investments were suddenly worthless. Banks collapsed, and many people lost their savings.

The Depression Worsens

Frightened American investors withdrew money from European markets, causing the collapse of European banks. By 1931, trade had slowed and jobs were scarce in both North America and Europe.

The U.S. government hired photographer Dorothea Lange to call the public's attention to the struggle of the rural poor. Her portrait of a migrant mother is probably the most famous photograph taken in the American Depression.

▶ **CRITICAL THINKING**
Making Connections Why do you think that the government paid writers and photographers to record the Great Depression?

depression a period of low general economic activity marked especially by rising levels of unemployment

Academic Vocabulary

ensure to make sure, certain, or safe

During the Great Depression, President Franklin D. Roosevelt would often address the nation on the radio. His "fireside chats" became a beacon of hope for many suffering Americans.

The Great Depression brought misery to millions of people. In 1932, one out of four American and British people and two out of five German people had lost their jobs. Hungry people begged for food on the streets or waited in lines for meals at government or charity soup kitchens. More and more people became homeless and built huts of tin or cardboard for shelter.

Democratic governments in Europe and North America responded to the economic crisis in different ways. Britain provided workers with benefit payments and government-supported housing. In France, the Great Depression hit later and was less severe. The French government focused on cutting back spending.

Roosevelt's New Deal

President Franklin D. Roosevelt believed that the U.S. federal government needed to boost the ailing economy and provide relief to the jobless. With the support of Congress, Roosevelt set up a government program called the New Deal.

Under the New Deal, the federal government created several different agencies to help people buy food, pay for housing, and find work. The Civilian Conservation Corps (CCC) gave jobs to many young people. They constructed facilities and planted trees in national parks. The Works Progress Administration (WPA) paid jobless workers to build hospitals, roads, bridges, and dams. In addition, the WPA gave work to artists and writers. Other new agencies assisted farmers and business leaders.

Roosevelt also worked with the federal government to carry out reforms. In 1935, Roosevelt had Congress pass the Social Security Act. This program gave pensions, or payments, to workers after they retired. It also provided workers with unemployment insurance. This meant that the government gave payments to jobless workers until they found another job. Roosevelt's New Deal **restored** Americans' hope for the future.

☑ PROGRESS CHECK

Explaining Why was the Dawes Plan introduced?

©Bettmann/Corbis

Reading**HELP**DESK

Reading Strategy: *Summarizing*
Read the three paragraphs that explain President Roosevelt's New Deal program. In three sentences, condense and explain those paragraphs.

Dictators in Italy and Germany

GUIDING QUESTION *Why did people in Italy and Germany support rule by dictators?*

The Great Depression spread fear and uncertainty all over the world. Despite weak economies, long-standing democracies such as the United States, Britain, and France remained strong. In Italy, Germany, and other newly democratic nations, citizens were less loyal to democratic ideas. When these countries' economies collapsed, people turned to strong leaders for help. These leaders became dictators who ruled their nations by force.

Under these dictators, a new form of government called totalitarianism arose. In a **totalitarian state** (toh·ta·luh·tehr·ee· uhn), political leaders try to totally control the way citizens live and think. During the 1930s, totalitarian leaders used print, radio, film, and the arts to enforce their views. People who disagreed were harshly punished.

Italian dictator Benito Mussolini started out as a reformer in Italy. Because of his experiences in World War I, he wanted to restore Italy to its past glory.

Mussolini's Italy

Italy was the first European country to become a totalitarian state after World War I. It had a huge debt to repay. Because Italy was an ally of Germany, it too had to pay reparations. Many people were jobless. The government was unable to deal with the rising discontent of its citizens.

As disorder spread, Benito Mussolini (buh·NEE·toh moo· suh·LEE·nee) created the Fascist Party. He pledged to restore order, fix the economy, and make Italy great. His followers brutally attacked their opponents in the streets. In 1922, the Fascists staged a huge march on Rome. To prevent bloodshed, Italy's king agreed to name Mussolini as head of government.

Mussolini was called *Il Duce* (eel DOO·chay), or "the Leader." He quickly ended democracy in Italy and banned all political groups except the Fascists. Personal freedoms and a free press were gone. Mussolini built up Italy's military and promised to restore the glory of ancient Rome.

Hitler's Germany

During the early 1930s, many German businesses failed, and millions of workers lost their jobs. Many Germans backed a political leader named Adolf Hitler.

A powerful speaker, Hitler appealed to people's fears about the economy and their bitterness about the Treaty of Versailles. He promised to create jobs and make Germany a world power.

totalitarian state government in which citizens are under strict control by the state

Academic Vocabulary

restore to put or bring back into existence

©Hutton-Deutsch Collection/Corbis

There's More Online! connected.mcgraw-hill.com

Hitler was the leader of the National Socialist (Nazi) Party. Hitler and the Nazis portrayed the Germans as a "master race" that was better than other people. Nazis were known for their anti-Semitism, or hatred of Jews. They blamed Jews for Germany's problems. Hitler presented these ideas in his book *Mein Kampf*, or "My Struggle."

By 1932, the Nazi Party had won a large number of seats in the German parliament. In 1933, Hitler was named chancellor, or prime minister of Germany. As chancellor, Hitler had the parliament pass a law that gave him all power to deal with the country's problems. The law provided a legal way for Hitler to become a dictator.

Hitler and his followers then began to build a totalitarian state. He banned all political parties except the Nazis and broke up labor unions. Citizens lost their rights of freedom of speech, assembly, press, and religion. The Nazi government took control of the country's radio and newspapers. It also took over the courts and set up a secret police and large prisons called concentration camps.

The Nazi government carried out Hitler's extreme anti-Semitism. In 1935, the Nuremberg Laws were issued. These laws stated that Jews were no longer citizens and had no political rights. The government also took control of Jewish businesses and jobs. Jews had limited access to medical care and could not attend state-run schools.

Nazis also tried to limit women's rights. Women, the Nazis claimed, were meant to be wives and mothers, not leaders. As a result, the government discouraged women from becoming lawyers, doctors, or professors. Instead, posters urged women to "get ahold of pots and pans. ..."

Adolf Hitler (below), who had been a corporal in World War I, led the Nazi Party to power in Germany. Formal parades showcased the "goose step" marching style of Nazi troops (above).

▶ CRITICAL THINKING

Analyzing Why might the German people have believed in and supported Hitler?

✓ PROGRESS CHECK

Comparing How were Mussolini and Hitler alike in their ruling methods?

Reading HELPDESK

Reading Strategy: *Identifying*

Read the paragraphs about Hitler's rise to power. In three sentences, identify factors that led to Hitler's control of the government.

collectivization an economic system in which a government controls production and distribution of all goods

The Soviet Union Under Stalin

GUIDING QUESTION *How did Stalin's rule affect the peoples of the Soviet Union?*

Totalitarian rule also came to Russia. By 1922, after revolution and civil war, the Communists had secured their power. Lenin served as leader of the new Communist state. In that year, the Union of Soviet Socialist Republics (USSR), or the Soviet Union, was formed. This huge territory included Russia and most lands of the old Russian Empire.

Stalin in Power

After Lenin died in 1924, two Communist leaders competed to rule the Soviet Union. They were Red Army commander Leon Trotsky and Communist Party head Joseph Stalin.

One of Stalin's jobs was to appoint party officials. This responsibility gave Stalin the support of the thousands of officials he had appointed. Their backing helped Stalin defeat Trotsky and seize power. By the late 1920s, Joseph Stalin had become dictator of the Soviet Union.

A Government-Run Economy

Stalin wanted to turn the Soviet Union from an agricultural country into an industrial power. To do this, he introduced a series of Five-Year Plans. These were programs that set economic goals for a five-year period. Under the Five-Year Plans, steel mills, power plants, and oil refineries were built and kept under government control.

Under Stalin's orders, the government also took control of all farming. Stalin's plans called for **collectivization** (kuh·lehk·tih·vuh·ZAY·shuhn). This meant combining small farms into large, factory-like farms run by the government.

Many peasants resisted collectivization. They destroyed their houses, cows, and pigs rather than become part of the government system. This resistance did not last long. Peasants who refused to cooperate were either shot or sent to prison.

By 1939, the Soviet Union was a major industrial power. Millions, however, suffered from miserable working conditions, low pay, and a lack of housing. Individual citizens were required to make sacrifices for the greater good of all. Those people who opposed Stalin's actions were killed or sent to remote prison camps. Many prisons were located in cold and remote Siberia, the most eastern region of the country.

Joseph Stalin built the Soviet Union into a superpower. At the same time, however, he destroyed the freedom of the Soviet people.

✔ **PROGRESS CHECK**

Explaining Why did Stalin force collective farms on Soviet peasants?

GEOGRAPHY CONNECTION

Japan conquered territory throughout East Asia to gain land and natural resources.

1 REGIONS At what point in time had the Japanese added the most territory?

2 CRITICAL THINKING
Summarizing What are some issues Japan faced as an island nation in the 1930s?

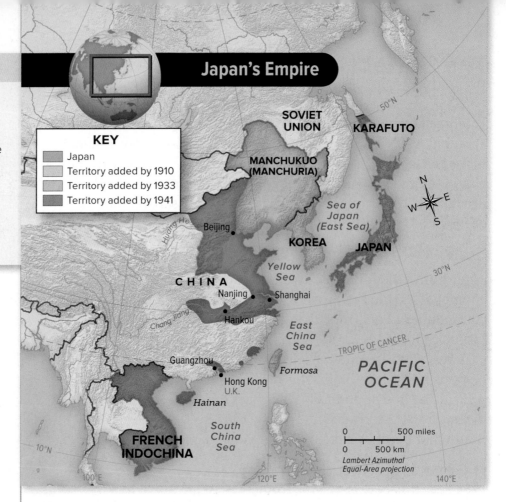

Military Rule in Japan

GUIDING QUESTION *Why did the Japanese turn to military rule and territorial expansion during the 1930s?*

While Stalin tightened his hold on the Soviet Union, military leaders took control of Japan. Japan's industrial power had grown by the early 1900s. Between 1872 and 1925, the nation's population more than doubled, from 25 million to 60 million.

An Industrial Society

The Japanese government emphasized manufacturing and trade. It hoped that new industries and markets would create jobs for its growing population. Government-controlled banks provided money to build factories, mines, and railroads. The government helped develop large private businesses called *zaibatsu*.

During the 1920s, Japanese goods had flooded world markets. Japanese factory managers and rural landowners had grown wealthy. Industrial workers and farmers, however, remained poor. Food prices rose rapidly, which led to riots.

Reading**HELP**DESK

Reading Strategy: *Listing*

List two factors that helped Stalin become dictator of the Soviet Union.

Military Expansion

When the Great Depression hit Japan, many workers lost jobs and some even faced starvation. The value of manufactured goods fell worldwide. Japan's military leaders blamed Japan's difficulties on the spread of American and European ideas. They felt that they only way for Japan to recover would be to return Japan to its old warrior traditions.

As Japan's trade declined, Japan's military leaders argued that Japan needed more land and natural resources to make its economy stronger. In 1931, without government approval, army leaders invaded Manchuria (man·CHUR·ee·uh), the northeast region of China. The use of calvary was their strongest weapon. When Japan's prime minister tried to stop the war, the military killed him. From then on, Japan's government did what the military wanted. Japan began making plans to build an empire in Asia even if it meant war with other countries.

Japan's army invaded Manchuria in 1931 and was able to control major cities in that country.

✓ PROGRESS CHECK

Analyzing Why do you think Japanese military leaders blamed Japan's problems on the spread of Western ideas?

LESSON 1 REVIEW

1. How did the stock market crash contribute to the *depression* of the 1930s?

2. What did Stalin's policy of *collectivization* mean to Russian farmers?

Answer the Guiding Questions

3. *Summarizing* How did President Roosevelt deal with the Great Depression in the United States?

4. *Explaining* What other regions of the world besides the U.S. were affected by the Great Depression?

5. *Identifying* What were the Nuremberg Laws issued in 1935 in Germany?

6. *Defining* What does the government try to control in a totalitarian state?

7. **ARGUMENT** Political tensions throughout the world led to the start of World War II. Which event do you think contributed the most to the beginning of this war? Write a persuasive essay in which you explain your choice.

LESSON 2

World War II Begins

ESSENTIAL QUESTION

• How does conflict develop?

IT MATTERS BECAUSE

For millions of people, World War II was the most destructive event in the twentieth century.

The Path to War

GUIDING QUESTION *How did European leaders respond to the demands Hitler made for territory?*

Many Germans believed that the Allies had unfairly punished Germany for causing World War I. They supported Adolf Hitler because he criticized the Treaty of Versailles. In his speeches, Hitler vowed that he would no longer obey the treaty.

The Treaty of Versailles greatly limited the size of Germany's military. Hitler stated that Germany would no longer accept this limitation. In March 1935, he announced that Germany would increase the size of its army and form a new air force.

The Treaty of Versailles also gave clear instructions about the Rhineland. This German region lay between the Rhine River and the French border. To protect France, the treaty stated that no German troops could be in the Rhineland. Taking a chance that France and Britain would not **intervene**, Hitler ordered German troops into the Rhineland in March 1936.

As Hitler expected, France and Britain did not use force, because neither was willing to risk a war. British leaders thought they could avoid conflict by accepting Hitler's demands—a policy known as **appeasement** (uh·PEEZ·muhnt). Because the French relied on British help, they also accepted his demands.

Reading **HELP**DESK

Taking Notes: *Identify*

On a chart like this one, list the main world leaders and their countries in 1939.

World Leaders in 1939

Country	Leader

Content Vocabulary

• **appeasement**

Hitler's Actions in Europe 1936–1939

5 1939 Hitler demands control of the Danzig Corridor and invades Poland.

3 1938 Hitler is given the Sudetenland by the British and the French.

4 1939 Hitler marches into, and takes over, Czechoslovakia.

1 1936 Hitler orders troops into Rhineland.

2 1938 Hitler takes over Austria after the Anschluss.

500 miles
500 km
Lambert Azimuthal Equal-Area projection

GEOGRAPHY CONNECTION

Hitler moved swiftly to regain lands that Germany had lost after World War I. He later went on to take other regions.

1 REGIONS What areas had Hitler acquired by August 1939?

2 CRITICAL THINKING
Assessing How were Hitler's conquests in Europe a form of nationalism?

Hitler and Mussolini

Hitler gained an ally in Italy's Benito Mussolini. In 1935, Italian troops invaded the African kingdom of Ethiopia. Britain and France opposed the invasion, but neither country acted to stop it. Hitler, however, fully supported Mussolini.

Next, the two dictators intervened in Spain. From 1936 to 1939, a destructive civil war divided that country. Germany and Italy helped a Spanish military leader, General Francisco Franco, overthrow Spain's new democratic republic. Like Hitler and Mussolini, Franco headed a strong government that demanded citizens' total loyalty. Soon after Franco's victory, Hitler and Mussolini formed an alliance. Franco did not join with them.

Meanwhile, Hitler grew bolder. He demanded that German-speaking Austria become part of Germany. The Austrian chancellor asked Britain and France for help, but once more the two democracies did nothing. In March 1938, Hitler sent German troops into Austria and took over the country.

appeasement trying to avoid war with an aggressive nation by giving in to its demands

Academic Vocabulary

intervene to come between in order to prevent something

Hitler next turned to Austria's neighbor, Czechoslovakia. He demanded that the Czechs give up the Sudetenland (soo·DAY·tuhn·land), a part of Czechoslovakia where many Germans lived. Czechoslovakia refused and was ready to fight to keep its territory. Britain and France, fearing a major war, preferred to hold talks. In September 1938, European leaders met in the German city of Munich (MYOO·nihk).

At the Munich Conference, British and French leaders agreed to Germany's demand for the Sudetenland. In return, Hitler pledged not to further expand German territory. Neville Chamberlain (nehv·uhl chaym·buhr·luhn), Britain's prime minister, promised that there would be "peace in our time."

Events soon proved Chamberlain wrong. In March 1939, German forces took over western Czechoslovakia and set up a Nazi-friendly state in the eastern part. Hitler then demanded control of Danzig, a German city located in Poland that was under League of Nations protection. Britain **responded** by promising to support Poland if the Germans invaded its territory.

✓ PROGRESS CHECK

Analyzing Why did Britain and France follow a policy of appeasement?

The Coming of War

GUIDING QUESTION *How did war in Europe develop into another world war?*

Hitler spent the summer of 1939 preparing to invade Poland. He was concerned, however, that Stalin would oppose him. Although bitter enemies, Hitler and Stalin signed a treaty in August 1939 promising not to attack each other. They also secretly agreed to divide Poland. Hitler now could attack.

Germany on the Attack

On September 1, 1939, German forces invaded Poland. Two days later, Britain and France declared war on Germany. Meanwhile, German planes bombed and machine-gunned Polish targets. Tanks and soldiers poured through the country's western defenses. Then, Soviet troops invaded eastern Poland. In less than a month, Germany and the Soviet Union divided Poland between them.

In April 1940, German forces moved north, attacking Denmark and Norway. Next, they turned west to invade the Netherlands and

German officers led by Hitler himself marched through Paris. The fall of France meant that Britain would now have to face Nazi Germany.

▶ CRITICAL THINKING
Drawing Conclusions Why do you think Hitler expected Britain to want peace after the fall of Paris?

Roger Viollet/Getty Images

Build Vocabulary: *Related Words*

The verb *declare* is a more forceful term than the verb *speak*. To declare something is to announce it officially and with emphasis. The noun *declaration* is a spoken or written announcement. Use a dictionary to find additional related words.

Belgium. The Germans then swept into northern France. Italy joined the war on the side of Germany, attacking France from the southeast. On June 14, German troops marched triumphantly into Paris. The French surrendered a week later.

The Battle of Britain

The fall of France meant that the Allies were down to one major power: Britain. Hitler expected the British to seek peace. Instead, Britain's new prime minister, Winston Churchill (wihn·stuhn chuhrch·hihl), defiantly declared:

" We shall defend our island, whatever the cost may be, we shall fight on the beaches, we shall fight on the landing grounds, we shall fight in the fields and in the streets, we shall fight in the hills, we shall never surrender. "

—Winston Churchill, from a speech to the British House of Commons, June 4, 1940

Hitler was now determined to invade Britain. In August, the German air force set out to destroy Britain's Royal Air Force (RAF) and take control of the skies. The Germans began bombing British airfields and aircraft factories. These attacks started an air battle that became known as the Battle of Britain.

A new technology called radar helped the RAF. Radar stations along the British coast tracked incoming German airplanes using radio waves and directed British fighter planes to stop them. As German air losses mounted, German planes started bombing British cities. They destroyed large areas of London and killed many civilians.

The attacks failed to break Britain's will to fight. By October 1940, Germany had not won control of the air, so Hitler canceled invasion plans. Britain escaped invasion thanks to a few hundred RAF pilots. Churchill told Britain's Parliament: "Never in the field of human conflict was so much owed by so many to so few."

The bombing of London itself during the Battle of Britain caused destruction and loss of life. It did not, however, defeat the British people.

PHOTO: ©Corbis
TEXT: Winston Churchill, "Speech before Commons", June 4, 1940. Reproduced with permission of Curtis Brown Ltd, London on behalf of the Estate of Sir Winston Churchill. Copyright © Winston S. Churchill.

Academic Vocabulary

respond to give an answer; to react

The United States Remains Neutral

At first, the United States was determined to stay **neutral**, or not taking sides in the war. In the 1930s, Congress had passed laws making it illegal for the United States to assist warring countries if the U.S. was not involved in the war itself. President Roosevelt, however, viewed Germany as a danger to the United States.

In 1940, Roosevelt convinced Congress to approve a policy that allowed the British to buy U.S. goods if they paid cash and carried the goods to Britain in their own ships. Congress passed the Lend-Lease Act in 1941. This law allowed the U.S. to lend weapons to Britain. Roosevelt also ordered U.S. naval protection for British ships sailing close to the United States.

Invasion of the Soviet Union

Failing to defeat Britain, Hitler turned his attention to taking over the Soviet Union. Hitler ignored the agreement that he and Stalin had made not to attack each other. German forces invaded the Soviet Union in June 1941. They destroyed most of its warplanes, disabled tanks, and captured half a million soldiers.

As the Germans advanced into Soviet territory, Stalin ordered a scorched-earth policy. Soviet troops and civilians burned cities, destroyed crops, and blew up dams.

When the rainy season began, muddy roads trapped the German army's trucks and wagons. Soon afterward the harsh Russian winter set in, catching the German invaders unprepared. On December 2, 1941, Hitler's army reached the outskirts of Moscow. The Soviets struck back, forcing a German retreat.

Pearl Harbor

While Hitler and Mussolini waged war in Europe, the Japanese launched new attacks in East Asia. Japan had taken over Manchuria in 1931. During the rest of the 1930s, the Japanese moved steadily southward into China. In December 1937, they seized Nanjing (nahn·jihng), the Chinese capital. China's leader, Chiang Kai-shek, retreated into China's interior. His government later joined the Allied powers.

Japan next moved into Southeast Asia. After France surrendered in 1940, Japanese forces seized the French colony of Indochina. The Japanese also wanted to seize the Dutch East Indies, British Malaya, and the Philippines. Their goal was to obtain badly needed food supplies, oil, and rubber.

Reading**HELP**DESK

Academic Vocabulary

neutral not taking a side

Reading Strategy: *Listing*

On a chart, list the actions Japan took before bombing Pearl Harbor.

In response to Japan's actions, President Roosevelt blocked Japanese efforts to withdraw money they had deposited in American banks. He also stopped sales of oil, gasoline, and other resources to Japan.

The American actions angered the Japanese, who decided to go to war against the United States. On December 7, 1941, Japan carried out a surprise air attack on the U.S. Pacific fleet at Pearl Harbor, Hawaii. The attack destroyed many battleships and planes and killed more than 2,300 soldiers, sailors, and civilians. It also enraged the American people.

The next day, President Roosevelt asked Congress to declare war on Japan. He called December 7 "a date which will live in infamy [disgrace]." On December 11, 1941, Germany and Italy declared war on the United States.

The Japanese attack on Pearl Harbor was so destructive because it took the U.S. fleet by surprise.

✅ PROGRESS CHECK

Identifying What was Stalin's scorched-earth policy?

LESSON 2 REVIEW

1. What effect did the policy of *appeasement* have on the European country of Austria?

Answer the Guiding Questions

2. ***Describing*** What did Hitler pledge at the Munich Conference?

3. ***Explaining*** What two-part treaty did Hitler and Stalin agree to in August 1939?

4. ***Summarizing*** What did the results of the Battle of Britain show about the British?

5. ***Explaining*** Why did the Japanese bomb Pearl Harbor?

6. **ARGUMENT** Before September 1939, Britain followed a policy of appeasement toward Germany. Do you think that policy helped prevent war or did it just delay war? Support your opinion with facts.

LESSON 3

Allies Win the War

ESSENTIAL QUESTION
- Why is history important?

IT MATTERS BECAUSE

An Allied victory over the Axis states was necessary for the survival of American and European democracies.

The Global Struggle

GUIDING QUESTION *How did the Allies gradually push back Germany, Italy, and Japan in World War II?*

World War II was a conflict fought on an enormous scale. On one side were the Allies—the United States, Britain, the Soviet Union, and China. On the other side were the Axis powers— Germany, Italy, and Japan. The war was fought in two major theaters, or battle areas—Europe and the Pacific. Winning battles required outstanding leaders and hundreds of thousands of troops. At home, civilians worked hard to provide resources and goods for the war.

War in Africa and Europe

The Allies developed a war strategy, or plan of action, for fighting the Axis powers. Allied leaders Stalin, Churchill, and Roosevelt decided to **focus** first on defeating Hitler. They would turn their attention to Japan later. This plan became known as the "Europe first" policy. Stalin wanted the British and Americans to attack Nazi-held Western Europe. Churchill, however, argued that the Allies were not yet ready to fight strong German forces in Europe. He wanted to attack the edges of the German-held territory, and Roosevelt agreed.

Reading**HELP**DESK

Taking Notes: *Listing*

In a graphic organizer like this one, list the territories the Allies regained in their early battles against Germany, Italy, and Japan.

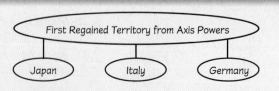

Content Vocabulary
- **D-Day**

At the end of 1942, American and British forces landed in Morocco and Algeria. Moving swiftly eastward, they joined British forces advancing west from Egypt to close in on the Germans. In May 1943, the Allies drove the Germans out of North Africa.

Allied troops then advanced into southern Europe. They took the Italian island of Sicily in the summer of 1943, and landed on Italy's mainland in September. U.S. general Dwight D. Eisenhower (EYE·zuhn·howr) directed the invasion. Another American general, George Patton, and British general Bernard Montgomery actually led the troops.

As the Allies advanced, the Italians overthrew Mussolini and surrendered. German forces in Italy continued the fight but could not halt the Allied move into central Italy. In June 1944, Allied forces finally entered Rome, Italy's capital.

While the British and Americans fought in North Africa and Italy, the Soviets battled the Germans on Soviet territory. In the spring of 1942, German forces advanced on Stalingrad, an industrial city in southeastern Russia. Soviet troops fought back and surrounded the city, cutting off German supply lines. Several months later, in February 1943, the Germans surrendered. The German defeat at Stalingrad marked a major turning point in the war.

Meanwhile, Allied leaders made plans for the world for after the war was over. Roosevelt, Churchill, and Stalin **convened** in Tehran, the capital of Iran, in late 1943. At this Tehran Conference, the leaders agreed to divide up Germany after Hitler was defeated. Stalin also agreed to help the United States defeat Japan and to join an international peace-keeping organization after the war.

Dwight D. Eisenhower was commander of the Allied armed forces. What action did Eisenhower direct in the summer of 1943?

At the Tehran Conference, Stalin, Roosevelt, and Churchill agreed to plans for the world for after the war.

▶ CRITICAL THINKING
Analyzing Why did leaders in the middle of a war talk about what would happen after the war?

Academic Vocabulary

focus to direct attention
convene to come together

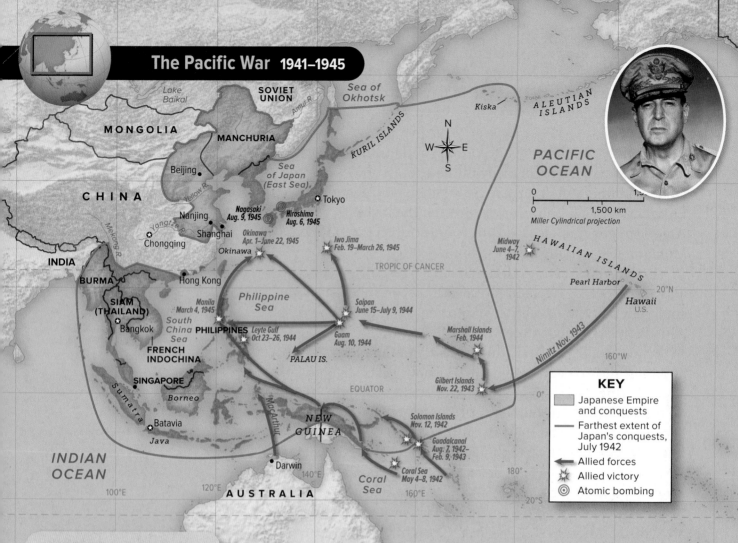

The Pacific War 1941–1945

Lake Baikal

MONGOLIA

SOVIET UNION

MANCHURIA

Amur R.

Sea of Okhotsk

Kiska

ALEUTIAN ISLANDS

KURIL ISLANDS

PACIFIC OCEAN

Beijing

CHINA

Sea of Japan (East Sea)

Tokyo

Nagasaki Aug. 9, 1945

Hiroshima Aug. 6, 1945

Nanjing

Shanghai

Yangtze R.

Chongqing

Yellow R.

Mekong R.

0   1,500 km

Miller Cylindrical projection

Okinawa Apr. 1–June 22, 1945

Okinawa

Iwo Jima Feb. 19–March 26, 1945

TROPIC OF CANCER

Midway June 4–7, 1942

HAWAIIAN ISLANDS

Nimitz Nov. 1943

INDIA

BURMA

Hong Kong

Philippine Sea

Pearl Harbor

Hawaii U.S.

20°N

SIAM (THAILAND)

Manila March 4, 1945

South China Sea

PHILIPPINES

Bangkok

Leyte Gulf Oct 23–26, 1944

Saipan June 15–July 9, 1944

Guam Aug. 10, 1944

Marshall Islands Feb. 1944

160°W

FRENCH INDOCHINA

PALAU IS.

SINGAPORE

Borneo

Sumatra

Batavia

Java

INDIAN OCEAN

MacArthur

NEW GUINEA

Darwin

100°E   120°E   140°E

EQUATOR

Gilbert Islands Nov. 22, 1943

0°

Solomon Islands Nov. 12, 1942

Guadalcanal Aug. 7, 1942– Feb. 9, 1943

Coral Sea May 4–8, 1942

180°

Coral Sea

160°E

20°S

AUSTRALIA

KEY

- ▢ Japanese Empire and conquests
- ── Farthest extent of Japan's conquests, July 1942
- ◀── Allied forces
- ✴ Allied victory
- ◎ Atomic bombing

GEOGRAPHY CONNECTION

To defeat Japan, the United States attacked Japanese-held islands. General MacArthur (above) regained the Philippines.

1 **REGIONS** What were two important island targets to capture from the Japanese?

2 **CRITICAL THINKING**
Analyzing Why was the battle at Midway Island important?

War in the Pacific

While war raged in Europe, the Allies fought Japan in the Pacific. By mid-1942, Japan had driven American troops out of the Philippines and seized many Pacific islands. The United States, however, soon recovered. In June 1942, American forces won a major sea and air battle at Midway Island. This battle stopped the Japanese advance and changed the course of the Pacific war in favor of the Allies.

During the next three years, U.S. commanders in the Pacific—General Douglas MacArthur and Admiral Chester Nimitz—carried out a plan called island-hopping. This plan called for attacking certain key Pacific islands. The United States then used these islands as stepping stones for moving closer to Japan.

By 1945, the Americans had recaptured the Philippines and destroyed much of Japan's air force and navy. As American forces closed in on Japan itself, the Japanese military fought to keep the Allies from reaching their homeland.

☑ **PROGRESS CHECK**

Contrasting How was the war in Europe different from the war in the Pacific?

The Holocaust

GUIDING QUESTION *Why is the Holocaust considered a dark chapter in human history?*

During World War II, Hitler and the Nazis set up a program of genocide (JEH·nuh·syd), or the deliberate killing of an entire group of people. As many as 6 million Jews were killed in what has become known as the Holocaust. Millions of others, including Slavs and Roma, or Gypsies, were also ruthlessly murdered.

The Nazis believed that the Jews were a threat to the "racial purity" of the superior German people. The Nazis also targeted other groups that they thought were inferior.

Nazi Persecution of the Jews

Beginning in the 1930s, Nazi laws had taken away the personal and political rights of the German Jews. On the night of November 9, 1938, the Nazis burned synagogues, destroyed Jewish shops, and killed many Jews. About 30,000 Jewish men were sent to concentration camps. Because the Nazis had shattered the windows of so many Jewish shops, this event became known as *Kristallnacht*, or the "night of broken glass."

During World War II, the Nazis mistreated the Jews in the lands they conquered. They forced Jews to wear a six-pointed yellow star on their clothing. In Poland and other parts of Eastern Europe, Jews were crowded into ghettoes, areas set aside for them in cities and towns. Eva Galler, who survived the Holocaust, describes life in the ghetto of Lubaczow, a town in Poland:

Plate glass windows of Jewish businesses were targeted in the *Kristallnacht* destruction.

PRIMARY SOURCE

❝ The ghetto was the size of one city block for 7,000 people. We slept 28 people in a room that was 12 by 15 feet. It was like a sardine box. People lived in attics, in basements, in the streets—all over . . . It was cold. We were not given enough to eat. . . . There was not enough water to drink. . . . Every day a lot of people died.❞

PHOTO: ©Bettmann/Corbis
TEXT: Eva Galler as told to John C. Menszer, Project Director at Holocaust Survivors website, www.holocaustsurvivors.org.

The Death Camps

The Nazis began the mass killing of Jews when the German army invaded the Soviet Union in 1941. Special Nazi forces accompanied the army. They sought out Jews, gathered them together, shot them, and dumped their bodies into mass graves.

In January 1942, German leaders agreed on what they called "the final solution" to destroy the Jews. Nazis rounded up millions of Jews and hundreds of thousands of other innocent people in the areas under their control. Crammed into railroad cars like cattle, the prisoners were taken to death camps, such as Auschwitz (OWSH·vihts) in Poland. At the camps, many people were killed in poison gas chambers. Others were worked to death or died of starvation. Still others were victims of cruel medical experiments performed by Nazi doctors. At war's end, Allied forces moving into Nazi-held areas saw firsthand the unspeakable horrors of the death camps. About two-thirds of Europe's Jewish population perished in the Holocaust.

The Holocaust had an impact on the world after World War II. The **consequences** of Nazi brutality made people aware of the importance of defending human rights and combating prejudice. Governments and international organizations also began to work to prevent and punish the crime of genocide. The inability of Jews to find shelter from Nazi terror increased demands for the Jews to have their own country in Palestine. Christians and Jews began to move toward greater understanding and cooperation.

Many people who were taken to Nazi concentration camps were killed soon after arrival. Others were kept as slave laborers. None were well-treated.

☑ PROGRESS CHECK

Analyzing Why do you think the Holocaust was a world human rights issue?

©Corbis

Reading**HELP**DESK

D-Day June 6, 1944, the day on which Allied forces began the invasion of France in World War II

Academic Vocabulary

consequence something following as a result or effect; outcome
transport to convey or carry

(t)Time & Life Pictures/Getty Images; (b)Archive Photos/Getty Images

Ending the War

GUIDING QUESTION *What actions did the Allies take to win the war?*

While the Holocaust was taking place, the Allies were focused on defeating the Axis countries. By 1944, the Germans and Japanese were retreating everywhere. The Allies were now preparing to invade Germany and Japan.

What Was D-Day?

For months, Allied forces under General Eisenhower had been preparing to invade Nazi-held France. June 6, 1944, was **D-Day**—the day of the invasion. Ships left Britain carrying troops and equipment across the English Channel to the French province of Normandy. When the battleships arrived at Normandy, their guns pounded German positions on shore. Meanwhile, Allied soldiers were **transported** from the ships to the beaches. There, they fought their way through German machine-gun fire. Despite heavy German resistance, the invasion was a success. Within a few weeks, a million Allied soldiers had landed in France.

From Normandy, the Allies launched an attack against the Germans. By early August, U.S. General Patton and his tanks were racing through northern France while General Montgomery's British troops moved along the coast into Belgium. Pressured on all sides, the German forces retreated and on August 25, French and American soldiers entered Paris.

American, British, and Canadian troops landed at five different beaches on D-Day. American troops coming ashore at Omaha Beach paid a high price. As the soldiers waded toward the beach, more than 2,000 of them were shot by German machine gunners.

The atomic bomb created a huge mushroom cloud. The American decision to use the atomic bomb ended the war, but at a terrible cost in human lives. The destruction of two cities was complete.

In December 1944, however, the Germans counterattacked in Belgium. German troops advanced, pushing back the Allied lines and creating a bulge. The attack later became known as the Battle of the Bulge. After weeks of fighting, the Americans won the battle and then moved into Germany.

By late 1944, the Soviets had driven the Germans out of Russia and across Poland. In February 1945, Soviet troops arrived on the outskirts of Berlin. On April 30, Hitler committed suicide in Berlin. The Germans surrendered on May 7, ending the war in Europe.

The Atomic Age Begins

By the end of 1944, an Allied victory over Japan seemed certain. In October, General Douglas MacArthur regained the Philippines. Then, in early 1945, American forces defeated the Japanese in bloody battles on the Pacific islands of Iwo Jima and Okinawa. With most of the Japanese air force and navy destroyed, American bombers began pounding Japanese cities. In desperation, the Japanese sent suicide pilots, known as kamikazes, against the Americans. The kamikazes crashed planes loaded with explosives into American ships. Despite setbacks, Japan's military leaders refused to surrender.

In April 1945, Franklin Roosevelt died, and Harry S. Truman (TROO·muhn) became president. Truman faced a difficult decision. Should he risk the lives of American troops by invading Japan? Or should he use the newly developed atomic bomb in hopes it would end the war?

Since 1941, American engineers and scientists had been building an atomic bomb at a secret laboratory in Los Alamos, New Mexico. The atomic bomb program was called the Manhattan Project.

American officials disagreed about using such a powerful weapon. Some opposed its use because it would kill thousands of Japanese civilians. Others wanted to warn the Japanese about the bomb. The final decision rested with Truman. He believed it was his duty to use every weapon available to save American lives. He demanded that Japanese leaders surrender unconditionally. The Japanese did not respond, and Truman ordered the use of the bomb.

On August 6, 1945, a plane named the *Enola Gay* dropped an atomic bomb on the Japanese city of Hiroshima. Between 80,000 and 120,000 people were killed in the explosion. Thousands more died afterward from burns and radiation sickness.

Reading**HELP**DESK

Build Vocabulary: *Word Parts*

The suffix *-ful* has many meanings. As part of a noun, it means "number or quantity that fills something," as in *handful*. As part of an adjective, it means "having the qualities of," or "full of," as in *joyful*.

Three days later, another American plane dropped a second bomb—this time on the city of Nagasaki. It killed between 35,000 and 74,000 people. Faced with such destruction, the Japanese government surrendered on August 15, 1945.

Effects of the War

More than 70 million people fought in World War II. The casualties were enormous. Altogether, more than 55 million people died during the war. These included 22 million Soviets, 8 million Germans, 2 million Japanese, and 300,000 Americans.

In addition to the human losses, World War II was the most expensive war in history. Some experts claim its financial cost would be equal to about $4.1 trillion today. Because of the use of deadly new weapons, World War II was also the world's most destructive conflict. The war also led to a dramatic change in the world's balance of power. Britain, France, Germany, and Japan ceased to be great military powers. In their place arose two superpowers—the United States and the Soviet Union.

Another effect was a greater commitment to world peace. Even before the war ended, the Allies had started a world organization. In April 1945, representatives from 50 countries drew up a charter for the United Nations (UN). The UN Security Council, part of the UN's General Assembly, would investigate international problems and propose settlements.

War crime trials were also held. Between November 1945 and September 1946, Nazi leaders were tried at Nuremberg, Germany, for "pursuing aggressive war" and for committing "crimes against humanity." Similar trials took place in Japan.

As another response to war crimes, the United Nations drew up the Universal Declaration of Human Rights in 1948. This Declaration set forth in detail the rights and freedoms of individuals. It also marked the first time the international community had recognized this issue.

President Truman made the final decision to drop the atomic bomb on Japan.

▶ CRITICAL THINKING
Analyzing What disagreements did American officials have regarding the atomic bomb?

 PROGRESS CHECK

Explaining Why did President Truman decide to drop atomic bombs on Japan?

LESSON 3 REVIEW

1. Why was *D-Day* an important event in the Allies' fight against Germany?

Answer the Guiding Questions

2. *Identifying* What happened in June 1942 at Midway Island in the Pacific?

3. *Describing* How did the Nazis persecute the Jews during World War II?

4. *Explaining* What did Allied leaders decide about Germany at the Tehran Conference in late 1943?

5. *Analyzing* What is the significance of the event at Hiroshima?

6. **INFORMATIVE/EXPLANATORY** Write three paragraphs that explain the effect World War II had on the world.

Archive Photos/Getty Images

There's More Online!

LESSON 4
The Cold War

IT MATTERS BECAUSE
The Cold War between the Soviet Union and the United States lasted for forty-five years and still influences our world today.

Cold War Beginnings

GUIDING QUESTION *How did the United States try to stop the spread of communism without going to war?*

The United States and the Soviet Union emerged from World War II as superpowers. The two disagreed, however, about what the world was to be like after the war. As the war ended, the Soviet Union forced communist rule on Eastern Europe. The Americans and the Soviets competed for world leadership. Their rivalry lasted from 1945 to 1990 and was known as the Cold War.

What to do with Germany?

In February 1945, the "Big Three" Allied leaders—Roosevelt, Churchill, and Stalin—met at Yalta, a Soviet port on the Black Sea. Postwar control of Germany was the most difficult issue. The three leaders finally decided to split Germany into four zones, or parts. The Soviet Union was to control eastern Germany, while the United States, Britain, and France were to hold zones in the western part. The capital of Berlin, located deep within East Germany, also was to be divided among the four. The leaders also agreed to free elections in countries released from Nazi rule.

In April 1945, President Roosevelt died. Vice President Harry S. Truman became president. The next month, American, Soviet,

Taking Notes: *Listing*

In a chart like the one here, list two aid programs that showed the U.S. was actively engaged in European political events.

U.S. Acts in Europe

Content Vocabulary

- **containment**
- **Truman Doctrine**
- **Marshall Plan**
- **racial segregation**

Europe During the Cold War

KEY
- Warsaw Pact member
- Communist nation outside Soviet bloc
- Neutral nation
- NATO member

0 500 miles
0 500 km
Lambert Azimuthal Equal-Area projection

NORWAY
FINLAND
SWEDEN
DENMARK
North Sea
Baltic Sea
SOVIET UNION
REPUBLIC OF IRELAND
UNITED KINGDOM
NETH.
GER. DEM. REP.
POLAND
FED. REP. OF GERMANY
BELGIUM
CZECHOSLOVAKIA
LUX.
ATLANTIC OCEAN
FRANCE
SWITZ.
AUSTRIA
HUNGARY
ROMANIA
Black Sea
YUGOSLAVIA
Adriatic Sea
BULGARIA
PORTUGAL
SPAIN
Corsica
ITALY
ALBANIA
TURKEY
Sardinia
GREECE
Crete
Cyprus (U.K.)
AFRICA
Mediterranean Sea
20°E
40°E
60°N
50°N
40°N

and British leaders met at Potsdam, Germany. Stalin demanded that the Germans pay high reparations for the destruction they had caused in the Soviet Union, which Truman firmly opposed. Still Stalin did not hold free elections in Eastern Europe. Instead, the Soviets set up Communist governments there and kept troops in the **region**. Europe eventually split into two armed camps—Communist Eastern Europe and largely democratic Western Europe.

The British leader Winston Churchill was concerned about **widespread** Soviet control. In a speech in 1946, Churchill described events in the region:

PRIMARY SOURCE

"From . . . the Baltic to . . . the Adriatic, an iron curtain had descended across the Continent [Europe]. Behind that line lie all the capitals of the ancient states of Central and Eastern Europe . . . in what I must call the Soviet sphere [area]. . . . Police governments are prevailing in nearly every case."

GEOGRAPHY CONNECTION

After World War II, Europe was divided into communist and non-communist nations.

1 PLACE Which communist country did not join the Soviet bloc?

2 CRITICAL THINKING *Contrasting* Which alliance had more members—NATO or the Warsaw Pact?

Academic Vocabulary

region a broad geographic area with similar features
widespread broadly extended or spread out

Winston Churchill (1874–1965)

Winston Churchill was first elected to the British Parliament when he was 26. During the 1930s, he warned of the dangers of German rearmament to Western democracies. However, politicians and the general public did not listen. Churchill became prime minister when Britain declared war on Germany. He was prime minister throughout the war, inspiring the British not to give up. He also served in this position from 1951 to 1955. For his service to his country and the Allies, Churchill received many honors at home and abroad. In 1963, he was made an honorary citizen of the United States.

▶ **CRITICAL THINKING**
Making Inferences Why do you think Churchill continued warning about German rearming?

In referring to an "iron curtain," Churchill meant that the Soviets had cut off Eastern Europe from the West. He warned that they might expand their control beyond Eastern Europe.

What Was Containment?

Like Churchill, American leaders worried about the Soviet threat. For an answer, they turned to the ideas of George F. Kennan, an American diplomat. Kennan claimed that war could be avoided and the Soviets stopped if the United States stood firm. Kennan's policy, called **containment**, stated that the U.S. had to "contain," or hold back, communism. This meant using military and other methods.

The U.S. soon put containment into effect. In March 1947, Truman presented a plan that was later named the **Truman Doctrine**. The Truman Doctrine pledged that the United States would help any nation threatened by a communist takeover.

The United States also feared a weak Europe would lead to the spread of communism. Secretary of State George C. Marshall proposed that the U.S. give economic aid to war-damaged Western European countries. The **Marshall Plan** brought an economic recovery that lessened the appeal of communism.

A Divided Germany

Meanwhile, the western Allies and the Soviet Union disagreed on Germany's future. President Truman believed that a reunited, thriving Germany was important for Europe. Stalin, on the other hand, feared a strong Germany would attack the Soviet Union.

In 1948, the United States, Britain, and France decided to unite their zones to form a new West German republic and combine their sections of Berlin.

In response, Soviet troops surrounded West Berlin and imposed a blockade that cut the city off from needed supplies. The West began a massive airlift of supplies that saved West Berlin. In May 1949, the Soviets ended the blockade.

Germany, however, and the city of Berlin remained divided. By the end of 1949, West Germany was allied with the United States, and communist East Germany was tied to the Soviet Union.

To contain the Soviets, the United States, Canada, and ten Western European countries **established** the North Atlantic Treaty Organization (NATO) in 1949. NATO is still in force today

©Corbis

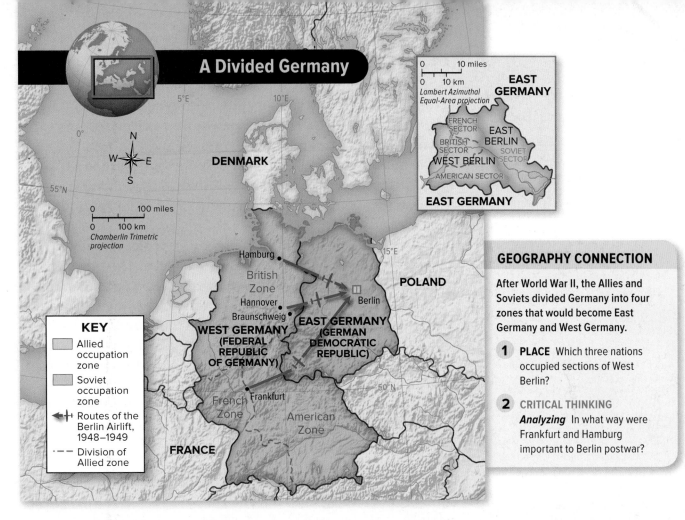

A Divided Germany

EAST GERMANY

FRENCH SECTOR
BRITISH SECTOR
AMERICAN SECTOR
WEST BERLIN
EAST BERLIN
SOVIET SECTOR

EAST GERMANY

0   10 miles
0   10 km
Lambert Azimuthal
Equal-Area projection

DENMARK

0   100 miles
0   100 km
Chamberlin Trimetric
projection

Hamburg

British Zone

Hannover

Braunschweig

WEST GERMANY
(FEDERAL
REPUBLIC
OF GERMANY)

EAST GERMANY
(GERMAN
DEMOCRATIC
REPUBLIC)

Berlin

POLAND

French Zone

Frankfurt

American Zone

FRANCE

KEY
- Allied occupation zone
- Soviet occupation zone
- Routes of the Berlin Airlift, 1948–1949
- Division of Allied zone

GEOGRAPHY CONNECTION

After World War II, the Allies and Soviets divided Germany into four zones that would become East Germany and West Germany.

1 PLACE Which three nations occupied sections of West Berlin?

2 CRITICAL THINKING
Analyzing In what way were Frankfurt and Hamburg important to Berlin postwar?

to police world situations. At the time, member nations agreed to aid any member that was attacked. In 1955, West Germany was allowed to form an army and become a NATO member. In response, the Soviets formed a military alliance with the Communist governments of Eastern Europe. It was known as the Warsaw Pact.

The Berlin Wall

After Stalin died in 1953, Nikita Khrushchev (nuh·KEE·tuh krush·CHAWF) led the Soviet Union. Khrushchev demanded in 1961 that the Western powers withdraw from Berlin. U.S. president John F. Kennedy rejected this demand.

The Soviets then built a concrete wall that separated Communist East Berlin from democratic West Berlin. People could not travel freely in and out of East Berlin. Guards on the wall shot anyone who tried to escape communist rule. For nearly 30 years, the Berlin Wall was an important **symbol** of the divisions of the Cold War.

The towering Berlin Wall reminded Germans in East and West Berlin of the divisions in their city and country.

The Arms Race

Nuclear weapons also played an important role in the Cold War. By the early 1950s, international tensions rose as the United States and the Soviet Union competed in a nuclear arms race. This meant both sides built more missiles and bombers.

The most dangerous Cold War dispute took place in Cuba, a communist island just 90 miles (144 km) south of Florida. There, in 1959, a new communist government came to power under a leader named Fidel Castro.

In October 1962, President Kennedy learned that the Soviets had placed long-range missiles in Cuba. The president immediately ordered the navy to blockade Cuba until the Soviets removed the missiles. Kennedy also warned that the U.S. would launch a **nuclear** attack on the Soviets if they fired the missiles. After five agonizing days, Soviet leaders agreed to withdraw their missiles from Cuba. The U.S. pledged not to invade Cuba. Nuclear war had been avoided.

✓ PROGRESS CHECK

Explaining Why did the Soviets place a blockade on West Berlin?

GEOGRAPHY CONNECTION

The Soviet Union set up missiles in Cuba that were capable of reaching the United States.

1 **LOCATION** About how far is Cuba from the U.S. mainland?

2 **CRITICAL THINKING**
Making Inferences Why do you think the Soviet Union wanted to place missiles in Cuba?

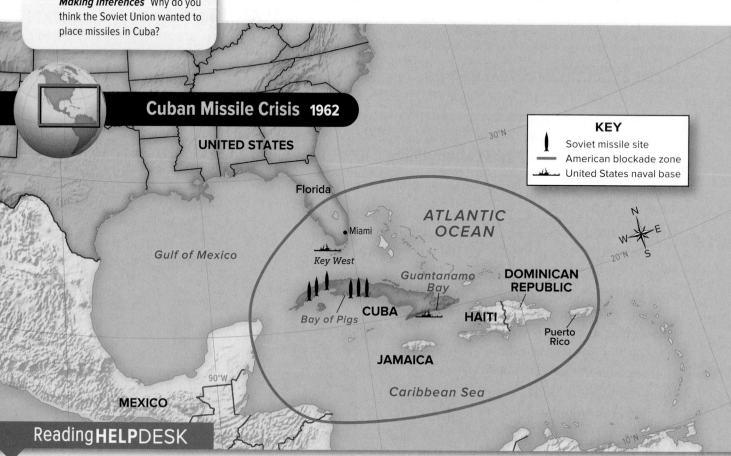

Cuban Missile Crisis 1962

KEY
| Soviet missile site
— American blockade zone
United States naval base

UNITED STATES

Florida

• Miami

Key West

Gulf of Mexico

ATLANTIC OCEAN

30°N

20°N

N
W E
S

Guantanamo Bay

DOMINICAN REPUBLIC

CUBA

Bay of Pigs

HAITI

Puerto Rico

90°W

JAMAICA

Caribbean Sea

10°N

MEXICO

ReadingHELPDESK

Academic Vocabulary

nuclear having to do with the nucleus of an atom, such as the energy created by a nuclear reaction

Vietnam Divided

[Map showing Vietnam, Laos, Cambodia, Thailand, Myanmar (Burma), China and surrounding region]

CHINA

Lao Cai • • Pingxiang

MYANMAR (BURMA)

Dien Bien Phu •

Hanoi • • Haiphong

RED RIVER DELTA

LAOS

NORTH VIETNAM

Gulf of Tonkin

Vientiane •

Mekong R.

DMZ (Demilitarized Zone)

17th Parallel

THAILAND

South China Sea

Bangkok •

CAMBODIA

SOUTH VIETNAM

Bay of Bengal

Tonle Sap

Phnom Penh • • Tay Ninh

Gulf of Thailand

Saigon •

MEKONG DELTA

0 — 200 miles
0 — 200 km
Mercator projection

TROPIC OF CANCER

20°N · 15°N · 10°N · 110°E · 105°E · 100°E

GEOGRAPHY CONNECTION

In 1954, Vietnam was divided into Communist North Vietnam and non-Communist South Vietnam. The two parts of Vietnam were not reunited until 1975 when South Vietnam fell under communist rule.

1 LOCATION What countries did North Vietnam border?

2 CRITICAL THINKING
Calculating How far apart were the capitals of North and South Vietnam?

The Cold War in Asia

GUIDING QUESTION *How did the Cold War affect countries in Asia?*

The Cold War also reached Asia. By the 1950s, communists ruled China and the northern parts of Korea and Vietnam. As a result, the United States applied its policy of containment to Asia.

Communism in China

During World War II, the Nationalist forces of Chiang Kai-shek (jee·AHNG KY·SHEHK) and the Communist troops of Mao Zedong (MOW ZUH·DUNG) joined together to fight the Japanese. After World War II, the Nationalists and Communists fought each other. In 1949, the Nationalists fled to the island of Taiwan (TY·WAHN). There, Chiang Kai-shek set up a Nationalist government that claimed to rule all of China. On the mainland, Mao Zedong headed the People's Republic of China. In the early 1950s, Mao's Communist government took over the country's businesses and industries.

The Korean War

At the end of World War II, the United States and the Soviet Union divided Korea. The communists set up a government in the north, and an American-backed government took over the south. On June 25, 1950, northern troops invaded the south.

Gaining the support of China's rural peasants, Mao began a successful communist movement to gain control of the country.

▶ **CRITICAL THINKING**
Analyzing Why did Mao work with Chiang Kai-shek in the 1930s?

AP Photo

There's More Online! connected.mcgraw-hill.com

Lesson 4 **773**

President Truman persuaded the United Nations to send troops to Korea. When UN troops advanced toward the Chinese border, the Chinese communists entered the conflict. They drove the UN forces back to South Korea. After that, neither side was able to gain a clear victory. In 1953, they signed a cease-fire ending the fighting. The two Koreas remained divided.

Japan's Dramatic Recovery

From 1945 to 1952, Allied military forces under General Douglas MacArthur **occupied** and ruled Japan. The American-led government greatly reduced Japan's **military**. Japan also adopted a new democratic constitution and a bill of rights. The United States poured billions into Japan's economy and sparked an economic boom in Japan. The Japanese government and its business leaders worked closely together to plan the country's industrial growth. By the 1970s, Japan was a major economic power.

☑ **PROGRESS CHECK**

Determining Cause and Effect Why did Chinese Nationalists create a government on the island of Taiwan?

The Cold War Era

GUIDING QUESTION *How did countries develop at home during the Cold War era?*

After World War II, the Soviet Union rebuilt its heavy industry and boosted its military might. In Soviet-controlled Eastern Europe, governments copied the Soviet system. Some countries rebelled against controls.

Prosperous Western Europe

The Marshall Plan helped Europe rebuild quickly. West Germany developed economically, becoming the most prosperous nation in Western Europe.

France, led by war hero General Charles de Gaulle from 1959 to 1969, became a major manufacturer of aircraft, weapons, and cars. In Britain, older industries were slowly replaced with new service industries.

In 1957, France, West Germany, Belgium, the Netherlands, Luxembourg, and Italy founded the European Economic Community (EEC). The EEC was seen as the first step in building a united Europe.

Reading**HELP**DESK

racial segregation the act of forcing a race to use separate facilities

Academic Vocabulary

occupy to seize and maintain control of by military force
military a country's armed forces

What Was Life Like in the United States?

During the 1950s, the United States had a prosperous economy. Advancing civil rights became a major cause during this time. In 1954, the U.S. Supreme Court ruled against **racial segregation** (seh·grih·GAY·shuhn), or separation of the races, in public schools.

During the 1950s, the civil rights movement, led by Dr. Martin Luther King, Jr., used nonviolent marches to focus attention on discrimination. He called for the elimination of unfair treatment of African Americans in public places, housing, and voting.

President John F. Kennedy supported new civil rights laws. Following Kennedy's assassination, his successor, Lyndon Johnson, convinced Congress to pass a new Civil Rights Act and a Voting Rights Act. Johnson also introduced government programs known as the Great Society. These were designed to end poverty, improve education, and provide medical care to the poor and elderly.

In the 1960s, women sought equal rights in the workplace. More women had become lawyers, doctors, and government leaders. However, women still received lower pay than men. In 1963, Congress passed the Equal Pay Act. It outlawed paying women less than men for the same work.

President Lyndon Johnson (right) met with civil rights leaders— including Dr. Martin Luther King, Jr. (center)—to iron out details of needed legislation.

☑ **PROGRESS CHECK**

Describing What was the Great Society?

LESSON 4 REVIEW

Review Vocabulary

1. What did the *Truman Doctrine* protect?

2. What did laws against *racial segregation* in schools in 1954 mean to the states?

Answer the Guiding Questions

3. ***Contrasting*** After World War II, what economic systems did the Soviet Union and the United States want to spread in the world?

4. ***Identifying*** What action did President Kennedy take after he learned the Soviets had placed long-range missiles in Cuba?

5. ***Defining*** What was Mao's Great Leap Forward?

6. ***Explaining*** What did the Marshall Plan hope to achieve?

7. **ARGUMENT** The policy of containment lasted more than thirty years. Do you think containment was a good policy, or did it cause increased political tension, such as the Cuban Missile crisis? Support your opinion with facts.

LESSON 5

The End of Empire

ESSENTIAL QUESTION

• How do new ideas change the way people live?

IT MATTERS BECAUSE
After World War II, European colonial empires broke up, and many new nations arose to help shape world affairs.

India Wins Independence

GUIDING QUESTION *How did Indians convince the British to give their country its freedom?*

After India came under British rule in the 1700s, the British set up a well-run government, but they did little for India's people. In 1885, a group of Indian leaders met in Bombay (now Mumbai) to form the Indian National Congress (INC). Many people in the INC were willing to remain in the British Empire, but they wanted Indians to have a role in ruling India.

Who Was Gandhi?

After World War I, protests against British rule swept India. The most popular leader was Mohandas Gandhi, also a member of the INC. He opposed the British with non-violent **civil disobedience**—the refusal to obey unjust laws using peaceful protest. Gandhi's followers led strikes and boycotted British goods, and were imprisoned many times. Hindus backed Gandhi's cause, but Muslims feared the Hindu majority.

Dividing British India

After World War II, the British realized they could not keep control in India. Giving Indians their freedom was difficult, however. Bitter conflicts divided Hindus and Muslims. Finally, in 1947, British India was split into two new countries: largely

Reading**HELP**DESK

Taking Notes: *Identifying*

Identify two major events that eventually led to India's independence.

India's Road to Independence

1947 India granted independence

Content Vocabulary

• **civil disobedience**
• **Pan-Africanism**
• **apartheid**

civil disobedience
a nonviolent collective means of forcing changes from the government

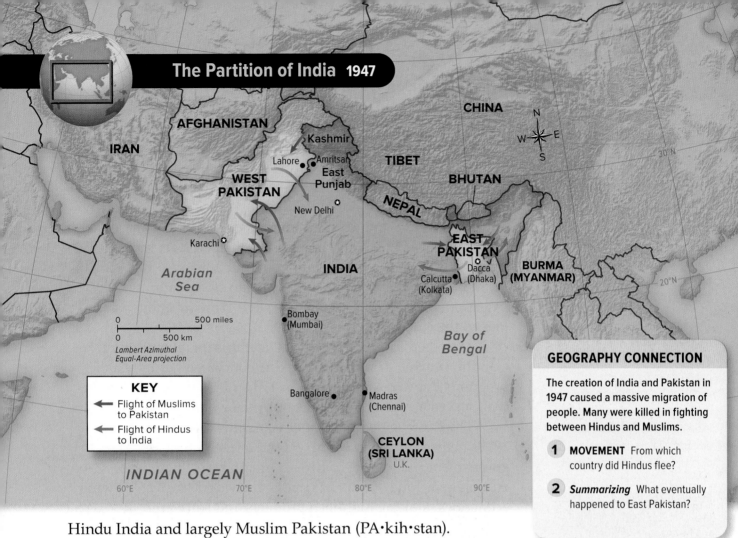

The Partition of India 1947

CHINA

AFGHANISTAN

IRAN

Kashmir

Lahore • • Amritsar

WEST
PAKISTAN

East
Punjab

TIBET

BHUTAN

NEPAL

New Delhi ⌖

Karachi ⌖

EAST
PAKISTAN

BURMA
(MYANMAR)

Arabian
Sea

INDIA

Dacca
(Dhaka) ⌖

Calcutta •
(Kolkata)

0   500 miles

0   500 km

Lambert Azimuthal
Equal-Area projection

Bombay •
(Mumbai)

Bay of
Bengal

KEY

⬅ Flight of Muslims
to Pakistan

⬅ Flight of Hindus
to India

Bangalore •

• Madras
(Chennai)

CEYLON
(SRI LANKA)
U.K.

INDIAN OCEAN

60°E   70°E   80°E   90°E

30°N

20°N

GEOGRAPHY CONNECTION

The creation of India and Pakistan in
1947 caused a massive migration of
people. Many were killed in fighting
between Hindus and Muslims.

1 **MOVEMENT** From which
country did Hindus flee?

2 *Summarizing* What eventually
happened to East Pakistan?

Hindu India and largely Muslim Pakistan (PA·kih·stan).
Pakistan was made up of two regions separated by 1,000 miles
(1,609 km) of India's territory. West Pakistan was northwest of
India, and East Pakistan was to the northeast.

When India and Pakistan became independent, many
Hindus in Pakistan fled to India. Many Muslims in India fled
to Pakistan. Fighting erupted, and more than 1 million people
were killed in this mass movement.

India-Pakistan Tensions

Tensions soon arose between India and Pakistan. Both countries
fought over the region of Kashmir (KASH·mihr). In 1949, the
war ended with most of Kashmir ruled by India. While fighting
India, Pakistan faced unrest within. In 1971, East Pakistan
declared independence, and it became known as Bangladesh
(bahng·gluh·DEHSH).

During the late 1980s, India and Pakistan fought more wars
over Kashmir. They built nuclear weapons, raising fears about
their fighting a nuclear war. In 2001, Muslim Kashmir terrorists
staged attacks in India. The two nations, however, held back
from fighting. Today, relations between India and Pakistan
have improved, but the dispute over Kashmir remains.

The Five-Year Plans that Nehru
used to guide India's economy
increased the growth of India's
industries within the first 10 years.

777

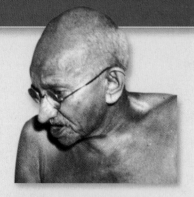

**Mohandas Gandhi
(1869–1948)**

The most popular Indian nationalist leader was Mohandas K. Gandhi (MOH • huhn • dahs GAHN • dee). As a young man, Gandhi was educated in Britain and later practiced law in South Africa. There, he led protests against unfair laws directed at South Africa's Indian population. After returning home to India, Gandhi used non-violent methods of protest to help India win its freedom from Great Britain. His beliefs and efforts later influenced civil rights leaders outside India, such as Dr. Martin Luther King, Jr.

Sequencing What did Gandhi do after returning home to India?"

India Modernizes

After independence, India was ruled by the Indian National Congress, renamed the Congress Party. The party's leader and India's first prime minister was Jawaharlal Nehru (juh·WAH·huhr·lahl NEHR·oo). A British-educated lawyer, Nehru had helped lead India to freedom. In 1948, Nehru lost a close ally when Gandhi was assassinated.

Under Nehru's guidance, India's government focused on building factories and strengthening industry. It also increased the amount of available farmland. This helped start India's Green Revolution to increase food production.

India's government also built dams to store water for irrigation. By 1979, Indian farmers were growing enough crops to feed the entire country.

Nehru died in 1964. Two years later, his daughter, Indira Gandhi, became prime minister. She continued her father's programs but was assassinated in 1984. Her son, Rajiv Gandhi, then served as prime minister until 1989 when he too was killed.

As India struggled politically, economic reforms in the 1990s helped move the country toward free enterprise. The government reduced its controls. Foreign investment was encouraged. Today, India has one of the world's fastest-growing economies, making high-tech products and software.

☑ PROGRESS CHECK

Explaining Why have India and Pakistan fought wars since independence?

New Nations in Southeast Asia

GUIDING QUESTION *How did nations in Southeast Asia become independent?*

Nationalism also emerged in Southeast Asia. After World War II, many Southeast Asian nations gained their independence from colonial rule. However, struggles between communist and non-communist groups brought political confusion and conflict.

Indonesia Gains Independence

In 1945, Achmed Sukarno and his nationalists declared the East Indies to be independent from the Dutch. They renamed their country Indonesia. The Dutch at first opposed independence. Then, Indonesia's communists staged a revolt. Fearing a communist takeover, the Dutch in 1949 accepted Sukarno's government.

Popperfoto/Getty Images

Reading**HELP**DESK

Academic Vocabulary

ethnic a group of people united by common racial, national, tribal, religious, linguistic, or cultural origin or background

Reading Strategy: *Compare and Contrast*

In two sentences, compare and contrast how India and Pakistan are alike and how they are different.

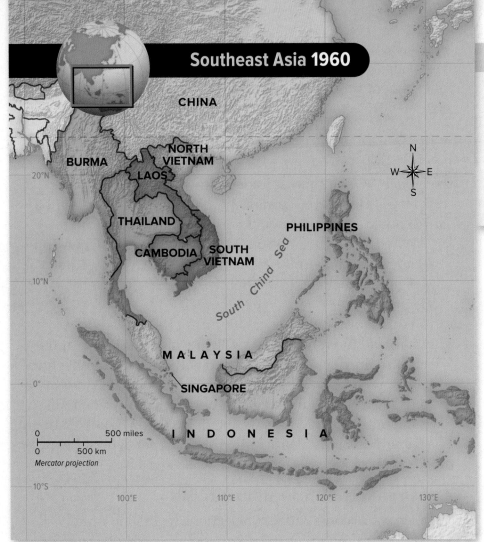

Southeast Asia 1960

CHINA

BURMA

NORTH VIETNAM

LAOS

THAILAND

CAMBODIA

SOUTH VIETNAM

PHILIPPINES

South China Sea

MALAYSIA

SINGAPORE

INDONESIA

0 500 miles

0 500 km

Mercator projection

20°N

10°N

0°

10°S

100°E 110°E 120°E 130°E

N W E S

GEOGRAPHY CONNECTION

Following World War II, the nations of Southeast Asia achieved self-rule.

1 LOCATION Where is Singapore located?

2 CRITICAL THINKING
Analyzing What nation in Southeast Asia covers the greatest area?

Sukarno did much to unite Indonesia. Most of Indonesia's people are Muslim, but they live on scattered islands and belong to different **ethnic** groups. Sukarno helped develop an official national language that put all Indonesians on an equal basis. However, he soon took away the legislature's powers and ruled as a dictator. Prices for food and other goods rose wildly.

In 1965, Indonesia's communists tried again to seize power. In a bloody crackdown, the Indonesian army killed about 300,000 people believed to be communist supporters. Then, the anti-communist General Suharto replaced Sukarno as dictator. In 1998, Suharto fell from power. By 2004, Indonesia became a democracy.

Myanmar and Malaysia

In 1948, Burma, now Myanmar, became free of British rule. In 1962, under military rule, Burma became a socialist country.

In 1990, the military leaders agreed to hold elections. Before voting took place, they arrested the key democratic leader, Aung San Suu Kyi (AWNG SAN SOO CHEE). She won the election, but Burma's military leaders rejected the results.

The British granted freedom to its colonies on the Malay Peninsula. In 1963, the territories united to form the independent Federation of Malaysia. The city of Singapore separated from the Federation and became independent in 1965.

France's Struggle for Vietnam

During World War II, the Japanese seized Indochina from the French. A Communist leader named Ho Chi Minh (HOH CHEE MIHN) formed a group called the Vietminh to drive out the Japanese.

When Japan gave up control of Indochina, Ho Chi Minh declared Vietnam independent. France, however, wanted to regain Indochina. In 1946, French troops fought the Vietminh.

Fearing the spread of communism, the United States gave military aid to French forces. The French could not beat the Vietminh. In 1954, they decided to withdraw from Indochina.

An agreement called the Geneva Accords divided Vietnam at the 17th parallel. Ho Chi Minh controlled North Vietnam. A government supported by the United States ran South Vietnam. The Geneva Accords also accepted the independence of two other countries in Indochina—Cambodia and Laos.

The United States in Vietnam

The Geneva Accords called for elections in 1956 to unite Vietnam. South Vietnam's leader, however, claimed the elections could not be fair.

After South Vietnam rejected elections, Ho Chi Minh decided to use force to unite Vietnam. He formed a guerrilla army known as the Vietcong. U.S. president Dwight D. Eisenhower did not want South Vietnam to come under communist control. He sent military advisers and aid to South Vietnam.

The United States became more directly involved in the fight for Vietnam in the 1960s. In August 1964, President Lyndon Johnson had Congress pass the Gulf of Tonkin Resolution. It gave Johnson broad powers to fight a war in Vietnam. In 1965, the U.S. began bombing raids against North Vietnam. Johnson also sent the first American combat troops.

By the late 1960s, many Americans at home actively opposed the war. Finally, in 1973, President Richard Nixon withdrew American forces from Vietnam. At least 2 million people, including 58,000 Americans, died in the conflict.

When Japanese forces captured the Dutch East Indies in World War II, they made Achmed Sukarno their adviser. In 1945, Sukarno seized his chance and proclaimed Indonesia's independence.

©Bettmann/Corbis

Reading**HELP**DESK

Academic Vocabulary

recover to get back, regain

U.S. troops land in the jungles of Vietnam. The difficult terrain made using helicopters necessary.

©Bettmann/Corbis

In 1975, North Vietnam's army defeated the South Vietnamese and united all of Vietnam under its communist government. That same year, communist forces also took control in neighboring Cambodia. During the 1980s and 1990s, changes came to Cambodia and Vietnam. The communists were overthrown in Cambodia, but the country still had not **recovered** from their rule. Meanwhile, Vietnam remained communist but faced a declining economy.

✓ PROGRESS CHECK

Analyzing Why did the United States become involved in the Vietnam conflict?

Independence in Africa

GUIDING QUESTION *How did Africans seek better treatment and independence from European rulers?*

In both world wars, black Africans had assisted the British and French military. Many of these colonial troops hoped their help would be rewarded with better treatment and some degree of self-rule. Instead, Europeans held on tightly to their African empires.

African Nationalism

Nationalism was strong among European-educated Africans. They were angered by the fact that Europeans supported democracy at home yet denied it to the people in their overseas colonies. This group provided the leaders who convinced Africans to demand their freedom.

Following World War I, more Africans became politically active. European governments responded by arresting protestors, yet they began making some reforms. Africans found such halfway steps unacceptable. They wanted independence.

After World War II, the European powers were weakened by the economic and military strains of the war. Scattered African protests grew into independence movements involving large numbers of people. The European countries did not have the resources to stop these movements.

North Africa

African independence movements had their first success in North Africa. In 1952, army officers overthrew Egypt's British-supported king, and Egypt became fully independent. Egypt's neighbor, Libya, won independence in 1951. In 1956, the French gave full independence to Morocco and Tunisia. France wanted to keep control of Algeria because many French people lived there. In 1954, Algerian Arabs began fighting the French in a bloody civil war. Algeria finally won independence in 1962.

Africa South of the Sahara

The desire for independence also swept through European colonies south of the Sahara. In West Africa, Kwame Nkrumah (KWAHM·eh ehn·KROO·muh) led a nationalist movement in Britain's colony of the Gold Coast. In 1957, the Gold Coast, renamed Ghana, became independent under Nkrumah. Britain's largest African colony—Nigeria—was granted independence in 1960. Other British colonies in Africa followed. In Rhodesia, the black majority won their struggle and renamed the country Zimbabwe.

In 1958, France offered its colonies south of the Sahara a choice. They could have limited self-rule with French aid, or become totally independent without aid. Fearing the colonies would choose help from the Soviet Union, France finally gave them all full independence and aid. The Belgian Congo was granted independence in 1960. Today the country is called the Democratic Republic of Congo.

Leaders of newly independent Ghana—including Kwame Nkrumah (third from left)—celebrate freedom from British rule.

▶ CRITICAL THINKING

Analyzing Why did many African nations seek independence from colonial rule?

©Bettmann/Corbis

Reading**HELP**DESK

Pan-Africanism a movement for the political union of all the African nations

apartheid racial segregation system enforced in South Africa

Portugal ruled its colonies of Angola and Mozambique harshly. When a revolution in Portugal overthrew that country's dictator, Portugal's new government freed Angola and Mozambique in 1975.

Some African leaders believed in **Pan-Africanism**—the unity of all black Africans. Ghana's Kwame Nkrumah was one of its earliest supporters. Thirty-two African nations founded the Organization of African Unity (OAU) in 1963. The OAU was the first step toward joining African nations. Today, an even more closely united organization known as the African Union (AU) has replaced the OAU.

Apartheid in South Africa

South Africa had been independent since the early 1900s. Most of its people were black Africans, but the smaller European population ran the government.

In 1912, black South Africans founded the African National Congress (ANC), hoping to gain political power. White South Africans, however, established a system known as apartheid. The policy of **apartheid** (uh·PAHR·tayt), or "apartness," separated ethnic groups and limited the rights of blacks. Black South Africans had to live in separate areas, called "homelands," where jobs and food were scarce. People of non-European background could not vote.

When black South Africans protested apartheid laws, the white government cracked down. In 1962, police jailed Nelson Mandela, the leader of the ANC. Protests against apartheid spread. The United Nations condemned apartheid, and many countries cut off trade with South Africa. Nearly 30 more years passed before South Africa ended the apartheid system.

Nelson Mandela spoke for the black majority as an early protestor of the apartheid policy in South Africa.

✓ PROGRESS CHECK

Explaining What African movement did Nkrumah and others work for?

LESSON 5 REVIEW

Review Vocabulary

1. What is *Pan-Africanism*?

2. What did the policy of *apartheid* mean to people in South Africa?

Answer the Guiding Questions

3. *Identifying* What was the name of Indonesia before World War II?

4. *Explaining* In opposing British rule, what policy did Gandhi urge the people of India to practice?

5. *Determining Cause and Effect* What was the result of the Gulf of Tonkin Resolution?

6. *Summarizing* What happened in British-controlled Egypt in 1952?

7. **INFORMATIVE/EXPLANATORY** In three paragraphs, explain the effect that the rise of nationalism after World War II had in Asian countries. Be sure to include facts.

CHAPTER 25 Activities

Write your answers on a separate piece of paper.

1 **Exploring the Essential Question**

INFORMATIVE/EXPLANATORY Write an essay that discusses how political ideas changed the way people lived after World War II. Focus on one continent, either Europe or Africa. Think about the spread of various political ideas, such as nationalism, democracy, and communism. Describe the effect these political ideas had on people's lives.

2 **21st Century Skill**

USING PRIMARY AND SECONDARY SOURCES Researching on the Internet, create a two-page report on the role the Marshall Plan had in bringing about change in Europe after World War II. Use primary source photos and information from reliable Internet sources such as the PBS and the Library of Congress websites. Analyze the effect of the Marshall Plan on European governments and society.

3 **Thinking Like a Historian**

SEQUENCING EVENTS Create a time line with markers every five years from 1939 to 1965. Place the following six events in the correct order on the time line:

Germany invades Poland
Warsaw Pact formed
U.S. sends troops to Vietnam

India gains independence
Atomic bomb dropped on Nagasaki
Nigeria gains independence

4 **GEOGRAPHY ACTIVITY**

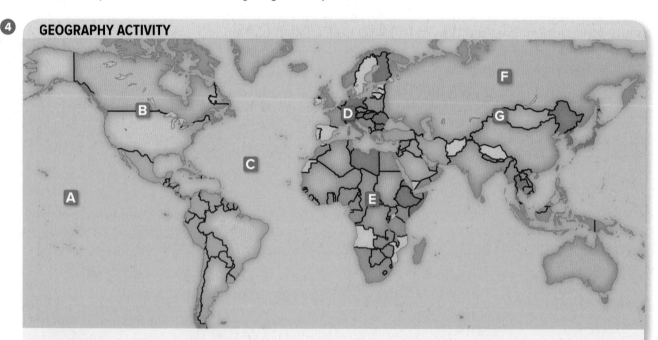

Locating Places

Match the letters on the map with the numbered places listed below.

1. Africa
2. Asia
3. Atlantic Ocean
4. Europe
5. North America
6. Pacific Ocean
7. Russia

Directions: Write your answers on a separate piece of paper.

CHECKING FOR UNDERSTANDING

1 Define each of these terms as they relate to World War II and the Cold War.

A.	depression	**G.**	Truman Doctrine
B.	totalitarian state	**H.**	Marshall Plan
C.	collectivization	**I.**	racial segregation
D.	appeasement	**J.**	civil disobedience
E.	D-Day	**K.**	Pan-Africanism
F.	containment	**L.**	apartheid

REVIEW THE GUIDING QUESTIONS

2 *Explaining* How did different industrialized countries in Europe, such as Britain and France, respond to the Great Depression?

3 *Specifying* What two problems did Italy face following World War I? How did they contribute to the rise of Mussolini's totalitarian government?

4 *Describing* What were some of the events that led to the war in Europe becoming another world war?

5 *Finding the Main Idea* Why was the Holocaust considered one of the worst crimes in human history?

6 *Summarizing* Briefly explain how the Allies were able to win the war.

7 *Discussing* What were some ways that Asian countries were affected by the Cold War?

8 *Listing* What were three developments that took place in the United States during the Cold War era?

9 *Describing* How did the Indians work to gain independence from Britain?

10 *Explaining* What major problem did Achmed Sukarno have when he took over leadership of Indonesia? How did he try to solve this problem?

11 *Identifying* How did Egypt obtain freedom from European control?

CRITICAL THINKING

12 *Sequencing* List in order the events that led to Japan's military taking control of its government in the early 1930s. Include at least six events in your list.

13 *Evaluating* Why do you think the British and French policy of appeasement was ineffective?

14 *Determining Cause and Effect* Why did the Japanese government decide to launch an attack on Pearl Harbor?

15 *Recognizing Relationships* How is the concept of Pan-Africanism related to the Organization of African Unity?

16 *Assessing* Which do you think was a better idea for preventing the spread of communism: the Truman Doctrine or the Marshall Plan? Explain your choice.

17 *Analyzing* Why did the Allies decide to begin attacking Hitler's forces in North Africa rather than first attacking them in Western Europe?

18 *Evaluating* Do you think President Truman used good reasoning when he decided to drop the atomic bomb on Japan? Explain your answer.

19 *Speculating* Why do you think France and Britain responded as they did when Hitler invaded Austria in 1938?

20 *Predicting Consequences* What do you think might have happened if the Soviet Union had not removed its missiles from Cuba during the Cuban Missile Crisis in 1962? Explain your reasons for your answer.

Need Extra Help?

If you've missed question	**1**	**2**	**3**	**4**	**5**	**6**	**7**	**8**	**9**	**10**	**11**	**12**	**13**	**14**	**15**	**16**	**17**	**18**	**19**	**20**
Review Lesson	1, 2, 3, 4, 5	1	1	2	3	3	4	4	5	5	5	1	2	2	5	4	3	3	2	4

DBQ SHORT RESPONSE

This excerpt comes from Franklin D. Roosevelt's Declaration of War on December 8, 1941.

"I believe that I interpret the will of the Congress and of the people when I assert that we will not only defend ourselves to the uttermost [extreme] but will make it very certain that this form of treachery shall never again endanger us."

—from *Address to Congress, Requesting a Declaration of War with Japan*

21 Briefly sum up the above statement in your own words.

22 Why do you think Roosevelt wanted to declare war on Japan?

EXTENDED RESPONSE

23 *Narrative* You are a person living in the United States when Japan bombs Pearl Harbor. Describe your feelings about the U.S. entrance into World War II. Do you think it is a good thing or a bad thing?

STANDARDIZED TEST PRACTICE

DBQ ANALYZING DOCUMENTS

This excerpt comes from *Mein Kampf* ("My Struggle"), by Adolf Hitler.

"[Germany's] task is not only to gather in ... the most valuable sections of our people, but to lead them ... to a dominant position in the world."

—Adolf Hitler, *Mein Kampf*

24 *Drawing Conclusions* Based on the excerpt, which statement do you think Hitler would agree with about the role of the German state?
   A. Germany should work to control other countries in the world.
   B. An international peace organization should be formed.
   C. Nations need to build a united, global economy.
   D. The people of Germany need to be given more educational opportunities.

25 *Finding the Main Idea* Which of the following is the main idea of the excerpt?
   A. "Valuable" German people should be encouraged to enter politics.
   B. "Valuable" people will help Germany dominate the world.
   C. Wealthy German people should be encouraged to lead German society.
   D. Germany should join an international peace organization.

Need Extra Help?

If You've Missed Question	**21**	**22**	**23**	**24**	**25**
Review Lesson	3	3	4	1	1

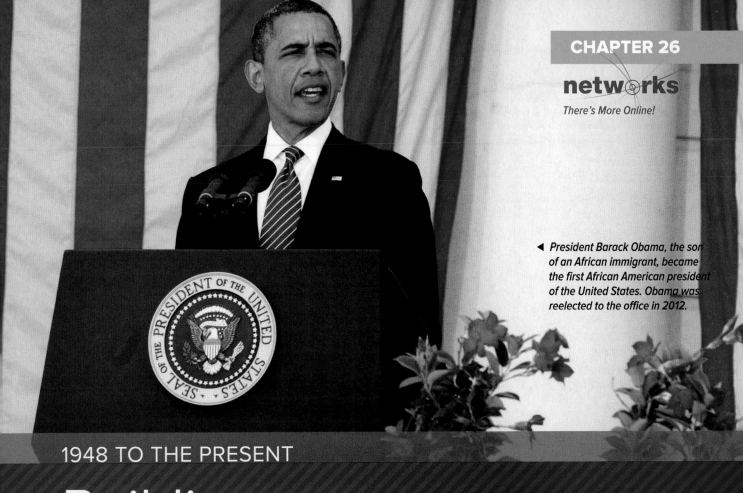

◄ *President Barack Obama, the son of an African immigrant, became the first African American president of the United States. Obama was reelected to the office in 2012.*

1948 TO THE PRESENT

Building Today's World

THE STORY MATTERS ...

On January 21, 2013, in front of the U.S. Capitol building, Barack Obama publicly took the oath of office for his second term as president of the United States. Then, before thousands gathered on the National Mall, Obama gave his Inaugural Address, highlighting the themes of his presidency. In his speech, the president called on Americans to work together, using "new ideas and technology to....empower our citizens with the skills they need to work harder, learn more, [and] reach higher." Globally, Obama stated, the United States must "be a source of hope to the poor,... the marginalized [neglected], [and] the victims of prejudice."

ESSENTIAL QUESTIONS

- How do governments change?
- Why does conflict develop?
- How do new ideas change the way people live?
- How does technology change the way people live?

DoD photo by Erin A. Kirk-Cuomo

Access to clean water is an important issue as the world's population grows. Some countries struggle to establish reliable and safe water systems. This map shows the percentage of people in a country that has access to drinking water using a safe water source. Examples of water sources include secure piped connections, protected dug wells and springs, and rainwater collection.

Step Into the Place

1. **LOCATION** Does South America or Africa have a higher percentage of people with access to a protected water source?

2. **REGIONS** What regions of Africa have the lowest percentage of people with access to a protected water source?

3. **REGIONS** Why might it be difficult to provide safe access to water in regions such as Southeast Asia?

4. **CRITICAL THINKING**
Analyzing What factors might affect a country's ability to provide safe water sources?

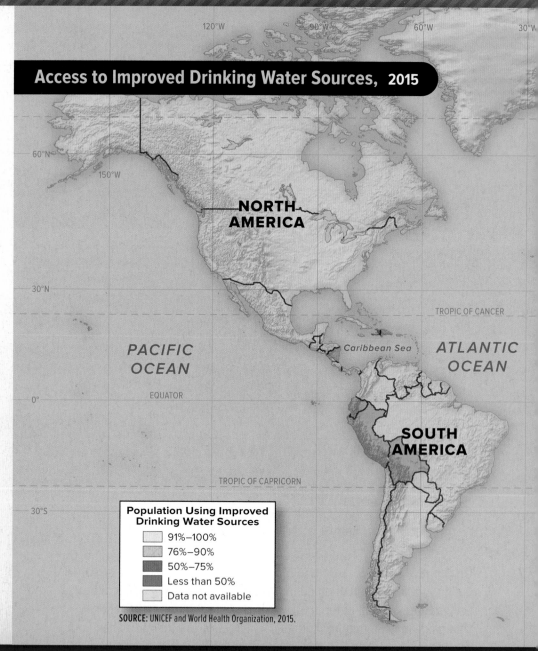

Access to Improved Drinking Water Sources, 2015

Population Using Improved Drinking Water Sources
- 91%–100%
- 76%–90%
- 50%–75%
- Less than 50%
- Data not available

SOURCE: UNICEF and World Health Organization, 2015.

Step Into the Time

TIME LINE Choose an event from the time line, and write a paragraph describing how it might connect to events you studied in previous chapters.

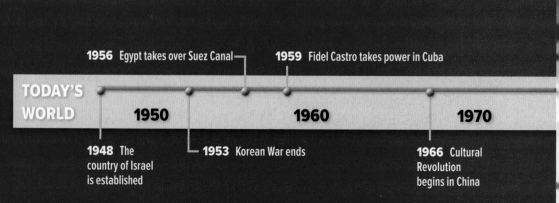

TODAY'S WORLD

1956 Egypt takes over Suez Canal

1959 Fidel Castro takes power in Cuba

1950

1960

1970

1948 The country of Israel is established

1953 Korean War ends

1966 Cultural Revolution begins in China

ARCTIC OCEAN

ARCTIC CIRCLE

EUROPE

ASIA

Mediterranean Sea

Persian Gulf

Red Sea

AFRICA

Sea of Japan

South China Sea

PACIFIC OCEAN

INDIAN OCEAN

AUSTRALIA

0   5,000 miles
0   5,000 km
Miller Cylindrical projection

N
W   E
S

1979 Revolution in
Iran overthrows shah

1993 European Union is formed

1991 Soviet
Union breaks up

1995 Dayton talks settle
Bosnian conflict

2015 Iran nuclear
agreement reached

1980

1990

2000

2010

Challenges in Latin America

ESSENTIAL QUESTION

• How do governments change?

IT MATTERS BECAUSE
Developments in Latin America affect U.S. trade and immigration.

Economic Developments

GUIDING QUESTION *What economic challenges have Latin America's people faced?*

Most of Latin America's countries won freedom in the 1800s. In these lands, rich landowners and businesspeople controlled social and political life. Poor farmers and workers, however, had little power.

Export Economies

During the late 1800s, Latin American countries depended on farming and mining. At this time, the United States and other industrial powers took control of Latin America's raw materials. Businesspeople from overseas exported Latin American goods, such as sugar, coffee, beef, copper, and oil.

As exports rose, some Latin American countries relied on only one or two key products. As the demand for these products rose, profits increased. Whenever demand decreased, however, prices dropped. Businesses then closed and workers lost jobs.

Latin America's reliance on exports brought benefits, too. Foreign investors built ports, roads, railroads, and factories there. Cities grew, and a middle class developed. Still, the wealthy few remained powerful; and most Latin Americans struggled to make a living.

Reading**HELP**DESK

Taking Notes: *Summarizing*

Use a table like this to show reforms put in place by Latin American leaders.

Leaders	Reforms
Cárdenas	
Calderón	
Allende	

Content Vocabulary

• **nationalize**   • **deforestation**
• **embargo**

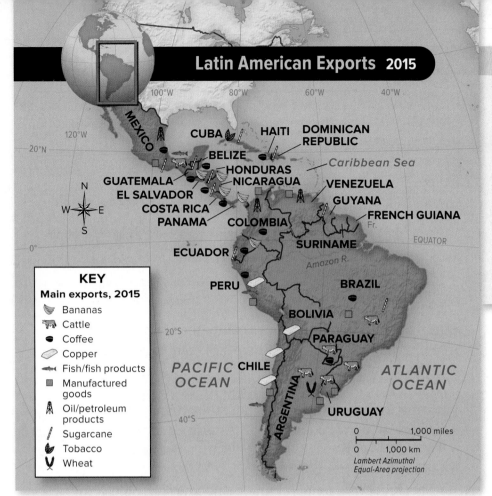

Latin American Exports 2015

KEY

Main exports, 2015

- Bananas
- Cattle
- Coffee
- Copper
- Fish/fish products
- Manufactured goods
- Oil/petroleum products
- Sugarcane
- Tobacco
- Wheat

0 — 1,000 miles
0 — 1,000 km
Lambert Azimuthal Equal-Area projection

GEOGRAPHY CONNECTION

The income of many Latin American countries came from the export of a narrow range of products.

1 PLACE What exports do Colombia, Venezuela, and Mexico have in common?

2 CRITICAL THINKING
Inferring Cattle are a chief export of Argentina, Paraguay, Uruguay, and Brazil. What geographic feature(s) would these countries have in common?

Latin America's Ties to the United States

During the 1900s, the United States greatly influenced Latin America. This was partly due to U.S. victory in the Spanish-American War of 1898. At war's end, Spain gave the United States control of the Caribbean island of Puerto Rico.

In 1903, Panama, with U.S. help, won freedom from Colombia. In return, Panama allowed the United States to build the Panama Canal. Over the next 30 years, U.S. troops were sent to guard U.S. interests in the Caribbean area.

Meanwhile, American companies grew in Latin America. The United Fruit Company owned land, railroads, and fruit-packing plants in Central America. U.S. companies also ran copper mines in Chile and oil wells in Mexico.

Many Latin Americans feared growing American influences. To improve U.S. ties with Latin America, President Franklin Roosevelt announced the Good Neighbor Policy in 1933. Under this policy, the United States agreed to settle any disputes peacefully and to aid the region's economies.

Debts and Reform

After World War II, agriculture was important in Latin America. Manufacturing, however, continued to grow there. Multinational corporations supplied some of the funding.

LATIN AMERICA'S ECONOMIC GROWTH 2000–2015

Latin America's economies have experienced significant economic changes since 2000.

1 **IDENTIFYING** In which 5-year period did Latin America experience the most economic growth?

2 **CRITICAL THINKING**
Making Generalizations
What economic challenges do Latin American countries face today?

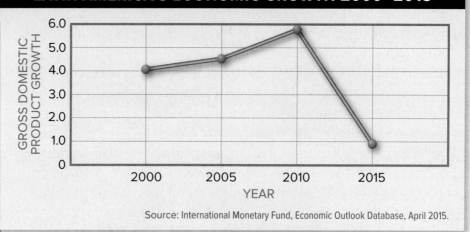

Source: International Monetary Fund, Economic Outlook Database, April 2015.

Multinational corporations are companies that do business in more than one country. Many U.S. companies are multinational.

Latin American leaders wanted to speed up economic progress. To get the needed funds, they turned to foreign banks. This borrowing weakened Latin America's economies, creating a debt crisis in the early 1980s. Within a decade, however, these economies had improved.

The debt crisis helped build democracy in some countries. Latin Americans had to make difficult changes to improve their economies. Several Latin American countries overthrew dictators and became democratic.

Today, Latin America's democracies face major challenges. The region's population is growing rapidly, but resources are limited. The divide between rich and poor creates social unrest. In addition, a growing trade in drugs has increased crime and corruption.

✓ **PROGRESS CHECK**

Determining Cause and Effect How did dependence on exports affect Latin American economies?

The Caribbean and Central America

GUIDING QUESTION *Why has progress been difficult in the Caribbean and Central America?*

In the 1900s, a few wealthy people largely controlled the Caribbean and Central America. Rebels fought against this group. The goal was to improve the lives of the poor.

Reading**HELP**DESK

nationalize to place private property under the control of a government

embargo a ban on trading or doing business with another country

Academic Vocabulary

revolution a sudden change, or an overthrow, of a government
immigrant one who moves to another country and settles there

Revolution in Cuba

After the Spanish-American War, Cuba became independent. However, during much of the 1900s, military dictators ruled the country. American companies held most of Cuba's wealth, based on sugar and mining. In 1959, Fidel Castro, a young lawyer, carried out a **revolution** and set up a new government.

Instead of forming a democracy, Castro made Cuba the first communist nation in the Americas. As a dictator, he drew Cuba close to the Soviet Union. Castro's government controlled the economy and society. It **nationalized** (NASH·uh·nuh·LYZD), or made itself owner of, American property in Cuba. This move damaged Cuba's ties with the United States. In 1960, the U.S. placed a partial trade **embargo** (ihm·BAHR·GOH) against Cuba. A trade embargo is a ban on trading with another nation.

In April 1961, Cubans with U.S. support tried and failed to overthrow Castro. This loss forced the United States to widen its trade embargo. The loss of trade, clumsy government planning, and poor harvests ruined Cuba's economy. Many Cubans fled to the United States. Most of these **immigrants** settled in Florida.

Castro relied on the Soviet Union for trade and financial aid. In 1991, however, the Soviet Union collapsed, and Cuba's economy weakened. Despite Cuba's poor economy, Castro remained in power until he became too ill to rule.

In 2008, his brother, Raul Castro, took over and started limited reforms. Meanwhile, relations between Cuba and the United States, which broke off in 1961, began to improve in 2015. By 2016, the first commercial airlines from the United States began flying to Cuba.

Haiti's Troubled Politics

In Haiti, another Caribbean republic, dictators have often ruled and ignored citizens' rights. In 1957, François Duvalier (frahn· SWAH doo·VAHL· YAY) was elected president. Once in office, Duvalier became a dictator who used terror to govern the country.

After Duvalier died in 1971, his son Jean-Claude Duvalier also ruled harshly until the military overthrew him in 1986.

In the 1950s, revolutionary leader Fidel Castro (center) led a band of 800 fighters against 30,000 Cuban government soldiers. After winning several battles, Castro was able to drive Cuban dictator Fulgencio Batista from the country in 1959.

▶ CRITICAL THINKING
Analyzing Why did Castro's new government come into conflict with the United States?

©Bettmann/Corbis

The Mexican Revolution began almost 100 years after the country had won its independence from Spain. In September 2010, Mexico celebrated the 200th anniversary of its independence and the 100th anniversary of its revolution.

▶ **CRITICAL THINKING**

Comparing How might a democratic revolution be similar to a war for independence?

In 1990, Haitians elected the reformer Jean-Bertrand Aristide (A·rih·STEED) as president. The military overthrew Aristide the next year. With U.S. help, Aristide returned to power in 1994 but was removed again ten years later. Haiti remains poor, and its people face many hardships. In 2010, a strong earthquake leveled much of Port-au-Prince, the capital, killing thousands of people. Despite help from abroad, Haiti was still suffering for years after the disaster.

Conflicts in Central America

During the 1970s and 1980s, civil wars divided Central America. Cuba's Fidel Castro wanted to spread communism throughout Latin America. The United States was determined to stop him.

In Nicaragua, Sandinista rebels overthrew dictator Anastasio Somoza in 1979. Nicaraguans called contras opposed the Sandinistas. With U.S. help, the contras fought Sandinista forces. In 1990, the Sandinistas lost power when Violeta Chamorro was elected Nicaragua's first woman president. Chamorro remained in office until 1997. In 2006, voters elected the Sandinista.

Guatemala also was torn apart by civil war. With U.S. support, Guatemala's government battled rebels from 1960 to 1996. About 200,000 people died, and the economy weakened.

Panama prospered because of the Panama Canal. In 1999, the U.S. gave the canal to Panama. Panama benefits from the fees that ships pay to use the canal. The canal also brings much trade and has made Panama a major banking center.

✓ **PROGRESS CHECK**

Identifying What nation was deeply affected by a U.S. embargo on trade?

Changes in Mexico

GUIDING QUESTION *How have political leaders dealt with the challenges facing Mexico?*

After 1945, Mexico set up new industries, and its economy grew. The government also improved life for Mexico's people. Despite these efforts, Mexico faced many challenges.

Revolution in Mexico

In the early 1900s, dictator Porfirio Díaz (pawr·FEER·yoh DEE·to acahs) ruled Mexico. Foreign investments benefited the wealthy. Peasants and workers faced hardships. In 1911,

Reading HELP DESK

Build Vocabulary: *Word Parts*

Contra is a Spanish word that means "against." It has the same meaning when used as a prefix in English. The word *contradict*, for example, means "to speak against" or "to say the opposite."

reformers overthrew Díaz. Revolution swept Mexico. In 1917, a new constitution set up a government led by a strong president.

During the 1920s, Mexico was officially democratic. However, only the Institutional Revolutionary Party was allowed to win elections. Mexican voters elected their leaders from this party.

In the 1930s, social reform swept Mexico. President Lázaro Cárdenas (KAHR·duh·NAHS) gave property to landless peasants. He also nationalized foreign-owned oil wells. This action angered owners, but most Mexicans approved.

Prosperity and Economic Change

Mexico's oil industry made gains after World War II. To build new industries, Mexico borrowed money from other countries. Then oil prices fell in the 1980s, causing economic hardships.

Mexico's weak economy cost the Institutional Revolutionary Party its support. In 2000 Vicente Fox became the first president in 70 years who belonged to a different party. Economic woes and rising drug-related crime turned many people against the government. In 2012 voters elected Institutional Revolutionary Party candidate Enrique Peña Nieto as president. Nieto pledged to fight crime and improve the economy.

Workers in Tijuana, Mexico assemble television sets at a manufacturing plant. As a member of **NAFTA**, Mexico was able to build more factories and create jobs for its people.

Meanwhile, Mexico boosted its international trade. In 1992, it signed the North American Free Trade Agreement (NAFTA) with the United States and Canada. Under NAFTA, Mexico built new industries. Many U.S. and other foreign companies have built *maquiladoras* (muh·KEE·luh·DOHR·uhs) in Mexico. In these factories, workers assemble products, using foreign-made parts. The finished products are then exported.

Despite the *maquiladoras*, many Mexicans cannot find jobs. Many have become migrant workers. These are people who migrate, or travel, to find work. Some migrant workers help plant or harvest crops. They legally and sometimes illegally enter the United States. Although the work does not pay well, migrant workers can earn more in the United States than in Mexico.

✓ **PROGRESS CHECK**

Identifying What changes did President Cárdenas bring to Mexico?

AFP/Stringer/Getty Images

Build Vocabulary: *Related Words*

Migrate (verb) means to move from one region or country to another. It also means to move periodically, particularly for work. A *migrant* (noun) is a person who migrates by moving periodically.

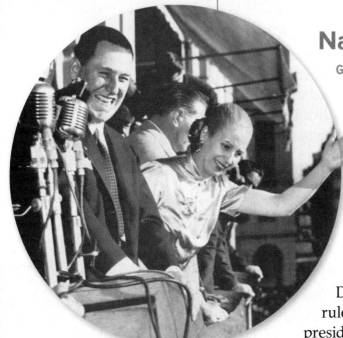

Support from working class voters helped Juan and Eva Perón stay in power. Eventually, the Perón government became corrupt and the army overthrew it.

▶ CRITICAL THINKING
Speculating How did Argentina's working class voters likely feel about Perón's corruption?

Nations of South America

GUIDING QUESTION *How has the desire for prosperity and democracy affected the recent history of South America?*

During most of the 1900s, South America was a region of contrasts. Cities had wealthy neighborhoods as well as sprawling slums. New industries arose, but many peasants still farmed. Governments were officially republics, but dictators ruled with the support of the wealthy.

Argentina and Brazil

During much of the 1900s, military leaders ruled Argentina. Juan Perón (pay·ROHN) became president in 1946. Perón and his wife Eva tried to improve the economy. Perón raised workers' wages, but his disregard of basic freedoms angered many people. In 1955, a military revolt overthrew Perón. In 1976, a new military group took control. In 1982, Argentina fought Britain over the Falkland, or Malvinas, Islands. Argentina's defeat in that war was a blow to the Argentine military. The country was able to become democratic. In 2007, Cristina Fernández became Argentina's first elected woman president.

Like Argentina, Brazil struggled politically. During most of the 1900s, the military ruled Brazil. The military gave up power in 1985, and within a few years, a federal republic emerged. Brazil is also a world economic leader. Economic activities, such as mining, agriculture, and manufacturing, have produced great wealth and a large middle class. These economic activities, however, have led to **deforestation,** or the cutting of forests without replanting. Brazil is now taking steps to preserve the rain forest.

Chile

During most of the 1900s, Chile was the region's most stable democracy. In 1970, Salvador Allende (sal·vah·DOR ah·YEHN·day) was elected president. Allende nationalized industry, raised wages, and gave land to the poor. Unhappy with the reforms, the military removed Allende from power in 1973.

AP Photo

Reading**HELP**DESK

deforestation the process of cutting down trees and forests in an area

Chile's next president, Augusto Pinochet (ah·GOOS·toh PEE·noh·CHEHT), was a ruthless dictator. In 1990, Pinochet was forced to resign. A free trade agreement with the United States in 2004 boosted Chile's economy. Two years later, voters elected Michelle Bachelet the country's first woman president.

Venezuela and Colombia

After 1945, Venezuela relied on oil as its major source of wealth. In 1998, former military leader Hugo Chávez (OO·goh CHAH·vehs) was elected president. Chávez's rule divided Venezuelans. Some groups supported his strong leadership, whereas others criticized his lack of concern for human rights. Meanwhile, Chávez tried to spread his influence overseas. He became friendly with Cuba's leaders and criticized the foreign and economic policies of the United States.

When Chávez died in 2013, Vice-President Nicolás Maduro (mah·DOO·roh) became president. Maduro continued Chávez's policies. Opponents who protested Maduro's government were arrested and jailed.

Beginning in the 1970s in Colombia, conflict among rival political groups and government forces caused many deaths. Even though peace talks to end the violence began in 2012, the conflict has continued.

Since the 1980s, the drug trade has been very powerful in Colombia. Instead of growing coffee, poor farmers raise and sell more profitable coca leaves to drug dealers. The leaves are then used to make the illegal drug cocaine. With U.S. help, Colombia's government has tried to break drug dealer's power. However, there has been little success.

✓ PROGRESS CHECK

Explaining What role did military forces play in South America's efforts to become democratic?

In 2011, Dilma Rousseff became Brazil's first female president.

▶ CRITICAL THINKING
Analyzing How has the change to a democratic government affected Brazilians?

LESSON 1 REVIEW

Review Vocabulary

1. How could an *embargo* on trade change the economy of a country?

2. Why might a country *nationalize* certain industries?

Answer the Guiding Questions

3. *Explaining* How did foreign companies affect Latin American countries?

4. *Generalizing* What role have military forces played in the governments of Latin America?

5. *Contrasting* How did Mexican rulers Díaz and Cárdenas try to help Mexico's economy?

6. *Determining Cause and Effect* What effect do crop prices have on the crops grown by farmers in Colombia?

7. **INFORMATIVE/EXPLANATORY** Why has it been difficult for many countries in Latin America to have democratic governments? Explain your answer in the form of a short essay.

LESSON 2

Africa and the Middle East

ESSENTIAL QUESTION
• Why does conflict develop?

IT MATTERS BECAUSE
Conflicts in Africa and the Middle East affect people around the world.

Nation-Building in Africa

GUIDING QUESTION *How have Africans tried to build nations after winning independence?*

After gaining independence, African nations faced many challenges. Governments and economies were often unstable. War, drought, and famine made it difficult to build modern societies. In South Africa, however, black South Africans won freedom and equality after years of hardship and resistance.

Conflicts and Independence

In the late 1800s, European nations divided Africa into colonies without concern for people living there. They tore apart once-united regions and threw together ethnic and religious groups that did not get along. After independence, many African countries kept the old colonial borders. As a result, conflicts divided people in several nations. Many people died in the civil wars that followed. Others became **refugees,** people who flee to another country to escape persecution or disaster.

In Somalia, fighting among rival warlords caused more than one million deaths. In Burundi and Rwanda, a struggle between Tutsi and Hutu ethnic groups erupted into genocide in the 1990s. In Rwanda more than 800,000 people were killed, most of them Tutsi. Two million more Tutsi became refugees.

ReadingHELPDESK

Taking Notes: *Listing*

Use a word web like the one shown here to list the political and social conflicts facing selected countries.

```
        South Africa
Sudan            Nigeria
        Conflicts
Israel            Iran
```

Content Vocabulary
• **refugee**   • **Intifada**
• **terrorism**

refugee a person who leaves a country because of war, violence, or natural disaster

Famine and Conflict in Africa

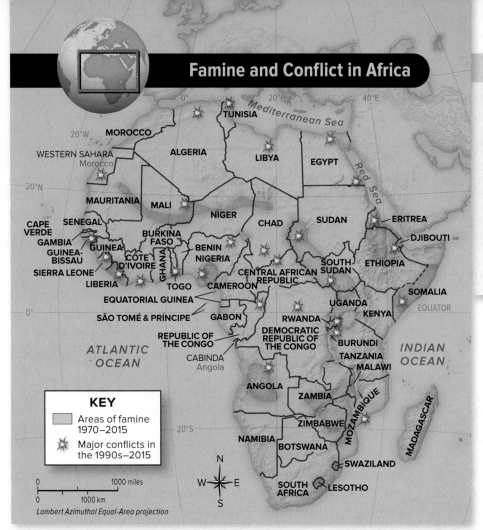

KEY

Areas of famine 1970–2015

Major conflicts in the 1990s–2015

0   1000 miles
0   1000 km

Lambert Azimuthal Equal-Area projection

GEOGRAPHY CONNECTION

Ethnic conflicts, drought, and famine have made economic development in Africa difficult.

1 PLACE Which countries in the south of Africa have not experienced famine or conflict?

2 CRITICAL THINKING
Analyzing Why might this time period have been particularly difficult for countries such as Angola, Ethiopia, South Sudan, and Sudan?

In Sudan, religious and economic issues erupted into a civil war in which nearly 2 million people were killed. After a peace agreement was reached, an election followed. Most voters in southern Sudan voted for independence. In 2011, South Sudan separated from Sudan and became independent. In Nigeria, Boko Haram, a violent Islamic group, has taken land and held many people captive.

Economic Challenges

African nations have also faced economic challenges. Africa is rich in mineral resources, such as oil, gold, and diamonds. These resources are unevenly distributed.

Most people in Africa farm or herd livestock. African farmers usually can grow only enough food to feed their families. Some farmers work on large, company-run farms that grow crops for export, including coffee, cacao, cotton, and peanuts. Like the nations of Latin America, many African countries rely on a single export crop to support their economy. When prices drop for these crops, incomes fall and people lose jobs.

Industry has played a small role in African economy. Colonial rulers did little to develop industry. After independence, African leaders encouraged the development of new businesses in urban areas. Some relied on foreign investors.

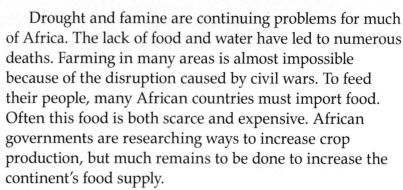

African and Western goods are available in outdoor markets that are located both in rapidly growing cities and in rural villages

Drought and famine are continuing problems for much of Africa. The lack of food and water have led to numerous deaths. Farming in many areas is almost impossible because of the disruption caused by civil wars. To feed their people, many African countries must import food. Often this food is both scarce and expensive. African governments are researching ways to increase crop production, but much remains to be done to increase the continent's food supply.

Ways of Life

Population growth and outside influences are changing everyday life in Africa. Africans, however, have tried to **maintain** many of their traditions. For example, family ties are very important.

About 70 percent of Africans reside in rural villages. Most villages are made up of a cluster of houses and shops, a medical clinic, or a schoolhouse.

African cities have grown rapidly in recent years. People have moved to cities to find jobs and to obtain an education. Most city dwellers have a higher standard of living than people in rural areas. City lifestyles **vary**, however. Some people are wealthy and live in luxury apartments or modern houses. Many residents are crowded into communities on the edge of cities. Often they have no water or electricity.

Rural and urban Africa face health care challenges. Millions of people there have been infected with the viruses that cause Ebola and AIDS. People with these diseases often cannot work to support their families. Governments struggle with these health emergencies because care and treatment are expensive. In addition, millions of children have become orphans due to these diseases.

South Africa and Apartheid

In South Africa, the white-run government ruled through a policy known as apartheid, or "apartness." Apartheid laws separated ethnic groups and limited the rights of blacks and other non-European South Africans. Protests within South Africa and abroad finally forced the government to end apartheid in the early 1990s. Protest leader Nelson Mandela was released from prison. South Africans, regardless of race, were declared equal under the law.

In 1994, South Africa held its first democratic election in which people of different races could vote. South Africans elected Nelson Mandela as their nation's first black president.

ReadingHELPDESK

Academic Vocabulary

maintain to continue
vary to show differences or undergo changes

successor one who follows, especially to an office, title, or throne

Mandela served as president until 1999. He worked to unite South Africans while rebuilding the country. His **successors,** Thabo Mbeki and Jacob Zuma, continued Mandela's policies.

✓ PROGRESS CHECK

Explaining Why do many African countries struggle to feed their people?

Thousands gather at a 2014 political rally in Soweto, South Africa. Since 1994, people of different races could vote in democratic elections in South Africa.

Identifying Who was South Africa's first black president?

The Arab-Israeli Conflict

GUIDING QUESTION *What issues have shaped the Arab-Israeli conflict?*

After World War II, independent nations replaced European empires in the Middle East. The discovery of oil brought wealth to several of these new nations. Disputes within the region affected the rest of the world. The reason for this was the global demand for oil and the Middle East's importance as a crossroads of trade.

Arabs and Israelis

Before and during World War II, Arab nations, such as Egypt, Iraq, Syria, and Jordan, won independence from European control. In 1948, a non-Arab nation also emerged in the Middle East.

The creation of Israel gave Jews their homeland and also provided shelter for Jews who had survived the Holocaust. In 1947, the United Nations voted to divide the British Palestine Mandate into separate Jewish and Arab countries. Jews accepted this decision, but the Arabs bitterly opposed it. In May 1948, the British left the area, and the Jews set up Israel. David Ben-Gurion (behn·gur·YAWN) became Israel's first prime minister.

After Israel's birth, Arab armies attacked the new nation. Israel's victory in this war brought changes. Many Palestinian Arabs fled to Arab lands. There, they lived in refugee camps, hoping to return someday. Also, many Jews from around the world settled in Israel.

There's More Online! connected.mcgraw-hill.com

Lesson 2 **801**

After its founding in 1948, Israel experienced much conflict with its Arab neighbors.

1 **LOCATION** Describe the relative location of the Sinai Peninsula to Israel.

2 **PLACE** In which areas is status yet to be determined?

3 **CRITICAL THINKING**
Explaining Jerusalem is located in the West Bank. Why is the city important to both the Israelis and the Palestinians?

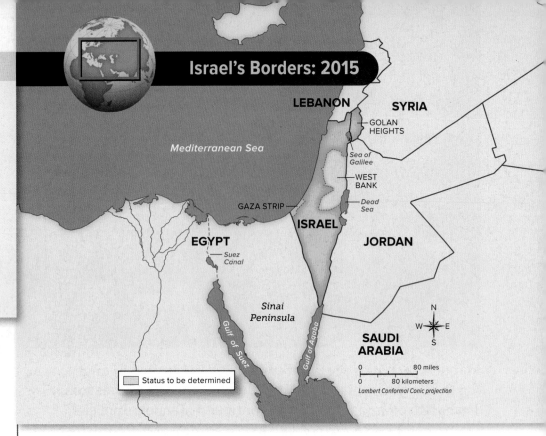

Israel's Borders: 2015

Status to be determined

After Israel was formed, many Arabs gave their support to President Gamal Abdel Nasser of Egypt. Nasser wanted to make Egypt a strong, modern nation. He also set out to reduce European influence in the Middle East.

In 1956, Egypt seized control of the Suez Canal from its European owners. Britain and France then joined Israel in invading Egypt. Britain and France hoped to overthrow Nasser and take back the canal. Israel wanted to end Egypt's military threat.

The United States and the Soviet Union both opposed the invasion. They forced the three nations to withdraw from Egypt. Egypt kept the canal and began accepting Soviet aid. Nasser emerged from the Suez crisis as a powerful Arab leader.

Continuing Conflicts

Tensions remained high between Israel and Arab countries. In June 1967, another war broke out. Egypt set up a naval blockade and placed troops near Israel's borders. Fearing an attack, Israel bombed Egyptian airfields on June 5. Syria and Jordan then joined the war against Israel. Within six days, Israel had destroyed the air forces of its Arab neighbors. Israeli troops moved into the Gaza Strip, Egypt's Sinai Peninsula, and Syria's Golan Heights. Israel also captured the old city of Jerusalem

ReadingHELPDESK

terrorism the use of violence against civilians to achieve a political goal

intifada the rebellion of Palestinians against Israeli occupation

Reading Strategy: *Using Context Clues*

If you do not know the meaning of a word, look for clues in the sentence and the paragraph where the word appears. Find the sentence "The talks led to the Camp David Accords." What word in the next sentence gives you a clue about the meaning of *accords*?

and the West Bank, the part of Jordan west of the Jordan River. This conflict, known as the Six-Day War, brought one million Palestinian Arabs under Israel's rule.

The 1960s also saw the rise of the Palestine Liberation Organization, or PLO, under its leader Yasir Arafat (ahr·uh·FAHT). The PLO's goal was to destroy Israel and take its land for the Palestinians. PLO members committed **terrorism** against Israel's people. Terrorism is the use of violence against civilians to achieve a political goal.

In 1973, Egypt's president, Anwar Sadat, ordered an attack on Israel. Egypt wanted to recapture the Sinai Peninsula. Eventually Israel, led by Prime Minister Golda Meir (may· IHR), forced the Egyptians back. The fighting ended with a cease-fire.

OPEC and Oil Prices

In 1960, major oil-producing nations, including many Arab countries, formed the Organization of Petroleum Exporting Countries, or OPEC. OPEC set out to control world oil prices by regulating how much oil each member nation produced.

During the 1973 war between Egypt and Israel, Arab members of OPEC refused to sell oil to countries that supported Israel. They also forced an increase in oil prices worldwide. These actions created an energy crisis and high inflation in Europe and the United States. In 1974, Arab nations finally agreed to sell oil to the United States again.

By the late 1970s, Egyptian president Sadat wanted peace. In 1978, he and Israeli prime minister Menachem Begin (BAY·gihn) joined U.S. President Jimmy Carter for peace talks at Camp David in the United States. The talks led to the Camp David Accords. Egypt recognized Israel's right to exist, and Israel agreed to give up the Sinai Peninsula. In 1994, Jordan also made peace with Israel.

Unresolved Issues

During the 1980s, Palestinian Arabs carried out an **intifada** (IHN·tuh·FAH·duh), or uprising. Israel, however, was able to keep control. In peace talks held in the 1990s, Palestinian Arabs accepted Israel's right to exist. In return, Israel gave Palestinians control of the Gaza Strip and areas of the West Bank. Angry about this peace plan, Palestinian fighters set off bombs in Israel. To keep out attackers, Israel in the early 2000s built a wall along its borders with Palestinian areas.

When Yasir Arafat died in 2004, Mahmoud Abbas became Palestinian leader. To further secure its borders, Israel left the Gaza Strip. Then Palestinians gave control of their legislature to Hamas—a militant party. In 2007, Hamas seized the Gaza Strip.

BIOGRAPHY

Golda Meir (1898–1978)

As Prime Minister of Israel, Golda Meir proved to be a strong and decisive leader. Anwar el-Sadat, the president of Egypt, once commented with humor that "the Old Lady [Meir] ... has guts, really."

Meir was born in Ukraine, but grew up in Wisconsin. She moved to Palestine in 1921. There she worked as a diplomat. In 1969, she became the first woman prime minister of Israel. While she was prime minister, eleven Israeli athletes were killed at the 1972 Olympic Games. Meir responded by demanding that Israel's secret service agency hunt down the murderers. A year later, she led her country to victory in the 1973 war with Egypt.

▶ CRITICAL THINKING
Explaining What acts show that Golda Meir was a strong, decisive leader?

In the United States, we use the color green as a symbol for saving the environment. In Iran, the color green means freedom. Mir Hossein Mousavi, one of the candidates who lost the 2009 election, used green as his campaign color. When he called the election unfair and asked for new voting, protesters filled the streets to support him. They wore green, carried green flags, and made green signs. Today, the different groups who are trying to bring political reform to Iran are called the Green Movement.

Since 2008, Israel's forces have entered Gaza to stop Hamas rocket attacks on Israel. In off-and-on peace talks, Israel and moderate Palestinians still disagree over old Jerusalem and Jewish settlements in the West Bank.

✓ PROGRESS CHECK

Determining Cause and Effect What were the effects of the Six-Day War?

Conflict in the Middle East

GUIDING QUESTION *How have revolution and war changed the Middle East?*

The Middle East faces many challenges. Much of the region's wealth belongs to a few people, while others struggle to survive. Some countries prosper because of oil. Others lack resources. Rapid population growth places demands on limited resources.

Islamic political movements have expanded as a result of these problems. These groups believe that strong Muslim societies require a return to traditional Islamic values.

Revolution in Iran

Iran (i·RAHN) was the first to experience an Islamic revolution. After World War II, Iran became a strong ally of the United States. Its shah, or king, was Mohammed Reza Pahlavi (rih·ZAH PA·luh·vee). With U.S. help, the shah worked to make Iran a modern industrial country. Many Iranian Muslims, however, disliked the shah's harsh ways and the changes in their society. They turned to their religious leaders for guidance.

The most respected Iranian ayatollah (EYE·uh·TOH·luh), or religious leader, was Ruhollah Khomeini (ru·HAWL·lah koh·MAY·nee). Khomeini organized protests against the shah and his rule. In 1979, as protests mounted, the shah and his family fled the country. Khomeini made Iran an Islamic republic.

In the 1990s, many Iranians demanded more freedom. The government, however, blocked reforms. Iranian president Mahmoud Ahmadinejad (mah·MOOD ah·MAH·dih·nee·ZHAHD) defended the policies of the religious leaders. In 2009, Mahmoud Ahmadinejad won reelection as president. Protestors did not believe the elections were run fairly and claimed voter fraud. In 2013, voters elected Hassan Rouhani, who promised more moderate policies.

Meanwhile, many countries suspected that Iran was developing nuclear weapons. Iran, however, claimed it needed nuclear energy to produce electricity. In 2015, several world powers and Iran reached an agreement. Iran would limit its nuclear program, and the other countries would end restrictions on trade with Iran.

Unrest in the Arab World

In 2011, protests swept the Arab world. Due to social media, protestors were able to organize and demand change. In Egypt, after massive protests, the 30-year rule of President Hosni Mubarack ended. The country's first free parliamentary elections were held, and the Islamic Mohamed Morsi was elected president. Fearing strict Muslim rule, the military forced him to resign. In 2014, former army chief Abdel Fattah el-Sisi was elected president.

In Libya, rebels overthrew dictator Muammar Qaddafi (kuh·DAH·fee). Fighting among rival groups has kept Libya in turmoil. Meanwhile, rebels in Syria fought dictator Bashir Hassad. Hassad held on to power, but the rebels controlled much of Syria. Recently, fighters from the Islamic State in Iraq and Syria (ISIS), a militant Islamic group, made major territorial gains in Syria and Iraq.

In 2011, Egyptian antigovernment demonstrators gathered in Cairo's Tahrir Square. They called for President Hosni Mubarak to step down. After weeks of protest, Mubarak gave up power.

▶ **CRITICAL THINKING**
Analyzing Why would citizens organize to remove their leader?

PROGRESS CHECK

Explaining What happened to Iran after the overthrow of the shah?

LESSON 2 REVIEW

Review Vocabulary

1. What type of event might cause a person to become a *refugee*?

2. Why do some groups choose to use *terrorism*?

3. What would a country experiencing an *intifada* be like?

Answer the Guiding Questions

4. ***Explaining*** What challenges did Africans face in building independent nations?

5. ***Determining Causes and Effects*** Why did Jews look for a homeland in Palestine after World War II?

6. ***Identifying*** What challenges does the government of Iran face?

7. **INFORMATIVE/EXPLANATORY** As in the Middle East, two countries want to control the same area. You are a diplomat asked to help solve the problem without warfare. Outline what steps you would follow to lead the countries to a peaceful solution.

There's More Online! connected.mcgraw-hill.com

LESSON 3

End of the Cold War

ESSENTIAL QUESTION

• How do new ideas change the way people live?

IT MATTERS BECAUSE
The end of the Cold War brought new democratic reforms and political upsets around the world.

The Collapse of the Soviet Empire

GUIDING QUESTION *Why did the Soviet Union and Eastern European Communist governments collapse?*

In the 1970s, relations began to improve between the United States and the two Communist giants—the Soviet Union and China.

More Peaceful Relations

During the 1970s, a new era in American-Soviet relations began. This period was called **détente**. *Détente* (day·TAHNT) comes from a French word that means "a relaxation of tensions." During the years of détente, the United States and the Soviet Union sought a better relationship with each other. The Soviets felt secure because they were now about equal to the Americans in nuclear arms. The United States was recovering from the Vietnam War. It wanted to improve relations with both the Soviets and the Chinese.

A major benefit of détente was a slowdown in the nuclear arms race. In 1972, U.S. President Richard Nixon and Soviet President Leonid Brezhnev signed SALT, or the Strategic Arms Limitation Treaty. The treaty put limits on an increase in the number of nuclear weapons by both nations.

Reading**HELP**DESK

Taking Notes: *Comparing and Contrasting*
Create a Venn diagram to list the characteristics of glasnost and perestroika.

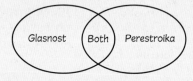

Content Vocabulary

• **détente**
• **glasnost**
• **perestroika**
• **ethnic cleansing**

The Cold War Heats Up

Despite high hopes, détente did not last. In 1979, Soviet forces invaded Afghanistan to support a failing Communist government. U.S. president Jimmy Carter opposed the invasion and reduced trade with the Soviets. In 1981, Ronald Reagan, an anti-Communist, became U.S. president. Calling the Soviet Union an "evil empire," Reagan increased America's military strength and began a new arms race with the Soviets. The costs weakened an already struggling Soviet economy. During Reagan's presidency, the United States backed groups in Africa and Central America trying to overthrow governments friendly to communism. American aid also went to Islamic groups fighting the Soviets in Afghanistan.

Gorbachev's Reforms

The Soviet Union's economic crisis brought a new leader, Mikhail Gorbachev (GAWR·buh·CHAWF), to power in 1985. He quickly changed the Soviet Union. Under a policy called **glasnost** (GLAZ·NOHST), or "openness," Soviet citizens were free to say and write what they thought without fear of government punishment. Another policy, known as **perestroika** (PEHR·uh·STROY·kuh), or "rebuilding," had the goal of reforming the Soviet economy. It gave factory managers more freedom and encouraged the creation of private businesses.

The Revolutions of 1989

Like the Soviet Union, communist Eastern Europe was economically weak. Eastern Europeans began to push for change. In 1989, Eastern Europe's communist governments fell one by one. Candidates opposed to communism were freely elected to lead new governments. Poland elected Lech Walesa (lehk vah·LEHN·suh), while Czechoslovakia chose Vaclav Havel (VAHT·slahf HAH·vuhl).

Scott Stewart/Associated Press

Gorbachev's reforms helped to improve Soviet-American relations. In 1985, Soviet president Gorbachev (right) and U.S. president Reagan (left) Gorbachev met in Geneva to discuss reducing supplies of nuclear weapons held by each nation.

---

détente a relaxation of tension, and increased understanding between nations

glasnost a Soviet policy allowing for free discussion of political and social ideas

perestroika a Soviet plan of reforming government and economic policies

ARCTIC OCEAN

East Siberian Sea

Laptev Sea

Barents Sea

Kara Sea

Bering Sea

EUROPE

Baltic Sea

Riga   Tallinn

LITHUANIA   ESTONIA

Vilnius   LATVIA

Minsk

BELARUS

MOLDOVA

Chisinău   Kiev

Moscow

RUSSIA

Sea of Okhotsk

UKRAINE

Black Sea

ASIA

Lake Baikal

GEORGIA   Tbilisi

ARMENIA   Yerevan

Baku

Aral Sea

Astana

KAZAKHSTAN

Lake Balkhash

Sea of Japan

AZERBAIJAN   Caspian Sea

TURKMENISTAN   UZBEKISTAN

Tashkent

Ashkhabad

Bishkek

Dushanbe   KYRGYZSTAN

TAJIKISTAN

0   1,000 miles

0   1,000 km

Lambert Conformal Conic projection

KEY
— Border of the former Soviet Union
— National boundary
⊙ National capital

GEOGRAPHY CONNECTION

The breakup of the Soviet Union led to the creation of 15 new nations.

1 LOCATION Identify the location of the new nations in comparison to Russia's location.

2 CRITICAL THINKING
Evaluating Which of the newly independent countries had the best chance of becoming economically successful? Why?

Finally, it was Germany's turn. On November 9, 1989, East German Communist leaders bowed to pressure. In a historic move, they opened the main gate in the Berlin Wall.

The next day, soldiers and civilians began tearing down the wall. East Germans could now move freely back and forth to West Germany. In 1990, the two parts of Germany were reunited after more than 40 years of separation.

The End of the Soviet Union

As communism ended in Eastern Europe, Gorbachev faced growing criticism from both hard-liners and reformers. Hard-liners wanted changes to stop, while reformers believed change was not fast enough. The reformers were led by Boris Yeltsin, who became president of Russia, the largest Soviet republic. In August 1991, hard-line Communists attempted a government takeover. Boris Yeltsin made the following address to the people:

Reading HELP DESK

Build Vocabulary: *Acronyms*

An acronym is a word formed using the first letters of a larger name or phrase. SALT is an acronym for "Strategic Arms Limitation Treaty." Earlier in the chapter, you learned about NAFTA, the "North American Free Trade Agreement." What other acronyms have you learned? What do they stand for?

❝ On the night of 18 to 19 August 1991 the legally elected president of the country was removed from power.... We call upon the citizens of Russia to ... demand that they [the Communists] immediately return the country to a normal path of constitutional development.... We appeal to the troops ... not to take part in this reactionary coup. We call for a general strike until ... these demands are met. *❞*

—Boris Yeltsin, August 19, 1991

Many Russians stood firm, and the hard-liners gave up. As a result, the Soviet Union collapsed in December 1991. Yeltsin and his successor, Vladimir Putin, introduced free enterprise reforms. However, as president, Putin limited citizens' rights. He restricted freedom of speech and assembly. Putin also promoted Russia's power. Russian forces defeated rebels in the breakaway region of Chechnya (chehch·NYAH). Putin believed that Ukraine's government was too friendly with Western Europe. In 2014, Putin seized Ukraine's Crimea region, which had a large Russian population. Next, he backed rebels fighting for Russian control in eastern Ukraine. In 2015, Putin extended Russian influence in Southwest Asia by supporting Syria's fight against the militant Islamic State in Iraq and Syria (ISIS).

What Changes Occurred in the Balkans?

In Europe's Balkan Peninsula, the fall of communism created a new wave of nationalism. National and ethnic rivalries exploded in the country of Yugoslavia.

Yugoslavia's problems began in 1980, when Communist dictator Josip Broz Tito died. Tito's iron rule had held the country's six republics together since the 1940s. With Tito's death, rival ethnic groups began a bitter power struggle.

In the early 1990s, Slovenia, Croatia, Bosnia-Herzegovina, and Macedonia declared their independence. The republic of Serbia used force to keep Yugoslavia under its control.

The heaviest fighting took place in Bosnia-Herzegovina, where Serbs fought Croats and Muslims. The Serbs carried out **ethnic cleansing**—removing or killing an entire ethnic group—against non-Serbs. Many civilians died or became refugees. In 1995, peace talks in Dayton, Ohio, led to the division of Bosnia-Herzegovina into Croat-Muslim and Serb regions.

As president, Vladimir Putin won praise for strengthening Russia's economy, but he also received criticism for holding too much power.

ethnic cleansing the use of force to remove or kill an entire ethnic group

In 2004, Serbia's government renamed the country Serbia and Montenegro. Two years later, the people of Montenegro voted to become independent. Kosovo, a largely Albanian Muslim territory, also decided to break away. Serbia and its ally Russia, however, refuse to accept Kosovo's independence. The former Yugoslavia now consists of as many as six countries.

✔ **PROGRESS CHECK**

Determining Cause and Effect What were the two new policies that Gorbachev introduced?

China Under Communism

GUIDING QUESTION *How have the policies of China's government changed since the 1960s?*

When China became Communist in 1949, its leaders wanted to create a modern country. By the mid-1960s, still far from this goal, they tried new ways to bring changes to China.

The Cultural Revolution

China's leader Mao Zedong (MOW·dzuh·DUHN) believed that China was losing its dedication to communism. In 1966, he began the Cultural Revolution. People viewed as "undesirable" were driven out of the Communist Party. Thinkers who wanted freedom to **promote** new ideas were arrested. Meanwhile, students called Red Guards accused leaders and ordinary citizens of not supporting communism.

The Cultural Revolution tore apart Chinese society. People stopped working, and factory production fell. Fighting broke out between Red Guards and other groups. The Chinese army finally was called out to use force to end the Cultural Revolution.

Economic Reforms

Mao Zedong died in 1976. China's new leader, Deng Xiaoping (DUHNG SHYOW·PING), was more interested in economic growth than in communist theories.

Under Deng, China began many free-enterprise reforms. Government eased its control over factories and farms. Foreigners were invited to set up businesses in special economic zones.

During China's Cultural Revolution, posters of Mao Zedong were used to influence the public. Mao's domination of China lasted until he died in 1976.

▶ **CRITICAL THINKING**
Analyzing Why do you think Mao was pictured as a smiling, happy leader?

敬祝毛主席万寿无疆

Cancan Chu/Getty Images News/Getty Images

Reading**HELP**DESK

Academic Vocabulary

promote to help bring into being
violate to break, to treat with disrespect

By the 2000s, these reforms had turned China into an economic power. China's economic growth, however, created problems. Its air and water pollution levels are among the highest in the world.

Demands for Political Change

Despite allowing economic freedoms, China's government limits political activities. In 1989, thousands of citizens gathered in Beijing's Tiananmen (TEE·EHN·AHN·MUHN) Square to call for democracy. Government troops broke up the protest, and many people were killed or injured. Around the world, China's action was called a **violation** of human rights, or basic freedoms. In 2010, Chinese officials did not allow Tiananmen protestor Liu Xiaobo (LOO SHAO·BOH) to receive the Nobel Peace Prize for his efforts to bring human rights to China.

China's leaders also were criticized for their actions in Tibet. China took over the kingdom of Tibet in 1950. The Dalai Lama (DAH·LY LAH·muh), Tibet's Buddhist leader, has asked world leaders to support political rights for Tibet's people. China refuses to give independence to Tibet.

During the 1990s, China regained Hong Kong and Macau, territories it had lost to Europeans in the 1800s. Both territories are centers of manufacturing, trade, and finance. Their citizens enjoy more freedoms than do people in the rest of China. China's government, however, still controls the choice of local officials. In 2014, Hong Kong protestors tried but failed to get the government to hold democratic elections.

China's communist government refused to make promised reforms in Hong Kong's elections in 2014. Protestors filled Hong Kong's streets, demanding the right to vote for all of Hong Kong's citizens. Calls for the government to change its position were unsuccessful.

EugeneHoHo/Getty Images

✅ **PROGRESS CHECK**

Identifying What was the Cultural Revolution in China?

LESSON 3 REVIEW

Review Vocabulary

1. How do countries get along if they practice *détente*?

2. Under the policy of *glasnost*, what could a reporter write about government leaders or officials?

3. How would *perestroika* help a business owner?

Answer the Guiding Questions

4. *Explaining* How did the arms race with the United States affect the Soviet Union?

5. *Contrasting* How did the policies of Deng Xiaoping differ from those of Mao Zedong?

6. **ARGUMENT** Mikhail Gorbachev, as a communist leader, brought many changes to the Soviet Union. Write a brief summary of his achievements as if you were his public relations manager.

There's More Online! connected.mcgraw-hill.com

The World Enters a New Century

networknavigation

There's More Online!

• How does technology change the way people live?

IT MATTERS BECAUSE

The world is developing into a global community. Modern technology has brought the countries of the world closer together.

A Changing World

GUIDING QUESTION *How has the world changed politically during the past 20 years?*

The global economy has brought many changes. Asia now plays a growing role in world affairs, and Europe is moving toward unity. The United States is still the world's major superpower, but it also depends on other countries in areas such as trade and foreign policy.

September 11 and al-Qaeda

Since the 1990s the world has seen a rise in terrorism. On September 11, 2001, a horrifying terrorist act was carried out in the United States. Terrorists seized four American passenger planes. They deliberately crashed two of the planes into the towers of the World Trade Center in New York City.

They flew a third plane into the Pentagon, the U. S. military headquarters in Washington, D.C. The fourth plane crashed in Pennsylvania killing all on board. The attacks together killed almost 3,000 people.

The terrorists belonged to al-Qaeda (al·KY·duh), a militant Islamist group led by a Saudi Arabian named Osama bin Laden (oh·SAHM·uh bihn LAH·duhn). Al-Qaeda at

Reading**HELP**DESK

Taking Notes: *Identifying*

Complete a table like this one to identify the name and purpose of each regional trade organization.

Name of Organization	Purpose of Organization

Content Vocabulary

• **interdependent** • **pandemic**

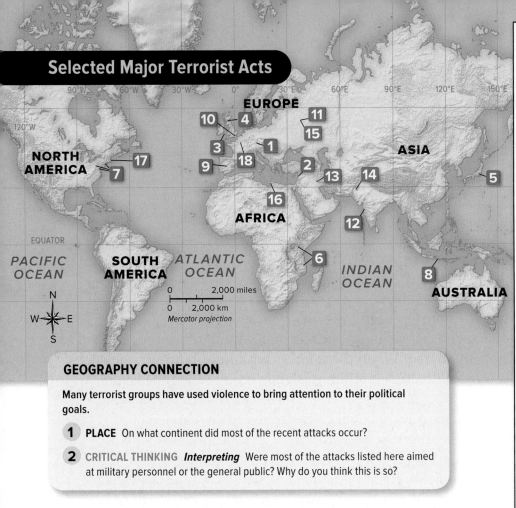

Selected Major Terrorist Acts

1. **1972** Eleven members of the Israeli Olympic team are killed at the Olympic Games in Munich, Germany

2. **1983** Bombing of U.S. Marine barracks in Beirut, Lebanon, kills 241

3. **1985** Bomb on an Air India 747 kills 329

4. **1988** Bomb on Pan Am flight 103 kills 259 in Lockerbie, Scotland

5. **1995** Nerve gas released in a Tokyo subway kills 12

6. **1998** Bombings at U.S. embassies in Kenya and Tanzania kill more than 200

7. **2001** Hijacked airliners crash into the World Trade Center, the Pentagon, and a field in Pennsylvania, killing thousands

8. **2002** Bombing at nightclub in Bali, Indonesia, kills 202

9. **2004** Bombing of Spanish commuter trains kills 191 and injures more than 1,400

10. **2005** Bombing of London subway trains and bus kills 52 and injures 700

11. **2005** Bombing by Chechen separatists in Moscow wounds 14 civilians, 1 child

12. **2006** Bombing of Mumbai commuter trains kills 207 and injures 700

13. **2009** Vehicles explode in Baghdad, Iraq, killing 155 and injuring more than 520

14. **2010** Attack in western Pakistan kills 104 and wounds more than 120

15. **2011** Bombing at Moscow airport kills 35 and injures 130

16. **2012** Attack on U.S. consulate in Benghazi, Libya, kills U.S. ambassador and three officials

17. **2013** Bombing at Boston Marathon kills three people and injures 260

18. **2015** Attacks throughout Paris leave over 100 people dead and 350 injured

GEOGRAPHY CONNECTION

Many terrorist groups have used violence to bring attention to their political goals.

1 PLACE On what continent did most of the recent attacks occur?

2 CRITICAL THINKING *Interpreting* Were most of the attacks listed here aimed at military personnel or the general public? Why do you think this is so?

first fought in Afghanistan against the Soviets. Bin Laden later turned al-Qaeda into a terrorist group aimed at the United States.

Following the 9/11 attacks, President George W. Bush vowed those responsible would be brought to justice. The United States and allied forces invaded Afghanistan. There, a militant Islamist government called the Taliban provided shelter to al-Qaeda. After the Taliban's overthrow, American and allied troops stayed in Afghanistan to fight Taliban and al-Qaeda forces.

In May 2011, U.S. Forces captured and killed Bin Laden who was hiding out in Pakistan. However, fighting continued in Afghanistan.

Iraq, Afghanistan, and Pakistan

In the 1980s, Iraq and Iran fought a bitter war over land near the Persian Gulf. Then, in 1990, Iraq seized its southern oil-rich neighbor, Kuwait (ku·WAYT). In response, U.S. and allied forces drove the Iraqis out of Kuwait. Iraq was defeated, and much of its army was destroyed. Iraq's dictator Saddam Hussein, however, remained in power.

In 2002, U.S. President George W. Bush sought to overthrow Saddam Hussein. He claimed that Hussein supported terrorists and was hiding deadly chemical and biological weapons.

BIOGRAPHY

U.S.-led forces bombed Baghdad in two wars—the 1991 Persian Gulf War and the Iraq War of the 2000s. This shows the bombing of the presidential palace in 2003.

Malala Yousafzai (1997–   )

Malala Yousafzai attended school in her village in Pakistan when the Taliban came to power. Opposed to education for women, Taliban officials closed all the girls' schools in the area. At age 11, Yousafzai blogged about her desire to return to school. When Pakistan's government regained control of the area, Yousafzai resumed her education. She continued to speak out, however, about the right of girls to be educated.

In 2012, a gunman shot her in the head on her way home from school, but Yousafzai survived. Her bravery won her support throughout the world. Malala Yousafzai, at only age 17, became the youngest person ever to receive the Nobel Peace Prize in 2014.

▶ **CRITICAL THINKING**
Explaining   Why has Malala Yousefazai become a spokesperson for girls' educational rights?

In 2003, U.S.-led armies invaded Iraq. No deadly weapons were found, but the invasion removed Hussein from power.

The United States found it difficult to create a democratic Iraq. Despite elections, Muslim groups fought for power or demanded self-rule. American troops **aided** in bringing some stability to Iraq. When these forces withdrew, however, violence broke out. In 2014, a militant Islamic group called the Islamic State in Iraq and Syria, or ISIS, seized large areas of Iraq and killed thousands of people. The United States carried out air strikes on ISIS bases, but ISIS forces steadily expanded throughout the region.

Fighting also took place in Afghanistan. There, the U.S.-backed government faced Taliban forces. American troops at first led in combat. Then, Afghan troops took on more of the fighting. In 2015, the Afghan government and Taliban officials began peace talks, but the conflict continued. Meanwhile, Afghanistan's Muslim neighbor, Pakistan, faced Taliban attacks on its citizens.

Asia's Economic Powers

India is rapidly becoming an economic power. Many American businesses now rely on workers in India and other countries to do certain jobs for them. This practice, called outsourcing, appeals to U.S. companies. In India, for example, wages are low and the country has many skilled, educated, English-speaking workers.

Japan was the first Asian country to become an economic giant. Other countries in East Asia have built strong, modern economies. These include China, South Korea, Taiwan, and Singapore.

(l)Steve Sands/Contributor/Getty Images; (r)RAMZI HAIDAR/AFP/Getty Images

Reading**HELP**DESK

Academic Vocabulary

aid to give help or assistance

Build Vocabulary: *Word Parts*

The suffix *-al* means "of, relating to, or characterized by." Chemical means related to chemistry. *Biological* means related to biology, or the study of life. What does *territorial* mean?

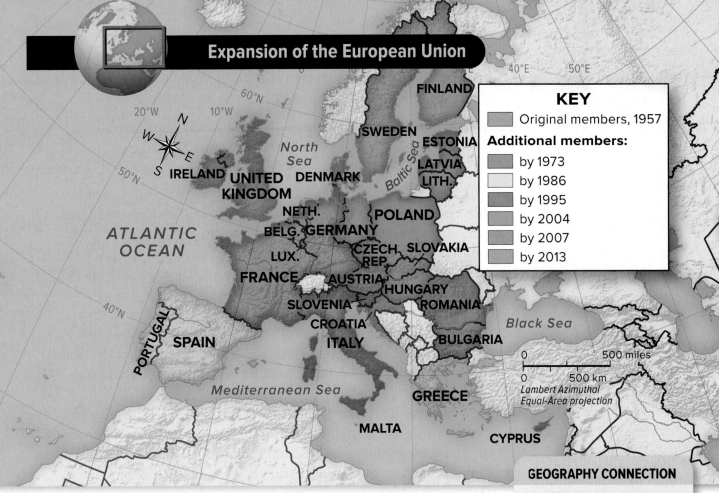

Expansion of the European Union

KEY

Original members, 1957

Additional members:

- by 1973
- by 1986
- by 1995
- by 2004
- by 2007
- by 2013

0 — 500 miles
0 — 500 km
Lambert Azimuthal Equal-Area projection

GEOGRAPHY CONNECTION

The European Union was formed to improve trade and to build European economies.

1 **LOCATION** Where are the European Union's newest members located?

2 **CRITICAL THINKING**
Analyzing How might banding together in the EU help European countries expand their role in the global economy?

In 2011, the economy of Japan received a crushing blow. A major offshore earthquake and gigantic tsunami, or tidal wave, destroyed much of Japan's coast. The economic struggles of Japan were felt all over the world. In addition, damages to a nuclear power plant raised fears about the leakage of dangerous levels of radiation.

European Challenges

During the early 1900s, European powers controlled large parts of the world. Although this is no longer the case, Europe still is a major economic and cultural center. By forming the European Union (EU), European nations have made their continent an economic superpower like the United States.

After World War II, Britain lost its colonies and faced steep economic decline. Since then, British voters have elected both Labour and Conservative governments. In 2010, the Conservatives under David Cameron came to power. Their major goal was to deal with Britain's economic challenges.

Like Britain, France lost its empire after World War II. However, it has modernized its economy. In recent decades, conservative and socialist governments have ruled under leaders such as Charles de Gaulle, Nicolas Sarkozy, and François Hollande.

Barack Obama (1961–)

Barack Obama came from a modest home. Overcoming challenges, Obama completed his education and graduated with highest honors from Harvard University law school.

After law school, Obama moved to Chicago. There, he organized voter registration drives that helped thousands of African Americans. He was elected to the Illinois Senate and gained national attention with his address to the National Democratic Convention in 2004. Obama's speech introduced an idea he called "the audacity [boldness] of hope." It encouraged Americans to hope for better days ahead. Obama served in the U.S. Senate before winning the White House in 2008. Four years later, Obama was elected to a second term as president.

▶ **CRITICAL THINKING**
Describing Describe Obama's career experience that prepared him to be president.

interdependent relying on one another for goods, information, and other resources

Reunited after the Cold War, Germany has Europe's strongest economy. Recently, a global economic downturn brought challenges to Germany. In 2005, Angela Merkel became the first female chancellor, or head of government.

What Was Happening in the United States?

During the 1980s, President Ronald Reagan brought about a conservative shift in the United States. Conservatives believe that a smaller government is less corrupt and more efficient. To reach those goals, Reagan cut social welfare programs and lowered taxes. Adopting a tough stand against communism and the Soviet Union, he strengthened the American military by increasing spending for tanks, ships, and nuclear missiles. As a result, the federal debt—the money the government borrowed and owed to banks—rose.

By the mid-1980s, the American economy was strong, but it stopped growing in the late 1980s. An economic recession occurred, which is a period of slow economic growth or decline. President George H.W. Bush, who followed Reagan, could not solve the problem.

Democrat Bill Clinton defeated Bush in the 1992 presidential election. Clinton, along with a Republican-controlled Congress, balanced the budget and reformed welfare. In 2000 and 2004, Republican George W. Bush, son of George H.W. Bush, was elected president. As president, Bush dealt with the war on terror and the U.S.-led war in Iraq.

Then a severe recession occurred beginning in 2007. Americans chose Democrat Barack Obama to be the nation's first African American president in 2008. Serving two terms, Obama signed into law a massive health care reform bill. Meanwhile, Republicans strongly opposed Obama. They blamed him for greatly expanding the size of government and increasing tax burdens on citizens.

✓ **PROGRESS CHECK**

Summarizing How did the downturn in the global economy affect governmental elections in Britain and France?

The Global Community

GUIDING QUESTION *How has the world become more connected in the early twenty-first century?*

Today, we live in a global community that has made people increasingly **interdependent.** This means that they **rely** on one

Courtesy of the White House

Academic Vocabulary

rely to depend on
contribute to provide an item or service

Build Vocabulary: *Word Parts*

The prefix *micro-* means "very small." A microprocessor is a very small computer chip. A microwave oven uses very small waves of radiation to cook food. What is microprint?

another for goods, information, and other resources. Because of interdependence, a drought, war, or oil spill in one region of the world can affect people in regions far away.

Technology Revolution

A major **contributor** to interdependence is the technology revolution. Driving this change is the computer. From the 1940s to the 1970s, scientists developed small devices, such as the transistor, microchip, and microprocessor, to efficiently control the flow of electricity.

In 1976, Stephen Wozniak and Steven Jobs built the first small computer for personal use. In the 1980s, Bill Gates developed software that tells computers how to do specific tasks. Soon an affordable personal computer was available.

Through personal computers, people are now able to go on the Internet. This is a huge web of linked computer networks. The Internet has made global communications almost instant.

Computers and other new technologies have benefited space exploration. In July 1969, American astronaut Neil Armstrong became the first human to step on the moon's surface. In the early 1980s, American scientists developed the space shuttle.

In the mid-1990s, the American space shuttle *Atlantis* docked with the Russian space station *Mir.* Japan, India, and the European Union are making plans for future human space missions. This international cooperation for space exploration is a significant change from the competition of the Cold War.

Global Economy

Today, countries have created organizations to encourage the international flow of goods and services. For example, the World Bank and the International Monetary Fund (IMF) make it easier for businesses to invest in other countries.

Many nations also have worked to make international trade free and easy. This has led to GATT (General Agreement on Trade and Tariffs) treaties. In addition, more than 150 nations now belong to the World Trade Organization (WTO). This group arranges trade agreements and settles trade disputes.

Some countries have set up regional trade groups. The European Union (EU), for example, which was formed in 2003, unites much of Europe both politically and economically.

Connections to
TODAY

The Presidency

George H. W. Bush and George W. Bush are the second father-son pair to serve as U.S. presidents. More than one hundred sixty years before the Bush presidencies, John Adams and his son John Quincy Adams each served a term as president. John Adams was in the White House from 1797 to 1801, and John Quincy Adams lived there between 1825 and 1829.

Computers in public libraries provide many people with access to the Internet.

Following Japan's earthquake, a child is tested for radiation exposure. He evacuated his village near a nuclear power plant.

▶ CRITICAL THINKING
Comparing What are the benefits and risks of nuclear power?

Some EU member nations have a common currency called the euro (YUR·oh). In the Americas, the North American Free Trade Agreement (NAFTA) creates a free-trade area.

In 2008, a major financial crisis shook the global economy. Banks and stock markets were hit hard by the collapse of the U.S. housing market. Investors suffered losses and hesitated to buy more stocks. Banks were unwilling to lend to other banks.

These events created the Great Recession, the worst economic crisis since the 1930s. By 2012, the worst of the crisis seemed to be over. National economies, however, continued to struggle toward recovery.

✓ PROGRESS CHECK

Explaining Why have countries in some world regions formed trade groups?

Global Challenges

GUIDING QUESTION *What challenges face the global community in the early 2000s?*

Developed and Developing Nations

A major global issue is the gap between developed and developing nations. Developed nations mix agriculture, manufacturing, and service industries. They have long been industrialized and use new technologies. Developed nations include the United States, Canada, Germany, and Japan. Newly industrialized countries depend more on manufacturing and less on agriculture. These countries are Brazil, Thailand, and South Korea.

Developing nations rely mostly on agriculture and have little industry. These include nations in Asia, Africa, and Latin America. Developing nations often depend on developed nations for economic aid.

Dealing With Nuclear Power

Nuclear proliferation (pruh·LIH·fuh·RAY·shuhn), or the spread of nuclear weapons, threatens all. In 2015, Iran agreed to limit its nuclear program. In return, other countries agreed to end their trade restrictions against Iran. Nuclear programs in

The Asahi Shimbun/Getty Images

ReadingHELPDESK

pandemic an outbreak of disease that occurs over a wide geographic area and affects an exceptionally high number of people

Academic Vocabulary

minimal the least possible

countries such as North Korea, Libya, Iran, India, and Pakistan, have been the focus of worldwide concern.

Nuclear power harnessed for nonmilitary uses is an issue that faces modern governments and also affects the environment. After a destructive earthquake hit Japan in 2011 and damaged nuclear reactors there, this concern increased. Leaking radiation threatened air and water quality, and the health and food sources in Japan and in neighboring countries as well.

Concern Over the Environment

In recent years, people have become more aware of threats to the environment. Many people fear that the world's growing population may soon be too large for the planet's resources to support. The use of natural resources also has hazards. In 2010, an oil drilling accident in the Gulf of Mexico killed 11 workers and created a massive oil spill that threatened coastal areas.

Most scientists think the Earth is getting warmer, possibly due to pollution. They believe global warming is changing weather patterns. These changing patterns then cause droughts and floods.

Global Health Care

Health care is a worldwide issue. **Pandemics** (pan·DEH·mix) are disease outbreaks that occur over a wide area and affect many people. In 2014, the Ebola virus spread throughout parts of West Africa and reached other continents. A new vaccine promises to halt the disease.

Meanwhile, new technologies advance medical science. Doctors use lasers to perform surgery with **minimal** discomfort to patients. In addition, organ transplants have now become much more common than before.

A pelican is examined after being evacuated from the 2010 oil spill along the Gulf Coast. The oil drilling accident polluted ocean waters and disrupted the habitats of Gulf wildlife. The oil drilling accident was an environmental disaster.

☑ PROGRESS CHECK

Contrasting How are developing countries different from developed countries?

LESSON 4 REVIEW

Review Vocabulary

1. How might *interdependence* contribute to a *pandemic*?

Answer the Guiding Questions

2. **Drawing Conclusions** How can war affect a country's global power?

3. **Making Inferences** Why might a drought in Asia affect people in Europe or North America?

4. **Making Generalizations** How have Asian countries developed strong economies?

5. **Explaining** Give examples of how new technologies have improved medical treatments.

6. **INFORMATIVE/EXPLANATORY** Examine the labels or packaging of three products to determine where they were produced. Then write a short paragraph that explains your findings and what they reveal about globalization.

Write your answers on a separate piece of paper

1 **Exploring the Essential Question**

INFORMATIVE/EXPLANATORY You travel back in time to 1980. How would you describe the fall of the Soviet Union if you were a newspaper reporter living in Moscow? Write a descriptive essay to explain how communist rule finally ended. Describe how these events are likely to affect the daily lives of Soviet citizens.

2 **21st Century Skills**

ANALYZING IMAGES Create a slide show presentation that highlights political leaders who fought for democracy in Latin America. Use photos that illustrate different events as well as the dictators, rebels, or democratically elected leaders. Share your findings with the class.

3 **Thinking Like a Historian**

SEQUENCING Create a time line that shows important events in the modern history of the Soviet Union.

4 **GEOGRAPHY ACTIVITY**

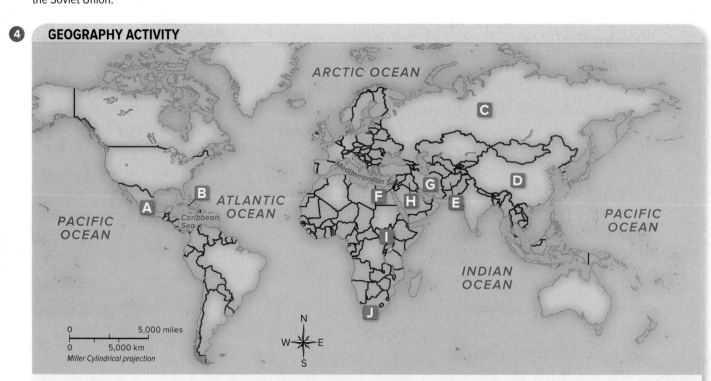

Locating Places

Match the letters on the map with the numbered places listed below.

1. Iran
2. Iraq
3. Cuba
4. Russia
5. China
6. South Sudan
7. South Africa
8. Mexico
9. Afghanistan
10. Israel

Directions: Write your answers on a separate piece of paper.

CHECKING FOR UNDERSTANDING

1 Define each vocabulary term as it relates to today's world.

- **A.** nationalize
- **B.** embargo
- **C.** deforestation
- **D.** refugee
- **E.** terrorism
- **F.** intifada
- **G.** détente
- **H.** glasnost
- **I.** perestroika
- **J.** ethnic cleansing
- **K.** interdependent
- **L.** pandemic

REVIEW THE GUIDING QUESTIONS

2 *Listing* What major challenges do Latin America's democracies face?

3 *Explaining* Why did the United States become involved in the civil war in Nicaragua?

4 *Identifying* What were some of the causes of the Cuban revolution?

5 *Summarizing* What was the purpose of NAFTA?

6 *Naming* What is the primary economic activity in most African countries?

7 *Explaining* How did social media impact the 2011 protests in the Arab world?

8 *Identifying Cause and Effect* What impact did the death of Josip Broz Tito have on Yugoslavia?

9 *Contrasting* How do the lives of the citizens of Macau and Hong Kong differ from those of other Chinese citizens?

10 *Explaining* Why did the United States send troops into Iraq in 2002?

11 *Defining* What is the euro? What is a possible benefit of the euro?

12 *Making Inferences* How might a pandemic affect a nation's economy?

CRITICAL THINKING

13 *Identifying Cause and Effect* How did the end of the Cold War in Europe impact Cuba?

14 *Defending* Do you believe U.S. military intervention in countries such as Nicaragua, Guatemala, and Cuba was justified? Why or why not?

15 *Evaluating* What has been an effect of economic growth in Brazil?

16 *Determining Cause and Effect* What do you think Arab members of OPEC hoped to accomplish when they refused to sell oil to countries supporting Israel in its 1973 war with Egypt?

17 *Predicting Consequences* How do you think the agreement regarding Iran's nuclear energy program will impact the Middle East over the next decade?

18 *Comparing and Contrasting* How is Russian president Vladimir Putin similar to former Soviet leader Mikhail Gorbachev? In what ways does Putin differ from Gorbachev?

19 *Assessing* Economic reforms in China have turned the country into a global economic power. Can China still be considered a Communist country? Explain your answer.

20 *Making Inferences* Why might groups such as al-Qaeda and ISIS choose to attack civilians?

Need Extra Help?

If You've Missed Question	**1**	**2**	**3**	**4**	**5**	**6**	**7**	**8**	**9**	**10**	**11**	**12**	**13**	**14**	**15**	**16**	**17**	**18**	**19**	**20**
Review Lesson	1, 2, 3, 4	1	1	1	1	2	2	3	3	4	4	4	1	1	1	2	2	3	3	4

DBQ SHORT RESPONSE

In 2003, Iranian Shirin Ebadi supported a peaceful Iran. She said,

"[Some Iranians] are trying to . . . deal with the problems . . . of the existing world by virtue of [with] the values of the ancients. But, many others . . . seek to go forth in step with world developments and not lag behind the caravan [flow] of civilization, development and progress."

    —Excerpt from Nobel Lecture by Shirin Ebadi, human rights activist

21 What does Ebadi say about how Iran is coping with modern problems?

22 Explain what Ebadi means by "not lag behind the caravan of civilization, development and progress."

EXTENDED RESPONSE

23 *Informative/Explanatory* You meet someone in a small village of Southwest Asia. People live in traditional ways and know little about modern technology. How would you explain how globalization connects people all around the world?

STANDARDIZED TEST PRACTICE

DBQ ANALYZING DOCUMENTS

Summarizing South African leader Nelson Mandela worked to end apartheid. He declared:

"During my lifetime . . . I have cherished [loved] the ideal of a democratic and free society in which all persons live together in harmony and with equal opportunities. It is an ideal which I hope to live for and to achieve. But if needs be, it is an ideal for which I am prepared to die."

    —Nelson Mandela, April 20, 1964

24 What best explains Mandela's opinion about race relations in South Africa?
- **A.** White Africans should rule black Africans.
- **B.** Black Africans should rule white Africans.
- **C.** Different races cannot live in harmony in South Africa.
- **D.** A country should provide equal opportunities for its citizens.

25 *Inferring* What does Mandela imply about his efforts?
- **A.** He is afraid of the South African police.
- **B.** He believes the court system is fair.
- **C.** He is willing to make a stand against unfair practices.
- **D.** He thinks he can convince people to set him free.

Need Extra Help?

If You've Missed Question	**21**	**22**	**23**	**24**	**25**
Review Lesson	2	2	4	2	2

World Religions Handbook

TERMS

animism—belief that spirits inhabit natural objects and forces of nature

atheism—disbelief in the existence of any god

monotheism—belief in one God

polytheism—belief in more than one god

secularism—belief that life's questions can be answered apart from religious belief

sect—a subdivision within a religion that has its own distinctive beliefs and/or practices

tenet—a belief, doctrine, or principle believed to be true and held in common by members of a group

A *religion* is a set of beliefs that help people explain their lives and the world around them. In many cultures, religious beliefs help people answer basic questions about life's meaning. People use religion to help them lead a meaningful life and to explain the mysteries of life, such as how and why the world was created. Religions explain what happens to people when they die or why there is suffering.

Religion is an important part of culture. Most religions have their own special beliefs, celebrations, and worship styles. They also have their own sacred texts, symbols, and sites. These beliefs and practices unite followers wherever they live in the world.

The religions in this handbook have sacred elements, celebrations, and worship styles. We can gain a better understanding of these religions by examining what sets them apart.

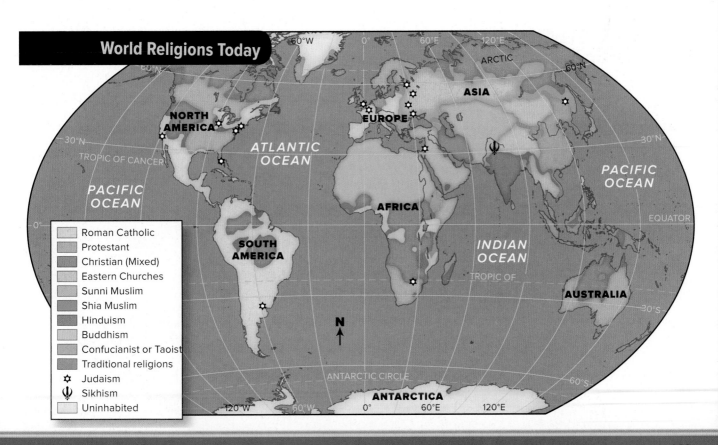

World Religions Today

Legend:
- Roman Catholic
- Protestant
- Christian (Mixed)
- Eastern Churches
- Sunni Muslim
- Shia Muslim
- Hinduism
- Buddhism
- Confucianist or Taoist
- Traditional religions
- ✡ Judaism
- ☬ Sikhism
- Uninhabited

We study religion because it is an important part of culture. Religion can determine how people interact with one another. Religion can also influence what people wear and eat.

There are five major world religions: Christianity, Islam, Hinduism, Buddhism, and Judaism. Some religions, including Hinduism, Sikhism, and Judaism, are related to a specific culture. Followers are usually born into these religions.

There are many ways that religion has spread throughout the world. When people migrate, they move from one place to another. People who migrate take their beliefs and customs with them. These beliefs and customs then influence other cultures around them.

Missionaries have also spread religion throughout the world. Missionaries are people who move to another area in order to teach their religion to those who are not followers.

Finally, religion has spread throughout the world because of trade and war. As people trade, they interact with each other, sharing their beliefs. Conquerors bring their culture, including their religions, to conquered areas.

Percentage of World Population

Islam: 23%
Christianity: 33%
Sikhism: 0.4%
Other religions: 4%
Buddhism: 7%
Hinduism: 14%
Judaism: 0.2%
Confucianism: 4%
Nonreligious or atheist: 16%

Note: Total exceeds 100% because numbers were rounded.
Sources: The World Factbook 2016; www.adherents.com.

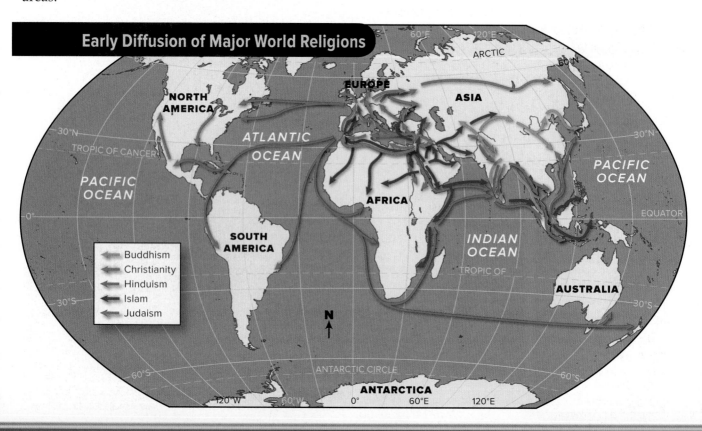

Early Diffusion of Major World Religions

Buddhism
Christianity
Hinduism
Islam
Judaism

Buddhism

PHOTOS: (t) Serg Zastavkin/Shutterstock.com (b) ©ArmandsPharyos/Alamy. TEXT: From THE SACRED BOOKS OF THE EAST, ed. F. Max Müller, Vol. X. The Dhammapada, trans. from Pâli by F. Max Müller; and The Sutta-Nipâta, trans. from Pâli by V. Fausböll, Oxford at the Clarendon Press, 1880.

Buddhism was founded about 2,500 years ago by Siddhartha Gautama. He grew up as a prince near the Himalaya. Today, this area is in southern Nepal. One day, Siddhartha Guatama left his palace to explore the world. As he traveled, he was shocked at the poverty he saw. He gave up all his wealth and became a monk. He meditated and taught about the meaning of life. Siddhartha Gautama later became known as the Buddha. His teachings became known as Buddhism.

The Buddha or "Enlightened One" taught that people suffered because they cared too much about fame, money, and personal possessions. He believed that wanting these things could lead to greed or anger. The Buddha taught his followers the Four Noble Truths. He believed these would help people seek spiritual truth. The fourth truth says that people can end suffering by following eight steps, known as the Eightfold Path. When people were free from all earthly concerns, they would reach Nirvana, or the state of perfect happiness and peace.

Buddhism spread throughout Asia. Several branches of Buddhism developed. The largest branches of Buddhism are Theravada and Mayhayana. Theravada Buddhism is practiced in Sri Lanka, Burma, Thailand, Laos and Cambodia. Mayayana Buddhism is practiced in Tibet, Central Asia, Korea, China, and Japan. Theravada means "teachings of the elders." Followers of Theravada view the Buddha as a great teacher, but not a god. Mahayana Buddhism teaches that the Buddha is a god.

Statue of the Buddha, Siddhartha Gautama

Sacred Text ▾

For Theravada Buddhists, the sacred collection of Buddhist texts is the Tripitaka ("three baskets"). This excerpt from the *Dhammapada,* a famous text within the Tripitaka, urges responding to hatred with love:

❝ For hatred does not
cease by hatred at any time:
hatred ceases by love, this is
an old rule. ❞

—*Dhammapada 1.5*

Sacred Symbol ▾

The *dharmachakra* ("wheel of the law") is an important Buddhist symbol. The eight spokes represent the Eightfold Path—right view, right intention, right speech, right action, right livelihood, right effort, right mindfulness, and right concentration.

Sacred Site ▲

Buddhists believe that Siddhartha Gautama achieved enlightenment beneath the Bodhi Tree in Bodh Gayā, India. Today, Buddhists from around the world travel to Bodh Gayā in search of their own spiritual awakening.

Worship and Celebration ▶

The goal of Buddhists is to achieve Nirvana, the enlightened state in which individuals are free from ignorance, greed, and suffering. Theravada Buddhists believe that monks are most likely to reach Nirvana when they reject worldly objects, behave morally, and devote their lives to meditation.

Christianity

Christianity has more members than any of the other world religions. It began with the death of Jesus in A.D. 33 in what is now Israel. Christianity is based on the belief in one God and on the life and teachings of Jesus. Christians believe that Jesus, who was born a Jew, is the son of God and that Jesus was both God and man. Christians believe that Jesus is the Messiah (Christ), or savior, who died for people's sins. Christians feel that when people accept Jesus as their savior, they will achieve eternal life.

The major forms of Christianity are Roman Catholicism, Eastern Orthodoxy, and Protestantism. In 1054, disputes over doctrine and the leadership of the Christian Church caused the church to divide into the Roman Catholic Church, headed by the Bishop of Rome, also known as the pope, and the Eastern Orthodox Church, led by patriarchs. Protestant churches emerged in the 1500s in an era known as the Reformation. Protestants disagreed with some Catholic doctrines and questioned the pope's authority. Despite their different theologies, all three forms of Christianity are united in their belief in Jesus as savior.

Stained glass window depicting Jesus

Sacred Text

The Christian Bible is the spiritual text for all Christians. It is considered to be inspired by God. This excerpt, from Matthew 5:3-12, is from Jesus's Sermon on the Mount.

Sacred Symbol

Christians believe that Jesus died for their sins. His death redeemed, or freed, people from their sins. The statue *Christ the Redeemer,* located in Rio de Janeiro, Brazil, symbolizes this important Christian belief.

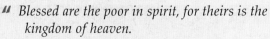

> *Blessed are the poor in spirit, for theirs is the kingdom of heaven.*
> *Blessed are those who mourn, for they shall be comforted.*
> *Blessed are the meek, for they shall inherit the earth.*
> *Blessed are those who hunger and thirst for righteousness, for they shall be satisfied.*
> *Blessed are the merciful, for they shall obtain mercy.*
> *Blessed are the pure in heart, for they shall see God.*
> *Blessed are the peacemakers, for they shall be called sons of God.*
> *Blessed are those who are persecuted for righteousness' sake, for theirs is the kingdom of heaven.*
> *Blessed are you when men revile you and persecute you and utter all kinds of evil against you falsely on my account.*
> *Rejoice and be glad, for your reward is great in heaven, for so men persecuted the prophets who were before you.* ❞

Sacred Site ▶

The Gospels are books in the Christian Bible that describe the life and teachings of Jesus. The Gospels state that Bethlehem was the birthplace of Jesus. Because of this, Bethlehem is very important to Christians. The Church of the Nativity is located in Bethlehem. Christians believe that the church sits on the exact site where Jesus was born.

Worship and Celebration ▼

Christians participate in many events to celebrate the life and death of Jesus. Among the most widely known and observed events are Christmas, Good Friday, and Easter. People attend Christmas church services to celebrate the birth of Jesus. As part of the celebration, followers often light candles to symbolize their belief that Jesus is the light of the world.

Confucianism

Confucianism began more than 2,500 years ago in China. Although considered a religion, it is actually a philosophy. It is based upon the teachings of Confucius.

Confucius believed that people needed to have a sense of duty. Duty meant that a person must put the needs of the family and the community before his or her own needs. Each person owed a duty to another person. Parents owed their children love, and children owed their parents honor. Rulers had a duty to govern fairly. In return, the ruler's subjects had to be loyal to the ruler and obey the law. Confucius also promoted the idea that people should treat others the same way that they would like to be treated. Eventually, Confucianism spread from China to other East Asian societies.

Students study Confucianism, Chunghak-dong, South Korea

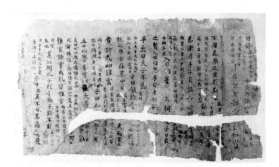

The Analects

Sacred Text ▾

Confucius was famous for his sayings. These teachings were gathered into a book called the *Analects* (see image above) after Confucius's death. Below is an example of Confucius's teachings:

❝ *To learn and to practice what is learned time and again is pleasure, is it not? To have friends come from afar is happiness, is it not? To be unperturbed when not appreciated by others is gentlemanly, is it not?* ❞

Sacred Symbol ▾

Yin-yang symbolizes the harmony offered by Confucianism. Black and white represent two energies. These energies are different from each other, but they also cannot be separated from one another. An example of a *yin-yang* relationship is night and day. Night looks and is different from day, but you cannot have night without day. Both rely on each other to complete each other. It is believed that the *yin* and *yang* act together to balance one another.

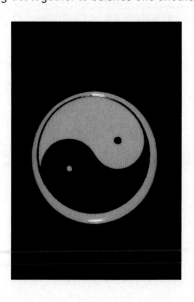

Commemorate the 2555th Anniversary of Confucius Birthday

Sacred Site ▲

The temple at Qufu is a group of buildings dedicated to Confucius. Confucius's family home was located here. It is one of the largest ancient architectural complexes in China. Every year, followers gather at Qufu to celebrate the birthday of Confucius.

Worship and Celebration ▶

Followers of Confucianism do not worship Confucius as a god. Confucius is their spiritual leader, and there are temples dedicated to him. Followers believe that Confucianism is a guide for living and effective governing.

Hinduism

Hinduism is one of the world's oldest religions. It is the world's third largest religion, after Christianity and Islam. Hinduism does not have a single founder or founding date. Hinduism grew out of the religious customs of many people over thousands of years in India. Hindus think of all their deities as different parts of one universal spirit. This universal spirit is called Brahman.

According to Hindu sacred texts, every living thing has a soul that is part of Brahman. The body is part of life on Earth. At death, the soul leaves the body and joins with Brahman. However, Hindus believe that the soul is not joined to the Brahman immediately after a person dies. Instead, a soul must pass through many lives, or be reincarnated, before it is united with Brahman. According to the idea of karma, the life into which a soul is reborn is determined by the good and evil acts performed in past lives. Dharma is the divine law that requires people to do their duties in the life that they are living in order to achieve a better life.

Sacred Text ▾

The Vedas are the entire collection of Hindu sacred writings. The Vedas are written in ancient Sanskrit. They are the oldest religious texts in an Indo-European language. The Vedas include Hindu hymns, prayers, and descriptions of rituals.

Statue of Vishnu, a Hindu deity

> *Now, whether they perform a cremation for such a person or not,*
> *people like him pass into the flame,*
> *from the flame into the day,*
> *from the day into the fortnight of the waxing moon,*
> *from the fortnight of the waxing moon into the six months when the sun moves north,*
> *from these months into the year, from the year into the sun,*
> *from the sun into the moon, and from the moon into the lightning.*
> *Then a person who is not human—he leads them to Brahman.*
> *This is the path to the gods, the path to Brahman.*
> *Those who proceed along this path do not return to this human condition.*
> —The Chandogya Upanishad 4:15.5

Sacred Symbol ▾

One important symbol of Hinduism is actually a symbol for a sound. "Om" is a sound that Hindus often chant during prayer, and rituals.

PHOTOS: (t) Dorling Kindersley/Getty Images; (b) Image Source/Getty Images; TEXT: THE EARLY UPANISADS translated by Olivelle (1998) 112w from Chandogya Upanisad. © 1998 by Patrick Olivelle. By permission of Oxford University Press, USA.

Sacred Site ▶

Hindus believe that when a person dies, his or her soul is reborn. This is known as reincarnation. Many Hindus bathe in the Ganges and other sacred rivers to purify their souls and to be released from rebirth.

Worship and Celebration ▼

Holi is an important North Indian Hindu festival celebrating the triumph of good over evil. As part of the celebration, men, women, and children splash colored powders and water on each other. In addition to its religious importance, Holi also celebrates the beginning of spring.

Islam

Followers of Islam, known as Muslims, believe in one God, whom they call Allah. The word Allah is Arabic for "god." The founder of Islam, Muhammad, began his teachings in Makkah (Mecca) in A.D. 610. Eventually the religion spread throughout much of Asia, including parts of India to the borders of China, and much of Africa. According to Muslims, the Quran, their holy book, contains the direct word of God, revealed to their prophet Muhammad. Muslims believe that God created nature. Without God, Muslims believe, there would be nothingness.

Muslims are expected to fulfill the Five Pillars of Islam, or acts of worship. Muslims must believe and declare that there is no god but Allah, and Muhammad is his prophet. Muslims must pray five times a day facing toward Makkah. Muslims must tithe, or give a portion of their income to the poor. Muslims must fast during the holy month of Ramadan, meaning that they must not eat from dawn to dusk. Finally, Muslims, if possible, should visit Makkah at least once in their lifetime.

Muhammad died in A.D. 632, and disagreement broke out about who should be the caliph, or the successor to Muhammad. Two groups with different opinions emerged. The Shia believed that the rulers should descend from Muhammad. The Sunni believed that the rulers only need to be followers of Muhammad. Most Muslims today are Sunni.

Sacred Text ▾

The Quran instructs Muslims about how they should live and treat others. The Quran also contains rules that affect Muslims' daily lives. For example, Muslims are not allowed to eat pork, drink liquor, or gamble. The Quran also has rules about marriage, divorce, and business practices. The excerpt below is a verse repeated by all Muslims during their five daily prayers.

> *❝ In the name of the merciful and compassionate God. Praise belongs to God, the Lord of the worlds, the merciful, the compassionate, the ruler of the day of judgment! Thee we serve and Thee we ask for aid. Guide us in the right path, the path of those Thou art gracious to, not of those Thou art wroth with, nor of those who err. ❞*
>
> —The Quran

The Dome of the Rock, Jerusalem

The Quran

Sacred Symbol ▾

Islam is often symbolized by the crescent moon. It is an important part of Muslim rituals, which are based on the lunar calendar.

Sacred Site ▶

Makkah is a sacred site for all Muslims. One of the Five Pillars of Islam states that all who are physically and financially able must make a hajj, or pilgrimage, to the holy city once in their life. Practicing Muslims are also required to pray facing Makkah five times a day.

Worship and Celebration ▼

Muslims believe that Muhammad received the Quran from Allah. They celebrate this event during the holy month of Ramadan. Muslims fast from dawn until sunset during the month. Muslims believe that fasting helps them focus on one's spiritual needs rather than one's physical needs. They also believe that fasting makes them aware of the needs of others. Ramadan ends with a feast known as Eid-al-Fitr, or Feast of the Fast.

Judaism

Judaism was the first major religion based on monotheism—the belief in one God. Jews trace their national and religious origins to Abraham. According to the Hebrew Bible—the Tanakh—God made a covenant, or agreement, with Abraham around 1800 B.C. If Abraham moved to the land of Canaan, which today is Lebanon, Israel, and Jordan, Abraham and his descendants would be blessed. Abraham's descendants would continue to be blessed as long as they followed God's laws. Jews believe that if they strive for justice and live moral lives, they will help create a new era of universal peace.

El Ghriba Synagogue, Jerba, Tunisia

Star of David, also known as the Magen David

The Torah scroll

Sacred Text ▾

Jews believe that God gave Moses the writings and teachings found in the Torah. The Torah includes the first five books of Moses in the Hebrew Bible. These books include Genesis, Exodus, Leviticus, Numbers, and Deuteronomy. They tell the story of the origins of the Jews and explain Jewish laws. The remainder of the Hebrew Bible contains the writings of the prophets, Psalms, and ethical and historical works.

> ❝ I am the Lord your God, who brought you out of the land of Egypt, out of the house of slavery; you shall have no other gods before me. ❞
>
> —Exodus 20:2

Sacred Symbol ▾

One of the oldest Jewish symbols is the menorah. The menorah is lit to celebrate Hanukkah. Hanukkah is an eight-day holiday. During Hanukkah, Jews celebrate the rededication of the Temple of Jerusalem following the victory over the Syrian-Greeks around 167 B.C. Another important Jewish symbol is the Star of David, also known as the Magen David, or Shield of David.

Sacred Site ◂

The Second Jerusalem Temple was a sacred building to Jews after they were freed from slavery in Babylon around 538 B.C. It was located in Jerusalem, the holiest city for Judaism. The Temple was destroyed by the Romans in A.D. 70. The Western Wall is the remains of the structure that surrounded the Second Jerusalem Temple. The wall quickly became a sacred site in Jewish religious tradition. Jews throughout the world pray facing Jerusalem in the morning, afternoon, and evening. Jews living in Jerusalem pray facing toward the Western Wall.

Worship and Celebration

The day-long Yom Kippur service ends with the blowing of the ram's horn (shofar). Yom Kippur is the holiest day in the Jewish calendar. During Yom Kippur, Jews do not eat or drink for 25 hours. The purpose is to reflect on the past year, repent for one's sins, and gain forgiveness from God. It falls in September or October, ten days after Rosh Hashanah, the Jewish New Year.

Sikhism

Sikhism emerged in the mid-1400s in the Punjab, in northwest India. Sikhism is a religion that arose out of the teachings of Guru Nanak. Sikh tradition says that Guru Nanak's teachings were revealed directly to him by God.

Sikhs believe in one God who is formless, all-powerful, and all-loving. One can achieve unity with God by helping others, meditating, and working hard. While about 76 percent of the world's 27 million Sikhs live in the Punjab, Sikhism has spread widely as many Sikhs have migrated to different regions throughout the world.

Sikh men often wear long beards and cover their heads with turbans.

Guru Nanak

Sacred Text

The primary sacred text for Sikhs is the Guru Granth Sahib. Collected from the mid-1500s through the 1600s, it includes contributions from Sikh Gurus, along with others also claimed as saints by Hindus and Muslims, such as Namdev, Ravidas, and Kabir.

> *Enshrine the Lord's Name within your heart. The Word of the Guru's Bani prevails throughout the world, through this Bani, the Lord's name is obtained.*
> —Guru Amar Das, page 1066

Central Symbol

Ek Onkar is one of the central Sikh symbols. It represents the belief that there is one God for all people, no matter what their religion, gender, race, or culture.

Sacred Site ▸

Darbar Sahib, also known as the Golden Temple, is located in Amritsar, Punjab. It is one of the most popular Sikh houses of worship. It is believed that Guru Nanak meditated along the lake that surrounds the temple.

Worship and Celebration ▾

Vaisakhi is a significant Punjabi and Sikh festival in April. Sikhs celebrate Vaisakhi as the day Guru Gobind Singh, the 10th Guru, established the Khalsa, the community of people who have been initiated into the Sikh religion. In Punjab, Vaisakhi is celebrated as the New Year and the beginning of the harvest season.

Indigenous Religions

There are many types of religions that are limited to certain ethnic groups. These local religions are found in Africa, as well as isolated regions of Japan, Australia, and the Americas.

Most local, or indigenous, religions reflect a close relationship between humans and the environment. Some groups teach that people are a part of nature, not separate from it. Animism is characteristic of many indigenous religions. Natural features are sacred, and stories about how nature developed are an important part of religious heritage. Although many of these stories have been written down in modern times, they were originally transmitted orally.

Africa Many people living in Africa practice a variety of local religions. Despite their differences, most African religions recognize the existence of one creator, in addition to spirits that inhabit all forms of life. Religious ceremonies are often celebrated with music and dance.

The Turkana from Kenya perform a traditional jumping dance.

Rituals are an important part of African religions. These Masai boys are wearing ceremonial dress as part of a ritual.

Masks are a component of ritual and ceremony in many African religions.

Japan Shinto, founded in Japan, is the world's largest indigenous religion. It developed in prehistoric times and has no formal teachings. The gods are known as *kami*. Ancestors are also worshipped. Shinto's four million followers often practice Buddhism, too.

Shinto shrines are usually built in places of great natural beauty to emphasize the relationship between people and nature.

This Shinto priest is presiding over a ritual at a Japanese temple. Shinto priests often live on shrine grounds.

Australia The Australian Aboriginal religion does not have any gods. It is based upon a belief known as the Dreaming, or Dreamtime. Followers believe that ancestors sprang from the Earth and created people, plants, and animals. Followers also believe that ancestors continue to control the natural world.

Aborigine women bless a newborn with smoke during a traditional ritual intended to ensure the child's health and good fortune.

Aborigines often paint their faces with the symbols of their clan or family group.

Indigenous Religions

Native Americans The beliefs of most Native Americans focus on the spirit world; however, the rituals and practices of individual groups vary. Most Native Americans believe in a Great Spirit who, along with other spirits, influences life on Earth. These spirits make their presence known primarily through acts of nature.

Good health, a productive harvest, and successful hunting often serve as the reasons for Native American rituals, prayers, and ceremonies. Native Americans also observe a person's passage into different stages of life. Rituals celebrate birth, adulthood, and death. Prayers, in the form of songs and dances, are offered to spirits.

Rituals are passed down from generation to generation. These Native Americans are performing a ritual dance.

There are many different Native American groups throughout the United States and Canada. This Pawnee is wearing traditional dress during a celebration in Oklahoma.

Totem poles, like this one in Alaska, were popular among the Native American peoples of the Northwest Coast. They were often decorated with mythical beings, family crests, or other figures. They were placed outside homes.

Assessment

Reviewing Vocabulary

Match the following terms with their definitions.

1. sect
2. monotheism
3. polytheism
4. animism
5. atheism

   a. belief that spirits inhabit natural objects and forces of nature
   b. belief in one God
   c. a subdivision within a religion that has its own distinctive belief and/or practices
   d. belief in more than one god
   e. disbelief in the existence of any god

Reviewing the Main Ideas

World Religions

6. Which religion has the most followers worldwide?

7. On a separate sheet of paper, make a table of the major world religions. Use the chart below to get you started.

Name	Founder	Geographic distribution	Sacred sites
Buddhism			
Christianity			
Confucianism			
Hinduism			
Islam			
Judaism			
Sikhism			
Indigenous			

Buddhism

8. According to Buddhism, how can the end of suffering in the world be achieved?

9. What is Nirvana? According to Buddhists, who is most likely to achieve Nirvana and why?

Christianity

10. In what religion was Jesus raised?

11. Why do Christians accept Jesus as their redeemer?

Confucianism

12. What is Confucianism based on?

13. What does yin-yang symbolize?

Hinduism

14. Where did Hinduism develop?

15. What role do Hindus believe karma plays in reincarnation?

Islam

16. What are the two branches of Islam? What is the main difference between the two groups?

17. What role does Makkah play in Islam?

Judaism

18. What is the Torah?

19. What is the purpose of Yom Kippur?

Sikhism

20. According to Sikhism, how does one achieve unity with God?

21. Why do Sikhs celebrate Vaisakhi?

Indigenous Religions

22. Why would local religions feature sacred stories about the creation of people, animals, and plant life?

23. Which of the indigenous religions has the largest membership?

Enrichment Activity

24. **Research Project** Use library and Internet sources to research the role of food and food customs in one of the world's major religions. Create a presentation to report your findings to the class.

- Content vocabulary words are words that relate to world history content.
- Words that have an asterisk (*) are academic vocabulary. They help you understand your school subjects.
- All vocabulary words are **boldfaced** or **highlighted in yellow** in your textbook.

abandon • **alphabet**

ENGLISH	A	ESPAÑOL

*abandon to leave and not return; to leave, often because of danger (p. 252; p. 456)

*abandonar salir y no regresar; dejar, con frecuencia debido al peligro (pág. 252; pág. 456)

abolitionism movement to end slavery (p. 687)

abolicionismo movimiento para poner fin a la esclavitud (pág. 687)

absolutism a political system in which a ruler has total power (p. 651)

absolutismo sistema político en el cual un gobernante tiene poder total (pág. 651)

*accompany to go with someone as a companion (p. 200)

*acompañar ir con alguien como compañero (pág. 200)

*accurate free from errors; in agreement with truth (p. 239; pp. 562–563)

*exacto sin errores; que se ajusta a la verdad (pág. 239; págs. 562–563)

accursed doomed, miserable (p. 597)

maldito condenado, miserable (pág. 597)

*achieve to succeed; to gain something as the result of work; to successfully complete a task (p. 187; p. 456)

*lograr tener éxito; obtener algo como resultado del trabajo; completar una tarea con éxito (pág. 187; pág. 456)

*achievement something gained by working for it (p. 512)

*logro algo que se obtiene trabajando por ello (pág. 512)

*acquire to get possession of something; to get as one's own (p. 124; p. 310)

*adquirir tomar posesión de algo; tomar como propio (pág. 124; pág. 310)

acupuncture originally, a Chinese practice of inserting fine needles through the skin at specific points to treat disease or relieve pain (pp. 296–297)

acupuntura práctica originaria de la China que consiste en insertar agujas delgadas en puntos específicos de la piel para tratar una enfermedad o aliviar el dolor (págs. 296–297)

*adequate enough for a particular requirement (p. 424)

*adecuado suficiente para un requisito en particular (pág. 424)

*administer to be lawfully in charge of (p. 342)

*administrar estar legalmente a cargo (pág. 342)

*affect influence; to cause a change (p. 179)

*afectar influir; ocasionar un cambio (pág. 179)

agora a gathering place; marketplace in ancient Greece (p. 180)

ágora sitio de reunión; plaza de la Grecia antigua (pág. 180)

*aid to give help or assistance (p. 814)

*auxiliar proveer ayuda o asistencia (pág. 814)

allies those who support each other for some common purpose (pp. 624–625)

aliados quienes se apoyan entre sí para un propósito en común (págs. 624–625)

alphabet a set of letters or other characters used to write a language (pp. 144–145)

abecedario conjunto de letras o de otros caracteres usados en la lengua escrita (págs. 144–145)

Glossary/Glosario

ambush a surprise attack (p. 626)

emboscada ataque sorpresivo (pág. 626)

anatomy the study of the body's structure (p. 344)

anatomía estudio de la estructura del cuerpo (pág. 344)

ancestor a person that someone is descended from (p. 282)

ancestro persona de la cual alguien desciende (pág. 282)

animism belief in spirits that are outside of the body (p. 518)

animismo creencia en espíritus que están fuera del cuerpo (pág. 518)

annul to declare invalid (p. 604)

anular declarar inválido (pág. 604)

anthropology the study of human culture and how it develops over time (pp. 8–9)

antropología estudio de la cultura humana y su desarrollo a lo largo del tiempo (págs. 8–9)

anti-Semitism hostility toward or discrimination against Jews (pp. 568–569)

antisemitismo hostilidad o discriminación hacia los judíos (págs. 568–569)

apartheid racial segregation system that was enforced in South Africa (pp. 782–783)

apartheid sistema de segregación racial que se implantó en Sudáfrica (págs. 782–783)

apostle Christian leader chosen by Jesus to spread his message (p. 377)

apóstol líder cristiano elegido por Jesús para difundir su mensaje (pág. 377)

appeasement trying to avoid war with an aggressive nation by giving in to its demands (pp. 754–755)

apaciguamiento tratar de evitar la guerra con una nación agresora cediendo a sus exigencias (págs. 754–755)

archaeology the study of objects to learn about past human life (p. 8)

arqueología estudio de objetos para conocer el pasado de la vida humana (pág. 8)

archipelago many scattered islands surrounded by an expanse of water (pp. 516–517)

archipiélago muchas islas dispersas rodeadas por una extensión de agua (págs. 516–517)

***area** the land included within a set of boundaries (pp. 422–423)

***área** terreno incluido dentro de un conjunto de límites (págs. 422–423)

aristocrat a member of an upper class of society, usually made up of hereditary nobility (p. 282)

aristócrata miembro de la clase alta de la sociedad o de la nobleza, por lo general formada por la nobleza hereditaria (pág. 282)

armistice a truce or temporary stop in battle; a cease-fire (pp. 734–735)

armisticio tregua o interrupción temporal en una batalla; cese al fuego (págs. 734–735)

artifact an object made by people (pp. 8–9)

artefacto objeto elaborado por las personas (págs. 8–9)

***assume** to take for granted to be true (p. 316)

***suponer** dar por hecho que algo es cierto (pág. 316)

astrolabe a tool that helps sailors navigate using the positions of the stars (p. 413)

astrolabio instrumento que ayuda a los marineros a navegar mediante la ubicación de las estrellas (pág. 413)

astronomer a person who studies planets and stars (p. 92)

astrónomo persona que estudia los planetas y las estrellas (pág. 92)

***authority** the right or power to give orders, make decisions, or control people; power over thoughts, opinions, and behavior (p. 125; pp. 400–401; pp. 572–573)

***autoridad** derecho o facultad de dar órdenes, tomar decisiones o controlar a las personas; poder sobre los pensamientos, las opiniones y el comportamiento (pág. 125; págs. 400–401; págs. 572–573) *available* ready to be used (p. 56)

awareness the state of having understanding or knowledge (p. 32)

disponible listo para usarse (pág. 56)

conciencia tener comprensión o conocimiento (pág. 32)

B

barbarians uncivilized people (p. 502)

bard someone who writes or performs epic poems or stories about heroes and their deeds (p. 178)

barter to trade by exchanging one good or service for another; to exchange goods without using money (p. 42)

bazaar a marketplace (p. 412)

behalf representing; in the place of (p. 518)

benefit to receive help; to gain (p. 310)

Bhagavad Gita a section of the Indian epic *The Mahabharata* (p. 269)

bias an unreasoned, emotional judgment about people or events (p. 12)

blockade the closing off of a port or harbor to prevent entrance or exit (pp. 732–733)

bourgeoisie the middle class in France (p. 673)

boycott to protest by refusing to do something (pp. 666–667)

Brahman the universal spirit worshiped by Hindus (pp. 257–258)

Bronze Age the period in ancient human culture when people began to make and use bronze (p. 67)

Buddhism a religion founded in ancient India by the religious teacher the Buddha (p. 260)

bureaucracy a group of non-elected government officials (p. 284)

bureaucrat a government official (p. 109)

bárbaros personas no civilizadas (pág. 502)

bardo persona que escribe o relata poemas épicos o historias sobre héroes y sus hazañas (pág. 178)

hacer trueque comerciar mediante el intercambio de un bien o servicio por otro; intercambiar productos sin usar dinero (pág. 42)

bazar mercado (pág. 412)

en nombre en representación; en lugar de (pág. 518)

beneficiarse recibir ayuda; obtener (pág. 310)

Bhagavad Gita sección de la epopeya india *el Mahabharata* (pág. 269)

parcialidad juicio emotivo o que no tiene fundamento racional acerca de personas o eventos (pág. 12)

bloqueo clausura de un puerto o espolón para evitar la entrada y la salida (págs. 732–733)

burguesía clase media francesa (pág. 673)

boicotear protestar negándose a hacer algo (págs. 666–667)

Brahmán espíritu universal adorado por los hindúes (págs. 257–258)

Edad del Bronce periodo de la cultura humana antigua en el cual las personas comenzaron a fabricar y usar el bronce (pág. 67)

budismo religión fundada en la antigua India por el maestro religioso Buda (pág. 260)

burocracia grupo de funcionarios del gobierno que no son elegidos (pág. 284)

burócrata funcionario del gobierno (pág. 109)

C

caliph a Muslim leader (p. 404)

califa líder musulmán (pág. 404)

Glossary/Glosario

***calligraphy** artistic handwriting (p. 486; p. 488)

*__calligraphy__ ...

*__caligrafía__ letra artística (pág. 486; pág. 488)

*__capable__ able, competent (p. 331)

*__capaz__ hábil, competente (pág. 331)

capital money and goods used to help people make or do things (pp. 38–39)

capital dinero y bienes usados para ayudar a las personas a hacer cosas (págs. 38-39)

caravan a group of merchants traveling together for safety, usually with a large number of camels; a group of traveling merchants and animals (p. 92; p. 400)

caravana grupo de mercaderes que viajan juntos por seguridad, usualmente con un gran número de camellos; grupo de mercaderes y animales que viajan (pág. 92; pág. 400)

cardinal directions north, south, east, and west (p. 35)

puntos cardinales norte, sur, este y oeste (pág. 35)

cash crops crops grown in large amounts to be sold for profit (p. 629)

cultivo comercial cultivo producido en grandes cantidades para venderlo y obtener ganancias (pág. 629)

cataract a waterfall or rapids in a river (p. 102)

catarata cascada o rápidos de un río (pág. 102)

cavalry part of an army in which the soldiers ride horses (p. 232)

caballería división de un ejército en la cual los soldados montan a caballo (pág. 232)

censor an official who watches others for correct behavior (p. 293)

censor funcionario que vigila el correcto comportamiento de otros (pág. 293)

census a count of the number of people in a country (pp. 499–500)

censo conteo del número de personas de un país (págs. 499–500)

*__challenge__ to invite the start of a competition; to present with difficulties (p. 130; pp. 432–433)

*__desafiar__ invitar para que se dé inicio a una competencia; presentarse con dificultades (pág. 130; págs. 432–433)

*__channel__ a straight or narrow sea between two land masses; a canal; narrow body of water between two land masses (p. 196; p. 280)

*__canal__ mar recto o estrecho que se encuentra entre dos masas continentales; masa de agua estrecha que se encuentra entre dos masas continentales (pág. 196; pág. 280)

checks and balances a system in which each branch of government limits the power of another branch (pp. 44–45)

equilibrio de poderes sistema en el cual cada rama del gobierno limita el poder de otra (págs. 44–45)

chivalry the system, spirit, or customs of medieval knighthood (pp. 549–550)

caballerosidad sistema, espíritu o costumbres de los caballeros medievales (págs. 549–550)

choropleth a special-purpose map that uses color to show population density (p. 36)

mapa de coropletas mapa temático que mediante colores muestra la densidad de población (pág. 36)

circumference the outer border of a circle; the measurement of that border (p. 239)

circunferencia borde externo de un círculo; medida de ese borde (pág. 239)

circumnavigate to go completely around something, such as the world (pp. 622–623)

circunnavegar rodear por completo algo, como por ejemplo el mundo (págs. 622–623)

city-state a city that governs itself and its surrounding territory (pp. 78–79)

ciudad-estado ciudad que se gobierna a sí misma y el territorio que la rodea (págs. 78–79)

civic duty the idea that citizens have a responsibility to help their country (p. 315)

deber cívico idea según la cual los ciudadanos tienen la responsabilidad de ayudar a su país (pág. 315)

*civil of or relating to citizens; relating to the state or government (p. 324; p. 476)

*civil relativo a los ciudadanos; relativo al Estado o al Gobierno (pág. 324; pág. 476)

civil service the administrative service of a government (p. 294)

servicio civil servicio administrativo de un gobierno (pág. 294)

clan a group of people descended from the same ancestor (p. 431)

clan grupo de personas que descienden del mismo ancestro (pág. 431)

clergy church officials (p. 384)

clero funcionarios de la Iglesia (pág. 384)

*code a set of official rules; a system of principles or rules (p. 87; pp. 549–550)

*código conjunto de leyes oficiales; sistema de principios o reglas (pág. 87; págs. 549–550)

collapse to break down; to lose effectiveness; complete failure, breakdown (p. 194; pp. 734–735)

colapsar derrumbarse; perder efectividad; el término en inglés "collapse" también significa "completo fracaso", "crisis" (pág. 194; págs. 734–735)

collectivization an economic system in which a government controls production and distribution of all goods (pp. 750–751)

colectivización sistema económico en el cual un gobierno controla la producción y distribución de todos los bienes (págs. 750–751)

colony a group of people living in a new territory who have ties to their homeland; a new territory (p. 179)

colonia grupo de personas que viven en un nuevo territorio y mantienen vínculos con su tierra natal; un territorio nuevo (pág. 179)

comedy a play or film that tells a humorous story (p. 217)

comedia obra de teatro o película que cuenta una historia humorística (pág. 217)

command economy an economic system in which a central government decides what goods will be made and who will receive them (p. 40)

economía planificada sistema económico en el cual un gobierno central decide qué bienes se producirán y quién los recibirá (pág. 40)

commandment a rule that God wanted the Israelites to follow (p. 143)

mandamiento regla que Dios quería que los israelitas cumplieran (pág. 143)

commerce an exchange of goods; business (p. 633)

comercio intercambio de bienes; negocio (pág. 633)

*commit to carry out or do (p. 261)

*cometer llevar a cabo o hacer (pág. 261)

*communicate to share information with someone; to exchange knowledge or information (p. 58; p. 156)

*comunicar compartir información con alguien; intercambiar conocimientos o información (pág. 58; pág. 156)

*community a group of people with common interests and values living in an area; people living in a particular area; an area (p. 157; pp. 174–175; p. 238; p. 381; pp. 436–437)

*comunidad grupo de personas con intereses y valores comunes que viven en un área; personas que viven en un área en particular; un área (pág. 157; págs. 174–175; pág. 238; pág. 381; págs. 436–437)

*complex having many parts, details, or ideas; made up of many related parts; complicated (pp. 90–91; p. 454; p. 586; p. 588)

*complejo que tiene muchas partes, detalles o ideas; que consta de muchas partes relacionadas (págs. 90–91; pág. 454; pág. 586; pág. 588)

*conclude to reach an understanding; to make a decision (p. 176)

*concluir llegar a un acuerdo; tomar una decisión (pág. 176)

Glossary/Glosario

conclusion a decision reached after examining evidence (p. 14)

concordat agreement between the pope and the ruler of a country (pp. 546–547)

***confirm** to prove that something is true; to remove doubt (p. 413)

***conflict** a battle or war; a fight or disagreement; a fight or battle (p. 203; pp. 218–219)

Confucianism a system of beliefs based on the teachings of Confucius (pp. 286–287)

conquistadors Spanish soldiers who conquered people in other lands (p. 622)

conscription citizens required to serve in the military of their country (p. 727)

***consequence** following as a result or effect (p. 764)

***consider** to give careful thought (pp. 183–184)

***considerable** large in size, quantity, or quality (p. 626)

***consist** to be made up of (p. 80)

***constant** always happening (p. 58)

constitution basic laws of a state that define the role of government and guarantee its obligation to the people; a document that describes how a country will be governed and guarantees people certain rights (p. 518; p. 666)

constitutional monarchy a political system in which the head of state is a king or queen who rules according to a constitution (p. 652)

***construct** to build by putting parts together; to build; to create (pp. 56–57; p. 115; p. 188; pp. 214–215, p. 714)

consul head of a government, usually with a limited term in office (p. 313)

***contact** communication or connection; interaction with other people (p. 344; pp. 438–439)

containment preventing the spread of communism beyond its existing borders (p. 770)

***contrast** the act of comparing by looking at differences (p. 330)

conclusión decisión que se toma luego de examinar evidencias (pág. 14)

concordato acuerdo entre el papa y el gobernante de un país (págs. 546–547)

***confirmar** demostrar que algo es verdadero; despejar dudas (pág. 413)

***conflicto** batalla o guerra; lucha o desacuerdo; lucha o batalla (pág. 203; págs. 218–219)

confucianismo sistema de creencias basado en las enseñanzas de Confucio (págs. 286–287)

conquistadores soldados españoles que conquistaron pueblos en otras tierras (pág. 622)

reclutamiento requisito que deben cumplir los ciudadanos de servir en el ejército de su país (pág. 727)

***consecuencia** que se da como resultado o efecto (pág. 764)

***considerar** pensar detenidamente (págs. 183–184)

***considerable** de gran tamaño, cantidad o calidad (pág. 626)

***constar** estar formado de (pág. 80)

***constante** que siempre sucede (pág. 58)

constitución leyes básicas de un estado que definen la función del gobierno y garantizan su obligación con el pueblo; documento que describe cómo será gobernado un país y garantiza a las personas algunos derechos (pág. 518; pág. 666)

monarquía constitucional sistema político en el cual el jefe de Estado es un rey o una reina que gobierna de acuerdo con una Constitución (pág. 652)

***construir** formar uniendo las partes; edificar; crear (págs. 56–57; pág. 115; pág. 188; págs. 214–215, pág. 714)

cónsul jefe de un gobierno, por lo general durante un tiempo limitado en el cargo (pág. 313)

***contacto** comunicación o conexión; interacción con otras personas (pág. 344; págs. 438–439)

contención evitar la expansión del comunismo más allá de sus fronteras actuales (pág. 770)

***contrastar** acción de comparar observando diferencias (pág. 330)

*__contribute__ to give or donate something (p. 269)

*__convene__ to come together (p. 761)

*__convert__ to accept a new belief; to bring from one belief to another (pp. 432–433; p. 502)

*__cooperate__ to work together for the good of all (pp. 560–561; pp. 698–699)

*__cooperation__ working together (p. 163)

__corporation__ a type of company that sells shares in the company to investors (p. 694)

__cottage industry__ making goods in workers' homes (p. 634)

__coup d'etat__ a change of government in which a new group of leaders seize power by force (p. 676)

__covenant__ an agreement with God (p. 142)

*__create__ to make or produce something; to bring something into existence; to produce by a course of action (pp. 230–231; p. 374)

__credentials__ something that gives confidence that a person is qualified for a task (p. 19)

*__crucial__ important or significant (p. 110)

*__culture__ the set of beliefs, behaviors, and traits shared by a group of people (pp. 36–37; pp. 140–141; p. 408; p. 629)

__cuneiform__ writing developed by the Sumerians that used wedge-shaped marks made in soft clay (p. 82)

*__currency__ something, such as coins or paper money, that is used as a medium of exchange; money in the form of coins or paper (p. 293; p. 586)

*__contribuir__ dar o donar algo (pág. 269)

*__congregarse__ reunirse (pág. 761)

*__convertir__ aceptar una nueva creencia; llevar de una creencia a otra (págs. 432–433; pág. 502)

*__cooperar__ trabajar juntos para el bien de todos (págs. 560–561; págs. 698–699)

*__cooperación__ trabajar juntos (pág. 163)

__sociedad anónima__ tipo de compañía que vende acciones de la compañía a inversionistas (pág. 694)

__industria casera__ fabricación de bienes en casa de los trabajadores (pág. 634)

__golpe de Estado__ cambio de gobierno en el cual un nuevo grupo de líderes se hace al poder por medio de la fuerza (pág. 676)

__alianza__ acuerdo con Dios (pág. 142)

*__crear__ hacer o producir algo; hacer que algo exista; producir mediante una serie de acciones (págs. 230–231; pág. 374)

__credenciales__ algo que brinda confianza con respecto a las cualificaciones de una persona para una tarea (pág. 19)

*__crucial__ importante o relevante (pág. 110)

*__cultura__ conjunto de creencias, comportamientos y características que comparte un grupo de personas (págs. 36–37; págs. 140–141; pág. 408; pág. 629)

__cuneiforme__ sistema de escritura desarrollado por los sumerios que consta de marcas en forma de cuña hechas sobre arcilla blanda (pág. 82)

*__moneda__ algo que se usa como medio de intercambio, como las monedas o el papel moneda; dinero en forma de monedas o billetes (pág. 293; pág. 586)

D

__Dao__ Chinese system of beliefs which describes the way a person must rule (pp. 284–285)

__Daoism__ a Chinese philosophy concerned with obtaining long life and living in harmony with nature (p. 288)

*__data__ information, usually facts and figures (p. 20)

__Tao__ sistema chino de creencias que describe la manera en que una persona debe gobernar (págs. 284–285)

__taoísmo__ filosofía china que se interesa en la forma de obtener larga vida y vivir en armonía con la naturaleza (pág. 288)

*__datos__ información, por lo general hechos y cifras (pág. 20)

Glossary/Glosario

D-Day June 6, 1944; the day on which Allied forces began the invasion of France in World War II (pp. 764–765)

Día D 6 de junio de 1944; el día en que las fuerzas de los Aliados empezaron la invasión de Francia durante la Segunda Guerra Mundial (págs. 764–765)

*decade a group or set of 10; period of 10 years (p. 5; p. 202)

*década grupo o conjunto de diez; periodo de diez años (pág. 5; pág. 202)

*decline to become weaker; to move toward a weaker condition; to decrease in importance (pp. 126–127; p. 177; p. 268; pp. 721–722)

*decaer debilitarse; moverse hacia una condición de mayor fragilidad; perder importancia (págs. 126–127; pág. 177; pág. 268; págs. 721–722)

deforestation cutting down trees and forests in an area (p. 796)

deforestación eliminación de árboles y bosques en un área (pág. 796)

delta a fan-shaped area of silt near where a river flows into the sea (p. 102)

delta área cenagosa en forma de abanico cercana al punto donde un río desemboca en el mar (pág. 102)

demand the amount of something that a consumer wants to buy (p. 39)

demanda cantidad de algo que los consumidores quieren comprar (pág. 39)

democracy a government by the people (p. 184)

democracia gobierno del pueblo (pág. 184)

depression a period of low general economic activity marked especially by rising levels of unemployment (p. 747)

depresión periodo de poca actividad económica general, marcado especialmente por altos niveles de desempleo (pág. 747)

descendant future member of a family (p. 349)

descendiente miembro futuro de una familia (pág. 349)

*design to skillfully plan or create something (p. 692)

*diseñar planear o crear algo con destreza (pág. 692)

*despite in spite of; regardless of (p. 222)

*a pesar de pese a que, sin tener en cuenta (pág. 222)

détente a relaxation of tension and increased understanding between nations (pp. 806–807)

distensión alivio de las tensiones y mayor entendimiento entre las naciones (págs. 806–807)

*devote to give one's time, effort, or attention earnestly (p. 309)

*dedicar brindar tiempo, esfuerzo o atención sinceramente (pág. 309)

*devotion dedication, a strong commitment (p. 163)

*devoción dedicación, compromiso sólido (pág. 163)

dharma a person's personal duty, based on the individual's place in society (pp. 258–259)

darma deber individual de una persona, de acuerdo con su lugar en la sociedad (págs. 258–259)

dhow sailboat using wind-catching, triangular sails (pp. 428–429)

dhow velero que usa velas triangulares para atrapar el viento (págs. 428–429)

Diaspora groups of Jews living outside of the Jewish homeland (pp. 160–161)

diáspora grupos de judíos que viven fuera de su territorio natal (págs. 160–161)

dictator a person with absolute power to rule (p. 314)

dictador persona con poder absoluto para gobernar (pág. 314)

din loud noise (p. 497)

bulla ruido alto (pág. 497)

diplomacy the practice of conducting negotiations between countries (p. 586; p. 588)

diplomacia práctica que consiste en realizar negociaciones entre países (pág. 586; pág. 588)

direct democracy a form of democracy in which all citizens can participate firsthand in the decision-making process (pp. 198–199)

disciple student (p. 497)

*****display** to place an object where people can view it (p. 387)

*****distort** to twist out of shape or change the size of (pp. 30–31)

*****distribute** to divide into shares and deliver the shares to different people; to give or deliver to members of a group (p. 109; p. 330; p. 464)

doctrine official church teaching (p. 384)

*****document** an official paper used as proof or support of something; a piece of writing (p. 166; p. 558; p. 666)

domesticate to adapt an animal to live with humans for the advantage of the humans (pp. 62–63)

*****dominate** to control or influence something or someone; to rule over, govern, or control (pp. 174–175; p. 728)

dominion rule, control (p. 719)

downtrodden people who are poor or suffering (p. 349)

drama a story written in the form of a play (p. 217)

dynasty a line of rulers from one family (pp. 106–107)

democracia directa forma de democracia en la cual todos los ciudadanos pueden participar directamente en el proceso de toma de decisiones (págs. 198–199)

discípulo estudiante (pág. 497)

*****exponer** colocar un objeto donde las personas puedan verlo (pág. 387)

*****distorsionar** deformar o cambiar el tamaño de algo (págs. 30–31)

*****distribuir** dividir en partes y repartirlas entre diferentes personas; dar o repartir a los miembros de un grupo (pág. 109; pág. 330; pág. 464)

doctrina enseñanza oficial de la Iglesia (pág. 384)

*****documento** texto oficial que se usa como prueba o respaldo de algo; escrito (pág. 166; pág. 558; pág. 666)

domesticar adaptar a un animal para que viva con los seres humanos para provecho de estos (págs. 62–63)

*****dominar** controlar o ejercer influencia sobre algo o alguien; reinar, gobernar o controlar (págs. 174–175; pág. 728)

dominio gobierno, control (pág. 719)

oprimidos personas pobres o que están sufriendo (pág. 349)

drama historia escrita en forma de obra de teatro (pág. 217)

dinastía línea de gobernantes de una familia (págs. 106–107)

E

*****economic** the system in a country that involves making, buying, and selling goods (p. 176)

*****economy** the system of economic life in an area or country; an economy deals with the making, buying, or selling of goods and services (p. 64; p. 572)

.edu the ending of a URL of a Web site for an educational institution (p. 20)

elements substances that consist of atoms of only one kind (p. 648)

ellipses shapes like stretched circles; ovals (pp. 644–645)

*****económico** sistema de un país que implica la elaboración, compra y venta de productos (pág. 176)

*****economía** sistema de la vida económica en un área o un país; la economía se relaciona con la elaboración, compra y venta de productos o servicios (pág. 64; pág. 572)

.edu parte final del URL (por sus siglas en inglés) del sitio web de una institución educativa (pág. 20)

elementos sustancias formadas por átomos de un solo tipo (pág. 648)

elipses figuras semejantes a círculos estirados; óvalos (págs. 644–645)

embalming the process of treating a body to prevent it from decaying (p. 111)

embalsamamiento proceso que consiste en tratar un cuerpo para evitar que se descomponga (pág. 111)

embargo a ban on trading or doing business with another country (pp. 792–793)

embargo prohibición del comercio o los negocios con otra nación (págs. 792–793)

embrace to hug someone (p. 85)

abrazar estrechar entre los brazos a alguien (pág. 85)

*emerge to come into being or become known (p. 252; pp. 278–279)

*surgir llegar a ser o darse a conocer (pág. 252; págs. 278–279)

*emphasize to attach a sense of importance to something; to express the importance of something (p. 203)

*poner énfasis dar importancia a algo; expresar la importancia de algo (pág. 203)

empire a large territory or group of many territories governed by one ruler (pp. 86–87)

imperio gran territorio o grupo de muchos territorios a cargo de un gobernante (págs. 86–87)

*enable to make possible (p. 326)

*permitir hacer posible (pág. 326)

*ensure to make certain or make sure of (pp. 146–147; p. 518)

*asegurar tener certeza o garantizar (págs. 146–147; pág. 518)

entente a formal agreement between two nations to cooperate for specific purposes (p. 728)

entente acuerdo formal de cooperación entre dos naciones para propósitos específicos (pág. 728)

entrepreneur one who organizes, pays for, and takes on the risk of setting up a business (p. 633)

empresario persona que organiza, paga y asume el riesgo de establecer un negocio (pág. 633)

entrepreneurship the act of running a business and taking on the risks of that business (pp. 38–39)

espíritu empresarial acción de dirigir un negocio y asumir los riesgos de ese negocio (págs. 38–39)

envoy a government representative to another country (p. 123)

enviado representante de un gobierno ante otro país (pág. 123)

ephor a high-ranked government official in Sparta who was elected by the council of elders (p. 186)

éforo funcionario del gobierno de alto rango en Esparta a quien elegía el consejo de ancianos (pág. 186)

epic a long poem that records the deeds of a legendary or real hero (pp. 82–83)

epopeya poema largo que registra las hazañas de un héroe legendario o real (págs. 82–83)

Epicureanism the philosophy of Epicurus, stating that the purpose of life is to look for happiness and peace (p. 238)

epicureísmo filosofía instaurada por Epicuro, la cual afirmaba que el propósito de la vida es la búsqueda de la felicidad y la paz (pág. 238)

era a large division of time (p. 5)

era gran división de tiempo (pág. 5)

*establish to start; to bring into existence (p. 544; p. 770)

*establecer iniciar; hacer que exista (pág. 544; pág. 770)

estate a social class in France before the French Revolution (pp. 672–673)

estado una de las clases sociales en Francia antes de la Revolución francesa (págs. 672–673)

*estimate to determine an approximate value, size, or nature of something (p. 262)

*estimar determinar el valor, el tamaño o la naturaleza aproximados de algo (pág. 262)

*ethnic a group of people united by common racial, national, tribal, religious, linguistic, or cultural origin or background (pp. 778–779)

*etnia grupo de personas unidas por compartir su origen o su entorno racial, nacional, tribal, religioso, lingüístico o cultural (págs. 778–779)

ethnic cleansing the use of force to remove or kill an entire ethnic group (p. 809)

limpieza étnica uso de la fuerza para eliminar o asesinar a todo un grupo étnico (pág. 809)

*****eventual** taking place at an unnamed later time; later; final or ultimate; (p. 266; p. 308; p. 688)

*****final** que ocurre en un tiempo futuro indeterminado; posterior o último (pág. 266; pág. 308; pág. 688)

evidence something that shows proof or an indication that something is true (pp. 10–11)

evidencia algo que proporciona pruebas o indicios de que algo es cierto (págs. 10–11)

excommunicate to declare that a person or group is no longer a member of the church (p. 389)

excomulgar declarar que una persona o un grupo ya no son miembros de la Iglesia (pág. 389)

executive branch the part of government that enforces laws (pp. 44–45)

poder ejecutivo rama del gobierno que hace cumplir las leyes (págs. 44–45)

extended family a family made up of several generations (pp. 436–437)

familia extendida familia compuesta por varias generaciones (págs. 436–437)

Exodus the departure of the Israelites out of slavery in Egypt (p. 142)

éxodo salida de los israelitas de Egipto que puso fin a su esclavitud (pág. 142)

exile a forced absence from one's home or country (pp. 152–153)

exilio ausencia obligada del propio hogar o país (págs. 152–153)

*****expand** to enlarge; to spread out; to increase the number, volume, or scope (p. 162; pp. 352–353; p. 644)

*****ampliar** agrandar; extender; aumentar el número, el volumen o el alcance (pág. 162; págs. 352–353; pág. 644)

*****expert** a skilled person who has mastered a subject (p. 41)

*****experto** persona cualificada que domina una materia (pág. 41)

export a good that is sent from one country to another (p. 42)

exportación producto enviado de un país a otro (pág. 42)

*****extract** to remove by a physical or chemical process (p. 145)

*****extraer** eliminar mediante un proceso físico o químico (pág. 145)

extraterritoriality legal practice of foreigners living in a country who are not subject to the laws of that country (p. 721)

extraterritorialidad práctica legal de los extranjeros que viven en país, quienes no están sujetos a las leyes de ese país (pág. 721)

F

fable a story meant to teach a lesson (p. 216)

fábula historia que busca enseñar una lección (pág. 216)

feat achievement, success (p. 597)

hazaña logro, éxito (pág. 597)

*****federal** referring to an organized union of states under one government (pp. 670–671)

*****federal** relativo a una unión organizada de estados bajo un gobierno (págs. 670–671)

federal system a government in which power is divided between central and state governments (pp. 44–45)

sistema federal gobierno en el cual el poder está dividido entre el gobierno central y los gobiernos estatales (págs. 44–45)

feudalism the system of service between a lord and the vassals who have sworn loyalty to the lord; political order; under feudalism, nobles governed and protected people in return for services (p. 523; pp. 548–549)

feudalismo sistema de servicio entre un señor y los vasallos que le han jurado lealtad; orden político; en el feudalismo, los nobles gobernaban y protegían a las personas a cambio de sus servicios (pág. 523; págs. 548–549)

Glossary/Glosario

Glossary/Glosario

fief a feudal estate belonging to a vassal (p. 549)

filial piety the responsibility of children to respect, obey, and care for their parents (pp. 290–291)

*finite limited; having boundaries (p. 14)

fjord a narrow inlet of the sea between cliffs or steep slopes (p. 544)

*focus to place all of one's attention on something; direct attention (p. 260; pp. 760–761)

fossil plant or animal remains that have been preserved from an earlier time (pp. 8–9)

*found to create or set up something such as a city; to set up or establish; established or took the first steps in building; (p. 6; p. 151; p. 307; p. 686)

feudo propiedad feudal perteneciente a un vasallo (pág. 549)

piedad filial responsabilidad que tienen los hijos de respetar, obedecer y cuidar a sus padres (págs. 290–291)

*finito limitado; que tiene límites (pág. 14)

fiordo entrada estrecha del mar entre acantilados o pendientes empinadas (pág. 544)

*enfocar poner toda la atención en algo; dirigir la atención (pág. 260; págs. 760-761)

fósil restos vegetales o animales que se han preservado desde una época anterior (págs. 8–9)

*fundar crear o instituir algo, como una ciudad; establecer o formar (pág. 6; pág. 151; pág. 307; pág. 686)

G

*generation a group of individuals born and living at the same time; the time span between the birth of parents and the birth of their children (p. 295; pp. 648–649)

genocide the deliberate killing of an ethnic group (p. 735)

geocentric an Earth-centered theory; having or relating to the Earth as the center (p. 643)

gladiator in ancient Rome, a person who fought people or animals for public entertainment (p. 341)

glasnost a Soviet policy allowing for free discussion of political and social ideas (p. 807)

*global involving the entire Earth (pp. 626–627)

globalization the growth in free trade between countries (pp. 42–43)

Glorious Revolution the overthrow of King James II of England (p. 652)

*goal something that a person works to achieve; aim (p. 566)

gospel the accounts that apostles wrote of Jesus' life (pp. 384–385)

.gov the ending of an Internet URL of a government Web site (p. 20)

*generación grupo de individuos que nacen y viven en la misma época; periodo de tiempo entre el nacimiento de los padres y el nacimiento de sus hijos (pág. 295; págs. 648–649)

genocidio exterminio deliberado de un grupo étnico (pág. 735)

geocéntrico teoría centrada en la Tierra; que tiene o se relaciona con la Tierra como el centro (pág. 643)

gladiador en la antigua Roma, alguien que se enfrentaba a una persona o a un animal para entretener al público (pág. 341)

glasnost política soviética que permitió el libre debate de ideas políticas y sociales (pág. 807)

*global que implica toda la Tierra (págs. 626–627)

globalización crecimiento del libre comercio entre los países (págs. 42–43)

Revolución Gloriosa derrocamiento del rey Jacobo II de Inglaterra (pág. 652)

*meta algo que una persona se esfuerza por alcanzar; objetivo (pág. 566)

evangelio relato que los apóstoles escribieron sobre la vida de Jesús (págs. 384–385)

.gov parte final del URL de un sitio web del gobierno (pág. 20)

grand jury a group of citizens that meets to decide whether people should be accused of a crime (p. 558)

gravity the attraction that the Earth or another celestial body has on an object on or near its surface (pp. 646–647)

griot traditional storyteller (pp. 426–427)

guarantee to promise (p. 432)

*guarantee something that is assured or certain (pp. 652–653)

guerrilla warfare a form of war in which soldiers make surprise attacks on the enemy (pp. 684–685)

guild a group of merchants or craftsmen during medieval times; a group of merchants or craftspeople (p. 524; pp. 554–555)

guru a teacher (p. 254; p. 256)

gran jurado grupo de ciudadanos que se reúne para decidir si se debe acusar a una persona de un crimen (pág. 558)

gravedad atracción que la Tierra u otro cuerpo celeste ejerce sobre un objeto que se encuentra en su superficie o cerca de esta (págs. 646–647)

griot narrador tradicional (págs. 426–427)

garantizar prometer (pág. 432)

*garantía algo que se asegura o es cierto (págs. 652–653)

guerra de guerrillas forma de guerra en la cual los soldados lanzan ataques sorpresivos al enemigo (págs. 684–685)

gremio grupo de mercaderes o artesanos durante la Edad Media; grupo de mercaderes o artesanos (pág. 524; págs. 554–555)

gurú maestro (pág. 254; pág. 256)

H

heliocentric having or relating to the sun as the center of the solar system (p. 644)

Hellenistic Era the time period following the death of Alexander during which Greek culture spread through the known world (pp. 234–235)

helot enslaved person in ancient Sparta (p. 185)

hemisphere a "half sphere," used to refer to one-half of the globe when divided into North and South or East and West (p. 29)

hereditary having title or possession by reason of birth (p. 284)

heresy ideas that go against Church teachings; a religious belief that contradicts what the Church says is true (pp. 568–569; p. 607)

*hierarchy an organization with different levels of authority; a classification into ranks (p. 383)

hieroglyphics a writing system made up of a combination of pictures and sound symbols (p. 105)

Hinduism a major religion that developed in ancient India (pp. 257–258)

heliocéntrico que tiene o se relaciona con el Sol como centro del sistema solar (pág. 644)

Época helenística periodo posterior a la muerte de Alejandro, durante el cual la cultura griega se difundió por todo el mundo conocido (págs. 234–235)

ilota persona esclavizada de la antigua Esparta (pág. 185)

hemisferio "media esfera"; término usado para referirse a la mitad del planeta al dividirlo en Norte y Sur, o en Este y Oeste (pág. 29)

hereditario que tiene el título o la posesión debido a su nacimiento (pág. 284)

herejía ideas que van en contra de las enseñanzas de la Iglesia; creencia religiosa que contradice lo que la Iglesia dice que es cierto (págs. 568–569; pág. 607)

*jerarquía organización con diferentes niveles de autoridad; clasificación en categorías (pág. 383)

jeroglíficos sistema de escritura formado por una combinación de imágenes y símbolos que representan sonidos (pág. 105)

hinduismo religión de gran importancia que se desarrolló en la antigua India (págs. 257–258)

Glossary/Glosario

Hippocratic Oath a set of promises about patient care that new doctors make when they start practicing medicine (pp. 226–227)

Juramento Hipocrático conjunto de promesas acerca del cuidado de los pacientes que los nuevos médicos hacen cuando empiezan a ejercer su profesión (págs. 226–227)

hogan a square wooden home of Native Americans (pp. 466–467)

hogan casa cuadrada de madera de los indígenas americanos (págs. 466–467)

hostage someone held against his or her will in exchange for something (p. 626)

rehén alguien retenido en contra de su voluntad a cambio de algo (pág. 626)

humanism an emphasis on worldly concerns; belief in the worth of the individual and that reason is the path to knowledge (pp. 589–590)

humanismo énfasis en las preocupaciones terrenales; creencia de que la razón es el camino al conocimiento, y en el valor del individuo (págs. 589–590)

I

Ice Age a time when glaciers covered much of the land (p. 60)

Era de Hielo tiempo en el cual los glaciares cubrían la mayor parte de la Tierra (pág. 60)

icon a representation of an object of worship (p. 387)

ícono representación de un objeto de adoración (pág. 387)

iconoclast originally: a person who destroys icons; today: a person who criticizes traditional beliefs (p. 387)

iconoclasta originalmente, persona que destruye íconos; hoy, persona que critica las creencias tradicionales (pág. 387)

ideograph a symbol in a writing system that represents a thing or idea (p. 282)

ideograma símbolo en un sistema escrito que representa un objeto o una idea (pág. 282)

*immigrant one who moves to another country and settles there (pp. 792–793)

*inmigrante persona que se traslada a otro país y se establece allí (págs. 792–793)

imperialism policy of one nation directly or indirectly controlling the political or economic life of other nations (pp. 710–711)

imperialismo política en la cual una nación controla directa o indirectamente la vida política o económica de otras naciones (págs. 710–711)

import a good brought into a country from another country (p. 42)

importación producto que entra a un país procedente de otro (pág. 42)

*impose to establish by force or authority (p. 602)

*imponer establecer mediante la fuerza o la autoridad (pág. 602)

incense a material that produces a pleasant smell when burned (p. 123)

incienso material que produce un aroma agradable al quemarlo (pág. 123)

*individual a single human being; human being; person (pp. 40–41; p. 223; p. 287)

*individuo un solo ser humano; ser humano; persona (págs. 40–41; pág. 223; pág. 287)

indulgence a pardon, or forgiveness, of a sin (pp. 598–599)

indulgencia perdón, o exoneración, de un pecado (págs. 598–599)

industrialism an economic system where machines do work that was once performed by animals or humans (pp. 690–691)

industrialismo sistema económico en el cual las máquinas realizan el trabajo que antes realizaban los animales o las personas (págs. 690–691)

inflation a continued rise in prices or the supply of money; a period of rapidly increasing prices (p. 41)

inflación aumento continuo de los precios o de la oferta de dinero; periodo de rápido aumento de los precios (pág. 41)

***innovation** the introduction of something new (pp. 316–317)

***innovación** introducción de algo nuevo (págs. 316–317)

***inspect** to look over carefully (p. 329)

***inspeccionar** examinar de una manera cuidadosa (pág. 329)

institution a custom or practice that many people accept and use (pp. 532–533)

institución costumbre o práctica que muchas personas aceptan y usan (págs. 532–533)

***integral** essential, necessary (pp. 4–5)

***integral** esencial, necesario (págs. 4-5)

***intensify** to become stronger (pp. 316–317)

***intensificar** hacerse más fuerte (págs. 316–317)

interdependent relying on one another for goods, information, and other resources (p. 816)

interdependientes que dependen unos de otros para obtener productos, información y otros recursos (pág. 816)

***interpret** to explain the meaning of (p. 375)

***interpretar** explicar el significado de algo (pág. 375)

***interpretation** an explanation of the meaning of something (pp. 14–15)

***interpretación** explicación del significado de algo (págs. 14–15)

***intervene** to come between in order to prevent something (pp. 754–755)

***intervenir** interponerse para evitar algo (págs. 754–755)

intifada the rebellion of Palestinians against Israeli occupation (pp. 802–803)

intifada rebelión de los palestinos contra la ocupación israelí (págs. 802–803)

***invest** to give money to a company in exchange for a return, or profit, on the money; to put money in new businesses or other money-making projects (p. 633)

***invertir** dar dinero a una compañía a cambio de rendimientos, o ganancias, sobre el dinero; colocar dinero en nuevas empresas y otros proyectos lucrativos (pág. 633)

***investigate** to observe or study by examining closely and questioning systematically (pp. 224–225)

***investigar** observar o estudiar examinando detenidamente y formulando preguntas de manera sistemática (págs. 224–225)

***involve** to include (p. 307)

***involucrar** incluir (pág. 307)

irrigation a system that supplies dry land with water through ditches, pipes, or streams (p. 77)

irrigación sistema que abastece de agua los terrenos secos mediante zanjas, tuberías o corrientes (pág. 77)

Islam a religion based on the teachings of Muhammad (pp. 398–399)

islam religión basada en las enseñanzas de Mahoma (págs. 398–399)

***isolate** to separate from others; to separate from other populated areas; to set apart from others (p. 102; p. 399; pp. 516–517)

***aislar** separar de otros; separar de otras áreas pobladas; apartar de otros (pág. 102; pág. 399; págs. 516–517)

***issue** a concern or problem that has not yet been solved (p. 46)

***asunto** inquietud o problema que aún no se ha resuelto (pág. 46)

isthmus a narrow piece of land linking two larger areas of land (p. 450)

istmo porción estrecha de tierra que une dos áreas más grandes de tierra (pág. 450)

Glossary/Glosario

J

Jainism a religion of ancient India that does not believe in a supreme being, but emphasizes nonviolence and respect for all living things (p. 263)

jainismo religión de la antigua India que no cree en un ser supremo sino que enfatiza en la no violencia y el respeto a todos los seres vivos (pág. 263)

judicial branch part of government that interprets laws (p. 45)

poder judicial rama del gobierno que interpreta las leyes (pág. 45)

*jury a group of people sworn to make a decision in a legal case (pp. 45–46)

*jurado grupo de personas que prestan juramento para tomar una decisión en un caso legal (págs. 45–46)

K

kaiser emperor of Germany (p. 686)

káiser emperador de Alemania (pág. 686)

karma a force that decides the form that people will be reborn into in their next lives (pp. 258–259)

karma fuerza que decide la forma en que las personas renacerán en sus próximas vidas (págs. 258–259)

knight a mounted man-at-arms serving a feudal superior (p. 549)

caballero hombre armado que cabalga y sirve a un superior feudal (pág. 549)

kosher prepared according to Jewish dietary law (p. 158)

kosher preparado de acuerdo con la ley judía sobre la alimentación (pág. 158)

L

*labor the ability of people to do work; work; the tasks that workers perform (pp. 38–39; pp. 112–113; pp. 522–523)

*mano de obra capacidad de las personas para trabajar; tareas que los trabajadores realizan (págs. 38–39; págs. 112-113; págs. 522–523)

labor union an organization of those employed who work together to improve wages and working conditions (p. 700)

sindicato organización de empleados que trabajan juntos para mejorar sus salarios y condiciones laborales (pág. 700)

laity regular church members (p. 383)

laicado miembros regulares de la Iglesia (pág. 383)

language family a group of similar languages (p. 253)

familia lingüística grupo de idiomas semejantes (pág. 253)

latifundia large farming estates (p. 321)

latifundios propiedades agrícolas de gran tamaño (pág. 321)

latitude imaginary lines that circle the Earth parallel to the Equator (p. 30)

latitud líneas imaginarias que rodean la Tierra en dirección paralela al ecuador (pág. 30)

*legal of or relating to the law (p. 362)

*legal relativo a la ley (pág. 362)

legalism a Chinese philosophy that stressed the importance of laws (p. 289)

*legalismo filosofía china que resaltaba la importancia de las leyes (pág. 289)

legion large groups of Roman soldiers (p. 310)

legion grupos numerosos de soldados romanos (pág. 310)

legislative branch the part of government that passes laws (pp. 44–45)

poder legislativo rama del gobierno que aprueba las leyes (págs.44–45)

*****legislature** a group of people who make the laws (p. 313)

*****asamblea legislativa** grupo de personas que hace las leyes (pág. 313)

liberalism a political philosophy based on the Enlightenment ideas of equality and individual rights (p. 698)

liberalismo filosofía política basada en la Ilustración y en las ideas de igualdad y derechos individuales (pág. 698)

limited government a government whose powers are restricted through laws or a constitution (pp. 670–671)

gobierno limitado gobierno cuyos poderes los restringen las leyes o la Constitución (págs. 670–671)

*****link** a connecting element or factor; to connect; to join (p. 298; pp. 452–453)

*****vínculo** elemento o factor que conecta; el término en inglés "link" también significa "conectar"; "unir" (pág. 298; págs. 452–453)

*****locate** set up in a particular place (p. 65)

*****localizarse** establecerse en un lugar en particular (pág. 65)

longitude imaginary lines that circle the Earth from the North Pole to the South Pole, measuring distance east or west of the Prime Meridian (p. 30)

longitud líneas imaginarias que rodean la Tierra desde el Polo Norte hasta el Polo Sur, que miden la distancia al este o al oeste del meridiano principal (pág. 30)

M

*****maintain** to keep in the same state; to continue (p. 432; p. 800)

*****mantener** conservar en el mismo estado; continuar (pág. 432; pág. 800)

maize corn (p. 454)

maíz elote (pág. 454)

mandate a territory that was officially controlled by the League of Nations but is governed by a member nation (pp. 736–737)

mandato territorio controlado oficialmente por la Sociedad de Naciones pero que lo gobierna otra nación miembro (págs. 736–737)

Mandate of Heaven the belief that the Chinese king's right to rule came from the gods (p. 284)

mandato divino creencia de que el derecho de gobernar del emperador chino venía de los dioses (pág. 284)

*****manual** involving physical effort; work done by hand (p. 118; p. 254; p. 256)

*****manual** que implica esfuerzo físico; trabajo elaborado a mano (pág. 118; pág. 254; pág. 256)

maritime related to the sea or seafaring (p. 530)

marítimo relacionado con el mar o los marineros (pág. 530)

Marshall Plan U.S. program that gave aid to European countries to help them rebuild after the war to prevent Soviet expansion (p. 770)

Plan Marshall Programa estadounidense de auxilio a los países europeos que ayudó a su reconstrucción después de la guerra para evitar la expansión soviética (pág. 770)

martial arts sports that involve combat and self-defense (pp. 524–525)

artes marciales deportes que implican combate y defensa personal (págs. 524–525)

martyr a person who is willing to die for his or her beliefs (p. 382)

mártir persona dispuesta a morir por sus creencias (pág. 382)

mass religious worship service for Catholic Christians (p. 568)

misa culto religioso de los cristianos católicos (pág. 568)

Glossary/Glosario

matrilineal tracing descent through mothers rather than fathers (p. 437)

matrilineal linaje que se traza teniendo en cuenta la línea materna, no la paterna (pág. 437)

***medical** relating to the practice of medicine (p. 344)

***médico** relativo al ejercicio de la medicina (pág. 344)

***meditate** to focus one's thoughts to gain a higher level of spiritual awareness (p. 260)

***meditar** enfocar los pensamientos para alcanzar un nivel más elevado de conciencia espiritual (pág. 260)

mercantilism an economic theory that depends on a greater amount of exports than imports in order to increase a country's supply of gold and silver (p. 632)

mercantilismo teoría económica que depende de una mayor cantidad de exportaciones que de importaciones para aumentar la oferta de oro y plata de un país (pág. 632)

mercenary a soldier who fights for money rather than loyalty to a country (p. 584)

mercenario soldado que combate por dinero y no por lealtad a un país (pág. 584)

***method** a way of doing something; a procedure or process (p. 56; p. 239; p. 484; p. 633)

***método** manera de hacer algo; procedimiento o proceso (pág. 56; pág. 239; pág. 484; pág. 633)

***migrate** to move from one place to another (p. 252)

***migrar** desplazarse de un lugar a otro (pág. 252)

migration the movement of people from one place to another place (p. 36)

migración desplazamiento de personas de un lugar a otro (pág. 36)

militarism a support for war and military power (p. 727)

militarismo apoyo a la guerra y al poderío militar (pág. 727)

***military** of or relating to soldiers, arms, or war; the armed forces (p. 87; p. 185; p. 281; p. 549; pp. 656–657; p. 774)

***militar** relativo a los soldados, las armas o la guerra; las fuerzas armadas (pág. 87; pág. 185; pág. 281; pág. 549; págs. 656–657; pág. 774)

minaret the tower of a mosque from which Muslims are called to pray (pp. 414–415)

alminar torre de una mezquita desde la cual se convoca a los musulmanes a orar (págs. 414–415)

***minimal** the least possible (pp. 818–819)

***mínimo** lo menos posible (págs. 818–819)

missionaries people who are sent by a religious organization to spread the faith (p. 546)

misioneros personas enviadas por una organización religiosa a difundir la fe (pág. 546)

mobilization assembling armed forces into readiness for a conflict (pp. 728–729)

movilización proceso de reunir las fuerzas armadas y prepararlas para un conflicto (págs. 728–729)

monarchy a government whose ruler, a king or queen, inherits the position from a parent (p. 68)

monarquía gobierno cuyo jefe, un rey o una reina, hereda el cargo de uno de sus padres (pág. 68)

monastery a religious community (p. 389)

monasterio comunidad religiosa (pág. 389)

monotheism a belief in one God (pp. 140–141)

monoteísmo creencia en un solo Dios (págs. 140–141)

monsoon seasonal wind, especially in the Indian Ocean and southern Asia (p. 249)

monzón viento estacional, especialmente en el océano Índico y el sur de Asia (pág. 249)

mosaics images created by an arrangement of colored glass or stone (p. 364)

mosaicos imágenes creadas con vidrios o piedras de colores (pág. 364)

mosque a Muslim house of worship (p. 412)

mezquita casa musulmana de culto (pág. 412)

myth a traditional story that explains the practices or beliefs of a people or something in the natural world (pp. 212–213)

mito historia tradicional que explica las prácticas o creencias de un pueblo, o algo en el mundo natural (págs. 212–213)

N

nationalism the desire of people with the same customs and beliefs for self-rule (pp. 682–683)

nacionalismo deseo de autogobierno de las personas con las mismas costumbres y creencias (págs. 682–683)

nationalize to place private property under the control of a government (pp. 792–793)

nacionalizar poner propiedad privada bajo el control de un gobierno (págs. 792–793)

neo-Confucianism a new form of the ideas of the philosopher Confucius; included Buddhist and Daoist beliefs (p. 480)

neoconfucianismo nueva forma de las ideas del filósofo Confucio; incluía las creencias budistas y taoístas (pág. 480)

Neolithic Age relating to the latest period of the Stone Age (pp. 62–63)

Era Neolítica relativo al último periodo de la Edad de Piedra (págs. 62–63)

*network a connected group or system; a system where all parts are connected (p. 297; p. 530)

*red grupo o sistema conectado; sistema donde todas las partes están conectadas (pág. 297; pág. 530)

*neutral not taking sides or not getting involved (pp. 728–729; p. 758)

*neutral que no toma partido ni se involucra (págs. 728–729; pág. 758)

nirvana in Buddhism, a state of perfect happiness and peace (p. 261)

nirvana en el Budismo, estado de felicidad y paz perfecta (pág. 261)

nomads people who move from place to place as a group to find food (pp. 54–55)

nómadas personas que viajan de un lugar a otro en búsqueda de alimento (págs. 54–55)

novel a long fictional story (p. 500)

novela historia de ficción larga (pág. 500)

*nuclear having to do with the nucleus of an atom, such as the energy created by a nuclear explosion (p. 772)

*nuclear que tiene que ver con el núcleo de un átomo, como la energía creada por una explosión nuclear (pág. 772)

O

oasis a green area in a desert fed by underground water (pp. 398–399)

oasis área verde en el desierto que se alimenta de agua subterránea (págs. 398–399)

obstacle something that stands in the way (p. 85)

obstáculo algo que se interpone en el camino (pág. 85)

*obtain to gain something through a planned effort; to acquire or receive something; to take possession of (p. 118; p. 191; p. 620)

*obtener conseguir algo mediante un esfuerzo planificado; adquirir o recibir algo; tomar posesión de (pág. 118; pág. 191; pág. 620)

*occur to happen (p. 308)

*ocurrir suceder (pág. 308)

ode a lyric poem that expresses strong emotions about life (pp. 346–347)

oda poema lírico que expresa fuertes emociones acerca de la vida (págs. 346–347)

oligarchy a government in which a small group has control (p. 184)

oligarquía gobierno en el cual un grupo pequeño tiene control (pág. 184)

ongoing continuously moving forward (p. 502)

en curso que se mueve continuamente hacia delante (pág. 502)

opportunity cost what is given up, such as time or money, to make or buy something (p. 40)

costo de oportunidad lo que se entrega, como tiempo o dinero, para hacer o comprar algo (pág. 40)

oracle a sacred shrine where a priest or priestess spoke for a god or goddess (p. 214)

oráculo templo sagrado donde un sacerdote o una sacerdotisa hablaba en nombre de un dios o una diosa (pág. 214)

oral history stories passed down from generation to generation (p. 438)

historia oral historias transmitidas de generación en generación (pág. 438)

oral tradition the custom of passing along stories by speech (pp. 216–217)

tradición oral costumbre de transmitir historias verbalmente (págs. 216–217)

orator a public speaker (p. 349)

orador persona que habla en público (pág. 349)

.org the ending of an Internet URL for an organization (p. 20)

.org parte final del URL de una organización (pág. 20)

*__overseas__ across the ocean or sea (pp. 618–619; pp. 678–679)

*__ultramar__ cruzando el océano o el mar (págs. 618–619; págs. 678–679)

P

Paleolithic relating to the earliest period of the Stone Age (pp. 54–55)

Paleolítico relativo al periodo más antiguo de la Edad de Piedra (págs. 54–55)

paleontology the study of fossils (pp. 8–9)

paleontología estudio de los fósiles (págs. 8–9)

Pan-Africanism a movement for the political union of all African nations (pp. 782–783)

panafricanismo movimiento por la unión política de todas las naciones africanas (págs. 782–783)

pandemic an outbreak of disease that occurs over a wide geographic area and affects an exceptionally high number of people (pp. 818–819)

pandemia brote generalizado de una enfermedad que ocurre en una amplia área geográfica y afecta un número de personas excepcionalmente alto (págs. 818–819)

papyrus a reed plant that grows wild along the Nile River (pp. 104–105)

papiro planta hueca que crece a lo largo del río Nilo (págs 104–105)

parable a short story that teaches moral lesson (p. 375)

parábola historia corta que enseña una lección moral (pág. 375)

*__parallel__ moving or lying in the same direction and the same distance apart (p. 77)

*__paralelo__ que se mueve o se extiende en la misma dirección y a la misma distancia (pág. 77)

*__participate__ to take part (p. 356)

*__participar__ tomar parte (pág. 356)

patriarch an older male figure of authority, often within a religious community (p. 497)

patriarca figura masculina de edad mayor que representa la autoridad, con frecuencia dentro de una comunidad religiosa (pág. 497)

patricians the ruling class of ancient Rome (pp. 312–313)

patricios clase gobernante de la antigua Roma (págs. 312–313)

Pax Romana Roman peace (pp. 328–329)

Pax Romana paz romana (págs. 328–329)

peninsula a piece of land nearly surrounded by water (pp. 174–175)

perestroika a Soviet plan of reforming government and economic policies (p. 807)

***period** a division of time that is shorter than an era (p. 150)

persecute to treat a group of people cruelly or unfairly (pp. 664–665)

***perspective** a way of showing the relationship between objects in a drawing to give the look of depth or distance (p. 592)

phalanx a group of armed foot soldiers in ancient Greece arranged close together in rows (p. 182)

pharaoh ruler of ancient Egypt (pp. 108–109)

philosopher a person who searches for wisdom or enlightenment (p. 199)

***philosophy** the study of the basic ideas about society, education, and right and wrong; basic beliefs, concepts, and attitudes (pp. 286–287; p. 344)

physical map a map that shows land and water features (p. 34)

pictograph a symbol in a writing system based on pictures (p. 282)

pilgrim a person who travels to holy sites (p. 268)

plagiarize to present someone's work as your own without giving that person credit (pp. 20–21)

plague a disease that spreads quickly and kills many people (p. 570)

plane geometry a branch of mathematics centered around measurement and relationships of points, lines, angles, and surfaces of figures on a plane (p. 240)

plantation a large estate or farm that used enslaved people or hired workers to grow and harvest crops (pp. 628–629)

plateau an area of high and mostly flat land (p. 424)

plebeians ordinary citizens in ancient Rome (pp. 312–313)

península espacio de tierra que está casi completamente rodeado por agua (págs. 174–175)

perestroika plan soviético de reforma de las políticas gubernamentales y económicas (pág. 807)

***periodo** división de tiempo más corta que una era (pág. 150)

perseguir tratar a un grupo de personas de manera cruel o injusta (págs. 664–665)

***perspectiva** modo de mostrar la relación entre los objetos en un dibujo para dar un aspecto de profundidad o distancia (pág. 592)

falange grupo de infantería armada en la Grecia antigua que se organizaba en filas muy cerradas (pág. 182)

faraón emperador del antiguo Egipto (págs. 108-109)

filósofo persona que busca la sabiduría o la iluminación (pág. 199)

***filosofía** estudio de las ideas básicas sobre la sociedad, la educación y el bien y el mal; creencias, conceptos y actitudes básicas (págs. 286–287; pág. 344)

mapa físico mapa que muestra los accidentes geográficos terrestres y marítimos (pág. 34)

pictograma símbolo usado en un sistema de escritura que se basa en imágenes (pág. 282)

peregrino persona que viaja a lugares santos (pág. 268)

plagiar presentar el trabajo de otra persona como propio sin darle ningún crédito a esa persona (págs. 20–21)

plaga enfermedad que se extiende rápidamente y mata a muchas personas (pág. 570)

geometría plana rama de las matemáticas que estudia las medidas, las propiedades y las relaciones entre los puntos, las rectas, los ángulos y las superficies de las figuras en un plano (pág. 240)

plantación gran propiedad o granja en la cual los esclavos o personas contratadas cultivaban y recolectaban las cosechas (págs. 628–629)

meseta área alta y en su mayoría plana (pág. 424)

plebeyos ciudadanos comunes en la Roma antigua (págs. 312–313)

Glossary/Glosario

point of view a personal attitude about people or life (p. 12)

polis a Greek city-state (p. 180)

political map a map that shows the names and borders of countries (p. 34)

polytheism a belief in more than one god (pp. 78–79)

pope the title given to the Bishop of Rome (pp. 384–385)

popular sovereignty the idea that government is created by the people and must act according to people's wishes (pp. 670–671)

porcelain a ceramic made of fine clay baked at very high temperatures (p. 483)

praetors Roman government officials who interpreted the law and served as a judge (p. 313)

*precise exact (p. 6)

predestination a religious belief that God has already decided who will go to heaven and who will not (pp. 602–603)

*predict to describe something that will happen in the future (p. 460)

*primary most important; first (p. 622)

primary source firsthand evidence of an event in history (pp. 10–11)

*principle an important law or belief; rules or a code of conduct (p. 407; p. 480)

proconsul a governor (p. 329)

*professional relating to a type of job that usually requires training and practice (p. 322)

*prohibit to forbid something; to make something illegal (pp. 723–724)

projection a way of showing the round Earth on a flat map (pp. 30–31)

proletariat the working class (p. 700)

*promote to encourage the doing of something; to help bring into being (pp. 266–267; p. 810)

punto de vista actitud personal acerca de la vida o las personas (pág. 12)

polis ciudad-Estado griega (pág. 180)

mapa político mapa que muestra los nombres y las fronteras de los países (pág. 34)

politeísmo creencia en uno o más dioses (págs. 78–79)

papa título dado al obispo de Roma (págs. 384–385)

soberanía popular la idea de que el gobierno es creado por el pueblo y debe actuar de acuerdo con sus deseos (págs. 670–671)

porcelana cerámica elaborada con arcilla fina cocida a temperaturas muy elevadas (pág. 483)

pretores funcionarios del gobierno romano que interpretaban la ley y actuaban como jueces (pág. 313)

*preciso exacto (pág. 6)

predestinación creencia religiosa según la cual Dios ya ha decidido quién irá al Cielo y quién no (págs. 602–603)

*predecir describir algo que sucederá en el futuro (pág. 460)

*principal lo más importante; primero (pág. 622)

fuente primaria evidencia de primera mano de un hecho histórico (págs. 10–11)

*principio ley o creencia importante; reglas o código de conducta (pág. 407; pág. 480)

procónsul gobernador (pág. 329)

*profesional relativo a un tipo de trabajo que por lo general exige capacitación y práctica (pág. 322)

*prohibir impedir algo; declarar algo ilegal (págs. 723–724)

proyección manera de mostrar la forma redonda de la Tierra sobre un planisferio (págs. 30–31)

proletariado clase obrera (pág. 700)

*promover estimular la realización de algo; ayudar a que algo exista (págs. 266–267; pág. 810)

Glossary/Glosario

propaganda biased information used to influence public opinion (pp. 730–731)

propaganda información parcializada usada para influir en la opinión pública (págs. 730–731)

prophet a messenger sent by God to share God's word with people (pp. 140–141)

profeta mensajero enviado por Dios para compartir su palabra con las personas (págs. 140–141)

*__protect__ to defend from trouble or harm (pp. 342–343)

*__proteger__ defender de problemas o daños (págs. 342–343)

protectorate a relationship in which a nation has its own government, but its military is controlled by another government (pp. 710–711)

protectorado relación en la cual una nación tiene su propio gobierno, pero su ejército lo controla otro gobierno (págs. 710–711)

proverb a wise saying (p. 150)

proverbio refrán sabio (pág. 150)

province a territory governed as a political district of a country or empire (p. 88)

provincia territorio gobernado como distrito político de un país o imperio (pág. 88)

psalm a sacred song or poem used in worship (p. 149)

salmo canción o poema sagrado que se usa en el culto (pág. 149)

*__publish__ to produce the work of an author, usually in print (p. 414)

*__publicar__ producir la obra de un autor, por lo general de manera impresa (pág. 414)

*__pursue__ to follow in order to capture or defeat (pp. 232–233)

*__perseguir__ seguir para capturar o derrotar (págs. 232–233)

pyramid a great stone tomb for an Egyptian pharaoh (pp. 112–113)

pirámide gran tumba de piedra para los faraones egipcios (págs. 112–113)

Q
---

quipu a tool with a system of knots used for mathematics (p. 465)

quipu instrumento con un sistema de nudos usado para las matemáticas (p.465)

Quran the holy book of Islam (pp. 402–403)

Corán libro sagrado del Islám (págs. 402–403)

R
---

rabbi the official leader of a Jewish congregation (p. 166)

rabino líder oficial de una congregación judía (pág. 166)

racial segregation the act of forcing an ethnic group to use separate facilities (pp. 774–775)

segregación racial acción de obligar a un grupo racial a usar instalaciones físicas separadas (págs. 774–775)

*__radical__ extreme or far-reaching; in favor of making wide-ranging changes (pp. 674–675)

*__radical__ extremo o de largo alcance; que apoya los cambios muy diversos (págs. 674–675)

raja an Indian prince (p. 254)

rajá príncipe indio (pág. 254)

*__range__ the limits between which something can change or differ (p. 590)

*__intervalo__ límites entre los cuales algo puede cambiar o diferir (pág. 590)

rationalism the belief that reason and experience must be present for the solution of problems (pp. 648–649)

racionalismo creencia en que la razón y la experiencia son necesarias para la solución de problemas (págs. 648–649)

recession a period of slow economic growth or decline (p. 41)

recesión periodo de crecimiento económico lento o descendente (pág. 41)

Reconquista the Christian effort to take back the Iberian Peninsula (pp. 574–575)

Reconquista esfuerzo cristiano por recuperar la Península Ibérica (págs. 574–575)

*recover to get back again; regain (pp. 780–781)

*recuperar volver a tomar; recobrar (págs. 780–781)

Reformation a religious movement that created a new form of Christianity known as Protestantism (pp. 598–599)

*Reforma movimiento religioso que creó una nueva forma de cristianismo conocida como protestantismo (págs. 598–599)

reforms changes to bring about improvement (p. 352)

reformas cambios para obtener mejoras (pág. 352)

refugee a person who leaves a country because of war, violence, or natural disaster (p. 798)

refugiado persona que deja un país debido a la guerra, la violencia o un desastre natural (pág. 798)

*regime rulers during a given period of time (pp. 493–494)

*régimen gobernantes durante un periodo determinado (págs. 493–494)

*region a broad geographic area with similar features (p. 90; pp. 380–381; p. 769)

*región área geográfica amplia con características similares (pág. 90; págs. 380–381; pág. 769)

reincarnation the rebirth of the soul (p. 258)

reencarnación renacimiento del alma (pág. 258)

*reinforce to strengthen (p. 352)

*reforzar fortalecer (pág. 352)

*reject to refuse to accept or consider (p. 221; p. 387)

*rechazar negarse a aceptar o considerar (pág. 221; pág. 387)

*reluctance resistance, unwillingness (pp. 721–722)

*renuencia resistencia, falta de voluntad (págs. 721–722)

*reluctantly hesitantly or unwillingly (p. 315)

*a regañadientes con vacilación o de mala gana (pág. 315)

*rely to depend on someone or something; to be dependent; to count on for help; to contribute to (pp. 128–129; p. 281; p. 462; pp. 624–625; p. 816)

*confiar depender de alguien o de algo; ser dependiente; contar con la ayuda de alguien (págs. 128–129; pág. 281; pág. 462; págs. 624–625; pág. 816)

Renaissance a renewal or rebirth of interest in Greek and Roman arts (pp. 582–583)

Renacimiento renacer del interés en las artes griegas y romanas (págs. 582–583)

reparations payments for war damages made to winning countries by defeated ones (p. 735)

reparaciones pagos por los daños de la guerra que las naciones perdedoras hacen a las naciones ganadoras (pág. 735)

representative democracy a form of democracy in which citizens elect officials to govern on their behalf (pp. 198–199)

democracia representativa forma de democracia en la cual los ciudadanos eligen a los funcionarios para que gobiernen en su nombre (págs. 198–199)

representative government government in which citizens elect officials who administer its policies (pp. 44–45)

gobierno representativo gobierno en el cual los ciudadanos eligen a los funcionarios que administran sus políticas (págs. 44–45)

republic a form of government in which citizens elect their leaders (p. 310)

república forma de gobierno en la cual los ciudadanos eligen a sus líderes (pág. 310)

*reside to be present continuously or have a home in a particular place; to live (p. 111; p. 252)

*residir estar presente de manera continua o tener un hogar en un lugar determinado; vivir (pág. 111; pág. 252)

*resource something that is useful; a ready supply of something valuable (pp. 38–39; p. 630)

*respond to give an answer; to react (pp. 756–757)

*restore to bring something back to an original state; to bring something back to an earlier or better condition (p. 362; p. 476; pp. 604–605; p. 748)

resurrection the act of rising from the dead (p. 377)

*reveal to make information public; to tell a secret; to make known (p. 221)

*revolution a sudden change, or an overthrow, of a government (pp. 792–793)

rhetoric the art of public speaking and debate (p. 221)

ritual words or actions that are part of a religious ceremony (p. 213)

*role the function or part an individual fills in society; something that plays a part in the process (p. 116; pp. 540–541)

rouse to stir up or excite (p. 597)

*recurso algo que es útil; una provisión constante de algo valioso (págs. 38–39; pág. 630)

*responder dar una respuesta; reaccionar (págs. 756–757)

*restaurar volver a dejar algo en su estado original; volver a dejar algo en una condición anterior o mejor (pág. 362; pág. 476; págs. 604–605; pág. 748)

resurrección acción de levantarse de entre los muertos (pág. 377)

*revelar hacer pública una información; contar un secreto; dar a conocer (pág. 221)

*revolución cambio repentino, o derrocamiento, de un gobierno (págs. 792–793)

retórica arte de hablar y debatir en público (pág. 221)

ritual palabras o acciones que forman parte de una ceremonia religiosa (pág. 213)

*rol función o papel que un individuo cumple en la sociedad; algo que desempeña un papel en el proceso (pág. 116; págs. 540–541)

despertar provocar o suscitar (pág. 597)

S

Sabbath a weekly day of worship and rest (pp. 154–155)

sahib title meaning "sir" or "master" in India (p. 719)

saints people considered holy by followers of the Christian faith (p. 364)

salvation the act of being saved from the effects of sin (pp. 378–379)

samurai a warrior who served a Japanese lord and lived by a strict code of loyalty (p. 521)

Sanskrit the first written language of India (p. 254)

satire verse or prose that pokes fun at human weakness (pp. 346–347)

satrap the governor of a province in ancient Persia (p. 191)

satrapy the territory governed by an official known as a satrap (p. 191)

sabbat día semanal de culto y descanso (págs. 154–155)

sahib título que significa "señor" o "maestro" en India (pág. 719)

santos personas que los seguidores de la fe cristiana consideran sagradas (pág. 364)

salvación acción de salvarse de los efectos del pecado (págs. 378–379)

samurai guerrrero que servía a un señor japonés y vivía de acuerdo con un estricto código de lealtad (pág. 521)

sánscrito primera lengua escrita de la India (pág. 254)

sátira verso o prosa que se burla de la debilidad humana (págs. 346–347)

sátrapa gobernador de una provincia en la antigua Persia (pág. 191)

satrapía territorio gobernado por un funcionario llamado sátrapa (pág. 191)

savanna a flat grassland, sometimes with scattered trees, in a tropical or subtropical region (pp. 128–129; p. 423)

sabana pradera llana en una región tropical o subtropical, algunas veces con árboles dispersos (págs. 128–129; pág. 423)

scale a measuring line that shows the distances on a map (p. 35)

escala línea de medición que muestra las distancias en un mapa (pág. 35)

scarcity the lack of a resource (p. 40)

escasez falta de un recurso (pág. 40)

schism a separation or division from a church (p. 389)

cisma separación o división de una Iglesia (pág. 389)

scholarly concerned with academic learning or research (p. 14)

erudito relacionado con el aprendizaje académico o la investigación (pág. 14)

scholasticism a way of thinking that combined faith and reason (p. 565)

escolasticismo forma de pensar que combinaba la fe y la razón (pág. 565)

scientific method the steps for an orderly search for knowledge (pp. 648–649)

método científico pasos para una búsqueda de conocimiento ordenada (págs. 648–649)

Scientific Revolution a period from the 1500s to the 1700s in which many scientific advances changed people's traditional beliefs about science (p. 644)

revolución científica periodo entre los siglos XVI y XVIII en el cual muchos avances científicos cambiaron las creencias tradicionales de las personas sobre la ciencia (pág. 644)

scribe a person who copies or writes out documents; often a record keeper (p. 82)

escriba persona que copia o escribe documentos; con frecuencia, quien lleva los archivos (pág. 82)

scroll a long document made from pieces of parchment sewn together (p. 155)

rollo documento largo elaborado con pedazos de pergamino unidos (pág. 155)

secondary source a document or written work created after an event (p. 11)

fuente secundaria documento o trabajo que se escribe después de que ocurre un evento (pág. 11)

sect a religious group (pp. 524–525)

secta grupo religioso (págs. 524–525)

secular related to worldly things (pp. 582–583)

secular relacionado con las cosas terrenales (págs. 582–583)

*secure free from danger (pp. 564–565)

*seguro libre de peligro (págs. 564–565)

*seek to look for or try to achieve; to search for (pp. 45–46; p. 237)

*buscar indagar o tratar de alcanzar; investigar (págs. 45–46; pág. 237)

seminary a school for religious training (pp. 606–607)

seminario escuela para la formación religiosa (págs. 606–607)

separation of powers the division of power among the branches of government; a government structure that has three distinct branches: legislative, executive, and judicial (pp. 44–45; pp. 652–653)

separación de poderes división del poder entre las ramas del gobierno; estructura de gobierno que tiene tres ramas distintas: legislativa, ejecutiva y judicial (págs. 44–45; págs. 652–653)

serf a member of the peasant class tied to the land and subject to the will of the landowner (pp. 550–551)

siervo miembro de la clase campesina atado a la tierra y sujeto a la voluntad del terrateniente (págs. 550–551)

shadoof a bucket attached to a long pole used to transfer river water to storage basins (p. 104)

cigoñal cubeta atada a una pértiga larga que se usa para pasar agua del río a vasijas de almacenamiento (pág. 104)

shamanism belief in gods, demons, and spirits (p. 511)

chamanismo creencia en dioses, demonios y espíritus (pág. 511)

shari'ah Islamic code of law (pp. 402–403)

sharia código jurídico islámico (págs. 402–403)

sheikh the leader of an Arab tribe (p. 399)

jeque líder de una tribu árabe (pág. 399)

Shia group of Muslims who believed the descendants of Ali should rule (p. 407)

chiíta grupo musulmán que creía que los descendientes de Alá debían gobernar (pág. 407)

shogun a military governor who ruled Japan (p. 522)

sogún gobern ante militar que reinaba en Japón (pág. 522)

shrine a place where people worship (p. 66)

templo lugar donde la gente rinde culto (pág. 66)

silt fine particles of fertile soil (p. 77)

limo partículas finas de suelo fértil (pág. 77)

*similar having things in common; having characteristics in common (p. 287; p. 440)

*similar que tiene cosas en común; que tiene características en común (pág. 287; pág. 440)

sinkhole a depression or hollow where soil has collapsed (pp. 459–460)

sumidero depresión u hoyo donde el suelo ha colapsado (págs. 459–460)

smallpox a disease that causes a high fever and often death (p. 625)

viruela enfermedad que produce fiebre alta y con frecuencia, la muerte (pág. 625)

smith craftsperson who works with metal (p. 349)

herrero artesano que trabaja los metales (pág. 349)

*social class a group of people who are at a similar cultural, economic, or educational level (p. 289)

*clase social grupo de personas con un nivel cultural, económico o educativo similar (pág. 289)

social contract an agreement between the people and their government (p. 652)

contrato social acuerdo entre el pueblo y su gobierno (pág. 652)

socialism the means of production are owned and controlled by the people, through their government (pp. 698–699)

socialismo medios de producción de propiedad de las personas y controlados por ellas a través de su gobierno (págs. 698–699)

Socratic method philosophical method of questioning to gain truth (p. 221)

método socrático método filosófico que consiste en hacer preguntas para conocer la verdad (pág. 221)

solid geometry a branch of mathematics about measurement and relationships of points, lines, angles, surfaces, and solids in three-dimensional space (p. 240)

geometría sólida rama de las matemáticas que estudia las medidas, las propiedades y las relaciones entre los puntos, las líneas, los ángulos, las superficies y los sólidos en el espacio tridimensional (pág. 240)

Sophists Greek teachers of philosophy, reasoning, and public speaking (p. 221)

sofistas maestros griegos de filosofía, razonamiento y retórica (pág. 221)

*source a document or reference work (pp. 10–11)

*fuente documento u obra de referencia (págs. 10–11)

soviet a committee to represent the concerns of the Russian people (p. 738)

sóviet comité que representaba los intereses del pueblo ruso (pág. 738)

special-purpose map a map that shows themes or patterns such as climate, natural resources, or population (pp. 34–35)

mapa temático mapa que muestra temas o patrones como el clima, los recursos naturales o la población (págs. 34–35)

specialization the act of training for a particular job (p. 66)

especialización acción de capacitarse para un trabajo específico (pág. 66)

species a class of individuals with similar physical characteristics (pp. 8–9)

especie clase de individuos con características físicas semejantes (págs. 8–9)

sphere of influence a region where only one imperial power had the right to invest or trade (pp. 710–711)

esfera de influencia región donde solo una potencia imperial tenía derecho a invertir o comerciar (págs. 710–711)

spiritual a gospel song (pp. 440–441)

espiritual canción de música gospel (págs. 440–441)

*stability the condition of being steady and unchanging (p. 186)

*estabilidad cualidad de estar fijo o ser inalterable (pág. 186)

*status a person's rank compared to others (pp. 258–259)

*estatus posición de una persona en comparación con otras (págs. 258–259)

steppe flat, dry grassland (pp. 489–490)

estepa sabana plana y seca (págs. 489–490)

Stoicism the philosophy of the Stoics who believed that people should not try to feel joy or sadness (p. 238)

estoicismo filosofía de los estoicos, quienes creían que las personas no debían tratar de sentir alegría ni tristeza (pág. 238)

*strategy a careful plan to achieve a goal (p. 712)

*estrategia plan cuidadoso para alcanzar una meta (pág. 712)

*structure a building or other built object (p. 270)

*estructura edificio u otro tipo de construcción (pág. 270)

stupa a Buddhist shrine, usually dome-shaped (pp. 266–267)

estupa templo budista, por lo general en forma de domo (págs. 266–267)

stutter an uneven repetition of sounds and words (p. 85)

tartamudeo repetición irregular de sonidos y palabras (pág. 85)

*style a distinctive form or type of something (pp. 218–219; pp. 530–531)

*estilo forma o tipo característicos de algo (págs. 218–219; págs. 530–531)

subcontinent a large landmass that is smaller than a continent (pp. 248–249)

subcontinente gran masa continental más pequeña que un continente (págs. 248–249)

*successor one that comes after; one who follows, especially to an office, title, or throne (p. 332; pp. 800–801)

*sucesor persona que sucede a otra; quien sigue, especialmente en un cargo, un título o un trono (pág. 332; págs. 800–801)

*sufficient enough (p. 202)

*suficiente bastante (pág. 202)

sugarcane a grassy plant that is a natural source of sugar (pp. 438–439)

caña de azúcar planta herbácea que es una fuente natural de azúcar (págs. 438–439)

sultan Seljuk leader (p. 408)

sultán líder seléucida (pág. 408)

Sunni group of Muslims who accepted the rule of the Umayyad caliphs (p. 407)

sunita grupo musulmán que solo acepta el mandato de los califas Umayyad (pág. 407)

supply the amount of a good or service that a producer wants to sell (p. 39)

oferta cantidad de un producto o servicio que un productor quiere vender (pág. 39)

surplus an amount that is left over after a need has been met (p. 78)

excedente cantidad que queda luego de satisfacer una necesidad (pág. 78)

*survive to continue to live; to live through a dangerous event; to continue to function or prosper (p. 152; pp. 434–435)

*sobrevivir seguir viviendo; vivir luego de haber tenido una experiencia peligrosa; continuar funcionando o prosperar (pág. 152; págs. 434–435)

Swahili the unique culture of Africa's East Coast and the language spoken there (pp. 434–435)

swahili cultura exclusiva de la costa este de África y lengua que se habla allí (págs. 434–435)

*symbol a sign or image that stands for something else; something that stands for or suggests something else (p. 35; p. 701; pp. 770–771)

*símbolo signo o imagen que representa otra cosa; algo que representa o sugiere algo más (pág. 35; pág. 701; págs. 770–771)

synagogue a Jewish house of worship (pp. 154–155)

sinagoga casa judía de culto (págs. 154–155)

systematic agriculture the organized growing of food on a regular schedule (pp. 62–63)

agricultura sistemática cultivo organizado de alimentos de acuerdo con un calendario habitual (págs. 62–63)

T

*technology the use of advanced methods to solve problems; an ability gained by the practical use of knowledge (pp. 38–39; p. 56;)

*tecnología uso de métodos avanzados para solucionar problemas; habilidad obtenida mediante el uso práctico del conocimiento (págs. 38–39; pág. 56)

*temporary not permanent; lasting for a limited period (pp. 464–465)

*temporal que no es permanente; que dura un periodo limitado (págs. 464–465)

tenant farmer a farmer who works land owned by someone else and pays rent in cash or as a share of the crop (p. 295)

agricultor arrendatario agricultor que trabaja la tierra que pertenece a otro y le paga una renta ya sea en efectivo o con parte de sus cosechas (pág. 295)

*tensions opposition between individuals or groups; stress (p. 164)

*tensiones oposición entre individuos o grupos; presión (pág. 164)

terror violent acts that are meant to cause fear in people (pp. 490–491)

terror actos violentos que buscan atemorizar a las personas (págs. 490–491)

terrorism the use of violence against civilians to achieve a political goal (pp. 802–803)

terrorismo uso de la violencia contra los civiles para alcanzar una meta política (págs. 802–803)

*text words written down in a particular form, such as a book (p. 254)

*texto palabras escritas en un formato específico, como un libro (pág. 254)

textile woven cloth (pp. 132–133)

textil tela tejida (págs. 132–133)

*theme a topic that is studied or a special quality that connects ideas (p. 32)

*tema materia que se estudia o cualidad especial que conecta ideas (pág. 32)

theocracy a government of religious leader(s) (pp. 108–109)

teocracia gobierno de uno o más líderes religiosos (págs. 108–109)

theology the study of religious faith, practice, and experience (p. 565)

teología estudio de la fe, la práctica y la experiencia religiosas (pág. 565)

*theory an explanation of how or why something happens (pp. 642–643)

*teoría explicación de cómo o por qué sucede algo (págs. 642–643)

Torah teachings that Moses received from God; later became the first part of the Hebrew Bible (p. 143)

Tora enseñanza que recibió Moisés de Dios; llegó a ser la primera parte de la Biblia hebrea (pág. 143)

Glossary/Glosario

totalitarian state a form of government in which citizens are under strict control by the state (p. 749)

Estado totalitario forma de gobierno en la cual los ciudadanos están bajo estricto control del Estado (pág. 749)

*tradition a custom, or way of life, passed down from generation to generation (pp. 154–155)

*tradición costumbre, o forma de vida, que se transmite de una generación a otra (págs. 154–155)

traditional economy an economic system in which custom decides what people do, make, buy, and sell (p. 40)

economía tradicional sistema económico en el cual la costumbre decide lo que las personas hacen, producen, compran y venden (pág. 40)

tragedy a play or film in which characters fail to overcome serious problems (p. 217)

tragedia obra de teatro o película en la cual los personajes no pueden superar problemas graves (pág. 217)

*transfer to copy from one surface to another by contact (p. 484)

*transferir copiar de una superficie a otra por contacto (pág. 484)

*transform to change the structure of; to bring about a large and widespread change (p. 322; p. 634)

*transformar cambiar la estructura; provocar un cambio grande y generalizado (pág. 322; pág. 634)

transformation a complete change (p. 497)

transformación cambio total (pág. 497)

*transport to transfer or carry from one place to another; to convey or carry (pp. 424–425; pp. 764–765)

*transportar transferir o llevar de un lugar a otro; comunicar o llevar (págs. 424–425; págs. 764–765)

trial jury a group of citizens that decides whether an accused person is innocent or guilty (p. 558)

jurado grupo de ciudadanos que decide si un acusado es inocente o culpable (pág. 558)

tribe a social group made up of families or clans (p. 142)

tribu grupo social conformado por familias o clanes (pág. 142)

tribune an elected Roman official who protects the rights of ordinary citizens (p. 313)

tribuno funcionario romano elegido que protege los derechos de los ciudadanos comunes (pág. 313)

tribute payment made to a ruler or state as a sign of surrender; payment to a ruler as a sign of submission or for protection (p. 88; pp. 514–515)

tributo pago hecho a un gobernante o Estado en señal de rendición; pago a un gobernante como señal de sumisión o para obtener protección (pág. 88; págs. 514–515)

triumvirate three rulers who share equal political power (p. 323)

triunvirato tres gobernantes que comparten el mismo poder político (pág. 323)

Truman Doctrine granted aid to countries threatened by communist takeover after World War II (p. 770)

Doctrina Truman ayuda conferida a los países amenazados por la expansión comunista después de la Segunda Guerra Mundial (pág. 770)

tsunami a huge ocean wave caused by an undersea earthquake (p. 529)

tsunami enorme ola oceánica causada por un sismo subacuático (pág. 529)

tyrant an absolute ruler unrestrained by law; harsh ruler (pp. 183–184; p. 719)

tirano gobernante absoluto que actúa sin control por parte de la ley; gobernante cruel (págs. 183–184; pág. 719)

U

*unify to bring together in one unit; to join; to make into one group (pp. 106–107; pp. 292–293; pp. 608–609)

*unificar juntar en una unidad; unir; formar un grupo (págs. 106–107; págs. 292–293; págs. 608–609)

*unique one of a kind; different from all others (pp. 100–101; p. 431)

*exclusivo único en su clase; diferente de los demás (págs. 100–101; pág. 431)

urban having to do with a town or city rather than a rural area (p. 583)

urbano relativo a un pueblo o una ciudad, no a un área rural (pág. 583)

urbanization the increase in the proportion of people living in cities rather than rural areas (pp. 696–697)

urbanización aumento en la proporción de personas que viven en las ciudades y no en áreas rurales (págs. 696–697)

URL the abbreviation for uniform resource locator; the address of an online resource (p. 20)

URL abreviatura de uniform resource locator (localizador uniforme de recursos); dirección de un recurso en línea (pág. 20)

utilitarianism belief that society should provide the greatest happiness for the largest number of people (p. 699)

utilitarismo creencia de que la sociedad debe brindar la mayor felicidad al mayor número de personas (pág. 699)

V

*vary to show differences or undergo changes (p. 800)

*variar mostrar diferencias o experimentar cambios (pág. 800)

vassal a person under the protection of a lord to whom he has vowed loyalty; a low-ranking noble under the protection of a feudal lord (p. 523; pp. 548–549)

vasallo persona bajo la protección de un señor a quien ha jurado lealtad; noble de baja categoría bajo la protección de un señor feudal (pág. 523; págs. 548–549)

vault a curved ceiling made of arches (p. 345)

bóveda techo curvo compuesto por arcos (pág. 345)

Vedas ancient sacred writings of India (p. 254)

Vedas antiguos escritos sagrados de la India (pág. 254)

vernacular the everyday spoken language of a region (p. 566)

vernácula lengua hablada en una región (pág. 566)

*version a different form or edition; a translation of the Bible (p. 161)

*versión formato o edición diferentes; traducción de la Biblia (pág. 161)

veto to reject (p. 313)

vetar rechazar (pág. 313)

vigil the night before a religious feast (p. 597)

vigilia la noche anterior a una fiesta religiosa (pág. 597)

vile morally low (p. 597)

vil de baja moral (pág. 597)

*violate to disobey or break a rule or law; to break, to treat with disrespect (pp. 20–21; pp. 810–811)

*violar desobedecer o incumplir una regla o ley; romper, tratar de manera irrespetuosa (págs. 20–21; págs. 810–811)

volcano a mountain that releases hot or melted rocks from inside the Earth (pp. 528–529)

volcán montaña que libera rocas calientes o fundidas desde el interior de la Tierra (págs. 528–529)

*volume amount included within limits (p. 452)

*volumen cantidad incluida dentro de los límites (pág. 452)

*voluntarily by choice or free will; willingly (p. 231)

*voluntariamente por elección o voluntad propia; con gusto (pág. 231)

W

warlord a military commander exercising civil power by force, usually in a limited area (p. 281)

caudillo comandante militar que ejerce el poder civil por la fuerza, usualmente en un área limitada (pág. 281)

widespread frequent in many places, common; broadly extended or spread out (p. 673; p. 769)

*generalizado frecuente en muchos lugares, común; ampliado o muy difundido (pág. 673; pág. 769)

Z

ziggurat a pyramid-shaped structure with a temple at the top (p. 80)

zigurat estructura en forma de pirámide, en cuya punta se encuentra un templo (pág. 80)

Zoroastrianism a Persian religion based on the belief of one god (p. 192)

Zoroastrismo religión persa que se basaba en la creencia en un dios (pág. 192)

Index

Index

Index

Index

Index

K

L

Index

Index

Index

Index

Index

Index